AMERICAN
ECONOMIC HISTORY

HARPER'S HISTORICAL SERIES

Under the Editorship of

GUY STANTON FORD

HAROLD UNDERWOOD FAULKNER

Dwight W. Morrow Professor of History, Smith College

AMERICAN
ECONOMIC
HISTORY

SEVENTH EDITION

HARPER & BROTHERS PUBLISHERS, NEW YORK

To My Mother

HELEN UNDERWOOD FAULKNER

CONTENTS

PART IV. THE INDUSTRIAL REVOLUTION

PART V. A NEW SOCIETY

MAPS

GRAPHS AND CHARTS

ILLUSTRATIONS

These pictures follow page 488

Freight Transportation by Land—A Conestoga Wagon
The *"DeWitt Clinton"*—First Railroad Train in New York
Engines of the Civil War Days
Meeting of a Local Grange in the Early 1870's at the Height of the Agrarian Crusade
Anti-Railroad Cartoon of the 1870's
Wheat Threshing, Cheyenne County, Nebraska, About 1900
Thirty Horses Pulling a Combine, Harvesting Wheat in the Northwest
Communication on Lower Broadway, 1889
Elevated Railroad at 110th Street and Columbus Avenue, New York
America's New Labor Force—A Group of New Arrivals at Ellis Island Early in the Twentieth Century
Labor in the Textile Mills Was Largely Women and Children

These pictures follow page 584

Labor Union Meeting at the Time of the Cloakmaker's Strike in New York in 1912
Samuel Gompers, President of the American Federation of Labor
Train of the Camden and Amboy Railroad Reconstructing the Delaware and Raritan Canal About 1866 at a Time When Canal Transportation Was Declining
Completion of the First Transcontinental Railroad at Promontory Point, Utah, May 10, 1869
Poster Advertising the Opening of the Union Pacific Railroad
Union Pacific's First Locomotive
A Crack Pullman Train of the Early Twentieth Century Running Along the Bank of the Chesapeake and Ohio Canal
Alfred Stieglitz Has Beautifully Photographed in "The Terminal" Horse Car Transportation in New York in the 1890's
Charles Duryea in His First Horseless Carriage
The Wright Brothers' First Flight Near Kitty Hawk, North Carolina
Black Maria—The First Moving Picture Studio Set Up by Edison for His Experiments
Mechanized Agriculture—Twelve McCormick-Deering Sixteen-Foot Threshers
Mechanized Agriculture—A Caterpillar Diesel Tractor Pulling a 14-foot Drill and a 14-foot Land Roller in Tandem
Displaced by Drought and Mechanized Agriculture, the Small Farmer Moves on in Search of Work

These pictures follow page 680

Modern Industry—Automobile Body Assembly Line
Assembling Component Parts for the Electron Gun

EDITOR'S INTRODUCTION

THE trailing clouds of glory that lay around our nation's youth have begun to fade away. With the war we reached middle age at a bound. We are now counting our resources, human and material, as we never did before. The results of the inventory are not wholly reassuring, and we are checking up our waning natural resources, our political institutions, our education, our social philosophy, to find where there is waste and lost motion. Mankind may not be at the crossroads, but it is dimly conscious that the road ahead is not the broad and happy highway of the past. It is more necessary than ever before that we should study our national history from every standpoint, and especially the economic. I think this book will be counted among the most useful of the aids yet provided for such study.

It may be well to point out that he who writes the economic history of any age or land undertakes a difficult task. If it be an economic history of the United States, as this volume is, the task is not less but rather more difficult. His subject is a country where nature has been bountiful and the exploitation of natural wealth has been less trammeled by old institutions and social customs than in Europe. Here the political individualism of a pioneer people has given freer play than ever before in human history to all the acquisitive impulses of men and groups of men. The faith of a youthful people that it lived in a land of inexhaustible resources and that nothing could happen to it that had happened to older lands where soil and forests became exhausted and the mineral wealth dissipated has opened the door for a material development unparalleled in the history of nations. How easy then for him who starts with the point of view implied in the title "economic history" to forget that the history of significant men and nations is, in its end results, but the charted field of a battle between their inherited ideas and unrealized ideals, on the one hand, and the material circumstances of their physical environment, on the other. I believe the author has written an account of our economic history free from the errors of one-sided materialism.

It is the achievement of this book that it is American history seen whole and sturdily, though from the given standpoint of its title. The reader has presented to him the picture of success and error in the discharge of an implied trusteeship. It is done dispassionately, without disproportion or vain glorification. Those who study it can draw their own conclusions and, if they master it, will find themselves in possession of the essential equipment necessary to a citizenship that will face in the next generation more complicated social and economic problems than it has in the past.

The student of economic history should be warned that he must face and master many facts. It is not a simple matter to grasp such data and wring their meaning from them. I believe that here, too, the author has given skillfully all the aid that any self-respecting student should require. He has gathered and integrated into an account that does not halt a remarkable and significant mass of tables, figures, and graphs. He has labored patiently that the student may read intelligently and be armed to test old conclusions or draw new ones. This is a difficult task for any author, but an essential one in an economic history. If an editor may not voice an opinion he can at least express his confidence that classroom use will prove that the author has achieved a large measure of success in writing a narrative that makes statistics an asset to teaching.

Neither teacher nor text writer is content to have a student think one book is the subject. A bibliography of material that will amplify, supplement, and enforce the text is essential. Such an aid to scholarship has been, as I can testify, one of the writer's chief concerns.

Guy Stanton Ford.

PREFACE TO THE FIFTH EDITION

THE third and fourth editions of this book were largely concerned with keeping it up to date. This is the first time since 1931 that the volume has been entirely reset. This has given the author a chance to rearrange or consolidate certain of the material, to make numerous deletions, particularly in the early part of the book, and to add new and pertinent information. It has made it possible for the publishers to design a new and more attractive format and for the author to improve the educational equipment by adding new maps and charts and to trace our economic development through forty pages of illustrations. Above all, this revision has afforded an opportunity to include and acknowledge the results of much significant research done in recent years by scholars in this field. So much fine work is being done in American economic history that any effort to integrate or interpret it has become increasingly difficult but at the same time an increasingly exacting and challenging task.

The author is very grateful that enough teachers have found this volume sufficiently useful to warrant another edition. Only through an understanding of our economic past can we plan wisely for the future; it is hoped that this and similar volumes may contribute in some slight way to the knowledge of our country so necessary in meeting the problems of the critical years ahead. The author is also grateful for the criticisms, suggestions, and help of many kinds he has received from scholars since the book was first published. Most textbooks which have gone through one or more revisions tend to become the cooperative result of many minds. For this aid, acknowledged in the preface of previous editions, the author again expresses his thanks.

HAROLD U. FAULKNER

Northampton, Mass.
  December 1, 1942

PREFACE TO SEVENTH EDITION

THIS is the first time since the fifth edition of 1943 that the entire text of *American Economic History* has been reset. By deleting certain minor sections in the early part of the book and some fringe discussions touching political and social history, the volume has been brought down to date without substantially increasing its size. When necessary, revisions and additions have been made in the graphs, maps, and illustrative material. As in earlier editions this one has profited from the suggestions and criticisms of scholars in the field, particularly those made by Dr. Clarence H. Danhof. For all of these the author is grateful. It is hoped that whatever usefulness this book may have had will be continued in the new edition.

HAROLD U. FAULKNER

Northampton, Mass.
February 12, 1954

PART I

THE BACKGROUND

CHAPTER 1

PHYSIOGRAPHIC FACTORS AND NATURAL RESOURCES

PHYSIOGRAPHIC INFLUENCES

THE study of history, particularly economic history, must begin with a knowledge of the physical outline and resources of the unit under observation. Civilization has been defined as the process of conquering nature, but in that process nature has reacted quite as much on man as man on nature. "Thus," says Buckle, "we have man modifying nature, and nature modifying man; while out of this reciprocal modification all events must necessarily spring."[1]

Physical environment determines to a large extent where man shall live, what kind of work he shall do, what he may produce, and the routes over which he must travel and transport his products. Because of its influence upon his economic life, physical environment goes far to determine man's social and political point of view, his habits and desires, and even his physical frame.[2]

The history of the United States, written so largely in terms of the conquest of the continent, shows physiographic influence at every step. The contour of the coast fixed the place of the first settlements, the river valleys and mountain gaps pointed the routes westward, while the formation of the soil and the nature of its products determined the occupation of the settler after he had reached the new country.

GEOGRAPHIC DIVISIONS OF THE UNITED STATES

The North American continent forms a rough triangle approximately 3000 miles across at the north and tapering to a width of but a few miles at

[1] Henry T. Buckle, *History of Civilization in England* (1862), I, 15.
[2] See Franz Boas, *Changes in Bodily Form of Descendants of Immigrants* (1912), compiled from *U.S. Immigration Commission Reports*.

the Isthmus of Panama. Facing three oceans, it is influenced by each. The Pacific sends a stream of warm water against the western coast, which makes it habitable as far as Alaska, although, because of the Cordilleras, the effect is limited to the fringe of seacoast. The Gulf Stream of the Atlantic provides rainfall for the lower Mississippi and Gulf states, and its influence can be seen as far north as New England. The Arctic, where it touches America, cut off from the currents of both Atlantic and Pacific, is icebound and so makes unfit for habitation a large part of the northern half of the continent. A vast mountain range, the Cordilleras, traverses the western portion of the continent from Alaska to Panama. At its widest point, around the 40th parallel, this system has a breadth of about 1000 miles, with many of its peaks attaining a height of 14,000 feet. On the east the Appalachian system, bordering a fringe of seacoast and interspersed with fertile valleys, extends from Newfoundland to Alabama. It is nowhere as high as 7000 feet. Between these two mountain ranges lies an immense plain which, with the exception of a few patches of low mountains, stretches from the Gulf of Mexico to the Arctic. The drainage of this great plain is carried off by three main outlets: (1) the Mississippi and its tributaries, notably the Missouri, Ohio, Arkansas, and Red rivers, emptying into the Gulf of Mexico; (2) the Great Lakes, draining into the St. Lawrence and the Atlantic; and (3) the MacKenzie, and the numerous streams running into Hudson Bay.

On this continent, roughly between the 25th and 49th parallels, lies the United States of America. In area it contains 3,026,789 square miles—over two-thirds the size of Europe. It has been divided geographically into six more or less distinct parts.

1. The eastern lowlands, or coastal plain, lying between the shore and the Appalachians. This region includes the eastern fringe of the states facing the Atlantic. Although the soil is generally not so fertile as that farther west, it is suitable for ordinary garden vegetables and for wheat, corn, and tobacco. It fortunately provided the first settlers with two indigenous plants—their chief cereal, corn, and their chief export, tobacco. As the agricultural center shifted westward, the future of the coastal plain became more and more concerned with manufacturing and commerce, the former made possible by the highly developed water power of the fall line, and the latter by the excellent harbors of the frequently indented coast. Two strings of cities mark the boundaries of the coastal plain; on the west the cities of the fall line—Montgomery, Augusta, Macon, Columbia, Raleigh, Richmond, Trenton, Hartford; on the east the seacoast ports—Savannah, Charleston, Norfolk, New York, Boston, Philadelphia, and Baltimore.

2. The Appalachian region, directly to the west, composed of parallel mountain ranges, including the Blue Ridge and the Alleghenies. The Ap-

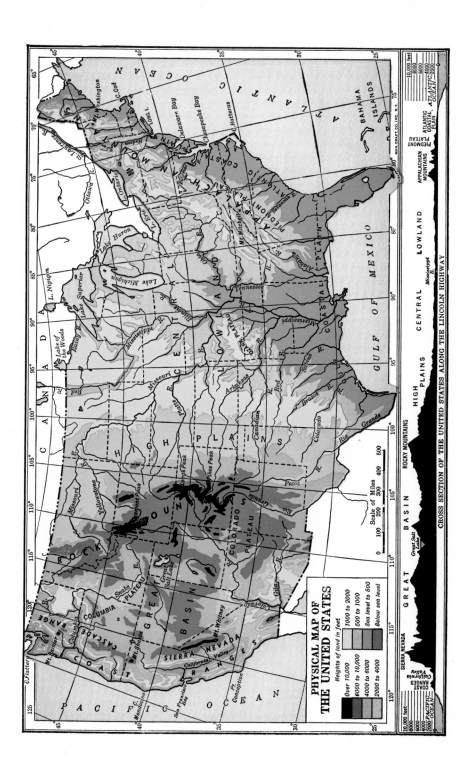

PHYSICAL MAP OF
THE UNITED STATES

Heights of land in feet

Over 10,000
6000 to 10,000
4000 to 6000
2000 to 4000
1000 to 2000
500 to 1000
Sea level to 500
Below sea level

Scale of Miles
0   100   200   300   400   500

CROSS SECTION OF THE UNITED STATES ALONG THE LINCOLN HIGHWAY

palachians extend from Newfoundland to Alabama, rising to heights of over 6000 feet in the White Mountains of New Hampshire and the Black Mountains of North Carolina. Between these mountain ranges, extending a distance of 600 miles from New Jersey to Georgia, are to be found many fertile valleys. On both sides of the mountain systems, and especially to the west, are wide tablelands, merging gradually into the plains. In all, this section comprises some 300,000 square miles, only 12,000 of which are untillable, and contains in its fertile piedmonts and valleys, notably the Shenandoah, Cumberland, and Tennessee, some of the finest farming lands in America. The position of natural resources has given rise to a pronounced geographic localization of industries. Thus the nearness of the mountains to the coast in New England causes a rapid fall in the streams and produces the water power which early made of New England a manufacturing center; the coal and iron deposits of Pennsylvania and the southern Appalachian states have given rise to the great iron and steel cities of Pittsburgh and Birmingham.

3. Lowlands of the Gulf states. This region includes Florida, southern Georgia, Alabama, Mississippi, Louisiana, and eastern Texas, where the rich black alluvial soil and the hot climate form an excellent combination for the staple crop, cotton, and for the vegetables and semitropical fruits which have become an increasingly important factor in the agriculture of this area

4. The great plain of the Mississippi Valley. The Mississippi Valley consists of a relatively small delta section of alluvial soil, some twenty to thirty thousand square miles in area, and the great tablelands of the Appalachians and the Rockies. The wide fertile prairies and river valleys of this region make it the agricultural heart of North America. It is here that immense crops of wheat and corn are raised; in the Mississippi delta, as in the Gulf states, cotton is king. The "Father of Waters" and its tributaries, the Ohio and the Missouri, furnish excellent natural transportation facilities which are augmented to the north by the Great Lakes and their connecting canals.

5. The Cordillera region. Although fertile valleys are to be found here and bits have been made artificially arable by irrigation, the greater part (at least nineteen-twentieths) is useless for agriculture. The great value of this region in the past has come chiefly from its mineral deposits of copper, iron, silver, and gold. As contrasted with the great Mississippi Valley which has the potential capacity to support an enormous population, the Cordillera region will probably always be sparsely populated, especially when its mineral resources are exhausted. Nevertheless, the increasing attention devoted to irrigation projects and dry farming is slowly laying the foundation for a permanent prosperity. Moreover, the vast projects at Boulder Dam, Grand Coulee, and elsewhere, designed to provide not only water for irrigation

but also hydroelectric power, may well lay the foundation for light industries in the future.

6. A narrow region of low mountains on the extreme western coast. Of great fertility and extremely even and temperate climate, this section has developed enormously the production of fruit and vegetables. Although the Pacific coast is unfortunate in that it possesses but few natural harbors, the opening of the Panama Canal and the commercial importance of the Far East point to the increasing use of such facilities as are offered at the Golden Gate, Puget Sound, the Columbia River, and the artificial harbor at Los Angeles. Gold brought the first large influx of English-speaking settlers to California, but its great present and future wealth depends upon other products, notably oil, fruit, and vegetables.

In the preceding paragraphs the emphasis has been placed upon *geographic* divisions. At the same time an effort has been made to point out their economic significance from the point of view of *human use*. For the economic historian the human-use region or division is much more valid for a proper understanding of the unit of land under study than the geographic.[3] Enough has been said, however, to make clear the close relationship between physiography and human use and to make possible their simultaneous discussion. In this connection it is suggested that one of the factors that tends to make political history confusing is the fact that political boundaries are often quite artificial and have no relationship to economic boundaries. As Turner has emphasized, the United States is a federation of economic and cultural sections rather than a union of states.[4] It is through a study of these different economic sections, the interests of which are often in conflict, that we reach an understanding of the nation's economic and political history.

GEOGRAPHIC INFLUENCE UPON COLONIZATION

Although the American continent is accessible on its western side and the ancestors of the aborigines undoubtedly entered it from Asia, it was most fortunate that when the white man came to these shores he approached them from the east. Had the continent been turned around, its history would have been different, for the rugged Cordilleras would have presented to the pioneer a difficult barrier. The accessibility of continents is largely determined by the navigability of their rivers, and in this respect the American continent in its eastern area was most favored. After the forbidding Atlantic had once been crossed, the European found a land the ingress to which was simple. The St. Lawrence Valley connecting with the Great Lakes, the

[3] J. R. Smith and M. O. Phillips, *North America*, pp. 38–39.
[4] F. J. Turner, *Significance of Sections in American History* (1933).

Hudson River opening through the Appalachians, and the Mississippi with its innumerable tributaries penetrating the very heart of the continent pointed the way inland and made possible a more rapid settlement. Particularly was this true in the South, where innumerable little rivers flowed into the sea, too small for the large freighters of today, but navigable for the tiny ships of the seventeenth century. To the north the Delaware, the Hudson, and the Connecticut rivers cut the coastal plains as far as the Appalachians and formed the natural highways for the early settlers.

Along these rivers settlements were planted, and down them were floated furs and tobacco, the two products that first linked the colonies with the markets of Europe. It is estimated that there are over 26,000 miles of navigable rivers in the United States, not counting the 2760 (meandered length, 4329) miles of shore line on the Great Lakes. Including indentations, the coast line on both oceans amounts to over 64,000 miles, with at least two-thirds of this directly accessible to Europe on the Atlantic and the Gulf of Mexico. With numerous rivers and an indented coast, good harbors were to be expected. The Atlantic and Gulf states show excellent examples of each harbor type: New York and Baltimore, of the drowned valley; Galveston, Provincetown, and many little harbors on the Carolina, Florida, and New Jersey coasts, of harbors formed from barrier reefs; New Orleans and Philadelphia, of river harbors. These and numerous other natural ports and river towns povided the points at which the raw materials for export could be gathered and the manufactured products of the mother country received and marketed.

CLIMATE AND RAINFALL

The territory now embraced in the United States was eminently fitted for those European races destined to settle and conquer the American continent. It lies between the lines of 40 and 70 degrees average annual temperature, representing a climate similar to that in the portions of Europe producing the most energetic and civilized races. Ellsworth Huntington and other students have found a close relationship between civilization and climate, and between physical and mental activity and climate.[5] A climate favorable

[5] "Changes in the barometer," asserts Huntington, "seem to have little effect. Humidity, on the other hand, possesses a considerable degree of importance, but the most important element is clearly temperature. The people here considered [groups of factory operatives and college students] are physically most active when the temperature is from 60 to 65 degrees, that is, when the noon temperature rises to 70 degrees or even more. This is higher than many of us would expect. Mental activity reaches a maximum when the outside temperature averages about 38 degrees, that is, when there are mild frosts at night. Another highly important climatic condition is the change of temperature from one day to the next. People do not work well when the temperature remains constant. Great changes are also unfavorable. The ideal conditions are moderate changes, especially a cooling of the air at frequent intervals." Ellsworth Huntington, *Civilization and Climate* (1925), p. 8. Some of these findings have been challenged.

to the rapid development of man must have a warm season long enough to grow plenty of food and a cold season severe enough to make men work to lay up surplus food for the winter; it must in addition provide reasonably healthful surroundings. This combination the settlers found in most of the present United States.

Fundamental also in its effect upon the well-being of people is the amount of rainfall. Wheat, for example, man's most important food, can generally not be grown when the annual rainfall is less than 10 inches or more than 45. The average annual rainfall of the United States is 26.6 inches, varying from 5 inches in southern Utah to over 60 in the western valley of northern California, Washington and Oregon, and on the Gulf coast. The Pacific coast has a damp, insular climate which becomes drier toward the mountains, until in the great arid plateau moisture is almost lacking. The rainfall gradually increases, however, as we approach the Gulf of Mexico and the Atlantic. East of the Appalachians it averages from 30 to 50 inches a year. Since 20 inches is essential for agriculture and from 30 to 50 inches for ideal soil moisture, conditions for agricultural production are here most favorable. While the variations of both temperature and rainfall are greater than in Europe, the climate as a whole is essentially the same.[6]

In American economic history the subject of rainfall is of primary importance. The United States (except for some areas of the Pacific coast) is roughly divided into two parts: one east of the 100th meridian where rainfall averages more than 20 inches a year, and the other west of that line where rainfall averages less. East of this meridian agriculture is reasonably safe; there is rarely a drought lasting an entire season or covering any large area. West of it the average is less than sufficient. There are seasons when rainfall there is adequate for corn or wheat but these may be followed by seasons when droughts destroy crops, and winds whip up the dry pulverized soil, destroy the land, and sometimes drive the inhabitants out of the area. Lack of adequate rainfall on the Great Plains is the essential factor in the economic history of that region and an important influence in understanding our national policy in currency, banking, transportation, and other fields of economics.[7]

Adaptability of Europeans to American climate and conditions seems well established. Observations which have been made on groups of both Teutons

[6] Interesting graphs showing the correlation between physical environment, on the one hand, and wealth, occupations, income, intelligence, education, etc., on the other hand, are given by Huntington in Jerome Davis and H. E. Barnes (eds.), *An Introduction to Sociology* (1931), Book II, pp. 191–304.

[7] Interesting data on the importance of rainfall can be found in J. R. Smith and M. O. Phillips, *op. cit.,* pp. 7–8 and chap. 23. How rainfall delimits the corn belt is noted in O. E. Baker, *Economic Geography* (1925), p. 499; and in J. R. Smith and M. O. Phillips, *op. cit.,* p. 366 n.

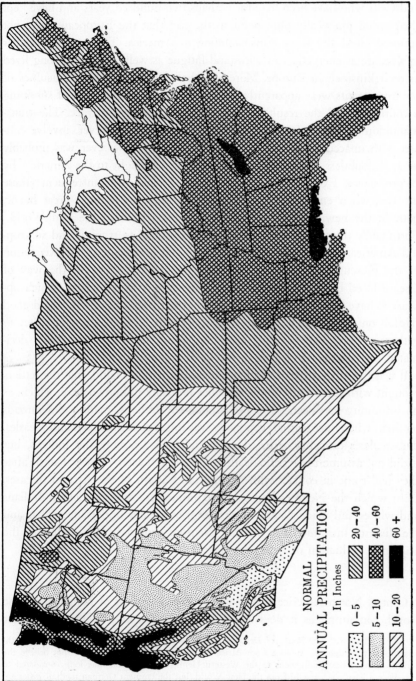

NORMAL
ANNUAL PRECIPITATION
In Inches

20 − 40

40 − 60

60 +

0 − 5

5 − 10

10 − 20

(From H. H. McCarty, *The Geographic Basis of American Economic Life*, Harper & Brothers.)

and Celts who have been here for perhaps two hundred years and have kept
their strain practically pure point to the fact that the Europeans have not
suffered physically from transplantation to America. They are no smaller
in size, are as energetic, can withstand fatigue as well, and are as long lived
as their kinsmen in Europe. Moreover, the energy and creative faculties of
the immigrants were apparently challenged by the mighty task of subduing
a continent, and the result was a sturdy and resourceful race. The transplantation of European civilization to America did, however, involve contact with unaccustomed diseases. To Europeans yellow fever was probably
new; it doubtless originated in Africa and was brought to the Americas by
Negro slaves. Except in southern Europe, malaria was infrequent; these
diseases, when encountered by colonists in America, created great havoc,
both in the new settlements and when carried back to the Old World.[8]
Fortunately these pestilences were largely confined to tropical and subtropical America, and they did not in the long run greatly delay the occupation
of the present United States. Probably the greatest curse in the way of
disease faced by the white settlers in this country was malaria, which appears to have been the most persistent frontier disease. Level lands and good
rainfall on the Atlantic and Gulf coastal plains allowed stagnant water to
gather and provided breeding spots for mosquitos; the disease often decimated early settlers and kept them out of certain sections.

It was the misfortune of the aborigines, on the other hand, that the settlers
brought with them Old World maladies probably unknown here, which, as
no immunity had been developed among the Indians, made rapid inroads
on them when once started. Especially was this true of smallpox and measles.
Tuberculosis probably occurred in sporadic cases among the Indians, but
it did not assume the terrific death-dealing role it later possessed until after
they had come in contact with civilization. Certain of the African diseases,
from which the Negroes had achieved immunity, devastated both Indians
and whites and made Negro slavery seem of greater importance. That and
the diseases introduced by African Negroes should be considered in the
economic evaluation of American slavery.

SOIL

Central North America is perhaps the choicest block of homeland in the
world, containing as it does arable soil, minerals, and facilities for water

---

[8] P. M. Ashburn, *The Ranks of Death,* pp. 99–140. Hookworm, that scourge of the South,
was probably brought to America from Africa by slaves; present authorities do not believe the
parasite to have been indigenous to the Western Hemisphere. Syphilis was long considered to
have been a legacy to the Old from the New World, but the eminent German medical historian,
Karl Sudhoff (followed by Ashburn), concluded from his researches that sporadic cases had
existed in Europe and Asia from remote antiquity. Syphilis did, however, appear in greatly increased and aggravated form in Europe during the fifteenth and sixteenth centuries, giving rise
to the contemporary and subsequent belief that it came from America.

transportation. Only 40 per cent of the land is arable, but the different types of soil and divergencies in climate make it possible to raise a variety of crops, and the area is so large that a severe food shortage has never been experienced. The significance of soil texture upon our history has never been fully appreciated by the general historian, but a close correlation between qualities of the soil in a section and its prosperity is clearly discernible to the student. Intensive studies of even small areas, such as Alabama, show a close relationship between soil fertility and the distribution of crops, prosperity, races, and culture.[9] The Connecticut Valley, with its many colleges, its old publishing concerns, its famous newspapers, and its prosperous towns and villages, is also the most fertile strip of land in New England.

Economic history, in fact, might most logically commence with a study of the formation of soils and the varying resulting textures.[10] In North America particularly, such a study should include some reference to the glacial activity which occurred thousands of years before the white man came to America. Time and again glaciers a mile or more thick covered the northern part of the continent, affecting the future of mankind in both beneficent and detrimental ways. As the glaciers moved southward they leveled off ancient mountains, filled valleys with debris, scooped out the Great Lakes and thousands of others, turned the course of rivers, and scraped off the surface soil leaving bare rocks and pastures strewn with boulders in some places and in others rich deposits to form the basis for future agriculture. Six times continental ice sheets advanced and retreated across the corn belt, mixing the subsoil with the surface soil and producing those rich limestone areas where agricultural productivity reaches its highest development. In other places they left swamps or sandy outwash plains indicating terminal moraines. The continental ice sheets at one time or another covered New England, the Lake states, most of North Dakota, and parts of Montana.[11] Certain regions of Wisconsin, Minnesota, Iowa, and Illinois were not covered by these glaciers, and a comparison of the civilization in the glaciated regions with that in the "driftless area" established a connection between geologic history and economic and cultural development which the student of history should carefully consider. Destroyer and creator, glacial action of bygone millenniums is still a potent factor in human lives.

INFLUENCE OF NATIVE PRODUCTS ON THE EARLIER SETTLERS

One of the great influences upon our history, next to topography, natural routes of travel, and climate, is the part played by the character and distribu-

---

[9] E. Huntington and F. E. Williams, *Business Geography,* chap. 5.

[10] An excellent introduction to the story of how the interaction of plants, wind, water, and weathered rocks produced various types of soil is given in C. E. Kellogg, *The Soils That Support Us* (1941). See also, F. A. Shannon, *The Farmer's Last Frontier,* chap. 1.

[11] For maps, see Kellogg, *op. cit.,* p. 28, and Shannon, *op. cit.,* pp. 10 and 12.

tion of the vegetable products. Presence or absence of forests, fertility and adaptability of the soil, and similar factors have determined both where the settler would erect his cabin and by what method he would support himself. The great variation in climate and soil has made it possible to raise in some part of our country practically every food product of importance, whether native or imported. In fact, the majority of plants of great economic value today have been of foreign origin.

The most pressing immediate need of the colonists was food. Even where the motive for colonization was the discovery of gold and silver, the practical question of keeping alive until the precious metals could be found intruded at once. Apparently it cost the Jamestown settlers years of suffering and the loss of many lives before they realized that the food supply should be their first concern. Lack of sufficient and proper nourishment was the greatest cause of the heavy mortality of the early years in Virginia, a fact that seems almost inexplicable when we consider the richness of the native food resources. The forests held an abundance of deer and other edible animals; the woods, bays, and marshes were plentifully supplied with every variety of wild fowl known to Englishmen; fish, both salt-water and fresh, were everywhere abundant. In the midst of such plenty the "starving time" in Virginia must be accounted for not by any scarcity of native food but by the ignorance of the settlers as to how to gather and utilize the native products (for many of them were neither hunters, fishermen, nor farmers) and by their neglect of the cultivation of food crops—a neglect due to the hope of quick riches by other means.

Wood is vital to man's existence, especially in a primitive civilization, where it provides shelter, fuel, means of conveyance on land and water, and even a considerable element of food. The early comers to the Atlantic seaboard found it thickly wooded; not an unmixed blessing, since land must be cleared of trees and underbrush before it can be made suitable for most agricultural uses. Far from unimportant was the forest as a source of food. The maple furnished sugar—in many cases the only sweetening except honey that was available. Beech, hazel, and hickory nuts, chestnuts, walnuts, and butternuts were found here. Most of the varieties of fruit trees have been imported, but the wild plum, cherry, persimmon, and mulberry were native to some parts of the Atlantic seaboard.

Among the edible plants, either growing in a wild state or cultivated by the Indians when white settlers arrived, were maize, or Indian corn, pumpkins (or pompions, as they were called at first), squash, beans, rice, tomatoes, peanuts, Jerusalem artichoke, peppers, American aloe, sweet potatoes, watermelons, huckleberries, blackberries, strawberries, black raspberries, cranberries, gooseberries, and grapes. Vegetables and food-bearing plants of all kinds were imported, some of them entirely foreign and others European varieties of products native to America.[12]

To the Indian and early settler the animal life of the continent was of vast importance. Besides being a constant and oftentimes chief source of food supply, it furnished materials for clothing, shelter, and other necessities. Of the native animals, probably the most valuable to the aborigines were the deer east of the Mississippi and the buffalo which swarmed the great western plains, neither of which have any present economic significance. After the white settler appeared and the fur trade commenced, the smaller animals, such as the weasel, sable, badger, skunk, wolverine, mink, otter, and sea otter, became important. There was a demand also for such fur-bearing rodents as the squirrel, hare, muskrat, and beaver. With the exception of the llama and the alpaca, which were used locally in South America as beasts of burden, and the dog, the American Indian never succeeded in domesticating any of the native fauna. Almost from the beginning, however, such common farm animals as horses, cattle, sheep, and swine were imported; the climate was found suitable for European livestock, and the vast grazing areas and easily grown food supported a rapid increase in numbers. Poultry of all kinds was introduced from Europe, and one variety of the innumerable wild fowl frequenting the American woods, the wild turkey, was taken to Europe, domesticated, and later brought back. The turkey was the one American contribution to domestic poultry, but the original native wild turkeys were in reality much larger than the barnyard product today, weighing as they did thirty or forty pounds. Such splendid birds sold for a shilling apiece, and so ruthless was their destruction that within a century after the settlement of America they had practically disappeared from the settled areas of the country.

The New World could furnish fish not only for the settlers but for all Europe. In his *New England Rarities* (1672) Josselyn enumerated over two hundred kinds of fish that were caught in New England's waters; Gosnold records that his ships in 1602 were "pestered with cod." Not only the ocean and bays, but the rivers, lakes, and brooks teemed with fish; often they were struck and killed with a stick and scooped up in frying pans. Besides their value as food and export, fish had worth to the early settler as fertilizer. As a consequence the fisheries were destined to assume a place of economic importance in the commercial life of New England.

GEOGRAPHIC INFLUENCE UPON OCCUPATIONS

In addition to the favorable elements for easy and rapid colonization produced by rivers, harbors, and a long indented coast line, there should be

[12] Lyman Carrier, *The Beginning of Agriculture in America*, p. 41.

noted especially the part played by the two greatest plants which America gave to the world—maize and tobacco. Maize yielded twice as much food per acre as the smaller grains, was less dependent upon seasons, could be cultivated without plowing and with the crudest implements, and was grown with a minimum of labor. It provided a new and cheaper source of food, and the stalks furnished a more valuable forage than those of other grains. This plant largely helped to fix the early settlements in North America. Although the tobacco plant did not aid settlement in the same sense as did Indian corn, the fact that it soon furnished the basis of wealth to a large part of the country must be considered among the factors which contributed to the rapid transplanting of the European race.

In later years our history was influenced by the climatic adaptability of certain regions to certain products. Thus the southern states were found suitable for cotton culture, and that plant became, after the invention of the cotton gin, the great southern staple. It fastened slavery on the South, and in the train of slavery came many of the developments leading to the Civil War. The fertility and climate of the upper Mississippi Valley made it ideal for the cultivation of corn, and hastened settlement. Where mineral resources were at hand, economic life turned to them, so that in the Wyoming Valley of Pennsylvania, in the Rockies, and in the oil fields whole communities have been built up around the extraction of minerals.

The harbors and rivers along the eastern coast not only fostered colonization but gave a turn to the occupation of the people. The barren soil of New England turned the settler's interest toward an easier means of livelihood than farming, and the nearby fishing made of the colonial and nineteenth-century New Englander a follower of the sea. New England became the center of colonial shipping and retained that position in later years during the heyday of the American merchant marine. With the passing of shipping as their leading industry, New Englanders turned to the abundant water power and found an outlet for their energies and a source of wealth in manufacturing. In the central Atlantic states, where fertile farm lands were combined with good harbors, rivers, and water power, the activities of the people were more diversified and spread over the major occupations.

One more section may be used to illustrate the effect of environment upon occupation. The first settlers in the Old Northwest (Ohio, Indiana, Illinois, Michigan, and Wisconsin) were chiefly farmers. The rest were rivermen, merchants, or others who took care of the needs of the farmers. Since much of the soil is fertile and particularly favorable to the growing of corn, large areas remain today an important part of our agricultural domain. The Old Northwest, however, had other wealth besides fertile soil. All the states in this region have soft coal. Oil, gas, and clay in Ohio, limestone in Indiana, and other valuable minerals are scattered through this section. With such wealth, it was not long before part of the people turned to mining and to the manufacture of products depending on minerals. Eastern Ohio and the region bordering on Lakes Erie, Huron, and Superior have become one of

(From H. U. Faulkner, Tyler Kepner, and E. H. Merrill, *History of the American Way,* McGraw-Hill.)

the great manufacturing centers of the nation. At Youngstown and Cleveland, Ohio, at Gary, Indiana, at Chicago, Illinois, and in many other cities, great smelting plants turn iron into steel and other factories manufacture the steel into a thousand different commodities. In this region, with Detroit as the center, are produced almost all the American automobiles, and at Akron, Ohio, the rubber used in them is processed. The region is also important in processing agricultural products, particularly Chicago, the great meat-packing center of the world.

VARIETY OF PRESENT RESOURCES

Geographic influences are as powerful today as they have been in our past history. Furthermore, the present natural products of the country and the undeveloped resources will determine to a large extent our future in the political as well as the economic field. Let us examine briefly the natural products and resources of the United States.

In the variety of natural resources this country is rich beyond any European nation. Where most countries have two or three such assets, the United States leads the world in many. Her size and the variations of climate and physiographic factors endow her with a rich variety of natural products, animal, vegetable, and mineral. Britain, for example, has sufficient coal and iron for her needs, but her economic activities necessitate the importation of grains, meats, leather, cotton, certain minerals, including oil, and many other commodities essential to her industries and to the maintenance of life in her population. Italy and Norway have water power and foodstuffs, but must import iron and coal. France, although her resources and climate are varied, cannot supply her own needs in many essential products, such as petroleum, copper, and raw cotton.

The United States, on the other hand, with the exception of several minerals, such as chrome and tin, of relatively minor importance, and of natural rubber, and coffee, produced in the 1920's most products necessary for her own consumption and manufacture, and much to export. Food necessities of all kinds she has in abundance, enough to support a much larger population than her own, as was shown during the two world wars and as could be increasingly demonstrated were more intensive methods of cultivation profitable. The United States exports food to many parts of the world, and although she imports various foods, such as coffee, tea, sugar, spices, and tropical fruits, such imports are luxuries rather than absolute necessities. During the boom period of the late twenties we produced about 70 per cent of the world's oil, nearly 50 per cent of the copper, 38 per cent of the lead, 42 per cent of the zinc, 42 per cent of the coal, 46 per cent of the iron, 54 per cent of the cotton, and 62 per cent of the corn; we possessed 36 per cent of the developed horsepower of the world; yet the continental United States had only about 6 per cent of the world's population and land area.[13]

[13] *Commerce Yearbook, 1930*, Vol. II, Part II, "Comparative World Statistics." Percentages compiled from averages over several years, mostly 1925–1929. The United States leads all other countries in the world in the production of oats, barley, tobacco, and hogs, as well as in all the commodities mentioned above. These percentages, of course, vary with different years and differing economic conditions. During the depression years they dropped considerably. In 1936,

FOREST RESOURCES

At the present time the United States, with its 434,000,000 acres of forest, produces and uses one-half of the sawn lumber manufactured in the world. The forest belt of the American continent covers roughly the region east of a line drawn from the western shore of Hudson Bay south to Texas, a large area in the highest regions of the Rocky Mountains, and the Pacific forest in the Sierra Nevada and the coast ranges. For convenience in classifying the products, the timbered areas may be divided roughly as follows: (1) The Northeast has as its most important species the conifers, or soft woods, including white pine, spruce, and hemlock, although the various hard woods such as hickory, oak, and maple are found here also. (2) The South has four general types, varying with the altitude: cypress and hard woods in the swamps and lower sections of the river valleys of the Atlantic and Gulf states; yellow pine in the rest of the coastal plain from Virginia to Texas; hard woods on the lower slopes of the Appalachians; and conifers higher up in the mountains. (3) The Great Lake region contains, in the southern part, considerable hard wood; in the northern section pine, tamarack, cedar, and hemlock predominate. (4) The Rocky Mountain division is chiefly noted for the western yellow and lodgepole pines. (5) The Pacific coast produces soft woods; there is an abundance of Douglas fir, hemlock, pine, cedar, and redwood. The most important, the Douglas fir, attains its best development in the Puget Sound region, where it reaches a height of from two to three hundred feet.

Because of the enormous waste in clearing the land and the destruction of large areas by forest fires, the lumber industry has ceased to be important in most of these regions and has been continually shifting. The northeastern states, which seventy-five years ago produced more than one-half of all the lumber, now contribute less than one-tenth of the whole. Likewise, the pine forests of Michigan and Wisconsin, states which in the late 1880's produced over two-thirds of the lumber, have rapidly declined. The Pacific states have long been the largest producers, with the southern states ranking second. Most of the lumber comes from Oregon, Washington, North Carolina, Alabama, and Mississippi. The chief hard woods are oak, yellow poplar, red gum, and maple. The soft woods comprise over three-fourths of the total production, with Douglas fir, yellow pine, ponderosa pine, and hemlock valued in the order named. It is estimated that originally the American forests covered 822,000,000 acres, with a stand of marketable saw timber of

---

for example, the United States produced about 61 per cent of the world's oil, 23 per cent of the copper, 24 per cent of the lead, 40 per cent of the coal, 34 per cent of the pig iron, 30 per cent of the zinc, 41 per cent of the cotton, and 51 per cent of the corn.

5,200,000,000,000 square feet; by the early 1920's this had been reduced to 461,000,000 acres with a stand of 2,215,000,000,000 square feet. "Stated in other fashion," says R. S. Kellogg, "nearly 60 per cent of the merchantable saw timber of the United States has been utilized or destroyed, and the bulk of it has gone in the past fifty years."[14] There is much less today. Conservative estimates suggest that we are consuming wood almost twice as rapidly as it is being replaced by natural growth, and it is obvious that unless strenuous and far-reaching methods are adopted to insure replacement the United States will be dependent upon imports for a large proportion of her supply. American production reached its maximum in 1909, when 44,000,000,000 board feet were produced; this had declined to 38,000,000,000 in 1950, and we are now importing large amounts from Canada.

The lumber supply of the future is dependent not alone upon replacement through scientific forestry but also upon the careful conservation of the remaining forests. Although three-fourths of the forest area is now given some kind of protection, the losses from fire are still great. In the decade that ended in 1950 more than 1,824,000 forest fires occurred in the United States, or an average of 500 a day. They burned over an average of 21,622,000 acres each year. Better protection has brought some decline in fires in recent years. Preservation of wood also rests in part upon less wasteful methods of cutting and marketing. Much less than half of the wood taken from the forests reaches the retailer in marketable form.

AGRICULTURAL RESOURCES

Although the value of manufactured goods surpasses that of agricultural, agriculture continues to be a basic industry of the United States. Its products are the basis upon which many of our most important industries are built, and one-eighth of the labor force of the country is still employed in it. The leading crops in value in 1951 were corn, cotton, hay, wheat, tobacco, oats, and potatoes. Of vegetable foodstuffs, cereals are the most important, and of these maize, or Indian corn, takes first place. In 1946 the yield was over 3,000,000,000 bushels—in that year over 90 per cent of the world's crop. Corn is grown extensively in the cotton belt of the South, but three-fourths of our supply is raised in the so-called "corn belt" of the upper Mississippi Valley, which includes the states of Kansas, Nebraska, Illinois, Iowa, Ohio, Indiana, and Missouri. Here are to be found the ideal conditions for its growth—heavy rains which alternate with much sunshine, and a soil which is drained easily and does not cake.

Wheat in the United States has only about half the acreage of corn and a valuation of less than half, but its position as one of the chief foods of man-

[14] R. S. Kellogg, *Pulpwood and Wood Pulp in America* (1923), p. 148.

kind makes it in some respects more important than corn. Introduced from the Old World by the earliest settlers, it has spread so widely that for some years prior to 1930 we led in its production.[15] In 1915, under the impetus of war needs, the production mounted to over a billion bushels, the largest yield in our history up to that time, but, like corn, the production fell off until World War II increased it again. Whereas about four-fifths of the corn produced is consumed on the farm and only about one-fifth is offered for sale, almost all of the wheat is sold and converted into flour. Wheat is grown in forty states, but the leading states in 1951 were North Dakota and Kansas. Although these states lead in total production, the yield per acre in Washington is sometimes almost double.

The United States has led the world not only in the production of corn and wheat but also in that of oats and barley. The annual production of oats is over 1,300,000,000 bushels, about three-fourths of which comes from the North Central States. These states also produce about three-fifths of the barley and three-fourths of the rye.

Among the crops used for human foods which are grown in the United States should be mentioned rice and sugar, white and sweet potatoes. The center of American rice production is Louisiana, where it is grown mainly by irrigation, but a considerable amount is also produced in Texas, Arkansas, and California. Practically all of the cane sugar produced in the United States comes from Louisiana, but it furnishes only a small fraction of the sugar used in this country, most of which is imported from Cuba, Puerto Rico, Hawaii, and the Philippines. The cultivation of sugar beets, however, has increased rapidly during the last few years.[16] Cultivation of white potatoes, the value of which in 1951 was over $497,000,000, is carried on in every state of the Union, but conditions are more favorable in the northern and northeastern sections. Sweet potatoes are grown extensively in the southern states.

In spite of the rapid substitution of motor power for animal power, the production of hay, curiously enough, was 15,000,000 tons greater in 1939 than in 1919. This may be explained by the fact that more hay is fed per animal unit, that a reduction in other farm crops usually results in greater hay production, and that more legume hay is being raised to improve the land by crop rotation.[17] In 1939 the value of the hay crop was second only to that of corn; in 1951 it was third, with at least 15 per cent of the improved farm land given over to its production.

Ranking second in value among American crops (1951), but the greatest of all crops in the South and still the greatest single item of export, is cotton. In

---

[15] Recent figures on production of wheat in Russia show that country as the leader after 1930.
[16] The United States produces about one-tenth of the world's sugar beets, ranking third among the nations in this crop.
[17] *Yearbook of Agriculture, 1930,* pp. 308–310.

1951 the cotton yield was 15,290,000 bales, valued at over $2,878,000,000. This approximated nearly three-fifths of the world's crop, British India and Egypt ranking second and third, respectively. The cotton belt lies in a strip 1450 miles long and 500 miles wide, south of the 37th parallel, including all the southern states from North Carolina to Texas and California. About twenty-three million acres were given over to this staple in 1939. A superior type, known as Sea Island cotton, but representing in amount only about one per cent of the total product, is grown on the sea islands of South Carolina and the interior counties of Georgia and Florida. Before the First World War almost two-thirds of the cotton crop was exported, but now we are using nearly half of it at home.

Tobacco is grown east of the Mississippi in seventeen or more states, mainly in the eastern coastal plain, the Appalachian region, and the Mississippi Valley plains. The total product in 1951 was over 2,282,000,000 pounds, and the chief centers of production were in North Carolina, Kentucky, and South Carolina. Tobacco now ranks only fifth in value among the agricultural crops of the United States, although this country leads the world in its production and (including the crops of the insular possessions) furnishes about one-quarter of the world's crop. About three-fifths of the domestic growth is consumed here.

The great importance of the native animal life on this continent to the early settlers and pioneers has been mentioned. Possessing as it does the necessary requisites of temperate climate and immense pasturage areas, this country was destined to take its place as a leading source of animal products. It ranks first in the number of swine produced, second in cattle, and third in sheep. The best grazing lands for cattle are in the Great Plains and the Rocky Mountain tablelands and their eastern slopes. The centers for milk production, however, are near the great cities, with Wisconsin, New York, California, and Pennsylvania as the leading states for dairy products. The swine country is, with the exception of Texas, identical with the region of the greatest corn production. While sheep are to be found in every state in the Union, the chief wool centers are Texas and the far-western states. The most important horse and mule markets are East St. Louis and Kansas City, both in the center of the horse-raising area. Mules are more numerous than horses in the southern states, because they can better endure the hot climate and hard usage. Owing to the fact that corn is the best cereal for fattening poultry, the center of the poultry industry is in the North Central States, from which comes over one-half of the billion-dollar annual yield of eggs and chickens.

Although the resources of the sea do not play as important a part in our economic life as they did in the colonial and early national period, they still provide a livelihood for some 157,000 wage earners, and foodstuffs valued at around $365,000,000 annually (1950). The United States and Alaska still lead the world in this industry. The western Atlantic from Newfoundland to the Chesapeake is one of the two most important fishing areas in the world. The haddock, mackerel, cod, herring, halibut, tuna, and oysters on the Atlantic coast supply in value about half of the annual haul of the United States, including Alaska. The salmon fishing of Alaska and

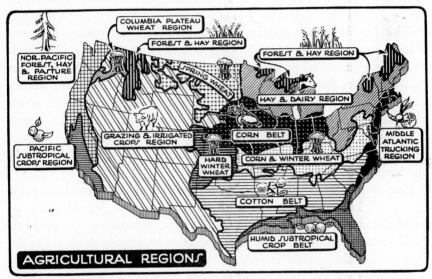

(From H. U. Faulkner, Tyler Kepner, and Hall Bartlett, *The American Way of Life,* Harper & Brothers.)

the west coast is the most important phase of this industry on the Pacific coast, the fisheries of which yield a catch worth annually $39,300,000 (1949). The Great Lakes supply herring, whitefish, trout, yellow perch, and many other varieties valued annually at about $11,458,000 (1949).

As in the case of lumber and certain other resources, the fishing industry has been characterized by tragic waste and disregard of the future. This is particularly true of the salmon fishing on the west coast, where methods based upon momentary profits have reduced the haul and driven the fish farther and farther north.

MINERAL RESOURCES

In 1860 the value of the products of the mines and quarries (metallic and nonmetallic) of the United States was placed at $90,000,000; in 1949 it had increased to $10,580,000,000. Of all the minerals, metallic or nonmetallic, petroleum ranks first (1949) with a value of $4,674,000,000 or about two-fifths of the total valuation for all minerals. Although oil was produced originally to satisfy lighting needs, its field of usefulness has been widened until by distillation and other processes such commercial products as kerosene, benzine, gasoline, naphtha, heavy and lubricating oils, paraffin, and asphalt are manufactured. With the continued extension of the manufacture of gasoline motors and oil-burning engines, the value of petroleum in industry has constantly increased. Oil was first discovered in the Appalachian area, extending from New York to Tennessee, and originally most of the oil came from this region. It is found in many places, but the three chief fields today are (1) the mid-continent regions, including western Missouri, Kansas, and Oklahoma; (2) the California field, and (3) the Gulf field, comprising the coastal plains of Texas and Louisiana. Although the United States produces about one-half of the world's output, large amounts are imported from Venezuela and elsewhere. The tremendous speed with which this country is consuming its oil resources has led certain geologists to sound frequent warnings and to predict that the peak of production has been reached. Fortunately new and important sources have been opened up in the Near East since the last war.

Next to petroleum, coal is the most important of the minerals in point of value.[18] The anthracite deposits of the United States, located chiefly in northeastern Pennsylvania, are by far the most important in the world in both quality and quantity. The most important bituminous fields are in the Appalachian Mountains, extending from Alabama to Pennsylvania, but rich deposits are also to be found in many states of the Mississippi Valley and elsewhere. The aggregate coal areas of this country approximate 500,000 square miles, or about 13 per cent of its area.[19] The fact that these beds are well distributed is significant, for the expense of transportation of this essential commodity to industrial and commercial development is a big item in its ultimate cost. Also important is the fact that the richest deposits are within a few hours' haul of the great ports of New York and Philadelphia, and but a little farther from the manufacturing states of southern New England. If this had not been the case, the history of the northeastern United States after the Industrial Revolution might have been different. Moreover, the large deposits of coal in the Old Northwest have contributed greatly to make that area a great manufacturing center. On the other hand, it is extremely unfortunate that the production and use of this basic mineral are accom-

[18] The anthracite production in 1949 was valued at $344,000,000 and bituminous at $2,126,-000,000.

[19] To these fuel resources the future historian will add the present peat swamps as yet almost wholly neglected; of these there are seven million acres in Minnesota alone. See E. K. Soper, *The Peat Deposits of Minnesota*, Bulletin 16, Minnesota Geological Survey (1919).

panied by so much waste,[20] and that the industry, especially since the expansion of mine capacity between the two world wars, has been harassed by overproduction and by a chaotic labor market. A world-wide decrease in the demand for coal has been occasioned chiefly by the substitution of oil and gas for coal, by the development of hydroelectric power, and by technical improvements in converting coal into steam and electric power. The coal industry has been slow to adapt itself to all these changes; it has been a classic example of unscientific production. Nevertheless, man-hour output in bituminous coal mining has increased more than 50 per cent in the last quarter-century. And this, despite the relatively small amount spent in research.

Next to coal and petroleum, the most valuable nonmetallic products of the mines are cement and natural gas. The value of the latter in 1950 was estimated at about $408,500,000. Little used before 1870 except for lighting purposes, and allowed to go to waste in large quantities, it has since come to be recognized as ideal for heat and power and is now conserved as fully as conditions permit. Production has more than doubled since 1922, but here again some geologists predict exhaustion before many years. Only one-fifth is used for domestic light and heat; the remainder is used in industry. A notable development has been the invention of a process whereby gasoline may be extracted from the natural gas without injuring its utility for heating purposes.

The most valuable, most widely distributed, and cheapest of the metals in the United States is iron. It is also the most important material used for machinery, tools, buildings, and other materials of industry which play so vast a part in an age of iron and steel. Iron is found in practically every state, but the great bulk of the ore produced comes from the Lake Superior district, including Minnesota, Michigan, and Wisconsin; the only other important source is the Birmingham region of Alabama and Tennessee. The Lake Superior region not only contributes almost nine-tenths of the iron ore but contains at least three-fourths of the available deposits. The ore is, moreover, of distinctly superior grade to that of the Appalachians and Rockies. The advantageous situation of Pittsburgh and Birmingham as regards both coal and iron gave them a start in the iron and steel industry, but the eventual predominance of the Lake Superior ores created a tendency for the manufacturing center of the iron and steel industry to shift to such Lake shore points as Buffalo, Cleveland, Chicago, and Gary. The United

[20] It is estimated that only about 50 per cent of the bituminous coal is actually extracted from the mine, while another 10 per cent is lost in preparation and marketing. This says nothing of the waste in consumption. It should be noted, however, that the maximum recovery in coal is far below 100 per cent.

States is particularly fortunate with regard to this metal, for her known iron resources appear to be nearly equal to those of all the rest of the world. But the Superior ores are being depleted, and the United States is already importing iron from Venezuela, Canada, and elsewhere. Moreover, certain alloys of iron of growing significance in our industrial life—manganese, nickel, vanadium, chrome, tungsten, and the like—are found here in small quantities or not at all.

Copper preceded iron in its use in primitive times. This metal is so ductile and easily worked that the ancient world became exceedingly proficient in turning it to a variety of uses. Since the harnessing of electricity for man's use, and the invention of the telegraph and telephone, copper, because of its excellent properties as a conductor, has assumed a new importance. Its use is also widened by the fact that when combined with zinc it forms brass, and combined with tin it makes bronze. Improvements in extracting the metal, and the greater demands for it, have made possible the increase of the world's annual output from 9000 tons in 1801 to about 2,350,000 in 1951. Of this the United States contributes about one-third,[21] the states of Arizona, Utah, New Mexico, and Montana producing almost three-fourths of the whole. The annual copper output of Arizona alone exceeds that of any foreign nation. The purest deposits in the country are in the glacial districts of upper Michigan, but the greatest are in Arizona, which supplies over one-third of the American copper. The deposits in Montana, Nevada, and Utah have made possible the cities of Butte and Anaconda in Montana, Bingham in Utah, and the four Arizona towns of Bisbee, Morenci, Globe, and Jerome.

In the production of zinc, a comparatively new industry in this country (our first records of production are of 1873), the United States and Germany rank as the two largest sources of supply. The metal is used chiefly as an alloy of copper and tin, in paints, and also for galvanizing iron and steel to protect them from rust. Although twenty states mine zinc-bearing ores, over two-fifths come from the region known as the Joplin, comprising southwestern Missouri, southeastern Kansas, and northeastern Oklahoma.[22]

Lead is another metal in whose production the United States leads, supplying over one-third of the world's total. Twenty-one states and Alaska produce it, but the output of most of them is small. Missouri, Idaho, Utah, and Colorado yield three-fourths of the smelter production of lead. Advancing industrialization has increased the use of lead in its pure form and in its numerous alloys, and, like most metals, its production was greatly stimulated by the First and Second World Wars. One-third of the lead in times of

[21] The United States is not only the leading producer of copper but also the leading refiner, importing as she does much copper ore from other nations for refining. Chile, exporting chiefly to the United States, is the second largest producer of copper ore.

[22] The production of zinc in 1950 was 623,000 short tons valued at about $179,000,000.

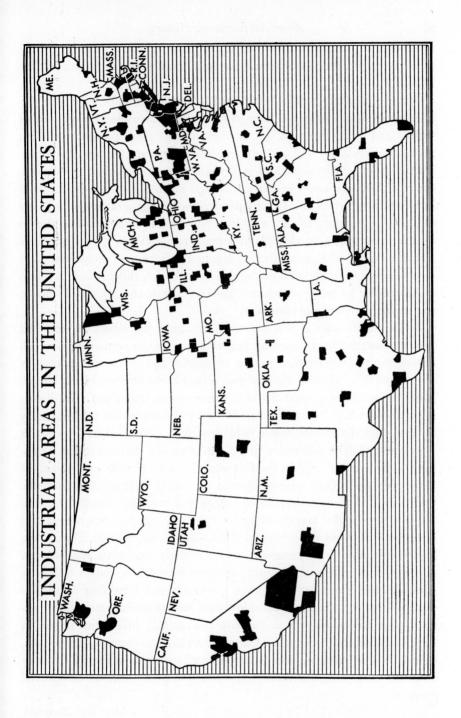

INDUSTRIAL AREAS IN THE UNITED STATES

peace goes into white lead for paint. Like other industrial minerals, the increase in its production has been spectacular, from 15,600 short tons in 1860 to 430,678 in 1950.

Of the remaining metals, aluminum has become the most important. Because of its firm texture and strength, but at the same time its lightness of weight and non-rusting quality, it is superior to other metals for certain purposes, particularly for cooking utensils and airplanes. Bauxite, the principal ore from which aluminum is derived, is mined chiefly in Arkansas, Georgia, Alabama, and Tennessee, although much of it in normal times is imported from British and Dutch Guiana. The bauxite is often shipped long distances to be processed into a whitish powder called alumina and this in turn is shipped to reduction plants located where electric power is cheap. The production of bauxite and its eventual reduction to aluminum have increased tremendously with the Second World War; this advance has been made possible by new hydroelectric power developments on the Tennessee and Columbia rivers and elsewhere.

Of less significance in our industrial life, gold and silver, the so-called "precious metals," have played an important part in our economic and social history in promoting the migration of peoples and the founding of new commonwealths.[23] Before 1848 the gold mined in the territory of the United States was not large (a total of 1,187,170 fine ounces, 1792–1847). The discovery of deposits in California in 1848, however, quadrupled the world's supply by 1852, and the United States held first place until surpassed by South Africa in 1898. The production in California rapidly declined in the sixties, but the discovery of gold in the Comstock Lode in Nevada in 1859 helped to keep up the nation's supply. During the height of production from the Comstock Lode (1859–1869) the annual output averaged almost three million fine ounces; this average declined in the seventies and was not reached again until the gold discoveries in Alaska in the late nineties. During the first two decades of the present century the yearly production was between three and four million fine ounces, declining thereafter to only a little over two million in 1929. Artificial prices imposed by the New Deal legislation during the period of currency manipulation have sufficiently stimulated production to push it upwards to over five and one-half million fine ounces in 1939. The chief sources of gold in this country are now South Dakota, Utah, California, and Nevada. About two-thirds of the metal is used for money or to maintain value for money; the rest is used for various commercial purposes.

Silver production had its great spurt in this country after the discovery of the Comstock Lode. Although the commercial needs for silver have, of

[23] Below, chaps. 10, 18.

course, increased, its decline as a monetary medium after the nineties caused its price to fall steadily. The production of silver was about 503,000 fine ounces for the decade 1850 to 1860; during the 1920's yearly production ranged from 53,000,000 to 73,000,000. As in the case of gold, the government placed artificially high prices on silver and thus stimulated production in the late thirties.[24] Silver for all practical purposes is no longer a precious metal. If it were not for the fact that Senators from seven silver states sit in Congress to protect the price and future of this relatively unimportant mineral, the price would be less and its economic usefulness in industry much greater, to the benefit of the nation.

WATER RESOURCES

The importance of water in our economic history and in our present economic life can scarcely be overestimated. Water is valuable not only as the habitat of fish and certain fur-bearing animals, and as a cheap and convenient highway of commerce, but also as an important supply of power which can be harnessed so as to fill an infinite variety of human needs. Outside of the use of water for power production, it must be remembered that large quantities of water are required in many types of manufacturing, at least 75 per cent for cooling. Over thirteen barrels of water are needed to make one barrel of oil, 65,500 gallons to make one ton of steel, and 67,000 gallons to make one ton of sulfate paper. Water is neither limitless nor inexhaustible and the problems of its conservation will become more pressing as the size of industry and of the population increases.

During the colonial period, rivers were the chief highways of inland commerce and continued so until the coming of railroads. In the early decades of the Industrial Revolution, water supplied the chief motive power for factories,[25] but during the eighties power derived from steam surpassed that from water, and by 1900 over three-fourths of the power used in manufacturing plants came from steam. This was due chiefly to the development of the coal resources which made it possible to locate factories at the most convenient points. The situation has changed greatly, however, during the last five decades. The rapid development of electricity and the inventions which have made possible the transportation of electric power over large areas have encouraged a return to water as a primary power.

Most electricity, however, is not produced by water power, but by coal or gas. Nevertheless, the use of water power for this purpose has grown tremendously. The project of "harnessing Niagara" was undertaken in the late nineties, and the success attained there has encouraged other stupendous

---

[24] Production in 1950 was approximately 42,406,000 ounces valued at $38,380,000.
[25] Below, chap. 13.

projects, until today a network of giant power cables extends over the more thickly settled regions. Hydroelectric development has already gone far, notably in four sections: the North Atlantic, on the Merrimac, Connecticut, and Hudson rivers; the St. Lawrence region, on the Niagara and other rivers, running into the Great Lakes; on the Catawba and other rivers of the Carolina Piedmont; and on the rivers of the north Pacific. Nearly 25,-000,000 horsepower, approximately one-half of the world's developed horsepower, was produced in this country by 1935, but the possibilities of water power are still in their infancy. The great new power projects which have come into operation at Boulder Dam on the Colorado, at Bonneville and Grand Coulee on the Columbia, and at various points on the Tennessee give some indication of the vast possibilities of electric power in this country. Probably less than half of the potential water power has yet been tapped.

A REAPPRAISAL OF NATURAL RESOURCES

No nation in history has been endowed with natural resources as great as those existing in the United States. Most of the important minerals necessary to a great manufacturing nation she has had in abundance. In her fertile valleys and broad plains she can produce foods, of both temperate and semi-tropical varieties, sufficient to support a population much larger than the present. In addition to her sources of power from coal and petroleum she still has vast reserves of water power. For three centuries the United States has comprised an economic world in itself. Today she is not only the most wealthy and prosperous of nations, displaying a higher standard of living than any other, but a country in which the real wages of work—food, fuel, shelter, and clothing—are higher and more abundant than elsewhere.

But the raw-material basis upon which this wealth and prosperity have rested is rapidly changing. The plethora of raw materials has led to wasteful exploitation. Much soil has been ruined, forests have been carelessly destroyed, and minerals have been wasted. The cream has long since been skimmed. Our national economy has already grown up to its resource base; in many important respects it has outgrown it. From a nation with a surplus of raw materials we have shifted to a deficit nation. Once huge exporters of copper, lead, and zinc, we have become the world's largest importers of these metals. Once self-sufficient in iron and petroleum, we now depend on foreign nations for a growing portion of our needs. Today we are partially dependent upon foreign nations for all metals but two—magnesium and molybdenum. From a net exporter of lumber we have become a net importer. A century ago we exported raw materials and foodstuffs; today we import them. In 1820 over 60 per cent of our exports were crude materials, in the late 1940's but 15 per cent; finished manufactured goods amounted to 6 per cent in 1820 and are over 50 per cent today. An opposite change occurred in imports.

What of the future? For decades the normal needs of an increasing population can be met in foodstuffs and in power resources, particularly power furnished by coal and water. Moreover, many industrial needs, particularly those based on agricultural products, can be fulfilled. But even these are dependent upon every method of conservation known to science. The development of synthetic products can also ease the strain on certain raw materials and take care of many demands. As for minerals, including petroleum and iron, the two great hallmarks of early self-sufficiency, we must look elsewhere for at least part of our raw materials. The era of absolute self-sufficiency has ended. The future is one of closer relationship with the rest of the world.

NOTE ON STATISTICS

In any work dealing with economics, wide use must be made of statistics, the nature of which should be better understood. "One of the prime objects of statistics," says W. I. King in his *Elements of Statistical Method* (p. 22), "is to give us a bird's-eye view of a large mass of facts, to simplify this extensive and complex array of isolated instances and reduce it to a form which will be comprehensible to the ordinary mind." To accomplish this, involved mathematics are often used to develop economic formulas and scientific statistics, which then interpret the descriptive statistics compiled by the census and other agencies.

A word should be added as to the accuracy of statistical tables. Absolute accuracy in the material with which we are dealing is probably never possible, but since the aim is better comprehension of an entire field, relative and not absolute accuracy is the main objective. Statistics are estimates rather than exact enumerations. It is impossible, for example, to obtain more than an approximate estimate of the number of bushels of wheat produced. Furthermore, statistics of varying kinds differ greatly in relative reliability. For instance, the number of deaths reported is relatively accurate, as the returns are required by law, but a tabulation of the causes of death may be far from correct. Above all, students should be warned in the use of certain types of financial statistics. Wages, for example, have little meaning unless interpreted in relation to current prices. It should also be kept in mind that the use of round numbers sometimes gives a more accurate impression than the figures carried out, because when attention is directed to the digits the main point being demonstrated may be lost, especially in comparisons.

For a concise account of the manner in which facts for statistical study are collected, see *The Review of Economic Statistics,* Sept., 1920—Jan., 1921. Prefatory sections contain valuable material on methods employed and sources of information. For a clear and not too technical account of the nature of statistics, read Willford I. King, *Elements of Statistical Method* (1913), Parts I and II. Suggestive essays on the function of statistics in economics, history, political science, and sociology by E. R. A. Seligman, H. U. Faulkner, J. A. Fairlie, and W. F. Ogburn, respectively, can be found in W. F. Ogburn and Alexander Goldenweiser (eds.), *The Social Sciences and Their Interrelations* (1927).

Most of the statistical information in this book is obtained from government sources. The federal departments have statistical divisions that compile elaborate reports, and the Bureau of the Census maintains a permanent staff that collects information. A large amount of data is conveniently reprinted in *The Statistical Abstract of the United States,* published annually by the Bureau of the Census of the Department of Commerce. The more important material of interest to historians has been collected by the Bureau of the Census in *Historical Statistics of the United States, 1789–1945* (1949). *The Abstract of the Census of Manufacturers* and *The Abstract of the Census* are less bulky to use than the *Census* and condense the most valuable material of each census.

SELECTED READINGS

McCarty, H. H., *The Geographic Basis of American Economic Life,* chap. 1.
Semple, E. C., and Jones, C. F., *American History and Its Geographic Conditions,* chaps. 1–3.
Hulbert, A. B., *Soil and Its Influence on the History of the United States.*
Kellogg, C. E., *The Soils That Support Us,* chaps. 1–3, 9, 16, 18.
Huntington, E., and Williams, F. E., *Business Geography,* chap. 5.
Smith, J. R., and Phillips, M. O., *North America,* chap. 1.
The President's Materials Policy Commission, *Resources for Freedom,* Vol. I.

CHAPTER 2

ECONOMIC BACKGROUND
OF COLONIZATION

THE RISE OF MERCHANT CAPITALISM

THE discovery of America was brought about by a train of circumstances extending back through centuries of European history and culminating at the end of the fifteenth century. Intellectual, political, and, above all, economic factors contributed to make this a turning point in world history. The fifteenth century and the beginning of the sixteenth marked the height of the Renaissance, a period of inquiry and dissatisfaction with the old order. In political life the modern state was being erected on the ruins of feudalism; with the national state came a cessation of the private warfare of the Middle Ages, greater protection to travelers and merchants, and fewer tolls. More settled conditions encouraged the extension of trade and commerce, and the revived economic life led naturally to exploration and discovery. The latter was aided by the compass and astrolabe, by that time in general use, and by the improvement in the charts and maps; the news of scientific and commercial progress was disseminated by means of the printing press, invented about the middle of the fifteenth century.

Although the influences just mentioned all contributed to the great era of European expansion, particular emphasis should be placed upon the development of merchant capitalism, which transformed feudalism into a capitalist economy and gave a tremendous impetus to colonization and the development of overseas trade. Despite the condemnation of the church, moneylending continued throughout the late Middle Ages. Great private bankers, like the Medici of Florence and the Fuggers of Augsburg, accumulated surpluses as merchants and then turned to moneylending. By the end of the fifteenth century Flemish speculators were operating an exchange at Antwerp where commodities and the shares of joint-stock companies were bought and sold. These merchant princes and bankers helped to finance the struggle of kings against their feudal lords and contributed much to the eventual establishment of the great national states. Above all, this capital accumulation contributed to the development of medieval industry and commerce which formed the immediate background for the discovery of America.

As the chaos of feudal society gave way to national monarchical states, a new impetus was given to the expansion of trade and the development of merchant capitalism. Internally conditions became more stabilized, to the benefit of trade and industry. In need of money to strengthen their position at home and their prestige abroad, the new monarchs encouraged industry within their realms and granted trading monopolies to groups of adventurers willing to risk their fortunes in foreign commerce. The new merchant and trading class was encouraged at the expense of the old nobility. At the same time the Protestant Revolt weakened the prestige of the Catholic Church, which had frowned on interest-taking and excessive profit-making and had emphasized the doctrine of the "just price" with ultimate reward in the world to come.[1] In many ways the foundations were being laid for a great expansion.

TRADE WITH THE EAST

As for the immediate impetus to the discovery of America none was more important than the desire on the part of Europeans to find a quicker and cheaper route to the East. From the dawn of commerce Europe had been dependent upon Asia for most of her luxuries and many of her necessities. The importance of spices in the Middle Ages is difficult to appreciate today, when meat is kept fresh by cold storage or curing; but the monotonous diet and coarse food of those times made spices and condiments so desirable that they were frequently sent as gifts of honor from one sovereign to another. Pepper from the Malabar coast of India was a staple import during the Middle Ages and was used by all who could afford it. Cloves, cinnamon, nutmegs from the Moluccas, and sugar from Arabia and Persia were more expensive and less commonly used, but in great demand. Apothecaries obtained many of their drugs from Asia, among them rhubarb, balsam, gums, aloes, cubebs, and camphor. The precious stones which adorned the persons of the upper classes in Europe came almost exclusively from the East.

Trade with the East, however, was not confined exclusively to such luxuries as spices, drugs, and precious stones. An important class of wares which served manufacturing industries, namely, dyestuffs, found their source there. Indigo was a chief staple of Bagdad, and brazilwood, producing a red dye,

---

[1] R. H. Tawney, *Religion and the Rise of Capitalism* (1926), discusses this aspect in detail.

came from India. Alum, considered indispensable for fixing colors in dyeing and one of the most desirable products of the Levant trade, was procured mainly in Asia Minor. Manufactured products, superior in workmanship, material, and design to anything known in Europe, came also from the East: glass and cutlery from Damascus, Samarkand, and Bagdad; porcelain from China; a great variety of cottons and silks from India, China, Persia, and Asia Minor. Persian rugs, Cashmere shawls, taffeta silk, damask linen, and japanned ware all testify to the Eastern nomenclature and origin of the most sought-after textiles, rugs, tapestries, and household luxuries.

In return for these products Europe could offer only woolen fabrics and such metals and minerals as arsenic, antimony, quicksilver, tin, copper, and lead. Although these products were much valued in the East, their weight and bulk made transportation on the long overland routes an arduous and unrewarded task. Gold and silver, on the other hand, were more easily transported and were consequently used freely to make up the balance. This movement of the precious metals from Europe to Asia was made possible by the fact that the monetary system of Europe in the Middle Ages was not highly developed. The continued movement of gold and silver to Asia, however, undoubtedly caused a scarcity of these metals in Europe, which was not relieved until the opening of mines in Mexico and Peru.

While trade with the Near and the Far East was a leading factor in the economic life of the Middle Ages, little was known by Europeans of Asia or the routes thereto. Trade had flourished in ancient times, but during the barbaric invasions of the fifth century and the succeeding conflicts this commerce had been largely broken up. A general awakening of economic life in the eleventh century set in motion with renewed vigor the intercourse with the East, a movement greatly aided by the Crusades (1095–1270). Not alone did the Crusades enlarge the vision and knowledge of Europeans by introducing them again to the learning and products of Asia, but they laid the foundations for the prosperity of the Italians in this trade. Towns at the extreme south of the Italian peninsula sprang into importance, as did Amalfi on the Bay of Naples, Genoa at the head of the Tyrrhenian Sea, and Venice at the head of the Adriatic.

MEDIEVAL TRADE ROUTES

The products of the East reached Europe over three main trade routes, of which the oldest and most important during the greater part of the Middle Ages was the central passage. Merchandise was gathered from India and the Far East and brought to Ormuz at the mouth of the Persian Gulf, and thence to Bossorah (Bozra) at the mouth of the Tigris, and up the valley to Bagdad. From Bagdad the routes spread like a fan either north to Tabriz, westward to Antioch, Damascus, or Jaffa, or west and then south to Alexandria. The southern route was chiefly a sea route leading from India across the Arabian Sea to the Red Sea. The cargoes in most cases were landed on the western coast and transferred to caravans, which carried them to the Nile, upon which they were floated down to Cairo. This route, although attended by difficulties of navigation, was the cheapest and quickest, and at the close of the Middle Ages the most important. The northern route, which was entirely overland, was in reality a system of routes leading from the inland provinces of China and India to the Caspian and up the Volga to central Russia and the Baltic, or to the Black Sea and thence to Europe.

The terminal points, then, of the eastern trade were such cities as Trebizond on the Black Sea, Constantinople on the Bosphorus, Antioch, Beirut, Tripoli, Laodicea, and Jaffa on the Syrian coast, and Alexandria at the mouth of the Nile. At these cities, and even in such inland points as Damascus and Aleppo, merchants from Spain, France, and Italy met the caravans and purchased what goods had escaped destruction from the elements and confiscation by pirates. The bulk of the Levant trade during the five hundred years from 1000 to 1500 rested in the hands of the Italians, and the three cities of Venice, Genoa, and Pisa struggled for supremacy in this trade, while Florence became a banking and manufacturing center. From the Italian cities the Oriental merchandise was distributed to northern and central Europe through two main channels. German merchants handled the overland reexport trade from Venice and Genoa. Through the St. Gothard Pass to Basel, Constance, Strasbourg, and down the Rhine, or over the Brenner Pass to Munich, Nuremburg, or Frankfort were the usual routes. In addition to the overland passages through the Alps, a large amount of trade was carried on by sea with Lisbon, Bruges, and London. As far as northern Europe was concerned, it was in the Low Countries—at Antwerp, Bruges, Ghent, and other towns—that the lines of medieval commerce finally crossed. Here the goods of the Mediterranean and the Baltic were sent to be distributed later throughout England and France.

THE COMMERCIAL REVOLUTION

Our task so far has been, first, to point out the importance of the Eastern trade[2] to the Europe of the Middle Ages and, second, to show that the center

---

[2] To show that the question of Eastern trade routes is still a vital one it is necessary simply to call attention to the history of the Suez Canal and the attempt of Germany to cut in on this route by means of the Berlin-Bagdad Railway. The importance of this was never lost sight of during the First World War, as the campaigns in Palestine and the Euphrates Valley demonstate. Two decades later Britain's life line was again threatened when Italy, anxious to dominate the Mediterranean, entered the Second World War to break British control of Gibraltar, Egypt, and the Suez Canal.

of European medieval commerce lay in the Mediterranean basin. How this trade center shifted from the Mediterranean to the Atlantic, producing a Commercial Revolution, remains to be shown. The story involves the discovery both of new trade routes to the East and of the American continents.

Of the many factors operative in bringing this about, one stands pre-eminent—the eagerness of Europe for the products of Asia, coupled with the difficulty and expense of obtaining them over the existing trade routes. This made imperative the discovery of quicker and cheaper means of travel to the East. The old explanation that the capture of Constantinople by the Ottoman Turks in 1453 and the extension of their control over Syria and Egypt virtually closed the old trade routes and thus hastened the discovery of new routes is no longer accepted. The routes through Syria and Egypt did not, in fact, come under the control of the Ottoman Turks until a quarter-century after Columbus discovered America. That the Turks raised the fees for foreign merchants and increased tariffs and tolls there can be no doubt, but the trade of Venice and other Italian cities continued to flourish throughout the sixteenth century. Moreover, investigations by Professor Lybyer have shown that there was no serious interference in Eastern trade and no rise in the prices of Eastern commodities in Europe after the Turkish conquests. He contends, on the other hand, that motives "related to religion, crusading, conquest, and adventure probably outweighed the seeking of spices in the minds of the great explorers and their royal supporters," and there is much to be said for this explanation.[3] If the Turkish interference is entirely discounted, there still remain the disadvantages of the old trade routes, which provided an important impetus for the burst of exploring activity in the fifteenth and sixteenth centuries.

Although such Italian travelers as Carpini and the three Polos had added much to the European knowledge of Asia, and the Italian cartographers led in the accuracy of their maps, it was left to the Portuguese to discover the new way to the East. Always a seafaring nation to whom the Atlantic coast of North Africa was not wholly unknown, they were spurred on by the enthusiasm of Prince Henry "the Navigator," a member of the Portuguese ruling family and a man in whom rare business ability was combined with the instinct of the explorer and the zeal of the missionary. One expedition after another was sent by him to explore the west coast of Africa. It was not, however, until 1487 that Bartholomew Diaz discovered what he called the Cape of Storms and what King John II of Portugal later christened the Cape of Good Hope. Ten years later Vasco da Gama rounded the cape, pushed up the east coast, and in 1498 reached India. The new sea route to India was

[3] A. H. Lybyer, "The Influence of the Ottoman Turks upon the Routes of Oriental Trade," in the *Annual Report* for 1914 of the American Historical Association, I, 125–133.

complete and trade was rapidly established. The strategic position of Portugal, combined with lowered cost of transportation over the new route, threw the Eastern trade into the hands of the Portuguese, who took immediate advantage by laying the foundations of an Eastern empire which they ruled until the crowns of Spain and Portugal were joined. With the opening of the new route to the East the center of the world's trade shifted from the Mediterranean to the Atlantic. Venice, it is true, continued a prosperous and important shipping center for another century, but the loss of her Eastern trade was a severe blow. Merchants trading in Eastern wares deserted the Rialto for the bustling harbor of Lisbon, and the glory that had belonged to Venice now passed to the Atlantic seaports.

THE DISCOVERY OF AMERICA

Portugal was not the only nation where men were dreaming of riches through quicker routes to the Indies. Before Da Gama had made his epochal voyage to India, Ferdinand and Isabella of Spain, fresh from their conquests over the Moors, had paused in their building of a great Spanish state to promise aid to the Italian navigator Columbus in his projected westward voyage. Columbus, believing with all educated astronomers and philosophers that the earth was round, thought that by sailing due west he could reach the Indies. "I have always read that the world," said he, "comprising the land and the water, is spherical, as is testified by the investigations of Ptolemy and others, who have proved it by the eclipses of the moon and other observations made from east to west as well as by the elevation of the pole from north to south." His thesis was of course correct and not new; his mistake was in conceiving the world to be a smaller sphere than it turned out to be. The greatness of Columbus lay not in the originality of his conception but in his courage in venturing the unknown seas and in his pertinacity in pursuing his project. Sailing west in 1492 with his three little ships, he at length ran into what was probably one of the Bahamas. He believed that he had discovered outlying islands of the Indies, and returned three times, only to meet with disappointment in his efforts to get through to India.

The efforts of Columbus were emulated by John Cabot, the Italian navigator in the service of Henry VII of England, who sailed due west in quest of Cipango, only to land on the barren shore of Labrador. Even after Balboa (1513) had discovered the great western ocean and Magellan's ship *Victoria* had circumnavigated the globe (1519–1522) in that greatest feat of navigation of all time, explorers continued for a hundred years to seek for channels leading through or around America to Asia. This quest for a passage to the Indies led to the explorations of Verrazano (1524), Cartier (1534), Frobisher (1576–1578), Davis (1585–1587), and Hudson (1609). Although no natural opening through the American continents to Cathay was ever discovered, these voyages gave to Europeans their first knowledge of what is now the coast of the United States and of the two great rivers of the eastern coast, the St. Lawrence and the Hudson.

The Commercial Revolution, including as it did the discovery of America, had incalculable effects upon economic history. Only a few of the most important can be suggested here. The comparative cheapness of water transportation over the new routes to the Indies reduced the cost of Oriental goods and made possible their more general use. Long ocean voyages developed the construction of stronger and taller ships which could profitably carry to Europe the bulky commodities hitherto unknown, such as tea, coffee, Indian corn, and tobacco. All the influences tending to the development of merchant capitalism and economic imperialism were accentuated. The growth in business developed better methods of carrying on trade, new industries sprang into existence, manufacturing increased—all of which tended to break down the antiquated guild system. Even agriculture responded to the stimulus of new crops and the necessity of supporting a greater population which came with enlarged commercial activities. The slave trade was revived to provide the labor necessary to work the plantations of the New World. Not the least effect of the discovery of America was the plunder of Mexico and Peru. The flow of gold and silver from the mines of the New World put Europe definitely on a money economy and gave merchant capitalism a new lease on life. Trade with the Far East, which had been declining as Europe was gradually stripped of her precious metals, revived and flourished. The sudden flow of precious metals pushed prices upward. Since wages and rents lagged behind,[4] enormous profits were reaped by merchants, industrialists, and other entrepreneurs. This in turn stimulated commerce and industry and the results have permeated almost every phase of economic and social life.

One over-all interpretation of the effects of the Commercial Revolution and the discovery of new worlds has recently been emphasized.[5] It involves western Europe (the metropolis) in its relations to a new frontier, which brought to western Europe new products, new wealth, a new and greater trade, and a new outlet for its products and population. Economically Europe at the end of the fifteenth century was by modern standards a static civilization. Its area was "saturated with people," its labor supply was glutted, and its population pressed hard on the means of subsistence. Commodities were in scant supply and the standard of living was low. Then came the discovery

[4] Adam Smith, writing in 1776, insisted that "the discovery of the abundant mines of America, seems to have been the sole cause of this diminution [between 1570 and 1640] in the value of silver in proportion to that of corn." *Wealth of Nations* (Cannan ed., London, 1904), I, 191.

[5] Walter Prescott Webb, *The Great Frontier*.

of the Americas, of South Africa, of Australia and New Zealand, all areas with a small and retarded native population that could be brushed aside by migrating peoples from Europe. This produced an economic, social, and intellectual revolution in the metropolis and a boom period which has lasted 400 years. From it may be deduced a thousand ramifications of modern history. Today the world is living at the tail end of this long economic boom and many of its problems rest upon this fact.

With regard to political and imperial history a word may be added. Upon one class in Europe the Commercial Revolution had its greatest influence. While kings and nobles fought over colonial empires, the bourgeoisie or townsfolk, that new middle class just emerging, reaped the benefits. In every country the number of those dependent upon commerce and trade grew rapidly and the long process of the exaltation of the middle class politically and economically at the expense of the landed aristocracy began. In the arena of imperial politics the Commercial Revolution inaugurated a series of struggles for colonial possessions and commercial power during which maritime supremacy passed from Portugal to Spain and then, during the Dutch rebellion, to Holland. But England and France were both growing in national spirit and sea power and both made war upon the wealthy but diminutive republic until they had effectually crippled her. With Holland eliminated, England and France engaged in a series of seven great wars extending from 1689 to the overthrow of Napoleon, which left Great Britain supreme upon the sea and the foremost colonial power. All of these nations, however, while relinquishing their maritime supremacy, retained certain parts of their colonial empire.

MOTIVES FOR THE COLONIZATION OF AMERICA

As the idea was gradually brought home to Europeans that the new-found land was not the Indies but two mighty continents, not only did statesmen dream of new empires, and knights and merchants of new sources of riches, but the common man began to think of a new home across the seas where he might escape from the religious, political, and economic tyranny of the Old World. The motives for colonization were varied—religious, political, and economic being often inextricably combined.

The age of the Reformation was one in which the religious motive was strong. Prince Henry sent his ships to find not only the Indies but also the fabled Christian kingdom of Prester John. "We come in search of Christians and spices," said Vasco da Gama. In the breasts of the early Spanish conquerors and explorers a consuming passion for gold was fused with a strong crusading spirit. "Gold is most excellent," said Columbus. "Gold is treasure, and he who possesses it does all he wishes to in this world, and succeeds in helping souls into paradise."[6] French Jesuit priests threaded the lakes and rivers in advance of the fur trader, baptizing as they went. The religious impulse moved even the more prosaic English. Drake and Hawkins scoured the Spanish Main[7] to fight Catholics as well as collect booty. Later many felt with the Virginia Company managers that the first object of that plantation was "to preach and baptize into *Christian Religion,* and by propagation of the *Gospell,* to recover out of the arms of the Divell, a number of poore and miserable soules, wrapt up unto death, in almost invincible ignorance."[8]

While the work of the priests in opening the routes for settlers should not be underestimated, even more important than the crusading spirit in promoting settlement was the desire for freedom from religious persecution at home. Separatists and Puritans founded New England to obtain religious liberty; but Puritan intolerance in turn drove Roger Williams and his followers to Rhode Island and banished Anne Hutchinson. Puritanism drove Cavaliers to Virginia and English Catholics to Maryland. French Protestants found refuge in the Carolinas, while Quakers, Mennonites, Moravians, and other sects found a home in Pennsylvania, New Jersey, and elsewhere.

Political motives also played their part. Each nation would secure for itself as much of the new land as possible. Settlements in the thirteen colonies were encouraged to check the northward advance of the Spanish and the southward and eastward pressure of the French. The four-cornered struggle for empire between Spain, France, England, and Holland during the sixteenth and seventeenth centuries contributed much in hastening the occupation of America. Divergence in political ideas, often derived from religious tenets, also sent many to the New World.

More important than the religious and political were the economic motives. It was the search for new routes to the Far East that led in the first place to the discovery of America, and during the next century it was the desire to find an opening through the continent that led to the explorations of Cartier, Frobisher, Davis, and others. When gold and silver were discovered in abundance by Cortez (1519) in Mexico, and by Pizarro (1531) in Peru, the dominating impulse of Spain was the exploitation of this source of income. The foundations of New Spain rested during the early years on the precious metals. Nor was the hope of quick riches through the discovery of gold and silver absent from the minds of the early English explorers,

[6] Fourth Voyage. Letter to Ferdinand and Isabella, written July 7, 1503. Original Narratives of Early American History Series, *The Northmen, Columbus, and Cabot,* p. 412.

[7] The term "Spanish Main" properly means the coasts bordering on the Caribbean Sea but is sometimes applied to the Caribbean itself.

[8] From "A True and Sincere declaration of the purposes and ends of the Plantation begun in Virginia . . . Set Forth by the authority of the Governors and Councillors established for that Plantation." Given by Alexander Brown, *Genesis of the United States* (1890), I, 339.

whose appetites had been whetted by the good fortune of their Spanish rivals.

In time Europe came to realize that gold was not the only product of value which might be obtained from America. It is believed that even before the discovery of Columbus fishing vessels from England and France had sailed out to the west until they found fish in plenty. Certainly in the fifteenth century the fishing fleets of many nations drew wealth from the Grand Banks. The fur trade came soon to rival in value even that of gold. Sugar, tobacco, cocoa, and many other products, including timber and naval stores (tar, pitch, rosin, cordage, masts, and lumber), demonstrated the value of the Americas to Europe as a source of raw materials. As a counterpart to the growth of manufactures in Europe came the appreciation of colonial settlements as a market for the finished products of the looms and workshops of the mother countries. In enumerating the benefits which England would derive from the establishment of colonies beyond the Atlantic, Sir George Peckham wrote that it would revive and promote especially the trades of "Clothiers, Woolmen, Carders, Spinners, Weavers, Fullers, Shearmen, Dyers, Drapers, Cappers, Hatters," and would repair "many decayed towns."[9] A pamphleteer, writing prior to 1606 on "Reasons for raising a fund for the Support of a Colony at Virginia," speaks of it as a place "fit for the vent of our wares."[10]

The economic motives so far mentioned involve to some extent state as well as private interest and participation. Other economic impulses concerned the individual more directly. The desire to escape the economic restrictions of the governmental guild regulations, the hope of bettering his fortunes upon a new soil where land might be acquired easily and the fruits of labor saved from a feudal lord, appealed to the poor but ambitious man. Younger sons of the nobility and impoverished gentlemen saw a chance in the New World to found a fortune or commence life anew.

There was also a belief in the sixteenth and seventeenth centuries that England was overpopulated, as, in fact, she was, and that the colonies would provide a natural outlet for the surplus population. Contemporary writers stress the dangers of overpopulation and unemployment. The author of *Nova Britannia* speaks of "our land abounding with swarms of idle persons, which having no means of labor to relieve their misery, do likewise swarm in lewd and naughty practices, so that if we seek not some ways for their foreign employment, we must provide shortly more prisons and corrections for their bad conditions. It is no new thing but most profitable for our state, to rid our multitudes of such as lie at home pestering the land with pestilence

[9] Sir George Peckham, *A True Reporte of the Late Discoveries . . . of the Newfound Lands,* a rare pamphlet published in 1583, reprinted in *Magazine of History with Notes and Queries,* Extra Number 68 in Vol. XVII, Extra Numbers (1920), p. 43.

[10] E. D. Neill, *Virginia Vetusta,* p. 30.

and penury, and infecting one another with vice and villainy worse than the plague itself."[11] A statute of 1572 follows the precedent of half a century in complaining that England was "with rogues, vagabonds and sturdy beggars exceedingly pestered."[12] It is estimated that in Elizabeth's reign there were as many as ten thousand tramps, hundreds of whom were hanged every year, and many more inflicted with severe punishment.

Many factors contributed to make unemployment widespread over a long period. Among them were the disbanding of feudal retainers under Henry VII, the gradual breakup of the medieval manorial system, the dissolution of the monasteries and cessation of monastic charity, the inclosures of farm land into sheep pastures, and the close of the Elizabethan wars. Enormous numbers thus deprived of their customary occupations became highwaymen, beggars, or public charges. To men of this type America held out hope, and those in authority were in no wise loath to part with them.[13]

It is not easy in going through contemporary documents to determine with any accuracy the proportion of weight to be given to the various influences leading to American colonization. Individuals differed in their motives, and influences which carried weight in one period may have been of little importance in another. The numerous propaganda pamphlets written to encourage colonization attempted to include all arguments and to appeal to all men. In the end, however, it is safe to say that the underlying motive for interest in America on the part of the great majority—whether king, noble, or commoner—was the economic. On the part of the merchant adventurer it was profit, on that of the humble emigrant a chance to find in the New World opportunities for a better life.

SELECTED READINGS

Cheyney, E. P., *European Background of American History*, chaps. 1–4, 7, 8.
Packard, L. B., *The Commercial Revolution*.
Nettels, Curtis, *The Roots of American Civilization*, chaps. 1–5.
Hacker, L. M., *The Triumph of American Capitalism*, chaps. 1–7.
Webb, W. P., *The Great Frontier*, chap. 1.

[11] *Nova Britannia* (1609), reprinted in *American Colonial Tracts*, Vol. I, No. 6.
[12] 14 Eliz., Chap. 5. Extract given in George W. Prothero, *Select Statutes*, pp. 67–69.
[13] See Frederick W. Tickner, *Social and Industrial History of England* (1915), and Henry D. Traill (ed.), *Social England* (1910), Vol. III, index under "Beggars."

CHAPTER 3

THE COLONIZATION

OF AMERICA

COLONIAL SYSTEM OF SPAIN

Four nations—Spain, France, Holland, and England—strove to dominate the North American continent. Each nation had settlements in what is now the United States, and each nation in its efforts to reproduce on American soil a New Spain, a New France, a New Netherlands, or a New England, as the case might be, left here the imprint of its civilization. Although the statesmen of each of these four countries believed thoroughly in the regulation of the economic life of the colonies, nowhere was the idea carried to such extremes as in the treatment of the Spanish colonies by the home government. From 1503 until 1717 most of the commerce to and from the colonies was required to pass through the city of Seville. At the American end of entry of goods to the mainland during most of this period was limited to the two ports of Vera Cruz on the Mexican coast and Porto Bello on the Isthmus of Panama, the former receiving goods for Mexico and the latter for South America.

By 1561 the development of piracy along the Spanish Main led the government to establish the system of yearly fleets which lasted nearly two centuries. Once a year two fleets would form under the protection of warships and sail to the West Indies, where they would separate, one proceeding to Vera Cruz and the other to Porto Bello. The arrival of the fleet at Porto Bello marked the period of the annual fair, when the silver wedges from the Peruvian mines which "lay like heaps of stones in the street without any fear or suspicion of being lost" were exchanged for wines, figs, olives, cloth, iron, quicksilver, and luxuries from Spain. Besides gold and silver, which formed the chief item in the return voyage, cochineal, sugar, hides, and drugs were taken back.

This commerce was further restricted by the granting of monopolies on gunpowder, salt, tobacco, and quicksilver, by excises levied on goods sold, by export and import duties averaging perhaps 15 per cent, and by the king's royalty of one-fifth on the yield of the gold and silver mines. In the colonies the culture of olives, vineyards, tobacco, and hemp was forbidden, and inter-colonial trade was restricted. The entire system was highly artificial and was seriously undermined by the wholesale smuggling after the English and Dutch had obtained a foothold in the West Indies and England had, through the Asiento (1713), secured the monopoly of the African slave trade with Spanish America.

A disproportionate emphasis may easily be placed on the part played by gold and silver in the economic life of Spanish America.[1] Although they formed the chief items of export, the Spanish government was not indifferent to the establishment of agricultural colonies, nor were the colonists wholly occupied with extracting the precious metals. A great majority of the population lived by farming and ranching, the products of which, including hides, corn, the American aloe or agave, sugar, cocoa, vanilla, and cochineal, were more valuable than those of the mines. Around the two basic industries, mining and agriculture, was built up a prosperous and even wealthy civilization while the English and French to the north were still struggling to maintain a bare existence.

The economic unit of early Spanish America was the *encomienda,* a grant of land carrying with it the authority to command the services of a certain number of Indians. Begun by Columbus in the West Indies, it was later extended and applied almost universally on the continent. Under this system the Indians were forced to till the crops, tend the cattle, and work the mines for their Spanish overlords. While efforts were made to limit the duration of the *encomienda* system and detailed regulations were issued concerning the treatment of the Indians, forbidding their enslavement and advising their conversion to Christianity, it was to be expected that under such a system the natives would degenerate into serfs and often be subjected to the most cruel treatment. The conquest of a large territory with a backward native population by a comparatively few adventurous soldiers bent on rapid accumulation of wealth made inevitable the transplanting of the only system of government known to these men—the feudal system of Europe.

---

[1] The effect on Europe, however, was extremely important. The influx of the precious metals, not only from Latin America but from other newly discovered lands, both revolutionized the price structure and speeded economic development in many ways. Webb, in *The Great Frontier,* p. 19, estimates the value of gold and silver production, 1493–1940, at $47,382,316,-252. He reaches this figure by valuing gold produced up to 1701 at $20.67 an ounce and silver at $1.38 an ounce. From 1701 to 1934 he uses the market value of the metals, and after that date $35 per ounce for gold and $0.8958 for silver.

Instead of exterminating or driving away the Indians as did the English settler, the Spaniard made serfs of the majority of them. In 1574, scarcely three generations after the conquest of Mexico, there were in the New World, according to Velasco (historian to the Council of the Indies), two hundred Spanish cities, towns, and mining settlements, containing 160,000 Spaniards, of whom about 4000 were *encomenderos* (lords of Indian serfs); the rest were settlers, miners, traders, and soldiers, controlling an approximate Indian population of 5,000,000 in eight or nine thousand villages. This was a half-century before Plymouth was founded. Settling side by side, the Spaniard and Indian have eventually become so intermingled that a large proportion of the Spanish-American population are a mixture of the two races.

Although the influence of Spanish civilization has been felt primarily in "Latin America," that influence has not been lacking in the region of the present United States. It was the Spanish who started the culture of citrus fruits in Florida and California, the manufacture of sugar in the West Indies, and cattle ranching and sheep raising in the Southwest; and their influence upon law and architecture can be traced. In all this the most important role was usually played by the missionaries who composed the cultural element of the Spanish vanguard. Spain was also responsible for the first permanent white settlements and the first explorations in the United States.

FRANCE IN AMERICA

Almost a century elapsed after the voyage of Verrazano before the first permanent French settlement was made at Quebec in 1608, but the genius of the French for exploration, and their talent for dominion, were notably demonstrated in the succeeding years. Dominated by patriotism, missionary zeal, and a desire to open up more territory to their traders, priests and explorers pushed their canoes up the St. Lawrence, along the Great Lakes, and down the Mississippi, until by the end of the century French posts extended from New Orleans at the mouth of the Mississippi to Fort Radisson near the western end of Lake Superior, and east to Nova Scotia.

The success of the French as colonizers did not measure up to their attainments as explorers and missionaries. The French as a whole cared little for colonization, while the persecuted Protestants, who might have furnished a valuable element for immigration, were forbidden to come. The most important cause of failure, however, was probably due to the source of economic wealth. The economic backbone of New France was the fur trade. To the Frenchman with initiative the harsh climate and stubborn soil of the St. Lawrence Valley made little appeal. The back country was rich in furs, and in the pursuit of these he penetrated ever farther into the interior. Adaptable in the extreme, he would often affect the manners and dress of the Indians, lead them on the warpath, live with them, and intermarry. This won to the French not only the bulk of the fur trade but the friendship of practically all of the Indian tribes, with the exception of the Iroquois. If wealth was to be gained in New France it must be through furs, and noble and peasant alike engaged in the business. At least a third of the population was occupied in gathering and transporting furs.

As the fur trade was the principal source of wealth, so it proved also to be the chief cause of weakness for the colony. So long as greater profits were to be made in peltries, it was difficult to interest settlers in agriculture, and the safest basis for a permanent colony was thus lacking. Instead of the 1,300,000 inhabitants which the English colonies boasted in 1754, more than nine-tenths of whom were engaged in agriculture, compactly settled along a fringe of seacoast and firmly established, the French had only about 80,000 scattered along the rivers and Great Lakes from the Mississippi to Nova Scotia. Beyond the barest necessities of subsistence, agriculture was neglected. There was some attention to fisheries, but practically no manufactures other than household in New France.

From 1600 to 1663 the efforts of the French to colonize and exploit the American mainland were in the hands of commercial companies, the most famous of which was known as the Hundred Associates. After that date the administration was taken over by the crown, and a government characterized by extreme absolutism and centralization was set up. To make complete the replica of the autocratic system of France in the New World, an order of nobility was created by Richelieu in the charter of the Hundred Associates. To induce members of the lesser nobility to remain in America, seigniories were granted them along the lake and river fronts. When the seigniories were inhabited at all the peasant settlers usually lived on a road perhaps a half-mile back of the river or lake, with their fields sloping down to the water on one side and back into the forest on the other. These grants were usually four arpents (768 English linear feet) on the water front and ten arpents (1920 feet) deep. This long, narrow holding, peculiar to the French, had a twofold *raison d'être*. Comparative freedom from Indian raids made it unnecessary for the French to huddle in fortified villages, but their sociable nature inclined them toward living near one another.

With the seigniories went the rest of the paraphernalia of feudalism. The tenant was expected to pay rent to the seignior—trifling, to be sure, and generally in produce—to work for the lord a certain number of days a year, patronize his grist mill, present to him one fish out of every eleven caught, and render other feudal dues. Although remnants of this system outlasted the English conquest by half a century, the conditions in New France, in contrast to the situation in Spanish America, were not such as feudalism would thrive on. With plenty of vacant land and the fur trade to beckon them on, any attempt to impose a strict feudal system upon the inhabitants was doomed to failure, and the duties of the peasant to the seignior became more nominal than real. The lords themselves, hardly more prosperous than their tenants, were forced to till the fields with their own hands or take to the life of a fur trader. With the seigniorial system and despotic government went paternalism. Taught to depend not upon themselves but upon the home government, the settlers soon lost initiative in economic problems. With their trade shackled by petty restrictions and controlled by government monopoly, it is little wonder that private enterprise in industry was smothered and Canada never prospered under France. This institutional and economic background goes far to explain the eventual conquest of New France by the British.

THE DUTCH IN AMERICA

The efforts of the Dutch to participate in the profits of the American trade led eventually to their settlement of the Hudson Valley. Henry Hudson in the interests of the Dutch East India Company had explored in 1609 the river which bears his name, and a trading post called New Amsterdam had been established in 1614 by some enterprising merchants of Amsterdam. In 1621 Dutch interests in America were taken over by the Dutch West India Company, a great private corporation to which the States-General of Holland granted a monopoly of the trade not only of the American seaboard but also of the coast of Africa south of the Tropic of Cancer. This corporation, interested in trade in gold, slaves, and tropical products, equipping hundreds of privateers, supporting an army and a large navy with which it made war upon Spain and Portugal, found the fur trade of the Hudson Valley but a small item in its numerous enterprises. The valley consequently absorbed but a small part of the interest of the directors. This attitude is well expressed in the remonstrance of the company to the States-General against a peace with Spain, when they maintained that their object was not "trifling trade with the Indians nor the tardy cultivation of uninhabited regions," but "acts of hostility against the ships and property of the King of Spain and his subjects."[2]

In spite of the company's lack of interest in the Hudson Valley, much was done there in the way of trade and colonization. Fort Orange, upon the site of the present Albany, was built in 1622, a village on Manhattan Island was founded in 1623, and settlements were made later not only in the Hudson Valley but in the Mohawk Valley, on Long Island, and along Delaware Bay.

[2] J. R. Brodhead, *Collection of Documents*, I, 62.

The West India Company, however, intent upon accumulating dividends, was not interested primarily in settling the country. The greatest profits were to be made in furs, and upon the promotion of the fur trade the chief energies of the company and its representatives were bent. Later shipbuilding was carried on to some extent, and eventually prosperous agricultural communities grew up.

The first farming in New Netherlands seems to have been done not by tenants but by servants working for the company, which owned both the land and the stock upon it. After trading posts had been established the company became more interested in stimulating settlement, and a scheme of landed proprietors was introduced in 1629. Any member of the company who would bring over fifty persons at his own expense would receive a tract of land reaching sixteen miles along the river all on one bank, or half on one bank and half on the other, with no limit as to width; and under this impetus a number of wealthy Dutchmen, including the Amsterdam jeweler, Killian Van Rensselaer, carved out huge estates in the Hudson Valley. Upon these grantees, or patroons, were bestowed both proprietary rights and subordinate jurisdiction. The patroons could hold manorial courts, with the right reserved for the tenants to appeal to the company, could found townships and appoint officials for them. Upon their estates they had the monopoly of weaving and certain exclusive trading privileges. Here, too, as in New France and New Spain, an attempt was made to graft on the New World the feudal system of Europe. Under this system the most influential members of the company soon gained control of the choicest lands in the Hudson Valley. Here we have the origin of the large landed estates which existed in New York until well into the nineteenth century. Their influence can be seen in the economic history of New York State and was the cause of the "anti-rent wars" of the 1830's and 1840's.

The Dutch, who had never accepted the feudal system in its entirety as had other Europeans, chafed under the unaccustomed rule of the company and manor barons. The patroon system was exceedingly unpopular from the start, and in 1640 the company attempted to modify it by reducing the extent of the patroonships and introducing a class of smaller proprietor who was to hold 200 acres tilled by five men brought over at his expense. Again in 1650 a further effort was made to increase the number of small farmers. A tract of land with implements and stock was granted to the settler, with the understanding that he pay a fixed rent and return the stock or an equivalant at the end of six years. In general the agricultural products and life were not unlike that found in New England, although the big plantations along the Hudson and Delaware Bay, where tobacco was a favorite crop, resembled those of Virginia.

The centralized despotism of the government of New Netherlands in the period before 1629 was modified after the introduction of the patroon system with its almost independent jurisdiction, but the principle of representative government was not recognized in New Netherlands until the closing years of Dutch occupation. At the same time the loss in efficiency and unity of control under a semifeudal patroon system made the colony more susceptible to foreign conquest. Driven like a wedge between the English colonies in New England and the South, the strategic territory of New Netherlands was naturally gazed upon with covetous eyes by Great Britain. In fact, English settlers were beginning to filter in from the east, many seeking that religious toleration which the Dutch were the first to recognize in America and which Englishmen had sought for in vain in all New England except Rhode Island. This influx of English, combined with the lack of interest on the part of the company at home, the corrupt and despotic government in the colony, and the growing sea power of Great Britain, led to its final conquest in 1664. When the English captured New Netherlands, it contained a population, according to the estimate of Stuyvesant, of about 10,000. Nineteen languages were spoken in New Amsterdam at that time, the city thus early partaking of the cosmopolitan tone which ever since has been a distinguishing feature.

EARLY ENGLISH COLONIZATION

England in the age of Elizabeth was ripe for exploration and colonization. The strong Tudor monarchy had destroyed the strength of the feudal nobility, broken the political and economic power of the church, and admitted to titled rank men whose minds were occupied with trade and commerce. With the growing strength of her national government and with a rapidly expanding economic life there developed an independent, self-reliant population eager for gain and commercial development, keen to challenge the maritime domination of Spain, and full of confidence in the destiny of England. While English sea captains like Sir John Hawkins and Sir Francis Drake roamed the Spanish Main to bait their enemy, capture his bullion, and sack his cities, more serious imperialists were dreaming of establishing plantations in the western wilderness. Men like William Hakluyt preserved the voyages of English sailors, wrote pamphlets to point out the social, economic, and political advantages of foreign possessions to England, and inflamed the minds of rich and poor with prospects of comfort and wealth to be gained by adventure abroad.

Just as private individuals had borne the burden of propagandizing for English expansion, so English colonization was accomplished by private initiative and with little or no aid from the British crown. The Tudors, Henry VII and Elizabeth, favored overseas expansion but did little more.

The Stuarts, James I and Charles I, living in a period of rising prices, were always in need of funds and engaged in a continuous wrangle with their Parliaments over the question of taxes. They were, nevertheless, sincerely interested in colonization if it could be carried on without cost to them. The English kings held to the theory that title to and political jurisdiction of newly discovered or settled lands were vested with the sovereign. To preserve this title, but at the same time to encourage expansion, they were willing to grant to properly accredited persons (usually favorites of the crown) royal patents or charters to settle and exploit the new lands. This arrangement might serve to protect their rights and to increase the power and wealth of the nation and themselves, but at the same time it involved no direct cost to themselves or their government.

From the first patent granted to John Cabot in 1496 down to the Pennsylvania settlement in 1682, this was the general policy followed. Cabot, whose voyages (1497–1498) laid the foundation for England's claim to North America, was financed by Bristol and London merchants. To Cabot and his sons and heirs was given the right of a monopoly to whatever trade he might develop with the regions discovered except that the king was to receive a fifth of the profits. When Englishmen almost a century later (1578) again turned their attention to colonization, Elizabeth granted to that model knight, Sir Humphrey Gilbert, the exclusive right to "inhabit and possess at his choice all remote and heathen lands not in the possession of any Christian prince," but the crown was to receive "the fifth part of all the oare of golde or silver" that might be obtained. Gilbert made two voyages. His first expedition was scattered by a storm; his second in 1583 planted a small colony in Newfoundland which soon disappeared.

In the charter issued in 1584 Elizabeth passed on to Gilbert's half brother, Sir Walter Raleigh, the rights conferred in the early charter. Raleigh dispatched five expeditions to America and spent £40,000 of his personal fortune, but his efforts resulted in failure. His third expedition in 1587 actually planted a colony on Roanoke Island off the coast of Virginia. This colony vanished, however, because of failure in England to support the infant enterprise. His efforts, nevertheless, were not entirely lost. At least he proved that the initial stage of colonization was a task beyond the personal fortune of any single Englishman.

Raleigh's failure resulted in the next effort's being made by a group of capitalists through the medium of a joint-stock company. These men, inflamed by the success of the East India Company, dreamed of establishing an outpost in America where traders and gold hunters might duplicate the success attained in India. The Virginia charter of 1606 created two companies, one consisting of "certain Knights, Gentlemen, Merchants, and other

Adventurers, of our city of London and elsewhere"; and the other of "Sundry Knights, Gentlemen, Merchants, and other Adventurers, of our cities of Bristol and Exeter, and of our town of Plymouth." These two groups of stockholders, the big businessmen of their day, were known as the London and Plymouth companies. Upon them the king bestowed the coast of the present United States—to the first-named company the region between parallels 34 and 41, and to the second that between parallels 38 and 45, with the region between the 38th and 41st open to either on condition that neither settled within one hundred miles of the other. Attempts at colonization were immediately made by both companies, unsuccessfully by the Plymouth group on the Kennebec River in Maine, and permanently by the London Company, whose expedition planted a settlement in 1607 thirty miles up the James River.

The London and Plymouth companies, it should be pointed out, were by no means the first groups to whom European monarchs granted monopolies of trade with privileges of colonization and government. At least seven, beginning with the Muscovy Company in 1554 and going down through the East India Company in 1600, had appeared in England alone. It was the practice of the monarchs of northwestern Europe, as we have noted, to dodge financial risk by granting monopolistic inducements to private companies.

The difficulties of the first Jamestown settlers were due in part to the inadequate financial strength of the original group of entrepreneurs and in part to the fact that the company's interest was in trade, of which there was little, and in gold, of which there was none. The first difficulty was overcome by a new charter in 1609 which (in addition to separating the London and Plymouth companies) converted the Virginia enterprise into a true joint-stock company. All were invited to purchase stock at a par value of £12 10s., the cost of transporting and equipping one settler, and all stockholders were entitled to dividends and a land grant. The capital thus raised was to be used to send settlers to America who were to work for the company for seven years. At the end of this period the improved land was to be divided among the stockholders, 100 acres for each share of stock.

At the same time the rights of the company were specifically stated. They included complete control of the natural resources of the country and the levying of export and import duties up to a certain amount. For twenty years the company was granted exemption from paying duty on goods imported in Virginia, and for all time it was to pay only 5 per cent upon goods brought into England. In return it was expected to colonize the country and to pay to the king one-fifth of all gold and silver acquired. Even these allurements did not produce enough capital, and in 1612 in a third charter the king authorized the company to raise further funds through lotteries. Eventually the Virginia Company sought to promote settlement by granting land to groups or individuals who would send over settlers or come at their own expense. In this way larger numbers were induced to migrate.

From the first arrival until the company went bankrupt and lost its charter in 1624 most of the settlers were servants whose way had been paid. The colony was a true plantation. But the shiploads of lumber and other forest products gathered and sent to England paid only a small fraction of the expenses incurred by the company to found the Virginia Plantation. For the stockholders in England the Virginia Company represented only a heavy financial loss, but in world history its role was important, for it laid the foundations of the English world empire and the American nation.

The next permanent English settlement in the New World was that of the Separatists at Plymouth. Impelled by the hope that they might find in America an opportunity both for economic betterment and for the worship of God after the dictates of their own hearts, they negotiated with the Virginia Council for patents to settle in their land. A charter was eventually granted by the Virginia Company, now under the control of Sir Edwin Sandys and the Puritan faction, giving the earnest little group the right to found a plantation and govern it by laws of their own in accordance with those of England. The Virginia Company would not finance the settlement and the Separatists had to find assistance elsewhere. Eventually seventy London merchants subscribed £7000, a sum sufficient for the purpose. Under the terms of the "Articles of Agreement of Plymouth Plantation" each share was to be reckoned at £10. For "adventuring himself" each emigrant was counted as holding one share and was permitted to purchase as many more as he was able. For seven years all wealth produced by the colonists was to go into the common stock, and from this and supplies sent by the London merchants the colonists were furnished food, clothing, and other necessities. At the end of seven years "ye capitall & profits, viz. the houses, lands, goods and chatles, be equally divided betwixte ye adventurers, and planters; wch done, every man shall be free from other of them of any debt or detrimente concerning this adventure."[3] Those who came to the colony before the expiration of the seven years were to share proportionately, according to the time spent. Whereas the settlers in Virginia, whose transportation was paid by the company, were merely servants of the company who were to receive at the end of the seven years nothing but their freedom, the Plymouth colonists were stockholders in a company for which they all worked and the profits of which they would all share. In addition, their efforts were to be directed by officials of their own choosing and not by representatives sent

[3] William Bradford, *History of Plymouth Plantation* (Commonwealth of Massachusetts edition), pp. 56–58.

from England, as in the case of the Virginia Company. The whole plan was a far more generous arrangement than that under which the Virginia Plantation struggled during its early years.

The merchants who had subscribed their money expected immediate and large returns, but the wringing of a mere subsistence from the stubborn soil demanded practically the entire time of the colonists. It is true that some wealth was secured by furs and fisheries, but never enough to return any profit to the stockholders. On their side, the London stockholders were not able to send over supplies in any degree sufficient for the needs of the suffering settlers. As in Virginia, a serious hindrance to success was the common store and the plan of co-operative industry. When famine threatened in the third year the system was abolished as far as agriculture was concerned, and land was allotted to each man for temporary use only. By 1627, the year in which the agreement with the London merchants ended, the colony was firmly established. Desiring to sever relations with the London merchants in a manner different from that prescribed originally, the colonists made arrangements whereby the interests of the London stockholders were bought out for £1800, to be paid in nine annual installments of £200 each. In return the merchants surrendered all claims upon the colony. The money was paid chiefly through profits in the fur trade.

Plymouth was eventually absorbed by the strong Massachusetts Bay Company, whose charter had been obtained in 1629 for commercial purposes, and whose stockholders were chiefly Puritan merchants. The pronounced High Church tendency of Charles I and his attempt at tyrannical government, which began in earnest in 1629 with the dissolution of Parliament and the imprisonment of men prominent in opposing his policies, gave to the activities of the company a different turn. To many of the leading Puritans, Massachusetts appeared as an ideal refuge from the hostile policies of the king. Since they belonged to the ruling classes at home, they were unwilling to emigrate as the servants of a plantation company. Consequently they bought up the stock of the Massachusetts Company, pledged themselves to emigrate, and took over their charter with them. Thus we find Massachusetts Bay settled by the controlling members of the company itself and its form of government in the early years comparing rather strikingly to that of a modern corporation. The freemen, for example, may be compared to the stockholders, and the governor, deputy governor, and eighteen assistants may be compared to the president, vice-president, and board of directors. The place of meeting was not stipulated in the charter, so that it was possible to transfer the whole corporation to America. The great migration of 1630–1640, which brought to America over 20,000 settlers, including some of the best stock in England, has left a deep impress upon the whole political, social, and economic fabric of American life.

LATER ENGLISH COLONIZATION

Virginia and Plymouth were, as we have said, colonized by commercial companies. They bore the brunt of settling a strange land far from the base of supplies. Subsequent English colonization was not attended with the hardships endured by the Pilgrim Fathers and the companions of the doughty Captain Smith. Later colonists could profit by the mistakes of their less fortunate predecessors, and it was now possible for private individuals to colonize with success. Later English settlements were founded not only by chartered companies but also by two other agencies—(1) migrating groups from existing colonies and (2) wealthy proprietors. Examples of the first of these are Connecticut, Rhode Island, and parts of New Hampshire and Maine.

The little fishing settlements of Maine and New Hampshire were colonized in part by emigrants from England under the protection of Sir Fernando Gorges and Captain John Mason, who had received patents for this region, and in part by inhabitants of Massachusetts Bay, who by 1652 were successful in extending the government of the last-named colony over the new country. The colonies of Rhode Island and Connecticut were offshoots of Massachusetts Bay, the former settled by religious exiles and the latter by pioneer farmers in search of more fertile land. Roger Williams established in 1636, on lands purchased from the Indians, a democratic commonwealth where for the first time in America religious freedom was put in practice. Windsor, Connecticut, was founded in 1635, and Hartford in the following year, by dissatisfied groups from Massachusetts. The settlers of neither Rhode Island nor Connecticut had a legal title to the land under English law, being simply squatters on the king's domain; but both succeeded eventually in securing charters confirming their occupation.

Under the proprietary system the king granted a single individual (or a group, as in the Carolinas) estates in America which might be colonized and held by him practically as a feudal lord under the king with very extensive powers and rights, but in most cases with the restraining provision that he must make laws "by and with the consent of the freemen." Land was granted in this way to a number of men, of whom Gorges and Mason have been mentioned. The most important experiments, however, were those of William Penn in Pennsylvania and the Calverts in Maryland. New York for a time (1665–1685, with the exception of 1673–1674, when it was recaptured by the Dutch) was a proprietary colony of the Duke of York, who handed over New Jersey to his two friends Sir George Carteret and Sir John Berkeley. The last-named province, most of which came under the control of the Quakers until taken over as a crown colony in 1702, was settled chiefly by men attracted from the surrounding regions by the liberal land offers. The Carolinas were occupied either by Virginia frontiersmen pushing south or by immigrants direct from England. They were granted (1663) by Charles II to eight proprietors, the most active of whom was Anthony Ashley Cooper, later Earl of Shaftesbury. John Locke (his former tutor) worked out a highly elaborate model state with a feudal hierarchy, but it was not adaptable and was never put in actual operation. Proprietary rule in the Carolinas came to an end in 1729. Georgia, the last of the thirteen colonies, was founded in 1733, partly as a result of the desire of the British government to set up a buffer state against the Spanish in Florida, and partly through the philanthropic desire to help English debtors commence life anew. For these reasons a charter was given to a group of trustees in 1732, who were to be in control for twenty-one years. But few of the class for whom the colony was founded came, and the population grew slowly.

LAND TENURE IN THE COLONIES

The story of colonization raises for the first time (but by no means the last) the whole problem of land tenure. Despite Indian occupation, European monarchs assumed that the land belonged to them. In turn they granted it under certain conditions to joint-stock companies, to individual proprietors, to a group of proprietors as in the case of the Carolinas, or to a group of trustees as in Georgia. It was inevitable, as we have seen in New France, New Netherlands, and New Spain, that attempts would be made to transplant aspects of the feudal system to America. It was the existing land system in Europe and the only system the colonists knew. It was also clear that such a system in the long run was bound to fail in the new settlements. For one thing, the country was too vast; any system which would restrict the amount of land held was certain to be unsuccessful, for there was too much vacant land which could be obtained by mere occupation. The country was too sparsely settled to be controlled effectively and the authority of the proprietor or crown was too distant or too weak to enforce obedience. Moreover, the competition among proprietors for settlers was so great that it was impossible to impose onerous feudal dues. Furthermore, men who braved the dangers of frontier life demanded actual ownership. As a consequence, the quitrents of the proprietors were collected intermittently and with great difficulty, while laws restricting the amount of land which any single individual might own were generally evaded.

After attempts at co-operative agriculture failed in both Virginia and Massachusetts, they were followed by the parceling out of land. Eventually in Virginia, 100 acres were given in fee simple to each stockholder for each share owned upon the first division and another 100 acres per share when the grant was "seated." A shareholder also received as a "head right" 50 acres for every person he might transport. This privilege was later extended to all residents. After 1705 the crown granted 50 acres for five shillings on condition that a house be built and three acres of land cultivated within three years. Thousands of acres were granted for meritorious service or through favoritism. The Virginia law was so easily evaded that by 1700 the average plantation was 700 acres. In Massachusetts Bay every adventurer who emigrated or paid the passage of an emigrant was to receive 50 acres. The usual system in New England, however, was settlement under the group plan, in which a number of prospective settlers would secure from the General Court a grant commonly of 36 square miles, upon which they would lay out the village, assign plots for homes and gardens, and later divide the arable and the pasture land. The land outside that owned in common was held ordinarily in fee simple (absolute ownership).[4]

Penn and Baltimore, dominated as they were by altruistic motives, imposed small quitrents, but the competition for settlers in any event kept the quitrents low. This form of rent had originated in Europe as a money commutation of other services, and was looked upon as a boon. In America, small as it might be, it was considered an unjust relic of a hated system. Penn offered 500 acres to anyone who would transport and "seat" his family, and was willing to sell 5000-acre tracts for £100 and throw in 50 acres for each servant brought, but he reserved a quitrent of one shilling per 100 acres. In Maryland a settler was given 100 acres for himself, 100 more for his wife and for each servant, and 50 for each child. They were freehold grants subject to a rent of ten pounds of wheat per 50 acres. Anyone who would bring over five settlers was granted 1000 acres, subject to a quitrent of twenty shillings a year. For bringing over more men, larger grants were made which might be divided up and sublet under the manorial usage. A man with a musket and six months' provisions might receive 150 acres in New Jersey, with a like amount for each servant or slave, and 75 additional acres for each woman—conditions so liberal that many came in from the near-by colonies. Somewhat similar offers were made in other colonies.

In spite of quitrents and other feudal regulations, the system of land disposal, as it actually developed, did not greatly hinder the normal expansion of the cultivated area. Nor did it prevent wide ownership of land among the population. It was, nevertheless, a source of much friction and discontent. The rent rolls of the crown and proprietors at the opening of the Revolution

[4] For further comments on the New England system, see below, p. 65.

amounted to £37,500 annually, and about half of it was actually collected. The difficulties which arose over this and other phases of feudal tenure were a constant source of friction which contributed to the Revolution. Fortunately, primogeniture, entails, quitrents, and other appurtenances of the feudal system which prevailed in many of the colonies were mostly abolished during or shortly after the Revolution.

The most unfortunate aspect of the colonial land system was the fact that it favored the building of large estates. It was by no means as democratic as might appear. Early arrivals obtained the best land; the rest had to take what they could get on the frontier. In New England, as we shall see, influential favorites of the legislature often secured the choicest land with little effort or expenditure. This was a great era of land speculation which favored the man close to the government, particularly if he had some capital with which to start. The ill effects of the land system were particularly accentuated in the South. Here it promoted social inequality and political corruption, and developed a landed aristocracy, at the same time hindering the westward advance of settlement. Landownership might be widely distributed but it was so uneven in amount that a class society existed from the start.

SELECTED READINGS

Nettels, Curtis, *The Roots of American Civilization,* chaps. 6, 8.
Bourne, E. G., *Spain in America,* chaps. 14–20.
Munro, W. B., *Crusaders of New France,* chaps. 8–11.
Weeden, W. B., *Economic and Social History of New England,* Vol. I, chaps. 1–5.
Bruce, P. A., *Economic History of Virginia in the Seventeenth Century,* Vol. I, chap. 1.

PART II

THE AGRARIAN AGE

CHAPTER 4

COLONIAL AGRICULTURE

AND LABOR

ECONOMIC PREVIEW OF THE FIRST TWO CENTURIES

FOR the first two centuries after the English colonists settled in America, the economic life was essentially agricultural. It was based on a simple technology brought from Europe with some native additions derived from the Indians. Except for a relatively few large plantations, mainly in the South, it was based on the small farm. Although the agricultural units were by no means self-sufficing, the markets except for a few commercial agricultural products were of small volume. In this simple agricultural civilization, faced by a scarcity of labor and capital, intercolonial commerce was small, and industry, except in the home and small shop, was virtually nonexistent. On the other hand, international commerce was relatively large. Exports from New England were chiefly products of the sea and the forest; from the Middle Atlantic colonies, flour, wheat, and other foodstuffs of the farm; and from the southern area, tobacco and a few commercial crops with a market in Europe. The towns were few and small; more than nine-tenths of the population earned their living on the farms. Inland commerce and economic life were restricted by lack of an adequate monetary system and transportation facilities.

Although there were substantial differences in the distribution of income and wealth, the standard of living for most was low. Patterns of consumption were correspondingly frugal. Except for a few wealthy merchants engaged in the export trade, venture capital, except in the later years of the period, hardly existed. Education was slight, and the hours of labor were long. By the time of the Revolution there were perhaps 2,500,000 inhabitants in the colonies, but they were thinly spread over a large area. In relation to modern times it was a primitive civilization.

EUROPEAN BACKGROUND

Like most aspects of American life, colonial agriculture was based on the knowledge and methods which the colonists brought from Europe, modified and influenced by American conditions. European agriculture of the seventeenth century was extremely primitive. The tools were few and crude; a plow, harrow, hoe, rake, spade, and sickle, with possibly a cart, represented the equipment of the most prosperous farmer. Little was known of stock breeding and this little could be rarely practiced for cattle and sheep were herded together in a common pasture. Since there was little food for animals during the winter, most of them were slaughtered in the fall. The lack of adequate care and of knowledge meant that cattle and sheep were smaller than they are today.

The use of land was likewise primitive. The more advanced farmers practiced a crude rotation of crops on a two- or three-field system. Under the latter one strip was planted with wheat, rye, or some other crop sown in the fall and harvested in the spring; a second strip was planted with oats, barley, peas, or some other crop planted in the spring and harvested in the summer or fall. The third field was allowed to lie idle in the hope that it would recover some measure of its fertility. When fertilizing was done, it was accomplished by turning the livestock into the stubble after the crops were harvested.

Until the eighteenth century little progress had been made over the methods of ancient times. In that century, however, important agricultural advances occurred in England. Jethro Tull and Charles Townshend showed that clover and other crops would renew the soil more adequately than allowing it to lie idle. Turnips, it was found, provided winter forage for animals, allowing the farmer to keep his stock through the cold months and improve his breed. Another great farmer, Robert Bakewell, experimented successfully with methods of stock breeding and actually doubled the size of his sheep.

American farmers of the eighteenth century came to know of these improvements but adopted them very slowly. There was little in the American environment to encourage their use. Rich virgin soil, with an inexhaustible supply to the west, was no incentive to scientific farming. The value of manure was hardly appreciated, crop rotation was rare, and "land butchery" was the usual practice. One observer said that the colonial farmer seemed to have but one object—the plowing up of fresh land: "The case is, they exhaust the old as fast as possible till it will bear nothing more, and then, not having manure to replenish it, nothing remains but to take up new land in the same manner."[1]

[1] *American Husbandry*, I, 144.

Considerable attention was given by farmers in the early years to experimenting with the environment. It was soon found that most of the common grains, vegetables, and fruits of northwestern Europe were suitable to American soil and climate, as were the various farm animals. But efforts to introduce subtropical fruits of the Mediterranean countries failed. The same was true of repeated attempts to raise silkworms and produce silk. These early efforts were often doomed to failure not so much because the climate was unsuitable as because the scarcity and high cost of labor made production impracticable. Success in some cases came in later years when knowledge of plant breeding and scientific agriculture had made greater progress.

AGRICULTURAL ACHIEVEMENTS OF THE AMERICAN INDIAN

It is erroneous to picture the American Indian as a nomad, destitute of a permanent home and intent solely upon hunting and fighting. The Indian was the first American farmer, and agriculture played a large part in the economic life of the tribe. Cartier and Champlain saw fields of corn on the banks of the St. Lawrence, De Soto on the Mississippi, and Coronado in the Southwest. The first settlers in the Ohio Valley found cornfields extending for miles along the river bank. General Wayne wrote in 1794 that he had never "before beheld such immense fields of corn in any part of America, from Canada to Florida." Regardless of where the warpath or hunting expedition might lead him, the warrior would return in the planting season and harvest time. Indications point to the fact that the villages built near these fields were often permanent, as in the case of the Pueblo Indians, or semipermanent, as with the Iroquois of New York.

The extent to which the Indians practiced agriculture is difficult to determine with exactness. It varied, of course, with the different tribes and in different parts of the country, ranging from tribes like the Apaches, who practiced it to a limited extent, to the southwestern Indians, who constructed reservoirs, irrigation system, and permanent cities, and hunted very little. The Atlantic coast Indians from Maine to Florida, with whom the English first came in contact, were farmers as well as hunters, and during the first years their corn helped keep the colonists alive. It is the testimony of explorers that the Indians in most parts of the United States relied upon corn and other cultivated products for their principal subsistence.

Indian agriculture in the main was built up around the cultivation of corn and tobacco. To prepare the ground, the Indian first girdled the trees or scotched the roots until they were dead. The dead trees and stumps, as well as brushwood, were then burned. With his stick or crude implement he then dug shallow holes three or four feet apart, into which he dropped a few grains of corn and beans. Between the hills he planted pumpkin and squash.

As the corn came up it was hilled, and after the harvest much of it was dried and stored away in pits or caves lined with bark or in corncribs, so as to protect it from rotting bacteria or fungi. Recent developments in agriculture have added little to the essential methods of raising corn practiced by the Indians. Like corn, tobacco was widely used by the Indians from the West Indies to Canada. It was cultivated in separate fields, but it also grew wild along the Atlantic coastal plain. Compared to the present product, the Indian tobacco was of an inferior grade. Nevertheless, Indian methods of cultivation were followed by the white man, as well as Indian methods of curing by the sun or open fire.

The third native American plant, destined in the years to come to be of world importance and to rank as one of the world's greatest four foods (the others were wheat, corn and rice), was the white potato. It is not possible to locate definitely its original habitat, but it is thought to be Peru or Chile. When introduced in England, this vegetable was called Virginia potatoes, but the careless nomenclature of those days (as evidenced by calling the great American bird the turkey) is no proof that Virginia was its original habitat. The potato was cultivated in various parts of Europe, but gained popularity first with the Irish, hence the colloquial name "Irish potatoes." Carried back to the New World, it found little favor in New England until the Irish settlers of New Hampshire encouraged its culture. Sweet potatoes, a native product in the South, were at once adopted by the English settlers and cooked in many ways. Though white potatoes were produced in very small amounts before the Revolution, large crops of sweet potatoes were characteristic of southern agriculture practically from the beginning.

The tools of the Indians were of the crudest: the shoulder blade of an antler or deer, a flat stone (usually flint) chipped and tied by thongs to a stick, a clean shell, sometimes a mere stick, were their implements of agriculture. Most of the work was done by the old men, women, and children, but it was not uncommon for the younger men to go into the fields at planting or harvesting time. The work at such periods was often co-operative and accompanied by ceremonies and festivals.

The chief contribution of the Indian to the white man was in agriculture. Owing perhaps to the fact that his only domesticated animal was the dog, he had not advanced far, but he had made considerable progress. He understood the bringing of wild plants under control and the breeding of plants by seed selection. He had grasped the idea of fertilization and of working the soil. He practiced multiple cropping. He knew how to preserve foods— berries and fruits with syrup or honey, and fruit, vegetables, and meat by artificial or sun drying. The New England farm, cleared by tree girdling, with its rows of corn twined with bean vines, interspersed with squash and pumpkin and protected by scarecrows, was a counterpart of the Indian field. The Indian gave to the white man both his chief food and his principal export and taught him how to cultivate them.

NEW ENGLAND AGRICULTURE

As in other areas, the first settlers depended on English supplies. As soon as crops could be raised, they turned to corn, pumpkins, squash, and beans, the cultivation of which they learned from the Indians. They also raised peas, parsnips, turnips, and carrots from seeds which they brought with them. Wheat, introduced from England, was not immediately successful, but they had greater success with rye and buckwheat. Barley, oats, and other European grains were introduced generally and thrived, but other products experimented with were found unsuitable. Many berries and fruits grew wild in New England—cranberries, huckleberries, blackberries, and raspberries; and cherry and plum trees. Apple trees were imported at once, and were especially successful in New England and the middle colonies. In his *Wonder-working Providence,* Johnson, writing of 1642, said that the settlers already had "apples, pears, and quince tarts instead of their former Pumpkin Pies."[2] Orchards were a part of every farm and the large apple crops caused them to be "reckoned as profitable as any other part of the plantation."

Since the Indians had no domesticated animals, the settlers immediately imported them and they multiplied rapidly. Cattle were brought in as early as 1624 and formed the basis of rapidly increasing herds and successful dairying. Hogs were raised in great numbers in New England, and a considerable export trade was developed in barreled pork. Horses of a very hardy variety were raised, particularly in Rhode Island, and exported in large numbers to the West Indies. Sheep were early introduced into Massachusetts and Rhode Island, where they were successfully developed and exported to the other northern colonies. Though these sheep were the old unimproved breeds, able to forage for themselves and to withstand hardships, conditions were at first hard for them, and special legislation was necessary to encourage sheep raising. Usually the sheep of the entire settlement grazed in common, under the care of a paid herder.

While the New England farmer of colonial times could with hard work obtain a living from the soil and might even become very prosperous, his methods were of the crudest and most primitive type. The great improvements in English agriculture which, as we have pointed out, led to the introduction of turnips, clover, and better grasses, to the more scientific rotation of crops, and to the abandonment of the three-field system, did not come

---

[2] Edward Johnson, *Wonder-working Providence of Sion's Saviour in New England 1628–1651.* Original Narratives Series, p. 210.

until the eighteenth century and then interested Americans but little. What slight knowledge of improved agricultural methods the immigrant might have he was likely to discard when confronted with an abundance of virgin soil. A harrow, a spade, a fork, all clumsily constructed of wood, were his chief farm tools. In the early days few could afford a plow; a town often paid a bounty to anyone who would buy one and keep it in repair. For twelve years after the landing of the Pilgrims there were no plows in Plymouth, and in the Massachusetts Bay Colony in 1637 there were only thirty-seven. One plow would do the work for a considerable territory.

Such a thing as scientific farming was unknown, and even rotation of crops was rarely practiced. The land was used until its fertility was exhausted, and was then allowed to lie fallow or planted with natural grasses until it recuperated. Owing to the small size of the farms and the settlement in villages, "land butchery" was not practiced in New England to the extent that it was in the South, but methods were bad enough. Even to a contemporary observer tillage in New England was "weakly and insufficiently given: worse ploughing is nowhere to be seen, yet the farmers get tolerable crops; this is owing, particularly in the new settlements, to the looseness and fertility of old woodlands, which with very bad tillage, will yield excellent crops."[3]

Bad as their agricultural methods were, their treatment of livestock was worse. The same observer maintained that in all that concerned cattle the farmers in New England were "the most negligent ignorant set of men in the world. Nor do I know any country in which animals are worse treated. Horses are in general, even valuable ones, worked hard, and starved: they plough, cart, and ride them to death, at the same time that they give very little heed to their food; after the hardest day's work, all the nourishment they are like to have is to be turned into a wood, where the shoots and weeds form the chief of the pasture; unless it be after the hay is in, when they get a share of the after-grass."[4] During the early days when food was scarce, laws were passed forbidding the feeding of corn to animals.

With the exception of a few dollars' worth of salt and iron, many a New England farmer was practically self-sufficing. From his field he obtained grains, from his orchard fruits, and from his pasture land meat and dairy products. Flax from the field and wool from the sheep were spun and made into clothing by his wife and daughters. From honey and maple sap he obtained ingredients to sweeten his food; corn whisky and cider furnished him with strong drink. Every farmer had to be a Jack-of-all-trades, and his wife had to be just as able to turn her hand to anything. The New England

[3] *American Husbandry*, I, 81.
[4] *Ibid.*, I, 80.

farmer may have been self-sufficing, but it was not from desire. All who could, raised a surplus, mainly for the West Indian market. The New England soil as a whole may not have been too fertile, but it was often good enough for intensive farming. It was not so much the soil as the greater ease of making money in industry and commerce that turned New Englanders to other pursuits.

The early settlements in New England were made under agreements whereby every shareholder or settler was entitled to a certain amount of land. Further expansion usually occurred in the following manner. As vacant land near the seacoast grew scarce, groups or congregations would obtain a grant from the General Court, to which they would move in a body and found a town. The grants, commonly thirty-six square miles, were owned by these proprietors and eventually divided among them. From the center of the town, where the meetinghouse stood, a wide street was laid out, and along it house lots with perhaps six acres of garden land were assigned. Eventually the rest of the land was distributed, each settler receiving a share in the upland, meadow land, and marsh land, and rights in the commons. This system, in combination with the rocky soil, the rigorous climate, and the land laws which allowed division among several heirs, was not conducive to the development of great landed estates. The New England farm continued to be a comparatively small affair; the New Englander lived in a village and tilled the land with his own hands.

The New England villages, with their houses and gardens grouped compactly, with the village commons and the rights in the remaining land, are reminiscent of the English manor. Much of the land was held in common, although cultivated separately, and the town meeting was the center where plans were worked out and the cowherds, swineherds, and other officers who cared for the village property were elected. The system described was transitory. As the towns grew larger and the danger from Indians lessened and as labor became diversified, the inhabitants were often glad to sell their scattered strips, and the compact farm with its buildings and land together appeared, resembling rural New England as we know it today. The ease with which new land might be acquired, and an independent living assured, practically precluded for many years a non-landholding labor class and necessitated much co-operation among the farmers. Houses were raised, fences built, corn husked, and fields plowed by co-operative effort, and the gatherings were made the occasion of revelry as well as hard work.

AGRICULTURE IN THE MIDDLE COLONIES

With the exception of the Hudson Valley, where the patroon system of large landed proprietors was started by the Dutch and continued by the

English, the land system of the middle colonies resembled that of New England in the sense that the holdings were generally small. There were large plantations on the Chesapeake shore of Maryland, but even in this area the situation was much the same. Between the Hudson and the Potomac the settlers found the soil and climate much closer to that of their native lands than did those of New England. The soil of New Jersey was so rich, said Peter Kalm, the Swedish traveler, in 1749, that it made the settlers careless husbandmen. "They had nothing to do but to cut down the wood, put it up into heaps, and to clear the dead leaves away. They could then immediately proceed to plowing, which in such loose ground is very easy; and having sown their grain, they get a most plentiful harvest. This easy method of getting a rich crop has spoiled the English and other European settlers, and induced them to adopt the same method of agriculture as the Indians; that is, to sow uncultivated grounds, as long as they will produce a crop without manuring, but to turn them into pastures as soon as they can bear no more, and to take on new spots of ground, covered since ancient times with woods, which have been spared by the fire or the hatchet ever since the Creation."[5] In the fertile soil the wheat and barley often grew so rank that it reached a height of six or seven feet, with little grain in the heads. An observer in the Mohawk Valley in 1665 wrote that he had seen fields in which wheat was raised for eleven years in succession on the same field, and farms which had not been manured for nine years. The same traveler mentions the irrigation of meadows in Pennsylvania, but such care was rare.

Although nine-tenths of the New Englanders were farmers, the inhabitants of the middle colonies were even more predominantly agricultural in their economic life. With the exception of furs and lumber, the exports of this section seem to have been almost entirely agricultural. Judging from the export statistics,[6] wheat must have been the chief export, the average acre yielding from twenty to thirty bushels, a larger crop than was common in England at that time. Corn was raised throughout these provinces, providing the bulk of food for cattle in the winter. Rye, barley, buckwheat, and oats were also generally grown, the latter with great success. Fruits suitable to a temperate climate grew in great abundance—apples in New York, peaches and melons in the sandy soil of New Jersey and Delaware. "Peaches are of a fine flavor," says the author of *American Husbandry,* "and in such amazing plenty that whole stock of hogs on a farm eat as many as they will, but yet the quantity that rot under the trees is astonishing. . . . Watermelons are in such plenty that there is not a farmer or even a cottager without a piece of ground planted with them."[7] Large herds of cattle grazed on the coastal

---

[5] Adolph B. Benson (ed.), *Peter Kalm's Travels in North America,* I, 308.
[6] See below, chap. 5.
[7] *American Husbandry,* I, 139.

lowlands of Long Island, New Jersey, and elsewhere; hogs were abundant, running wild in the woods; and sheep were plentiful in Pennsylvania.

The agriculture of the middle colonies was somewhat influenced by the heterogeneous population. English, Dutch, Germans, Swedes, and other nationalities had their settlements, imported their particular strains of live-stock, farmed with their own methods, and raised their favorite crops. Even with the unscientific and wasteful methods of the time, a rude abundance was easily obtained. For the European peasant it was a veritable land of promise.

SOUTHERN AGRICULTURE

The settlers in Virginia found the soil too rich and the climate too warm for English wheat. But they soon discovered in tobacco a staple crop with a growing market upon which they could concentrate their energies. Although prices declined in later years, its growth was a profitable business, and the crop grew to 130,000,000 pounds by 1790. Since tobacco was raised for exportation, it was necessary that the plantation be located on the river banks where the tiny ships of colonial days could sail up and load a cargo from each farmer's wharf. The land was accordingly rapidly taken up along the many Virginia rivers, then along the Chesapeake inlets, and then south into the Albermarle and Pamlico districts of North Carolina. When the lands along the rivers were entirely occupied, the late comers were forced to set off a tier of farms immediately back of the river plantations and get the tobacco to their neighbors' wharves as best they might.

Tobacco, it was found, quickly exhausted the richest soil and necessitated the continual use of fresh land. Three years under the most favorable circumstances was the age of a tobacco field, after which it was turned over to other crops. White labor was scarce and costly, and gradually Negro labor was substituted. Supervision was essential for slave labor and it was believed that an overseer was too expensive unless he had twenty Negroes under him. This situation encouraged large plantations. Sometimes the great plantations had 1000 acres under actual tobacco cultivation besides land for other crops, a cattle range, and woodland. Many Virginia tobacco plantations were 5000 acres or over in size. These factors, combined with the ease with which the title to new land was acquired, are the chief causes for the large holdings in the South. Mere occupation and the payment of a small fee or quitrent were sufficient to establish ownership. "Head rights," or the granting of land to those who imported settlers, grants for meritorious service, and purely personal grants all contributed to the swelling of the large estates.

The very ease, however, with which land could be acquired tended to make labor scarce and thus to a certain extent retarded the development of large estates. The typical southern holding, while much larger than the New

England farm, was still moderate in size and the average southern white was a small farmer. Methods of agriculture, the emphasis upon the one staple, tobacco, and the geography of the country all tended to a system of settlement which prevented the growth of towns and promoted a distinctly rural life of scattered plantations in contrast to New England, where occupation usually began by founding a town.

Next in importance to the plantation system, which was undoubtedly the basic feature of southern commercial agriculture, was the cattle range. Shifting arable land and large plantations made inclosures impracticable; the vast unoccupied regions could readily be utilized for cattle ranges. Cattle, horses, and swine roamed in droves, subsisting on roots and herbage, branded when possible, but wild and often hunted as wild beasts. Each settler had his "right in the woods," which gave him a share in the unbranded cattle. Although the technique of ranching in the West was derived from the Spaniard, the western cattle ranch, nevertheless, with its roundup and brandings, was a replica on a much larger scale and at a later date of cattle ranching during the early days in Virginia and the Carolinas. The treatment of such livestock as was domesticated was even more unscientific than in the North. It was believed by many that housing and milking cows in the winter would kill them!

Passing south from Maryland and Virginia into the Carolinas, one found different conditions. Although cattle ranching was a feature in both North and South Carolina, in the first-named colony the farms were likely to be small and the products diversified, while the plantations of South Carolina were given over to the production of rice and indigo on a large scale. The farmers of North Carolina, most of whom were emigrants from Virginia— poor men, often former indentured servants or debtors—raised chiefly tobacco and corn on small farms.

Experimentation with rice began in South Carolina in the late 1600's and it became profitable with the importation of Negro slaves who were able to work in the hot, swampy coastlands. By the time of the Revolution, Charleston was exporting annually about 125,000 barrels. After Parliament granted in 1748 a bounty of sixpence a pound on indigo (a blue dye), that product also became an increasing source of wealth until displaced by cotton soon after the Revolution. Other efforts to raise semitropical products, however, usually failed.

CHARACTERISTICS OF COLONIAL AGRICULTURE

To lay down with exactness the characteristics of a period extending from 1607 to 1781 is difficult, owing to changing conditions in such an extended time. Certain general facts, however, can be stated. First of all, it is evident that colonial economy was predominantly agricultural. Although fish and naval stores were important export items, they were of far less value than the agricultural products shipped abroad. The economic life of the South came to rest upon large land grants, slave labor, and the export of such staples as tobacco, rice, and indigo. Nevertheless, it is important to remember that while the plantation system determined the economy of the South and the planters were the dominant influence in the government, they were at all times outnumbered by the smaller farmer. It has been maintained by a leading southern historian that "nine-tenths of the South's landowners at any period in her history were small proprietors."[8] The dependence of the prosperity of this section on the success or failure of a single crop and upon the fluctuation of a foreign market led to repeated efforts on the part of colonial assemblies to stimulate a greater production of foodstuffs. In this movement the small farmer played a large part, so that by 1736 foodstuffs and flax were produced in sufficient quantity for both home needs and exportation, and by 1760 sufficient livestock for local consumption. In contrast to the South, northern agriculture was based upon limited land grants, free labor, and food crops designed chiefly for a home market, although much was exported.

If one is to understand colonial agriculture, or, for that matter, any phase of colonial economic life, he must always remember that he is dealing with a world dominated by a mercantilist philosophy. *Laissez faire* was utterly foreign to the minds of seventeenth- and eighteenth-century rulers. The products of America were to supplement, not to compete with, those of the home countries. Tariff regulations prevented the selling of certain agricultural commodities, particularly foodstuffs, to England. Other laws required that sugar, tobacco, cotton, wool, indigo, and other products be sent only to that country. This might give the colonists a monopoly of the English market, but it also to that extent limited the foreign market. At the same time both the English and colonial governments at one time or another encouraged by bounties the production of tobacco, flax, hemp, indigo, and other crops. It was an age in which innumerable laws restricted or encouraged, as the case might be, the normal development of colonial agriculture.

It is also easy, as we shall see in the next chapter, to overemphasize the isolation and the self-sufficient aspect of the American farm. It is true that transportation facilities were poor and the typical small farmer had little ready money. At the same time there were always certain basic needs such as iron, salt, firearms, and ammunition common to all farmers, and innumerable other commodities which he greatly desired. There were taxes, mortgage payments, and other expenses. Even the small frontier farmer strove to raise

[8] W. E. Dodd, *The South in the Building of the Nation,* V, 74.

a surplus which he could market, while the plantation owners of the South were primarily engaged in raising staple crops for export. That the small farmer was more self-sufficing than he was after the Industrial Revolution is obvious, but it is also clear that every effort was being made to escape that situation.

COLONIAL LABOR

In Europe during the seventeenth and eighteenth centuries there appeared to be an abundance of labor but a dearth of resources. In America the reverse was true. The Europeans who settled North America found a virgin continent still unexploited, with a wealth of raw materials awaiting the hand of man. Labor and capital were both scarce and from the earliest times the problem of obtaining a sufficient supply was most difficult. This is perhaps a partial explanation of the American philosophy of the glorification of work and of the Puritan hatred of idleness, as exemplified in many colonial laws. The supply of labor from the native population was practically negligible, for the Indian in the region of the present United States preferred to live his old life rather than to subordinate himself to the white man. The European, possessing enough initiative to pioneer in a new land, was not the type that would readily submit to the authority of others when the chance of becoming a free landowner was so easy and the inducement to strike out for oneself so alluring. The need for labor was greater in the South, where the staple crops were raised on large plantations, and less in the North, where the farmer and his family cultivated a small farm. There were consequently more servants of all types in the South, but in all sections the demand for them was keen.

In the North the scarcity of labor was partially met by co-operation. When an extraordinary situation arose, as at the time of a house raising or a ship launching, the neighbors were called upon and the project was accomplished by the associated efforts of the group. What laborers there were in the North were of two classes—free and non-free. Although there were always some of the former, their number was small, for a man with any capacity could with little difficulty become a landowner and attain a degree of independence.

The non-free laborers were of two classes—indentured servants[9] and slaves. The indentured servants were also of two classes—voluntary and involuntary. The voluntary indentured servant[10] was one whose servitude was based upon a free contract. Many a person, eager to start a new life in America,

[9] The name "indenture" comes from the form of the contract, which was written in duplicate on a large sheet, the halves being separated by a wavy or jagged cut, called an indent.

[10] "Commonly call'd Kids," says Hugh Jones, *The Present State of Virginia* (1724), reprint by Sabin (1865), p. 53.

gladly sold himself for a period of from three to seven years to shipmasters or emigration brokers in payment of his passage to America, his length of service depending on his ability to pay part of the passage money or his success in disposing of himself advantageously. A few Germans and others voluntarily indentured themselves in order to learn the language and obtain funds to start life more advantageously. The voluntary free servant was ordinarily entitled to two weeks to find a purchaser, but, as he was not allowed to leave the ship, this right was of restricted value.

The second class of indentured servants, those suffering involuntary servitude, were usually debtors, vagrants, or criminals deported by the courts. The vagrancy laws since the days of Elizabeth had been extremely harsh in England. In addition, there were the various laws prohibiting the free movement of labor from one parish to another, because of fear that paupers might be thrown upon the parish for support. It was easy to fall into debt during hard times, and the penalty for debt was imprisonment. Over 300 crimes in the seventeenth century were punishable in England by death. With the courts and prisons crowded with paupers, vagrants, debtors, and petty criminals, it seemed the most humanitarian as well as the most practical policy to ship them over to the colonies. In this way England was relieved of a burden and America supplied with much-needed labor. If these prisoners could pay their own passage money they were free to do as they pleased; otherwise (and this was true of almost all), they were sold for from seven to ten years. In spite of the scarcity of labor, "His Majesty's Seven Year Passengers," as they were called, were far from welcome, the colonists much preferring their room to their company,[11] but the protests of the colonies against being made a dumping ground for criminals were of little avail.

The group of indentured servants was also recruited by the professional "spirits" or crimps who picked up thousands of children and adults and sold them to shipmasters engaged in the colonial trade. So extensive was this kidnaping in the latter half of the 1600's that Parliament passed legislation to curtail it, but the need for labor in the colonies was so great that the authorities showed little interest in enforcing the prohibition. This attitude changed somewhat in the 1700's as Britain became a great commercial and industrial power. The desire to deport criminals increased, but Britain preferred to keep her skilled workmen at home. In 1765 Parliament forbade the emigration of skilled workers.

The rights of servants were to a certain extent protected. They were entitled to food, clothing, shelter, and medical attendance when sick, and they might own property. At the end of their service they were usually given an outfit and in some cases fifty acres of land. Although protected by law from

[11] *Ibid.*

unjust cruelty, the age was a hard one and the lot of the indentured servant, especially the involuntary, was exceedingly unenviable. On the one hand, the cost and need of labor were an incentive to considerate treatment, but on the other hand, the desire to obtain as much labor as possible in the number of years covered by the indenture was a spur to excessive driving. In many cases the lot of the slave was superior to that of the indentured servant, for the loss to the owner of an able-bodied slave was greater, and hence conducive to better treatment. Most of the servants in the North were recruited from indentured servants, as were those in the South during the seventeenth century, for slaves were at first unpopular and slavery grew slowly. In 1681 there were 6000 white servants in Virginia and but 2000 slaves. Thousands of "free-willers" came each year during the latter part of the seventeenth and early part of the eighteenth century, but the number gradually decreased until by the Revolution their immigration had practically ceased.

Of the white immigrants to the colonies during the colonial period, probably half came as indentured servants. It is estimated that in Pennsylvania, Maryland, and Virginia possibly three-fourths of the white population at the time of the Revolution were of this stock. Although most of the population growth during the colonial period came from natural increase rather than from immigration, it is evident that the indentured servants and their offspring formed an important element in the early population of America.

The system of indentured servants helped to solve two problems: It enabled poor men to escape from Europe with a chance of starting life anew in a land of greater opportunities and it provided America with much-needed immigrants and laborers. For the average European laborer immigration on his own resources was impossible. Transportation to America cost from £6 to £10 and this amounted in money wages to three or four years' income for the pitifully underpaid English laborer. In terms of the wages obtainable in Europe, the indentured servant in America often sold his services at a reasonable price. Free workers in America obtained wages 30 to 100 per cent higher than in England. Cruel as the system was, it was not without its defenders. George Alsop, himself an indentured servant, wrote home that "The servants of this Province [Maryland], which are stigmatiz'd for slaves by the clapper-mouth jaws of the vulgar in England, live more like Freemen than the most Mechanick apprentice in London, wanting for nothing that is convenient and necessary, and according to their several capacities, are extraordinarily well used and respected."[12] It should be remembered that the voluntary indentured servants in most cases represented men and women who had the courage and stamina to seek escape from an en-

[12] George Alsop, *A Character of the Province of Maryland*, p. 94.

vironment for which they were not responsible and which held out no hope. A good proportion who survived the ordeal in America achieved the better life which they sought and many rose to positions of importance in their communities.

It should be noted, of course, that colonial labor was by no means limited to indentured servants from Europe or slaves from Africa. Families in the colonies were large and child labor was used to the utmost. The common practice in Europe of throwing debtors in jail was not followed in the colonies. Labor was too scarce, and debtors were allowed to work out their obligations to their creditors, while lawbreakers could also work out their fines by indenture. Moreover, the system of "apprenticeship" was widely practiced by which youths bound themselves until the age of eighteen or twenty-one to work for and live with a master in return for learning a trade and to read and write.

COLONIAL SLAVERY

Today economic expansion is often carried on by moving investment funds to the labor supplies, for that form of capital is concentrated in North America and Europe, whereas cheap labor is to be found in Asia, Africa, and South and Central America. Our forefathers, equipped with resources of land and raw materials, needed labor, and a partial solution was found in slavery. The reason why American farmers, chiefly plantation owners in the South, turned from white indentured servants to slaves was the conviction that they were cheaper than any form of labor obtainable. An indentured servant cost on an average from £2 to £4 a year in capital investment; an able-bodied slave could be purchased for from £18 to £30. For this the slave owner received a lifetime of service, with the possibility of gain from increase in the slave's family.

During the fifteenth century Portuguese traders began to import into Europe Negroes from the "Slave Coast," the part of the west coast of Africa extending from Cape Verde on the north to Cape St. Martha on the south. From the time of the first Portuguese settlement in Africa in 1482 the traffic became regular, lasting for about four hundred years. The slaves were purchased from native brokers living in the coast towns, who obtained them from the tribes in the interior. The latter, well supplied with guns and ammunition, turned over their prisoners of war and the fruit of their raiding parties to be imprisoned in the slave pens along the coast until they could be shipped away.

The first Negro slaves were brought to America and sold at Jamestown in 1619 by a Dutch privateer; within a few years they were to be found in all of the colonies. Slaves were unpopular at first, notwithstanding the scarcity of labor; hence their number grew slowly and for half a century Negroes composed only a small fraction of the total population. The slave trade was in the 1600's largely a monopoly of the Dutch until their power was broken in the 1660's. After that the Royal African Company of England took over until 1698. Then the traffic was thrown open and expanded rapidly. Bancroft estimated the number of slaves in the American mainland colonies in 1714 at 59,000, and in 1754 at 263,000. The first census (1790) showed over 697,-000. At this time they formed two-fifths of the total southern population, varying from a small percentage of the total in Maryland and North Carolina to over twice the white population in South Carolina.

The slave trade to the English colonies was soon monopolized by British and American ships. The latter proved to be especially efficient. The usual procedure for the Yankee slaver was to load up with rum and other commodities in New England, sail for the Slave Coast and exchange his goods for Negroes, dispose of the latter in the West Indies or the mainland, and take on a cargo of sugar, molasses, and tobacco for the North. The voyage between Africa and the West Indies, known as the "Middle Passage," shows slavery in its gloomiest aspect and the slave dealers at their worst. Crowded in the smallest possible space and chained to the ships, the Negroes suffered untold agonies during the slow weeks of the Atlantic passage; if they fell sick, they were thrown overboard, lest they contaminate their fellows. But our ancestors were hardened to suffering and had few compunctions about slavery.

A slave economy was adopted on the tobacco plantations of the South as the easiest way to fill the need for labor, and on the rice plantations of South Carolina as the only labor that could endure the climatic conditions on the hot, muggy rice fields. Slavery fulfilled an economic need, and as long as this continued it prospered. Toward the time of the Revolution, when the tobacco farms were wearing out, it fell into disfavor, only to be revived a few years later by the invention of the cotton gin.

SELECTED READINGS

Gray, L. C., *History of Agriculture in the Southern United States to 1860,* chaps. 1, 14–16.

Carrier, Lyman, *The Beginnings of American Agriculture,* chaps. 3–7, 9, 10–25.

Bidwell, P. W., and Falconer, J. I., *History of Agriculture in the Northern United States Before 1860,* chaps. 1–10.

Wertenbaker, T. J., *The First Americans,* chap. 3.

Phillips, U. B., *American Negro Slavery,* chaps. 1–7.

Bogart, E. L., and Thompson, C. M., *Readings in the Economic History of the United States,* pp. 28–40, 82–95.

CHAPTER 5

COLONIAL COMMERCE

AND INDUSTRY

CONDITIONS OF COLONIAL COMMERCE

THE American colonies from the beginning were destined to develop a large and thriving commerce. The whole theory of mercantilist economy envisaged the colonies as producers of commodities needed by the home country and in turn as purchasers of the latter's goods and services. This of necessity developed active commercial relations. Certain products of the forest and field were wanted in England, and the colonists in a new country desired the manufactured goods of the more advanced nations. Even the tariff laws passed by the British government to prevent the importation of foodstuffs and other colonial commodities sometimes reacted to encourage commerce, for they forced the colonists, in need of money to purchase English manufactured goods, to find other markets for their products.

In the development of commerce the American colonists were particularly blessed by physiographic conditions. Excellent harbors dotted the coast of New England and the middle colonies. Coastal bays, indentations, and rivers in the middle and southern colonies made commerce easy. "The accessibility of continents," it has been said, "is determined by the navigability of their rivers,"[1] and this is especially true of a newly settled region. Numerous small rivers in the South allowed the tiny vessels of the period to sail directly to the private wharves of the planters. "None of the plantation houses, even the most remote," commented a Frenchman traveling in Virginia in 1686, "is more than 100 or 150 feet from a 'crik' and the people are thus enabled not only to pay their visits in their canoes, but to do all their freight carrying by the same means."[2]

[1] E. C. Semple, *American History and Its Geographic Conditions*, p. 20.
[2] Durand, *A Frenchman in Virginia* (1923), p. 23.

75

Until the days of the railroad and automobile it was much easier to carry on commerce by water than by land. This was particularly true in a new country where roads were few and generally poor. It was not until the last third of the eighteenth century that regular stagecoach travel was established between a few of the larger centers. In 1771 the famous "flying machine" actually reduced the time between Philadelphia and New York to little more than a day and a half. As late as 1794 it took a week under the most favorable circumstances to travel by coach from Boston to New York.[3]

Under such conditions it was natural that most colonial commerce was carried on by water. Even so, the conditions were hard enough to give pause to a modern mariner. The boats were small and dependent on wind and weather, and the time consumed in crossing the Atlantic was exasperatingly long. The Pilgrims were at sea over two months between England and Cape Cod, and Peter Kalm more than a century later asserts that "it was common in winter time to be fourteen, nineteen or more weeks in coming from Gravesend to Philadelphia."[4] The weariness of such a voyage, the monotony of the diet, the discomfort in the cramped quarters, the misery in bad weather, the sickness from scurvy and contagious diseases which often accompanied a long passage can easily be imagined. If the dangers on the high seas were safely passed, there were still the hazards of sand bars and reefs, many of which were not even charted in those early years; and the few lighthouses which existed before the Revolution were of but limited service.

Other factors also continuously harassed colonial commerce. Not the least of these was the lack of a convenient medium of exchange. As the balance of trade between England and the colonies was always against the latter, what little currency found its way to British North America was quickly drained away. Such currency as existed came chiefly through trade with the Spanish and French colonies or drifted in through the medium of privateering or even piracy. A contemporary writer noted that money from the West Indies "seldom continues six months in the province before it is remitted to Europe." Barter was complicated by the fact that the amount of precious metals in the foreign coins varied, and also by the fact that although English coins were rarely seen, business was carried on in terms of pounds, shillings, and pence.

Conditions, of course, were not quite so bad as they might seem. International trade was conducted by drafts and bills of exchange; domestic trade, largely by barter of the stable commodities—beaver skins, corn, wheat. "The term bills of Students at Harvard College," says Dewey, "were for many

---

[3] Edmund Quincy, *Life of Josiah Quincy*, pp. 47–48. Colonial travel is further developed in chap. 14.

[4] Adolph B. Benson (ed.), *Peter Kalm's Travels in North America*, I, 14.

years met by payments of produce, livestock, meats, and 'occasionally with various articles raked up from the family closets of student debtors.' One student, later president of the college, in 1649 settled his bill with 'an old cow,' and the accounts of the construction of the first college building include the entry 'Received a goat 30s plantation of Watertown rate, which died.' "[5]

Efforts by the colonists to provide substitutes for metallic currency and barter were continuous. In Virginia and Maryland warehouse receipts for tobacco which had been deposited were successfully used. In 1690 Massachusetts issued bills of credit to pay the soldiers who took part in the expedition against Port Royal and Quebec, and this experiment in paper money was followed by all the colonies in the hope that such currency would fill a very evident need in commercial life. Acceptable at a premium over silver for the payment of taxes and generally specifying the date for payment, the early issues held up well, but as they became larger and the credit upon which they were based weaker, the result was disastrous. Depreciation followed excessive issue and the numerous emissions with their uncertain value hindered as much as they helped business. So-called "loan banks" in Massachusetts and Pennsylvania issued loan bills on real estate, personal security, and merchandise, but little is known of them. Disapprobation in Great Britain of these monetary issues led to an act of Parliament in 1751 forbidding the further issuance of legal tender bills of credit in New England, a prohibition extended to the other colonies in 1764. Although bitterly resented, this legislation was far from being wholly effective. It is estimated that $22,000,000 in paper was still in circulation at the time of the Revolution.

Another source of more or less continuous annoyance to colonial commerce was the existence of piracy and, in time of war, privateering. Wars were frequent in the seventeenth and eighteenth centuries, particularly after the beginning of the "Second Hundred Years' War" between England and France in 1689. In theory the difference between a pirate, a robber on the high seas, and a privateer, legally commissioned to war upon an enemy, was very wide. In practice it was sometimes exceedingly thin. The famous Captain Kidd started as a privateer and ended as a pirate. Despite the difficulties from pirates and privateers during the long years of warfare, their activities were not a complete loss to the colonists. Their booty and treasure had to be disposed of, and they were often smuggled into the colonies and sold at cheap prices. Prominent merchants and even government officials connived at the practice. The Rhode Islanders were particularly active in it. One report in 1736 to the Board of Trade asserts: "These practices will never be put an end to till Rhode Island is reduced to the subjection of the British

[5] D. R. Dewey, *Financial History of the United States*, p. 19.

Empire; of which at present it is no more a part than the Bahama Islands were when they were invaded by the Bucanners."[6] In any event the booty from this illicit traffic was large. Sober estimates suggest that New York alone for many years secured on an average of £100,000 in treasure annually in this way and that up to 1700 the greater supply of specie in the colonies was thus obtained.

THEORY OF COLONIAL TRADE

Reserving for a later chapter a more detailed discussion of British colonial policy, we need here merely outline its general purpose and effect. As we have already suggested, the theory behind the mercantilist policy was the subservience of the colonies to the political and economic welfare of the home country. This was the consistent and continuous policy followed for two centuries, clearly understood and repeatedly stated. The first Lord Sheffield once declared that "the only use and advantage of American colonies or West Indies islands is the monopoly of their consumption and the carriage of their produce." A member of the Board of Trade made this even clearer when he wrote in 1726:

Every act of a dependent provincial government ought therefore to terminate in the advantage of the mother state unto whom it owes its being and protection in all valuable privileges. Hence it follows that all advantageous projects or commercial gains in any colony which are truly prejudicial to and inconsistent with the interests of the mother state must be understood to be illegal and the practice of them unwarrantable, because they contradict the end for which the colony had a being and are incompatible with the terms on which the people claim both privileges and protection. . . . For such is the end of the colonies, and if this use cannot be made of them it will be much better for the state to do without them.

Could anything be clearer! After all, what was the use of an empire anyway? The only problem that remained was to determined how colonies in the long run could be made most valuable to the home country. Nor were those bodies of the British government which had supervision of colonial affairs (particularly the Lords of Trade and its successor, the Commissioners of Trade and Plantations) without definite ideas as to how this should be done. The commodities produced in the colonies and desired by England were encouraged by bounties and a monopoly of the home market. Those that came into competition with goods produced in England were kept out by high tariffs. Manufacturing in the colonies whose products competed with English products was discouraged or forbidden. Colonial efforts to ease the financial system by paper money—a system which forced the colo-

[6] Quoted by M. W. Jernegan, *The American Colonies, 1492–1750,* p. 380.

nists to buy dear and sell cheap—were forbidden. Colonial laws to curtail the slave trade, a source of immense profit to British slave traders, were vetoed. Every possible attempt was made to center colonial trade in the home country where British capital might reap the profits of the carrying trade, of insurance, and of middlemen's commissions.

Although British mercantilism as a whole operated to the detriment of colonial economic interests and was probably the most potent influence in bringing on the American Revolution, it did not, curiously enough, discourage colonial commerce. For this there were three main reasons. First of all the colonies, being a new country where land and resources were plentiful and labor scarce, were normally producers of raw or semifinished materials. They naturally fitted into the imperial system in which the colonies supplied the raw materials and the home country the manufactured products. In the second place, the colonies that produced commodities competing with those of Great Britain discovered other markets, particularly in the West Indies and southern Europe. Thus they secured means with which to purchase British manufactured goods. Finally, when British laws came in conflict with colonial interests they were evaded. Despite the British Navy, already the most powerful on the sea, smuggling was rampant, and trade with nations forbidden by British law flourished.

ROUTES AND COMMODITIES OF COLONIAL TRADE

The chief markets for colonial products were England, the West Indies, and southern Europe. By an act of 1660 certain "enumerated" commodities raised on the British mainland colonies were required by law to be sent only to England—tobacco, cotton, wool, and indigo. To these were later added naval stores (tar, pitch, turpentine, hemp, masts, yards), rice, copper, iron, lumber, furs, pearl ashes, and other commodities. As the export staples of the southern colonies were largely tobacco, rice, and indigo, and to a lesser extent naval stores and furs, most of the export trade of these colonies was a direct trade with England. In return they imported drygoods, hardware, furniture, and other types of manufactured goods.

In New England and the middle colonies the situation was quite different. These colonies had certain commodities—such as naval stores, lumber, furs, and metals—that were desired in the mother country, but their great staples —fish, grain, and other foodstuffs—were kept out of England by high tariff. Their export trade with her was therefore relatively small and they were forced to find other outlets for their chief products. These outlets were primarily in the West Indies and to a lesser extent in southern Europe. To them New England sent mainly pickled and dried fish, pickled beef and pork, horses and livestock, and various kinds of building material. The exports to these regions from New York and Pennsylvania were chiefly flour and wheat. By the opening of the eighteenth century the West Indian islands had been turned largely into sugar and tobacco plantations unable to support themselves without the importation of cheap food for slaves and lumber for homes and for casks to transport sugar, molasses, and tobacco. In return the mainland colonies obtained molasses which they could turn into rum for the fishing fleet, the slave trade, or domestic use. They also obtained specie or various commodities which could be used to purchase manufactured commodities from Britain. The extent of this trade may be seen from contemporary estimates. One puts the average annual exports from New England (1763–1766) at £485,000, over half of which were products of the sea; from New York at £526,000; and from Pennsylvania at £705,500, more than half of the last two being flour and wheat.[7]

The whole course of colonial commerce provides an interesting study in international trade and balance of payments, to say nothing of the ingenuity of the colonial merchant and sea captain in finding an outlet for the products of his region in the face of mercantilist restrictions. In addition to a certain amount of intercolonial commerce and the direct trade to and from Britain and to and from the West Indies, there developed various phases of the famous triangular trade. The imports of New England and the middle colonies from Britain were in some years eight or more times their exports. This trade was maintained in various ways. New England and the middle colonies exported their grain, meat, fish, and lumber to southern Europe, then carried wine, fruit, and other commodities to England where they were exchanged for manufactured products. Another triangular route was the carrying of the products of the New England and the middle colonies to the West Indies where they were exchanged for sugar, molasses, and other commodities; these were taken to England to be exchanged for manufactured goods that were brought back to the northern mainland colonies. As already pointed out, these manufactured goods from England were in part paid for by coin or bills of exchange on London obtained by the direct trade between the northern mainland colonies and the West Indies, a condition made possible partly by the fact that the exports from the West Indies to Great Britain were almost three times the imports.

No one ever made this clearer than Benjamin Franklin himself, testifying as the agent of Pennsylvania before a committee of the British House of Commons in 1766. After pointing out that Pennsylvania imported £500,000 worth of goods each year from Britain and exported to her but £40,000, he was asked, "How then do you pay the balance?"

[7] *American Husbandry,* I, 59, 124, 181.

The balance [he replied] is paid by our produce carried to the West Indies, and sold in our own islands, or to the French, Spaniards, Danes and Dutch; by the same carried to other colonies in North-America, as to New-England, Nova-Scotia, Newfoundland, Carolina and Georgia; by the same carried to different parts of Europe, as Spain, Portugal and Italy: In all which places we receive either money, bills of exchange, or commodities that suit for remittance to Britain; which together with all the profits on the industry of our merchants and mariners, arising in those circuitous voyages, and the freights made by their ships, center finally in Britain, to discharge the balance, and pay for British manufactures continually used in the province, or sold to foreigners by our traders.

Still another phase of the triangular commerce was the African slave trade, which grew enormously during the 1700's. The causes were: (1) the

TRIANGULAR TRADE I.

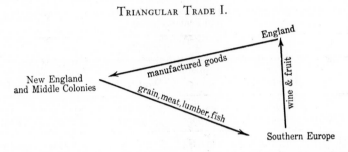

demand for cheap labor on the plantations of the islands and mainland, and for household servants in the northern colonies, and (2) the large profits which accrued from the trade to English interests and colonial shipowners.

TRIANGULAR TRADE II.

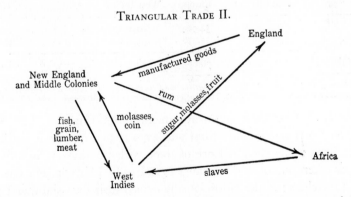

Not only were the shipping interests in New England concerned in the slave trade, but also the rum manufacturers who supplied the chief commodity used in the purchase of the Negroes. Until the Revolution almost all the Negroes were taken to the West Indies, and from there a certain portion were later brought to the mainland. From 25,000 to 30,000 slaves a year were transported to these islands, and perhaps 10,000 a year were taken from there to the continental colonies.

Considering the primitive conditions in America, such as lack of good transportation facilities and of liquid capital, and the other disadvantages, foreign commerce in the colonial period was extremely active and showed a high per capita value. Throughout the period there was a healthy increase that reached its apex in the decade of the 1760's. Although statistics are by no means dependable, a rough estimate for one of the later years enables the student to obtain a fairly clear picture of the amount and direction of this commerce. It will be noted, first of all, that northern commerce was more evenly distributed than that of the South. The colonies south of Penn-

COLONIAL EXPORTS AND IMPORTS, 1769
(In Pounds Sterling)

Exports from	To				
	Great Britain	Southern Europe	West Indies	Africa	Total
North	284,269	335,810	555,612	19,584	1,195,275
South	1,247,245	216,923	192,292	690	1,657,150
Total	1,531,514	552,733	747,904	20,274	2,852,425

Imports to	From				
	Great Britain	Southern Europe	West Indies	Africa	Total
North	504,614	54,909	594,421	877	1,154,821
South	1,100,367	21,770	195,326	151,120	1,468,583
Total	1,604,981	76,679	789,747	151,997	2,623,404

Figures from E. R. Johnson *et al.*, *History of Domestic and Foreign Commerce of the United States*, I, 92, and F. A. Shannon, *America's Economic Growth*, p. 32. The North in this table includes all colonies north of Maryland.

sylvania carried on their commerce mainly with England. The North's discrepancy between imports from and exports to England is particularly evident. This unfavorable balance of trade with the mother country, however, was taken care of in the manner described by Franklin. For one thing, colonial merchants in the North usually owned their own ships, and profits from the carrying trade alone contributed much to even the balance. Of all the commerce, that with southern Europe was most important in maintaining an approximate balance, and this was true of both North and South. Although the year 1769 showed a balance of trade in favor of the South, this was generally not the case. When it did occur, it was deceptive, for the profits

of the English middlemen and the shipowners more than made up the difference and in the long run tended to throw the plantation owners into a
chronic state of indebtedness.

CONDITIONS OF COLONIAL INDUSTRY

The pre-eminence of agriculture in colonial economy has been stressed
again and again. Factory production as we know it today did not exist.
Even the "putting out" system—a method of production in which the capitalist gathered the raw material, distributed it to individual workmen in
their homes, and later collected and sold the finished product—was rare.
Nevertheless a certain type of crude and somewhat primitive industry was
widespread. First of all, there was the typical household manufacturing.
On the average farm the housewife spun and wove the wool, flax, or cotton
for clothes, smoked and salted meat, dried and preserved fruit and vegetables. She made her own soap and candles and brewed her own beer.
Leather for shoes, gloves, and work clothes was produced and processed on
the farm. From his own wood lot the farmer procured timber for his house
and hard wood for his tools, furniture, and casks. The hard labor involved
in manufacturing all these necessities of living was not expended by preference. The colonial farmer, like the farmer of today, would have much preferred to exchange his surplus for manufactured goods. The typical farm of
the colonial period, however, was small, surpluses were meager, and transportation was poor. The farm family manufactured its own goods by necessity.

Another type of household industry existed, the products of which were
designed not for the home but for the outside market. During their spare
time in the winter months many farmers manufactured nails, shingles, barrel staves, or casks which found a ready market in the West Indian trade
or in the local fish and rum industry. In fact, by the end of the colonial
period this type of industry had often expanded into small local shops. This
form of industry—industry that was an adjunct of, or supplementary to,
agriculture and commerce—was typical of much colonial manufacturing.
The products included tools for farming, ships for the widespread commerce, naval stores and other ship supplies, and casks and containers for
tobacco, rum, molasses, and fish. Like industry on the farm, it was one of
necessity, stimulated at times by bounties, such as those on naval stores,
offered by the British government for commodities wanted in the home
country.

Another type of manufacturing which may be described as village industries appeared as communities grew to a size that could support them.
Most settlements of any size had a sawmill where the farmers could have

their lumber prepared, a gristmill where their corn or wheat could be ground, and a fulling mill where cloth could be smoothed and dyed after it was woven. Such communities, if large enough, also supported a shoemaker, a tailor, a cabinetmaker, or other highly trained artisans who produced goods on order.

Delay in the development of colonial manufacturing for export and the general trade was not due to lack of resources. These existed or could be produced in abundance. It was not due to lack of capital. This could be obtained in England or from the surpluses of prosperous merchants, of whom there were many by the late colonial period. Nor was it due in the last analysis to lack of labor, scarce as that might be. The colonial population by 1776 was one-fourth that of England. Newly arrived immigrants, deprived of good land in the East, might have been induced to enter manufacturing; indentured servants and slaves were available. The lack of development was the result, among other factors, of the belief that greater profits were to be obtained in agriculture, commerce, and land speculation. Above all, it resulted from the opposition of the British government. British mercantilism looked upon the colonies as a source of raw materials and a market for manufactured goods. Manufactured commodities that came into competition with British goods either in the colonies or in international trade were to be discouraged. At the same time every encouragement should be given to an economic system which would bind the colonies more closely to the needs of British mercantilism.

Even the most cursory survey of the actions of the Board of Trade and other groups in the British government or of their representatives in America during the century preceding the American Revolution bears out this contention. The policy can be seen in specific legislation to curtail the development of a colonial woolen or iron industry. Complaints of British manufacturers, for example, that the colonists were exporting woolens led to the act in 1699 forbidding the shipment of wool, woolen yarn, or cloth produced in the colonies to any other plantation or country. In 1732 the exportation of hats was similarly prohibited. A law of 1750, while it permitted the entry of bar iron in England, prohibited in the colonies the erection of slitting or rolling mills, and plate, forge, or steel furnaces. Since it did not prohibit casting furnaces, the colonists could still make cannon, kettles, salt pans, and other utensils. This policy is also evident in the instructions to colonial governors to prevent the levying of duties on British goods brought to America or anything else that would in any way give preferential treatment to colonial manufactured products. It is apparent in the innumerable vetoes of colonial laws passed to encourage local manufacturing. It is clear in the veto of laws passed by southern legislatures to curtail the slave trade, for it was the business of the British government to perpetuate in the colonies the plantation system that was so profitable to the commercial and shipping interests of the home land. Far from being accidents of politics, say the Beards, such acts, instructions, and vetoes "were the matured fruits of a mercantile theory of state which regarded colonial trade as the property of the metropolis, to be monopolized by its citizens and made subservient in all things to their interests."[8]

INDUSTRIES OF THE FOREST

To the pioneer farmer the rich forest lands of America seemed only an obstruction to be cleared as quickly as possible in order to open up his farm. It was not long, however, before he discovered in the forests a valuable commodity for trade. Four industries were dependent upon the forest—lumbering, shipbuilding, the manufacture of naval supplies, and the making of potash. In addition, of course, there was the lucrative fur trade. Lumbering and shipbuilding were particularly active in the northern colonies where the rivers extended well up into the forests and sawmills could be run by water power at the fall line. There was a steady and profitable market in the West Indies and southern Europe, and many a farmer was able to attain prosperity by part-time work preparing wood for the market.

With an abundance of white pine, fur, and oak close to the water's edge and a ready supply of pitch pine for tar and turpentine, the colonists had at hand the raw products for shipbuilding. The cheapness of the raw materials overcame the high cost of labor, and the need for ships stimulated the industry from the start. Most of the shipbuilding was centered in New England, where construction was 30 to 50 per cent cheaper than in Europe. By 1760 the colonies were building from 300 to 400 boats a year, and one-third of the tonnage sailing under the British flag was American built. Besides lumber and ships New England produced certain naval stores, notably tar, pitch, rosin, turpentine, and water-rotted hemp. These commodities, needed by the British Navy and merchant marine, were imported chiefly from Sweden, Poland, and Russia, but after 1705 they were stimulated, particularly in the Carolinas, by British bounties.

Throughout the colonial period the fur trade was an important forest industry and a valuable source of income for all of the colonies. Many types of furs were secured, but the basic pelts were beaver skins in the North and deer skins in the South. For these the colonists traded guns, rum, knives, axes, cloth, kettles, and other commodities. Sale of the first two was forbidden in most of the colonies, but since it facilitated trade, the laws were generally evaded. The high profits of the early years declined as the Indians

[8] C. and M. Beard, *Rise of American Civilization*, p. 193.

grew wiser and as colonial traders came in competition with the French and Spanish, but the annual export of furs from the British mainland colonies amounted by the end of the colonial period to well over £200,000.

The fur trade, however, has a much deeper significance in American history than its commercial and industrial phase. The fur trader pressing after the retreating game supply blazed the trail for the missionary and settler and pointed the way to the West. But though he opened the western routes and brought material prosperity, his unscrupulous treatment of the red men often resulted in Indian wars with their horrors and devastations. It also brought him in continuous competition with the French fur traders (*coureurs de bois*), whose relations with the Indians were more successful, but whose commodities were more costly and had to be carried farther. As the furs declined on the eastern coast and the traders pushed west of the Alleghenies, the competition became more bitter. Moreover, the founding as early as 1670 of the Hudson's Bay Company, to which the English king gave a grant to trade in the regions draining into Hudson Bay, was a direct stroke at the political and economic interests of France. From then on, as far as the colonies were concerned, competition for the fur trade played an important part in the colonial wars and in the ultimate decision as to whether Britain or France would dominate the continent.

INDUSTRIES OF THE SEA

Whether it was the chronic state of hunger under which Europe suffered during the Middle Ages or the desertion of the western coast of Europe by the food fish that drove the fishermen to push westward for their supply is uncertain. By 1300 they had reached Iceland, and at least a hundred years before there was an English settlement in New England, European fishermen were sailing regularly to the "Banks." By 1500 the deep-sea fisheries were in full operation and the Newfoundland waters were frequented by ships of England, France, Spain, and Portugal. To preserve the fish on the long trip home they had to be cured, and for this it was necessary to land and spread them out in the sun where the moisture could evaporate and the salt "strike in." The mystery which hangs over these early trips to the fishing banks, possibly because a great deal of the product was smuggled in on the return voyage, makes it impossible to determine at what date Europeans first began to land upon various parts of the coast to cure their fish. The Portuguese alone in 1550 had 400 fishing vessels in American waters; England in 1610 was said to have derived an income of $10,000,000 from the sale of surplus fish. In consequence, European governments early in the seventeenth century awoke to the importance of possessing lands close to the fishing banks. This necessity provided one impetus to North American exploration, and resulted in disputes over lands close to the fishing grounds which have continued almost to the present day.

The demand for fish was widening in Europe, especially in Catholic countries. New England, close to the fishing grounds and with an abundance of shipbuilding materials at hand, was in a strategic position to profit. After 1650 her prosperity was closely connected with fishing, and by 1675 over 600 vessels and 4000 men were engaged in cod fishing. By the end of the colonial period the industry was worth £225,000 a year. As the market developed, New Englanders divided their fish in three classes. The largest and fattest, because they were the most difficult to cure thoroughly, were consumed locally. The second class, smaller and more easily cured, was exported to the Continent. The third class, too small for the European or American market, was sold in the West Indies as food for slaves, usually in exchange for molasses. The latter was brought back and converted into rum. In addition to the manufacture of rum, which was a result of the fishing industry, the demand for salt was stimulated, and salt vats were erected at various points along the shore, where sea water could be evaporated. Fish, molasses, rum, and salt all contributed to make the cooperage industry one of the liveliest in the colonies.

Almost as important as fishing during the last hundred years of the colonial era was the whaling industry. Spermaceti, sperm oil, whalebone, and ambergris were in great demand. Whales were abundant off the New England coast and after 1700 New England seamen began to put off and harpoon the unwieldy monsters when they came up to breathe. When the whales were driven off the coast, the whalers followed them to other regions. After 1732 an annual bounty of twenty shillings a ton (doubled in 1747) was paid on vessels of 200 tons or upward engaged in whaling, and the consequent increasing values of the products spurred on the hunters. The most skillful whalers in the world came from New England and that area practically monopolized the business. Over 300 vessels and 4000 sailors were engaged in it at the outbreak of the Revolution, most of them hailing from Nantucket, New Bedford, Marblehead, and Provincetown. Upon the basis of spermaceti a candlemaking business of some importance grew up.

INDUSTRIES OF THE HOME AND WORKSHOP

Mention has already been made of household industries, but it may be worth while again to emphasize the importance of this phase of colonial manufacturing. Few homes were without a spinning wheel and a hand loom, and the larger part of the textiles used in the colonies were produced in the home. Most of this cloth was either wool or linen or a mixture of the two. Sheep were more commonly raised on farms in this period than in later years and flax was more widely grown. Hemp cloth or linen of varying degrees of fineness was the chief colonial textile; it served nearly all of the purposes for which cotton is used today. While the British government did what it could to discourage the production of woolen goods which came in competition with its own manufacturing, it was eager to encourage the growth and use of hemp and flax. Several colonial assemblies offered bounties for the growing of these two commodities and others required that they be grown. Little cotton was grown in the mainland colonies until after the 1790's. Some was imported, but being a difficult fiber to work, it was generally mixed with linen or wool before spinning. Not only was spinning and weaving a universal household industry, but by the time of the Revolution the faint beginnings of the factory system could be seen in the grouping of several weaving machines under the same roof. Such shops could be found in certain of the larger towns such as Philadelphia and Lancaster.

It was impossible to produce iron utensils on most farms. The cost of importing them was so great, however, that ironworks appeared in Massachusetts at Lynn and Taunton as early as the 1640's to exploit the bog iron common in those regions. In the eighteenth century the industry moved farther from the coast to use the rock ores in the uplands of New Jersey and Pennsylvania. Some copper was also mined in Connecticut, New York, and New Jersey.

The purpose of the iron mines was chiefly to supply the immediate needs of the colonists for wagon and sleigh tires, mill spindles, anvils, pots, kettles, forged plates, weights, bells, chains, anchors, guns, and cannon. In conjunction with these mines and smelting establishments, casting works were usually found. Slitting mills furnished iron rods from which the farmers manufactured nails on winter evenings by means of a small furnace in the chimney corner. The colonial smelting furnaces generally were small and crude, producing from a dozen to twenty tons a week.

The development of iron foundries was not what the British wanted. Pig iron might be produced in the colonies, but the colonials must not compete with the home manufacturers. By 1750 the casting of iron had reached such proportions that Parliament prohibited the erection of any slitting or rolling mill, plating, forge, or steel furnace, under a penalty of £200. Although iron manufacturing was restricted, the production of pig and bar iron was encouraged after 1757 by permitting their admission into the port of London free of duty. Exports under this stimulus grew to 7525 tons in 1771, valued at £20 a ton.

From the amount of furniture and other household utensils exhibited in antique shops as "colonial," one might gain the impression that most of our forefathers were engaged solely in this type of manufacturing. Most of the "antiques" date from the years after the Revolution. Nevertheless a large amount of household furnishings was manufactured either in the home or on order by local cabinetmakers. Some of it even entered the intercoastal trade. The loadings of New England vessels trading with the southern colonies and the West Indies show frequent items of furniture for export to these regions. Some glass was also manufactured. One experiment, that of the famous Baron Stiegel, who set up a feudal state and glassworks at Mannheim, southwest of Lancaster, produced excellent glassware but otherwise proved unsuccessful.

An almost universal industry, household and otherwise, was the making of many kinds of liquor. It throve especially in the coast towns of New England, where the West Indian molasses was distilled into rum, particularly for the slave trade and the fishing expeditions. At one time twenty distilleries in Newport alone were engaged in the business. Not only rum but also beer, ale, and cider were exported to the West Indies. It must not be thought, however, that this liquor business was concerned entirely with exports; our forefathers were hard drinkers and a large proportion was consumed at home.

EXTENT OF COLONIAL INDUSTRY

It would be the merest guesswork to attempt even an approximate statement of the extent of colonial industry at various periods. Contemporary accounts are either inadequate or exaggerated for the purpose of influencing prospective settlers or setting at rest the fears of the home government. The colonists' attempt at the time of the Stamp Act to free themselves from dependence upon British industry brought in 1766 and 1768 letters from the Lords of Trade to the colonial governors demanding an annual report on manufactures in their provinces. Though inadequate, these reports are a valuable source of information.[9] The general tenor of the replies was to depreciate the extent of colonial industry and to emphasize the dependence of the colonists upon Great Britain. While specific industries were mentioned, it was maintained that the wealthier classes bought imported goods and that the lure of the land turned the mechanic into a farmer, to the detriment of the development of manufacturing. Governor Bernard of Massachusetts went so far as to declare, "I do not think it necessary to send an annual account where I have nothing to inform of."

These reports, apparently aimed to reassure the British government that

[9] A summary of these letters is given in Victor S. Clark, *History of Manufactures in the United States, 1670–1860,* pp. 207 ff.

the colonists were in no position to become economically independent, belittled unduly the real condition of colonial manufacturing. A truer impression is given by an English writer who stated in 1774 that

the inhabitants in the Colonies . . . do make many things, and export several manufactures, to the exclusion of English manufactures of the same kinds. The New England people import from the foreign and the British Islands very large quantities of cotton, which they spin and work up with linen yarn into a stuff, like that made in Manchester, wherewith they clothe themselves and their neighbours. Hats are manufactured in Carolina, Pennsylvania and in other Colonies. Soap and candles, and all kinds of wood-work, are made in the Northern Colonies and exported to the Southern. Coaches, chariots, chaises, and chairs, are also made in the Northern Colonies and sent down to the Southern. Coach harness, and many other kinds of leather manufactures, are likewise made in the Northern Colonies, and sent down to the Southern; and large quantities of shoes have lately been exported from thence to the West India Islands. Linens are made to a great amount in Pennsylvania and cordage and other hemp manufactures are carried on in many places with great success: and foundry ware, axes, and other iron tools and utensils are also become articles of commerce, with which the Southern Colonies are supplied from the Northern.[10]

When the colonist could afford it, he undoubtedly preferred to buy the finest grade of manufactures from abroad; but the essentials could be obtained here, and the nonintercourse agreements prior to the Revolution demonstrated Franklin's contention that the colonist could supply himself with what was absolutely needed without recourse to Great Britain. To do so, however, at that time was abnormal, for colonial economy was primarily agricultural.

SELECTED READINGS

Hacker, L. M., *The Triumph of American Capitalism*, pp. 136–158.
Nettels, Curtis, *The Roots of American Civilization*, chaps. 9, 10.
Johnson, E. R., *et al.*, *History of Domestic and Foreign Commerce of the United States*, Vol. I, chaps. 1–6, 9–11.
Dewey, D. R., *Financial History of the United States*, chap. 1.
Tryon, R. M., *Household Manufacture in the United States, 1640–1860*, chaps. 1–6.
Clark, V. S., *History of Manufactures in the United States, 1607–1860*, chaps. 1–9.
Bogart, E. L., and Thompson, C. M., *Readings in the Economic History of the United States*, pp. 42–80, 96–105.

[10] *Interest of the Merchants and Manufacturers of Great Britain in the Present Contest with the Colonies Stated and Considered* (London, 1774; reprinted in Boston), p. 12.

CHAPTER 6

FRONTIER EXPANSION BEFORE
THE REVOLUTION

SIGNIFICANCE OF THE WESTWARD MOVEMENT

CONFLICTING influences have contributed to the formation of American character and ideals. On the one hand, proximity to the ocean and intercourse with Europe retarded the development of a distinctly American civilization, while on the other the westward movement and frontier life continually worked to efface the European influence and to stimulate the growth of a new nation. The Appalachian barrier and the lack of transportation facilities, until the opening of the nineteenth century, kept the great majority of the people east of the mountains. As late as 1830 the center of population was still on the Atlantic coast. Nevertheless, even before this date, as afterward, one of the most important factors in the life and history of the people was the continued westward advance. The movement inland commenced almost immediately after the first settlements were made and lasted until after 1890, when the frontier lines moving west and east joined. "Up to our own day," said Professor Turner in 1893, "American history has been in a large degree the history of the colonization of the Great West. The existence of an area of free land, its continuous recession, and the advance of American settlement westward, explain American development."[1]

Leaving until a later time a more detailed discussion of the validity of the Turnerian thesis and the effects which the westward movement has had, we need here simply point out by way of introduction some of its important influences suggested by Turner. The exigencies of pioneer life forced the settler, if he was to survive, to adapt himself to changed conditions; and although he carried with him the ideas and training of his youth, the influence of his European cultural background became progressively less. As settlers of

[1] F. J. Turner, *The Frontier in American History*, p. 1.

various races were thrown together in a similar environment, there gradually evolved a composite type of American. The never-ending struggle against the forces of nature, against hostile Indians and wild beasts, developed a self-reliant, aggressive, individual type, characterized by antipathy to control and to any attempt to abridge his independence—what Burke called "a fierce spirit of liberty." The comparative equality of wealth in a new community, where each man stood upon his own feet, made it easy to forget the artificial customs of an old world and developed a more democratic outlook. The West, as a result, has often been the most democratic part of America, and our history has been full of the struggles between the democratic frontiersman and the more conservative Easterner. The elements which have gone to make up the life of the frontiersman have produced intellectually a type that is restless, energetic, and practical, and at the same time buoyant and optimistic.

For our political life the growth of the West with its different interests has meant the emergence of sectionalism and the demands of the Westerner for legislation promoting his own interests—internal improvements, free land, and an inflated currency. At the same time, however, his need for many things which only the national government could give him has been a potent factor in the growth of nationalism. In the technique of government the drive of the West has been toward such democratic innovations as the direct election of United States Senators, woman suffrage, and the initiative, referendum, and recall. Economically, the growth of the West brought, at least until recent years, virtual industrial independence for the nation, along with sectional specialization.

STAGES OF WESTWARD ADVANCE

Even during colonial times rather clearly marked stages of westward advance were in evidence. The first was usually marked by the activities of the hunter, trader, or missionary. Traders and trappers like Daniel Boone and Jedediah Smith, and missionaries like Father Marquette and Marcus Whitman are typical of the pathfinders who blazed the way. The trail of the hunter followed that of the wild animal and the Indian and eventually became a highway of civilization, and the trading posts erected at convenient points on the western trails grew into such cities as Albany, Pittsburgh, Chicago, and St. Louis. Following the trapper and the trader came the rancher, who occupied the land to exploit the grasses. Of all farm products, livestock was in those days the easiest moved, and from the "cow pens" of seventeenth-century Virginia and the Carolinas to the great modern ranches of the western prairies the frontier ranchman has generally marked the farthest westward advance.

Close on the heels of the rancher came the farmer, the first wave dispersing in sparsely settled communities and wastefully exploiting the soil. This preliminary farming stage was in turn succeeded by more or less intensive farming in denser settlements. Where conditions were favorable, the farming stage gave way to the final stage—urban life with its manufacturing and commercial activities.

These stages through which most of our country has passed—the hunting, the ranching, the farming, the industrial—have all played their part in its development, and for almost three centuries this process has been repeated and the drama re-enacted, coloring our history and determining our civilization. All these stages, of course, were not inevitable, nor did they always occur in the order named. Sometimes representatives of all the four groups landed pell-mell in a new region and contributed simultaneously to its development.[2] In general, however, the recurring stages so vividly portrayed by Professor Turner marked the outstanding epochs in our economic advance.

The Atlantic frontier was compounded of fisherman, fur trader, miner, cattle-raiser, and farmer. Excepting the fisherman, each type of industry was on the march toward the West, impelled by an irresistible attraction. Each passed in successive waves across the continent. Stand at Cumberland Gap and watch the procession of civilization, marching single file—the buffalo following the trail to the salt springs, the Indian, the fur trader and hunter, the cattle-raiser, the pioneer farmer—and the frontier has passed by. Stand at South Pass in the Rockies a century later and see the same procession with wider intervals between. The unequal rate of advance compels us to distinguish the frontier into the trader's frontier, the rancher's frontier, or the miner's frontier, and the farmer's frontier. When the mines and cow pens were still near the fall line, the traders' pack trains were tinkling across the Alleghenies, and the French on the Great Lakes were fortifying their posts, alarmed by the British trader's birch canoe. When the trappers scaled the Rockies, the farmer was still near the mouth of the Missouri.[3]

ROUTES OF WESTWARD MIGRATION

Navigable streams marked the first routes of westward migration. The hope of finding a passage through the newly discovered lands to the riches of Cathay led the earliest explorers to probe the innumerable rivers and estuaries with their tiny boats. Later the rivers and lakes offered to the fur trader the readiest access into the interior, and decades, even centuries, before the settler followed him he had clearly pointed out the routes of travel. Twelve years before the Dutch made their famous purchase of the island of Manhattan they had established a trading post at Albany; by 1627 merchants

[2] C. W. Alvord, in the *Mississippi Valley Historical Review*, VII, 403–407 (March, 1921).
[3] F. J. Turner, *op. cit.*, p. 12.

of Jamestown were trading with Indians of the upper Potomac and Susquehanna. The French, who had stumbled upon an easy route into the interior and had been forced by circumstances into the development of the fur trade, had discovered long before the opening of the eighteenth century the best routes between the basin of the Great Lakes and the Mississippi. There they had used the key portages which the Indians make known to them.

South of the St. Lawrence were four leading routes through the Appalachian barrier. The most northerly and the best, that by way of the Hudson and Mohawk to the Lakes, was closed to early settlers by the Iroquois. To the south was a second route leading from the headwaters of the Mohawk to the upper Allegheny. The third led across southern Pennsylvania to the Monongahela and thence to the Ohio, a line later followed by the Cumberland Road. The fourth and most important to the pre-Revolutionary settlers was southward down the great Appalachian Valley and out through the Cumberland Gap or the Tennessee Valley. A possible route around the south of the Appalachians was closed by the Cherokees. While these routes were known to fur traders long before the Revolution, it was not until the latter part of the eighteenth century that settlers in any numbers followed them. Before that time the need of keeping in close touch with the European market had kept the white man near the rivers, and hostile French and Indians as well as the natural mountain barrier had all contributed to limit settlement east of the Appalachians.

THE FIRST FRONTIER

As already noted, Virginia's first frontier was a string of farms and plantations located on the numerous rivers, from which their great staple, tobacco, could be shipped. As the land along the rivers was pre-empted, the inland region was tapped, but the tendency to stay close to the rivers made early Virginia like a federation of peninsulas. It also perpetuated a rural environment despite efforts of the government to control the frontier movement by grouping frontiersmen into towns at the first falls of the rivers. The frontier of Virginia pushed south as well as west, and by 1700 the region of the Carolinas north of Albemarle Sound and east of the Chowan River had been occupied.

Unlike the somewhat haphazard westward migration of the Virginia colonists, the New England colonial governments attempted very definitely to superintend the founding of towns and prescribe their limits. Whereas the migration in Virginia was by individuals, that in New England was by groups and towns (pp. 55, 65). But control went farther than that. An order of the Massachusetts General Court in 1636 directed that none go to the new plantations without the permission of a majority of the magistrates, an order which was probably evaded. On the other hand, the danger from French and Indian attack led the General Court in 1694, after enumerating certain "Frontier Towns," to forbid the inhabitants to desert these outposts on pain of imprisonment and confiscation of their land. The closeness of the New England frontier to the older settlements and the constant danger of enemy attack made the position and status of the frontier towns a matter of the most earnest concern. Other New England colonies followed the same system.

Settlement by townships by approved groups of men had many advantages, particularly in affording maximum protection against the Indians, but it also opened the way for controversies between the proprietors who received the grant and the nonproprietors who came in later and who might have no rights in the common or undivided lands. As the nonproprietors were often more numerous and gained control of the local government, the opportunities for friction were great.

The beginnings of Dutch settlement can be traced to trading posts on the Delaware River and at the mouth and upper reaches of the Hudson. Schenectady at the rapids of the Mohawk was begun in 1661, and in the succeeding years the intervening land along the two rivers was taken up under the patroon system and allotted to tenants by the patroons or the New Amsterdam officials. New Jersey, Pennsylvania, Delaware, and Maryland were settled under the early proprietors through individual land grants or sales to settlers. Although the settlers moved westward rapidly, villages and towns early developed. The Carolinas in 1700 boasted two patches of settlement, the northern around Albemarle Sound, in reality an extension of Virginia, and the southern extending from the Santee River south, with Charleston as its center. The southern colony, founded in 1670 under the patronage of eight proprietors, was commercially bound to the West Indies, whence most of the inhabitants came. Settlement was hindered at first by the attempt to impose an artificial system of government—the Grand Model of John Locke—but after that plan had been discarded the movement up the river was rapid. Excellent additions to the population were furnished by the Scotch-Irish and by 500 Huguenots who left France after the revocation of the Edict of Nantes and took up 50,000 acres along the Santee.

It is evident even from this brief review of early settlement that by 1700 the American population had already taken on the heterogeneous character which has distinguished it to our own day. Most of the immigrants during the seventeenth century came from England, but there was also a sprinkling of people from other parts of the British Isles and from the nations of western Europe. This trend, as we shall see, was to be even more pronounced in the eighteenth century, when the great majority of immigrants came from

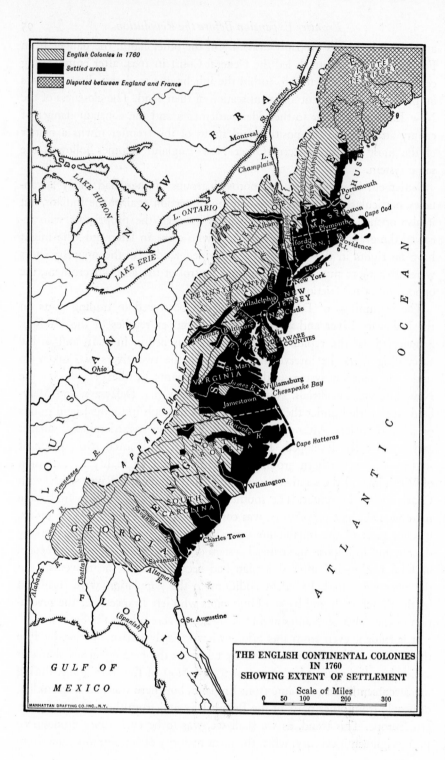

Legend:
- English Colonies in 1760
- Settled areas
- Disputed between England and France

THE ENGLISH CONTINENTAL COLONIES
IN 1760
SHOWING EXTENT OF SETTLEMENT

Scale of Miles
0   50   100   200   300

MANHATTAN DRAFTING CO. INC., N.Y.

Ireland and Germany. As a matter of fact, migration in the seventeenth century was not large; the population in all of the English mainland colonies in 1700 was probably not more than 250,000. Of this number, New England had about 80,000, Virginia 60,000, and Maryland 30,000; the remainder was concentrated along the Hudson and Delaware rivers and in various areas in the Carolinas. Small as the population was, it was enough to occupy the coastal plains and to extend the area of settlement to the fall line of the rivers. It was the eighteenth century that was to widen the area to include the foothills of the Appalachian range.

INDIANS AND THE EARLY WESTWARD MOVEMENT

The insignificance of the Indian in the United States today in numbers and power[4] makes it easy to underestimate his role in American history. It should be remembered that the Indian, in a sense, prepared the way for the European settler. Indian trails generally marked the routes inland taken by the white men from the earliest days to the era of railroads. The clearings made by the Indian for his crude farming were among the first occupied by the newcomers, who not only used his land but adopted his methods of agriculture. Furthermore, the Indians spurred on the white advance by the temptations which they held out to the fur trader. The latter, returning with tales of the rich western lands, continually whetted the desires of the land-hungry settlers.

On the other hand, however, every frontier had an Indian barrier to dispose of, and the problem of removing the red man, by purchase of land or forcible ejection through warfare, was a continual difficulty for almost 300 years. The Indian held possession of strategic passes and gaps in the mountains, and was able temporarily to hold up immigration into the West. Again should be noted the effect of the Indian barrier upon the life and character of the people; frontier life meant danger from the Indians, which necessitated courage and self-reliance. Although the main burden of defense against the Indians rested upon the frontiersman, the latter naturally demanded aid from the more populous East. This provided a distinct trend toward nationalism. Indian dangers also developed more community life and less scattered settlement than would have occurred otherwise.

By the end of the seventeenth century the lands back to the fall line had been pretty well cleared of Indians, who were driven into the Piedmont

[4] F. E. Leupp, *The Indian and His Problem* (1910), p. 350, estimates the number of Indians in 1492 in the continental United States area as between eight and nine hundred thousand; the article "Indians" in the *New International Encyclopedia* quotes James Mooney, United States government expert, as estimating the Indian population of the continent north of Mexico at that time at 1,115,000. The Indian population of continental United States in 1950 was about 400,000.

region.[5] But this first foothold was not achieved without war and suffering. With the exception of Penn's colonies, where treatment of the Indians according to the golden rule kept the settlers relatively free from molestation, friction with the red men was frequent. The most serious of the seventeenth-century conflicts was with the Pequots in 1675, when all New England joined in one of the bloodiest Indian wars in our history. King Philip's War broke the power of the New England Indians, but their descendants, driven northward, continued in later years to aid the French in harassing the frontier settlements. How the Indian danger drove the settler toward nationalism and unity may be seen in the New England Confederation of 1643, when Plymouth, Massachusetts Bay, Connecticut, and New Haven joined together for military defense. It was a forerunner of the famous Albany Congress of 1754, in which an attempt was made to bring the colonies together for united action, chiefly with reference to Indian problems.

THE ADVANCE INTO THE PIEDMONT

With the tidewater settlements fairly well secured, the colonists during the years from 1700 to the conclusion of the French and Indian War in 1763 pushed into the Piedmont region to take up the lands between the fall line and the Alleghenies. In New England this process was hastened when the old method of carefully guarded township grants to approved men was replaced by the plan of locating towns in advance of settlement and then auctioning them to land speculators. During these years most of the land between the Housatonic and the Connecticut was taken up, and by 1737 Connecticut had disposed of her unlocated lands. In New Hampshire settlement proceeded up the Merrimac and some distance up the Connecticut. The taking up of lands was also encouraged by the grants of Governor Wentworth of 121 towns west of the Connecticut in what was later Vermont. Although the New England expansion of this period was toward the north, it had all the essential characteristics of the westward movement.

A large and influential element in this frontier advance was furnished by immigrants from North Ireland, who with questionable accuracy have been commonly termed "Scotch-Irish,"[6] a race well adapted to the rigors of pioneer life and *"par excellence* the Indian fighters."* The act of 1699 prohibiting the exportation of Irish wool from Ulster, the enforced payment of tithes to the Anglican Church, and the fact that between 1714 and 1718 many of the

---

[5] The term "Piedmont," literally foothills, in American physiography designates that part of the Atlantic coastal plain lying between the low coastal plain proper and the Appalachian highlands. See chap. 1.

[6] The non-Irish population who had settled in Ulster and other parts of North Ireland came from England as well as Scotland. Of those who came from Scotland, the great majority were Lowland Scots whose blood may have been more English than Scotch.

leases granted to the original settlers expired, all contributed in the early years of the eighteenth century to bring about a great migration of Scotch-Irish to America. So rapid was the influx into New England that the authorities shipped the newcomers to the frontier, where they settled in Worcester, moved on to the Connecticut Valley, and following the river northward, settled in Windsor, Orange, and Caledonia counties in Vermont, and Grafton County in New Hampshire.

Hemmed in by the Catskills to the west and with the Mohawk pass into the interior blocked by the Iroquois, New York during this period showed little expansive vitality. Nothwithstanding the richness of the soil, the cultivation of the narrow ribbon of land along the two rivers proceeded slowly, largely because of the fact that the Dutch system of huge manorial grants was continued under British rule. With millions of acres of the choicest lands under the control of a handful of men who wanted to settle tenant farmers upon their lands, it was little wonder that the tide of immigration moved elsewhere. New York caught some of the first wave of the German-Swiss immigration, which, commencing in 1683, continued throughout the first half of the next century. This inflow, which came mostly from the upper Rhine Valley and Switzerland, resulted from religious persecution, political discontent, and economic disorganization following the continental wars. In New York most of them moved to the Mohawk Valley, where they settled in the country between Fort Hunter and Palatine Bridge. The Scotch-Irish moving on from New England mingled with the Dutch in the Mohawk region and entered the Cherry Valley in 1738.

Pennsylvania's reputation as a home for persecuted sects under Penn's magnanimous rule brought to her shores as permanent settlers, between 1700 and the Revolution, at least 100,000 Germans from the Palatinate and surrounding regions, the ancestors of the present "Pennsylvania Dutch"; 100,000 more were scattered along the frontiers of the other colonies from the head of the Mohawk to Georgia. The Pennsylvania frontier of this period was also the center of the great Scotch-Irish migration which brought to this country between 1730 and 1770 close to half a million. Probably one-third of Pennsylvania's population at the time of the Revolution was composed of Germans from the Rhineland, and another third of immigrants from northern Ireland. The cost of land in Pennsylvania in 1719 was ten pounds per hundred acres and two shillings quitrent; the price was raised in 1732 to fifteen pounds and a quitrent of a halfpenny an acre. But with the rapid influx of immigrants the management of the lands fell into confusion and a large proportion was occupied by squatters without title. James Logan, agent of the Penn family, disgustedly asserted that the Irish settled in "an audacious and disorderly manner," alleging that "it was against the laws of God and nature, that so much land should be idle while so many Christians wanted it to labor on and to raise their bread."[7] The Germans spread out in eastern Pennsylvania, and the Scotch-Irish, coming a little later, planted their outposts in the Cumberland, Juniata, and Susquehanna valleys.

From Maryland to Georgia the story of the occupation of the Piedmont is much the same. As population increased and the rich lowlands were exhausted, more and more land was taken up until the fall line was reached. Then there moved up into the Piedmont a stream of newcomers, mostly of the poorer classes, to claim lands under head rights, or settlers brought in by wealthy speculators to satisfy the requirements for obtaining their vast estates. Efforts were made by each of these colonies, for the purpose of protection, to lure men to the frontier by cheap or free lands and by exemption from taxation. For the same reason attempts were made to prevent the growth of large estates and to stimulate communal life. These efforts were only partially successful, for an aristocratic planter group occupied the Piedmont along with a yeomanry of small farmers. By 1730 settlers from the coast had spread from thirty to fifty miles into the Virginia Piedmont, but in the Carolinas and Georgia the foothills had scarcely been touched.

After 1730 this westward movement from the coast was augmented by a steady stream of Germans and Scotch-Irish from the northeast. The Blue Ridge Mountains of Virginia and the pine barrens of the Carolinas abruptly checked the advance from the coast, but beyond these barriers lay rich lands in the great valleys of the Appalachians to which ready access could be had from the north. Impetus was given also by the fact that the best land in Pennsylvania was already taken up, whereas land in Maryland could be obtained at a cheaper price and in Virginia it was practically free. Accordingly, a steady stream of pioneers flowed through the Cumberland, Hagerstown, and Shenandoah valleys into the great mountain trough, and finally out through the passes east into North Carolina or west some years later into Kentucky and Tennessee. By 1760 they had reached the uplands of Georgia. In the Piedmont were mingled the settlers of these two converging streams, the vanguard being usually the sturdy and venturesome Scotch-Irish.

Before the Revolution there had developed in the back country a society distinct from that in the tidewater regions. The men of the Piedmont were generally small farmers and trappers, destitute of wealth but well equipped with courage and initiative. Democratic and individualistic, they resented their political and economic subservience to the minority of the coastal plain. From the beginnings of the westward advance a distinct antagonism between the interior and the coast seems to have developed, and during this

---

[7] Quoted by H. J. Ford, *The Scotch-Irish in America*, pp. 271–272; also by C. A. Hanna, *The Scotch Irish*, p. 63.

period it can be clearly seen in controversies between the plantation owners of Virginia and the small farmers of the Piedmont, between the backwoodsmen of Pennsylvania and the wealthy Quakers of the East, and between the frontiersmen of New England and the coast-town aristocracy. This antagonism was evident in the contests between the debtor class of the interior and the property-holding class of the coast, in the demands for a more democratic and representative government in which the frontier might be more justly represented, in the dissatisfaction over the defective administration of government and law under which the back country suffered, and finally in the different moral and intellectual outlook of the two regions.

Absentee landlordism was a curse of the early West. The hope of making fortunes in western land soon developed, and most of those who enjoyed means or influence speculated in land. "You may be pleased to know," said a Deerfield petition of 1678, "that the very principle & best of the land; the best for soile; the best for situation; as lying in yᵉ centre & midle of the town: & as to quantity, nere half, belongs unto eight or 9 proprietors each and every of which, are never like to come to a settlement amongst us, which we have formerly found grievous & doe Judge for the future will be found intollerable if not altered."[8] While the actual settlers cleared the land and bore the brunt of Indian wars, the proprietors profited financially in the security of the tidewater country. As the frontiersmen were the debtor class and as specie was difficult to obtain, they demanded paper money and the payment of taxes in kind—demands which were generally opposed by the older communities. The frontiersman was inclined to feel that his contribution to the defense of the colony exempted him altogether from the burden of taxation. Politically he felt that he was discriminated against by means of property qualifications and careful allotment of representation.

The aristocracy of the tidewater and coast towns, although outnumbered, managed until the Revolution to keep control of the governments in their own hands. The counties of Chester, Bucks, and Philadelphia elected twenty-six delegates to the Pennsylvania legislature, and the five frontier counties only ten. Jefferson complained that 19,000 men below the falls legislated for more than 30,000 living elsewhere, as well as appointing their chief executive and judicial officers. The desire to escape from eastern control led to efforts to form such new states as Franklin and Vermont. Dissatisfaction over the administration of the government was keen. Officials were corrupt, and justice was expensive and slow, for the counties were large and it was sometimes necessary to travel long distances to court. Aid in time of war was uncertain. Finally, the intellectual outlook was different. In religious matters the frontiersman was likely to be a Dissenter or neglect the means of grace

[8] George Sheldon, *History of Deerfield, Massachusetts* (2 vols., 1896), I, 189–190.

entirely. The social and economic conditions under which he lived made him democratic and in most cases opposed to slavery. These differences in point of view accentuated the more pressing causes of antagonism.

This antagonism led to armed uprisings in at least two cases before the Revolution. When Governor Berkeley of Virginia failed to prosecute vigorously operations against the Indians, frontiersmen under Nathaniel Bacon took the matter in their own hands. Thereupon Berkeley (1676) declared Bacon and his followers rebels and attempted to arrest them. The backwoodsmen and small planters rose in rebellion behind Bacon, forced Berkeley to make concessions, gained control of the legislature, and inaugurated numerous democratic reforms. At the high tide of success Bacon died and the rebellion collapsed. Berkeley, with the backing of the tidewater aristocracy, was able to revoke the reform legislation and take cruel revenge. Almost a century later (1769) rebellion broke out in South Carolina when the backwoodsmen, under the name of Regulators, demanded reforms and attempted to take the law into their own hands. Although they met the government party in arms on the Saluda, hostilities were averted when their demands were complied with. Two years later the Regulators of North Carolina and the militia of Governor Tryon clashed in the battle of the Alamance. The frontiersmen were defeated, and the reins of government were held by the conservatives until the new constitution of 1776 recognized the rights of the interior. The failure on the Alamance was one influence that drove the first pioneers across the Alleghenies.

THE FRENCH BARRIER

Since 1604 the French had maintained permanent settlements in the New World and during the seventeenth century had explored and laid claim to the region of the St. Lawrence, the Great Lakes, and the Mississippi. The English fur traders had disputed their possession of the Hudson Bay country, and competition between English and French fur traders had begun in the Mohawk Valley, soon to extend into the region of the Ohio and Mississippi. The area in America, however, was so vast that competition for land on which to settle did not develop until the 1700's and then the Indians were often drawn in when armed conflict came.

In 1689 began the second Hundred Years' War between France and Britain, which continued with brief intervals until 1815 and comprised sixty years of actual fighting. Six of the seven wars were fought in America as well as Europe. The underlying cause was the rivalry for commercial and colonial supremacy. For Americans the economic interest was in land and furs, and the battle was for control of the Ohio, Mississippi, and St. Lawrence valleys.

When this struggle reached its climax in the French and Indian War

(1754–1763), the French were handicapped by lack of numbers, for the 80,000 inhabitants of New France were overwhelmingly outnumbered by the 1,300,000 English. Furthermore, they were not compact but scattered throughout a vast area. These disadvantages were partially compensated for by their centralized government, which functioned infinitely better in time of war than the disconnected colonial governments of the English, and by the fact that they already held the strategic points in the territories under dispute. However, the stronger economic strength of the English colonies, the superior sea power of Great Britain, the driving force of the elder Pitt, and the persistence of the British soldiers, Amherst and Wolfe, proved in the end victorious and the great colonial empire of France passed largely to England. By the Treaty of Paris in 1763, France ceded to England all of Canada and the land east of the Mississippi; of her vast American empire she retained only the islands of St. Pierre and Miquelon off the coast of Newfoundland, to be used for drying fish, and the sugar islands of Martinique, Guadeloupe, and St. Lucia. From Spain England took Florida, and France ceded to Spain New Orleans and the country west of the Mississippi.

THE SPANISH BORDER

Spain remained a factor in the colonization of the present United States long after France had been eliminated, and the gradual advance northward of the Spanish frontier brought her into conflict with England, France, and the United States in turn. The first permanent white settlement in the limits of the present United States was made by the Spaniards at St. Augustine, Florida, in 1565, after they had destroyed a French colony fifty miles northward. With the cessation of French attempts to settle the Carolinas, no further impetus was given to the Spanish advance northward in Florida until the British settled Georgia in 1733. Hostilities commenced during King George's War, but the Peace of Aix-la-Chapelle made no change in the Georgia-Florida frontier. The Peace of Paris at the conclusion of the French and Indian War, however, transferred Florida to Britain, in whose hands it remained until 1783, when it was returned to Spain.

In the meantime the Spanish frontier was gradually pushing northward from Mexico; the motive was the lure of fabled riches and the desire to win souls to Christianity, and missionaries, soldiers, and fur traders led the way. It was in 1598 that Juan de Oñate entered New Mexico with the definite intent to settle. Santa Fe, founded in 1609, became the capital of the new colony, whose limits were extended during the century as the Franciscans and Jesuits established new missions among the Indians. By 1680 there were more than 2500 Spaniards in the colony, and by the end of the century they had practically subjected the Indians.

Eastern Texas, which had been temporarily occupied, 1690–1693, was re-entered in 1716 by an expedition which founded San Antonio in that year. The expedition into Texas had been undertaken principally as a counter-move against the French, who were making trading expeditions westward from Louisiana and establishing relations with the Indians of Texas and Arkansas. When war broke out in 1719 between France and Spain, the contest spread to the colonies, where it was waged along the whole border from Pensacola to the Platte River. An expedition into Texas (1720–1722) clinched Spain's hold on the new province, although the territory in dispute between France and Spain continued to extend from the Trinity to the Mississippi. By 1700 Spanish ranches were to be seen in Arizona, but the Spanish advance into California did not occur until later. The Portola ex-pedition founded San Diego in 1769, and the next year a post at Monterey was established. The year of the Declaration of Independence saw the be-ginnings of San Francisco; San Jose was founded in 1777 and Los Angeles in 1779. At the conclusion of the Revolution the land now encompassed by the United States was under the control of two nations, the infant American Republic and Spain, with Great Britain and Russia disputing the northern boundary line.

BRITISH WESTERN POLICY, 1763–1775

In the intercolonial wars just discussed, the Indians usually sided with the French, and the reason is fairly obvious. The French were chiefly interested in furs and provided a market where the Indian could dispose of the pro-ceeds of the hunt; the English, on the other hand, wanted land above all else, and their occupation of it meant an end to the furs. "Are you ignorant of the difference between the king of England and the king of France?" asked Duquesne of the Iroquois. "Go see the forts that our king has estab-lished and you will see that you can still hunt under their very walls. . . . The English, on the contrary, are no sooner in possession of a place than the game is driven away. The forest falls before them as they advance, and the soil is laid bare so that you can scarce find the wherewithal to erect a shelter for the night."[9] The Indian understood this, and as an aftermath to the French and Indian wars Pontiac, chief of the Ottawas, greatest of Indian warriors and friend of the French, organized a confederation of tribes in the Northwest and during the years 1763 and 1764 attacked the frontiers of Virginia and Pennsylvania and the British forts west of the mountains.

The inability of the colonies properly to handle Indian affairs led the home government to formulate a policy under which a definite boundary should be established between the lands to be settled by white men and those re-served for Indians. In order to carry out this policy the Proclamation of 1763

[9] Quoted by F. J. Turner, *op. cit.*, p. 14.

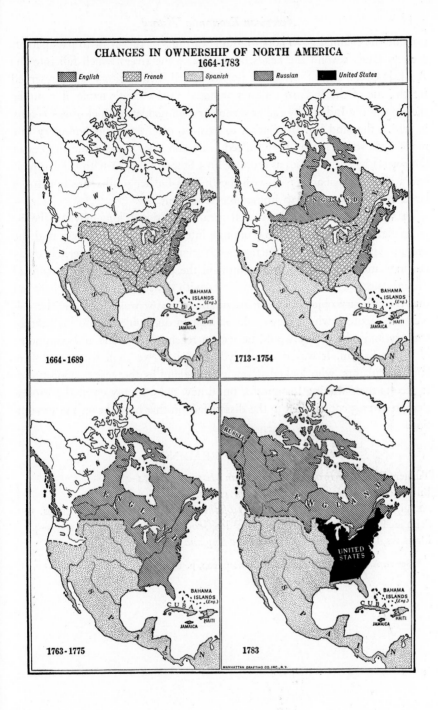

CHANGES IN OWNERSHIP OF NORTH AMERICA
1664-1783

English   French   Spanish   Russian   United States

1664-1689

1713-1754

1763-1775

1783

MANHATTAN DRAFTING CO. INC., N.Y.

forbade the colonial governors to grant warrants of survey or to pass patents for any lands beyond the heads or sources of the rivers which fall into the Atlantic Ocean from the west or northwest, all such territory being reserved for the use of the Indians unless purchased in the king's name at a public meeting of the Indians by the governor or commander-in-chief of the colony in which the land lay. In relation to existing conditions this boundary line made little sense. It was later shifted (in some cases west of the sources of the rivers) by such treaties as those at Fort Stanwix (1768) with the Iroquois and at Fort Lochabar (1770) with the Indians farther south, thus opening a large extent of territory to immediate settlement.[10]

This policy, no matter how well meant, could not long obviate the irreconcilable differences in the economic interests of the white man and the Indian. Although in actual practice the Proclamation did not materially delay the movement westward, the attempt on the part of the British to control this advance was received in the colonies with dissatisfaction. Many believed that the primary object of the Proclamation of 1763 was to confine the colonists to territory where they could be kept in due subjection to the mother country and where they would be within reach of the trade and commerce of Great Britain. It was particularly resented, as we shall see, by wealthy land speculators, who looked upon western land as the easiest opportunity to recoup their waning fortunes or build new ones. In any event the Proclamation of 1763 contributed to the dissatisfaction that brought on the Revolution.

SELECTED READINGS

Turner, F. J., *The Frontier in American History*, chaps. 1–4.
Billington, R. A., *Westward Expansion*, chaps. 3–7.
Akagi, R. H., *The Town Proprietors of the New England Colonies*, chaps. 1–7.
Semple, E. C., *American History and Its Geographic Conditions*, chaps. 4–6.
Mathews, L. K., *The Expansion of New England*, chaps. 1–5.

[10] See R. A. Billington, *Westward Expansion*, map, p. 147.

CHAPTER 7

ECONOMIC CAUSES OF THE
REVOLUTION

BRITISH MERCANTILISM APPLIED TO THE AMERICAN COLONIES

LIKE all revolutions, the revolt in America against British rule can be explained by no simple formula. It came from an interplay of many forces—economic, political, and social. Like most revolutions, however, that in America resolves itself in the final analysis mainly into a conflict between the economic interests of two groups. But it was more than a single conflict between the economic interests of Britain and her mainland colonies; it was in many ways a revolt against a social and political system no longer applicable to conditions in America.

The economic conflict, as already suggested,[1] rested upon a general economic theory popular in the sixteenth, seventeenth, and eighteenth centuries and known as mercantilism. It was followed by all colonial powers of those years, and the system which developed from it has often been called Colbertism after Jean Baptiste Colbert (1619–1683), Finance Minister of Louis XIV, who pushed the theory to its farthest extent. Mercantilism was a policy aimed at building strong, wealthy, and independent national states, which would be achieved by promoting economic independence and a favorable balance of trade. This was the essence of mercantilism.

Specifically, its exponents hoped to achieve this, first of all, by encouraging native shipping and thus avoiding dependence upon foreign ships to carry native products. This would also contribute to the development of an efficient navy and well-trained seamen in time of war. Native shipping would also reserve to the nation the profits of the carrying trade. Second, the mercantilists would protect and stimulate home industry in order to be self-sufficing industrially and provide employment to citizens; third, they

[1] Above, pp. 78 f.

would protect and aid home agriculture to provide both foodstuffs and sufficient raw materials to manufacture; and finally, they would maintain a
favorable balance of trade in order to amass and keep in the country as large
an amount of metallic currency as possible. The nation which had the most
gold and silver, they believed, enjoyed the most favorable and strategic position. It was not that mercantilists did not understand other forms of wealth,
but they felt that the precious metals were particularly important because
with them they could purchase any desired products from any place.

Mercantilism had many advocates in its period and is not without its
proponents today. But like other theories of economics, it is a reflection of
the age in which it was popular. It was a reaction from the chaos and disorder of the Middle Ages, and a natural result of the Commercial Revolution, the revival of a money economy, and the rise of the national state. But
mercantilism had its faults. It laid too much emphasis upon the advantage
of the precious metals in comparison to other commodities. It overestimated
commerce in relation to agriculture and industry, and it was wrong in believing that a favorable balance of trade meant a benefit in the long run or
that the gain of one nation was a loss to another.

The mercantile policy, it is obvious, was essentially concerned with the
welfare of the mother country. If colonies were acquired, their purpose was
to round out the economic life of the home country. It was their business to
produce commodities not obtainable at home, chiefly raw materials, and
to use manufactured goods produced in the mother country. Colonies were to
offer opportunities for the development of a large merchant marine, profits
to shipowners engaged in the carrying trade, wealth to importers and exporters, and opportunities for the investment of capital. In brief, they were to
subserve the interests of the mother country. If, in this process, the interests
of the colonies were also served, well and good. If there was a conflict, it
must be resolved to the benefit of the home country. Under no conditions, if
it could be avoided, were colonies to be competitors.

Although the roots of British mercantilism were planted during the sixteenth century, it was not until the days of Cromwell and after that the great
statutes were enacted upon which British mercantilism rested. By that time
England had become a maritime power of importance and was beginning to
build a colonial empire. The most famous of her Navigation Acts, passed in
1651, provided that: (1) No goods of the growth or manufacture of Asia,
Africa, or America shall be imported into England or the dominions thereof,
except in ships of which the proprietor, master, and a major part of the
mariners are English; (2) no goods of the growth or manufacture of Europe
shall be imported into England or the dominions thereof, except in English
ships and in such foreign ships as do belong to that country where the goods
are produced and manufactured; (3) no goods of foreign growth or manu-

facture, that are to be brought into England, shall be brought from any other place than the place of growth and production, or from those ports where alone the goods can be shipped or whence they are usually shipped after transportation. The intent of this act was to give to English or colonial shippers a monopoly of the carrying trade.

This act was strengthened in 1660 by an "Act for the Encouraging and Increasing of Shipping and Navigation" (2 Charles II, Chap. 18), which provided that goods carried to and from England must be transported not only in English-manned ships but in English-built ships or ships built in the English colonies. The act of 1660, besides providing for the protection of shipping and thus the development of the merchant marine, sought to regulate the trade of the colonies so as to add to the monopoly of navigation that of colonial commerce and markets. It was enacted that "no sugars, tobacco, cotton-wool, indigo, ginger, fustick, or other dyeing woods, of the growth, produce, or manufacture of any English plantations in America, Asia or Africa" should be shipped to any place whatsoever except England. This list was expanded in 1706 by the addition of the naval stores—tar, pitch, turpentine, hemp, masts, and yards; by rice in 1705–1730; by copper ore, beaver, and other furs in 1721; by molasses in 1733; by whale fins, hides, iron, lumber, raw silk, and pearl ashes in 1764. The nonenumerated articles, chief of which were fish, grain, and rum, could be exported anywhere until 1766, but after that date exportation was confined to nations south of Cape Finisterre. The latter provision virtually excluded the colonies from direct export trade with any country of northern Europe except England.

Not only did England seek to control colonial exports, but by an act of 1663 she sought to monopolize the handling of imports into the colonies. This act prohibited by high duties the importation into the colonies of any European goods unless brought via England and in English (including colonial) -built and -manned ships, an act which allowed duties and commissions to be collected in England before European goods reached America, and limited the profits of carrying such commodities to British or colonial merchantmen. Exceptions were made in the case of salt from Spain for the New England fisheries, wine from Madeira and the Azores, and provisions and horses from Ireland and Scotland. The laws of 1660 and 1663 were both evaded, the former by shipping such enumerated articles as sugar and tobacco directly to European ports without taking them first to England, under the pretense that the commodities were destined for another colony. In an effort to make this unprofitable, Parliament in 1673 enacted a law (reaffirmed and interpreted in 1696) levying a tax on enumerated articles shipped from one colony to another, equal in amount to the import taxes levied on the articles in England.

The British mercantilist policy was concerned not only with control of the carrying trade and the regulation of imports and exports, but also with control of the few manufacturing enterprises in the colonies. To prevent colonial manufacturing from coming into competition with the home industry, colonial governors were instructed "to discourage all manufactures and to give accurate accounts of any indications of the same." That representatives of the crown well understood the British attitude and were only too sympathetic with it may be seen in the words of Lord Cornbury, governor of New York, 1702–1708, who wrote to the Board of Trade:

> I am well informed, that upon Long Island and in Connecticut, they are setting up a woollen Manufacture, and I myself have seen serge made upon Long Island that any man may wear. Now if they begin to make serge, they will in time make course cloth, and then fine; we have as good fullers earth and tobacco pipe clay in this Province, as any in the world; how farr this will be for the service of England, I submit to better judgements; but however I hope I may be pardoned, if I declare my opinion to be, that all these Colloneys, which are but twigs belonging to the main Tree (England,) ought to be kept intirely dependent upon and subservient to England, and that can never be if they are suffered to goe on in the notions they have, that as they are Englishmen, soe they may set up the same Manufactures here, as people may doe in England; for the consequences will be that if once they see they can cloath themselves not only comfortably but handsomely too, without the help of England, they who are already not very found of submitting to Government, would soon think of putting in execution designs they had long harboured in their breasts. This will not seem strange when you consider what sort of people this Countrey is inhabited by. . . .[2]

In actual practice it was impossible for either British or colonial governments completely to control household industries or even those of the small shop. If Great Britain had been willing to import the fish and agricultural commodities of the northern colonies a greater importation of British manufactured goods might have been effected. Since she would not, a certain amount of colonial manufacturing was bound to develop.

There were two industries, however, that Britain guarded with a jealous eye—woolens and iron. England had already become a leading manufacturer of woolens and one-half of her exports to the colonies were woolen goods. So hostile were home manufacturers to competition that as early as 1699 a Woolen Act was passed providing that no woolen goods might be exported from the colonies or sent from one colony to another, and in the following year the duty on woolens imported into the colonies from England was removed. As a result of this legislation the manufacture of cloth for sale was checked and the hold of the English woolen merchants upon the American

---

[2] Letter to Secretary Hedges in 1705, in E. B. O'Callaghan (ed.), *Documents Relating to the Colonial History of New York*, IV, 115.

trade was prolonged for a century. The abundance of beaver gave the colonist a decided advantage in the manufacture of beaver hats. A petition in 1731 from a company of feltmakers caused Parliament to institute an inquiry which disclosed that 10,000 hats a year were manufactured in New England and New York. Thereupon an act containing the following provisions was passed: (1) that after 1732 no hat should be put on board a ship or cart for exportation to England, or for transportation from one colony to another; (2) that no one should make felt hats unless he had served an apprenticeship for seven years. No master should have more than two apprentices, and they could not serve for less than seven years, nor could they be Negroes. The penalty for violation was £500.

The iron industry, which had commenced in 1643 with John Winthrop's smelting furnace near Lynn, had grown by 1750 to healthy proportions. England was in need of iron, and conflicting interests until 1750 had prevented adverse legislation. To encourage the production of raw material but discourage the manufacture of iron products, a law was passed in 1750 providing (1) that bar iron might be imported duty free to the port of London, and pig iron to any port in England; and (2) that no mill or other engine for rolling or slitting iron, no plating forge to work with a tilt hammer, nor any furnace for making steel should be erected in the colonies. In 1757 it was provided that bar iron might be imported into any British port free of duty.

These restrictions upon manufacturing may not have seriously impeded American economic development, but the fact that England was so quick to protect the interests of her citizens at home as against those in the colonies did not go unnoticed. "A colonist cannot make a button, a horse shoe, nor a hobnail," complained a Boston newspaper in 1765, "but some sooty ironmonger or respectable buttonmaker of Britain shall bawl and squall that his honor's worship is most egregiously maltreated, injured, cheated, and robbed by the rascally American Republicans."[3] To the disgust of the colonists, these bawls and squalls were seriously considered by the British government.

Not the least among the economic conflicts between Britain and her colonies was the friction that arose over the currency policy. What metallic currency appeared in the colonies, whether English, Portuguese, or Spanish, was soon drained off to England because of the unequal balance of trade.[4] In their need to carry on the normal demands of trade, the colonists had resorted to the use of wampum, warehouse receipts, and other devices. In the end it was inevitable that various types of paper money should be tried. Massachusetts began it in 1690 when she issued paper money (without me-

[3] Boston *Gazette*, April 29, 1765. Quoted by C. and M. Beard, *Rise of American Civilization*, I, 195.
[4] Above, p. 76.

tallic backing) to pay her soldiers returning from the unsuccessful expedition against Quebec. It was the origin of paper money in America, and the money was kept near par by making it payable for taxes at 5 per cent advance over coin. Encouraged by the success of the first issue, she authorized a second in 1709. Connecticut, New Hampshire, Rhode Island, New York, and New Jersey followed before 1711, and other colonies later. Depreciation generally ensued, for this paper money was soon issued in excess of the domestic monetary demand at gold prices. In the meantime in 1704 the so-called "loan banks," designed to issue paper money on mortgages and real estate, were established in Massachusetts; but before these schemes could go far, Parliament intervened in 1741 and applied the Bubble Act of 1720, which put an end to these banks. In 1751 Parliament forbade the issue of bills of credit as legal tender in New England, and in 1764 extended the prohibition to the remaining colonies.[5]

These acts curtailing the right of the colonies to issue paper money were passed by the British Parliament mainly to safeguard the English creditor. Along with them went an act of 1752 making the lands, tenements, and slaves of American debtors subject to levy in England for obligations of their owners. In America, however, the problem of paper currency went far deeper than any protection of the English creditor. Here both the small debtor farmer and the plantation owner realized the opportunity afforded by an inflated currency to ease the situation in which they found themselves. These groups who were interested in paper currency were usually opposed by the wealthier creditor merchants of the towns. British laws forbidding American paper money, in fact, came from petitions of wealthy colonists as well as British merchants.[6] In any event, British restrictions helped to alienate the great mass of small farmers and even the debtor plantation owners of the South. England's attitude on this matter did much to sow the seeds of discontent.

EFFECT OF THE "OLD COLONIAL SYSTEM"

In surveying the period from 1650 to 1763 to determine the actual effect of the mercantile system as applied to the British mainland colonies, it is evident that, while the policy was essentially selfish and the interests of the colonists were sacrificed to those of the home country, its effects were by no means disastrous. On the whole, the American colonists enjoyed an economic

---

[5] These restrictive acts, says Dewey, "did not entirely suppress colonial paper money; under the exceptions prescribed, temporary treasury notes as well as notes of loan banks which had not been suppressed continued to circulate; so that in 1774 it was estimated that $12,000,000 were in current use." *Financial History of the United States* (8th ed., 1922), p. 30. Harlow (*American Historical Review*, XXXV, 47 Oct., 1929), puts the figure probably more accurately at $22,000,000.

[6] Curtis Nettels, *The Roots of American Civilization*, pp. 530–537.

prosperity and a political liberty unusual in the eighteenth century. British rule, as Adam Smith correctly stated, was "less illiberal and oppressive than that of any other European nation."

The explanation of this prosperity rests primarily on three facts. First of all, the interests of the colonists often ran parallel to those of the mother country. It was fundamentally sound for them to devote themselves to extractive industries. In the second place, although the bounties offered by England for various products in some cases produced artificial conditions, in others they aided a logical development and were a source of wealth for the colonists. Typical of these were the substantial bounties offered on naval supplies and indigo, and the preferential tariff treatment given in England to tobacco, lumber, iron, whale oil, and pot and pearl ashes. It should also be noted that the duty on commodities bound for the colonies via England was generally refunded so that in many cases the colonists could purchase these commodities cheaper than could the English.

The third reason, and perhaps the most important of all, why British mercantilism did not press more heavily was the fact that the most harmful legislation was either evaded or not enforced. During the first half of the eighteenth century England followed the policy of Robert Walpole, who took for his motto *"Quieta non movere"* ("Let sleeping dogs lie"). It was during this period of "salutary neglect" that the West Indian trade reached such great proportions and that evasion of the act of 1663 requiring European goods to be imported via England was so prevalent. Colonial merchants also evaded the act of 1663 by loading various enumerated articles without giving bond that they would be delivered in England, by loading or unloading at other than ports of entry, or by collusion with British customs officers. It was estimated that in 1700 one-half of the trade of Boston was in violation of the law. The evasion of the law continued actively until the 1760's, particularly in the case of the Molasses Act of 1733. As we have seen, much of New England's prosperity was based upon the importation of specie and molasses from the West Indies and the manufacture from molasses of rum for the fur trade, the slave trade, and the fishing industry. This molasses the New Englanders could purchase from the French, Dutch, and Spanish islands more cheaply than from the British islands. At the behest of British plantation owners in the West Indies, Parliament in 1733 placed duties on goods imported from foreign plantations. This effort to protect British sugar planters to the detriment of New England trade fortunately remained a dead letter until 1763.[7]

---

[7] David A. Wells, writing on the "American Merchant Marine" in Lalor's *Cyclopædia of Political Science* (I, 75), says of the colonial merchants, "Nine-tenths of their merchants were smugglers. One-quarter of all the signers of the Declaration of Independence were bred to

In view of these facts, it appears that up to 1763 the colonists did not suffer severely from the "Old Colonial System" of England but on the contrary had grown rapidly in population and wealth. But it must still be remembered that the mercantile system embodied procedures that were likely to be detrimental to colonial economy. Disadvantages to the colonists were: (1) Monopoly of the carrying trade by English and colonial shippers removed foreign competition, which may have had a tendency to make freight rates higher. (2) A middleman's profit had to be paid to the English merchant, since most of the colonial products had to pass through his warehouses. (3) The colonies were regarded as a source of cheap raw material for the English manufacturer, and at the same time as a market for selling the finished product at his own price. (4) The colonists' supply of gold and silver with which to pay for these manufactured goods was small and constantly being exported to England; yet Britain tried to close to them one of their greatest sources of gold, the Spanish, Dutch, and French West Indies. (5) Colonial efforts to ease the currency and credit situation were disallowed by the British government.

BRITISH POLICY AFTER 1763

Enough has been said to make clear the inherent clash between British capitalism and the expanding economic interests of American merchants, plantation owners, and farmers. While the colonies were young and the laws evaded, British mercantilism did not press too heavily. But in 1763 more than a century had passed since the first great Navigation Act of Cromwell. The colonies had grown in population and wealth and the disadvantages of the British colonial system were pressing more heavily upon them. To a certain extent colonial economic life had adjusted itself to these disadvantages, but further pressure was bound to cause trouble. It was the increasing of this pressure after 1763 which deepened the clash of interests and brought to a climax the forces leading to the Revolution.

Essentially there was no fundamental change in British policy after 1763 beyond strengthening and enforcing a policy already a century old—a policy based on protecting British interests and keeping the colonies in a subservient economic position. It is true that after the defeat of France in 1763 the great statesman, William Pitt, sought to weld more firmly the bonds which held the empire together. But these were essentially the old bonds by which the

---

commerce, to the command of ships and to contraband trade. Hancock, Trumbull (Brother Jonathan), and Hamilton were all known to be cognizant of contraband transactions and approved of them. John Hancock was the prince of contraband traders, and, with John Adams as his counsel, was appointed for trial before the admiralty court in Boston, at the exact hour of the shedding of blood at Lexington, in a suit for $500,000 penalties alleged to have been incurred by him as a smuggler."

empire served the interests of British merchant capitalism. It was the protection of British sugar interests rather than dreams of a great empire that decided Pitt to take Canada instead of the French Islands of Guadeloupe, Martinique, and St. Lucia at the end of the French and Indian War. It was, in fact, this clash between the sugar interests of the British West Indies and those of the northern colonies that brought the first measures leading directly to the Revolution.

The great commodity of colonial trade in the eighteenth century was sugar. By the 1760's British investments in Jamaica, Barbados, and other sugar islands amounted to the enormous sum of £60,000,000, six times the amount of British investments in the mainland colonies. Seventy "sugar lords" sat in the British Parliament to protect these interests. But absentee ownership, worn-out soil, inefficient management, and a high export tax at the island ports had put the British growers at a distinct disadvantage in comparison with those in the French islands. Colonial importers were buying their sugar and molasses at 25 to 40 per cent less from the French, and the British islands were supplying only one-eighth of the needs of the mainland colonists. Angered that this trade between the mainland colonies and the French islands continued even during the French and Indian War to the great advantage of the French, Pitt ordered the Navy in 1761 to stamp out smuggling in the foreign West Indian trade. In the same year colonial courts were ordered to issue writs of assistance (general search warrants) to aid in apprehending smugglers. That the colonists thus early understood the significance of this policy of tightening control is clear. James Otis thundered against the writs of assistance so eloquently that John Adams later called his speech the "opening gun of the Revolution."

With the end of that war, Grenville, the new Prime Minister, and Townshend, president of the Board of Trade, backed by George III, determined to end the policy of "salutary neglect." Believing that the American colonies should be brought under more direct supervision of the crown and that the colonists should help pay the war debts incurred in their defense, they decided (1) to enforce more strictly the laws of trade and (2) to raise revenues in the colonies by means of the Molasses Act. It was this attempt to enforce the old commercial policy, along with the new imperialism, that was the greatest of all the causes of the Revolution. England's policy now became a real grievance and one which to the commercial interests seemed to spell ruin. Their opposition was immediate and strenuous.

The first measure under the new regime was the Sugar Act of 1764, designed to provide for the defense of the colonies. It cut in half the duties of the Molasses Act of 1733, in the hope that the removal of the prohibitive rates might induce merchants to be more honest and that some revenue might be raised. On the face of it this act, which reduced the import duties on foreign molasses from sixpence to threepence a gallon, seemed more liberal than the act of 1733, but the British government intended to enforce the new act. British naval officers were to collect the customs duties, and cases arising from indictments for smuggling were to be tried by British admiralty courts. In addition, duties were laid on sugar, indigo, coffee, wines, silks, and calicoes, and at the same time the number of enumerated articles was increased. Economic depression was felt at once in New England and the middle colonies, and the reaction from it was apparent in the South.

The Sugar Act was supplemented in 1765 by the Stamp Act, which provided that stamps varying in cost from a halfpenny to £10 be affixed to licenses, contracts, deeds, wills, newspapers, pamphlets, almanacs, and other papers. The Stamp Act, following the Sugar Act so closely, created an excitement unparalleled in the colonies. When petitions and remonstrances failed, a boycott of English goods was inaugurated, merchants binding themselves to import no British goods until the act was repealed. In England merchants and manufacturers were affected to such an extent that in 1766 the Stamp Act was repealed and the Sugar Act revised downward, although the concessions were accompanied by a Declaratory Act asserting the legal right of Parliament to legislate for the colonies "in all cases whatsoever."

Rejoicing followed the repeal of the Stamp Act, and opposition to the British government might have subsided had not the imperial authority in 1765 passed a Quartering Act, declaring that the colonists should provide for the light, lodging, and fuel of garrisons to be placed in specified districts. In 1767 Charles Townshend, who was now the leading spirit in the Cabinet, forced through Parliament the Townshend Acts, one of which imposed duties on glass, paper, painters' colors, red and white lead, and tea. Though not high, these tariffs fell on articles of general consumption and raised the cost of living. More dangerous than the duties were other features of the Townshend Acts which called for a reorganization of the customs service, with courts of admiralty established in the colonies to expedite cases of smuggling, and which provided that the money raised be used to pay the expenses of the civil government. The latter provision was particularly obnoxious because it would have removed from the colonists their chief weapon in their conflict with British officials. A special act suspended the New York Assembly because it had refused to comply with a law of 1765 calling for the adequate quartering of soldiers. Irritating also was a part of one of the acts that reaffirmed the legality of the writs of assistance.

Immediately following the passing of the Townshend Acts the colonists again resorted to their policy of nonintercourse. The boycott of 1768–1769 was more than a voluntary movement; it was backed and encouraged by political bodies, and it was much more thorough and universal than the nonimportation movements following the Stamp Act. The value of English goods imported into New England and the middle colonies dropped from £1,363,000 in 1768 to £504,000 in 1769. While imports from England slightly increased in the southern colonies, the falling off for the whole country was over £500,000, sufficient to cause enough economic unrest in both England

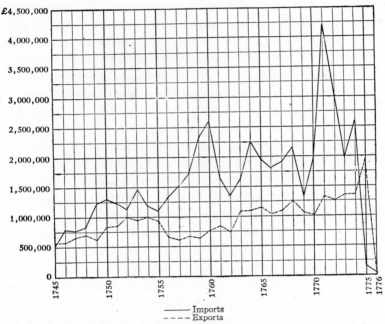

————— Imports
– – – – Exports

(From E. R. Johnson *et al., History of Domestic and Foreign Commerce of the United States,* I, 120.)

TRADE BETWEEN GREAT BRITAIN AND THE AMERICAN MAINLAND COLONIES, 1745–1776.

and America to bring about the partial repeal of the Townshend Acts in 1770.

As a matter of principle, in order to assert the power of the crown over the colonies, a tax of 3*d.* a pound on tea was retained, but a refund of 12*d.* a pound was allowed on tea exported from England to America, so that America was offered cheaper tea than could be purchased in England. Although the most tyrannical and objectionable aspects of the Townshend Acts, including the tax on tea, remained on the statute books, opposition to British policy collapsed rapidly after 1770. Nonimportation broke down, trade was resumed, and prosperity returned. Imports, which had fallen to £1,604,000, jumped to £4,200,000 in 1771. Prosperous merchants, now making money in spite of import duties, turned their backs on radical political leaders and on the mobs they had so freely used against British policy, and sought to quiet agitation.

Any hope of ironing out the difficulties with the British government, however, was prevented by revolutionary agitators at home and by the stupid maintenance of her old colonial policy by Britain and her colonial agents. In Massachusetts Samuel Adams kept up a running fight with the governor in an effort to keep the revolutionary spirit alive. With others of similar mind, like Patrick Henry and Thomas Jefferson, he organized committees of correspondence throughout the colonies to exchange views and information. In the end it was the British government, unwittingly perhaps, that ended possibilities of reconciliation. The climax came in an effort to save the East India Company from bankruptcy. That famous company, which had long exploited the great riches of India with little interference, had fallen on evil days through extravagance or mismanagement. Its bankruptcy would drag with it a horde of British politicians and capitalists and must therefore be prevented. The company had 17,000,000 pounds of surplus tea stored in its warehouses. Among the measures adopted to save the company was one that gave it the right to sell directly to America and remitted the customary duty imposed on imports of tea brought into England. This would help the company find a market and at the same time provide the colonists with cheaper tea than they had ever enjoyed. Before the Tea Act of 1773 the colonists paid four profits—to the East India Company, the English middleman, the American middleman or importer, and the local shopkeeper. Allowing the company to import directly to the colonies eliminated two groups of middlemen as well as two profits. Furthermore, such an arrangement would inevitably give it a monopoly to import tea into the colonies. If the company could be given a monopoly on tea, why not on other commodities that it transported from India? If a monopoly could be conferred upon the East India Company, a similar monopoly on other commodities might be granted to any company. Obviously, other principles besides that of taxation were involved. Instantly the most powerful class in the seaport towns was aroused. Merchants like Hancock, who had been importing and paying the duty on tea, now strenuously opposed the Tea Act, and their opposition, in conjunction with the activities of the radical politicians, led directly to the break with Great Britain.

When the tea arrived in American ports vigilance committees usually destroyed it or refused to allow it to be landed. In Boston a group of citizens disguised as Indians boarded the vessels and dumped the cargo of 342 chests of tea into the water. The "Boston Tea Party" was a direct challenge to British authority and Parliament responded by four disciplinary measures, known as the "Intolerable Acts." These acts closed the port of Boston until the tea should be paid for, revised the Massachusetts charter so as to remove some of its liberal features, provided for the trial in England of colonial agents accused of violence in executing their duty, and revived the Quartering Act of 1765 for the purpose of stationing soldiers in Massachusetts. By another act which had nothing to do with the Boston situation but was the result of long study over the problem of Canadian administration, the territory between the Ohio and the Great Lakes was annexed to the Province of Quebec. This last act was not intended as a retaliatory measure, but it was resented as extinguishing the claims of Virginia, New York, Connecticut, and Massachusetts to these regions and placing them under an autocratic government in which the Roman Catholic Church was recognized by law.

With the passing of these acts, events leading to the Revolution followed in quick succession. Immediately a third boycott was organized, encouraged by the different colonial assemblies and by the Continental Congress on December 1, 1774. The colonial merchants, made wiser by their serious losses in the former embargo period and unwilling to strengthen the hands of the non-merchant radicals, were loath to embark upon this project again, but public opinion carried all before it and the third boycott was more strictly enforced than either of the other two. English imports into the colonies dropped from £2,590,000 in 1774 to £201,000 in 1775. This shrinkage, enormous for the period just at the dawn of the Industrial Revolution, was a stunning blow to English factory towns and seaports, and Parliament was flooded with petitions. The king and his ministers would not yield, and in March, 1775, Massachusetts was declared to be in a state of rebellion; the fishermen of New England were forbidden the Grand Banks, and the trade of the New England colonies (extended in April to most of the other colonies) with other countries than Great Britain, Ireland, and the British West Indies was interdicted. Nine months later all intercourse with the colonies was prohibited.

From what has been said it is obvious that the economic causes of the Revolution emanating from the commercial policies of Great Britain were far from being "accidents of politics, conceived in the heat of controversy." They were, on the other hand, "the matured fruits of a mercantile theory of state which regarded colonial trade as the property of the metropolis, to be monopolized by its citizens and made subservient in all things to their interests,"[8] and this policy had been consistently followed by Puritan and Cavalier, by Stuart and Hanoverian, by Whig and Tory. Fallacious in theory and disastrous in practice, mercantilism in Europe was in the saddle; and it was left to the mainland colonies of England in America to strike the first blow against it.

[8] C. and M. Beard, *op. cit.*, I, 103.

THE PROBLEM OF WESTERN LAND

Among the major causes of friction between Britain and her mainland colonies was the changing policy after 1763 with respect to western land. Up to that time, as Professor Nettels makes clear, Britain had pursued a land policy which "reflected the purposes of British merchant capitalism."[9] The object was not to obtain revenue for the crown itself through land sales and quitrents; it was rather to promote settlement to provide markets for British goods and profits for British merchants. Small plots were granted to bona fide settlers and larger grants were made to speculators on condition that they settle a designated number of families on them. A rapid settlement of the frontier was also encouraged as a means of protection against the French and Spanish menace and for the promotion of the fur trade.

With the removal of the French menace in 1763 one necessity for promoting frontier settlement had ended. Uprisings of Indians under Pontiac in the same year which decimated the frontier of Virginia and Pennsylvania[10] also indicated a possible need for a change in frontier policy. Various factors entered into any consideration of the British policy. With the great Canadian fur trade now in British hands it seemed wiser to many that further settlement of the West be discouraged or kept well under control lest the frontier destroy this lucrative business. British merchants also argued that further advance would extend beyond the mountains and be out of their reach. This advance would draw off settlers in the East and endanger the seaboard area where British capitalists had substantial investments. Moreover, if there was to be any development of the trans-Allegheny region it should be under the direct control of the British government so that British land speculators might have better access to the profits. A definite revival of interest in colonial land speculation was evident in England after 1763. Nor was the British government oblivious to the possibility of income from land sales and quitrents. These might provide funds for colonial administration which would both ease the burden of British taxpayers and at the same time free British colonial officials from dependence on colonial legislatures for financial grants.

In 1763 the British government issued the famous proclamation which forbade colonial governors to warrant surveys or grant patents "for any lands beyond the heads or sources of any of the rivers which fall into the Atlantic Ocean from the West or Northwest." Its immediate cause may have been to pacify the Indians, but all the considerations outlined above form part of its background. From the point of view of the colonists it was

[9] Curtis Nettels, *op. cit.*, p. 602.
[10] Above, p. 104.

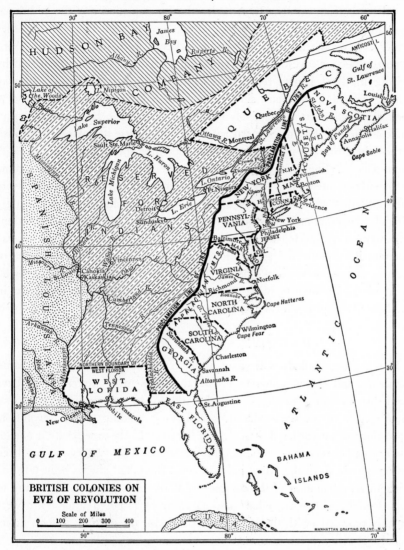

BRITISH COLONIES ON EVE OF REVOLUTION

Scale of Miles
0   100   200   300   400

a new departure, but from that of the British colonial policy it represented
the old subservience of American interests to those of British merchant
capitalism.

Whatever the motives, the Proclamation of 1763 was bitterly resented in
America. The resentment was strengthened when the crown in 1774 issued
new regulations with regard to ungranted lands in certain of the old colonies
and in the rest of the western lands. Quitrents on new grants were to be
more than double the usual charge; there were to be no further free gifts
of lands by the governors, and all tracts were to be sold at auction at not

less than sixpence an acre. In America the Proclamation and the additional regulations cut across the interests of two groups—the bona fide frontier settler ever on the move to the West, and the large land speculator. With opportunities for investment by American merchant capitalists restricted by various kinds of British regulations, land speculation was the easiest way out. It was the natural and simplest way to make money quickly and few men of wealth were not actively engaged in it. While land speculators in the colonies that had no western land were not averse to having the British rather than the colonial governments supervise speculation in this land, there was a feeling on the part of all that the new regulations were a blow at American interests. Those who felt them most severely, perhaps, were the southern plantation owners. Many of them were finding it increasingly difficult to operate profitably under the restrictions of mercantilist regulations and many were sinking deeper into debt to British investors. The one way out was investment and speculation in western land. With this avenue of escape cut off, many were ripe for revolution. This helps to explain why great plantation owners in the South joined the patriot cause, whereas in the North a majority of the wealthy were Tories.

BACKGROUND OF THE REVOLUTION

Mercantilist regulations as they applied to shipping, commerce, manufacturing, and currency, together with the problem of western land, have been discussed in some detail. But they do not by any means give a complete picture of the economic and social causes leading to the Revolution. Historians of an earlier day made much of the battle over taxation and of the cry of "no taxation without representation." This, we know, has been overemphasized. In the literal political sense there had always been taxation without representation of the colonies by Parliament from the beginning of colonization. Moreover, what new taxes were imposed after 1763 were quickly repealed (with the exception of a minor tax on tea) as soon as colonial opposition became strong.

There was, nevertheless, a psychological antipathy to taxation, both colonial and imperial, which must be recognized, and which undoubtedly played a part in the final break. No one has better summarized America's attitude toward taxation than Callender:

It was the fact that social conditions in the colonies were such as to render all taxation except for purely local purposes extremely unpopular. In the unorganized, dispersed society of the colonies it was impossible for men to recognize any connection between most of the governmental expenditures, which occasioned taxation, and their own interests and welfare. Taxes were a burden and did not seem to be justified by necessity, especially after the French had been expelled from the continent. That a great reluctance to pay taxes existed in all the colonies, there can be no doubt. It was one of the marked characteristics of the American people long after their separation from England. Down to the time of the Civil War it constituted one of the difficulties American statesmen always had to face. It was the principal rock upon which the confederation split, and Hamilton recognized it as the chief problem to be solved in the establishment of the new government. Until the Civil War it was strong enough to prevent the establishment of a respectable revenue system in either federal or state finance. It was this unwillingness to bear the burden of taxation that caused nine of the states to default in the payment of interest on their public debts in the early forties, and at least one of them to repudiate the debt altogether. It was fear of this also that caused so long a delay in levying adequate taxes to support the government during the Civil War. Here we have an explanation of that extravagant and, to us now, somewhat incomprehensible opposition to the slight burden of taxation which England proposed to levy upon the colonies.[11]

Undoubtedly one potent cause in bringing about the separation was the period of depression or "hard times" which preceded the Revolution. This was in part a letdown from the artificial prosperity of the French and Indian War. It was also partly, but not entirely, the result of the commercial and financial legislation of the period 1763–1765 and the resulting economic dislocation. Other factors were at work to produce this economic depression, nor was it confined to the colonies. It was the period in England of both the industrial and the agricultural revolutions, with the unrest and instability attendant upon these phenomena. With the introduction of the factory system and industrial capitalism on a big scale came what was perhaps the first of the great cyclical fluctuations which in recent years have become so common.[12] The depression was accentuated by poor crops in England between 1765 and 1774.

The hard times in England were reflected in America; decreased buying power in England combined with the enforcement of the mercantile system was disastrous to the commercial classes of New England and the middle colonies, where commerce was the chief source of private fortunes. The revision and enforcement of the Molasses Act threatened ruin to the prosperity of merchants and shippers, and their misfortune reacted upon the southern colonies. The exports of New England in the ten years 1765–1775 reached the 1765 total only in 1768 and 1771. In the five years following 1765 her imports failed to reach that year's figure, although they were higher after 1770. Imports from England into New York reached the 1764 figure only once

[11] G. S. Callender, *Selections from the Economic History of the United States, 1765–1860,* p. 123. Quoted by permission of the publishers, Ginn and Company.
[12] See chap. 29.

(1771) before the end of the Revolution. Exports from Virginia and Maryland did not reach the 1763 figure until 1775. The South as a whole did not feel this general economic recession as did the North, but the fluctuations in trade were indicative of increasing economic instability.

This depression, nevertheless, was felt not by the merchants alone; the farmers were also affected. The tobacco planters were discovering that a century and a half of wasteful methods had worn out their lands, and the poor crops in 1758 and later years brought a sharp decline in the amount of tobacco exported. The exportation of pig and bar iron reached its high point in colonial times in 1771 and decreased rapidly thereafter. Similar reductions in the production of other commodities could be traced, although some products, such as flax, that were covered by a substantial bounty showed decided prosperity. The business unrest and depression were accentuated both in England and in America by the three attempts to bring Britain to terms through nonintercourse. The Townshend duties on the necessities of life, the closing of the port of Boston, and the closing of the Grand Banks to New England fishermen were imperial mistakes that hastened colonial rebellion. Hard times have always produced some kind of political unrest in our country; Bacon's rebellion represents an earlier instance in colonial history, and the pre-Revolutionary depression is another conspicuous example.

Although wealthy plantation owners in the South and many prominent merchants in the North supported rebellion, the American Revolution was not without its class and sectional struggles. Frontiersmen complained of injustice and the domination of colonial legislatures by the aristocrats of the older communities and believed that these were the men most loyal to England. The Revolution was in part a frontier uprising against eastern Tories. Both on the frontier and in the tidewater sections there was resentment on the part of the poor and the lower middle class against political disfranchisement, land laws such as primogeniture and entail which maintained an aristocratic class, a land system which favored wealthy speculators, and a social and economic system which everywhere pressed against them. Among the disfranchised and less favored there was a strong desire to diminish the power and prestige of the local aristocracies as well as the power of the British government. As one historian has aptly put it, "The Revolution was not merely a question of 'home rule'; it was also a question who should rule at home."[13]

One hundred and fifty years had passed since the first Englishman had settled in America, a continent separated from the home land by 3000 miles of ocean and weeks of weary sailing. Under such conditions abiding loyalty after the first generation could hardly be expected if the strain became great.

[13] Carl Becker, in *American Historical Review*, Vol. XXIX, No. 2, p. 345.

Perhaps one-fourth of the population emanated not from England but from Holland, Germany, Sweden, Ulster, and South Ireland, many of the latter with an innate hostility toward Great Britain. Even in New England, where the majority were of English descent, the bulk of the people, said a contemporary historian, "knew little of the mother country, having only heard of her as a distant kingdom, the rulers of which had, in the preceding century, persecuted and banished their ancestors to the woods of America."[14] These factors, augmented by the aggressive and independent life of a new community, tended to develop self-reliance and to minimize the need of English protection, especially after the end of the French and Indian War. There was a gradual weakening of the ties and a growth of an independent social consciousness. The mere possibility, for instance, of the Church of England's extending its authority in the colonies aroused a storm of protest, and the efforts of Great Britain to circumscribe the power of the colonial governments were looked upon almost as an infringement of the rights of a sovereign people. The settlers in America had up to the Revolution worked out their own destinies with little aid or interference from the outside. They were perfectly justified in feeling that they had a right to continue to do so, and they were in no mood to brook any change in status.

The most cursory examination of the factors in the controversy leading to the Revolution, as suggested in this chapter, leads one to discard quickly the old theory that the Revolution occurred because an English despot was seeking to regain his lost powers, as well as the other explanation that it was fought in protest to taxation without representation.[15] Deep-seated causes of long standing were behind it, and it is easy to agree with the Beards, when they say: "Considered in the light of the English and provincial statutes spread over more than a hundred years, in the light of the authentic records which tell of the interminable clashes between province and metropolis, the concept of the American Revolution as a quarrel caused by a stubborn king and obsequious ministers shrinks into a trifling joke. Long before George III came to his throne, long before Grenville took direction of affairs, thousands of Americans had come into collision with British economic imperialism, and by the middle of the eighteenth century, far-seeing men, like Franklin, had discovered the essence of the conflict."[16] The development of a psychology which made independence desirable was a long process. "The Revolu-

---

[14] David Ramsay, *History of the American Revolution* (1811 ed.), I, 43–44.

[15] Louis Hacker in a brilliant article develops the thesis that the chief cause of the Revolution was the mercantilist restrictions placed by the British government on expanding colonial merchant capitalism. This policy, which caused little annoyance in the seventeenth century, worked progressively in the eighteenth to imperil the prosperity of the mainland colonies. L. M. Hacker, "The First American Revolution," *Columbia University Quarterly,* XXVII, 259–295 (1935).

[16] C. and M. Beard, *op. cit.,* I, 201.

tion," as John Adams asserted many years later, "was effected before the war commenced." It was "in the minds and hearts of the people."[17]

SELECTED READINGS

Beard, C. and M., *Rise of American Civilization,* chap. 5.
Nettels, Curtis, *The Roots of American Civilization,* chaps. 22–24.
Hacker, Louis, *The Triumph of American Capitalism,* chaps. 11–12.
Van Tyne, C. H., *The Causes of the War of Independence,* chaps. 1, 3, 5, 7, 10, 11.
Beer, G. L., *British Colonial Policy 1754–1765,* Introduction, and chaps. 1, 13, 14, 15.
Johnson, E. R., *et al., History of Domestic and Foreign Commerce of the United States,* Vol. I, chap. 3.

[17] *Works,* X, 292.

CHAPTER 8

ECONOMIC ASPECTS OF THE REVOLUTION

CLASS AND SOCIAL DIVISIONS

IN spite of fundamental differences between the home government and the colonists, and long-continued friction, Americans were far from unanimous in demanding independence. The Tories, who supported the crown policy, were undoubtedly in the majority at the outbreak of hostilities but after 1776 they were probably in the minority. John Adams thought that at least one-third of the colonists remained loyal to Great Britain. Speaking generally, it may be said that the groups composing the Tories were: (1) the personal, political, or business followers, dependents, or friends of the royal governors; (2) the non-smuggling merchants of New England and the middle colonies whose interests were engrossed in the type of trade which could prosper without running counter to the English law; (3) many of the rich planters of the southern colonies; (4) the clergy attached to the Church of England and many of the rank and file of that denomination in the North; and (5) many of the most prosperous among the professional classes. In addition there was that great mass of the people from natural conservatism or inertia opposed to change and habitually content with conditions as they are. The most cultivated, the most influential, and the wealthiest inhabitants of the coast towns from Boston to Charleston, Carolina, were likely to be loyalists.

Although the Whigs, or Patriots, were led by rich merchants like Hancock, able bankers like Morris, and aristocratic planters like Washington, the great strength of the rebellion came from the middle and poorer classes, "the plain people, as distinguished from the aristocracy."[1] So evident is this that some observers have seen in it "not so much a split between the colonies and the English government, as it was one aspect of a war between different

[1] J. F. Jameson, *The American Revolution Considered as a Social Movement*, p. 25.

127

divisions of the English people on both sides of the Atlantic," and "in reality but a battle in a great world-wide struggle between contending social classes."[2] The warm support of the Revolution by the great majority of the frontiersmen was to some extent a challenge by an agrarian and frontier people to both a waning feudalism and a rising capitalism, and the influence of the more radical western ideals was one of the potent internal forces that brought the separation.[3] An intensely earnest minority, knowing its mind and active in its propaganda, took the lead and achieved independence. There was, as Ramsay says, "an animation in the friends of Congress which was generally wanting in the advocates for royal government."[4]

The most unfortunate page in the history of the Revolution was the civil war in which neighbor attacked neighbor. From 30,000 to 50,000 Tories enlisted in the British Army and Navy, New York alone furnishing 15,000. Those to whom regular service did not appeal organized companies of militia under commissions from the crown which co-operated with the Indians in the cruel and useless warfare, of which the crowning examples were the Wyoming and Cherry Valley massacres. Loyalist privateering, of which New York was the center, somewhat balanced the depredations of the Patriots engaged in similar occupations. Governor Tryon's expedition in July, 1779, against the coast towns of Connecticut, which laid Fairfield and Norwalk in ashes, was the most serious Tory undertaking of the war. Wherever Patriots confronted Tories, there the fighting was fiercest.

The lot of the Tories not under the protection of the British Army was likely to be a hard one. Denounced and deprived of citizenship under the new state constitutions, they had no legal redress for their troubles. Laws forced them to pay for a cause they hated and at the same time denied them liberty to speak or write their opinions. Tarring and feathering, imprisonment, banishment and the appropriation of property, death—any of these might await the man whose loyalty to the Patriot cause was suspected. Whole communities of loyalists were driven into the back country to prevent their giving aid to the British Army on its approach. Eleven hundred Tory refugees sailed away with Howe's army to Halifax in March, 1776, and 3000 left with Clinton from Philadelphia in 1778. At least 35,000—some believe 100,000—eventually reached Canada and laid there the foundations of a new English commonwealth. The makers of British Canada were the Tories who left the thirteen colonies during the war.

[2] A. M. Simons, *Social Forces in American History*, p. 70.
[3] The career and philosophy of Patrick Henry illustrate clearly the opposition of interests between the interior and the coast regions. See W. W. Henry, *Patrick Henry: Life, Correspondence and Speeches* (3 vols., 1891).
[4] David Ramsay, *History of South Carolina from Its First Settlement in 1670 to the Year 1808* (2 vols. in one, 1858), I, 147.

To carry on a war efficiently with such a division of sentiment was impossible. Not only was there no unanimity as regards separation from England, but there was no unity among the colonies. Thirteen provinces jealous of one another and with separate interests made impossible a close political union or the formation of a body with sufficient powers to carry on a revolution. Only a common cause and a common enemy developed enough cooperation to keep an army in the field. The Continental Congress took over the prosecution of the struggle, but it had little authority. It could not impose taxes; it simply voted levies and asked the states to meet them. Efforts to draw up a plan for a united government which would grant legal power to a central body were blocked until 1781. The states on their part either ignored the requests of Congress for money or handed over what they saw fit. At the same time most of them insisted on maintaining their militia at home for their own defense. Though the success of the war depended on the Continental Army, it was recruited and supported under the aegis of a delegation of state representatives intrusted with insufficient authority to carry on the task.

ECONOMIC AND SOCIAL CHANGES

The American Revolution effected an economic as well as a political revolution. As the French Revolution of 1789 and the Russian Revolution of 1917 broke up the big landed estates and brought a radical change in the agrarian economics of these two nations, so the years 1775–1781 in the thirteen colonies introduced changes in the land system as real if not as spectacular. Whatever institutions were not indigenous to the soil were bound to disappear in the upheaval. For a century and a half Europeans had endeavored to transplant to America the feudal system of the Old World, and vast estates were to be found in most of the colonies. As late as 1769 five-sixths of the population of Westchester County, New York, lived on manor lands. The exodus of the Tories not only removed the most conservative class in the country, thereby throwing the local governments into the hands of a new group, but made possible the breaking up of the large landholdings. In November, 1777, Congress recommended that the states confiscate and sell the loyalist property and invest the proceeds in Continental loan certificates. The idea found immediate favor. New Hampshire confiscated twenty-eight estates, including that of Governor Wentworth. Massachusetts confiscated the land of all who fought with England, including the Pepperell estate containing thirty miles of coastland. In New York State the 50,000-acre manor of Sir John Johnson, the Philipse manor of 300 square miles, the Morris estate, and many other large holdings were broken up and sold, usually in parcels of not over 500 acres. Everywhere crown and proprietary properties were confiscated. The Penn estate taken over by Pennsylvania was valued at nearly one million pounds sterling,[5] and the State of New York received about 3,160,000 Spanish dollars for forfeited real estate. As in France during the Revolution, "country lawyers and newly rich merchants swarmed over the seats of the once proud aristocracy, so in the United States during and after the cataclysm a host of groundlings fresh from the plow and counting house surged over the domains of the Jessups, De Lanceys, and Morrises."[6]

Although the confiscation of crown and Tory estates did something to break up large landholdings, it by no means ended the great estates. Nor did it end the mania for land speculation so widespread in the years before the Revolution. This was true in both East and West. States with western lands gave land bounties to soldiers, which in turn were bought and consolidated into large holdings. Virginia's practice of selling vacant lands as a means of paying state debts increased during the war and also stimulated speculation. Bending the state laws to their purpose, says Nettels, "promoters obtained great tracts in the West. They purchased at a discount the bounty warrants of soldiers unable or unwilling to migrate; they sent out servants to secure preemption rights; and they converted state certificates of indebtedness (which represented the values of depreciated currency) into claims upon the land. Estates as large as 140,000 acres came into being."[7] So much land, in fact, had thus been obtained beyond the Alleghenies that settlers pushing westward found it difficult to secure titles for reasonable amounts.

Along with the confiscation of land and its division into smaller parcels went a social revolution effected by a change to more democratic land tenure. Quitrents were the first to disappear. By 1786 every state but two had abolished entail, and by 1800 primogeniture had gone, the new laws providing in some form or other for equality or inheritance. Jefferson's act of 1776 probably released from half to three-quarters of the entire "seated" area of Virginia.[8] The significance of these laws in the development of a democratic society is, of course, obvious; one should also note the fact that this action was taken in many cases after the fighting had ceased. The war might be over, but the American Revolution, in a sense, had just begun.

The Revolution had been ushered in with much condemnation of the autocratic methods of the British government. Consequently the new state

---

[5] Pennsylvania later granted the Penn family £130,000 in compensation.

[6] C. and M. Beard, *Rise of American Civilization*, I, 294. The Tories put their losses at $40,000,000, and the British government finally granted them $15,000,000.

[7] Curtis Nettels, *The Roots of American Civilization*, p. 684.

[8] Thomas Jefferson in a letter to John Adams, dated Monticello, Virginia, October 28, 1813, dwells with pride upon the fact that the laws of Virginia abolishing entails and primogeniture, "drawn by myself, laid the ax to the root of pseudo-aristocracy." Paul Leicester Ford (ed.), *Writings of Thomas Jefferson* (1898), IX, 427.

constitutions reflected this feeling in the emphasis which they placed upon the so-called "natural rights of man"—life, liberty, and the pursuit of happiness; freedom of speech, of the press, and of worship; no taxation without the consent of the governed; jury trial; and so forth. In theory democracy had made great headway, but in practice it was otherwise. Most of the common devices by which an aggressive democracy could be checked were in use. The right to vote and hold office was limited to those who owned land or considerable taxable property; probably not one white man in five had even the franchise. Notwithstanding the illiberal provisions in the new constitutions, indications were not wanting that social readjustments were in progress. The Tory exodus decreased the power of the conservatives and strengthened the hands of such frontier radicals as Jefferson. The antislavery movement grew rapidly during the war, and by the end of the century a majority of the states had forbidden the importation of slaves, while all the New England states, with New York and Pennsylvania, had provided for abolition or gradual emancipation. The leavening force of the Revolution also played its part in religion. In 1770 there was an established church in most of the colonies, but during the war and in the years soon after, disestablishment took place, although religious tests of various kinds were still exacted from officers and legislators.

FRONTIER ADVANCE DURING THE REVOLUTION

The military events of the Revolution have overshadowed to a great extent the story of the frontier advance which went on simultaneously. Although the Proclamation of 1763 had forbidden settlement west of the Alleghenies, it was impossible to hold back the land-hungry settlers impatient to escape the restrictions of the conservative eastern counties. During the year of the Proclamation the first settlers pressed forward and established themselves on the upper Yadkin; six years later James Robertson and John Sevier led a band of Virginia frontiersmen to the Watauga Valley. There they drew up the first written constitution adopted west of the mountains by American-born frontiersmen, and Watauga acted as an independent political community until incorporated as part of North Carolina in 1778.

The hunting trips of Daniel Boone and others had served to make known the wonders of the Kentucky country, and after 1769 settlers began to filter in, only to be driven out by the Indian attacks of 1774. In the following year Judge Richard Henderson founded the Transylvania Company, which purchased from the Indians the land between the Kentucky and Cumberland rivers. Boone led the first settlers into the area, and the Transylvanian pioneers, after drawing up a democratic constitution, petitioned Congress for statehood. Virginia refused to recognize their independence and Congress refused the petition. In 1779 Robertson led an exodus of the most restless of the Watauga settlers into Tennessee and planted a colony at Nashboro at the bend of the Cumberland. Still another group of frontiersmen around the headwaters of the Ohio organized the independent state of Westsylvania and petitioned Congress unsuccessfully for statehood. These attempts at state making illustrate only too clearly the lack of sympathy between the frontiersmen and their eastern neighbors, and the backwoodsmen's associations of Watauga, Boonesboro, and Nashboro exemplify the "social compact" in its simplest forms and are in marked contrast to the undemocratic features of the state constitutions being set up almost simultaneously.

Although the winning of the "Old Northwest" by George Rogers Clark by ousting the British from the old French posts on the Mississippi and Wabash had little or nothing to do with obtaining this land at the end of the war,[9] it makes clear the fact that the Revolution was also a frontier phenomenon. An appreciable part of the destinies of the Revolution lay in the hands of the frontiersmen—in Vermont under Ethan Allen, in New York under Gates and Herkimer, and in the Carolinas under Marion and Sumter—many of whom were not English but Scotch-Irish, German, and Welsh. As the influence of the upland country became greater, the westward migration of the state capitals began and continued in the years following the war: in Virginia from Williamsburg to Richmond; in South Carolina from Charleston to Columbia; in North Carolina from Edenton to Raleigh; in Georgia from Savannah to Louisville, thence to Milledgeville and after the Civil War to Atlanta; in New Jersey from Burlington to Trenton; in New York from New York City to Albany; in Pennsylvania from Philadelphia to Lancaster and later to Harrisburg; and in New Hampshire from Portsmouth to Exeter. One of the demands of Shays's Rebellion was that the capital of Massachusetts be moved westward. The frontier, says Professor Turner, was the "vanguard of the Revolution and the advance guard of colonization."

EFFECT OF THE WAR ON AGRICULTURE

At the opening of the Revolution the population of the United States is estimated to have been in the neighborhood of 2,750,000. Of men between eighteen and sixty there were about 700,000, but at no time during the war was more than one-eighth of this number under arms in the colonial armies, and during most of the period probably no more than one-sixteenth. Con-

[9] Clark's exploit was probably not the deciding factor in the acquisition of the Northwest, although there is now definite reason to believe that it was fully known to American and therefore to British negotiators. See letter from Sargé to Franklin, edited by Lewis J. Carey, in the *Mississippi Valley Historical Review*, XXI, 375–378 (Dec., 1934). The matter was primarily a diplomatic problem in which Great Britain chose to favor the United States rather than France or Spain.

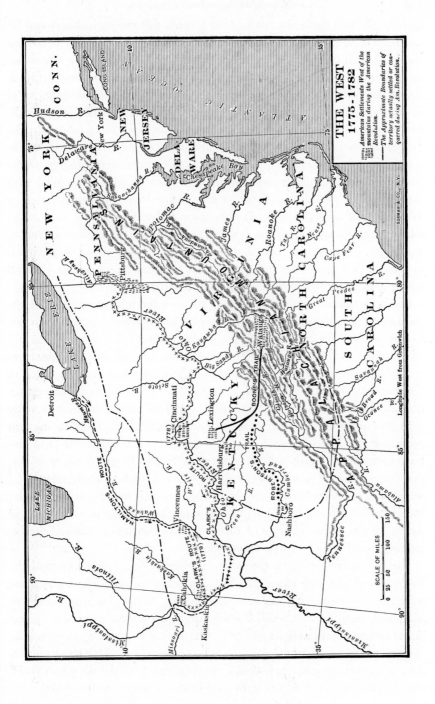

THE WEST
1775-1782

American Settlements West of the mountains during the American Revolution.

The Approximate Boundaries of territory actually settled or conquered during the Am. Revolution.

SCHNAKE & CO., N.Y.

NEW YORK   CONN.

Hudson R.

LONG ISLAND

A T L A N T I C

O C E A N

New York

Delaware R.

NEW JERSEY

PENNSYLVANIA

DELAWARE

Chesapeake Bay

Susquehanna R.

Potomac R.

Pittsburg

Shenandoah R.

James R.

Roanoke R.

MARYLAND

VIRGINIA

The R.

Neuse R.

Cape Fear R.

NORTH CAROLINA

Peedee

Great

Savannah R.

Longitude West from Greenwich

SOUTH CAROLINA

Broad R.

Oconee R.

LAKE ERIE

Allegheny R.

Detroit

LAKE MICHIGAN

Miami R.

Ohio River

Big Sandy R.

Scioto R.

Cincinnati (1778)

Lexington

Kentucky R.

BOONE'S TRAIL

Watauga

Clinch R.

Holston R.

Nolichucky R.

French Broad R.

A P P A L A C H I A N

HAMILTON'S ROUTE

Vincennes

Wabash R.

CLARK'S ROUTE

Harrodsburg

KENTUCKY

Ohio R.

Green R.

ROBERTSON'S TRAIL

Cumberland R.

Nashboro

ROBE

Alabama

Illinois R.

Kaskaskia R.

Cahokia

Missouri R.

CLARK'S ROUTE (1779)

Kaskaskia

Mississippi River

Tennessee R.

Mississippi R.

SCALE OF MILES
0 25 50   100   150

cerning the war there was widespread apathy, and the agricultural and industrial life of the people went on much as usual. After the first year New England, with the exception of the occupation of Newport and a few minor raids upon the coast, was free from the British. Agriculture was hardly affected. In New York, New Jersey, and Pennsylvania the depredations of both armies were to a great extent compensated for by the liberal prices the French and British paid the farmers in gold for supplies of all kinds; the farmers seemed only too willing to double their prices for the French and to sell their produce to Howe, while Washington's men shivered and starved at Valley Forge. That the colonies must have been plentifully supplied with profiteers and "sunshine patriots" we may gather from the words of George Washington: "Such a dearth of public spirit and want of virtue, such stockjobbing, and fertility in all the low arts to obtain advantage of one kind or another . . . I never saw before, and I pray God I may never be a witness to again. . . . Such a dirty mercenary spirit pervades the whole that I should not be at all surprised at any disaster that may happen."[10]

Blockade runners were always ready to carry the tobacco of the Virginia plantations to a waiting market in Europe. Comparatively speaking, the last twenty years of the century were the golden age for tobacco, for it was still the leading southern product. The production of leaf tobacco rose from 101,800,000 pounds in 1774 to 130,000,000 in 1790, at which time over half of the southern population was either engaged in or dependent on its production. In the Carolinas the cultivation and export of rice went on, apparently with little interruption. In 1778 the first water mill adapted to cleaning and preparing rice for the market, and the model upon which subsequent improvements were based, was erected on the Santee River. While it is true that many phases of southern agriculture were not fundamentally affected by the war, at the same time it should not be forgotten that Patriot plantation owners suffered from the British raids and lost heavily by the confiscation of slaves. Likewise, the cessation of British bounties on indigo marked the beginning of the end of an important industry.

The interference in trade caused by nonimportation agreements and the first years of the war stimulated the production of wool throughout the colonies. The same was true of cotton in the South. The legislatures of Maryland, Virginia, and South Carolina urged upon their farmers the growing of cotton so effectively, apparently, that Hamilton, writing in 1775, said, "Several of the Southern colonies are so favorable to it that, with due cultivation, in a couple of years they would afford enough to clothe the whole continent."[11] American agriculture with its primitive wasteful methods was stim-

---

[10] George Washington, *Writings* (Ford ed.), III, 246, 247.
[11] H. C. Lodge (ed.), *Works of Alexander Hamilton* (1885), I, 153.

ulated as a whole rather than injured by the war. Moreover, knowledge of European improvements was spread by the foreigners whom the war brought into the country.

EFFECT OF THE WAR ON INDUSTRIAL LIFE

American manufactures were more directly affected by the war than American agriculture. The Revolution enfranchised American industry by ending the annoying restrictions which the English Parliament under the influence of mercantilism had imposed when it sought to confine the colonies to the production of raw materials. During the boycotts preceding the outbreak of hostilities, the colonists refused to purchase English goods, and great efforts were made to stimulate the manufacture of such necessities as woolens and linens which had formerly been imported in large amounts. Large numbers of people pledged themselves not to eat lamb or mutton or to buy from butchers who sold it, that the wool might be saved for clothing; women of all classes turned to the production of cloth as a domestic business. The southern planters employed their poorer white neighbors at spinning or weaving or themselves built loom houses and trained their slaves to this work. Homespun was worn by the wealthiest. The necessity for wool cards led Connecticut to lend Nathaniel Niles, of Norwich, £300 for four years to make wire for card teeth. Massachusetts in 1777 granted a bounty of £100 for the first 1000 pounds of "good merchantable card wire" produced in any water mill in her own territory from iron made in the American states. This activity in spinning and weaving during the early years of the war declined after the cargoes captured by the privateers began to be thrown on the market and importation was resumed.

The manufacture of munitions and necessaries of war was, of course, stimulated. The life in the colonies which made everyone a hunter had developed skilled locksmiths, and small gun factories sprang up in Massachusetts, Connecticut, and Rhode Island. Connecticut in 1775 offered a bounty of 1s. 6d. for each gunlock manufactured, and 5s. for each complete stand of arms to the number of 3000. Congress in 1778 founded works in Springfield where cannon were cast—the predecessor of the present national armory established there in 1794. The casting and forging of guns and camp kettles was carried on in Pennsylvania and on the Hudson; new furnaces were built in many places in New England and the middle colonies. Rhode Island and Maine granted bounties for the manufacture of steel.[12] It is claimed that Jeremiah Wilkinson of Cumberland, Rhode Island, turned out in 1777 the first cold cut nail in the world. Massachusetts offered bounties on sulphur extracted

---

[12] *Rhode Island Colony Records*, VIII, 240. Also see Victor S. Clark, *History of Manufactures in the United States*, I, 219–232.

from native ores, and Rhode Island for powder, but most of the powder used was imported. Attempts at mining and refining lead were made in Connecticut and at Cheswell, Virginia, but most of that used was obtained from abroad or from melting down lead roofs, window weights, and other commodities.

A very real shortage of many of the necessities was felt until 1777 in all parts of the country, but it was in part overcome. The increase in newspapers during the war from thirty-seven to over one hundred brought an increase in paper mills. Small establishments were set up to manufacture various commodities formerly imported. Shipbuilding, however, an industry which had been stimulated by the Navigation Acts, was greatly restricted during the war. Limited as was the manufacturing, it is remarkable that so much was carried on. Labor, always scarce and expensive in the colonial period, became increasingly so during the war. Enlistments in the Army and on privateers, and the emigration of loyalists with their servants, decreased the supply. Wages of skilled and unskilled labor doubled from 1774 to 1784, not only because of scarcity of labor, but also because of the rising cost of living and the increased amount of money in circulation.

COMMERCE AND PRIVATEERING

The Revolution favored maritime activity in two ways: first, in the opening of colonial ports to the world, and second, in stimulating privateering. The nonimportation agreements of the years preceding the war had exhausted the country of English goods; as a consequence, the merchants of Spain, Holland, and France eagerly welcomed the new markets, discovering means of evading the British warships and privateersmen to such purpose that by 1777 there was little lack of foreign merchandise. Lists of imports during the war reveal items distinctly in the class of luxuries—such finer textiles as velvets, linens, silks, and broadcloths, as well as teas, coffees, spices, and wines. Ports occupied by the British were opened to English goods and considerable quantities were imported through New York. The articles were paid for mainly by exports of flour, tobacco, and rice, and by the money which found its way to the colonies through the medium of foreign loans and British quartermasters. These exported staples also had to run the gantlet of the British fleet and privateersmen. Although the British admirals reported the capture of 570 vessels between 1776 and 1779, exportation was sufficiently lucrative to continue with little abatement throughout the war. Twenty-four million pounds of tobacco alone were recorded in 1777–1778 by the British customs officials, about one-third of the ordinary consumption, received possibly under the pretense that it came from neutral ports, for the Dutch island of St. Eustatius and the French island of Martinique served as ports where cargoes could be transferred and neutralized.

Hand-power Farming—Agricultural Tools in 1790.

Harvesting Wheat Before the Invention of the Reaper.

Stocking Frame—Spinning and Weaving (Eighteenth Century).

Farming at the Beginning of the Nineteenth Century. These Crude Engravings from the *Farmer's Almanac* Show Hand Power Agriculture, as in Reaping and Threshing.

From O. Turner, Pioneer History of the Holland
Land Purchase of Western New York (1850)

Four Stages of the Frontier.

Pioneering by Train (Currier and Ives Conception).

Sod House on the Prairies—The First Home of Many Farmers on the Great Plains.

Photo by Brown Brothers

Pawhuska, Oklahoma—A Typical Frontier Town of the Late 1880's.

Courtesy of Northern Pacific Railroad

Homesteaders Carrying Supplies From Railroad Station at Mandan, North Dakota.

Model of Whitney's Cotton Gin in the United States National Museum.

Eli Whitney, Inventor of the Cotton Gin and of Machinery to Make Interchangeable Parts. Yale University Library.

The Country Fair. Painting by J. A. Woodside.

Mechanized Farming in the Middle Nineteenth Century. (Currier and Ives.)

Of almost equal magnitude with wartime commerce were the operations carried on by privateers. It has been estimated that 2000 privateers were commissioned, of which the great majority came from Massachusetts.[13] Salem, which had been mainly a fishing town before the war, had 59 privateers carrying 4000 men in 1781, and probably 180 during the war. Nearly 200 commissions were issued by Rhode Island, where privateering became so popular that the Assembly found it necessary to check it and pass laws to limit the size of the crews. Newburyport sent out twenty-two vessels, and the Connecticut towns of New London, Hartford, and New Haven also engaged in the lucrative business, although more closely watched by the British fleet. Most of the operations were carried on from the smaller New England towns, for New York, Boston, Philadelphia, Newport, and Charleston were at one time or other under British control.

With his usual routine voyage cut off, the American seaman found a natural outlet in privateering. Daring was necessary and the risk great, but the spice of adventure and the lure of profits drew the keenest and coolest. It was customary for the owners to split half and half with the crew, according to rank. Captured prizes were either taken to European ports, sold, and the money invested in merchandise to be brought home, or else, if the capture was effected off the American coast, brought in at once. More than 445 prizes were brought in by the Salem fleet. Elias Hasket Derby, the chief shipowner and the enterprising genius of this little town, died in 1799, worth about $1,000,000 realized chiefly from privateering profits, a stupendous fortune for those days. In the year 1776 alone, English West Indiamen to the number of 250 were captured, entailing a loss of £1,800,000, and insurance rates from the West Indies to England rose to 23 per cent. "Probably as many as ninety thousand Americans were, first and last," says Jameson, "engaged in these voyages, a number of men almost as great as served in the army, and greater than that of the army in any single year save one."[14]

Silas Deane in 1777 wrote Robert Morris that as American privateers and cruisers "sailed quite around Ireland and took or destroyed seventeen or eighteen sail of vessels, they most effectually alarmed England, prevented the great fair at Chester, occasioned insurance to rise, and even deterred the English merchants from shipping goods in English vessels at any rate, so that in a few weeks forty sail of French ships were loading in the Thames on freight, an instance never before known."[15] He adds that "even the packet

[13] "Six hundred and twenty-six letters of marque were issued to Massachusetts vessels by the Continental Congress, and some thousand more by the General Court." S. E. Morison, *Maritime History of Massachusetts*, p. 29.

[14] J. F. Jameson, *op. cit.*, p. 103.

[15] The Deane Papers, II, 108, New York Historical Society Publications. Letter, dated "Paris, 23rd. August, 1777," to Robert Morris, who was a member of the Secret Committee of Congress. This entire letter, pp. 106–111, is well worth reading for its account of the activities of "American ships of war, private as well as public."

boats from Dover to Calais were for some time insured." A witness before a special parliamentary inquiry in 1778 stated that the losses suffered by British merchants from American privateers "could not be less than two million two hundred thousand pounds." Privateering served the purpose not alone of harassing the enemy but of keeping alive the maritime spirit and holding capital to the shipping industry. It also increased the unpopularity of the war in England.

FINANCING THE REVOLUTION

The most difficult task which Congress had to handle was providing funds for carrying on the war. No power was given to it to levy taxes, and if such power had been given, it is doubtful whether legislation would have been practicable, owing to the colonists' hatred of any form of taxation. The entire cost of the war measured in gold was only about $104,000,000, a sum which should have been easily raised. As a matter of fact, the generation which fought the war paid about half the cost, chiefly on account of the depreciation of the paper money which had been issued in lieu of taxes. Under the circumstances the resort to paper money seems quite natural. As England's control over currency had been one of the colonists' grievances, they expected that, with the restraining hand of the mother country withdrawn, recourse would be made immediately to fiat money.

The war had scarcely commenced when Congress (June 22, 1775) issued bills of credit for $2,000,000, to be redeemed for Spanish milled dollars by the states in proportion to population at a time and place not specified. From then until November 29, 1779, Congress authorized forty-two emissions of paper money to the amount of $191,552,380. To complicate the situation, the states began issuing competing paper currency; by 1783, eleven states had authorized paper to the amount of $246,366,941.[16] This was altogether more than the new nation had any need for, and as its value rested ultimately on the success of the struggle and the willingness of the states to redeem the paper, it was natural that depreciation should set in. In ringing proclamations Jay and others urged in the name of patriotism that all good citizens accept it in trade. Patriots were exhorted and Tories forced to receive it. Buoyed up by the French and Spanish subsidies, the dollar held up fairly well until September, 1777, when it began to depreciate rapidly; in March, 1780, the Continental dollar sold for 2.45 cents, a value it held until the end of the war. In 1781 it took $100 in paper money to buy a pair of shoes, $40 to purchase a bushel of corn, $90 for a pound of tea, $1575 for a barrel of flour. "Not worth a continental" became the synonym of worthlessness. People with

---

[16] These computations were made by Professor Lewis J. Carey from tables in R. V. Harlow, "Aspects of Revolutionary France," *American Historical Review*, XXXV, 46–68 (Oct., 1929).

fixed incomes suffered, but it was the heyday for the speculator and the debtor.

Chaotic as was the currency situation during the Revolution, its effect on economic life must not be overemphasized. The evils of fiat money in a primitive self-sufficing community, when barter is common, are mitigated because relatively few people are forced to use much of it. Furthermore, the loss was distributed because the depreciation did not all come at once. The influx of European gold during the war, which brought in more metallic currency than the colonies had ever known, helped to ease the situation, even if the gold did not remain long in circulation. The issuing of paper money was probably the only means by which the war could be financed.

In addition to the issuing of paper currency, almost every other means was used to obtain funds. Certificates of indebtedness were issued by quarter-masters in payment for supplies which they requisitioned. Domestic loans were floated first at 4 per cent and later at 6 per cent, but without great success. Equally discouraging was the result of the requisitions made upon the states. Because of unwillingness to tax their own citizens and jealousy or distrust of their sister commonwealths, the states failed to respond adequately to the demands of the Continental Congress. Lotteries were set up and prize money was taken from the sale of captures made by government privateers. Gifts were obtained from private individuals abroad, and loans and gifts from foreign governments. Including the expenses incurred by the states in maintaining their own militia, the cost of the Revolution in gold (in round numbers) has been estimated by Professor Seligman as follows:

Paper money	$41,000,000 (approx.)
Certificates of indebtedness	16,708,000
Loan-office certificates	11,585,000
Foreign loans	7,830,000
Taxes (requisitions upon the states)	5,795,000
Gifts from abroad	1,996,000
Miscellaneous receipts	856,000
State debts	18,272,000
	$104,042,000[17]

ECONOMIC REORGANIZATION AFTER THE WAR

As usually happens after a war, the American Revolution was followed by an economic reorganization that carried in its wake a period of uncertainty and hard times. During the conflict, labor and investment had been diverted from agriculture and legitimate trade to manufacturing and privateering. Men had gone into unwonted occupations which ceased when the war ended.

[17] For a discussion of the payment of this debt, see below, pp. 153 ff.

Lowered prices resulting from the cessation of war demands, in combination with the importation of the cheaper manufactured goods of Europe, were fast ruining such infant manufacturing concerns as had sprung up during the war. The reabsorption of the disbanded army into economic life required time. So also did the replenishment of the stock of slave labor in the South, where thousands of Negroes had been taken off by the British and fleeing loyalists. South Carolina and Virginia had felt severely the ravages of war in the later years; New England had seen her fishing industry and the resulting West Indian trade ruined. Other states found business stagnant and conditions depressed.

Another factor which made the situation even more distressing was the British Navigation Acts. The American Revolution had been fought for freedom of commerce and in repudiation of the whole economic policy of Great Britain as it applied to the colonies. Instead, however, of remedying the situation, the War for Independence made matters worse. The only clause in the treaty of peace (1783) concerning commerce was a stipulation guaranteeing that the navigation of the Mississippi should be forever free to the United States. Jay at this time tried to secure some reciprocal trade provisions with Great Britain, but without result. Pitt in 1783 introduced a bill into the British Parliament providing for free trade between the United States and the British colonies, but instead of passing it Parliament enacted the British Navigation Act of 1783, which admitted only British-built and manned ships to the ports of the West Indies and imposed heavy tonnage dues upon American ships in other British ports. This was amplified in 1786 by another act designed to prevent the fraudulent registration of American vessels, and by still another in 1787 which prohibited the importation of American goods by way of foreign islands.

The favorable features of the old Navigation Acts which had granted bounties and reserved the English markets in certain cases to colonial products were gone; the unfavorable alone were left. The British market was further curtailed by the depression in Britain after 1783. Although the French treaty of 1778 had promised "perfect equality and reciprocity" in commercial relations, it was found impossible to make a commercial treaty upon this basis. Spain demanded as her price for reciprocal trading relations that the United States surrender for twenty-five years the right of navigating the Mississippi, a price which the New England merchants would have been glad to pay. France (1778) and Holland (1782) made treaties, but not on even terms; Portugal refused our advances. Only Sweden (1783) and Prussia (1785) made treaties guaranteeing reciprocal commercial privileges.

To make matters more galling, Americans needed European commodities, especially the manufactured goods of England, which they were accustomed to from long usage. So necessary were they that in 1784 goods to the approximate value of £3,700,000 were imported and only £750,000 worth of goods sent in return; this meant paying the balance in specie or in other credits extended by foreigners to buyers in this country. John Adams was sent to England in 1785 and remained for three years in a futile effort to negotiate a commercial treaty; he argued unsuccessfully that "it is England's interest to cherish her trade with America, and if a hard policy is adopted America will trade elsewhere or build her own factories." There were not a few in Great Britain who realized the soundness of Adams' contention, but powerful mercantile interests prevented concessions. Under the leadership of Lord Sheffield[18] the British government took the position that the interests of the loyal colonies should be protected and that the American trade could be kept even if the old navigation laws were retained.

The weakness of Congress under the Articles of Confederation prevented retaliation by the central government. Power was repeatedly asked to regulate commerce, but it was refused by the states, upon whom rested the carrying out of such commercial treaties as Congress might negotiate. Eventually the states themselves attempted retaliatory measures, and during the years 1783–1788 ten states levied tonnage dues upon British vessels or discriminating tariffs upon British goods. Whatever effect these efforts might have had were neutralized by the fact that the duties were not uniform; they varied in the different states from no tariffs whatever to duties of 100 per cent. This simply drove British ships to the free or cheapest ports and their goods continued to flood the market. As Washington wrote to Lafayette in 1788, ". . . It would be idle to think of making commercial regulations on our part. One state passes a prohibitory law respecting some article, another state opens wide the avenue for admission. One assembly makes a system, another assembly unmakes it."[19]

WEAKNESS OF THE CENTRAL GOVERNMENT AND DISSENSION AMONG THE STATES

It was the lack of a strong central government that tied the hands of Adams and Jay in their negotiations with foreign nations for reciprocal commercial treaties and made it possible for certain states to nullify the retaliatory measures of the others against England. Under the Articles of Confederation (1781–1789) each state "retained its sovereignty, freedom, and independence," granting to Congress only such rights as could not be easily exercised by the individual states, such as the right to conduct foreign affairs,

[18] His pamphlet, *Observations on the Commerce of the American States* (1784), was of great influence in this controversy.
[19] George Washington, *op. cit.,* IX, 254.

declare war, raise an army and navy, borrow money, and emit bills of credit. The right to levy taxes was not granted; Congress had merely the right to make "requisitions" which the states might or might not meet. A government without power to raise taxes was without power to provide for a standing army to enforce treaties, if they could be made. As a consequence, the government under the Articles of Confederation was one without power at home and without standing abroad. England openly violated the Treaty of 1783 by refusing to surrender the northwest trading posts; Spain trafficked with the western frontiersmen in an attempt to instigate a rebellion against the United States; and Barbary pirates levied blackmail on American merchant ships.

At home the union brought about by the Revolution seemed rapidly breaking up. Instead of one nation presenting a united front, there were again thirteen bickering states wrapped up in their old selfish provincialism, intent upon their own ambitions and problems. Pennsylvania attacked the Connecticut settlers in the Wyoming Valley as if they had been an intruding war party of Indians, and Connecticut and New York fought over the region of Vermont. These boundary-line disputes were only dramatic examples of the hostility which was ever present in commercial relations between the states. A classical example of these commercial wars occurred in 1787 when New York levied import duties and placed other hindrances in the way of New Jersey and Connecticut farm products, which had hitherto largely supplied the New York City market. New Jersey replied by levying a tax of $1800 a year upon a Sandy Hook lighthouse recently purchased by New York and essential to the safety of the harbor; and a mass meeting of businessmen in New London pledged themselves under penalty of $250 not to send goods to New York for a period of twelve months.

Spectacular as these commercial wars sometimes were, their importance should not be exaggerated. Recent students have insisted that the process of commercial recovery was not greatly retarded by interstate jealousy and cutthroat commercial laws.[20] Discriminatory duties were exceptional after 1783, when it was usual to exempt the produce of American states from import duties and give preferential tonnage rates to American-owned vessels over foreign ships.

CHAOS IN THE CURRENCY

Even more disastrous to economic life than foreign trade restrictions, a weak central government, and interstate rivalries was the chaos in the currency. Congress and the several states during the war had issued $437,919,321 in paper money, and in addition there had been much counterfeiting. The

[20] R. A. East, *Business Enterprise in the American Revolutionary Era*, pp. 249–250.

paper money of the states had depreciated in varying amounts, and the money issued by Congress, the Continental paper, had become practically valueless, simply a commodity in the hands of speculators. Since this money gradually passed from circulation as worthless, business again became dependent upon English, French, Spanish, and Portuguese coins. The innumerable varieties of money complicated barter. The appearance of foreign coins, however, did not wholly remedy the situation, for, as in earlier years, they were exported to pay for imports. With such a scarcity of currency and after two exceedingly trying years, it was to be expected that the old cry for paper money would again be renewed during the depression of 1785–1786, particularly by the farmer class, the debtors, and the poor generally.

The business interests, realizing the effects of more paper money on trade, resisted the demand stubbornly. As their legislatures were again under the control of the large planters or wealthy merchants of the coast towns, Massachusetts, New Hampshire, Connecticut, Delaware, Maryland, and Virginia succeeded in escaping further paper money, but only after severe struggles. A mob crying out for paper and threatening the lives of the legislators surrounded the meetinghouse at Exeter, New Hampshire, and were dispersed by the militia. The farmers of central and western Massachusetts, strong for paper money and hot against the aristocrats of Boston who had gained control of the government through the conservative constitution in 1780, revolted under Daniel Shays and were put down only after Governor Bowdoin had sent a good-sized army against them. The other seven states yielded to the demand; but neither laws nor threats of bodily harm could in some cases make merchants take the money. The most exciting case in the judicial history of Rhode Island was fought on this question, when a certain John Weeden, a butcher, refused to accept scrip for meat. The judges held the statute unconstitutional and were summoned before the legislature and reproved, but their decision stood.

Important as was the question of paper money at this time from an economic point of view, its social significance was even greater. It served as a tangible issue around which social discontent could rally. The close of the Revolution found the old ruling aristocratic class weakened by the emigration of the Tories. The former middle class had pushed to the front and the small farmer was more of a factor. Dominated by more democratic ideals, this group opposed bitterly such projects as the promise of Congress to grant officers half pay for life and the founding of the Society of the Cincinnati. Their fear of an aristocratic class is seen in the abolition of primogeniture and entail, and the seizure of the rights of the proprietors in Pennsylvania and Maryland; their fear of a king, in the restrictions built around the executive in the new state constitutions.

But a counterrevolution had already set in. A new ruling class had possession of most of the state legislatures, a group whose economic interests were at variance with those of the small farmers. The latter, harassed by heavy debts, the scarcity of specie, and the depression of 1785-1786, were in no mood to see their welfare ignored by a new ruling class out of sympathy with the common man. Economic unrest and class antagonism reached their climax in Massachusetts in the rebellion of 1786, but the hard-pressed farmers who followed Daniel Shays only expressed more vigorously the feelings of thousands of small farmers in each of the states. Hundreds, disheartened, emigrated to the West, only to receive further evidence of the weakness of the central government. For there the Spaniards had closed the mouth of the Mississippi to their products, thus preventing their reaching a market. It was in this social structure and these conditions that the project of a new constitution and a stronger central government was launched.

HOW CRITICAL WAS THE "CRITICAL PERIOD"?

From what has been said it is clear enough that the years between York-town and the adoption of the Constitution were difficult. Problems of readjustment after any war are serious. Whether these years were as "critical" as earlier historians have pictured them, however, is open to question.[21] Recent research has tended to emphasize the enlarging business activity during this period. First of all should be noted the rapid revival of commerce until it soon reached prewar levels. It is true that under the Navigation Act of 1783 the British West Indies were closed to American ships, but the demand for lumber and foodstuffs in these islands was so great that ways of evading the act were quickly discovered. One method was to ship products to the French, Dutch, or Spanish islands whence they found their way to the British islands. The fact that half of the shipments to the West Indies from the United States reached Jamaica is alone ample proof of this. By the middle 1780's the navigation acts of the French, Spanish, and Dutch had been sufficiently relaxed to allow an active trade with their colonies. Moreover, trade with France and Holland developed beyond prewar levels since these nations took certain "enumerated" products which during the colonial period could be shipped only to Great Britain. By 1787-1789 the trade with Holland had become more than 50 per cent as important as that with England, with a balance probably in favor of America. This revival of commerce brought in its wake, of course, a revival of the fishing and lumbering industries and a demand for foodstuffs, tobacco, and other agricultural commodities.

During the Revolution the slave trade passed into other hands and the

---

[21] In 1888 the historian-philosopher, John Fiske, published a volume, *The Critical Period in American History, 1783-1789*, and many subsequent writers have followed his lead in emphasizing the darkness and chaos of these years.

three-cornered route became a thing of the past. The Yankee, however, soon found other opportunities for trade in the Baltic countries, the Near East, and the Far East. It was in 1785 that the *Empress of China* entered New York from Canton and in 1787 that the *Grand Turk* sailed into Salem from the same port; of forty-six foreign vessels entering Canton in 1789, eighteen were American. It was also during these years that the first New England mariners reached the northwest coast in search of furs. Captain Gray's famous voyage to Oregon and China (1787-1790) opened the New England–Northwest-China trade, a lucrative traffic whereby the New Englander traded manufactured products to the northwest Indians for furs, and then sailed for China to trade the furs for Oriental goods.

Commerce was by no means the only field in which a vigorous spirit of business enterprise was evident. With British restrictions now lifted, the Bank of North America was established in 1781, the Bank of New York and the Massachusetts Bank of Boston in 1784. Throughout the country merchant capitalists, hitherto held in restraint by British mercantilism, were pooling their capital and organizing companies to exploit the West, to build turnpikes, bridges, and canals, and to promote manufacturing. The issuing of charters to American concerns was almost unknown in the colonial period, but between 1781 and 1785 state legislatures issued eleven and between 1786 and 1790 at least twenty-two more.

Americans were particularly loath to sacrifice such gains in manufacturing as they had made during the war. Many of these industries kept going. During this period the first cotton factory in the United States was built (1787) at Beverly, Massachusetts, and two years later Slater built his mill at Pawtucket. In 1788 a woolen factory was established at Hartford, with a capital of £1280, raised by subscription to shares at £10 each. Before the end of the period many of the large New England towns had commenced their manufacturing careers. At Philadelphia John Fitch and others who were experimenting with the steam vessel produced one that ran eighty miles a day. It was a period when society was alive not only to political changes but to the economic possibilities of the new nation.

It is true that the country suffered a depression in 1785 and 1786, but the letdown was due as much to overtrading and expansion as to any weakness of government. It did not last long and in the two years preceding the adoption of the Constitution economic activity, as suggested by some of the dates in the preceding paragraphs, was again in full swing. Commenting on this activity, a leading authority on the period writes:

High rentals, building activity, and luxurious living actually impressed Franklin on his return to America in 1785. Stagecoach routes and facilities were steadily being increased in various regions. The paper industry continued to grow, and important companies were organized for iron and woolen manufacturers in 1786 and 1788. Above all, it is significant that capital was much sought after everywhere during the "critical" years. Interest rates were high in 1784. New York merchant-capitalists were even invited to New Jersey and Connecticut, being promised liberal treatment. . . . And if it be argued that all this merely emphasized a great lack of capital, rather than a general demand for it, it can be pointed out in reply that there was no difficulty in securing subscriptions of specie value for large amounts of bank stock in 1784 in Philadelphia, Boston and New York.[22]

THE STRUGGLE FOR THE CONSTITUTION

That the economic and social conditions of the 1780's presented many reasons for a stronger central government there can be no doubt. American economic expansion needed a more unified economic program, freedom of interstate commerce, a more stabilized currency, and other benefits which a strong central government could provide. Nevertheless, the student of American history must be on his guard not to overemphasize the effects of the weak government under the Articles of Confederation. "The defects of the old confederation," as Callender well says, "were then in no way responsible for the hard times. It had not produced them, nor could the best government in the world have removed them."[23] To no small extent it was the economic conditions that prevented government from functioning rather than poor government that caused the depression.

Nevertheless, the movement for a constitution was supported most eagerly by those whose economic interests were most seriously affected by the weakness of the central government under the Articles of Confederation. It was also supported by many of the new ruling class who were frightened by the restlessness of the small farmers, particularly after Shays's Rebellion. Moreover, investors in manufacturing and shipping desired a government strong enough to protect them against foreign discrimination, and this despite the economic expansion of the 1780's. Capital was also being continually attacked by the debtor class, who were endeavoring to push stay laws and paper-money acts through the legislatures, and who sometimes in the local courts showed a disconcerting lack of interest in the rights of absentee capital. While shipowners and manufacturers wanted protection from a strong central government, domestic merchants were anxious to demolish the barriers to interstate traffic and longed for a stable and uniform currency.

But among the most ardent advocates of the Constitution were naturally all those who held claims against the Confederacy. These included owners of Continental bonds, certificates of indebtedness, and paper money, who knew

[22] R. A. East, *op. cit.*, p. 242.
[23] G. S. Callender, *Selections from the Economic History of the United States, 1765–1860*, p. 182.

that a strong central government would be able not only to redeem its own securities but to tone up the state paper. Much of this paper, of course, was no longer in the hands of the original owners but had long since shifted into the possession of speculators. The foreign debt being excluded, it has been conservatively estimated that the increase in the value of Continental securities which resulted from the adoption of the Constitution and the sound financial policies of the new government was at least $40,000,000, which in value represented one-tenth of the total taxable value of the land in the thirteen colonies—obviously no mean stake to play for.[24] Another type of speculator eager for a strong government was the investor in western land; his group included a large number of the wealthy and prominent men of the time.

Behind the movement for a new Constitution, then, were the commercial, financial, creditor, and speculating classes, who were eager to safeguard and strengthen the rights of property. To be sure, these groups were in a minority, but they contained many men of ability, integrity, and broad vision who were powerful, active, and easily organized, for they were concentrated in the towns and represented in each state. With such a group behind the movement, it was to be expected that the document would be conservative in nature and the rights of private property and vested interests would be carefully safeguarded. The Constitutional Convention itself could hardly have been better picked to serve these interests. The left-wing radicals of the Revolution were notable for their absence, while more than half the delegates were either investors or speculators in public securities which would be benefited by the new Constitution. Much attention has been given by historians to the differences in the Convention and the great compromises which it wrought, but, as a matter of fact, its members were in pretty close agreemnt on essentials, and their facility in effecting compromises was due to their unity on the fundamentals.

Under the circumstances, opposition to ratification was bound to be extremely bitter, and it was long doubtful whether the Constitution would be accepted. The opposition came mostly from the agricultural districts and debtor areas. "I believe it to be a fact," said Patrick Henry, "that the great body of yeomanry are in decided opposition to it."[25] Whether the people desired it or not it is impossible to know, for no more than one-fourth of the adult males voted in the election for delegates to ratifying conventions and probably not more than one-sixth of the adult males ratified it. As Professor Beard well says, "The Constitution was not created by 'the whole people,'

---

[24] C. A. Beard, *An Economic Interpretation of the Constitution of the United States,* pp. 34 ff.
[25] W. W. Henry, *op. cit.,* III, 578. Speech, June 24, 1788, in the Virginia Convention of June, 1788, convened to consider the question of the adoption of the United States Constitution.

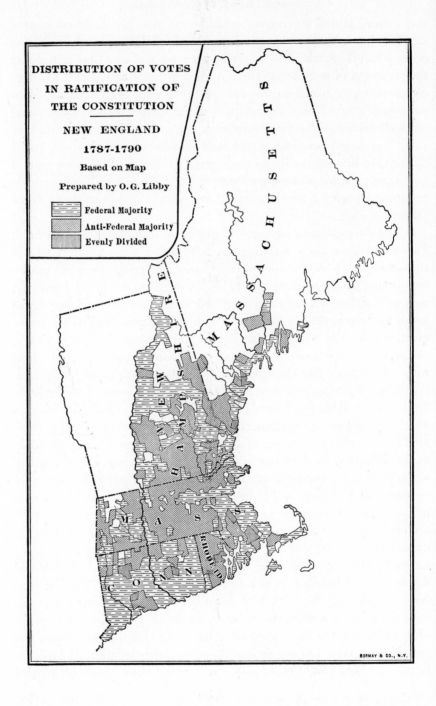

DISTRIBUTION OF VOTES
IN RATIFICATION OF
THE CONSTITUTION

NEW ENGLAND
1787-1790

Based on Map
Prepared by O. G. Libby

Federal Majority
Anti-Federal Majority
Evenly Divided

BORMAY & CO., N.Y.

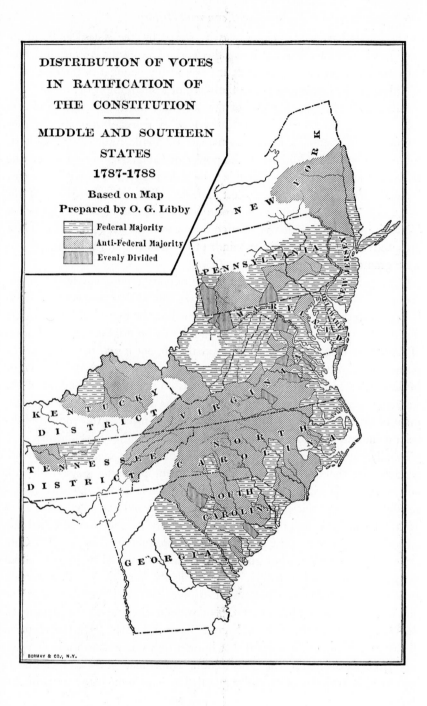

DISTRIBUTION OF VOTES
IN RATIFICATION OF
THE CONSTITUTION

———

MIDDLE AND SOUTHERN
STATES
1787-1788

Based on Map
Prepared by O. G. Libby

Federal Majority
Anti-Federal Majority
Evenly Divided

BORMAY & CO., N.Y.

as the jurists have said; neither was it created by 'the states,' as Southern nullifiers long contended; but it was the work of a consolidated group whose interests knew no state boundaries and were truly national in their scope."[26]

Although the Constitution was the work of a small minority, its adoption meant the elimination of many of the economic ills under which industry and commerce had struggled since the war. A reorganization of the government was essential and the immediate economic results were salutary. Its most important additions to the power of Congress were those relating to finance and commerce—it enabled the federal government to levy taxes, regulate trade, coin money, protect industry, direct the settlement of the West, and, as later events proved, to establish credit and redeem its securities. Under it freedom of trade was insured throughout the young republic. These prospective benefits were in the minds of the framers, and adequate powers were granted.[27]

Giving all due recognition to the many salutary economic effects brought about by a stronger central government, we should note at least three facts in respect to the Constitution. It was designed, in the first place, for a society distinctly agricultural and mercantile, and drawn up primarily by the leaders of these economic groups. Not only was this so, but it was the intent of the framers to protect these interests in case the structure of society might change in the future. In the second place, there was no intention on the part of the framers to set up an unmodified democracy. As a consequence, the readjustment of the Constitution a hundred years later to meet a great industrial development and more democratic conditions was fraught with difficulty.

Finally, the feeling was strongly expressed during the campaigns over ratification that the Constitution was a document primarily concerned with bolstering up the rights of private property, especially that invested in personality, and not sufficiently interested in the generally accepted "Rights of Man." To make it more palatable and to secure its adoption, the first ten amendments, known as the Bill of Rights, were submitted by the first Congress and duly ratified. They guaranteed such fundamental rights as freedom of speech, press, and assembly, religious liberty, jury trial, and protection against unreasonable searches and excessive bails and punishments. The ninth and tenth amendments gave blanket protection aganst usurpations by the federal government of the rights of citizens and states. With the adoption of these amendments, it seemed that human rights as well as those of property had been covered by the Constitution. Unfortunately, these amendments have not always been so carefully guarded as have some other parts of this important document.

[26] C. A. Beard, *An Economic Interpretation of the Constitution,* p. 325.
[27] Most of the economic clauses in the Constitution are in Article I, Sections 8, 9, and 10.

SELECTED READINGS

Jensen, Merrill, *The New Nation,* chaps. 8–17.

Jameson, J. F., *The American Revolution Considered as a Social Movement,* chaps. 1–3.

East, R. A., *Business Enterprise in the American Revolutionary Era,* chaps. 10–12.

Hacker, L. M., *Triumph of American Capitalism,* chaps. 13–14.

Billington, R. A., *Westward Expansion,* chap. 9.

Shultz, W. J., and Caine, M. R., *Financial Development of the United States,* chaps. 3–4.

Clark, V. S., *History of Manufactures in the United States,* Vol. I, chap. 10.

Beard, C. A., *An Economic Interpretation of the Constitution of the United States,* chaps. 2, 3, 6, 10, 11.

Callender, G. S., *Selections from the Economic History of the United States, 1765–1860,* pp. 122–177.

Flügel, F., and Faulkner, H. U., *Readings in the Economic and Social History of the United States,* pp. 3–38.

CHAPTER 9

FINANCE AND TARIFF

FISCAL POLICY OF THE NEW GOVERNMENT

IN spite of the widespread opposition to the adoption of the Constitution, the new government, when it commenced its labors in 1789, was comfortably controlled by the friends of that document. Eleven of the twenty-four Senators in the first Congress had helped to draft it, and a strong group of framers and ratifiers, led by James Madison, were in the House. The first Cabinet was in no sense a coalition; all the members but Jefferson ardently supported the Constitution and he gave it general approval. Although certain concessions, as in the case of the first ten amendments, were made to the opponents, the early laws of the new republic were framed to meet the wishes of the conservative economic interests which had been responsible for its framing and adoption. They were essentially Federalist in policy.

Of the numerous problems which confronted the new government, none were more important than the financial. In fact, the chief items of legislation during the twelve years of the Washington and Adams administrations had to do with financial matters. Since a major principle of the Federalist doctrine was a strong central government, one necessity was an ample income to establish and maintain such a structure. It was clear that the chief expenses would be the maintenance of an army and navy, the payment of principal and interest on the national debt, and the support of the so-called "civil list." Protection of the merchant marine, defense against the Indians, and preservation of the infant republic in the face of foreign aggression necessitated a military establishment. Debts must be paid if the credit of the new government was to be maintained. The general running expenses of the civil government must be met. As it turned out, about 50 per cent of the cost of government during the Federalist period went to the Army and Navy, about 30 per cent to the public debt, and the rest to the civil list and other expenses.

Washington offered the post of Secretary of the Treasury to Robert Morris, famous as the financier of the Revolution, but upon his refusal he appointed Alexander Hamilton. Under the latter's able leadership a fiscal policy was inaugurated which established the new government on a firm financial basis. Duties on exports were forbidden by the Constitution, and it was natural to turn to tariffs on imports as the proper and easiest source for revenue. The act of July 4, 1789, the first tariff act under the new government, was designed primarily for revenue, but it recognized the protective feature. There were eighty-one enumerated articles, upon over thirty of which specific duties were levied; the remainder called for ad valorem (appraised by value) rates varying from 7½ to 15 per cent. Upon most imported articles not enumerated a 5 per cent ad valorem duty was levied. Although the rates were exceedingly low, the average being not over 8½ per cent, some protection was given. The debates on the tariff brought out the conflicting interests of the various sections of the country. Duties were imposed to help the steel and paper mills of Pennsylvania, the brewers of New York and Philadelphia, the glass manufacturers of Maryland, the iron workers and rum distillers of New England. The by-products of the farmhouse were also aided by duties on nails, boots and shoes, and ready-made clothing. Luxuries, such as tea, coffee, sugar, and wines, were more heavily taxed. It was soon found, however, that the tariff of 1789 did not provide enough revenue, and increases were made in 1790, 1792, and 1794.

One of the last acts of the first session of Congress, which adjourned on September 29, 1789, was to request Hamilton to make a report on the state of the finances. In compliance with this he submitted four reports: the first on January 14, 1790, which dealt with the public debt; the second on December 13, 1790, which recommended an excise; the third on the same date, recommending a national bank. The fourth, on December 5, 1791, was his famous report on manufactures advocating production.

In his first report Hamilton showed that the total foreign debt to France, Spain, and Holland, with arrears of interest, amounted to $11,710,378; the domestic debt with arrears at 6 per cent amounting to approximately $40,414,086 and the existing state debts of about $25,000,000 totaled altogether $77,124,464. He proposed that the national government take over this debt of the states which had been incurred to aid the Revolution and that both state and national debt be refunded at par. This was necessary, he said, to place the credit of the government on a firm basis. There was but slight opposition to the principle of paying the foreign and federal domestic debt, but the proposal that the federal government assume the state debts aroused violent controversy. It was justly charged that the speculator was favored at the expense of the patriot, and certain states at the expense of others. Certain southern states, where the debts relative to the population were less than in the North, strongly opposed assumption of state debts, and many who had parted with their depreciated paper for a song bitterly resented the payment at par to speculators.

On speculation the honest but suspicious Republican Senator from Pennsylvania, William Maclay, comments in his diary in January, 1790: "This day the 'budget,' as it is called, was opened in the House of Representatives. An extraordinary rise of certificates has been remarked for some time past. This could not be accounted for, neither in Philadelphia nor elsewhere. But the report from the Treasury explained all. . . ." The following day he writes: "I call not a single house or go into any company but traces of speculation in certificates appear"; and a few days later: "Hawkins, of North Carolina, said as he came up he passed two expresses with very large sums of money on their way to North Carolina for purposes of speculation in certificates. Wadsworth has sent off two small vessels for the Southern States, on the errand of buying up certificates. I really fear the members of Congress are deeper in this business than any others."[1]

Hamilton finally prevailed against bitter opposition (1790). His arguments were both economic and political. Refunding and assumption would establish the credit of the federal government, consolidate behind it the commercial and financial interests, and provide sound securities which might answer the purposes of money in business operations. "If all the public creditors," he urged, "receive their dues from one source, distributed by an equal hand, having the same interests, they will unite in support of the fiscal arrangements of the government." Washington's approval helped, as did the personal interests of many congressional holders of state and federal paper. Jefferson also co-operated by promoting a political deal by which the advocates of the measure, in return for southern votes, permitted the national capital to be located on the Potomac. Two years later he wrote disgustedly to Washington that he had been "duped" into this "by the Secretary of the Treasury, and made a tool for forwarding his schemes, not then sufficiently understood by me. . . ." It seems doubtful if the shrewd Virginian was as innocent as he claimed. His home state received one-sixth of the total assumption expenditure, a windfall which wiped out not only her entire Revo-

---

[1] E. S. Maclay (ed.), *Journal of William Maclay* (1890), pp. 177–179. In its details the bill was extremely complicated and not financially advantageous to the federal government. An interesting feature of the Funding Act of 1790 was the provision for cleaning up the Continental currency. In 1780 Congress had recommended to the states that the notes be taken up at forty to one, and $119,400,000 were received and canceled. Under the Funding Act of 1790 some $6,000,000 were taken in at the United States Treasury at the rate of one hundred to one in payment for government bonds. The rest were lost, destroyed, or never redeemed.

lutionary debt but also most of her other debts. Whatever may have been the circumstances surrounding the passage of the bill, Hamilton's plan was sound in principle.

Hamilton's advice that an excise tax be levied was in like manner followed by Congress, but only after most strenuous opposition. It was his belief that an excise would both provide revenue for the national government and bring home to the most remote frontiersman who operated a still the power of that government. The tax accomplished its purpose, but it rested heavily and, it was felt, unjustly upon the frontiersmen, whose bulky products could be marketed only when reduced to the more concentrated form of whiskey. The opposition of the Pennsylvania frontiersmen to the tax in the "Whiskey Rebellion" of 1794 demonstrated both the hatred toward it and the strength of the new government in crushing disobedience. Other internal revenue taxes were also levied by the Federalists, but under Jefferson all of them, including the whiskey tax, were repealed.

Hamilton's third recommendation was the establishment of a national bank. This was to be modeled after the Bank of England, a great institution privately owned but publicly controlled. In one respect Hamilton deviated from the English model by suggesting that the federal government own one-fifth of the stock. He urged the bank on the ground that (1) it would provide a much-needed paper currency, (2) it would furnish a safe place for keeping public funds, (3) it would benefit both the government and business by providing banking facilities for the carrying on of commercial transactions, and (4) it could act as a fiscal agency for the government in such transactions as the sale of bonds. There was a real need for such a bank, for at the time of the adoption of the Constitution there were only three banks in the United States—the Bank of North America in Philadelphia, the Bank of New York, and the Bank of Massachusetts in Boston. Furthermore, under the new Constitution the states were not allowed to issue money. That the proposed bank would have tremendous influence over the nation's currency and credit and the power virtually to dictate federal fiscal policies was obvious. This, however, was no drawback to the Federalist capitalists who at the moment controlled the national government and presumably would soon own most of the bank.

To Jefferson and his followers, who advocated a strict construction of the Constitution,[2] the bank bill seemed highly dangerous. He saw in it the crea-

---

[2] By "strict construction" is meant a limiting of the powers accorded to the national government by the Constitution to the exact letter of that document; by "loose construction," the broad interpretation of certain clauses of the Constitution and "the general welfare" phrase in Article I, Section 8, to include an extension to implied powers not specifically prohibited. H. S. Commager (ed.), *Documents*, I, 156–160, has the arguments both of Hamilton and Jefferson.

tion of a financial monopoly in the hands of seaboard capitalists which might operate unfairly and to the detriment of state banks. He argued that the bill was unconstitutional, and when he failed to prevent its passage, he organized a political party which drove the Federalists out of office in the campaign of 1800. Despite strong opposition the bank was chartered in 1791 for twenty years with a capital of $10,000,000, of which amount the government might subscribe $2,000,000 and private investors $8,000,000, one-fourth in specie and three-fourths in government bonds. The notes of the bank were to be limited to the amount of the capital stock and were to be receivable in taxes as long as they were redeemable at the bank in specie. Reports were to be made to the Secretary of the Treasury, who was authorized to inspect the affairs of the bank at any time. In spite of this strict government regulation, the bank was in reality chartered as a private corporation and as such met bitter opposition.

The first Bank of the United States was nevertheless a salutary influence in the financial operations of the early republic, fulfilling amply the expectations of its advocates. Aided by the credit of the government, it was able to do business in a conservative fashion and acted as an efficient agent of the Treasury Department. During its twenty years it loaned the federal government $13,500,000 and when the government sold its stock it realized a profit of $700,000. But beyond all that it provided a safe paper currency. As a creditor of many state banks and by its policy of refusing the notes of non-specie-paying banks, it drove out fiat money and kept the paper at par.

The currency of the new bank was issued in terms of the dollar, the unit already adopted by the Congress of the Confederation. In 1792, after a report from Hamilton, Congress passed its first currency act, placing the valuation of the new American dollar at 24.75 grains of gold, the value of the Spanish milled dollar, and establishing the decimal system.[3] In the belief that a grain of gold was equal to 15 grains of silver, it was provided that a silver dollar should contain 24.75 times 15, or 371.25 grains of pure silver, the smaller coins to be of proportional weight. Free and unlimited coinage of both gold and silver was provided for in the act, and both were made full legal tender. Although a mint was established in Philadelphia which in 1794 began the coinage of silver and in 1795 that of gold, little metal was brought in to be coined, partly because the amount of precious metals mined in this country during those years was small, and partly because silver was slightly over-valued at the ratio of 15 to 1. Thus the coinage of gold was discouraged, for under the working of Gresham's Law cheap money drives out the better

[3] The basic ideas for the American currency system were actually presented first by Jefferson in a report to Congress under the Articles of Confederation. Hamilton advised little that was new except to decrease slightly the amount of silver in the dollar.

currency.[4] What gold was coined was speedily sent out of the country, and the nation was soon reduced to a silver standard. But the silver situation continued unsatisfactory because American silver dollars were exported to the West Indies, where they were accepted in exchange for Spanish milled dollars of slightly greater value. The latter were brought in, reduced to bullion, and presented to the mint for coinage. This was profitable to the importers of Spanish dollars but it provided no currency for the United States, and Jefferson ended the coinage of silver dollars in 1806. From then until 1836 no silver dollars were coined. In fact, the currency situation, as far as the precious metals were concerned, was quite inadequate during this early period. The unequal balance of trade with Britain which drained these metals out of the country was one of the causes. Until the coinage system was changed in 1834, paper money, coins of small denominations, and foreign coins comprised the currency.

The recommendations of Hamilton and the laws which followed were designed not only to end the financial chaos but to strengthen the federal government. Their implication was political as well as economic, and in the controversies over their adoption the group opposed to them speedily developed into the Republican party, destined before many years to assume under Jefferson the reins of government. As already suggested, these measures were especially heartening to the commercial and financial interests, but the settlers west of the Alleghenies also felt the benefits and strength of the new government. This was particularly true of the Treaty of 1795 with Spain, by which the "right of deposit" at New Orleans was obtained, a right which gave to the Westerners the privilege of landing their products and reshipping without the payment of duties.

It has long been the habit to attribute the success of the new federal government to the excellence of the Constitution and the soundness of the Hamiltonian economics, but this is only part of the story. The federal government was hardly organized before Europe was plunged into a war which brought new markets to American shippers, industrialists, and agrarians alike. The Constitution was launched on a wave of prosperity, and in the good times which followed the opposition to it rapidly disintegrated.

THE SECOND BANK OF THE UNITED STATES

Hamilton's idea of a banking system, modeled after that of Great Britain, in which a great bank under the joint control of private bankers and the government might regulate the currency and act as the fiscal agent of the

[4] When two or more currencies of unequal value are in concurrent circulation, each being available for money payments, the poorer tends to drive the better out of circulation. The ratio 15–1 was accurate in 1792, but new discoveries of Mexican silver reduced the value of silver.

government, was followed successfully in the first Bank of the United States. So useful was the bank that by the time its twenty-year charter expired (1811) many Republicans who had at first opposed it had been won to its support. Secretary of the Treasury Gallatin himself strongly advised its continuance. The House voted by a majority of one to renew the charter, but the Senate vote was a tie and Vice President George Clinton cast the deciding vote against it. The opposition of the West and of the state banks everywhere, along with the old Republican suspicion of the power and monopoly of the bank, ended its career.

With the restraining hand of a specie-paying national bank removed, numerous state banks sprang up, the number increasing from 88 to 246 in five years, and the money in circulation from $45,000,000 to $100,000,000. Their various notes circulated at a discount, sometimes as great as 50 per cent. The disorganized state of the currency was accentuated by the War of 1812, which the government financed with great difficulty. More than a year passed after war was declared before Congress summoned enough courage to increase the internal taxes, and the war was largely paid for by loans approximating $80,000,000 and Treasury notes to the amount of $36,680,794. The latter usually bore interest and were receivable in all payments to the United States, but had no legal tender qualities. Owing to the opposition of New England, these loans were floated chiefly in the Middle Atlantic States and with the exception of the first loan were sold at discounts running as high as 20 per cent.

The disastrous financial experience of the Treasury during the war and the chaotic condition of the currency led Secretary Alexander Dallas to urge the creation of a new United States bank. With the lessons of the war still fresh, the Republicans, who so long had denounced the earlier institution, now chartered the second Bank of the United States in 1816 for twenty years. It provided that one-fifth of the $35,000,000 capital should be subscribed by the government and that five of the 25 directors should be appointed by the President. The notes of the new bank were to be acceptable in payment of federal taxes. It was also expected that the notes, redeemable in specie on demand, would force the state banks to resume specie payment or drive their notes out of circulation.

Although badly mismanaged during its first three years, the bank was restored to soundness under the direction of Langdon Cheves (1819–1823) and during most of its subsequent history adequately fulfilled its function as a commercial bank, as a fiscal agent of the government, and as a producer and protector of sound paper currency. But it was always under attack in various parts of the country. When it expanded its operations by establishing branches, it encountered the jealousy of the local state banks; when it contracted its operations, it met the opposition of the same banks, who had borrowed money from it. Certain of the states attempted to tax branch banks out of existence, but Chief Justice Marshall in two famous decisions (McCulloch *v.* Maryland, 1819, and Osborn *v.* United States Bank, 1824) declared the acts unconstitutional, asserting that what the Constitution permitted the national government to set up no state might destroy.

Although the brilliant Nicholas Biddle, who succeeded Cheves in 1823, used the bank effectively in easing the strain in the economic crises of 1825 and 1828, he later used its great power unscrupulously to play politics. Nor could there be any question as to the reality of Biddle's power. "I never saw such a Board of directors," wrote Henry D. Gilpin, one of the federal directors. ". . . We know absolutely nothing. There is no consultation, no exchanges of sentiments, no production of correspondence. . . . We are perfect cyphers."

Andrew Jackson, true son of the West, feared the bank as a dangerous monopoly prejudicial to the common man. He was, in fact, a "hard money" man, suspicious of the power of any bank to issue paper money. In his first message Jackson questioned both the constitutionality and the expediency of the bank, but committees in both the House and the Senate reported favorably upon it. The supporters of Henry Clay (candidate of the National Republican party in 1832), scenting a political issue which they believed would carry them to victory in 1832, prevailed upon the bank to petition for the renewal of the charter four years before the existing charter expired, and Biddle, convinced that such a move would be successful, did so. Jackson vetoed the bill; the question of the bank was made an issue in the presidential election of 1832, and the victory of the Democrats spelled the doom of the bank.

In an effort to frighten the nation into support of the bank, Biddle in 1833 ordered a contraction of loans and produced a credit stringency known as "Biddle's Panic." Instead of accomplishing the desired result, he merely convinced the people, including many conservative business leaders, that Jackson was right and that the powers of the bank were dangerous to the nation. Jackson fought back by refusing to deposit government funds in the second Bank of the United States. He had to remove two Secretaries of the Treasury before he could find one who would follow this policy, but in the end he dealt staggering blows to the bank before its charter expired in 1836.

In the long controversy over this struggle, historians and economists have generally agreed on the usefulness of such a bank, if used wisely, as an agent of the government, as a protector of the currency, as an instrumentality to exercise over-all control over speculation and overexpansion, and as an aid in economic recessions. But the second Bank of the United States was in reality a private bank with tremendous economic privileges and irresponsible power run essentially for the profits of its stockholders. It was by no means a responsible central bank; rather it was a great commercial bank which made loans as did other banks and thus came in competition with state banks.[5]

BANKING AND CURRENCY, 1834–1862

The failure to recharter the second Bank of the United States was a victory for the West, and it ended the attempt to control the currency by means of a central bank. Depositing government funds in selected institutions ("pet banks," as Jackson's political opponents called them) was far from satisfactory, encouraging as it did overexpansion of bank notes and laying the government open to the charge of favoritism. Arguing that it was not the business of the government to assume the management of domestic or private exchange or to engage in any kind of banking business, Van Buren proposed that the government establish an independent treasury to care for its own funds. By means of subtreasuries the government would collect its revenues in specie and make all disbursements in specie through its own officials. By this plan it was intended not only to divorce the government entirely from the business of banking but also, by paying only specie, to promote the use of specie and thereby lessen the demand for bank notes. This independent treasury system was established after much opposition by the Democrats in 1840, discontinued by the Whigs in 1841, and then re-established by the Democrats in 1846 (continuing until merged with the Federal Reserve System in 1913 and finally ended in 1921). In the meantime, the Whigs endeavored unsuccessfully to re-establish a central bank, and their failure ended until 1863 the circulation of paper money sanctioned by the federal government.

The independent treasury system proved safe and efficient in handling the government funds, and also appeared to have had some success in restraining overexpansion of bank notes and in promoting the circulation of specie. Moreover, it prevented a financial crisis from tying up federal funds. One weakness was that it withdrew a portion of the nation's specie from circulation. As long as federal balances were small, no trouble might follow; but if the balances were large, the effect might be disastrous. The end of the second Bank of the United States and the establishment of the independent treasury system did not, as we shall see, solve the fundamental question of control of credit. Whether this should be a function of government, of private bankers, or of a combination of both still remains a subject of controversy.

In spite of his frontier background, Jackson was a hard-money man, and

[5] G. R. Taylor, *The Transportation Revolution*, pp. 305–311.

in the furtherance of this policy legislation was enacted in the hope of restoring an American metallic currency. The act of 1792, which established free and unlimited coinage of gold and silver at 15 to 1, overvalued silver, and under Gresham's Law gold disappeared. The silver dollar, it will be remembered, had been discontinued in 1806, leaving a miscellaneous collection of foreign coins as practically the only metallic currency. By an act of 1834 (slightly amended in 1837) the ratio was changed from 15 to 1 to 15.98+ to 1, or approximately 16 to 1. At the same time, the weight of the gold dollar was reduced from 24.75 grains of pure gold to 23.22, while the weight of the silver dollar remained the same, that is 371.25 grains of pure silver. Under this new ratio, gold was overvalued and came into circulation again, while silver failed to appear. The overvaluation of gold was even more evident after the discoveries in California in 1848 reduced the price of that metal. It was only by debasing the fractional silver in 1853 that subsidiary silver was kept in circulation.

In addition to the metallic currency coined by the federal government, there was an increasing number of bank notes of various denominations issued by the state banks. The number of such banks increased from 307 in 1820 to 1601 in 1860, their capital from $102,000,000 to $422,000,000, and their note circulation from about $16,600,000 to $207,000,000. As these banks were authorized by the states and in some cases their president and directors chosen by the legislature, the question of the constitutionality of their note issues was a pertinent one.[6] This question came before the courts in 1824 and was not definitely settled until 1837 when the Supreme Court made a distinction between bills issued on the credit of a state and those issued by an institution in which the state might be the sole stockholder;[7] the latter were held constitutional. In the earlier cases Marshall had attempted to restrict narrowly the note issues of state banks, but the states'-rights court under Roger B. Taney gave them wide leeway.

The issues of these banks obviously depended chiefly upon the safeguards provided by the states. In Massachusetts as early as 1809 a penalty of 2 per cent a month was placed upon banks which failed to redeem their notes on demand, and all banks incorporated after 1829 were restricted in their note circulation to one and one-fourth times the capital. The "Suffolk System," a method by which the city banks stood ready to redeem note issues and the country banks were required to establish redemption agencies in Boston, kept the New England bank notes at par. New York established a "safety fund" whereby each bank had to pay to the treasurer of the state an amount equal to one-half of one per cent of its capital stock until the payments

[6] Article 1, Section 10. "No State shall . . . coin money; emit bills of credit," etc.
[7] Briscoe *v.* The Commonwealth of Kentucky, 11 Peters 257.

should amount to 3 per cent, this fund to be used to redeem the notes of any bank which failed. These safety devices, however, were unusual. The legislatures were inexperienced and the pressure for easy money was great. The result was that the notes of hundreds of banks were in circulation, the value of which even an expert banker could hardly determine. Furthermore, counterfeiting was relatively easy. The difficulty of carrying on business under such handicaps can easily be imagined.

THE SPECIE CIRCULAR AND THE PANICS OF 1837 AND 1857[8]

With the downfall of the second Bank of the United States came a rapid expansion in the number, capital, and note circulation of the state banks. An orgy of speculation followed which was aided by the distribution among the states in 1837 of the government surplus to the amount of about $28,000,000.[9] It was likewise spurred on by the mania for internal improvements and the inordinate speculation in western land. The income from the sale of public lands jumped from $1,880,000 in 1830 to over $20,000,000 in 1836. Jackson, who was far from an expert on finance, clearly saw the essential unsoundness of the situation when he said in a message to Congress, "It was perceived that the receipts arising from the sales of the public lands were increasing to an unprecedented amount. In effect, however, these receipts amounted to nothing more than credits in bank. The banks lent out their notes to speculators. They were paid to the receivers [land agents] and immediately returned to the banks, to be lent out again and again, being mere instruments to transfer to speculators the most valuable public lands and pay the Government by a credit on the books of the banks. . . . The spirit of expansion and speculation was not confined to the deposit banks, but pervaded the whole multitude of banks throughout the Union and was giving rise to new institutions to aggravate the evil."[10] The bubble of speculation was enlarged by the utterly reckless manner in which the states borrowed here and abroad for internal improvements and the prodigality with which they loaned their credit to unsound institutions.

The panic of 1837 was presaged by the crop failure of 1835. This prevented the farmers from meeting their obligations to the land speculators and merchants, and the latter could not pay their loans at the banks. The crop failure eventually produced a balance of trade against the United States, a with-

[8] For a general discussion of panics, see chap. 29.

[9] The national debt was paid off in 1835, and during the next two years, for the only time in our history, the federal government was out of debt. The surplus which accumulated during this period was distributed to the states in the form of a loan, but it was understood at the time that it was to be an outright gift, and not a dollar has been recalled.

[10] Eighth Annual Message, December 5, 1836, in Richardson's *Messages and Papers of the Presidents* (1909 ed.), II, 1468.

drawal of foreign credits, and a need of specie to pay foreign creditors. In the midst of these accumulated difficulties Jackson hastened the crisis by issuing on July 11, 1836, his Specie Circular, an order which directed that future payments for public land had to be made in gold and silver. This served as a wet blanket to dampen the ardor of speculation in western land and shook the confidence in the circulating bank notes. The situation was further complicated by the failure of important mercantile houses in England toward the end of 1836, involving many English manufacturers and cutting down the demand for American cotton.

The panic which ensued was the worst that the nation had experienced up to that date. By the end of May, 1837, every bank in the country had suspended specie payment. The bank-note circulation contracted from $149,-000,000 in 1837 to $58,000,000 in 1843, and the sale of public land fell off from $20,000,000 in 1836 to $1,000,000 in 1841. In that year Congress passed a special bankruptcy law under which 39,000 persons canceled $441,000,000 worth of debt. The depression continued to be severe for five or six years, holding back the expansion of both manufactures and agriculture.

Eventually recovery set in, and with the revival of business the country again experienced a period of remarkable growth. Spurred on by rising prices, due chiefly to the discovery of gold in California in 1848, railroad building was pushed on rapidly, new manufacturing establishments were set up, and the westward movement was accelerated. A temporary halt was called by a third panic in our history, that of 1857. Overspeculation in the future of the country and overinvestment in railways upon which an adequate return was largely an expectation of the future, and in mineral resources, produced a setback, the causes of which closely resemble those of other American panics. As Schouler points out: "Premature railroads at the West had fostered premature cities, teeming with premature traffic for a premature population; and while canals and railroads had conspired to reduce the mileage rate of transportation, the dispersion of American farmers over a vastly wider area counterbalanced that advantage."[11] The failure of the Ohio Life Insurance and Trust Company in August, 1857, precipitated the panic, which was primarily financial and affected chiefly the financial centers and the speculative western railroad investments. Recovery was quick and the opening of the Civil War found the nation on the upgrade of a new cycle of prosperity.

TARIFF POLICY TO THE CIVIL WAR

Although the first American tariff was passed scarcely two months after the inauguration of Washington, the various tariff acts until 1816 had been

[11] James Schouler, *History of the United States of America Under the Constitution,* V, 384.

primarily for revenue and had afforded only incidental protection. It is true that Alexander Hamilton in his *Report on Manufactures* had given classic expression to the arguments for protection, but a strong movement for a protective tariff waited upon the War of 1812 and its effects. The collapse of prices in land and agricultural products following the deflation of 1815–1818, and the fear that the dumping of European goods set free by the close of the war might snuff out the infant manufacturing, aroused an active interest in protection. In the years of ardent nationalism following the War of 1812, statesmen and economists, to say nothing of manufacturers, rang all the changes on the argument for protection of "infant industries." Still influenced by the war, all sections of the country united in supporting the tariff of 1816. The bill was introduced by William Lowndes of South Carolina, and John C. Calhoun, later a most uncompromising opponent of protection, led the fight for its enactment. It placed duties ranging from 7½ to 30 per cent ad valorem, giving special protection to cottons, woolens, iron, and other manufactured commodities stimulated by the recent war.

From 1816 until 1833 the movement for protection grew steadily. It developed first of all from the writings of Daniel Raymond, who attacked the free-trade teachings of Adam Smith and others, then dominant in Europe, insisting that they did not apply to the American economic environment. Men like the publicist, Mathew Carey, and the editor, Hezekiah Niles, formulated and popularized the arguments,[12] and the popular political idol, Henry Clay, took the leadership in advocating it. To the "infant industries" argument Clay now added and emphasized the need for manufacturing to provide home markets for agricultural products and raw materials. In a famous speech in March, 1824, he pointed out the loss of European markets which the American farmer had suffered as a result of the close of the Napoleonic Wars, and asserted that only by developing industrial cities could the American farmer find a market for his surplus. In later speeches he tied up the movement for internal improvements with his plea for the tariff, showing that better transportation facilities were necessary for the exchange of products between the farmer and industrialist. Such an economic development, he believed, would free America from dependence on European markets, and to his program he gave the name "American System."

While Clay was urgently advocating his "American System," diverse interests began to make themselves felt and to line up definitely the sections of the country on one side or the other. The center of the early movement for protection was in the middle and western states of that period—New York,

[12] While the men just noted were advocating protection, others, particularly in the South, urged the continuation of a low tariff system. Among those who gave intellectual leadership to this group were Thomas Cooper of the University of South Carolina, Thomas R. Dew of William and Mary, and George Tucker of the University of Virginia.

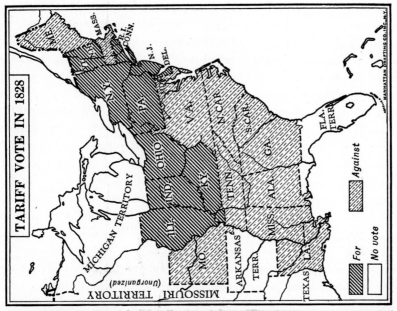

TARIFF VOTE IN 1828

MICHIGAN TERRITORY

MISSOURI TERRITORY
(Unorganized)

ME.
MASS.
R.I.
CONN.
N.Y.
N.J.
PA.
DEL.
OHIO
IND.
ILL.
MO.
ARKANSAS TERR.
KY.
TENN.
VA.
N.CAR.
S.CAR.
GA.
ALA.
MISS.
FLA. TERR.
TEXAS LA.

MANHATTAN DRAFTING CO.INC.-N.Y.

For ▨
Against ▨
No vote ☐

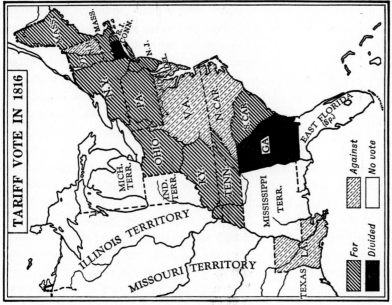

TARIFF VOTE IN 1816

ILLINOIS TERRITORY

MISSOURI TERRITORY

MICH. TERR.
AND. TERR.
ME.
MASS.
R.I.
CONN.
N.Y.
N.J.
PA.
DEL.
OHIO
KY.
TENN.
VA.
N.CAR.
S.CAR.
GA.
MISSISSIPPI TERR.
EAST FLORIDA (Sp.)
TEXAS LA.

For ▨
Against ▨
Divided ■
No vote ☐

New Jersey, Pennsylvania, Ohio, and Kentucky. They had felt keenly the disturbing effects of the war, and were eager to develop a home market to dispose of their agricultural products. The South, on the other hand, was desirous of obtaining her manufactured articles cheaply and, with her chief market in Europe, naturally opposed protection. Manufacturing was being successfully carried on in the South, but it was relatively small in amount, and the great majority of the influential classes were convinced that her future lay in agriculture. New England at first was divided. The manufacturing interests, not yet powerful, were in favor of protection, whereas the shipping group and the merchants feared that a tariff would injure their business. As a consequence, she split her votes on the tariff until about 1830, when the manufacturers won control and lined her up on the side of protection. This change may be seen in the attitude of Daniel Webster, who opposed the tariff of 1816 but supported that of 1828. On the other hand, Calhoun, who had ardently backed the tariff of 1816, now led the opposition to the protective system.

In 1818 further protection was given to iron, and the duty of 25 per cent on cotton and woolens was extended until 1826. An effort to raise duties in 1820 was lost in the Senate by one vote. A general revision was undertaken after the election of 1824, at which time all the candidates had advocated protection. Not only was additional protection given to manufacturers of woolen goods, lead, glass, and iron, but 25 per cent was now granted to hemp manufacturers, and wool growers were specifically aided. This tariff received the support of the iron interests of Pennsylvania, the wool growers of Ohio and the middle states, the hemp growers of Kentucky, and the manufacturers everywhere, but it incurred the disfavor of the northern shipper and the bitter hostility of the South, where much wool was used for Negro clothing.

The tariff of 1828 was the result of the agitation of the woolen interests for increased protection, aided and abetted by the Jacksonian politicians, who thought they saw a chance of promoting the interests of their candidate in the coming election. It was their intention to propose a bill so obnoxious that it could not pass, although the Jackson men of the North might vote for it and thus pose in the next election as the true friends of domestic industry. By increasing the duties on raw wool, sailcloth, and molasses it was expected that New England would line up with the South to oppose the measure. John Randolph sarcastically observed that "the bill referred to manufactures of no sort or kind, except the manufacture of a President of the United States."

To the surprise of all, this bill, which raised the general tariff rates to the highest level before the Civil War, was passed. But it was so unpopular that it was speedily dubbed the "Tariff of Abominations." It was on the statute books only four years, but during that time it aroused a storm of opposition, especially in the South. In 1832 a new bill removed many of the abominations and practically restored the tariff to the basis of 1824. Nevertheless, the bill was still essentially protective, and South Carolina in November, 1832, passed the famous Nullification Ordinance declaring the "tariff law of 1828 and the amendment of the same in 1832" to be null and void and not binding upon the people of South Carolina. President Jackson's uncompromising stand for national unity left South Carolina little hope of success, and in 1833 both sides agreed to a compromise tariff introduced by Henry Clay. The outcome was a victory for the nationalists under Jackson, but a lowering of the tariff in favor of the South. The act of 1833 provided for a decrease of all duties exceeding 20 per cent in the tariff of 1832; this reduction was to be very gradual until 1842, when a sudden lowering was to create a uniform ceiling rate of 20 per cent. This 20 per cent level, however, remained in force but a few weeks, from July until the passage of the more strongly protective tariff of 1842 in August.

The tendency of the tariff rates from 1832 to the Civil War was generally downward, although the principle of protection was never relinquished. The panic of 1837 so depleted the income of the national government that the protectionists were successful in restoring the duties in 1842 almost to a level with those of 1832. Passed by the Whigs, this act was speedily repudiated when the Democrats returned to power in 1845. The Walker tariff of 1846 classified imported commodities under schedules, A, B, C, D, etc. Luxuries were put into Class A and a tariff of 100 per cent was imposed; semiluxuries into Class B with a 40 per cent tax; commercial products into the remaining classes, with duties varying from 30 down to 5 per cent. The Walker tariff changed the system from specific to ad valorem duties and introduced the warehousing system of storing goods until the duty was paid, an innovation permanently retained. The duties, while maintaining protection, were radically lowered by this tariff, and the tendency toward reduction was continued in 1857, when the free list was enlarged and the rates of the Walker tariff were generally lowered. The reductions of 1857 were the result of a treasury full to overflowing from the immense expansion of business from 1846 to 1857. From the latter date until 1861 the United States more closely approached a free-trade basis than at any time since 1815.

It is extremely difficult, if not impossible, to determine the effects of the tariff system during the years preceding the Civil War. Undoubtedly the tariff legislation of the first seventy years of our history aided the growth of manufacturing and industry; it is equally true, however, that the emergence of the United States as an industrial nation was inevitable. The effect of the tariffs was chiefly artificial stimulation of a natural development. It is also true that the policy of protection was to a certain extent detrimental to the South, as southern leaders contended. But it should be remembered that the South won in the tariff battle of the 1830's and that from then on until the Civil War the trend of tariff rates was generally downward. The tariff was but one of a number of causes which brought the economic decline of the seaboard South. Nevertheless, Southerners channeled much of their economic discontent into opposition of the tariff, and its psychological influence was important in bringing secession. Of one aspect of the tariff system, at least, the student of economic history can be certain. It was receipts from the tariff that mainly supported the federal government during this period. Except for one year (1836) such receipts were higher—usually from five to ten times —than all other sources of income put together.

SELECTED READINGS

Taylor, G. R., *The Transportation Revolution,* chaps. 14–15, pp. 352–367.

Shultz, W. J., and Caine, M. R., *Financial Development of the United States,* chaps. 5–11.

Taussig, F. W., *Tariff History of the United States,* Part I.

McGrane, R. C., *The Panic of 1837,* chaps. 1–2.

Schlesinger, A. M., Jr., *The Age of Jackson,* chaps. 7–10.

Callender, G. S., *Selections from the Economic History of the United States, 1765– 1860,* chaps. 10, 11.

Bogart, E. L., and Thompson, C. M., *Readings in the Economic History of the United States,* chaps. 10, 15.

Flügel, F., and Faulkner, H. U., *Readings in the Economic and Social History of the United States,* chaps. 3 and 9.

CHAPTER 10

WESTWARD EXPANSION FROM THE REVOLUTION TO THE CIVIL WAR

THE WEST AT THE CLOSE OF THE REVOLUTION

Wʜᴇɴ the thirteen British colonies won their freedom in 1783, their territory included the area between British Canada on the north and Spanish Florida on the south as far west as the Mississippi. Of settlers from the British colonies only two or three hundred had broken through the mountain passes of the Alleghenies by 1776. At the conclusion of peace, however, some 25,000 were scattered along the head of the Cumberland, on the Kentucky River, on the Holston and French Broad, and in groups as far west as the Mississippi. Peace merely accentuated the movement of population, which during the next half-century swarmed into the region west of the mountains.

This westward movement of population continued despite the intrigues and opposition of the Spanish, French, British, and Indians. Spanish agents intrigued with the Indians of the Southwest to stem the advance of settlers from the East, and fostered the movement for independence among these settlers in order to erect buffer states between the thirteen original states and the Mississippi. This did not subside until Kentucky was admitted to the Union in 1792 and Tennessee in 1796, and until the Treaty of San Lorenzo. This treaty, negotiated by Pinckney in 1795, brought the evacuation of Spanish posts on the east bank of the Mississippi and the free use of that river with the right of deposit at New Orleans.

France had ceded her vast claims west of the Mississippi to Spain in 1763, but regained the area in 1800. Then, with his dreams of a new colonial empire collapsing, Napoleon suddenly sold Louisiana to the United States in 1803 for a paltry $15,000,000. But the fate of the Mississippi Valley was not fully determined until 1815, when the outcome of Waterloo laid to rest any further dreams of a French empire in America and the War of 1812 definitely eliminated Great Britain. Although Britain had agreed in the Treaty of 1783 to relinquish the forts along the Great Lakes, she continued to hold them in the interest of the fur trade, the annual value of which was estimated at £100,000.[1] She agreed again to evacuate them by the Jay Treaty of 1795, but her emissaries kept the Indians stirred up until the War of 1812 ended her active interference in the Middle West. The Second War of Independence was nominally fought over seamen's rights, but in reality it was a war of the West. Clay and the western "War Hawks" had pushed it in Congress, and the Westerners, hungry for a greater empire, unsuccessfully sought to annex Canada. With greater success the frontiersmen of the South had cleared the Creeks from southern and western Alabama and won the only notable land victory of the war at New Orleans. The war may have been a military stalemate but it ended British intrigues with the Indians in the Mississippi Valley and made the annexation of Florida inevitable. The results of the war were of interest chiefly to the West.

THE ORDINANCE OF 1787

For three centuries the settlement and development of land was the most important business of the American people. The story of their occupation deserves a full discussion even when the political as well as the economic aspects are involved. Among the first problems which confronted Congress on the cessation of hostilities in 1781 was the disposition of the western territory. Under the vague but inclusive wordings of the original charters Georgia, South Carolina, North Carolina, and Virginia claimed that their boundaries extended west to the Mississippi. The Northwest was in dispute between Virginia, Connecticut, Massachusetts, and New York; six states—Maryland, Pennsylvania, Delaware, New Jersey, New Hampshire, and Rhode Island—had no claims on western land. Fear that the greater expansion of the states with western claims might impair their own relative importance, and jealousy because the fortunate states could use the western lands to pay off war debts, motivated these six states to repeated demands that the trans-Allegheny region be turned over to the national government. The fight was led by Maryland, who had demanded as early as 1779 "that a country unsettled at the commencement of this war, . . . if wrested from the common enemy by the blood and treasure of the thirteen States, should be considered as common property, *subject to be parcelled out by Congress into free, convenient, and independent governments,* in such manner and at

---

[1] James M'Gill to Lt. Gov. Hamilton, Aug. 1, 1785. R. G. Thwaites (ed.), *Collections of the State Historical Society of Wisconsin*, XII, 72.

such times as the wisdom of the assembly shall hereafter direct."[2] Later she refused to ratify the Articles of Confederation until the states with claims promised to give them up. This they eventually did, though it was not until 1802 that Georgia, the last state, turned over her lands.

In 1784 Thomas Jefferson proposed a plan for dividing the Northwest Territory into a number of states with high-sounding classical names (Sylvania, Assenisipia, Metropotamia, Polypotamia, etc.), whose inhabitants were to enjoy most of the rights of the citizens of the older states and which were eventually to be admitted to the Union on equal terms as soon as their population warranted admittance. This plan was amplified in the more famous Ordinance of 1787, which provided (1) that not less than three nor more than five states were to be erected out of the territory, (2) that until the population numbered 5000 free male inhabitants the territory should be ruled by a governor and three judges appointed by Congress, who were to determine the local officers and make the laws, subject to veto by Congress; (3) that after the population reached 5000 the territories could have a two-house legislature, the lower appointed by the people and the upper a legislative council of five men selected by Congress from ten nominated by the lower house. The legislature could send a delegate to Congress with right to debate but not to vote. During this territorial stage the governor had power to veto; political rights were based on graduated ownership of land; a man owning 50 acres had the right to vote for a representative, but to be eligible for the lower house he must own 200 acres, for the upper house 500, and for the governorship, 1000 acres; (4) when any of the territories should have 60,000 inhabitants it might form a permanent constitution and state government and its delegates be admitted into Congress "on an equal footing with the original states in all respects whatever." This Ordinance laid down the principles of procedure which have since been generally followed in regard to new territory.[3]

Because the Northwest Ordinance of 1787 laid down the procedure upon which new states might organize, it has rightly received great emphasis from political historians. But it also had social and economic results of great importance. It established for the first time in history the principle that colonies

---

[2] Instructions of Maryland to her delegates, read in Congress May 21, 1779. Quoted by H. B. Adams, *Maryland's Influence upon Land Cessions to the United States* (1885), Johns Hopkins Studies, III, 26.

[3] "The so-called Ohio or Northwest Ordinance of July 13, 1787," said Eduard Fueter, the Swiss historian, "has been called one of the most important laws of the United States (from the point of world history it is perhaps the most important). . . . Thus the principle was abandoned that the welfare of the colonies ought to be subordinated to that of the mother country; rather was the principle established that colonies which are settled by a people are to be regarded as an extension of the mother country and are to be put on an equal footing in every respect." *World History,* trans. by S. B. Fay (1922), p. 105.

were to be considered as an extension of the mother country and were to be put on an equal footing in every respect. The old mercantilist idea that they existed simply for the benefit of the mother country was abandoned. The Ordinance abolished slavery; guaranteed life, liberty, property, and religious freedom; and encouraged education. It did much to encourage millions to move westward.

EARLY LAND POLICY OF THE REPUBLIC

Even before the famous Ordinance of 1787 had been passed, the Congress of the Confederation was giving attention to the problem of land disposal and laying the foundations of an American land policy. Despite a century and a half of experience, the problem was a difficult one. The Congress first of all had two objectives: it was eager to promote settlement but at the same time to derive an income from the sale of public land. As most settlers were poor men with little or no capital, the two desires were hardly compatible. If the land was to be sold, should it be disposed of in large tracts or small ones? Sale in large tracts would play into the hands of wealthy land speculators; sale in small lots would benefit bona fide settlers, who were generally poor. From the point of revenue, however, there were arguments against small sales. It might cost as much to survey the land as it was worth; buyers would purchase only the good land and leave the rest. The small-scale arrangement would tend to scatter the settlers rather than promote the compact settlements necessary for defense against the Indians. There was also the problem of settlement requirements. Should actual occupation of the land be required? Such a regulation would minimize speculation and favor the small buyer, but it might depress the value of the land. There were, of course, the important problems of price, of whether the land should be sold for cash or for credit (or both), and of where the land offices should be set up.

Since all this involved the method by which a large part of the American continent was to be transferred from the government to private ownership, it was obviously a matter of primary significance. To the westward-moving settler the land policy of the government was of fundamental importance. Forced by necessity to tackle the problem, the Congress under the Articles of Confederation made a beginning in the Land Ordinance of 1785. This provided (1) for a rectangular land survey by the government, (2) for the setting aside of one-thirty-sixth of the land for educational purposes, and (3) for the establishment of land offices for the sale of public lands at low prices. After a north and south line, known as the "prime meridian," had been established (the first one set up being the present boundary line between Ohio and Indiana), an east-west base line was laid down to intersect it at right angles. From the intersection of the prime meridian and the base line the surveyors ran out perpendicular lines at six-mile intervals. The crossing of these lines divided the land into squares containing thirty-six square miles. Each of these squares was to be a township and was subsequently to be subdivided into thirty-six squares each one mile square (640 acres), known as sections, Section 16 being reserved for the support of common schools. Most of the states admitted after 1842 also reserved Section 36

LAND DIVISION BY TOWNSHIP AND SECTION

SECTIONS OF A TOWNSHIP   SUBDIVISIONS OF A SECTION

6	5	4	3	2	1
7	8	9	10	11	12
18	17	16	15	14	13
19	20	21	22	23	24
30	29	28	27	26	25
31	32	33	34	35	36

HALF-SECTION 320 ACRES

QUARTER-SECTION 160 ACRES

HALF QUARTER-SECTION 80 ACRES

QUARTER QUARTER-SECTION 40 ACRES

QUARTER QUARTER-SECTION 40 ACRES

A TOWNSHIP IS 6 MILES SQUARE AND CONTAINS 36 SQUARE MILES

A SECTION IS 1 MILE SQUARE AND CONTAINS 640 ACRES

(From H. U. Faulkner, Tyler Kepner, and E. H. Merrill, *History of the American Way,* McGraw-Hill.)

for school purposes, thus setting aside for education one-eighteenth of the land surveyed. An attempt was made to reserve Section 15 from each township for religious purposes, but it was voted down. In the history of American land policy the Ordinance of 1785 proved as fundamental as the Ordinance of 1787 did in the political life of the new West. The method outlined in 1785 was generally followed during the next century.

It was in the methods of disposal rather than survey that policies changed. Uncertain whether to follow the New England system of grants by townships or the Virginia system of individual sales or grants, Congress in 1785 provided for both; half of the townships were to be sold entire and the other half in sections of 640 acres. The land was to be sold at auction, with a minimum price of $1.00 an acre. An act of 1796 raised the price to $2.00 an acre but introduced a credit system that allowed a year for payment. As few pioneers could command $1280, the demand arose immediately that the law be changed to favor the settlers. As the political power of the West increased, this demand was successful. In 1800 the minimum amount of land that could be purchased was reduced to 320 acres and in 1804 to 160 acres. The time for payment in the latter act was extended to five years. New legislation in 1820 again reduced the amount to eighty acres and cut the price to $1.25 an acre. Inordinate speculation culminating in the panic of 1819, however, influenced the Congress to abolish the credit system.

Perhaps the most important concession obtained by the West in the years before the Civil War was the right of pre-emption, secured in 1841. For years settlers had moved onto the public lands, cleared the forest, and laid out farms without the formality of a purchase, only to find that they were illegal intruders on government land; sometimes the land was sold over their heads or they were driven off by federal troops. Settlers demanded the right to take up the land that they wanted, whether it had been surveyed or not, and then purchase it at the minimum price free from competitive bids. In practice they had sometimes succeeded in doing this before the law of 1841 made it legal. Actual settlers would select their land and improve it and then organize squatters' protective associations. These protective associations would appear at the land auctions and make perfectly clear to any outsider that he had better not bid on their land—that is, if he valued his personal safety. The Pre-emption Act of 1841 was an important concession, but it was by no means the ultimate goal of the western frontiersmen. But the next step, free land to actual settlers, was not taken until the famous Homestead Act of 1862.

From this brief résumé of the more important land acts, it is evident that the land policy of the federal government became more liberal as time went on. It is also clear that under it the West was settled, mainly by relatively poor men. Nevertheless, the whole policy was by no means as just or as democratic as might appear. One historian insists that "the liberalization of the land laws, after 1820, must not be regarded as much more than a pious gesture."[4] The chief weakness was the fact that in actual practice the laws tended to favor the wealthy speculator rather than the poor settler. Three reasons (until the Homestead Act of 1862) were responsible: the government charged a price for the land beyond the capacity of the average settler, it set no limit on the amount that could be acquired, and it did not require actual settlement on, or improvement of, the land. Instead of promoting by such means a democratic society of small farmers, it threw the public domain into the hands of speculators. It is true that the government gave some land away —large grants to transportation companies, as in the case of the Illinois Central, and land bounties to veterans of Indian Wars and soldiers of the Mexi-

[4] Louis Hacker, *The Triumph of American Capitalism,* p. 209.

can War. But the railroads sold their land to settlers or speculators and the veterans seldom actually settled on their land, preferring to sell their bounties at a small price to speculators. As the average settler did not have the money to purchase from the government for cash, he was forced to borrow from eastern capitalists at absurdly high rates or to buy from land speculators who had already bought the better land from the government. Even when he pre-empted the land he could not buy it except by borrowing. In many cases the pioneer worked himself out of debt; in others he improved the land, sold it to a newcomer at an advanced price, and then moved westward to take up a new farm which he might own free of mortgage. There were many sections where the land policy drove pioneer farmers into a state of tenancy rather than encouraged a democratic pattern of ownership.[5]

THE SETTLEMENT OF THE OLD SOUTHWEST

The first great trans-Allegheny migration, as we have seen, was south of the Ohio into Kentucky and Tennessee. This went on steadily during the Revolution, the first census, of 1790, showing over 70,000 in Kentucky, and 35,000 in Tennessee. This migration had been undertaken chiefly by the yeomen farmers of the upcountry of the South who had originally found their way down the Great Valley from Pennsylvania, or by the small farmers who had been pushed out by the wealthier planters of the tidewater.

The Industrial Revolution, and especially the invention of the cotton gin in 1793, provided an apparently insatiable market for raw cotton and suddenly turned the eyes of the South to the development of a new staple. The tidewater lands of Virginia and the Carolinas seemed to be wearing out; this drove the southern planters to look westward for new and richer fields. The demand for cotton was the chief determining factor in the second stage of the settlement of the Southwest, and as the importance of cotton increased, the planter pushed on behind the small farmer, who had first pioneered across the mountains.

By the side of the picture of the advance of the pioneer farmer [says Turner] bearing his household goods in his canvas-covered wagon to his new home across the Ohio, must therefore be placed the picture of the southern planter crossing through forests of western Georgia, Alabama, and Mississippi, or passing over the free state of Illinois to the Missouri Valley, in his family carriage, with servants, packs of hunting dogs, and a train of slaves, their nightly camp fires lighting up the wilderness where so recently the Indian hunter held possession.[6]

---

[5] P. W. Gates, "Land Policy and Tenancy in the Prairie States," *Journal of Economic History,* I, 60–82 (May, 1941).

[6] F. J. Turner, *Rise of the New West,* p. 92.

Or as Timothy Flint describes it:

The southern settlers who immigrate to Missouri and the country southwest of the Mississippi, by their show of wagons, flocks and numbers create observation, and are counted quite as numerous, as they are. Ten wagons are often seen in company. It is a fair allowance, that a hundred cattle, beside swine, horses and sheep, and six negroes accompany each. The train, with the tinkling of an hundred bells, and the negroes, wearing the delighted expression of a holiday suspension from labor in their countenances, forming one group; and the family slowly moving forward, forming another, as the whole is seen advancing along the plains, presents a pleasing and picturesque spectacle.[7]

This was a new type of migration.

Just as the eighteenth-century frontier farmer could not withstand the advance of the southern planter, so now the pioneer of the Southwest was in turn displaced. Unable to refuse the high prices which the planter offered him for his land, and outbidden in the competitive land sales, the small farmer had the option of adopting the slave plantation economy, of retreating to the less desirable soil of the mountains, or of again striking north or west for new lands. Hindered by poverty from adopting slavery, these pioneers left the rich black soil of the Southwest to the planters, retreating to the mountains to become the "poor whites" of the South, or pushing north of the Ohio or across the Mississippi to become again the founders of new states.

With the decline of the yeoman farmer the Southwest fell under the control of the cotton aristocracy and cotton became in truth king. The invention of the cotton gin had increased production in South Carolina from 1,500,000 pounds in 1791 to 20,000,000 in 1801, and in Georgia from 500,000 pounds to 10,000,000. A similar increase was now to be seen in the new states. Tennessee, which raised 1,000,000 pounds in 1801, produced 45,000,000 in 1834. Louisiana, which raised practically none in 1801, produced 62,000,000 pounds in 1834; the output of Mississippi and Alabama was even more. The ranking states in the production of cotton in 1820 were South Carolina and Georgia, but before 1834 Alabama and Mississippi pushed to the front. Cotton was clearly the staple of this region, and its importance is seen by the fact that after 1830 it furnished about one-half to the total value of the exports of the United States. It had the effect of confirming slavery as an apparently permanent institution. With the lessening of the Indian danger, settlement went on rapidly. Louisiana became a state in 1812, Mississippi in 1817, Alabama in 1819, and Missouri in 1821.

As the Old Southwest began to fill up it was inevitable that American

---

[7] Timothy Flint, *The History and Geography of the Mississippi Valley*, I, 191.

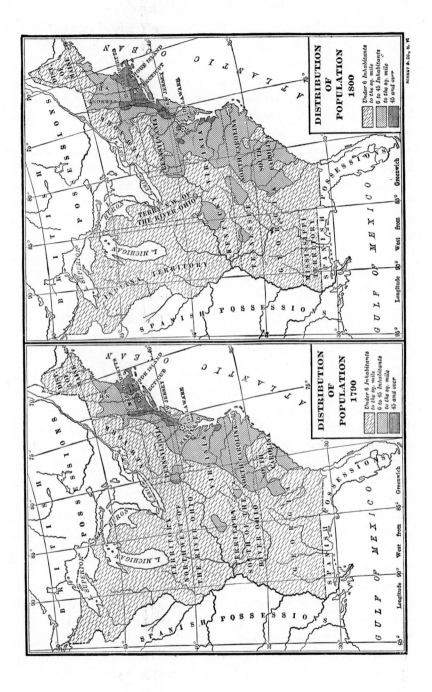

expansion would clash with Spain. The Pinckney Treaty of 1795 had opened the navigation of the Mississippi to American ships and obtained the right of deposit at the mouth and recognition of our ownership of the disputed land between the Yazoo and the 31st parallel. When Louisiana was purchased from France the territory governed by Spain extended west to the Mississippi north of the parish of Iberville. Nevertheless, at various times attempts were made to incorporate West Florida with United States territory. By 1810 the advance to the Southwest had brought enough Americans into the region practically to control it. In that year they demanded from Spain a remodeling of the government, but shortly after declared their independence and applied for annexation to the United States. Orders were immediately issued by President Madison to take military possession of West Florida as far as the Pearl. In 1819 Spain saw that it was useless to attempt to ward off further American aggression and agreed to give up East Florida. The United States assumed claims against Spain amounting to $5,000,000 and gave up all claims to Texas.

THE SETTLEMENT OF THE OLD NORTHWEST

The Land Ordinance of 1785 and the more famous Ordinance of 1787 prepared the way for opening to settlement the Old Northwest, the region north of the Ohio and east of the Mississippi. When this land was turned over to Congress, Connecticut, in order to foster religion and education and to reimburse those of her inhabitants whose homes had been burned by British raids during the Revolution, reserved a stretch of land 120 miles wide between the 41st parallel and Lake Erie which was known as "The Connecticut Western Reserve." In like manner, to redeem her military bounty certificates Virginia reserved 6000 square miles, known as the Virginia Military District, between the Scioto and the Little Miami, and Congress for the same reason reserved a block of land between the Scioto River and the Seven Ranges. The rest of the territory, with the exception of the lands sold to the Ohio and Scioto companies and to Judge Symmes, was surveyed and sold by Congress to settlers under the existing laws.

Hardly had the Ordinance of 1787 been passed before the Ohio Company, composed chiefly of Massachusetts speculators under the leadership of the Reverend Manasseh Cutler, had purchased 2,000,000 acres of land north of the Ohio with depreciated soldiers' certificates, and in December of that year the Company's first settlers left Ipswich, Massachusetts, for the Muskingum River.[8] In the spring of 1788 they founded Marietta, where the Muskingum

[8] The history of the methods and negotiations by which the Ohio Company secured their land is an amazing story, which throws a flood of light upon the political morality of the period. See R. A. Billington, *Westward Expansion*, pp. 212–220.

joins the Ohio. The Marietta settlers were followed in the same summer by a group from New Jersey under the leadership of Judge John Cleves Symmes, who settled Columbia and Cincinnati on part of the million acres between the Great Miami and the Little Miami which he and others had purchased. Some small French settlements at Detroit and in Illinois and Indiana already existed, but the pioneers of the Ohio Company and of the Symmes Purchase marked the first large entrance of Americans into the Northwest. The year 1790 saw the coming of Virginians into the Virginia Military District and the attempted settlement of groups of French, lured to America by the rosy promises of that most dubious of land speculative organizations, the Scioto Company, which was composed, according to Cutler, of "many of the principal characters of America." Connecticut, finding it difficult to induce individual buyers to take up land in the Western Reserve because of danger from Indians and the difficulty of access, finally sold most of the Reserve to the Connecticut Land Company, whose agent, General Moses Cleaveland, led a small party in 1796 to the site of the city now named for him.

These settlers opened the way for the multitudes which began to pour into the Northwest in the thirty years following 1790. In the meantime western New York was being rapidly taken up. Mountains, tangled underbrush, and hostile Indians had dammed up the white man in the valleys of the Hudson and the lower Mohawk. It was not until after the Revolution that pioneers from Pennsylvania and New Jersey followed the Susquehanna and Tioga north to Seneca Lake and into the heart of the state, while from the east New Englanders, pushing across from Massachusetts and Vermont, laboriously ascended the Mohawk or struck directly west by land. A few log huts were to be found in this area, but the census of 1790 showed scarcely more than 1000 people in western New York. West of Seneca Lake the land had been sold by Robert Morris to the Holland Land Company; east of it the state had reserved 1,700,000 acres for military bounties. But the plots were soon broken up as the immigrants, chiefly from New England, took up the rich lands on the Tioga, Chenango, Genesee, and Mohawk, streams upon which were shortly to arise cities whose names harked back to classic Greece and Rome.

A combination of causes contributed to the amazingly rapid settlement of the Old Northwest. Immigration of home seekers from Europe, which had amounted to some four or five thousand a year, increased rapidly after the War of 1812, the number entering from 1815 to 1830 amounting to half a million. In the North the economic depression during the period of the Embargo and Nonintercourse acts, the War of 1812 and immediately after, greatly stimulated the exodus to the West. In the South the planters deserted the worn-out tobacco lands of Virginia and North Carolina for the fresh alluvial soil of the Southwest, driving ahead of them the small pioneer farmer, who often moved on north into the Ohio Valley. Not only was immigration stimulated by economic causes, but the discontent, especially in New England, against the old religious and political oligarchy was potent in the movement. The gradually increasing liberality of the government in its western policy encouraged the taking up of new lands, and the extinction of the Indian titles between 1812 and 1830 opened up much new territory. The victories of William Henry Harrison in the Northwest and Andrew Jackson in the Southwest over the Indians marked the beginning of the rapid elimination of the red man from these regions.

After 1811, when the *New Orleans* was launched on the Ohio at Pittsburgh, the growth of the Northwest was aided by steam navigation. Before the advent of railroads the rivers formed the great avenues of travel and traffic, and upon them the immigrant or his products floated downstream in flatboats. By 1820 sixty steamboats plied on the western waters, and the succeeding years marked the golden age of the river boat. It took the old flatboat months to make the journey downstream from Louisville to New Orleans, but the steamboat could cover the same distance in a few days. Besides these various economic influences speeding the westward movement there was, of course, the constant advertising which the West received during these years from the Louisiana Purchase, the Lewis and Clark exploration and the publication of their journal, the expeditions of Aaron Burr, Pike's book on New Mexico, and the Indian victories of Harrison and Jackson—all of these kept the West vividly before the eyes of prospective settlers.

The influx into the Northwest was rapid from the start. The year that Marietta was founded (1788) saw 10,000 float down the river past this point; by 1803 the population of Ohio was sufficient for its admission as a state. While the prosperity of the East during the early Napoleonic Wars held back somewhat the exodus to the West, the movement was again stimulated by the embargo and the commercial difficulties preceding the war with Great Britain. An observer in Robbstown, Westmoreland County, Pennsylvania, a village on the highway to Pittsburgh, claimed that in one month toward the end of 1811, 236 wagons, with men, women, and children, and 600 merino sheep passed through to the West. Said McMaster,

Old settlers in central New York declared they had never seen so many teams and sleighs loaded with women, children, and household goods traveling westward, bound for Ohio, which was then but another name for the West. One account describes the roads passing through Auburn as thronged all winter long "with flitting families from the Eastern states." Another from Newburg, in New York, declares that during one day in July six wagons with seventy persons, all from Massachusetts, entered and left the village for Ohio, and that scarcely a week

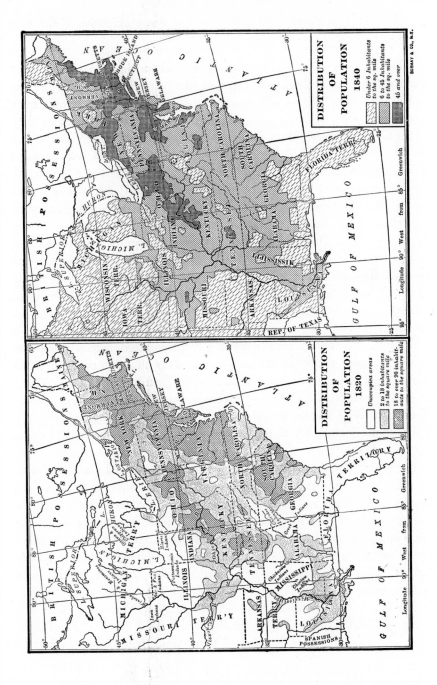

DISTRIBUTION
OF
POPULATION
1840

Under 6 Inhabitants
to the sq. mile
6 to 45 Inhabitants
to the sq. mile
45 and over

DISTRIBUTION
OF
POPULATION
1820

Unoccupied areas
2 to 18 inhabitants
to the square mile
18 to over 90 inhabit-
ants to the square mile

BO(R)MAY & CO., N.Y.

passed without its citizens "witnessing more or less immigration of the same kind."[9]

"Old America seems to be breaking up and moving westward," wrote Morris Birkbeck, an English observer, in 1817, while journeying on the National Turnpike. "We are seldom out of sight, as we travel this grand track toward the Ohio, of family groups behind and before us."[10] The population of the Old Northwest (Ohio, Indiana, Illinois, Michigan, Wisconsin), which at the opening of the Revolution was composed of but a few thousand French, by 1810 numbered 272,324, and by 1860 amounted to 6,926,884. Indiana was admitted into the Union in 1816, Illinois in 1818, and Michigan in 1837. By 1830 Ohio had over one million people, more than Massachusetts and Connecticut combined. Indiana in the decade 1810 to 1820 grew from 24,000 to 147,000. That this increase in population seriously drained the East is seen by the fact that Virginia and Massachusetts during the decade 1820 to 1830 remained almost stationary while the western states grew at a rate of 100 to 150 per cent. Chicago, a mere fur-trading station in 1830, increased to over 100,000 by 1860; Cleveland, with only 6070 in 1840, numbered 43,-000 in 1860. The chief cities of the West about 1830 were Cincinnati, or "Porkopolis," a meat-packing center in a rich farming district, with a population of 25,000; Pittsburgh, already an iron city with 12,000 people near the head of navigation of the most popular route (before 1825) to the West;[11] St. Louis with 6000, the point of exchange between the fur traders of the North and West and the steamboat trade of the Mississippi; and New Orleans, at the mouth, where the inland products were transferred to ocean boats.

The principal route over which influx traveled was the old road that Forbes had cut during the French and Indian War from Philadelphia to Pittsburgh by way of Lancaster and Carlisle.[12] Upon reaching Pittsburgh the immigrant transferred his effects to a flatboat and continued the journey down the Ohio and upon one of its tributaries to his chosen spot. Another important route was from Albany up the Mohawk to the Genesee turnpike, then to Lake Erie and Ohio. After the Erie Canal was completed in 1825 this route became more popular and contributed not only to the settlement of the Ohio Valley but to that of western New York. Another New York route was along the Catskill turnpike to the headwaters of the Allegheny. From Baltimore the traveler followed a turnpike to Cumberland, where began the

[9] J. B. McMaster, *History of the People of the United States*, IV, 383.
[10] Morris Birkbeck, *Notes on a Journey in America*, p. 31.
[11] The real head of navigation was Old Fort Redstone above Pittsburgh, from which point many embarked.
[12] The present Lincoln Highway.

National Road across the mountains to Wheeling on the Ohio, with branches leading to Pittsburgh. The wagon road from Virginia into central Kentucky was the chief southern route; from Kentucky and Tennessee many routes led to the Ohio in the region of Cincinnati or Louisville.

Although New Englanders founded Marietta and Cleveland, the majority of the population came from elsewhere. New England up to 1820 was still settling her own northern frontier and that of western New York. In Ohio the most numerous groups came from the central states of Pennsylvania and New Jersey, with Cincinnati as their commercial center. Next in importance were immigrants from Virginia, who outnumbered the New Englanders of the Western Reserve. Indiana and Illinois received in their northern counties some accessions from New England but were mainly settled by the yeomen farmers of the upcountry of Virginia and North Carolina and by the restless pioneers of Kentucky and Tennessee who had been pushed out by the wealthier planters. From this stock came Abraham Lincoln. Many of these immigrants from the South were Scotch-Irish, the "Hoosier" element of Indiana coming chiefly from North Carolina. The native stock which settled the Mississippi Valley was preponderantly from the South.

Nevertheless, the Northwest did not take on the tone of southern civilization. The poor whites of the South, with their Presbyterian and Quaker background, mingling with the pioneers from New England and the central states, developed communities of small farms rather than plantations, where slavery was forbidden and democracy was strong. The chief strain of direct immigration from Europe into the Old Northwest was German. Over half a million came between 1830 and 1850, and in the next decade another million took up lands in central Ohio around Cincinnati, in the Wisconsin counties along Lake Michigan, as well as in Indiana, Illinois, Michigan, and other states in the Mississippi Valley.

FRONTIER LIFE

The first task of the immigrant, whether he came by foot, horseback, crude wagon, or by river boat, was to decide upon a place to live. If he was a squatter his chief interest was to find some land distant from settlement where water was abundant and where a stream would furnish him a chance to reach a market for his produce and to purchase salt and the few necessities he might need during the year. If he intended to comply with the law, either he had purchased before going west or else, providing he had been lucky enough to avoid the land speculators who swarmed the western towns, he filed a claim at the land office upon paying the price of the land. Arriving at the site he had chosen, usually with wood and water as prime elements in his choice, he built a rude log cabin, often with the help of neighbors. His next task was to clear away the underbrush and girdle the trees on enough land to plant the first year's corn. The fertility of the fresh soil would ordinarily yield fifty to sixty bushels per acre the first year, and further clearing normally produced seventy to a hundred the second year. The cattle, hogs, and horses could easily pick up enough food during most of the year, and with little attention his garden produced sufficient for the table. A rude plenty was thus provided, and by the third or fourth year the settler was in a position further to improve his house and to sell surplus products. If the site was good other settlers would soon appear, and in their wake might come a tanner or the builder of a sawmill, then possibly a professional innkeeper. The nucleus of a town having been formed, work was to be had for a blacksmith, carpenter, wheelwright, or saddler, and eventually one or more stores would grow up.

This process of town development was noted in 1818 by Morris Birkbeck:

On any spot where a few settlers cluster together, attracted by ancient neighbourhood, or the goodness of the soil, or vicinity to a mill, or by whatever cause, some enterprising proprietor finds in his section what he deems a good scite for a town: he has it surveyed and laid out in lots, which he sells, or offers for sale by auction.

The new town then assumes the name of its founder:—a store-keeper builds a little framed store, and sends for a few cases of goods; and then a tavern starts up, which becomes the residence of a doctor and a lawyer, and the boarding-house of a store-keeper, as well as the resort of the weary traveller: soon follow a blacksmith and other handicraftsmen in useful succession: a schoolmaster who is also the minister of religion, becomes an important accession to this rising community. Thus the town proceeds, if it proceeds at all, with accumulating force, until it becomes the metropolis of the neighbourhood. Hundreds of these speculations may have failed, but hundreds prosper; and thus trade begins and thrives, as population grows around these lucky spots; imports and exports maintaining their just proportion. One year ago the neighbourhood of this very town of Princeton [Illinois] was clad in "buckskin," now the men appear at church in good blue cloth, and the women in fine calicoes and straw bonnets.

The town being fairly established, a cluster of inhabitants, small as it may be, acts as a stimulus on the cultivation of the neighbourhood: redundancy of supply is the consequence, and this demands a vent. Water mills, or in defect of water power, steam mills rise on the nearest navigable stream, and thus an effectual and constant market is secured for the increasing surplus of produce. Such are the elements of that accumulating mass of commerce, in exports, and consequent imports, which will render the Mississippi the greatest thoroughfare in the world.[13]

Later, as the resources of the community grew, there would come the demand for canals and better roads. The distance of the dwellings from one

[13] Morris Birkbeck, *op. cit.*, pp. 103–105.

another made social intercourse highly valued, and husking bees, quilting parties, house "raisings," and even revival services contributed a boisterous but stimulating change from the day's drudgery.

Not all the settlers by any means remained upon the claims which they first selected. The large amount of unoccupied land and the ease with which it could be acquired developed a restless, moving people. Markets were usually at a distance and, prior to canals and railways, almost impossible to reach. In consequence, money was a scarce commodity of which the backwoodsman saw little in the course of his life. The quickest method of acquiring specie was to sell the partly cleared farm to a newcomer and "clear again for the tall timber." Some men repeated this process a half-dozen times in the course of their lives—almost professional pioneers, who broke the way for more permanent home builders. As the population grew the latter were in turn followed by the capitalist.

The frontier stages have been well described in a much-quoted passage from J. M. Peck's *A New Guide for Emigrants to the West,* published in Boston in 1837.

Generally, in all the western settlements, three classes, like the waves of the ocean, have rolled one after the other. First comes the pioneer, who depends for the subsistence of his family chiefly upon the natural growth of vegetation, called the "range," and the proceeds of hunting. His implements of agriculture are rude, chiefly of his own make, and his efforts directed mainly to a crop of corn, and a "truck patch." The last is a rude garden for growing cabbage, beans, corn for roasting ears, cucumbers and potatoes; a log cabin, and, occasionally, a stable and corn-crib, and a field of a dozen acres, the timber girdled or "deadened" and fenced, are enough for his occupancy. It is quite immaterial whether he ever becomes the owner of the soil. He is the occupant for the time being, pays no rent, and feels as independent as the "lord of the manor." With a horse, cow, and one or two breeders of swine, he strikes into the woods with his family, and becomes the founder of a new county, or perhaps State. He builds his cabin, gathers around him a few other families of similar taste and habits, and occupies till the range is somewhat subdued, and hunting a little precarious; or, which is more frequently the case, till neighbors crowd around, roads, bridges, and fields annoy him, and he lacks elbow room. The preemption law enables him to dispose of his cabin and corn-field to the next class of emigrants, and, to employ his own figures, he "breaks for the high timber," "clears out for the New Purchase," or migrates to Arkansas or Texas, to work the same process over.

The next class of emigrants purchase the lands, add field to field, clear out the roads, throw rough bridges over the streams, put up hewn log houses, with glass windows, and brick or stone chimneys, occasionally plant orchards, build mills, school houses, court houses, &c., and exhibit the picture and forms of plain, frugal, civilized life.

Another wave rolls on. The men of capital and enterprise come. The "settler" is ready to sell out and take the advantage of the rise of property—push farther into the interior, and become, himself, a man of capital and enterprise in turn. The small village rises to a spacious town or city; substantial edifices of brick, extensive fields, orchards, gardens, colleges and churches are seen. Broadcloths, silks, leghorns, crapes, and all the refinements, luxuries, elegancies, frivolities and fashions, are in vogue. Thus wave after wave is rolling westward:—the real *el dorado* is still farther on.

A portion of the two first classes remain stationary amidst the general movement, improve their habits and condition, and rise in the scale of society.[14]

While this picture by Peck was fairly accurate for those regions which were destined to a bright future, it was, of course, not universal. Many regions barely passed beyond the pioneering stage. In the Old Southwest particularly, there was in many sections a sharp differentiation from the steady advance described by Peck. The first or pioneering stage was the same; but in the second phase, instead of improved houses, better farms, and the accumulated evidences of thrift and plenty, there entered in the South the cotton planter who bought up the clearings of the pioneer, consolidated the farms, and replaced the small white farmer with Negro slaves. The second phase thus often saw the country with a smaller population, certainly a smaller population of whites, than the first. After the steady cropping of the land without renewal and with inefficient labor came the third phase—that of general decline and gradual exodus. Said a prominent citizen of Alabama in 1855:

In 1825 Madison county cast about 3000 votes; now she cannot cast exceeding 2300. In traversing that country one will discover numerous farm houses, once the abode of industrious and intelligent freemen, now occupied by slaves, or tenantless, deserted, and dilapidated; he will observe fields, once fertile, now unfenced, abandoned, and covered with those evil harbingers—fox-tail and broomsedge; he will see the moss growing on the mouldering walls of once thrifty villages; and will find "one only master grasps the whole domain" that once furnished happy homes for a dozen white families. Indeed, a country in its infancy, where, fifty years ago, scarce a forest tree had been felled by the axe of the pioneer, is already exhibiting the signs of senility and decay, apparent in Virginia and the Carolinas; the freshness of its agricultural glory is gone; the vigor of its youth is extinct, and the spirit of desolation seems brooding over it.[15]

TRANS-MISSISSIPPI ADVANCE BEFORE 1860

By 1800 white settlers from the East had crossed the Mississippi, lured by the land laws of the Spaniards and the rich fur trade. By that time St. Louis

[14] Pp. 119–121.
[15] F. L. Olmstead, *A Journey in the Seaboard Slave States* (1856), p. 577.

had become a market for furs and lead which were floated down the Missouri and the Mississippi. However, the first real knowledge of the size and resources of the Louisiana Purchase came from the famous expedition of

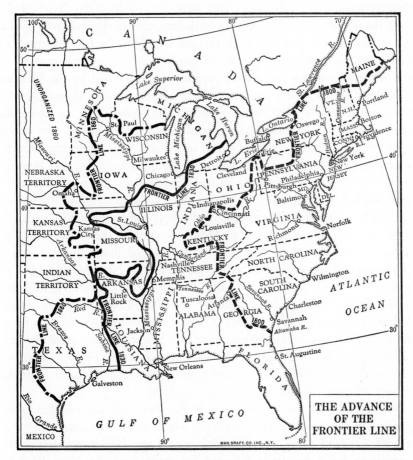

THE ADVANCE
OF THE
FRONTIER LINE

MAN. DRAFT. CO. INC., N.Y.

Technically, according to the census reports, the frontier is a region of more than two and less than six people per square mile. Because of the careful studies made by the census enumerators it is possible to reproduce with relative accuracy the frontier line for each decade up to 1890. The above map showing the frontier lines over thirty-year periods give a picture of population advance to the Civil War. It should be remembered, of course, that by 1860 the discovery of gold in California and of silver in Nevada, and the penetration of settlers into Utah, Oregon, and elsewhere in the Far West had developed a frontier line far beyond that shown here.

Meriwether Lewis and William Clark (1804–1806) who reached the Pacific by way of the Columbia River. Further information was added by the explorations of Captain Zebulon Pike, who, in 1805 and thereafter, explored the Mississippi practically to its source and the Arkansas and Red rivers, and penetrated into the Rockies to the mountain which bears his name.

As the fertility and resources of the new purchase became better known, pioneers crossed the Mississippi and ascended the Missouri. Toward the south the cotton planters, hungry for fresh land, crossed the river into Louisiana. Ahead of them were the cattle rangers, who from the first settlement of Jamestown had extended west of the line of permanent settlements. The first Americans under Stephen F. Austin were welcomed by the Mexican authorities, but as American cattle rangers began to collide vigorously with the Spanish frontier cattlemen extending northward, and as numerous causes for friction—racial, political, and economic—developed, it was only a question of time before rebellion would take place. Not to be denied, American rangers and cattlemen rose against the Mexican Republic, won their independence in 1836 (recognized by the United States and many European countries, but not by Mexico), and petitioned for annexation to the United States. This was eventually consummated (1845) and led almost immediately to the Mexican War of 1846–1848. Mexico recognized the independence of Texas to the Rio Grande and ceded to the United States the vast region which includes the present states of California and New Mexico, most of Arizona, Nevada, and Utah, and parts of Colorado and Wyoming. Eighteen million dollars was paid for it, and five years later $10,000,000 more for the Gadsden Purchase in order to push the boundary line south of the Gila River and in this manner insure the possibility of a southern transcontinental railway in United States territory. This was the conclusion of the long-cherished designs on Texas, New Mexico, and California, which extended from the fantastic intrigues of Burr to the actual conquest.

Oregon makes an interesting study in the westward advance, for its acquisition involved almost every influence which might stimulate settlement. In 1788 Captains Gray and Kendrick visited the Northwest, laying the foundations for a fur trade followed for many years by New England merchants. On a second voyage in 1792 Captain Gray discovered the Columbia River, and claim to the Columbia Valley was further strengthened in the years 1804–1806 by the famous expedition of Lewis and Clark. In the meantime, the two English fur companies, the Hudson's Bay Company and the Northwest Company, had commenced to penetrate the region, but their domination was soon disputed by John Jacob Astor and his American Fur Company, which founded Astoria in 1811 as a basis of operations. During the War of 1812, Astor's interests were sold to the Northwest Company, and the latter was soon absorbed by the Hudson's Bay Company, which under the able leadership of Dr. John McLoughlin controlled Oregon for the next quarter-century.

Gradually a new wave of interest developed in Oregon, this time among prospective settlers rather than fur traders. The great propagandist for the settlement of Oregon was Hall J. Kelley, a New England schoolmaster who published his *Geographical Sketches of Oregon* (1829),[16] organized a society

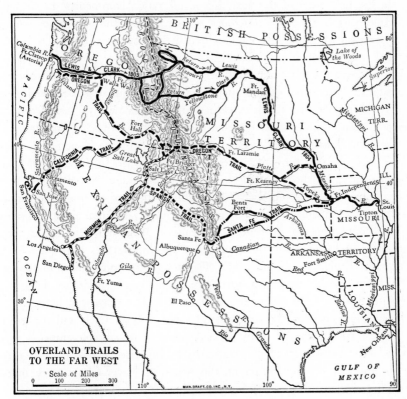

OVERLAND TRAILS
TO THE FAR WEST
Scale of Miles
0   100   200   300

The map above shows both the famous route taken by the Lewis and Clark expedition of 1804–1806 and the more common overland trails which developed to Oregon and California as settlers sought the fertile land of the Pacific coast and prospectors the gold and silver deposits of the mountains. A glance at the transportation maps on pages 482 and 495 will make clear that the same routes or variations of them were later followed by the great transcontinental railways.

to promote emigration to that region, and journeyed there himself in the early thirties. Businessmen of the type of Nathaniel J. Wyeth of Cambridge, Massachusetts, were again dreaming of commercial exploitation, and the Methodist Church in 1833 arranged to send missionaries to the Indians of

[16] A second edition (1831) of this pamphlet is reprinted in *Magazine of History with Notes and Queries,* Extra No. 67, Vol. XVII, and Kelley's *General Circular to all Persons of Good Character who wish to emigrate to the Oregon Territory* is reprinted as Extra 63, in Vol. XVI.

the Northwest. The Far West was also receiving a certain amount of literary exploitation from Washington Irving and others, and letters from the missionaries began to spread the news of the fertile lands of the great Northwest. Only a handful of American settlers had trickled into Oregon in the thirties, but in the first years of the next decade migration commenced in earnest. In 1846 an agreement was concluded with England, the only other nation now seriously claiming the land, whereby the boundary line of the 49th parallel was continued to the Pacific.

Profits from the fur trade and the lure of fertile lands were mainly responsible for the American occupation of Oregon, but it was the religious motive, so potent two centuries earlier in the settlement of America, that led to the founding of Utah. Persecuted and driven from one community to another, the Mormons, under their great leader, Brigham Young, left Nauvoo, Illinois, in 1846 for some retreat in the Far West. In the next year the advance guard reached the Salt Lake basin, and there the settlement was made. Sobriety, thrift, and skillful leadership, combined with an integration resulting from a unified religious purpose, quickly brought prosperity and plenty. Population was recruited by means of missionaries in the eastern states and in Europe, and the expenses of the immigrants were paid by a "Perpetual Emigration Fund." The efficiency of the migration and the rapidity with which a desert was turned into a thriving community mark the Mormon settlement as one of the most successful in American history.

Hardly had the Mormons established themselves in Utah and the great Southwest been acquired from Mexico before a remarkable impetus was given to the occupation of the west coast by the discovery of gold in 1848 on the millrace of John Sutter on the American River, about forty miles from Sacramento. There was already a handful of American farmers in California, but now from the four corners of the earth prospective gold diggers flocked to the new land. By the end of 1848 at least 6000 had arrived, while in the next year probably 35,000 came by sea and 42,000 by land; the population in 1850 was 92,597, more than that of the state of Delaware. The sea routes were either around the Horn or to the Isthmus of Panama, overland to the Pacific, and up the coast. Engineers were sent out in 1849 to plan a railroad across the Isthmus; this was completed with great difficulty five years later and did an enormous business until the first transcontinental line was completed in 1869.

Overland there were two chief routes. The northern and shorter route, known as the Oregon Trail, led from St. Joseph or Independence near the Missouri along the Platte River to Fort Laramie, and through the South Pass to Fort Bridger, where the traveler had a choice of two routes to the California Trail. The gold seeker traveling by way of the Southern, or

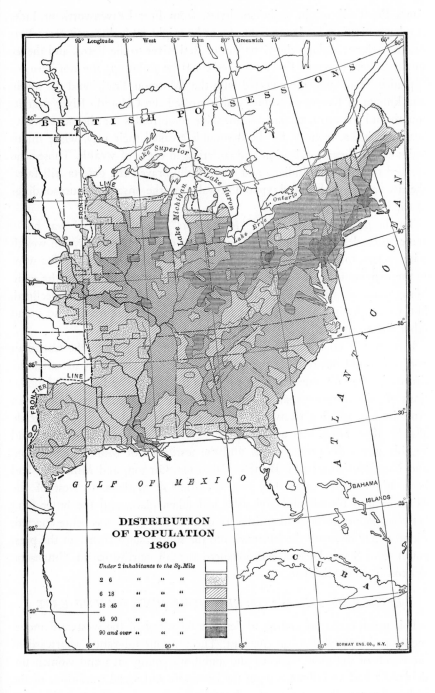

95° Longitude 90° West 85° from 80° Greenwich 75° 70° 65°

B R I T I S H   P O S S E S S I O N S

Lake Superior

Lake Michigan

Lake Huron

L. Ontario

Lake Erie

FRONTIER LINE

FRONTIER LINE

A T L A N T I C   O C E A N

G U L F   O F   M E X I C O

BAHAMA ISLANDS

C U B A

DISTRIBUTION
OF POPULATION
1860

Under 2 inhabitants to the Sq. Mile		
2 6	"	" "
6 18	"	" "
18 45	"	" "
45 90	"	" "
90 and over	"	" "

BORMAY ENS. CO., N.Y.

Santa Fe, Trail, might strike southwest from Fort Leavenworth or Independence via Fort Dodge to Santa Fe or he might push due west from Fort Smith, Arkansas, along the Canadian or Red River to the Pecos, and thence to Santa Fe. At Santa Fe two routes could be followed: the northern, or "Spanish Trail," which connected with the "Mormon Trail," and the southern, known as Kearney's Route, which crossed the Colorado River near its mouth and led north to San Diego. Over these routes for the next twenty years "prairie schooners" by the thousands creaked their way, while multitudes endured every privation and suffering in quest of wealth. Those who escaped trouble with Indians and successfully braved the deserts still faced the risks of the cholera and typhoid prevalent in the unsanitary surroundings of the boom mining towns.

To the great majority of the "forty-niners" the lure of gold was but a snare and a delusion. True, a minority of the early gold seekers won wealth with pickax and cradle, but even in these early years the great profits went to the merchant, the hotelkeeper, the transportation company, and the gambling house proprietor. After a few years the exportation of gold declined, but a more lasting prosperity was founded upon agriculture, industry, and other wealth-producing activities.

In 1850 it is no longer possible to draw a line south from the Canadian border to point out roughly the western frontier. In the two years after the discovery of gold thousands jumped across the prairies and laid the foundations of new commonwealths. Since 1848 there have been two frontiers in America, one moving westward and the other eastward. During the decade 1840 to 1850 Texas was annexed; the territories of Iowa, Wisconsin, and Florida were admitted as states, and the territories of Minnesota, Oregon, and New Mexico created. By 1860 California, Oregon, and Minnesota had been admitted as states. The first extension of settlements west of the Missouri into Kansas and Nebraska had taken place, and the bitter feud between the proslavery and antislavery groups for control was being enacted. Pioneers had crept up the Missouri into the southeastern corner of the present state of South Dakota and advanced steadily northward in Minnesota, Wisconsin, and Michigan.

EFFECT OF THE WESTWARD MOVEMENT ON THE EAST

It is much easier, of course, to describe the effect of the westward movement on the West than on the East. The constant migration westward of thousands of the most vigorous and ambitious young men and women undoubtedly had an influence upon the economic and social conditions of the seaboard states. Since the westward movement was primarily an agricultural expansion it eventually, when transportation facilities were developed, brought the products of the rich western soil into competition with those of the East. This, in combination with the declining fertility of the seaboard states, tended, as we shall see, to weaken the position of eastern agriculture and depress the value of eastern farm lands. Eastern farmers were glad that in the West their children might find new opportunities, but the effect upon their own position was often difficult.

To determine the effect of the westward movement upon the rising American manufacturing industries is more difficult. Eastern manufacturers were convinced that the exodus of labor to the West kept the wage level high in the East and discouraged industrial development. There seems to be little foundation for this belief. There was always a large movement of farm boys and girls to the growing eastern cities as well as to the West. Each year tens of thousands of immigrants from Europe stopped in the eastern cities, thus providing a large labor force. The decline of wages in the 1840's and 1850's along with increasing unemployment during these decades weakens this argument. Just who went West during the first half of the nineteenth century is by no means as clear as might be supposed. The results of the most recent research indicate that the movement was essentially one of farmers and their children rather than one of city laborers.[17] There are few data to show that factory workers left the mills to migrate to the West. The fact that thousands of farm boys and girls preferred to go West rather than to the eastern factories, thus removing *potential* wage earners, may have had its effect on wage scales. But in view of the declining wage scales, this could not have been serious in its long-run effects on industrial development.

In any event, as the valleys of the Ohio and Mississippi filled up, eastern manufacturers found a market for their products. This promoted geographic division of labor and the interplay of commerce. As the years passed, the East became more and more a manufacturing section, the West a food-growing reigon, and the South a producer of cotton. During the first decades of the century the East shipped manufactured goods to the West, but the West sold most of its food products to the South, sending them via the river routes. The South in turn sold most of its produce to Europe, or sent it north. After the completion of the Erie and Pennsylvania canals, and especially after the opening of railroads, western products began to move east as well as south, and before the Civil War railroad iron had securely connected the region north of the Ohio with the economic interests of the Northeast.

Farmers, manufacturers, and merchants of the seaboard states might view with consternation the rapid development of the West, but not so the capitalist with a surplus with which to speculate in western land or in trans-

---

[17] Carter Goodrich and Sol Davison, "The Wage Earner in the Westward Movement," *Political Science Quarterly*, L, 161–185 (June, 1935) and LI, 61–116 (March, 1936).

portation facilities. This was probably the chief area of activity for American capital, particularly in the years which preceded the panics of 1819, 1837, and 1857. Writing of Illinois, Professor Gates sums up neatly the role of the speculator, but his description would apply to almost any region in the Middle West: "The rôle of the speculator has been one of profound importance in the history of Illinois. He preceded the settler, selected the choice locations, purchased them with land warrants or cash, surveyed and located them and then sought to turn immigration into his section. He was foremost in the advocacy of canals, railroads, plank roads and river improvements; to secure these his influence was exerted on the legislature, on county and city organizations and on Congress. As a factor in politics his influence cannot be overestimated."[18]

INFLUENCE OF THE WEST UPON EARLY AMERICAN POLITICS

Fear that the frontiersman with his radical ideas of democracy and strong tendency toward nationalism would upset the equilibrium of the nation and undermine the work of the founders was widespread in the East. Eastern fear of western democracy, in fact, has been a constant factor in American politics from the days of Bacon's Rebellion to the present time. Softening this fear was the widespread belief among statesmen, students of American conditions, and leaders of American thought that the West provided a "safety valve" against political and social discontent. As long as there was unoccupied land to which men might move when political, social, or economic conditions in the East became too hard, the nation would at least be saved from a revolutionary explosion. "Whenever social conditions tended to crystallize in the East," says Turner, "whenever capital tended to press upon labor or political restraints to impede the freedom of the mass, there was this gate of escape to the free conditions of the frontier." The West might be dangerous politically, but at the same time it was a safety valve. This theory lasted as long as the frontier.

Whether the West really acted in this way to any important extent is more than doubtful. The movement of dissatisfied eastern laborers, as has been suggested, was small. The cost of westward migration was too great for the poorer wage earner, and he knew little about farming. As a result those in the East who suffered most from the economic system were practically prevented from escaping it. Moreover, population statistics appear to show that migration to the West was much greater during prosperity than in depression. Waves of economic discontent were often evident while there was an abundance of unoccupied land. This unrest seems to have been quite as strong since the disappearance of the frontier. Furthermore, social discon-

[18] P. W. Gates, *The Illinois Central Railroad and Its Colonization Work*, p. 119.

tent seems frequently to have been more acute on the frontier than in eastern cities.

Whether the West acted as a safety valve or not, there can be no doubt as to its strong influence upon American politics. In state politics the aggressive frontiersmen demanded the rewriting of the state constitutions in the interest of democracy, as, for example, in New York in 1821 and Virginia in 1830. Gerrymandering and other devices were employed to ward off the growing power of the new communities, but with only temporary success. The buoyant and intense spirit of the New West was not to be denied. In national politics the story was the same. The Federalists, representing the eastern aristocracy and what manufacturing and business interests there were at the time, lost control of the executive and legislative branches at the end of Adams' administration. With the accession of Jefferson, himself a Piedmont farmer, the influence of the western agriculturists was more in evidence, an influence which steadily increased as the representatives of one new state after another, elected by universal manhood suffrage, took their seats in Washington.

During the period of the Republican presidents (Jefferson, Madison, Monroe, and John Quincy Adams) the spirit of the West was shown in the growth of strong national policies. The War of 1812 was a western war. The demands of the new communities led to the building of the National Road, notwithstanding the objections of the strict constructionists. The tariffs of 1816, 1824, and 1828 were passed only by the support of Kentucky and the Northwest, influenced chiefly by the arguments of Henry Clay, whose "American System" conceived of a manufacturing East as the logical market for the agricultural West. The famous decisions of the arch-Federalist, Chief Justice Marshall, while bitterly resented by the Westerners, were generally in line with the nationalism so strong in the West. After 1820 there came a reaction from the nationalism of the previous years, which encompassed the South and West and swept Andrew Jackson into the Presidency in 1828. With his sincere belief in the ability and right of the masses to rule, Jackson, a true representative of the New West, bitterly fought privilege and vested wealth as he saw them in the second Bank of the United States. Although strongly grounded in the idea of states' rights, his frontier training gave him a vision which made him stand firm against the nullification of South Carolina. Even the Whig party, in a sense a resurrected Federalist party, which opposed him was led by a Westerner, Henry Clay.

SELECTED READINGS

Turner, F. J., *The Frontier in American History,* chaps. 4–7, 13.
Taylor, G. R. (ed.), *The Turner Thesis* (Amherst Series).
Bond, B. W., Jr., *The Civilization of the Old Northwest,* chaps. 1, 2, 10.

Billington, R. A., *Westward Expansion*, chaps. 11–30.

Webb, W. P., *The Great Plains*, chap. 5

Mathews, L. K., *The Expansion of New England*, chaps. 6–10.

Coman, K., *Economic Beginnings of the Far West*, Parts III and IV.

Hacker, L. M., *The Triumph of American Capitalism*, chaps. 15, 16.

Callender, G. S., *Selections from the Economic History of the United States, 1765–1860*, chap. 12.

Flügel, F., and Faulkner, H. U., *Readings in the Economic and Social History of the United States*, chaps. 5, 11.

CHAPTER 11

THE AGRICULTURAL ERA

EFFECT OF THE WESTWARD MOVEMENT ON AMERICAN AGRICULTURE

For almost three centuries one of the great influences on American agriculture was the existence of an area of unoccupied land to which settlers were continually moving. This influence was particularly important in the century after the Revolution as the westward movement became more rapid and was stimulated by the increasing liberality of the federal land policy, the growing tide of immigration, and the development of improved transportation facilities. That it was by no means easy to migrate to the West without at least a small backlog of capital and some knowledge of farming is evident. Nevertheless, there were few men endowed with strength, ambition, and willingness to work who were unable to acquire land and make a new start in life. An ordinary laborer in the new country might save enough in a year to purchase his eighty acres, while a skilled mechanic or schoolteacher, both in great demand on the frontier, might purchase in less time. The proceeds from the sale of two horses or eight cattle would buy a quarter-section. During the years 1783–1860 most of the land between the Alleghenies and the Mississippi was taken up, and the advance tide of migration swept into Texas, covered Missouri, and penetrated Kansas and Minnesota. The Mormons were carrying on agriculture around the Great Salt Lake and farms were rapidly developing on the Pacific slope.

Perhaps the greatest effect of this easily acquired land was to perpetuate the old-fashioned and criminally wasteful methods. The treatment of land in Virginia is thus described by Washington in a letter to Arthur Young, the great English proponent of scientific agriculture:

The cultivation of tobacco has been almost the sole object with men of landed property, and consequently a regular course of crops have never been in view. The general custom has been, first to raise a crop of Indian corn (maize) which

197

according to the mode of cultivation, is a good preparation for wheat; then a crop of wheat; after which the ground is respited (except from weeds, and every trash that can contribute to its foulness) for about eighteen months; and so on, alternately, without any dressing, till the land is exhausted; when it is turned out, without being sown with grass seeds, or any method taken to restore it; and another piece is ruined in the same manner.[1]

The tobacco grower, when his land wore out, found it cheaper to take up new land than to care for the old, and tobacco culture advanced westward into Kentucky. The same was true a little later of cotton, this factor contributing to the rapid occupation of Alabama, Mississippi, and eastern Texas. Northern agriculture was influenced in a similar way. Why, asked the farmer, must I cultivate intensively a small farm in Massachusetts or New Hampshire when an abundance of richer soil awaits the plow in central New York or the Ohio Valley?

After the pioneer had reached the new country the temptation was always present to skim the cream from the fresh land and then sell out and try his fortune farther on. Said an observer in Missouri in 1849, "Farming is here conducted on the regular skinning system . . . most of the farmers in this country *scratch* over a great deal of ground but *cultivate* none,"[2] a system which of course amazed the European traveler. Said Birkbeck in 1818, "The idea of exhausting the soil by cropping, so as to render manure necessary, has not yet entered into the estimates of the western cultivator. Manure has been often known to accumulate until the farmers have removed their yards and buildings out of the way of the nuisance. They have no notion of making a return to the land, and as yet there seems no bounds to its fertility."[3] Before the development of rapid water and steam transportation the pioneer farmer was handicapped by a lack of markets, which naturally lessened the incentive to improve his holdings. Enough could easily be raised to support his family without calling forth the latent possibilities of the new farm.

Even more harmful to agriculture than the ease of acquiring fresh lands after the old had been ruined was the fever of land speculation that seized the American people and continued decade after decade during this period. Exaggerated, to be sure, but with elements of truth is the picture drawn by an Englishman:

Speculation in real estate has for many years been the ruling idea and occupation of the Western mind. Clerks, labourers, farmers, storekeepers, merely fol-

---

[1] W. C. Ford (ed.), *The Writings of George Washington*, XI, 178 ff.

[2] *Cultivator*, New Series VI (1849), p. 302, quoted in P. W. Bidwell and J. I. Falconer, *History of Agriculture in the Northern United States, 1620–1860*, p. 272.

[3] Morris Birkbeck, *Letters from Illinois* (1818), p. 18.

lowed their callings for a living, while they were speculating for their fortunes. There are no statistics which show how many Yankees went out West to buy a piece of land and make a farm and home, and live and settle, and die there. I think that not more than one-half per cent of the migration from the East started with that idea: and not even half of these carried out the idea. The German immigrants, indeed, were better entitled to be called settlers; but all classes and people of all kinds became agitated and unsettled, and had their acquisitiveness perpetually excited by land speculations in some shape or other—new railways, roads, proposed villages and towns, gold mines, water-powers, coal mines—some opportunity or other of getting rich all at once by a lucky hit. . . .

In the United States, vast numbers of the population became excited with dreams of sudden wealth, and the idea of a life of labour was scouted as the suitable destiny of mere timid, non-enterprising, weak people, or plodding Dutch or English, but altogether beneath the notice of Young America. . . .

By convenient laws, land was made as easily transferable and convertible as any other species of property. It might and did pass through a dozen hands within sixty days, rising in price at each transfer; in the meantime producing buffaloes and Red Indians. Millions of acres were bought and sold without buyer or seller knowing where they were, or whether they were anywhere; the buyer only knowing that he hoped to sell his title to them at a handsome profit.[4]

Speculating on the progress of the country entered into the very soul of the pioneer and was part of his being.[5] In picking out a site for his claim the first consideration was its situation in respect to a possible rise in value. The typical frontiersman of these days was a man who laid out his claim, erected a rude cabin, and worked the land only until he could sell out at a profit. Upon the eastern farmer the effect of all this was demoralizing. He, too, imbibed the spirit of land speculation, and many an eastern farm was put up for sale by the proprietor, who was eager to unload and try his fortune elsewhere. This trading on the progress of the country gave the American farmer a migratory tendency which was impossible under Old World conditions and unusual in a group which by its very occupation moved slowly. It broke down local attachments and discouraged intensive improvements; the farmer was building not for his descendants but for the first possible opportunity to sell.

Eastern agriculture was further demoralized by western competition. After canals and railroads had provided an outlet for the bulky agricultural products of the West, the farmer of New England and the middle states found it difficult to compete successfully in the raising of grain and meat and was forced to reorganize his economy to that of truck farming, fruit raising, dairying, or tobacco culture. Only the most favorably located or

[4] D. W. Mitchell, *Ten Years in the United States* (1862), p. 325.
[5] See quotation from Peck, above, p. 185.

most fertile of the grainfields in the East could continue to compete with western grain. This reorganization took time and was attended with difficulties. Farming in the East was further handicapped by difficulty in obtaining sufficient labor. Higher wages and greater opportunities drained off to the near-by cities or the West the best of the farm hands.

RISE OF COTTON

Undoubtedly the most striking feature in the agricultural history of the first half-century of the Republic was the rise of cotton. During the colonial period little progress had been made in cotton culture. Lack of a market and the overshadowing importance of tobacco discouraged its growth, despite the efforts of colonial governments to the contrary. Some cotton was raised to be woven into cloth, but its use was confined to the poorer classes. Interruption of trade with Great Britain during the Revolution, which cut off the importation of foreign fabrics, turned the minds of Southerners to the production of cotton as a means of filling the need, and the legislatures of Maryland, Virginia, and South Carolina urged its possibilities upon their people. The chief difficulty with which the cotton grower had to contend was the separation of the seeds from the cotton fiber, a costly process even with slave labor.

The years 1790–1830 witnessed a veritable revolution in southern agriculture as far as the chief product was concerned. By the latter date cotton had become the principal southern crop and the largest single item of export from the country. This rapid development was occasioned, first of all, by the equally sudden opening of an available market. In England between 1767 and 1780 Hargreaves, Arkwright, and Crompton had constructed devices which were destined to eliminate hand spinning and substitute water power and later steam. In 1785 similar improvements in weaving were developed by Cartwright; the result was an Industrial Revolution well under way in the early decades of the nineteenth century. Eventually the designs of these machines were brought to America[6] and factories established here. "In 1775, the cotton manufacture in England," says Adam Seybert, "was ranked 'amongst the humblest of the domestic arts'; the products of this branch were then almost entirely for home consumption; in 1797 it took the lead of all other manufactures in Great Britain, and in 1809, gave employment to 800,000 persons."[7]

Rapid and cheap manufactures reduced prices and created demand. Any amount of cotton could now be manufactured; the problem was to obtain the raw material. In the year 1786 almost by accident "sea-island" cotton was

[6] See chap. 13.
[7] Adam Seybert, *Statistical Annals . . . of the United States* (1818), p. 92.

introduced from the Bahamas and was found to thrive along the seacoast. Because it had a longer fiber than the "short staple" variety, it was possible to separate the seeds by running the fiber between rollers turned in opposite directions. The demand for it abroad was immediate and its cultivation spread rapidly among the seacoast farmers. The planters were the more ready to take up the cultivation of cotton because the tobacco lands were wearing out and the market for indigo and rice had been injured by the separation from Great Britain. The South badly needed a new crop at the same time that the factory owners of England were clamoring for the raw product.

The impetus for cotton culture was undoubtedly present. Only the difficulty of separating the seeds from the cotton held back expansion. Climatic conditions restricted the sea-island cotton to the coastal lowlands; the short-fibered upland cotton, upon which the greater part of the South had to depend, could be cleaned only with painful slowness at an average of about a pound a day per slave. The problem was solved in 1793 by Eli Whitney, a wide-awake Yankee and a mechanical genius, who had gone south to teach school immediately after graduating from Yale.

Whitney's contraption, in its crudest form, consisted of a cylinder, equipped with teeth projecting through strips of metal which drew in the cotton fiber leaving the seeds behind, and a second roller, equipped with brushes to free the teeth from the lint, that revolved in the opposite direction. Operated by hand, the machine would clean fifty pounds a day; with water power, a thousand. Said the inventor in a letter to his father:

I made one before I came away which required the labor of one man to turn it and with which one man will clean ten times as much cotton as he can in any other way before known and also cleanse it much better than in the usual mode. This machine may be turned by water or with a horse, with the greatest ease, and one man and a horse will do more than fifty men with the old machines. It makes the labor fifty times less, without throwing any class of People out of business.[8]

EFFECTS OF THE COTTON GIN

Whitney's cotton gin was the first important American agricultural invention and was largely the production of one man's genius. Its effects were immediate and far reaching. Cotton came to be the greatest commercial crop of the South and the largest single export of the nation. With the exception of 1808, the year of the Embargo Act, and 1812–1814, the war years, the growth of cotton culture was rapid and steady. Production in 1790 was 4000 bales of 500 pounds; in 1860 it was 3,841,416 bales. About 22 per cent of the value of the total export in 1810, it reached 57 per cent in 1860 while the

[8] "Correspondence of Eli Whitney," *American Historical Review*, III, 100.

value of cotton exports increased during the same years from $66,758,000 to $333,576,000.[9] Its importance in the export trade explains the source of southern wealth, the South's attitude on the tariff, her overconfidence at the beginning of the war, and her eventual failure.

The invention of the cotton gin and the rise of cotton culture were important in the opening up of the Southwest. Beginning in Georgia and South Carolina, cotton growing after 1800 spread into North Carolina and southeastern Virginia and across the mountains into Tennessee. After men realized that the rich alluvial soil of Alabama and Mississippi was better suited to cotton than the uplands, prospective growers entered in a steady stream, pushing before them Indians, Spaniards, and cattle ranchers. Crossing the Mississippi, they drove the cattlemen into Texas, contributed in bringing about the Mexican War and its resulting annexations, and by 1860 had pre-empted the coastal regions of Texas. The exhausting methods of early cotton culture, as with tobacco, wore out the soil and impelled the planter to search for further virgin land. As late as 1820 over half the cotton grown in the country was raised in Georgia and South Carolina. By 1850 Alabama had taken first place, with Georgia second, Mississippi third, and South Carolina fourth. In 1860 Mississippi, Alabama, and Louisiana raised over half the total product, and the yield from Texas now surpassed that of South Carolina. The most pronounced periods of expansion in the Southwest were in the flush years preceding the crisis of 1837, and in the period immediately following the annexation of Texas. With the shifting of the center of cotton culture went a shift in the centers of trade, of wealth, and of political power. The importance of Charleston and Savannah declined, while Memphis, Mobile, and New Orleans rose as commercial centers. In

[9] AVERAGE ANNUAL PRODUCTION AND EXPORTS OF AMERICAN COTTON FOR FIVE-YEAR PERIODS, 1791–1865, AND AVERAGE ANNUAL PRICES FOR MIDDLING UPLANDS COTTON IN NEW YORK AND LIVERPOOL

Years	Average Annual Production in the United States in Pounds	Average Annual Exports from the United States in Pounds	Percentage of Crops Exported	Average New York Prices for Middling Uplands— Cents	Average Liverpool Prices for Middling Uplands— Pence
1791–1795	5,200,000	1,738,700	33.43	31.7	No data
1801–1805	59,600,000	33,603,800	56.38	25.0	15.4
1811–1815	80,000,000	42,269,400	52.83	14.8	20.5
1821–1825	209,000,000	152,420,200	72.93	16.2	9.2
1831–1835	398,521,600	329,077,600	82.57	11.9	8.0
1841–1845	822,953,800	691,517,200	84.03	7.7	4.7
1851–1855	1,294,422,800	990,368,600	76.51	9.6	5.4
1861–1865	No data	No data	No data	58.9	19.1

Source: *The South in the Building of the Nation*, V, 211.

the decade 1850–1860 New Orleans handled about half the cotton crop. By that time the center of the cotton kingdom had shifted to the Southwest.

The effects of the invention of the cotton gin permeated the whole social as well as the economic life of the South by fastening upon it the system of slavery. Slavery as an institution was decidedly under fire in the years immediately following the Revolution. Intelligent planters were bginning to question the economic soundness of the entire slave system as it operated in the South at that time. Wrote Washington in 1794: "Were it not that I am principled against selling negroes as you would cattle in the market I would not in 12 months be possessed of a single one as a slave. I shall be happily mistaken if they are not found to be very troublesome species of property ere many years have passed over our heads."[10] Men like Washington and Jefferson, at their death, freed their slaves and with other prominent Southerners urged the abolition of the whole iniquitous system. In the North the movement to end slavery was making rapid progress.

The trend toward abolition was halted by the invention of the cotton gin. Cotton was a crop pre-eminently adaptable to slave labor. Almost the entire Negro family could work in the cotton fields during the greater part of the year. A single overseer could supervise a large number of slaves, and cotton culture as a whole was suitable to the crude and wasteful methods of ignorant slave labor in a country where large stretches of fresh land could be taken up as the old wore out. Although the number of slaves increased from approximately 698,000 in 1790 to almost 4,000,000 in 1860, the increase was not rapid enough to meet the demand, and as larger regions were brought under cultivation the demand for slaves grew. Before the cotton gin was invented a good field hand brought $300; twenty years later the price had doubled. The average value was around $800 in 1830, $1200 in 1850, and from $1400 to $2000 in 1860. Abolition sentiment died away not only in the South but also in certain of the border states, where it had been strongest. The movement of cotton production to the West and South left a surplus of slaves in the border states, particularly Virginia, and their disposal became an active business. At the same time the law prohibiting the slave trade was openly evaded along the whole coast. Fearful of the increasing criticism of the system, the slaveowners, ably represented in Congress, met attacks boldly and worked unceasingly to extend the slave area.

In the North the effects of the rise of cotton were also felt. The infant textile industries of New England were stimulated; and north of the Ohio the farmers found a market for their pork, corn, flour, and whiskey. This stimulated agriculture and brought prosperity to the Middle West, but it

[10] Quoted in W. H. Mazyck, *George Washington and the Negro* (1932).

also favored the rapid extension of slavery and the development of the plantation system in the Southwest.[11]

OTHER ASPECTS OF SOUTHERN AGRICULTURE

By far the greatest southern product during the colonial period was tobacco. The last decade of the century saw it at the height of its importance, when over half the population of the tobacco states was engaged in or dependent on its cultivation. It headed the list of exports in 1791, when more than $4,590,000 worth was shipped abroad. Still the leading export in 1800, it declined rapidly in importance, owing to the disastrous effects of the Embargo Acts and the War of 1812, the competition of Cuba, Colombia, and Sumatra, high import taxes imposed on it by foreign countries, the gradual exhaustion of the land, and the rise of cotton. The effect of the shifting of land and slaves from tobacco to cotton was distinctly noticeable; the industry remained practically stationary until 1840, when exports again equaled the amount shipped in 1790. The substitution of flue curing for the old-fashioned charcoal fire and the introduction of a new yellow-leaf species so improved the product as to give the industry a new life; the population increase widened the home market. Between 1850 and 1860 the production more than doubled, so that at the opening of the war the South continued to be the greatest producer of tobacco in the world. Although Virginia and Kentucky produced half the crop at this time, the center was moving westward. About half the crop raised at this time was exported to England and Germany.

Sugar cane was early imported but it was not until about 1800 that refining had advanced sufficiently to make it an important product. Louisiana was the center, and by 1860 it produced 280,000 hogsheads with the work of 180,000 slaves.

Rice, which had been a leading colonial crop along the seacoast of South Carolina and Georgia, continued to be successfully grown, the production more than tripling from 1820 to 1850. The high-water mark was reached in 1850, after which a decline set in. Until that year South Carolina raised more than half the crop, with Georgia producing most of the rest. The rice grower as a class was undoubtedly the most scientific farmer in the prewar South. Forced by necessity to use the same soil continually, his attention was early turned to the use of fertilizer and the reclamation of swampy land. The fact that only the moist soil was suitable for rice resulted in plantations of diversified products quite different from the cotton and tobacco plantations. The rice grower was encouraged in his efforts by a steady market and the acknowledged fact that the Carolina product was the best in the world. His chief problem was to meet the acute competition for slave labor produced

[11] P. W. Bidwell and J. I. Falconer, *op. cit.*, chap. 13.

by the rapidly developing cotton and sugar plantations in the southwestern states.

Another crop of considerable importance in certain sections of the South was hemp. The beginnings of this industry were almost simultaneous with the settlement of Kentucky. Hemp became as important here in the early years as tobacco had been in early Virginia. It was used principally for bagging and rope for cotton bales and for cloth for Negroes, but the market extended to the North and East. From Kentucky hemp growing spread into Tennessee, Arkansas, and Missouri, where it was an important factor in winning the latter state to slavery. Henry Clay, the champion of the "American System," was, it should be noted, the representative of the Kentucky hemp growers. Kentucky in 1850 produced 17,787 tons of hemp, Missouri 16,028, and Tennessee 595.

Although the economic life of the South was dominated by the commercial crops already described, other crops were raised, chiefly for home consumption. In addition to the usual garden vegetables, cereals were produced in 1859 as follows: Indian corn, 433,067,000 bushels; wheat, 49,158,000 bushels; oats, 32,163,000 bushels; rye, 4,070,000; and barley and buckwheat in small amounts. The southern soil was more adaptable to corn than the other cereals, and it served as the chief food for the slaves. The crop, however, was barely half that raised in the five states north of the Ohio and was not adequate for southern needs. These crops, nevertheless, occupied the attention of a majority of the small farmers, who far surpassed the plantation owners in number. In the animal industry the South, particularly Kentucky, was famous for the excellent speed horses bred there. Kentucky was also noted for breeding shorthorn cattle and Hampshire hogs. Virginia's pre-eminence in sheep raising during these years can be traced back to Washington's interest and the subsequent efforts of agricultural societies. That the activity of the South in livestock was not confined to fancy breeding is evidenced by the estimated value of all livestock, which the census of 1860 placed at $381,778,601.

AGRICULTURAL ADVANCE INTO THE REGION OF THE OLD NORTHWEST

Quite as significant in the history of American agriculture as the rise of cotton was the opening to agriculture of the region between the Ohio River and the Great Lakes, westward into the prairies of Iowa and Kansas. The lands of western New York and northern Ohio, probably at one time covered by water, are endowed with a fine rich soil, free of boulders and easy to cultivate, and blessed with a climate tempered by the expanses of water. Nearly 100,000 square miles of water surface furnish the finest inland navigation in the world, facilities augmented by a natural outlet through the Mohawk Valley to the eastern coast. Tributaries of the Ohio and the Missouri allowed the produce of the North Central States to be carried by way of the Mississippi to the markets of Europe and the southern states. Natural highways were supplemented in the early decades by the Erie Canal, the Pennsylvania Canal, and the Cumberland Road, and after 1840 by the railroads which were easily built in this region.

The first settler, pressing into the wooded stretches bordering the Ohio and its tributaries, found the problems much the same as on his New England or Kentucky farm. It was a case of clearing the forest and duplicating the old crops. As the land was taken up and the advance pushed into Indiana, Illinois, and Iowa, the pioneer found himself in a different type of country with new problems to be faced. Here was to be found prairie land without forest, which made building expensive and firewood scarce. Frequent absence of water was a deterrent. The tough prairie soil was extremely hard to break with the early wooden plows, and at first there was a mistaken idea that it was not fertile. Occupation of the prairies was sometimes held up by the lack of transportation facilities, which made it impossible to market the surplus profitably. When the real richness of the soil was realized, especially after the improvement of the steel plow and other farm machinery, and after artificial transportation facilities had been developed, the land was quickly put under cultivation. Occupation was the more rapid because the land needed little preparation for sowing. Practically no clearing was necessary; the soil was simply broken with a plow or ax, and a crop of corn planted. The first crop usually broke up the sod sufficiently to let it rot, and in the second year a crop of wheat was possible.

The development of the Lake region and prairies depended largely upon markets and transportation. The Industrial Revolution was turning western Europe into an urban manufacturing civilization and was beginning to make itself felt in America in an increased demand for foodstuffs. This was particularly true after the repeal of the Corn Laws in 1846, which opened Great Britain to American foodstuffs. An important market also developed in the South, where the planters believed it more profitable to purchase food and turn the entire labor energy of the slaves to raising the staple crop. As a consequence, the North Central States developed into a great food-producing region, whence the products moved eastward by canal and railroad and south by steamboat and rail in two continuous streams. Western New York and northern Ohio became interested in fruitgrowing and dairying, while the rest of the Middle West produced chiefly meat and cereals.

What little exportation of foodstuffs there had been from this region prior to 1825 had been in the form of beef, pork, and mutton on the hoof. Before the era of canals and railroads and the development of the packing industry, the farmers of the western counties of Pennsylvania, Maryland, Virginia, and Ohio annually took great droves of cattle and hogs along the highways leading to Philadelphia and Baltimore. "During the summer and autumn, along these lines of travel, so many drovers passed that an observer, a mile or more away, could know of the passing of stock, for far up in the air he could see long moving lines of rising dust."[12] Livestock raising has always been a leading frontier occupation, for every frontier has provided animal food at low cost. In the Middle West, where hog growing was destined to become a great industry, conditions were especially favorable. Hogs at first could find maintenance on the mast[13] and herbage of the forests on the fringe of civilization; later on, corn, their principal food, was found especially adaptable to the soil and soon became the leading crop.

About 1818, meat packing as an industry came into existence west of the Alleghenies. The development of markets, of transportation, and of banking facilities, and the growth of a sufficient population to provide a steady supply of animals had progressed far enough by this time to build up a considerable meat-packing industry in Cincinnati. In the early years meat was preserved by salting and smoking, and, as this process did not require large capital, packing establishments sprang up in many of the larger towns. Nevertheless, Cincinnati retained the leading position until 1860, although the center moved continually westward. As Chicago grew in size, its superior transportation facilities, combined with its nearness to the new pork states, enabled it to take the lead. Upon the meat industry and the manufacture of such by-products as leather goods, fertilizers, glue, candles, soap, lard, salt, and barrels the early prosperity of both Cincinnati and Chicago rested. This industry is still basic in these centers.

The chief stimulus for cereal production in the early years came from the need for food for animals and ingredients for the manufacture of whiskey. Corn was too bulky to transport, but it could be fed to animals, which in turn could be driven many miles to the market. Corn and rye could easily be reduced to the less bulky and more concentrated form of spirituous liquors. It was this fact that made whiskey a characteristic pioneer product and explains the opposition of the frontier farmer of Pennsylvania to Hamilton's excise tax. Corn during this entire period remained by far the chief agricultural product, although little found its way out except in the form of whiskey or meat.

After the opening of the Erie and Pennsylvania canals and the growth of

---

[12] I. F. King, "The Coming and Going of Ohio Droving," *Ohio State Archæological and Historical Society Quarterly*, XVII, 249 (1908).

[13] Fruit of the oak and the beech or other forest trees.

railroads it was possible to ship cereals east as well as south, and there was a great impetus to other lines of cereal production. Wheat was consigned either to millers at Cincinnati, Louisville, and St. Louis to be prepared for local and southern consumption or to the east via Buffalo and Pittsburgh. Some eventually reached Europe via New York or New Orleans. The Middle Atlantic States in 1850 still produced more wheat than the North Central, but in the next decade western production increased 125 per cent to 15.5 for the Middle Atlantic. As the western wheat grew in importance, the milling center shifted from the coast streams to Rochester on the Erie Canal, then to Chicago and St. Louis, and eventually to the great mills of the Northwest.

BEYOND THE MISSISSIPPI

The extension of agriculture beyond the Mississippi into Missouri, Minnesota, Iowa, Kansas, and Nebraska was a continuation of the frontier experience of the states north of the Ohio, with essentially the same products and civilization. Farther south in Louisiana and Arkansas, the fringe of settlements was pushed beyond the Mississippi before the region east had been fully occupied, and tobacco, cotton, sugar, and cereals were grown. American advance into Spanish territory began in 1821, when Moses Austin, a native of Connecticut, obtained a grant from the Spanish government upon which to plant a colony of settlers from the United States, and in the next year his son, Stephen, established the first Anglo-American settlement in the Brazos and Trinity valleys. Probably 30,000 Americans followed Austin's band in the next fifteen years, taking up land mainly along the rivers between San Antonio and Nacogdoches and the coast. Most of them were Southerners who either brought their slaves and raised cotton or engaged in ranching.

The reason for their migration was the opportunity to obtain better land at less cost than was possible in the United States, where the best land in the South was already pre-empted and the minimum price of what remained was $1.25 an acre. This immigration took place during the revolutionary epoch when Mexico was winning her independence from Spain. Welcomed at first by both Spaniards and Mexicans, the new settlers soon provided cause for friction. Attempts by the Mexican government to prevent further immigration, to abolish slavery, and to eliminate home rule were but a few of the causes which led inevitably to insurrection. The land-hungry Americans revolted, won their independence from Mexico in 1836, and were annexed to the United States in 1845.[14] By 1860 Texas had a population of 604,000 living on 42,891 farms and raising 405,100 bales of cotton, in addition to her extensive ranching industry.

It should also be remembered that American farmers by 1860 were laying

[14] Above, p. 188.

the foundations for a great agricultural empire on the Pacific coast. The population of California had increased from 92,000 in 1850 to 380,000 in 1860, providing a growing demand for the products of local agriculture. At the same time placer mining was giving out, and many of the forty-niners, who had been farmers before their migration to California, began to see great agricultural opportunities in the new state. Already the Pacific region was occupied with large-scale ranching—both cattle and sheep—and was raising substantial crops of barley, wheat, and other cereals.

EFFECT OF THE INDUSTRIAL REVOLUTION AND WESTERN AGRICULTURE UPON THE EAST

In rural New England during the first half of the century changes were enacted which brought about a veritable agricultural revolution. As in colonial days, farm life in 1800 was characterized by self-sufficiency. With few markets for his produce, the farmer was unable to buy from without; what he needed in the way of food, clothing, and tools was raised or manufactured mainly on the farm. After 1810 this condition began to change gradually as the Industrial Revolution slowly transformed New England into a manufacturing center.

The urban population, which in 1860 amounted to about one-third of the total population of southern New England, provided a market for agricultural products. Farming, which had been general, began to give way to specialization: intensive farming of root crops in the regions adjacent to the cities, wool growing in the hilly country, and the fattening of beef cattle in the Connecticut Valley. New markets created new interest in farming, which was strengthened by agricultural societies and by the use of improved machinery after 1830, particularly the iron plow.

No sooner had the New England farmer accustomed himself to the new conditions than a second readjustment was forced upon him by the growth of railroads. Cheap transportation made it impossible for him to compete with western wool, beef, and pork; in consequence, although corn continued to be the agricultural backbone of New England, the production of beef and pork declined. Attention was turned to dairying and truck gardening, and on the rich bottom lands of the Connecticut in the three decades after 1840 there developed a spectacular extension of tobacco culture as the increasing use of cigars provided a market for the superior wrappers grown there. This agricultural upheaval brought striking changes to rural life. The self-sufficient domestic system broke down before the factory system. Markets for agricultural products brought ready money to the rural districts, new comforts to the farmer, and a higher standard of living. Women released from household industries sought work in the factories. At the same time many men, discouraged by the uncertainties of this period of readjustment, followed the lure of new opportunities in the cities or of richer lands in the West. The whole situation was further complicated by a readjustment of land values usually, but not always, detrimental to the farmer.

What was happening in New England was taking place to a lesser extent in the middle states. The richer farm land in this region enabled it to compete for a longer period with the products of the West and it remained an important agricultural section throughout these years. Nevertheless, developing industry in the Hudson and Delaware valleys and in growing seaport towns furnished an increasing local market for foodstuffs and brought an agricultural readjustment to meet the demand. The seaboard South, on the other hand, had little to compensate her for the competition of western cotton and other products. No important industrial development created large cities, and cotton found its outlet in New Orleans and other Gulf cities. Like New England the seaboard South was dotted with deserted farms, but unlike New England it was unable to adjust itself or turn its energy into new channels. Southern leaders like John Taylor of Caroline and Edmund Ruffin urged diversification of crops and conservation of soil by scientific agriculture, but their call fell on deaf ears. With his capital tied up in land, his soil wearing out, and labor draining off to the Southwest, the eastern plantation owner seemed able to do little. It is this situation which explains in part the discontent leading to secession.

TECHNICAL ADVANCES IN AGRICULTURE

The period from 1830 to the Civil War witnessed the beginnings of revolutionary changes in American agriculture. Fresh agricultural labor as well as enlarged markets was provided by the rapidly increasing population resulting from (1) natural growth in a civilization conducive to large families, (2) immigration which amounted during these years to over 4,500,000, and (3) the growth of the factory system with its increase of the urban population. The rapid building of railroads after 1850 stimulated the farmer by bringing both the products and the markets of the world to his door. The discovery of gold in California and an increased demand for foodstuffs due to the repeal of the English Corn Laws in 1846 both helped to raise prices. Scientific agriculture made rapid strides, but especially to be noted was the invention and adoption by the American farmer of labor-saving machinery. This development was slow in the quarter-century after the Revolution but gathered speed in the years from 1810 to 1840 and thereafter proceeded with almost lightning-like rapidity.

In a nation where land was plentiful but labor scarce, it was to be expected that the first great advances would come in labor-saving rather than in land-saving devices. "In Europe," said Jefferson, "the object is to make the most of their land, labor being abundant: here it is to make the most of our labor, land being abundant." American farming implements were designed to increase the yield per man rather than the yield per acre; in the latter we have not kept up with more thickly populated countries. For years after 1800 a farmer's equipment consisted usually of a crude wooden plow, harrows, hoes, shovels, forks, and rakes, poorly constructed and often homemade. The first great improvement was the metal plow, which came into general use after 1825. Colonial plows had been covered with strips of iron, and as early as 1790 Charles Newbold of New Jersey was working on the idea of a cast-iron plow, which he finally patented in 1797. But Newbold's plow was ineffective and many farmers would have none of it.

The conception of an improved plow was not lost sight of, men like Jefferson and Webster making studies of types and materials. Eventually Newbold's plow—one solid piece of cast iron—was improved by others, including Jethro Wood of New York, who in 1819 patented a plow, the different parts of which interlocked and could be replaced if broken. Manufacturers and inventors infringed his patents, but the farmer profited. Eventually moldboards were designed, more adaptable to breaking the matted grasses of the prairies, the sticky soil of which also necessitated a smoother surface. This was provided by the all-steel plow of John Deere and the chilled-steel plow of James Oliver, which eliminated blowholes and made the metal less brittle. After the thirties the metal plow was adopted rapidly by the farmer, particularly after quantity production lowered prices. Improved plows not only effected a saving in the labor of men and animals but by stirring the soil more deeply lengthened its productivity.

Simultaneously with the improvement in plows came the invention of the mowing and reaping machines to keep pace with the increased production which the new plows made possible. Just as in manufacturing, the improvement of one stage of agricultural production forced the development of others. The grain cradle had come into use about 1800 and had considerably facilitated both the cutting and the gathering of the grain, but harvesting was still a painfully slow process. Many men experimented during the following years on the problem of a reaper, and many minds contributed to the eventual machine. A patent for a mowing machine had been granted to William Manning of New Jersey in 1831, but the two men who succeeded in building a practical reaper were Obed Hussey and Cyrus McCormick, whose patents were dated, respectively, 1833 and 1834. Hussey's machines, which could mow fifteen acres a day, were good enough to demonstrate the possibilities of a reaper and he had little competition for almost a decade. His poverty and mistakes in policy, however, prevented large-scale produc-

tion and in the end other manufacturers were to reap greater fame and fortune. The greatest success was experienced by Cyrus McCormick, of Scotch-
Irish ancestry, who had emigrated from Pennsylvania into the Shenandoah
Valley and who inherited from his father a mechanical genius and an interest
in farm machinery. Turning his attention to the development of a practical
reaping machine, he continued, after securing his first patent, to manufacture
reapers in his workshop on the Virginia farm and to perfect further improvements. Believing his machines would be more practical on the level
land of the West, he moved in 1845 to Brockport, New York, on the Erie
Canal, and three years later to Chicago, where by 1860 he was turning out
4000 machines a year.

The principle of these early mowers and reapers was the same—a number
of blades or "wipers" swept the grain against the cutting surface, after which
it was pushed on to a receiving table and automatically shoved off when
enough had been gathered to make a sheaf. Laborers following the machine
tied the sheaves. These early machines, clumsy as they were, showed their
superiority over hand labor and improvements came rapidly. By 1855 nearly
10,000 were in use. At the International Exposition at Paris in that year an
American reaper cut an acre of oats in twenty-one minutes, one-third of
the time consumed by the foreign makes. By this time also the most serious
disadvantages, such as side draft, clogging, and inability to begin in standing
grain, had been practically eliminated. Moreover, new features such as the
header, invented by George Esterly of Wisconsin, were being added to increase the usefulness of the machines. In the succeding years the reapers were
widely introduced, a fact which explains the great crops in spite of the labor
shortage during the Civil War.

A necessary further improvement was furnished when a satisfactory
thresher was added to the mechanical devices upon which the farmer could
depend. With the old-fashioned hand flail progress was painfully slow; from
eight to sixteen bushels a day was the average production per man. Experiments went on in both Europe and America in an attempt to devise flails
which could be attached to cylinders and driven by horse or steam power,
but it was not until 1850 that the separator was attached to the thresher and
the whole process of threshing and winnowing was carried on in the same
machine. In America Hiram and John Pitts took the leadership in developing a successful thresher, securing their first patent in 1837.

The invention and improvement of other farming implements accompanied the greater inventions. The horse hayrake, which did the work of
from eight to ten men, came into use about 1820, and the curing of hay
was aided years later by the invention of the tedder. In the decade of the
forties seed drills for sowing wheat were introduced, and between 1840 and

1860 came the corn planter and various types of cultivators which by the latter date had been widely adopted.

Wide-awake farmers of the time were not unaware that a revolution in agricultural methods was under way. As early as 1839 Jesse Buel, a prominent agitator for scientific farming, wrote:

The disparity between the old and new implements of culture is great, not only in the time employed, but in the manner in which they do their work, and in the power required to perform it. The old plow required a four-cattle team, and two hands, to manage it, and the work ordinarily was but half executed. The improved plow is generally propelled by two cattle, requires but one man to manage it, and, when properly governed, performs thorough work. Harrows and other implements have undergone a like movement. Besides, new implements, which greatly economize the labor of tillage, are coming into use, as the roller, cultivator, drill-barrow, etc., so that a farm may now be worked with half the expense of labor that it was wont to be worked forty years ago, and may be better worked withal.[15]

This remarkable development which Buel described in 1839 was but the beginning. A much more important period of agricultural transformation came in the next two decades, the years which witnessed the introduction of seed drills, corn planters, cultivators, and many other types of machinery, particularly the mower and the reaper. Said the Census of 1860:

By the improved plow, labor equivalent to that of one horse in three is saved. By means of drills two bushels of seed will go as far as three bushels scattered broadcast, while the yield is increased six to eight bushels per acre; the plants come up in rows and may be tended by horse-hoes. . . . The reaping machine is a saving of more than one-third the labor when it cuts and rakes. . . . The threshing machine is a saving of two-thirds on the old hand flail mode. . . . The saving in the labor of handling hay in the field and barn by means of horserakes and horsehayforks is equal to one-half."

It was doubtless this saving in labor which made possible the great added expense to the farmer of the new machinery.

SCIENTIFIC FARMING

In England the work of Arthur Young, Jethro Tull, Viscount Townshend, Robert Bakewell, and others in the eighteenth century had demonstrated to Englishmen what might be done in the way of scientific farming. Little interest was shown in agricultural improvements in the colonies, and

[15] *The Farmer's Companion* (ed. of 1839), p. 123, quoted by P. W. Bidwell and J. I. Falconer, *op. cit.*, p. 281. Harry Carman (ed.), *Jesse Buel*, contains many excerpts from *The Farmer's Companion*.

it was not until after the Revolution that many wealthy American farmers became interested in better methods. The lead was taken by planters like Washington and Jefferson, who were farmers on a large scale and intensely interested in agricultural experiments. Washington, who has been described as "not only the greatest man, but the greatest agriculturist of the period," turned from tobacco raising to an intensive cultivation of other products. He was the founder of the mule-raising industry in the country, the fine Kentucky breed of later years descending directly from the best asses of France and Spain sent him as presents by Lafayette and the king of Spain. His experiments in sheep raising, continued by George Washington Parke Custis, did much to better the breed of sheep in the South. A few of the excellent merino sheep had been smuggled out of Spain, but it was not until the Napoleonic Wars that it was possible to obtain them in large numbers. Jefferson and Robert Livingston were especially interested in the introduction and wide distribution of merinos, a mania for which swept the country in the years 1810–1816. A "strange and incomprehensible infatuation," commented Birkbeck. "There is not a district, scarcely a spot that I have travelled over, where a flock of fine wooled sheep could be kept with any prospect of advantage, provided there were even a market for the carcase. Yet by the ragged remains of the merino family, which may be recognized in many places, I perceive that the attempt has been very general."[16] The importation of merinos and other breeds nevertheless greatly improved the stock.

A similar improvement also took place in the quality and size of cattle. English shorthorn or Durham cattle were imported into Kentucky in 1817, and in succeeding years great numbers were bought by farmers who desired to better their stock. Henry Clay in 1817 imported the first Herefords, but this breed did not develop rapidly until it was found adaptable to the Texas ranges in the seventies. Other standard breeds were imported and farmers came to take more interest in bettering their herds. Since the usual mode of travel, at least until 1840, was by horseback, excellent horses were imported and developed in this country. Kentucky early became the great center of horse raising and there the breeders specialized in a good saddle horse with easy motion and a rapid walk.

Knowledge of these superior breeds, of the new inventions, and of the improved methods of tillage was disseminated by five means: agricultural societies, agricultural fairs, farm periodicals and literature, agricultural schools, and government aid. The beginnings of all of these are to be found in this period. The Philadelphia Society for Promoting Agriculture was founded in 1785 and included in its membership Washington and Franklin. Similar so-

[16] Morris Birkbeck, *Notes on a Journey in America*, pp. 87, 88.

cieties were founded in five other states before 1800.[17] The first half of the
century saw other organizations springing up all over the country, whose
purpose was to spread information, lend mutual aid, and stimulate improved
methods by holding fairs and offering prizes—pioneers in the great task of
agricultural education.

A distinguishing feature of American agricultural life is the county fair.
The first agricultural fair was held in Washington in 1804, but the idea took
root chiefly through the influence of Elkanah Watson, who in 1807 exhibited
two merino sheep in the public square of Pittsfield, Massachusetts, and who
three years later persuaded some of his neighbors to join him in an exhibition
of livestock on the village green. From this exhibition came the Berkshire
Agricultural Society, the first permanent fair association in America. Watson
pushed his idea in other states and similar societies were rapidly founded.
The first state aid for agricultural fairs was granted by New York in 1819,
when $20,000 was appropriated for two years. The United States Patent Of-
fice in 1858 printed a list of over 900 agricultural societies, most of which
were state or county organizations that existed for the purpose of holding
fairs. The interchange of ideas, the new information obtained, and the rivalry
promoted by these fairs made them of great importance, especially during
this period, in demonstrating the worth of the new machinery.

Agricultural journalism sprang up along with the associations and fairs.
Its real beginning dates from 1819, when John S. Skinner founded *The
American Farmer* at Baltimore, a weekly paper which enjoyed continuous
publication until 1833—a venture quickly imitated in other parts of the
country. Of these papers, perhaps the best in the East was *The Cultivator*
(1834–1853), founded in Albany by Jesse Buel, and in the West *The Prairie
Farmer,* founded in 1840.

Agricultural education in America undoubtedly had its start with special
instruction in the existing schools, perhaps the first being the establishment
in 1792 of a professorship of natural history, chemistry, and agriculture at
Columbia University. The first institution devoted principally to the teaching
of agriculture was the Gardiner Lyceum, established in 1822 at Gardiner,
Maine, which for the next ten years maintained its distinctive agricultural
character. Other schools were founded with the same purpose in view, but
agricultural education had to wait on state aid before it became a real factor.
The state constitution of Michigan, adopted in 1850, provided for a college

[17] The Philadelphia Society for Promoting Arts, "mainly for improving agriculture," had
been founded twenty years before, as well as a similar society in Pennsylvania, but little is known
of their activities. The New Jersey Society for Promoting Agriculture, Commerce and Arts
was established as early as 1781. See Carl Raymond Woodward, *The Development of Agriculture in New Jersey, 1640–1880* (1927), pp. 51–52.

of agriculture. In accordance with this provision the legislature appropriated $40,000 for buildings, instruction, and maintenance, and in 1857 a state college of agriculture was opened, the first institution of its kind in America. Two years later Maryland and Pennsylvania followed the example of Michigan in establishing state-supported institutions. The great growth of agricultural education, however, followed the passing of the Morrill Act in 1862.

National aid to agriculture began in 1839, when Congress appropriated $1000 to be expended by the Commissioner of Patents for the collection of statistics and investigations for the promotion of agriculture. After 1842, with the exception of one year, gradually increasing appropriations were made for this purpose. Annual agricultural reports were printed after 1854. Agricultural matters were handled by the Patent Department until 1862, when a separate Bureau of Agriculture was set up. These modest beginnings of federal and state interest in the problems of the farmer hardly presaged the immense government activity in recent years.

AGRICULTURAL TRENDS, 1783–1860

In this brief review of American agriculture during the period from 1783 to the outbreak of the Civil War three great developments stand out. First of all there was the great expansion of the farming area which was to cover the larger part of the Mississippi Valley and turn America into the greatest agricultural region in the world. In the second place there was a rapid development of agricultural specialization in which specialized commercial agriculture in well-defined areas was taking the place of the self-sufficient farm. Finally there was the real beginning in America of scientific agriculture and the mechanization of farm methods.

In many ways these years were the brightest in American agricultural history. This was an era of confident expansion in which the future seemed secure. Widening markets in Europe kept pace with expanding farm areas in this country. Factories abroad and at home absorbed the cotton crop and industrial centers purchased foodstuffs. Except for panic periods prices were generally higher and farmers were able in turn to buy the products of forge and factory. In the South slaves, the chief property of the plantation owner, rose in value, and in the Old Northwest the rapid settlement combined with good prices pushed up the value of lands. In such a situation it was natural that the talent of the nation should turn to scientific improvements, to the invention of farm machinery, and to agricultural education. Agriculture was the nation's primary interest. Transportation facilities were developed and industry was organized to serve its needs. The period, in truth, was America's agricultural era.

SELECTED READINGS

Bidwell, P. S., and Falconer, J. I., *History of Agriculture in the Northern United States, 1620–1860,* chaps. 11–25.

Gray, L. C., *History of Agriculture in the Southern United States to 1860,* chaps. 27, 39.

Hutchinson, W. T., *Cyrus Hall McCormick,* chaps. 3, 4, 7, 8.

Edwards, E. E., "Agriculture—The First Hundred Years," *Yearbook of Agriculture, 1940,* pp. 190–232.

Hammond, M. B., *The Cotton Industry,* chaps. 1–3.

Flügel, F., and Faulkner, H. U., *Readings in the Economic and Social History of the United States,* pp. 153–187.

CHAPTER 12

THE MERCHANT MARINE AND
FOREIGN COMMERCE

POSTWAR REVIVAL

THE significance of the maritime industries and foreign commerce in the colonial period has already been stressed, as have the activities of privateers during the Revolution. Note has also been made of the opening of the three-cornered China trade in the 1780's.[1] Commerce with the Far East ushered in the golden age of American shipping, but it was not the Canton market alone which lured the venturesome and aggressive sea captains in the decades after 1790. Merchantmen from the coast towns carried the American flag into every port where Yankee ingenuity could secure access or trading ability secure profits. These were the years before foreign commerce had developed the complicated structure of later times. Merchant capitalists largely dominated coastwise and foreign trade; they purchased the commodities to be sold, built and owned their own ships, and sent them out under their own agent, the captain or the supercargo, who traded back and forth wherever profits seemed most likely. These trips were important ventures, sometimes lasting two or three years.

Sensitive in the extreme as merchant shipping is to outside influences, the favorable reaction occasioned by the adoption of the Constitution, by tonnage taxes imposed on foreign vessels, by the establishment of public credit, and by increased demand for American products resulting from the European wars was nevertheless astonishing. The tonnage registered for foreign trade jumped from 123,893 in 1789 to 981,000 in 1810. The imports carried in American bottoms—the most important method of determining the real prosperity of a merchant marine—increased during the same period from 17.5 per cent to 93 per cent, and exports in American bottoms from 30 to 90 per cent.

[1] Above, p. 145.

Shipping interests had been among the most ardent in supporting the new Constitution, and the first Congress hastened to their protection. The first act passed by the first Congress (with the exception of a formal statute with reference to the taking of oaths) was the act of July 4, 1789, which, although designed for the "encouragement and protection of manufacturers" and for obtaining revenue, gave real aid to shipping by allowing a discount of 10 per cent in the tariff duties on imports brought to this country in ships built and owned by American citizens. In order to encourage the newly developed trade with the Far East, this same act allowed a reduction in the duty on tea imported direct from the East. This made the tariff paid by the American ship less than half that of the foreign vessel, and at the same time dealt a blow to the East India Company by placing high duties on tea bought in Europe, even if imported in American ships. The next act of the same Congress, that of July 20, 1789, imposed a duty of six cents a ton on American-built ships owned by Americans upon entering our ports, but charged thirty cents a ton on American-built ships owned by foreigners and fifty cents a ton on foreign-built and -owned ships. It was provided at the same time that American ships in the coastwise trade should pay tonnage duty only once a year, while foreign ships must pay it at every entry. This act presaged the early absorption of the coastwise trade by American ships.

An act of 1790 on the government and regulation of seamen provided a code of law in advance of the time. It stipulated that a written contract must be entered into between master and seamen specifying the voyage and rate of wages; without this no master could have full control of his men. He was also required to pay them the highest current wages, with the ship itself as a guaranty. Masters were liable to severe penalties for abandoning American sailors in a foreign country (often evaded), and seamen who signed articles and deserted their ship might forfeit their wages and be brought back under compulsion. With but few changes, this was the basis of the law covering seamen until the salutary modifications of the La Follette Act of 1915. The development of a strong merchant marine was also aided by the creation in 1798 of an American Navy, which repeatedly gave a good account of itself in the succeeding years.

Much of the remarkable growth in shipping was absorbed in the first years of this period in the Far Eastern trade, but when the energies of the European nations were taken up with the Napoleonic Wars, American merchantmen were to be found wherever business was to be obtained. "The unfolding of the great West," says Marvin, "had scarcely begun. . . . Not only did most of the American people live within reach of the ocean, but the ocean everywhere seemed to be the nearest, the most natural, and the most inviting field of adventure. It was true of many more American towns than tide-encircled Boston that 'Each street leads down to the sea.' Down these streets went most of the young men who had dreams in their heads and iron in their blood, and they always found ships waiting."[2] It was the day when "the streets of London, the quays of Lisbon, and the Hong of Canton were more familiar sights to the merchants of the coast than were the somber forests and stump-studded clearings of Western America."[3] "At the end of 1793," says Ugo Rabbeno, "the tonnage of the United States exceeded that of every other nation except England; their foreign trade ranked in point of value next to that of England, and, proportionally to the population, the United States was the first commercial nation of the world."[4] Between 1795 and 1801 the average annual net earnings of the American merchant marine were believed to exceed $32,000,000.

The two decades after 1789 were not, however, years of peaceful and uninterrupted development. During practically the entire period we were in difficulties with our chief rivals, England and France, and between 1801 and 1805 our tiny Navy engaged in war with Tripolitan pirates in defense of our merchant marine. In 1792 war broke out between France and Austria, a war which was eventually to involve all Europe and to continue, with but two short interruptions, until 1815. The superiority of the British Navy was soon apparent and it was not long until the merchantmen of France and her allies had entirely disappeared from the sea. The result was to throw the carrying trade of France into the hands of American merchantmen flying the flag of the only neutral nation of importance on the ocean. While all Europe was engaged in a life-and-death struggle, Yankee merchants and shipowners reaped handsome profits from transporting the products of the French, Dutch, and Spanish colonies, as well as trading with Britain and France.

Britain, eager to break up the trade with her enemies and weaken her new rival on the sea, forbade trade with her enemies' colonies. Especially irritating was her claim that British sailors found on American ships might be taken and forced to serve on British men-of-war. In the later years of the war, as seamen became scarcer, she became more and more unscrupulous in her use of this alleged right; the State Department believed that in 1806 and 1807 as many as 6000 American seamen were serving under compulsion in the British Navy. As to the number of impressed seamen who were American-born it is impossible to know. English sailors, intrigued by higher wages and better conditions, were deserting by the thousands. "Every English vessel," says Henry Adams, "which entered a Virginia port was at once abandoned by her crew, who hastened to enter the public or private ships of the United

[2] W. L. Marvin, *The American Merchant Marine*, p. 43.
[3] C. and M. Beard, *Rise of American Civilization*, I, 400.
[4] Ugo Rabbeno, *The American Colonial Policy*, p. 141.

States. The captain of any British frigate which might happen to run into the harbor of New York, if he went ashore, was likely to meet on his return to the wharf some of his boat's crew strolling about the town, every man supplied with papers of American citizenship."[5] As England at this time did not recognize the alienation of nationality, she resented this on legal as well as practical grounds.

Although the chief trouble was with Britain, the first actual fighting was with France. Believing that under the Treaty of 1778 we were duty bound to help her in her war with Great Britain, she resented Washington's neutrality proclamation, violated our neutrality, and insulted our government. The result was an undeclared war (1798–1800) with naval engagements and the capture of many French privateers. Despite interference from British warships, French privateersmen, and Tripolitan pirates, the years 1792–1807 were exceedingly prosperous, not only for the merchant marine, but for the nation as a whole. The rapid increase in exports was made up chiefly of provisions, a market for which had been created by the war. Europe, too busy fighting to raise sufficient foodstuffs, called increasingly upon America to furnish grain and meat, as well as such raw materials as cotton, wool, and leather. While the prices of foodstuffs and raw materials soared, farmers reaped a golden harvest, shared by the shippers who transported the products and the merchants who during these prosperous years were able to dispose of increasing amounts of imported goods. Sailors' wages rose from eight to thirty dollars a month and foreigners became naturalized in order to partake of the huge profits of American shipowners. The whole situation was remarkably similar to the early years of the First World War, 1914–1917, when the United States as the great neutral profited from supplying foodstuffs and other products to the warring nations.

This period of prosperity ended in 1807. In the European war France was master of the Continent and Britain mistress of the sea. Britain between 1804 and 1807 declared a blockade of northern Europe from the Elbe to Brest and forbade neutral vessels' landing at the ports of France or her allies without touching and paying duties at an English port. Napoleon replied by decrees declaring the British Islands under blockade and threatening ships who stopped there liable to seizure. Largely a paper blockade by France and but inadequately enforced by Britain, the loss to Americans, nevertheless, was severe. This utter disregard of neutral rights accompanied by such virtual acts of war as the firing on the American frigate *Chesapeake* by a British man-of-war finally aroused Jefferson to action.

Anxious to preserve peace, Jefferson believed that Europe could be brought to terms by an embargo. On his advice Congress in December, 1807, passed

[5] Henry Adams, *History of the United States of America*, II, 334–335.

an Embargo Act which prohibited American ships from sailing to foreign ports and permitted coasting trade only under condition that the owner give bonds double the value of the cargo that it would be relanded in the United States. Instead, however, of starving Great Britain into submission, the act bade fair to ruin our own shipping. American exports dropped from $108,-343,150 in 1807 to $22,430,960 in 1808; imports, from $138,500,000 to $56,990,-000. New York, said a British traveler at that time, "was full of shipping, but they were dismantled and laid up. Their decks were cleared, their hatches fastened down, and scarcely a sailor was to be found on board. Not a box, bale, cask, barrel, or package, was to be seen upon the wharves. Many of the counting houses were shut up or advertised to be let; and the few solitary merchants, clerks, porters, and laborers that were to be seen, were walking about with their hands in their pockets. . . . The coffee-houses were almost empty; . . . The streets near the waterside were almost deserted; the grass had begun to grow upon the wharves. . . ."[6] The testimony of this traveler may not have been unprejudiced, but McMaster estimates that 55,000 sailors and 100,000 mechanics and laborers were thrown out of work and that during the period of the Embargo Act ships lost $12,500,000 in net earnings. The customs revenues sank from $16,000,000 to a few thousand.

The losses sustained by the shipping interests as a result of the Embargo Act were colossal, especially in New England, where 100 Massachusetts towns adopted resolutions against it. Smuggling was rampant and from certain New England ports "loaded vessels literally fought their way to the sea," for New Englanders found that they could carry on a prosperous commerce notwithstanding the many adverse factors. In spite of widespread opposition, Jefferson's theory of an economic boycott was a sound one, and there is evidence pointing to the fact that, if it had been continued long enough, it might have accomplished the desired result. Subsequent nonintercourse or embargo measures did bring success. Britain repealed her Orders in Council in 1812, unaware that this country had declared war a few days earlier.[7]

The pressure of the shipping interests, however, was so strong that in March, 1809, the Embargo Act was repealed, and for it was substituted the Nonintercourse Act, which prohibited trade only with Great Britain and France and their possessions. This act was repealed in 1810, and new legislation, called the Macon Bill, was enacted; this provided that as soon as either England or France withdrew her decrees against our shipping, the Nonintercourse Act would be revived against the other country. Napoleon immediately announced (August 5, 1810) that his decrees were repealed, and Madi-

[6] John Lambert, *Travels Through Canada and the United States of North America in the Years 1806, 1807 and 1808* (1810), II, 65.

[7] This is told in full in W. W. Jennings, *The American Embargo* (1921), and L. M. Sears, *Jefferson and the Embargo* (1927).

son issued a proclamation reviving the Nonintercourse Act against England if she did not repeal the Orders in Council before February 2, 1811. She ignored the proclamation and Napoleon, in spite of his announced repeal of the decrees, continued, as before, to seize and rob American ships wherever he could lay hands on them. Nevertheless, the years 1809 and 1810 showed increases in both imports and exports and the registered tonnage in foreign trade reached 981,019 tons in 1810, a mark not equaled again until 1847. In spite of all the setbacks and discouragements, it had been a period of remarkable growth and prosperity, the worst blow being the Embargo Act imposed by our own government.

THE WAR OF 1812

The year 1811 found the United States fast drifting into a war with England. Although France and England had both apparently vied with each other in heaping insults upon our government and bringing losses upon our shipping, it was the latter nation that was in a position to enforce her attitude and to cause the most trouble. In order to give merchantmen a chance to reach a safe harbor, Congress imposed a third embargo in the spring of 1812 and on June 18 declared war. The causes, as reviewed by Madison in his message of June 1, were violations of our flag on the high seas, confiscation of our ships, illegal impressment of seamen, blockade of our ports, the obnoxious Orders in Council, and the inciting of Indians against our borders. All but one of them had to do with violations of the rights of American merchantmen; yet it was the young "War Hawks" of the South and West, led by Henry Clay, who urged the war in Congress, and the representatives of western farmers and plantation owners whose votes made it possible. Agriculture, like shipping, had suffered from interference with commerce, for the produce of the farms and plantations comprised a large part of our exports. It was the decline of the prices of agricultural commodities that was the all-important underlying cause and for this farmers and planters rightly held Great Britain responsible.[8] But it was also the Indian menace and the desire to annex Florida and Canada that fed the flames of the war spirit rising along the whole frontier. "Agrarian cupidity," cried John Randolph, "not maritime right urges the war. Ever since the report of the Committee on

[8] The causes of the War of 1812 have been discussed at length in J. W. Pratt, *Expansionists of 1812* (1925). While he proves an overwhelming desire to conquer Canada, he attributes the reason to an anxiety to eradicate the Indian menace rather than to mere "land hunger." He fails, however, to take into adequate consideration the influence of the agricultural depression, a factor which has been emphasized by George R. Taylor in "Agrarian Discontent in the Mississippi Valley Preceding the War of 1812," *Journal of Political Economy*, XXXIX, 471–505 (Aug., 1931). Conflicting theories of the causes are discussed in W. H. Goodman, "The Origins of the War of 1812: A Survey of Changing Interpretations," *Mississippi Valley Historical Review*, XXVIII, 171–186 (Sept., 1941).

Foreign Relations came into the House, we have heard but one word—like the whip-poor-will, but one eternal monotonous tone—Canada! Canada! Canada!"[9]

On the other hand, New England, which had been most disastrously affected by the British acts, bitterly opposed the war, many believing that it "originated in hatred to *New England* and to commerce; in subservience to the mandate of the Tyrant of *France.*"[10] Federalist statesmen believed that new agrarian empires arising in the West as a result of the war would further jeopardize the waning influence of the seaboard states. Not only did New England in certain instances refuse to fight or lend money to carry on the war, but she actually rendered aid to the British and made preliminary movements toward secession. In England the result of the embargoes had been to raise the cost of food. With war in sight the Orders in Council were withdrawn five days after war had been declared in the United States. Modern cables might have prevented the conflict.

The War of 1812 was primarily a war on the sea. With the exception of the battle of New Orleans, which was fought after peace had been signed, the conflicts on land were of minor importance and were usually unsuccessful to American arms. Before the declaration of war both Clay and Calhoun had talked glibly of the ease with which the militia would capture Canada, but all attempts to invade that region met with utter failure. On the other hand, the American Navy of but twenty-three vessels of all classes gave an excellent account of itself, capturing 254 naval and merchant ships of the enemy before being destroyed or shut up in American harbors. By the end of the war the British Navy, numbering at that time about 1000 ships, had effectually blockaded the American coast and captured some 1400 merchant vessels and fishing boats. Exports dropped from $61,317,000 in 1811 to $6,927,000 in 1814; imports during the same period from $53,400,000 to $12,965,000. The most effective work on the American side was done by the privateersmen, who took 1300 prizes valued at $39,000,000. The self-reliant American seaman, realizing that he was fighting his own battle, was at his best aboard a privateer.

To Britain, concerned mainly with the last efforts of the Napoleonic Wars, the American struggle was a side issue. But the war had occupied much of her Navy, her losses from American privateers had been tremendous, and the lack of American commodities had pushed food prices in England to fantastic heights. The war, in fact, was a stalemate, and peace was signed December 27, 1814. The treaty made no mention of the causes of the war—

[9] *Annals of Congress,* 12th Cong., I, 533.

[10] Declaration of a Barnstable County Peace Convention, quoted by S. E. Morison, *The Maritime History of Massachusetts,* p. 198.

impressments, right of search, or blockades—but with the removal of the causes and the record our seamen had made in asserting their rights, it seemed unlikely that the latter would soon again be called into question. What immediate gains there were came to the West, where the Indian power in the Northwest and Southwest was effectually broken and the way prepared for the annexation of Florida and a rapid extension of the frontier.

The natural reaction after the war was immediately felt. The conclusion of peace released shipping and the registered tonnage for foreign trade went up from 674,600 in 1814 to 824,300 in 1815. Exports increased from $6,927,400 in 1814 to $93,281,100 in 1818; imports from $12,965,000 in 1814 to $147,103,000 in 1816. This sudden prosperity was not entirely healthy. The flood of imports glutted the market and forced many manufacturing concerns which had been established during the war to suspend operations. This, combined with the disturbed and unsettled financial condition, brought in 1818 a sharp decrease in tonnage registered in foreign trade, and in 1819 a marked decrease in both exports and imports.

The years immediately following the war marked the beginning of legislation to establish commerce on the principle of reciprocity. The act of March 3, 1815, provided that all discriminating duties imposed by former laws on the tonnage of foreign vessels or the goods imported therein would be repealed in the case of any foreign nation that abolished its discriminating and countervailing duties against us. On the other hand, an act was passed in 1817, in imitation of the European navigation laws, forbidding the importation of goods from any foreign port except in American vessels or vessels of the country from which the goods came, and at the same time closing the coasting trade to foreign vessels, but providing for repeal in the case of nations that removed such restrictions upon our vessels. An act of 1828 provided for reciprocity with foreign nations in the indirect carrying trade. The result of these three acts was a long series of reciprocal treaties with foreign nations, commencing with the treaty of July 3, 1815, with Great Britain, which abolished differential duties with respect to direct trade between the two countries. This was followed by treaties with France in 1822 and Prussia in 1828, guaranteeing reciprocal liberty in commerce, and in the succeeding years with most of the countries of Europe and Central and South America It was not until 1830 that England opened the West Indian ports to the United States commerce, and the restrictions of the act of 1817 against her were removed.

REVIVAL AND DECLINE

The years 1820 to 1830 witnessed a second period of remarkable growth and prosperity. Although the amount of tonnage registered in foreign trade did not equal that of 1815–1817 or the figures of the next two decades, the proportion of American carriage in the foreign trade reached 92.5 per cent in 1826, a larger percentage than has been attained before or since. J. R. Soley maintains that "in every respect we may say that this period represents the most flourishing condition of shipping in American history."[11] Not only were we carrying practically all of our own goods, but the reputation of Yankee

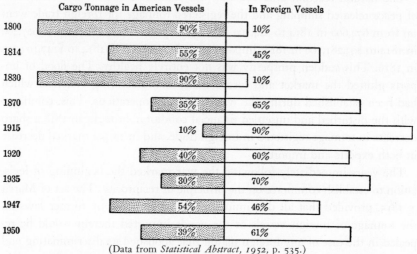

(Data from *Statistical Abstract, 1952,* p. 535.)

CARGO PERCENTAGE OF EXPORTS AND IMPORTS IN AMERICAN VESSELS.

The proportion of a nation's commerce carried in its own merchant marine is a good index of the prosperity of that merchant marine. The golden era of our shipping was before the Civil War, after which came a rapid decline. Shortages occasioned by both the First and Second World Wars brought a new revival.

shipbuilders for turning out models which in speed, strength, and durability surpassed any vessels to be found brought about the sale between 1815 and 1840 of 540,000 tons of shipping to foreigners. A fully equipped 500-ton sailing vessel cost $37,500 in America and $43,000 in England. Generations of New England shipbuilding had produced the most skilled artisans in the world, and northern Europe had lost many of her shipwrights, drawn here by higher wages. To man these ships there were the aggressive and intelligent Yankee sailors, who appeared equally at home on the cod banks, in the whaling ships, or on the rigging of a transatlantic packet. Notwithstanding higher wages, it cost less to run an American vessel, for a smaller crew was carried.

[11] In N. S. Shaler (ed.), *The United States of America,* chapter, "The Maritime Industries of America," I, 539.

It was during this decade that the development of the packet ship occurred. The first line of sail packets, the Black Ball Line, had been founded in 1816 between New York and Liverpool. A second line to Liverpool began operation in 1822, and soon other lines to London and Le Havre. These packets, larger and better than the ordinary merchant ships, specialized in high-grade freight and passenger traffic. They made their trips regularly, sometimes in eighteen or twenty days, and were especially designed for transatlantic work. They were the predecessors of the present steam lines and their service was so excellent that they remained in operation long after the steamship became dominant.

With all this prosperity it should be remembered that tonnage in foreign trade was less in 1830 than in 1820, and that with the increasing population there was a relative falling off in per capita tonnage from 12.54 cubic feet in 1807 and 13.43 in 1810 to 4.25 in 1839 and 8.63 in 1855, the date marking the highest point of the clipper-ship era. Most of the elements which contributed to the later rapid decline were already making themselves felt.

In the history of ocean navigation the decades from 1830 to 1860 marked the most important advance that the world had yet seen. By this time the Industrial Revolution was well under way and world tonnage increased rapidly, as did the size of ships. The typical merchant ships of the 1850's were three times the size of those built in the 1820's. Farsighted shipbuilders turned from wooden to iron ships and equipped them with steam power rather than sails. These years were also significant in the history of the American merchant marine. Although registered tonnage in foreign trade increased, the percentage of our trade carried in American bottoms fell.[12] The American merchant marine was definitely on the decline.

Robert Fulton had demonstrated the practicability of steam as a motive force for propelling ships in his memorable voyage up the Hudson in 1807, and steam craft were on the Mississippi as early as 1812.[13] Notwithstanding the fact that the *Savannah,* a 300-ton vessel built in New York and equipped with steam as well as sails, had made a twenty-seven-day trip across the Atlantic in 1819, eighty hours of which she traveled under steam, it was generally considered that steamboats were adaptable only for river and coast navigation. A chief difficulty was the space required for fuel. The utilization of anthracite coal and the invention of the screw propeller, both of which occurred in the thirties, hastened an inevitable development.

Englishmen had been experimenting with steam packets on short services to Rotterdam, Hamburg, and Gibraltar for a number of years before the *Sirius* and the *Great Western* in 1838 made the trip to New York by steam

[12] See graph, p. 226.
[13] See chap. 14.

only in seventeen and a half and fifteen days, respectively. These records proved that wooden side-wheeled steamers could make the trip in a shorter time than the fastest sailing packet. The British government was farsighted enough to realize that the motive power of the immediate future was steam, and in 1839 it heavily subsidized the Cunard Company, which began its career in 1840 with four side-wheeled wooden ships. This policy of subsidization, which has been continued to the present time by Great Britain, aided materially not only in giving her maritime interests a start in the new type of ships but in helping them win and hold supremacy on the ocean.

Almost as revolutionary as the gradual substitution of steam for sailing vessels was the very gradual substitution of iron and later steel ships for those of wood. With an abundance of coal and iron close to the sea, with skilled mechanics and cheap labor, and with a metallurgical industry developed far in advance of ours, Great Britain forged ahead from the start. By 1853 one-fourth of the total tonnage built there were steamships, and more than one-fourth were made of iron. In the same year 22 per cent of our tonnage was constructed for steamships, but scarcely any iron ships were built here. The Yankee shipbuilder, overconfident in the recognized superiority of his inimitable clipper ship, was blind to the fact that the future of the sea was for the nation which could build the cheapest and best iron steamships. The clipper was fast but uneconomical. Built of wood, it could not be expanded indefinitely. Moreover, steamships in the long run were to prove safer and even faster than the beautiful clipper.

The thirty years from 1830 to 1860 were characterized by extremely rapid production in shipbuilding. The 538,136 tons registered in foreign trade in 1831 increased to 2,496,894 in 1862, a figure that represented the culmination of our shipbuilding tonnage until surpassed in World War I. From 1848 to 1858 shipbuilding was maintained at an average of 400,000 tons a year. This construction was caused, in the first place, by the development after 1845 of the above-mentioned justly famous American clipper ship, the fastest sailing ship afloat, an extraordinary product of decades of shipbuilding and the intense rivalry between steam and canvas. Designed for speed, the clipper was built on sharp lines and carried a maximum of canvas. She was intended primarily for long voyages and was used especially for the California and Far Eastern trade. Given a fair breeze, she could outdistance a steamship. It was not uncommon for a clipper to sail over 300 miles a day; the *Flying Cloud* on a ninety-day run to San Francisco made 374 miles on one day. The *Comet,* on an eighty-day voyage from San Francisco to New York, averaged 210 miles a day. Records of eighty-six days from Singapore to New York and eighty-four from Canton to New York were made between 1851 and 1853. It appeared that the American shipbuilder, before he relinquished his supremacy, was intent upon demonstrating the heights of efficiency and speed to which a sailing ship could attain.[14]

In the second place, there was an increased demand for shipping. This was occasioned chiefly by the discovery in 1848 of gold in California. The overland routes were slow and perilous, and the demand for passage and shipments to the Golden Gate swamped accommodations. The Yankee packet could make the trip around the Horn in about three months, thus giving a prolonged lease of life to the building of sailing ships. The wars between Great Britain and China in 1840–1842 and 1856–1860 threw a part of the China trade into American hands. The revolutionary outbreaks of 1848 interrupted European trade, with a resulting benefit to Americans; and the Crimean War, for which many European boats were engaged in transporting troops and supplies, gave new openings to American ships. In addition, the natural increase in commerce due to the growth in population, wealth, and production necessitated increased shipping. Our exports increased from $19,-012,000 in 1791 to $333,576,000 in 1860, almost two-thirds of which was cotton. Imports increased during this same period from $29,200,000 to $353,616,-000. Increasing immigration also contributed to the demand for shipping facilities.

Notwithstanding these demands, there was a decidedly unhealthy element in this remarkable activity in shipbuilding. In the first place the demand from Europe resulting from the Crimean War was abnormal; between 1854 and 1859 the European nations were buying here 50,000 tons of shipping as against 10,000 tons in normal years. Furthermore, the increase in the building of sailing ships unfortunately came at a time when their days were numbered, for between 1850 and 1860 the share of ocean freight carried by steamers increased from 14 to 28 per cent. When the abnormal demand for sailing ships abated, as it did in 1858, it meant that shipyards built and equipped to produce wooden ships and shipwrights trained for a type no longer in demand would be idle, and that foreign shipyards already engaged in building iron steamships would be in a superior position. The panic of 1857 precipitated the crash. In 1858 the shipbuilding output, which had been maintained for the preceding ten years at an average of 400,000 tons a year, dropped to 244,-000 and in 1859 to 156,000. At the same time the combined imports and exports carried in American bottoms were steadily declining, only 65.2 per cent being carried in 1861 as against 92.5 per cent in 1826.

[14] It is believed that the lines of the clipper ship were originally derived from a type of Chinese coasting vessel known as the "Singapore fast boat," a half-block model of which (now in the Clark Collection at the Massachusetts Institute of Technology) was brought from China by Captain R. H. Waterman. The first clipper in this country, the *Rainbow,* was designed by John W. Griffiths and built in New York. The greatest of the clipper ships, including the *Flying Cloud,* were built in Massachusetts by Donald McKay, a Nova Scotian trained in the shipyards of Isaac Webb in New York.

The decline of the American merchant marine was by no means due solely to British subsidies and the technological superiority of iron steamships. Many other factors were involved. In the first place the importance of certain of the old trade routes declined. The great revival of the carrying trade after the Revolution was to no small extent the result of the opening of the China trade and of the Napoleonic Wars. The wars were over by 1815. The China trade declined with the disappearance of the sea otter, with the substitution in America of European porcelain for Chinese pottery, and with the change in the styles of men's clothes which no longer demanded large quantities of silk. Only tea remained as an important article of Far Eastern commerce and its importance was waning as Brazilian coffee replaced tea as the national drink. Even the West Indian trade which had been the backbone of colonial commerce fell off. Nor did the Treaty of 1830, which opened the British West Indian ports to American ships, revive it. As opportunities lessened, profits became smaller and more uncertain. Great fortunes had been made in the Far Eastern trade in the early years of the century and profits were fair a half-century later in the California trade, but as a whole commerce and shipping no longer offered outstanding opportunities.

As chances for profit declined in shipping, capital found new and more profitable fields for investment. Manufacturing, which grew rapidly after the War of 1812, absorbed some of it; and considerable amounts were drawn into such internal improvements as canals and railways. The minds of the venturous and ambitious turned from the sea to the unexploited West, and capital turned from shipbuilding and the carrying trade to the development of natural resources. The elements contributing to the decline of the merchant marine were already apparent before the Civil War, and the result would undoubtedly have been the same if that conflict had not occurred. The war, however, accentuated a tendency already existing and dealt a blow from which the merchant marine failed to recover until artificially revived during the First World War. In 1861 registered American tonnage in foreign trade amounted to 2,496,894 tons and in 1865 to 1,518,350, and the percentage of imports and exports carried in American ships dropped in the same years from 66.2 to 27.7. The decrease of some 900,000 tons in the war years was due chiefly to two causes. The first was the loss sustained from Confederate cruisers such as the *Alabama,* built and fitted out in England contrary to the laws of warfare. The second and more important was the sale during the four years 1862–1865 of 751,595 tons of shipping abroad, occasioned by lack of confidence, the decline in profits caused by continual Confederate captures and high insurance rates, and the decline in the export business resulting from the cessation of cotton shipments abroad.

WHALING AND FISHING

The whaling industry was definitely retarded during the Revolution and the Continental wars, 1775–1815, but revived after Napoleon's final defeat. The recorded tonnage had increased from practically nothing in 1814 to 35,-000 tons in 1820, and then steadily, during the golden age of the industry, to 198,000 in 1858. After that year the decline set in. Before 1791 whaling had been confined to the Atlantic, but gradually cruises were extended into other oceans; after 1835 the industry was largely confined to the Pacific. Almost the entire whaling fleet hailed from New York and New England. Sag Harbor, New York, boasted sixty-three vessels in 1846, though the great center was New Bedford, Massachusetts, and the smaller towns close by; their fleet numbered over 200 vessels in 1857 and employed over 10,000 seamen. Nantucket ranked second and New London third as whaling ports during this period, the former relinquishing her colonial supremacy because of the shallow harbor which prevented the entrance of the large vessels. Many of the coast towns engaged in the traffic on a smaller scale and derived rich profits. Boston and New York were the chief exporting centers; the leading foreign markets for sperm oil were the West Indies, South America, and northern Europe; and for whalebone France, England, and the Baltic region. The larger part of the oil product was absorbed in the domestic market. During the height of its prosperity the products of the whaling industry surpassed in value those of all the rest of the fishing industry combined. In New England whaling ranked next to textiles and boots and shoes. The average annual production from 1835 to 1860 was 118,000 barrels of sperm oil, 216,000 barrels of whale oil, and 2,324,000 pounds of whalebone, with an average annual value of about $8,000,000. After 1850 the decline was rapid, owing partly to the growing scarcity of whales but chiefly to the increased use of mineral oils and gas as illuminants.

The cod-fishing industry suffered the same early setbacks as whaling experienced during the two wars of independence, but eventually recovered after the passage of a series of laws that remitted most of the duty on the imported salt which was used. The registered tonnage engaged in cod fishing increased from 25,000 in 1790 to 136,700 in 1860. In that year close to 2500 vessels with crews numbering 18,000 were fishing for cod, the annual value of which was about $3,000,000. After 1818 an increasing number of vessels went out after mackerel, the maximum tonnage before 1860 reaching 73,800 in 1849. During this period, also, commercial fishing for herring, halibut, and oysters began. Maine and Massachusetts monopolized the cod fishing, the catch being about evenly divided between them. The two chief centers were

Portland and Castine, Maine, and Gloucester and Marblehead, Massachusetts. The latter state sent out the major part of the mackerel fleet. Despite the expanding fishing fleets and large catches, the fishing industry never attained the relative economic importance that it held throughout the colonial period.

COMMODITIES AND PAYMENTS

Foreign commerce quickly re-established itself in the decade after the Revolution and by 1790 its value amounted to more than three times that of the 1760's. As a result of the increased European demand for foodstuffs and raw materials during the Napoleonic Wars, its value had again more than

IMPORTS AND EXPORTS BY DECADES

Year	Total Exports	Total Imports
1790	$ 20,200,000	$ 23,000,000
1800	70,972,000	91,253,000
1810	66,758,000	85,400,000
1820	69,692,000	74,450,000
1830	71,671,000	62,721,000
1840	123,609,000	98,259,000
1850	144,376,000	172,510,000
1860	333,576,000	353,616,000

Compiled from *Statistical Abstract, 1921*, Table 482, p. 836.

trebled by 1800. Interrupted by the embargo, the War of 1812, the postwar readjustment, and other factors, foreign trade declined in money value from the high figures of 1807 and did not reach them again until 1835. After that the trend was generally upward. In examining the value table of exports and imports the student should note the great decline in domestic prices after the panic of 1819. Although in value foreign trade declined in the 1820's, in amount it increased.[15]

During this entire period, about 50 per cent of the imports comprised manufactured goods ready for consumption. Textiles, metals, and earthen goods were imported from England and the Continent; wines from France; molasses, sugar, rum, and coffee from the West Indies; specie and bullion from Mexico; hides, indigo, and coffee from South America; and tea, silks, china, and spices from the Orient. England supplied the greater part of the imports, but as the years went on trade with continental Europe, especially France, increased, while the West Indian trade declined. In return for imports, as the accompanying table shows, we sent our raw materials for use in manufacturing, and foodstuffs.

[15] G. R. Taylor, *The Transportation Revolution*, pp. 192–193.

In the South, tobacco and rice gave way to cotton, which, after the invention of the gin, became our largest single export. By 1860 it comprised 60 per cent of our exports. Along with rice, tobacco, and refined sugar, approximately three-fourths of our exports were produced in the Southern states. As for foodstuffs, particularly wheat and packed meat, Americans found but a small market in Europe, except during periods of crop failures. This was true even after the repeal of the Corn Laws. Competitive conditions for foodstuffs were better in the West Indies and South America and these areas were our principal markets. Of manufactured exports, which amounted to only about 12 per cent of total exports at the end of the 1850's, cotton goods after 1830 were the most important. Its principal markets were China, Mexico, and

EXPORTED MERCHANDISE BY GROUPS, PERCENTAGES OF TOTALS

Year	Crude Materials	Manufactures for Further Use in Manufacturing	Manufactures Ready for Consumption	Foodstuffs in Crude Condition— Food Animals	Food stuffs Wholly or Partially Manufactured
1820	60.46	9.42	5.66	4.79	19.51
1830	62.34	7.04	9.34	4.65	16.32
1840	67.61	4.34	9.47	4.09	14.27
1850	62.26	4.49	12.72	5.59	14.84
1860	68.31	3.99	11.33	3.85	12.21

Compiled from *Statistical Abstract, 1921*, Table 482, pp. 848–849.

the West Indies. Other important exports were pot and pearl ashes (from which potash is derived), wood, iron and steel, distilled spirits, and manufactured tobacco. During the period after 1820 Great Britain took about half our exports, with Europe as a whole purchasing from two-thirds to three-fourths. European purchases were almost entirely raw materials; our manufactured exports went to the rest of the world, chiefly Canada, Mexico, the West Indies, South America, and the Orient.

A word should also be said concerning re-exports, which during some years of the Napoleonic Wars were more valuable than the exports of domestic production. This trade, however, had dropped to one-fourth of our total exports in the 1820's and to one-twelfth in the 1860's. Most of our re-exports to the Western Hemisphere and Asia came from Britain, notably cotton goods. To Europe, particularly Great Britain, we exported the tropical commodities of Latin America, such as sugar, molasses, and coffee, and tea from China. Our chief re-export market in the 1850's was British North America, to which we re-exported not only British commodities but also Canadian flour to the maritime provinces, because of superior transportation facilities across the United States. In the end most of the re-export trade was lost to Great Britain and primarily for the same reasons that our merchant marine declined.

Commerce was carried on mainly through New York, Philadelphia, Baltimore, Boston, and New Orleans, although Salem, Newburyport, Plymouth, and many other seaport towns were important trade centers in the earlier decades. Pre-eminence in foreign trade depended in the end on communication with the interior, and the building of the Erie Canal made New York's position secure as the leading commercial city on the Atlantic seaboard. The activities of Philadelphia, Baltimore, Boston, and other seaport towns in pushing canals and railroads were based on the hope that western products might be shipped to Europe through them. So successful had New York become by the time of the Civil War that she handled three-fourths of the re-export trade and, as we shall shortly see, became the center of the "cotton triangle."

Except for the 1840's, American imports from Europe from 1815 to 1860 were larger than our exports. In the balance of international settlements the huge debits in this country were offset in the main by the freight profits earned by the merchant marine, by the commissions of merchants in the re-export trade, by investments of European capital in the United States, and by the movement of specie and bullion. Smaller credit items came from the sale of ships and money brought in by immigrants. Until 1849 this specie movement was made up in the main of gold and silver coin and bullion from the Latin American trade; the United States tended to use the quantities she received in excess of domestic monetary requirements as an export item to Europe. After 1849 this country became the greatest gold-producing country in the world, and consequently an important part of the balance of international payments consisted of this commodity. Even so, the balance of trade for the entire period was against the United States. Estimates put foreign holdings in federal, state, railroad, and other securities at about $400,000,000 in 1860.

No account of either commerce or the merchant marine would be complete without some mention of the coastwise traffic. Legislation in 1789 favored the American merchant marine to an extent that virtually excluded foreign vessels from participation.[16] The coastwise trade to the South was concerned with distributing northern or European goods among the southern coastal towns. The northward movement consisted mainly in loading western foodstuffs at New Orleans, or cotton, sugar, tobacco, and other products at New Orleans, Mobile, Charleston, and elsewhere, and bringing them to the northern cities for use or export. The most important aspect of this trade was the so-called "cotton triangle." Vessels carried cotton directly from

[16] Above, p. 219.

a southern port to Europe, returned to New York with freight or immigrants, and sailed southward on the coastwise run with freight or ballast. An alternative route used only two sides of the triangle. Coastwise vessels picked up southern cotton and brought it to New York, whence most of it was shipped to Europe. European goods in return were first brought to New York and then distributed throughout the South. After the discovery of gold the intercoastal trade grew in importance as hundreds of vessels each year plied between California and the eastern seaboard. That the coastwise trade was of extreme significance may be seen from one estimate which put the value of commodities thus transported in 1852 at $2,600,000,000 as against $374,425,000 for foreign commerce. The value of the commodities carried in the coastal traffic was more than double that carried on either canals or railroads.[17]

SELECTED READINGS

Johnson, E. R., *et al., History of Domestic and Foreign Commerce of the United States,* Vol. I, chaps. 12–14 and 19 (by T. W. Van Metre).

Marvin, W. L., *The American Merchant Marine,* chaps. 4–14.

Taylor, G. R., *The Transportation Revolution,* chaps. 6, 9.

Morison, S. E., *The Maritime History of Massachusetts, 1783–1860,* chaps. 3 ff.

Albion, R. G., *The Rise of New York Port,* chap. 6.

Hutchins, J. G. B., *The American Maritime Industries and Public Policy, 1789–1914,* chaps. 8–11.

Flügel, F., and Faulkner, H. U., *Readings in the Economic and Social History of the United States,* pp. 194–206, 208–219, 680–682.

[17] E. R. Johnson *et al., History of Domestic and Foreign Commerce of the United States,* I, 344.

PART III

THE COMING OF THE
FACTORY SYSTEM

CHAPTER 13

THE RISE OF THE FACTORY
SYSTEM

THE DEVELOPMENT OF A NEW ECONOMY

The improved agricultural technology discussed in a previous chapter was indicative of a new society developing in the United States. It was part of a generally expanding technology which brought, particularly in the Northeast, the development of the small factory and, in the years after the Civil War, a full-fledged Industrial Revolution. Agriculture continued to be operated on the small unit rather than the large farm. It was constantly improved by new machinery and, after the late nineteenth century, by government aid in research and education. In later years it received similar assistance in marketing and in the maintenance of a price structure to insure profitable operation.

On the other hand, industry experienced a more fundamental revolution. Continually improved machinery brought the factory system, and the factory system a large group of wage laborers, with separation between the owners of the machinery and those who worked it. All this was based on the development of artificial power, such as water, steam, and electricity, and a constantly growing system of internal transportation. With the growth of the factory system, of transportation facilities, and of large-scale commerce, greater aggregations of capital appeared with a financial structure to handle it. The growth of industry and capitalism went hand in hand. This resulted in a far more complex structure of society. The change was particularly rapid after the Civil War in the breaking down of old relationships, the revolutionizing of many aspects of the old society, and the bringing into this country of the stresses already experienced in western Europe with the coming of the Industrial Revolution.

The years 1790 to 1860 witnessed the gradual rise of the factory system and the foundations in America of the Industrial Revolution. This was also the

239

period when the United States passed from a condition of economic dependence on Europe to one in which the ordinary wants of manufactured goods could be supplied at home. These years may be divided into three periods.[1] The first, 1790–1815, was characterized by economic dependence on Europe for the finer type of manufactured goods. But also during this period international disturbances brought succeeding crises in our economic life, interferences with international trade, and the birth of the factory system. In the second period, 1815–1840, small factory production grew gradually and manufacturing made an aggressive entrance into political controversies. During these years manufacturing was largely dependent upon water transportation for the distribution of its products.

The third period, 1840–1860, profited from the discovery that the use of coal was practical for iron smelting and steam power. It was marked by the rise of railroads, which greatly facilitated transportation, and by the introduction of many new improvements in machinery, which quickened and diversified manufacturing enterprises. These were the years when manufacturing grew rapidly and the little mills began to take on some of the characteristics of the modern factory. In other words, they ceased to be adjuncts of merchant capitalism and became definite integrated units where skilled managers supervised the machine production of standardized products by labor that had been removed from the home or small shop. Factory owners were no longer merely merchants or commission men; they became actual manufacturers with factory production as their chief interest. In these years America began definitely to feel the effects of the Industrial Revolution.

In the whole period from 1790 to 1860 agriculture still continued to occupy the chief energies of the people. Nevertheless, household manufacturing, outside the field of food preparation, declined after 1815. For the next twenty years the decrease of household manufacturing in the East was offset by a considerable expansion of it on the frontier. After that the decline was general and rapid, dependent, of course, upon the development of transportation facilities. The small shop was still an important producer, but household manufacture had largely disappeared by 1860. Milling and meat packing, industries closely allied to agriculture, rose first, followed by textiles and then by the metal industries. Unoccupied public land across which the frontier advanced was a determining factor in the history of manufactures, as it was in agriculture, especially as it affected the type of product.

ECONOMIC DEPENDENCE ON EUROPE

The Revolution, as we have seen, brought political independence but by no means economic independence. Products of the colonial period which

[1] These divisions follow in general those of Victor S. Clark in his *History of Manufactures in the United States, 1607–1860*, chap. 11.

had been exported to Europe still found a market there and we continued to import European manufactured commodities. Manufactures which had grown up during the Revolution were smothered by the cheaper British goods thrown onto the American market on the resumption of peace. Moreover, certain industries which had thrived in the old "three-cornered traffic" were largely destroyed by the prohibition of trade with the British West Indies. There was every indication that America would again sink into a subservient position, producing the raw materials which Europe needed and taking the latter's goods in return. Competition with England in the production and sale of maufactured goods seemed out of the question.

It was not only the difficulty of competing with Europe that held back the development of manufactures; internal factors were of equal importance. After two hundred years of settlement there still remained an apparently exhaustless supply of unoccupied land; the lure of an independent life with profits to be secured both from agriculture and from rising land values attracted the average man more than existence as an industral laborer. Agriculture was still the primary industry, the one from which most people believed the greatest returns were to be obtained. Unoccupied western land was the main cause of the scarcity and consequent high cost of labor, an important deterrent to the growth of manufacturing. Marketing the agricultural products seemed the most important problem to be solved, and what liquid capital remained from agriculture and commerce was drawn into schemes for turnpikes, canals, and railroads. In particular the infant manufacturing industry had to compete for capital with the shipping industry on river and ocean during the golden era of the merchant marine. Net earnings of the latter between 1795 and 1801 were estimated at $32,000,000 a year, three-fourths the total value of agricultural exports during the same years; the tonnage built in American dockyards increased from 202,000 in 1789 to 1,425,000 in 1810. Nor were American carriers content with transporting their own produce; they scoured the seas in search of business. In some years during the first decade of the century the foreign goods transported exceeded domestic products in value, and the re-export trade was extremely active. This competition for capital, of course, kept interest rates high, making it difficult for manufacturers to borrow money for operating expenses or expansion. It was the age of merchant capitalism in which the credit and transportation facilities were geared to the needs of the merchant rather than of the manufacturer.

Rising manufacturing had to contend—except during the periods of the first and second Banks of the United States—with inadequate banking facilities and a currency situation that was fantastic. Furthermore, after about 1830 it had to operate under a federal government that was dominated by southern plantation owners little interested in the development of manufacturing. This group opposed a protective tariff, a strong central banking system, a transcontinental railroad built in the North, free land for homesteaders, and a government immigration plan. With the Supreme Court under their domination, legal decisions gave little encouragement to the type of capitalist enterprise necessary for the rapid development of the factory system.

In the face of these contending factors, it is a source of wonder that any progress whatever was made. Yet it was during the years most discouraging to industrial life that the birth of the factory system took place and American manufactures established themselves. The chief contributing causes were (1) the partial shutting off of European imports during the Revolution (1775–1783), the Embargo and Nonintercourse acts, and the War of 1812–1814; (2) the existence of an abundance of raw materials, especially cotton, iron, and fuel, and of water power; (3) the immigration of skilled and unskilled European laborers in continually increasing numbers, in many cases persons unused to agriculture and willing to engage in industry; (4) government aid through protective tariffs; (5) the versatility and genius of a resourceful people; and (6) the appearance of small amounts of accumulated capital. To make possible the use of these small accumulations, the states began to charter corporations.

Certain other factors also must be considered as part of the background for the growth of manufacturing. There were savings in freight rates which tended to overcome the higher cost of labor in this country. There was the discovery of gold in California which made it possible for the United States to have an unfavorable commodity balance in international trade and yet purchase abroad iron, machinery, and other products needed to develop manufacturing. Underlying all of these factors, however, was the phenomenon of a rapidly expanding domestic market that was being made ever more available by the continued improvement in transportation facilities.

Although the small amount of surplus capital in the country was largely drawn into other fields, sufficient was attracted to maufacturing after 1815 to give the latter a start. Considerable amounts came from commercial firms who withdrew their capital from commerce during the uncertain years preceding and following the War of 1812. Similarly shipowners and sea captains during the same period turned from the carrying trade to cotton manufacturing. With the decline of the East Indian trade, capital in Salem and Providence shifted to manufacturing, as did that in New Bedford with the passing of the whaling industry. Merchants with surpluses, especially those who wished to assure themselves of a supply of the finished product, invested actively in manufacturing.

In a sense, many of these merchants were already manufacturers. As had been done in England in the years before the Industrial Revolution, they had gathered the raw materials, distributed them to the farmhouse and small shop to be turned into manufactured goods, and then collected them for sale in the markets. But undoubtedly the largest number of establishments originated from small shops and water mills whose owners reinvested their accumulations until their enterprises assumed respectable proportions. The profits from manufacturing were normally large, affording both new capital for extension and a stimulus to outsiders to invest. From the inaccurate and inadequate census estimates it is probable that the capital invested in manufacturing was about $50,000,000 in 1820 and $1,000,000,000 in 1860.

EUROPEAN BACKGROUND—THE INDUSTRIAL REVOLUTION IN ENGLAND

The Industrial Revolution in America was preceded and made possible by a similar transition in England. For thousands of years economic processes had been carried on in essentially the same manner. Thread was spun and cloth woven by hand; this was true of other manufactured articles. These handicraft operations were usually carried on either in the home as a by-industry to farming or in a little shop attached to the house where the master craftsman, surrounded by his journeymen and apprentices, laboriously turned out his products. During the eighteenth century and the first quarter of the nineteenth, various inventions were made which were destined to revolutionize the world, changing the everyday life of mankind more profoundly than had anything in any previous age. England, the first of the European nations to free herself from the shackles of guild regulations, possessed of a thriving commerce and accumulated capital, free from the internal devastation of the European wars, and rich in coal and iron, was the logical starting point for this great advance.

The Industrial Revolution, the result of the work of thousands of experimenters, began in the textile industry. In 1733 John Kay invented the "fly-shuttle," a device by which a weaver, instead of reaching across to throw the shuttle back and forth, could jerk a string to accomplish the same purpose. This simple contrivance allowed the weaver to work on a much wider piece of cloth and with greater rapidity. The speeding up of weaving brought increased demand for thread; but it was not until 1770 that James Hargreaves, a Lancashire weaver, patented an improvement on the old-fashioned spinning wheel whereby eight spindles connected by a band to a horizontal wheel, and turned by a crank, could spin eight threads at a time. While Hargreaves was still working on his "spinning jenny," Richard Arkwright, a barber of Preston, patented a machine in 1769 which drew the carded cotton through a series of rollers, each set revolving at a greater velocity than the preceding set, and turned out cotton thread strong enough to be used as warp. His original patent called for a machine worked by horses, but in 1771 water power was used and his "water frame" made the manufacture of cotton thread a commercial possibility and himself a wealthy man. A further improvement in spinning was made in 1779 by Samuel Crompton, who combined Hargreaves' "jenny" and Arkwright's "water frame" in a machine called a "mule," which turned out a better thread at quicker speed and enabled England to compete with India in the finer textiles.

Since the spinners were now far ahead of the weavers, it was quite logical that the next advance should be in weaving. The invention, strange to say, was the result of the labors of a Kentish clergyman, Edmund Cartwright, who knew absolutely nothing of machinery when he first set to work on the problem. By 1785 he had constructed a power loom for weaving, propelled first by horses and then by steam. The demand for cotton was now so great that increasing numbers of southern planters were turning from raising tobacco to cotton, a transition made possible by Eli Whitney's cotton gin. These inventions in cotton machinery were but the beginning of the revolution in textiles. Other inventors followed with machinery for other fabrics.

Simultaneously with the improvements in textile machinery came the practical steam engine. The properties of steam had been known to the ancient Egyptians, and interesting experiments had been made toward the end of the seventeenth century. Thomas Newcomen patented an engine in 1705 to pump water out of the mines; it was capable of doing the work of fifty men but was slow and expensive to operate. In 1763 James Watt, a Scottish engineer, was given a model of one of Newcomen's engines to repair. In 1769 he patented an improved engine which effected a great saving in fuel and time by drawing off the steam into a separate condenser, thus keeping the cylinder continually warm and making it possible by automatic controls to use the same steam in forcing the cylinder both ways. In company with Mathew Boulton, a wealthy manufacturer, Watt began the commercial manufacture of steam engines. To a man of his genius it was not difficult to apply the backward and forward motion of the piston to the turning of wheels or the driving of a steam hammer. Industry was now to a great extent emancipated from water power and factories sprang up in the large cities. These engines not only facilitated the mining of coal and iron but provided a greater market for both materials.

The improvements in manufacturing, which brought increased production, were followed by striking advances in the methods of distribution. The years of the Industrial Revolution saw great progress in road building under the direction of such men as Telford and McAdam. James Brindley constructed the Bridgewater Canal, opened in 1761, for the purpose of carrying coal from

Worsley to Manchester. The success of this canal led in the next decade to a wave of canal building, similar to that in the United States after 1825, which connected most of the principal rivers and centers in England. Machinists since the 1780's had realized the possibilities of connecting the piston of the steam engine to a wheel revolving in water, but it was not until 1803 that William Symmington demonstrated the practicability of the steamboat on the Clyde and 1807 that Robert Fulton demonstrated this for Americans. In that year a Watt engine drove the *Clermont* from New York to Albany, a distance of 150 miles, in thirty-two hours. Before many years similar experiments were being made in ocean travel. What Fulton accomplished for water traffic the Englishman George Stephenson, building on the work of Trevithick and others, did for land transportation. In 1829 Stephenson's engine, "The Rocket," in a trial test between Liverpool and Manchester attained a speed of twenty-nine miles an hour, demonstrating beyond doubt the feasibility of steam railroads.

With the substitution of power-driven machinery for hand labor and the utilization of steam in factories and for transportation purposes, the Industrial Revolution was well under way. Its results are the civilization in which we live. The introduction of machinery produced an immense increase in production, with a corresponding increase in wealth and a general transformation of business methods to take care of this increase. It enhanced enormously the wealth, power, and numbers of the rising middle class. At the same time it brought into being what was virtually a new class, that of the industrial wage earner. Most of the added wealth produced by the Industrial Revolution was absorbed by the middle class. On the other hand, the industrial wage earners, separated from the land and concentrated in the slums of the new cities which sprang up around the factories, were reduced to extremes of poverty and degradation.

The sharp distinction in wealth and opportunity in the new era was soon felt in politics. The middle class, leaning on the *laissez-faire* philosophy of their own economists, Adam Smith, Ricardo, and others, demanded and won a commanding position in the government. To the industrial worker the displacement of the landed aristocracy by the middle class brought no immediate advantage. Stirred to wrath by legislation which discriminated against their interests, workmen followed the example of their industrial masters and agitated for political rights. This agitation, commencing with the Chartist Movement (1838–1848) and continuing to the present day, has resulted in political democracy and in a long list of acts promoting social betterment. Machinery has cheapened the process of printing, a factor which, combined with the growth of the urban population, has quickened intellectual life and progressive thought. Upon international relations the Industrial

Revolution has had an immense influence. The search for raw products, the scramble for new markets and for a place to invest some of the surplus wealth created by machines became acute. The result was a new imperialism, a new militarism, and the conquest of economically backward peoples.

BEGINNINGS OF THE AMERICAN FACTORY SYSTEM

In America industry went through somewhat the same evolution as in England, but much more rapidly. Self-sufficing manufacture for household needs had developed there into the handicraft or domestic stage where the work might be done at home, but the products were sold elsewhere by retail or wholesale. In the later years of this stage work was sometimes done in the home but it was on a commission basis, the merchant capitalist distributing the raw materials to be worked up. In the United States household manufacture for family needs was general everywhere at the end of the eighteenth century, except, perhaps, in some plantation districts, and this type of manufacture continued in the frontier regions long after it had disappeared from the seacoast. Household manufacture for the general market was also carried on at this time, the craftsman sometimes working on the raw material supplied by the merchant capitalist. The manufacturing artisan who had confined his energy to custom work was extending his operations to a general market, and some mills and furnaces were operating on a scale that approached factory production. At the same time itinerant artisans wandered from house to house making shoes and doing other skilled work beyond the ability of the family. In other words, all these stages of industry—the household, the domestic, the small mill or shop, and their various modifications—were contemporary in America on the eve of the Industrial Revolution. Although the United States passed from "mother-and-daughter power to water-and-steam power" in a short period of some seventy years, almost all phases of the household and domestic stages continued during these years. Rapid as was the transition, it would have come even more quickly had not the poverty and remoteness of the frontier held it back.

Since the Industrial Revolution had taken place first in England, that country had become the workshop of the world. This advantage she was loath to lose, and attempts were made to keep the secrets of the new machinery from spreading. Between 1765 and 1789 laws were passed prohibiting the migration of skilled workers in textiles and machinery, and the exportation of textile machinery, plans, or models. But the measures did not materially delay the introduction of such machinery into this country after interest had once been aroused.

The years from the close of the Revolution to 1800 were a period of experimentation. Factories in which the jenny was used were established in

1787 at Philadelphia, at Beverly, Massachusetts, and in succeeding years at other places in New England and New York—undoubtedly the first cotton mills in America. None of them long survived. The first successful Arkwright mill was built in 1789 by Samuel Slater, an English emigrant who had served an apprenticeship in one of Arkwright's factories at Belper and had been induced to come to America by bounties offered here for the improved machinery. Through the influence of Moses Brown, a Quaker merchant of Providence, Slater came to Rhode Island, and in 1790 his mill, erected at Pawtucket, spun the first machine-made cotton warp in America. The beginnings of the American factory system can truly be traced to Slater and his Pawtucket mill. "The first attempt systematically to develop an extensive water-power for general manufacturing purposes," says Clark, "was probably the conception of Alexander Hamilton," whose initiative resulted in the incorporation in 1791 of a company in New Jersey for the manufacture of textiles on the falls of the Passaic.[2] The company itself was short-lived but it founded Paterson, which eventually became an important textile city.

The first spinning machines set up were run either by hand or by horsepower. Later, water power was used extensively, and for a while almost exclusively, both for spinning and weaving and for other types of production. Steam was probably first used in America for pumping mines in New Jersey and Rhode Island during the last decades of the eighteenth century; it is believed that it was first applied to mill machinery in a sawmill in New York in 1803. In the years following, either the imported low-pressure engines of the Boulton-Watt type or the high-pressure engines of Evans were introduced in sections where water power was inadequate or fluctuated greatly. The latter was true in the Ohio Valley, and it was in this region that steam power in manufacturing was first widely used. Moreover, steam power was superior in the heat-using industries, such as glass and ironmaking, centered in western Pennsylvania and Ohio. Another impetus to the use of steam engines was provided as good water-power sites in New England were no longer obtainable and as manufacturing began to center in cities. Although steam power increased rapidly after 1840, water remained the chief source of power as late as 1860.

When manufacturing by machinery was once firmly established, American inventors enthusiastically took up the ideas of European engineers, adapted them to conditions here, and contributed new improvements. Labor scarcity did much to stimulate inventions, but ignorance as to what had been done in England led to duplication. Of American contributions, perhaps the most famous was that of Eli Whitney, who not only invented the cotton gin but in the late 1790's applied the principle of standardization of parts and inter-

[2] *Ibid.*, I, 404.

changeable mechanism in the manufacture of firearms. Another notable American advance was the Goulding condenser, which greatly simplified and quickened the carding of wool. The first successful power loom for weaving in America was constructed by a Boston merchant, Francis Cabot Lowell, who on a trip to England in 1810–1812 had made a careful study of textile machinery. With the aid of a mechanical genius, Paul Moody, Lowell designed and constructed a new set of spinning machinery and a power loom which were set up at Waltham in 1814. Here, for the first time in the world, it is believed, all the processes of spinning and weaving were brought together in the same factory. In concentrating all the processes in one factory the "Waltham system" took a long step toward modern factory production. In the succeeding years many American inventors, of whom perhaps John Thorp, Samuel Batchelder, and William Mason are the best known, invented the "ring spinner," which raised spindle speed to three times that of the Arkwright spindle, and perfected machines for knitting and lacemaking, and for manufacturing linen and cotton in figured designs.

Not only in textiles were American machinists making progress. Oliver Evans of Philadelphia invented a high-pressure steam engine which was used successfully. Rumsay, Fitch, and Fulton made notable experiments in the application of steam to water transportation, and John Stevens of Hoboken directed his attention to a railroad engine. Geissenhainer in 1830 successfully smelted iron ore with anthracite coal, and in 1851 William Kelly of Kentucky independently discovered the principle of the Bessemer method of decarbonizing molten metal by forcing air through it. Elias Howe in 1846 invented the sewing machine, a machine equally suitable to the home and the factory and one that not only proved an immense boon to women but revolutionized the clothing and shoe industry. The work of Morse in introducing the magnetic telegraph effected a similar revolution in methods of communication. These men and hundreds of other inventors must be given the chief credit for the establishing of American manufacturing. The Patent Office, which reported an average of seventy-seven inventions annually from 1790 to 1811, recorded 544 patents in 1830. In the decade 1841–1850, it issued 6460 patents, and in the next decade 25,250.

While due credit is given to the work of the inventors, recognition should also be accorded that remarkably large and brilliant group of entrepreneurs and capitalists who built upon the labors of the technicians, men who planted little factories in out-of-the-way places which became the foundation for important industries and thriving cities. Among the many who quickly come to mind are Nathan Appleton and Abbott Lawrence, who were leaders of the group responsible for the manufacturing development of Lowell and Lawrence; Edmund Dwight, who played a similar role in Chicopee and

Holyoke; and William Gregg of Graniteville, South Carolina. One of the ablest of them was Patrick Tracy Jackson (1780–1847), whose activities exemplify the entrepreneur at his best. Apprenticed to a Newburyport merchant at the age of fifteen, he became a sea captain in his early twenties, retired from the sea at twenty-eight to engage in the exporting and importing business, and with the curtailment of his shipping interests by the War of 1812 found an outlet for his energy in the manufacture of cotton. Joining his brother-in-law, Francis C. Lowell, he aided in the establishment of the famous Waltham factory and managed it in its early years. When the local power resources were exhausted Jackson and his associates moved to the Merrimac and erected mills around which grew the city of Lowell, the "Manchester of America." Finding transportation facilities from his new mills to Boston inadequate, Jackson turned a ready ear to the reports of steam railroads and was chiefly responsible for the first one in New England. Sailor, merchant, manufacturer, railroad builder—his life epitomizes the economic history of New England during the first half of the nineteenth century.[3]

The development of the Industrial Revolution, of course, followed no fixed rule. Some factories were merely the extension of tiny mills already in existence; some were the work of inventors or technicians who also had capital, as in the case of Lowell; others were established by businessmen who had little or no technical knowledge but could obtain capital. Some were personally managed by the owner or his friends, while many, particularly in the large centers of New England, were controlled by absentee owners and conducted by resident managers. Each type of industry had to develop its particular technique of production and distribution. In at least one industry the expanding market produced by the Industrial Revolution was met by the expansion of old methods rather than by new machinery. The shoe industry, for example, did not introduce new machinery until after 1860, but in the meantime the little hand shop increased in size until a more minute division of labor became necessary. In the shoe centers of New England there appeared the main "factory," where the cutting, packing, and shipping were done, and many little shops or even private homes about the town where specialized operations, such as binding, stitching, soling, and lasting, were

---

[3] The number of these businessmen of great ability during this period is amazing. Besides Appleton, Lawrence, Lowell, Dwight, and Jackson, the student is referred to the sketches of Nathan P. Ames, Benjamin Talbot Babbitt, Richard Borden, Charles Goodyear, Ward Cheney, Jonas Chickering, Alvah Crocker, Samuel Downer, Arthur M. Eastman, Charles Tillinghast James, and scores of others included in the *Dictionary of American Biography*. A study of the lists of directors of New England banks, insurance companies, and railroads, as given by Vera Shlakman, *Economic History of a Factory Town*, Appendix A, shows the small and closely knit group of financial and industrial entrepreneurs who promoted the economic development of New England during the first half of the nineteenth century.

carried on—the whole an excellent example of a primitive industry expanding to meet changed conditions without new machinery. Not until power was applied to shoe machinery did shoe production become in reality a factory industry.

THE TEXTILE INDUSTRY

The Industrial Revolution and the development of the factory system in this country started in the cotton textile industry. Following Slater's success at Pawtucket, spinning mills sprang up at various points in southern New England and were later given an impetus by the embargo and the War of 1812. But these little mills were operated chiefly by women and children, and the weaving was done in the home by the "putting out" system. Factory production began with the Boston Manufacturing Company established during the war years by Lowell and his associates at Waltham, where all the processes, including weaving, were done in a single establishment.

Scores of the little mills were destroyed by the return of peace and the flooding of the American market by the pent-up English goods. But the Waltham mills survived, and, with the tariff of 1816, new labor-saving devices, and a world-wide business revival, new mills rose on the ruins of the old. Boston investors spread the Waltham system in other towns (some of which they created) north of Boston, in western Massachusetts, and in New Hampshire and Maine, while another group, centered in Providence, followed their example in Rhode Island and southern Massachusetts. Companies specializing in the manufacture of textile machinery were established, and the manufacture of cotton spread into other areas of the country. Sixty-nine per cent, however, was centered in New England. Well established and thriving by 1840, cotton textiles increased in value 150 per cent in the next twenty years, amounting in 1860 to $115,682,000. The industry employed about 122,000 workers.

Although the Census of 1860 showed the woolen industry in capitalization and value of products a little over half the size of the thriving cotton industry, the United States was still dependent on Britain for quantities of both raw wool and manufactured goods. The manufacture of woolens developed more slowly than that of cotton, notwithstanding the fact that woolen cloth was used from the time of the early settlements and the adaptability of large parts of the country to sheep raising was thoroughly demonstrated. There were several causes. English statesmen, acting under the policies of mercantilism, had discouraged in every possible way the manufacture of woolens in America. Great Britain excelled in the colonial period, as she still does, in the manufacture of woolens, and it was difficult to compete even after the assistance rendered by the tariffs following the War of 1812.

Furthermore, a far larger number of farms produced wool than cotton and this tended to prolong the household production of woolen cloth.

Nevertheless, the manufacture of woolen cloth slowly passed from the home to the factory. Colonial sheep produced wool suitable only for coarser cloths; but after 1790 improved breeds were gradually introduced from Spain, Ireland, and England, and these, bred with the existing stock, bettered the product and made possible the manufacture of excellent woolens from domestic sheep. Simultaneously with the growing of improved wool came the gradual shift from household to factory manufacture. Little weaving had been done outside the home before the Revolution, and household weaving had undoubtedly increased during the troubles with Britain. Just as Samuel Slater had evaded the British law and brought to America knowledge of the cotton machinery, so two brothers, John and Arthur Scholfield of Yorkshire, emigrated in 1792 and aided in establishing small mills in Massachusetts in 1793, and later in Connecticut, where the most improved woolen machinery was set up. But mill production was almost entirely in carding, spinning, and finishing. The War of 1812 gave woolen manufacturing its first real foothold, the new factories turning out military equipment, cloths for the Negroes, and even fine woolens. The fact that about this time knee breeches were no longer worn also brought a wider demand for woolen goods. It was estimated at the conclusion of peace that $12,000,000 had been invested in woolen mills, the product of which was valued at $19,000,000.

The conclusion of the war and the subsequent heavy importation of accumulated European goods ruined many of these mills and was a potent influence in bringing about the tariff of 1816, in which a 25 per cent ad valorem rate was imposed on most woolen goods. The postwar depression had in like manner affected the farmers, thus lengthening the life of household manufacturing; as late as 1830, even in the leading textile states of New England, more woolen cloth was woven at home than in the factories. There was some improvement in the decade of the twenties with the introduction of power looms for weaving, but as a whole it was a precarious period for the industry. After 1830 normal prosperity returned and woolen manufacturing firmly established itself, securing control in certain lines of the domestic market. It is not until the decade of the forties that it can truly be said that the factory-made product had the upper hand and that the domestic industry was in a decline. Although the production of worsteds remained small and the manufacture of broadcloths declined, the industry as a whole showed healthy progress during the next twenty years, with an increasing output of cassimeres, satinets, flannels, blankets, felts, and carpets.

In comparison to cottons and woolens the production of other textiles was small. Before the introduction of the factory system flax held first place in homespun products, but machinery for the manufacture of cotton and wool cut the price of these fabrics and displaced flax. Factories for the manufacture of cordage, sailcloth, and the finer grades of flax goods existed, but their number was few, their life precarious, and their output, though of good quality, not large. The use of hemp in the manufacture of bagging and bale cloth was a minor but active industry in Kentucky and Missouri producing 9,540,000 yards in 1860. Unsuccessful efforts had been made in the Connecticut and Willimantic valleys to produce silk in the early decades of the century, but lack of cheap labor and indifferent success in cultivating mulberry trees held back the development until about 1840. About that time the Cheney brothers started their factory at Manchester, Connecticut, and John Ryle took over a small mill at Paterson, New Jersey, where they spun raw silk imported from the Orient. But silk manufacturing was still in its infancy in 1860 when the census reported forty-two mills in the Northeast. Only one of them, however, produced woven goods.

THE HEAVY INDUSTRIES

The development of modern industry is closely bound up with the story of iron, a substance which now enters into the construction of machinery, buildings, ships, and the innumerable needs of an "iron age." In the seventeenth and eighteenth centuries, when charcoal was used for smelting, the virgin forests of America provided cheap fuel at almost the same time that the supply was being exhausted in England. When the possibility of using anthracite coal for smelting was discovered in the nineteenth century, the existence of iron and coal in close proximity was again advantageous to American smelters. The rapidly growing manufactures and population provided an expanding market which was partially protected by tariffs.

Before the close of the Revolution iron was smelted from bog iron in all the thirteen colonies except Georgia. Bog iron was gradually supplemented by iron from the rich magnetic ore belt extending from the Berkshires in Massachusetts and the Salisbury district in Connecticut across the Hudson through Orange County, New York, and into Morris County, New Jersey. Slowly the smelting industry pushed westward. By 1810 ironmaking had extended up the Susquehanna, into the Juniata Valley, and up the Lehigh. Farther south it had crossed the mountains into Tennessee and Kentucky, where a considerable quantity of high-grade ore was later produced in an agrarian slave economy. The Census of 1810 reported 153 furnaces producing 53,908 tons of iron. The production of iron was also stimulated by the embargo and the War of 1812 but suffered a severe setback in the years immediately following. The Census of 1820 gives little information of value, but in the following decades the industry grew up in western Pennsylvania and the Ohio Valley, extending by 1860 as far as the region of Lake Superior, where smelting was carried on in northern Michigan and near Detroit. The use of coal after 1840 revived the smelting of iron east of the Alleghenies, especially in Pennsylvania and those points in New Jersey and New York reached by canal.

In the colonial period and the early decades of the nineteenth century iron products were likely to be made in the same little smelting mill that produced the raw material, or else the iron was smelted to be sold to near-by blacksmiths. Thus household utensils and the few metal tools in use were generally either custom-made or turned out on a very small scale. It was not until the 1820's that specialization in metal products developed to any great extent, and even then the foundries and factories generally remained close to the source of supply. The use of the steam engine in water transportation after 1808 favored specialization in this type of ironwork and brought into being engine works on such important arteries of traffic as the Hudson, Delaware, and Ohio, although for many years engines were made only to order. With the advent of railroads, locomotives were built at many machine shops, but by 1860 their construction tended to concentrate at Philadelphia, the home of the Baldwin and Norris plants (founded in 1832 and 1834, respectively), and at Paterson, New Jersey. With the increased demand for new kinds of metal goods, rolling mills, which in the early years had been devoted chiefly to rolling and slitting nail plates, turned their attention to other products such as iron rails and tires. In the fifties the iron straps used for railroads were gradually discarded for the heavy solid iron rail, a transition which brought into existence a specialized form of the industry centered in eastern Pennsylvania.

One of the earliest of the metal industries to become specialized was the making of stoves. At first the plates were cast at the furnaces and assembled by the merchants, but eventually the whole process was carried on in the same establishment. The use of anthracite coal greatly increased the demand for the iron range, and by 1850 the annual production was over 300,000 stoves, valued at around $6,000,000. These were manufactured chiefly in Philadelphia, New York, Albany, Cincinnati, Providence, and Pittsburgh.

For the smaller metal products, in some of which steel and iron were used, the center of manufacturing was New England. Iron axes, springs, bolts, wire, firearms, and clocks were largely made there. The factory system brought into being the manufacture of textile machinery, half of which in 1860 was constructed in Massachusetts. Likewise half of the edge tools and three-fourths of the cutlery produced in the country in that year came from New England, chiefly Connecticut. Berlin became a center for tinware and the Naugatuck Valley for brassware. The manufacture of sewing machines, the output of which reached 110,000 in 1860, was divided principally among the Singer factory at New York, the Wheeler and Wilson Company of Bridgeport, and the Grover and Baker Company of Boston.

The Industrial Revolution not only created new markets and made new demands upon the iron industry but revolutionized the industry itself. In becoming the basic heavy industry, it underwent many important changes. New techniques, as in rolling, puddling, and the use of coal in blast furnaces, were introduced. Local supplies of ore and crude iron were assembled in urban areas for further manufacturing. Quite as important was the replacement of an essentially agricultural demand for iron by one coming from the industrialization of manufacturing and from the needs of transportation. The contemporary revolution in agriculture in the early years probably was responsible for the first important market for ironware, and the hundreds of factories turning out plows and other agricultural machinery laid the foundations for the rapidly developing industry. Until about 1859, as Professor Hunter has pointed out,

. . . the manufacture of iron was controlled and conditioned by the needs and requirements of a pioneer agricultural population, which were met to a large extent by forges and rolling mills without the mediation of manufactories of finished iron products. The principal function of the manufacturers of wrought iron was to supply the country iron workers, blacksmiths by profession or necessity, with bar iron to be shaped to meet the needs of farmer, wagoner and mill owner. . . . In the period which followed the iron manufacturer gradually ceased to serve the agricultural population directly. The demand for iron came increasingly from industries engaged in the production of finished iron goods and the machinery of industry and commerce. . . . The agricultural era gave way to what might be termed the *industrial era*.[4]

PROCESSING OF AGRICULTURAL PRODUCTS

The processing of foodstuffs, particularly the grinding of flour and the packing of meat, had been a household industry from the earliest colonial times. It was also among the first forms of manufacturing outside the home to be found in a frontier community. Although gristmills, as Clark has pointed out, were "relatively smaller employers of labor than were sawmills and iron furnaces, and their owners were to a less extent industrialists, nevertheless they employed considerable capital and in the aggregate played an equally important part in the economic life of the community."[5] One reason for the smaller number of men employed was the early improvement in machinery. In the late eighteenth century Oliver Evans had perfected devices

[4] L. C. Hunter, "The Influence of the Market upon Techniques in Iron Industry in Western Pennsylvania to 1860," *Journal of Economic History*, I, 241–281 (1929).
[5] Victor S. Clark, *op. cit.*, I, 180.

by which every step of milling from cleaning to barreling could be done by mechanical means. It is possible, as one student has suggested, that this may have been the first instance of an uninterrupted process of machine manufacturing from raw material to the finished product in the history of industry. By 1800 mills existed which could turn 100,000 bushels of grain a year into flour. With the increasing population and the exportation of foodstuffs along with the invention of the reaper and other agricultural machinery, the milling of flour grew in importance. At the same time the wheat belt moved across the Alleghenies and was followed by the wheat processors. Early centers were Baltimore, Richmond, and Rochester; later milling moved westward to Chicago, St. Louis, and the principal towns of the Ohio Valley.

Colonial farmers had found a market for their surplus meat in the coast towns, the West Indies, and other foreign countries. In the succeeding years the growing cities and the plantations of the South provided additional markets. Meat packing in earlier times was essentially a seasonal industry. At certain periods it required a considerable labor supply, and also banking and shipping facilities. Thus it was forced to concentrate in large centers where such facilities could be supplied. These centers were at first the seaport towns, but the packers followed the frontier and by 1850 Cincinnati was the chief center, packing 27 per cent of the meat products of the West. Also growing in importance were Louisville, Chicago, and St. Louis. Meat was preserved in the earlier years principally by salt, but by the middle of the nineteenth century the method of sterilizing by heat and enclosing in airtight receptacles was widely used. Meat packing had additional importance because of the numerous by-products—glue from hoofs; oils, candles, and soaps from the fats; bristles from hair; and fertilizers from other parts. Until the Civil War most meat packing was still done at home, but factory packing had made such headway that with the stimulation of the war it soon became the leading American industry in value of products. Knowledge of how to can other foods as well as meat had also been developed by the middle of the century, climaxed by Gail Borden's discovery in the early 1850's of a "process of evaporating milk in a vacuum."

Such products as leather and tobacco could receive a crude processing in the farmhouse, but a better grade demanded tanneries and tobacco factories. The same was true of the important distilling industry. The growth of the farming population in the West led to the decline of rum as the national drink and the substitution of whiskey distilled from rye or corn. The chief center of the industry in 1810 was Pennsylvania, but it soon shifted to New York, Ohio, and Kentucky. By 1850 Cincinnati was the largest whiskey market in the world, and factories were capable of producing 2,000,000 gallons a year. Although whiskey maintained its pre-eminence until well past the middle of the century, there was an increased production and use of malt beverages.

Ranked by value added by manufacturing, the industrial products in 1860 were cotton goods, lumber, boots and shoes, flour and meal, men's clothing, iron (cast, forged, rolled, and wrought), machinery, woolen goods, carriages and wagons, and leather. The three highest in value of product were flour and meal, cotton goods, and lumber. The three industries employing the largest number of workers were boots and shoes, cotton goods, and men's clothing.

DISTRIBUTION OF INDUSTRY

The location of American industries was determined by chance in some cases, but more commonly by economic factors. The Northeast asserted her leadership in manufacturing in colonial times and continued to hold first rank. New England, with little good agricultural soil but gifted with abundance of water power, an active commerce, and a thrifty, energetic, closely settled population, was especially fitted for manufacturing, though the area lacked important raw materials. The Middle Atlantic States were favored by more varied mineral resources, by direct routes to the interior, and by a greater supply of capital and labor but were handicapped by competing agriculture and the constant draining off of her population to the West. Nevertheless, important centers for textiles and other manufactures arose near the water power furnished by the Mohawk, the Hudson, and the Delaware, and in such cities as New York, Newark, Paterson, Philadelphia, Rochester, and Pittsburgh, which were located on routes of travel or accessible to coal and iron. The early years of the century also gave promise of considerable manufacturing in the Piedmont regions of Virginia and the Carolinas, but the absorbing interest in agriculture prevented any great development until after the Civil War, although such successful enterprises as Gregg's cotton mills at Graniteville, South Carolina, and the Tredegar ironworks at Richmond proved that this handicap might be overcome.

Far more important than the South was the region of the Ohio River, where, prior to 1860, considerable manufacturing existed. Pittsburgh specialized in many forms of ironware; Cincinnati, until 1850 the only town west of the Alleghenies with a population of 100,000, was a great center for meat packing and the manufacture of machinery, clothing, whiskey, and other commodities; Louisville produced cordage, bagging, and clothing, and Chicago was developing large milling and packing interests. The products of New England and the middle states in general were of a type requiring detailed manufacturing with finer mechanisms and involving higher labor costs. Thus textiles, boots and shoes, rubber goods, clothing, glassware, pot-

tery, and cutlery were centered here. The following figures from the Census
of 1860 give a comparison of the sections in manufacturing:

MANUFACTURING BY SECTIONS, 1860

Sections	Number of Establishments	Capital Invested	Average Number of Laborers	Annual Value of Products
New England	20,671	$ 257,477,783	391,836	$ 468,599,287
Middle states	53,387	435,061,964	546,243	802,338,392
Western states	36,785	194,212,543	209,909	384,606,530
Southern states	20,631	95,975,185	110,721	155,531,281
Pacific states	8,777	23,380,334	50,204	71,229,989
Territories	282	3,747,906	2,333	3,556,197
Total	140,533	$1,009,855,715	1,311,246	$1,885,861,676

Eighth Census, *Manufactures*, III, 725.

INFLUENCE OF TRANSPORTATION ON MANUFACTURING

The location of the early manufacturing plants was dependent not only
on access to water power but on transportation facilities as well. The development of manufactures went hand in hand with the development of cheaper
and more rapid means of transportation. Until overland routes were opened
up, the settlers kept close to the coast line or the numerous rivers which cut
inland in a northerly or northwesterly direction, and it was on the coast or
along these rivers that the first tiny manufacturing plants were to be found.
Many of the early industries were concerned with shipbuilding, another
factor that determined location. As the westward movement progressed and
the various trans-Allegheny routes came into use, industrial life frequently
made its appearance at key points on the rivers, such as Pittsburgh, Cincinnati, Louisville, and St. Louis. At such points factories were established to
build ships and engines and to manufacture cordage and other necessities in
navigation, as well as nails, kitchen utensils, and furniture for the passing
immigrant. As the newcomers filled up the surrounding country there also
appeared packing plants, mills, breweries, and distilleries, where the products of the settlers could be turned into less bulky form for shipment. In a
similar manner, points like Wheeling on the Cumberland Road were given
a start toward an industrial life, as were other towns, like Lexington, close
to but not on the main line of travel. Although overland transportation was
severely limited until the advent of canals and railroads, the improvement of
wagon roads and the building of turnpikes were an important stimulus to
both industry and commerce.

About the middle of the eighteenth century two Irish tinsmiths, William
and Edgar Pattison, had settled in Berlin, Connecticut, and commenced to
peddle their manufactured wares from house to house. As they prospered,

others imitated them, until Connecticut became the center not only of tin manufacture but of brass products, clocks, and other small but desirable commodities; other New England towns manufactured cheap jewelry and novelties for the peddlers. Each spring New England capitalists and manufacturers supplied their agents with a stock of goods, and the agents set out on horseback, returning with their profits in the fall. The coming of the turnpike enabled the peddler to extend his operations, establish depots and operatives at distant points from which he might replenish his wares, and cover effectively almost every accessible settlement. "I have seen them," said Timothy Dwight, "on the peninsula of Cape Cod, and in the neighborhood of Lake Erie; distant from each other more than six hundred miles. They make their way to Detroit, four hundred miles farther; to Canada, to Kentucky; and, if I mistake not, to New Orleans and St. Louis."[6]

With the completion of the Hudson and Lake Champlain Canal in 1823, and the more important Erie Canal two years later, a mania for canal building ensued which opened up new and quicker routes from east to west, vitally affecting the growth of manufacturing. The fall in freight rates made it possible for eastern manufacturers to get their wares into the hands of the frontiersmen at prices within reach, and for the Westerner to ship his iron, lead, wool, leather, flour, and meat back east cheaply enough to find a market. The cheaper canal rates tended (1) to discourage the growth of the finer types of manufacturing on the frontier and to give added impetus to the growth of such industries in the Northeast, and (2) to stimulate production in the West and discourage manufacturing, other than putting frontier products—meat, leather, grain, and iron—into shape for transportation. The more regular deliveries and the better information obtainable in regard to markets made it possible to conduct business on a surer foundation and a larger scale. As manufacturing towns had grown up on the rivers, the canals in a similar manner brought into existence manufacturing cities like Rochester or greatly stimulated industrial life in such terminal cities as New York, Buffalo, Philadelphia, and Pittsburgh. Even before the advent of railroads artificial water routes had so supplemented river navigation that it was possible to tap the resources of most of the settled regions.

The tendencies in manufacturing set in motion by the canals were further accentuated by the rapid building of railroads after 1840. Inland freight rates declined during the canal-building period, and dropped still further with the coming of the railroads. Transportation east and west was now as practical as from north to south. Industry was no longer dependent upon the seasons, for goods could be shipped in the winter months; hence the necessity of closed mills, idle workmen, and unproductive capital because of

[6] Timothy Dwight, *Travels in New England and New York* (1823), II, 54.

inability to move goods was largely eliminated. Railroads could be built more cheaply than canals, and to many points impossible of access by the latter, all of which tended to reduce the final cost of manufactured products. The railroads quickened the settlement of the frontier, and the consequent increase in population created new and greater markets; they also made it possible for different sections to specialize in the occupations favorable to them. Although for some years railroad building absorbed much of the available capital and thus impeded manufacturing other than that concerned in railroad supplies, the setback was temporary.[7]

SELECTED READINGS

Clark, V. S., *History of Manufactures in the United States, 1607–1860*, Vol. I, chaps. 11–21.
Tryon, R. M., *Household Manufacture in the United States, 1640–1860*, chaps. 7, 8.
Keir, Malcolm, *Manufacturing*, chaps. 3–7.
Taylor, G. R., *The Transportation Revolution*, chaps. 10, 11.
Callender, G. S., *Selections from the Economic History of the United States, 1765–1860*, chap. 9.
Bogart, E. L., and Thompson, C. M., *Readings in the Economic History of the United States*, chaps. 8, 9.
Flügel, F., and Faulkner, H. U., *Readings in the Economic and Social History of the United States*, chaps. 2, 8.

[7] Economists have also pointed out the influence of transportation on labor organization. Greatly extended market areas brought severer competition among employers which resulted in wage cuts and speeded the organization of labor.

CHAPTER 14

INTERNAL TRANSPORTATION
AND COMMUNICATION TO 1860

SIGNIFICANCE AND PROBLEMS OF AMERICAN TRANSPORTATION

THE ever-westward movement of population and the rapid conquest of a continent have made the matter of transportation one of the most vital problems facing both government and people since our history began. As the first settlers along the seacoast were dependent upon ocean transportation to market their raw materials in Europe and obtain manufactured products in return, so later waves of advancing settlers were in like manner dependent upon rivers, roads, canals, and railways in disposing of their products. Especially was the question acute in an essentially agricultural community, like that of the United States before the Civil War, where the commodities to be transported were likely to be bulky and in some cases perishable.

Not only was the economic life of the new settlements dependent largely upon transportation, but their location and existence were in many cases determined by it. The first settlements were usually made on rivers or harbors, and the advance inland followed the numerous rivers which ran into the Atlantic and provided the easiest facilities for transportation. As the best land was taken up along the rivers, the new settlers were forced to occupy the back country and to get to the rivers by crude roads. These roads often followed existing trails, for the paths of the deer and buffalo in their quest of water became the trails of the Indian hunters and the wagon roads and railroads of the white man.[1]

[1] "The New York Central and the Lake Shore follow the old Lake Shore Trail; the Pennsylvania follows the old Mahoning Trail; the Toledo and Ohio Central follows the Monongahela Trail; the Baltimore and Ohio follows the Great or Big Trail; another Pennsylvania line follows the Moravia-Scioto-Beaver Trail; the Hocking Valley, the Sandusky-Richmond Trail; the Norfolk and Western follows the Scioto Trail; the Cincinnati, Hamilton and Dayton follows the Miami Trail; the Lake Erie and Wheeling, the Muskingum Trail." B. H. Meyer (ed.), *Transportation in the United States, 1860,* p. 6.

Where rivers met the ocean and formed good harbors, where one river ran into another, or where trails connected with rivers, particularly at the head of navigation, there were the strategic points at which towns and cities sprang up. After 1850 railroad building went on so rapidly that railroads often preceded the settlers and, like the rivers in earlier years, pointed to inevitable routes. Gradual improvements in transportation did much to weaken economic sectionalism and in turn political sectionalism. When our national government was founded, the trip from Boston to New York by the fastest stage route required a week; today one can go by air from New York City to Los Angeles, California, in less than twelve hours. Railroads bound the East and West together at the time of the Civil War and have contributed greatly to the specialization of industry in certain sections and the mutual interdependence of economic groups and geographic sections.

Two great transportation problems have faced the American people. The first was that of bringing the bulky agricultural products to the markets. Except for farmers who lived on or near navigable rivers, this was never adequately solved until the coming of the railroads. Moreover, while farmers might float their corn or cotton down the river, the difficulties of bringing back return cargoes of manufactured goods were not met until the river steamboat appeared.

Even after the steamboat had greatly facilitated river commerce, there remained the problem of those who lived far from water transportation. Although the United States is unusually well supplied with national waterways, a glance at the map will show that most of her rivers run generally from north to south. The population on the other hand has usually moved from east to west; hence the real transportation needs were for facilities which would allow an east-west movement rather than one from north to south. A survey of the history of American internal transportation makes this clear. The first important artificial highways were in most cases roads reaching westward into the back country from the seacoast or from rivers. In some cases they were designed to connect the headwaters of navigable rivers running into the Atlantic or into the Mississippi, thus establishing a route westward. This was also true of most of the canals. With the coming of the railroads this problem was solved, for a railroad could free itself from the river valleys and cut westward at will, except where its route might be determined by mountain passes. Reference to a railroad map (p. 278) will establish the fact that with a few exceptions the important trunk lines run from east to west. A glance at a highway map or a map of air routes will also illustrate this point.

Improvements in transportation facilities before the Civil War fall roughly into three groups: (1) turnpikes and improved roads, (2) canals and improved rivers, and (3) railroads. Simultaneously came the introduction and rapid development of the river steamboat, an important feature of the transportation history of these years. Throughout this period, as in earlier and later years, the movement for better transportation facilities was impelled by certain fundamental motives. Among them were the demands of farmers for better transportation to market their products, demands that were supported by the inhabitants of coast towns who desired cheaper foodstuffs and by exporters who wanted larger amounts of commodities at cheaper prices. At the same time importers and eastern manufacturers hoped to widen their markets. When transportation facilities were privately built there was the hope of dividends and always the lure of speculation, for a turnpike, canal, or railroad was bound to affect the value of adjacent land. The building of transportation facilities inevitably went hand in hand with land speculation.

THE TURNPIKE ERA

At the opening of the national period the main towns along the seacoast were connected by roads of a most rudimentary type, constructed before the technique of modern roadbuilding was understood. Choked with mud in the spring, thick with dust in the summer, and often heavy with snow in the winter, the overland routes were fraught with the most arduous labor and hardship, frequently with real danger. The risk was increased by the fact that until long after the Revolution there were no bridges over the principal rivers. In addition there were trails leading westward—two cut during the French and Indian War to Pittsburgh, and another farther south through the Cumberland Gap. Traders in New York had also opened the Mohawk Trail to the Genesee Valley and Lake Erie. As yet they were merely routes for westward-moving settlers and the pack trains of fur traders.

In the 1790's an intense interest developed in improved road transportation, particularly in the building of turnpikes, that is, roads upon which tolls were charged. This seems to have been caused primarily by the rapid westward movement and by the increased prosperity and growing foreign commerce resulting from the European wars. The inadequacy of the existing roads, built largely for local needs, and the need for better-constructed highways designed for through traffic became more evident. A later impetus developed from the difficulties of moving troops and supplies during the War of 1812.

The lead in the movement for better roads was taken by private individuals who organized companies to build these turnpikes. The first in America was the pike from Philadelphia to Lancaster, built from 1792 to 1794 at a cost of $465,000. Well constructed in a populous area, it was financially successful from the start. Wrote Francis Baily in 1797: "There is, at present, but one turnpike-road on the continent, which is between Lancaster and

Philadelphia, a distance of sixty-six miles, and is a masterpiece of its kind; it is paved with stone the whole way, and overlaid with gravel; so that it is never obstructed during the most severe seasons."[2]

So successful was the Lancaster Pike that a mania for building turnpikes spread over the country. During the next thirty years hundreds of charters were issued by the states and thousands of miles of roads were built. Many state governments contributed by purchasing substantial amounts of shares in these companies. Moreover, the building of toll roads also gave an impetus to the construction of many toll bridges. The spending of millions of dollars for highways resulted in a great improvement in American transportation. But few of them approached the Lancaster Pike in excellence. The mania itself eventually died down, not so much because of the rivalry of canals and railroads as because they were financially unsuccessful. The cost of maintenance and collection of tolls exceeded the income. Only a few of the best located paid dividends in their most profitable years. A tiny minority operated at a profit.

Turnpikes improved transportation but did not solve the problem. The cost was too high. The freight per ton from Philadelphia to Pittsburgh by an all-land route was $125, and the average through the country for general merchandise, according to McMaster, was $10 per ton per hundred miles, making it out of the question to transport such bulky articles as grain and flour more than 150 miles. (At this time, the freight on a ton coming from Europe was 40 shillings.) These rates were kept high not only by poor roads but by high tolls. The average toll in New England was 12½ cents per wagon for each two miles. In New Jersey it was one cent per mile for each horse; the Pennsylvania rates varied according to the width of tire and number of horses. Nor did improved roads solve the problem of passenger transportation. Travel on the new turnpikes was faster and more comfortable, but the time consumed was still great and the average cost was 6 cents a mile.

FEDERAL PARTICIPATION

In the movement for transportation improvement the demand for federal aid soon followed that for state participation. Government aid and control had been a normal procedure during the colonial period, and loose constructionists, ardent nationalists, and those who would benefit financially insisted that the "general welfare" clause of the Constitution gave such power. They also pointed to Article I, Section 7, which gave the national government power to establish post offices and post roads and to regulate interstate com-

[2] Francis Baily, *Journal of a Tour in Unsettled Parts of North America in 1796 and 1797,* p. 107.

merce. Strict constructionists considered this interpretation too broad, and their group was augmented by those who claimed that it was unfair to tax the whole country for the benefit of certain sections.

The discussion brought forth on April 4, 1808, the famous report on internal improvements made by Albert Gallatin at the request of Congress. Gallatin pointed out that in more developed countries where capital was plentiful transportation facilities could be built by private initiative without direct aid from the government. In America, however, this was largely prevented by the high cost of labor and the unusual demand for capital. Federal aid, he argued, was advisable since improved transportation would unite the country, provide an important aid in military defense, raise the value of western land, and contribute to the economic development. He urged that the peninsulas jutting into the Atlantic be cut by canals—across Cape Cod, across New Jersey, and between the Delaware and the Chesapeake. Further communication north and south should be provided by a great turnpike running from Maine to Georgia. East and west transportation might be improved by building roads that would join the headwaters of certain eastern rivers with the headwaters of other rivers running into the Ohio. He suggested that one method of paying for this might be the sale of public lands.

By private or state efforts Gallatin's plan was eventually completed. But for the moment, the chief result of the demand for internal improvements at the expense of the national government during these early years was the Cumberland Road. Ohio was admitted to the Union (1803) under an agreement whereby federal lands sold within her borders were exempt from taxation for five years; in return the federal government was to appropriate 5 per cent of the proceeds from the sale of such lands for the building of roads, three-fifths of which was to be expended within the state for state roads and two-fifths by Congress in building roads to and through the state. Similar agreements were later made with Indiana, Illinois, and Missouri. This allowed even the strict-construction Republicans a loophole, and during Jefferson's administration, on March 29, 1806, Congress authorized the building of such a road. The first contract, however, was not signed until 1811, and the first stretch of 130 miles to Wheeling, West Virginia, was not completed until 1818.

The road was continued from Wheeling almost due west through Zanesville, Columbus, and Springfield, Ohio; Richmond, Indianapolis, and Terre Haute, Indiana; to Vandalia, Illinois; it reached Columbus in 1833 and Vandalia in 1852. The road to Wheeling was especially well built: "Its numerous and stately stone bridges, with handsome stone arches, its iron mile posts, and its old iron gates, attest the skill of the workmen engaged in its construction, and to this day remain enduring monuments of its grandeur and solidity."[3] The road was supported by western Congressmen, whose influence went far in bringing about the passing of more than thirty acts for its construction and maintenance between 1806 and 1838. It cost the federal government $6,821,200.

Until the coming of railroads the 834 miles of the "National Pike" provided one of the chief avenues to the West. "As many as twenty four-horse coaches have been counted in line at the time on the road, and large, broad-wheeled wagons, covered with white canvas stretched over bows laden with

(From H. U. Faulkner, *Economic History of the United States*, by permission of
The Macmillan Company.)

THE NATIONAL PIKE.

merchandise and drawn by six Conestoga horses, were visible all the day long at every point, and many times until late in the evening, besides innumerable caravans of horses, mules, cattle, hogs and sheep. It looked more like the leading avenue of a great city than a road through rural districts."[4]

The Cumberland Road not only furnished a great highway for emigration but reduced transportation costs between Baltimore and the Ohio and brought great prosperity to the regions through which it ran. Communication between East and West was quickened by the Great Western Mail which followed it and by the express coaches of the rival transportation companies, which developed incredible speed. So beneficial was the road that numerous local turnpikes were projected which it was hoped the national government would sponsor. No less than 111 surveys and plans for roads, canals, railroads, and river improvements were before Congress in 1830 when Jackson called a halt by his veto of the Maysville Road Bill, a proposed turnpike from Maysville to Lexington, sixty miles in length, entirely in the state of Kentucky. Jackson held it to be unconstitutional for the government to use money for such enterprises confined wholly to individual states. This veto contributed much to throwing future internal improvements into state hands.

[3] T. B. Searight, *The Old Pike*, p. 16.
[4] *Ibid.*

The excitement over turnpikes died down as the nation turned to canals, but there has never been a time in our history when there has not been continuous roadbuilding as the country has expanded. During the fifties, for example, interest blazed up again in a fever for building plank roads, and several thousand miles were constructed. These were built by laying parallel stringers on the ground about four feet apart and nailing planks across them eight feet long and three or four inches thick. At a cost of $1200 to $1500 a mile these roads were relatively inexpensive, but they wore out quickly and were soon forgotten in the railroad boom of the 1850's.

THE RIVER STEAMBOAT

While turnpike projects were being pushed with feverish haste, experiments were being made with the steam engine that were destined to give longer life and renewed importance to river traffic. A number of American engineers, including Oliver Evans, John Fitch, James Rumsey, John Stevens, and others, had been experimenting with the steam engine in water transportation and had successfully propelled vessels, but it was left to Robert Fulton to make steam navigation commercially successful. After many discouragements, but with the backing of Robert R. Livingston, Fulton in 1807 built the *Clermont,* a 160-ton side-wheeler, which he navigated to Albany, a distance of 150 miles, in thirty-two hours. "My steamboat voyage to Albany and back," said Fulton in a letter, "has turned out rather more favorably than I had calculated. The distance from New York to Albany is one hundred and fifty miles. I ran it up in thirty-two hours, and down in thirty. I had a light breeze against me the whole way, both going and coming; and the voyage has been performed wholly by the power of the steam-engine. I overtook many sloops and schooners beating to windward, and parted with them. The power of propelling boats by steam is now fully proved."

Fulton's epochal voyage in 1807 inaugurated a revolution, not only in river traffic but in ocean commerce as well. He and Livingston immediately obtained a monopoly of the waters of New York State for twenty years, and soon afterward a similar monopoly of the waters of the lower Mississippi in the territory of New Orleans. Several steamboats were in operation on the Hudson before the two men established a shipyard at Pittsburgh in 1811 and launched the *Orleans,* the first steamboat on the Ohio. This boat descended the Ohio and Mississippi in the winter of 1812, but could not return against the swift current. It was three years (May, 1815) before a steamboat succeeded in ascending the rivers from New Orleans to Louisville, a feat accomplished in twenty-five days by Henry Shreve, the greatest of the western navigators.

The development of steam navigation was held up temporarily until the monopolies in New York and Louisiana were broken by the Supreme Court decision in Gibbons *v.* Ogden (1824). This decision held that river transportation could not be monopolized by any one state, but that the regulation of interstate traffic came under the powers of Congress. The success of the steamboat was demonstrated by the fact that the time from New Orleans to Pittsburgh was soon reduced from 100 to thirty days. By the 1850's the fastest steamboats were making the upstream journey from New Orleans to Louisville in less than five days; freight and passenger rates were cut to a fraction of their former cost. Profits, nevertheless, were high and river steamboats were built rapidly. It is believed that in the late forties the steamboat tonnage on the western rivers was greater than that of the entire British Empire. Profiting from her position, New Orleans during the 1830's grew more rapidly in population and wealth than any city in the country.

The early experiments had been made in the East, but it was upon the western waters that the river steamboat was to play its greatest role. In 1816 Shreve, throwing precedents aside, used a flat-bottomed keelboat as his model, placed the engine on deck with the cylinders in a horizontal position, and built a second deck over the first. This flat-bottomed model, developed by Shreve and others was particularly suited to overcome the danger of river navigation, and it was the forerunner of those speedy and gorgeous palaces that plied between the western ports in the golden days of river navigation. Steamboats on the eastern rivers specialized in passenger traffic, those on the western rivers in freight.

The loss of large numbers of steamboats because of bars and snags led to the appropriation between 1822 and 1860 of over $3,000,000 by the national government for bettering traffic conditions on the Mississippi, Ohio, Missouri, and Arkansas rivers. The commerce of the Mississippi Valley in 1852 was estimated at $654,000,000, a large proportion of which was made possible · by the steamboat, which not only aided in the marketing of bulky foodstuffs and cotton but thereby stimulated a more rapid settlement of the region.

ERA OF CANAL BUILDING—THE ERIE

The river steamboat was an immense boon to the river towns, but it did not solve the problem of east-west transportation. The "National Pike" had helped, but costs were too high, and the population of the trans-Allegheny West had grown so large as to demand greater facilities. The center of population by 1850 had almost reached the Ohio in the western part of the present West Virginia. River transportation had in part met the needs of southwestern cotton planters, but not those of the farmers north of the Ohio.

As the limitations of roads became evident, and the needs for eastern outlets more intense, attention was drawn to artificial waterways. On the eastern coast some efforts had been made to improve facilities from inland areas to the tidewater by canals, and there were dreams of connecting the trans-Allegheny West with the eastern coast in the same manner. The success of James Brindley in England in constructing the Bridgewater Canal (opened 1761) and in later projects had stimulated great canal activity in that country and was reflected here in continuing interest. The Erie was the most notable artificial waterway built in this country, but it was not the first. Small canals had been constructed in Virginia, North Carolina, and Massachusetts, the most successful being the Middlesex Canal, twenty-seven miles long and extending from the Merrimac River to the Charles in Massachusetts. Long before the Erie Canal was begun the superiority of canals over turnpikes was demonstrated. The chief advantage lay in the fact that a horse could drag through dead water a load fifty times heavier than on land. Against this advantage was the greater cost of building canals and the greater difficulty of surmounting changing levels. In the North freezing weather temporarily closed canals to traffic, and in all parts of the country washouts often rendered them useless.

If water transportation was to be achieved to the trans-Allegheny West, the most obvious and best route was a connection between the Hudson and Lake Erie where the rise was only 630 feet. Agitation for such a canal began in the 1780's, but it was 1817 before New York State, urged on by Governor Clinton, undertook to build without outside aid. The chief engineer of the Erie Canal was Benjamin Wright, but the mechanical genius who circumvented so many difficulties was Canvass White, a young man who had walked 2000 miles along the towpaths of England studying every detail of canal construction there. White was the exception, for many of the engineers in the early days of canal building in America had never even seen a canal before they commenced to construct one. Fifteen miles of waterway between the towns of Utica and Rome were opened in 1819, and on October 26, 1825, cannon stationed at intervals along the canal announced from Buffalo to Albany the opening of the entire length and the departure of the first boats. Some weeks later, from the decks of the *Seneca Chief,* which had headed the procession of vessels, Governor Clinton poured the contents of a cask filled with water from Lake Erie into New York Harbor to signify the wedding of the waters.

As originally built, the Erie Canal was 363 miles long. It was constructed at an average cost of $20,000 a mile, the total amounting to approximately $7,000,000. Typical of other canals of the period, the Erie was forty feet wide and four feet deep (later widened to seventy and deepened to seven) and could accommodate thirty-ton barges. It followed the Mohawk to Rome, and

thence westward through the present cities of Syracuse, Rochester, and Lockport to Buffalo by way of the Tonawanda and Niagara rivers. Subsidiary
canals connected it with Lakes Ontario, Champlain, and Seneca. Eventually
New York had 906 miles of artificial waterways.

The success of the Erie was immediate. Tolls exceeded the interest charge
before it was finished and during the first nine years amounted to $8,500,000
—more than the initial cost. Nineteen thousand boats and rafts passed West
Troy in the Erie and Champlain canals during 1826. The first and greatest
effect of "Clinton's ditch" was in providing an all-water route to the West,

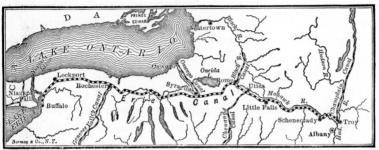

(From H. U. Faulkner, *Economic History of the United States,* by permission of
The Macmillan Company.)

THE ERIE CANAL.

thus furnishing an outlet for the bulky products of the interior. Freight
from Buffalo to New York dropped from $100 to $15 per ton, and the time
from twenty days to eight. Farm produce of western New York doubled in
value and that of the states north of the Ohio was increased; this rise carried
in its wake a corresponding rise in land values. If the Old Northwest was
mightily stimulated, the regions immediately adjoining this "great blood
vessel of the state" fairly boomed. Utica, Syracuse, and Rochester became
thriving towns, and the terminals—Buffalo, Albany, and New York—took
on new life. The last-named city doubled its population between 1820 and
1830 and took from Philadelphia its leadership as the first American seaport.
The Lake cities of Buffalo, Cleveland, Detroit, and Chicago entered a period
of rapid growth and began to rival Pittsburgh, Cincinnati, St. Louis, and
New Orleans, as the produce of the western farmers was drawn through the
northern route. To a large and important area the Erie Canal opened a
period of unprecedented prosperity. Passenger packets made the distance
from Albany to Buffalo in four and a half days, and over this route passed
a continually increasing stream of western immigrants. The Old Northwest
seemed firmly bound to New York through the Erie, for the distance to the
sea was shorter this way than through either the Mississippi or the St. Lawrence Valley.

OTHER EASTERN CANALS

The success of the Erie Canal and the consequent prosperity of New York led to similar projects in other eastern states. These were of three types. First, other efforts were made to link the Atlantic states with the Ohio River Valley. Second, canals were built to improve transportation between the up-country and tidewater. And third, canals were built to improve transportation north and south along the coast.

Of the first the Pennsylvania Canal was the only one that was successful. That state, fearful lest her western trade be drawn off to New York, was first caught in the mania for canal building, and rapidly constructed (1826–1834) a system of canals and portages from Philadelphia to Pittsburgh, following the Susquehanna, Juniata, Conemaugh, and Allegheny rivers. A horse railroad led from Philadelphia to Columbia on the Susquehanna where the canal began; from here the route was along the east bank of the Susquehanna and the west bank of the Juniata to Hollidaysburg. The mountains between Hollidaysburg and Johnstown were crossed by a portage railway thirty-three and a half miles long, upon the inclined planes of which it was possible to raise a boat 1399 feet in less than ten miles and lower it 1171 feet. The Pennsylvania Canal with its connecting railways was 394 miles long and was constructed at a cost of over $10,000,000. Although state-owned, the government did not operate either cars or boats; it simply charged a toll for their use. To build this route to the West it had been necessary to surmount an altitude of almost 2300 feet as against a rise of 630 feet on the Erie Canal. Not so satisfactory as the Erie, this route was yet successful in its purpose and through it a share of the western trade reached Philadelphia.

Not to be outdone by their northern neighbors, the citizens of Maryland and Virginia took up with renewed vigor an old plan to connect the eastern coast and the Ohio River by means of a canal running along the Potomac. The Potomac Company, with Washington as its first president, had been incorporated in 1785, but it was not until 1828 that the Chesapeake and Ohio Canal was commenced. Originally planned to extend from Georgetown, as its eastern terminal, to Cumberland, and thence by a tunnel across the range to the Youghiogheny, it was never pushed farther than Cumberland. It was completed in 1850 after many discouraging setbacks, at a cost of $11,000,000, of which $7,000,000 was contributed by the state of Maryland, $1,500,000 by the terminal cities, and $1,000,000 by the United States government. The Chesapeake and Ohio Canal was unsuccessful, owing largely to the fact that it did not cross the mountains and to the bitter opposition and competition of the Baltimore and Ohio Railroad, which was built simultaneously over the same route.

Numerous canals were built to connect the upcountry with the tidewater. In New England the Cumberland and Oxford (Sebago Pond to Portland) in Maine survived railroad competition until 1870. The Blackstone from Worcester to Narragansett Bay lasted twenty years. The New Haven and Northampton, finally opened in 1835, never developed enough business to cover operating expenses. In the middle states were the various subsidiary canals to the Erie and Pennsylvania, but more important, the canals built to bring anthracite coal to the coast. Of these the principal canals were the Delaware and Hudson, from Honesdale, Pennsylvania, to the Delaware and Hudson rivers, and the Lehigh, from White Haven and Mauch Chunk to Easton on the Delaware where it connected with the Delaware Division Canal to Philadelphia and the Morris Canal to Jersey City. The 102-mile Morris Canal cut through northern New Jersey to carry coal to the New York market.

Of the canals to facilitate north-south traffic the most important were the Delaware and Raritan and the Chesapeake and Delaware. The first, which ran from New Brunswick on the Raritan to Bordentown on the Delaware, was completed in 1838 and improved traffic from New York to Philadelphia. The Chesapeake Canal, thirteen and a half miles long, cut through from the Delaware to Chesapeake Bay and was completed in 1829.

CANALS IN THE MIDDLE WEST

The success of the Erie Canal stimulated interest also in the Middle West, and projects were immediately formulated to connect the Ohio with Lake Erie and thus provide a continuous inland waterway from New York to New Orleans. In 1825 Ohio authorized the building of two canals, one, known as the Ohio and Erie, to extend from Portsmouth on the Ohio along the course of the Scioto, Muskingum, Tuscarawas, and Cuyahoga to Cleveland; the other, the Miami and Erie, to extend from Cincinnati through Middletown, Dayton, and Defiance to Toledo, following the course of the Miami and Maumee rivers. Governor Clinton, the "father of the Erie Canal," turned the first spadeful for the Ohio and Erie. It was finished in 1833, so that Ohio by that date had over 400 miles of navigable canals. By 1850 this had extended to over 1000 miles. Although no great volume of through traffic appeared on the Ohio canals, a large local traffic and traffic of local goods for out-of-state markets developed. This reached its peak in the early 1850's, only to disappear rapidly with the coming of the railroads.

Indiana, caught with the same enthusiasm for internal improvements, commenced in 1832 (completed in 1843) the Wabash and Erie, which connected Lake Erie with the Ohio River. The route led through the Miami and Erie to Defiance, entered Indiana in Allen County, and then went southwest along the Wabash to Terre Haute and south to Evansville on the Ohio. Over 450 miles in length, it was the longest canal ever built in America. That part north of Terre Haute was kept open until 1872, when, like the Ohio canals, it succumbed to railroad competition. Indiana also built the White Water Canal from Hagerstown, Wayne County, mostly along the White Water River, to Lawrenceburg on the Ohio. Illinois, still sparsely settled, built the Illinois and Michigan Canal (1836–1848), connecting Lake Michigan with the Mississippi by an artificial waterway from Chicago to La Salle, the head of navigation on the Illinois. Wisconsin attempted to join Green Bay, an arm of Lake Michigan, with the Mississippi by means of a canal between the Fox and Wisconsin rivers, but the project was not completed until 1856. Lakes Huron and Superior were connected in 1855 by a canal around St. Marys Falls. Constructed originally by Michigan, it was later turned over to the United States government and has become one of the most important artificial waterways in the world. Navigation on the Ohio was furthered by a short canal around the falls at Louisville. Canal mileage in the United States was estimated at 1270 in 1830, 3320 in 1840, and 3700 in 1850.

EFFECT OF THE PANIC OF 1837

Much of the canal mileage had been built by the several states. Constitutional objections had tied the hands of the national government, although considerable aid had been rendered by donations of 4,000,000 acres of public lands and by the purchase of stock, as in the case of the Chesapeake and Ohio. Private capital proved inadequate, but the credit of the states in the prosperous days of the late twenties and early thirties seemed inexhaustible. Land speculators and bona fide settlers encouraged expenditures out of all proportion to the existing wealth and population of the states, and wrote into the state constitutions of the period directions "to encourage internal improvements within the state." Rivalries between states and cities contributed to the mania. State debts, which had amounted to only $12,790,728 in 1820, had increased to $200,000,000 in 1840, most of which had been incurred for banks, roads, canals, and railroads. A good share of the money for canals had been borrowed from England. The confidence placed in the United States Bank, the high standing of our national credit, the high interest rates on American securities—combined with ignorance of conditions here—easily induced Europeans to buy American stocks and bonds.[5] Only seven states (Connecticut, Delaware, Georgia, New Hampshire, North Carolina, Rhode

---

[5] See R. C. McGrane, "Some Aspects of American State Debts in the 'Forties," *American Historical Review*, XXXVIII, 673–686 (July, 1933), and his *Foreign Bondholders and American State Debts* (1935).

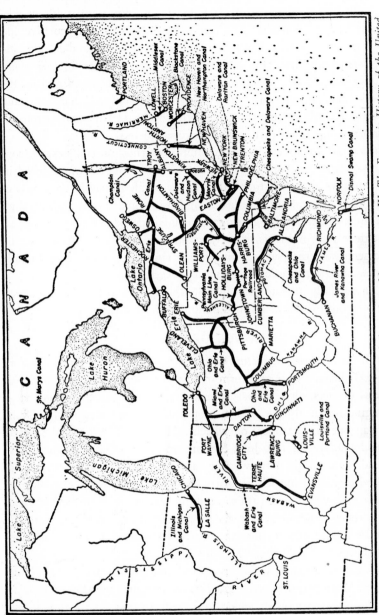

(From George Rogers Taylor, *The Transportation Revolution, 1815–1860,* p. 35, vol. IV, *The Economic History of the United States,* Rinehart & Company.)

PRINCIPAL CANALS BUILT BY 1860.

Island, and Vermont) had not contracted debts for these purposes. Much of this work had been undertaken in an era of enthusiasm without adequate knowledge of difficulties and costs. The projects were speculative and in some cases unnecessary. Furthermore, in spite of the grandiose expectations of canal enthusiasts, the canals remained largely local in their commercial significance. In 1840 only one-seventh of the freight carried on the New York canals originated outside the state. Despite what has been said, many of these canals at one time or another were relatively prosperous; it was railroad competition that chiefly destroyed them.

This too rapid investment in internal improvements, especially canals, contributed largely to the panic of 1837, and when the bubble was pricked in that year most of the states found themselves unable to pay interest or continue the work. Several of them, including Mississippi, Louisiana, Maryland, Pennsylvania, Indiana, and Michigan, repudiated their debts. Nearly all sold out their improvements to private concerns and ceased to aid public improvements, and the people, going to the opposite extreme, now forbade in the new state constitutions the use of government credit for such purposes. Consequently, private individuals and corporations largely shouldered the work during the era of railroad building which was just dawning.

SIGNIFICANCE OF RAILROADS

The full flush of prosperity for canals had scarcely been reached before they were challenged by a new form of transportation. Simultaneously with the success of steam-driven boats, the idea had come to engineers that a steam engine might also be used to propel wheeled vehicles. Oliver Evans in 1804 had put his steamboat on wheels and driven it through the streets of Philadelphia, and in 1820 John Stevens, on his estate at Hoboken, New Jersey, had built a little narrow-gauge railroad upon which he ran a locomotive and cars with himself a passenger. When in October, 1829, George Stephenson's *Rocket* pulled a train weighing thirteen tons on the Liverpool and Manchester Railroad at an average speed of fifteen miles an hour, the practicability of steam railroads was clearly demonstrated. The advantages of railroads over canals were soon realized.

Railroads were cheaper to construct, and transportation over them was more rapid. Moreover, they were not confined to comparatively low districts on account of water supply or subject to the expense and delay of locks; they could be laid to reach almost any part of the country, including the back doors of factories. They were not as seriously affected as canals by change of seasons, droughts, floods, or freezing; all sections could benefit at all times. The rivers ran mostly north and south, but the new railroads could strike directly west. Where railroads did follow in general the course of rivers, there were opportunities for short cuts which appreciably reduced the distance between points. The effect of the railroads in opening up the West, in providing transportation for western products, in stimulating eastern manufacturing, in speeding labor organization (note, p. 259), in binding the sections together, in disseminating information and education to remote sections provides a story intertwined with every phase of our economic, social, and political life.

Although steam railroads were first developed in Britain, they expanded more rapidly in this country. Within a decade our mileage far surpassed that of Europe. The demand in a large country for cheap, fast, and flexible transportation was an underlying cause. Contributory, of course, was the fact that there were no restrictive political boundaries or customs barriers. Moreover, land was much cheaper (later federal and state governments gave land to the railroads) and the opposition of vested interests was less keen, although railroads did meet the bitter opposition of canals.

EARLY AMERICAN RAILROADS

"England," says Dunbar, "had been building railways for nearly two hundred years, had made iron rails since 1738 and steam locomotives since 1804."[6] But these components were not satisfactorily combined in a steam railroad until 1829. In America wooden rails for local roads to move iron and stone had been used in various places early in the century. The best known of these were the three-mile road from Quincy, Massachusetts, to Neponset, opened in 1826, and the Mauch Chunk Railway in Pennsylvania completed in the next year. The first railroads designed for passenger service were those built to supplement the canal system, such as the road from Philadelphia to Columbia and from Hollidaysburg to Johnstown.

The first spadeful of earth for the track of the Baltimore and Ohio was turned on July 4, 1828, by Charles Carroll of Carrollton, the last surviving signer of the Declaration of Independence. This was the first railroad in the modern sense in America; the first division of it, thirteen miles long, was opened in 1830. Even the builders of this road were not sufficiently convinced of the value of steam, and the motive power for the first vehicles was horsepower. On a trial trip in 1830 Peter Cooper's engine, *Tom Thumb*, made the thirteen miles from Baltimore to Ellicott's Mills in an hour, and the management turned definitely to steam.

The first attempt to run a steam railroad locomotive in this country (barring the demonstration by Stevens) was made in 1829 on the Carbondale and Honesdale Railroad (now part of the Delaware and Hudson), but the nine-horsepower *Stourbridge Lion*, imported from England and set up here,

[6] Seymour Dunbar, *History of Travel in America*, III, 906.

was found too heavy for the rails and trestles of the road and was discarded. Meanwhile a charter had been granted for a road from Charleston to Hamburg, South Carolina, and over this line in 1830 the *Best Friend of Charleston,* the first locomotive made in America for regular and practical use, was put in operation; it attained a speed of thirty miles an hour when traveling alone, and from sixteen to twenty-one miles with four loaded cars. When this line was completed to Hamburg in 1833 it covered 136 miles and was the longest railroad at that time in the world. In 1826 the New York legislature granted a charter to the Mohawk and Hudson Railroad Company, the earliest forerunner of the New York Central. Construction was started in 1830, and in 1831 the *De Witt Clinton* on a trial trip made the seventeen miles from Albany to Schenectady in an hour. The first link in the present Pennsylvania system, a strip of road connecting Philadelphia with the Susquehanna, was completed in 1834.

The practicability of the new transportation having been established, the nation turned to railroads to settle the great problem of communication with the same enthusiasm which a few years previously it had shown toward canals. Some railroads were built, as were canals, primarily to carry specific commodities to the seacoast, others because of a general desire to improve transportation; but everywhere was the hope that almost any village, if it could be touched by the magic influence of the rails, might duplicate the astounding development of a Syracuse or Buffalo. By 1860 more than 30,000 miles had been built.

The rivalry of the seaboard cities in their hope of tapping the western region sprang up anew, and such cities as Boston, Charleston, Savannah, and Baltimore, which had been excluded from the race during the canal-building period, joined with the rest in projecting gigantic plans for routes into the interior. As the years went by, the railroads passed from the stage in which they were built merely as feeders for canals and connecting links between rivers and artificial waterways to that of great trunk lines dependent upon themselves alone. Before 1850 only one line of railroad had been completed between the tidewater and the great interior basins of the country, but a passenger on it, as he crossed New York, was carried by sixteen different companies. Freight was restricted by the payment of tolls and by frequent transfers due to different-gauge roads. The first consolidation on this road, the New York Central, was effected in 1853, after which this route took its place as one of the two great railroad systems leading to the interior. This was also the year that saw the first rail service from New York to Chicago. Between 1850 and the opening of the Civil War eight other great lines were completed between the seaboard and the western system of lakes and rivers. They included the present Erie, a rival of the New York Central, completed to Dunkirk on Lake Erie in 1851, the Pennsylvania, which reached Pittsburgh in 1852, and the Baltimore and Ohio, which reached Wheeling in the next year.

Similar activity was evident in the South. In 1850 the Western and Atlantic Railroad of Georgia reached the Tennessee River and, with the opening of the Nashville and Chattanooga in 1854, connected Atlanta with the river and rail system of the Northwest and became the distributing agency for western grain and meat in the eastern cotton belt. By 1858 the Central Virginia, running west from Richmond, and the Southside Railroad, running west from Petersburg, had made connections with the Southwest, and by 1859 with the Mississippi River. Efforts of the southeastern seaboard cities to tap the Mississippi Valley were centralized inevitably at Chattanooga because of the superior topography of that location. From here railroads branched southward to touch the Gulf at Mobile, westward to the Mississippi at Memphis, and northward into the Old Northwest.

As the products of the Southwest, which had formerly flowed through New Orleans and Mobile, began to be diverted eastward, the merchants of the Mississippi and Gulf ports were stirred to action. The citizens of Mobile organized the Mobile and Ohio, which, with the aid of federal land grants, reached Cairo, Illinois, in 1859, and in the same year New Orleans opened connection with Jackson, Tennessee, by building the New Orleans, Jackson and Great Northern. In the meantime, the Illinois Central, also bolstered by gifts of federal land, had bridged the gap between Cairo and Chicago. Between 1850 and 1860 about 8000 miles of railroad were built in the Southwest and that region had rail connections not only with the Atlantic coast but with the Ohio Valley. These herculean efforts saved much of their earlier traffic for the Gulf ports, but relatively their position declined. The new railroads between New York, Philadelphia, Baltimore, and other northern ports and the Northwest not only spurred the economic life of the Ohio Valley but tended more and more to drain the western products eastward. The bands of steel which held these two sections together did much to hold the Northwest to the Union at the time of the Civil War.

By the opening of the Civil War the region east of the Alleghenies was equipped with a skeleton railroad system which was to grow rapidly in the years to come. As the primary passes of the Alleghenies were penetrated and the original tracks of the great railway system east of the Mississippi were laid down, the chief seaboard cities established connections with the West and the flow of commerce between these sections was immensely speeded.

PROBLEMS OF EARLY RAILROAD BUILDING

Because steam locomotion was in its infancy, the early American railroad builders, like the early canal builders, had to meet and solve innumerable problems. The decades of the forties and fifties were pre-eminently years of experimentation. Some ideas were obtained from England, but different conditions, such as long-distance passenger traffic and bulkier freight, soon made it apparent that developments in the two countries would not be closely parallel.

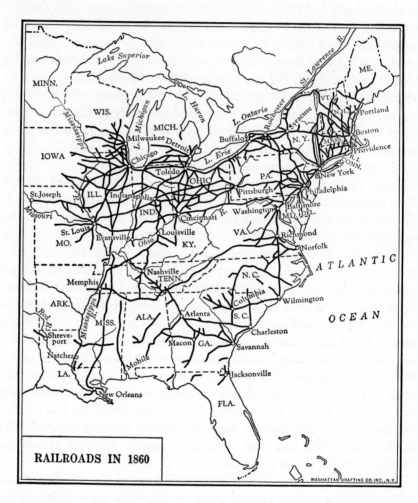

RAILROADS IN 1860

Problems of track construction, gauge, friction of the wheels on the rails, bridges, brakes, coupling apparatus, safety devices, lighting, and heating all had to be worked out. Although decades passed before they were finally mastered, astonishing progress was made from the start. The first rails consisted of strips of iron laid longitudinally upon wooden beams attached to ties. These iron strips had the unfortunate faculty of coming loose and curling up, sometimes protruding through the floor of the coach and making it necessary for the engineer to stop the train and mend the track. It was not until the early fifties that iron rails came extensively into use. There was no uniform gauge at first, the distance between the rails ranging in width from four feet three inches on the Delaware and Hudson to six feet on the Delaware, Lackawanna, and Western. This lack of uniformity increased expenses in shipping freight and eventually necessitated the relaying of large portions of the roadbed. The early engines were not equipped with cabs until after 1842. Wood furnished the fuel for both engines and heating, and, until coal came into use, the destruction caused by escaping sparks that started forest fires and ignited the wooden coaches, to say nothing of their effect upon the passengers' clothing, was a serious problem. Although passenger coaches during the first twenty-five years of railroad history were near the last word in discomfort, they as well as the engines were usually brightly painted, highly ornate, and emblazoned with high-sounding names. The early trains averaged only about fifteen miles an hour, but they marked a new era in speed of transportation. The first passenger coaches were little more than the bodies of stagecoaches equipped with wheels adapted to the tracks. Gradually they were lengthened to cars more nearly resembling the modern type, with openings at each end and with seats in two rows separated by an aisle. The original brakes were identical in principle with those used in stagecoaches—blocks of hard wood brought into contact with the wheels by levers operated by foot power.

Inadequate and flimsy construction characterized most of the American railroads before the Civil War. As the roadbeds began to wear out and a greater strain was put upon them by the introduction of heavier rolling stock, accidents became increasingly frequent. Complications were often caused by the failure to fence off the right of way. During the decade of the fifties and even later, a railroad passenger literally took his life in his hands. The day of the air brake, the automatic coupler, the block system of signals, and scientifically constructed roadbeds was still in the future. An accident was considered an "act of God" rather than negligence on the part of the railroad. The departure and arrival of trains were matters of pure conjecture, and timetables were hardly taken seriously until the forties. Nor was there any uniformity in rates or fares. In the late forties passenger fares ranged from 1.5 cents a mile in New York to 5.35 cents in Mississippi, and freight from 4 cents a ton-mile in Vermont to 24.39 cents in Mississippi. Charges depended largely on existing competition.

FINANCING THE EARLY RAILROADS

Hardly less important than the problems of engineering were those connected with raising sufficient funds to construct the 30,000 miles of railroad in operation before the Civil War. Railroad promoters had financial difficulties from the start, difficulties which were not lessened by the fact that the new railroads must necessarily come into competition with turnpikes, plank roads, canals, and interests vested in these enterprises.[7] There was the fundamental difficulty inherent in the problem of financing a railroad in new unsettled country where an adequate return on the investment could be realized only by the expected growth of the area. Such a condition does not offer the prospective investor an immediate return; he has only a speculative possibility of future income if people move to the sections tapped by the road. While investments in railroads in the more thickly populated East frequently paid large dividends, the prospect of returns on the projected railways in the more sparsely settled West and South was uncertain. In any event, the investor might wait years before dividends came in. In spite of these difficulties, over $1,250,000,000 was invested in railroads between 1830 and 1860. Much of this was obtained from abroad, where financiers had already forgotten their unfortunate experiences in the panic of 1837 and the repudiations incidental thereto, and were willing to speculate again on the economic possibilities of the New World. Some capital was drawn from New England, where accumulated capital had been released by the declining whaling industry; this was to be augmented in the years to come by a similar decline in shipping. Merchants and farmers in the terminal cities and along the routes subscribed, often influenced not so much by the desire for dividends as by the expectation of profit from increased business and the rise in land values.

Where private capital was insufficient, city, state, county, and national aid was freely given. Except in Massachusetts, where loans were extended to certain railroads, little state aid was given in New England. Elsewhere the situation was quite different. Pennsylvania, Michigan, South Carolina, and Georgia undertook to finance their first railroads. Georgia, in fact, not only built a railroad from Atlanta to Chattanooga herself but continued to operate it until 1870. New York loaned $6,000,000 to the New York and Erie to help build a railroad across the southern section of the state. Maryland purchased $3,000,000 of Baltimore and Ohio stock; Virginia subscribed three-fifths of the stock of many railroads and by 1860 had contributed some $21,000,000. Michigan, Illinois, and Indiana also pioneered in railroad construction. One student estimates that states in the fifteen years before 1840 borrowed $90,000,000 for railroad construction. Others estimate that county and

[7] A leading argument against railroads in these early years held that they were more monopolistic than turnpikes or canals. Benjamin Wright, engineer of the Erie Canal, wrote in a letter appended to a congressional document: "I consider a long line of railroad . . . as being odious in this country, as a monopoly of the carrying, which it necessarily must be. A canal, on the contrary, is open to any man who builds a boat." *House Ex. Doc.* No. 18, 1831–32, 22nd Cong., 1st Sess., I, 174.

municipal contributions amounted to more than those of the states, at least one-fifth of the total costs. What these funds amounted to in actual mileage may be estimated by the cost of construction, which in the 1850's varied from $25,000 to $50,000 a mile.

Constitutional scruples held back direct federal gifts for railroad construction. But it did not prevent aid by means of government surveys and through tariff reductions until 1843 on iron used in railroad construction. Moreover, the demand for railroad transportation became so great and the inability of the western states to finance the new projects so obvious that direct aid was finally given. It began in 1850 with a grant of over 2,500,000 acres of public land to the state of Illinois, the land lying in alternate sections along the projected route of the Illinois Central. This grant was turned over by the state to the railroad with the stipulation that 7 per cent of the company's gross earnings be reserved for the state. In similar manner lavish gifts were made to Mississippi, Missouri, Michigan, Wisconsin, Minnesota, Iowa, Arkansas, Alabama, Florida, and Louisiana, amounting by 1861 to approximately $31,000,000.

As it was to the advantage of the railroads to dispose of the public lands to provide cash for themselves and to increase the population along their routes, these grants had a part in speeding settlement as well as in promoting railroad construction. This was particularly evident in the case of the Illinois Central, which worked energetically to bring immigrants to its region. Although the effort to bring about government regulation of railroads did not come until the late 1860's, some faint beginnings are to be found in these early years when the states were so generous in extending aid. Some states attempted to limit charges, to put a ceiling on dividends, and to reserve the right to purchase the railroad after a certain date. But these efforts accomplished little for the time being.

STREET RAILWAYS

The increasing concentration of the population in cities developed in the fifth decade of the century a distinctly urban passenger problem. From the beginning of railroads it had been necessary in some cases to run them over city streets, but these were not street railways in the proper sense. The idea of the sunken rail which would not obstruct wheeled traffic had to be developed before such roads could be practical.

The first vehicle used for periodic transportation of the city population was the omnibus, a modification of the stagecoach. One was operating in New York City before 1828 between Wall Street and Greenwich Village. The first omnibus in Philadelphia appeared in 1831. In the fifties the sunken rail came into use, and from then until the days of the electric tramways various types of horsecars, some of which had two stories, handled the demands of city traffic as best they could.

TRANSPORTATION IN THE TRANS-MISSISSIPPI WEST

A glance at the railroad map (p. 278) makes it clear that railroad construction prior to 1860 was largely limited to the region east of the Mississippi. Except for a few prongs of steel extending westward from St. Louis and other points along the river and a few tiny railroads in California, the trans-Mississippi West was as yet dependent upon rivers and dirt roads. Despite these inadequate facilities this vast region was not devoid of a lively commerce. From the early years of the century fur traders working out of St. Louis had covered the valleys of the upper Mississippi and Missouri and had floated their pelts down the rivers to make St. Louis the great fur center of the nation. Moreover, these traders had discovered the routes followed in later years by the immigrants along the Oregon, California and Santa Fe trails and subsequently by the first transcontinental railroads.

Long before the first covered wagons started for Oregon or California in the early forties, an active commerce had developed over the Santa Fe Trail. In 1821 a trading party setting out from the Missouri took their way to Santa Fe over the route now generally followed by the Atchison, Topeka and Santa Fe and found there a ready market for their goods. It was discovered that it was actually cheaper to transport goods up the Missouri to Independence and from there by pack train or freight wagon to Santa Fe than to bring them up through Mexico from Vera Cruz. This opened the Spanish Southwest to American traders and in the succeeding years there was a continuous movement of textiles, cutlery, and other commodities to Santa Fe, where they were exchanged for furs, mules, and gold and silver bullion. Measured by modern standards the Santa Fe trade was not large. In only one year, 1843, when the eastern goods sent southward amounted to $450,000, did its value exceed $250,000. But the importance of the trade was greater than its value. It inflamed the national imagination and aroused interest in the Southwest years before the annexation of Texas. "The Santa Fé trail," says Paxson, "was the first beaten path thrust in advance of the western frontier."

With the discovery of gold in California in 1848 the whole history of trans-Mississippi transportation took on new life. Stage traffic from Independence to Santa Fe was begun in 1849 and in the same year a monthly mail to Salt Lake City was established. Although steamship and clipper communication between the east coast and California either around the Horn or by way of Panama was exceedingly brisk throughout the fifties, it was not until 1858 that the federal government awarded to John Butterfield a contract to carry mail overland from Memphis and St. Louis to California. In the fall of that year Butterfield started a semiweekly passenger and mail service through Preston, El Paso, and Fort Yuma to the Pacific coast which made the trip in about twenty-five days.

Others followed, including the famous firm of Russell, Majors and Waddell, which traveled over other routes and developed a large freight and passenger service. This was an extensive business in the early sixties; the above firm was reputed to have had 6250 wagons and 75,000 oxen in the freight business alone. In 1860 William H. Russell organized the pony express which by relays of horseback riders carried mail from St. Joseph, Missouri, to Sacramento, California, in about ten days. It was probably the fastest transportation of its kind yet known, but it brought financial ruin to Russell, Majors and Waddell. The bankrupt firm was bought in by Ben Holladay in 1862 and in turn sold by him to Wells, Fargo & Company, which controlled much of this traffic until the first transcontinental railroad was completed. The pony express ended with the coming of the first transcontinental telegraph line in 1861.

DEVELOPMENT OF EXPRESS TRANSPORTATION

The entrance of Wells, Fargo & Company into western transportation gives some indication of the early development of transportation. The founder of express transportation was William Francis Harnden, a former conductor and ticket agent on the Boston and Worcester. Taking his cue from the methods by which gold and silver were transferred, Harnden in 1839 conceived the idea that a similar business might be developed in the rapid and safe transportation of small packages and valuable papers. Harnden himself carried the first express in a carpetbag between New York and Boston, but the business grew so rapidly that he took in a partner, and the firm of Harnden & Company's Express was founded in 1840. Agents were hired, the business was extended in 1841 to include Philadelphia and Albany, and European agencies were opened to look after the transportation of immigrants.

Harnden's success brought Alvin Adams into the field, and a rival express business was started between New York and Boston. With Ephraim Farnsworth as a partner, Adams & Company was founded; by 1843 its business extended as far west as St. Louis and New Orleans. In 1854 Harnden & Company was merged with the new Adams Express Company, leaving the latter supreme in the Northeast for the time being. In the meantime, Henry Wells, Harnden's agent at Albany, had left Harnden and formed Wells, Fargo & Company, which by 1845 connected the East with Chicago, Cincinnati, and St. Louis. In that year Wells, Fargo sold out to the American Express and moved to the Pacific coast. It was here, curiously enough, that the express service, scarcely more than a decade after its birth, achieved its greatest triumph, when Wells, Fargo & Company carried the mail and gold of the forty-niners, and where, according to Samuel Bowles, "the first three establishments set up in a mining town were a restaurant, a billiard saloon, and a Wells & Fargo office."[8]

COMMUNICATION BY TELEGRAPH

Samuel F. B. Morse (1791–1872), trained as an artist, and professor of the literature of the arts of design in New York University, evolved the idea of the electromagnetic telegraph in the early 1830's. With the aid of Alfred Vail he had constructed a practical instrument by 1837. Although his invention was repeatedly demonstrated and undoubtedly contained immense future possibilities, it was impossible to interest private entrepreneurs. Forced to seek government aid, Morse and his friends besieged Congress for six years before that body in 1843 finally appropriated $30,000 for the construction of a line from Baltimore to Washington. This line was completed by May of the following year in time to transmit to the capital information from the Whig and Democratic conventions which met in Baltimore that spring. A private company was then formed, and with great difficulty funds were obtained for a line from Philadelphia to Newark. It was opened in 1846 and was later extended to Jersey City, from which point messages were transmitted to New York by ferry.

The practicability of the telegraph once established, its extension was rapid. Ezra Cornell, who had been associated with Morse in constructing the first line and had demonstrated the superiority of the overhead wire, became the organizing genius of the rapid expansion which set in. In comparison to a railroad the cost of construction per mile was less, and the problems to be met were fewer. In 1846–1847 New York was connected with Boston, Albany, and Buffalo, and in the next year with Cleveland, Toledo, Detroit, and Chicago. Although forced to meet such new conditions as severe plain and mountain storms as well as hostile Indians, the Western Union, spurred on by government subsidies, extended its lines to the Pacific in 1861. In that year 50,000 miles of telegraph lines were in operation.

The rapid development of telegraphy was due in part to the close relations established early between railroads and the new invention. Railroads needed telegraphy to operate their roads efficiently and telegraph companies needed the railroad right of way to put up their lines. The possibilities of telegraphy once demonstrated, its usefulness in underseas communication was quickly

[8] Samuel Bowles, *Our New West*, p. 347.

realized. Cyrus Field completed the first transatlantic cable in 1858, but transmission was not successful until the cable was relaid in 1866.

SELECTED READINGS

MacGill, C. E., *et al.*, *History of Transportation in the United States Before 1860*, chaps. 2–11, 17.

Taylor, G. R., *The Transportation Revolution*, chaps. 2–5, 7, 13.

Harlow, A. F., *Old Towpaths*, chaps. 6 ff.

Gates, P. W., *The Illinois Central Railroad and Its Colonization Work*, chaps. 2, 5, 6.

Callender, G. S., *Selections from the Economic History of the United States*, chaps. 7, 8.

Flügel, F., and Faulkner, H. U., *Readings in the Economic and Social History of the United States*, chap. 10.

CHAPTER 15

POPULATION AND LABOR

POPULATION: INCREASE AND DISTRIBUTION

A STUDY of population statistics for the first seventy years of our history reveals three outstanding tendencies, quite normal under the circumstances: (1) a rapid increase, (2) a westward migration, and (3) a concentration in cities. The total population of the nation in 1790 was probably under four million, while that given in the Census of 1860 was 31,443,321.

POPULATION OF THE UNITED STATES TO 1860

Year	White	Colored	Total
1790	3,172,006	757,208	3,929,214
1800	4,306,446	1,002,037	5,308,483
1810	5,862,073	1,377,808	7,239,881
1820	7,866,797	1,771,656	9,638,453
1830	10,537,378	2,328,642	12,866,020
1840	14,195,805	2,873,648	17,069,453
1950	19,553,068	3,638,808	23,191,876
1860	26,922,537	4,441,830	31,443,321[a]

a Including Indians, Japanese, Chinese, and all others, who numbered 78,954.
U.S. Census, 1910, I, 127.

Until after 1820 most of this growth was attributable to the natural increase in a new land where large families were economically profitable. Said the Swedish traveler, Peter Kalm, who toured America about 1750: "It does not seem difficult to find out the reasons, why people multiply faster here than in Europe. As soon as a person is old enough he may marry in these provinces without any fear of poverty. There is such an amount of good ground yet uncultivated, that a new-married man can, without difficulty, get a spot of ground, where he may comfortably subsist with his wife and children. The taxes are very low, and he need not be under any concern on their account."[1]

[1] A. B. Benson (ed.), *Peter Kalm's Travels in North America* (2 vols., 1937), p. 211.

The conditions favoring large families which Kalm had observed in the late colonial period continued as long as this country remained pre-eminently an agrarian nation. In addition to the natural growth of population there was an immigration amounting to over 5,000,000 people between 1820 and 1860. Not only did the normal increase of births over deaths and the additions from immigration speed the population growth, but the effects of the Industrial Revolution and the expansion of commerce created new wealth and new possibilities of employment in trade and industry, and so provided a source of livelihood for additional people. The population growth during each decade averaged about 34 per cent, the population almost doubling every twenty years.

Even more striking than the increase in actual numbers was the distribution. In 1790 over 94 per cent lived on the Atlantic slope of the thirteen original colonies, with less than a quarter of a million west of the Alleghenies. By 1820 the proportion had distinctly changed. The census of that year showed about 73 per cent living on the Atlantic slope and 27 per cent west of the mountains. The southern group of states was still the most populous, but New York could boast of the greatest population of any single state. The population beyond the mountains now outnumbered that of New England. During the decade 1810 to 1820 New York added 413,000 to her numbers, more than any other state; Ohio came next, with 351,000. But the ratio of increase had been greatest in the new western states; one eastern state, Delaware, had remained practically stationary. In the thirty years from 1790 to 1820 the seaboard states had contributed almost two and one half millions to the population of the West.

The Census of 1850 revealed that almost half of the population (45 per cent) now lived west of the Alleghenies. Professor Channing has pointed out[2] that in the thirty years from 1820 to 1850 the number of inhabitants of the region west of the Appalachians more than doubled by five millions, while the population of the seaboard states, notwithstanding the immigration from Europe, failed to double by two millions. Assuming that the population should double by natural reproduction in thirty years, it seems probable, he believes, that during these three decades the East contributed at least four million to the population of the West.[3]

The South furnished the largest proportion of this western migration. Two-fifths of the inhabitants of South Carolina, one-third of those of Virginia and North Carolina, and nearly one-quarter of those of Georgia emigrated west of the mountains to form almost the entire population of the

[2] Edward Channing, *History of the United States,* V, 49.

[3] Between 1820 and 1830 the population increased 32.5 per cent and the settled area 24.4 per cent; between 1830 and 1840 the figures were 32.5 and 27.6 per cent, respectively.

Old Southwest and the predominating element in the Old Northwest. A continual stream of New Englanders moved toward the west, sometimes pausing for a generation in Vermont or western New York, but in most cases pushing on eventually to the new country and giving a distinct New England tone to the northern tier of counties in Ohio and Indiana. There was also a large movement from the middle states into the Northwest, in actual numbers greater than that from New England.

In addition to this movement across the mountains, there was the exodus, particularly in New England, from the farms to the cities. This was, in fact, the period in American history of the most rapid urbanization. Both of these movements must have placed a severe strain upon the rural population, and both are illuminating in any attempt to study the social and economic cross-currents of life in the seaboard states during the first half of the nineteenth century. The causes of the cityward migration were many, chiefly attributable to the Industrial Revolution—the growth of the factory system, the development of internal transportation, and the economic processes which took people from the farm and allowed them to live by manufacturing, commerce, trade, or finance. The population of the seaboard cities was largely augmented after 1820 by immigrants, many of whom were ill adapted by training for farm life and went no farther. The development of the means of communication by canals and later by railroads allowed a greater distribution of agricultural produce and an expanded foreign commerce, leading to the growth of cities at collecting and transfer points.

The market for agricultural products speeded the westward movement, which in turn added to the population of important points on the routes of travel. The competition of western agriculture became so keen as to discourage eastern farmers, especially in the less fertile regions, and to accentuate a movement toward the cities which the growth of manufacturing favored. In 1780 there were only five towns of over 8000 population—Philadelphia, New York, Boston, Charleston, and Baltimore, containing 2.7 per cent of the population of the country. Of these, Philadelphia alone had over 20,000. The Census of 1840 showed 44 cities over 8000, with New York, now the largest, containing 312,710. By 1860 there were 141 towns of over 8000, comprising 16.1 per cent of the population. In that year New York, as now constituted,[4] had a population of about 1,175,000; Philadelphia, 566,000; and Baltimore, 212,000.

By 1810 New York City had forged to the front and after the completion of the Erie Canal speedily became the great American metropolis, acting as a shipping center for a large part of the western produce. The city was forced to meet the competition of other seaboard cities and even of New

[4] The population of New York as then constituted was 813,669 (Borough of Manhattan).

Orleans for the products of the rich grain section of the Great Lakes. But her excellent harbor and strategic geographic position, aided by canals and then railroads, in combination with an able group of restless leaders who had developed a large coastwise trade, won unquestioned supremacy for her. Philadelphia and Baltimore, leading colonial towns that were favored by rich agricultural and mineral hinterlands, sought, by building turnpikes and competing systems of canals, to tap the western areas and draw to themselves a share of the produce, but their success was indifferent until the advent of railroads. Boston, a normal center for trade east of the Connecticut River

GROWTH OF CITY POPULATION, 1780–1860

Year	Number of Cities Having a Population of					Percentage of Total Population in Cities
	8000 or Over	8000 to 20,000	20,000 to 75,000	75,000 to 250,000	250,000 or Over	
1780	5	4	1	..	..	2.7
1790	6	4	2	..	..	3.3
1800	6	1	5	..	..	4.0
1810	11	6	3	2	..	4.9
1820	13	7	4	2	..	4.9
1830	26	19	4	3	..	6.7
1840	44	28	11	4	1	8.5
1850	85	56	21	6	2	12.5
1860	141	96	35	7	3	16.1

and aided by a hinterland of thrifty and resourceful people, had played an important role in the great maritime days of the Republic, but as Americans turned their interests from the sea to the development of the West she was severely handicappd by her geographic position. Her commercial importance was now overshadowed by that of New York, and only the coming of the Industrial Revolution served to support her continued development as a trading center. A crescent of satellite textile, leather, and metal towns, including the thriving cities of Nashua, Lowell, Waltham, Lynn, Worcester, New Bedford, and Fall River, grew up behind her to bring a new era of prosperity.

As New England turned to manufacturing, colonial towns like Providence, New London, Hartford, and New Haven became important cities, and hundreds of obscure villages grew into thriving towns or small cities. "In 1840," says Bidwell, "it would have been difficult to find 50 out of 479 townships in Southern New England which did not have at least one manufacturing village clustered around a cotton or a woolen mill, an iron furnace, a chair factory or a carriage shop, or some other representative of the hundred miscellaneous branches of manufacturing which had grown up in hap-

hazard fashion in every part of these three states."[5] Although the early factories were small, they were widely dispersed, and the growth of the factory
system was accompanied by a growth of urban population. Only three towns
in New England in 1810 boasted over 10,000 inhabitants—Boston, Providence, and New Haven, with a combined population of 56,000—whereas in
1860 there were twenty-six such cities with a population of 682,000.

Pittsburgh, located at the head of navigation on the Ohio where East met
West, in a position to tap vast regions, and in the midst of a rich coal and
iron district, became a city of note as early as 1800. The situation of Cincinnati and Louisville on the same river insured their future. St. Louis collected
the commerce of the Missouri and upper Mississippi, and Mobile and New
Orleans were the shipping points on the Gulf. Chicago, Detroit, Cleveland,
Buffalo, the shipping ports of the Great Lakes, had begun by 1860 to show
the promise of their subsequent greatness and to foretell the relative decline
of the Ohio river towns. At other points too numerous to mention, natural
advantages or fortuitous circumstances led to urban growth.

In the South, however, many of the cities, such as Williamsburg, Charleston, and Savannah, went back absolutely or relatively. The drain of population westward, the shift of the center of cotton production, the natural outlet
of cotton culture across the mountains, the drawing of western produce to
Baltimore and Philadelphia rather than to the southern seaports, and the
lack of manufacturing development—all contributed to the relatively small
growth of urban life in the South Atlantic States. South of Mason and
Dixon's line there were in 1860 only twenty-seven towns or cities with a
population above 4000.

IMMIGRATION BEFORE 1860

The preliminary report of the Eighth Census estimated from a "survey of
the irregular data previous to 1819" that from 1790 to 1800 about 50,000
Europeans arrived here, from 1800 to 1810 about 70,000, and from 1810 to the
end of 1820 about 114,000. To determine the actual settlers, a deduction of
14.5 per cent from these figures should be made for transients. After 1819
official records were kept which are approximately correct. Immigration up
to 1825 amounted to less than 10,000 a year, but gradually increased thereafter
until by 1832 about 60,000 annually were coming, an increase due in part to
prosperity here and political disturbances in Europe. This swelled to 79,000
in 1837, only to be cut in half the next year by the panic. The flow of immigration again increased to over 100,000 in 1842, to be reduced again in the
next year by the financial depression. The five years from 1845 to 1850

[5] P. W. Bidwell, "The Agricultural Revolution in New England," *American Historical Review*, XXVI, 686 (1921).

showed a tremendous gain, because of the severe winters of 1845 and 1846 on the Continent, the subsequent spring floods which affected agriculture adversely, the potato famine of 1845 and 1846 in Ireland, and the revolutions of 1848 and 1849. Never before or since, in fact, has the number of immigrants been so great in proportion to the American population.

Economic and political influences abroad were not alone in driving hundreds of thousands to the New World; the discovery of gold in California

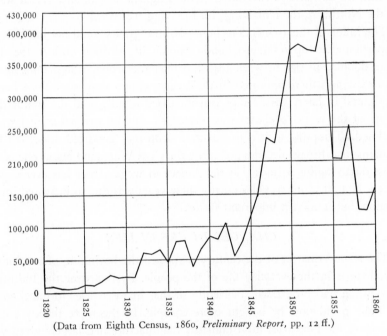

(Data from Eighth Census, 1860, *Preliminary Report,* pp. 12 ff.)

IMMIGRATION INTO THE UNITED STATES, 1820–1860.

lured many more. Immigration amounted to 427,833 in 1854 but dropped in the next year to less than half that number; in 1860 it amounted to only 153,640. This decline has been attributed to the Crimean War and troubles in India, which absorbed some of the excess population and increased the demand for agricultural and manufactured goods. The Civil War at first affected immigration adversely, but the war prosperity, combined with the allurements of the Homestead Act, renewed the flow of alien settlers. More than half of the immigrants prior to 1860 came from the British Isles, particularly Ireland, and one-third from Germany. The five leading occupations as stated by male immigrants during these years were: laborers, 872,317; farmers, 764,837; mechanics, 407,524; merchants, 231,852; and miners, 39,967. In 1860 there were about 4,000,000 foreign-born settlers in the United States.

As regards distribution it is possible to speak only in general terms. At least five-sixths of the Irish immigrants remained east of the Appalachians, most of them in the cities, where they formed the bulk of the unskilled labor. On the other hand, the German immigrant of this period was more likely to be a farmer, and at least half of the Germans took up lands west of the mountains, not a few on the Wisconsin and Texas frontiers. The large majority of the Scandinavians pushed west to find homes in Illinois, Wisconsin, or Minnesota. Perhaps two-thirds of the English, Scotch, and Welsh stayed in the Northeast, the remaining third moving westward.

The influx of this tremendous horde of immigrants could not but have an important effect upon the social and economic life of the period. As the older cities doubled in size between 1840 and 1860 and scores of new ones sprang into existence, there appeared in the larger centers slum conditions hardly duplicated in later years. Pauperism increased rapidly, and the standard of living of the working classes was pushed steadily downward as real wages declined.[6] Tempting as it is to expatiate upon the "good old days," the fact remains that the two decades preceding the Civil War stand out as one of the most discouraging periods that the American wage earner has ever experienced. Not all of his troubles during these years was due to increased immigration, but it was an important factor.

CHANGES IN URBAN LIFE

The second quarter of the century witnessed the beginning of revolutionary changes in the everyday life of the people. By that time the Industrial Revolution had progressed sufficiently so that many articles formerly made at home could now be bought more cheaply. In the more thickly settled regions of the Northeast most domestic manufacture had largely given way to factory processes. This tendency brought greater specialization of work on the part of the men and more leisure for the women. Eventually it took many men and women away from agriculture and into factory work. Improved and factory-made machinery simplified and to some extent made agricultural labor easier, but most of the changes in actual living conditions came of necessity first to the city dwellers. After the twenties, candles as a means of lighting slowly gave way to oil and, in the larger cities, to gas. Street lighting by gas was adopted in Boston in 1822, in New York in 1823, and in Philadelphia in 1837. Anthracite coal had been known to exist in the Wyoming and Lehigh valleys since the late 1700's, and shipments had been made to Philadelphia as early as 1805; but it was not used for home heating until 1815. Its extensive use was delayed by the difficulties of transportation and the expense of installing grates and stoves. Canals and railroads solved the first problem, and the increasing cost of wood in the large cities made the

[6] See tables in N. J. Ware, *The Industrial Worker, 1840–1860*, pp. 27 ff.

solution of the second inevitable. By 1825 wood had been replaced by coal in a large number of homes in New York and Philadelphia. In the Northeast during the succeeding years kitchen fireplaces were closed up and iron ranges put in their place, while fireplaces in other parts of the house gave way to iron stoves. The drudgery of housekeeping was also lightened by the substitution of tinware for much of the older and heavier iron and copper, a boon brought to the housewife by the ubiquitous Yankee peddler.

The problem of water supply was naturally a pressing one in the growing cities. Until well into the century, most of the water for city dwellers was obtained from cisterns, house pumps, or various community pumps scattered throughout the city. After 1799 water from the Schuylkill River was raised by steam pumps to a reservoir and distributed through log pipes to a small part of Philadelphia. This system was improved and extended in 1822 by the opening of the Fairmount Waterworks, which conveyed the water by iron pipes through the entire city. Wooden pipes carried water to lower New York up to 1842,[7] when the aqueducts were finished and Croton water was brought to the city. By that year all the larger cities were supplied by artificial means.

While the conveniences of life were increasing, some advance was also made in providing for public safety. The old and inefficient night watch which lit the lamps, cried out the hours of the night, and gave the alarm for fires was superseded in 1845 by an organization of day and night watchmen more nearly approximating our police force of today. As a matter of fact, the modern police system extends back hardly more than ninety years. Up to the decade of the fifties organized fire fighting had been carried on by volunteer groups—at their best enthusiastic and efficient, but at their worst little better than gangs of city toughs more interested in fighting a rival gang than in extinguishing a fire. This decade saw the beginning of the end of the volunteer fire department in the larger cities.

Of great influence in stimulating the economic and social life of the people was the act of 1845 which introduced cheap postage. The charge on letters weighing not over a half-ounce and going less than 300 miles was now five cents; over that limit it was ten cents, with an additional charge for extra weight. Further reductions were made in 1851, when a half-ounce letter prepaid would be carried 3000 miles for three cents, or, if not prepaid, for five cents; for 3000 miles and over, the respective rates were six and twelve cents. By 1840 the penny newspaper had made its appearance

---

[7] The first effort to supply New York with water from a central reservoir was undertaken by the Manhattan Water Company, a concern created by a legislative bill proposed by Aaron Burr in 1799. In reality this company was a banking corporation disguised as a water company and was created to compete with Hamilton's Bank of New York. It did, however, develop a water system which it maintained until it sold it to the city in 1808. The concern continues today as the Bank of the Manhattan Company.

upon the streets, competing newspapers had commenced their keen rivalry for news, and the mass of Americans, from the unskilled laborer to the powerful capitalist, became the slave of the daily paper—an institution purporting to exist to carry news, but usually spreading propaganda for some interest, political or economic. The news-spreading function of the papers and their ability to keep the people cognizant of what was happening in the world at large were made possible by the invention of the telegraph and its introduction after 1844. The effect of the invention of the steamboat and the steam railway was also considerable in promoting travel, in breaking up intellectual isolation, and in modifying intellectual provincialism to a slight extent.

CONDITIONS OF LABOR

Scarcity of skilled labor is a normal condition in a new country. As a consequence the status of the American wage earner relative to that of similar workers in the industrial nations of western Europe was fairly high, at least until the decade of the forties. Victor Clark estimates that the wages of unskilled labor in this country were between one-third and one-half higher than in Great Britain and those of skilled workers somewhat less. While the lot of the skilled laborer might be tolerable, the unskilled laborer, although commanding greater wages than in Europe, barely made ends meet. His pay averaged about half that of skilled labor. Two shillings at the time of the Revolution was a day's pay; this increased to about 90 cents a day in 1800 and $1.00 in 1825, and remained around this point for many years, even during the activity of canal and railroad building. His condition at the opening of the century is gloomily pictured by McMaster:

Sand sprinkled on the floor did duty as a carpet. There was no glass on his table, there was no china in his cupboard, there were no prints on his wall. What a stove was he did not know, coal he had never seen, matches he had never heard of. . . . He rarely tasted fresh meat as often as once in a week, and paid for it a much higher price than his posterity. . . .

If the food of an artisan would now be thought coarse, his clothes would be thought abominable. A pair of yellow buckskin or leathern breeches, a checked shirt, a red flannel jacket, a rusty felt hat cocked up at the corners, shoes of neat's-skin set off with huge buckles of brass, and a leathern apron, comprised his scanty wardrobe. The leather he smeared with grease to keep it soft and flexible.[8]

Farm hands received from $7.00 to $15.00 a month, with board, depending upon season and locality; the general average tended from the lower to the higher figure as time went on. Without board, the compensation of agricultural laborers rose from 50 cents a day at the opening of the century to

[8] J. B. McMaster, *History of the People of the United States*, I, 96–97.

$1.50 and even $2.00 by 1860.[9] The wages of skilled labor, both agricultural and industrial, ran from $1.00 to $2.00 a day, although the minimum was often exceeded.

Factory workers also commanded higher wages than in Europe. Nevertheless, between 1830 and 1860 in Massachusetts, where wages were highest, men earned $5.00 a week, children between $1.00 and $2.00, and women from $1.75 to $2.00 a week, the latter figures including board. Wages were lower in Pennsylvania, New Jersey, and the southern states. Those who have studied the general problem of real wages during these years believe that they advanced from the twenties through the thirties and forties and declined in the fifties.[10] The advance was somewhat over 10 per cent.

In comparison with modern wage scales the above compensations seem small indeed. But wage scales, of course, have no meaning except in relation to prices. During the thirties men could obtain board and room for from $1.75 to $2.00 a week; for women the cost ran from $1.25 to $1.50. As both were earning double this amount a margin of half their salary was left for other expenses. This might be enough for single men or women, even enough for them to save something; but it was inadequate to support a family unless more than one member was working. In other words, the situation was not unlike that of the average wage earner in later years.

Foreign travelers were particularly impressed with the lack of poverty and with the opportunities which they believed existed for the wage earner. Said the Irishman, Thomas Mooney, in 1850:

The lowest wages going in the United States for a labourer's day's work is seventy cents, or about three shillings British money. This would be eighteen shillings for a week; and you can obtain good board, lodging and washing for a little less than ten British shillings, or two and a half dollars a week. So that you will be able to save seven or eight shillings a week to buy a farm, which farm you can buy for five shillings an acre. . . . Remember that, if you please, you can, as soon as you get a regular employment, save the price of an acre and a half of the finest land in the world every week, and in less than a year you will have money enough to start for the west, and take up an eighty-acre farm which will be your own forever.[11]

As is often the case, Mooney's deductions looked better on paper than in reality. In actual practice few immigrant wage earners escaped to the frontier by this route. And not many escaped a grinding poverty which, particularly in cities, was widespread in the forties and fifties. One fact that can be stated

[9] P. W. Bidwell and J. I. Falconer, *History of Agriculture in the Northern United States, 1620–1860*, pp. 275–277, 495.
[10] G. R. Taylor, *The Transportation Revolution*, pp. 294–295.
[11] Thomas Mooney, *Nine Years in America* (1850), p. 37.

with certainty is that the introduction of the factory system was not attended with the extreme horrors which accompanied the change in England. In America most of the cloth had either been purchased from Europe or been made by women on the farm as part of their household duties. The factory system therefore threw few men out of labor, and the factories for many years had to compete for labor with the more alluring prospects of independence on a frontier farm. Moreover, the early textile mills in New England were largely cotton mills; up to that time cotton had not been manufactured to any great extent at home. Hence no large group of hand operatives was thrown out of employment.

The early operatives in these mills were ordinarily girls or unmarried women who looked upon the chance of earning money and at the same time escaping from the drudgery and dependency of farm life, at least for some years, and as an opportunity rather than a misfortune, especially as working in the mills meant no loss of social standing. Many of the early millowners were men of humanitarian leanings who, partly from desire and partly from necessity, made efforts to provide boardinghouses, to safeguard the morals of their employees, and, through donations of money for churches and libraries, to stimulate high aspirations. European observers were amazed at the high caliber of the factory girls and their comfortable living conditions. To Anthony Trollope, Lowell seemed "the realization of a commercial utopia" where the operatives were "taken in, as it were, to a philanthropical manufacturing college, and then looked after and regulated more as girls and lads at a great seminary, than as hands by whose industry profit is to be made out of capital."[12]

Harriet Martineau, writing of conditions as she saw them at Waltham in 1835, describes the life of the factory operatives:

I visited the corporate factory-establishment at Waltham, within a few miles of Boston. The Waltham Mills were at work before those of Lowell were set up. The establishment is for the spinning and weaving of cotton alone, and the construction of the requisite machinery. Five hundred persons were employed at the time of my visit. The girls earn two, and some three, dollars a-week, besides their board. The little children earn one dollar a-week. Most of the girls live in the houses provided by the corporation, which accommodate from six to eight each. When sisters come to the mill, it is a common practice for them to bring their mother to keep house for them and some of their companions, in a dwelling built by their own earnings. In this case, they save enough out of their board to clothe themselves, and have their two or three dollars a-week to spare. Some have thus cleared off mortgages from their fathers' farms; others have educated the hope of the family at college; and many are rapidly accumulating an independ-

---

[12] Anthony Trollope, *North America* (1864), pp. 245, 247.

Threshing in the Age of Horse Power.

An Early McCormick Reaper—Probably the Second Type Invented by Him.

Haying by Hand and Horse Power.

"Forging the Shaft," Painting by John Ferguson Weir. An Iron Foundry
About 1860.

The Bettmann Archive

Early Gold Mining in California. One Miner Is Rocking the Cradle While
His Partner Brings the Results of His Diggings from a Nearby Stream.

Mather Photo from Drake Museum

Early Oil Wells—Loading Oil at Funkville, Oil Creek, Near Titusville,
Pennsylvania, About 1861.

A Typical River Steamboat—Steamboat *Natchez* Loading at a Mississippi River Port.

Model of John Fitch's First Steamboat.

South Street, New York, in 1855.

U. S. M. Steam Ship *Atlantic*. Typical Transatlantic Steamship of the Middle
Nineteenth Century. Lithograph by N. Currier.

Immigrants Arriving. A Drawing Made in 1851.

New England Factory Workers—"Bell Time." Drawing by Winslow Homer.

Yankee Peddler. An Important Phase of Early American Commerce.

Combined Locks on the Erie Canal at Lockport.

Typical Canal Transportation.

ence. I saw a whole street of houses built with the earnings of the girls; some with piazzas, and green venetian blinds; and all neat and sufficiently spacious.

The factory people built the church, which stands conspicuous on the green in the midst of the place. The minister's salary (eight hundred dollars last year) is raised by a tax on the pews. The corporation gave them a building for a lyceum, which they have furnished with a good library, and where they have lectures every winter,—the best that money can procure. The girls have, in many instances, private libraries of some merit and value.

The managers of the various factory establishments keep the wages as nearly equal as possible, and then let the girls freely shift about from one to another. When a girl comes to the overseer to inform him of her intention of working at the mill, he welcomes her, and asks her how long she means to stay. It may be six months, or a year, or five years, or for life. She declares what she considers herself fit for, and sets to work accordingly. If she finds that she cannot work so as to keep up with the companion appointed to her, or to please her employer or herself, she comes to the overseer, and volunteers to pick cotton, or sweep the rooms, or undertake some other service that she can perform.

The people work about seventy hours per week, on the average. The time of work varies with the length of the days, the wages continuing the same. All look like well-dressed young ladies. The health is good; or rather, (as this is too much to be said about health anywhere in the United States), it is no worse than it is elsewhere.

These facts speak for themselves. There is no need to enlarge on the pleasure of an acquaintance with the operative classes of the United States.[13]

This rosy picture of Miss Martineau's did not tell the whole story. While the condition of American operatives during the Industrial Revolution was undoubtedly much better than in Europe, it was not enviable. A paternalism in which the operatives lived in company houses, often spent their earnings in company stores, worshiped in company churches, and had to submit to excessive supervision of their private lives would be considered intolerable today, and the long hours would tax the strength of even the hardiest farm girl. Nominal wages at the opening of the Industrial Revolution, it is true, gradually rose. As in England, the increase of wealth due to machinery went largely into the hands of the capitalist class. The early mills were in most cases unsanitary and unhealthy places in which to work.

Hours of labor were excessively long. According to Professor Ely: "The length of actual labor [1832] varied from twelve to fifteen hours. The New England mills generally ran thirteen hours, but one mill in Connecticut ran fourteen hours, while the length of actual labor in another mill in the same State, the Eagle Mill at Griswold, was fifteen hours and ten minutes. The regulations at Paterson, New Jersey, required women and children to be at

---

[13] Harriet Martineau, *Society in America* (1837), II, 57–59.

work at half-past four in the morning."[14] A committee of the Massachusetts legislature, investigating the hours of labor of children in factories as affecting their education, reported in 1825: "It appears however that the time of employment is generally twelve or thirteen hours each day, excepting the Sabbath," and added, "which leaves little opportunity for daily instruction."[15] As late as 1845 the average hours of labor in the Lowell mills varied from eleven hours and twenty-four minutes in January to thirteen hours and thirty-one minutes in April, practically from sun to sun. While the strain in the early factories could not have been so great as in later years, the hours were too long for workers of any age.

Children were at first not used in the Massachusetts mills to the extent that they were in England. The need of gathering workers together from the surrounding country and building quarters and boarding houses involved special problems with children. Nevertheless, as time went on the evil became widespread and was unchecked by law. This was particularly so in Rhode Island, southern New England, and elsewhere where is was common practice for manufacturers to contract for the labor of whole families rather than of individual adults. In 1820 the proportion of child workers in Massachusetts cotton mills was 45 per cent and in Rhode Island 55. These percentages by 1832 had declined to 21 and 41. In woolen mills the percentage was much less. A report of a convention of New England mechanics and workingmen held at Boston in 1832 estimated that the children employed in manufactories constituted about two-fifths of the total number of workers. The *Mechanics' Free Press* for August 21, 1830, prints the following statement regarding children in the Philadelphia factories:

It is a well-known fact, that the principal part of the helps in cotton factories consists of boys and girls, we may safely say from six to seventeen years of age, and are confined to steady employment during the longest days of the year, from daylight until dark, allowing, at the outside, one hour and a half per day [for meals] . . . and that too with a small sum, that is hardly sufficient to support nature, while they [the employers] on the other hand are rolling in wealth of[f] the vitals of these poor children every day. We noticed the observations of our Pawtucket friend in your number of June 19, 1830, lamenting the grievances of the children employed in those factories. We think his observations very correct, with regard to their being brought up as ignorant as Arabs of the Desert; for we are confident that not more than one-sixth of the boys and girls employed in such factories are capable of reading or writing their own name.[16]

Possibly too much attention has been given to factory labor. It should be remembered that other types of labor surpassed in numbers those employed

[14] R. T. Ely, *Labor Movement in America*, p. 49.
[15] J. R. Commons *et al.* (eds.), *Documentary History of American Industrial Society*, V, 59.
[16] *Ibid.*, V, 61–62.

in factories. This was true even in New England, where the domestic system persisted in rural areas and where shoes, hats, and other commodities were manufactured in the homes for an outside market. There were the skilled workers in the building and printing trades, who were often able to maintain wages more easily than factory workers. There were also, of course, the large number of unskilled workers, mainly immigrants, who built the canals and railroads. The latter were lucky to get $8 to $10 a month with "keep," and they often worked under unhealthy and incredibly bad conditions.

While conditions for large groups of workers were relatively good during the early years of the Industrial Revolution, the situation changed notably in the forties. Immigration increased rapidly in that decade, crowding the cities and bringing a competition among laborers which speedily brought wage reductions. Beginning with the panic of 1837, practically every trade experienced radical reductions at a time when the cost of living, especially in the cities, was increasing. Horace Greeley estimated that the cost of provisions in New York City rose 50 per cent between 1843 and 1850, and in 1851 he estimated a minimum weekly budget for a family of five at $10.37. Yet at that time carpenters, plasterers, and bricklayers were averaging around $10.00 a week, and the majority of painters, hatters, cabinetmakers, and other skilled workmen were getting $4, $5, and $6 a week. One observer estimated in 1845 that one person in seven in New York City was a pauper. All of this existed at a time when the housing problem in the cities was desperate, for the cities were flooded with immigrants more rapidly than houses could be built. Almost the only tinge of light in an otherwise black picture was the fact that the agitation for a shorter working day had cut down the workday in some mills to as low as eleven hours.

In the textile mills of New England and elsewhere conditions grew worse in the forties as wages were reduced and employers bound themselves more closely together by agreements as to wages, hours, and black lists, and extended their paternalism to intolerable lengths. Labor agents of textile manufacturers were still scouring the back country of New England for farm girls, but the "golden age" of the girl operative had passed. By 1850, says Ware, "the white-gowned girls who marched to welcome Presidents, who talked so intelligently to foreign visitors, who wrote poetry and stories filled with classical allusions, were no longer found in the cotton mills. They had been driven out by a prolonged and fruitless struggle to protect their standards."[17] They had also been driven out by the flood of Irish immigrants who were

[17] The degradation of the worker during this period has been effectively discussed by N. J. Ware, *op. cit.*, particularly in chaps. 4 and 7. See also Vera Shlakman, *Economic History of a Factory Town*, chaps. 5 and 6.

rapidly becoming a new labor force in the New England mills. Labor papers as well as reformers constantly and correctly complained that the condition of workers was growing worse, and resented the optimistic comments of foreign visitors.

EARLY LABOR ORGANIZATIONS

Three factors are chiefly responsible for the development of labor organizations in America—the coming of the Industrial Revolution, the concentration of labor in urban areas, and the changing economic position of the worker. Prior to the advent of the factory system most manufactured goods were produced in the home or small shop, and the products were the result of well-trained and skilled work. The typical workman learned his trade by serving as an apprentice, gained experience by working for wages for some years as a journeyman, and finished his career as a master workman. A laboring class, in the sense of people who spent their lives working for wages as employees, hardly existed in the colonial period. With the coming of machinery and the factory system this situation began to change. As machinery took the place of hand tools, the long training of the skilled craftsman became less necessary. The workman learned to run a machine rather than to produce by hand. Not only this, but he learned to handle just one type of machine; for specialization became characteristic of the new type of production. Moreover, the new machinery was expensive. Only the man with capital could afford to own it, and the worker must seek its owner if he wanted a job. Although hand production continued for many decades after the invention of machinery, the ability of machines to produce more cheaply doomed it in the end.

The necessity for the worker to seek the machine and to sell his services for wages created for the first time in this country a large wage-earning class. This tendency was undoubtedly speeded during the latter part of the eighteenth century and the early years of the nineteenth by the domination of the merchant-capitalist. He was the central figure in the nation's economic life during these years. He was essentially a wholesaler, an importer and exporter, who bought where it was cheapest and sold where he could secure the best prices. Sometimes he financed the individual worker or the small shop; often he expanded his business into manufacturing for himself. In any event, he increased competition among manufacturers, forced prices down, and speeded the separation of master workmen and their employees. In this bitter competition for markets, and under the goad of the merchant-capitalist, employers saw no way of reducing prices except through lower wages and longer hours.

Under this pressure associations of master employers, hitherto chiefly interested in training apprentices and maintaining standards of workmanship and products, shifted their interests to reducing costs and increasing profits. Workingmen in turn slowly began to organize for their own protection. Short-lived local craft organizations appeared in the 1780's and more permanent unions in the 1790's. The Philadelphia shoemakers, for example, organized in 1792 and the New York printers established the Typographical Society in 1794. These societies were purely local, although organizations in the same trade were sometimes established in other cities and there was communication between them. Like unions in later years, these early organizations were primarily interested in obtaining higher wages, shorter hours, and better working conditions through collective bargaining, but they were also interested in sick and funeral benefits.

Although this early labor movement developed slowly and was localized in a few of the larger towns, it is interesting to note that even this early many of the techniques of later labor struggles were discovered and used. *Collective bargaining* was employed as early as 1799 by the Philadelphia shoemakers to effect a compromise in a wage dispute and was continually resorted to by many unions thereafter. *Strikes,* although not common, were recorded as early as 1786, when the printers of Philadelphia struck against their employers. *Walking delegates,* or *business agents* as they are called today, were appointed to see that agreements were lived up to. The *closed shop* goes back to 1794 when the Philadelphia shoemakers compelled each employer to hire only union members. Strikers often instigated *boycotts* against a firm which they were fighting, and on numerous occasions established control over apprenticeship to safeguard both their own wages and the quality of workmanship. The New York Typographical Society, for instance, complained in 1809 that "a superabundance of learners, runaway apprentices and half-way journeymen as well as adults who had served less than half-time at their trade, had a depressing effect upon the wages of full-fledged workers." On the other hand, *employers' associations* were organized early for the purpose of protecting their own interests and opposing unions.

This technique of labor action, the student should be warned, came slowly, certainly as far at it was used on any large scale. The complexity of achieving national organization with full-time officers, dues, strike funds, and the concentration upon demands that could be won by strike action retarded development. And, as we shall note later, labor was as interested, and as excited, over various reforms as were Owen, Greeley, Brisbane, Evans, and others, who have been criticized for leading labor astray from their main objective. In reality, labor organization was largely a reform movement up to the Civil War. Union organization was still in an embryonic stage.

One of the most difficult problems faced by labor organizations was that of legal status. Under the English common law any combination of workmen formed to raise wages was a conspiracy against the public welfare. In the absence of statute law governing this point in America, the problem arose as to whether the English common law applied in this country. Between 1806 and 1815 six separate conspiracy trials were held, four of which were decided against the workers. Certain of the trials seemed to transcend the question at issue and to involve the political philosophy of Federalists and Republicans, which advocates of the Federalists upholding the English common law and Republicans insisting that it had no standing here. In such an economic, political, and class conflict, the courtrooms were not without bias. Said the Federalist judge in the first trial: "In every point of view, this measure [the strike] is pregnant with public mischief and private injury, . . . tends to demoralize the workmen, . . . destroy the trade of the city, and leaves the pockets of the whole community to the discretion of the concerned. . . . A combination of workmen to raise their wages may be considered from a two-fold point of view: one is to benefit themselves, . . . the other is to injure those who do not join their society. The rule of law condemns both."[18] As time went on, however, the courts shifted their attention from the question as to whether a union of workers was a conspiracy to the means employed by labor to obtain its ends. The right of workers to join unions was finally recognized in a famous decision in 1842,[19] but for many years strikes, boycotts, and other labor weapons were subjects of legal action.

If any date can be set for the origin of the American labor movement, as we understand such a movement today, it is 1827 when the Philadelphia carpenters struck for a ten-hour day. They were immediately joined by the painters, glaziers, and bricklayers, and with this as a nucleus a Mechanics' Union of Trade Associations was organized which eventually included fifteen unions. Following the lead of Philadelphia, local unions sprang up in the leading cities, both on the eastern seacoast and in the Middle West, and more than a dozen city trade associations, like the Mechanics' Union of Trade Associations, appeared. Not only did this movement toward city-wide organization develop, but at least five unions—shoemakers, comb makers, carpenters, hand-loom weavers, and printers—established national organizations. The first national convention of labor representatives was held in 1834. This enlargement of union organization until it finally reached national proportions was made possible by increased population, growing urbanization, improved transportation facilities, and wider competition in industry.

LABOR IN THE REFORM MOVEMENT

Labor organizations in America, it will be noted, began not in the factories but among the skilled workers in the trades. These men had spent years in

---

[18] J. R. Commons *et al.* (eds.), *op. cit.,* III, 230–233.
[19] Commonwealth *v.* Hunt, 4 Metcalf 111 (1842).

acquiring their skills and they represented the more highly trained and alert group of workers. Their demands went beyond shorter hours and better working conditions to include free schools, abolition of imprisonment for debt, restriction of child labor, mechanics' lien laws, equal taxation, direct election of public officials, and various other political and economic reforms.[20] In these they were often joined by reformers of various kinds and by workers and middle-class people unaffiliated with union organizations. So wide, in fact, was the reform program of these early unions that it could be achieved only through political action. Such action was now possible because of the wide extension of the suffrage in the new or revised state constitutions. In 1828 the Mechanics' Union of Trade Associations in Philadelphia proposed to the several unions in that city that they join in nominating candidates "to represent the interests of the working classes." This they did, and several of their candidates backed by the Jacksonian and other parties were elected. Other cities followed Philadelphia's example. In at least fifteen states local labor parties were formed and fifty labor papers founded. The strength of labor's first political effort was in the Northeast.

This first excursion into labor politics was brief and the results were local and temporary. The workers were new at the game of politics and confused by the skillful attacks of the old parties, and by 1832 the movement had virtually disappeared. Likewise this first wave of labor organization largely disintegrated with the panic of 1837. This temporary collapse of the labor movement left the field open to politicians and reformers of various kinds who hoped to rally labor to their reform schemes. The reforms advocated in the twenties were revived in the forties and new ones proposed. Of particular interest to labor as well as to other large elements in the country were the various projects for co-operative living advocated during these years. Utopian socialism had beeen brought to America in the 1820's by Robert Owen, who tried his experiment at New Harmony, Indiana. His project collapsed, but renewed interest was apparent in the late thirties and early forties after Horace Greeley and Albert Brisbane gave wide publicity to the co-operative organization advocated by the Frenchman, Charles Fourier. Unlike Owen, who stressed the overwhelming importance of environment on the character of human beings, Fourier emphasized the economy and efficiency that would result if mankind were organized into groups of from 300 to 1800 people (phalanxes) living in a central building (phalanstery), the group being to a large extent economically self-sufficing. Scores if not hundreds of "communities" of one kind or another were established in this country between 1820

---

[20] Other reforms sometimes advocated by one group of labor or another included temperance, abolition of lotteries, abolition of capital punishment, abolition of monopolies, prohibition of private banks, abolition of compulsory military service, and votes for women.

and 1850, the most famous being Brook Farm, near Boston, where many of the best-known New England intellectuals resided at various times.

Through the influence of George Henry Evans, who had been prominent in the labor movement in New York, labor was also drawn closely into the activities of the "Agrarian League" and the land reform movement. Evans' program called for ending the sale of public land to companies and speculators and apportioning it in small amounts to actual settlers without charge. His agitation caught the attention of many in the dark days following the panic of 1837 and undoubtedly hastened the Homestead Act of 1862. Of more immediate value to labor than Evans' program was the progress toward a ten-hour day. What was left of organized labor after the panic made this an essential demand. Government employees obtained a ten-hour day in 1840, and gradually in the late forties and early fifties a few of the states began to pass ten-hour acts, in some cases only for women and children.

Although the efforts of organized labor during these years to improve the political and economic life of the worker seem slight, they were by no means fruitless. Many reforms which they advocated were eventually achieved; in this their co-operation played a part. The ten-hour day, for example, was widely accepted by the opening of the Civil War; this was only one type of legislation that labor had advocated. The important part labor played in the agitation for free public education has been admitted but probably not fully recognized. Almost all of the needed changes advocated during this great era of reform were part of the labor program.

During the fifties labor shifted from a policy of generally advocating reform to one of "old-line unionism." As the influence of the "reformers" declined, new leaders appeared to strengthen the new trend. Discovery of gold in California, the rapid building of railroads, and other developments brought prosperity and higher prices. Labor responded by taking on new life and organizing new locals and at least ten national unions. The latter included the Typographical Union founded in 1850, the Hat Finishers in 1854, the Stone Cutters in 1855, and both the National Union of Machinists and Blacksmiths and the National Moulders Union in 1859. Not only was unionization rapidly extended but it was organized upon a more practical, businesslike, solid basis. The panic of 1857 hit organization another blow. Only three nationals survived, but this time labor was in a better position than it had been before to meet an economic depression, and a new development of organization soon set in.

SELECTED READINGS

Channing, E., *A History of the United States,* Vol. V, chap. 2.
Stephenson, G. M., *History of American Immigration,* chaps. 1–12.

Hansen, M. L., *The Atlantic Migration*, chaps. 11–13.

Taylor, G. R., *The Transportation Revolution*, chaps. 12, 13.

Commons, J. R., *et al.* (eds.), *History of Labor in the United States*, Vol. I, pp. 169–230.

Beard, Mary, *A Short History of the American Labor Movement*, chaps. 1–6.

Ware, N. J., *The Industrial Worker, 1840–1860*, chaps. 10–15.

Bogart, E. L., and Thompson, C. M., *Readings in the Economic History of the United States*, chap. 16.

Flügel, F., and Faulkner, H. U., *Readings in the Economic and Social History of the United States*, pp. 251–259, 397–412.

CHAPTER 16

ECONOMIC CAUSES OF THE
CIVIL WAR

GROWTH OF SECTIONALISM

Tʜᴇ fact that the political controversies preceding southern secession centered largely around the question of the further extension of the slave system
and that one important result of the Civil War was the end of chattel slavery
has often led historians to overemphasize this factor. That slavery was one of
the chief causes leading to the conflict of arms, no one will deny. That it was
the "single cause," as Rhodes once asserted,[1] is an interpretation hardly warranted by facts. The Civil War was essentially a conflict of economic sections. It was by no means the first sectional conflict in our history, nor was it
the last. During the War of 1812, New England leaders, for example, talked
of secession at the time of the Hartford Convention. Twenty years later the
South Carolina legislature passed an Ordinance of Nullification declaring
the Tariff Acts of 1828 and 1832 not binding on the people of that state. The
conflict of economic interests between the North and South had become so
acute by 1860 that secession might have resulted without the complication of
slavery.

The basic conflict between the two sections lay in the fact that the South
was primarily agricultural and the North was becoming increasingly industrial. It was a friction between a plantation economy and a rising industrial capitalism. The agricultural life of colonial times, founded on the
plantation system and perpetuated by the introduction of cotton, tended to
make the South an agricultural and exporting section with little manufacturing. On the other hand, the North was steadily developing a commercial
and manufacturing life. The opposition of interests first made itself felt on

[1] J. F. Rhodes, *Lectures on the Civil War*, p. 2.

306

the question of the tariff. In the wave of nationalism following the War of 1812, southern leaders combined with northern in passing the protective tariff of 1816; but by 1824 their attitude changed, and they vigorously opposed this and succeeding tariffs. The western states, desiring to build up a home market, had supported the tariffs of 1816, 1824, 1828, and 1832, but the growth of the southern market for their products brought some shift in their attitude. The doctrine of nullification, or state sovereignty, which had been earlier set forth by Kentucky in protest against the Alien and Sedition Acts and by New England in opposition to the War of 1812, was now reaffirmed by South Carolina against the "tariff of abominations" of 1828 and the tariff of 1832; the doctrine was never lost sight of and finally resulted in actual secession. The compromise tariff of 1833 registered a victory for the South, and her representatives, with the aid of the West, were able to prevent the adoption of the protective principle on a large scale until the Morrill Bill of 1861.

A similar battle was waged over the banking and currency system. The South in general, as a debtor region with a lack of liquid capital, favored easy banking laws and an expanded currency. In alliance with the frontier West she managed to destroy the second Bank of the United States and to determine the banking system from 1836 until secession.

The South was victorious over the North not only in regard to tariff, currency, and banking, but also with respect to the public land policy and western expansion. Southern agriculture, tied up as it was with cotton and slavery, needed room for rapid expansion. Northern manufacturers, on the other hand, desired a more concentrated population and hence opposed measures which might encourage migration to the West. The South favored rapid sale of western lands in large tracts at low prices, while the North advocated smaller and more restricted sales at higher prices. These conflicting views resulted in a compromise in 1841, a pre-emption bill which provided for sales to actual settlers at a very low price. In actual practice, however, the southern planter found this law liberal enough for his needs, and in the fifties he vigorously opposed further liberalization of the land laws because such a policy would benefit the small white farmer and promote the rapid extension of free territory.

The same differences were to be seen in opinions on territorial expansion. Cotton production as practiced under slavery needed a constant supply of fresh land, and the demand for new slave territory was literally pushed on by its own weight. Furthermore, as the North began to surpass the South in population and wealth, it became more essential to the South to maintain a number of Senators sufficient to control the Senate and protect her interests. Southern leadership had largely favored the acquisition of Louisiana,

Florida, Texas, and the lands won from Mexico, as well as the conspiracies to annex Cuba. Opponents of the Mexican War were against expansion of the slave power rather than extension of territory.[2]

As long as the states of the Northwest found a market for their agricultural products in the South, they were inclined to support that section; but the building of canals and railroads eventually provided the trans-Appalachian states north of the Ohio with both an eastern and a European market. Quite as important, however, in linking the Old Northwest with the eastern seaboard states rather than with the South was the promise of free homesteads made by the Republican party. The alliance in the Republican party of 1860 of eastern manufacturers seeking high tariffs and western farmers demanding free lands was to the Southerner an unholy and malicious plot, and it meant the eventual defeat of the South. Southern leaders saw the issue clearly. Jefferson Davis openly declared that it was not the dictates of humanity or the desire to benefit the slaves that impelled the free-soil agitators to oppose the further extension of slavery.

Not at all [said he]. . . . It is that you may have an opportunity of cheating us that you want to limit slave territory within circumscribed bounds. It is that you may have a majority in the Congress of the United States and convert the government into an engine of northern aggrandizement. It is that your section may grow in power and prosperity upon treasures unjustly taken from the South, like the vampire bloated and gorged with the blood which it has secretly sucked from its victim. . . . You desire to weaken the political power of the southern states; and why? Because you want, by an unjust system of legislation, to promote the industry of the New England states, at the expense of the people of the South and their industry.[3]

SOUTHERN ECONOMY

The words of Jefferson Davis reflect with a fair degree of accuracy the attitude of the great majority of the cotton, tobacco, rice, and sugar planters of the South. Although, as we have seen,[4] the great mass of southern whites were small farmers, it was the plantation lords who dominated the economic, social, and political life of the South. "There was never in America," asserts Dodd, "a more perfect oligarchy of business men than that which ruled in the time of Jefferson Davis and Alexander Stephens."[5] These were the men whose opinions were followed in the South. They believed that the economic

[2] J. D. P. Fuller, "The Slavery Question and the Movement to Acquire Mexico, 1846–1848," *Mississippi Valley Historical Review*, XXI, 31–48 (June, 1934), argues convincingly, on the other hand, that many Southerners opposed annexation because the region was not suitable for slavery.

[3] Quoted by C. and M. Beard, *Rise of American Civilization*, II, 5–6.

[4] Above, pp. 67–68, 69.

[5] W. E. Dodd, *The Cotton Kingdom*, p. 121.

troubles of their section were the result of northern domination and that their problems could be solved only by political independence. It was the same belief that led plantation owners to favor independence from Great Britain in 1776. That the power of northern capitalism bore heavily upon them there can be no question. But that independence would have solved their problem is more than doubtful.

There is something inherent in a plantation economy that puts it in a dependent position in a capitalist world. Except under a system of central regulation almost unknown in the nineteenth century, southern plantation owners had no more control over national production or prices than the wheat farmer in the 1920's. The price of cotton was determined by the world market. If it was sufficiently high so that a profit was realized, there was a tendency to increase production. In the South this meant investment of profits in land and slaves. If prices were low and the year's crop was sold at a loss, the planter had to borrow to carry himself until the next year, and he pledged his future crop as security for the loan. In either case he was left without liquid capital. It was easy under such a situation to fall into debt and to be overcharged by the bankers who lent him money and the commission men who marketed his crop. He began with no control over prices or total production and ended by dependence upon those who financed his operations.

How this operated in the prewar South is not difficult to describe. To meet the expense of raising his crop the planter borrowed from his factor[6] at interest rates of from 8 to 12 per cent, pledging his future crop. If there was a surplus, the factor sold it at the prevailing price, charging a commission of from one-half of one per cent to 2.5 per cent. Hauling, storage, freight, weighing, and insurance cost an additional 2.5 to 4 per cent. To protect himself against loss it was customary for the factor to stipulate a minimum number of bales to be delivered and to make a penalty charge for failure. This, with other conditions, tended toward overproduction and resulting low prices.

The funds which financed this production came largely from British and northern banks. Payments were made in 120-day New York drafts or 60-day sterling bills of exchange which were discounted by southern banks. If there was a demand for these drafts or for sterling exchange in New York, the discount rates favored the planter. If there was little demand, he was at a disadvantage. Moreover, the price of cotton was inevitably influenced by exchange rates. This hazard was particularly acute during the panic of 1857 when exchange rates dropped, cotton buying slowed down, and the price of cotton fell. The South lost heavily during that year in a situation over which she had no control. This panic brought home more clearly than ever before

[6] In this case, a combination of banker's representative and commission merchant.

the fact that New York had become a bottleneck through which flowed the greater part of the financial transactions of the South and that southern prosperity might be dependent upon the condition of the money market in New York.

One important effect of the investment of a large proportion of southern wealth in land and slaves for the production of commercial crops was the one-sided economic life which it produced. Although many slaves became skilled mechanics, slave labor as a whole was too ignorant for large-scale industrial development. Whether it was or was not fitted for industry, the fact remains that the slaveowner believed his labor was more profitable when expended in agriculture. Skilled white mechanics in general avoided the South. Although water power and cotton were both at hand, there was little liquid capital to invest in manufacturing, and the planter preferred to send his products to the mills of New England or Europe. The great industrial progress which encompassed the North in the two decades before the war largely passed by the South. Except in cotton manufacturing and iron founding, development was trivial.

COTTON MANUFACTURING IN NEW ENGLAND AND THE SOUTH, 1840–1850

	Census	Plants	Capital	Operatives
Southern states	1840	248	$ 4,331,078	6,642
	1850	166	7,256,056	10,043
New England	1840	674	34,931,399	46,834
	1850	564	53,832,430	61,893

The paucity of industrial development in the southern states was only too well illustrated after the war broke out, when the Confederacy found itself hopelessly dependent upon the outside for the simplest manufactured products. The planters of the Southwest even imported their corn and bacon from north of the Ohio in order to devote their whole plantation to cotton. The one-sidedness of southern economic life is thus pessimistically described by Helper, who produced the most scathing indictment to come from the pen of a Southerner:

In one way or another we are more or less subservient to the North every day of our lives. In infancy we are swaddled in Northern muslin; in childhood we are humored with Northern gewgaws; in youth we are instructed out of Northern books; at the age of maturity we sow our "wild oats" on Northern soil; in middle life we exhaust our wealth, energies and talents in the dishonorable vocation of entailing our dependence on our children and on our children's children, and, to the neglect of our own interests and the interests of those around us, in giving aid and succor to every department of Northern power; in the decline of life we remedy our eye-sight with Northern spectacles, and support our infirmities with Northern canes; in old age we are drugged with Northern physic; and, finally, when we die, our inanimate bodies, shrouded in Northern cambric, are stretched upon the bier, borne to the grave in a Northern carriage, entombed with a Northern spade, and memorized with a Northern slab.[7]

Lack of space forces us to leave to economics textbooks the arguments pro and con as to whether a region should specialize in the type of production best fitted for it or whether it should attempt to develop a well-rounded and self-sufficient economic life. The South was pre-eminently fitted to produce certain subtropical staples, which she did, at the same time purchasing her manufactured commodities from Europe and the North and considerable foodstuffs from the Old Northwest. Conditions being what they were, it was quite unlikely that she would or could have done otherwise.

Nevertheless, the situation proved detrimental to the South. Whether the Southerners sold their staples at a good or poor price, they ordinarily bought their manufactured goods at a high price. For this they blamed the tariff. The effects of the tariff upon the South were probably less bad than was generally believed. She won the tariff fight in 1833 and except for brief periods the rates continued downward until the Civil War. Certainly, after 1857 tariff rates were low.[8] More valid, perhaps, was the resentment of Southerners over the fact that, as an importing section, they paid a disproportionate amount in taxation to support the federal government. They argued correctly that a shift of policy from indirect to direct taxation would bring larger contributions from the North and so bear more equitably upon the whole country.

More detrimental to the South than the tariff was the costly system through which she purchased her manufactured commodities. Manufactured goods from the North were financed by northern bankers, brought to the South in northern ships, and distributed by northern jobbers or middlemen. Between the South and Europe there was little direct trade. A large proportion of southern cotton was shipped to New York and then to Europe. The return cargoes of manufactured goods went to northern ports and were then distributed throughout the South in the coastwise trade. This "cotton triangle" involved higher transportation costs and added commissions to middlemen. There is no doubt that the South would have benefited by the

[7] H. R. Helper, *The Impending Crisis of the South*, pp. 22–23. Helper was a middle-class Southerner from North Carolina who believed that slavery was ruining the South both economically and socially. His famous book, based largely on the Census of 1850, was and still is considered by Southerners a strongly biased picture. See his biography in the *Dictionary of American Biography.*

[8] Richard Hofstadter, "The Tariff Issue and the Civil War," *American Historical Review,* XLIV, 50–55 (Oct., 1938).

development of direct trade with Europe. There is great doubt, on the other hand, that the elimination of all tariffs would have greatly changed the existing trade routes or the system of distributing imported commodities. But Southerners believed that it would, and this fact is important in understanding their discontent. In history, unfortunately, belief is often more important than fact.

DEVELOPMENT OF SLAVERY

Although the rivalry of economic interests was fundamental in explaining the Civil War, it is impossible to escape the important part played by the slave system. In the first place, slavery accentuated the economic differences between the South on the one hand and the North and the Northwest on the other, and, in the second place, the political means whereby the South sought to protect herself from the growing strength of her economic rivals became closely related with the extension of slavery. It is for these reasons, as well as the fact that the economic life of the South was strongly colored by the slave system, that the development and effects of slavery should be studied closely.

Slavery, which had flourished in the colonial South, was on the defensive at the close of the Revolution. Losses incurred by the planters in the War of Independence, the exhaustion of the soil in the coast states, and the influx of white settlers from the North into these regions all tended to make the system less profitable. These influences, augmented by the Revolutionary theories unfavorable to slavery, led many Southerners to question its economic and moral basis. Nevertheless, it was still firmly entrenched in 1781 in the rice and indigo fields of the Carolinas and Georgia, although its hold on the tobacco plantations had been weakened. The factors which contributed beyond all others to revive an apparently dying institution were the introduction of sea-island cotton and the invention of the cotton gin (1793) simultaneously with the coming of the Industrial Revolution. The first gave the planters of the coast regions an opportunity to recoup their waning fortunes, the latter made it possible to raise profitably the inland short-fibered variety; and both led to the rapid extension of cotton culture into the uplands and westward.

In cotton the South found a crop that apparently paid with slave labor, for the requisite conditions necessary to make it profitable seemed ideally combined. The first of these was simplicity of operation; slavery thrives under a one-crop system of agriculture, the methods of which can be learned and mechanically repeated year after year. Cotton is a comparatively easy plant to raise, and the labor of the Negro could be adapted to it. Few tools and little equipment were needed, so that small loss was sustained even from inefficient labor. Cotton culture extends over three-fourths of the year, and in its production, more than in that of many other staples, it was possible to give employment to women and children, thus obtaining the maximum return from an entire family.

Still another advantage was the fact that the slaves could be more compactly massed in raising cotton than in producing many other products. A single laborer could work only three acres of rice and only five to ten acres of cotton, while he might cultivate thirty or forty acres of corn, a significant fact when it is appreciated that the labor of slaves is usually secured only under compulsion and that constant supervision is necessary. Supervision, moreover, was expensive. "To diminish the inducement for overdriving," says Professor Phillips, "the method of paying the overseers by crop shares, which commonly prevailed in the colonial period, was generally replaced in the nineteenth century by that of fixed salaries."[9] An overseer's salary in 1863 was about $1300, a considerable amount of cash for that time. The high cost of white overseers contributed in an important way to shift slave labor to large cotton plantations.

A further condition necessary to the profitable employment of slave labor is cheapness and ease of subsistence. The expenditure for shelter, fuel, and clothing was naturally not great in the warm climate of the cotton belt. The slave's chief food was bacon and corn; consequently some corn was usually raised on the plantation to provide food for slaves and hogs, although in later years considerable corn and pork were obtained from the states north of the Ohio. The cost of maintaining a slave ranged from $15 a year under the most favorable conditions to from $30 to $40 in the border states. The average was about $20 a year.

Important also in fastening slavery on the South was the abundance of unoccupied land in the West. Slave labor, incompetent and ignorant as it was, condemned the cotton planter to a one-crop system. Although cotton was less destructive to the soil than other staples, especially tobacco, its uninterrupted growth without the use of fertilizer meant the wearing out of the soil. As land was cheaper than slaves, the tendency was to "butcher the land" by planting crops of cotton until it was exhausted and then pushing on to new and fertile fields and repeating the process. This procedure was aided by the fact that most of the land was suitable for cotton. Thus slavery was dependent on a one-crop economy, which in turn, under the agricultural methods pursued, depended on the opening up of new lands. These facts explain in part the rapid westward advance of the cotton planter and the apparently insatiable hunger of the slaveholder for new land. They also explain why it was possible even with declining cotton prices and inefficient labor to continue to raise cotton at a profit. Until the fresh cheap land was

[9] Ulrich B. Phillips, *American Negro Slavery* (1918), p. 281.

exhausted, slavery seemed able to hold its own against the competition of free labor.

The southern states during the first half-century produced about seven-eighths of the world's cotton supply. The demand for it was steady and increasing. Whoever had slaves or could buy them turned more and more to raising cotton. DeBow estimated in 1850 that 2,500,000 of the 3,204,313 slaves were engaged in agriculture, and of these 72.6 per cent (1,815,000) were employed on cotton.[10] As the cotton planter pushed westward into the fertile lowlands of Alabama and Mississippi and a continually greater area was put under cultivation, the demand for slaves increased.[11] The wealthy planters were able to obtain the choicest lands, thus driving the poor whites to the small and less fertile farms where they raised food crops. These farmers would not or could not compete with slave labor, carried on as it was upon the big plantations. Not only were the efforts of the poor native whites largely withdrawn from cotton raising, but the labor situation in the South repelled the immigrant. The slaveholding states contained 378,205 foreign-born in 1850, the non-slave states 1,866,397; this constituted 3.91 per cent and 13.89 per cent, respectively, of the aggregate population of the sections.

The demand for slaves was met by natural increase and by importation from Africa, though the latter was illegal after 1808. There was also considerable internal slave trade. The surplus Negroes in the border states and the eastern Carolinas were shipped southwest for sale to the cotton planters of the new states. The natural increase of the slave population on the cotton plantations was very slight; on the sugar plantations of Louisiana it was less than the waste of life. On the other hand, the border states developed a hardy type of Negro, longer lived and more prolific, so that the population increase on the Virginia farms amounted frequently to 20 per cent. With the growing demand for Negroes there was a corresponding rise in the price. The average value of slaves in 1798 has been estimated at about $200; in 1815, at $250; in 1840, at $500; and in 1860, at $700. "Prime field hands," however, who sold for $200 in 1780 brought from $350 to $500 in 1800, $700 to $1000 in 1818, $1400 to $1800 or $2000 in 1860.[12] The increase was not steady, but varied

[10] J. D. B. DeBow, *Statistical View of the United States . . . Being a compendium of the Seventh Census* (1854), p. 94, note.

[11] The approximate Negro population, 1740–1860, is as follows. The estimate is taken from *The South in the Building of the Nation*, V, 111, note.

1740	140,000	1820	1,777,000
1776	300,000	1830	2,328,000
1790	750,000	1840	2,873,000
1800	1,002,000	1850	3,638,000
1810	1,380,000	1860	4,441,000

[12] *Ibid.*, V, 127.

with periods of prosperity and depression, which in turn were dependent on the price of cotton.

Not only was it now possible for the border states of Virginia, Maryland, and Kentucky to get rid of their surplus laborers, but it became more and more profitable for the slaveholders there to raise Negroes to "sell south." Professor Dew of William and Mary College asserted in 1832 that Virginia was "a *negro* raising State for other States; she produces enough for her own supply, and six thousand for sale,"[13] and Olmsted estimated that in the ten years preceding 1860 the annual export of Negroes from the border states was about 25,000. Negroes formed 50 per cent of the population of Virginia in 1782 and only 37 per cent in 1860. Regarding this aspect of the slave trade the fact should be emphasized that there was little if any intentional breeding for the slave trade. Certain sections where the land had deteriorated and where slavery had become unprofitable found themselves with a surplus of Negroes. Hard pressed economically, masters were forced to dispose of their slaves in the southern market, often against their own wishes. The following figures presented by Cairnes illustrate the constant draining off of slaves from the border states by the internal trade, as well as the decline of the system in the border states.

PERCENTAGE INCREASE OF POPULATION IN THE
DECADE ENDING 1850

State	Whites	Slaves
Virginia	20.77	5.21
Maryland	31.34	0.70
Kentucky	28.99	15.75
Arkansas	110.16	136.26
Mississippi	65.13	58.74
Louisiana	61.23	45.32

John F. Cairnes, *The Slave Power* (2nd ed., enlarged, 1863), p. 130.

To explain adequately the importance which southern leaders attached to the slave system, one further point should be emphasized. Southern wealth was invested primarily in cotton, land, and slaves. The value of cotton declined especially in the forties as greater quantities were thrown upon the market (see p. 338), and the value of the land simultaneously decreased under the wasteful methods then employed. Regions could be seen in the Southwest which in less than fifty years had advanced from a howling wilderness to a profitable agricultural economy, and then had declined to uninhabited

[13] Thomas R. Dew, in *The Pro-Slavery Argument* (1852), p. 359.

wastes.[14] While cotton and land values declined, the price of slaves continued to mount. Thus, the one form of southern wealth that became more valuable as the years passed was investment in slaves. Under such circumstances it is not surprising that the Southerner placed an exaggerated value on this form of property, and that the perpetuation of the slave system seemed essential to southern prosperity.

Some southern economists went even further and asserted that land values in the older states were dependent upon the institution of slavery. "It is, in truth, the slave labor in Virginia," said Professor Dew, "which gives value to her soil and her habitations;—eject from the State the whole slave population, and we risk nothing in the prediction, that on the day in which it shall be accomplished, the worn soils of Virginia would not bear the paltry price of the government lands in the West, and the Old Dominion will be a waste howling wilderness."[15]

The decade before the war saw both the maximum expansion of slavery and the early indications of its decline. Of the 12,000,000 people (in round numbers) in fifteen slave states, about one-third were slaves. The production of cotton, the great staple of the South, was closely tied up with the institution, and the border states, whose land was exhausted or not adaptable to cotton, were unwittingly joined to the system as breeding grounds for slaves. At the same time, it was evident that the progress of slave labor was practically at a standstill in most of the South and was actually declining on the Atlantic seaboard and in the border states. Throughout the South white farmers and free laborers were increasing faster than slaves. The more rapid growth of the white population presaged even in the South an approaching struggle between white and slave labor, a contest in which slavery would be at an increasing disadvantage as the better land was absorbed.

SLAVERY IN THE SOUTH

The census in 1860 gave the white population of the slave states at 8,099,-760 and the slaves at 3,953,580. The slaves were owned by only 384,000 whites, of whom 107,957 owned more than ten slaves, 10,781 owned fifty or more, and 1733 owned a hundred or more. Over 6,000,000 southern whites were not interested directly in slaveownership. Nevertheless, the fact that the great staple upon which the wealth and prosperity of the South depended was raised largely by slaves under a plantation system gave the institution an importance which the number of slaveholders would not seem to warrant. The slaveholding aristocracy produced able politicians who so molded opinion in

[14] See above, p. 186; also F. L. Paxson, *History of the American Frontier,* p. 206, and G. S. Callender, *Selections from the Economic History of the United States,* pp. 765–767.

[15] Thomas R. Dew, *op. cit.,* p. 358.

the South that when the break came in 1860 the great majority of whites were behind the secession movement. There is no better example in modern history of the shaping of public opinion by a handful of the ruling class so as to bring on a war to preserve an institution which benefited themselves alone.

As three-fourths of the slaves were engaged directly in agriculture and most of them in the production of cotton, the typical life of the slave was life on the plantation. The most intelligent and trusted Negroes, often those with a mixture of white blood, were employed as household servants. On the plantation there were often Negro carpenters, blacksmiths, and drivers, but the great mass of slaves—men, women, and children—were occupied in the fields. The owner was usually his own overseer on the smaller plantation, but on the larger he was forced to turn over the direct management to hired white overseers. These were in turn assisted by drivers, trusty Negroes who set the pace or supervised small groups. Work on a plantation was carried on in one of three ways: by the task system, in which a definite amount of work for the day was assigned to each slave according to his ability; by the gang system, in which a good driver set the pace and the rest followed; or simply by setting the slave to work with no incentive but the fear of the lash.

Absentee ownership was not widely prevalent in the South, but where it existed it was a great curse, involving as it did the employment of a hired overseer. Good overseers were scarce. Ordinarily of the poor-white class, they were not recognized as the social equals of their employers; often they were working temporarily as overseers to obtain money to become slaveowners themselves. They were but one step removed from the professional slave dealer, and socially in an inferior position. As the overseer was judged chiefly by his ability to produce a large crop, the typical overseer was likely to drive the slaves to the limit and to abuse the land more than an owner who directly supervised his plantation. Where the plantation was supervised by the owner, and especially on small plantations, the condition of the slaves was likely to be better.

Speaking broadly, the economic condition of a slave was not far above that of a well-kept farm animal of the present day. Likewise, it was not far different from that of the poorer laborers of the North. House servants inherited the cast-off clothing of the master's family and had enough to eat, but few comforts. The field hands worked usually from sunrise to sunset, cooked their own meals, and were lodged in cabins to the rear of the plantation, where furniture and cleanliness were notable by their absence. The ordinary food was corn bread and bacon. More humane masters sometimes allowed the slaves to cultivate a small garden patch and to keep a few chickens or a pig, varied their diet at times, and gave them holidays and presents. The more intelligent owners and those whose plantations were conducted most

scientifically exerted great care with respect to the sanitation and health of
the slaves and made some provision for their amusement and spiritual welfare. While teaching the Negro to read and write was forbidden in five states
in the belief that it made him discontented, religious instruction was often
given. Although he undoubtedly delighted in religious expression, any attempt to inculcate, through religious teaching, habits of honesty and chastity
in men and women who did not own their own bodies or the fruit of their
labors was not easy. A marriage ceremony was often performed, although
none of the states recognized slave marriage by law.

The abolition literature of the time gave much attention to the cruelties
practiced upon the slaves. In a system in which absolute ownership of certain
human beings rests in others, and labor is rendered chiefly because of fear
of the lash, flogging naturally existed and wanton cruelty was sometimes
perpetrated. It was not, however, the general practice, certainly not with the
house servants. Conditions were worst on the sugar plantations of Louisiana,
the rice fields of Georgia and South Carolina, and the large cotton plantations of the lower South, where gangs of slaves worked under the direction
of white overseers whom Patrick Henry described as "the most abject, de-
graded, unprincipled race." Certain other forms of cruelty which went with
the system, in particular the separation of families and their disposal on the
auction block, were more often seen in the border states, where slaves were
sold for the southern market.

On the other hand, there were many estates whose slaves were comparatively happy and contented, where kindly relations existed between master
and slave, and where the economic condition of the Negro was undoubtedly
better than after emancipation. Manumission was restricted as dangerous,
but many masters set their slaves free. The incomplete figures of the Census
of 1860 put the number of slaves manumitted in that year at 3018, a ratio
of one to every 1309 slaves. In that year there were about 262,000 free Negroes
in the slave states. With regard to the whole question of the treatment of
slaves, Professor Phillips' comment seems reasonable. "The theory of rigid
coercion, and complete exploitation," he says, "was as strange to the bulk
of the planters as the doctrine and practice of moderation was to those who
viewed the régime from afar and with the mind's eye."[16]

ECONOMIC ADVANTAGES AND DISADVANTAGES OF SLAVERY

The advantages of slave labor, which had been questioned before the introduction of cotton culture, were more and more reaffirmed as the century
progressed. It was maintained that the absolute ownership of the workmen
by the employer was advantageous to the latter because it allowed him to en-

[16] Ulrich B. Phillips, *op. cit.*, pp. 293–294.

joy the entire fruit of the product of labor, to organize his labor force as he thought best, and to control his workmen through his single will to a definite end. The control of the full time of men, women, and children seemed to be the last word in the elimination of waste power. After the initial purchase, in case this was necessary, the only expense was to keep the slave healthy and strong. It was furthermore sincerely believed that Negro labor under slavery was the only kind that could be employed in the unhealthy work on the rice fields.

While some enlightened Southerners believed that cotton could be raised with free labor, the great majority were convinced that only by means of slaves could large-scale cotton production be carried on; in fact, cotton culture seemed providentially designed to enhance the advantages of slave labor. Southern writers argued, not without grounds in some localities, that the slave in the South was better housed, better fed, and happier than the free unskilled laborer in either Europe or the northern states. Not only was the slave better off, they contended, but the master and his family, freed from the necessity for manual work, could devote their abilities to the amenities of life and to intellectual development, a contention often borne out in the case of the ten thousand families who were able to live in luxury on the labor of Negroes. As attacks upon slavery grew stronger, the institution was defended upon the authority of Scripture, upon the theory of the inferiority of the colored race which doomed it to economic dependence, and finally, as necessary to the safety of the whites, for Southerners declared that the revolt in Haiti and spasmodic disturbances in this country plainly showed what would happen to the future civilization of the South if the slaves were freed.[17]

The advantages of slave labor were more apparent than real. In the first place, the labor was given reluctantly and without interest. There was small incentive to increase production, for this meant a greater expectation on the part of the owner; therefore, the slave tended to hide his true ability and to render less labor than he was capable of. The continued supervision of the overseer and the fear of the lash were necessary to produce results. The hired overseer was expensive as regards both salary and methods, for his business was to turn out a big crop, and this he was tempted to do to the detriment of both land and slaves. The labor of the Negro slave was essentially unskillful. Since he was not far removed from African barbarism, had small incentive for intellectual growth, and was brutalized in character by the system under which he lived, it is little wonder that his labor lacked versatility and was limited to the simplest tasks. He could use only the simplest tools, and or-

---

[17] For further contemporary arguments, see C. F. McCay in *Eighty Years' Progress*, pp. 119 ff., and Thomas R. Dew in *op. cit.*

dinarily it was difficult to train him to use machinery. The average slave had to be kept at work on operations constantly repeated. Furthermore, although the cost of clothing and feeding a slave was small, when to this is added the interest on capital, depreciation, taxation, and insurance against sickness, flight, and death, the yearly expense for an able-bodied slave was not far from $135. Slaves were hired out in Georgia before the war at from $140 to $150 a year, but afterward, under a system of free labor, Negroes could be obtained for $120 a year with board.

As a whole, the weight of evidence points to the fact that slave labor under the conditions present just before the Civil War was economically unsound. Certain plantations efficiently managed and located on excellent land made good profits, and they did so despite slave labor, high interest rates, factors' commissions, and a generally disadvantageous economic system. When all the conditions were favorable, reasonable profits could be made. But all the conditions were rarely favorable and the average plantation operated on so close a margin that it was lucky in many years if it could show even a slight profit.[18] One thing is certain—the general prosperity of cotton production under the plantation system was declining in the years before the war, and slave labor was one of the contributing causes, not alone because it was inefficient, but also because of the increasing price of slaves.

Operating as he did under numerous handicaps, the cotton planter discovered a partial outlet in an unlimited extent of extremely fertile soil. Consequently, as already pointed out,[19] the planter, fortified with the wealth of the South, appropriated the richest land, used it up, and traveled on to new land. Whatever the immediate gains might be, the eventual effect was bound to be disastrous and out of all proportion to the gains. The extent of unused and exhausted land was very great in the seaboard states, almost resembling the havoc wrought by an invading army. Dickens, who was strongly anti-slavery, asserted in 1842 that the soil between Fredericksburg and Richmond had been "exhausted by the system of employing a great amount of slave-labour in forcing crops without strengthening the land, and it is now little better than a sandy desert overgrown with trees." He continues, with a touch of exaggeration, "In this district, as in all others where slavery sets brooding . . . there is an air of ruin and decay abroad which is inseparable from the system."[20] The proportion of undeveloped land was great in the South, for only the best land could be made to pay.

Under such conditions it is quite likely that the exhaustion of new land

[18] Some typical examples are given in Louis Hacker, *The Triumph of American Capitalism*, pp. 318–320, taken from R. B. Flanders, *Plantation Slavery in Georgia*, pp. 221–223, and C. S. Sydnor, *Slavery in Mississippi*, pp. 196–197.

[19] Above, pp. 175 ff.

[20] Charles Dickens, *American Notes* (1842), chap. 9, p. 51.

might in itself have forced a reorganization of the southern economy and doomed the slave system.[21] Such a situation, however, had not become acute by 1860. There was still plenty of land upon which to expand and the development of railroads was opening up still more. The problem was whether cotton culture on fresh lands could overcome all the handicaps including slavery. As Louis Hacker has well put it:

The pinch came, however, when reduction of rent cost by transference to new areas of operations was not sufficient. For while prices of necessaries needed for farm and home were going up, and the price of cotton was fluctuating critically, the price of field hands was also advancing. Why was this? It was due to the fact that superior methods of organization and their locations in new planting regions made it possible for lower South farmers to tempt away the slaves from the interior, the Border States, and the tidewater. That is to say, by the late 1850's, with scarcity in the available unfree labor supply, slave prices were based on their productivity under ideal conditions. To a large company of Southern planters, therefore, it was of the utmost importance that this form of capital costs also be reduced; and it could be done only by the legal reopening of the oversea slave traffic. The heart of the southern program was to be found at this point.[22]

THE DILEMMA OF THE SOUTH

By the 1850's the full effect of a plantation economy concentrating on one crop and operated by slave labor was apparent. The characteristic tendency of commercial planting regions to stress maximum current money income, to expand recklessly, and to live extravagantly when income was high had prevented the accumulation of liquid capital and kept the South in an inferior economic position. "That the South in general," says Lewis C. Gray, "and particularly the lower South, was continuously a debtor region was partly due to the requirements for new capital on account of the exigencies of expansion. But the relative poverty of the South, as compared with the North, was largely the result of a system of rural economy characterized by extravagance both in production and consumption, a system which concentrated a large proportion of the money income in the hands of a relatively small proportion of the population."[23]

In brief, a situation had developed in which the commercial and financial life of the section was directed and controlled from the outside. Charges for commercial services were high; interest rates were exorbitant. At the same time, the cost of labor, the chief expense in raising cotton, was mounting as the price of slaves increased. During the 1850's, moreover, the price of cotton

[21] C. W. Ramsdell, "The Natural Limits of Slave Expansion," *Mississippi Valley Historical Review*, XVI, 151–171 (Sept., 1929).

[22] Louis M. Hacker, *op. cit.*, pp. 281–282.

[23] L. C. Gray, *History of Agriculture in the Southern United States to 1850.* I, 460.

fluctuated in the neighborhood of 10 to 11 cents a pound, a price high enough to insure profits for the well-managed plantation on the richer soil but only a precarious living and a debtor status for the great majority of planters.

It should also be added that the concentration of wealth in the hands of the large plantation owners was producing detrimental social as well as economic effects. Particularly to be noted was the deteriorating effect on the small farmer. Unable to compete in raising cotton with slaves on the richer low-lands and unable to resist the prices offered for his land by the rich plantation owners, he was gradually driven to the less desirable locations. Typical of what was going on all over the South was the process described by a southern observer, quoted in a country newspaper.

The cotton-growing portion of the valley of the Mississippi, the very garden of the Union, is year by year being wrested from the hands of the small farmer and delivered over to the great capitalists. The white yeoman, the class which has contributed more of the blood and devotion, and good sense and enterprise which have made this country what it is than any other, are either forced into the sandy pine-hills or are driven West to clear and prepare the soil for the army of Negroes and Negro-drivers which forever presses on their heels, to make their industry unprofitable, and their life intolerable.[24]

Keen-minded Southerners were well aware of the economically disadvantageous situation in which their section found itself and there were no lack of remedies offered. Many students of agriculture condemned the extravagance and wastefulness of the existing plantation system and urged a greater degree of self-sufficiency for the plantations. This would enable the farmer to avoid making heavy purchases of food and equipment from the outside, reduce the necessity of borrowing money, and still allow him to raise large amounts of cotton. Said one advocate of better methods:

We cannot compete with the planters of Alabama and Mississippi, in a wild and destructive system, by which even they have sunk under embarrassment and ruin, with all their advantages of soil and climate. We can make up for our inferior soil and climate only by a superior system of husbandry. While they are exhausting their soil and preventing the natural increase of their slaves by a reckless system of pushing and driving, let us improve the fertility of the one, by resting and manuring it, and increase the number of the other, by moderate working and by providing everything necessary for their health and comfort.[25]

Other reformers urged escape from economic dependence by developing manufacturing in the South. Raw materials, they pointed out, existed in

[24] Quoted by F. L. Olmsted, *A Journey in the Back Country* (1860, reprinted 1907), chap. 8, pp. 329–330 (1860 ed.), and also in G. S. Callender, *op. cit.*, p. 767.

[25] Address of General George McDuffie before the State Agricultural Society of South Carolina in 1840. Quoted by L. C. Gray, *op. cit.*, I, 460.

abundance and a labor supply might be obtained from either slaves or poor whites. "As long as we are tributaries," said a writer in the Charleston *Mercury*, "dependent on foreign labor and skill for food, clothing and countless necessaries of life, we are in thraldom."[26] Under the whip of widespread propaganda some progress toward manufacturing was made during the forties and fifties, but lack of liquid capital, competent managers, and trained labor, as well as other handicaps, prevented its rapid development. In 1860 the South contributed only 8 per cent of the country's $1,886,000,000 of manufactures.

The disastrous effects of the panic of 1857 emphasized particularly the desirability of direct trade with Europe. Despite encouragement given by the southern states, efforts to develop a southern-owned merchant marine and direct trade with other nations proved unsuccessful. Much greater success was attained in internal improvements. As in the North, southern states, counties, and towns were lavish in their contributions for the building of railroads. The state of Georgia, for example, built and operated a railroad from Atlanta to the border near Chattanooga. By 1860 the South had constructed over 9500 miles (about one-third of the nation's total) at a cost of about $237,000,000, raised almost entirely in that section.

For the purpose of discussing and publicizing the various schemes to improve the economic position of the South, more than twelve commercial conventions were held between 1837 and 1860 in the southern states. Some of these conventions reflected little more than the ambitions of certain cities to promote their own interests or of fire-eating politicians to attack northern oppression. As a whole, however, they represented an effort to face the economic problems of the South. Speakers repeatedly urged the development of manufacturing, the establishment of direct trade with Europe, the abolition of the tariff, a Pacific railroad built by southern capital, and internal improvements constructed with federal aid. Frequent demands, particularly in the later years, were made for the revival of the African slave trade in order to reduce the cost of plantation labor. The South was by no means unanimously for this last. Slaveowners in the border states who sold their excess Negroes south and the great plantation owners who made profits under the existing system had no interest in reopening the slave trade. It was the small and middle-class planter who needed cheaper labor that backed this demand. It was this group, in fact, that was most vocal against what it believed to be northern oppression.

The South may have accomplished little in revising or improving her economic status in the decades preceding the Civil War, but she was pre-eminently successful in defending her interests in the political arena. The small

[26] *Niles Weekly Register*, April 19, 1845.

southern oligarchy which ruled the economic, political, and social life of the
South also dominated the federal government. During the thirty-two years
between the election of Jackson and Lincoln it controlled the Presidency and
the Senate for twenty-four years, the Supreme Court for twenty-six years, and
the House of Representatives for twenty-two years. During these years it
reduced the tariff until it was no longer a heavy burden. It revoked the subsidies to the merchant marine which had enabled northern shipowners to
meet the intensified competition of Great Britain. It prevented an extension
of federal subsidies for internal improvements except where they were of direct benefit to the South. It had been the chief influence in precipitating the
war with Mexico, which added large areas to the plantation domain.

Against a rising antislavery movement southern politicians opened to slavery in the Compromise of 1850 all the region obtained from Mexico except
California. Four years later in the Kansas-Nebraska bill they repealed the
Missouri Compromise and opened to popular sovereignty the great territories
of Kansas and Nebraska. Finally, in the Dred Scott case (1857), a Democratic states' rights Supreme Court declared the Missouri Compromise unconstitutional by denying the authority of Congress to legislate concerning
slave property in the territories. Fearful that a westward movement of small
farmers would create new areas hostile to slavery, the South had enough influence to prevent the final enactment of the Homestead Act until after secession.

These "amazing acts of mastery," as the Beards describe them, "—legislative, executive, judicial—committed by the federal government in the decade
between 1850 and 1860 changed the whole political climate of America."
They were accomplished not by the southern oligarchy alone but by southern
Democrats in alliance with those of the North and Northwest. By the end of
the fifties many influences were at work to weaken this alliance. First of all
was the rising antislavery movement in the North. Its chief strength was
exerted not toward emancipation but rather in opposing the further extension of the slave system. Its backing came from the small farmers of the
North and Northwest who looked forward to the extension of small farms
freed from the rivalry of the plantation system. This opposition became
stronger in the fifties as immigration flowed into the Old Northwest under
the stimulus of improved transportation facilities and the new lands opened
up by the Illinois Central Railroad.

In the second place, the economic and political bonds between the South
and the Old Northwest, which had kept the Democrats in power for so long,
were ready to snap by 1860. The agricultural produce of the regions north of
the Ohio, which for decades had supported the plantations of the southern
Mississippi Valley, now moved toward the Atlantic seaports as the trans-

Allegheny railroads penetrated the Northwest. A desperate effort to save the old trade routes was made by lavish land grants to the Illinois Central, but it failed. As the outlet for the produce of the Northwest shifted to the Northeast and to Europe, the Northwest became more sympathetic toward a tariff system which would promote industrial cities and enlarge the eastern market. A southern writer in *DeBow's Review* had seen this clearly as early as 1847: "A contest has been going on between the North and South not limited to slavery or no slavery—to abolition or no abolition, nor to the politics of either whigs or democrats as such, but a contest for the wealth and commerce of the great valley of the Mississippi—a contest tendered by our Northern brethren, whether the growing commerce of the great West shall be thrown upon New Orleans or given to the Atlantic cities."

This new economic alignment was quickly reflected in politics. In the middle fifties the new Republican party sought to integrate the dissatisfaction with the Democratic party as controlled by southern plantation owners. By opposing the extension of slavery it drew to itself both antislavery idealists who were against slavery on principle and the small farmers who sought the extension of free agriculture. By favoring donation of public lands and a transcontinental railroad it won the adherence of prospective western settlers. By advocating a higher tariff it held out a beckoning hand to the rising industrial interests of the East. The strength of the platform was evident in 1856 and even more so in 1860. Together with a split in the Democratic party in 1860, the platform carried the Republicans to victory. The victory was by no means complete—the Republicans had won the Presidency, but the Democrats still had control of Congress. Nevertheless, the slaveholding South interpreted the results of 1860 as portending the doom of her national control. There remained only political and economic submission or secession. She chose the latter. In the light of history this decision was a mistake. But there was no question that, as Seward put it, the issues involved an "irrepressible conflict." The economic forces unloosed by the Industrial Revolution were finding full play and were beating irresistibly upon the one-sided and somewhat static civilization of the South. At such a time in world history there could be but one result—a victory for free labor, *laissez faire,* and industrialization.

SELECTED READINGS

Phillips, U. B., *Life and Labor in the Old South,* chaps. 11–15.
Nevins, A., *Ordeal of the Union,* Vol. I, chaps. 13–15.
Channing, E., *History of the United States,* Vol. V, chap. 5.
Dodd, W. E., *The Cotton Kingdom.*
Hacker, L. M., *The Triumph of American Capitalism,* chaps. 21–23.

Gray, L. C., *History of Agriculture in the Southern United States to 1860,* Vol. I, chaps. 20–24.

Callender, G. S., *Selections from the Economic History of the United States, 1765–1860,* chap. 15.

Flügel, F., and Faulkner, H. U., *Readings in the Economic and Social History of the United States,* pp. 413–447.

CHAPTER 17

THE CIVIL WAR

THE SIGNIFICANCE OF THE CIVIL WAR

WHETHER we approach the Civil War from the point of view of economic, political, or social history, it is difficult to overemphasize its significance. It marks a definite break midway in the development of the nation. Its effects upon our industrial, financial, and commercial history were profound and will be developed in succeeding chapters. In the long story of the American worker this war not only marked the end of chattel slavery but speeded the national integration of the organized labor movement. In it the great sectional conflict based upon economic interests reached its climax. Economic sectionalism has remained, but no part of the country has since been strong enough to resort to arms. Politically the war for southern independence established the ultimate supremacy of the federal government. It also marked a division point in American social history. The great reform movement which characterized the decades of the thirties, forties, and fifties finally burned itself out in the slavery issue, and it was another half-century before the nation again turned seriously to the quest for social justice.

A comparison of resources makes it clear that the South was bound to lose in a long war. The total population of the eleven seceding states was less than 9,000,000, of which 3,500,000 were slaves; the population of the states remaining in the Union numbered over 22,000,000, and their labor force was recruited by continued immigration during the war. Of the real property of the nation, estimated in 1860 at about $16,000,000,000, the South, including slaves valued at more than $2,000,000,000, had about one-third. Of the $3,736,-000,000 wealth produced in 1859, the seceding states accounted for about one-fourth. Quite as important in considering the superiority of the North in fighting a long war was the fact that she controlled over 90 per cent of the manufacturing industry. If this was not sufficient, her possession of the merchant marine and the Navy enabled her to import needed supplies. The

South based her hopes primarily upon two factors: first, the fact that she was engaged in a defensive war on her own territory, which would help to neutralize the disparity in men and resources; and second, the importance of her cotton production, which she believed would finance the struggle and bring foreign interference in her behalf. The first hope was rendered futile by overwhelming northern superiority. The second failed because of the North's blockade of southern ports and Europe's failure to interfere. Only the incredible inefficiency and mismanagement of the federal government prevented an earlier end to the conflict.

DEPRESSION OF 1861

The first economic effect of the war was to throw the North and West into a severe panic. At the outbreak the agricultural South owed northern merchants close to $300,000,000, practically all of which was a total loss. Uncertainty as to the future and the forebodings incident to the beginning of the war brought about a wave of retrenchmeint and economy, and the banks were caught with cash reserves far too small to meet such an emergency. All of these factors united in bringing on the depression of 1861. The Dun reports listed in 1861 nearly 6000 failures of northern firms for sums of $5000 or more (a larger number than in the panic year of 1857), and a larger number of failures for sums under that amount.[1] The northern banks in general were able to maintain specie payment until the latter part of December, 1861, when they were forced to suspend, followed almost at once by the federal government. In the South, except in New Orleans, suspension occurred immediately after the opening of the war and continued until the end. The wildcat banks in the West were especially hard hit, not only because of their methods of banking, but also because of their more intimate relations with the South. In Illinois, eighty-nine out of 110 banks failed, while in Wisconsin thirty-nine and in Indiana twenty-seven went under.

REVIVAL OF AGRICULTURAL PROSPERITY

The depression of 1861 gave way in the following spring to a revival of prosperity in the North and West. Although thousands of farmers were drawn into the Union Army and thousands more deserted agriculture for the mines of the Far West, the effect was offset by the work of women in the fields, by the influx of immigrants from Europe, and by the use of labor-saving machinery. Many eastern farmers, finding that they could not compete in certain crops with the Westerner, emigrated to take up lands in the West, a movement stimulated after 1862 by the Homestead Act,[2] which

[1] Emerson D. Fite, *Social and Industrial Conditions in the North During the Civil War*, pp. 105–106.
[2] See chap. 18.

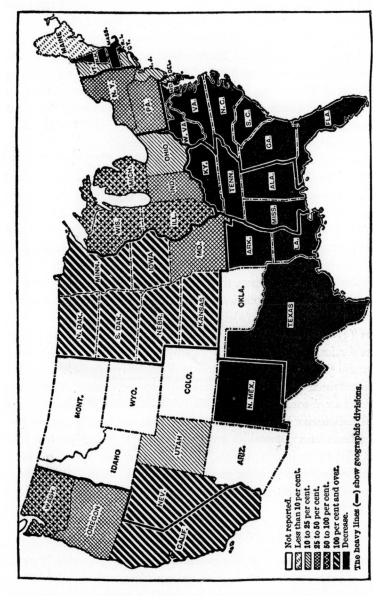

(From the *Statistical Atlas of the United States*, 1924.)

PERCENTAGE OF INCREASE OF ALL FARM PROPERTY, BY STATES, 1860–1870.

granted 160 acres free to almost anyone who would live on them for five years. Immigrants flocked from abroad during the war to take advantage of this act or to settle on the areas made available by the large railroad grants; upon arrival in New York, 45,000 declared their intention of continuing to Illinois, and 23,000 to Wisconsin.[3] There was also a considerable exodus to the western farm lands from the harassed border states. Never was such interest displayed in labor-saving farm machinery, now the center of attention at county fairs. The number of mowers manufactured increased from 20,-000 in 1861 to 70,000 in 1865, and a similar story could be told of horse rakes, grain drills, threshers, and other improved machinery.

Not only were the crops saved, but there was considerable increase in agricultural production. The wheat crop was greater during the war than at any time previous. Corn production, although it fell off slightly for the country as a whole, showed a remarkable increase in the western states. More hogs were put on the market than before the war; wool production rose from 40,-000,000 to 140,000,000 pounds, and the number of sheep on the farms doubled.

The principal factors which brought about this agricultural prosperity were (1) the necessity of feeding and clothing an army which at the close of the war numbered a million men; (2) the increasing population of the country as a whole; (3) the prosperity of the North, which made possible a greater expenditure for farm products; (4) the rapidly growing industry which employed increasing numbers in nonagricultural pursuits; (5) the stimulation of high prices which came from an expanding paper currency; and (6) the heavy demand from foreign countries. This demand came particularly from England, where the harvests of 1860, 1861, and 1862 had been below normal. As regards the British demand, it was freely asserted during the war, and with much foundation in fact, that the food supplies of the North and West were influential in preserving the neutrality of Great Britain.[4] When England had to choose between cotton and wheat there could be only one logical decision.

MANUFACTURING IN THE NORTH

Manufacturing, stimulated by war needs and liberally protected by tariff acts passed at every session of Congress, prospered enormously during the last three years of the war. Although the record is stained with the usual story of the sale of inferior goods to the government at high prices, of speculation, of lobbying, and of the amassing of fortunes by the so-called "shoddy aristocracy" out of the needs of the soldiers and the exigencies of war, it is still a significant fact that the period marked a notable advance in American

[3] Emerson D. Fite, *op. cit.*, p. 11.
[4] Below, p. 339.

manufacturing. There had been a wide extension of the factory system in the Northeast during the previous half-century, but it was the Civil War that turned the factory system into a full-fledged Industrial Revolution. In only one important industry, cotton manufacturing, did production decline. Southern statesmen expected that the cutting off of the cotton supply would bring Europe to their aid and the North to her senses, but they were mistaken. Surplus stock, already in the North at the beginning of the conflict, and a certain amount which found its way there through illicit traffic or from captured areas of the Confederacy, enabled many cotton maufacturers to run their mills on part time, and the higher prices of cotton goods made for considerable profits.

Perhaps no industry received a greater impetus from the war than the manufacture of woolen cloth. Anything that looked like wool was purchased by the government for uniforms. At the height of the war over 200,000,000 pounds of wool per year were being woven, as against 85,000,000 in times of peace, and annual dividends of from 25 to 40 per cent were frequent. Simultaneously came the rapid development of the ready-made clothing industry made possible by the sewing machine invented by Elias Howe and patented in 1846. The leather industry was also stimulated by war needs and it in turn was aided by the application of the sewing machine to leather through the patents of Lyman R. Blake and Gordon McKay. It was during the war that Chicago took the lead in pork packing and Pittsburgh increased enormously the manufacture of iron.

The production of machinery of all kinds must have been extensive, for the increase in manufacturing and transportation facilities during these years was unprecedented. Philadelphia, the largest manufacturing center in the country, boasted of fifty-eight new factories in 1862, fifty-seven in 1863, and sixty-five in 1864, and other large cities showed similar progress. Even the government went into shipbuilding and the manufacture of implements of war. The fact that a government rifle made at Springfield in 1860 cost $9 while a similar product made by private contractors cost $20 throws light both on the success with which government embarked in industry and on the profits of the munition makers. The war apparently contributed to the development of the nation's inventive genius, for the number of patents issued yearly more than doubled between 1860 and 1866.

The two basic mineral products, coal and iron, more than held their own in production during the war years. Michigan continued to turn out copper at the rate of about 6000 tons per year, and it became the "premier copper district of the world." The striking of oil in 1859 on the Drake farm at Titusville, Venango County, Pennsylvania, was the beginning of a great industry which went through the first stages of its development during the war. Thousands of wells were soon bored along Oil Creek in northwest Pennsylvania, as well as near Wheeling, West Virginia, and in Ohio. By 1862 production amounted to 128,000,000 gallons. Coincident with the excitement in the oil fields was the speculation in the cities, where 1100 oil companies with a capital stock of $600,000,000 sold $90,000,000 worth of securities. Not only was the production of petroleum the most important of the new industries developed during the war, but by 1865 oil had become an appreciable item in our foreign trade. The value of the petroleum exported rose from nothing in 1860 to almost $16,000,000 in 1865, when it ranked sixth in our exports.

In 1859 the famous Comstock Lode of gold and silver was discovered in Nevada, and the Gregory Lode of gold in Colorado; these mines and others must have produced at least $8,000,000 worth of the precious metals during the war. The rush for the mining towns, which began in 1859 with the announcement of the discovery of new deposits, continued during the war years. The population of Colorado jumped from 32,227 in 1860 to about 100,-000 in 1864. The year 1863 alone brought over 30,000 to Idaho. Virginia City, Nevada, grew from nothing to 18,000 in a short time, and the population of the state grew from 6857 in 1860 to 42,491 in 1870. The overland routes during the summer months were marked by a continuous stream of prairie schooners. One traveler on the Kansas route in 1863 testified to meeting on a sixteen-day journey an average of 500 wagons a day. In 1864 Omaha, the great point of exodus, saw 75,000 emigrants pass through toward the golden West.

LABOR AND THE COST OF LIVING

Reserving until a later chapter the discussion of the methods by which the Union government financed the war,[5] let us note here merely the cost of living, particularly as it affected the wage earner. The successive issues of legal-tender notes (greenbacks) and of short-term Treasury notes, which filled the country with a paper money fluctuating in value, tended, along with the increased demand for commodities, to drive prices up. According to the "Aldrich Report,"[6] the relative course, measured in currency and in gold, of wholesale prices and of money wages was as follows:

Year	Prices in Currency	Prices in Gold	Money Wages in Currency	Money Wages in Gold
1860	100.0	100.0	100.0	100.0
1861	100.6	100.6	100.8	100.8
1862	117.8	114.9	102.9	100.4
1863	148.6	102.4	110.5	76.2
1864	190.5	122.5	125.6	80.8
1865	216.8	100.3	143.1	66.2

[5] Below, chap. 24.

[6] Senate Reports, 52nd Cong., 2nd Sess., 1892–1893 (special session, March 4, 1893), Vol. III, Part I, pp. 9, 13, 14, 99.

Labor, which had enjoyed fair wages in the years immediately preceding the war, was hard put to it to make ends meet in the face of the rapidly rising cost of living. It has been estimated that the cost of sixty articles of prime necessity, aggregated according to quantities of such articles consumed, increased 125 per cent during the four years of the war.

The whole problem of determining real wages during the Civil War is a difficult one, as is the effort to compare wages during the war with scales which preceded it. The suspension of specie payments immediately eliminated gold from ordinary trade and put prices on the basis of greenbacks, and the value of the latter apparently fluctuated not according to the amount issued or the prosperity of the North but rather according to confidence in the success of the northern cause. A victory of the North pushed the value of the greenbacks up; a defeat sent it skidding. When to this is added the fluctuating value of gold, the unreliability of price estimates is apparent.

While commodities measured in paper money doubled in price, wages lagged behind. During the first two years of the war, wages in paper money had advanced only about 10 per cent over the average for 1860, but prices (in currency) had increased nearly 50 per cent. This big jump in prices came in 1863, and the winter of 1863 and 1864 saw both the beginning of trade-unionism on a larger scale and numerous desperately fought strikes. Up to this time any wage increases had been staved off by means of labor-saving machinery, by the employment of women and children, and by the systematic importation of cheap European labor. But capital was now forced to give in, and wages generally went up. During the war 800,000 immigrants entered the United States, a number sufficiently large to fill a big part of the gap which the war had made in the country's labor force. This heavy immigration goes far to explain the slight disturbance in the labor market and the failure of wages to rise materially until 1863. Professor Fite believes that the average advance in wages during the war amounted to 60 per cent, a point which left the laborer worse off at its conclusion than he had been in 1860.[7]

Those most severely affected by the rising cost of living were, as usual, the professional classes, particularly clergymen and teachers, government employees, and women. The pay of soldiers remained at $13.00 a month until July 20, 1864, when it was advanced to $16.00. Many of the most efficient government officials in civil occupations were forced to sever their connections with the government because of low pay. Women, especially seamstresses, were also unable to keep up with the rising cost of living; the average wage of women in 1865 working for contractors on army clothing was $1.54 a week. The low wages of women in the industrial world were sometimes eked out by soldiers' pay, a part of which was often sent home, by military

[7] Emerson D. Fite, *op. cit.*, p. 185, note.

bounties, and by charitable aid given to soldiers' families. The increased buying capacity of the nation during the last years of the war, the sale of luxuries, and the prosperity of popular amusement enterprises demonstrate, on the other hand, that labor shared to some extent in the flush times.[8] Some light is thrown both on the rapid advance in manufacturing and on the demand for labor by the census figures of 1869, which place the number of industrial establishments in that year at 252,148, an advance of 79.6 per cent and the greatest increase for any decade in our history. The number of wage earners in industrial establishments advanced from 1,311,246 to 2,053,996, an increase of 56.6 per cent which was not equaled even during the decade of the First World War.

NORTHERN CAPITAL

Although labor maintained itself with difficulty, capital found itself in a most flourishing position. Before the war the millionaires of the country might have been counted on the fingers of both hands; at its conclusion there were scores. War taxation favored the larger industry; and the process of consolidation, so marked in subsequent years, had its beginning during the war in the union of various telegraph lines and transportation companies. The American Telegraph Company and the United States Telegraph Company, the last important rivals of the Western Union, were acquired by the latter in 1866, giving it control of 75,000 miles of telegraph lines. In like manner, numerous smaller railroad companies in various parts of the country were brought under a single direction. The tendency toward centralized control of railroads was doubtless emphasized by the increased need of transportation facilities occasioned by the war and by the rivalry of different cities to be termini or collecting points for produce. The conduct of the war was hampered by the frequent transference of freight necessitated by the many little independent systems with different-gauge tracks and different types of rolling stock. The Pennsylvania, Lehigh, Erie, and other important roads absorbed the minor companies just before, during, or immediately after the war and laid the foundations of the great railroad systems of today. Of particular importance was the acquisition by the Pennsylvania system of the Pittsburgh, Fort Wayne and Chicago, which completed the first through connection under single ownership between Lake Michigan and the seacoast. It was also during these years that Commodore Vanderbilt joined the many little lines between New York and Buffalo into a single system which became the New York Central.

In addition to the consolidation of various units, the war witnessed considerable activity in railroad building. The longest railroad constructed during the war was the Atlantic and Great Western, now part of the Erie

[8] For the further history of labor during the war, see below, chap. 22.

system, which ran from Salamanca, New York, to Dayton, Ohio. By means of the Erie in the east and the Ohio and Mississippi in the west, it linked New York and St. Louis with a one-gauge railroad. This road, constructed at the rate of a mile a day by English capital and imported labor, demonstrated both the tireless business energy of the nation and the faith of northern and European financiers in the future, whatever might be the outcome of the conflict. By giving New York the first single-gauge track extending west to the Mississippi, it afforded her a distinct advantage over rival eastern seaports. Important also was the Philadelphia and Erie, completed in 1864, which connected the new oil fields with Philadelphia. Massachusetts, hoping to save part of the western trade, in 1863 took up the unfinished work on the Hoosac tunnel of the Troy and Greenfield and pushed to completion the connection between Albany and Boston. Other pieces of railroad construction were completed or planned, including the laying of the first rails for the Union Pacific, the first of the transcontinental lines to be built.

Never had the railroads been so prosperous. The Erie, the Hudson River, the Cleveland and Pittsburgh, and the Illinois Central, none of which had ever paid dividends, were paying 8 per cent or over by the end of the war, and many railroads sought to camouflage their real earnings by stock dividends. Capital was fully alive to its power and possibilities. The value of monopoly was understood, and the railroads began to tighten their grip on the coal producers in the anthracite region. In the cities, capitalists were indefatigable in planning street railway monopolies and pressing for long-term franchises in the legislatures. In twenty-seven cities streetcars appeared for the first time.

Although the cost of building almost doubled, the decline in construction for the whole country was very slight, a striking difference from conditions during the First and Second World Wars. In cities like Philadelphia, Chicago, and San Francisco, where population was rapidly mounting, or in cities like Lynn and Springfield, Massachusetts, where industry was immensely stimulated by war needs, there was extensive building. The Capitol at Washington was completed during the war, as were many state and municipal buildings. "On every street and avenue," said the Chicago *Tribune* on October 8, 1863, "one sees new buildings going up, immense stone, brick, and iron business blocks, marble palaces and new residences; everywhere the grading of streets, the building of sewers, the laying of water and gas pipes, are all in progress at the same time."

SOCIAL ACTIVITIES IN THE NORTH

The unprecedented war prosperity plunged many of those who benefited into a riot of extravagance and pursuit of pleasure. More charitable obsevers might attribute this to an attempt to forget the horrors of war and to keep up a brave front, but the true explanation was the accumulation of sudden wealth in the hands of those unused to it. The race tracks were crowded and stakes offered on a scale never before seen. Athletics were enthusiastically patronized, and the leading actors played to packed houses. The most expensive jewelry, clothing, and furniture found the readiest sale.

To picture the life of those who remained at home in the North as a mad scramble for wealth to be spent in extravagant living while the "boys in blue" were fighting and dying for the Union would be far from correct; high living was largely confined to certain classes and to the cities. Furthermore, if the Northerner was wholehearted in his spending, he was often wholehearted in his giving. At least fifteen colleges were founded during the sixties, including Vassar, the first institution of collegiate rank exclusively for women, the Massachusetts Institute of Technology, Cornell, Lehigh, Swarthmore, Bates, and the state universities of Kansas and Minnesota. Private benefactors contributed heavily to endowment funds and financed new buildings in many of the already existing institutions. Voluntary contributions of at least $5,000,000 to education are recorded. That the minds of the national legislators were turned to educational needs, even during the terrible strain of war, is demonstrated by the Morrill Act of July 2, 1862, by which the national government gave to each state 30,000 acres of public land for each of its Senators and Congressmen, the income from which was to be devoted to mechanical and agricultural schools, with provision for military training to be made in their curriculums.

Sanitary and welfare work among the soldiers, taken care of in subsequent wars by the Red Cross and other organizations, was consolidated chiefly under two bodies—the United States Sanitary Commission and the United States Christian Commission. The former, approved by the government to supplement the medical department of the Army, affiliated the local societies engaged in soldier welfare work. Through their instrumentality clothing, bandages, medicines, food, and tobacco to the value of $25,000,000 were distributed to the soldiers. The Commission's most important service was that rendered on the battlefield and in the actual campaign, but the other phases of its work were very valuable. These included twenty-five soldiers' homes maintained in the leading cities, where passing soldiers might find meals and lodging; agencies to advise and help soldiers in regard to back pay, bounties, and pensions; convalescent hospitals; the publishing of a hospital directory; and innumerable other measures to make the soldier's lot easier. Newspapers collected funds for the Commission; huge sanitary fairs were held in the large cities; theaters contributed from their receipts, as did public service utilities. Even school children gave entertainments and contributed their pennies. The spiritual welfare of the soldiers (in addition to the work of the regular chaplains) was taken care of by the United States Christian Commission, which sent clergymen and Bibles as well as hospital supplies and food.

Larger than the amounts given for soldiers' welfare work were the donations and bounties to the dependent families of the soldiers, made by the state, county, and local authorities and by individuals. The Provost Marshal General of the United States estimated that $600,000,000 was distributed by national, state, and local authorities in bounties, and $100,000,000 more by individuals. Probably half of this found its way back to the dependent families. Municipalities contributed generously to the support of needy relatives, Philadelphia having at one time 9000 on its list at an annual expenditure of $600,000. Considerable sums were also raised in the North for the support of Negroes and southern refugees, and for the relief of the starving cotton operatives in Lancashire. The story of this wholehearted generosity and sacrifice goes far to offset the more sordid details of war speculation, profiteering, and extravagance.

"KING COTTON"

To no small extent the South rested her hope of success upon the world's need of cotton. Said Senator James H. Hammond of South Carolina in a famous speech in 1858: "Without firing a gun, without drawing a sword, should they make war on us, we could bring the whole world to our feet. . . . What would happen if no cotton was furnished for three years? I will not stop to depict what every one can imagine, but this is certain: England would topple headlong and carry the whole civilized world with her save the south. No, you dare not to make war on cotton. No Power on the earth dares to make war upon it. Cotton *is* King."[9] This was the slogan that so powerfully affected southern economic thinking.

That events did not bear out these sanguine hopes was due to two chief causes: first, to a surplus of cotton on hand, resulting from overproduction; and second, to the European need of northern wheat and her desire to export to the North. The decade 1840 to 1850 was one of overproduction, but during the next decade both planters and manufacturers "enjoyed a period of unexampled prosperity."[10] In 1860 a record crop was produced, "which the southern planter marketed with unusual haste on account of the threats of trouble, England taking 1,650,000 bales before the war broke out. The British market was glutted to such an extent that many of the mills actually shut down in 1861 and prices remained practically stationary. The blockade,

[9] Quoted by James A. B. Scherer, *Cotton as a World Power*, p. 239.
[10] James L. Watkins, *Production and Price of Cotton for One Hundred Years*, U.S. Dept. of Agriculture Bulletin No. 9, Miscellaneous Series (1895).

when it came, was laughed at as a paper blockade; and indeed it seemed to be so, for it is estimated that 3,127,568 bales were exported during the year ending August 31, 1861. Mill owners, it was reported, even longed for an effective blockade to relieve the glut of the market."[11] The blockade saved English middlemen from actual bankruptcy. The North also had stock, and "in the first year the American mills ran on two-thirds time, the next year

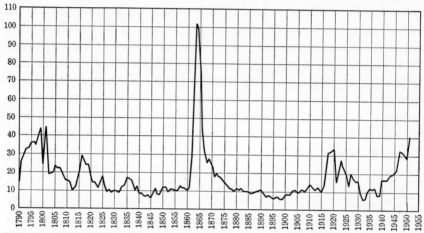

(Data from M. B. Hammond, *The Cotton Industry*, Appendix I; *Statistical Abstract, 1921*, p. 878; *ibid., 1940*, p. 729; *ibid., 1952*, p. 289. The prices up to 1921 are those that obtained on the New York market; after that year they are the general average prices in the chief cotton markets throughout the country.)

AVERAGE ANNUAL PRICES FOR MIDDLING UPLANDS, 1790–1950.

on from one-quarter to one-half time, in these two years consuming cotton that remained over from the heavy purchases of 1860."[12] Thus the cutting off of the supply of cotton was at first a benefit to cotton manufacturers, for it enabled them to dispose of their surplus stock and to keep up prices. When the mills in the North lowered production, operatives readily found employment in war industries.

In England there was unemployment and great distress among factory operatives. But the operatives realized that their battle as free laborers was being fought in the terrific struggle in America, and they stood stanchly by the side of the North, opposing any recognition of the Confederacy by the British government. The North understood the value of their good will, and showed appreciation by fitting out three ships with relief supplies for the Lancashire sufferers. In any event, northern mills were obtaining considerable supplies of southern cotton toward the end of the war as the northern

[11] James A. B. Scherer, *op. cit.*, p. 265.
[12] Emerson D. Fite, *op. cit.*, p. 86.

armies occupied larger areas of the South (table, p. 341), and Great Britain was developing sources of raw cotton in other parts of the world.

A second deterrent to English aid to the Confederacy was her dependence upon northern wheat because of poor crops at home from 1860 to 1862. England, says S. J. Chapman, "was helpless in the matter of the cotton supply. Interference would probably have proved futile; for America lay far away, and any action to bring in cotton might conceivably have operated in keeping back corn."[13] This fact was plainly pointed out in Parliament at the time. Professor Fite, in summing up the balancing of British interests between wheat and cotton in the Civil War, says: "At this distance it may safely be concluded that while the need of grain would not have prevented England from defending herself from a war of aggression by the United States, it was doubtless one of the factors, and an important one, in preventing aggressive demonstrations by England in favor of the Confederacy and against the United States."[14]

Whether the need for American wheat actually kept England neutral it is difficult to say. A recent student of Civil War diplomacy believes that it was not so much wheat per se that kept her neutral as the desire for war profits.[15] Great Britain, he points out, could obtain plenty of wheat elsewhere. She bought wheat from the United States, first, because it was cheaper and more convenient to purchase it here, and second, because she could exchange arms and ammunition for it. For the moment at least, Britain's economic interests seemed more closely identified with the North than with the South.

THE SOUTHERN BLOCKADE

The effect of the war upon the North had been to speed earlier economic developments. In the South the whole economic life was turned upside down. In the ante-bellum days the South had been a great agricultural region, with tobacco and cotton as the staple crops; these two commodities had been exchanged in the North and in Europe for manufactured goods. With his wealth tied up in cotton and slaves, the southern planter imported much of his foodstuffs from the states north of the Ohio. The very life of the South depended upon external trade, and the first effect of the war was to break up this trade. Northern as well as southern statesmen realized that "cotton is king," and at the beginning of the war an iron ring was thrown around the South, growing tighter each year as the Union armies pushed south and

[13] S. J. Chapman, *The Cotton Industry and Trade* (London, 1905), p. 66.

[14] Emerson D. Fite, *op. cit.*, p. 21. See also L. B. Schmidt, "The Influence of Wheat and Cotton on Anglo-American Relations During the War," *Iowa Journal of History and Politics* (July, 1918).

[15] F. W. Owsley, *King Cotton Diplomacy*, pp. 567 ff.

east, and as the Navy grew more efficient until finally it literally strangled the Confederacy into submission. The blockade acted detrimentally upon the South in three ways. In the first place, it cut off the outlet for her cotton and tobacco; and without a market it was impossible to establish commercial credit abroad with which to purchase supplies. The loss of markets and credit undermined the whole economic structure. Second, the blockade prevented the importing of the many kinds of manufactured goods upon which the agricultural South was dependent. Third, it forced slave labor into unaccustomed occupations and resulted in a tremendous decline in the value of both land and slaves.

The South strove heroically to counteract the effects of the blockade. Arms, ammunition, shoes, blankets, medicines, and various luxuries were shipped from Europe to various ports in the West Indies; from there low-built, lead-colored side-wheeled steamers slipped into the ports of Wilmington, Charleston, Savannah, Mobile, or Galveston. The profits were enormous and attracted a disproportionate amount of capital; £30,000 each way was a not uncommon profit on a voyage. Although captures were frequent and the chances of success grew smaller as the war drew to a conclusion, the fact that two successful voyages compensated the owners for total loss on a third made blockade running still a good gamble. Even the state governments invested in companies operating blockade runners. The North Atlantic blockading squadron reported the names of fifty runners captured between August 1, 1863, and September 30, 1864, but a large volume of business must have been carried on if southern sources are to be believed. According to the Secretary of the Treasury of the Confederate States, forty-three runners entered the ports of Wilmington and Charleston in May and June of 1864.

The temptation of excessive profits from certain types of imports was more than the patriotism of some could stand, and the Confederate government finally passed an act (February 6, 1864) forbidding the importation of such luxuries as wines, spirits, laces, carpets, toys, furniture, and jewelry. By later laws the government sought to control for its own use a certain amount of space in incoming and outgoing boats. It is impossible to determine accurately the amount of goods exported and imported by blockade runners. In 1862, 1863, and 1864 the exportation of cotton to Europe was probably less than one-tenth that of the prewar years. The comparatively small amount exported reached its destination either through the medium of blockade runners or by way of Matamoras, Mexico, to which point considerable cotton was taken overland through Texas.

Southern cotton found its way to the markets of the North by other routes than those of the blockade runner. The first policy of the Confederate government was to prevent any cotton whatsoever from reaching the North, on the theory that its lack would bring the war to a speedy conclusion. In furtherance of this policy it passed an act on May 21, 1861, prohibiting exportation of cotton except through seaports. This plan broke down under the exigencies of the situation, and contraband trade in the staple was carried on all through the war. There were times when the Confederate armies were provided with food obtained in exchange for cotton. This widespread illicit trade was a source of demoralization to civilians and officers both of the North and of the South, and brought numerous protests from commanders in the field to their respective governments. The overland cotton trade to the North during the years 1862 to 1865[16] amounted to about 1,108,-000 bales, an amount larger than that obtained by Great Britain from block-

RECEIPTS AND SHIPMENTS OF COTTON FROM NEW ORLEANS DURING THE WAR (In Bales)

Year	Receipts	Total Exports	Export to Liverpool	Export to Havre	Export to New York	Export to Boston
1859–60	2,235,448	2,214,296	1,348,163	303,157	62,936	131,648
1860–61	1,849,312	1,015,852	1,074,131	384,938	29,539	94,307
1861–62	38,880	27,678	1,312	472	4,116	109
1862–63	22,078	23,750	2,070	1,849	17,859	1,418
1863–64	131,044	128,130	1,155	4,023	109,149	12,793
1864–65	271,015	192,315	31,326	5,952	144,190	15,993

M. B. Hammond, *The Cotton Industry*, p. 263.

ade runners. This trade was more essential to the South than to the North, of course, and helped to prolong the war. The accompanying table shows the cotton movement at New Orleans, the principal port of the Confederacy.

MANUFACTURING IN THE SOUTH

The amount of cotton run through the blockade or smuggled through the lines, and the manufactured goods and gold received in return, softened but slightly the grip of the iron ring. The one-sided civilization of the South put the Confederate states at a decided disadvantage. Manufacturing concerns were comparatively few, and many of those existing were destroyed by the Union armies. Up to the opening of the war practically all the machinery had been imported, and the rich coal and iron deposits of the South had scarcely been tapped. It is true that cotton to the value of $7,000,000 was spun in the South in 1860 and that cotton manufacturers, although handicapped by depreciating machinery, continued production during the war and made extensive profits. Nevertheless, most of the large-scale manufacturing was carried on by the Confederate government itself, which took over and operated factories producing whiskey, salt, guns, small arms, gunpowder,

[16] Freedom of trade was restored in May, 1865.

and other munitions of war. After the first two years of the war when the factories were in practical operation, the Confederate armies did not suffer for these essentials. Except for immediate war needs, manufacturing production as a whole declined.

In general, there was a reversion to hand industry. The hand looms and spinning wheels were brought out and much of the clothing and shoes for civilian and soldier were plantation-made. The sacrifice and painstaking labor of the women of the South who worked at these unaccustomed tasks were as heroic as the labor of the slaves was faithful, and both were in bright contrast to the speculation and extravagance all too evident in such cities as Charleston, Mobile, and Richmond. This rapid return to household production was like turning the hands of civilization backward, an undoing of the Industrial Revolution. The development of war manufacturing was severely handicapped by the lack of surplus capital. Previously most of the excess wealth had been invested in land and slaves, and much of the liquid capital on hand during the war years was attracted almost exclusively to blockade running, where profits were enormous. "Fifty or sixty millions of dollars," complained the president of a manufacturers' convention in Augusta in 1864, "have gone into blockade-running, while scarcely a new dollar has gone into manufacturing."[17] Speculation, in fact, was as widespread in the South as in the North, and with greater damage to her cause. "The passion for speculation," asserted President Davis in 1863, "has seduced citizens of all classes from a determined prosecution of the war to a sordid effort to amass money."[18]

AGRICULTURAL PRODUCTION AND THE COST OF LIVING

There was a decided reluctance on the part of many planters to substitute grain crops and meat production for cotton, but this change became more and more necessary as the war progressed. In this respect an agricultural revolution was to a certain extent temporarily brought about by the war. The cotton crop of 1862 was only a little over one-quarter that of 1861, and that of 1864 only about one-eighth, while the production of cereals, especially corn, increased yearly. Nevertheless, the price of bread and meat, measured in gold, mounted steadily, and in many parts of the South there was a distressing lack of food at various times, a lack that was especially acute in 1864. The pinch was greatest in the cities, for the farmer could worry along somehow. "Meal is the only food now obtainable except by the rich," commented an observer in Richmond on February 23, 1864, and he added: "We look for a healthy year, everything being so cleanly consumed that no gar-

---

[17] Quoted by J. F. Rhodes, *History of the United States*, V, 396, from the Augusta *Chronicle* May 26, 1864.

[18] *Ibid.*, V, 424, from *Official Records*, Vol. XXX, Part I, p. 212.

bage or filth can accumulate."[19] In the early months of 1864, when one dollar of gold was worth $22 in Confederate money, flour sold in Richmond at $300 a barrel Confederate money, and shoes at $150 a pair. There were bread riots in Atlanta, Mobile, and other places.

The food scarcity was caused not so much by absolute lack as by poor distribution, for there was no failure of crops during the war. There were over 6000 miles of railroad in the seceding states, sufficient at that time to distribute the food under normal conditions. But the rolling stock and rails wore out rapidly under the severe strain to which they were subjected by war needs, and it was impossible to replace them. The government used the iron mills for other work, and commandeered much of the rolling stock for military purposes. Necessarily, all but the main lines were abandoned. The result was that corn sold in Virginia for fifteen times its price in Georgia. The Union forces eventually obtained control of a large portion of the southern railways, thus further reducing the food supply. Sherman's sixty-mile swath of destruction in Georgia and the desolation left by Sheridan in the Shenandoah Valley added to the woe of the South and the scarcity of provisions.

FINANCING THE CONFEDERACY

When the war broke out the southern states were in debt both to the North and to Europe, and it was thus almost impossible to obtain further credit from the outside. Of surplus capital there was little. There was some metallic currency, of course, but it was difficult for the government to secure possession of it, and specie payment was suspended almost immediately after the outbreak of the struggle. In addition to taxation, the Confederate government endeavored up to 1863 to support itself by bond issues and fiat money in the form of treasury notes. Of the latter, close to one billion dollars were issued. With only the credit of a rebel government behind them, they speedily depreciated in value until on February 17, 1864, the Confederate Congress passed an act providing for either the compulsory funding of these notes into 4 per cent bonds or the exchange of all notes under $100 for new notes at the rate of three dollars' worth of the old for two of the new.[20] This

---

[19] J. B. Jones, *A Rebel War Clerk's Diary at the Confederate Capitol,* II, 186.

[20] G. C. Eggleston in *A Rebel's Recollections* (p. 84) quotes a friend as saying: "Before the war I went to market with the money in my pocket, and brought back my purchases in a basket; now I take the money in the basket, and bring the things home in my pocket." By the end of 1864 there were probably over one billion dollars in treasury notes in circulation, "but the issues grew so enormously," says Rhodes (*op. cit.,* V, p. 344), "that apparently no exact account of them was made public; it is even possible that the treasury department itself did not know the amount afloat." One gold dollar, according to a table given by Schwab (p. 167), would purchase sixty-one Confederate paper dollars. These figures, of course, do not seem impressive when compared to the inflation following World War I in central and eastern Europe. See J. C. Schwab, "The Confederate Foreign Loan: An Episode in the Financial History of the Civil War," *Yale Review,* I (1893).

amounted to virtual repudiation and drove the people to primitive methods of barter during the final months of the war. The situation was made more hopeless by the state, municipal, and corporation issues of paper which passed as currency.

A $15,000,000 loan, floated in Europe early in 1863 by the French firm of Erlanger & Company, and secured by cotton purchased by the Confederate government, was designed to supply the specie with which to purchase naval and military supplies in Europe. Although the bonds maintained a surprisingly high value, the actual return to the South was slight; $5,000,000 was expended on vessels that were never delivered, $6,000,000 in attempting to keep the market price of the bonds higher, another million in the three semiannual drawings for redemption of bonds. Considering these expenditures, says Professor Schwab, and the fact that "the government had to go heavily into debt at home and wrecked the currency in order to gain the necessary cotton on which to base the foreign loan, the net gain from the loan sinks to an insignificant sum."[21] On their return from Europe, the Confederate agents reported to the Richmond government that "the loan was unsuccessful as a source of revenue, but very successful as a political demonstration." Professor Schwab says that "as late as September 7, 1864, the London *Times* considered the holders of the cotton bonds better off than those of Federal securities."[22]

In 1863 the Confederate Congress, realizing that the financial system was weakened beyond repair, passed a law providing for a levy of one-tenth on agricultural products and authorized any officer of the Army to seize such property within certain limits. Without specie, without credit abroad, with her foreign trade cut off, and with a virtually worthless paper currency, the South was forced to levy on agricultural products. It was the agricultural resources freely given or forcibly taken that provided the chief economic strength of southern resistance in the last two years.

ECONOMIC EFFECTS OF THE CIVIL WAR

In contrast to its effect in the North, the Civil War did not bring in its wake financial prosperity or a period of booming business for the South. Instead of inaugurating a new epoch of unprecedented expansion, it marked a period of destruction in which the old economic life was torn up by the roots. It is true that the fiat money made it a heyday for the speculator, that some fortunes were made by blockade runners, by merchants, and others

[21] *Ibid.*, p. 185.
[22] *Ibid.*, p. 183. He goes on to give the reasons for this optimism; it was largely due to the idea of investors that cotton for redeeming the bonds was certain to be forthcoming, and that there would be no repudiation of the debt.

in the cities, and that for those who had gold there was plenty of the best to be obtained, at least during the earlier years of the war. To the average Southerner the war meant the sacrifice of luxuries and many necessities, in addition to the distress and bitterness entailed by the disastrous outcome; to the economy of the South it meant destruction and chaos, and eventually a fresh start. In summarizing the war Woodrow Wilson said truly:

On the part of the North it was a wonderful display of spirit and power, a splendid revelation of national strength and coherency, a capital proof of quick, organic vitality throughout the great democratic body politic. . . . But its material resources for the stupendous tasks never lacked or were doubted; they even increased while it spent them. On the part of the South, on the other hand, the great struggle was maintained by sheer spirit and devotion, in spite of constantly diminishing resources and constantly waning hope. Her whole strength was put forth, her resources spent, exhausted, annihilated; and yet with such concentration of energy that for more than three years she seemed as fully equal to the contest as the North itself. And all for a belated principle of government, an outgrown economy, an impossible purpose.[23]

In the economic history of the United States the Civil War was extremely important. In the South it put an end to Negro slavery and, to a large extent, to the plantation system. In the North it speeded the Industrial Revolution and the development of capitalism by the prosperity which it brought to industry. The secession of the states'-rights agrarian representatives of the South opened the way for protective tariff legislation and for a more rapid development of the West through the Homestead Act and large railroad grants. The exigencies of war needs brought inflation and new types of paper currency; it brought a new effort on the part of the federal government through the National Bank Act to extend its influence in the banking activities of the nation, and an aggressive move to build a transcontinental railway—all of which were to have an important influence in later history. But, above all, the federal government passed from the control of the agrarian slavocracy of the South to that of the rising industrial plutocracy of the North.[24]

SELECTED READINGS

Schwab, J. C., *The Confederate States of America,* chaps. 9–12.
Dewey, D. R., *Financial History of the United States,* chaps. 12, 13.
Fite, E. D., *Social and Industrial Conditions in the North During the Civil War.*
Rhodes, J. F., *History of the United States,* Vol. V, chaps. 27, 28.
Randall, James G., *The Civil War and Reconstruction,* chaps. 27, 28.

[23] Woodrow Wilson, *Division and Reunion* (rev. ed., 1898), p. 239.
[24] These and other effects of the conflict will be developed more fully in succeeding chapters.

Cole, A. C., *The Irrepressible Conflict,* chaps. 14, 15.

Owsley, F. L., *King Cotton Diplomacy,* chaps. 5, 19.

Jones, J. B., *A Rebel War Clerk's Diary,* chaps. 29, 30.

Flügel, F., and Faulkner, H. U., *Readings in the Economic and Social History of the United States,* pp. 447–483.

CHAPTER 18

THE LAST FRONTIER

THE TRANS-MISSISSIPPI ADVANCE

THE population of the United States according to the Census of 1860 was approximately 31,443,000. By that year the region bordering the west bank of the Mississippi had been admitted to statehood: Minnesota (1858), Iowa (1846), Missouri (1821), Arkansas (1836), and Louisiana (1812). West of that tier of states only three areas had sufficient population for admission: Texas, with 602,000 in 1860, Oregon with 52,000, and California with 380,000. By the 1860's two frontiers had been established—an eastward-moving one along the Pacific coast and a westward-moving one extending unevenly along the 97th meridian. The latter fringe of settlement ran southward through central Minnesota and Iowa, through eastern Kansas, and along the western boundary of Arkansas, and then bulged westward to include a large area of eastern Texas (maps, pp. 187, 191). In the region between this line and the fringe of settlement along the west coast lay approximately half the territory of the United States, but in 1860 this area contained only one per cent of the population. This intervening territory was America's "last frontier."

More than two centuries had elapsed between the founding of the first permanent white settlement within the boundary of the present United States and the extension of the frontier line west to the 97th meridian. The rest of the nation was largely occupied in the three decades 1870–1890. It was peopled chiefly by miners, ranchers, and farmers, lured by discoveries of rich deposits of minerals and by opportunities to exploit free grass and to open fertile farming areas. The process was speeded by favorable land laws, by a rapidly increasing immigration, and particularly by the building of the great transcontinental railroads, the invention of barbed wire, and the quantity production of windmills.

347

THE MINERS' FRONTIER

The search for minerals, which had played such a major role in the early exploration and settlement of the American continent, again became an important influence in the settlement of the "last frontier." Missionary activity and ranching had brought the first permanent white occupation of California. But the handful of Mexicans was quickly submerged in the flood of gold seekers who overran the country in 1849 and created from it an American state in 1850. Only a small percentage of the "forty-niners" actually acquired wealth from the metal, but a large number remained to exploit the possibilities in commerce, agriculture, and lumber. With thousands of white settlers in California and a scattered population of farmers and trappers in Oregon, America's possession of the Pacific coast was beyond dispute.

Some beginnings of actual settlement had already been made east of the Sierras, by Mormons around the Salt Lake basin and by Spanish ranchers pushing north from Mexico. The discovery of gold in California was of course followed by the activities of numerous prospecting parties in many parts of the Rockies. Rumors that the precious metal was to be found in the Pikes Peak region were confirmed in 1859, and that year saw a great exodus to what later became the state of Colorado. Professional prospectors and miners of the West hastened to the scene, their ranks augmented by thousands from the East who had felt the pinch of the depression following the panic of 1857. "Pikes Peak or bust," was the motto of the "fifty-niners," and not far from 100,000 reached Colorado during the rush of the first year. Although half returned "Busted! By Gosh!" those who remained laid the foundations of a new state eventually admitted in 1876. The Colorado deposits, unfortunately for the early gold seekers, were embedded in quartz lodes that required heavy machinery and large capital for working; hence they could not be developed immediately. Although agriculture now surpasses in importance the products of the mines, for decades minerals played a leading role in the development of the state. The mines at Leadville have yielded over $300,000,000 worth of silver and those at Cripple Creek a similar amount of gold.

The rush which laid the foundations of Colorado was but one of a series of booms which planted mining camps on many a lonely creek and forbidding hillside in the Rockies. Small desposits of gold had brought about the founding of Carson City in 1858 at the extreme western part of the Territory of Utah, close to the California border line and near the old overland route from Salt Lake City to San Francisco. The discovery of the famous Comstock Lode in the next year on the eastern slope of Mount

Davidson, not far from Lake Tahoe, brought an influx of immigrants who transformed the region into the Territory of Nevada (formerly part of the Territory of Utah) in 1861 and into a state three years later. The great silver deposits were easily accessible, located as they were on the main route to California, and Carson Valley was speedily entered from both the west and the east. From 1860 to 1890 the Comstock Lode yielded $340,000,000 worth of silver, and was the economic backbone of the region during those years. The yield declined rapidly after 1890. However, new discoveries of gold, silver, and copper in 1906 and the following years at Tonopah, Goldfield, and other places renewed industry and brought a fresh influx of population. Copper was not mined in large quantities until after 1908, but today its annual production has a value almost double that of all other minerals produced in the state.[1]

Handicapped by climate and inaccessibility, the western part of the Territory of New Mexico (now Arizona) was prospected slowly, and individual miners found it difficult to operate successfully. Mining companies, however, with laborers recruited from California, opened up a few deserted shafts near the old Spanish town of Tucson soon after the Gadsden Purchase was consummated. The Civil War closed the Tucson mines for the time being, but further discoveries in 1862 and 1863 along the east bank of the Colorado near Bill Williams Fork brought a new outburst of gold enthusiasm. Arizona was made a territory in 1863 (a state in 1912), but for over ten years after territorial government was set up troubles with the Apaches made mining a dangerous occupation. Gold and silver, which drew the first prospectors to Arizona, have since become a small part of her mineral production. She now leads the Union in copper production.

Just as the influx of gold diggers had brought sufficient population to create the new Territories of Colorado, Nevada, and Arizona, so discoveries of the precious metal led to the organization of Idaho Territory in 1863. The Territory of Washington had already been separated from the Oregon Territory in 1853, because of the inconvenience of administering the distant settlements on Puget Sound, but Washington was not admitted as a state until 1889. In 1860 gold was discovered on the reservation of the Nez Percé Indians near the juncture of the Clearwater and Snake rivers. "To attempt to restrain these miners," reported the Superintendent of Indian Affairs, "would be like attempting to restrain the whirlwind," and in the next year thousands poured into these river valleys; the town of Lewiston sprang up as a center. The discoveries here were followed by others on the Salmon River, at Boise, and in the Owyhee district, south of the great bend of the Snake. The trappers

---

[1] Fortunately Samuel L. Clemens (Mark Twain) went to Nevada in 1861 and in *Roughing It* (1871) has given to posterity unforgettable descriptions of the boom days in Virginia City.

of the Hudson's Bay and the American Fur Companies had first roamed over this country, and the farmers who followed McLoughlin and Whitman were the first serious settlers; but it was the gold seekers of '61 and '62 who gave Washington new life and founded Idaho. As gold had brought in 1861 the development of the present western Idaho, so new discoveries in 1863 gave birth to Alder Gulch, to Virginia City, and to a new group of mines in eastern Idaho. Ten thousand came to Virginia City in 1864 and the same year saw the founding of Helena, "the last of the boom towns of the period." Such an ingress of miners to these points caused the cutting away of northeastern Idaho into the Territory of Montana in 1864, and the organization of Wyoming Territory in 1868. The discovery of gold in 1882 at Coeur d'Alene brought a new rush to Idaho; but the production of gold relative to that of other metals has not been large. Her next-door neighbor, Montana, produces copper in the Butte region in an amount which is surpassed only by Arizona and Utah (1937).

The decade of the sixties saw the Rockies at least partially occupied from Mexico to the Canadian border, with most of the population scattered on the mining claims which dotted the hillsides and valleys or gathered into the raw towns which had sprung up near the more valuable deposits. Frederick L. Paxson, historian of the frontier, has caught the spirit of the picturesque but demoralizing life of the mining frontier:

The shifting population which inhabited the new territories invites and at the same time defies description. It was made up chiefly of young men. Respectable women were not unknown, but were so few in number as to have little measureable influence upon social life. In many towns they were in the minority, even among their set, since the easily won wealth of the camps attracted dissolute women who cannot be numbered but who must be imagined. The social tone of the various camps was determined by the preponderance of men, the absence of regular labor, and the speculative fever which was the justification of their existence. The political tone was determined by the nature of the population, the character of the industry, and the remoteness from a seat of government. Combined, these factors produced a type of the life the like of which America had never known, and whose picturesque qualities have blinded the thoughtless into believing that it was romantic. It was at best a hard, bitter struggle, with the dark places only accentuated by the tinsel of gambling and adventure.

A single street meandering along a valley, with one-story huts flanking it in irregular rows, was the typical mining camp. The saloon and the general store, sometimes combined, were its representative institutions. Deep ruts along the streets bore witness to the heavy wheels of the freighters, while horses loosely tied to all available posts at once revealed the regular means of locomotion, and by the careless way they were left about showed that this sort of property was not likely to be stolen. The mining population centering here lived a life of contrasts.

The desolation and loneliness of prospecting and working claims alternated with the excitement of coming to town. Few decent beings habitually lived in the towns. The resident population expected to live off the miners, either in way of trade or worse. The bar, the gambling house, the dance hall have been made too common in description to need further account. In the reaction against loneliness, the extremes of drunkenness, debauchery, and murder were only too frequent in these places of amusement.[2]

Yet upon such unpromising foundations were laid the beginnings of many of our far-western states. The search for minerals brought the first important white migration to the present California, Nevada, Arizona, New Mexico, Colorado, Idaho, and Montana.

THE RANCHERS' FRONTIER

Between the eastern frontier line and the mining settlements of the West there stretched from Texas to Manitoba a vast territory of rolling land. Grass-covered but lacking in rainfall, this country was believed by many to be unfit for cultivation and unlikely ever to be occupied. It was in the 1860's that it was found that cattle not only could withstand the severe winters of northern Nebraska but would thrive on the pasturage of wild grass there. This discovery opened the country almost immediately to cattlemen and ranchers, who occupied it for the next two decades until largely driven aside by the advancing frontier of farmers.

Since the days of the Spaniards cattle had been bred on the Texas plains, where, exposed to the weather and running free on the wide ranges, a sturdy stock had developed. Heretofore there had been little incentive for ranchers to market their cattle, for the farmer of the Mississippi Valley and the Atlantic coast had easily been able to supply the local need. Moreover, a slowly developing southern market had been cut off by the Civil War, leaving the Texas range overstocked at the end of the conflict. But the rapidly growing population of the East and the railroads advancing to the very doors of the cattle ranch now offered both a market and the means of transportation, opportunities quickly taken advantage of by the Texas cattlemen. At the same time the slaughter of the buffalo had made way for the cattle. Without the buffalo, which provided subsistence for them, the plains Indians were rendered helpless and easily pushed back into reservations useless even for the grazing of cattle.

On the southern ranges there were two roundups. The first came in May, when the young cattle were marked with the owner's brand according to the existing customs and laws. The second, a beef roundup, came in July or August, when the mature animals, particularly the yearling steers, were sep-

[2] F. L. Paxson, *The Last American Frontier* (1910), pp. 170–172.

arated from the rest and started on the long trail north to Kansas, Nebraska, or Wyoming to be fattened and sold. The remainder were turned back on the range to multiply. At Abilene, Kansas, on the newly built Kansas Pacific, and at Dodge City on the Atchison, Topeka and Santa Fe there grew up during the seventies the greatest of the early cattle towns. At Ogallala, Nebraska, there was another great cattle center, and 400 miles northwest of there, at Miles City, Montana, still another center developed for the Northwest.

On their arrival at these points the herds were usually fattened for the market and then sold for immediate slaughter or for shipment to the stockyards of Kansas City, Milwaukee, or Chicago. As time went on and competition became keener, thought was given to experimental breeding and to the production of the most profitable type for this method of disposal. Stock growers' associations appeared for mutual protection against lawbreakers and thieves, and to guard as best they could against the contamination of their herds by Texas fever, hoof and mouth disease, and other ailments.

The ranchers' frontier lasted about two decades, from the late sixties to the late eighties. It was characterized by the long drives which sent some 4,000-000 Texas cattle northward to be slaughtered or to stock the northern ranges, and by the rapid spread of cattle ranches over the vast area of unenclosed government land. It was also characterized by large profits resulting from an expanding market and low overhead costs. Chiefly responsible for the latter was the opportunity to graze cattle free on government land. By the middle eighties, however, overexpansion had ended the high profits and shifted the ranchers' frontier to a more stabilized industry. Moreover, the great drives were now a thing of the past. Transient as this period was, the hard but romantic life of the cowboy has become immortalized as part of our history through Theodore Roosevelt's association with the cow country, the novels of Owen Wister and others, and the pictures of Frederic Remington. The "dime novel" and the moving picture have made it a part of American folklore.

Production of cattle for the market has continued as an important industry of the Great Plains, but the characteristics of the ranchers' last frontier are gone. Of all the factors which put an end to the open range and the long drive, the most important was the advancing farmers' frontier. This in turn, as we shall see, was speeded by the building of the transcontinental railroads and their subsidiaries. The railroads which had made the ranchers' frontier possible contributed to hasten its end. Railroads may have brought the farmer to the frontier, but it was the invention of barbed wire which really enabled him to take possession and hold the land against the range cattle. In the end it also helped the cattlemen. Under the severe competition the scrub stock and the longhorn had to give way to better breeds which required more care. The new stock could not fend for itself, but had to be enclosed. As the ranchers witnessed the farmers' frontier eating into the open range, the more farsighted hastened to enclose land. Much of this enclosure was illegal; the estimates of it in 1888 run as high as 8,000,000 acres. The increasing inroads of both farmers and ranchers on the public land soon changed the economic picture of the West. The shift of the cattle industry from the open range to the pasture was also hastened by the appearance of cattle diseases and the quarantine laws passed by northern states against southern cattle. Two other factors tended to stabilize the industry under the new conditions: the severe winters of the early eighties which destroyed many cattle, and the overexpansion during this period which brought collapse and ruin to many cattlemen.

Short as was the life of the ranchers' frontier, it left definite influences upon our history. Above all, it helped to open to settlement the vast area between the 100th meridian and the Rockies. The clamor of both ranchers and farmers for more land forced the opening of Oklahoma to settlement. With the growth of the ranchers' frontier, the packing industry moved westward to center in Chicago, St. Louis, Kansas City, and Omaha, where it quickly became a monopoly in the hands of Armour, Hammond, Morris, and Swift. Packing and refrigeration processes were forced upon the industry by the transportation factor. With these problems solved, the exportation of meat became increasingly important. The conflict between the cattlemen on the one hand and the packers and railroads on the other for the profits of the industry contributed to the economic and political controversies of the time and to the rising tide of agrarian unrest.

THE FARMERS' FRONTIER

Pressing rapidly on the heels of the ranchers came the vanguard of farmers who succeeded by 1890 in virtually closing the American frontier. Many factors explain the rapid occupation of this vast area. First of all were the land laws. The long agitation for free land finally achieved its objective. The first bill was passed in 1860 and vetoed by Buchanan, but a second, sponsored by the Republican party in the election of that year, was signed by Lincoln on May 20, 1862. The Homestead Act granted a quarter section (160 acres) free to the head of a family or to a person over twenty-one who was a citizen of the United States or who had filed his intention of becoming one and who had not borne arms against the United States. Residence of five years was required; good faith was to be evidenced by cultivation. After six months,[3] however, the entry might be commuted by the payment of $1.25 an acre.

[3] Raised to fourteen months in 1891.

Later amendments have further liberalized the act by permitting Union veterans of the Civil War and the veterans of all succeeding wars to count the time served in the Army against the five-year required residence period.

Other acts which followed tended either to liberalize the Homestead Act or to make other land available at low cost. The Timber Culture Act of 1873, for example, allowed a homesteader to apply for an additional 160 acres which would become his if he planted at least one-fourth to trees within four years. The Desert Land Act of 1877, a result of lobbying ranchers, gave a tentative title to 640 acres in the Great Plains upon the initial payment of 25 cents an acre, proof of irrigation within three years, and payment then of an extra dollar an acre. The Timber and Stone Act of 1878 opened to citizens at the appraisal value, but in no case at less than $2.50 an acre, 160 acres of public lands valuable chiefly for timber and stone and "unfit for cultivation" at the date of sale. The Dawes Act of 1887 provided for individual instead of tribal ownership of small amounts of land by the Indians and thus opened up large areas of reservations to settlers. An act passed in 1909 provided for enlarged homesteads of 320 acres of nonirrigable land where dry farming was necessary, one-fourth of which had to be cultivated in two years. In 1912 the five-year residence was reduced to three, and an act to allow 640 acres for stock raising further liberalized the system in 1916.

The Homestead Act of 1862 has often been described as opening a great new era in the history of our national land policy. In a sense this is true, although free land was obtainable in the colonial period[4] and by special acts in later years. Upon closer examination, however, the significance of the act tends to diminish. First of all, the Homestead Act was superimposed on the old laws and was later restricted by new ones. The Pre-emption Act of 1841, allowing a person to buy choice lands by pre-emption, continued in effect until 1891. The old system of sale by auction and cash was still in existence, as, for example, in the Timber and Stone Act. Moreover, much of the best land had been given away and was not available for free homestead occupation. Through the Morrill grant for agricultural colleges and other legislation to foster education over 200,000,000 acres had been given away by 1930. Between 1850 and 1871 another 200,000,000 acres were given to aid in the building of railroads, although this was later reduced to 137,000,000 when the railroads failed to meet the requirements of the law. Much of the land obtained by treaties with the Indians was reserved for sale rather than for free distribution. The government likewise held for sale the alternate sections which it had reserved in the railroad grants. Since the railroad and educational grants, as well as much of the best land owned by the government, could be obtained only by purchase, the homesteader on the great plains was often forced to

[4] Above, p. 55.

take second-best lands and those at a distance from transportation facilities. It is not surprising, therefore, to find that up to 1890 only 48,225,736 acres were granted under the Homestead Act to 372,659 families, and only about one-third of these claims were finally proved. It is doubtful if more than 1,000,000 people out of a population increase of 30,000,000 between 1860 and 1890 actually profited from this act.[5] Interestingly enough it was in the years after 1890 that the greatest expansion under the Homestead Act took place. From 1862 to 1926 the government issued 1,391,128 patents for approximately 226,159,000 acres.

Not only were the homestead laws limited in their benefits, but their intention was often frustrated by evasion and misuse. Their intention may have been to provide free land for migrant settlers and to cover the West with small freeholds, but the results were often far different. At one time it was possible for a settler to secure 1120 acres of land—160 acres under the Homestead Act, 160 acres under the old Pre-emption Act, 160 acres under the Stone and Timber Act, and 640 acres of desert land. By collusion with individuals it was a simple matter for mining and lumber companies to secure immense holdings by violating the intent, if not the letter, of the law. This was done through the privilege of commuting, a feature of the Homestead Act which allowed the homesteader at any time after six months of filing his claim to obtain his land by paying $1.25 or $2.50 an acre for it. Thus in six months large corporations acting through their agents might, at a small cost, obtain lands worth many times the amount paid. It is estimated that from 1881 to 1904, 23 per cent of the land transferred from government to private ownership under the Homestead Acts was obtained by commuting. In North Dakota during the first decade of the present century more acres were commuted than were obtained by five years' residence.[6] An agent of the land office asserted that "actual inspection of hundreds of commuted homesteads shows that not one in a hundred is ever occupied as a home after commutation."[7]

The situation respecting the public lands became so notorious that in 1879 Congress appointed a commission to examine and report on the land system, but the suggested reforms were ignored. Until the rise of the conservation movement after 1900 only the courageous stand of Arthur and Cleveland can be taken as real evidence of a national desire to enforce the existing laws. A New Public Land Commission appointed by Roosevelt submitted elaborate reports and suggested salutary reforms along the same line as the previ-

[5] The limitations of the Homestead Act are clearly shown in P. W. Gates, "The Homestead Act in an Incongruous Land System," *American Historical Review*, XLI, 652–681 (July, 1936), and in F. A. Shannon, "The Homestead Act and the Labor Surplus," *ibid.*, pp. 637–651.

[6] B. H. Hibbard, *A History of the Public Land Policies* (1924), p. 387.

[7] Quoted in *ibid.*, p. 389.

ous commission, but again little was done. The policy of the government as regards public land has remained essentially as before and (according to the National Conservation Commission of 1909) is far from subserving the best interests of the nation.

Not only has our land policy been open to the criticism that the laws have been criminally evaded and negligently enforced, but the wisdom of the whole system itself has been questioned. Has it been to the best interests of the nation to give away its heritage of land so rapidly and so freely that it has encouraged wasteful methods of farming, glutted the market with foodstuffs, and decreased the value of the agricultural lands in the East? As opposed to these criticisms it is argued that farms have been provided for many settlers from the East and for multitudes drawn from Europe by the prospect of free land. The policy has enormously stimulated the rapid occupation of the trans-Mississippi country and the founding of new commonwealths. This, in fact, was the main purpose of the Homestead Act, and the intention was that settlement should proceed under a democratic system. The Public Land Commission said of the act, "It protects the government, it fills the state with homes, it builds up communities and lessens the chances of social and civil disorder by giving ownership of the soil, in small tracts, to the occupants thereof." These hopes were but partly realized. Ownership of small tracts, as originally contemplated, was often frustrated by the fraudulent evasion of the acts; the result was large holdings and landless workers. Moreover, it is doubtful if free land under the Homestead Act ever played an important part as a "safety valve" for labor. The last three decades of the nineteenth century were years of discontent and strife among eastern wage earners and of acute economic and political unrest in the agricultural West.

Quite as potent as the Homestead Act in promoting the advance of the farming frontier was the construction of the transcontinental railways. After exhaustive government surveys, twenty years of agitation, and arduous labor, the last spike in the roadbed connecting the Union Pacific and the Central Pacific was driven on May 10, 1869, at Ogden, Utah, and the first railway across the continent was completed. Other transcontinental lines were authorized in the sixties, and the years from the close of the war until the panic of 1873 were characterized by feverish railroad building which was renewed with the revival of business after 1878. Under the direction of Henry Villard, the Northern Pacific was completed in 1883, and the same year saw the linking of the Atchison, Topeka and Santa Fe and the Southern Pacific in a southern route to California. In 1882 the Texas Pacific and the Southern Pacific met at El Paso and connections were thus made between the Pacific and New Orleans or St. Louis. By the middle eighties there were at least four main routes to the Pacific, and such roads as the Kansas Pacific, completed

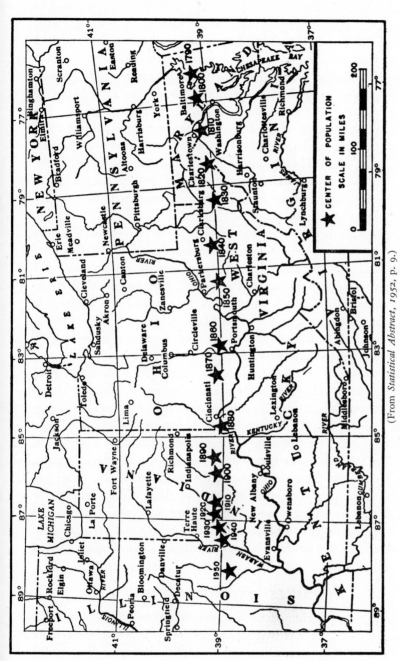

(From *Statistical Abstract, 1952*, p. 9.)

WESTWARD MOVEMENT OF THE CENTER OF POPULATION.

"Center of Population" is that point which may be considered as center of population gravity of the United States or that point upon which the United States would balance, if it were a rigid plane without weight and the population distributed thereon with each individual being assumed to have equal weight and to exert an influence on the central point proportional to this distance from the point.

to Denver in 1870, and the Chicago, Burlington, and Quincy, completed to the same point in 1882, opened up much additional territory to immigrants.

The Union Pacific had been looked upon as a national project and had been aided lavishly by the government, a policy which until 1871 was generally followed with other prospective western roads. Approximately 137,000,-000 acres have been granted by the national government to states or to private corporations for internal improvements, of which the larger part has gone to the transcontinental roads. In fact, all the western roads just mentioned were recipients of large public land donations, except the Chicago, Burlington, and Quincy. These grants included a right of way and alternate sections on each side of the track, ranging from five sections per mile to as high as forty for the Northern Pacific. The remaining sections were reserved by the government for later sale.

Whether the land belonged to the railroads or the government, it was essential for the railroads to populate it. Their literature and advertisements were printed in many languages and distributed over the eastern states and Europe. Agencies were established in Europe and America, and their representatives carried on propaganda wherever the field seemed ripe. In the East veterans' organizations were canvassed for likely immigrants, and influential men were obtained to lead groups of Scandinavians to the Northwest. Transportation rates were reduced, reception houses established, and liberal credit inducements offered for the purchase of land. The roads which were particularly active in this work, such as the Northern Pacific, overlooked few known methods of encouraging immigration. In a debate on the admission of the Dakotas in 1884, Benjamin Harrison correctly observed: "Conditions of emigration have changed. The emigrant who is seeking a home in the West does not now use as his vehicle a pack-train, a Conestoga wagon, or even a broad-horn. The great bulk of the people who have gone into Dakota have gone upon the steam-car, many of them within sight of the home which they were to take up under the homestead laws of the United States . . . whereas in the case of the state of Indiana it was thirty years after the admission of that state into the Union before a single line of railroad was built in its territory."[8]

WINDMILLS AND BARBED WIRE

Important as were the Homestead Acts and the railroads, there were other significant factors in the rapid settlement of the Great Plains. The more permanent problem facing the farmer who settled in the region between the 98th meridian and the Rockies was the inadequate rainfall. In this section, says its greatest historian, "the scarcity of moisture is the subject that fur-

[8] 48th Cong., 2nd Sess., *Congressional Record,* Vol. XVI, Part I, p. 109 (Dec. 9, 1884).

nishes the greatest amount of thought and talk; in fact, it is the crux of the whole problem of conquering the Great Plains."[9] Its history has been largely determined by the search for water. Efforts to solve this problem extend from the dug wells of the first pioneers to the great irrigation projects of the federal government at Hoover Dam and Grand Coulee. They include experiments in dry farming and the importation and adaptation of drought-resisting wheat and corn. For the average prairie farmer, however, the supply of water depended on pumping up the ground water with a windmill; hence the development of quantity production of small metal windmills went hand in hand with frontier expansion into the Great Plains. Adapted to the almost continuous delivery of small amounts of water, the windmill was perhaps the most important mechanical aid in the occupation of this area.

Without the windmill the settlement of the prairies might have been indefinitely delayed; without barbed wire the plains might still be in possession of the cowboy and the roaming herds of cattle. Until the sixties, fencing material was primarily wooden rails, rocks, and hedge growth. This was sufficient until the pioneer left the timbered region and moved into the prairies. At first he avoided the open land, although it was often more fertile; when he finally struck into it he tried frantically to find substitutes for the old fencing materials. Solution of the problem came in the middle seventies when patents for practical barbed wire were taken out by two Illinois farmers, Joseph F. Glidden and Jacob Haish. Never did inventors find a more receptive market. The production and sale of barbed wire which amounted to 10,000 pounds in 1874 jumped to 80,500,000 six years later. Quantity production reduced the price from $20 a hundred pounds in 1874 to a low mark of $1.80 a hundred in 1897.

The way was now open for rapid expansion. Said an old settler in Texas: "It was not until about 1875 that the black lands really became available for agricultural purposes. The development of those lands had lagged for lack of the means of fencing them at moderate cost. They were so far from timber as to make rail fences out of the question. The want was supplied by the Glidden barbed wire, which, beginning about 1875, was shipped into the state, not by the carload but by the trainload. After that immigrants ceased to stop in East Texas, and the black lands came into their own."[10] Ranchers might descend upon the outlying farms and cut the wire to pieces, but it was a losing battle. Barbed wire not only enabled the farmers to win the battle but it forced the ranchers to change the methods of their own industry.[11] "It was barbed wire," says Webb, "and not the railroads or the home-

[9] W. P. Webb, *The Great Plains* (1931), p. 322.
[10] *Ibid.*, p. 317.
[11] Above, p. 353.

stead law that made it possible for the farmers to resume, or at least acceler-ate, their march across the prairies and onto the plains. Even the fertile Prairie Plains were but sparsely settled until after the advent of barbed wire."[12]

A phase of the occupation of the last frontier, upon which it is unnecessary to enter in detail, is the dispossession of the Indians. Until 1861 the trans-Mississippi Indians were generally on friendly terms with the United States, notwithstanding the fact that their lands were continually traversed by sur-veyors and miners. Driven to desperation by the obvious fact that the end was near, the Indians made their last stand against encroaching civilization. The Sioux uprising in 1862 was followed by that of the Cheyenne and other tribes in the sixties, and the Indian struggle culminated in the Sioux war of 1876 and the defeat of their chieftain, Sitting Bull. In the elimination of the western Indian, it is only fair to say that the outstanding feature was not the treachery of the red man but rather the ruthless greed of the white invader backed by the regular Army, whose rifles gave way on the plains to the more deadly six-shooter. A subsequent chapter of this long-drawn-out tragedy was written in 1887 in the Dawes Act, in which the government sought to hasten the Indians' acceptance of the white man's civilization by abolishing the tribal ownership of land and allotting to the head of each family a quarter section of 160 acres, an eighth section to single adults and orphans, and a sixteenth to each dependent child. To protect the new owner, the right to mortgage or dispose of the land was withheld for twenty-five years, and it was to be tax-free for that period. The Dawes Act carried with it the right of citizenship for those Indians who voluntarily left their tribes and took up homesteads under its provisions. It failed to solve the problem of the Indian, but it was instrumental in opening much land to white settlers.

END OF THE FRONTIER

By 1890 the frontier (technically, a region with more than two and less than six people per square mile) had vanished. Most of the good arable land had been taken up by that time. The farmers' frontier had met and expro-priated much of the ranchers' cow country and now reached the mining country in the Rockies. Fertile farming land to the west of the Sierras on the Pacific coast was now yielding more than the precious metal ever had. In 1904 the government still owned 700,000,000 acres of land, but most of it was valueless except for dry farming, irrigation, or drainage projects. Economically this great region between the Mississippi and the mountains is primarily agricultural, the newly populated territories separating roughly into the wheat country of Montana and the Dakotas; the corn belt of Kansas,

[12] W. P. Webb, *op. cit.*, p. 317.

Iowa, and Nebraska; and the cotton fields and grazing lands of Arkansas and Texas. Occupation and economic development were followed by admission to statehood—North Dakota, South Dakota, Montana, and Washington in 1889, and Idaho and Wyoming in 1890. The abandonment of polygamy by the Mormon church in 1890 paved the way for the admission of Utah in 1896; Oklahoma became a state in 1907, and New Mexico and Arizona in 1912.

With the passing of the frontier one era in American history ended. More than any other factor, the existence of a large area of unoccupied land and a constantly moving frontier had differentiated the underlying economic conditions of the United States from those of western Europe. The frontier had provided an outlet for restless groups from the East and a home for millions of immigrants from Europe. It had shaped the content and direction of foreign trade and the type and location of domestic industry. It had laid its mark on our monetary system and our railroad history. Not only had it been of primary importance in our economic history but it had reacted upon our social and political development and gone far to mold American psychology and American philosophy.

Historians and economists in recent years have been greatly interested in pointing out the influence of the frontier and in predicting the changes which may follow its disappearance. A word of caution, however, should be interjected. Good free land might be gone, but after 1890 there was still a large amount of inferior land which, with modern methods, might be made productive, and an abundance of cheap land was still obtainable.[13] For those who still desired high-grade free land, it was possible, as thousands did, to emigrate to Canada. The twentieth-century immigrant might have to pay for his land, but he might also escape many of the hardships of the earlier settlers.

Nevertheless, as the twentieth century enters its sixth decade, certain effects of the passing of the frontier seem evident. An impetus has been given to conservation, reclamation, and scientific agriculture. Manufacturing has become less a simple supplement to extractive industry; rather, by greater use of improved machinery it is carrying its processes further. Commerce, which was early concerned with the exportation of agricultural and of raw or semimanufactured products, and the importation of manufactured goods, has gradually become concerned with the importation of agricultural commodities and of raw materials and the exportation of manufactured goods, thus laying the foundations for an economic expansion similar to that of western Europe. What effect the passing of free land will

---

[13] As already pointed out, three times as much land was patented under the Homestead Act after 1890 as before.

have upon the growth of the tenant system, upon the development of organized labor, and upon the growth of class consciousness it is too early to predict; but it is obvious that it portends a new group of economic and social problems whose solution will tax the best intelligence of the next century.[14]

SELECTED READINGS

Billington, R. A., *Westward Expansion,* chaps. 30–36.

Osgood, E. S., *The Day of the Cattleman,* chaps. 4, 5.

Webb, W. P., *The Great Plains,* chaps. 5–8.

Shannon, F. A., *The Farmer's Last Frontier,* chap. 9.

Gates, P. W., "The Homestead Law in Incongruous Land System," *American Historical Review,* XLI, 652–681 (July, 1936).

Hedges, J. B., "The Colonization Work of the Northern Pacific," *Mississippi Valley Historical Review,* XIII, 311–342 (Dec., 1926).

Flügel, F., and Faulkner, H. U., *Readings in the Economic and Social History of the United States,* pp. 741–764.

[14] C. W. Wright, "The Disappearance of Free Land in Our Economic Development," *American Economic Review,* XVI, 265–271 (Supplement, March, 1926), reprinted in F. Flügel and H. U. Faulkner, *Readings in the Economic and Social History of the United States,* pp. 758–764.

PART IV

THE INDUSTRIAL REVOLUTION

CHAPTER 19

THE AGRARIAN REVOLUTION

AGRICULTURE DEVELOPMENT, 1860–1910

So significant has been the industrial advance since 1860 that it has obscured an agricultural development quite as momentous. The half-century from 1860 to 1910 witnessed an agrarian revolution which included both the introduction of agricultural machinery and the increased adoption of scientific farming. It saw the rapid growth of government interest and aid to agriculture and a widespread movement toward agricultural education. Spurred on by the Homestead Act, by migration from Europe, and by all the influences which have advanced our frontier, the agricultural domain was pushed westward until most of the usable land was pre-empted. The entire population of the United States in 1860 was 30,000,000, but in 1910 there were 50,000,000 living on farms and in villages supported by agriculture, and the number of farms had grown from 2,000,000 in 1860 to 6,000,000 in 1910. During this half-century over 500,000,000 acres of new land had been brought under cultivation, an area almost as large as that of western Europe, providing new homes for millions of people, freight for railroads, and food for the increasing industrial classes in Europe and America.

This development was, perhaps, too rapid, for it drove the prices of foodstuffs down to a point in many cases below the cost of production. It was accompanied by circumstances which brought hardship and discontent to the farmers and which were reflected in political and economic unrest. The end of the frontier, however, eventually stimulated interest in conservation, in irrigation projects, and in scientific farming. With rising prices for products and land values from 1899 to 1920, and with better roads, electric trolleys, automobiles, and farm machinery, the economic condition of the farmer improved and rural life became more satisfying. Nevertheless, these years saw a constant increase in urban population and manufacturing, and a relative decline in agricultural population and wealth.

365

AGRARIAN DISCONTENT

Although the period since the Civil War was one of great agricultural expansion, it was not one of uninterrupted prosperity. On the contrary, the period from 1867 to 1897 was one of uncertainty and discontent. During the flush period of the war when prices soared as the result of greater demand for foodstuffs and an inflated currency, many farmers extended their operations by increasing their holdings and equipment. Ex-soldiers, tradesmen, and mechanics, encouraged by the Homestead Act and railroad propaganda, hastened to take up land; but all of them usually lacked sufficient money and tools, and the land was mortgaged to provide for the necessary equipment. All went well until the inflated war prices collapsed. The government's policy of calling in some of the greenbacks and ultimately raising the paper currency to a parity with gold put the farmers at a disadvantage, for the American farmer was predominantly a debtor and consequently was injured by a decline in the general price level. Unable to meet his interest payments, which continued at the old rate while prices fell and the value of money increased, he was often forced to see his mortgage foreclosed and the results of years of labor wiped out. He had the option of going into industry, entering the ranks of the tenant farmer or agricultural laborer, or again moving on to the frontier.

It was not only the problem of deflation and the lack of adequate credit facilities which harassed the farmer, but the fact that he found himself at a disadvantage in his relations with the rapidly developing railroad and industrial monopolies. The railroads upon which he was dependent for marketing his products were often careless and inefficient, discriminating in their favors to industries at the expense of the agricultural sections. Where there was no discrimination, freight rates might still be needlessly high because of dividend payments on heavily watered stock. Throughout the last decades of the nineteenth century, the development of big business and monopolies proceeded rapidly. "Never in our history," said the Greenbackers in prefacing their platform in 1884, "have the banks, the land-grant railroads, and other monopolies been more insolent in their demands for further privilege—still more class legislation. In this emergency the dominant parties are arrayed against the people and are the abject tools of corporate monopolies."

While the prices of farm commodities declined, those of manufactured products, dominated by monopoly practices, remained high or did not decline proportionately. Monopolies in meat packing and other processing industries were often able to hold the prices of farm commodities artificially low while they profited by the high prices charged to consumers. Moreover, the holders of patent monopolies on such essential farm commodities as barbed wire or well machinery were often able to harass and overcharge the farmer.[1] At the same time the farmer felt that an undue share of the profits was taken by the middlemen and by the speculators on the grain and cotton exchanges. While he bore the hardships of a lonely and arduous frontier life, eastern capitalists deprived him of the profits of his toil. "There are three great crops raised in Nebraska," said one of the farmers' papers in 1890. "One is a crop of corn, one a crop of freight rates, and one a crop of interest. One is produced by the farmers who by sweat and toil farm the land. The other two are produced by men who sit in their offices and behind their bank counters and farm the farmers."[2]

This feeling of bitterness over an exploitation which, in fact, existed, was particularly strong in the sections where the pinch was greatest, particularly on the wheat farms of the West. Minor elements in the prevailing unrest in that region were the conflict between the land-hungry pioneer farmers and the cattle raisers, and the fraudulent methods employed by individuals and companies in obtaining large blocks of land. But the trans-Mississippi West was not the only section that suffered from declining prices and the exploitation of railroads, monopolies, and middlemen. In the South the situation was equally discouraging. Here the whole economic structure had crashed with the Civil War, and a new economy was being painfully reconstructed on the ruins. Bankrupt planters, ignorant colored labor, and declining cotton prices were the elements from which the new system must be erected. In the Northeast, deflation and western competition severely affected the agricultural interests, accentuated the movement to the cities, and increased the area of deserted farms. Throughout the country the general decline in land values was a factor in the agrarian discontent; for the American farmer, it must be remembered, was a land speculator as well as an agriculturist. Added to all this was the high tariff of the Civil War, continued during the years of peace, which aided the manufacturing interests and at the same time increased the cost of living and jeopardized the foreign market for foodstuffs.

The farmers fought back against economic tendencies and specific grievances, and for three decades after the Civil War the agrarian sections were in an almost continuous condition of revolt. This revolt took the form of political pressure exerted through farmers' organizations and political parties, and various co-operative efforts in the field of business in an attempt to help themselves. It was directed against their chief difficulties—monetary deflation, railroad abuses, and monopoly practices. From the late 1860's until the end of the century the farmers fought bitterly the deflationary policies of

---

[1] Earl W. Hayter, "The Western Farmers and the Drivewell Patent Controversy," *Agricultural History*, XVI, 16–28 (Jan., 1942).

[2] *Farmers' Alliance*, August 23, 1890. Quoted by John Hicks, *The Populist Revolt*, p. 83.

the federal government. They organized the Greenback party in an effort to bring about inflation by fiat paper money, and the Populist party to achieve the same end by restoring free and unlimited coinage of gold and silver at 16 to 1. Both parties directed their attacks against monopolies as well as against deflation. The first great farmers' organization of the West, the Patrons of Husbandry, exerted its greatest influence in promoting state legislation to control railroad abuses. Although the farmers' revolt failed to bring inflation it was very influential, as we shall see,[3] in initiating anti-monopoly and anti-railroad legislation in the states and eventually in the federal government. It was also influential in such banking reform as the Federal Reserve Act, and in bringing the Federal Farm Loan Act and other legislation to improve the credit facilities of the farmer.[4]

In addition to political pressure, the farmers sought relief by entering the field of business for themselves. Examples of these attempts are co-operative buying and selling organizations, and farmers' insurance companies, promoted by the Grangers, the Farmers' Alliance, and, more recently, by state legislation in the Dakotas, and by federal legislation. The movement has been notably strong in the control of grain elevators, 4000 of which, it is estimated, are owned by 400,000 farmers. It appears to be the almost unanimous opinion of agricultural experts that consolidation of interests on the part of the farmers is essential to their prosperity. This point of view was eventually given official sanction in the Agricultural Marketing Act of 1929.[5] It should also be noted here that many laws to promote agricultural education and scientific agriculture have been passed. For them to have the desired results requires both government aid and personal initiative, and both have been forthcoming.

After recovery from the panic of 1893, agricultural conditions improved as a result of currency inflation and the fact that the demand for agricultural products was catching up with the supply. The first two decades of the new century were years of expansion and prosperity when new buildings, fresh equipment, and improved roads demonstrated even to the casual observer that a better day had come. The total value of crops in 1899 was $2,998,704,-000; in 1909 it was $5,487,000,000. The value of all farm property, including land, increased from $20,440,000,000 in 1900 to $40,991,000,000 in 1910, about 100.5 per cent. The value of the land alone increased from an average of $15.57 per acre in 1900 to $32.40 in 1910, or 108.1 per cent, an increase greater than that in all previous years since the discovery of America. World War I

---

[3] The fight for inflation will be discussed more fully in chap. 25, that for railroad legislation in chap. 23, and that for monopoly control in chap. 21.

[4] Below, pp. 397 ff.

[5] Below, p. 628.

with its inflated prices brought continued prosperity, but no group felt the subsequent depression more keenly than the farmer.[6]

MECHANIZATION OF THE FARM

Large farms and scarcity of labor, the two forces which heretofore had directed the development of farm machinery, continued to be influential after the Civil War. The first great improvements in the plow, reaper, and thresher had already demonstrated their practicability before 1860, but it was the war that widened their use. When the federal government mobilized the largest army that the world had yet seen, those who remained on the farm turned of necessity to labor-saving machinery. The rapid adoption of farm machinery was also encouraged by the fact that the type of country occupied during these years was adaptable to large-scale farming and to machine operation. It is therefore correct to say that the agricultural revolution in America, as far as machinery is concerned, came in the half-century after 1860.

The climate in the wheat regions of the Middle West necessitated rapid harvesting when the crop was ripe, and the amount planted was dependent upon the farmer's ability to harvest before the grain spoiled. Consequently the attention of inventors was directed most of all toward methods to speed up harvesting. Already in 1858 C. W. and W. W. Marsh had patented the "Marsh harvester," a reaping machine which, by means of an endless apron, delivered the grain upon a table where two men could bind it. This reaper almost doubled the amount of grain that could be harvested in a given time. Even more important was John F. Appleby's invention in 1878 of a "twine binder," a machine which took the place of the crude and unsatisfactory wire binders in use and increased eightfold the speed in harvesting. "The invention of the twine binder, therefore," says Professor Carver, "by increasing the amount which a farmer could harvest, increased by that precise amount the quantity which he could profitably grow. In other words, it was the twine binder more than any other single machine or implement that enabled the country to increase its production of grain, especially wheat, during this period. The per capita production of the country as a whole increased from about 5.6 bushels in 1860 to 9.2 bushels in 1880."[7] Further improvements were made by the addition of a bundle carrier and, in dry climates, of a header. On the great wheat farms of the West were to be found "combines" drawn by a score or more of horses or later propelled by gasoline

---

[6] The average value of farm land per acre increased to $57.36 in 1920, decreasing to $35.40 by 1930; the estimated gross income from farms increased to $13,566,000,000 in 1920, decreasing to $9,414,000,000 in 1930; the value of all farm property increased to $77,924,000,000 in 1920, decreasing to $57,246,000,000 in 1930. *Statistical Abstract, 1933*, pp. 535, 565.

[7] T. N. Carver, *Principles of Rural Economics*, p. 99.

tractors which could cut, thresh, clean, sack, and weigh the grain without the touch of human hands.

Improvements in machinery for planting and cultivating appeared simultaneously with those for harvesting. During this period there came into use the straddle-row cultivator, the sulky plow, spring-tooth sulky harrows of various types, and seeders that plant, cover, and fertilize at the same time. This type of agricultural machinery, which helped to speed up the process of planting and thus put it on a par with harvesting, was rapidly adopted after 1875 in the Red River wheat country and the Far West. The lister, which plows and plants the seed at the same time, was introduced in 1880. The mowing machine has been perfected, and improvements in haying have included the spring-tooth sulky rake and machines for loading, stacking, and baling. Hand shelling of corn gave way after 1850 to machine shelling. The failure of the hay crop several times in the eighties, when the dairying industry was being rapidly developed, directed attention to corn raising, and the combined work of many inventors resulted in a machine with which one man can cut and bind from six to ten acres a day. This enables the farmer to cut his fodder corn green with the juice still in the stock and store it in the silo for winter food, whereas before he was often forced to leave it standing in the fields to dry.

The first stage in the mechanization of the farm was the general displacement of men by horses as the motive power for agricultural energy. This commenced long before the Civil War but developed most rapidly between 1860 and 1910. It was accompanied by a tremendous increase in the number of draft animals on the farm. The substitution of horsepower for manpower, however, had hardly begun before manufacturers of farm machinery were considering the possibility of substituting mechanical power for that of animals. On the large prairie farms experiments were soon being made with steam tractors for planting and preparing the land. By 1910 the gasoline engine had been applied to farm machinery and was so obviously superior to either steam or horsepower that in the next decade it rapidly replaced both on large farms. Almost as revolutionary in its effects has been the use of the gasoline truck and pleasure car, which have brought the farmer into closer touch with urban life and thus facilitated both marketing and purchasing. Not only the automobile but gasoline pumping and lighting outfits have helped to bring the advantages of the city to the farmer and to decrease household drudgery. Where the farm is close to an electric supply, much of the smaller indoor machinery, such as milk separators, churns, and washing machines, is operated by electricity. Since electrical facilities expanded rapidly after the early 1930's in rural areas, the use of electricity on farms has greatly increased.

As a result of the mechanization of agriculture, the value of farm machinery in this country more than doubled between 1860 and 1890 and between 1890 and 1930 increased from $500,000,000 to $3,600,000,000. It is estimated that the amount of power used on farms increased eight times between 1900 and 1935. One of the important effects of this mechanization was the increased productivity of farm labor; the best estimates indicate an increased productivity per worker of about 400 per cent. One effect of this has been the creation of greater wealth. Some of this wealth has undoubtedly remained in the hands of the farmer, who has thus been enabled to buy machinery and improve his economic condition, but at the same time mechanization has had a tendency to concentrate wealth in the hands of the proprietor class who are in a position to buy expensive machinery. This can be seen in the relative increase of agricultural laborers in the leading cereal states even before the turn of the century.

SEVEN LEADING CEREAL STATES
(Illinois, Iowa, Kansas, Nebraska, Minnesota, North and South Dakota)

	1880	1900	Percentage of Increase
Proprietors (owners or tenants)	836,967	1,073,911	28
Agricultural laborers	363,233	631,740	74

In the country as a whole, the percentage of increase for the two classes was about the same, because of the growth of tenant farming in the South. The man with capital was obviously at an advantage in the cereal states, where expensive machinery was becoming the order of the day. As a result, the poorer farmer was reduced to the status of a tenant or an agricultural laborer. The development of a landless agricultural proletariat has been the most unfortunate result of the agricultural revolution, and has become characteristic of America as well as Europe.

Summarizing, we may say that machinery on the farm has (1) released men for other work; (2) increased the production of agricultural products and the output per capita; (3) eliminated a certain amount of drudgery from farm life; (4) allowed the cultivation for other purposes of many acres which had hitherto been used to produce fodder for horses; (5) enlarged the real income of proprietors. On the other hand, the new machinery has undoubtedly (6) increased relatively the landless agricultural laborer by making it more difficult for the man without capital to engage in agriculture; and (7) contributed to bring about the great overproduction of agricultural commodities characteristic of much of the period (excepting World War I), from 1873 to 1941.

SCIENTIFIC FARMING

The mechanization of agriculture is but one aspect of a developing interest in scientific farming which has been evident in recent decades. Scientific farming began in the Netherlands as a revival of Roman practice and spread into England during the eighteenth century, but the abundance of unoccupied land and rich virgin soil as well as the scarcity of labor held back its development in the United States. There were a few gentlemen farmers— among them Washington, Jefferson, Livingston, and Clay—who sought through experimentation to improve methods, and there were agricultural societies and county fairs that attempted to distribute information and encourage better agriculture.[8] But the typical American farmer continued to "butcher" his land and neglect his livestock, following the careless methods of earlier years. During the last decades of the nineteenth century, however, certain factors were beginning to operate which inevitably aroused greater interest in scientific agriculture. Better transportation facilities made it possible to enlarge markets and gave an impetus to the improvement of the quality of the product. Declining prices during much of this period produced greater competition which in turn developed improved and cheaper methods of farming. The gradual disappearance of unoccupied arable land also heightened the interest in scientific farming.

Although private initiative, expressed through individual farmers, farm papers, and farm organizations, has continued to urge scientific methods, it has been chiefly the federal and state governments which have stimulated it. Unlike the great industrialists, the small individualistic farmer has little capital and operates on too small a scale to finance experimental research. If such research is to be done, it must be undertaken largely by government agencies.

Since the 1860's the American farmer has not lacked aid from either the state or the national government. This is attributable to three reasons. In the first place, the fundamental importance of agriculture has always been recognized. Although the estimated annual value of agricultural products averaged (1919–1929) only about $11,000,000,000 and that of manufactured products $60,000,000,000, more than half of the important manufacturing industries—for example, slaughtering and meat packing, milling, the production of cotton and woolen cloth, boots and shoes, and many others—are dependent upon agriculture. Farm products are also an important, in some sections the most important, item of railroad freight. Agriculture still remains the foundation of much of our economic life. In the second place, during most of our history the farmer has exerted a potent influence on the legislative branch of the government. As late as 1880, 49 per cent of the gain-

[8] Above, chap. 11.

fully employed population was engaged in agriculture. Although this had fallen off in 1910 to 32.5, and in 1930 to 21.4 per cent,[9] the fact that the industrial population is largely centralized has given the farmer special weight in the upper house, where southern and western Senators are naturally very susceptible to the demands of agriculture. The so-called "agricultural bloc" in both houses has been quick to coalesce when the farmers' interests are at stake. In the third place, the policy of *laissez faire,* so strong during the first decades of the Industrial Revolution, has been gradually breaking down, and nowhere has this change of attitude been more apparent than in the relations of the government to agriculture. This has been due not alone to the political strength of the farmer but to the realization of the economic importance of agriculture, of the farmer's handicaps in dealing with other economic groups, and of his consequent special need of protection. Moreover, large agricultural exports were needed, at least until after World War I, to pay the costs of borrowing from abroad. Consequently, government aid has taken three forms: first, research and education; second, protection by legislation against other groups; and third, help in reclamation and irrigation.

Some mention has already been made of government aid to education and the scientific study of agricultural problems. The work of the schools and experiment stations is augmented and to a certain extent directed by the activities of the Department of Agriculture. George Washington as President recommended a governmental board, but it was not until 1839 that Congress voted $1000 to the Commissioner of Patents for the "collection of agricultural statistics and other agricultural purposes." In 1862 these activities were removed from the Patent Office and a Commissioner of Agriculture was created to direct a bureau whose duty was "to acquire and diffuse among the people of the United States useful information on subjects connected with agriculture in the most general and comprehensive sense of the word, and to procure, propagate, and distribute among the people new and valuable seeds and plants." In 1889 this bureau was elevated to the rank of the other departments, and its head made a Secretary and a member of the Cabinet.

The educational and research activities of the Department of Agriculture have extended into many fields and gradually been divided into separate bureaus. The Bureau of Animal Industry has charge of meat inspection and animal quarantine. It has done remarkable work in studying and checking such animal diseases as cattle fever, pleuropneumonia, hoof and mouth disease, and hog cholera. The Bureau of Plant Industry is engaged in combating plant disease, in studying better agricultural methods and plant acclimatization, in distributing seed, and in similar activities. More than 34,000

---

[9] Figures for 1880 included those engaged in lumbering and fishing. *Statistical Abstract, 1930,* p. 60; Census, 1930, *Population,* V, 39.

new plants have been brought into the country, notably kaffir corn, durum wheat, drought-proof alfalfa, and new varieties of subtropical fruits. Closely allied to the last-named Bureau is the Bureau of Entomology and Plant Quarantine, which studies insects and thus directs the work of combating pests and of introducing beneficial insects. Campaigns have been waged against the Hessian fly, the gypsy and browntail moth, the boll weevil, the corn borer, the Japanese beetle, and the Mediterranean fruitfly.[10] The Bureau of Agricultural Chemistry and Engineering investigates the chemical and physical properties of soils, fertilizers, and agricultural products and conducts research in farm machinery and equipment.

Other bureaus or divisions concentrate on the study and preservation of trees, on the problems of the dairy industry, on marketing problems, agricultural credits, home economics, and the collection and publishing of agricultural statistics. In fact, it would be difficult to find any phase of agriculture in which the Department of Agriculture is not active in giving serious study and sound advice. Moreover, other departments of the government are contributing to agriculture. For example, the Department of Commerce since 1940 has taken over the investigations in meteorology, climatology, and seismology formerly carried on by the Weather Bureau of the Department of Agriculture.

On a much smaller scale most of the states, through departments of agriculture, financial appropriations, and protective legislation, have sought to aid agriculture after the manner of the federal government. Some have gone to the extent of offering subsidies to encourage the production of certain agricultural products; for example, Kansas has tried to promote the growing of beet sugar. Perhaps the crowning example of state resources applied to the interests of the farmer was the North Dakota legislature's sanction in 1919 of the complete program of the Farmer's Non-Partisan Political League, which, among other things, called for state-owned flour mills and terminal elevators, a state-owned and -operated bank, and state loans to home builders and land purchasers. Opposition of eastern financial interests, the agricultural depression after 1920, and political reaction within the state largely ended these experiments.

Scientific farming, of course, has been given tremendous impetus by agricultural education, and this in turn has received its greatest stimulus from the federal and state governments. The decade of the fifties saw a rapidly growing interest in agricultural education which found vent in the establishment of several state agricultural schools. Impetus to the movement was given by the passage of the Morrill Act in 1862. Introduced by Justin S. Morrill in 1857 and vetoed by President Buchanan, it was brought up again

[10] *Yearbook of Agriculture, 1930,* pp. 50–60.

during the war and passed. The act provided that 30,000 acres of public land be given to each state for each Senator and Representative in Congress, the funds from the sale of these lands to be accumulated and the interest used to support, endow, and maintain "at least one college where the leading object shall be, without excluding other scientific and classical studies, and including military tactics, to teach such branches of learning as are related to agriculture and the mechanic arts, in such manner as the legislatures of the states may, respectively, prescribe, in order to promote the liberal and practical education of the industrial classes in the several pursuits and professions of life."

This first "land-grant" act constituted the greatest single piece of legislation ever passed in the interest of agricultural education, and under its provisions institutions were gradually established in each of the states and in Hawaii and Puerto Rico. In some states the agricultural or mechanical schools are attached to the state universities or other colleges. In Massachusetts, the income was divided to help found two schools, the Massachusetts Agricultural College[11] and the Massachusetts Institute of Technology. There were sixty-eight land-grant colleges teaching agriculture in 1916. The Morrill Act has been extended by subsequent legislation, notably in 1890 and in 1907, when additional appropriations were voted to increase to $50,000 the annual income of each school subsidized by the government. The Hatch Act of 1887, which provided funds for experiment stations in the various state colleges, turned the attention of these schools to investigation as well as to teaching.

Almost as valuable as the actual instruction given in the colleges and the scientific research carried on there is the diffusion of information among those not regularly attending. The scope of the agricultural colleges has been extended to include special short-term winter courses and extension work. The latter is carried on by correspondence, by publications, by lectures, by itinerant schools sometimes conducted in special trains, by farmers' institutes, by farm demonstration experiments, and by co-operation with farmers' organizations wherever possible. The value of this work was recognized by Congress in the Smith-Lever Extension Act of 1914; under its provisions $480,000 was appropriated, to be divided equally among the states, and an additional $600,000 was granted, to be increased annually by $500,000 until at the end of seven years the annual appropriation by the national government for this purpose would amount to $4,580,000.

Agricultural education is also carried on by the United States Department of Agriculture, which is engaged in the twofold task of experimentation and dissemination of information. The latter is accomplished by means of more

[11] Now the University of Massachusetts at Amherst.

than a dozen publications, among which are the *Yearbook of Agriculture,* the *Farmer's Bulletin,* the *Journal of Agricultural Research,* the *Monthly Crop Reporter,* and the *Weekly News Letter.* The state agricultural departments, which exist in most of the states, function in a somewhat similar way. The educational influence of the county and state fairs is still potent. Hundreds of agricultural societies have grown up to promote knowledge and spread information on almost every conceivable phase of plant and animal culture. One or more of their organs or of the general farm journals, of which nearly 500 are published, reach almost every farmer. Several of these have a circulation of over 500,000. Agricultural instruction, aided by federal funds first granted in the Smith-Hughes Vocational Education Act of 1917, is gradually being introduced into high schools, and in several states it is required in the rural schools. Both federal and state departments of agriculture conduct regular educational programs by radio. As the channels for the diffusion of agricultural information have grown, the interest of practicing farmers in scientific agriculture has also increased. Until the early years of the present century few American farmers had much interest in what they called "book-farming." Since the First World War this attitude has changed.

So much attention has been given to the part played by the federal government in agricultural education and research that it is easy to overlook the work of the experiment stations in the land-grant colleges. The United States surpasses every other nation in the extent of her agricultural research and most of it is done in these experiment stations. The first agricultural experiment station in this country was established under the direction of Professor W. O. Atwater in 1875 at Wesleyan University, Middletown, Connecticut, through appropriations of the state and donations by Orange Judd, proprietor of the *American Agriculturist.* The notable work accomplished here encouraged Congress to pass the Hatch Act of 1887. Under its terms experiment stations have been established in each of the states, where scientists often specialize in some problem connected with their particular section— for example, diseases and improvement of the cotton plant in Alabama and the pineapple in Florida, the proper feeding of cattle in Texas, new varieties of sugar cane in Louisiana, rust-resisting wheat in Minnesota, and diseases of potatoes in Vermont. Agricultural research has increased the annual value of crops by hundreds of millions, but there is still much to be done in this direction. The average yield of wheat per acre in America is only half that of England, Germany, or Holland, although the fields in those countries have been cultivated for centuries. Again it should be pointed out that we fail to equal western Europe in yield per acre not because less is known here of scientific agricultural methods but because our uppermost interest is to produce more per unit of labor rather than per acre.

Especially interesting have been the effects on scientific agriculture of the pressure of the population on land. As the arable land was occupied, settlers pressed westward into the semiarid country between the region of adequate rainfall and the Rockies. This movement was stimulated by a series of wet years in the early eighties. In later years, when normal weather returned, a partial solution for the lack of rainfall was provided in dry farming. The principles of dry farming call for plowing the land deep after harvest, disking deep after each rainfall, pulverizing the topsoil and keeping it free from weeds, and in alternate years tilling through the summer without raising a crop—all of them expedients to lessen evaporation. To aid in this type of farming the Department of Agriculture has imported drought-resisting species of wheat, corn, and other plants from the dry regions of Asia and Africa. Dry farming has opened up a great deal of land to agriculture, but it has also helped to destroy much land. Heavy winds have blown away millions of acres of topsoil and sometimes rendered the land useless for agriculture.

IRRIGATION AND RECLAMATION

As the farmer pushed into the Great Plains and the foothills of the Rockies it became increasingly clear that his primary problem was lack of water. Cheap metal windmills and dry farming offered only partial solutions. From the early settlement days there was the continuous hope that much could be accomplished by irrigation. Although the federal government was giving away 160 acres of fertile land under the Homestead Act, it authorized under the Desert Land Act in 1877 the purchase of 640 acres at $1.25 per acre (25 cents down and $1.00 within three years) on condition that a certain amount be irrigated within three years. A holding of this size might be necessary for dry farming, but irrigation was better adapted to a small acreage intensively cultivated. In any event, this legislation accomplished little except to stimulate land frauds. But propaganda for irrigation through federal aid continued unabated during the late eighties and the nineties. In 1888 Congress provided for an irrigation survey and in 1894 passed the Carey Act. Under it the states in the arid region might receive 1,000,000 acres of public land and authorize irrigation through private enterprise; but they had to reserve authority to pass on the plans submitted and on the charges for water rates. The land was generally sold at 50 cents an acre, and the water rights of these projects averaged from $30.00 to $40.00 an acre, paid for usually in ten annual installments; the irrigation companies retained control of reservoirs, dams, and other equipment until full payment had been made.

Artificial irrigation, however, proceeded slowly, chiefly for two reasons. In the first place a large amount of capital was involved. This meant that when the country finally committed itself to large-scale projects only the federal government could command the necessary resources. In the second place, only a relatively small area can be irrigated. Federal participation finally came in the Reclamation Act of 1902, which provided for the setting aside of proceeds from the sale of public lands in sixteen designated states, to be used as a fund for irrigation projects. When money is available, the Secretary of the Interior may award contracts for such works. The farmers, who have taken up the land either by purchase or under the Homestead Act, defray the cost of the work by annual payments, thus perpetuating the fund. Under this act and subsequent appropriations over $300,000,000 has been spent in the examination, construction, and operation of projects for the reclamation of arid regions. By 1950 over 2,275,000 irrigated acres were in cultivation. The value of the crops produced on them amounts to over $250,000,000 annually.

Completion of the score or more projects now under construction by the Bureau of Reclamation of the Department of the Interior will add several million more acres to the irrigated area. Among the most noted of the irrigation projects are the Roosevelt Dam in Arizona, the Arrowrock Dam in Idaho, the Elephant Butte Dam in New Mexico, the Boulder Dam on the Colorado River, and the Grand Coulee in Washington. The latter alone, it is estimated, will irrigate more than 1,000,000 acres, about as much land as in the state of Delaware. Although considerable valuable farm land has been reclaimed in this way, too much cannot be expected from this in the future. Only limited areas of the Great Plains—probably not more than one-sixteenth at the most—are located where water is available. This water the federal government is rapidly conserving and putting to use. The cheap electric power provided by federally built dams (at present with a kilowatt capacity of over 4,000,000) may in the end prove as valuable as the irrigation projects.

THE BATTLE FOR ECONOMIC EQUALITY

Faced with overproduction and declining prices, the farmers during the last four decades of the nineteenth century kept up a ceaseless struggle to share more fully the rising level of living of society as a whole. Their battle against railroad abuses culminated in state and federal regulation and their fight against monopoly prices brought state and federal legislation. Their struggle for inflation and fair interest rates, on the other hand, made little progress up to 1890. Probably the Populist platform of 1892 comes as close as any thing to stating the farmers' program at the end of the century. Among its important economic and political demands were a flexible currency divorced from any banking control; loans at 2 per cent interest; free and unlimited coinage of gold and silver at 16 to 1; a graduated income tax; postal savings banks; government ownership of railroads, telegraph, and telephones; a secret ballot; direct election of Senators; and the initiative and referendum. There was also an undercurrent of opposition to monopoly. This program (most of which has long since been attained) was considered essential to re-establish economic and political equality. The story of the

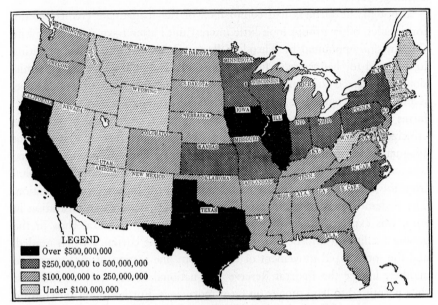

LEGEND
■ Over $500,000,000
▨ $250,000,000 to 500,000,000
▨ $100,000,000 to 250,000,000
□ Under $100,000,000

(From *Statistical Abstract, 1940*, p. 670.)

GROSS FARM INCOME BY STATES, 1939.

Rental and benefit payments are not included in the income shown on the map.

conflict as it related to railroads, trusts, and currency will be told in succeeding chapters. It is sufficient here to note only one aspect of it, the effort to obtain improved credit facilities.

Since the West was largely developed on borrowed money, it was normally in its earlier years a debtor region. When in need of capital it was forced to borrow from eastern moneylenders, often at exorbitant rates of interest. While 6 or 7 per cent might be the usual rates (including all costs) on eastern farm mortgages, farmers in the West were paying 8 or 10 and sometimes as high as 15 per cent. This discrepancy was due in part to the greater risks involved in frontier loans and in part to the inadequate banking facilities in the West. Although the situation improved after 1900 as more banks were established in that section and as insurance companies extended their investments in farm mortgages, the general credit situation continued to be disadvantageous for the farmer. The natural reaction of the debtor farmer was to demand a monetary and banking system that would provide cheap and easy money. This explains the western farmers' opposition to the first and second United States Banks, their opposition after the Civil War to greenback contraction, and their advocacy of free and unlimited coinage of gold and silver at 16 to 1. It also explains their demand for more liberal banking laws.[12]

Although the farmers had complained of the inadequate credit facilities for decades, other groups took little interest until after 1900. A Country Life Commission appointed by Theodore Roosevelt in that year called attention to the need for better credit facilities, and the National Monetary Commission familiarized this country with the farm mortgage systems of Europe. Republicans, Progressives, and Democrats all promised action in their platforms in 1912. The existing national bank system, established in 1863, was criticized specifically by the farmer on two grounds: first, that it did not adequately serve small communities because the minimum capital required was too great; and second, that it encouraged the flow of accumulated capital from the country to the city, where it was used for industry or speculation. The Federal Reserve System, established by a Democratic administration in 1913, was expected to be of particular aid to the agricultural class in the greater facilities it afforded for the expansion of the currency when needed, and the more rapid movement of funds from one section of the country to another. Under the Federal Reserve Act national banks were for the first time permitted to lend money on farm mortgages. Furthermore, agricultural paper running six months could be rediscounted at the Federal Reserve bank, whereas commercial paper, to be eligible for rediscount, must mature within three months.

More direct in its application to farmers was the system established under the Federal Farm Loan Act of 1916. This act had two main objectives; the first was to make it easier for farmers to obtain loans for periods of six months or more, and the second was to enable them to secure funds at a lower rate of interest. The act authorized the establishment of twelve Federal Land banks, with an initial capitalization fixed at $750,000 each, under the supervision of a Federal Farm Loan Board appointed by the President. These banks did not lend directly to individuals, but rediscounted for co-operative borrowing groups known as "National Farm Loan Associations." These Associations had to have at least ten members and to borrow at least $20,000. Loans were not to exceed 50 per cent of the value of the land and 20 per cent of the value of the permanent improvements. The Federal Land banks were to secure funds beyond the initial capitalization by selling bonds

[12] On farm credit after 1897 see H. U. Faulkner, *Decline of Laissez Faire*, pp. 358–365.

based on the mortgages obtained from the farmers. As these bonds were exempt from taxation (except inheritance taxes) and were considered a safe form of investment it was hoped that money would be easily forthcoming to lend to farmers at low rates of interest.[13] The Federal Farm Loan Act also created Joint-Stock Land banks (subsequently liquidated under the Farm Credit Act of 1933), similar to the Federal Land banks, to be incorporated by private individuals; they obtained funds by selling first-mortgage, tax-exempt farm-loan bonds on the market. These banks could deal directly with the farmer instead of through associations.

Even the credit facilities provided by the legislation just described did not prove entirely satisfactory. Emphasis had been placed on long-term credits, but in the early 1920's farmers also realized their need for better facilities for short-term borrowing. These were provided by the Agricultural Credits Act of 1923, which established twelve Federal Intermediate Credit banks (as adjuncts to the existing Federal Land banks). They do not deal with individual borrowers or lend directly on land security, but are banks for rediscount of agricultural and livestock paper for periods of six months to three years. Five millions of capital for these banks was furnished by the United States Treasury.

Under this legislation the farmer was now able to borrow money at reasonable rates of interest for any length of time. He was on the road to freedom from oppressive interest rates, and had virtually achieved the demands of the earlier Populists. Nevertheless, the entire agricultural credit structure was reorganized, extended, and liberalized, as we shall see, by the Farm Credit Act of 1933,[14] for by this time it was clear that more than easy credit was necessary to save farmers from bankruptcy.

RECENT AGRICULTURAL TENDENCIES

Speaking broadly, the history of American agriculture until about 1890 was chiefly the story of the westward movement and the continuous opening of new land for speculation and production. In detail this story has been modified by the invention of new machinery, by the necessary adaptation of crops to new soil, and by the gradual shifting of production to new regions whose superiority severely handicapped older communities. The placing of large areas of new land under cultivation was in turn attended by a decline in agricultural prices and by the production of a surplus for export.

With the opening of the twentieth century, American agriculture entered a new period in its history, radically different from the old. As most of the

---

[13] Subscription was open to the public, but so little interest was shown that the federal government was forced to subscribe $8,891,270 of the $9,000,000 necessary for the twelve banks.

[14] Below, p. 664.

land immediately available for farming had been pre-empted by 1900, further additions to arable land have come from dry farming, from irrigation or drainage, or from putting into use woodland or other unimproved land on the farm. While the farm area increased by 15,000,000 acres a year for the thirty years previous to 1900, the increase from 1900 to 1910 was only 4,000,-000 acres a year, or 4.8 per cent. The decade 1910 to 1920, however, showed an increase of 8.8 per cent in farm acreage and of 5.1 per cent in improved land; this can be accounted for by the unusual stimulus of the war. The percentage of the land area of the United States included in farms increased throughout our history up to 1920, when it reached 50.2; by 1925 it had decreased to 48.6, but by 1930 it reached 51.8. There was also a decline after 1920 in the number of farms (from 6,448,343 in 1920 to 5,382,162 in 1950), a phenomenon caused chiefly by scarcity of labor, consolidation of farms due to the introduction of new machinery, and the boll weevil.

Until 1910 American agriculture was still extensive in its nature and there was no hesitancy in sacrificing land to labor. The farmer resembled the miner, who took out riches from the soil without giving anything in return. The increasing value of farm products and of land has turned the farmer to more intensive agriculture. This movement seemed well under way during the first decade of the century but was not so pronounced during the next ten years when the demands of the First World War opened new land to cultivation. Nevertheless, large areas of corn, barley, and buckwheat have been turned over to more intensive crops, and the increasing use of fertilizer demonstrates more careful husbandry. While the production percentages in the 1920 Census did not keep pace with the increase in the acreage devoted to many of the products, this may not by any means mean less intensive farming. In view of the poorer land brought under cultivation, the opposite may be true.

Although agricultural increase during the first two decades of the present century was not as rapid as that in industry and mining, it was nevertheless notable. Total production, for example, between 1897 and 1917 increased 30 per cent. The early twentieth century, however, showed some shifts in production. Citrus fruits, sugar, oil crops (cottonseed, peanuts), and poultry and eggs moved ahead most rapidly, while hay, grains, wool, and meat animals showed the slowest advance. The production of buckwheat and flaxseed actually declined. The United States had long been the largest tobacco-exporting nation, but the chief cause for the increased output during these years was the growing domestic consumption, the result in part of the shift to cigarette smoking during the war and the growth of cigarette smoking by women. Cotton production experienced between 1897 and 1914 a period of notable expansion as production moved westward into Oklahoma and western Texas. Later production was held up by destruction from the boll weevil, by decline in exports, and by greater competition from abroad. Although the United States continued to import four-fifths of her sugar from abroad, domestic production was increasing, chiefly in beet sugar rather than cane. One of the most interesting dietary shifts during these years was that to citrus fruits, grown chiefly in California and Florida.

An outstanding factor in agricultural life has been the decided movement of population toward the cities; neither rural population nor farm production has advanced as rapidly as the increase in urban population. As late as 1910 the urban population (that is, those living in towns of 2500 or more)

POPULATION AND AGRICULTURE

	1880	1900	1910	1920	1930
Rural population[a] (in millions)	32,950	39,313	41,637	42,437	44,637
Percentage rural	65.0	51.7	45.3	40.1	36.4
Percentage of increase over preceding census	..	9.5	5.9	1.9	2.6
Percentage of increase of population as a whole over preceding census	30.1	20.7	21.0	14.9	7.7
Acres of improved land per capita of total population	5.7	5.5	5.2	4.8	4.3

[a] Defined in this table as population outside incorporated places.
Commerce Yearbook, 1932, I, 132, 133.

was still in the minority (45.8 per cent); but in 1920 it had mounted to 51.4 per cent, and in 1930 to 56.2 per cent. On the whole this tendency has been for the best. As one government statistician aptly puts it:

A century or more ago some four-fifths of the population was engaged in agriculture, which means that most of the people had to give their time to producing practically bare necessities. Ever since, there has been a rapid decline in this proportion, representing the freeing of larger and larger numbers to produce commodities and services of a less essential character, thus raising the standard of living. This shift has been due largely to advances in the productivity of agriculture itself, resulting in part from the opening up of better lands, but much more from improvements in methods of production.[15]

To this statement should be added the obvious fact that many food-processing activities formerly performed on the farm have been transferred to the town or city.

Agriculture has steadily lost ground in percentage of population, of gainfully employed, and of national wealth. The proportion of our population engaged in agriculture is now smaller than in most of the countries of the world. Argentina, Belgium, Holland, Switzerland, England and Wales, and (somewhat surprisingly) Australia are the only countries reporting a lower

[15] *Commerce Yearbook, 1932,* I, 31.

proportion in the years since the First World War.[16] Truly, the United States
has become an industrialized nation.

The rapid occupation of the West under the stimulus of the Homestead
Act and the building of the transcontinental railroads increased the production of foodstuffs beyond normal needs, and from the end of the Civil
War until the late nineties American agriculture suffered from overproduction. Toward the end of the century the demand for foodstuffs began to
overtake the supply, and from then until the opening of World War I the
farmers enjoyed their first real period of prosperity of any length since the
Civil War. A hectic boom period characterized the World War years, and

PERCENTAGE OF ALL FARMS OPERATED BY TENANTS, 1880–1930

	1880	1890	1900	1910	1920	1925	1930
United States	26	28	35	37	38	39	42
New England	9	9	9	8	7	6	6
Middle Atlantic	19	22	25	22	21	16	15
East North Central	20	23	26	27	28	26	27
West North Central	21	24	30	31	34	38	40
South Atlantic	36	38	44	46	47	44	48
East South Central	37	38	48	51	50	50	56
West South Central	35	39	49	53	53	59	62
Mountain	7	7	12	11	15	22	24
Pacific	17	15	20	17	20	16	18

Yearbook of Agriculture, 1930, p. 1008; *Statistical Abstract, 1933*, p. 548.

then came deflation and depression. The natural result of many of these
factors up to 1920 was a sudden and enormous rise in land values during the
first two decades of the twentieth century. Between 1900 and 1920 the value
of farm lands and crops increased more than fourfold, and the prices of farm
products nearly threefold (value changes due only in part to the rise in the
price level), although the mass of crop production during the same period
increased less than 50 per cent. The deflation of the postwar years wiped out
part of this advance, but the figures for 1930 still showed a decided gain
over those for 1910.[17]

Curiously enough, no matter whether the period was one of depression
or prosperity, farm tenancy seemed to increase. While many reasons have
been offered to explain this phenomenon, probably the most important has
been the rising value of lands in areas whose products require expensive
machinery. In such a situation it was beyond the ability of the poor man
to meet the costs. Government economists talked much of the "ladder theory," that is, the climbing of the agricultural laborer through tenancy to
farmownership, but statistics seemed to show that more descended the ladder

[16] *Ibid.*, II, 662–664.
[17] The agricultural depression of the 1920's and 1930's will be discussed in chap. 28.

than climbed it. In any event the tendency reversed itself about 1935. Since then the farms operated by tenants have declined to 26.8 per cent.

Of all the influences which affected American agriculture in the half-century after the Civil War, none was more important than foreign trade. Agriculture cannot move beyond the self-sufficing stage unless there is a market for its surplus. For the American farmer this market was provided during the last half of the nineteenth century and the early years of the twentieth in the rapidly growing population of western Europe. Agricultural exports increased more or less steadily from 1860 until around the turn of the century, when the high point was reached. Fifteen years later they were artificially stimulated by the First World War. The peak year for corn exports was in 1897, when 212,000,000 bushels were exported; for wheat, in 1901, with 239,000,000 bushels exported. Meat and meat products, which had been relatively insignificant as exports before the Civil War, soon ranked third in importance, with a value of $179,000,000 in 1900.

The effect on Europe was to disorganize the agricultural structure and to speed industrialization. As one Austrian economist has suggested, this flow of agricultural produce had an effect upon the economy of the Old World comparable to that produced by the flow of gold and silver after the discovery of America. For America, this market speeded the advancing frontier, the occupation of new land, the flow of immigration, and the improvement and enlargement of transportation and marketing facilities. At the same time the agricultural surplus helped to pay the unequal balance of trade between Europe and America and made possible large-scale borrowing from Europe. This in turn led to the development of industry in America, artificially stimulated by a protective tariff system. When the export of agricultural commodities began to decline after 1900 the United States had become sufficiently urbanized to take up the slack. It was not the decline of the European market between 1900 and 1915 that injured the American farmer; it was the artificial revival of that market during the First World War and its decline in the 1920's.

GEOGRAPHIC DISTRIBUTION

Although the frontier had officially ended in 1890, the movement of agriculture continued westward. It is true that the production of wheat had begun to decline in California by the 1890's, but production increased in the Red River Valley, the Kansas-Nebraska area, the Dakotas, and the Oregon-Washington area. Like wheat, the corn belt also showed a movement toward the west, followed by hog production and the slaughtering of hogs. In the Northeast beef cattle declined in the face of a growing dairy industry, but increased on the Great Plains. The latter years of the nineteenth century saw a tripling of cotton production in Texas and a few years later a similar advance in Oklahoma. While areas on the east coast and in the Middle West near the great concentrations of population maintained or increased their truck gardening and fruit growing, the great advance came in Florida and California.

The Northeast. Influences which were at work even before the Civil War to modify agricultural conditions in the Northeast have since been active in an increasingly greater degree. A century ago New England and the Middle Atlantic States were agriculturally self-sufficient. Today New England imports 80 per cent of her food. Competition of western products made possible through the development of transportation facilities, and the growth of industrial life, have radically altered the nature of agricultural products. Raising livestock for wool and meat has given place to dairying and to vegetable and fruit growing. The most fertile lands in New England are the rich bottom lands of the Connecticut Valley, largely given over to onions and tobacco, and the Aroostook Valley in Maine, where one-tenth of the potatoes sold in the country are raised. Where this type of farming is impossible, the competition of the West has often forced the poorer land out of cultivation. In New England between 1860 and 1910 farm land under cultivation decreased by over 5,000,000 acres, or 42 per cent, resulting in the thousands of deserted farms to be seen in this section. During these years cattle decreased from 56 to 20 per 100 of the population, and sheep from 60 to 4. Although the number of farms in New England has continued to decline during the decades 1920–1950, there appears to be no diminution in the agricultural products of the region. While rural population declined relatively, the whole population increased by 110 per cent. The richer soil in New York, Pennsylvania, and New Jersey has kept a greater amount of land under cultivation than in New England, but there has been the same transition to truck farming, dairy products, and fruits. This is the result of a nearby and ever-increasing urban market.

The South. Before the Civil War the South was almost entirely agricultural, engaged in raising some foodstuffs but dependent chiefly upon the great staple, cotton, which was produced on large plantations by the labor of Negro slaves. The war and the freeing of the slaves changed the system. The products remained the same, but the manner of production was altered. Ruined by the war, the great planter had neither resources nor equipment to continue the old plantation under a wage system. Some manner of livelihood, however, had to be found for him and for the new freeman. The result was the gradual breaking up of the large holdings into small farms ranging from twenty to fifty acres, which are operated by Negroes, usually as sharecroppers or tenant farmers. While in some cases (about one-fourth) cash rentals are paid, in most the farms are let out under a system by which the owner furnishes the tools and sometimes the seeds and a mule, and in return takes one-half of the corn and cotton raised.

The effect of this system has been almost as destructive to the soil as that of the old plantation system. There was actually less improved land in the South Atlantic division in 1900 than in 1860. Not only has this tenant farming been ruinous to the soil, but it has tended to perpetuate the one-crop system. The owner of the land or the local merchant who provides tools and supplies and in return takes a lien on the future crop insists that it be cotton, because that is the most salable product. It is, in fact, the crop which the Negro has been trained for generations to raise, and the simplicity of its production, as in slave days, fits in with the stage of his agricultural advancement. While it might be an overstatement to say that slavery in the South was followed by a period of serfdom in which the Negro was held in bondage by being constantly in debt to the landowner or cotton factor, it would not be far from the truth. This was the evolution in southern society—a development made inevitable after the war by the economic situation, by the intellectual status of the Negro at that time, and by the failure of the North to make possible for the Negroes a more rapid adjustment to a free society.

In considering southern agriculture it should be remembered that thousands of poor whites as well as the Negro have fallen victims to the system of sharecropping. The Negro, in fact, during recent decades has shown greater ability than the white to push up from this status. It is estimated that nearly 200,000 Negroes own their own farms, aggregating 20,000,000 acres and valued at over $500,000,000. But the tenant system for both blacks and whites is still predominant (it actually increased during the thirties), with the yield per acre discouragingly small and the average annual income of the tenant farmer before the last war only about $150. The methods are still crude and wasteful, and so little cereal and meat are raised that this agricultural region still imports foodstuffs. The salvation of the southern farmer has been the usually steady demand and the high price paid for cotton. The cotton crop increased from 3,841,000 bales (500 pounds) in 1860 to 14,828,000 in 1929, the South still producing from 60 to 65 per cent of the world's yield. This supremacy has been challenged by the northward advance of the boll weevil, but this has not been an unmixed curse, for it has forced certain sections to turn from one staple to diversified farming.

The center of cotton production continues to be west of the Alleghenies, with Texas the largest producer. The center of tobacco culture, on the other hand, has moved back east of the mountains, with North Carolina far in the lead of the producing states. Sweet potatoes, peanuts, pecans, garden vegetables for the northern market, and semitropical fruit are now being grown in rapidly increasing amounts, bringing new prosperity to Georgia, Florida, and the Gulf states. There has also been a considerable development of truck farming and dairying near industrial centers for the local market. The potential agricultural possibilities of the South are enormous, and many students believe that the greatest agricultural progress in the future will come south of the Ohio and the Mason and Dixon's line.

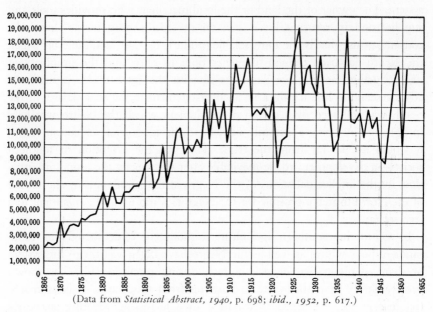

(Data from *Statistical Abstract, 1940*, p. 698; *ibid., 1952*, p. 617.)

PRODUCTION OF COTTON IN THE UNITED STATES BY 500-POUND BALES, 1865–1951.

The Upper Mississippi Valley. By 1890 the frontier line of farms had pushed west until practically all the arable land was occupied. In this great region between the Alleghenies and the Rockies has arisen the most productive agricultural area in the world. Its chief products are corn, wheat, and livestock. The central states from Ohio to Iowa were found well adapted to corn, and its production has laid the foundation for the raising of hogs, cattle, and poultry. While the center of corn production has to a certain extent remained fixed since 1860,[18] the center of wheat has moved steadily west. In 1860 most of the wheat was grown east of the Mississippi, but by 1939 almost 50 per cent was raised in the five states of Kansas, North Dakota, Oklahoma, Montana, and Washington. The westward advance was accel-

[18] In 1859 over 70 per cent of the corn was raised in Illinois, Ohio, Missouri, Indiana, Kentucky, Tennessee, Iowa, Virginia, Alabama, and Georgia. In 1929 some 67 per cent was raised in the ten states of Iowa, Illinois, Nebraska, Indiana, Ohio, Missouri, South Dakota, Kansas, Texas, and Kentucky (listed in the order of their importance).

erated by certain inventions in flour manufacture, notably the "middlings purifier" of La Croix and the substitution of rollers for stones in crushing the grain. These inventions allowed the production of fine white flour from the hard spring wheat, the type best grown on the Minnesota and Dakota prairies. Under the liberal policy of the government large claims were staked out, and often through actual fraud immense farms were built up where the soil was worked for wheat alone by the wonderful new machinery. These "bonanza farms" of a thousand acres or more not only wore out the soil but glutted the market with wheat and drove prices down.

The growing value of farm land (particularly marked from 1900 to 1920) which has necessitated more intensive cultivation, the wearing out of the land, and the immigration of farmers into the Northwest have all helped to break up the large holdings and in many cases to substitute other kinds of agriculture. In Wisconsin, where twenty years ago wheat was the chief product, the farmers have turned to other cereals, to livestock, and particularly to dairying; this state leads all others in the value of dairy products. In 1929 she produced 60 per cent of the cheese made in this country. Though not so well situated, Minnesota has taken from Wisconsin the lead in the production of butter. By 1929 over half the nation's creamery butter was produced in Minnesota, Iowa, Wisconsin, Nebraska, and Ohio. At the same time, the competition of Canadian wheat is turning the attention of Dakota farmers to dairy products. As the reaper and binder have made possible the great wheat farms of the West, so have the Babcock tester and the power churn and mixer made possible the rapid expansion in butter and cheese production.

The Far West. It was the gold stampede of 1849 that first brought large numbers to the Pacific coast, but the great wealth of this region was destined to be agricultural. The agricultural income of California today far outstrips her combined income from oil and mining, and the production cost more than triples that of the motion-picture industry. With the exception of Texas, she surpasses all the other states in the value of her agricultural products. She produces nearly one-half of the country's fresh fruit, about 95 per cent of its dried fruit, a third of its truck crops, and nearly a third of its canned fruits and vegetables. Only the scarcity of water prevents an even greater production from this incredibly fertile soil. Although California supports a large dairy industry, made possible by the large production of tame hay and the rapidly increasing population, her chief agricultural products are fruits, of both the subtropical and temperate varieties, and vegetables. In the Imperial Valley of southeastern California, in the Great Central Valley that stretches northward for hundreds of miles, and along the seacoast there have developed great farms where highly specialized commercial agriculture is carried on. If the future of agriculture is to resemble the "factory in the field," the future is already in evidence here. Huge farms, manned by migrant labor and often, as in large-scale business, controlled by the banks, are the general pattern. Two per cent of California's farms, it is estimated, control one-fourth of the acreage, produce nearly one-third of the crop value, and pay more than one-third of the bill for hired labor. Large-scale agriculture has been typical of this region since the days of the Mexican ranches. It has come down through the huge wheat fields which characterized California in the seventies and eighties and remains in the more recent development of fruit growing and truck farming. The seasonal and migrant agricultural labor which has received so much attention in recent years has been a serious economic and social problem in California since the earliest days.

In Oregon and Washington, where there is a greater variety of climate, agriculture is not specialized; fruit, wheat, dairy products, and wool are all produced in considerable quantities. Farther east the valleys and foothills of the Cordilleras, which hitherto had been supposed unarable, have been brought under cultivation by dry farming or irrigation. The introduction of durum wheat, kaffir corn, and a different type of alfalfa, all suitable to dry soil or cold climate, has helped to vegetate these regions. Huge irrigation projects now in the process of construction will undoubtedly considerably increase the productive area.

SELECTED READINGS

Everett, E. E., "American Agriculture—the First 300 Years," *Yearbook of Agriculture, 1940,* pp. 221–276.

Shannon, Fred, *The Farmer's Last Frontier,* chaps. 4–8, 11, 12.

Faulkner, H. U., *The Decline of Laissez Faire,* chaps. 13–14.

Hammond, M. B., *The Cotton Industry,* chaps. 4–6.

Buck, S. J., *The Agrarian Crusade.*

Flügel, F., and Faulkner, H. U., *Readings in the Economic and Social History of the United States,* chap. 17.

CHAPTER 20

DEVELOPMENT OF THE
INDUSTRIAL REVOLUTION

GROWTH OF INDUSTRY

THE factory system in America obtained its first real foothold during the period of the embargo and the War of 1812 and in the mills which sprang up in the succeeding years. Nevertheless it seems safe to say that "until about the year 1850, the bulk of general manufacturing done in the United States was carried on in the shop and the household, by the labor of the family or individual proprietors, with apprentice assistants, as contrasted with the present system of factory labor, compensated by wages, and assisted by power."[1] Since 1850 our economic life has been revolutionized as we followed in the wake of western Europe in substituting factory-made products for those made by hand labor. The development of the factory system has been continuous, but the process was immensely hastened by the demands of the Civil War. If the War of 1812 introduced the factory system, the Civil War brought an Industrial Revolution, and it is this development of the Industrial Revolution which was the outstanding feature of American economic life in the half-century after 1860.

More and more America turned to factory-made goods and to large-scale industry, and Americans occupied themselves increasingly with manufacturing. Until the decade of the eighties agriculture was the principal source of wealth, but the Census of 1890 showed that manufacturing had forged to the front, and ten years later the value of manufactured products was more than double that of agricultural.

The increasing value of manufactured over agricultural products is reflected in the concentration of population. The Census of 1920 reported, for the first time in our history, the urban population (those living in towns

[1] Twelfth Census, VII, liii.

of 2500 or over) as more than the rural, the percentages being 51.4 and 48.6, respectively. The percentage of people living in towns of over 8000 increased from 16.1 in 1860 to 43.8 in 1920. In 1950 the percentage of the urban population was 59; that of towns of 8000 or more was 49.3 in 1940. While the population from 1850 to 1900 trebled (from 23,192,000 to 75,995,000) and the products of agriculture nearly trebled ($1,600,000,000 to $4,717,070,000), the value of manufactures increased eleven-fold ($1,019,107,000 to $11,406,-927,000). From 1859 to 1914 the value of American manufactures increased eighteen-fold, and from 1859 to 1919 thirty-three-fold. Naturally this increase stands out when a comparison is made with foreign nations. M. G. Mulhall, in his *Industries and Wealth of Nations* (1896), shows how the United

COMPARISON OF THE VALUE OF AGRICULTURAL AND MANUFACTURED PRODUCTS

Value of Products	1889	1899	1909	1919
Agricultural	$2,460,107,000	$ 4,717,076,000	$ 8,498,311,000	$23,783,200,000
Manufactured (including those based on agriculture)	9,372,379,000	11,406,927,000	20,672,052,000	62,418,079,000

Statistical Abstract, 1921, pp. 862, 868. This table has not been continued in the *Statistical Abstract* for recent years, but the gross farm income of all crops including government payments for 1939 is estimated at $9,769,000,000 (*Statistical Abstract, 1940*, p. 668). The decline since 1919 represents the deflation from the prices of the First World War. The value of the products for all industry in 1937 was approximately $61,000,000,000 (*ibid.*, p. 805).

States, which had ranked fifth in the value of manufactured products in 1840 and fourth in 1860, had taken first place in 1894. At that time she produced twice as much as Great Britain and half as much as all Europe together.

The Census of Manufactures in 1909 gave the value of manufactured products as over $20,000,000,000. This figure may be compared with the Census of 1907 in Great Britain, which reported $8,000,000,000 for that nation, and with the estimate for Germany in 1913, which reported between $11,000,000,000 and $12,000,000,000. The United States, however, consumed a larger proportion of her manufactured goods at home than either of these nations, although there was a great actual increase in exports. In the normal years before the First World War, while Great Britain exported one-fourth, we exported less than one-tenth of our manufactured products, a proportion changed temporarily by the war.

Manufacturing was progressing favorably in the fifties when the panic of 1857 halted its development. The impetus to production given by the Civil War increased the number of establishments 79.6 per cent during the decade of the sixties, and the number of wage earners 56.6—the largest relative advances in any decade in our history. The severe panic of 1873 again retarded manufacturing, especially in the founding of new establishments, but before the decade had run its course recovery set in and a healthy progress was evident. The eighties showed the largest increase in manufacturing up to 1909 in capital invested and in wages paid, the growth during the decade amounting to 133.8 per cent for the former and 99.5 for the latter. Despite the depressing effect of the panic of 1893 on industry, figures for 1899 evidenced substantial gains. They pale into insignificance, however, before the enormous strides in the twentieth century, the second decade of which, including as it did the period of the First World War, surpassed all others in our history in percentage of increase in capital, wages, and value of products. This increase was, of course, partly discounted by the decrease in the purchasing power of the dollar.[2] While capital, wages, and value of products advanced 95, 158, and 157 per cent respectively from 1914 to 1919, the number of wage earners increased only 29.3 and the number of establishments only 5.2 per cent. More detailed statistics on the development of manufactures over a period of eighty-eight years are given in the table on the next page.

In a study of the development of manufacturing it is interesting to note the changes in the rank and importance of various industries. In 1860 the first four groups in value of products were dependent upon either agriculture or lumbering, while in 1914 four and in 1919 three groups (including the first) out of the first six were still dependent upon these sources. Although manufacturing from agricultural raw materials predominated, iron and steel manufacture had advanced by 1914 from fifth place to second; and foundry and machine-shop products, which in 1860 were included with crude iron and steel, ranked fourth as a separate division. Two new groups appeared among the first ten—car construction and repairs, and automobiles, both transportation products. Even among the great manufacturing groups the rank is not static, and no list long remains the same. For instance, between 1900 and 1914 automobile manufacture became so important that it was separated from machine-shop products and was in the eighth place. By 1929 it ranked first, exclusive of bodies and parts, but it dropped to second place in 1937. The products of the industry standing twenty-fifth in rank in 1914 (silk goods, including throwsters) had a higher value ($254,011,000) than those of the industry ranking first in 1860.

In the following tables, the industries are arranged according to value of products, not always a satisfactory measure of the importance of a given industry "because only a part of this value is actually created within the industry. Another part, and often a much larger one, is contributed by the value of the materials used."[3] Statistics for both cost of materials and value of products include a large amount of duplication because of the use of the products of some establishments as materials by others. The value added by

[2] Below, p. 580.
[3] *Census of Manufactures, 1929*, I, 35.

MANUFACTURES: SUMMARY, 1849 TO 1937

	Number of Establishments (in Thousands)	Percentage of Increase or Decrease (−)	Wage Earners (Average for the Year) (in Thousands)	Percentage of Increase or Decrease (−)	Wages (in Millions of Dollars)	Percentage of Increase or Decrease (−)	Cost of Material Supplies, Fuel, and Power (in Millions of Dollars)	Percentage of Increase or Decrease (−)	Value of Products (in Millions of Dollars)	Percentage of Increase or Decrease (−)	Value Added by Manufacture (in Millions of Dollars)	Percentage of Increase or Decrease (−)
Factories and hand and neighborhood industries:												
1849	123	—	957	—	237	—	555	—	1,019	—	464	—
1859	140	14.1	1,311	37.0	379	60.0	1,032	85.8	1,886	85.1	854	84.1
1869	252	79.6	2,054	56.6	620	63.8	1,991	93.0	3,386	79.5	1,395	63.3
1879	254	0.7	2,733	33.0	948	52.8	3,397	70.6	5,370	58.6	1,973	41.4
1889	355	40.0	4,252	55.6	1,891	99.5	5,162	52.0	9,372	74.5	4,210	113.4
1899	512	44.1	5,306	24.8	2,321	22.7	7,344	42.3	13,000	38.7	5,656	34.3
Factories, excluding hand and neighborhood industries and establishments with products valued at less than $500:												
1899	205	—	4,510	—	1,895	—	6,441	—	11,103	—	4,662	—
1909	265	29.3	6,273	39.1	3,210	69.3	11,876	84.3	20,068	80.7	8,191	75.6
1919	210	−20.7	8,431	34.4	9,673	201.3	36,283	205.5	60,053	199.2	23,770	190.1
1929	207	−1.4	8,380	−0.6	10,910	12.7	37,441	3.1	68,178	13.5	30,737	29.3
1937	167	−19.3	8,569	2.2	10,112	−7.3	35,539	−5.0	60,713	−10.9	25,174	−18.0

Census of Manufactures, 1937, Part I, pp. 18 f. Percentages since 1899 determined by the author.

RANK OF LEADING INDUSTRIES, 1860, 1914, AND 1929

Rank	1860 Industry	Value of Products (in Thousands)	1914 Industry	Value of Products (in Thousands)	1929 Industry	Value of Products (in Thousands)
1	Flour and meal	$248,580	Slaughtering and meat packing	$1,651,965	Motor vehicles	$3,722,793
2	Cotton goods	115,726	Iron and steel, steelworks, and rolling mills	918,665	Meat packing, wholesale	3,434,634
3	Lumber planed and sawed	104,928	Flour-mill and gristmill products	877,680	Iron and steel, steelworks, and rolling mills	3,365,789
4	Boots and shoes	91,889	Foundry and machine-shop products	866,545	Foundry and machine-shop products	2,791,462
5	Iron founding and machinery	88,648	Lumber and timber products	715,310	Petroleum refining	2,639,665
6	Clothing, including furnishing	88,095	Cotton goods	676,569	Electric machinery	2,300,916
7	Leather, including morocco and patent leather	75,698	Cars and general shop construction and repairs by steam railroad companies	510,041	Printing and publishing, newspapers, and periodicals	1,738,299
8	Woolen goods, including yarn, etc.	65,706	Automobiles	503,230	Clothing, women's	1,709,581
9	Liquors	56,588	Boots and shoes	501,760	Motor vehicles, bodies and parts	1,537,930
10	Steam engines	46,757	Printing and publishing, newspapers, and periodicals	495,906	Bread and bakery products	1,526,111
11	Iron, cast	36,638	Bread and other products	491,893	Cotton goods	1,524,177
12	Iron, forged, rolled, and wrought	36,537	Clothing, women's	437,888	Lumber and timber products	1,273,472
13	Provisions (beef, pork, etc.)	31,986	Clothing, men's	458,211	Car and general construction and repairs, steam railroads	1,184,435
14	Printing (book, job, etc.)	31,063	Smelting and refining copper	444,022	Cigars and cigarettes	1,066,909
15	Carriages	26,849	Liquors, malt	442,149	Flour and other grain-mill products	1,060,269

Figures for 1860 compiled from Census of 1860, volume on *Manufactures*; for 1914, from *Abstract of Census of Manufactures, 1914*, Table 220, pp. 516 ff.; for 1929, from *Abstract of Census of Manufactures, 1929*, I, 21, 35.

RELATIVE IMPORTANCE OF LEADING INDUSTRIES FOR THE UNITED STATES, 1937

	Number of Establishments	Wage Earners		Cost of Materials, Fuel Purchased, Energy, and Contract Work		Value of Products		Value Added by Manufacture	
		Average for the Year	Rank	Amount in Thousands of Dollars	Rank	Amount in Thousands of Dollars	Rank	Amount in Thousands of Dollars	Rank
All industries	166,794	8,560,231		35,539,333		60,712,872		25,173,530	
Steelworks and rolling mills	6,410	479,342	1	1,833,745	4	3,330,491	1	1,496,747	1
Motor vehicles	131	194,527	8	2,394,269	1	3,069,219	2	701,949	5
Meat packing, wholesale	1,160	127,477	15	2,386,090	2	2,787,358	3	401,267	13
Petroleum refining	365	83,182	22	2,064,307	3	2,546,746	4	482,439	10
Motor vehicles, bodies and parts	936	284,814	4	1,275,073	5	2,080,018	5	804,945	4
Electrical machinery, apparatus and supplies	1,435	257,660	5	642,867	10	1,622,098	6	979,232	3
Bread and bakery products	17,193	239,388	6	727,022	7	1,426,163	7	699,141	6
Printing and publishing, newspapers and periodicals	9,244	135,215	14	393,021	18	1,396,031	8	1,003,010	2
Cigarettes	34	26,149	70	771,522	6	968,927	9	197,405	30
Cotton woven goods	677	336,104	2	525,947	13	967,110	10	441,163	12
Machinery not otherwise classified	2,298	146,712	11	375,647	20	964,151	11	588,504	7
Paper	647	110,809	17	567,449	11	957,940	12	390,491	15
Chemicals not otherwise classified	601	78,951	25	455,062	16	932,750	13	477,688	11
Flour and other grain-mill products	2,238	26,390	69	722,711	8	856,310	14	133,600	41
Lumber and timber products	7,647	323,948	3	345,800	24	848,481	15	502,681	9

Abstract of Census of Manufactures, 1937, pp. 34-36.

manufacture gives a more accurate idea of the importance of the industry; most significant of all, particularly when unemployment becomes widespread, is the average number of wage earners employed. In these tables the Census of 1937 has been used rather than more recent figures because this was the last census taken under approximately normal conditions before the Second World War. Changes between 1929 and 1937 in the relative value of the first fifteen industries have not been important. It should be noted, however, that paper and chemicals entered this group. Cigarette manufacturing had been separated from cigars in the census, but nevertheless had advanced from fourteenth to ninth place.

The remarkable expansion in manufacturing has been attended by a corresponding growth in economic independence. During the colonial period and the years before the Civil War we were largely dependent upon Europe for much of the better class of manufactured goods; our exports consisted chiefly of our surplus of food and raw materials. The high tariff walls, and the influx of immigration from Europe that provided cheap labor, made it possible to exploit our unsurpassed mineral and agricultural wealth. Except for certain rare metals, we have the materials to manufacture almost anything we need at home. The First World War broke even the great chemical monopoly of the Germans. Imports now consist to a large extent of luxuries, tropical fruits, rubber, sugar, coffee, and manufactured goods involving much hand labor. But they also include certain commodities, for which substitutes would have to be found in case of an indefinite blockade. However, such a blockade would not seriously interfere with our ability to live and carry on the economic functions, particularly since the development of synthetic rubber.

CAUSES OF THE GROWTH OF MANUFACTURE

Undoubtedly a strong impetus was given to the growth of manufacturing by the imperative needs of the Civil War and by the stimulation of high prices resulting from war demands and the printing of fiat money. The real causes of the long upward swing are more fundamental. The United States became a great manufacturing nation first of all because of her unsurpassed natural resources. Rich agricultural products, such as livestock and cotton, have formed the basis of some of her most important manufacturing industries. Moreover, iron, coal, oil, copper, and other minerals have been obtainable in large quantities. In addition to raw materials, manufacturing is dependent upon labor and a market. Labor was secured by the natural rapid increase of population in an undeveloped country and by millions of immigrants, many of whom were unfitted by training and environment for other than factory work. American manufacturers could not look to the older countries for a large market, but had to build one at home in competition with foreign products. Such a market was partially supplied by the continued growth of the population, but particularly by the needs of the great agricultural South and West. During the three decades 1900–1930 the domestic market was increasingly supplemented by a growing export trade as the United States embarked aggressively upon a program of extending her foreign commerce and investment.

The high tariffs which began with the Civil War became a fixture in our system and have undoubtedly stimulated manufacturing, both by the large profits allowed to well-established industries and by the protection given to infant enterprises. That the United States would have experienced a marvelous development of manufacture without a protective tariff there is no reason to doubt, but it is equally evident that high tariff walls have considerably speeded the growth of certain industries. Under Republican and Democratic administrations alike, the government has ordinarily sought to promote industrial prosperity.

In contrast to the system of high protective tariffs, the internal policy of the government, at least until the 1930's, has been largely *laissez faire*. The lack of government interference during the period of great growth undoubtedly imparted a spirit of confidence amounting sometimes to recklessness on the part of the entrepreneur. Even after attempts to exercise control were made in 1887 and 1890, for a long time these efforts met with slight success. Manufacturing has also been aided by the freedom of interstate commerce, a factor which was instrumental in the acceptance of the Constitution and amply justified it. "The mainland of the United States," it has been said, "is the largest area in the civilized world which is thus unrestricted by customs, excises, or national prejudice, and its population possesses, because of its great collective wealth, a larger consuming capacity than that of any other nation."[4] "It is the enjoyment of free-trade and protection at the same time," asserted James G. Blaine, "which has contributed to the unexampled development and marvelous prosperity of the United States."[5] Both have undoubtedly helped, particularly the former. The newness and freedom of the country have reacted upon the character of both capitalists and laborers. The former have generally been inventive, resourceful, ready to take risks and to seize whatever advantages offered; the latter have developed a mobility unknown elsewhere, and have been freer to desert the old hand processes for the new machinery than in older countries where there were fewer opportunities for change.

[4] *Twelfth Census of the United States*, VII, lvii.

[5] James G. Blaine, *Twenty Years of Congress*, I, 211. Unfortunately this freedom of interstate trade has been significantly modified in recent years by state legislation generally upheld by the Supreme Court. See below, pp. 531–532.

Without transportation facilities, manufacturing, other than purely local, would be well-nigh impossible. The 26,000 miles of navigable rivers, the Great Lakes, the roads, and the canals helped in the early years of the introduction of the factory system, but it was not until the construction of a network of railways that large-scale manufacturing became practicable. The latter definitely took transportation out of the local stage. More recently the railroad facilities have been augmented by the enlarging of some of the old canals, and by the invention of the automobile and the resulting highway construction. Manufacturing and transportation have helped to create wealth which has been constantly available for reinvestment in similar projects.

As the Industrial Revolution has progressed, new inventions have made possible many new manufacturing industries which have been stimulated by the purchasing power of the American consumer. Among these important industries may be mentioned the manufacture of transportation equipment; electrical supplies used for telephone, telegraph, radio, lighting, and household equipment; bicycles, automobiles, and airplanes. In addition to agricultural machinery this country has contributed many famous scientific advances since 1865, advances which have done much to stimulate industry. Among them might be mentioned the loading coil for long-distance telegraphy and telephony (Michael Pupin); high-speed tool steel (F. W. Taylor and J. M. White); airplane mechanics (Charles M. Manly and the Wright brothers); synthetic resins (Leo Baekeland); Audion tube (Lee De Forest); automatic bottle machine (Michael Owens); tungsten filament light (William D. Coolidge); alternating current motor (Nicola Tesla); the loom invented by James H. Northrup and George A. Draper, and the contributions of Thomas A. Edison, George Westinghouse, Elihu Thompson, Charles P. Steinmetz, E. F. W. Alexanderson, Irving Langmuir, and many others. The distribution of the products made possible by the work of these great scientists and many others has been aided, of course, by the development of large-scale advertising and salesmanship. It has also been stimulated by the relatively high wage scale of American workmen.

In discussing the causes for the development of manufacturing the application of science to industry, particularly in recent years, cannot be overemphasized. No longer do large industries depend upon the findings of individual inventors or scientists working independently; rather they support staffs of research workers whose business is to discover methods of producing a better product more cheaply or to develop an entirely new one. Large-scale industrial research had come slowly in this country. It had been held back partly because of the fact that much of American manufacturing was concerned with the simple process of reducing the raw materials to a form for the export market and for further use in manufacturing, all of this giving little encouragement for elaborate organized research. Large and well-organized laboratories waited upon large-scale industry able to support such undertakings. Moreover, brilliant individual inventors had so far been able to keep ahead of industrial entrepreneurs. After 1900 the situation changed, and industry, taking its cue from government laboratories and those of technical schools, began to develop this type of work. Led by the Bell Telephone System, the Du Pont Company, the General Electric Company, and Eastman Kodak, industrial research was well under way by the time of the First World War. Spurred on by the federal government, this expansion went on far more rapidly in the 1920's.

Some progress also has been made to apply science to labor. Led by Frederick Winslow Taylor and his disciples, "scientific management" began to be introduced into factories in the second decade of the century and after the First World War was almost universally adopted. Taylor was convinced that careful studies of time and methods of work would reveal the quickest and most efficient manner of doing the job, after which it could be pitched to the standard of the most efficient. By eliminating the incompetent and by stimulating the best workers through wage systems believed to be psychologically sound, greater production might be obtained and higher wages paid. Although "scientific management" has become a commonplace in American industrial practice, it has been bitterly opposed by labor, which insists that it is the forerunner of the "speed-up" and the "stretch-out."

Any discussion of the causes of the development of American manufacturing would be incomplete without mentioning the part played by the entrepreneurs, who often were neither scientists nor, strictly speaking, manufacturers or industrialists. These were men like Andrew Carnegie in steel, Philip D. Armour in slaughtering and meat packing, John D. Rockefeller in oil refining, and J. P. Morgan in finance. Through their skill in integration, finance, or salesmanship these men were able to create great enterprises which reduced manufacturing costs, created new markets, and stimulated industrial development. Far more numerous were the small manufacturers who were often a combination of engineer, inventor or scientist, and businessman, and who were the original entrepreneurs or builders of American manufacturing.

CHARACTERISTICS OF AMERICAN MANUFACTURING

Manufacturing in America has been influenced in its development by several factors which differentiate it from the European system. Foremost among these is the scarcity of labor, prevalent during much of our history and inevitably directing the inventive genius of the nation to the creation of labor-saving machinery. American products are pre-eminently machine-made, not hand-made, a characteristic not wholly favoring quality, since the substitution of machine for hand products has meant a certain sacrifice of the artistic, the delicate, and the beautiful for the sake of large-scale production. With certain notable exceptions, such as shoes and automobiles, it would probably be correct to say that European consumption goods are generally finer in quality and more artistic than ours, whereas our production goods (machinery, etc.) are generally finer than the Europeans.

Scarcity of labor also helped to develop earlier in America than in any other country the standardization of machinery and parts, permitting the rapid production of complicated mechanisms in large quantities, each part of which is made separately, the whole being assembled later. This makes possible easy replacement of parts and keeps down expenses in running machinery.

Another characteristic attributable partly to the scarcity of labor and partly to the character of the raw materials (particularly true in earlier years) is that much of our manufacturing produces small changes, and the value added by manufacture forms a relatively small proportion of the total value of the product. "Thus the slaughtering and meat-packing industry," said the *Census of Manufactures,* "which ranks first (1914) in gross value of products, and the flour-mill and gristmill industry, which ranks third in that respect, both hold a comparatively low rank in regard to number of wage earners and value added by manufacture."[6] This form of manufacturing is likely to be located close to the supply, whereas more complicated forms, like the metal and textile industries of New England, are often far from the raw material. The dependence of many of our leading manufactured products upon agriculture should again be emphasized. Of the fifteen leading industries summarized in the table of industries for 1937, at least five are directly dependent on agriculture. It should be remembered, however, and this will be noted in the next section, that American manufacturing became increasingly dependent on and concerned with mineral products.

Closely allied with the scarcity of labor has been the enthusiastic adoption of any power other than hand. Most of our factories are operated by steam, water, or electricity. Since 1870 mechanical power in the United States has increased from 2,346,000 horsepower to 42,931,000 in 1929. Whereas in 1870 the horsepower contributed by waterfalls and steam was about equal, the tendency during the next four decades was definitely toward steam. With the development of electricity and the increasing cost of coal there has been a swing back to water power. As electrical engineers have perfected the means for transporting power over long distances, it has been possible

[6] *Abstract of the Census of Manufacturers,* 1914, p. 27.

to manufacture electricity by water power rather than by coal, and manufacturers have found it advantageous to purchase power from hydroelectrical
companies or to build their own power stations.[7] Whether produced by
water or by coal, the development of electricity for manufacturing as well as
for lighting and other purposes has been an important aspect of the recent
history both of manufacturing and of the electrical industry. The extent of
electrification of factory power equipment has grown from 33 per cent in
1914 to 74 per cent in 1929, and is constantly increasing. "Practically all of the
increase in factory power equipment since 1914 has been in electric motors
operated by current from central stations."[8]

Some note has already been made of an outstanding characteristic of
American manufacturing—freedom from tradition. Our rapid development
may be traced to some extent to the freedom from inherited ideas, leaving
our industries unhampered to seek the best and quickest way. The surviving influences of guild regulation and the medieval legislation of town
and nation were not felt. Furthermore, American labor is intelligent, quick
to comprehend and to adopt new methods. Environment has made the
American a jack-of-all-trades and has nurtured his inventive genius. Nowhere have new methods of machine production been more enthusiastically
sought. Liberal patent laws have aided; the 276 patents granted in the
decade 1790–1800 grew to 25,200 in the decade 1850–1860 and to 234,956 in
the decade 1890–1900. In 1911 the total number of patents issued since 1790
reached the million mark. In the single year of 1951 the number issued and
reissued amounted to 48,719. In a typical year of the late thirties more than
70,000 patents were applied for and over 40,000 granted. The greatest manufacturing plants now maintain laboratories devoted exclusively to the development of new devices, and it has become a regular practice to offer
substantial awards to workers for suggestions regarding improvements in
production. The mere recitation of some of the great patents issued in the
field of electricity or gas engines would provide a thumbnail sketch of the
recent development of American manufacture and of technical advancement.

MASS PRODUCTION

One of the most important characteristics of American industry has been
the development of mass production. Along with this came an advance in the
output of manufactured goods almost double that of the production of raw
materials. At the same time there was a growing emphasis upon goods
needed for use in capital equipment (machines, tools, and implements for

[7] C. O. Ruggles, "Problems in the Development of a Super-Power System," *Harvard Business
Review*, II, 161 ff.; reprinted in part in F. Flügel and H. U. Faulkner, *Readings in the Economic
and Social History of the United States*, pp. 501–511.
[8] *Commerce Yearbook, 1930*, I, 268.

further production) rather than for human consumption. The machine-tool industry fell into the category of durable goods, a type of commodity in which the average annual rate of increase in physical production far exceeded that in non-durable goods. It should be noted that during the first two decades of the present century the horsepower capacity in manufacturing tripled while the horsepower per wage earner increased from 2.11 to 3.24.[9] This development was summarized by two economists: "We resort increasingly to the factory, and within the factory, increasingly to the machine. Inventions, technical improvements, new industrial processes make for continued change. Labor is displaced by machinery; old machines are rapidly displaced by new—all of which calls for larger and larger output of industrial materials and equipment."[10]

"Mass production," according to Henry Ford, one of its leading exponents, "is the focussing upon a manufacturing product of the principles of power, accuracy, economy, system, continuity and speed . . . and the normal result is a productive organization that delivers in quantities a useful commodity of standard material, workmanship and design at minimum cost."[11] Mass production rested primarily upon the principle of standardization of parts and interchangeable mechanism, an idea well known since the 1790's when it was applied by Eli Whitney in the manufacture of guns. Beyond interchangeable mechanism, the development of mass production depended upon progress in technology and inventions, the availability of adequate capital, and a national market big enough to absorb the product. Mass production was based upon mass consumption, and by 1900 such consumption was possible.

By the early 1900's technology had reached a stage where standardization and technology could join hands. The situation was based on the development of the machine-tool industry, which in turn was largely the result of the research of Frederick Winslow Taylor and J. Maunsel White in developing a new high-speed carbon steel. The new steel doubled the productivity of machine tools and the whole machine-tool industry rapidly improved. At the same time Taylor agitated for the improvement of management and a more scientific and efficient use of the worker's time. With better machine tools and "scientific management," industry was prepared for mass production.

Leadership in the development of mass production was taken by the Ford Motor Company. This concern was pre-eminently fitted for experimentation in assembly technique. The automobile in its early years was largely a business of assembling parts made in various machine shops and collected at

[9] Harry Jerome, *Mechanization in Industry*, pp. 216–225.
[10] E. E. Day and Woodleif Thomas, *The Growth of Manufactures, 1899–1923*, pp. 90–91.
[11] Henry Ford, "Mass Production," *Encyclopaedia Britannica*, 13th ed., Supp. Vol. II, p. 821.

an assembly point. Not only was Ford the largest producer (1000 cars a day by 1913), but from 1908 to 1927 he had manufactured the same car without important modification. Ford began with the system developed in earlier years with guns, sewing machines, bicycles, and other products—that of the stationary assembly. The component parts were brought to the worker, who then put them together. In 1913 Ford began to experiment with "moving assembly." He began with small parts but soon moved into the assembly of the chassis. It was now only a matter of time and experimentation before workers could specialize in small tasks and upon work delivered at predetermined speed. The radical reduction in time and expense quickly turned industry to the new system. The base price of the Model T Ford, for example, dropped from $950 to $290. At the same time Ford increased the minimum daily pay to $5 and reduced the workday from nine to eight hours (1914).

WESTWARD MOVEMENT OF MANUFACTURING

Like population and agriculture, the movement of manufactures has been steadily westward. A map published in the Twelfth Census[12] shows the center of manufacturing in 1850 (computed upon the gross value of products) near the center of Pennsylvania, forty-one miles northwest of Harrisburg. In 1860, 1870, and 1880 it moved to western Pennsylvania, and by 1890 nearly to the center of Ohio, a few miles southwest of Canton; the next census shows a further progress westward to a point southeast of Mansfield. During the forty years from 1850 to 1890 the westward movement of the center of manufacturing was 225 miles, and the westward movement of the center of population 243 miles, indicating the close relationship of the two movements.

The westward movement of manufacture has been caused primarily by the filling up of the West, which has provided labor and a market, and secondarily by the desire to be near raw materials. It has been retarded by the scarcity of labor in the new communities and by the concentration of capital in the older ones. It has likewise been forced to wait upon the development of transportation facilities. Although manufacturing has lagged behind both agriculture and population in the westward advance, it has usually followed the raw material as fast as labor could be obtained. Thus flour milling moved west from the coast rivers to Rochester on the Erie Canal, then to Chicago, and finally to Minneapolis and Kansas City. The meat-packing industry had its trans-Allegheny beginnings about 1816 at Cincinnati, but it moved to Chicago and Kansas City. Lumbering is an excellent example of an industry forced to follow the source of supply. The Northeast originally furnished most of the lumber, but at present it is obtained

[12] Twelfth Census of the United States, *Statistical Atlas*, plate 170.

largely from the Northwest and South. As in the case of milling and meat packing, the manufacture of agricultural machinery moved westward. Most of the factories shifted from their original home in central New York to Illinois and Wisconsin, following both the hickory forest and the farmer. In a similar manner, the present century has shown a strong tendency for the cotton industry to move southward toward the source of cotton.

As a whole, American industry has been largely centered in a manufacturing belt which included New England, the Middle Atlantic States and the East North Central States. At the opening of the century three-fourths of the manufacturing was centered in this region bounded by the Great Lakes and the St. Lawrence in the north, the Mississippi River in the west, and the Ohio and Mason and Dixon's line in the south. This is still the great manufacturing area, although its proportion to the total has declined to two-thirds. As a whole, manufacturing has moved westward into the West Central States and to the west coast but there has also been a large industrial development in the South Atlantic and East South Central States, where today at least one-ninth of our industry is situated.

LOCALIZATION OF INDUSTRY

Although the center of manufacture has moved westward, this tendency has been hampered as well as aided by the many influences making for localization. The Twelfth Census has ably summed up the general causes for the localization of industry as follows: (1) nearness to materials, (2) nearness to markets, (3) nearness to water power, (4) a favorable climate, (5) supply of labor, (6) capital available for investment in manufactures, and (7) the momentum of an early start. Any one of these, or a combination of several, explains the location of most of our manufacturing.[13]

The nearness to materials explains the concentration of milling in the Twin Cities and Kansas City; of meat packing in Chicago, Omaha, and Kansas City; of fruit and vegetable canning in California, central New York, and Baltimore; of fish canning in Oregon and on the New England coast; and of tobacco in North Carolina. It also explains, in part, the recent migration of many cotton mills to the South.

The nearness to market is an influential factor in the localization of industry, especially in the production of bulky and heavy articles. Four of the eight states ranking highest in value of manufactured products—New York, Pennsylvania, Illinois, Michigan, Ohio, New Jersey, California, and Massachusetts—are in the Northeast; they contributed (1950) approximately 50 per cent. The other area of industrial concentration is in the well-popu-

[13] Twelfth Census, VII, *Manufacturing*, Part I, pp. ccx–ccxiv; also in F. Flügel and H. U. Faulkner, *op. cit.*, pp. 495–503.

lated region of the East North Central States of Ohio, Indiana, Illinois, Michigan, and Wisconsin. The localization of the manufacture of such luxuries as jewelry at Providence, silk at Paterson, and furs at New York, and the localization in the Northeast of factories producing certain high-grade necessities is due to the fact either that originally the primary market was east of the Alleghenies or that the principal market remains there. Transportation costs, especially before the days of railroads and automobiles, were naturally a powerful factor in locating industries in thickly populated communities or on rivers and highways leading directly thereto.

Before the introduction of the steam engine, manufacturing was largely dependent upon water or hand power. The pre-eminence of New England and eastern New York as manufacturing communities is in no small degree due to the water power furnished by the Hudson, the Mohawk, the Connecticut, the Housatonic, the Merrimac, and scores of other streams. Industries like cotton and wool, founded in the early days on water power, have continued to depend upon it. In New England this has been partially due to the distance from the coal supply. The utilization of coal has made manufacturing in many districts independent of water power, and has caused the centering of many industries near the coal fields; as a result the horsepower generated by coal has until recently increased with greater rapidity than that obtained from water. As already pointed out, however, the ability to transport electric power over long distances (whether manufactured by coal, gas, or water power) has had a tendency to minimize the importance of both sources of power in determining the location of industry.

Along with water power, a favorable climate has helped to determine the geographic position of the textiles. High humidity and an even temperature have fitted Fall River and New Bedford for cotton manufacturing. The invigorating air of the North is more suitable for labor than the enervating climate of many parts of the South, and seems to be a permanent factor that tends toward the industrial development of the North. However, air-conditioned factories have tended to overcome even this disadvantage.

Industries naturally tend to establish themselves where there is a supply of labor. While American labor is undoubtedly more mobile than that of other nations, the expense of moving and the attachment to home and friends are likely to keep it relatively fixed. The decline of the merchant marine and the meager profits from agriculture freed much labor in New England for manufacturing, a supply augmented by women and children coming in from the farms. Immigrants who were factory workers at home drifted to the factory towns to swell the available labor force. An industry of a certain type draws or provides skilled labor in that particular line, thus giving a further impetus to the establishment of new factories. As an industry becomes concentrated, future skilled labor must be trained in this center, an influence which keeps it from spreading. Four-fifths of women's clothing is made in New York State, three-fourths of the plated ware in Connecticut, and almost all of the carpets in Philadelphia, Thompsonville (Connecticut), and Yonkers and Amsterdam (New York.) Industries employing women and children often follow those that employ men; thus textile mills are often set up in foundry and mining towns. It is easier to move capital than labor, and the human factor must always remain vital in the establishment of an industry.

In recent years most large enterprises have secured their capital from the great financial centers. This, however, is usually a second stage. Before financiers step in to reorganize or enlarge a manufacturing plant, the industry has ordinarily been established by the enterprise and capital of local business-men, illustrating "the tendency of a town to own itself in the early stages of its industrial life."[14] The early development of the textile industry in the South is a good example. Outside capital can be attracted more easily to a prosperous town and to an industry in which local people have invested. The rapid rise of textiles in New Bedford and other New England cities was due in part to the capital set free by the decline of whaling and the merchant marine. Fall River is an excellent illustration of a town which has specialized in one industry, the control of which has largely been retained in the community.

The momentum of an early start can be given as a leading cause for the localization of industry. It has been said that if the population of New England were suddenly wiped out it would be doubtful if its future would be other than that of a summer resort, its natural advantages for manu-facturing as against its disadvantages being so slight. Johnstown and Gloversville, New York, the greatest glove center in America, originally drew glovers because they were advantageously located to make use of deer skins. As skilled labor gravitated there it has continued to produce leather, kid, and cloth gloves. An early carpet factory in Amsterdam, a few miles to the south, has drawn to it skilled weavers who have made it the second largest carpet city in the country. The chance settlement of a skilled shoe-maker at Lynn in 1750 made it the leading shoe town and kept it so, notwith-standing its distance from the source of raw materials. A similar early set-tlement of jewelers in Providence made it a center in that industry. The habit of industrial imitation is great, for the average man has not the courage to be an industrial pioneer; with skilled labor at hand and success-ful industries already in operation, he is likely to follow the line of least re-sistance.

[14] Twelfth Census, VII, *Manufacturers*, Part I, pp. ccxi–ccxii.

Most industries, of course, are influenced not by one but by several of these factors. Thus the development of silk manufacturing in Paterson, New Jersey, was due to an early start, to the existence of skilled labor, to the special qualities of water required, and to this industry's need for certain climatic conditions. What has been said of industry in general is true to a limited extent of the concentration in certain districts of the great cities of middle-men, such as stockbrokers, textile wholesalers, fur merchants, and others.

The Northeast (New England, New York, Pennsylvania, and New Jersey) from the beginning of our industrial history has been the most important manufacturing region, the value of its products in 1950 amounting to over one-third of the total. Almost all of the factors which influence localization have been operative here—markets, labor, capital, transportation facilities, and the impetus of an early start. The streams of New England and the coal of Pennsylvania provided ample power. In certain raw materials alone was this section handicapped. In the small-scale industries of the early years a sufficiency of raw materials such as iron, wool, and hides could be found at home, but later these had to be imported to a large extent. The other advantages, however, not only preserved to this region its supremacy in many types of metal, leather, and textile manufacturing, but created cotton mills and sugar refineries, the raw materials for which are entirely imported. The Northeast surpasses all other sections in the value of output per person, the percentage of people engaged in manufacturing, and the number and variety of such enterprises.

Of the eight states which lead in the value of manufactured products, New York, Pennsylvania, New Jersey, and Massachusetts are in this region. The five most valuable manufactured products of New York State in 1950 were men and women's clothing, printing and publishing, food processing, and machinery. In Pennsylvania (1950) steelworks and rolling mills were by far the chief industry, followed by foundry and machine-shop products, electrical machinery, and printing and publishing. The principal industries of New Jersey were chemicals, electrical machinery, food processing, machinery, and textiles. Turning to New England, we find Massachusetts primarily interested in electrical machinery, textiles, boots and shoes, and clothing. The remainder of the new England states, like Massachusetts, excel in textiles and also in the manufacture of smaller metal products. Connecticut leads in the production of brass, bronze, and copper objects, clocks, firearms, and silverware; and Rhode Island, until recently, in jewelry. The distance from raw materials has turned the Northeast to the manufacture of smaller commodities in which the labor cost is higher, the transportation cost lower, and the value added by manufacture greater.

The Middle West (East North Central and West North Central States) had to wait upon immigration and settlement before sufficient labor and capital could be accumulated for manufacturing. The wealth of raw materials, both agricultural and mineral, destined this section to an industrial future. As the greatest corn country in the world, she has naturally created a slaughtering and meat-packing industry and has drawn manufacturers of vehicles and farm machinery. The bituminous coal of Ohio, Illinois, and Michigan provided power; the iron of Ohio, Missouri, and the Lake Superior region of Minnesota furnished raw materials for foundries, and petroleum formed the foundation of other industries. In this section are located Ohio, Illinois, and Michigan, the third, fourth, and fifth states respectively in the value of manufactured products in 1950. At that date the most important manufactured products in the point of value were: Illinois, machinery and meat packing; Ohio, steelworks and rolling mills; Michigan, motor vehicles; Wisconsin, machinery; Missouri and Iowa, food processing.

The economic life and the manufactures of the Pacific States are founded primarily upon agriculture and lumbering. In both Washington and Oregon the preponderant industry is lumber and timber products; flour and other grain-mill products and meat packing are important. California leads the nation in canning and preserving fruits and vegetables, although her leading industry in point of value is aircrafts and parts, a recent development. Shipbuilding, which in each of these states ranked among the first five industries in 1919, sank to a position of relative unimportance in the 1920's, only to be revived during the Second World War.

It is customary to think of the eight Mountain States as interested fundamentally in the extraction of minerals, and of their manufactures as closely connected with smelting and refining. This impression is not always borne out by the facts, for the value of the agricultural products of these states is nearly double that of the mineral. The chief industry (1950) in value of products in Idaho was lumber and timber products; in Colorado, meat packing; in Nevada, copper. It is interesting to note that one of the chief industries in the Mountain States is car and general shop construction and repairs by steam railroads. In Arizona and Utah agriculture is the chief industry and in New Mexico, petroleum. In Wyoming agriculture and the production of petroleum stand first and in Montana agriculture and the production of copper are outstanding.

In the South (East South Central and West South Central States) the Civil War ended forever the popular belief that the future of that section lay wholly in agriculture. Without capital, the great plantations were broken up to be tilled by tenant farmers; the remnants of the planter class largely pursued their fortunes in the cities. It was not until the decade of the eighties that manufacturing made much headway. By that time the South had re-

covered sufficiently to accumulate local capital, and northern investors began to pause in their exploitation of the West to see the latent possibilities
in the South. This section was still and probably always will be primarily
agricultural; but the great crops of cotton and tobacco needed preparation
before marketing, and the cheap labor available from the Negroes and "poor
whites" made it likely that factories would be set up close to the raw materials. Until recent years her lumber and mineral resources had scarcely been
tapped, but both have provided inviting fields for outside capital.

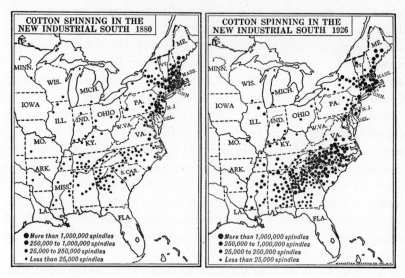

The most spectacular development which any southern industry has experienced occurred in lumbering. The interest of the South in forest products
goes back to colonial days, but her important position dates only recently
from the partial depletion of the northern forests. In 1869 the northeastern
states produced 35.7 per cent and the Lake states 28.2 per cent of the lumber
cut in the United States, and ten years later these two regions still produced
60 per cent of the total, although the Lake states were now in the lead. By
1899 the southern states (including the Carolinas and Virginia) had taken
the lead, and continued to hold it until 1930, when the Pacific States assumed first rank. Southern production still amounts to over one-third of
the total cut.

Since 1880 New England's monopoly in the manufacture of cotton has
been broken by the southern states, in particular by North and South
Carolina. Nearness to the source of raw materials and cheap labor, combined
with increased taxation and labor costs in New England, have been the chief
causes. Lack of child labor legislation was another. The South also profited
from the tremendous development of hydroelectric power on the Piedmont

rivers and the fact that its textile machinery was new. The chief advantages left to New England were the supply of skilled labor and the nearness of markets.

This southern movement forced the New England manufacturer to turn his attention to the production of the finer grades of cloth and has left the coarser grades of sheeting and ducks to the South. By 1950, however, this differentiation had been largely ironed out. In 1880 there were less than 500,-000 spindles in North Carolina, South Carolina, and Georgia, with a product

SUMMARY OF MANUFACTURERS BY GEOGRAPHIC SECTIONS, 1939

| | Number of Establishments | Wage Earners (Average Number) | In Millions of Dollars | | | | Percentage of Total Value of Products |
			Wages	Cost of Materials, Containers, Fuel, and Power	Value Added by Manufacture	Value of Products	
New England	16,135	952,873	1,024	2,459	2,430	4,889	8.6
Middle Atlantic	56,300	2,249,683	2,689	8,667	7,370	16,037	28.2
East North Central . .	40,419	2,196,388	2,951	9,778	7,775	17,553	30.9
West North Central . .	14,947	382,354	428	2,453	1,363	3,816	6.7
South Atlantic	17,316	986,526	826	3,153	2,237	5,390	9.5
East South Central . .	7,279	357,827	291	1,130	828	1,959	3.5
West South Central . .	10,021	262,585	238	1,735	832	2,567	4.5
Mountain	4,011	69,339	82	545	275	820	1.4
Pacific	17,816	429,667	561	2,198	1,601	3,798	6.7
Total for the United States	184,244	7,887,242	9,090	32,118	24,711	56,829	100.0

Preliminary Report, Census of Manufactures.

valued at scarcely $13,000,000, while there were over 8,500,000 spindles in New England. By 1910 over half of the raw cotton was manufactured in the South, and by 1951 over four-fifths. As notable as the increase in cotton manufacture has been the development in the utilization of the by-products. Cottonseed, formerly thrown away, is now fed to cattle or manufactured into cooking oil; the value of cottonseed products rose from $12,000,000 in the eighties to $265,000,000 in 1929.

Abundant supplies of coal and iron in Tennessee and Alabama led to the establishment, especially in Alabama, of extensive iron and steel works. The production of pig iron in Alabama increased from 347,000 tons in 1880 to 8,241,000 in 1949. The city of Birmingham grew from 3000 to 326,037 in 1950, and is one of the steel centers of the United States. More recently the discovery of oil wells in Texas and Louisiana has laid the foundations of a great new southern industry and a new prosperity. On the heels of the oil development has come an expansion in the chemical industry.

The value of southern manufactured products has increased from $338,-791,898 in 1880 to $9,916,000,000 in 1939; nevertheless, the southern states in 1939 produced but 17.5 per cent of the total manufactures of the nation, measured in terms of value.[15] The future must necessarily see a further industrial development in the South, but it will be handicapped by unskilled labor, an enervating climate, and the superior possibilities of agriculture.

BASIC INDUSTRIES

The basic industries in the United States coincide closely with the basic needs of the people—food, clothing, and metals for machinery, transportation,[16] and other uses.

Manufacture of Food. When the position of the United States as a food-producing nation is taken into account, it is not at all surprising to find that, of the eight industries in 1937 whose output was valued at over one billion dollars per year, two were foodstuffs; meat packing, wholesale, ranked third, and bread and other bakery products ranked seventh. A glance at the table on page 396 will show that the relative importance of the manufacture of foodstuffs was even greater in earlier decades. Of the group of industries as rated by the Census of Manufactures of 1937 and of 1949, food and kindred products stood first in value of products. The slaughtering of animals, the preserving of food, and even the grinding of grain were at one time largely household industries. The entrance of women into industry and professions, the multifarious activities of the modern housewife, the increasing scarcity of household servants, the growth of urban life, and the cheapness of manufactured products have all tended to take the preparation of food in the processing stages out of the home. Baker's bread, prepared breakfast food, and canned meat, vegetables, fruit, fish, and milk are all indications of this tendency.

Much of this manufacturing, it is true, is of a simple kind and has depended for its development rather on increased production of foodstuffs than on new inventions. Nevertheless, the invention of modern methods of refrigeration in the seventies immensely stimulated cattle raising and the transportation of fresh meats, and the roller process of making flour permitted the utilization of spring wheat and so put under cultivation the wheat fields of the Dakotas, Montana, and Minnesota. The development of "deep freeze" units in the 1940's has widened the use of refrigeration in the

---

[15] The value added by manufacturing in the southern states in 1950 is estimated at $15,740,-000,000. The percentage of the nation's total, however, has changed little since 1939.

[16] The development of the automobile industry is discussed above, p. 403; below, p. 500.

home. Innumerable patents have made possible the use of old staples in new forms. In like manner, manufacturing processes have introduced new but valuable foods, such as cottonseed oil and peanut butter. The total value added to food by manufacture is estimated in 1950 at $10,095,000,000, about 11.2 per cent of the total value added to manufactures in the country.

In comparison with other nations America is a large consumer of meat. In value of products, meat packing has ranked near the top for over forty years, although 85 per cent of this value is in raw materials, and less than 2 per cent is added by manufacture. The industry, as before suggested, has followed the westward movement of the corn belt. From 1816 to 1860 its center was in Cincinnati and the cities of Ohio, but it has now shifted west to Chicago, St. Louis, Omaha, and Kansas City. In addition to the introduction of refrigeration and canning, the industry has profited by the utilization of an ever-increasing number of by-products which are now the chief source of profit. No part of the animal is wasted; fertilizer, leather, glue, wool, and many other products are derived therefrom. The packing industry has grown from 259 establishments in 1859, the value of whose output was $29,441,000, to 1160 in 1937, with products valued at almost $3,000,000,000.

According to the estimates of 1950, food processing in point of value was headed by beverages, followed by baking products, meat products, miscellaneous food preparations, canning, preserving and freezing, and grain-mill products. Like meat packing, the primary processing of grains had followed the wheat fields into Kansas, Minnesota, Texas, and Missouri. By the First World War, however, Buffalo had regained its position as the leading flour-milling city. This was due chiefly to the fact that freight rates on the Great Lakes were more favorable to wheat than to flour, to the development of cheap hydroelectric power on the Niagara River, to Buffalo's favorable position as a distributing point, and to the ability to import Canadian wheat under bond and export the flour. Although the west coast is far in the lead in canning and preserving, that industry exists in almost every state in the Union. The same is true of such ubiquitous industries as bakery products, soft beverages, confectionery and ice cream, and even milk and its products.

Few manufacturing industries have undergone more radical changes in the past half-century than the food industries. This fact has been particularly noticeable in recent years in the retail food field. The development of urban life has made it impractical to purchase food in large quantities and has hastened the decline of baking, canning, preserving, and other forms of food preservation in the home. As a result, bread and other bakery products are largely processed out of the home, and flour and butter are largely retailed in small quantities. The market for canned fruit, vegetables, and meat has grown tremendously. The retailer now handles chiefly package goods in small units, and industries that manufacture cartons and cans have developed to large proportions.

Textiles, Shoes, and Clothing. The textile industry is primarily concerned with the manufacture of cloth and clothing. In 1950 it ranked second among the great groups of industries, with a value added by manufacture of $9,789,000,000 and an average number of employed of 2,368,000. Cotton was the first American industry brought into the factory and was the largest and most prosperous of the textile industries before the Civil War. The abnormal demand for woolens during the war and the interruption in the supply of raw cotton had pushed cotton back temporarily. It was not until 1900 that it again attained its leadership among the textiles. The position of cotton and to a lesser extent wool was challenged after the First World War by rayon, and in the 1940's and 1950's by other synthetic fibers such as nylon, dacron, and orlon.

The great competition in cotton manufacturing has brought astounding progress since 1860. Although the fundamental patents were taken out before the Civil War, notable achievements, particularly in labor-saving devices, have been made since then, so revolutionary that the large concerns have been forced to replace their machinery two or three times. Among the most famous of the improvements are the ring spinner, the Northrop loom, the Barber warp-tying machine, and the automatic seamless knitting machine. The first three have doubled the production per operative. The ring spinner does not turn out as even or soft a thread as the old mule spinner, but its greater production speed has won it an assured place in American mills, where labor is costlier and scarcer. The Northrop loom is almost human in its ability to stop if the warp breaks or the shuttle gets out of place, and in inserting the colored warps at the proper time. The Barber machine ties the ends of the threads together, and the Bronson knitting machine knits stockings complete in every detail.

Woolen manufacturing has also grown tremendously since 1860 and with it the tendency toward consolidation. Because of special conditions the American manufacturer has until recently carried out all the processes of manufacture in a single plant, carding the short fiber for woolens, combing the long fiber for worsteds, spinning the thread, weaving the cloth, and dye-ing it. In Europe, on the other hand, different plants have specialized in these processes and thus skilled labor has been concentrated on certain phases. This partially accounts for the frequent superiority of British wool-ens. Our manufacturers lead the field in the grade and variety of flannels and blankets, but their greatest output in quantity consists of the cheaper wool-ens that are consumed by the wholesale clothing houses. The manufacture of expensive woolens has been too small in this country for profitable large-scale production. The manufacture of worsteds dates from about 1870 and is rapidly growing at the expense of other woolens, but expansion has been retarded by the greater amount of labor necessary. The development of woolen machinery has been less rapid than that of cotton, and the inventions have been mostly English in their origin, as has also the machinery itself.

The most spectacular advance in the woolen branch of textiles in America has occurred in the manufacture of carpets. Until after the Civil War carpets were largely hand woven. Most of the inventions have been the work of Americans, who have made the United States the greatest carpet-producing nation in the world and the products the finest obtainable, except the hand-loom rugs of the Orient. The prosperity and wealth of the nation permitted a high domestic consumption; in 1937, we produced 65,346,000 square yards of carpets and rugs. Factory production of carpets begin in 1841 when Erastus B. Bigelow of Boston adapted the power loom to the weaving of ingrain carpets and a few years later to the weaving of Wiltons and Brussels. His work was supplemented in 1864 by Smith & Skinner of Yonkers, who applied the power loom to Axminsters. The value of manufactured carpets and rugs rose from $7,857,000 in 1860 to $475,000,000 added by manufacturing in 1950. The mills then operating were located chiefly in New York, Pennsylvania, and Massachusetts.

In hosiery and knit goods the United States also leads the world. Hosiery was knit in the home until 1832, when Egbert Egberts at Cohoes, New York, successfully applied the principles of knitting by power; thereafter the manufacture of hosiery gradually shifted to the factory. Owing to the variety of products, the tendency toward comparatively small mills with moderate capital has been marked in this industry. Until the First World War hosiery was largely produced from wool and cotton with the luxury trade in silk. Rayon came in during the 1920's and nylon in the 1930's. The latter has superseded all other materials for women's stockings. The war with Japan cut off the raw silk and silk hosiery virtually disappeared. The industry is largely centered in Pennsylvania and the South.

The most remarkable advance in textiles in America was in the silk industry. This was the more astonishing because this industry was built up on raw material which must be imported from a great distance and in competition with the long-established and well-equipped mills of France. The success was due to tariff protection, to the enterprise of manufacturers, and to the nation's wealth, which created a market. With these favoring factors but against great odds, the value of silk products became larger than that of any other nation, with over 90 per cent for domestic consumption. As with hosiery the recent war dealt a severe blow to the domestic silk industry, but even before the war the value of rayon, or synthetic silk, manufactured exceeded that of pure silk. Nylon and other synthetics have further curtailed the industry. John Ryle of Paterson, New Jersey, and the Cheneys of South Manchester, Connecticut, founded the industry when they began the manufacture of thread and ribbons; they branched out eventually into piece goods. Paterson became the center of the silk and rayon industry, with Pennsylvania, New Jersey, New York, Connecticut, and Massachusetts the principal producing states.

Following closely upon the heels of textile development came that of ready-made clothing. This was stimulated by the demands of the Civil War and made possible by the invention of the sewing machine. Labor was provided by women and children and by the steady influx of foreigners, first the Irish, and after 1876 the Polish Jews and Italians. The application of factory methods to ready-made clothing is comparatively new; until about 1914 the industry was cursed by sweatshop methods under which operatives worked for a miserable pittance in their own homes, often in the most unhealthy surroundings. Considerations of humanity, of public health, and of business have gradually eliminated sweatshop clothing both voluntarily and through legal means. Some modern clothing factories are as up to date as any in other industries, though much clothing is still manufactured in small factories sometimes little better than sweatshops. New York City is far in the lead in the production of both men's and women's clothing, but her production of men's clothing is greatly augmented by other metropolitan centers such as Chicago, Philadelphia, Rochester, and Baltimore. New centers for women's clothing have developed in Los Angeles and St. Louis.

Until 1845 shoemaking was a hand trade usually carried on in the home. The change to the factory began in that year with the invention of the leather roller, which hastened the preparation of hides. Then came the Blanchard lasting machine, which could turn out lasts of standardized sizes. Soon J. B. Nichols, a Lynn shoemaker, adapted Howe's sewing machine to the sewing of uppers, and just before the Civil War Lyman R. Blake invented the McKay machine for sewing the uppers to the soles. Shoe machinery is among the most ingenious in the world; an average factory uses sixty kinds of machines. A peculiarity of the industry is the control of the most important patents by a single company, the United Shoe Machinery Company, who lease the principal machines and are paid a royalty upon each pair of shoes manufactured.[17]

"The American shoe of today is the standard production of the world," said the Census of 1910, and this still holds true. The centers of manufactur-

[17] The United Shoe Machinery Company was prosecuted by the government on the grounds that their "tying clause," which requires that one machine shall be used in conjunction with another, was in violation of the Clayton Act, a contention upheld in 1922 by the Supreme Court. United Shoe Machinery Corp. *et al. v.* U.S., 258 U.S. 451.

ing are in the vicinity of Boston, New York, and St. Louis. The boots and shoes produced in three New England states—Maine, Massachusetts, and New Hampshire—represent over one-third of the total for the United States, and Massachusetts still holds first rank among the states, with New York second, and Missouri third.

Iron and Steel. It is impossible to overestimate the importance of iron and steel in modern life. We live in an age of machinery which rests upon iron and steel, as do our transportation system and our large structures. In steel rails, railroad coaches, automobiles, and an infinite variety of tools and machinery, the basic metal enters intimately into our everyday life. The rapid rise in output is accounted for chiefly by the increased demand, by the substitution of coke for anthracite coal in smelting, and by revolutionary inventions which have facilitated and cheapened production. Iron and steel and their products have long since ranked among the leading industries of the nation. The group includes many industries, such as blast furnaces, steelworks, rolling mills, and other iron and steel manufacturing; but it excludes machinery, transportation equipment on land and water, and railroad repair shops, each of which forms a separate division in the census.

The manufacture of iron and steel falls into two divisions: the production of pig iron and its conversion into commercial iron and steel. Until after the Civil War, steel was a rare commodity that was used chiefly in cutlery and the finer grade of tools. Iron was the chief metal in use, and until 1839, when anthracite coal was introduced, it was for the most part smelted with charcoal. After the Civil War, bituminous coal, chiefly in the form of coke, was introduced in smelting, a factor that enabled the industry to distribute itself so widely that in 1880 iron was manufactured in thirty states. The greatest event in the history of iron and steel occurred in the 1850's, when an American, William Kelly, and an Englishman, Henry Bessemer, independently discovered a method, known as the Bessemer process, by which a blast of cold air is forced through the molten pig iron to oxidize the foreign substances; after this such quantities of carbon and other elements may be introduced as will make the desired quality of steel. By cheapening production it made the use of steel universal and relegated iron to a position of comparative unimportance.[18]

The Bessemer process has its limitations. It is not suitable for ore of high phosphorus content, and this has led to its being supplanted by the open-hearth, or Martin, process, which makes possible the use of lower-grade ores. Because the ore in the Lake Superior region was high-grade, the Bessemer method was widely used until 1906, but since then it has been largely superseded by the open-hearth method. Some advance has recently been made in

[18] Steel rails, cheaper and more durable than iron, influenced transportation tremendously.

smelting through electrical processes. With greater production and better smelting methods there have appeared other improvements. The furnaces have doubled in size and tripled in heating capacity since 1850; the average output of fifty tons a day per furnace in 1870 increased to a capacity of over 450 tons a day (1929). By 1951 the United States produced over 105,000,000 tons of steel, almost four times the amount produced in 1935. It represents over half the world's supply.

The chief domestic centers of iron ore are Minnesota, Michigan, and Alabama, a factor which had also influenced the location of steel production and its movement toward the west. After a half-century of exploitation the Lake Superior iron has begun to decline. The result is that the United States now imports iron ore from a dozen other countries, and the westward movement of steel production has ended. The recent building by United States Steel of its monster plant at Morrisville on the Delaware is for the use of Venezuelan ore.

Other Basic Manufacturing. Although much emphasis in the preceding discussion has been on the production of iron and steel, the importance of the nonferrous metals and their alloys in our industrial system should not be underestimated. These metals include copper, lead, aluminum, zinc, tin, gold, and silver. Their importance in the manufacture of intricate machinery, electrical apparatus, and small metal goods is obvious. In wartime they rank second only to steel, and of them copper, lead, and aluminum are by all odds the most important.

The manufacture of electric supplies is another industry which depends on metals—copper, lead, zinc, and aluminum, as well as steel. Although the telegraph was in use in the forties and the telephone in the eighties, the general development of the industry has taken place during the past forty years. The electrification of railroads and the spectacular development of radio and household appliances have enormously stimulated this industry. In fact, the application of electricity to telegraphy, telephony, wireless communication, lighting, motors, and motion pictures has influenced economic and social life more powerfully than any group of mechanical inventions since those which ushered in the Industrial Revolution.

The birth of the petroleum industry, it will be remembered, took place during the Civil War.[19] So important was this product as a lubricant and illuminant that within six years after the boring of the first well it ranked sixth in American exports. The industry developed steadily as petroleum replaced other illuminants, but its great era of expansion waited upon the invention of the internal-combustion engine and the Diesel engine. The hundred-million-barrel mark in production was reached in 1895, but with

[19] Above, p. 331.

the invention of the automobile around the turn of the century this figure jumped to five hundred million in 1917 and one billion in 1923. By that time the United States was producing approximately two-thirds of the world's supply, and the chief centers had moved southwest to Texas, California, and Oklahoma. The history of the industry was often complicated by chaotic overproduction until the Second World War, by a long period of monopoly in refining, and later by government control. Since 1941 the chief problem has been inability to keep up with the growing demand for oil in heating and transportation. This with the fact that domestic resources are limited ,has turned the attention of American producers to resources in other parts of the world. To the numerous uses of petroleum in America the Second World War added the manufacture of synthetic rubber.

SELECTED READINGS

Clark, V. S., *History of Manufactures in the United States,* Vol. II, chaps. 1, 6, 13, 14; Vol. III, chaps. 1, 22.

Faulkner, H. U., *Decline of Laissez Faire,* chaps. 6, 7.

Twelfth Census of the United States, Vol. VII, chap. 2.

Ise, John, *United States Oil Policy,* chaps. 2–5, 12–18.

Wolfe, H. and R., *Rubber: A Story of Glory and Greed,* pp. 421–506.

Clemen, R. A., *The American Livestock and Meat Industry,* chaps. 8–21.

Kennedy, E. D., *The Automobile Industry,* chaps. 1–6.

Flügel, F., and Faulkner, H. U., *Readings in the Economic and Social History of the United States,* chap. 13.

CHAPTER 21

CONSOLIDATION OF BUSINESS

THE CULMINATION OF LAISSEZ FAIRE

THE half-century following the Civil War saw both the culmination of the economic philosophy of *laissez faire* and the reaction against it. All the processes of the American Industrial Revolution were immensely speeded by the war; but in the rapidly growing industrial and agricultural life unbridled freedom and competition reigned supreme. The *laissez-faire* doctrine of Adam Smith and his successors had been accepted as final by the great majority of Americans in the years immediately following the war, and a fitting capstone had been put upon the theories by the first section of the fourteenth amendment.[1] Although this had supposedly been incorporated in the Constitution to protect the Negro, the increasing pressure of corporations upon the courts eventually led to an interpretation which went far to restrain the interference of state legislatures in the operation of business. To the rising capitalist and, in fact, to the average citizen, it seemed not only unnecessary, but bad economics, to regulate private capital. Capital should be aided, not impeded, in the development of the vast natural resources of which, it was believed, there was a sufficiency for all—a theory that was given practical application through the control of the federal government by the business interests during four decades after 1860. This point of view was further strengthened by the pioneer individualism of a frontier people who demanded the utmost freedom of action. As a consequence, competition and *laissez faire* were the order of the day.

These were the years when millions of acres were given to the railroads and charters bestowed with a free hand. The most valuable of the oil, lum-

---

[1] "No State shall make or enforce any law which shall abridge the privileges or immunities of citizens of the United States; nor shall any State deprive any person of life, liberty, or property without due process of law; nor deny to any person within its jurisdiction the equal protection of the laws." See below, p. 488.

ber, and metal lands were occupied under federal land acts, bought in, or obtained by fraud. Although there was indeed plenty for all, victory went to the strongest and the most unscrupulous. The same was true in the struggle for markets. The home market, which had been freely supplied with manufactured goods from abroad during the early decades of the century, was buying 89 per cent of its manufactured commodities from domestic producers by 1860, and 97 per cent by 1900. In the struggle for these resources and markets legislatures were bribed, the people were robbed,[2] many types of illegal methods were used, and even armed force was resorted to upon occasion. As late as 1910 a well-known British journalist aptly likened the United States to "an enormously rich country overrun by a horde of robber barons, and very inadequately policed by the central government and by certain local vigilant societies."[3]

In a famous passage written in 1776, Adam Smith made the assertion: "Every individual is continually exerting himself to find out the most advantageous employment for whatever capital he can command. It is his own advantage, indeed, and not that of society, which he has in view. But the study of his own advantage naturally, or rather necessarily, leads him to prefer that employment which is most advantageous to society."[4] This roseate prediction made at the dawn of the Industrial Revolution as to the beneficial results of *laissez faire* upon the welfare of society was hardly borne out in the decades following the Civil War. Unbridled competition as it developed not only destroyed many manufacturers but in the end brought consolidation which often worked harm both to producers of raw materials and to consumers. With unrestrained competition and *laissez faire,* however, came evils which to a certain extent applied their own curb. The public finally reacted against the wasteful exploitation of the country's resources and the illegal methods so commonly used, and cutthroat competition was so disastrous to business itself that some way out had to be found. Business consolidation and government regulation have been the inevitable outcome.

GROWTH OF BUSINESS CONSOLIDATION

The years before the Civil War saw the golden age of the small manufacturing business, the period when the typical concern was owned by a single entrepreneur, a family, or a small handful of stockholders. Since the seventies the tendency has been to consolidate. Economists at opposite ends of the scale

[2] M. N. Orfield, *Federal Land Grants to the States with Special Reference to Minnesota,* Bulletin of the University of Minnesota (1915), shows how the public lands, forests, and mineral wealth of one richly endowed state passed into private hands.

[3] William Archer, "The American Cheap Magazine," *Fortnightly Review,* LXXXVII, 930 (1910).

[4] Adam Smith, *Wealth of Nations,* Book IV, chap. 2, fourth paragraph.

of economic thought have agreed that the consolidation of smaller units into larger is an inevitable result of the conditions brought about by the Industrial Revolution. Whether this trend is inevitable or not, it has been very marked in our economic life. Most of the witnesses appearing before the Industrial Commission in 1899 believed that "competition so vigorous that profits of nearly all competing establishments were destroyed"[5] was the chief motivating force for business combinations, and this appears to have been the immediate cause which led many to unite to escape being driven to the wall. The bitter rate wars of the railroads during the early seventies had driven fares and rates between competitive points below the cost of transportation. Competition was so excessive in the refining of sugar, for example, that eighteen out of about forty refineries had failed before consolidation was begun.

Added to the losses from price cutting were the inherent losses of competition due to costs of advertising and salesmen, and the many disadvantages which a small industry must suffer in comparison with a large one in utilizing by-products, securing the best management, and bargaining with labor, bankers, and transportation companies. The desire to eliminate needless costs went hand in hand with the eagerness to reap greater profits, which were particularly available when the business, as in the case of Standard Oil, was large enough to effect a monopoly. Other causes for consolidation, of course, included control of basic patents, and the huge promoters' profits possible through new organization.

While these were the immediate causes, certain results of the Industrial Revolution made big business possible. Thus the history of consolidation and of the growth of big business are closely interwoven. The invention of labor-saving machinery made large-scale production profitable, the heavy fixed investment in expensive machinery and apparatus discouraged competition, and the very growth in the size of the nation and of its business tended, as in the case of the railroads, to inevitable consolidation. Gradually smaller inventions, such as the typewriter, adding machine, and many other appliances, contributed necessary elements to the age of big business. This development was greatly aided by the adoption of the corporate form, under which most large industrial units were organized. Likewise it should be remembered that concentration was a characteristic of the nineteenth century. It was to be seen not only in business but also in labor in the formation of unions, and in the political world in the unification of Italy and Germany.

Laissez faire may have dominated American economic policy during the last half of the nineteenth century, but there was one notable exception to its sway. Under the influence of her developing industry the United States com-

[5] *Preliminary Report of the Industrial Commission*, p. 9.

mitted herself in 1861 to a system of high protective tariffs which in general she has maintained ever since. This deviation from *laissez faire* seems also to have aided in the development of big business and monopoly. Henry O. Havemeyer, president of the Sugar Trust at the time of its formation, asserted that "the tariff is the mother of trusts," and there were many who agreed. Although many monopolies, such as the Standard Oil Trust and the American Tobacco Trust, owed little or nothing to the tariff, there were others, like the Sugar Trust, that did. In any event the tariff allowed monopoly profits.

"A calculation of the flat averages of the returns from all the leading industrial lines for which figures are given since 1850," assert Jenks and Clark, "gives almost startling demonstration of industrial concentration in the United States during the past two generations. Such a calculation shows that in thirteen leading lines of industry in the United States, the average manufacturing plant in the sixty years from 1850 to 1910 multiplied its capital by more than thirty-nine, its number of wage earners by nearly seven and the value of its output by more than nineteen."[6] This tendency continues to be an outstanding feature of American industry, as can be seen in the accompanying table. By 1923 the census had ceased to tabulate data for establishments whose annual output was less than $5000. From 1914 to 1929, small establishments doing a business of $5000 to $20,000 declined in relative numbers from 48.9 per cent to 32.9, while all the larger units increased; in percentage of wage earners these small units decreased from 6.0 to 2.3, and in value of products, from 3.7 to 1.1. It is interesting to compare these figures with those for establishments doing a business of one million dollars or over, which showed enormous increases. Although in 1929 this class constituted only 5.6 per cent of the total, it employed 58.3 per cent of the workers and produced 69.2 per cent of the value of products.

ADVANTAGES AND DISADVANTAGES OF THE CORPORATE FORM

As the size of the business unit increased and competition became more reckless and exacting, the old-fashioned methods of conducting a business by means of individual ownership or partnership became inadequate. The funds needed for buildings, equipment, and stocks were too great for individuals to supply, and the risk was too great to be undertaken singly. As a consequence, the corporate form of business was adopted after the Civil War to suit the new needs. Before that time it was used chiefly in the formation of banks, the building of turnpikes and railroads, or the launching of some project necessary for the public good, perhaps of such magnitude that the risks had to be widely distributed. It was generally looked upon as a danger-

[6] Jeremiah W. Jenks and Walter E. Clark, *The Trust Problem* (7th ed., 1917), p. 17.

ous and undemocratic form associated with the idea of monopoly, and one to be carefully supervised. In New York, for example, state incorporation under general laws was not permitted until the constitution of 1846.

MANUFACTURES: ESTABLISHMENTS CLASSIFIED BY VALUE OF PRODUCTS 1914–1929

Class of Establishments According to Value of Products	Establishments		Wage Earners		Value of Products	
	Number	Per Cent Distri- bution	Average Number	Per Cent Distri- bution	Amount	Per Cent Distri- bution
$5,000 and over[a]						
1929	210,959	100.0	8,838,743	100.0	$70,434,863,443	100.0
1925	187,390	100.0	8,384,261	100.0	62,713,713,730	100.0
1921	196,267	100.0	6,946,570	99.4[a]	43,653,282,833	99.7[a]
1919	214,383	100.0	9,000,059	99.5[a]	62,041,795,316	99.8[a]
1914	177,110	100.0	6,896,190	98.2[a]	23,987,860,617	99.1[a]
$5,000 to $20,000						
1929	69,423	32.0	202,958	2.3	771,417,436	1.1
1925	55,876	29.8	156,373	1.9	628,373,403	1.0
1921	71,075	36.2	224,852	3.2	782,977,433	1.8
1919	79,699	37.2	227,977	2.5	866,086,290	1.4
1914	86,587	48.9	423,829	6.0	893,459,166	3.7
$20,000 to $100,000						
1929	75,225	35.7	693,155	7.8	3,587,697,276	5.1
1925	68,951	36.8	660,309	7.9	3,272,196,872	5.0
1921	72,251	36.8	746,024	10.0	3,330,350,409	7.6
1919	75,627	35.3	773,701	8.6	3,487,756,280	5.6
1914	56,557	31.9	995,743	14.2	2,540,949,405	10.5
$100,000 to $500,000						
1929	44,153	20.9	1,672,983	18.9	10,023,771,653	14.2
1925	42,209	22.5	1,675,911	20.0	9,576,090,022	15.3
1921	38,027	19.4	1,629,573	23.3	8,405,758,540	19.2
1919	39,477	18.4	1,712,854	18.9	8,929,364,110	14.4
1914[b]	30,147	17.0	3,000,612	42.7	8,759,391,117	36.2
$500,000 to $1,000,000						
1929	10,395	4.9	1,121,547	12.7	7,294,860,945	10.4
1925	9,771	5.2	1,131,439	13.5	6,870,112,293	11.0
1921	7,581	3.9	966,559	13.8	5,296,720,583	12.1
1919	9,197	4.2	1,112,815	12.3	6,457,485,019	10.4
1914[b]						
$1,000,000 and over						
1929	11,763	5.6	5,148,100	58.3	48,757,116,133	69.2
1925	10,583	5.7	4,760,229	56.7	42,366,941,140	67.5
1921	7,333	3.7	3,379,562	48.4	25,837,475,868	59.0
1919	10,413	4.9	5,172,712	57.2	42,301,103,617	68.0
1914	3,819	2.2	2,476,006	35.3	11,794,060,929	48.7

[a] Small percentages for establishments doing a business less than $5000 omitted.
[b] Figures include data for two groups, $100,000 to $1,000,000.
Statistical Abstract, 1933, p. 693.

A corporation, according to an excellent definition, is "a voluntary autonomous association formed for the private advantage of its members, which acts with compulsory unity and is authorized by the state for the accomplishment of some public good."[7] In other words, a corporation is an organization or association created by law under a charter which authorizes it to do certain things. Although not a person, a corporation is an artificial being which like a person may carry on business, break the law, sue and be sued. It has many advantages which explain its almost universal adoption. (1) It makes easier the raising of large amounts of capital. Under the terms of the charter, corporations are allowed to capitalize their holdings and issue stock. This stock may be brought by many persons who often contribute comparatively small amounts to build up a great business. Thus the American Telephone and Telegraph Company boasted in 1952 of 1,220,000 stockholders, General Motors of over 488,800, and Standard Oil of New Jersey of over 269,000. A cor- poration may also borrow money and issue bonds, so that it has access to large resources of capital. (2) By owning corporate stocks, many people may share in the development of the country and in the profits of the largest concerns often managed by men of great ability, without themselves contributing anything but money. (3) The risk of the stockholders is limited by the law of the state. (4) The shares may usually be bought and sold; thus a person is allowed voluntarily to enter or leave a concern as his private interests dictate. (5) The corporation has great advantages in that it is not disrupted by the death or retirement of its members.

On the other hand, the corporate form has disadvantages. Where the number of stockholders is large and scattered, it is impossible for them to exercise any real control over their delegated agents, the directors elected at the annual meetings. The irresponsibility of the directors is accentuated by the legal attitude that a corporation is a separate legal person and that the directors are the agents of the corporation and not of the stockholders, which makes it useless for a stockholder or a minority to sue a director or his agents for loss incurred through fraud or negligence. The lack of control of the stockholders over their directors has often encouraged the latter to use their position to promote personal interests or to indulge in speculative management, fradulent promotions, and overcapitalization, which have in the end worked havoc to the stockholders, who are not inclined to inquire too closely as long as dividends are unimpaired.

From the point of view of the investor the numerous stock and bond issues so common to corporations are confusing, and only an expert can work out

---

[7] L. H. Haney, *Business Organization and Combination,* p. 82. A more famous definition is that of Chief Justice Marshall in the Dartmouth College case: "A corporation is an artificial being, invisible, intangible, and existing only in contemplation of law. Being the mere creature of law, it possesses only those properties which the charter of its creation confers upon it, either expressly, or as incidental to its very existence. . . . Among the most important are immortality, and, if the expression may be allowed, individuality; properties, by which a perpetual succession of many persons are considered as the same, and may act as a single individual." Dartmouth College *v.* Woodward, Vol. IV, Wheaton's Reports, 518, p. 636.

their true valuation. From the broader outlook of public policy, corporations seem to promote monopoly, for stock ownership facilitates interlocking directorates and interlocking ownerships. Whatever its disadvantages may be, however, the corporation has become the dominant form of business organization today. Although in 1919 corporations numbered only 31.5 per cent of the total establishments, they employed 86 per cent of the wage earners and produced 87.7 per cent of the total value of the products.[8] There is plenty of evidence to show that their relative importance has increased during the last two decades.

EVOLUTION OF CONCENTRATION

While some large concerns have achieved their size by internal growth and natural expansion, many more have come to their present greatness through the consolidation of industries engaged in the production of similar commodities. Attempts like those of the salt producers in western Virginia after 1830 to restrict output and thus control prices had been made before the Civil War, but it was not until after the panic of 1873 that the movement toward consolidation became important. The periods through which the consolidation movement has passed can be divided roughly according to the forms which it has taken: (1) pools, (2) trusts, (3) holding companies, (4) amalgamations and mergers, and (5) "community of interest."

Pools. Pools appeared after the panic of 1873 and the movement continued until about 1887. A pool is an organization of business units whose members seek to control prices by apportioning the available business in some way. This form was especially popular among the railroads, for the bitter rivalry between competitive points was fast leading to ruin. Although forbidden in the Interstate Commerce Act of 1887, the practice was continued, especially in the South, where the transportation of cotton was for a long time apportioned and the freight rates fixed by common consent. Pooling is now legal with railroads, if permission is granted by the I.C.C. In addition to traffic pools there have been "output" pools, illustrated by the agreement between the powder manufacturers in 1886 which sought to eliminate "ill-regulated and unauthorized competition" by mutual understanding in regard to output and price. Informal apportionment of business among different units of the same industry undoubtedly still persists to some extent. Another form of pool is that in which territory and market are allotted. A typical example was the agreement entered into in 1902 between the Imperial Tobacco Company of Great Britain and the American Tobacco Company, giving the former exclusive control of the British Isles, and the latter control

---

[8] *Abstract of the Census of Manufacturers, 1919,* Table 195, p. 340. Classification according to ownership was omitted between 1919 and 1925.

of the United States, her colonies, and Cuba; a new corporation, the British-American Tobacco Company, Limited, was to handle the business in the rest of the world. A more recent marketing pool was made shortly after the First World War when the British Marconi Company and the Radio Corporation of America attempted to divide between them the radio business of the world. Still another type of pool occurs when a certain part of profits or income is deposited with a central body to be distributed later.

Trusts. Pools in railroads were declared illegal in 1887 by the Interstate Commerce Act, and again in 1897 by the Supreme Court in the case against the Trans-Missouri Freight Association. Pooling declined after 1887, but was by no means abandoned. In its place came a new form of understanding which appeared to be legal and at the same time much more efficient. From that year until 1897 the trust was the most favored form of combination. A trust is a form of organization in which the stockholders under a trust agreement deposit with a board of trustees a controlling portion of their stock and receive trust certificates in return. Unlike a pool this is no mere federation; it is an actual consolidation of interests. It is a case of using the old legal idea of a trusteeship to create a monopoly, and was introduced as early as 1879 and 1882 by the Standard Oil Company. This was followed by the formation in 1887 of the "Whiskey Trust" (Distillers' and Cattle Feeders' Trust), the "Sugar Trust" (Sugar Refineries Company), the "Lead Trust," the "Cotton-Oil Trust" (1884), and by others in succeeding years. The trust form, which gave absolute power to the trustees, created a monopoly, opposition to which produced antitrust laws on the part of various states in 1889 and later, and the Sherman Antitrust Act on the part of the national government in 1890. The early prosecutions by the federal courts under the Sherman Act were generally unsuccessful, but the dissolution of the North River Sugar Refining Company by the New York Court of Appeals in 1890 and of the Standard Oil Trust by the Ohio courts in 1892 put a decided damper upon this method of consolidation. Interestingly enough, these cases were decided on the grounds that the creation of a trust had violated rights granted in the charter and not on the grounds that monopolies had been created.[9] In any event the decisions were accepted by the corporations. Moreover, the panic of 1893 and the succeeding years of depression held up for the time being further aggressive moves toward consolidation.

Holding Companies. The antitrust legislation led to the adoption of a new form of consolidation, namely, the holding company. Although outright mergers and fusions continued, the holding company was the dominant form used during the greatest period of business consolidation, the years from 1897 to 1904. A holding company is an organization created to dominate

[9] H. R. Seager and C. A. Gulick, Jr., *Trust and Corporation Problems* (1929), pp. 51–55.

other corporations by owning or controlling a portion of their stocks. Although this device had been employed before this time by the Pennsylvania Company and the American Bell Telephone Company, it was now adopted rapidly, Standard Oil, as with the trust form, again taking the lead. The movement toward the holding company was greatly facilitated by the complacent laws of a number of states, particularly New Jersey, West Virginia, Delaware, and Maine, which permitted the organization of pure finance corporations under a general statute allowing the widest powers to these corporations. Their obligations were so slight that merely the maintenance of a dummy office and the submission of a meager annual report complied with the law. New Jersey, because of her position, was able to outbid the other states, and the providing of head offices to which directors might journey from New York to hold their annual meetings became an important industry in Jersey City.

Between 1897 and 1904 over $6,000,000,000 worth of securities were marketed; in 1897 alone, new corporations were organized with a nominal capital of $3,512,000,000, of which at least one-fourth was "water." In 1904 John Moody listed 318 greater or lesser industrial trusts representing consolidations of nearly 5300 distinct plants and capitalized at over $7,000,000,000, of which 236 (with five-sixths of the capital) had been incorporated since January 1, 1898, 170 of them under New Jersey law.[10] In fact, most of the great corporations of today were formed during those years, including what for many years was the greatest of them all—the United States Steel Corporation.

This huge holding company, with its eleven constituent companies, controlling some 170 subsidiary concerns, was the handiwork of J. P. Morgan and Elbert H. Gary and in a sense marked the climax of the trust movement. The underlying impetus for its organization was the bitter competition in the iron and steel business and Andrew Carnegie's threat of even keener warfare in the future. Carnegie, anxious to retire, finally succeeded in unloading his vast steel properties upon Morgan, who merged them with a number of steel concerns in which he was already interested, and certain others that were brought in, the whole constituting the United States Steel Corporation. The actual value of the tangible property of this new corporation was estimated by the Commissioner of Corporations at $682,000,000; yet it was capitalized at $1,402,846,000, of which $510,205,000 represented preferred stock, and $508,-

[10] John Moody, *The Truth About the Trusts* (1904), p. 486. Seven of the greater trusts which he lists—the Amalgamated Copper Company (1899), the American Sugar Refining Company (1891), the American Smelting and Refining Company (1899), the Consolidated Tobacco Company (1901), the Standard Oil Company (1899), the U.S. Steel Corporation (1901), and the International Mercantile Marine Company (1902)—boasted an aggregate capital of over $2,500,-000,000; with a single exception they were all formed after 1898, and all were incorporated under New Jersey law.

227,000 common.[11] Obviously all of the common stock and an appreciable
share of the preferred represented "water," but so powerful and so successful
was the enterprise that with the exception of three years it paid dividends on
its common stock until 1932. From the point of view of promotors and
original investors it has proved one of the most successful of the great consolidations.

Mere size, as many investors discovered, did not necessarily mean profits.
Such consolidations as the International Mercantile Marine Company and
the United States Shipbuilding Company[12] brought losses rather than gains,
and the speed with which consolidation proceeded filled the market with
what Morgan called "undigested securities." By 1904, most of the important
industries had been consolidated to a greater or lesser extent, and for the time
being there were few remaining fields to conquer. Furthermore, when the
holding company constituted a monopoly its position was no safer than that
of the trust. In 1904 the Roosevelt administration secured the conviction and
dissolution of the Northern Securities Company, an organization formed to
hold the stock of the three great railroads tapping the Northwest. The courts
affirmed that, while a holding company was legal under the laws of the in-
corporating states, it was illegal when the obvious intent was to effect a
monopoly. In the same tenor subsequent decisions dissolved the Standard
Oil and American Tobacco holding companies.

Mergers and "Community of Interests." The holding company is still the
most significant type of corporate organization in the United States and in
recent years it has been carried to new refinements by means of "voting
trusts" and pyramided holding companies (below, p. 613 ff.). Nevertheless,
other methods of consolidation have supplemented it. Amalgamation and
merger or the outright purchase of one organization by another is one
method. Likewise antitrust laws have stimulated new methods of achieving
monopoly through "community of interest," usually through the purchase
of stock by individuals, holding companies, corporations, investment trusts,
or "voting trusts." One company can buy a sufficient quantity of another
company's stock to make its influence felt, and representatives of one company may thus sit on another's board. True, the Clayton Act forbids interlocking directorates in competitive companies engaged in interstate business
whose capital, surplus, and undivided profits aggregate more than $1,000,000;
but even here the same persons, as stockholders, may exercise great influence
through "dummy" directors. So extensive was the "community of interest"
in the oil companies that the dissolution of the trust in 1892 and of the hold-

[11] *Report of the Commissioner of Corporations on the Steel Industry* (1911), Part 1, pp. xvii–
xxiv; also in F. Flügel and H. U. Faulkner, *Readings in the Economic and Social History of the
United States,* pp. 566–573.
[12] H. R. Seager and C. A. Gulick, Jr., *op. cit.,* chap. 12.

ing company in 1911 made little difference. The railroads have been under the questioning eye of the people for so long that they especially have resorted to consolidation through "community of interest." To such an extent has the purchase of stock been consummated between the railroads that it is comparatively easy to divide them into seven or eight different groups according to their controlling financial interests, a situation which has softened competition in certain sections served by these systems.

THE STANDARD OIL COMPANY

The history of the oil business is of particular significance in the study of industrial combinations, for the rise and progress of the Standard Oil Company illustrates practically every phase in the development and methods of monopoly under American conditions. It serves, in fact, as the classic story of monopoly in this country. Successful drilling for oil commenced in 1859 in the vicinity of Titusville, Pennsylvania, after the discovery of the Drake well. While the business of drilling wells and refining oil expanded rapidly during the war, the production in 1865 was behind the demand and the whole industry was severely handicapped by lack of transportation facilities and efficient refining machinery. The fact that transportation was the great problem and the chief expense of the expanding oil industry made it quite evident to the most able men in the business that success would come to the large concern with enough capital to install the best machinery for large-scale production and sufficient output to force favorable railroad rates. In 1867, while the industry was still in its infancy, John D. Rockefeller united the refineries of William Rockefeller & Co., Rockefeller and Andrews, Rockefeller & Co., S. V. Harkness, and H. M. Flagler into the firm of Rockefeller, Andrews & Flagler. "The cause leading to its formation," he said, "was the desire to unite our skill and capital in order to carry on a business of some magnitude and importance in place of the small business that each separately had theretofore carried on."[13] Further capital was needed, and in 1870 the company was reorganized into the Standard Oil Company of Ohio, with a capital of $1,000,000 and a refining capacity in its Cleveland plant of about 600 barrels a day. This amounted, however, to only 4 per cent of the oil refined in the United States, and the Standard plant was not even then the largest in the country.

Up to 1879 competition among oilmen had been largely in production. In the succeeding years it was a competition for transportation facilities and favorable rates, a bitter war which left the Standard Oil Company in complete control. This victory may be attributed largely to the business acumen of Rockefeller and his associates, to favorable freight rates, and to the un-

[13] *Preliminary Report of the Industrial Commission*, p. 95.

scrupulous methods to which these men resorted to destroy competition and win favorable concessions from railroads and legislatures. Their desire to secure cheap transportation rates was aided by the railroads, chiefly the Erie, the New York Central, and the Pennsylvania, which were in competition for the oil business. In keeping with the policy of the time, the roads lowered their rates at competitive points and to promising concerns. In all the dickering with the railroads, no group of refiners was so successful as Standard Oil. Its success, however, must be attributed to greater administrative ability rather than to deeper guilt. Its favorable location at Cleveland was, to be sure, a factor in this success, since it freed the concern from complete dependence on the railroads by affording water transportation to the seaboard by way of the Great Lakes and the Erie Canal.

The most notorious of the rate agreements was made through the South Improvement Company chartered by the Pennsylvania legislature in 1871 with the widest powers, including authority "to construct and operate any work, or works, public or private, designed to include, increase, facilitate, or develop trade, travel, or the transportation of freight, livestock, passengers, or any traffic by land or water, from or to any part of the United States."[14] This company, 900 of whose 2000 shares were held by Rockefeller and his close associates, was actually organized by the railroads seeking business, not the refiners seeking cheap transportation. Nevertheless the company made contracts with the Pennsylvania, the New York Central, and the Erie, whereby it agreed to ship 45 per cent of all the oil transported by it over the first-named railroad and to divide the remainder between the other two roads. In return the railroads agreed to allow rebates on all petroleum shipped by the company and to charge all others the full rates, and in addition to furnish the South Improvement Company waybills of all petroleum and its products transported over their lines. Each road also agreed "at all times to cooperate, as far as it legally may, with the party hereto of the first part against loss by injury or competition, to the end that the party hereto of the first part may keep up a remunerative, and so a full and regular business, and to that end shall lower or raise the gross rates of transportation over its railroads and connections, as far as it legally may, for such times and to such extent as may be necessary to overcome such competition." The South Improvement Company aroused such a storm of opposition that its charter was revoked after three months. The story is told here simply to point out how far the system of rebating might go. Despite the end of the South Improvement Company, rebates and favorable discriminations were continued. Standard Oil gradually extended its operations to include the ownership of pipe lines; by 1879 it

[14] *Ibid.*, p. 608. The charter of the South Improvement Company is given on p. 607 and the contract with the Pennsylvania on p. 610.

controlled from 90 to 95 per cent of the oil refined and was able in turn
virtually to dictate its rates to the roads. The "Hepburn Committee," reporting to the New York legislature in January, 1880, said:

It owns and controls the pipe lines of the producing regions that connect with
the railroads. It controls both ends of these roads. It ships 95 per cent of all oil.
. . . It dictates terms and rates to the railroads. It has bought out and frozen out
refiners all over the country. By means of the superior facilities for transportation
which it thus possessed, it could overbid in the producing regions and undersell
in the markets of the world. Thus it has gone on buying out and freezing out all
opposition, until it has absorbed and monopolized this great traffic, this great
production which ranks second on the list of exports of our country. The parties
whom they have driven to the wall have had ample capital, and equal ability in
the prosecution of their business in all things save their ability to acquire facilities
for transportation.[15]

In order to dominate the situation more completely, the Standard Oil
Company of Ohio worked out a scheme in 1882 by which the stockholdings
of fourteen companies and the majority of holdings of twenty-six others were
placed in the hands of nine trustees having irrevocable powers of attorney.
The stockholders received trust certificates in return. The par value of these
certificates amounted to $70,000,000, of which $46,000,000 was owned by the
nine trustees who dictated the policies of the constituent companies. The
public in general had no difficulty in understanding the purpose of this new
organization. A wave of state antimonopoly legislation followed, and the
courts of Ohio in 1890 broke up the Standard Oil Trust into twenty constituent companies. Trust certificates were replaced by proportionate shares
of stock in the new companies.

In 1899 a second attempt was made to bring the entire properties under
single control by the formation of the Standard Oil Company of New Jersey,
a holding company as well as an operating company, formed with the intention of transferring to it the stock of the different corporations so that in
time one concern might own and direct the whole industry. The new company's position as a holding company was gravely imperiled by the decision
in the Northern Securities case (1904)[16] and was finally made untenable by
the Supreme Court order of dissolution in 1911.[17] The business since then has
been carried on by corporations chartered by the several states, which for
years usually acted harmoniously and exercised a dominant influence through
a "community of interest" brought about by the ownership by certain individuals of controlling stock in the several companies. By 1904 Standard Oil

[15] New York Assembly Document No. 38, 1880.
[16] Below, p. 441.
[17] Below, p. 441.

controlled about 85 per cent of the domestic and 90 per cent of the export trade. Its earning capacity had increased from $8,000,000 in 1882 to $57,459,-356 in 1905, and its dividends from 5¼ per cent in 1882 to 30 per cent in 1898. In recent years the various Standard Oil companies have stretched into foreign fields, notably in Latin America and the Middle East.

Increased motor traffic has added impetus to production and stimulated the formation of many new and powerful companies, such as the Texas, the Gulf, and the Shell companies, which have effectively undermined the almost complete monopoly enjoyed fifty years ago by the Standard Oil groups. The latter, however, continue to be dominant in the transportation and refining of oil and still overshadow their rivals.[18] Before leaving the discussion of the oil monopoly it should be emphasized again that Standard Oil achieved its long pre-eminence through monopoly in refining. Others produced the oil; Standard refined it. In later years as competition developed, the Standard companies, along with their competitors, were forced into transportation through oil pipes, into retailing as well as wholesaling, and into exploration and production as well as refining.

COMBINATIONS AND MONOPOLIES

The discussion so far has been largely concerned with the combination movement and the various forms it has taken. It should be remembered, however, that a pool, a holding company, or even a trust may be organized without effecting a monopoly. But the desire for a monopoly and its advantages has ordinarily been in the minds of the organizers, for a virtual monopoly may be brought about by controlling an important percentage of the product. So obvious was it that the trusts were organized to eliminate competition and to control products that the term "trust" has been commonly used in America to designate any large combination which approaches a monopoly, and it is sometimes even applied indiscriminately to any big business.

There are a number of different kinds of monopolies with which we are familiar. There may be *personal* monopolies in which an individual possessing special talent or knowledge may be able to drive out competitors. There are *legal* monopolies: public, such as the post office in America, or private, such as those based on patents, copyrights, or franchises. Another important group is the *natural* monopoly of situation or organization, as illustrated by a street railway or bus company, by gas or electricity works, or by anthracite coal mines. *Labor* monopolies resulting from combinations of skilled laborers often control the labor supply. But of special interest to us here are the *capi-*

---

[18] For a brief review of Standard Oil history, see H. R. Seager and C. A. Gulick, Jr., *op. cit.*, chaps. 6 and 7, and H. W. Laidler, *Concentration of Control in American Industry*, chap. 2.

talist monopolies or monopolies of organization which, by the concentration of large aggregations of capital and the unification of a sufficient number of production units, have been able to exercise a monopoly.

Even a cursory consideration of these types brings home the fact that certain forms of monopoly are inevitable and that others are encouraged for the sake of the public welfare. Personal talent or a steam railway is often an inevitable monopoly. A government post office system and a franchise creating a street railway may be monopolies established for the public good; broad social welfare is considered in the granting of patents. On the other hand, capitalist monopolies and monopolies of labor lead at once into controversial fields. But even here modern conditions prevent us from taking too dogmatic an attitude. The cost of erecting a sugar refinery or a steel mill is so great that absolute free competition is almost automatically cut off, and labor's prefectly laudable determination to secure better conditions through a stronger bargaining organization cannot be condemned too hastily.

CAPITALIST MONOPOLIES—ADVANTAGES AND DISADVANTAGES

Large-scale monopolistic production has always had its strong advocates as well as its critics. The former have emphasized in particular the savings in both production and marketing. As to production, they hold that the large resources make it possible to use only the best-located plants and the most efficient machinery, especially in slack times; that large-scale production allows more complete utilization of by-products and economies in the division of labor; that it permits the specialization of production at the different plants; that administrative expenses can be saved by the elimination of duplicated high-salaried positions and at the same time the best talent in the field can be secured. They also point out that research can be pursued on a larger scale; that waste and ineffective methods can be more easily detected through careful comparison of different plants that produce the same article; and that there is greater strength in dealing with labor. As to marketing, it is maintained that expenses are reduced by the elimination of salesmen and advertising, by the elimination of cross-freights, since orders can be filled from the nearest plants, and by the development of greater strength in the export business. The argument is also advanced that control of the market price of both a raw commodity and the finished article helps to stabilize prices and production and thus exerts a healthy influence upon economic life. During periods of rapid monopolistic development, the evils of competition were always emphasized and the motto "competition is the death of trade" was kept well to the front.[19]

[19] A. J. Eddy, the leading proponent of trade associations, epitomized this by the caption, "Competition is War, and 'War is Hell,' " across the title page of his book, *The New Competition* (1914).

On the other hand, it is argued that while a monopoly may manufacture more cheaply, the savings are not passed on to the consumer, for a monopoly is usually formed to enhance profits, and there is conclusive evidence that in many cases the public has been gouged by unwarranted charges. It was the belief of the Industrial Commission in 1902, after a most exhaustive study, "that in most cases the combination has exerted an appreciable power over prices and in practically all cases it has increased the margin between raw materials and finished products. Since there is reason to believe that the cost of production over a period of years has lessened, the conclusion is inevitable that the combinations have been able to increase their profits."[20] A little earlier, Professor Jenks had come to the conclusion that "the fact that the power to increase the margin temporarily at least, somewhat arbitrarily, and the fact that the margin has been increased in specific cases, seems to be clearly established." The crux of the argument rests largely not so much on whether prices have been lowered as on whether they have been sufficiently reduced to take care of the lower costs of large-scale production.[21]

While the price to the consumer has often been kept higher than necessary, the producers of the raw materials, such as cattlemen, sugar raisers, and others, have suffered from the lack of competition among buyers. Furthermore, monopoly has often resulted in inefficient and careless service to the consumer, and he has been forced to accept what was given him. Whatever might be the gains of monopoly from a purely scientific point of view, it was quite obvious that both the producer of the raw material and the consumer of the finished product were pretty much at the mercy of the manufacturer if the manufacturing processes constituted a monopoly.

In a comparison of the advantages and disadvantages, it should be pointed out that many of the alleged advantages of monopolies are similarly applicable to any large-scale industry where there is no monopoly. Steady consolidation of business has gone far, and there is every reason to believe that in most industries the process will continue. Nevertheless, monopoly as such has generally been distrusted as both an economic and a social evil, and persistent efforts either to restore competition or to control monopolies have been undertaken through legislative means.

EARLY ANTITRUST MOVEMENT

Notwithstanding the dominance of *laissez faire* and the enthusiasm with which business consolidation proceeded, there developed a strong opposition to the movement. This came first from the deep-seated antipathy to monopoly inherited from the old English common-law conception, a dislike which

---

[20] *Final Report of the Industrial Commission*, XIX, 621.
[21] Jeremiah W. Jenks, *Trusts and Industrial Combinations*, Department of Labor Bulletin, No. 29, July, 1900, p. 765.

was undoubtedly stimulated by the misfortunes of those whose means of livelihood were injured by the new consolidations. Second, there was fear that the country's natural resources would be brought under the control of a few irresponsible men. By 1873 six corporations owned most of the anthracite coal deposits of Pennsylvania and the transportation facilities to carry the coal out, and in the succeeding years much of the bituminous field was appropriated. By 1882 thirty-nine refineries of Standard Oil controlled 90 per cent of the product. Said Henry Demarest Lloyd in 1894:

A small number of men are obtaining the power to forbid any but themselves to supply the people with fire in nearly every form known to modern life and industry, from matches to locomotives and electricity. They control our hard coal and much of the soft, and stoves, furnaces, and steam and hot-water heaters; the governors on steam boilers and the boilers; gas and gas-fixtures, natural gas and gas-pipes, electric lighting, and all the appurtenances. You cannot free yourself by changing from electricity to gas, or from the gas of the city to the gas of the fields. If you fly from kerosene to candles, you are still under the ban.[22]

By 1904 most of the great products of the country were in the control of big combinations, so large as to constitute monopolies. Not only were the people disturbed over the appropriation and consolidation of the resources of the country, but they were thoroughly aroused over the dishonest methods of competition which in many cases had brought success by open evasion of the law. The concern that did not want to join the trust was throttled by every unfair means known, among the least vicious of which was the obtaining of special railroad rebates, a practice which as much as anything else made possible the success of Standard Oil. Not only was there evasion of the law, there was tampering with the government; the unwholesome influence of big business upon politics was evidenced by the free distribution of railroad passes and still more by activities at election time. The supreme court of Michigan undoubtedly expressed the current feeling when it said in a case involving the Diamond Match Company, one of the most notorious of the trusts during the period: "Indeed, it is doubtful if free government can long exist in a country where such enormous amounts of money are allowed to be accumulated in the vaults of corporations, to be used at discretion in controlling the property and business of the country against the interest of the public and that of the people, for the personal gain and aggrandizement of a few individuals."[23]

Moreover, the financial practices incident to consolidation, the watering of stocks, the paying of enormous commissions to lawyers and banking houses, had helped to fleece the general public. And, finally, labor has found it more

[22] H. D. Lloyd, *Wealth Against Commonwealth*, pp. 9–10.
[23] Richardson *v.* Buhl *et al.*, 77 Michigan State Reports 658.

difficult to deal with the increased power of consolidated capital and has been among the severest critics of the trusts. Typical of this power was the United States Steel Corporation, which for more than thirty years prevented large-scale labor organization in its mills, and through its influence as the dominant concern in the industry also prevented organization in other companies.

This rapid growth of monopoly and the irresponsible use of the power which went with it were viewed with concern by many of the most thoughtful citizens. Among the literature calling attention to defects in the economic life of the time, three widely read books stand out. Henry George in 1879 published his *Progress and Poverty,* in which he advocated a single tax on land values as one solution for the problem of monopoly. Edward Bellamy's *Looking Backward* (1887), by glorifying the socialist state, pointed to another solution; and Henry Demarest Lloyd's *Wealth Against Commonwealth* (1894) was the ablest and most effective attack ever delivered against trusts. The opposition which developed had already made itself felt in political channels. Further grants to railroad corporations and monopolies had been opposed by both the major parties in 1872. The Greenbackers in 1880 and the Anti-Monopolists in 1884 had called for government action to prevent or control monopolies, and this was true in 1888 of the platforms of the four leading parties—the Republican, Democratic, Prohibition, and Union Labor. Although monopolies were already presumably banned under the common law, twenty-seven states and territories by the close of 1890 had passed laws intended to prevent or destroy them, and fifteen states had incorporated provisions in their constitutions for the same purpose. In that year the federal government also took action.

THE SHERMAN ANTITRUST ACT

By 1890 public opinion had become so aroused over the subject of monopolies that federal legislation was demanded to supplement state laws. Investigations undertaken in 1888 by a committee of the House of Representatives[24] and by a committee of the Senate of the State of New York[25] offered little in the shape of constructive suggestion but confirmed current beliefs as to the evils of monopolies. President Harrison in his message of December, 1889, urged legislation against trusts which partook of the nature of conspiracies.[26] A number of antitrust bills were introduced in the Senate in 1888, but two years of discussion ensued before a bill was finally passed. Its

[24] *Report of Investigation of Trusts,* House Reports, 50th Cong., 1st Sess., 1887–88, Vol. IX, Serial Number 3112.

[25] *Report of the Senate Committee of General Laws on Investigation Relative to Trusts,* March 6, 1888.

[26] Richardson, *Messages and Papers of the Presidents,* IX, 43.

enactment was in no small measure due to the willingness of conservative Republican Senators to trade their votes to secure a simultaneous enactment of the McKinley tariff.

The Sherman Antitrust Act of 1890[27] contained eight sections; the principle and theory of the act, however, appear in the following:

"Sec. 1.—Every contract, combination in the form of trust or otherwise, or conspiracy, in restraint of trade or commerce among the several States, or with foreign nations, is hereby declared to be illegal. . . .

"Sec. 2.—Every person who shall monopolize or attempt to monopolize or combine or conspire with any other person or persons to monopolize any part of the trade or commerce among the several States, or with foreign nations, shall be deemed guilty of a misdemeanor. . . ."

Fines and imprisonment were provided for violation, and the injured person might recover three times the damages sustained. The several circuit courts of the United States were invested with jurisdiction to prevent or restrain violations of the act, and the Attorney General was directed to institute proceedings in equity against such violations.

The Sherman Act was looked upon by many as an unnecessary blow at legitimate business and as futile opposition to an inevitable economic development. The committee who framed it maintained truly, however, that the bill was simply a restating of the usual English common-law principles and their extension to America. The act did not attempt to define "contract, combination, or conspiracy in restraint of trade"; it was purposely drawn in general terms for the courts to interpret, the intention being that no business legitimately carried on need fear interference.

Senator Cullom called the Sherman Act "one of the most important enactments ever passed by Congress," but it was decidedly ineffective for a long while, chiefly, in the early years, for three reasons: First, the economic depression in the 1890's deferred further large-scale consolidation for some time; second, the general terms in which the bill was stated required much legal interpretation to be effective; and third, the federal government evinced lack of interest in enforcing it. The panic of 1893 temporarily crippled business and made both national and state governments loath to increase their burdens. The political weakness of the Harrison administration, followed by the necessary affiliations of Cleveland with eastern capitalists during his second term, prevented aggressive legislation; and under McKinley the combination movement went on merrily, with little apparent desire on the part

[27] 26 Stat. 209. The texts of this act and the other federal antitrust acts mentioned in this chapter are to be found in Jeremiah W. Jenks and Walter E. Clark, *The Trust Problem,* in "Appendix F: Federal Trust Legislation in the United States." The various sections of the Appendix contain much valuable source material. See also F. Flügel and H. U. Faulkner, *op. cit.,* pp. 541 ff.

of the administration to interfere. Down to 1901 the government had instituted eighteen suits, but with discouraging lack of success. The spirit of *laissez faire* and the economic tendency during the period toward consolidation, combined with the difficulties of handling the technical questions involved in the trust and corporate form, hindered decisive and clear-cut judicial action.

The futility of the Sherman Act seemed indisputable when in 1895 the Supreme Court refused to dissolve the American Sugar Refining Company (which had just acquired four competing Pennsylvania plants, thus enabling it to control over 95 per cent of the sugar refined) on the ground that the Sherman law was applicable only to monopoly in restraint of trade and that the mere purchase of sugar refineries or the refining of sugar was not commerce in the strict constitutional sense.[28] This almost incredible decision was considerably weakened, however, four years later in the Addyston Pipe case, when the Court held that, although the members of the pool manufactured pipe, their agreements were concerned with buying and selling across state lines, and in this case were illegal.[29] Also the Court had already decided that the act applied to railroads and had held two railroad agreements illegal.[30] Although these cases made it possible to accomplish something under the Sherman Act, we must agree with Professor Jenks when he says, "A study of these statutes and of the decisions of our courts of last resort which have been made under them will show that they have had comparatively little, practically no, effect, as regards the trend of our industrial development."[31]

While the Sherman Act had little influence upon business consolidation, it is the irony of fate that capital succeeded in using it effectively against labor unions. The Pullman strike of 1894 was broken by the government acting through the courts, when the latter held the actions of the union a conspiracy in restraint of interstate commerce and issued an injunction to desist.[32] In the famous Danbury Hatters' case members of a labor union were held financially responsible under the Sherman Act to the full amount of their individual property for losses to business occasioned by an interstate boycott.[33] Certain courts actually went so far as to question the legality of trade unions per se, holding them, because of their restrictive rules and practices, as illegal combinations both at common law and under the Sherman

[28] U.S. *v.* E. C. Knight Company, 156 U.S. 1.
[29] Addyston Pipe and Steel Co. *v.* U.S., 175 U.S. 211 (1899).
[30] U.S. *v.* Trans-Missouri Freight Association, 166 U.S. 341 (1897), and U.S. *v.* Joint Traffic Association, 171 U.S. 505 (1898).
[31] J. W. Jenks, *The Trust Problem* (rev. ed., 1905), p. 218.
[32] *In re* Debs, 158 U.S. 564 (1894). See H. R. Seager and C. A. Gulick, Jr., *op. cit.,* pp. 374 ff.
[33] Loewe *v.* Lawlor, 235 U.S. 522 (1915).

Antitrust Act.[34] In the Clayton Act of 1914, as we shall see, Congress tried to exempt labor unions from the application of the antitrust acts just as it tried more effectively to control business, but in neither case were its efforts crowned with notable success.

THE MUCKRAKERS AND THE REVIVAL OF ANTITRUST ACTIVITIES

The tremendous revival of the combination movement in the prosperous years immediately following the Spanish-American War, coincident with the abuses and the high-handed disregard of public welfare as evidenced by the large corporate interests, brought a logical reaction. Beginning with the publication in 1903–1904 of Ida M. Tarbell's "History of the Standard Oil Company" in *McClure's Magazine,* there ensued a period in which many of the worst features of our economic and social life were aired before the public. Lincoln Steffens' *Shame of the Cities* (1904) exposed the rottenness of many of the local governments; Thomas Lawson's "Frenzied Finance," published in *Everybody's Magazine* (1905–1906), showed Wall Street at its worst; Upton Sinclair in *The Jungle* (1906) revealed the horrible filth and misery of the workers in the meat-packing industry; and Charles Edward Russell excoriated the "beef trust" in *Everybody's* in articles entitled "The Greatest Trust in the World." Winston Churchill in *Coniston* (1906) drew a picture of the subservience of the state legislatures to the railroads; other phases of the railroad problems were handled by Ray Stannard Baker in a series, "The Railroads on Trial," in *McClure's;* and B. J. Hendrick in the same magazine laid bare the illegal and crooked practice of the insurance companies in "The Story of Life Insurance" (1907). Other books and numerous magazine articles enlarged upon the lawlessness and greed of big business and the venality of politicians. In the campaigns of 1896, 1900, and 1904 the Democrats directed part of their artillery against the trusts.

Some of this "muckraking" was undoubtedly exaggerated, but most of it, unfortunately, was only too true. Whether exaggerated or not, it helped to stimulate a healthy reaction for reform, a movement in which President Theodore Roosevelt took the lead. On a campaign speaking tour in 1902 he attacked the trusts, and in the next year Congress passed three acts to control big business more effectively. The first of these, known as the Expediting Act, gave preference to federal suits brought under the Interstate Commerce Act and the Sherman Antitrust Act. The second was the Elkins Antirebate Act, which aimed to clarify the law and eliminate one of the worst practices of the railroads. The third created a Department of Commerce and Labor

---

[34] Kealy *v.* Faulkner, 18 Ohio Superior and Common Pleas Decision 498 (1908); Hitchman Coal and Coke Co. *v.* Mitchell, 202 Fed. 512 (1912).

with a subsidiary Bureau of Corporations to make "diligent investigation into the organization, conduct, and management of corporations." In the same year the President directed his Attorney General to institute proceedings against the Northern Securities Company, a New Jersey holding corporation designed to create a transportation monopoly in the Northwest by controlling the stock of the Great Northern, the Northern Pacific, and the Chicago, Burlington, and Quincy. The successful issue of this suit[35] in 1904 showed that the Sherman Act might not be a useless reed in the hands of an aggressive administration. Under Roosevelt nineteen civil suits and twenty-five criminal suits were instituted in federal courts, and under Taft the effort to enforce the Sherman Act was carried on even more aggressively. The Pure Food and Drugs Act of 1906 marked a distinct step forward in the policy of government intervention to protect the welfare of the public, as did the Meat Inspection Act passed a week later.

DISSOLUTION OF THE STANDARD OIL COMPANY AND THE AMERICAN TOBACCO COMPANY

The Taft administration believed that legitimate business might go on undisturbed and a solution to the trust problem be found by the voluntary federal incorporation of concerns, their charters to be approved by a projected corporation commission, with power reserved to Congress to revoke such charters. A bill to this effect was introduced, but public interest was never sufficient to push it through. As a consequence, the government continued to press the prosecutions already commenced, and succeeded in obtaining two notable decisions in 1911. The first of these, against the Standard Oil Company of New Jersey,[36] had been in the courts more than four years. The defendant argued that the Standard Oil companies were the natural products of the growth of a single business, that they had never competed with one another and consequently could not have conspired or combined in restraint of trade. Both the circuit and Supreme courts, however, affirmed the government's contention that the concerns had so conspired by many and devious methods to build up a monopoly. The dissolution was carried out by apportioning shares in the various constituent concerns pro rata to the stockholders of the holding company.

The case of the American Tobacco Company[37] was more complicated because the organization was not merely a holding company but an actual manufacturing concern, and one which was engaged in making a number of products, including chewing and smoking tobacco, snuff, little cigars, cig-

[35] Northern Securities Co. *et al. v.* U.S., 193 U.S. 360.
[36] U.S. *v.* Standard Oil Company of New Jersey *et al.,* 221 U.S. 1.
[37] U.S. *v.* American Tobacco Co. *et al.,* 221 U.S. 106.

arettes, and tin foil. The court attempted to restore competition by creating separate companies in each line; for example, the manufacture of smoking tobacco was divided among four companies, cigarettes among three concerns, plug tobacco among four, and tin foil between two. A proportionate distribution of stock in the new companies was made, corresponding to the holdings in the old. Each new company was enjoined from co-operating with, or holding stock in, another company.

Two interesting facts stand out in regard to these decisions. The first is that the dissolutions failed in this purpose. In form there was competition, in reality there was little. The distribution of stock created simply a community of interest among the various concerns which appeared to work as harmoniously together as when under a single management. The increase in value of Standard Oil stocks after the dissolution showed that no detrimental results were feared. After more than thirty years of operation and numerous court dissolutions and interpretations, the Sherman Antitrust Act appeared to have failed utterly in its purpose of preventing monopoly and restraint. The second point to be noted was the interpretation given to the act by the two decisions. The Trans-Missouri Freight case decision (1897)[38] had refused to see any difference between reasonable and unreasonable combinations in restraint of trade, but the judges in the two decisions in 1911 professed to see a difference and maintained that the only restraint of trade which was intended by the law was that which monopolizes or attempts to monopolize. In other words, they introduced the so-called "rule of reason" and tried to differentiate between "good trusts" and "bad trusts." Many believed the "rule of reason" was an unwarranted interpretation, an *obiter dictum,* and that it simply weakened the act. It certainly made further consideration of trust cases by the courts more complicated.

DEMOCRATS AND THE TRUSTS—THE CLAYTON ACT AND THE FEDERAL TRADE COMMISSION

For years the Democratic party had assailed the Republicans as the friends and allies of the trusts. In their platform of 1912 the Democrats demanded that the Sherman Act be made more stringent in order to restore free competition. Their candidate, Woodrow Wilson, in a remarkable series of campaign speeches, emphasized what he called "The New Freedom." While claiming not to be one of those who think that competition can be established by law against a world-wide economic tendency, he still believed that much of our old, free co-operative life could be restored. Without condemning big business as such, he laid the destruction of competition to the trusts. "American industry is not free, as it once was free," he said. "Amer-

[38] U.S. *v.* Trans-Missouri Freight Association, 166 U.S. 290.

ican enterprise is not free; the man with only a little capital is finding it harder to get into the field, more and more impossible to compete with the big fellow. Why? Because the laws of this country do not prevent the strong from crushing the weak."[39] To restore, if possible, some of the old competition appeared to be the purpose of the new administration, and it was obvious that after years of criticism some legislation would be passed.

If any added impetus was necessary to bring further antitrust legislation, it was furnished during the early months of the Wilson administration by the amazing revelations of the activities of the New York, New Haven and Hartford Railroad, under the direction of J. P. Morgan, William Rockefeller, Charles S. Mellen, and others, to effect a monopoly of transportation in New England. With reckless improvidence they had used the credit of the New Haven to gain control of the Boston and Maine, the Boston and Albany, and the New York, Ontario and Western; they had then bought up competing trolley lines, and finally gained virtual control of most of the coastal water transportation to and from New England. The details of the many transactions by which this monopoly was attained revealed, not only "a loose, extravagant and an improvident management,"[40] but corruption of legislatures, subsidizing of the press, the retention of powerful political bosses as attorneys who did no legitimate legal work, fictitious sales of stocks to boost market prices, payment of unitemized vouchers, dishonest use of corporate funds, and, in the words of the Interstate Commerce Commission, the erection of a web of entangling alliances "seemingly planned, created, and manipulated by lawyers expressly retained for the purpose of concealment or deception."[41] As this story came out through the government prosecutions, even the most naïve citizen could see that the demand for further antitrust and railroad legislation had some foundation.

In his campaign speeches Wilson affirmed that the trouble with the Sherman Act was that it was not definite enough and needed a more careful statement of unlawful practices, so that legitimate business might better know when it was within the law. These ideas Congress sought to embody in the Clayton Antitrust Act of 1914.[42] The following are the chief provisions:

1. The act forbids (a) any person to discriminate in price, either directly or indirectly, between purchasers of commodities whenever such discrimination lessens competition or tends to create monopoly, (b) a manufacturer to sell his goods to a dealer under conditions requiring the latter not to handle the products of competitors—a hit at the so-called "tying" agreements.

[39] Woodrow Wilson, *The New Freedom*, p. 15.
[40] *Interstate Commerce Commission Reports*, XXXI, 34.
[41] *Ibid.*, XXXI, 31. Excerpts in F. Flügel and H. U. Faulkner, *op. cit.*, pp. 577–583.
[42] 38 Stat. 730; reproduced in part in F. Flügel and H. U. Faulkner, *op. cit.*, pp. 543–547.

2. Corporations were forbidden to acquire stock in another concern where the effect was substantially to lessen competition. The holding of stock solely for investment was allowed.

3. Interlocking directorates were forbidden in concerns engaged in interstate commerce whose capital, surplus, and undivided profits aggregated more than $1,000,000, if such concerns were competitors.

4. It was made unlawful in the case of banks for one person to serve as director or officer in another if the deposits, capital surplus, and undivided profits of any of the institutions exceeded $5,000,000.

5. Labor unions and farmers' organizations were specifically declared not to be conspiracies in restraint of trade.

A few days earlier a Federal Trade Commission of five members had been created,[43] whose business it was to investigate persons or corporations (except interstate carriers and banks) subject to the antitrust laws, and present reports of its activities. It was also granted power to issue orders requiring the cessation of illegal practices, and if these were not obeyed it was to apply for federal action to the circuit court of appeals in the district where the alleged offense was committed. The commission took over the work of the old Bureau of Corporations and was designed to act for corporations along somewhat the same line as the Interstate Commerce Commission has done for interstate carriers.

In order that Americans might compete on more equal terms with great foreign concerns, the antitrust laws were modified in 1918. The Webb Export Act stated that nothing in the Sherman Act was to be construed as making "illegal an association entered into for the sole purpose of engaging in export trade and actually engaged solely in such trade," providing this association was not party to any attempt to restrain competition or control prices within the country. Furthermore, the Clayton Act under the same condition was not to be construed as forbidding the "acquisition or ownership by any corporation of the whole or any part of the stock or other capital of any corporation organized solely for the purpose of engaging in export trade." There seems to be little doubt that the Webb Export Act has stimulated both foreign trade and combination at home.[44]

FAILURE OF ANTITRUST LEGISLATION

Despite the fact that the great majority of the American people appear to favor the maintenance of competition, where such a system is possible, their efforts to preserve it have not been entirely successful. As we shall see

[43] 38 Stat. 717; quoted in part in F. Flügel and H. U. Faulkner, *op. cit.*, pp. 547–551.

[44] L. T. Fournier, "The Purposes and Results of the Webb-Pomerene Law," *American Economic Review*, XXII, 18–33 (March, 1932).

later (pp. 609–614), the people themselves have been negligent in times of prosperity, and big business has often promoted acts to exempt or weaken the existing antitrust legislation, as, for example, in the so-called "fair trade" acts to govern the price of trade-marked commodities. While competition of a certain type exists, consolidation has continued. In 1947 seven industries out of thirty-eight having a shipment value of one billion or over for their products, showed more than 50 per cent of their production turned out by four companies: cigarettes, 90.4 per cent; soap and glycerin, 79; tires and inner tubes, 76.6; blast furnaces, 67.3; copper rolling and drawing, 60.1; motors and generators, 58.6; and motor vehicles and parts, 55.7.[45] There are at least four other industries in which eight companies produce more than 50 per cent. There are, of course, many others, such as public utilities, where monopolies exist under franchises, or where control of underlying patents, as in the case of the United Shoe Machinery Company, establishes virtual monopolies.

With regard to the many industries dominated by a few large concerns, competition as far as the consumer is concerned is an illusion rather than a reality. As in the case of cigarettes, soap, gasoline, tires, and many other commodities, the competition is largely limited to advertising; the price and the quality remain approximately the same. This sort of thing has developed in part through trade associations, which inform the trade regarding prices and methods of trade in a manner that makes it possible to evade both the antitrust acts and competition in price and quality. Moreover, great industries have found it safer and in the long run more remunerative to divide the business rather than fight to get it all, particularly in face of the antitrust acts. The result is that we live in an age of administrative rather than competitive prices.[46] There might be, but by no means always is, competition in quality, service, and style, while prices remain stabilized.

As to the laws themselves, there were many other reasons why they failed. First of all, they were not fitted to the problem. As one student well put it, "When the need was to shape the future, it [Congress] looked to the past. On the eve of the greatest of industrial revolutions, the National Government was fitted out with a weapon forged to meet the problems of petty trade. . . . A rule of the common law, emerging from petty trade, was thus evoked to control affairs of industry."[47] Instead of recognizing increasing size and consolidation in a changing economic world and protecting the public through licenses and supervision, it sought to hold on to the past and deal with the situation through restraint of interstate traffic.

[45] *Statistical Abstract of the United States, 1952*, p. 755.
[46] H. U. Faulkner, *Decline of Laissez Faire*, pp. 171–175.
[47] Walton Hamilton, quoted in *ibid.*, p. 185.

One point which is sometimes forgotten is the fact that the Antitrust Division of the Department of Justice was never granted enough money to carry on adequately its work. Juries were often inadequately equipped to handle the problems with which they were confronted, and the lawyers themselves were often unable to deal with the mass of documents necessary for a convincing case. Moreover, the plaintiffs themselves were often not too helpful, since they did not "sit in" on the conspiracy which injured them. The enforcement of antitrust laws is largely determined by the attitude of the executive. Since 1900, with the exception of the McKinley administration and the period of the 1920's, the executives were usually interested in enforcing the law. Not only so, but the Supreme Court also seemed conscientious in interpreting the legislation. But the Court shifted its point of view and its interpretation so often that it confused the issues and weakened the possibility of doing much with existing laws. It is surprising that the legislation accomplished much of anything at all.

THE MONEY TRUST

No discussion of business consolidation would be complete without reference to the concentration of banking power. Parallel with the rapid but extensive consolidation of business has gone that of the banking interests. The increasing wealth of the country naturally enlarged the size of the banks, and the greater demands of their customers necessitated growth and consolidation in order to meet them. By the opening of the twentieth century, however, this concentration was so vast that there was a firmly grounded conviction among many that a small group controlled the financial resources of the land, lending and withholding funds where they pleased, thus holding in the hollow of their hands the fate of many businesses.

We shall see in Chapter 23 how the important lines of railroads through interlocking directorates and stockholdings were in the power of six influential groups dominated by a score of men. It was now asserted that the same men controlled the banking facilities. Around the Morgan-Rockefeller interests, wrote John Moody in 1904,

. . . or what must ultimately become one greater group, all other smaller groups of capitalists congregate. They are all allied and intertwined by their various mutual interests. For instance, the Pennsylvania Railroad interests are on the one hand allied with the Vanderbilts and on the other with the Rockefellers. The Vanderbilts are closely allied with the Morgan group, and both the Pennsylvania and the Vanderbilt interests have recently become the dominating factors in the Reading system, a former Morgan road and the most important part of the anthracite coal combine which has always been dominated by the Morgan people. . . . Viewed as a whole, we find the dominating influences in the Trust to be made up of an intricate network of large and small capitalists, many allied to one another by ties of more or less importance, but all being appendages to or parts of the greater groups, which are themselves dependent on and allied with the two mammoth, or Rockefeller and Morgan groups. These two mammoth groups jointly . . . constitute the heart of the business and commercial life of the nation.[48]

The concentration of capital was promoted by the fact that the Rockefeller and Morgan interests worked through banks which they controlled; thus the National City Bank, for some years the greatest of American banking institutions,[49] became the Rockefeller bank, while the Morgans controlled the First National, the Bankers' Trust (founded by the Morgans), and others. Wall Street and the insurance companies formed a community of interest in the joint direction of the great trust companies; hence the influence of Wall Street became dominant in the vast lending operations of the insurance companies.

The general belief was fully confirmed in the report of the Pujo Committee (1913), which pointed out that the concentration of control of money and credit had been effected chiefly through consolidations of competitive or potentially competitive banks and trust companies; through interlocking directorates and stockholdings; through the influence of the powerful banking houses, banks, and trust companies brought to bear on insurance companies, railroads, and producing and trading companies; and finally through partnership arrangements between a few of the leading banking houses in the purchase of security issues, which had the effect of virtually destroying competition. The Committee named J. P. Morgan & Co., the First National Bank of New York, and the National City Bank as the most powerful banking units, and placed their combined assets in New York City, as controlled through seven subsidiary banks, at over $2,000,000,000. In addition to the interests named, the Committee believed that Lee Higginson & Co., Kidder, Peabody & Co., and Kuhn, Loeb & Co. were the principal banking agencies through which the corporate enterprises of the United States obtained capital for their operations. Four allied financial institutions in New York City, it affirmed, held 341 directorships in banks and in transportation, public utility, and insurance companies, whose aggregate resources were $22,245,000,000.

If by a "money trust" is meant an established and well-defined identity and community of interest between a few leaders of finance which has been created and is held together through stockholdings, interlocking directorates, and other forms of domination over banks, trust companies, railroads, public service, and

[48] John Moody, *op. cit.,* p. 493.
[49] Through numerous consolidations, the Chase National Bank in 1930 finally surpassed the National City Bank in size. See p. 611. By the late 1940's the Bank of America of California became the largest bank in the world.

industrial corporations, and which has resulted in a vast and growing concentration of control of money and credit in the hands of a comparatively few men—your committee has no hesitation in asserting as a result of its investigation that this condition, largely developed within the past five years, exists in this country today.[50]

While it was true that to a considerable extent this growth and consolidation followed natural economic laws—as is illustrated by the consolidation of financial power in other countries—at the same time there was a real danger in a situation in which the economic lifeblood of the nation was controlled by a small group of men using their power for private ends. The report of the Committee contained a number of recommendations in regard to bettering the banking facilities, breaking up concentration, and supervising the stock exchange. Some of the best of these were incorporated in the law creating the Federal Reserve System, the adoption of which was undoubtedly furthered by this investigation; in the Clayton Act, which forbade interlocking directorates in large banks; and in the Esch-Cummins bill, which empowered the Interstate Commerce Commission to supervise plans and security issues in the reorganization of interstate railroads. Federal laws, however, had little if any real effect in preventing the consolidation of capital until the days of the New Deal.

By 1914 the problem of monopoly had been studied and discussed from almost every angle. For more than a quarter of a century both the state and federal governments had experimented with legislation designed to prevent or check monopolies not operating under government permission. Nevertheless, the nation was to see during the boom of the 1920's one of the most intensive and widespread eras of consolidation it had yet experienced. The subsequent history of this consolidation and the public's more recent attitude on this subject will be presented in a later chapter.

SELECTED READINGS

Faulkner, H. U., *The Decline of Laissez Faire,* chap. 8.
Jenks, J. W., and Clark, W. E., *The Trust Problem,* chaps. 3–5, 9, 13–15.
Seager, H. R., and Gulick, C. A., Jr., *Trust and Corporation Problems,* chaps. 5, 8–15.
Haney, L. H., *Business Organization and Combination,* chaps. 6–16, 23–27.
Ripley, W. Z., *Trusts, Pools, and Corporations,* Introduction.
Flügel, F., and Faulkner, H. U., *Readings in the Economic and Social History of the United States,* chap. 14.

---

[50] Report of the Committee Appointed to Investigate the Concentration of Control of Money and Credit, 62nd Congress, 3rd Sess., p. 130; quoted by Chester A. Phillips, *Readings in Money and Banking* (1916), p. 606. See also F. Flügel and H. U. Faulkner, *op. cit.,* pp. 597–600.

CHAPTER 22

THE LABOR MOVEMENT

TO 1914

BACKGROUND OF LABOR ORGANIZATION

OUR economic history from the earliest colonial days has been characterized by a "labor problem"; but a "labor movement"—that is, an organized continued effort on the part of wage earners to better their standard of living—necessarily waited upon conditions arising from the growth in population, the rapid increase in manufacturing, and the concentration of population in cities. These effects of the Industrial Revolution were delayed in this country for many reasons—scarcity of labor, lack of liquid capital, abundance of rich unoccupied farming land—all tending to direct the energies of the people into rural occupations and delay the era of manufacturing and urban life.[1]

Nevertheless, population grew rapidly, almost doubling every twenty years until 1860. The percentage of the total population living in cities of 8000 or over increased slowly before 1840 and then more rapidly; only 8.5 per cent of the people lived in such cities in 1841, but by 1860 the percentage had risen to 16.1 and by 1930 to 49.1. The years of most rapid growth as shown in the accompanying table correspond closely with the period of greatest activity on the part of labor. If the word "urban" is used, as it is in the census reports, to designate places of 2500 inhabitants or over, it is found that, in 1950, 54 per cent of the population lived in urban territory, as compared with 28.6 per cent in 1880.

Although the growth of the urban population has been nation-wide, it has been most notable in the manufacturing sections; in 1920 more than two-thirds was contained in three geographic sections—the New England, the Middle Atlantic, and the East North Central States. Rhode Island and

[1] Above, pp. 240 ff.

Massachusetts each showed over 90 per cent living in towns, New York over 80 per cent, and New Jersey over 70 per cent. The three sections noted above turned out almost three-quarters of the manufactured products of the nation, reckoned in terms of value. The Census of 1849 recorded 957,000 wage earners producing commodities to the value of $1,019,000,000; that of 1889 showed 4,252,000, whose products were valued at $9,372,000,000; the figures for 1914 placed the wage earners at 7,036,000 and the value of the

GROWTH OF CITY POPULATION

Year	Total Population	Places of 8000 Inhabitants or Over		
		Population	Number of Places	Per Cent of Population
1790	3,929,214	131,472	6	3.3
1800	5,308,483	210,873	6	4.0
1820	9,638,453	475,135	13	4.9
1840	17,069,453	1,453,994	44	8.5
1860	31,443,321	5,072,256	141	16.1
1880	50,155,783	11,365,698	285	22.7
1900	75,994,575	25,018,335	547	32.0
1920	105,710,620	46,307,640	924	43.8
1930	122,775,046	60,333,452	1208	49.1
1940	131,669,275	64,896,083	1323	49.3

Fifteenth Census, 1930, Vol. I, *Population*, p. 9.

products at $24,246,000,000; and those for 1929 at 8,839,000 and $70,435,-000,000.

The rise of a class of wage earners and their concentration in urban communities are the fundamental factors leading to the growth of the labor movement. The increase in manufacturing after the Civil War developed larger business units, and this accretion in the power of capital stirred the wage earners to action, especially those skilled workers whose occupations were imperiled by the invention of new machinery. The passing of the small industry, in which a close personal relationship could be maintained between employer and employee, and its replacement by the corporation, with its thousands of owners scattered throughout the country, tended to a lack of understanding between labor and capital.

If the new machinery and the growth of mighty business units affected the wage earner detrimentally, they also contained the elements of his salvation. Big factories brought the workers together in cities where they could mingle with their fellows, exchange their ideas more readily, and combine more easily for resistance. Improvements in paper manufacture and printing made it possible to spread their program, develop loyalty, and weld the local organizations more firmly together. An aggressive labor press, as it developed, not only contributed to the education of the worker in the problems involved, but in like manner made capital conversant with the aims of labor. The whole movement was accelerated by the diffusion of knowledge through our democratic system of education and was integrated by the development of railways and more rapid methods of communication.

Finally, the conditions under which labor worked provided a real impetus to the development of an organized movement. The truck system of payment, company stores, long hours, low pay, unsanitary conditions of work, the sweatshop evil, the unconscionable exploitation of women and children, the incredibly degrading rules in practice in many establishments, lack of effective labor legislation, and inability to obtain justice in the courts—these and many other aspects of the problem which existed in the decades following the Civil War help to make clear the need of such organizations as the Knights of Labor and the American Federation of Labor.[2]

EFFECT OF THE CIVIL WAR ON LABOR

Organized labor, as we have already pointed out, had a history extending back half a century before the Civil War.[3] Until the 1850's, however, organization was largely local and on a relatively small scale. The Civil War gave a distinct impetus to the American labor movement. The struggle resulted in a deeper consideration of economic and social matters, for the question of the liberation of the slaves could hardly be discussed without also involving the status of northern labor, especially when economists of the South maintained that the condition of a southern slave was preferable to that of a northern wage earner—a contention which, considering hours and factory conditions, was not without point. The increasing cost of living brought on by the war was not met by a parallel rise in wages, for a steady influx of immigrants and the adoption of labor-saving machinery helped to meet the scarcity of labor. Especially irritating to labor was an act of July 4, 1864, which enabled agents of employers to engage foreign laborers under a contract in which their transportation was to be paid by future wages.

War tariffs and war contracts brought a sudden accumulation of wealth to a handful of industrialists and at the same time accentuated the sharp contrast between rich and poor. On the one hand was a growing power in the hands of capital, and on the other a misgiving concerning the likelihood of a glutted labor market when the soldiers returned. Both factors strengthened the determination of labor to keep wages up after they commenced to rise during the last two years of the war. Numerous local unions and at least

[2] See excerpts from *Report of the Committee of the Senate upon the Relations Between Labor and Capital* (1885), in F. Flügel and H. U. Faulkner, *Readings in the Economic and Social History of the United States*, pp. 816–829.

[3] Above, pp. 300 ff.

ten national unions sprang into existence between 1863 and 1866. The first of the great Railroad Brotherhoods, the Brotherhood of Locomotive Engineers, was organized at Detroit in 1863 as the "Brotherhood of the Footboard"; their example was followed in 1869 by the founding of the Brotherhood of Locomotive Firemen. By 1870 there were in existence no less than thirty-two national trade unions, and each important city had its trade assembly, its labor press, and its workingmen's library.

THE KNIGHTS OF LABOR AND ITS FORERUNNERS

Before the impetus given by the Civil War had spent itself, at least one notable attempt had been made to bring all labor together in a single organization. Under the leadership of W. H. Sylvis, and on the basis of the city assemblies of trade unions, the National Labor Union was organized; it held seven annual conventions, beginning in 1866, and at the height of its power had a membership of 600,000. The idea that the future of the wage earner lay in co-operative enterprises rather than in militant trade-unionism was strongly held and numerous experiments were made. The National Labor Union, among other things, advocated Chinese exclusion, the eight-hour day, and the establishment of a government bureau of labor. But it was essentially a politico-reform organization rather than a true trade union, and it disappeared after it had organized the National Labor Reform party in 1872.

Another notable development immediately after the war was the growth of the Knights of St. Crispin,[4] founded in Milwaukee in 1867 and especially strong in the shoe-trade centers of Massachusetts. It throve from 1868 to 1870, when it became the "undoubted foremost trade organization of the world."[5] Participation in politics and the depression following the panic of 1873 smashed both of these groups as they did many others. The period 1873–1880 was characterized by business demoralization, unemployment, and desperate and usually unsuccessful strikes sometimes accompanied by violence and crime[6]—notably the great railroad strike of 1877—all of which left the labor movement disintegrated and to some extent discredited. Only 18 per cent of the national trade unions survived these years.

During this discouraging period labor turned wholeheartedly to political action and to secret organizations. One of these was destined to play an important role in the recuperative years of the early eighties. In 1869 Uriah S.

---

[4] So called after St. Crispin, the patron saint of shoemakers.

[5] G. E. McNeill, *The Labor Movement*, p. 200.

[6] The deeds of the "Molly Maguires" in the anthracite coal regions of Pennsylvania illustrate the labor lawlessness during this period. J. F. Rhodes, *History of the United States from Hayes to McKinley, 1877–1896*, pp. 52–87, tells the conventional story; J. W. Coleman, *The Molly Maguire Riots* (1936) gives a better-rounded picture.

Stephens, a Philadelphia garmentmaker, and six fellow craftsmen organized the Noble Order of the Knights of Labor. The high idealism of Stephens was written into the constitution and upheld by Terence V. Powderly, who succeeded him as Grand Master. Taking their motto from Solon, they affirmed, "That is the most perfect government in which an injury to one is the concern of all." Their aim was to secure to the wage earner the fullest enjoyment of the wealth he creates, and leisure for the development of his intellectual, moral, and social faculties. They favored the eight-hour day, a tax on incomes and inheritances, postal savings banks, workingmen's compensation for injuries received through lack of necessary safeguards, and the appropriation by the community of the unearned increment on land. That the socialism strong in Europe at that time had made some progress here is seen in their advocacy of the public ownership of such utilities as railways, gas plants, and waterworks. In addition they urged private co-operative organizations of workingmen to handle the production and distribution of goods.[7] The leaders and a minority of the order felt "that strikes are deplorable in their effect and contrary to the best interests of the order," and that success lay in "agitation, education and organization." "Without organization," said Powderly, "we cannot accomplish anything; through it, we hope to forever banish that curse of modern civilization—wage slavery."[8]

The order was secret at first; even the name was unknown. It was designated by five asterisks and usually spoken of as the "Five Stars." Growth was slow in the beginning. In 1869 only eleven tailors comprised the membership of Assembly No. 1, and in 1873 there were only six assemblies, all in Philadelphia. Two years later the organization had grown to eighty assemblies in the city and vicinity, and in 1875 a national convention was called at Tyrone, Pennsylvania, and an invitation extended to other labor organizations to join them. By 1883 the membership was 52,000; but within three years it had jumped to 700,000, and at the height of its career numbered close to a million. Widespread, though unwarranted, distrust of the organization led the Knights in 1881 to abolish its secret character. In make-up it resembled a "grand national union of industrial workers" rather than a federation of craft unions as exemplified later in the American Federation of Labor. Whether a local union or a group of craft unions, all were directly affiliated with the central governing body. Composed of both national trade unions and local assemblies, its composition was heterogeneous. At first it was open to all workers alike—skilled and unskilled, men and women, black and white—but later three-fourths of its members had to be wage

[7] C. D. Wright, "Historical Sketch of the Knights of Labor," *Quarterly Journal of Economics*, I, pp. 142–143 (Jan., 1887). See also F. Flügel and H. U. Faulkner, *op. cit.*, pp. 793–798.

[8] Speech before the annual convention in Pittsburgh, 1880.

earners. But even this rule gave access to all types of reformers; many of the assemblies included small businessmen and farmers. Under such conditions strong divergence of opinion as to policies was bound to arise.

Two main factions appeared, one favoring reform through political channels and the other advocating direct action. The latter group proved the more powerful and embarked the Knights on an aggressive campaign to raise the standard of living, thus involving them in many severe strikes. The most notable and successful of these was the one directed against the Gould railway system in 1885 which wrung concessions from one of the most powerful capitalists of the day. Writing in 1886 of the Knights of Labor, Professor Ely described them as "the most powerful and the most remarkable labor organization of modern times . . . established on truly scientific principles which involved either an intuitive perception of the nature of industrial progress, or a wonderful acquaintance with the laws of economic society."[9]

But the year 1886, which marked the height of their power, marked also the beginning of their downfall. Unsuccessful strikes in that year undermined their prestige and alienated public sympathy;[10] factional differences prevented united action; inadequate leadership handicapped them;[11] political activity hurt them; and overcentralization of power created suspicion. Besides all this, the rising opposition of a new organization, the American Federation of Labor, aided in their undoing. The decline of the order after 1888 was as rapid as had been its growth. Its brief but spectacular career, however, was not without results. Many weak unions had been reorganized and put on their feet through affiliation with the Knights, and others had been founded. A standing Committee of Labor was established by the House of Representatives in 1883, and in the following year a national Bureau of Labor was created to gather expert information. At the same time a rather thorough investigation by a Senate committee on the relations between capital and labor was undertaken in 1883.[12] Even President Cleveland, who little understood the significance of the labor disputes which filled his first administration, in 1886 sent to Congress the first presidential message devoted to labor, in which he advocated the creation of a board of labor commissioners to act as official arbiters in labor disputes. Congress followed

[9] R. T. Ely, *Labor Movement in America*, p. 75.

[10] The Haymarket riot of 1886, with the attendant bomb-throwing, also alienated public sympathy from the labor movement, although neither the Knights of Labor nor the American Federation of Labor had any connection with the anarchists who were responsible.

[11] This weakness is particularly emphasized in N. J. Ware, *The Labor Movement in the United States, 1860–1895* (1929). A more favorable impression of Powderly will be found in his autobiography, *The Path I Trod*, edited by H. J. Carman, Henry David, and P. N. Guthrie (1940).

[12] *Report of the Committee of the Senate upon the Relations Between Labor and Capital* (1885). Excerpts from this report are to be found in F. Flügel and H. U. Faulkner, *op. cit.,* pp. 816–832.

his suggestion halfheartedly in 1888 by enacting a law for the settlement of railway disputes by arbitration, provided both parties were willing. Perhaps the greatest contribution of the Knights was their re-emphasis of the dignity of labor and the need of organization and solidarity.

THE AMERICAN FEDERATION OF LABOR

The origin of the American Federation of Labor dates from 1881, when a joint call for a convention was issued by the Knights of Industry, an organization strong in the Middle West, and the Amalgamated Labor Union, an offshoot of the Knights of Labor. This convention called a second, which met at Pittsburgh in the same year and formed a union which was reorganized at Columbus in 1886 as the American Federation of Labor. Although the early platforms of the Federation embodied such demands as a protective tariff, anti-contract immigration, the abolition of conspiracy laws as applied to trade unions, and compulsory education, the trend of its policy has been away from direct political action to unionism pure and simple. In this it differed radically from the Knights of Labor.

The American Federation, as its name implies, was distinctly a federation of craft and industrial unions rather than a "one big union" affair, and its policy has been one of distinct liberality toward the autonomy of its constituent groups. In 1951 it was composed of the following elements:

1. National and international unions, of which there were 108, comprising 55,000 local unions. They had a total membership of over 9,000,000.
2. Local trade and federal unions, composed of seven or more wage earners whose trade and calling are not organized and who are not members of any body affiliated with the Federation. There are hundreds of such unions.
3. Fifty state federations (including Alaska and Puerto Rico), with which the labor groups inside the several states are directed to join.
4. City central bodies, numbering about 1000, to which the locals are expected to ally themselves, but the powers of which are limited by the American Federation and the various national trade unions.
5. The national and international unions are grouped more or less roughly into departments, according to the line of work followed, as the Building Trades Department, Metal Trades Department, Railroad Employees Department, and Union Label Trades Department. Over 700 local department councils supervise locally the work of the departments. Each of the four departments has its separate set of officers.

The officers of the Federation consist of a president, fifteen vice presidents, and a secretary-treasurer, who are elected at the annual convention and form a powerful executive body. The national and international unions have virtual self-government, but the power of the local union is distinctly circumscribed. By a per capita tax on all of the members, ample funds are obtained to carry on the work of the Federation, which has executive offices in its own building in Washington.

The growth of the American Federation was slow for a number of years, its membership numbering only 100,000 in 1890, and 278,000 in 1898. By 1900 this had grown to 548,000, by 1904 to 1,676,000, and by 1914 to 2,000,000. The years from 1898 to 1904 were, perhaps, the most successful which the A. F. of L. has experienced, years which one labor historian has called the "heroic" days of unionism,[13] a period in which idealism, self-sacrifice, and driving energy made organized labor an important factor in American economic life. It was also a period in which organized labor received wide recognition from employers, one which another historian has called a "honeymoon period of capital and labor."[14]

Not only did membership increase rapidly, but a helping hand was extended from such middle-class organizations as the National Consumers' League (organized 1898), the National Civic Federation (1901), the National Child Labor Committee (1904), and the American Association for Labor Legislation (1906), all committed to collective bargaining and, in the case of the last two, to far-reaching social legislation. "It was the harvest," said Gompers, "of the years of organizing work which was beginning to bear fruit."[15] These successful years, however, brought a stiffening of the lines of battle on the part of capital, and progress during the next decade was not so rapid.[16] This growing opposition to labor development was headed by the National Association of Manufactures (founded 1895) and its subsidiary organizations such as the American Anti-Boycott Association, which financed the legal battles in the Danbury Hatters' case and the Buck Stove and Range case. It was characterized by the extension and perfection of a technique for fighting labor which included the use of the injunction, the "yellow-dog contract," and the labor spy. Internally labor itself was weakened by the perpetual battle between those favoring industrial organization and those committed to craft unions, and between those favoring a distinct labor party and those who would continue the accepted political policy of the A. F. of L. Those who believed in political action were generally socialists who were eager to win organized labor to their movement. A second period of rapid growth occurred during the First World War, when

[13] L. L. Lorwin, *The American Federation of Labor*, p. 59, note.
[14] Selig Perlman in J. R. Commons *et al.*, *History of Labor in the United States*, II, 524.
[15] Samuel Gompers, *Seventy Years of Life and Labor* (1925), II, 105.
[16] See H. U. Faulkner, *Decline of Laissez Faire*, pp. 295–301, and F. Flügel and H. U. Faulkner, *op. cit.*, pp. 808–812.

the membership doubled from approximately 2,020,000 in 1914 to 4,078,000 in 1920, and a third great period of expansion occurred during the years of the New Deal and the Second World War.[17]

Although built primarily upon the basis of craft unions, certain large industrial unions like the United Mine Workers, the Western Federation of Miners, and the International Union of Brewery Workers affiliated without materially changing the complexion of the larger organization. On the other hand, certain important groups, notably the Railway Brotherhoods, have constantly refused to affiliate with the Federation. In recent years, as we shall see later, there have been important defections from the ranks of the A. F. of L. and a powerful rival organization, the Congress of Industrial Organizations, has appeared. Labor has never operated as a single unified group.

POLICIES OF THE AMERICAN FEDERATION OF LABOR

Broadly speaking, the purpose of the American Federation of Labor has been: (1) to agitate all questions looking toward the benefit of the working classes, in order to bring about the enactment of favorable measures and the repeal of oppressive laws in both state and national legislatures; (2) to use all possible means to remedy abuses under which the wage earner works and to uphold him in his just rights and privileges; and (3) to promote close and thorough organization to insure such results. More definitely, it has attempted to raise the standard of living by fighting for shorter hours, higher wages, and better working conditions. At the same time it has sought to protect its members by benefit and insurance schemes and by pushing union labor products.

The policies of the labor unions and the measure of success they have won during the past fifty years have been to no small degree due to their leaders. During these formative years American labor on the whole was fortunate in its leadership, and the long tenure of office which the best officials have had shows a realization of this fact on the part of the rank and file. Perhaps the most brilliant was John Mitchell (1870–1919). Starting work in the coal mines at thirteen, he joined the United Mine Workers of America on its organization in 1890 and nine years later, at the age of twenty-nine, was its president. Although there were only 43,000 members when he rose to power, so skillfully did he direct their uphill fight that he lived to see a membership of 400,000, probably the largest trade union of his time. At the age of thirty-two he led the miners through the spectacular and successful coal strike of 1902 in such superb fashion that his prestige became national.

[17] Below, pp. 677–681.

The most famous of the labor leaders during his period and the most valuable in his services to the wage earner was Samuel Gompers. Born in London in 1850 of Dutch-Jewish parentage, he emigrated to America at the age of thirteen and soon after joined as an apprentice the first cigar makers' union organized in New York. An active worker in the founding of both the American Federation and the Cigar Makers' International Union, he became president of the former in 1882, and with the exception of one year (1894) was annually re-elected until his death in 1924. Scores of other able leaders could be mentioned—the Railway Brotherhoods have been particularly productive of them—men whose contributions to the organization and integration of the 100 or more national and international unions are well known in the labor world.

These men, trained in the rough school of experience, have developed a hard-headed and practical, but at the same time aggressive, policy. Whatever may have been their attitude as to ultimate ends, they refused to allow any dreams of a millennium to stand in the way of fighting for what small gains could be attained at the moment. "We are all practical men," said Adolph Strasser, president of the Cigar Makers' Union, before a Senate committee in 1883. "We have no ultimate ends. We are going on from day to day. We are fighting only for immediate objects—objects that can be realized in a few years."[18] Samuel Gompers' insistence upon rather strict adherence to a policy of organization based on national craft or trade unions, upon frugality in money matters, and upon avoidance of radical economic theories enabled him with considerable success to bring the pressure of organized labor to bear on such practical demands as the eight-hour day, the Saturday half-holiday, federal child labor legislation, the restriction of immigration and alien contract labor, and workingmen's compensation. In brief, American labor under the leadership of Gompers and the A. F. of L. largely reverted to the type of old-line unionism followed in Great Britain for many decades after the collapse of Chartism.

While pleased with whatever can be obtained peaceably, the American Federation of Labor has not hesitated to back its constituent unions in the fierce warfare of strikes and boycotts. Ordinarily a local is forbidden to strike without the consent of the national, but, that consent once given, the national is responsible for the successful outcome. With the growth of the Federation has come a corresponding increase of strikes and lockouts, rather than a diminution, notwithstanding the improved methods for settling disputes adopted by many of the leading unions. The two chief ends hoped for in strikes have been wage increases and recognition of the union; it is interest-

[18] *Report of the Committee of the Senate upon the Relations Between Capital and Labor*, I, 460.

ing to note that the proportion of strikes attributable to the latter has constantly increased. Three-fifths of the strikes called in 1881, for example, were for higher wages and only one-sixteenth for recognition of the union, while in 1905 less than one-third were for higher pay and about an equal proportion for union recognition.[19] By means of the boycott the unions have attempted to put their stamp of disapproval upon the products of certain employers hostile to organized labor, as in the case of the Buck Stove and Range Company of St. Louis, and Daniel Loewe, hat manufacturer of Danbury, Connecticut. What amounts to an indirect boycott is the appeal to all friends of labor to use only goods bearing a union label. Other methods by which labor has sought to protect itself are many. Regulations are demanded regarding hours of work, relations of union to nonunion men in the shop, use of nonunion materials, number of helpers and apprentices, and many other matters of daily importance about which it seems advisable to have a definite understanding.

The most fundamental desire of the wage earner is for some sense of security as regards his work and wages. This, along with the growing strength of trade-unionism, has brought a rapid development in collective bargaining. John Mitchell believed that "the hope of future peace in the industrial world lies in the trade agreement,"[20] and it must be admitted that where given a fair trial collective bargaining has proved the most hopeful factor in lessening the possibility of serious labor strife. The trade agreement as it developed ranged from the simplest type to the more complicated forms taken by the International Typographical Union in its dealing with the American Newspaper Publishers' Association and the elaborate ones in the organized ready-made clothing industry. Some employers have become sufficiently enthusiastic over the stabilizing influence of these agreements to be reconciled to the closed shop.

INDUSTRIAL UNIONISM AND THE I.W.W.

Although craft unionism was undoubtedly in the ascendant from the 1880's until the late 1930's, it did not occupy the entire stage even in the early years. Industrial unionism persisted in such groups as the United Mine Workers of America, where every workman from slate picker to engineer belongs to one union, the International Longshoremen's Association, and the ready-made clothing unions.[21]

For practical reasons, industrial unionism survived even in the days when

---

[19] *Twenty-First Annual Report of the Commissioner of Labor, 1906, Strikes and Lockouts* (1907), p. 32. See also F. Flügel and H. U. Faulkner, *op. cit.*, pp. 832–835.

[20] John Mitchell, *Organized Labor* (1903), p. 347.

[21] Amalgamated Clothing Workers (men's clothing) and the International Ladies' Garment Workers' Union (women's clothing).

skilled craftsmen predominated. It was the logical form for an industry which has workmen in many different trades, or an industry like mining, that is often isolated from great centers. Moreover, as we shall see later, it was practically the only type that could be successful in the new mass industries, where labor-saving machinery was rapidly displacing skilled craftsmen.[22]

Militant industrial unionism never quite died out after the disintegration of the Knights of Labor, but it was not until 1905 that it seriously challenged the trade unions. A convention held in that year in Chicago under the influence of the Western Federation of Miners and the socialistically inclined American Labor Union, and dominated by such radicals as Eugene V. Debs, leader of the Socialist party, Daniel DeLeon, founder of the Socialist Labor party, and William D. Haywood, founded the Industrial Workers of the World. Declaring that the "universal economic evils affecting the working class can be eradicated only by a universal working-class movement," they demanded the formation of "one great industrial union, embracing all industries, providing for craft autonomy locally, industrial autonomy internationally and wage class unity generally." "It must be founded on the class struggle," said the manifesto, "and its general administration must be conducted in harmony with the recognition of the irrepressible conflict between the capitalist class and the working class." A new preamble affixed to their constitution in 1908 asserted that "a struggle must go on until the workers of the world organize as a class, take possession of the earth and the machinery of production and abolish the wage system."[23] Believing in the class struggle, they advocated direct action as the means to victory. Direct action included such tactics as the general strike, boycott, and sabotage. Sabotage might be peaceful, merely soldiering on the job, or it might involve such violent tactics as destruction of property. Enmity to the present order was fundamental in their philosophy, and their methods of warfare were those best suited to the moment. The I.W.W. was the American aspect of revolutionary socialism growing throughout the world.

The doctrines of the I.W.W. appealed to the great class of unorganized, unskilled workers generally, especially to certain groups of eastern factory operatives and to the migratory workers of the West who follow the harvest and cut the lumber. Although handicapped from the start by factional quarrels and overloaded with strong leaders, the I.W.W. from 1909 to 1917 was an aggressive organization. With great ability its agitators handled the Lawrence strike of 1912 and the Paterson strike of 1913, and kept the Northwest in a state of unrest. Their revolutionary language and violent methods

[22] Below, pp. 679–681.
[23] Quoted in P. F. Brissenden, *The I.W.W.*, Appendix II.

eventually aroused the hostility of the public and inclined it to condone the lawless and extralegal methods employed by communities in their efforts to rid themselves of this group. The opposition of the I.W.W. to the war in 1914 brought them into direct hostility to the government, which further curtailed their operations. Although its members at the height of its activity in 1916 probably did not number more than 70,000, the lack of numbers was counterbalanced by the enthusiasm and revolutionary ardor of its members. In the years after the war many of its members were largely absorbed in the Communist party.

Despite the disappearance of the I.W.W., its influence on the labor movement was strong. It strengthened the antagonism of the A. F. of L. toward dual unionism but at the same time made clear the necessity of doing something for the unskilled worker. It was the failure of the Textile Workers Union to take the leadership at Lawrence and Paterson that opened the way for the I.W.W. The I.W.W. was interested in the Negro and in the migratory unskilled worker and undoubtedly improved the condition of the latter. But above all it strengthened the tendency toward industrial unionism at a time when the new mass industries were creating millions of unskilled workers.

Before going further it may be well to note briefly certain criticisms of labor unions. The hostility of the public to a revolutionary organization of the I.W.W. type is easily understandable. But the American Federation of Labor and, in more recent years, the Congress of Industrial Organizations are neither radical nor socialist, so that the attack proceeds from a different angle. Many critics have assailed labor unions on the grounds of "authorized practices that destroy efficiency, limit output, increase costs enormously, produce a labor monopoly,"[24] and this arraignment undoubtedly includes the chief counts brought against them. The unions are accused of so minutely prescribing the amount of work to be done by their members and the manner in which the job shall be carried on, and of so arbitrarily limiting membership, as to show an utter indifference to other workmen and to the public welfare amounting almost to a conspiracy against society. The classic examples of this evil, it is pointed out, are found in the building trade, one of the great basic industries, where regional disputes, limitation of output, and arbitrary rules of all kinds are sometimes carried to absurd and wasteful extremes. Labor has also been bitterly criticized because of certain unscrupulous leaders who have used their power to rob both workers and employers. Although this type of racketeer is rare, enough of them have operated, particularly during the 1920's, to injure the reputation of a great and funda-

[24] F. L. Bullard, "Labor Unions at the Danger Line," *Atlantic Monthly*, Vol. CXXVI, No. 6 (Dec., 1923).

mentally honest movement. A frequent attack made in recent years is that organized labor has grown so strong as to unbalance the economic system. As long as labor is dependent upon others for a job, there is a certain speciousness about this argument.

LABOR AND POLITICS

As soon as the franchise was extended downward far enough to include the wage earners, it was inevitable that the demands of labor would become intertwined with politics. This was true of the first labor movement of the 1820's and 1830's, but inadequate facilities for communication, as well as the localization of manufacturing, prevented this first political effort from becoming national in scope. Workingmen's parties, nevertheless, were formed in New York State and workingmen's candidates presented themselves in Philadelphia, New England, and elsewhere. The depression following the panic of 1837 interrupted the political activities of labor, and until after the Civil War its efforts were directed along other channels.[25]

Although a Labor Reform party entered a presidential candidate in 1872, the radical labor vote during the next few years was absorbed in the Greenback party, which in 1878 coalesced with the Labor Reform group. The Greenback platform, in addition to its views on currency reform, included demands for the regulation of interstate commerce, a graduated income tax, prohibition of the importation of contract labor, and labor legislation. The support of the Greenbackers in 1880 and 1884 was drawn chiefly from the western farmers and eastern labor; the party disappeared in the election of 1888 and its place was taken by the Union Labor party, which drew its vote chiefly from the West and South. The strongest and most radical of the early third parties was the Populist or People's party, which polled over a million votes in 1892 on a platform which included free coinage of silver, a graduated income tax, postal savings banks, and the government ownership of railways, telegraphs, and telephones. Their convention declared itself in sympathy "with organized workingmen to shorten hours of labor" and maintained that "the interests of rural and city labor are the same, their enemies identical." This effort to tie up the political interests of the farmer and city laborer, which extended even to the Farmer-Labor party of 1920, the Progressive party of 1924, and subsequent left-wing efforts, is one of the most persistent and interesting developments in American political history.

With the passing of the Populist party and the growing strength of the American Federation of Labor, organized labor has been less ready to embark officially in politics. Samuel Gompers during his long period of control

[25] Above, pp. 303-304.

persistently and successfully opposed the formation of a distinct labor party, and his successor, William Green, pursued the same policy. Nevertheless, this policy of the Federation has been under the continued fire of the left-wing groups, some of whom insist upon independent political action, while others would secure from that body its endorsement of socialism. Daniel De-Leon, the early intellectual leader of the labor group, attempted unsuccessfully in the eighties to induce both the Knights of Labor and the American Federation of Labor to join the nucleus of a Socialist party. Failing in this, he organized rival bodies[26] and became the dominant figure in the Socialist Labor party. This party, however, never became strong and was pushed into the background after 1898 by the Social Democratic party (later called the Socialist party) led by Eugene V. Debs, Morris Hillquit, and Victor Berger. Although the Socialist party undoubtedly received considerable backing from the liberal middle class, the large proportion of its votes must have come from labor. The fact that its popular standard-bearer, Debs, received almost 900,000 votes in 1912 and 918,000 in 1920[27] shows that up to that time, in reality, a labor party was already in existence that might have become exceedingly powerful if it had officially received trade-union support.

The failure to work through a distinct labor-party movement does not mean that the labor unions hesitate to throw their political influence where it may be of the most benefit. Holding the balance of power in numerous instances, they have endorsed candidates favorable to labor, have often elected them, and by aggressive lobbying have influenced much labor legislation. Furthermore, the American Federation has not hesitated to take an official stand on issues involving political action; it has endorsed proposals for the initiative, the referendum, and the recall, the direct election of Senators, woman suffrage, government ownership or regulation of public utilities, restriction of immigration, the establishment of state and national labor bureaus and a national department of education, abolition of child labor, and all manner of legislation protecting the life, health, and future of the worker. Gompers concisely summed up his own philosophy: "I have always sought to use political situations for labor's advantage."[28]

Although the "full dinner pail" argument which the Republicans have advanced to reconcile workmen to their party has been powerful, labor in general has been inclined to divide its vote among opposing parties. When the Democratic organization in 1896 absorbed the Populist party and at the same time severely criticized the Supreme Court decision on the income tax

[26] First the Socialist Trade and Alliance, and years later the I.W.W.

[27] The votes in 1920 were cast for Debs in spite of the fact that he was in prison at the time for alleged violation of the Espionage Act.

[28] Samuel Gompers, *op. cit.*, II, 77.

and the use of the injunction, the appeal to labor was strong. In 1908 labor appealed to both conventions for an anti-injunction plank. The "Republican reactionists," said Gompers, "told Labor to go to Denver," where the Democrats were to meet.[29] There the Democratic party put itself on record as opposed to the use of injunctions in labor disputes, and after that Gompers and other leaders worked unofficially but openly for both Bryan and Wilson. Through the medium of this party two of their greatest legislative victories were obtained—the Adamson Act and the Clayton Act. In 1924 labor momentarily deserted its time-honored policy when the A. F. of L. officially endorsed its lifelong friend, La Follette. From then until 1952, when it endorsed Adlai E. Stevenson, the A. F. of L. resumed again its official neutrality. Nevertheless, it is clear that labor as a whole has supported the Democratic party and the "New Deal."

LABOR AND THE COURTS

While the wage earner has been able to influence state and national legislatures and to make distinct progress in his dealings with his employer, his experience with the judiciary has not been so fortunate. Under the American system of checks and balances, in which a judiciary (by its very nature generally conservative and not representative of the working class) passes on the constitutionality of legislation, it is not at all surprising that progress has been slow. Labor has had to struggle not only against a conservative judiciary but also against legal theories and economic philosophies whose origin antedated the Industrial Revolution.

Labor unions had scarcely been formed before they were haled into court on the ground that, in the absence of a statute or legislation on the point, the old common law of England applied in America, and a combination of workmen to raise wages was a conspiracy against the public and, as such, illegal. Decisions during the first two decades of the nineteenth century were generally against the workmen, but gradually the attitude of the courts shifted. Mere combining was no longer taken as conspiracy, and the judiciary now directed its attention rather to the methods employed by the unions to gain their ends. For years, however, the right to strike, to boycott, and to picket was questioned in the courts.

The fifth amendment to the Constitution asserted that no one could be "deprived of life, liberty, or property without due process of law," and most of the state constitutions contain similar statements. The idea was again incorporated in the first section of the fourteenth amendment when the same restrictions were placed upon the states. Although Justice Holmes once asserted that this amendment did not write *laissez faire* or any other economic

[29] *Ibid.*, p. 202.

doctrine into the Constitution, his belief was not generally held by the sturdy exponents of that economic doctrine, who interpreted many labor laws as an infringement of liberty, an abridgment of contract, or class legislation. With such a background, it is not surprising that many labor laws have been declared unconstitutional. Legislation which has come under the ban of the courts at various times includes laws fixing the hours of labor engaged on public works, laws designed to protect the health of adult male workers by limiting the hours of labor in private industries, laws prohibiting the payment of wages in scrip or the enforced dealing at company stores, laws prohibiting the manufacture of such commodities as cigars in tenement houses, laws forbidding employers from holding back wages, workingmen's compensation laws, and minimum-wage laws.

To many observers the courts have seemed to stretch their ingenuity to the limit to hamper organized labor. The use of picketing has been narrowly restricted;[30] laws to prevent an employer from discharging a man on account of membership in a union have been thrown out;[31] laws forbidding an employer to compel a worker to sign a nonunion card ("yellow-dog contract") have been set aside;[32] and at the same time unions have been enjoined from inducing workers who have signed such a contract to join a union.[33] In fact, almost every type of social legislation or laws protecting union activities has at some time or other been held unconstitutional.

Notwithstanding the long list of adverse decisions, labor has been insistent in affirming the constitutionality of labor legislation under the police power given the state to look after the health and safety of the people. This power has been generally, although not always, upheld by the courts in the case of laws governing the hours and conditions of work of women, and the position of guardian which the state maintains toward children has allowed protective legislation for minors. In the case of adult males there has been much judicial interpretation. Where the laws have obviously been designed to protect the health and safety of the community, such as those limiting the hours of employment on public carriers, they have generally been upheld. In the case of laws governing hours of labor in private industries intended to protect not so much the safety of the public as the health and safety of the workers, the courts have been more dilatory. In 1895, for example, the Illinois supreme court declared unconstitutional an eight-hour day for women;[34] the Colorado supreme court in 1899 acted similarly on an eight-hour law for the smelting industry as "an unwarrantable interference with

[30] Truax *v.* Corrigan, 257 U.S. 312 (1921).
[31] Adair *v.* U.S., 208 U.S. 161 (1908).
[32] Coppage *v.* Kansas, 236 U.S. 1 (1915).
[33] Hichman Coal & Coke Co. *v.* Mitchell, 245 U.S. 229 (1917).
[34] Ritchie *v.* People, 155 Ill. 98 (1895).

the right of both the employer and employee in making contracts";[35] the United States Supreme Court in 1905 declared the Lochner ten-hour law fixing the hours of work in bakeshops in New York as one which "reached and passed the limit of police power";[36] the New York supreme court in 1907 nullified a law prohibiting night work for women;[37] and as late as 1923 the United States Supreme Court declared a minimum-wage law in the District of Columbia unconstitutional.[38]

Eventually through the insistence of progressive public sentiment there came a reversal of earlier decisions, and there is now little doubt of the right of a state to regulate hours of labor under the police power.[39] Legislation respecting safety and sanitation in factories is now generally held to be constitutional, and the courts have come to be more liberal in rewriting the old common law and in placing more responsibility upon employers in case of accident.

The national government's control over interstate commerce has aroused hope that something might be accomplished here in the field of labor legislation. In 1913 a separate Cabinet department was created for labor; in 1914 an effort was made in the Clayton Act to exempt labor unions from prosecution as conspiracies in restraint of trade; in 1915 the La Follette Seaman's Act went far to insure decent conditions for American sailors. The Adamson Act of 1916, which provided for a basic eight-hour day on interstate carriers, was a great victory and was upheld by the Supreme Court.[40] On the other hand, the Palmer-Owen bill, passed in 1916 to prohibit interstate commerce in the products of mines or quarries of children under sixteen, and in manufactured products produced by children under fourteen, was declared unconstitutional in 1918.[41] An attempt in 1919 to accomplish the same object by the imposition of a 10 per cent tax on the net profits of factories employing children under fourteen years of age met the same fate (May 18, 1922).[42]

No judicial activity has been so bitterly opposed by labor as the use of the injunction in labor disputes.[43] Designed originally as a powerful weapon

---

[35] *In re* Morgan, 26 Colo. 415; 58 Pacific 1071 (1899).

[36] Lochner *v.* New York, 198 U.S. 45 (1905).

[37] People *v.* Williams, 189 N.Y. 131 (1907).

[38] Adkins *v.* Children's Hospital, 261 U.S. 525 (1923).

[39] Holden *v.* Hardy, 169 U.S. 366 (1898); Bunting *v.* Oregon, 243 U.S. 240 (1917); Ritchie *v.* Wayman, 244 Ill. 509 (1910); People *v.* Charles Schweinler Press, 214 N.Y. 395 (1915).

[40] Wilson *v.* New, 243 U.S. 322 (1917).

[41] Hammer *v.* Dagenhart, 247 U.S. 251 (1918).

[42] Bailey *v.* Drexel Furniture Company, 259 U.S. 20 (1922).

[43] "An injunction," says Professor Watkins (*An Introduction to the Study of Labor Problems,* p. 324), "is an order issued by a court of equity for purpose of preventing injury to a person or property or of preseving the existing conditions until the final determination of rights." In theory it is an extraordinary expedient, to be used when property and personal rights are imperiled, and when there are no other remedies at law adequate to meet the emergency. A viola-

in the hand of the crown to be employed only rarely against threatened lawlessness and riotous outbreaks, it has come in recent years in America to be used quite commonly by the courts to limit the activity of labor during strikes. The imprisonment of Eugene V. Debs and others for violating a federal injunction during the Pullman strike of 1894, and the sentencing to prison of Gompers, Mitchell, and Morrison for ignoring the Buck Stove and Range injunction are two striking incidents in the more or less free use made of this instrument. "Government by injunction" has been denounced as a one-sided and unjust use of power, and labor succeeded in writing into the Clayton Act of 1914 a clause which prohibits the use of restraining injunctions in cases between employers and employees "unless necessary to prevent irreparable injury to property, or to a property right, of the party making the application, for which injury there is no adequate remedy at law." As might be expected from the looseness of the phraseology of this prohibition, little actual change was effected. In 1932 a federal anti-injunction act (Norris-LaGuardia Act) again prohibited labor injunctions in federal courts as well as prohibiting the use of "yellow-dog contracts." In the postwar years, however, the Taft-Hartley Act has again strengthened the use of the injunction.[44]

PROGRESS OF THE WAGE EARNERS

With the exception of the long and bitter depression of the 1930's, the standard of living of the American wage earner has improved since 1865. During the Civil War prices rose faster than wages, and at its conclusion real wages were still below the level of 1861. After the war, prices declined, but wages tended to remain near the point of 1865 or higher. Between that year and 1890 real wages rose at least 100 per cent in industry and somewhat less in agriculture. From 1897 to 1914 wages continued to advance, but so also did prices, with the result that during these years many wage earners gained but slightly, if at all, as far as real wages were concerned. The same was true during the period of World War I, but from 1920 to 1929 there appears to have been a distinct advance in real wages.[45] The problem of labor income and real wages is, of course, significant, for it immediately raises the question whether labor is receiving its fair share in the increase

tion of an injunction is punished as contempt of court without jury trial and may involve fine or imprisonment. In earlier years the injunction was used by the courts only in extraordinary situations. In recent years it has become a common instrument in labor cases. The development of the free use of the injunction has a twofold significance. In the first place, it has enormously increased the power of the judiciary. In the second place, the original theory of the injunction has been strained greatly to fit labor cases, and has been developed chiefly as a weapon to be used against labor.

[44] Below, pp. 720–722.
[45] Below, pp. 593–594.

of wealth due to the unprecedented productivity of the nation's industries.

On the other hand, it should be pointed out that real wages tell only part of the story of the condition of the working classes. It is possible for real wages to decline, as they probably did for some groups between 1897 and 1919, but at the same time for the standard of living to improve. Through public works and charity a certain portion of the national income may find its way back to the people as a whole; likewise, inventions of various kinds

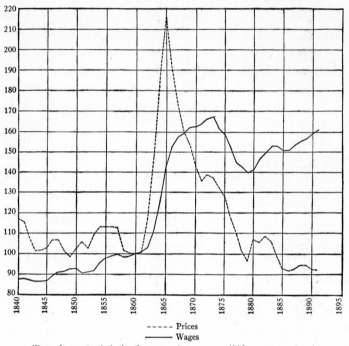

- - - - - Prices
———— Wages

(Data from *Statistical Abstract, 1899,* p. 92; *ibid., 1921,* p. 854.)

WAGES AND PRICES, 1840–1891.

and labor-saving devices may become available for the masses through large-scale cheap production. Furthermore, social legislation may improve the conditions of work. Real progress, for example, was made in decreasing the length of the working day. Operatives in cotton mills in the 1840's sometimes worked thirteen and fourteen hours. By 1860 the average day for all labor was eleven hours—this after an agitation for a ten-hour day which extended over thirty years. Though inadequate, the best figures obtainable for the period 1840–1890 are from the Aldrich Report; this gives the average in 1844 at eleven and one-half hours a day, in 1865 eleven, with a gradual reduction until 1890, when the average was ten hours. Since its organization the American Federation of Labor has steadily advocated the eight-hour day. This with a Saturday half-holiday, making a forty-four-hour week, has been the great demand of labor. By 1920 the unions had achieved this in most of the highly organized industries,[46] but the great majority of the wage earners worked a longer day. In certain hazardous occupations fewer hours had been obtained by legal enactment. Beginning with Utah in 1896, thirty states by 1916 had placed an eight-hour day for miners upon the statute books. Some impetus was given to the movement by a law passed by Congress in 1892 providing for an eight-hour day for government employees. During the First World War the labor shortage gave momentum to this demand, and a majority of trades using skilled labor worked under this schedule. In recent years many trades in certain areas have introduced the five-day week, at the same time retaining the existing wage scale. In fact, the weekly hours of factory work in 1951 averaged slightly over forty.

Organized labor and certain liberal middle-class organizations[47] have fought strenuously against the exploitation of the labor of women and children, and in this they have received aid from many outside their own ranks. It is obvious that the effects of excessive labor on the part of women and children cause physical degeneration and thus menace the future of the race and nation. For the male worker the labor of women and children imperiled not only his wage scale but in some cases his job. Before much could be done, however, it was necessary to undermine the old-fashioned belief that the factory was a God-sent protector against the evils into which idleness might lead children, to break the influence of the doctrine of *laissez faire,* and to counteract the influences of greed which fattened upon such labor. The early textile mills were largely worked by women and children, and this situation continued in certain sections until the 1930's. Although the number of children at work increased in the years before the First World War, relatively there was a decline. The Census of 1870 reported 739,164 children between the ages of ten and fifteen engaged in gainful occupations, and the Census of 1910 reported 1,990,225, not quite half of whom were girls. This amounted to 5.2 per cent of all those gainfully employed and was a decrease of 0.8 per cent since 1900. The proportion of gainfully employed children to the total number of children, however, increased from 16.8 in 1880 to 18.8 in 1910. While a majority of those listed were engaged in agriculture or other nonindustrial pursuits, it was still discouragingly true that thousands were to be found in factories in 1914, especially in the southern states where northern capital had often helped to build large textile mills. It is true that agricultural labor up to a certain extent may not be physically deleterious to a child of immature years, but this can hardly be said of factory or sweatshop

---

[46] In the 1930's, in an effort to check the evils of the speed-up and to spread the available work, a number of unions agitated for and obtained the six-hour day.

[47] Such as the National Consumers' League, founded in 1899, and the National Child Labor Committee (1904).

work. Certainly the reports of conditions of child labor throughout the nation were bad enough during these years to shame the most callous government into action.[48]

Attempts to do away with child labor have taken the form of laws limiting the working hours, setting an age limit below which children may not be gainfully employed, prohibiting night work, and providing for compulsory education. Legislation in regard to child labor started in Massachusetts in 1836, when a law was passed regulating the instruction of children employed in manufacturing establishments. In 1842 the working day for children under twelve was limited to ten hours (considered a great advance!), and acts of 1866 and 1867 forbade the employment of any child under sixteen for more than sixty hours a week. In 1873 the length of the school year was extended to twenty weeks and the age of attendance to twelve years, and ten years later all towns of more than 10,000 population were compelled to establish evening schools. A law of 1888 excluded children under thirteen from factories, workshops, and mercantile establishments, and those under fourteen except during vacation; other indoor work was forbidden children under thirteen unless they had attended school twenty weeks. The age of compulsory attendance was raised in 1889 to fourteen years and the school year to thirty weeks. In this hesitating manner Massachusetts, a state always in the forefront of labor legislation, tackled the evil of child labor, and by much the same methods other states have taken up the problem.

Although as late as 1914 six states (all in the South) had no laws making school attendance compulsory, all the states had some form of child labor legislation on the statute books by the 1930's. In 1914 the minimum age of lawful employment varied from twelve to fourteen years, depending on the economic background and the social consciousness of the states. New Mexico, for example, had no law except one prohibiting children under fourteen from working in mines; in Utah and Wyoming only mines and dangerous occupations were forbidden to children; and in four of the southern states there was no minimum age for employment in stores. With few exceptions, the states now limit the working day of a child under sixteen to eight hours, and the majority of the states and the District of Columbia prohibit night work. Laws of this type, combined with vigorously enforced legislation for compulsory education and with appropriate penalties for infringement, are necessary to eliminate this curse. Child labor has been most common in the families of newly arrived immigrants and among the "poor whites" of

---

[48] See John Spargo, *The Bitter Cry of the Children* (1906); Mrs. John Van Vorst, *The Cry of the Children* (1908), and such government bulletins as "Child Labor in Canneries," *Child Labor Bulletin*, Vol. I, No. 4 (Feb., 1913).

certain sections of the South, where economic pressure was sufficient in many cases to cause the parents to co-operate with the employer in ignoring existing laws.[49]

Aroused by the agitation against child labor during the early years of the century, the federal government also engaged in the battle. In 1912 Congress added a Children's Bureau to the Department of Labor and at various times passed legislation to ban child labor in the District of Columbia. In 1916 and again in 1919, as we have pointed out, Congress attempted to curtail child labor throughout the nation, only to have the laws declared unconstitutional by the Supreme Court. To overcome this check, a constitutional amendment to permit the prohibition of child labor under eighteen was submitted to the states in 1924, but only twenty-eight had ratified it by the end of 1953. However, certain New Deal legislation, including the National Industrial Recovery Act, the Walsh-Healey Government Contracts Act, and the Fair Labor Standards Act, has sought to accomplish this purpose.[50] Since the constitutionality of the last act has been upheld, child labor in industry has largely disappeared. Nevertheless, the Bureau of the Census estimated that in 1951 close to 2,000,000 young people from fourteen to seventeen years were working in various occupations, although some only on a part-time basis. Several hundred thousand below fourteen years were also working, at least half of them for pay.

The factory system and other results of the Industrial Revolution have thrown open to women innumerable new opportunities to earn a livelihood. Many of the old home occupations, such as clothmaking, soapmaking, and fruit and meat preserving, have passed to the factory and women have followed. Often unorganized, living at home and looking upon their work as temporary, they have been subject, like children, to economic exploitation. They were, particularly in earlier years, the victims of the "sweated industries," where work was contracted out to be done in the home. In recent years the number of women employed outside the home has increased faster than the total population, but the advance has come in middle-class occupational groups rather than among factory workers. Also noticeable is a relative decline in the number of women employed in such traditionally feminine occupations as waitresses, general servants, and seamstresses. The number of women engaged in manufacturing industries in 1914 was 1,500,000 and in 1950 about 3,545,000.

The two great evils attendant upon the employment of women which legislation has attempted to mitigate are insufficient pay and physical injury,

[49] A summary of child labor laws as they existed in 1933 is given in Publication 197, *Child Labor Facts and Figures* (revised to October, 1933), published by the Children's Bureau of the Department of Labor.

[50] Below, p. 675.

both of which may have deleterious effects extending to society as a whole. The feeling has gradually spread that women, like children, need the protection of the state, and especially that their physical well-being as mothers of future citizens is a concern of society. In certain of the states commissions have been instituted to study the cost of living and to decide upon minimum-wage scales, which in some cases are compulsory. The first minimum-wage law in the country was passed in Massachusetts in 1912. Although the First World War drew thousands of women into industry under supposedly advantageous circumstances, many students in close touch with labor conditions insisted that the wages of women relative to those received by men were hardly bettered. Of 117 plants investigated in 1919 in New York State, twenty-nine paid women less than $12 a week, and sixty-nine less than $14.[51] The Consumers' League in 1919 claimed, on the basis of statistics compiled by the U.S. Bureau of Labor Statistics, that only one out of fourteen industries in New York City which employed large numbers of women paid a living wage.[52] While it is true that women are still underpaid in most occupations, the conditions under which they work have been bettered. Numerous laws improving factory conditions have been passed; practically all the states limit the hours of labor for women, and several have laws that prohibit night work.

Although the percentage of accidents among workmen is larger in the United States than in any of the other great industrial nations, we have been the last to recognize that these accidents should be borne by industry rather than wholly by the workman. Until within the last forty years the law worked on the theory that responsibility for an accident could be placed upon some person and he must bear the loss. This responsibility was almost always placed upon labor rather than capital, on the ground that the workman knew the risk he must run if he accepted a job, or that the accident was caused by contributory negligence on his part or that of a fellow worker. If the employer could prove that he had exercised reasonable precautions, he was ordinarily relieved of responsibility.

Eventually the point of view of society changed. It was realized that the old common law which might have fitted conditions before the Industrial Revolution was no longer adequate. Under modern conditions it became impossible to prove anyone's negligence in many accidents; obviously they were due to the inevitable risks of industry. In reality, industry was the guilty party, not the workman. Following in the footsteps of Germany (1884) and England (1897), various American states, beginning with Mary-

[51] *The Industrial Replacement of Men by Women*, bulletin issued by the Industrial Commission of New York, March, 1919.

[52] *Survey*, April 17, 1920. The percentage for the entire state was even more striking. "Nineteen per cent of the workers received less than $11 a week, 71 per cent received less than $14, and 88 per cent received less than $16."

land in 1902, began to pass workingmen's compensation acts. The first compensation laws of Maryland (1902), Montana (1909), and New York (1910) were declared unconstitutional, but after 1911 laws were framed which stood the tests of the courts. By 1942 all the states but Mississippi, together with the territories of Alaska, Hawaii, and Puerto Rico, had workingmen's compensation laws, as did the District of Columbia and the United States government for its civilian employees. Most of these laws, besides cutting away the old common-law defenses of the employer, provide for (1) the payment, in case of death or permanent disability, of a maximum amount in weekly allotments extending over a period of from 300 to 500 weeks, (2) in the case of temporary disability the payment of doctors' bills and for a certain period a percentage of the regular wages, and (3) in the case of certain specified industries the payment of a fixed lump sum. Usually agricultural laborers and domestic servants are excluded, as are commonly those employed in establishments that hire less than five men. Provisions for the payments required by the law are usually met by some form of insurance, through either state or private companies. It is now decidedly to the advantage of the employer as well as the employee to avoid accidents, and the salutary effect of these laws is increasingly evident. As a rule, their operation is supervised by special tribunals which pass on the claims for compensation. The widespread adoption of workingmen's compensation was probably the greatest legislative victory won by labor during the years just prior to the First World War.

Progress is evidenced not only by the laws protecting women and children and providing for workingmen's compensation, but also by other important pieces of social legislation designed to ameliorate conditions of work and to raise the standard of living of the wage earners. Their children have better milk as the result of city or state laws, playgrounds in the cities, medical inspection in the schools, and improved education. Better tenement house laws have improved their living quarters, and better-lighted and more sanitary factories, resulting in part from state legislation and in part from efforts by management to achieve greater production, have made their working hours easier. Initial steps have been taken for mothers' pensions, and before 1914 there was active propaganda for sickness and unemployment insurance and for old-age pensions. These and other new types of social legislation came with the depression and the New Deal legislation of the 1930's. With it also came a shifting of such legislation from the state to the federal government.

IMMIGRATION

Closely allied with the labor problem but containing elements of significance to all phases of our political, social, and economic life is the problem of immigration. Between 1860 and 1920 close to 28,500,000 foreigners sought our shores to enter our labor force permanently or temporarily, a number almost equal to the total population of the country in 1850. This incoming tide of labor as it rose and fell corresponded quite closely with the periods of prosperity and depression. Thus we find the peak years in 1873 with 459,803 arrivals, in 1882 with 788,922, in 1892 with 579,663, in 1907 with 1,285,349, and in 1914 with 1,218,420. While in actual numbers immigration increased in each decade up to the opening of the First World War, emigration and the normal growth of population kept the proportion of foreign-born to the whole population at about 14 per cent. It was slightly under this in 1860, and slightly over in 1910.

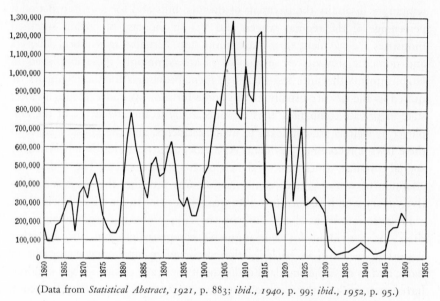

(Data from *Statistical Abstract, 1921*, p. 883; *ibid., 1940*, p. 99; *ibid., 1952*, p. 95.)

IMMIGRATION INTO THE UNITED STATES, 1860–1950.

As before the Civil War, the hope of economic betterment or the desire for greater political and religious freedom has been the compelling motive in the minds of the immigrants themselves. Nevertheless, the impetus has been partially supplied from without. Professor Commons is of the opinion that "the desire to get cheap labor, to take in passenger fares, and to sell land have probably brought more immigrants than the hard conditions of Europe, Asia, and Africa have sent."[53] Capital seeking renewed supplies of cheap labor and land-grant railroads desirous of peopling their territory and selling their real estate have co-operated with steamship companies in scouring Europe for prospective immigrants.[54] Until recent years, relatives and

[53] J. R. Commons, *Races and Immigrants in America*, p. 108.
[54] Above, p. 358.

friends in America in at least one-fourth of the cases sent back the cost of transportation. Emigration ceased to be a hazardous undertaking limited to the strong and self-reliant.

As emigration from Europe became easier, the source of immigration changed. Up to 1896 Great Britain, Ireland, and Germany contributed the greater number—aggressive and forceful men, and often skilled artisans and farmers, not radically different in blood and characteristics from the people already here. During the decade 1851–1860 these three countries sent 88 per cent of the immigrants, while Austria-Hungary, Italy, Russia, and Poland sent four-tenths of one per cent. In 1891–1910 the above three northern European nations sent 31.6 per cent, while the four nations in southern and eastern Europe furnished over 50 per cent. By the latter date the "new immigration" constituted over four-fifths of the total. This flow from south and eastern Europe brought a different type, hard-working and thrifty to be sure, but generally unskilled and accustomed to political and economic autocracy.

The mere size of the "new immigration," which amounted to over 13,000,-000 in the years 1900 to 1914, developed opposition and a demand for curtailment. It came chiefly from two sources: (1) a large part of organized and unorganized labor, who held that the continued inflow of cheap labor kept wages low and prevented a rise in the standard of living; and (2) many ardent Americans who believed that ideals and standards were being jeopardized by a too rapid addition to the "melting pot" of those who did not readily "melt." On the other hand, the advocates of comparatively easy immigration laws were represented until the First World War by capital, which argued that a continued supply of cheap labor was necessary to develop the nation's resources and to fill the jobs avoided by the native American. For this contention there was much to be said, for without doubt our economic structure has been reared to no small extent upon the rough labor of newly arrived immigrants. Yet it was a question whether tireless search for cheaper and cheaper labor was not bringing undesirable accessions to our shores more rapidly than they could be absorbed. That it is possible to maintain industry without fresh supplies of labor from abroad, even during periods of great demand, was proved during the First World War; the widespread unemployment in times of depression hardly pointed to the need of a greater labor force. Cheap labor is usually the most expensive in the long run, and it is quite probable that the nation might profit more by being forced to develop greater efficiency in the labor that is here than by importing unskilled and consequently low-paid wage earners.

Until recently, whatever restrictions were put on immigration were the result chiefly of the demands of labor. A number of acts culminating in 1882 finally prohibited Chinese immigration, and subsequent agreements with

Japan aimed at a similar exclusion of her citizens. With the act of 1882 the first step in federal control of immigration was taken. It placed a head tax of fifty cents on those entering, excluded certain undesirable classes of aliens, and provided for co-operation between the states and the federal government in the enforcement of the act. Under the influence of the Knights of Labor, laws were enacted in 1885 and 1889 prohibiting bringing over immigrants under contract to labor; these laws were generally evaded. The office which corresponds to the present Commissioner-General of Immigration was created in 1891. In the acts of 1891, 1893, 1907, and 1917 the policy was developed to exclude those morally, mentally, and physically unfit, and those afflicted with physical and mental diseases; vagrants, paupers, anarchists, and contract laborers were also debarred. For bringing in immigrants illegally, steamship companies are liable to fine and to the necessity of returning them, nor may they encourage or solicit immigrants.

In an effort to devise new methods of exclusion Congress enacted a literacy test but it was vetoed by Cleveland, Taft, and Wilson. Finally in 1917 such a test was passed over Wilson's veto. As a result of war conditions and because of apprehension that we might be deluged by an inflow from the war-torn nations of Europe, agitation for further restriction was strong at the conclusion of World War I. Not only labor but the general public, particularly many organizations who posed as super-patriotic (although their ancestors were all immigrants), favored restriction, and the 1920's saw a determined and successful effort to restrict radically the flow of alien immigrants.[55]

SELECTED READINGS

Daugherty, C. R., *Labor Problems in American Industry* (rev. ed.), chaps. 11–13.
Lorwin, L. L., *The American Federation of Labor.*
Ware, N. J., *The Labor Movement in the United States,* chaps. 1–9.
Faulkner, H. U., *The Decline of Laissez Faire,* pp. 101–114, chaps. 11, 12.
Brissenden, P. F., *The I.W.W., a Study in American Syndicalism,* chaps. 1–5.
Fitch, J. A., *The Causes of Industrial Unrest,* chaps. 2–5.
Parker, C. H., *The Casual Laborer and Other Essays,* chaps. 2–3.
Flügel, F., and Faulkner, H. U., *Readings in the Economic and Social History of the United States,* chap. 18.

[65] Below, pp. 634–635.

CHAPTER 23

TRANSPORTATION AND
COMMUNICATION, 1860–1914

RAPID RAILROAD EXPANSION

THE importance of railroad expansion in American history in the half-century after 1860 can hardly be overestimated. Our industrial and agricultural development was largely dependent upon internal transportation, of which the major part was furnished by the railroad. The very settlement of large sections of the West was promoted by the railroads, built in many instances through unoccupied regions with the settlers following in their wake. In 1860 the railroad mileage amounted to 30,625, most of which had been constructed in the prosperous years preceding the panic of 1857. The effect of the Civil War upon the railroads was both disastrous and stimulating. While the rolling stock and other equipment in the South either depreciated or was destroyed, the war spurred the North to fresh construction.[1] It was during the midst of the conflict and partially as a war measure that the first transcontinental railroad was begun. Most of the construction during the decade, however, came after 1865, the mileage in 1870 amounting to 52,922.

In the succeeding decades the increase was rapid and, except in periods of acute depression, continuous. Thirty-three thousand miles were built between 1867 and 1873, before the first great spurt had played itself out and the panic temporarily halted further construction. The panic of 1873 was itself partly attributable to overbuilding and overcapitalization of railroads. The period from 1860 to 1875 witnessed not only the construction of the first transcontinental line but also the extension of four great railroads from the Atlantic seaboard to Chicago—the New York Central, the Pennsylvania, the Baltimore and Ohio, and the Grand Trunk. After the recovery from the depression, the country entered another phenomenal period of railroad growth. The

---

[1] Above, pp. 334–335.

mileage, in 1880 totaling 93,261, rose to 167,191 in 1890—an increase of over 70,000 miles in one decade. The panic of 1893 again hampered construction, but it picked up in the prosperous years after 1898, and for twelve years thereafter new mileage averaged 5000 a year (2 per cent annual increase). Railroad miles in operation amounted in 1900 to 198,964 and in 1920 to 263,821.

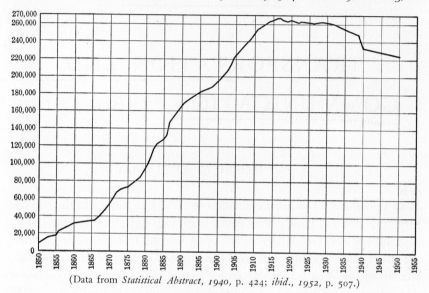

(Data from *Statistical Abstract, 1940*, p. 424; *ibid., 1952*, p. 507.)

MILES OF RAILROAD IN OPERATION, 1850–1950.

This growth far exceeded that of the population; since the Civil War the population has trebled, whereas railroad mileage has grown eightfold. In 1860 there was one mile of road to every 1087 people; in 1920 one mile to every 417. In 1914 the United States boasted more mileage than all Europe, and more than one-third that of the entire world.

On the other hand, by 1914 the country seemed to have approached a point of saturation. While the average construction was over 3000 miles a year between 1910 and 1913, it declined rapidly thereafter until in 1920 only 314 miles were built. Between 1916 and 1920 more mileage was abandoned than built, and this tendency has continued to the present time.[2] Many causes have contributed: (1) the competition of gasoline motor traffic, (2) economies of wartime, (3) low railroad profits and the precarious financial condition of many of the roads, which have suffered in the adjustments to higher costs, (4) the approach to the saturation point. From 1920 to the present time (except during the war), the weak roads exerted all their efforts to keep alive,

[2] Mileage, which reached the high point of 254,037 in 1916, dropped to 223,427 in 1951. Railroads reported the abandonment of 1370 miles in 1932 and 1149 miles in 1943, the twelfth consecutive year that abandonment exceeded 1000 miles.

while the prosperous companies improved their equipment rather than lengthened their lines.

The economic significance of railroads is far wider than merely that of transportation. It is impossible to gauge the social significance of facilities which have tended to break down rural isolation and link up the benefits of city and country. In our financial system railroad securities for decades were the most important single group and formed an integral part of the activities of the investment market and the credit world. In 1921 the railroads were capitalized (par value of stocks and bonds) at $21,891,450,785 and valued in 1920 by the Interstate Commerce Commission at $18,900,000,000. Ten years later the Commission set the valuation as of December 31, 1930, at $21,691,-000,000, and the net book value at $23,518,000,000. It can be reasonably deduced from available figures that the capital tied up in rail transportation before the First World War constituted probably about one-tenth of the total wealth of the nation, estimated in 1912 at $187,739,071,090. In 1910 the railroads furnished employment to 1,700,000 persons, 4.4 per cent of the gainfully employed.

THE TRANSCONTINENTAL ROADS

The idea of a transcontinental railroad seems to have originated in the lure of Oriental trade, but the discovery of gold in California in 1848 and the rapid settlement of that region gave the idea great impetus and led Congress in 1853 to provide for a survey of possible routes from the Mississippi to the Pacific.[3] The exigencies of the Civil War, political and military as well as economic, led eventually to the construction of the first line. The Union Pacific Railroad Company was created by Congress in 1862 for the purpose of building a road from Nebraska west to California; and the Central Pacific, under the leadership of Leland Stanford, Collis P. Huntington, and other famous railroad men, was organized to build from the Pacific coast eastward to meet the Union Pacific. Both railroads were granted subsidies of $16,000 a mile for construction on the level country, $48,000 a mile through the mountain ranges, and $32,000 for the sections between the ranges, the government taking a second lien on the property. Land grants of alternate sections contiguous to the railroads were offered in addition. Stimulated by loans and land grants and urged on by the great popular interest, both roads built frantically toward each other in the hope of obtaining as much of the subsidy as possible. Neither expense, hostile Indians, nor the severity of the mountain winters was permitted to hold up the work. Twenty thousand men

[3] In the East it was the merchant Asa Whitney who spent many years in agitating for such a road; in the West it was Theodore D. Judah who surveyed routes and interested the Sacramento merchants, Stanford, Huntington, Crocker, and Hopkins, in the project. Both died before the road was actually begun.

were laying two miles of track a day in the concluding weeks of an effort which brought the two roads together at Promontory Point, Utah, on May 10, 1869. There Leland Stanford drove the last spike of California gold while telegraph wires received the taps of the hammer and transmitted them to a rejoicing nation. The joining of these roads brought to its culmination the greatest transportation project in American history since the completion of the Erie Canal.

Hardly less romantic in its conception, but less successful in its immediate realization, was the effort to construct the Northern Pacific. Chartered by Congress in 1864 and subsidized with land grants larger than the combined area of the six New England states, it was finally begun in 1867 through the financing of Jay Cooke & Company. Five hundred miles had been built when the road was thrown into receivership by the failure of Jay Cooke. Eventually aggressive construction was resumed and, largely through the genius of Henry Villard, backed by German capital, the road was completed in 1883. The Atchison, Topeka and Santa Fe obtained from the national government in 1863 a grant of 6400 acres for every mile built; but construction did not begin until 1869 and had proceeded no farther than the eastern boundary of Colorado when it was stopped by the panic of 1873. Construction was resumed in 1880, following in general the old Santa Fe Trail, and in 1884 the tracks reached the Pacific coast.

In 1878 James J. Hill, a man who later became one of the greatest of railway executives, but at that time an unknown storekeeper in St. Paul, interested influential Canadians in a bankrupt little 200-mile railroad without any apparent future, known as the St. Paul and Pacific and described as "a streak of rust running through a desert." The Canadian capitalists were interested in the road only as a link in the freight operations of the Hudson's Bay Company between the Mississippi and Winnipeg, but under Hill's direction it was pushed to the Pacific and developed into the Great Northern system. In the meantime the group who had built the Central Pacific began to consolidate various little railroads running south out of San Francisco and during the seventies pushed them through Arizona and New Mexico to El Paso, Texas, where in 1882 communication with the East was secured. By the middle eighties the chief lines to the Pacific had been constructed.

FINANCING AND GOVERNMENT AID

Not the least interesting phase in the history of American railroads is the story of their early financing, which can be merely touched upon here. The urgent need for internal transportation, the remarkable success of the Erie Canal, sectional rivalries, and the scarcity of private capital were chief among the causes leading the states to finance many of the early projects. State aid was overdone and was brought to a disastrous close by the panic of 1837, an event which prevented what might have been a normal development in this country of state-owned transportation facilities. Thereafter, although government aid was rendered, particularly in the case of the transcontinental roads, the financing and management of internal transportation were largely in the hands of private capital.

An appreciable share of the yearly surplus of wealth, at least until 1916, was invested in railroads. The fundamental fact that transportation was essential to the building up of the nation was apparent, and nowhere was the American willingness to speculate on the country's progress better seen. But before private capital went into railroads, the government was expected to do much to make the way easy. Railroads were built under charters voted by the state legislatures; all of them contained valuable rights and concessions and many were obtained by corrupt means. The right of eminent domain—that is, the power to lay out a road and condemn the land needed if impossible to obtain it otherwise—was invariably granted. In certain cases a monopoly or protection against competition was conferred, as were special banking privileges to aid in raising money. Tax exemption was permitted in some charters forever, in others for a stated period, and in still others until the dividends should reach a certain percentage.

On the other hand, even in these free-and-easy early railroad charters, sections were sometimes inserted providing for a reduction in rates when the dividends exceeded a normal yield. The attitude of the legislatures and the public was that transportation should be encouraged by every possible means, and the charters reflected this attitude. The charter having been secured, the railroad was built by money or credit obtained through national, state, county, municipal, or private subscriptions. National aid was rendered by (1) tariff remission on rails, (2) land grants, and (3) direct financial aid. Almost 200,000,000 acres were originally granted, but this was reduced to 137,000,000 by forfeitures resulting from inability to meet the requirements of the law. These land grants included one-fourth of the states of Minnesota and Washington, one-fifth of Wisconsin, Iowa, Kansas, North Dakota, and Montana, one-seventh of Nebraska, one-eighth of California, and one-ninth of Louisiana. In all, 242,000 square miles, a region larger than Germany or France, was given to the railroads. Of the individual donations, the Northern Pacific received 44,000,000 acres, the Southern Pacific 24,000,000, the Union Pacific 20,000,000, the Santa Fe system 17,000,000. National bonds to the amount of $64,623,512 were also issued on the security of second mortgages to help certain of the western lines—loans eventually almost entirely repaid.

Aid on the part of the various states were rendered chiefly by (1) subscrip-

tions to the capital stock, a method resorted to by a number of states, (2) the
loan of state credit by such methods as direct purchase of railroad bonds or
endorsement of construction bonds, (3) state land grants, (4) bearing the ex-

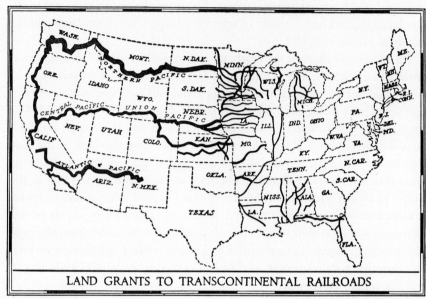

LAND GRANTS TO TRANSCONTINENTAL RAILROADS

(From H. U. Faulkner and Tyler Kepner, *America, Its History and People,* McGraw-Hill.)

pense of survey. Close to 55,000,000 acres were turned over by the states to
transportation companies. Counties and municipalities followed the states in
encouraging construction by subscribing for stock, by exchanging municipal
or county bonds for railroad securities, or by actually donating money and

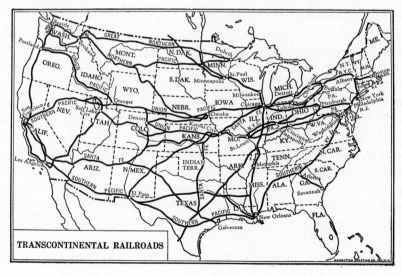

TRANSCONTINENTAL RAILROADS

land. In New York State 294 cities, towns, and villages contributed $29,978,-206 to railroads, and fifty-one counties gave subsidies or amounts varying from $5000 to $3,000,000. In Massachusetts, 171 towns and cities had issued bonds to aid railroads up to 1871.[4] This public aid should not be forgotten in the subsequent discussion of railroad abuses and the demand for public regulation.

The sum total of these various aids, amounting in most cases to outright subsidies, was very large; nevertheless, private backing has been even greater. Two classes of speculators have purchased railroad securities—those buying for dividends and a market rise, and those buying to promote building through their own region. This latter group in their enthusiasm were glad to exchange labor, land, and money for stock which often proved worthless. A considerable amount of financing was done in Europe, where American transportation securities have been exceedingly popular. In 1907 over one-fourth of the entire value of the roads was owned in Europe, mostly in Great Britain. In 1914 the *Wall Street Journal* estimated $3,400,000,000 worth of bonds, one-third of the outstanding railroad mortgage indebtedness, as held abroad; but the First World War brought many of these securities back to America, rendering our railroads for the first time virtually independent of foreign capital.

CHAOTIC CONDITIONS AND EARLY ABUSES

In a period of such rapid extension a chaotic situation was likely to develop, and abuses to creep in. Especially was this probable in an age in which business morality was at a low ebb. For some years the demand for transportation was so insistent that little attention was given to anything else; but by the early seventies railroad abuses had transformed hearty co-operation on the part of the people to a feeling of distrust and to a demand that the transportation companies be curbed. The abuses were many. In the first place, there was complaint that money was being wasted in unneeded and purely speculative enterprises. In their enthusiasm for railroad building, the American people apparently believed that the country could support an unlimited mileage. Roads were laid parallel in direct competition and driven into uninhabited country whose future was doubtful.

While some excuse might be made for overconstruction, none whatsoever can be discovered for the reckless graft practiced by the promoters through the medium of construction companies. These companies in themselves were

[4] D. P. Locklin, *Economics of Transportation,* pp. 56, 57. The experience of a typical New England town with the coming of various new types of transportation facilities is told in Ellen E. Callahan, *Hadley: A Study of the Political Development of a Typical New England Town from the Official Records (1659–1930),* in Smith College Studies in History, Vol. XVI, Nos. 1–2 (Oct., 1930–Jan., 1931).

not necessarily bad. In fact, there was considerable justification for them, since the rapid extension of railroads in the South and West, where the promise of adequate returns was not sufficient to attract capital, made it necessary to build them through organizations willing to take land and railroad securities in payment. The trouble was that there was little or no competition in awarding the bids, for the construction companies were generally made up of the group who controlled the projected railroad and who voted to themselves, as members of the construction company, contracts to build the roads. As the future of the roads was uncertain, the temptation to take all the profits possible in construction was ever present, and some of the roads thus built were so heavily loaded with debt at the start that bankruptcy was inevitable. The cost of building the Central Pacific was $58,000,000, but a construction company was paid $120,000,000 for the work; the profits of building the Union Pacific were estimated at between forty and fifty millions.

The most famous of these companies was the Crédit Mobilier, formed to build the Union Pacific. To prevent any interference which might arise because of the aid received from the federal government, Oakes Ames, a representative from Massachusetts and prominent in the Crédit Mobilier, was given 343 shares of stock, to be distributed among Congressmen where they would "do the most good." Ames's activities resulted in an investigation which showed that he had sold stock below its actual value to a number of Congressmen to influence their votes, and that the trail of bribery reached as high as the Vice President. The exorbitant and reckless expenditures as exemplified by the construction companies were typical of methods in many channels of railroad finance, but it is only fair to say that some railroads condemned these practices.

Even more exasperating than the wasteful and irresponsible methods of construction were the reckless manipulations of the finances of the roads, once built. Railroad magnates of the early decades looked upon the whole matter as a private business for personal gain. Apparently no feeling of public responsibility swayed them, and their conception of common honesty was exceedingly flexible. The attitude is illustrated by the famous story about Cornelius Vanderbilt, perhaps the greatest of the early railroad builders, who is alleged to have replied to a remonstrance regarding the feelings of the public over an arbitrary act, "The public be damned." Men like Jay Gould and Daniel Drew controlled railroads not to serve the public, improve the property, and make legitimate profits, but to manipulate the stock to build their fortunes.

No industry has suffered more from stock watering than the railroads, for time and again an expanded capitalization was placed upon a road without an equivalent addition in actual equipment. This has been done chiefly to pay expenses which the roads did not want to carry under regular expenditures, and to camouflage earnings. In many cases the increasing valuation of the properties has soaked up the water, but in more cases watered stock lies like an inert weight upon the real earnings, and stockholders clamor for dividends that can be paid only by unreasonably high charges. It was estimated that of the $7,500,000,000 indebtedness of the railroads in 1883, as much as $2,000,000,000 represented water. In four years, 1868 to 1872, Erie stock was watered from $17,000,000 to $78,000,000 in market speculation. In 1897 only 29.9 per cent of the country's railroad stock paid dividends; in the prosperous year 1890 less than 50 per cent; and even in the war year 1918 only 58.09 per cent. In the words of Charles Francis Adams, Jr., a railroad president, "The system was, indeed, fairly honeycombed with jobbery and corruption."[5]

An abuse which struck at the very foundation of our democracy was the continued assault upon the integrity of the government by the railroad interests. The Crédit Mobilier scandal was notorious and famous because it implicated the highest legislators in the land, but similar activities on a smaller scale were common. Pressure upon legislators to grant favorable charters, and upon courts to interpret them broadly, was exerted by every means. The pass system in the height of its glory (or infamy) took care of many influential persons. The most powerful of the legislators were frequently employed as counsel at large salaries. Where this was not sufficient, many roads followed the example of the Erie, which in one year expended $700,000 as a corruption fund and for legal expenses, the amount being carried on the books as the "india-rubber account." The general attitude was much like that of the railroad magnate who was reported as saying that in Republican counties he was a Republican and in Democratic counties he was a Democrat, but everywhere he was for the railroad. The low political as well as low business morality of the period made corrupt practices possible, and the blame rests not alone with the roads.

More closely concerned with the general prosperity were the straits to which competition had reduced the railroads. Rate wars had lowered transportation costs between competitive points to ruinous figures. Passenger fares between Cleveland and Boston in August, 1876 were down to $6.50; cattle in the same year were carried from Chicago to New York for a dollar a carload. While the shippers at competitive points (especially where there was an option of water transportation) profited at the expense of the roads, the farmers suffered from the railroads' general practice of raising their tariffs at noncompetitive points to recoup their losses. The same causes led to another form of discrimination equally galling, the custom of charging more for a short haul than for a long. Still another unfair practice which was ex-

[5] C. F. Adams, Jr., *Railroads: Their Origin and Problems*, p. 126.

ceedingly prevalent was the granting of rebates on freight charges. Where competition was bitter or the shipping concern strong, substantial refunds were obtained. Thus Standard Oil and other large shippers procured rebates that gave them an advantage the smaller organization failed to obtain and, like the farmer, the smaller concerns had to pay higher freight rates to make up for the losses of the railroads.

Cutthroat competition led eventually to the system of "pooling," by which the available business was allotted proportionately at agreed rates. Although the railroads broke the pooling agreements almost as soon as they were made, the mere attempt to make them was looked upon as unfair, monopolistic, and contrary to the common law. A mere enumeration of the grievances against the railroads in the decade of the seventies enables one to understand the strong reaction against them which culminated in the "Granger movement." While many of these abuses have been eliminated and others softened, the old distrust on the part of the public has never entirely died out.[6]

THE GRANGER MOVEMENT AND THE RAILROADS

The first strong agitation against the railroads occurred in the early seventies among the farmers, especially those of the middle-western states of Illinois, Minnesota, Iowa, and Wisconsin. This activity is known as the "Granger movement," a name originating from the "Granges," or local lodges, of the Patrons of Husbandry. The significance of the Grange lies in the fact that through it the isolation of the farmer broke down to some extent, and he was able to voice his grievances. "We are not enemies of railroads," asserted the Grange, and "We wage no aggressive warfare against any other interest whatever."[7] Whatever the Grangers may have said, they counted the railroad abuses among their grievances; the first laws passed in the agricultural states in an effort toward better control and regulation of common carriers were popularly known as "Granger laws," and the legal cases arising from them as the "Granger cases." The attack on the railroads, which was waged fiercely from 1869 to 1875, was but one phase of a mighty movement of agrarian unrest which was inaugurated by the Granger movement and surged through the West for many years.

Inasmuch as early legal decisions, such as that in the Dartmouth College case, had interpreted a charter as a contract, the western states had been careful to insert in their constitutions provisions declaring that laws creating

---

[6] The *First Annual Report of the Interstate Commerce Commission*, reprinted in part in F. Flügel and H. U. Faulkner, *Readings in the Economic and Social History of the United States*, pp. 609–618, reviews in some detail the causes for the passing of the Interstate Commerce Act of 1887.

[7] See excerpt from the *Seventh Session of the National Grange*, as given in *ibid.*, pp. 741–744.

corporations might be altered or repealed, or to specify in the charters that railroad rates must be equal and reasonable. Backed by these specific rights and by the common-law conception that a business which was a public calling came under the regulatory power of the state, the representatives of the farmers passed laws in an attempt to control the railroads. The first act was passed in Illinois in 1869 and limited the roads to "just, reasonable, and uniform rates." In the new Illinois state constitution of 1870 the legislature was ordered to "pass laws to correct abuses and to prevent unjust discrimination and extortion in the rates of freight and passenger tariffs." Laws of 1871 attempted to do this by providing maximum fares and freight rates, by regulating warehouses and the transportation of grain, by establishing a board of railway and warehouse commissioners, and by providing for the enactment of a general railway incorporation act.

Minnesota followed in the same year with laws fixing freight and passenger schedules and providing for a railroad commission. Iowa and Wisconsin passed similar acts in 1874, the latter state enacting the Potter law, the most radical of the Granger laws. During this decade the demand for the regulation of railroads spread, and there seems to be no doubt that the aggressive activity of the "Granger states" of the upper Mississippi Valley gave an impetus to the whole movement for control which in some states was not consummated until the next decade. Most of the states passed some kind of railroad legislation; and in practically all of the new or rewritten state constitutions of the decade provisions were inserted making it the duty of the legislatures to regulate rates and prevent discrimination, and declaring the railroads public highways and the companies common carriers.

As a whole, the Granger laws sought (1) to establish, either by direct legislation or through a commission, schedules of maximum rates, (2) to prohibit a greater charge for a short haul than for a long one, (3) to preserve competition by forbidding the consolidation of parallel lines, and (4) to eliminate the evil of free passes for public officials. "Several of the principal features of American railroad legislation," says Professor Buck, "can be looked upon as primarily Granger in their origin."[8] Subsequent federal legislation sought to correct the same abuses against which the Granger states had legislated. Where railroad legislation was passed it was customary to set up commissions of experts. These were of two kinds: the strong commission, as in Illinois, with power to regulate rates and enforce the law; and the weaker commission, as in Massachusetts, with merely advisory powers and the duty of making reports to the legislature.

These first attempts to regulate the railroads were of course vigorously opposed by the companies and immediately fought in the courts. In general, the

[8] S. J. Buck, *The Granger Movement*, p. 205.

railroad laws were attacked from two angles. It was maintained, first, that the exclusive power to regulate interstate commerce rested with Congress, and that, as the bulk of the commerce was interstate, the national government should legislate if it was necessary. Second, the effort to regulate rates was maintained to be contrary to that portion of Section I of the fourteenth amendment which declares, "No state shall make or enforce any law which shall abridge the privileges or immunities of citizens of the United States; nor shall any state deprive any person of life, liberty, or property, without due process of law; nor deny to any person within its jurisdiction the equal protection of the laws."

The first of the so-called "Granger cases" was that of Munn *v.* Illinois, decided by the Supreme Court in 1876 and involving the Illinois law of 1871, which declared grain elevators to be public warehouses and established maximum charges. The plaintiffs sued on the ground that (1) warehousing was not a public calling and the business was therefore not within the regulatory power of the state; (2) the fixing of rates deprived the owners of the power to establish higher rates and thus deprived them of their property without due process of law. They further maintained that if the courts did decide that their business was a public calling it was the work of the judiciary and not the legislature to determine a fair charge. All of these contentions were thrown out by the decision of Chief Justice Waite, who held that this section of the Constitution did not invalidate the old English common law that was generally accepted when the amendment was passed. "Property," said he, "does become clothed with a public interest when used in a manner to make it of public consequence, and affect the community at large. When, therefore, one devotes his property to a use in which the public has an interest, he, in effect, grants to the public an interest in that use, and must submit to be controlled by the public for the common good." He further held that the fixing of rates was a legislative and not a judicial matter, asserting that "it has been customary from time immemorial for the legislature to declare what shall be reasonable compensation under such circumstances."[9]

The firm attitude of the court in the Munn case was maintained in the case of Peik *v.* the Chicago and Northwestern Railway Company, handed down in the same year. The contention of the railroads that state regulation was an infringement of interstate commerce (and thus unconstitutional), since most of the railroad traffic crosses state boundaries, was thrown out. Ignoring the effect of such laws upon those outside the state, the court declared that "until Congress acts in reference to the relations of this company to interstate commerce, it is certainly within the power of Wisconsin to regulate its fares, etc., so far as they are of domestic concern."[10] The contention of the

[9] Munn *v.* Illinois, 94 U.S. 113.
[10] Peik *v.* Chicago and Northwestern Railroad Co., 94 U.S. 164.

Freight Transportation by Land—A Conestoga Wagon.

The "DeWitt Clinton"—First Railroad Train in New York.

Engines of the Civil War Days. Railroad Yards, City Point, Virginia,
October 21, 1864.

Meeting of a Local Grange in the Early 1870's During the
Agrarian Crusade.

Culver Service

Anti-Railroad Cartoon of the 1870's.

Wheat Threshing, Cheyenne County, Nebraska, About 1900.

Thirty Horses Pulling a Combine, Harvesting Wheat in the Northwest.

Communication on Lower Broadway, 1889. The Small Pictures at the Bottom Are of Samuel F. B. Morse, Inventor of the Telegraph (*left*), and of Alexander Graham Bell, Inventor of the Telephone (*right*).

Elevated Railroad at 110th Street and Columbus Avenue, New York, About 1898 When Steam Power Was in Use.

America's New Labor Force—A Group of New Arrivals at Ellis Island Early
in the Twentieth Century.

Labor in the Textile Mills Was Largely Women and Children. Picture
Taken About 1900.

railroads that the courts and not the legislatures should fix charges was like-wise dismissed. "Where property has been clothed with a public interest," said the Court, "the legislature may fix a limit to that which shall be in law reasonable for its use. This limit binds the courts as well as the people. If it has been improperly fixed, the legislature, not the courts, must be appealed to for the change." The decisions in the Munn and Peik cases were supposed to have settled the main points of constitutional law involved in railway regulation; hence it was a matter of surprise when, ten years later (1886), in the case of the Wabash, St. Louis, and Pacific Railway *v.* Illinois,[11] the Su-preme Court reversed itself. The case arose over the violation of a law for-bidding a greater charge for a short haul than for a long one, when it was discovered that railroad rates were higher on freight from Gilman to New York than from Peoria to New York, although the latter point was eighty-six miles farther away. The decision now held that no state could exercise any control over commerce beyond its limits. Three years later in the "Min-nesota Rate case"[12] the railroads won the victory for which they had long struggled, when the Supreme Court took the stand that the reasonableness of rates was ultimately a judicial question. The Wabash and Minnesota cases made federal rather than state regulation the inevitable development.

DEVELOPMENT OF FEDERAL CONTROL

The Granger attack upon the railroads brought with it the demand for federal as well as state regulation. At the recommendation of President Grant in 1872 a committee was appointed under the chairmanship of William Windom of Minnesota which made a report[13] in 1874 advising government construction and extension of transportation facilities in order to reduce rates by making the government a competitor to private roads. The "Regan bill," aiming to abolish some of the worst abuses of the railroads, passed the House in 1878 but was not acted on in the Senate, and the question of railroad legis-lation lay dormant until 1885. In that year a Senate committee was appointed, headed by Shelby M. Cullom of Illinois, an indefatigable worker for rail-road regulation. In its report the following year[14] it reviewed carefully the various methods by which a remedy for the situation might be found, and endorsed some form of federal regulation and control to end the greatest evil, "unjust discrimination between persons, places, commodities, or particular descriptions of traffic."

In 1887 federal regulation of railroads was inaugurated as a compromise between government ownership and unrestrained private operation. Al-

[11] 118 U.S. 557.
[12] Chicago, Milwaukee, and St. Paul Railroad Company *v.* Minnesota. This decision was fore-told in 1886 in the case of Stone *v.* Farmers' Loan and Trust Co.
[13] *The Windom Report,* Senate Report No. 307, 43rd Cong., 1st Sess.
[14] *The Cullom Report,* Senate Report No. 46, 49th Cong., 1st Sess., Vol. II.

though passed during the Cleveland administration, the Interstate Commerce Act was supported by both parties and backed by urban as well as agricultural groups. It (1) provided that all charges should be just and reasonable, (2) forbade personal discriminations in the form of special rates, rebates, or otherwise, (3) forbade discriminations between localities, classes of freight, and connecting lines, (4) forbade a greater charge for a short haul than for a long, (5) prohibited pooling, and (6) ordered that all rates and fares should be printed and publicly posted, and no advance be made except after ten days' notice. The administration of the law was placed in the hands of an Interstate Commerce Commission of five members, which was given power to collect data from the carriers, call witnesses, hear complaints, and render decisions. If the commissioners believed that the law was violated and the roads refused to abide by their decisions, it was their duty to institute proceedings in the circuit courts. They were required to submit annual reports to Congress.

The passage of the Interstate Commerce Act was strongly opposed by the railroad officials, who predicted dire results; and their continued opposition and evasion, aided by various judicial decisions, effectively pulled the teeth from the act. The railroads successfully avoided giving full testimony until 1896, when the Commission eventually obtained compulsory power of investigation.[15] In 1897 the Supreme Court rendered the Commission virtually powerless when in the Maximum Freight Rate case it held "that the power to prescribe rates or fix any tariff is not among the powers granted to the Commission," thus limiting the latter's power over rates to deciding what was unfair, without the right to prescribe fair rates.[16] As if this was not enough, the Court cut the heart out of other sections of the act, notably Section 4, which forbade a greater charge for a short haul than a long one when made under "substantially similar circumstances." In the Alabama Midland case the Court ordered that the words "substantially similar circumstances" be interpreted literally—an impossible thing to do.[17]

The greatest weakness in the position of the Commission, however, was the fact that its decisions were not compulsory and that upon it rested the burden of initiating action in the courts. The attitude of the railroads and courts prevented the Interstate Commerce Act of 1887 from receiving a fair trial. Of sixteen rate cases appealed to the Supreme Court for enforcement between 1887 and 1905, fifteen were decided in favor of the carriers and only one sustained in part for the Commission. The average duration of railroad cases during this early period was close to four years; there were certain

---

[15] Brown *v.* Walker, 161 U.S. 591.

[16] Interstate Commerce Commission *v.* Cincinnati, New Orleans, and Texas Pacific Railway Company, 167 U.S. 479.

[17] 168 U.S. 144.

instances when litigation lasted nine years. In such a situation the Commission was soon reduced to a position so subordinate to the courts that its role became merely that of instituting proceedings and appearing as complainant.

Although some good work was done in securing rate publicity and in reducing the number of freight classifications, the act was important chiefly in its educational value and in introducing federal legislation, the system which has been in effect until the present time. That the Supreme Court itself knew that it had deliberately nullified a widespread desire on the part of the people to regulate interstate traffic and end long-standing abuses, there can be no doubt. Said Justice Harlan, dissenting in the Alabama Midland case:

> Taken in connection with other decisions defining the power of the Interstate Commerce Commission, the present decision, it seems to me, goes far to make that Commission a useless body for all practical purposes, and to defeat many of the important objects designed to be accomplished by the various enactments of Congress relating to interstate commerce. The Commission was established to protect the public against the improper practices of transportation companies engaged in commerce among the several states. It has been left, it is true, with power to make reports, and to issue protests. But it has been shorn, by judicial interpretation, of authority to do anything of an effective character.[18]

That the Interstate Commerce Act of 1887 had achieved no solution of the problem was apparent to all. Both the letter and the spirit of the act had been evaded, the Industrial Commission reporting in 1900 "that the railways still make discriminations between individuals, and perhaps to as great an extent as ever before."[19] The development of the Progressive movement in politics under the leadership of such men as Roosevelt and La Follette, however, meant a new effort to strengthen federal control.

The Elkins Act of 1903, aimed at the practice of rebates, declared deviation from published rates to be discrimination, and held both giver and receiver guilty. The Expediting Act of the same year gave preference in the circuit courts to cases arising under the Interstate Commerce Act of 1887 and the Sherman Antitrust Act of 1890, on the theory that such cases were "of general public importance." An important amendment to the legislation of 1887 was the Hepburn Act of 1906, which enlarged the scope of the Interstate Commerce Act to include express and sleeping-car companies, pipe lines, switches, spurs, tracks, and terminal facilities. The Commission, now increased to seven, of whom only four could be of the same political party, was empowered to determine just and reasonable rates and to order the carrier to adhere to them, leaving to the latter the burden of initiating court action.

---

[18] 168 U.S. 176 (1897).
[19] *Report of the Industrial Commission on Transportation*, IV, 5. See F. Flügel and H. U. Faulkner, *op. cit.*, p. 618.

On the face of it this change seemed small, but in practice it was almost revolutionary. From then on the Commission was an important body. The act also instructed the Commission to prescribe methods of bookkeeping for the railroads, and made their adoption compulsory. To end a certain type of discrimination, railroads were forbidden to carry commodities which they had themselves produced, except timber and goods needed in the conduct of their business. Free passes were forbidden, and rates had to be published thirty days before change. Although the part of the act respecting the right of railroads to carry commodities in which they had an interest has been nullified in part by court action, in general the court has limited itself to determining the legality of the Commission's orders rather than their wisdom or expediency. The Hepburn Act went far to eliminate the faults of the act of 1887, and since 1906 the Commission has been a responsible and powerful body.

In 1910 the Mann-Elkins Act was passed. It clarified the short- and long-haul clause of the Interstate Commerce Act and enlarged the powers of the Commission by granting to it the right to suspend for ten months the operation of a new scale of rates to allow time for an investigation. It set up a special Commerce Court to hear railroad cases arising from the Commission's activities; this was considered a much-needed innovation, for there was an obvious necessity for railroad cases to be tried by judges who were experts in such questions.[20] Of the subsequent legislation, mention may be made of the amendment of 1913 to the Interstate Commerce Act, requiring the Commission to report the value of all property owned or used by all the common carriers. Without such information, it was virtually impossible to set fair rates. Also came the Newlands Act of 1913 (amending the Erdman Act of 1898), providing for voluntary settlement of railroad disputes. In 1916 in the Adamson Eight-Hour Act the government entered into a new sphere of activity in regulating the hours of labor in interstate traffic. During these same progressive years several of the states, notably Iowa, California, and Wisconsin, moved aggressively to break the political power of the railroads by new legislation.

The opening of the First World War found the principle of government regulation firmly established and the railroad industry stabilized as never before. At the same time, inefficient management and the inevitable results of early excesses, coupled with dislike of government regulation, had helped to instill in many units of the industry a feeling of disquiet and uncertainty as to the future. Furthermore, railroad labor was becoming more restless and the public more exacting. Petitions by the railroads for higher rates and fares

[20] The Progressives in Congress distrusted the Commerce Court as a body of conservative judges biased in favor of the railroads, and discontinued it in 1912 by failing to appropriate funds for its maintenance.

were eventually granted, but too slowly to give adequate aid to the railroads. All factors pointed to further developments in federal regulation when war broke out.

RAILROAD CONSOLIDATION

Parallel to the combination of capital in other lines of industry there also developed a consolidation of railroads. This took place primarily to insure greater efficiency and savings, to eliminate competition, and to secure larger profits. It took two courses—that of uniting railroads to form a continuous line of travel, and that of consolidating the roads in a given geographic division. The first type of consolidation began before the Civil War and continued for many years. It is best exemplified by Vanderbilt's work in combining (1853) eleven little roads, which hitherto had most inefficiently handled the traffic between Albany and Buffalo, into the New York Central, and in adding five more roads to the system between 1855 and 1858.

As already noted, the late sixties and the decade of the seventies were a period of disastrous and unbridled railroad competition. By this time the through lines had taken form and were fighting bitterly for traffic. As this competition bade fair to ruin the roads, repeated efforts to eliminate it were made by means of pools or traffic associations, which sought to apportion the available business arbitrarily among the roads at rates mutually agreed upon. Such methods proved inadequate because the railroads did not keep their own agreements, and they became illegal after the Interstate Commerce Act forbade "any contract, agreement, or combination . . . for the pooling of freights of different and competing railroads," a clause later upheld by the Supreme Court in the case against the Trans-Missouri Freight Association (1897), when the decision asserted that the agreements entered into by this association violated the Sherman Antitrust Act of 1890 as agreements "in restraint of trade and commerce."

With pooling forbidden by law, the railroads, like other industries, turned again to consolidation to save themselves from the evils of too great competition. During the eighties, and again from 1898 to 1904, consolidation went on rapidly. By purchase, by lease, by the ownership of a majority of the stock, the larger railroads absorbed many of the smaller competing lines, which were thereafter often operated as separate but subsidiary companies. The period of rapid consolidation was brought to a halt after 1904 by the Supreme Court decision in the Northern Securities case. In 1901 the Harriman interests, which dominated the Union Pacific and the Southern Pacific, and the Morgan-Hill interests, which dominated the Great Northern, engaged in a battle royal for control of the Northern Pacific, which in turn controlled the Burlington system with an entry to Chicago. Having driven Northern Pacific common from around $100 to $1000 in a few days, the giants discovered that the fight had reached a stalemate, whereupon they reconciled their differences and organized the Northern Securities Company, a holding company to acquire the stock of the Great Northern and the Northern Pacific and thus control the Burlington system. Such an organization meant the elimination of competition in the Northwest. Scarcely three months after its formation the reviving storm of antitrust agitation broke upon it. The federal government instituted suit under the Sherman Act, and in 1904 the Supreme Court ordered its dissolution. "If Congress has not," said the Court, "by the words used in the Act, described this and like cases, it would, we apprehend, be impossible to find words that would describe them."[21]

By the time this great era of railroad consolidation reached its climax in 1906, the division of ownership and territory had been pretty clearly laid down. Of the 228,000 miles of railroad in that year, about two-thirds were in the hands of seven groups. The Vanderbilt roads with over 22,500 miles controlled the northern routes from New York to Chicago; the Pennsylvania interests (20,000 miles) dominated the roads to the West emanating from Pennsylvania and Maryland; the Morgan roads (18,000 miles) and their affiliates dominated the Southeast; the Gould roads (almost 17,000 miles) and the Rock Island system (almost 15,000 miles) were powerful in the Mississippi Valley. Beyond the Mississippi the Hill roads with over 21,000 miles had a monopoly of the Northwest, and the Harriman roads dominated the central and southern transcontinental routes. Although two-thirds of the mileage by this time had been divided among seven groups, in reality consolidation was even more far-reaching. These seven groups, for example, controlled 85 per cent of railroad earnings. Moreover, certain of these groups were closely allied through the same banking interests, and through interlocking directorates and stock ownership in the same concerns. Although the situation was by no means static since new alignments and new shifts were made under the pressure of one or another group of railroad speculators, the picture had not changed essentially up to the opening of the First World War. "The working out of the higher strategy in railroad consolidation," comments a leading authority of that period, "was the most significant feature of American transportation history in the decade of 1910. Within this brief period what now promises to become more or less permanent financial and operating groups, evolved out of the competitive chaos of the period of depression 1893–97."[22]

---

[21] Northern Securities Co. *et al. v.* U.S., 193 U.S. 360.

[22] W. Z. Ripley, *Railroads: Finance and Organization* (1915), p. 459.

In 1921 Senator La Follette charged that twenty-five directors linked together ninety-nine Class I roads, operating 211,280 miles, or 82 per cent of the country's transportation system, and that these were likewise closely allied with the leading equipment companies. The truth of these charges would support the belief that consolidation through community of interest has continued unabated. *Congressional Record,* March 14, 1921, with diagrams.

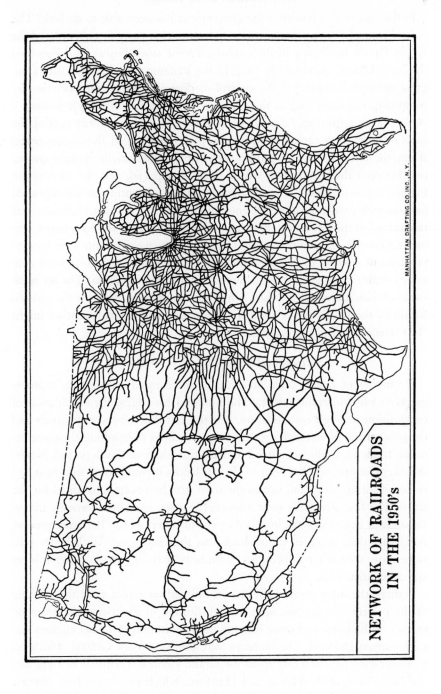

NETWORK OF RAILROADS
IN THE 1950's

MANHATTAN DRAFTING CO. INC., N.Y.

In the face of this tendency the government has been able to do little. The federal courts broke up the Northern Securities Company (1904), ordered the Union Pacific to dispose of its Southern Pacific stock (1912), and dissolved the New Haven monopoly in 1914. In the Panama Canal Act of 1912 Congress attempted to prevent the control of domestic water transportation by competing railroads, and in the Clayton Antitrust Act of 1914 it forbade a corporation's acquiring, "directly or indirectly, the whole or any part of the stock or other share capital of another corporation engaged also in commerce, where the effect of such acquisition may be to substantially lessen competition between the corporation whose stock is acquired, and the corporation making the acquisition." The apparent futility of preventing an accomplished fact, as well as the greater efficiency often achieved by consolidation, was recognized in the Transportation Act of 1920, which gave the Interstate Commerce Commission power to permit the carrier to acquire control by lease or purchase of another carrier in any manner which did not involve their consolidation into a single system of ownership and management. The act went further when it empowered the Commission to prepare plans for the consolidation of the roads into a number of systems in which competition might "be preserved as fully as possible."[23]

RAILROAD SERVICE AND COSTS

A number of factors have prevented a more rapid advance in improvements to railroad rolling stock. The financial hardships, the elimination of competition through consolidation, and the fact that express companies and the government have taken over the responsibilities of handling the more exacting traffic have all contributed to delay this phase of development. Nevertheless, great progress has been made, but before it could come steel rails had to be substituted for iron, just as the solid iron had been substituted for the strips. The first steel rails were imported in 1863, and their domestic manufacture was begun in 1865, impelled by the discovery of the Bessemer process. After that date much of the mileage was thus equipped. With better rails came more scientific roadbeds, and with heavier rolling stock, better bridges and other structures.

Perhaps the most notable advance in railroad operation since the opening of the present century has been the substitution of electricity for steam on certain of the lines, and more recently the substitution of Diesel engines and oil for steam and coal. The pioneers were the New York Central, which began operating by electricity from the Grand Central Terminal in 1906, and the New York, New Haven and Hartford, which two years later inaugurated complete electric service from the same terminal to Stamford, Con-

[23] Below, pp. 615–617.

necticut. The Norfolk and Western used electric power for heavy freight, and the Chicago, Milwaukee and Pugent Sound for long-distance traffic. The electric engine was found to be cheaper, faster, cleaner, and much better adapted to the crowded conditions of enclosed city terminals, as well as more dependable in zero weather. Only the precarious financial condition of many roads and the outbreak of the First World War prevented more rapid electrification. In the postwar years, however, came a new era of improved service characterized by Diesel engines, streamlined cars, greater comfort, and faster speed.

Freight earnings are over three times as great as passenger earnings on American roads, and there are forty freight cars to one passenger car. Most of the freight consists of heavy bulky products, such as iron and steel commodities, coal, grain, and timber, a factor of great influence in the development of rolling stock. In contrast to European equipment—which is light and small, designed to carry compact freight for short hauls—monster engines and large cars, built to carry heavy freight for long distances, have been the rule in America. Passenger coaches have followed this tendency in size, and our more democratic customs have prevented the adoption of the European compartment train. The tremendous weight of engines and cars has put a continually increasing strain on roadbeds, but the abundance of raw materials has held down the expense of keeping them in repair.

The comfort of passengers goes far beyond the dream of earlier travelers. Better springs, heating and lighting facilities, Pullman day and sleeping coaches and dining cars have all contributed to this. With the completion of the South Station in Boston in 1898, an era of huge station construction began, culminating in such beautiful and luxurious structures as the Washington depot (completed 1907), the Pennsylvania Station in New York (1910), and Grand Central (1913)—marvelous combinations of aesthetic qualities with utilitarian needs. Many safety devices have considerably eliminated the old danger for both passengers and workmen. Air brakes, block signals, the automatic coupler, and steel cars have furthered safety. Nevertheless, the loss of life on American railroads is great, and railroading continues among the most hazardous occupations. In 1920 the roads reported 6958 killed and 168,309 injured in accidents; of employees 2578 were killed and 149,414 injured; of trainmen, one in every 391 was killed and one in every eleven was injured.[24]

Equitable and fair freight rates are essential in a country whose economic life depends upon the transportation of large amounts of freight. Railroad

---

[24] The figures for 1951 show an appreciable reduction in casualties; the roads in that year reported 371 employees killed and 19,855 injured. By then passenger casualties were few and railroad travel had become the safest of any of the important facilities.

transportation is a business that ought to yield increasing returns, for the first cost is highest, and with the growth of population business should automatically increase without proportionate new expenditure. This, of course, is particularly true of a new and developing country like the United States. As the population has grown and new industries have been begun, transportation has been stimulated, resulting in more efficient service, the use of improved machinery, and the construction of better roadbeds. These factors, together with competition, kept freight rates on the decline until 1899, but since then government regulation has been necessary to keep them as low as possible. The average freight receipts per ton-mile measured in gold were 1.92 cents in 1867 and .724 in 1899. Since then they have increased—.766 in 1905 and 1.094 in 1928. By 1950 they had increased to 1.329. These changes, it should be noted, roughly followed the changes in general prices during this period.

Passenger fares have not decreased to the same extent, but travelers have benefited by improved service. The average revenue per passenger per mile was 2.63 cents in 1871 and 1.94 in 1910. Fares were increased during the First World War by the United States Railroad Commission and in 1920 by the Interstate Commerce Commission. The average receipts per passenger per mile on Class I carriers was 2.76 cents in 1920 and 2.60 in 1951.

The old theory of charging "all that the traffic will bear" was modified, first by the desire not to antagonize public opinion further, and later by government interference. The present rate-making policy as exemplified by the Transportation Act of 1920 is to allow rates high enough to give a fair return on the actual value of the property. Farmers, miners, and other producers of raw materials have been the great gainers from decreased freight rates, although the people as a whole have also profited.[25]

ELECTRIC RAILWAY TRANSPORTATION

The development of electric railways has taken place almost entirely in the last sixty years. It is part of the long story of the effort to solve the urban transportation problem, which seems always a little beyond the capacity of the rapidly growing cities. The first practical overhead trolley line was built in Kansas City in 1884, and by 1888 there were thirteen electric railways with forty-eight miles of track in the United States. After 1890 progress was extremely rapid, when inventors like Charles J. Van Depoele, Stephen D. Field, Frank J. Sprague, and Elihu Thompson turned their genius to this field. At the same time financiers and entrepreneurs, such as Thomas F. Ryan, Charles T. Yerkes, and William L. Elkins, entered as enthusiastically and as

[25] For a discussion of railroads since 1914, see pp. 614–618.

ruthlessly upon the building of trolleys as the "robber barons" of half a century earlier had taken up the construction of steam railroads. As with railroads, an early glamour surrounded the electric trolleys, for a town's pretensions to cityhood depended upon possession of a streetcar system.

There were numerous street railways before 1890, but the motive power was chiefly animal and steam. Electricity was rapidly substituted. New York, Chicago, and Boston all had elevated systems by 1901, but not until the latter date was electricity first used on the New York elevated. Electricity not only greatly facilitated traffic on the railways but made it possible to build subways. Boston, the pioneer in American subways, completed her first unit in 1898, and New York began construction in 1900. By 1905 trains were running under the East River to Brooklyn and, three years later, under the North River to New Jersey. Single-track mileage of street and electrical railways amounted in 1920 to 47,705; since then it has dropped to 19,602 in 1940 and 10,813 in 1950. This decline, of course, does not mean less transportation facilities; buses have been substituted for rails.

The electric railroads have supplied an important economic need made imperative by the growth of urban life. So far their chief business has been the transportation of passengers in thickly populated sections. Their freight possibilities, discouraged by the competition and hostility of the steam railroads, have never been fully exploited. The type of traffic thus handled has had an important significance, social as well as economic. The trolley in its day helped to break down the isolation of country life, decrease its disadvantages, and improve the economic and cultural opportunities of regions near the cities, and it afforded greater opportunity for the city population to reach the country. In this way it has done more than anything else except the automobile to unite suburban and urban communities.

Electric railways under certain conditions and in certain areas have been able to compete with steam roads quite successfully for passenger traffic. Greater cheapness in construction and operation has made lower fares possible, and the ability to run single cars has allowed frequent service and thus greater facilities and convenience. Built ordinarily in densely populated regions, they have an advantage over a railroad which is forced to carry the burden of long stretches of thinly peopled country. Nevertheless, the history of electric railways has been checkered. The rising costs of fuel and equipment, combined with the constant introduction of improvements rendered necessary in many cases by municipal ordinances, have made operation more expensive. The habit of the five-cent fare, which had become grounded in custom and law, was difficult to break. High financing, overoptimism in construction, and the growth of gasoline motor traffic all added to the discomfiture of electric roads. Between 1900 and 1913 a considerable portion of the street railways passed through either financial reorganization or actual receivership.

The attitude of the people in regard to street railways has been a repetition of their attitude toward the steam carriers—first a period of encouragement and aid through liberal franchises and stock subscriptions, then a period of dissatisfaction and criticism, in many cases justly deserved, and finally realization that the roads are an essential means of transportation that must be preserved and regulated for the benefit of the whole community. The competition of electric urban and interurban railways has been met by the railroads in two ways: first, by purchasing and operating the trolleys themselves, and second, by electrifying their own lines. The New Haven and the New York Central, both operating in congested regions, have used these methods. Since the Second World War, the railroads have largely by-passed electric transportation and have replaced the steam engines by Diesel oil-burning engines. Almost all railroad engines now being built are of this type.

THE AUTOMOBILE AND THE RENAISSANCE OF ROAD BUILDING

Of greater significance for the future than electric street railways was the gasoline-driven motor vehicle. After a century of experimentation, mostly with steam, practical cars were produced in 1893, but until 1903 the industry was in an experimental and unstable position. The early experimentation was done largely in Europe, where the automobile had been considerably developed before there was much interest in America; but at least one American —George B. Selden, of Rochester, New York, had built, as early as 1877, a vehicle equipped with a gasoline engine, a patent for which he finally obtained in 1895. As the news of the "horseless carriages" reached America in the nineties, many tinkering mechanics like Charles E. Duryea, Ransom E. Olds, Elwood Haynes, and Henry Ford succeeded in putting together contraptions which would run, some of them driven by electricity, by gasoline, by steam, by carbonic acid gas and alcohol.[26] The Selden patent failed to prevent a rapid development,[27] and after 1900 there ensued a period of intense competition in which the automobile was quickly made practical. The popularity of the automobile was undoubtedly increased by the improvement in design which took the engine from underneath and placed it in front, making the car look less like a horseless carriage, and by innumerable technical improvements which made it possible for persons without mechanical train-

[26] When the National Automobile Chamber of Commerce in 1925 determined to honor the American pioneers in the industry, it conferred medals upon John D. Maxwell, Edgar L. Apperson, A. L. Riker, John S. Clarke, Rollin H. White, H. H. Franklin, Charles Duryea, Charles B. King, Elwood Haynes, Alexander Winton, and R. E. Olds.
[27] W. Kaempffert, *A Popular History of American Invention* (1924), chap. 4.

ing to operate automobiles. Gasoline cars could be run in reverse by 1900, and by 1913 a practical self-starter had been invented. Furthermore, the price, under Ford's impetus, had been reduced by 1914 to a figure within the reach of at least the upper middle class. In that year the production of automobiles was about 569,000, the vehicles registered numbered 1,711,339, and the capital invested in manufacturing them amounted to over $400,000,000. The great expansion and the great influence of the motorcar were to come in the next fifteen years.[28]

One of the most important effects of the automobile was the renaissance of road building, reminiscent of the turnpike era of the closing years of the eighteenth and the early years of the nineteenth centuries.[29] The bicycle craze of the nineties, the introduction of the rural free delivery in 1896, the desire to bring rural transportation on a par with urban, and finally the advent of the motor inaugurated a widespread movement for improved highways. Better-roads organizations were formed, culminating in 1910 in the American Association for Highway Improvement. The lead in the movement was taken by New Jersey in 1891 and quickly followed in the succeeding years by other states, particularly in the East. They began by making small contributions for the improvement of town and county roads, but gradually extended their appropriations and their supervision until by 1914 some of them had laid out trunk lines and were appropriating millions of dollars to improve and keep them in repair. Under the strain of motor traffic the old dirt, gravel, or "water-bound macadam" surfaces were found inadequate, and some form of bituminous macadam or bitulithic pavement was gradually substituted. Stretches of concrete also were being laid by 1914, a material used extensively in the new bridges which were laid simultaneously with the new roads. Roadways, whose economic significance had declined with the advent of railroads, by 1914 were rapidly achieving their former position of primary importance, but the great period of highway construction, like the great period of automobile expansion, was to come in the next fifteen years.

AVIATION

Although commercial aviation, which has grown so rapidly in the last three decades, had made no progress in this country before the First World War, the science of aviation had sufficiently advanced to make its development possible, and American inventors were primarily responsible. Experiments in the construction of airplanes had been made in the nineties in England and France, but nothing came of them; the chief interest in aviation at the turn of the century concerned ballooning. The brilliant scientist of the Smith-

[28] Below, pp. 622, 623.
[29] Above, p. 622.

sonian Institution, Samuel P. Langley, was busy in the nineties devising steam-driven models which made successful flights. Finally, by means of an appropriation from the War Department he built a man-size airplane which in 1903 his assistant, Charles M. Manly, tried twice unsuccessfully to fly over the Potomac. Langley claimed that the trouble was not with the airplane but with the failure to launch it properly, and his belief was in part vindicated in 1914 when Glenn Curtiss installed a more powerful engine and flew the plane successfully.

While the public press was still jeering over the failure of the Smithsonian scientists, two mechanics from Toledo, Ohio, Orville and Wilbur Wright, were making the first successful flights in the history of the world with a heavier-than-air machine carrying a man. These flights at Kittyhawk on the lonely Carolina coast were the result of years of experimentation which were continued until 1908, when the Wrights began their demonstration in Europe and America. Although enthusiasm was widespread, the advance during the next few years occurred chiefly in Europe. America, however, had one further contribution of importance to make before 1914 in the hydroaeroplane designed by Glenn H. Curtiss and flown by him at San Diego in 1911. It was the military possibilities of the airplane in the First World War that gave aviation its first great impetus. The rapid development of commercial aviation began in the 1920's.[30]

INTERNAL WATER TRANSPORTATION

It is estimated that there are 260 streams available in the United States for commercial transportation, with over 26,000 navigable miles. These streams together with the Great Lakes give this country the finest natural system of internal waterways available to any nation in the world. Despite this fact and the large annual federal grants for the improvement of river channels, the importance of internal waterways has declined since the advent of the railroads. Only upon the Great Lakes has the tendency been otherwise. While the tonnage carried by the railroads has increased enormously, river tonnage has shown an absolute as well as a relative falling off. This is true even of the Mississippi traffic. The high-water mark of river transportation for the lower Mississippi came in 1880, when over 1,000,000 tons were received and shipped at St. Louis from and for the lower Mississippi; the figure fell to 141,000 in 1905. Receipts and shipments at St. Louis to and from the upper Mississippi declined from 340,000 tons in 1870 to less than 70,000 in 1905. Cotton receipts by river at New Orleans were reduced from 1,087,000 bales in 1880 to 231,000 in 1906. On the Ohio, however, there has been an absolute increase because of coal shipments, but a relative decline.

[30] For a further discussion of aviation, see below, pp. 623–625.

What is true of rivers holds even more for canals. Of the 4633 miles of canals built in the United States before 1909, 2444, or over half, have been abandoned. Of all artificial waterways, the Erie Canal in New York State has been the most important, and the statistics for this canal are indicative of the general tendency. The annual tonnage carried on it increased to a high point of over 4,600,000 tons in 1880, only to decline to 2,400,000 in 1906 and to 891,000 tons in 1920; this, too, in spite of the fact that tolls were abolished in 1882 and the canal has been enlarged and improved since 1903.[31] The tonnage of the Erie Railroad in the same state increased by 1905 to over 30,000,000, and that of the New York Central to over 40,000,000. In 1853 the New York State canal system carried 81 per cent of the total traffic; in 1873 it carried 35 per cent, and in both 1906 and 1908 only 3 per cent. The traffic which waterways still carry is largely bulky and low-class freight—iron, coal, lumber, grain, and building materials. The Sault Ste Marie connecting Lakes Superior and Huron, and in amount of tonnage carried the most important American canal, reported for the year 1908 iron ore as 59.6 per cent of its traffic, coal 23.9 per cent, and wheat 7.7 per cent. Over half the Mississippi River traffic and over three-fourths of that of the Ohio in recent years has been coal. The tonnage on the Monongahela, Allegheny, and Kanawha is similar. Nearly 90 per cent of the entire tonnage of the Chesapeake and Ohio Canal during the last years of its operation was coal.

The causes for the decline of water transportation in the United States are many. While ordinarily transportation by water is cheaper than by land, this advantage has been lost because of other factors. In the first place, American railroads have also been designed to handle large bulky traffic. As they were improved and enlarged, they have been able in many instances to lower their rates to a point approximately as low as those charged for water transportation. Where this has been impossible, the roads have obtained possession of the steamship lines and canals, and either operated or discontinued them. The speed of the railroads and their superiority in handling high-class freight have been influential in diverting traffic to them, for America as a nation likes speed. Their many branch lines touch an infinite number of points inaccessible to canals. Some of the early canals were unwisely located, others are too short to be used for through freight, and still others were built in regions where the original products, such as lumber, have become exhausted. The cost of transshipment often eats up the advantages that might accrue from cheaper rates. Furthermore, with the exception of the New York Barge Canal, the service and facilities of the canals have not been improved to meet the demands of present-day traffic. The difficulty of river navigation, owing to shifting sand, snags, and other impediments, to say nothing of winter

[31] In recent years this has increased, the total freight for 1950 being 5,211,472 tons.

freezing, has discouraged development. The large rivers, furthermore, flow in a southerly direction, whereas the bulk of the traffic moves east and west.

In spite of the decline in water traffic and the coming of the automobile and airplane, interest in canal and river transportation has revived since 1900, and persistent agitation in its behalf developed. Any temporary inability of the railroads to handle freight, or an increase in rates, invariably turns the attention of shippers to water facilities. River towns, hoping for a brighter future, promote almost continuous propaganda for improved waterways. Considerable stimulus was given to the interest in artificial waterways by the building of the Panama Canal, the greatest transportation project which the federal government has embarked upon. The victorious battles which Colonel William C. Gorgas fought against tropical disease, and which Colonel George W. Goethals waged against almost insurmountable natural barriers to accomplish a dream of centuries, thrilled the American people, as well they might, and turned their attention again to canals. A little later the problem became tied up with the conservation movement, and in 1907 Roosevelt appointed an Inland Waterways Commission to survey the entire subject. The agitation resulted in the appropiation of 1911 of approximately $10,000,000 to improve navigation on the Ohio; it also resulted in the state of Illinois's undertaking the first link in the projected "Lakes-to-Gulf Deep Waterway," and in a revival of the old scheme, first broached by Gallatin, for an intra-coastal waterway along the Atlantic. In 1909 a private company started a canal across Cape Cod which was completed in 1914. The most tangible result of this agitation, however, was the improvement and enlargement of the New York canal system, which involved 440 miles of improvement or new construction and the canalization of 350 miles of lakes and rivers. An initial appropriation of $101,000,000 was made in 1903, and New York again looked forward to the day when the products of the Great Lakes basin would pass over her waterways.

While river and canal traffic has diminished, that on the Great Lakes has increased. Here the ordinary advantages of water transportation are evident, and in addition long-distance conveyance is provided during a larger part of the year than is possible on canals in the same latitude. The cost of maintenance is smaller, too, than that of canals and rivers. This is seen in the freight rates, which in 1900 were 4.42 cents per bushel of wheat from Chicago to New York by lake and canal and 9.98 by railroad, and in 1920 were 14.60 and 16.68 cents respectively. Furthermore, the freight is especially suitable to water transportation, being composed almost entirely of bulky raw material. Anthracite and bituminous coal is transported north and west, and the return shipments are composed of flour, grain, iron ore from the Lake Superior mines (Mesabi Range), and lumber. The tonnage of the Great Lakes trade increased from 467,700 in 1860 to 169,881,000 in 1950. At the same time the tonnage of vessels passing through the Sault Ste Marie Canal rose from 403,- 659 in 1860 to 106,140,000 in 1950.

TELEPHONY, TELEGRAPHY, AND WIRELESS

The closing years of the nineteenth century saw a rapid expansion in the use of the telephone, an invention of epoch-making significance in the history of communication. Although a number of experiments had been made in transmitting the human voice by electricity, not until 1876 did Alexander Graham Bell successfully carry on a conversation with his assistant, Thomas A. Watson, over a line which he had erected between Boston and Cambridgeport, Massachusetts. Bell's first patent, which was taken out in that year, marked the beginning of the telephone industry, largely American in its origin[32] and improvements. Today this nation has approximately 60 per cent of the telephones in the world. In 1880 there were 34,305 miles of telephone wires in the United States; in 1952 the American Telephone and Telegraph Company, the huge holding company that controls most of the important American systems, reported about 159,000,000 miles under its direction. It boasted 855,000 telephones in 1900 and 9,172,000 in 1915, by which time the telephone had become standard equipment for a middle-class home. In 1952 it controlled about 39,414,000. Long-distance telephony began with the opening of a line between New York and Philadelphia in January, 1887, but it was not until 1915 that Bell spoke into an exact reproduction of his original instrument and was clearly heard by Watson in San Francisco. In the meantime the large research staff maintained by the American Telephone and Telegraph Company had developed technical improvements which were to make the next fifteen years a period of spectacular advance.

While telephony was revolutionizing our methods of communication, telegraphy also made important progress. Spurred on by the Civil War, a telegraph line was strung across the continent in 1862, and since that time the growth of telegraphy has been rapid. In 1945 there were in the United States 276,084 miles of telegraph lines, a substantial percentage of the world's telegraph service, over which about 236,453,000 telegrams were sent. Not only has the industry grown enormously, but numerous inventions have enabled it to expand in various ways. Beginning with J. B. Stearns's invention in 1872 of the duplex method by which two messages can be sent simultaneously in the same direction, the wires were further utilized by the discovery of the quadruplex system of transmitting four messages simultaneously, two each way, and later by multiplex telegraphy. Submarine telegraphic communication was achieved temporarily by Cyrus Field in 1858 and finally in 1866.

[32] Bell himself was a Scotchman who came to America in early manhood.

The significance of cable communication is too obvious to need comment. Printing telegraphy has been developed, as exemplified in the stock ticker, and various forms of writing telegraphy have been put in operation. Practically all of the telegraph lines in the United States are privately owned, and since the merger of the Western Union Telegraph Company and Postal Telegraph, Inc., in 1943, the business is carried on under the first-named company. The telegraph and cable business reached its high point about 1927. Since then it has suffered from telephone and wireless competition.

The most spectacular development in telegraphy came with wireless in the first decade of the present century. Many experimenters had worked on the principles underlying wireless, but it was left to the Italian, Guglielmo Marconi, to make it a practical thing. Marconi took out his first English patent in 1896 and gradually extended the range of his operations until in December of 1901 he caught at St. Johns, Newfoundland, the signal sent from Poldhu Station, Cornwall. By the opening of the First World War wireless installations had become standard equipment on every ship of any size, huge wireless stations were being erected, commercial wireless was an accomplished fact, and the way was open for the development of wireless telephony and radio.

THE POST OFFICE

One of the most important social and economic functions of government in modern times is the proper collection and distribution of mails. So important is this considered than any interference with the mails is a criminal offense. The great development of the postal system has occurred since 1860. The postal law of 1816, which was in effect until 1845, charged six cents for one piece of paper going not over thirty miles, prepayment being optional. In 1847 the rates were lowered and postage stamps of five- and ten-cent denominations introduced; prepayment was required. The rates were again reduced in 1861 to three cents per half-ounce for distances under 3000 miles and in 1883 to two cents an ounce for all first-class mail. The registration of letters was begun in 1854, and during Lincoln's administration the free delivery of mail (1863), the railroad post office (1862), and the money-order system (1864) were started. Under McKinley in 1896 the rural free delivery was established, with eighty-seven routes, the number of which had grown by 1950 to 32,619, covering 1,493,365 miles. In 1838 the country declared every railroad a mail route, but the post office pushed ahead and beyond the railroads, its operations in the sparsely settled West of the pioneer days forming a romantic and inspiring story. Always alert for new opportunities, the federal government began the transportation of mail by air in 1918 when Army planes carried the first mail from New York to Washington.[33]

[33] Below, p. 624.

In recent years the activities of the government have been extended into both the express and the banking businesses, although its entrance in both cases was bitterly fought by the interests affected. A postal-savings system was inaugurated in 1910 to provide absolute safety at low interest for the comparatively poor man. The interest of 2 per cent upon a full year's deposit was in fact so low that the amount placed was relatively small. Of more general use, the domestic parcel-post system, introduced in 1913 after successful operation in Europe, has been an immense blessing to the people, permitting as it does the transportation of small packages more rapidly, cheaply, and safely than does any other means. Some industries, the most notable of which are the great mail-order houses of Chicago, base the large bulk of their business upon its facilities. Again the farmer has been the great gainer. On the other hand, the federal government, presumably to promote the cultural and economic life of the nation, carries a great deal of second-class mail, particularly newspapers and magazines, at much less than cost. While this objective is to some extent achieved, the policy also results in subsidizing advertising and the transportation of much material that degrades rather than elevates the cultural level—all at the expense of the taxpayers. Some indication of the development of the post office may be seen from the fact that the gross postal revenues increased from $8,518,000 in 1860 to $1,603,628,-000 in 1950.

SELECTED READINGS

Moody, John, *The Railroad Builders.*
Riegel, R. E., *Story of Western Railroads,* chaps. 1–8.
Jones, Eliot, *Principles of Railway Transportation,* chaps. 5–15 (survey of legislation).
Daggett, Stuart, *Principles of Inland Transportation,* chap. 6 (street and interurban railroads).
Moulton, H. G., *Waterways vs. Railways,* chaps. 1–5, 15, 19.
Faulkner, H. U., *Decline of Laissez Faire,* chaps. 9–10.
Flügel, F., and Faulkner, H. U., *Readings in the Economic and Social History of the United States,* chap. 15.

CHAPTER 24

FINANCIAL HISTORY

SINCE 1860

FINANCING THE CIVIL WAR

No phase of American economic history was more directly affected by the Civil War than public finance. The effects of this conflict upon the financial structure of the nation were, in fact, revolutionary in their scope. The needs of war financing enormously increased the rates of the protective tariff of 1861, created a new federal banking system, injected fiat paper money into the currency, and inaugurated a bitter half-century conflict between the currency inflationists and contractionists. The cost of the war was stupendous for that period, and much greater than was believed possible at the opening of the struggle. David A. Wells, Special Commissioner of the Revenue, estimated in 1869 that the total war expenditure of the national government in the eight and a quarter years of the war and postwar period was $4,171,-914,498.33. In addition, he pointed out, there should be reckoned the payment for pensions amounting to $2,000,000,000 and the further direct and indirect losses to Union and Confederate states of some $4,823,000,000. "These estimates, which are believed to be moderate and reasonable," said Wells, "show an aggregate destruction of wealth, or diversion of industry, which would have produced wealth, in the United States since 1861, approximating *nine* thousand *millions* of dollars. . . . It is three times as much as the slave property of the country was ever worth. It is a sum which at interest would yield to the end of time twice as much as the annual slave product of the South in its best estate."[1]

In four years the government expenditures amounted to more than during

---

[1] *Report of the Special Commissioner of the Revenue, 1869*, Executive Document No. 27, House of Representatives, 41st Cong., 2nd Sess., p. vi. Up to 1951 Civil War pensions amounted to over $8,169,506,000.

the whole previous history of the nation. In an effort to meet these expenses, Congress used every known device for obtaining revenue. Since the tariff had supplied most of the federal income up to that time, it was regarded as the most important source. A new tariff, framed largely by J. S. Morrill, was passed by the Senate on March 2, 1861, just before Lincoln's inauguration; it aimed to supplant the low rates of 1857 and restore the general level of the Walker tariff of 1846, the average rates of which were about 25 per cent. But the Morrill tariff did not produce the income anticipated, and legislation during succeeding years gradually raised the average of duties until in 1864 it reached 47 per cent.

The continued tariff increases had been enacted to balance in some degree the high internal taxes imposed upon a wide variety of manufactured articles and business transactions. The method of distributing the excises was likened by Wells to the advice given the Irishman at Donnybrook Fair: "Whenever you see a head, hit it; whenever you see a commodity, tax it."[2] By the end of the war the internal revenue was yielding twice as much as the tariff. Another form on taxation, a tax upon incomes, was levied for the first time in our history in 1861, when 3 per cent was imposed on incomes above $800. Increased in 1862 and 1865 until incomes between $600 and $5000 were taxed at 5 per cent and those above $5000 at 10 per cent, this tax yielded about $347,000,000 before it was abolished in 1872.

While taxes were levied with a free hand, a large proportion of the income derived therefrom was not received until the later period of the war. In the meantime the conflict was prosecuted upon borrowed money obtained first through the flotation of short-time loans and later, when it became evident that the war would not be over in a few months, by long-term borrowing. On September 1, 1865, the public debt reached its highest point until 1917; it amounted to $2,846,000,000, and was made up of many types of notes. In June, 1866, the "interest-bearing debt consisted of loans bearing five different rates of interest and maturing at nineteen different periods of time."[3] Some were payable in coin and some in currency; eight-ninths of these were short-time notes.

One other method of financing the war expenses of the national government brought results which were to plague the country for decades. This was the issuance of paper money "on the credit of the United States." Treasury notes had been issued in times of stress earlier in our history, but they had been interest-bearing, had not been legal tender, had been issued for the most part in large denominations, and hence had had small circulation as currency. Other than these, no paper money had ever before been issued by the na-

[2] Quoted by F. W. Taussig, *Tariff History of the United States* (5th ed.), p. 164.
[3] D. R. Dewey, *Financial History of the United States* (10th ed.), p. 332.

tional government. Bank notes, supplied by some 1600 state banking institutions, and the metal coined by the United States Mint, together with the "old demand notes" issued in 1861,[4] made up the currency at the beginning of the war. The drain upon the metal in the Treasury occasioned the suspension of specie payments in December, 1861, first by the banks and soon afterward by the government. Metal currency was hoarded (except on the Pacific coast), and the issues of state banks were inadequate to meet the increased needs for a circulating medium.

GREENBACKS

On February 25, 1862, an act was passed authorizing an issue of $150,000,-000 in notes on the credit of the United States, and making them legal tender. Supplementary acts followed—altogether authorizing greenbacks to the extent of $450,000,000. They were legal payment for all debts public and private, except tariff duties and interest on the public debt. The colloquial term "greenbacks" originated from the green ink used in printing the backs of these notes. The greenbacks were supplemented by an authorization of $50,-000,000 for fractional currency in denominations as low as three cents, to replace the subsidiary coins that, as the war went on, had been hoarded and withdrawn from circulation. On September 1, 1865, $433,160,000 in United States notes was outstanding, besides $26,344,000 in fractional (paper) currency.[5] Other government obligations were also employed as currency, but were interest-bearing. The war left the country with the problem of fiat money still to settle and the greenbacks became a burning issue, both legally and financially.

Although the resources of the nation were quite adequate to finance the war and Congress seemed willing to increase taxation, the handling of Civil War finances as a whole was inept. Salmon P. Chase, Secretary of the Treasury until June, 1864, based his policy on the experience in earlier American wars—"finance your war costs on borrowed funds, and increase your taxes only for the purpose of covering service on the newly incurred debt." Sumner calls the financial maneuvers of 1861–1862 a "simple record of temporary makeshifts,"[6] but Sumner's opinion seems a little harsh, particularly when

---

[4] These notes, unlike the greenbacks, were receivable for customs duties and hence kept metal from flowing into the Treasury, thus hastening suspension of specie payment. *Ibid.,* pp. 279, 283.

[5] Earlier efforts to replace small coins by people who had to make change had resulted in the use of stamps, old Spanish quarter dollars, bank bills cut in halves or quarters, and the issuance of tickets, due bills, and other forms of obligation by individuals, firms, banks, and even municipalities. These were called "shinplasters." Congress interfered with this private issuance of money and first authorized the use of postage stamps; later, to prevent the inconvenience of using gummed stamps as currency, it authorized the Post Office Department to issue postal currency in denominations of five to fifty cents. By May 27, 1863, over $20,000,000 had been placed in circulation.

[6] W. G. Sumner, *A History of American Currency* (1876), p. 197.

the policies of Chase are compared with those of later wars. It is the opinion of most students that the weakest element in the financing of this war was the delay in applying effective taxation. Only slightly over one-quarter of the federal receipts during the four fiscal years 1862 through 1865 was obtained by this means.[7] *from taxation*

THE NATIONAL BANKING SYSTEM

After the second Bank of the United States ceased to exist in 1836, the federal government withdrew from any supervision of the nation's banking until the creation of the National Banking system in 1863.[8] For a time it deposited its money in state-chartered banks and then established an "independent treasury system" through which it paid its own bills and received money due it. With the restraining hand of the government removed, the state banks flourished like a green bay tree. What paper money existed was in the form of bank notes circulated by the state banks. As far as paper money was concerned, the chaos was almost indescribable. In 1862 there were about 1600 banks established under the laws of the various states whose notes circulated at a discount varying with the confidence in the bank and the distance from the bank of issue. "It was estimated," said A. Barton Hepburn, "that there were 7000 kinds and denominations of notes, and fully 4000 spurious or altered varieties were reported."[9] It was difficult to estimate the value of the various notes, and the annoyances and losses attendant upon doing business with them can easily be imagined. It was in part to eliminate this chaotic paper currency that the National Banking system was established, and it was one beneficial result of the war.

But the elimination of the state bank notes was not the only argument advanced for the creation of a national banking system. It was hoped that national banks would create a market for United States bonds, provide the country with a standardized paper currency, and tie up the financial interests more closely with the Union cause. The plan, in fact, had wide approval. A system of banks resting upon national rather than state authority, as Professor Dewey points out, "appealed to the growing feeling of nationalism; . . . it appealed to those who were jealous of the power of private corporations; it appealed to those who wished to relieve the government of distressing

[7] Customs receipts for these four years were $305,360,451; internal revenue and income taxes, $356,846,136; and loans including Treasury notes, $2,621,916,786. The ratio of loans to taxes decreased from $8.52 to $1 for 1861–1862 to $2.95 to $1 in 1864–1865. D. R. Dewey, *op. cit.*, p. 299.

[8] Above, p. 160.

[9] A. Barton Hepburn, *History of Coinage and Currency in the United States*, p. 177. An interesting old book compiled to aid in detecting spurious notes and published in New York in 1863 is *Hodge's Bank Note Safeguard; giving facsimile descriptions of upwards of ten thousand bank notes, embracing every genuine note issued in the United States and Canada.*

bargains, and who hoped the government would thus gain the ascendency in the control of capital; and finally it appealed to those who feared that further issues of United States notes would ultimately ruin both the government and private credit."[10]

The National Bank Act of 1863 (amended in 1864) granted charters to groups of not less than five stockholders (the amount of the capital stock being graduated for cities of different size), who must deposit with the federal government federal bonds equal in amount to one-third of the bank's capital, and not less than $30,000. In return the banks might receive bank notes up to 90 per cent of the current market value (not exceeding par) of the bonds. These notes were legal tender for all government dues except import duties and might be used by the government for all transactions except payment of principal and interest on the national debt. Numerous provisions, including reserve requirements, liability of stockholders, and strict national supervision, protected the depositor. Banks were slow in taking out charters, and in 1865 state bank issues were driven out by a 10 per cent annual tax. Supplementary legislation in 1900 liberalized the National Bank Act by permitting bank notes to be issued up to the full par value of the bonds; by reducing the capitalization of banks in cities of 3000 or under from $50,000 to $25,000; by refunding the existing national debt in thirty-year 2 per cent bonds; and by reducing the tax from one to one-half of one per cent per annum on all bonds yielding not over 2 per cent, if such bonds were deposited to secure circulation. The bank-note circulation, which reached $339,000,000 in 1873, declined to $168,000,000 in 1891 as the bonds fell due and were retired. Eventually further loans, issued to cover the Spanish-American War and other expenses, increased the note circulation by 1913 to $715,754,236, issued from 7473 national banks.[11]

RESULTS OF WAR FINANCING

In December, 1861, the northern banks, followed shortly after by the federal government, suspended specie payments. With the issuance of greenbacks, metallic money virtually disappeared. Under the impetus of Gresham's law,[12] greenbacks, the cheapest money, became the standard of value for ordinary commercial transactions. It would be incorrect, however, to attribute the rise in prices during the war to the legal-tender greenbacks alone. Contributing factors were the numerous short-term Treasury notes which

cheap money drives out valuable money

[10] D. R. Dewey, *op. cit.,* p. 321.

[11] By December 31, 1950, the number of national banks had decreased to 4965. As a result of the Federal Reserve Act and later of New Deal currency legislation, national bank notes have been largely replaced by Federal Reserve notes.

[12] Above, p. 157 n.

passed almost like money, and the enlarged issues of state bank notes. The Civil War boom and the increased demand for commodities of all sorts also influenced the prices of most commodities. But the issuance of nearly $450,-000,000 worth of irredeemable paper money at a time when prices were already on the rise greatly emphasized the movement. Measured in terms of gold, the greenbacks, as will be seen from the accompanying graph, at no time during the war reached par; in the summer of 1864 they dropped as low as 39. The fluctuations in their value were caused partly by speculation and partly by varying confidence in the government's credit and do not necessarily approximate the rise of living costs.

While the government during the Civil War gained as an employer of labor from the issuing of the greenbacks, it lost in the long run as a purchaser of commodities from the rise in prices. It has been estimated that the cost of the war was increased by over $500,000,000 by the decline in value of legal-tender money. Between 1860 and 1865 textiles quadrupled in price; groceries and flour doubled; meat, fuel, and rents increased over 50 per cent. At the same time real wages, especially for salaried men, lagged far behind.[13]

One of the legacies of Civil War finance was a thirty-year battle waged by the debtor groups, particularly the farmers, to prevent contraction of the currency and to maintain prices at the Civil War level when they had contracted many debts. Three factors were primarily responsible for the decline of prices in the postwar years. First of all was the cessation of the artificial demand for commodities produced by the war and accentuated by the disastrous panic of 1873. Second was the glut of foodstuffs, caused chiefly by the extreme rapidity with which the trans-Mississippi West was brought under cultivation. The third factor was the currency policy of the government, which looked toward the contraction of the paper currency and the resumption of specie payment.

The last of these was probably the most important. The government was contracting its paper currency at a time when there was a growing need for more money in business, a situation which was accentuated after the war by the fact that the area in which United States money was current was increased to include the South, the Confederate currency being replaced by that of the United States. This situation continued even after contraction was stopped. After the resumption of specie payments in 1879 and the reestablishment of the gold standard, prices continued to decline here until 1896, along with a general decline in world prices measured in gold. While the production of gold during the seventies and eighties remained about the same, the demand for it increased, owing to the adoption of the gold

[13] Above, pp. 332 ff.

standard by many new and large countries. This pushed up the price of gold and depressed the price of commodities.[14] The farmer fought bitterly and consistently against contraction. Any revolution in prices is bound to injure certain groups, and in this case it was the debtor farmer, chiefly in the West and South, particularly the Westerners who had pioneered during the war period of rising prices. This group now found it increasingly difficult to carry their mortgages and pay the debts incurred in buying stock and machinery. Declining prices of foodstuffs and a contracting currency had brought real hardship, and the debtor farmer put forth every effort to maintain or restore the former prices through currency inflation.

In its early stages the fight swung around the question of greenbacks. Three main problems pressed for settlement at the close of the war: (1) Had Congress the power under the Constitution to issue legal tender? (2) Should the existing issues be enlarged or contracted? and (3) Should specie payment be resumed? The first question was settled in 1871 by the Supreme Court in the case of Knox v. Lee[15] (overruling a previous decision in Hepburn v. Griswold, 1870),[16] when it affirmed that greenbacks could be presented to satisfy any debt contracted before the legal-tender acts were passed. The other questions reopened the conflict between inflationists and contractionists which has, to a certain extent, been ever present in our history. Before the constitutional questions were settled, the battle for inflation had started. The first move was to urge the payment in paper of both interest and principal upon all Civil War bonds unless the bond definitely specified gold. This plan, known as the "Ohio idea," was incorporated in the Democratic platform of 1868, but the election of Grant insured the payment of the debt in gold. Having lost this battle, the inflationists attempted not only to prevent the further contraction of the greenbacks but even to increase the amount. In 1864, $400,000,000 was fixed as a maximum, with a further reserve of $50,-000,000 to redeem a temporary loan. In 1866 the Treasury was authorized to retire the greenbacks, and Secretary McCulloch did withdraw about $77,-000,000, reducing the volume to about $356,000,000 when in February, 1868, further contraction was suspended. This amount remained practically constant for nearly five years. In 1874 Congress fixed the maximum at $382,000,-000. The Resumption Act (1875) provided for reducing the volume of United States notes to $300,000,000, but in 1878 the Greenbackers succeeded again in suspending further contraction. The amount then outstanding, $346,681,016, is the number of greenbacks still circulating today.

[14] F. A. Fetter, *Modern Economic Problems* (1916), pp. 48–54, 74 ff.

[15] Knox v. Lee, 12 Wallace 457.

[16] Hepburn v. Griswold, 8 Wallace 603. This decision is especially interesting inasmuch as it was delivered by Chief Justice Chase, who had been Secretary of the Treasury when greenbacks were first authorized, and who here passed adversely on the constitutionality of his own acts.

The fight now turned to the resumption of specie payments. The exchange of gold for paper by the government would bring the greenback to par, stabilize the currency, and raise the credit of the government. On the other hand, it was believed that this would further depress prices, and it was doubtful if gold in sufficient quantities could be obtained for the purpose. The defeat of the Republicans in the congressional election of 1874 caused

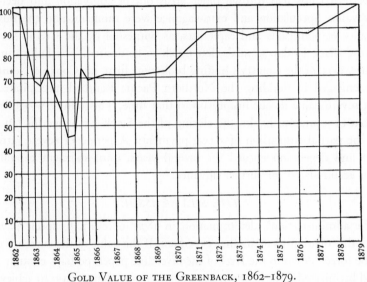

GOLD VALUE OF THE GREENBACK, 1862–1879.

that party to hasten through a Resumption bill in the following year, calling for the restoration of specie payments on January 1, 1879. This controversy over paper money, especially in its last phase, gave birth to a new political organization, the Independent National, or Greenback, party. Formed in 1876, it presented national tickets in three presidential campaigns and called for a number of reforms radical for that day, particularly the redemption of war bonds in paper and the nonresumption of specie payments. Its greatest strength was exhibited in the congressional elections of 1878, when it polled over a million votes. This, however, was no indication of the strength of the movement, for both major parties were shot through with sentiment for inflation.

THE PANIC OF 1873

In the meantime the distress of the debtors had been accentuated and the greenback movement stimulated by the panic of 1873. The feverish industrial and agricultural activity in the North during the Civil War, aided by the rising prices, had inaugurated a period of unprecedented prosperity. Immense regions in the West had been opened up to agriculture, and the easy profits of war prosperity had been invested freely in fixed forms of capital, notably transportation facilities. The prosperity had been too rapid, the expenditures too lavish, to be healthy; and the decade of the seventies opened with underlying conditions far from encouraging. Enormous amounts of capital had been sunk in railroads to finance the 30,000 miles built between 1867 and 1873, from which small immediate returns could be expected. The opening of western lands had thrown older areas out of cultivation and decreased their value. Speculation and extravagance were rampant, and the business morality of politicians and capitalists, as witnessed by the Crédit Mobilier and the Black Friday scandals, left much to be desired. The failure in September, 1873, of the country's leading brokerage firm, Jay Cooke & Company, then engaged in building the Northern Pacific Railroad, precipitated the most severe panic in our history up to that time. This failure was followed by that of numerous banks, the closing of the Stock Exchange for ten days, and the partial suspension of specie payments. A period of severe retrenchment and depression ensued for several years, until sufficient capital was again accumulated for further advance.[17]

THE SILVER ISSUE

The administration's determination in 1879 to return to specie payment drove the inflationists to another expedient. If the value of the currency could not be forced down to the level of inconvertible paper, perhaps enough silver could be injected into the monetary system at an inflated ratio to achieve the same end. It will be recalled that in acts of 1834 and 1837 the ratio of gold to silver, previously 15 to 1, had been changed to 16 to 1 (actually 15.98 to 1), the gold dollar thereafter containing 23.22 grains of pure gold and the silver dollar 371.25 grains of pure silver.[18] Since this overvalued gold slightly, silver, in accordance with Gresham's law, disappeared and gold came into circulation. In 1873 the silver dollar was worth $1.02 in gold and it was no longer profitable to coin it. So scarce was silver and so long had it been since any had been presented to the mints for coinage that Congress in 1873 dropped the further minting of the standard silver dollar.[19]

Far from a deep-dyed plot to demonetize silver, this act, later denounced as the "Crime of '73," was merely legislative recognition of the fact that silver dollars were not being coined. A congressional committee composed of a majority of silver men bitterly denounced this act three years later, pointing

---

[17] For a further discussion of panics and business cycles in our history, see chap. 29; and for two contemporary explanations, one American and one English, see F. Flügel and H. U. Faulkner, *Readings in the Economic and Social History of the United States,* pp. 688–695.

[18] Standard weight was 25.8 grains of gold nine-tenths fine and 412.5 grains of silver nine-tenths fine.

[19] The coinage of subsidiary silver under the act of 1853 was, of course, maintained and provision was made for a trade dollar.

out that while silver possessed the function of money it always stood guard against any considerable rise in gold. "To divest either metal of the money function because temporarily out of use," it asserted, was "reckless and unwise. . . . As well might the commander of an army while battle was raging disband and discharge his reserves because they were not engaged at the front. As well might the master of a ship cut loose and scuttle his lifeboats because the sky was clear and the sea calm."[20]

Well might the inflationists grow bitter when they contemplated the legislation of 1873, for the situation in regard to silver changed rapidly after that date. Germany in 1871, and Holland and the Scandinavian peninsula from 1873 to 1875, adopted the gold standard, and the Latin Monetary Union (France, Switzerland, Belgium, Italy, and Greece) in 1873 limited the coinage of silver. This threw a large supply of bullion on the market, which was augmented by the discovery of large deposits in Nevada. The price of silver dropped so sharply that in 1876 it was worth ninety cents, with the prospect of further decline. As silver grew cheaper, it was evident that if enough could be coined at the old ratio of 16 to 1, the working of Gresham's law would drive out the gold and reduce the currency to the value of silver. The demonetization of silver was now called the "Crime of '73," and the debtor West and South, backed by the silver states, demanded that the government "do something for silver."

The silver sentiment had grown so strong by 1876 that a commission was appointed to study the currency problem, but before it presented its report Richard Bland of Missouri in 1877 offered a bill for the free and unlimited coinage of silver at the old ratio of 16 to 1. In the more conservative Senate the bill was toned down to limit the purchase of bullion to not less than $2,000,000 and not more than $4,000,000 a month, to be coined into silver dollars of 412.5 grains. That such a bill had wide backing there could be little doubt. Said the chairman of the resolutions committee at a mass meeting in Chicago: "We would in this matter arouse the slumbering consciousness of the President and his advisers to some apprehension of the fact that there is a thunderstorm brewing in the West, and that unless they have a care, somebody is likely to be hit by the lightning of public indignation, unless they concede the just demands of the people."[21] In spite of this sentiment, Hayes vetoed the bill, but it was quickly passed over his veto, and during the twelve years of its operation 378,166,000 silver dollars were coined. The Bland-Allison Act of 1878 provided for the issuing of silver certificates in amounts of ten dollars and upward upon the deposit of silver dollars; but the metal money proved unpopular in business centers, and in 1886 the

[20] F. Flügel and H. U. Faulkner, *op. cit.*, pp. 695–697.
[21] Quoted by C. R. Williams, *Life of Rutherford B. Hayes*, II, 120.

denomination of the certificates was reduced to include one-, two-, and five-dollar bills.

To the great disappointment both of the silver interests and of inflationists the Bland-Allison Act failed to halt the decline in the value of silver or the downward trend of prices. Nor was there any indication that silver would drive out gold in accordance with Gresham's law. For this situation a number of factors were responsible. The nation was going through a period of tremendous industrial expansion; a larger amount of currency was necessary and the silver dollars and certificates were absorbed without difficulty. Moreover, there were several years during the eighties when the federal Treasury enjoyed a surplus. Part of this was stored in the Treasury and part was used to retire Civil War bonds. In either case the tendency was to reduce the circulating mediums and prevent inflation. Retirement of Civil War bonds reduced the bank-note circulation by $126,000,000 between 1886 and 1890. While one type of money was pushed into circulation another type was being withdrawn.

On the first of the year following the passing of the Bland-Allison Act the Treasury went back to specie payment. On January 2, 1879, Secretary Sherman had a slender supply of $140,000,000 in gold that had been accumulated with great difficulty, to meet the expected rush of holders of paper, but the soundness of the government's credit was demonstrated by the fact that only $125,000 was presented for gold, while $400,000 in gold was turned in for paper.

Although the Bland-Allison Act was in force for twelve years, it was unsatisfactory to both the inflationists and their opponents. The former looked upon it as simply an opening wedge to be pushed further if the purposes for which it had been passed failed to materialize. Prices of agricultural products continued to fall, and the distress of the debtor farmer who had borrowed on a fifty-cent dollar and must pay his debts with an eighty- or ninety-cent one became keener. By 1889 the silver in the dollar had declined to seventy-two cents, and hope persisted that if more silver was forced into the currency, inflation would take place. This was exactly what the gold advocates feared, and both President Arthur and President Cleveland urged the repeal of the act, the latter pointing out to Congress that the continued coining of silver dollars would eventually increase the currency beyond the needs of business, after which the unnecessary portion would be hoarded and thus the gold gradually eliminated.

Notwithstanding the opposition of the Chief Executive and the Treasury Department, the pressure for more silver became so great that the Republican party, as a matter of political expediency and as a means of insuring the passage of the McKinley tariff, sponsored and passed the Sherman Silver

Purchase Act in 1890. This bill required the Secretary of the Treasury to purchase 4,500,000 ounces of silver bullion a month and in payment for it to issue Treasury notes having full legal tender. These notes were to be redeemed in gold or silver at the discretion of the Secretary, "it being the established policy of the United States to maintain the two metals on a parity with each other," a provision later interpreted by the Executive as a promise to redeem all notes in gold. The amount of silver purchased under this act was practically the entire output of the American mines and was almost double that required by the Bland-Allison Act; it amounted to $155,931,002 in the three years of its operation. This proved to be more than the currency could stand without endangering the gold standard. The only saving feature of the bill was the provision to purchase by ounces rather than by dollars, which meant that the amount of silver bought by the government would be kept at a uniform level. If the law had provided for purchase by dollars (as in the Bland-Allison Act) rather than by ounces, a decline in the value of silver would automatically have increased the coinage of that metal. Since the value of silver fell steadily during the life of the act until it reached sixty cents in 1893, the significance of this provision is apparent.

THE PANIC OF 1893 AND THE ELECTION OF 1896

The decade of the nineties opened with the nation approaching the end of another business cycle. Railroad building during the eighties had been accompanied by inordinate speculation which had undermined supposedly strong organizations. Corporations on the verge of bankruptcy declared stock dividends and paid regular dividends out of capital. The failure of the Philadelphia and Reading and the National Cordage Company early in 1893 aroused the nation to its unhealthy industrial situation, which had already been foretold by financial conditions in Europe. A reaction from the highly speculative years through which the country had just passed was inevitable, but the panic of 1893 was precipitated to a small degree, at least, by the results of the presidential election of 1892, which presaged a modification of the government's tariff policy. Also there was the apprehension that the gold standard could not be maintained. Cleveland was elected that year on a Democratic platform committed to a reduction of the tariff, a prospect which manufacturers contemplated with dark forebodings. Cleveland himself believed in the gold standard, but his party was shot through with inflationary sentiment.[22]

From the point of view of those who would maintain the gold standard,

[22] Conflicting reasons for the panic advanced by contemporaries can be found in F. Flügel and H. U. Faulkner, *op. cit.*, pp. 710–717.

the federal Treasury was in a precarious situation. This was due to a number of causes. The amount of silver purchased under the Sherman Act was too large to be readily absorbed, and gold, by the operation of Gresham's law, began to be crowded out of circulation. The financial crisis in England in 1890 brought about liquidation there, which resulted in a net loss of $68,000,-000 in gold exported from the United States. The bumper wheat crop of 1891 coincident with a failure of European crops gave a temporary favorable balance of trade; but in 1893 the situation was reversed, with a net loss of $87,000,000 in gold exported. To complicate the difficulties of the Treasury Department, the surplus of the eighties had been wiped out by the extravagances of the Harrison administration and by the high McKinley tariff of 1890. By 1893 a Treasury deficit was impending.

An act of 1882 which authorized the Secretary of the Treasury to suspend the issue of gold certificates whenever the amount of gold coin or bullion in the Treasury reserved for the redemption of United States notes fell below $100,000,000 tacitly recognized the existence of a reserve and set a minimum safety point. Subsequent secretaries had not allowed the reserve to fall below this point, and so far it had been sufficient to maintain the gold standard even after the added strain imposed by the Sherman Silver Purchase Act of 1890. Wiping out the gold reserve would mean the suspension of specie payments or the substitution of silver for gold in the payment of paper presented under the act of 1890. Either would mean the elimination of the gold standard and the cheapening of money. While this would have brought joy to the inflationists, the mere possibility paralyzed with fear the holders of fixed capital and business in general.

When Cleveland was inaugurated the reserve was $100,982,410, and on April 22, 1893, it fell below the $100,000,000 mark, recovered temporarily in July, and then declined until in November it reached $59,000,000. Failures of well-known concerns had already shaken public confidence in the business structure, and the decline of the reserve set in motion a period of the severest liquidation yet experienced. During 1893 over 600 banking institutions failed, and during the summer seventy-four railroad corporations owning 30,000 miles of road passed into the hands of receivers. By the end of the next year 194 roads operating 39,000 miles had failed, including the Philadelphia and Reading, the Erie, the Northern Pacific, and the Union Pacific. More than 15,000 commercial failures involving liabilities of $346,000,000 were recorded for 1893. The production of iron and coal declined, and to add to the general distress there was a poor corn crop in 1894 and a decreased demand on the part of Europe for wheat. Unemployment, strikes, discontent, and much actual suffering characterized the winters of 1893 and 1894, a period which encompassed the Pullman strike in Chicago and the marching of "Coxey's army."

Cleveland, a firm believer in the gold standard, was determined to maintain it at any cost. Absolutely convinced that the Treasury's distress and the panic itself were "principally chargeable to Congressional legislation touching the purchase and coinage of silver,"[23] he called a special session of Congress on August 1, 1893, and demanded repeal of the Sherman Silver Purchase Act. A bill to this effect passed the House with little delay, but the Senate held it up until October 30, when it was granted by a sectional vote, with the West and South aligned against the North and East. If fear that the end of the gold standard would bring a panic was true, then the repeal of the Sherman Act came too late to be of any value. In January, 1894, the Treasury sold $50,000,000 of 5 per cent ten-year bonds to obtain gold, and in November resorted to an additional loan of $50,000,000. The gold obtained in this way soon drained out, for there was nothing to prevent the man who lent gold one day from presenting paper and demanding it back the next day. Borrowing on these conditions seemed useless; and when in February, 1895, the Treasury found itself with a reserve of only $41,000,000—and that declining at the rate of $2,000,000 a day—Cleveland negotiated with J. P. Morgan and a group of bankers for a loan of 3,500,000 ounces of gold, to be paid for in 4 per cent United States bonds. It was agreed that half the gold should be obtained abroad and that the bankers would exert every influence to prevent its withdrawal until the contract had been fulfilled. Cleveland's action in borrowing privately from the bankers brought down upon him a storm of abuse, and when, a year later (January, 1896), a fourth loan was resorted to, it was offered to the public. Liquidation by this time had run its course; the loan was several times oversubscribed, and during the year the gold reserve in the Treasury continued to mount.

The efforts of the inflationists to expand the currency, continuously evident since the close of the Civil War, reached their climax in the campaign of 1896. Agricultural prices, which had been on the decline since the sixties, touched bottom in the early nineties. Wheat in 1894 sold at 49 cents, corn in 1896 at 21 cents; in Kansas and Nebraska it was cheaper to burn it for fuel than to sell it. Against this situation the Populist party made organized protest, and in 1896 joined with the Democratic farmers of the West and South. The Democrats, incensed by Cleveland's hard-money stand, drove the gold-standard Easterners from control of their party, nominated William Jennings Bryan as their standard-bearer, and, with the Populists, engaged in one of the hardest-fought and most significant political campaigns in our

[23] Message on Silver, in *ibid.*, p. 707.

history. The chief issue of the campaign of 1896 was the free and unlimited
coinage of silver at a ratio of 16 to 1, but behind this demand was thirty years
of agrarian unrest and a cumulative protest against the currency and credit

(Data from *Statistical Abstract, 1930,* p. 769.)

BULLION VALUE OF 371¼ GRAINS OF SILVER (Contents of One United States
Silver Dollar) IN TERMS OF GOLD AT THE ANNUAL AVERAGE PRICE OF SILVER
EACH YEAR, 1866–1930.

system and against railroads and other monopolies which had borne hard
upon them. Their failure in this crusade left the federal government at the
opening of the new century in the control of conservative eastern capitalism.

THE CURRENCY ACT OF 1900 AND THE REVERSAL OF THE PRICE TREND

Although the campaign of 1896 settled the long controversy over bimetallism, the silver advocates were still so strong in the Senate that the gold
standard was not officially adopted until four years later. The Currency Act
of 1900 finally provided that the gold dollar of 25.8 grains nine-tenths fine
should be the unit of value and that all other forms of currency should be
maintained at parity with this dollar. To maintain this parity, provisions
were made to keep a gold reserve of $150,000,000 in the Treasury. Other
provisions of the act called for the retirement of the Treasury notes of 1890,

their replacement by silver certificates based on coined silver dollars, and the liberalizing of the laws governing national banks.

At the time the act was passed it was doubtful if in a severe crisis the $150,000,000 gold reserve could withstand the pressure of the existing redeemable money, which then amounted to $346,000,000 of greenbacks, over $484,000,000 of silver certificates, $76,000,000 of silver (coined or bullion), every dollar of which was worth only forty-seven cents in bullion, and the $331,000,000 of national bank notes based entirely upon the credit of the United States. The machinery for maintenance, though clumsy, proved sufficient, and the gold dollar as provided in 1900 continued to be the unit of value until changed by the currency legislation of 1933 and 1934.[24]

Fortunately for the nation, new discoveries of gold in South Africa, the Yukon, and Alaska, as well as the development of new processes for extracting the precious metal from the ore, flooded the world with gold during these critical years. The average annual coinage of gold, which had been $67,185,000 in the years 1891–1900, increased during the following decade to $101,022,000. This, with additions to the supply of bank notes, increased the per capita circulation from $23.85 in 1893 to $33.86 in 1907 and $34.20 in 1911. This had the effect not alone of enabling the government to maintain the gold standard but also of reversing the downward trend of prices. From the low point of 1896 to 1914 the general price level increased 40 per cent. The demand for inflation subsided as a leading political and economic issue and the debtor farmer enjoyed one of his few periods of economic prosperity. Gold, interestingly enough, had helped to provide an inflation which for years many believed could most easily be obtained through silver.

THE PANIC OF 1907 AND THE MOVEMENT FOR BANKING REFORM

In the campaign of 1896 McKinley had been heralded as the "advance agent of prosperity." In truth, liquidation had about run its course, and he entered office on a returning wave of prosperity which continued with but few interruptions until temporarily halted in 1907. The discovery of fresh deposits of gold, a succession of good harvests, the greater activity of American exporters in foreign fields, coincident with our embarkation upon a career as a colonial power, all served to stimulate business. Rising prices and confidence in the McKinley administration helped to promote rapid expansion and a great movement toward consolidation.

This prosperity continued with but slight interruption until 1907, when a brief and severe "bankers' panic" ensued. This panic was due chiefly to over-speculation in the large money centers and was the culmination of a long

[24] Below, pp. 656 ff.

struggle between the rapidly rising trust companies acting as commercial banks under inadequate reserve requirements and the more conservative and rigidly regulated commercial banks.[25] It was precipitated by the action of the Knickerbocker Trust Company in closing its doors on October 22 to prevent a run on the bank. Many of the speculative ventures crashed, but efforts by the government and by leading capitalists did much to prevent the panic from becoming general. It was limited largely to the cities and its effects were not widespread, a fact which gave it the name of the "rich man's panic." The panic of 1907 was laid by capital at the doors of the Roosevelt administration, whose meddling with business, it was claimed, had brought on the catastrophe. There was no basis for this charge; the fundamental and immediate cause was overexpansion and speculation by reckless and unscrupulous financiers, and inadequate banking facilities. Put in another way, it was tight money, declining confidence, and the tremendous strain put on the credit facilities of the New York banks.

The panic served one good purpose in that it brought out clearly the defects of the national banking system. Although the national banks had marked a long step forward by providing relatively safe banking facilities and a standard bank note based on the credit of the national government, further improvements were necessary. Probably the chief criticism brought against the system was its lack of elasticity. The Currency Act of 1900 had extended, under certain conditions, the issue of bank notes from 90 per cent to the full face value of the bonds upon which they were issued, but in times of emergency this did not provide sufficient currency. More could be obtained only by purchasing additional bonds, a fact which tied up the problem of paper money with the public debt and meant that the volume of national bank notes fluctuated with the monetary needs of the federal government and not with the currency needs of business. It was further maintained that the rigid reserve limits fixed by law made the credit facilities needlessly inelastic.

Another great weakness of the national banking system was its inadequacy in providing credit facilities for the rural agricultural regions. The Currency Act of 1900 had reduced the minimum requirements for bank capital from $50,000 for cities of 6000 or less to $25,000 for towns of 3000 or less, but even this reduction did not promote the establishment of adequate national banks in rural regions. Even when they did exist, their inability under the law to lend on real estate and their policy of extending commercial loans for sixty or ninety days did not fit the needs of the farmers. As a result, the rural communities were served, if banking facilities were available, largely by state

[25] J. G. Smith, *The Development of Trust Companies in the United States* (1927), pp. 345–352.

banks whose interest rates were high and whose financial condition was often precarious. The agricultural interests also complained that the whole banking system encouraged the flow of funds from communities where they had been accumulated to the large financial centers, where they were used for speculative purposes rather than for the legitimate needs of agriculture and industry. The efficiency of the system was hampered by the cumbersome and expensive exchange and transfer system and the decentralization of the gold supply. Many of these weaknesses had been evident for some time and agitation for improvement had been active for a decade before the 1907 panic.

Profiting from the lessons of the panic, Congress in 1908 passed an emergency measure, known as the Aldrich-Vreeland Act, making temporary provision for the issue of bank notes upon approved securities of states, cities, towns, or municipalities, and upon commercial paper, and providing for the formation of associations of national banks for the purpose of issuing notes, the act to be in force until June 30, 1914 (later extended another year). The same bill also called for the appointment of a National Monetary Commission to study banking conditions and report to Congress.[26] Much popular interest was now aroused, and both major parties were pledged to some kind of reform. The report of the Commission was submitted in January, 1912, with specific recommendations known as the "Aldrich plan." This plan did not suit either political group; but President Wilson, having disposed of the tariff, next pressed for banking legislation which took form in the Federal Reserve Act of December 23, 1913.

THE FEDERAL RESERVE SYSTEM

The act of 1913 (as amended in 1916 and in later years) did much to eliminate certain defects of the national banking system. It divided the country into twelve districts, and provided that a Federal Reserve bank was to be located in the principal banking city of each district—tacit recognition that the nation was fundamentally a group of economic sections rather than an agglomeration of states. The Federal Reserve cities decided upon were Boston, New York, Philadelphia, Cleveland, Richmond, Atlanta, Chicago, St. Louis, Minneapolis, Kansas City, Dallas, and San Francisco. Every national bank was required, and other banks were encouraged, to become members of the system by subscribing to the capital stock of the Federal Reserve bank in their district an amount equal to 6 per cent of their capital stock and surplus. In this manner each district Federal Reserve bank is owned by the various member banks scattered throughout the district. The

---

[26] *The Report of the National Monetary Commission* (1912), pp. 6–9, gives in detail the weaknesses of the old national banking system. See F. Flügel and H. U. Faulkner, *op. cit.,* pp. 719–721.

district banks were to be governed by a board of nine members, six chosen by the member banks and three by the Federal Reserve Board.

To direct the whole system, a Federal Reserve Board was set up at Washington; it consisted of eight members, including the Secretary of the Treasury, the Comptroller of the Currency, and six members appointed by the President. This board was to exercise supervisory powers and determine

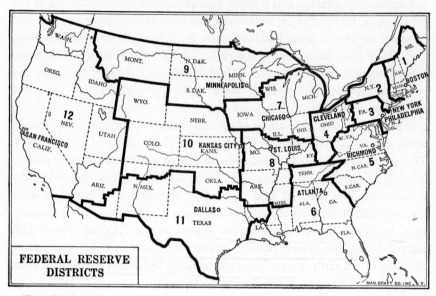

FEDERAL RESERVE
DISTRICTS

(From H. U. Faulkner and Tyler Kepner, *America, Its History and People,* McGraw-Hill.)

the larger questions of policy. A Federal Advisory Council, composed of one representative from each Federal Reserve bank, was created to consult with the board and help in unifying and carrying out the policies decided upon.

The Federal Reserve banks do no direct banking with individuals or business houses. They are simply bankers' banks, central agents for the member banks. Their duties include the rediscount of commercial paper for the member banks in the district, the purchase and sale of bills of exchange, the granting of loans to member banks on government securities as collateral, and other similar banking operations; and, in addition, they issue Federal Reserve notes. Furthermore the Reserve banks act as the fiscal agents of the government. Federal Reserve bank notes are issued, like national bank notes, upon the deposit of government bonds (also commercial paper since 1933), and were designed eventually to supplant the earlier notes. To provide a type of money which would expand and contract as needed, the Reserve banks were empowered to issue Federal Reserve notes on the security of short-term commercial paper. When this paper matures, the Federal Reserve bank (holder in due course) is paid largely with Federal Reserve notes. Hence the volume of these notes corresponds with the volume of commercial paper and the latter with the currency needs of business. Federal Reserve notes are receivable for taxes, customs, and all public dues, are obligations of the United States, and until 1933 were redeemable in gold on demand at the Treasury Department.

To safeguard the system, member banks were required (after 1917) to maintain with the district Federal Reserve bank 3 per cent of their time deposits and from 7 to 13 per cent of their demand deposits, depending on the population of the city. In turn the Federal Reserve banks were required to carry a 40 per cent reserve of gold (since 1933, gold certificates) against Federal Reserve notes outstanding, and a 35 per cent reserve of lawful money against deposits. Amendments to the original act have made it profitable for the state banks and trust companies to become members. At the same time this rapid extension has necessitated another amendment establishing branches of the Federal Reserve banks in a number of the larger cities.

The Federal Reserve system is generally conceded to mark a distinct advance over the old national banking system. It brought greater co-ordination under government control, improved facilities for carrying on banking over large areas, an elastic currency to meet the needs of expanding or contracting business, and needed liberalization of certain checks under the old system. Examples of the latter were authorizations for a member bank to make five-year loans on real estate up to one-quarter of its capital and surplus, and to accept drafts and bills drawn against it on foreign transactions based upon commodity imports and exports. By means of the elastic currency the new system helped to bring the nation through the First World War without excessive inflation from paper money or relinquishment of the gold standard.

Certain defects, nevertheless, soon became apparent. The Federal Reserve Act did not, for example, permit member banks to establish branches in the United States, a power later granted by the McFadden Act of 1923, which allowed branches in cities. The Banking Act of 1933 permitted them in states if the state banking laws permitted state banks to establish branches. Another defect was the failure to provide for medium-term credit; this was removed by the Intermediate Credits Act of 1923, which gave member banks the privilege of discounting nine-months' farm paper with the Federal Reserve banks for Federal Reserve notes. Perhaps the worst abuse which developed was the growth of security affiliates, brought to an end by the Banking Act of 1933. The elimination of security affiliates, the required insurance of deposits up to $5000, and other needed improvements, as we shall see, were later achieved by the New Deal in the Banking Acts of 1933 and 1935.[27]

RECAPITULATION

An effort has been made in this chapter to trace the financial history of the United States since 1860 primarily as it concerned banking and currency. The history of taxation during these years, essentially a problem of tariff policy, has been treated elsewhere.[28] Even from this brief résumé certain facts stand out clearly. First of all was the influence of Civil War financing upon both banking and currency. This financing created the national banking system, and at the same time introduced national bank notes and eliminated state bank notes. Civil War needs also brought the greenbacks into existence. The elimination of the paper currency existing at the opening of the war and the creation of two new kinds brought a fundamental change in our currency.

The effects of the war were apparent long after it ended. Efforts to restore the wartime price level lay behind the battles of debtor farmers and other inflationists to prevent the resumption of specie payment, to expand the greenback circulation, and to restore the free and unlimited coinage of gold and silver at a ratio of 16 to 1. This attempt at inflation by means of the Bland-Allison and the Sherman Silver Purchase acts added a large amount of silver or silver certificates to the currency system. This drive for inflation, it should be remembered, was interwoven with the whole American scene—economic, social, and political. It was in part a reaction against the decline of agriculture and the growing power of industrial capitalism. It was closely affected by the panics of 1873 and 1893 and it permeated political controversy for thirty years.

The long battle for inflation may have ended temporarily with the gold-standard Republicans in 1896, but the history of banking and currency reform and their interrelations did not. The national banking system was radically revised and improved by the Federal Reserve Act of 1913, and the currency system was changed by the addition of Federal Reserve bank notes and Federal Reserve notes. Although state-chartered banks continue, the system of nationally chartered banks goes back in direct lineage to the act of 1863. In a similar manner the currency is a conglomerate of the various kinds of money introduced, mainly since the Civil War. Treasury reports in 1953 still showed the following types of money in circulation: gold certificates, silver dollars, silver certificates and Treasury notes of 1890 (based in part on the Bland-Allison and Sherman Silver Purchase acts), subsidiary

[27] Below, pp. 659–660.
[28] Above, pp. 163 ff.

metal coins, United States notes (Civil War greenbacks), national bank notes, Federal Reserve bank notes, and Federal Reserve notes. Not even the important currency legislation of the New Deal has erased from our monetary system the imprint of the economic and political conflicts during the half-century from the first greenback legislation in 1862 to the passage of the Federal Reserve Act in 1913. The more recent history of banking and currency will be discussed in a later chapter.[29]

SELECTED READINGS

Dewey, D. R., *Financial History of the United States,* chaps. 12–22.

Shultz, W. J., and Caine, M. R., *Financial Development of the United States,* chaps. 13, 14, 16, 18, 20–25.

Hepburn, A. B., *A History of Currency in the United States,* chaps. 11–25.

Willis, H. P., *The Federal Reserve,* chaps. 1–8.

Lauck, W. J., *The Causes for the Panic of 1893.*

Bogart, E. L., and Thompson, C. M., *Readings in the Economic History of the United States,* chap. 20.

Flügel, F., and Faulkner, H. U., *Readings in the Economic and Social History of the United States,* chap. 16.

[29] Below, pp. 656 ff.

CHAPTER 25

DOMESTIC AND FOREIGN COMMERCE

ROUTES OF AND BARRIERS TO INTERNAL COMMERCE

As all sections of the country do not specialize in the growing or manufacturing of the same commodities, internal commerce is largely concerned with the distribution of commodities from the producing areas to consumers, wherever they may be. In earlier decades the routes followed mainly the rivers and canals. With the invention of the steam railroad and the automobile and the great improvement of roads the problem of mere physical distribution was largely solved. Since the general expansion of the population was essentially westward rather than north or south, artificial transportation facilities tended to follow the people; hence the chief routes of American commerce are east and west.

This general east-west movement is of course modified by sectional specialization and by the influence of metropolitan areas. The northeastern section of the country, for example, is largely concerned with manufacturing and the import-export trade. Foodstuffs or raw materials for manufacturing move from many sections toward this area to be processed or exported to the European or Latin-American market. Conversely, imports and manufactured goods move from the Northeast in all directions to supply consumers' needs. In the Old Northwest—that is, the states north of the Ohio and east of the Mississippi—is to be found the most self-sufficing section of the nation. Rich agricultural lands, abundant minerals, and intensive manufacturing make it possible for the population to buy largely at home. Despite this fact there is, of course, a steady stream of manufactured products, such as automobiles and steel, moving out and specialized products manufactured elsewhere coming in. From the earliest times the South has always specialized in the extractive industries—at first tobacco, later cotton and other agricultural products, and finally lumber and such minerals as chemicals and petroleum. A certain amount of these extractive commodities are shipped northward to be processed; but local manufacturing, stimulated by importations of northern capital, has increased in the past half-century. This is also true of the Far West. A region chiefly concerned during the nineteenth century with agriculture and the extraction of minerals, this section has also developed manufacturing. The rapid growth of the population on the west coast and the desire to save on freight rates has led many eastern manufacturers to establish branch factories in that area. Nevertheless, a large proportion of the Far West's manufactured goods is imported from the East in exchange for fruit, vegetables, and other agricultural products.

A certain modification in these main routes of commerce, as earlier suggested, is inherent in the fact that the surplus products of a section tend to gather in a central point where they are warehoused, wholesaled, financed, and later distributed to other parts of the country. This concentration has resulted in "metropolitan areas" which largely dominate the economic life of a section. When the Federal Reserve System was created in 1913 the government, as noted in the last chapter, divided the nation into twelve regions whose banking facilities centered in the cities of Boston, New York, Philadelphia, Richmond, Cleveland, Atlanta, Chicago, St. Louis, Dallas, Kansas City, Minneapolis, and San Francisco. These cities, in fact, are not only the financial centers but also the commercial centers of these areas. There are subsidiary metropolitan areas within the larger ones, but the center largely dominates commerce. Although a portion of a region's products are distributed and consumed in the immediate area, the surplus, usually the major part of the total, moves out of the area.

Economists have often stressed the advantage this country enjoys in freedom of interstate trade. The Constitution presumably insures this freedom, giving the federal government power to control interstate traffic. In recent years there has been, nevertheless, a growing tendency on the part of the states to find methods of evading the obvious purpose of the Constitution. The reasons are understandable and in some cases laudable—having to do with the protection of the economic and physical well-being of the citizens. A state often establishes quarantines to protect the health of its people or to prevent the spread of insect pests or animal diseases. Sometimes the purpose is to check the evasion of taxation. Usually it is plainly an effort to prevent competition and to protect the economic interests of the citizens. Although this tendency toward interstate barriers has grown rapidly in the past fifteen years, it has not yet become a major problem. These barriers are chiefly used to interfere with the interstate movement of agricultural products. Thus the milk farmers of one state will induce the legislature to establish certain standards and requirements of inspection which cannot be met easily by another state. Similarly, the dairy farmers who produce butter will do everything possible to have state laws impede the sale of margarine.

All types of ingenious regulations are devised to harass the merchant trucker from outside the state in order to aid the local truck farmer. Regulations regarding grading and labeling are often purposely designed to keep fruit, vegetables, or eggs from entering a particular commonwealth. Amendment XXI makes illegal the importation of intoxicating liquors into a state in violation of the laws of that state. Using this as a wedge, certain states have passed laws designed not to protect their inhabitants from the deleterious effects of alcoholic beverages but rather to help local brewers, distillers, or farmers. This has been achieved by requiring higher sales taxes on outside liquor, special licenses before an outside manufacturer can do business within the state, and other devices. Such practices often bring retaliatory measures until there develops a situation of state fighting state not unlike conditions during the period of the Articles of Confederation. Up to the present the Supreme Court has shown little interest in stopping this tendency.

TRENDS IN WHOLESALE AND RETAIL SELLING

Internal commerce has been largely influenced during the past half-century by the growth of the urban population and the improvement in transportation facilities. Increased urbanization has allowed more specialization in both wholesaling and retailing, and better transportation has had almost revolutionary effects upon rural buying. Population increase and concentration, for example, have enabled wholesalers to specialize in single commodities and made possible the development of the grain, cotton, coffee, and other exchanges whose operations are patterned after those of the stock market. Here the buying and selling of raw materials tends to set the price for the commodity. Urbanization has enabled not only wholesalers to specialize, but retailers as well. Sections given over to the wholesaling or retailing of specific commodities are often found in large cities.

Specialization in retailing is the normal practice in urban communities where there is enough business to make it possible. Interestingly enough, one persistent trend has been contrary to specialized retailing—the continued existence and even growth of the department store. Originally the department store as developed by Alexander T. Stewart in New York in the 1860's and in succeeding years by John Wanamaker in Philadelphia and Marshall Field in Chicago was little more than a glorified country general store. The convenience, particularly for suburban buyers, of making all the purchases under one roof rather than going from one store to another was sufficient to make a place for the department store. The business of many of these stores became so large that their various departments could be conducted as efficiently and on as large a scale as the specialized store.

Rural buying at the end of the nineteenth century was largely done in the country general store, which, like the city's department store, carried almost everything that the community needed. The old-fashioned peddler who traveled from door to door still existed, but his number was declining. Two developments of the 1890's did much to change this picture, the introduction of the rural free delivery and the invention of the automobile. The first of these made possible the rapid expansion of the mail-order house. Montgomery, Ward & Company was founded in 1872 especially to sell to the Grangers; Sears, Roebuck & Company was founded in 1895. Both grew rapidly in the late nineties and again after the inauguration of the parcel-post system in 1913. To the typical farmer and small-town American the mail-order purchase became as common as that from the country store. Revolutionary also was the automobile, which considerably extended the farmer's purchasing radius. Before its advent the average farmer bought from his country store and from mail-order houses, with possibly one trip to the city each year, if he was prosperous. The automobile made it possible to run into the nearest town every Saturday afternoon for shopping, even if the town was fifty or more miles away.

The automobile gave another blow to the country store, already forced to reduce its business to a few necessities; it forced the mail-order houses to change their technique. To catch the farmer's business on his frequent trips to the city, the mail-order houses beginning in 1926 opened retail outlets in many of the small and medium-sized urban centers. This made it possible through carload shipments to cut prices even further for the farmer, and at the same time it gave the mail-order houses a chance to enlarge their business to include the urban as well as the rural buyer. The establishment of these chain outlets was in line with a development which had been going on for years. The first and greatest of the chains goes back to the founding of the great Atlantic & Pacific Tea Company in 1858 which by 1930 had approximately 1600 branches and an annual business of $1,000,000,000. The success of the A. & P. led to the founding of many other chains in the grocery and other fields. The Woolworth Five and Ten Cent chain started in 1879 (1960 stores in 1952), the United Cigar Stores in 1892, and the Kresge system in 1897. In more recent years other successful chains have been built up, particularly in clothing, shoes, and drugs. Over fifty different lines of merchandise have been taken over by these chains and in some small towns they handle most of the retailing. In 1948 there were over 6000 different chains with 107,409 separate stores, and net sales of $30,425,000,000. They handled over one-fourth of the total retail sales of the country.[1]

Advertising of one kind or other probably goes back to the days when the first seller attempted to find a purchaser, but it waited upon the twentieth century to flower in its full glory. In the effort to sell commodities every human weakness and desire was exploited. If you had no interest in a commodity, you were made to desire it; if you already possessed it, you became convinced that yours was out of date and a new one was necessary; if you thought you were perfectly healthy, you were told about all the diseases you might have now or in the future, and so on. By suggestion, innuendo, or outright assertion one product was held up as superior to the next. The philosophy was largely based upon the old policy of *caveat emptor* —let the buyer beware. In the field of patent medicines and cosmetics this led to high-pressure advertising of commodities that were often absolutely worthless or harmful. A slight check was put on the sale of harmful medicines by the Pure Food and Drug Act of 1906, and a much stronger one by the Food, Drug, and Cosmetic Act of 1938. By the 1950's the advertising business had grown to tremendous proportions. Advertising expenditures at the opening of the decade were estimated at over $6,500,000,000, and this did not include direct advertising, door-to-door canvassing, and innumerable other methods of pushing a commodity. Newspapers and magazines were obtaining from two to three times as great an income from advertisers as from readers, a fact which tended to make the typical newspaper essentially an organ for advertisers. The radio and television chains also are largely supported by advertising.

There is no intention in these pages to discount the valuable aspects of advertising in acquainting the consumer with the merits of a new product or the advantages of a particular product, or the aid it contributes in developing the mass production of a useful commodity. Advertising without doubt increases one's desire to buy and thus increases business. Two difficulties arise. The first is a tendency to compete in advertising rather than to improve the product. The other is that advertising often stimulates a desire which the consumer can hardly afford. This dilemma was in part taken care of during the twenties and thirties by the tremendous expansion of installment buying—approximately 15 per cent of all goods were sold in this way. In recent years about 60 per cent of automobiles, 55 per cent of household appliances, and 50 per cent of furniture have been purchased on the installment plan. Credit is handled largely by small loan companies, by banks which have set up special departments in order to share in this lucra-

[1] *Statistical Abstract, 1952,* p. 899.

tive business, and in some cases by the manufacturer, as for example General Motors, which has organized finance companies to finance sales.

DISTRIBUTION AND COST OF GOODS

To trace and estimate the flow of goods in internal commerce and the distribution of costs in manufacturing goods is a difficult task. The Census of 1930 attempted to do this for the first time. The year 1929 was used, a year which represented the highest volume of internal trade up to that time in our history. As correlated by the Twentieth Century Fund,[2] it appears that in 1929 some $65.6 billion was paid for finished goods. Of this amount about $38.5 billion, or 59 per cent, represents the total cost of distribution. "On the whole, therefore," says the study, "it cost more to distribute goods in that year than it did to make them." It then suggests that the cost of distribution in the 1930's took an even larger share of the total cost of making goods and getting them into the hands of the buyers. In brief, it costs more to distribute goods than to produce them.[3] This throws considerable light on the important role played by various types of distributors in our economic system. It also indicates how small the actual costs of raw material and labor often are in the total cost of a commodity.

The realization that costs double or more from the time a commodity leaves the factory until it finally reaches the consumer has led to repeated efforts to cut the costs of distribution. Although the prices charged by individual distributors for an individual commodity usually appear reasonable, the costs of the complicated structure bear heavily upon the consumer. Important as are the distributing and marketing agencies, there is widespread belief that distribution has become too complicated and costly and constitutes too large a proportion of the total cost of a commodity. This in part explains the rapid development of consumers' co-operatives.

CAUSES OF THE DEVELOPMENT OF FOREIGN COMMERCE

The foreign commerce of the United States has grown tremendously since 1860. By 1920 exports had increased twenty-four-fold and imports sixteen-fold. In 1850 imports exceeded exports by $20,040,062, but in 1920 the excess of exports over imports was $2,880,114,000. During the same period per capita imports increased three-fold, and per capita exports increased seven-fold. The reasons for this great development are not hard to find. First of all was the continued and rapid expansion of the settled area of the nation, which opened to exploitation vast agricultural regions and new mineral resources. Along with this came the development of transportation facilities capable of han-

[2] *Does Distribution Cost Too Much?* (1939), chaps. 2 ff.
[3] *Ibid.*, pp. 62, 67–68, 117–118.

dling commerce as it expanded. In the second place, the unsurpassed natural resources of America combined with a rapidly growing population and a high protective tariff were gradually changing her from a nation whose interests were essentially agricultural to one predominantly manufacturing. The basic result of a situation in which an abundance of raw material is combined with continually improving machinery is the production of a surplus of manufactured goods which seeks an outlet abroad as well as at home. American industry needed foreign markets, and as industry developed, it necessarily promoted foreign trade.

Along with this there was the rapid development of all types of facilities tending to stimulate foreign trade. These included the expansion of the internal transportation system, technical improvements in communication such as the invention of cables and the wireless and transatlantic telephones, and improvement in banking and credit facilities. The principle of the telegraph was put into operation in undersea cables after 1852, the year in which a short line was laid from Dover to Ostend. Chiefly through the efforts of Cyrus Field, a successful transatlantic cable was finally achieved in 1866. By 1918 at least nine active cables connected North America with Europe, and the principal ports of the world were joined with 281,000 nautical miles of cable, enough to girdle the world thirteen times. Experiments by Heinrich Hertz in Germany after 1888, by Marconi in Italy, and by numerous inventors throughout the world perfected the wireless to such an extent that messages were sent across the Atlantic in 1903.[4] Within two decades after transoceanic wireless had been established, it was possible for anyone at small expense to receive by radio in his own home news flashes, stock quotations, and the commercial news of the day.

With the growth of foreign commerce has gone that of extended financial facilities. Some of our largest banks maintain branch offices in Europe, Asia, South America, and Africa which are able to furnish credit information, negotiate loans, issue bills of exchange, and in other ways aid commerce. In this connection the student of foreign commerce should keep in mind the aid continually given by various government facilities. This was particularly evident in the Department of Commerce under Secretary Hoover during the 1920's.

Foreign trade, of course, cannot be carried on long without commodities to export. During the last half of the nineteenth century, as in earlier years, American agricultural products supplied the chief commodities for the export trade—cotton to keep the textile mills of Europe humming and foodstuffs to feed the rapidly growing industrial population of western Europe. With

[4] On December 12 and 13, 1901, Guglielmo Marconi with the aid of a kite at St. John's, Newfoundland, caught the signal sent from Poldhu Station, Cornwall.

the turn of the century, however, manufactured products began to supplement and finally to surpass the agricultural value. American ingenuity, protected by patents, had evolved numerous types of labor-saving machinery so epoch-making in their significance that they found a ready sale abroad. Of

EXPORTS AND IMPORTS, 1860–1939

Year	Exports of Merchandise	Exports of Merchandise and Specie	Imports of Merchandise	Imports of Merchandise and Specie	Excess of Total Exports or Imports[a]
1860	$ 333,576,000	$ 400,122,000	$ 353,616,000	$ 362,166,000	$ 37,956,000
1900	1,394,483,000	1,499,462,000	849,941,000	929,771,000	569,691,000
1920	8,228,016,000	8,663,723,000	5,278,481,000	5,783,609,000	2,880,114,000
1929	5,240,995,000	5,440,985,000	4,399,361,000	4,754,950,000	686,035,000
1932	1,611,016,000	2,434,394,000	1,322,774,000	1,705,739,000	728,655,000
1939	3,177,176,000	3,192,314,000	2,318,081,000	5,978,047,000	2,785,733,000

[a] All figures in this column are excess of exports except those for 1939. The excess of imports over exports is due to the heavy flow of gold to America because of World War II.
Statistical Abstract, 1921, Table 482, pp. 840–841, 854–855; *ibid.*, *1940*, pp. 488–489.

these may be mentioned agricultural implements, sewing machines, typewriters, and cash registers. The United States also led the world in the development of mass production, and the low cost of commodities thus produced, notably automobiles, provided goods for the export market. Foreign commerce, of course, originates and is stimulated by the needs of one part of the world for the products of another. As we have repeatedly emphasized, no nation has been more fortunately situated in respect to resources than the United States; she has been in a position to furnish foodstuffs, raw materials, and eventually manufactured products to other parts of the world on most advantageous terms.

Importation has increased along with exportation, although the excess of exports over imports has grown since 1860 out of proportion to the increase of either exports or imports. Importation has resulted primarily from the desire for certain commodities such as coffee and natural rubber which we do not produce, and from the necessity of taking in exchange for certain of our commodities some products classed as luxuries and many others of minute and skilled workmanship which the cheaper labor costs and more artistic training of foreign artisans have enabled them to produce. It should be remembered also that the excess of exports over imports in value is partially compensated for (1) by large sums paid to Europeans (especially before the First World War) for marine freight and insurance, (2) by dividends and interest paid to foreign stock and bond holders, (3) by money sent home by immigrants, and (4) by American travelers, who were reported in those years as spending about $350,000,000 annually.

GOVERNMENT AID TO COMMERCE

Although it is a normal function of government to promote the trade and prosperity of its people, the extent to which this is actually done is sometimes not realized. Even in the United States, which, until recent years, was dominated by a *laissez-faire* theory as to the function of government, the federal government has been continually at work promoting commercial activity. This has been done chiefly through three methods: (1) construction and improvement of harbors, and measures to increase the safety of navigation, (2) efforts to make commerce more profitable, and (3) aid to the shipbuilding industry. Such aid originates in the first place from congressional legislation and is carried on either by bureaus of the executive departments or through independent agencies. This activity has been greatly extended since the rapid expansion of American commerce after the Spanish-American War, and especially since the division of the Department of Commerce and Labor into two executive divisions in 1913. A mere citation of the bureaus at present included under the Department of Commerce will give some idea of the extensive activity of that branch of the government: Coast and Geodetic Survey, to survey and chart the coasts; Bureau of Foreign and Domestic Commerce, to collect all data essential to the conduct of foreign and domestic trade; Inland Waterways Corporation, to promote, encourage, and develop inland water transportation; Weather Bureau, to provide weather forecasts for air transport, shipping, and other interests; Civil Aeronautics Authority and Civil Aeronautics Administration, to supervise and encourage air transport; Foreign-Trade Zones Board, to expedite and encourage foreign commerce in American ports of entry. There are also other bureaus designed to aid American business. Of great value also are the various bulletins, reports, and statistical material on trade published by the Department of Commerce.

Since 1802, when the first federal appropriation was made for rivers and harbors, over one billion dollars has been expended. This work is recommended and supervised by the Corps of Engineers of the United States Army, but owing to the fact that the appropriations are influenced to a considerable extent by political logrolling, not all of this money has been spent wisely. Safety in navigation has been promoted by the Bureau of Lighthouses, now part of the work of the Coast Guard under the Treasury Department, by the Coast and Geodetic Survey, and by the Weather Bureau, already mentioned. The Coast Guard divides its work between the maintenance of lighthouses and other safety devices, the Life Saving Service, which maintains over 250 active stations to warn ships of impending danger and help those in distress, and the Revenue Cutter Service, which aims not only to enforce the revenue laws but to supplement the work of the Life Saving

Service. Much of the work of the Coast and Geodetic Survey is supplemented by the Hydrographic Office of the Bureau of Navigation of the Navy Department, whose duty it is to provide accurate nautical charts, sailing directions, and manuals of instruction.

Efforts on the part of the government to make commerce more profitable have been exerted from the beginning of our history. Tonnage acts have been passed favoring American ships, and treaties negotiated to secure favorable treatment for American products. In addition to activities of the State, Treasury, and Post Office departments and various subsidiary bureaus in providing valuable information, there was instituted in 1912 the Bureau of Foreign and Domestic Commerce under the Department of Commerce, whose business it is "to develop the various manufacturing industries of the United States and markets for their products at home and abroad, by gathering and publishing useful information, or by any other available method." Through special agents and commercial attachés in foreign countries and by means of co-operation with the consular service of the State Department, data covering conditions and commercial opportunities abroad are gathered and distributed. As already stated, the work of this Bureau, particularly that of the special agents and commercial attachés, was greatly expanded during the years that Hoover was Secretary of the Department.

Special encouragement to foreign commerce was afforded in the Webb Export Act of April 10, 1918, which exempted associations entered into "for the sole purpose of engaging in export trade and actually so engaged" from the provisions of the Sherman Antitrust Act, on condition that such associations did not enter into a conspiracy to control prices or restrain competition. Corporations desiring to acquire part or entire ownership of such foreign trading associations were exempted from the provisions of the Clayton Act. During the 1930's, as we shall see, the Roosevelt administration took even more far-reaching steps to promote foreign commerce by trade agreements, loans to Latin-American nations, and new facilities provided through the Export-Import Bank.[5] This policy has continued since World War II.

THE MERCHANT MARINE

A merchant marine owned at home is not essential to an extensive foreign commerce. In fact, it may be cheaper to hire other nationals to handle the carrying trade than to participate in it directly. On the other hand, there are certain advantages, particularly during time of war, which may warrant aggressive government encouragement to the maintenance of a merchant marine. The Civil War dealt our once famous merchant marine a blow from which it never recovered. Destruction by Confederate privateers and

[5] Below, pp. 694–695.

large sales abroad decreased the tonnage. Delay in adopting iron steam-
driven ships gave British builders an advantage which they continued to
hold. But more important than all else was the fact that more profitable
investments in internal transportation and the exploitation of raw materials
in the great industrial age which dawned after the war drew capital away
from the sea. Lack of government interest helped complete the downfall
of American shipping.[6]

The five years following the Civil War showed a slight revival, but the

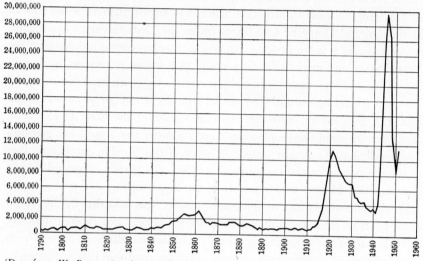

(Data from W. Bates, *American Marine*, pp. 462 ff.; *Statistical Abstract, 1940*, p. 463; *ibid.,
1952*, p. 565.)

TONNAGE OF THE UNITED STATES MERCHANT MARINE ENGAGED
IN FOREIGN COMMERCE, 1789–1951.

forces tending to a decline continued operative. American shipping engaged
in foreign trade and the fisheries, which amounted to 2,642,628 tons in 1870,
dropped to 826,694 tons in 1900. In 1860 the percentage of imports and
exports carried in American ships was 66.5, but this dropped in 1870 to 35.6,
in 1880 to 13, in 1890 to 9.4, in 1900 to 7.1. The merchant marine had a loyal
friend in Senator Frye to Maine, who in 1891 introduced bills to subsidize
mail steamers, freight steamers, and sailing vessels, but the encouragement
was insufficient. A subsequent bill introduced by him in 1901 was defeated
by the agricultural and manufacturing interests.

The La Follette Seamen's Act of 1915 was unjustly denounced by the
shipping interests as the final blow at a declining merchant marine, but its
backers claimed that it was a protection to American shipping and a simple

[6] Above, pp. 229–230.

act of justice to American seamen. Among other things it provided (1) that 75 per cent of the crew in American-owned and -operated ships should understand any order given by the officers; (2) that 64 per cent of the deck crews employed on American ships should ultimately be able seamen, having passed physical and professional examinations; (3) that half wages should be paid the crew in every port; and (4) that the crew of any vessel touching at an American port might quit the service. Other provisions regarding hours of labor in ports and the safety of seamen were looked upon as marking a long forward step in the legal code governing marine operations.

REGISTERED AND ENROLLED TONNAGE

Year	Tonnage Registered in Foreign Trade (Tons)	Tonnage Employed in Coastwise and Internal Trade (Tons)	Proportion of Imports and Exports Carried in American Vessels by Value
1910	782,517	6,668,966	8.7
1914	1,066,288	6,818,363	9.7
1915	1,862,714	6,486,384	14.3
1916	2,185,008	6,244,550	16.3
1917	2,440,776	6,392,583	18.6
1918	3,599,213	6,282,474	21.9
1919	6,665,376	6,201,426	27.8
1920	9,924,694	6,357,706	43.0
1921	11,077,000	7,163,000	35.7
1925	8,151,000	9,216,000	33.0
1929	6,906,000	9,526,000	33.1
1932	5,071,000	10,728,000	35.6
1939	3,312,000	11,228,000	35.8[a]

a This figure is for 1935, the last available percentage is given in the *Statistical Abstract* for 1940.

Statistical Abstract, 1921, p. 410; *1933*, pp. 377, 396; *1940*, pp. 463, 482.

There appears to be little or no evidence that this law providing decent treatment for American sailors has appreciably delayed the revival of the American merchant marine. In fact, indications were already evident that a revival was impending, which would have made progress without the artificial stimulation provided by the First World War. American manufacturers were able to produce steel plates cheaper than European, and there was surplus capital which might be enticed into the shipping industry. The elimination of the German merchant marine after the outbreak of war, and the rapid increase of exports due to war orders gave new stimulus to American shipyards.

Dependence upon European shipping from 1914 to 1916 demonstrated anew the need for a merchant marine, and in the latter year Congress approved the appointment of a United States Shipping Board to supervise ocean

freight rates, prevent unjust combinations and excessive charges, and advise
on methods to increase the merchant marine. When we entered the war the
Shipping Board organized the Emergency Fleet Corporation, which bent all
its efforts to turning out steel, wooden, and even cement ships. Congress
made $4,000,000,000 available for this work, and during the nineteen months
of the war 875 vessels of 2,941,845 gross tons were built. The sixty-one shipyards of 1917 with their 235 ways had increased by November, 1918, to 341
shipyards and 1284 launching ways, and the number of workmen had grown
from 45,000 to 380,000.

A large proportion of the gross tonnage in 1920 was owned by the government, and the question of its future was one which Congress was called upon
to decide. The bitter hostility of capital to government-owned transportation
presaged the government's retirement from the ocean carrying trade, an end
partially achieved in the Merchant Marine Act of 1920. Known as the Jones
Act, this legislation continued the United States Shipping Board and gave
partial recognition to the principle of subsidies to American shipping by
exempting companies from an excess profits tax up to a certain amount, and
by providing for government loans for construction to the amount of $25,-
000,000 a year for five years, the sum to be obtained from the sale of government ships. In a number of other ways it sought to stabilize and aid the
newborn merchant marine.

However, the effects of the Jones Act in promoting American shipping
were slight, and subsequent amendments and legislation, notably that of May
23, 1928 (Jones-White Act), sought to strengthen and liberalize it. Although
outright subsidies were avoided, the principle of indirect subsidies was recognized in loans for various purposes, in payments for carrying mail, in tax
exemption, and in government operation of ships at a loss. Discrimination in
tonnage and customs rates was provided by the act of 1920 but was opposed
by the administration and eventually repudiated. On the other hand, foreign-
owned ships were excluded from the coastwise trade altogether, government
ships were disposed of at ridiculously low prices, and the government co-
operated in many ways to encourage development. By 1929 the government
had succeeded in selling both its freight and its passenger liners on the Pacific
and its passenger boats on the Atlantic to private operators, thus largely re-
tiring from the shipping business.

In spite of this liberal policy and the definite effort on the part of the government to extend aid, the merchant marine declined relatively between the
First and Second World Wars. Tonnage engaged in foreign trade dropped
from 11,077,000 in 1921 to 3,312,000 in 1939, and the proportion of imports and
exports carried in American bottoms from 43 per cent in 1920 to 35.8 in 1935.[7]
The Shipping Board reported in 1927 that of $600,000,000 paid annually by

[7] See table above, p. 541.

shippers for freight, $480,000,000 went to foreign ships. Lloyd's register reported that for 1925 the tonnage constructed in America was less than one-eighth that built in Great Britain and Ireland, less than one-third that of Italy, and less than one-half that of Germany. In 1927 the Shipping Board reported that for every first-class merchant ship built in the United States since 1921 Great Britain had built forty-one, Germany twelve, Italy five, and France and Japan four each.[8] In that year the historic firm of William Cramp

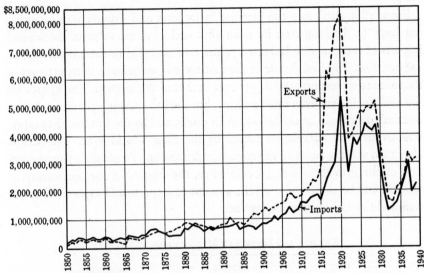

(Data from *Statistical Abstract, 1899,* p. 92; *ibid., 1921,* p. 854; *ibid., 1940,* p. 487.)

MERCHANDISE IMPORTED AND EXPORTED, 1850–1939.

and Sons withdrew from shipbuilding because of lack of business. The failure of American shipping to advance was attributed by government officials to the greater cost of building and operating, but undoubtedly other factors were contributing causes, including the artificial economic situation of the industry, the rapidity and newness of its development, and the competition of other industries for capital. In spite of all this, the artificial extension of the merchant marine had, by 1928, placed it second among the fleets of the world, with Great Britain first; the United States was followed by Japan, Italy, Germany, and France.[9]

TREND OF FOREIGN COMMERCE, 1860–1930

The Civil War profoundly affected foreign commerce. The high tariffs it inaugurated stimulated manufacturing. The cutting off of the southern trade

[8] In 1929 only 128,976 gross tons of shipping were built, as compared with 3,880,639 in 1920.

[9] The merchant marine under the New Deal and in the Second World War is discussed below, pp. 672–673, 703.

forced northern producers to seek other markets, with the result that between 1860 and 1865 there was an actual increase in exports other than cotton. The war temporarily ruined the cotton business of the South, and the amount of cotton exported did not reach the prewar level until 1875. This in turn cut down imports to the South. While the war ruined the merchant marine, it stimulated the building of railroads and further aided commerce by the concentration of capital and the better banking system which was introduced in 1863.

From 1865 until 1920 the increase in imports and exports was irregular, but large in the long run. Between 1870 and 1890 the value of the annual imports of merchandise increased 74 per cent and that of the annual exports 118 per cent. The first decade of the century saw an increase of 25 per cent in the value of the exports and 83 per cent in that of the imports. The figures for the next decade are even more striking, but the increases in value must be discounted to a certain extent by the rise in prices, and by the fact that they represent an artificial stimulation caused by the First World War. The decline after 1929 was the result of the economic depression. To obtain a true conception of the growth of foreign commerce, the figures in the accompanying table should be compared with the amount of imports and exports of certain commodities rather than their value.

EXPORTS AND IMPORTS OF MERCHANDISE BY DECADES

Year	Exports	Imports
1860	$ 333,576,157	$ 353,616,119
1870	392,771,768	453,958,408
1880	835,638,658	667,954,746
1890	857,828,684	789,310,409
1900	1,394,483,082	849,941,184
1910	1,744,984,720	1,556,947,430
1920	8,228,016,307	5,278,481,490
1930	3,843,181,000	3,060,908,000
1939	3,177,176,000	2,318,081,000

Fiscal years until 1920. Compiled from *Statistical Abstract, 1921*, Table 482, pp. 840–841, 854–855; *ibid., 1940*, p. 487.

Up to 1890 the leading exports were agricultural, including wheat, corn, and meat products and such processed agricultural commodities as flour, glucose, cotton and vegetable oils, butter, and cheese. Agricultural products amounted to 79.4 per cent of the country's exports in 1870, 83.3 per cent in 1880, 74.5 per cent in 1890, and 61 per cent in 1900. Manufactures ranked next to agriculture in importance, followed by forest products and minerals. Of individual commodities, exported grains took the lead, followed by cotton, meat and meat products, iron and steel, and mineral oil.

The percentages considered in connection with figures for valuation show a gradual decline in the relative importance of agricultural products in exports and an increase in that of partly or wholly manufactured commodities. Particularly is this to be noted during the last decade of the century. By far the greatest market was Great Britain, but there was a growing demand in all of the countries of northern Europe except Russia. Trade with southern Europe was stagnant; for South American trade, although the amount al-

DOMESTIC EXPORTS GROUPED ACCORDING TO SOURCES OF PRODUCTION

	1870		1880		1890		1900	
	Value[a]	Per Cent	Value[a]	Per Cent	Value[a]	Per Cent	Value[a]	Per Cent
Agriculture	$361,188	79.35	$685,961	83.25	$629,821	74.51	$ 835,858	60.98
Manufactures	68,280	15.00	102,856	12.48	151,102	17.87	433,852	31.65
Forests	14,898	3.27	17,321	2.11	29,473	3.49	52,218	3.81
Mining	5,026	1.10	5,863	.71	22,298	2.64	37,844	2.76
Fisheries	2,836	.62	5,255	.64	7,458	.88	6,327	.46
Miscellaneous	2,981	.66	6,689	.81	5,141	.61	4,665	.34
Total	$455,209	100.00	$823,935	100.00	$845,293	100.00	$1,370,764	100.00

a In thousands of dollars.
Monthly Summary of Commerce and Finance, p. 3249 (April, 1903).

most doubled between 1870 and 1900, the percentage of the total was less. Healthy progress was made in the Asian, Australian, and African markets. In 1870 the percentage of our total exports which went to Europe was 79.35, to North America 13.03, to South America 4.09, to Asia 2.07, to Oceanica .82, and to Africa .64. In 1900 Europe received 76.60 per cent, North America 13.45, South America 2.79, Asia 4.66, Oceanica 3.11, and Africa 1.79.

The figures for imports for 1870–1890 show foodstuffs, both in crude condition and partly manufactured, holding up well, and in the latter case actually increasing, with sugar as the leading single import. The group which advanced most rapidly was crude materials for use in manufacturing, including rubber, hides and skins, raw silks, and fibers. While Europe took 74.6 per cent of our exports, she sent us in 1900 only 51.8 per cent of our imports, most of which were in manufactured products. Relatively the import trade with North America declined greatly and that with South America increased slightly, while the imports from Asia, which had constituted 6.8 per cent of the total in 1870, advanced to 16.5 per cent in 1900.

By 1900 industrial development in the United States had advanced to the stage where there was an excess of manufactured products and minerals for export, and this, furthered by the impetus of the Spanish-American War, drove American capital and products into foreign markets. The same tendencies that were apparent in the last decade of the preceding century became more evident. Foodstuffs, which had led in exportation, gave place to manufactures. In 1900 all classes of foodstuffs constituted 39.80 per cent of our total exports; in 1910, only 21.58, with a decline in absolute value of nearly $177,-000,000. This decline is all the more marked because prices on the whole were rising. It will be noticed that while the value of foodstuffs exported increased nearly fourfold from 1900 to 1920, their percentage of total exports decreased from 39.80 to 25.18. During these twenty years manufactured exports increased nearly ten times in value and from 35.38 to 51.52 in percentage of total exports. Crude materials for further use in manufacturing were relatively in the same position in 1929 as at the opening of the century. Up to 1914 cotton, of which about two-thirds was exported annually, made up the bulk of this group and retained its position as the leading single American export. The decline of agricultural exports in comparison with manufactures is shown in the accompanying table.

EXPORTS OF UNITED STATES MERCHANDISE, BY ECONOMIC CLASSES

	Total Exports	Percentage of Total Exports				
		Crude Materials	Crude Foodstuffs	Manufactured Foodstuffs	Semimanufactures	Finished Manufactures
1900	$1,370,764,000	24.81	16.48	23.32	11.18	24.20
1910	1,710,084,000	33.57	6.42	15.16	15.66	29.19
1915	2,716,178,000	21.77	11.66	16.74	13.10	29.73
1920	8,080,481,000	23.30	11.36	13.82	11.86	39.66
1925	4,818,722,000	29.51	6.60	11.90	13.73	38.26
1929	5,157,083,000	22.15	5.23	9.40	14.13	49.09
1932	1,576,151,000	32.60	5.67	9.65	12.48	39.60
1939	3,123,343,000	17.44	3.55	6.48	19.17	59.21

Statistical Abstract, 1933, pp. 406, 411; *ibid., 1941*, p. 533.

As American manufactured articles have been exported in larger amounts, other nations have endeavored to keep them out by keen competition and high tariff duties. Although in 1914 our European exports amounted to 63.37 per cent of the total they consisted chiefly of cotton, wheat, flour, meat products, and tobacco. An outlet for manufactured products had to be found in other quarters. North American countries, especially Canada, have furnished the chief new markets, and exports to them have shown both absolute and relative gains. The first two decades saw an intensified rivalry in the Far East, complicated by the entrance of Japan; but the United States, at least until 1930, was fortunate in obtaining her share of the Asiatic trade. Particularly noticeable also has been the advance in South and Central American commerce, part of which was a normal development and part promoted by World War I. The relative importance of our export markets as shown by the percentage of exports in 1929 was as follows: to Europe, 44.7; to North America, 26.6; to Asia, 12.3; to South America, 10.3; to Oceanica, 3.7; and to Africa, 2.5. In contrast to our exports, more of our imports came from non-European countries. In 1929 less than one-third of our imports came from Europe and about the same amount from Asia; from North America came 22.3 per cent, and from South America, 14.5. From the latter we obtained coffee, which we are unable to raise at home, and from the Far East rubber and raw silk. At the same time our domestic supply of minerals, hides, chemicals, and tropical fruits was considerably augmented from these sources.

All this may be summed up by saying that in the years after the Civil War two-thirds of our exports were crude materials for use in manufacturing and more than four-fifths were crude materials and foodstuffs. By the end of the century this situation was changing rapidly, and by the 1920's foodstuffs partly or wholly manufactured, manufactures for use in further manufacturing, and manufactures ready for consumption comprised more than three-fifths of all our exports. This meant that the United States was no longer chiefly a source of raw materials for the European market but was herself scouring the world for raw materials and for new markets for her manufactured goods.

ORGANIZATION OF FOREIGN TRADE

The general organization of foreign trade has changed considerably during the past century. During the early decades of the nineteenth century importers and exporters were likely to deal in many commodities, to own their own ships, and themselves to provide the necessary services. In contrast to this, foreign trade in recent years has become much more specialized. Importers or exporters are inclined to limit their activities to certain lines. Instead of owning their own ships, they employ brokers to secure space in the vessels of some line that goes to the region in which they are interested. This is also true of the typical manufacturer; he merely wholesales his product to the exporter, and the latter in turn secures shipping space and sells the commodity to foreign retailers. In other words, a commodity may be manufactured by one corporation, exported through the medium of a group of commission men and brokers, and shipped on boats owned by a separate corporation.

Along with this specialization of trade activities there has developed in certain fields a considerable integration of activities. For example, the United Fruit Company owns its own plantations, railroads, and ships, and wholesales its tropical fruit. Similarly, some of the great oil companies, like Standard Oil, not only produce and refine their product but export it in their own tankers. Other concerns, such as General Motors, which do a large volume of export business, establish subsidiary corporations to handle their export trade through their own warehouses and distributing systems. The necessity of strengthening the position of American exporters, as we have already seen, led to the passage of the Exports Association Act (Webb Export Act) in 1918 to exempt organizations engaged in foreign trade from prosecution under the antitrust acts as long as their operations do not injure other Americans.[10]

TARIFF HISTORY SINCE 1860

The American system of high protective tariffs may be said to date from the Civil War. There had been protective tariffs, of course, before that time, but they had not been exorbitantly high and the tendency in the years immediately before the war was downward. The act of 1857 reduced the maximum protection to 24 per cent, and the general level of duties was reduced to the lowest point since 1815. This policy of tariff reduction, which in general had been in vogue during the period from 1833 to 1861, was completely reversed with the Morrill tariff of 1861, which inaugurated the subsequent high tariff system. The Morrill Act of 1861 was not passed as a war revenue measure, but it contributed to bringing on the conflict. Historians are far from unanimous as to the relative importance of southern fear and hatred of a high tariff in the rebellion, but there is a growing tendency to lay more emphasis upon it. This much seems evident: There was no widespread demand by manufacturers for a high tariff in 1860; Morrill himself admitted in later years that the tariff "was not asked for, and but coldly welcomed by manufacturers, who always and justly fear instability."[11] With the exception of the short period of the panic of 1857, the period from 1846 to 1861 was one of great economic prosperity. The Republicans, searching for issues to bind together the discordant elements in the North, evidently believed that the old Whig protectionists could be allied with the new Republicans if protectionism was offered them. The Morrill tariff with its high rates was introduced in the House of Representatives in the session of 1859–1860 and passed, but did not come before the Senate until the session of 1860–1861.

In the meantime the Republican convention met at Chicago, where high-protection industrialists and representatives of the frontier farmers demanding free homesteads jostled for recognition with the more idealistic free-soilers of '56 and '58. The Republicans went on record not only for free soil but for free homesteads and a protective tariff, and in the Middle Atlantic manufacturing states protection was the chief issue stressed. Curtin, Republican

---

[10] For the discussion of foreign trade in later years, see below, pp. 646–647, 691–695.

[11] Quoted by F. W. Taussig, *Tariff History of the United States* (7th ed.), p. 160; *Congressional Globe, 1869–1870*, p. 3295.

candidate for governor of Pennsylvania, did not even mention slavery in his acceptance speech but dwelt on "the vast heavings of the heart of Pennsylvania whose sons are pining for protection to their labor and dearest interests."[12] Between the time of the election and the inauguration of Lincoln the Senate acted favorably on the Morrill bill and the South had the most definite proof possible that the control of the government had passed from her own land-owning aristocracy to the rising plutocracy of the North. The Morrill tariff had hardly become law when Fort Sumter was fired upon. For the third time a high tariff played a part in an American rebellion.

The Civil War having begun, not only was the Morrill tariff retained, but there was no session of Congress which did not raise the rates. Money to carry on the war had to be obtained; war industries were demanding protection, and manufacturers were clamoring for higher rates to offset the vast system of internal excise taxes which were being levied. The most important of the war tariffs were those of 1862 and 1864. Earlier in 1862 an internal revenue bill had been passed and to compensate manufacturers added protection was granted. Under the guidance of strong protectionists and under the spur of war needs wholesale advances were again made in 1864. This latter act, says Taussig, "was in many ways crude and ill-considered; it established protective duties more extreme than had been ventured on in any previous tariff act in our country's history," yet "five days in all were given by the two houses to this act, which was in its effects one of the most important financial measures ever passed in the United States."[13] Among other things, it brought the average level of duties up to 47 per cent. This legislation of 1864, hastily drawn and crude as it was, and denying no protectionist request, remained for decades the basis of the American tariff system.

These war tariffs, unscientific and exorbitant as they were, naturally laid themselves open to the criticism of tariff reformers in the postwar years. David A. Wells, Special Commissioner of the Revenue, and Secretary of the Treasury McCulloch united in 1867 in urging reduction, but their bill failed. The act of 1870 aimed to reduce taxation, but the reductions affected almost entirely such purely revenue articles as tea, coffee, wines, and sugar. The growth of the Liberal Republican movement in 1872, which advocated a lower tariff, was strong enough to bring a 10 per cent reduction just before the election of that year, but the panic of 1873, and the loss of revenue resulting therefrom, afforded an excuse to restore the earlier levels. Throughout these reconstruction years the high-tariff lobby defeated practically every effort at reform; prosperity, when it existed, was attributed to the tariff, and the burdens of taxation were lifted by reducing the internal excises.

[12] Quoted and discussed by C. and M. Beard, *Rise of American Civilization*, II, 35.
[13] F. W. Taussig, *op. cit.*, pp. 167–168.

For almost a decade no further important attempt at tariff reduction was made. However, a Treasury surplus of $100,000,000 in 1881 and 1882 led President Arthur to suggest a general overhauling. A strongly protective commission was appointed which advocated reductions averaging 25 per cent, but the resulting bill of 1883 lowered the general level only 5 per cent. From the close of the Civil War until the eighties neither political party in its official pronouncements was clear on the tariff. The tariff reform clubs and the northern tariff reformers were as likely to be Republican as Democratic, and Republicans, like President Arthur, had taken the initiative in urging action. But in 1887 President Cleveland made the tariff a party issue when he devoted his entire message to it. Pointing out the dangers of a continuing Treasury surplus and declaring the existing tariff to be a "vicious, inequitable, and illogical source of unnecessary taxation," he demanded a general reduction. Following the President's lead, a bill was prepared under the direction of John G. Carlisle and passed the Democratic House. The Senate, on the other hand, passed a bill of its own, known as the Mills bill; but as neither could pass the other branch of Congress the matter waited upon the decision of the electorate in the campaign of 1888. For the first time in our history the tariff was the chief campaign issue and was given adequate discussion.

Although Cleveland received a majority of the popular votes, Harrison won in the electoral college, and in 1890 the Republicans, after revising the House rules to prevent dilatory tactics on the part of their opponents, passed the McKinley bill, which raised the average level to 49.5 per cent. High duties were placed on the finer grades of woolens, cottons, linens, and clothing, and on iron, steel, glass, and tin plate. To propitiate the farmer, tariffs were imposed on agricultural products; and to take care of the surplus, the duty on sugar was removed and a bounty of two cents a pound placed on the domestic product in order to protect the Louisiana producers.

This tariff was so quickly reflected in the higher cost of living that the Democrats were given possession of the House in 1890, and of the Senate and the Chief Executive's office in 1892. For the first time since the Civil War that party had control of the executive branch and both houses of the legislature. Since the campaign of 1892 had been fought over the tariff, some change was inevitable. Cleveland immediately pressed Congress for action, but his efforts toward a healthy reduction were foiled by an active lobby supported by Democratic protectionists. After denouncing the Wilson-Gorman tariff of 1894 as an example of party perfidy and dishonor, he allowed it to become law without his signature. It did, nevertheless, put wool, copper, and lumber on the free list and lowered the average level to 39.9 per cent. The decreased revenue was to be made up by a tax of 2 per cent on incomes over $4000, a feature of the act which was declared unconstitutional in 1895.[14]

[14] Pollock *v.* Farmers' Loan and Trust Company, 158 U.S. 429.

The campaign of 1896 was fought chiefly over the question of currency, and in 1897 there appeared to be little interest in the tariff or demand for change. McKinley, however, scarcely entered the White House before he called a special session of Congress to revise the rates. The Wilson-Gorman Act was speedily wiped from the statute books and the Dingley Act substituted; the latter not only restored the McKinley rates but raised the average level to 57 per cent, imposing high duties on raw and manufactured wool and restoring hides to the dutiable list.

Of the general tariff acts of the United States, the Dingley bill remained in force the longest. The deluge of prosperity which swept the country as it swung into the upgrade of a new business cycle in the years following the Spanish-American War gave it prestige with large groups, but this popularity was eventually undermined by the rising cost of living and the reviving anti-trust sentiment. The Republican platform of 1908 promised "revision" and the electorate interpreted the word as meaning downward. The disappointment which ensued after the Payne-Aldrich bill was passed in 1909 was a potent element in the Republican defeat in 1910 and the election of Wilson in 1912. President Taft in his Winona speech characterized the Payne-Aldrich Act as the best tariff bill the Republican party had ever passed, but this highly roseate view was not widely entertained.

Since the days of Cleveland the Democrats had bitterly denounced Republican high protectionism, and Wilson's victory made a new act inevitable. A "competitive tariff" had been emphasized; hence the Underwood-Simmons bill of 1913 put iron, steel, raw wool, sugar (the latter in 1916), and certain agricultural products on the free list and made large reductions on cotton and woolen goods, but raised the rates on chemicals and other products. The reduction in revenue was taken care of by an income tax, now constitutional under the sixteenth amendment. Whatever may have been the official stand of the Democratic party, its two attempts at tariff making resulted in acts which remained highly protective.

American tariffs in the making have been characterized by a most unscientific procedure of political give-and-take. The need of turning the question over to a group of experts was recognized in the creation of the Tariff Commission of 1882 and the Tariff Board of 1909. Neither of these was taken seriously by Congress, and the latter was legislated out of existence. In 1916 a new Tariff Commission of six members was created to investigate all questions with reference to tariffs and to submit reports to Congress. These tariff commissions, however "scientific" they are supposed to be, somehow take on a Republican complexion during a Republican administration and a Democratic complexion when that party is in power.

With the conclusion of the First World War and the return of the Republican party to power in 1920, a radical revision of the tariff was to be expected.

Two factors were dominant in its making: first, the agricultural distress following the collapse of the war boom; and second, the voice of economic interests, using the nationalism kindled during the war to give force to their demands, and clamoring for protection of the industries stimulated by the war. To prevent postwar dumping and to meet the demands of the farmers, an "emergency" tariff was rushed through a special session of Congress (May 27, 1921); it imposed duties on wheat, corn, meat, wool, and sugar and was to be kept on the statute books until a more detailed act could be framed. The latter, known as the Fordney-McCumber tariff (passed September 19, 1922), not only returned to the high duties of 1909 and earlier tariffs but surpassed them in the protection given. Agricultural products were protected to a high degree, although this protection was hardly needed and did not perceptibly affect the decline in prices. Hides, however, remained on the free list to off-set the effects of the absence of a tariff on boots and shoes, an omission insisted upon by the farmers. The duties on manufactured goods were fully as high as those on agricultural products, and of more significance. The duties on iron and steel, omitted in 1912, were reimposed, and those on textiles, especially silk, were increased. In response to the demands mentioned above, the act was particularly concerned with the so-called "war babies," especially with the chemical and dyestuff industries, and gave them ample protection. There was much talk during the passage of the act about equalizing "the differences in costs of production in the United States and the competing foreign countries"; and in fear that foreign competition might possibly injure the American producer, the President was given power to raise or lower duties not exceeding 50 per cent upon recommendation of the Tariff Commission. This power and the extreme protection conferred by the tariff are the outstanding features of the act.[15]

SELECTED READINGS

Faulkner, H. U., *The Decline of Laissez Faire,* chap. 3.
Twentieth Century Fund, *Does Distribution Cost Too Much?* chaps. 1–3.
Taylor, G. R., Bertis, E. L., and Waugh, F. V., *Barriers to Internal Trade in Farm Products.*
Zeis, P. M., *American Shipping Policy,* chaps. 1–11.
Taussig, F. W., *Tariff History of the United States* (7th ed.), Part II.
Dietrich, Ethel, *World Trade,* chaps. 1–6.

[15] For the tariff of 1930, see below, p. 647.

CHAPTER 26

ECONOMIC IMPERIALISM

THE "OLD IMPERIALISM"

IMPERIALISM, that national policy which tends toward the extension of political, economic, and cultural dominion over regions geographically situated beyond the national boundaries, is a phenomenon discernible from the earliest times in nations which have progressed to a position of wealth and power. In modern times the world has witnessed two distinct waves or outbursts of imperialism. The first of these, which has been called the Old Imperialism, began with the discovery of new trade routes to the East at the close of the fifteenth century and lasted until 1815, the end of the Second Hundred Years' War between France and England. Then ensued a lull in expansion, during which statesmen were little interested in extending their foreign dominions. The last third of the century, however, saw renewed interest and activity in foreign expansion on the part of many nations, a period begun in Britain by Disraeli (1874–1880) and by the embarkation of France and Germany after the 1870's upon new imperial efforts.

The old Imperialism operated in an epoch of mercantilism. It looked toward the migration of colonists who were to set up little Spains, little Englands, and little Hollands throughout the world to serve as sources of raw materials and markets for home products. Under the impetus of the Old Imperialism, North and South America, Australia, and Siberia were occupied by Europeans, and settlements and trading posts were established in South Africa, India, the East Indies, and elsewhere.

If the Old Imperialism is defined as the acquisition of land which is actually settled by those who acquire it, American expansion up to 1898 may be largely considered as such. Certainly until this time it consisted primarily of the migration of people into unoccupied or sparsely settled land. The area of the United States in 1800 was 892,135 square miles, sufficient in the belief of most men to accommodate the needs of its population for an indefinite period. But the restless, land-hungry spirit of the pioneer was so intense that it was only three years later that the Louisiana Purchase of 885,000 square miles was consummated. Florida, containing 59,600 square miles, was obtained from Spain in 1819; Texas, a region of 389,000 square miles, was annexed in 1845; and the Oregon territory (285,000 square miles) was secured by treaty in 1845. The Mexican War, fought for little else than to confirm the annexation of Texas and to extend our boundaries to the Pacific, added 529,000 square miles, augmented in 1853 by the Gladsden Purchase of 30,000 square miles. In the case of Florida, Texas, and Oregon, settlers had gone ahead of acquisition,[1] but in general the annexation of large stretches of land was made without any immediate expectation of use. This was true of Alaska, purchased in 1867 for $7,200,000; but in all cases settlers speedily entered to dominate and occupy. The prices paid were trivial in comparison to the value of the land, and where wars were fought they were neither difficult nor costly. The antiexpansionists were easily outmaneuvered by the frontiersmen or by the southern expansionists so generally in control of the national government before the Civil War. The Indian inhabitants were ruthlessly brushed aside; an inferior civilization in a sparsely occupied region inevitably gave way to an aggressive people possessed with energy and numbers to conquer, and resources to develop the land.

THE "NEW IMPERIALISM"

The new wave of imperialism which swept over the world after 1870 brought in its wake results more far-reaching than any other development since the Industrial Revolution ushered in modern times. In fact, the "New Imperialism" is a direct result of the Industrial Revolution. Its causes are principally economic. The epochal inventions in machinery increased production so enormously that new markets had to be developed to dispose of the surplus products, and the vast population of Africa and Asia was looked upon as potential customers. Improvements in transportation and communication by land and sea were of inestimable value in speeding up this search for new markets. As the Industrial Revolution increased the population and hence the markets at home, and as new markets were opened abroad, it was necessary to discover and develop new sources of raw material. Those interested in manufacturing and commerce believed that such sources were safer when controlled by the home government. In addition to these economic factors, a third was equally important. With the tremendous increase in manufacturing and transportation, there followed accumulations of capital

---

[1] True also of Utah, where the Mormons first settled while the Mexican War was in progress. In California there were probably fewer than 800 immigrants from the United States when this war broke out.

seeking investment. As the surplus of capital increased in Europe, interest rates declined and financiers were forced to go far afield for profitable investments.

As a result, European capital was invested heavily abroad. British foreign investments in 1914 were estimated by Sir George Paish at about $20,000,000,-000, approximately 23 per cent of the total capital investments of the nation.[2] British investments in India amounted to nearly $1,844,600,000, and in the United States before the First World War, close to $3,667,400,000.[3] In 1912 France had loaned abroad, chiefly in the Near East and Russia, over $8,000,-000,000, amounting to 37 per cent of the total personal securities of the French; and Germany was estimated to have about $6,500,000,000 loaned abroad at the beginning of that war. This money, invested in factories, mines, oil wells, railroads, and other public utilities, or loaned to foreign governments, had to be protected. It continually directed the eyes of capitalists and governments to foreign fields and served to weaken the independence of smaller powers as the wealthier nations gained economic control. It gave the tone to the "New Imperialism," which was in reality financial imperialism. As in the sixteenth, seventeenth, and eighteenth centuries the homeland sent out settlers to conquer and occupy, so now the capitalists of the nineteenth century sent out manufactured products and money. They were not interested in settlement, for the lands now exploited were generally already peopled.

In addition to the economic there were of course other motives. First, there was a sincere desire on the part of Christians to convert the followers of other religions—a course favored by imperialists of all kinds who realized that the missionaries blazed the trails which the soldier and merchant were only too ready to follow. The nineteenth century witnessed a remarkable effort on the part of both Catholic and Protestant missionaries, who sometimes sought the protection of their government to facilitate their work in foreign fields. Second, the argument that the colonies might absorb the products and even part of the surplus population of Europe was frequently advanced. Between 1870 and 1900 Great Britain added to her possessions (exclusive of spheres of influence) about 5,000,000 square miles with an estimated population of 88,000,-000; France added 3,500,000 square miles with a population of 37,000,000, and Germany 1,000,000 square miles with an estimated population of 14,000,000. Third, the whole movement was stimulated and condoned by the desire for national power and prestige. This new expansion was intimately connected with military and naval rivalry and forms part of the essential background of the world wars of the twentieth century.

[2] E. L. Bogart, *War Costs and Their Financing*, pp. 14–16.
[3] Cleona Lewis, *America's Stake in International Investments*, p. 531.

THE UNITED STATES AND THE NEW IMPERIALISM

Into this competition for extraterritorial possessions the United States entered—late, to be sure, but with vigor. Until 1898 there had been little reason for overseas expansion. Free land suitable for settlement had existed, and abundant opportunities for whatever free capital might be seeking investments. In fact, the usual scarcity of capital in a new country was so acute that European wealth to the extent of $7,000,000,000 (over half of which was British)[4] was still invested here in 1914. But the Spanish-American War marked a turning point. From a position of inferiority in 1860 we had advanced to a position of great economic importance. Our population had increased 97 per cent between 1870 and 1900; our agricultural products had doubled and our mineral products had soared fantastically. The nation had demonstrated that its resources were the greatest of any single country and that they were well in hand for exploitation. While approximately nine-tenths of the production was consumed at home, the other tenth, which was exported, amounted in 1898 to more than $1,000,000,000 and was sufficient to make important the matter of foreign markets.

By 1897 the necessity of calling upon Europe for continued loans to develop transportation and industry had largely ended. Although the flow of capital was inward until the opening of the First World War, for the most part the United States financed her own rapidly extending economic life, and even found a surplus for foreign investment. Her foreign investments (direct and portfolio) had reached about $684,500,000 million by 1897, an amount which had increased to over $2,500,000,000 at the opening of the First World War. How this was distributed will be pointed out later.

The Spanish-American War is generally considered as marking the definite embarkation of the United States upon a career of imperialism, but a gradual development can be traced from a much earlier period. The Monroe Doctrine in its stated intention—(1) to refrain from interference in European affairs, (2) to consider any attempt by the European powers to "extend their political system to any portion of either continent of America as endangering our peace and happiness," and (3) to warn that the era of colonization in the Americas was over—seemed rather to be a reaffirmation of Washington's policy of isolation than any move toward foreign power. Yet the Monroe Doctrine so expanded in importance and so broadened in interpretation that it eventually became a strong factor in American imperialism. It was an early indication of the region in which the interests of the United States would become keen and American financial expansion make its start. In a sense it preserved "America for Americans."

[4] *Ibid.*, p. 546.

That the United States had every intention of upholding the Monroe Doctrine was demonstrated by the opposition to French expansion in Mexico during the Civil War. On the other hand, whatever foundations the Monroe Doctrine laid in the Latin-American republics for confidence in our friendliness and unselfishness had already been largely sacrificed by our wholesale annexations at the end of the Mexican War. Latin Americans came to look upon the Monroe Doctrine as a policy of keeping out Europeans from regions which the United States intended to dominate. Nevertheless, the ideal of closer relations between the American republics first conceived by Clay was kept alive, notably through the efforts of James G. Blaine and the Pan-American Congress of 1889. Cleveland's aggressive championship of the South American republic in the boundary line dispute between Great Britain and Venezuela was a continuation of the same policy.

In the meantime, political developments in the Pacific were following economic penetration. The conquest of California and the purchase of Alaska definitely made the United States a Pacific power. Long before American settlers reached the western coast, Yankee sailors had built up a brisk trade with the Orient. Commodore Perry's famous voyage to Japan in 1854 was a natural sequel to developing commercial interests, as was our eventual appearance in the Samoan Islands. American control of Hawaii was presaged as early as 1875, when a treaty of reciprocity was arranged, which stipulated that none of the territory should be leased or sold to any other power. By the 1890's Hawaii had come largely under the control of foreign interests, chiefly American, and her prosperity was dependent mainly on the export of sugar to the United States. This prosperity, based upon reciprocity treaties with the United States, was suddenly upset by the McKinley tariff of 1890, which not only put sugar on the free list but provided a bounty of two cents a pound for American producers. Declining prosperity in conjunction with the accession of an autocratic and nationalistic queen stirred the foreign interests, mainly American, to revolt. The revolution was consummated with the active co-operation of the American minister and the presence of the United States Navy. Cleveland refused to sanction acquisition by such methods, but the Americans in Hawaii would not return to the old regime. The matter hung fire until 1898, when McKinley's administration under the stress of war brought annexation.[5]

THE SPANISH-AMERICAN WAR

The eyes of Americans had turned toward the control of Cuba for half a century before the Spanish-American War. Cuba occupied a strategic position controlling the entrance to the Gulf of Mexico. It would provide a

[5] J. W. Pratt, *Expansionists of 1898*, chap. 9.

natural extension for southern slavery, and its accession seemed a logical continuation of the policy which brought us Florida and the Southwest. American control of Cuba was a leading question from 1850 to 1861. "It is our destiny to have Cuba," said Stephen A. Douglas in 1858, "and it is folly to debate the question. It naturally belongs to the American continent."[6] With the overthrow of the slaveowning aristocracy in the Civil War, the matter of Cuban annexation became quiescent until the nation was prepared for overseas expansion. This situation had arrived by 1898.

Although the Spanish-American War marked a turning point in American foreign policy characterized by a definite trend toward economic imperialism, the war itself was not caused primarily by economic interests. It is true that American investments in Cuba had become important by 1898 and that the sugar interests were anxious for the United States to bring peace to that harassed island. Nevertheless, American business in general, desirous of promoting the reviving business prosperity, opposed the war.[7] It was primarily a "newspaperman's war" promoted by the so-called "yellow press," which strengthened American sympathy for the Cuban revolutionists and disgust for the policies of Spanish misrule, at the same time playing up every possible incident that might lead to a break with Spain. Behind the press was a small but powerful group led by Theodore Roosevelt, Henry Cabot Lodge, John Hay, and others, who were enamored of the philosophy of Captain Mahan and who welcomed the war as an opportunity for America to fulfill her "manifest destiny" in world affairs. They aimed, says Professor Pratt, "at no less than making the United States the indisputably dominant power in the western hemisphere, possessed of a great navy, owning and controlling an Isthmian Canal, holding naval bases in the Caribbean and the Pacific, and contesting, on at least even terms with the greatest powers, the naval and commercial supremacy of the Pacific Ocean and the Far East."[8]

The war left us with the Philippines, Puerto Rico, Guam, and the destiny of Cuba on our hands. The main problem faced was the future of the Philippines. Annexation, it was evident, meant the subjugation of an alien race in a remote tropical region and the definite embarkation upon the uncertain path of imperialism. The implications of this step were clearly seen by a strong anti-imperialist minority, who fought strenuously against annexation. They received some backing from tobacco, beet sugar, and other agricultural interests fearful of competition, and from labor leaders like Gompers who

[6] Speech in New Orleans, December 6, 1858; given in *Life of Stephen A. Douglas*, by "A Member of the Western Bar" (1860), p. 184.

[7] J. W. Pratt, *op. cit.*, chap. 7.

[8] J. W. Pratt, "The Large Policy of 1898," *Mississippi Valley Historical Review*, XIX, 223 (Sept., 1932).

feared the menace of cheap Oriental labor.[9] On the other hand, a large section of the business interests were finally won over to the idea that retention of the Spanish islands in the Far East would mean a rapid expansion of American trade. The administration was at first uncertain, but President McKinley, finally convinced that the majority of voters favored territorial expansion, insisted on annexation. The treaty was ratified February 6, 1899, by a margin of only one vote more than the required two-thirds majority.

There could be no mistaking the significance of the annexation of the Philippines. Nevertheless, McKinley insisted that it was a purely altruistic decision. "The Philippines, like Cuba and Puerto Rico," said he in 1899, "were intrusted to our hands by the war, and to that great trust, under the providence of God and in the name of human progress and civilization, we are committed. . . . We could not discharge the responsibilities upon us until these colonies became ours, either by conquest or treaty. Our concern was not for territory or trade or empire, but for the people whose interests and destiny, without our willing it, had been put in our hands."[10] In more realistic terms Senator Beveridge a year later expressed the attitude of the victorious imperialists: "The Philippines are ours forever, 'territory belonging to the United States,' as the Constitution calls them. And just beyond the Philippines are China's illimitable markets. We will not retreat from either. We will not repudiate our duty in the archipelago. We will not abandon our opportunity in the Orient. We will not renounce our part in the mission of our race, trustee, under God, of the civilization of the world."[11]

CARIBBEAN PENETRATION

American penetration of the Caribbean has been motivated by two primary interests. The first, and most important, is self-protection and involves the naval and air strategy of safeguarding the Panama Canal. The second is economic, the expansion of commerce and investments. These interests are obviously intertwined, and together they largely comprise the history of our relations in this region during the past half-century. Of the Caribbean Islands, Cuba is the most important and there American economic expansion has been the most intense. When war was declared against Spain, Congress in the Teller Resolution asserted that "the United States hereby disclaims any disposition or intention to exercise sovereignty, jurisdiction, or control over said Island, except for the pacification thereof, and asserts its determination, when that is accomplished, to leave the government and control of the Island

[9] F. H. Harrington, "The Anti-Imperialist Movement in the United States, 1898–1900," *Mississippi Valley Historical Review*, XXII, 211–230 (Sept., 1935).

[10] Speech in Boston, February 16, 1899, Boston *Herald*, Feb. 17, 1899, pp. 2–3.

[11] *Congressional Record*, January 9, 1900, 56th Cong., 1st Sess., Vol. XXXIII, Par. I, p. 704.

to its people." In spite of this resolution, American soldiers were kept in Cuba until 1902, and before they returned Cuba was forced to incorporate in a treaty and in her constitution the provisions of the Platt Amendment. By this she agreed that she would not enter into any treaty with a foreign nation that might impair her independence, that she would not assume any public debt for which her ordinary revenues were inadequate, that she would consent to the intervention of the United States "for the preservation of Cuban indepe-pendence, the maintenance of a government adequate for protection of life, property and individual liberty," and that she would lease or sell to the United States land sufficient for coaling and naval stations. This reduced Cuba to the status of an American protectorate, made possible repeated inter-vention in the island, and opened the way to a thorough economic penetra-tion.

In connection with Cuba, as well as with other Caribbean republics, it should be emphasized that the policy of the United States government has been concerned mainly with canal strategy. This has meant maintaining peace in the Caribbean and preventing the development of a situation which might give other nations an excuse to interfere in that area. Such a policy inevitably has prepared the way for economic penetration. Between the Platt Amendment and economic penetration this led in the case of Cuba to both political and economic dependence upon the United States. As far as politi-cal dependence was concerned, Franklin D. Roosevelt as part of his "good-neighbor policy" determined to end it, at least technically. A treaty with Cuba in 1934 abrogated the famous Platt Amendment and in the same year a tariff treaty under the Trade Agreements Act enlarged the American market for Cuban commodities.[12]

The social and economic history of Puerto Rico since American annexa-tion in 1898 has resembled that of Cuba. There has been a notable ad-vance in the sanitary and educational facilities of the island, an improvement in transportation facilities, and the building of public works. The wealth of the island has increased, from $100,000,000 to $650,000,000 or more, but, as in Cuba, it has come under the control of American capital, the land has been consolidated into large sugar and tobacco plantations, and the small farmer has been reduced to the status of a landless proletarian. Experts writing in the early thirties estimated that absentee owners controlled at least 60 per cent of the island's wealth. To complicate the situation even more, the island became essentially a two-crop country dependent upon the American market, and when that market collapsed, as it did in 1929, the economic situation be-came intolerable. At the depth of the depression in 1930, 60 per cent of the population were unemployed. Free trade with the United States since 1902

---

[12] Below, pp. 693–695.

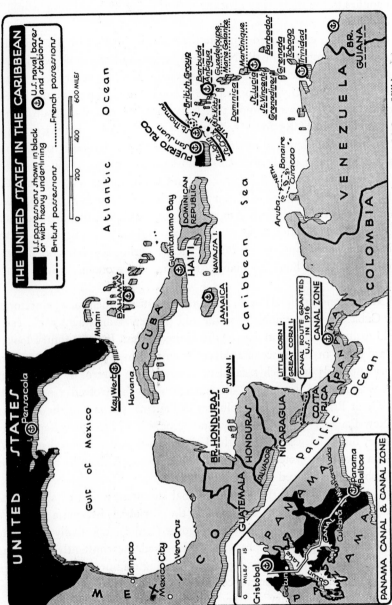

THE UNITED STATES IN THE CARIBBEAN

U.S. possessions shown in black or with heavy underlining
⊕ U.S. naval bases and stations
------- British possessions
········· French possessions

0   200   400   600 MILES

UNITED STATES
Pensacola
Key West ⊕
Miami
Havana
BAHAMA IS.
CUBA
Guantanamo Bay
Atlantic Ocean
DOMINICAN REPUBLIC
HAITI
JAMAICA
NAVASA I.
PUERTO RICO
San Juan
St. Thomas
St. Croix
VIRGIN IS.
British Group
Barbuda
Antigua
Guadeloupe
Marie Galante
Dominica
Martinique
St. Lucia
St. Vincent
Grenadines
Barbados
Grenada
Tobago
Trinidad
⊕

Gulf of Mexico
Tampico
Mexico City
Vera Cruz
MEXICO
GUATEMALA
SALVADOR
BR. HONDURAS
HONDURAS
NICARAGUA
SWAN I.
LITTLE CORN I.
GREAT CORN I.
CANAL ROUTE GRANTED U.S. IN 1916
COSTA RICA
CANAL ZONE
PANAMA
Caribbean Sea
Aruba NETH.
Bonaire
Curacao
COLOMBIA
VENEZUELA
BR. GUIANA

Pacific Ocean

PANAMA CANAL & CANAL ZONE
0   MILES   15
Cristobal
Colon
Gatun Locks
Gatun Lake
CANAL
Culebra Cut
Pedro Miguel Locks
Miraflores Locks
Panama
Balboa
PANAMA

(From H. U. Faulkner, Tyler Kepner, and E. H. Merrill, *History of the American Way*, McGraw-Hill.)

has been an advantage to Puerto Rico, but the American tariff system, which also applies to the island, has kept the cost of living higher than it would be otherwise.

Some aid was extended to mitigate the difficult situation by the relief and rehabilitation programs of the New Deal period, and economic activity was stimulated by the Second World War. Gains here, however, were partly nullified by the scarcity and high price of food caused in part by the lack of transportation facilities to import it. Important progress was made during the governorship of Rexford G. Tugwell (1941–1946) by the enactment of a minimum-wage law and other labor legislation. Of particular significance was the decision of the Puerto Rican legislature to enforce a law, passed by the United States Congress in 1900, to limit landholdings to 500 acres. The island legislature appropriated money to purchase such lands in the hope that a restoration of a small-farm economy might enable farmers to raise more foodstuffs for the better support of the population. The migration to the United States of thousands of Puerto Ricans during the war and postwar years first brought home to many Americans the economic plight of the islands.[13]

With the annexation of Puerto Rico and the establishment of a protectorate over Cuba it was inevitable that the old project of an interoceanic canal would assume new importance to the United States. If this country looked forward to the maintenance of an overseas empire, to say nothing of her own defense, not only was such a canal necessary but its control by our government was essential. In a series of maneuvers which involved a new treaty with Great Britain, aid to a revolution in Panama, puchase of the rights of the New Panama Canal Company, and recognition of the new Republic of Panama, the canal was built by the United States and completed in 1914.[14] Panama became a protectorate of the United States, although that position was technically removed by a new treaty in 1939.

With the building of the Panama Canal the preservation of the United States' interests in Central America and the Caribbean became a matter of even greater concern. The unstable governments, continually changing through forcible political upheavals, endangered the constantly increasing American investments and the rapidly developing commerce. Repudiation of foreign debts made the interference of creditor nations a constant danger and threat to the "canal policy" of the United States. To meet the situation the United States evolved a program somewhat as follows: First, the Monroe Doctrine must be maintained, a position demonstrated in 1902 when Roosevelt insisted that the Venezuelan debt controversy be submitted to arbitra-

[13] The Puerto Rican situation is discussed in R. G. Tugwell, *The Stricken Land* (1940).
[14] Much of this story is told in D. C. Miner, *The Fight for the Panama Route* (1940).

tion. Second, while our policy opposed the forcible collection of claims by European nations, it admitted that the recalcitrant countries should meet their just debts. Third, where this was necessary or where American interests were at stake, the policy of intervention and supervision might be adopted. In this manner a "Pax Americana" might be established in the Caribbean.

This policy, since known as the "Roosevelt Corollary" to the Monroe Doctrine, was first enunciated by Theodore Roosevelt in a message to Congress in 1904 and for two decades it dominated our relations with the small republics of the Caribbean and Central America.

If a nation [said Roosevelt] shows that it knows how to act with reasonable efficiency and decency in social and political matters, if it keeps order and pays its obligations, it need fear no interference from the United States. Chronic wrongdoing, or an impotence which results in a general loosening of the ties of civilized society, may in America, as elsewhere, ultimately require intervention by some civilized nation, and in the Western Hemisphere the adherence of the United States to the Monroe Doctrine may force the United States, however reluctantly, in flagrant cases of such wrongdoing or impotence, to the exercise of an international police power.

It was in Santo Domingo that the Roosevelt Corollary received its first practical application. Conditions there became so chaotic after the death of President Heureaux in 1899 that in 1904 the nation was bankrupt and unable to meet the interest on its debt. An executive arrangement was made in 1905 (later passed in treaty form in 1907) whereby the United States was to take over the administration of the customs houses and pay the Dominican government 45 per cent of the income for current expenses and 55 per cent for foreign claims. In 1908, Kuhn, Loeb & Company of New York refunded the debt of $20,000,000 under a treaty by which the United States was to collect the customs until the debt was paid. Furthermore, the public debt was not to be increased without the consent of the United States. Interference in the country's political life began in 1912, when Taft forced the resignation of a president, and culminated in the invasion of the marines in 1916. From then until 1924, when the marines were withdrawn, Santo Domingo remained under a military government conducted by the United States. In that year a new convention was drawn up validating earlier arrangements and extending the treaty of 1907 during the life of the bond issues, an arrangement which continued our control of Dominican finances and the power to intervene. In the meantime American interests had obtained control of the financial affairs of the country, one-third of the sugar industry, and other important resources.

In Santo Domingo the United States worked out a technique which was soon to be applied in Haiti on the western part of the same island. With its

3,000,000 inhabitants, Haiti is the most thickly populated of the West Indies and probably the richest in natural resources. For a number of years American bankers had been interested in Haitian finances, and the First World War gave an opportunity for government intervention. Professing to believe that Germany had designs upon Haiti and determined that no European nation should assume control of it, American troops invaded the island, forced through a treaty, and, despite armed opposition by the natives, occupied the country for almost twenty years. The treaty of 1915 imposed much the same conditions as applied to Santo Domingo: American aid in the development of natural and commercial resources, American receivership of customs and supervision of expenditures, an American financial adviser, and no cession of Haitian territory to any foreign nation. Thus another protectorate was added to the American empire and so it remained until softened by the removal of marines in the early 1930's. All this brought an improvement in the educational, sanitary, and transportation systems, but it also brought economic penetration.

With the construction of the Panama Canal, with American fruit interests active in Costa Rica and Honduras and virtually dominating the latter, the spread of American interests in Central America developed rapidly. Nicaragua was the most important of the Central American states to encounter American penetration, and her possession of a second route for an interoceanic canal was the primary cause. On a number of occasions United States marines had landed in Nicaragua at the request of her government, even before American participation in the revolution of 1912. At this time (figures for 1913) the United States handled 35 per cent of the imports and purchased 56 per cent of the exports of the country. Following this interference, American bankers, with the unofficial sanction of the State Department (after a treaty providing for intervention had failed to pass the Senate), reorganized the finances of the little country, established a national bank, and assumed control of the nation's finances. A treaty ratified by Nicaragua in 1914, and by the United States in 1916, provided that the latter should pay $3,000,000, receiving in return the exclusive right to build a canal on the Nicaraguan route, a ninety-nine-year lease on three small islands, and the privilege of constructing a naval base on the Gulf of Fonseca.

As far as the United States government was concerned, its main objective was achieved with the signing of the Bryan-Chamorro treaty. Nevertheless, the State Department continued to take an active interest in aiding American bankers with the agreements of 1917 and 1920, which continued outside financial control until the middle twenties. In like manner the Coolidge administration felt it necessary to send the marines back to Nicaragua during the revolutionary years after 1925 to protect American life and property, safeguard canal rights, and prevent foreign interference. The marines did not leave again until 1933.

Despite President Wilson's well-known opposition to territorial expansion, his administration offered to buy in 1916 the Danish West Indies, known as the Virgin Islands. The purchase of these islands had no direct economic significance. It was essentially a matter of naval strategy to safeguard the routes to the canal. Whatever the objectives, it was clear that by the end of the First World War the United States had achieved a "sphere of influence" in the Caribbean which virtually made that area an "American lake." Puerto Rico had been annexed, the Virgin Islands purchased, Cuba, Panama, the Dominican Republic, Nicaragua, and Haiti reduced to the status of protectorates, and naval bases scattered strategically at various points in the Caribbean. The development of this control had occurred during the two decades 1898–1918. Of the chief executives, only Theodore Roosevelt could be described as an expansionist. Taft was an exponent of "dollar diplomacy," on the theory that American economic penetration would be a distinct aid to less developed countries and a stabilizing influence. Wilson was neither an expansionist nor a dollar diplomatist, but his Caribbean policy differed little from that of his predecessors.

MEXICO

The most important exception to the hegemony of the United States in the region of the Caribbean and Central America was Mexico. Easy as it was to extend control over the diminutive republics of Haiti and Nicaragua, the problem of Mexico was more difficult, and relations with that nation have been exceedingly complicated since the revolution of 1910. Encouraged by thirty years of strong rule under Porfirio Diaz, United States oil drillers, silver miners, railroad builders, ranchers, and others had invested close to $1,000,000,000, and Europeans had interests aggregating half that amount. By 1910 approximately 80 per cent of investments in Mexican railroads was controlled by Americans, and 70 per cent of the oil was produced by American firms. After the outbreak of the revolution the United States government was under pressure to intervene for the protection of American capital, and at the same time European nations virtually forced us either to look after their interests or to allow intervention on their part, an action hardly in keeping with the Roosevelt Corollary. The Mexican revolution, itself largely an agrarian revolt by an exploited peasantry against the inordinately large accumulations of land, was accompanied by much banditry and considerable loss to the investments of American citizens, and it was further complicated by the fact that European and American interests often pulled the strings behind the scenes which gave impetus to the revolutionary activity.

On two occasions (1914 and 1917) armed forces entered Mexico but withdrew; probably only the European war prevented further outside interference. Since 1917 the diplomatic problems of the two nations have swung chiefly around the economic interests of American investors as affected by the Mexican Constitution of that year. This Constitution nationalized church property, secularized the schools, promised varied legislation, and declared that the soil and subsoil of Mexico belonged to the Mexican people. In the future only Mexicans might acquire ownership of Mexican land, except that Mexico might grant the same right to foreigners on condition that they agree "to be considered Mexicans in respect to such property, and accordingly not to invoke the protection of their governments to the same, under penalty, in case of breach, of forfeiture."[15] Under no condition might a foreigner acquire land within 100 kilometers from the frontier or 50 from the coast. Although theoretically this was not retroactive, it was bitterly opposed by American investors.

Relations with Mexico improved greatly during the late twenties through the tact of Ambassador Dwight W. Morrow, but deteriorated again a decade later when, as a result of a dispute over labor conditions, the Mexican government in 1938 nationalized foreign oil properties but promised indemnification. The American government, as it always had, conceded the right of expropriation; hence this phase of our relations with Mexico has been largely concerned since 1938 with securing a fair appraisal and adequate indemnification. Although neither was probably obtained (at least in the opinion of American claimants), Mexico in 1947 cleared off her liabilities to the amount of approximately $24,000,000. Generally speaking, the policy of the United States from Taft to Franklin D. Roosevelt has been to let the Mexicans work out their own salvation, but at the same time to exert pressure for more settled conditions and for protection of legitimate foreign interests.

THE FAR EAST

American economic interests in the Far East go back to the 1790's, when American merchants found in China a market for furs and other commodities and a source of tea and other Oriental goods.[16] As far as the United States had any policy in the Far East during the nineteenth century, it was the desire to keep the field open for free and equal commercial opportunities for all nations. In the furtherance of this objective this country made numerous contributions, including the opening of Japan in the 1850's, to foreign trade. This policy was continued and more definitely enunciated after 1899

---

[15] This is the so-called "Calvo doctrine" which has become increasingly a part of contracts signed between Latin-American governments and foreign investors.

[16] Above, p. 145.

as a result of the industrial development at home, the new spirit of economic imperialism, and three important developments in the Far East. The first was the annexation of the Philippines, which made the United States a power in the Far East; the second was the phenomenal emergence of Japan as a powerful nation; the third was the imperialistic designs of Japan and the great European nations upon the integrity of China.

The Philippines, as we have seen, were annexed in 1899 despite strong opposition at home and the necessity of overcoming the armed resistance of the Filipinos. Although many motives contributed to the annexation, the principal one seems to have been the hope of commercial expansion. Unlike American domination in Puerto Rico and certain other areas, American administration in the Philippines has generally been efficient, liberal, and essentially interested in the welfare of the natives. Civil government with native participation was established in 1901, partial home rule in 1907, and virtual home rule in 1916 with the Jones Act. Trade was promoted by an act of 1902 allowing Philippine commodities to enter the United States under a 25 per cent tariff reduction. Free importation was permitted in 1909, except for the admission of specified quotas of sugar and tobacco. After 1913 there was complete free trade.

From the beginning the Philippines have been a burden to American taxpayers rather than an asset. American trade with the islands increased—our exports from about $4,000,000 in 1901 to $83,400,000 in 1939, and imports from about $10,000,000 in 1900 to $92,000,000 in 1939. But this was by no means pure gain, for certain of the leading Philippine exports to the United States—sugar, tobacco, and coconut products—came into competition with American produce. Nor did the Philippines prove to be a fruitful field for investment. Total American investments in 1935 amounted to approximately $200,000,000, of which about one-sixth was in government bonds. The total was less than one-fifth the amount of capital that had flowed into Cuba. Moreover, it was difficult to see how ownership of the islands had contributed much to the development of the "fabulous trade" of the Orient. In any case a combination of three factors—Philippine demands for independence, the American farm bloc, and anti-imperialist Democrats—combined to bring passage of the Tydings-McDuffie Act of 1934, which granted Philippine independence after a period of ten years. But this was by no means all gain to the Filipinos. In return for eventual independence, immigration from the Philippines was to end and Philippine imports were to pay the regular American tariffs. Since the United States in 1934 took 87 per cent of Philippine exports, this was a high price. The greatest price was the danger of Japanese aggression and this, as it turned out, was paid before the United States retired from the islands.

With the invasion of the Philippines the picture quickly changed. The

United States recognized Philippine independence during the war (1943) and it was finally established on July 4, 1946. In the meantime Congress decided to ease the early years of transition to independence. The Philippine Trade Act (1946) granted eight years of free trade. After that, tariffs would rise 5 per cent annually for twenty years until they were in line with tariffs established on the goods of other nations.

American annexation of the Philippines was but one aspect of a great imperialistic movement which was to throw the Far East into a turmoil and which reached a climax in the Second World War. It began at the end of the Chinese-Japanese War in 1895, when Japan annexed Formosa and made Korea a sphere of influence. This was followed immediately by demands by France, Germany, Russia, and Great Britain upon China for long-term leases of important ports behind which they hoped to erect spheres of economic influence. In an effort to protect America's growing commerce, John Hay in September, 1899, addressed to the great powers interested in Far East exploitation essentially identical notes enunciating the new famous "open-door" policy. They requested that in its sphere of influence each nation give assurances (1) that all existing treaty ports and established interests in each sphere of influence would be unmolested, (2) that the Chinese tariffs and no others would be enforced and collected by Chinese officials, and (3) that no differentiation in port and railroad charges would be made between the citizens of any nation carrying on business. Russia declined; the others (except Italy) answered evasively; but Hay, ignoring the evasive replies, announced that in view of the favorable reception of his proposals, they would be regarded "as final and definitive."

This policy of encouraging China's economic integrity Hay expanded in the following year by an effort to maintain her political integrity. When a group of Chinese nationalists reacted against foreign aggression in the Boxer Rebellion of 1900, he reaffirmed the open-door policy and insisted that the rebellion should not be an excuse for the annexation of territory. This policy of attempting to maintain the economic and political integrity of China has continued to be the official policy of the United States for the past five decades. Although the *status quo* was upset by the Russo-Japanese War in 1904–1905 and again by the First World War, the United States succeeded at the Washington conference in 1921 in re-establishing it temporarily. Not until the Japanese invasion of Manchuria in 1931 did it completely collapse.

AMERICAN FOREIGN INVESTMENTS TO THE FIRST WORLD WAR

A glance at the accompanying table shows that American investments abroad increased five times between 1897 and 1914. It will also be noted that Mexico and Canada were the chief areas of American investment. Mexico had the largest total in 1897, and Canada in 1914. After that Canada maintained the lead until temporarily surpassed by Europe after the First World War.

American economic penetration of Canada began well before 1900. The causes were chiefly three: the desire to exploit the Canadian market, to obtain raw materials needed in the United States, and to escape Dominion tariffs on commodities that could be manufactured there. The penetration concentrated in the manufacture of automotive goods, rubber, electrical equipment, machinery, metals, chemicals, pulp, paper, and lumber. By the 1920's American investments surpassed those of Great Britain and by the

DIRECT AND PORTFOLIO INVESTMENTS BY GEOGRAPHIC AREAS
(In Millions of Dollars)

Areas	1897	1908	1914
Europe	151.0	489.2	691.8
Canada and Newfoundland	189.7	697.2	867.2
Cuba and West Indies	49.0	225.5	336.3
Mexico	200.2	672.0	853.5
Central America	21.2	41.0	93.2
South America	37.9	129.7	365.7
Africa	1.0	5.0	13.2
Asia	23.0	235.2	245.9
Oceanica	1.5	10.0	17.0
International, including banking	10.0	20.0	30.0
Total: Long-term credits	684.5	2,524.8	3,513.8

Cleona Lewis, *America's Stake in International Investments*, p. 606.

1930's controlled more than one-third of the mining industry, the electrical output, and at least one-fourth of the manufacturing. This penetration was largely in the form of branches of American manufacturing concerns set up to take care of the Canadian market rather than private investments in Canadian firms.

Almost the equal of our investments in Canada in 1914 were those in Mexico. During the Diaz regime American money flowed into Mexico at the rate of $40,000,000 a year. By 1914 the total amounted to about $850,-000,000, almost three times the amount of British investments. The investments covered many fields, but the chief concentration was in the mining and smelting of metals, in railroads, and, in the later years, in oils.[17] Despite the revolution and a decade of unrest, American investments continued to grow until the middle 1920's.

[17] The main items were estimated as follows: mining and smelting of precious metals, $140,-000,000; of industrial metals, $162,000,000; railroads, $110,400,000; and oil, $85,000,000. Other investments included agriculture, public utilities, manufacturing and selling organizations. Cleona Lewis, *op. cit.*, pp. 578–604.

As late as 1914 American investments in Mexico were as large as those in the West Indies and the rest of Latin America combined. But the great era of economic penetration in Mexico was approaching its apex, and that of the rest of Latin America was on the verge of a great expansion. In 1897 investments in the West Indies were about one-fourth of those in Mexico; in 1919 they were two-thirds. South America investments, trivial in 1897, were close to $800,000,000 in 1919. Of all the fields for investment, it was Cuba which probably grew the most rapidly in the two decades after 1897, and particularly after the beginning of the First World War. By the late 1920's American investments in that island amounted to over $1,000,000,000 in sugar, public utilities, railroads, mines, tobacco, and government securities, all fostered by branches of the National City Bank of New York and American brokerage houses. As already noted, over half the wealth of Puerto Rico was also soon concentrated in American hands. Despite protectorates and some artificial stimulations, American investments in other West Indian islands were relatively trivial in comparison to those in Cuba.

By 1914 investments in Central America, estimated at $90,000,000, were about one-third in railroads, one-third in tropical fruits, and the other third in the mining of precious stones, public utilities, and government loans. In South America, where United States investments had now started to expand rapidly, about two-thirds were in mining. Most of this was in copper, produced in Chile by the Anaconda Copper Company and the Braden Copper Company (controlled by Kennicott). A much smaller economic stake was concerned with the precious metals and stones. There was little interest in oils until after 1916. Compared with metals, American interest in railroads, public utilities, and manufacturing was small, but some $20,000,000 in 1914 was tied up in selling organizations and a similar amount in oil.

Despite the exaggerated dreams and rosy predictions of American imperialists, the Far East failed to become either an important trading center for American industrialists or a profitable field for American investments. American exports to all Asia were valued in 1897 at about $39,270,000 or 3.74 per cent of our total export trade. Twenty years later it was about $380,250,000 or 6.05 per cent. Of this about $37,150,000 went to China. The reasons for the relatively small amount are simple—the poverty of the mass of Orientals and the severe competition of European countries and later Japan. In capital investments the story is much the same. Total American investments (direct or portfolio) in Asia in 1897 have been estimated at $23,000,000, of which $20,000,000 was in oil-distributing organizations and other trading and sales corporations. By 1914 total investments in Asia, including the Philippines, amounted to $235,200,000. About half of this was in portfolio investments, largely the result of loans to the Japanese government.

Although little aid or encouragement was given by the federal government to economic expansion in Canada, Cuba, Mexico, and South America, the situation was quite different in the Far East, at least in China. Here, as we have seen, the American government made some efforts to effect an even opportunity to trade and to protect the Chinese economic and political future. From the McKinley to the Wilson administration, efforts were made to introduce American capital into Chinese loans for railroads and other projects. As a whole these were fruitless. The reasons were two: First, American capitalists were busy with investments elsewhere, including some reorganization of the American economic system. Second, Americans, as in the case of the Chinese trade, met the continuous, bitter, and successful rivalry of Japan and the European nations.[18]

TECHNIQUE OF IMPERIALISM

Enough has been said to give some idea of the manner in which imperialism is pursued. The New Imperialism of the past eighty years has generally been carried out by one of the following methods, or variations and combinations of them: (1) by means of military conquest, as in the case of the Boer War and the Spanish-American War; (2) by the appropriation, frequently by treaty consent from the natives, of certain regions not yet preempted by white men, as in large parts of Africa; (3) by means of lending money to weak or impoverished governments who eventually are unable to pay, after which the lending government steps in to enforce payment by taking over the customs, appointing a financial adviser, or actually establishing a protectorate—excellent examples are England in Egypt and the United States in Haiti and Santo Domingo; (4) by economic penetration, followed by friction with the natives and demand by the settlers for intervention and protection on the part of the home country. Hawaii is an example of this last.

The process of imperialism may be completed in one stroke, but it is more likely to run through various stages. The first may be missionary activity followed by economic penetration, which in turn may entail friction with the natives or danger to investments. Then may come intervention, with the establishment of a virtual protectorate. The last stage is actual annexation, but under modern conditions this is often unnecessary, for economic penetration can be carried on quite as effectively in a protectorate, and the expense and trouble of administration can be avoided. This is notably true in Cuba, where American investments were far greater than in all American colonies and protectorates combined.

While the technique of modern imperialism is obviously somewhat dif-

[18] American foreign investment is discussed in greater detail in H. U. Faulkner, *Decline of Laissez Faire,* chap. 4.

ferent from that of the seventeenth and eighteenth centuries, the underlying motive—economic benefit to the home or investing nation—is essentially the same. It should be pointed out, however, that the benefits have not been one-sided. American imperialism has sometimes meant the loss of political or economic independence, but it has generally brought greater prosperity and better living conditions. Improved transportation facilities, better sanitation, an aggressive attack upon tropical diseases, an extension of educational facilities, and a more efficient government have all followed in the wake of imperial-

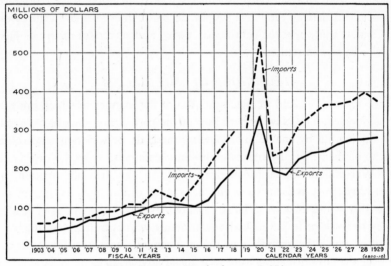

(From *Commerce Yearbook, 1930,* I, 88.)

FOREIGN TRADE OF CONTINENTAL UNITED STATES WITH ITS TERRITORIES
AND POSSESSIONS.

ism. Although this situation has not been due entirely to unselfish motives, the fact remains that the United States assumed "the white man's burden" in a serious mood. That the policy of economic imperialism has progressed simultaneously with the rapid expansion of our commerce with these dependencies may be seen from the accompanying graph. This is also true of the expansion of American trade and investments elsewhere in the world and in regions where there has been no political expansion or economic control. American economic investments in Japan, for example, amounted to $418,-000,000 in 1933, more than twice those in the Philippines.

One more comment on the technique of imperialism based on the experiences during the period since the Second World War should be made. The description so far given has been that of the technique of an expanding capitalism in western Europe and the United States. Since this appeared to be a natural development of a capitalist economy, it has been assumed by some that imperialism, whether it be economic, political, or cultural, would disappear under a different economic system. This, it seems, is not the case. While a capitalist nation such as the United States or a developing socialist country such as Great Britain has retreated from imperialism and relinquished colonies, Communist Russia has greatly expanded her territory and her spheres of influence. She has ended the independence of or reduced to the status of protectorates from eight to ten nations since 1939 and has moved in to dominate their political, economic, and cultural life. The technique has varied somewhat from that of capitalist expansion, but the results have been more far reaching.

RETREAT FROM IMPERIALISM

An effort has been made in the preceding pages to trace the development of our economic imperialism during the early decades of the present century. Although there has been a rapid expansion of commerce and investments in certain areas, as a whole the experience has not been happy or in certain aspects successful. The Philippine Islands did not prove to be a steppingstone to "China's illimitable markets." It was impossible to achieve the "open-door" policy without war, and as the years passed the United States seemed unwilling to precipitate a Far Eastern conflict to maintain this policy. When war finally came, it was Japan rather than the United States that began it. In the Caribbean the Roosevelt Corollary, which would make the United States the policeman of Latin America and the collector of debts owed to American citizens, proved impractical. Too many Latin-American states were disturbed by revolution, and too many had defaulted on their bond issues, for any one nation to police them all. Furthermore, American industrialists were eager to extend their foreign markets and could hardly do so without building up a spirit of good will among our southern neighbors. Finally, it was beginning to dawn on the American people that colonies and dependencies were more likely to be a source of trouble and financial loss than of gain. In brief, economic imperialism as supported by the Roosevelt Corollary had turned sour, and there was little appetite for further adventures.

With this as a background, there began a retreat from the type of imperialism evident after the Spanish-American War. Legislation in 1934 provided for Philippine independence after ten years. In Latin America a "good-neighbor policy" was gradually substituted for the Roosevelt Corollary. Military intervention ceased in Santo Domingo in 1924; the marines were withdrawn from Nicaragua in 1933 and from Haiti in 1934. Treaties with Cuba in 1934 and with Panama in 1939 helped to lift these nations from their status of technical protectorates. The new policy was made clear in a series of Pan-American conferences promoted by the United States. At Montevideo in 1933 the United States took a definite stand against "the intervention of any state of the American continent in the internal affairs of another state," and at Lima in 1938 she officially abrogated the Roosevelt Corollary. Closer economic relations for the benefit of all were to be promoted by reciprocal trade agreements and similar methods rather than by armed intervention. In the darkening clouds of a second world war the government of the United States hoped also to change the Monroe Doctrine from a policy promoted by herself alone to one in which all the American nations would co-operate in upholding a mutual program of hemisphere defense. Later conferences emphasized this policy and the United States has proved her sincerity by deeds as well as words.

SELECTED READINGS

Faulkner, H. U., *The Decline of Laissez Faire,* chap. 4.

Williams, B. H., *American Diplomacy,* chaps. 5–9.

Bemis, S. F., *A Diplomatic History of the United States,* chaps. 27–30, 35, 38–41.

Bemis, S. F., *The Latin American Policy of the United States,* chaps. 8 ff.

Griswold, A. W., *The Far Eastern Policy of the United States,* chaps. 1, 4.

Perkins, Dexter, *Hands Off,* chaps. 7, 9.

Flügel, F., and Faulkner, H. U., *Readings in the Economic and Social History of the United States,* chap. 19.

CHAPTER 27

AMERICA AND THE FIRST
WORLD WAR

*ECONOMIC TRENDS ON THE EVE OF THE WAR—DECLINE OF
LAISSEZ FAIRE*

Iɴ the last eight chapters an effort was made to trace the economic development of the United States from the conclusion of the Civil War to 1914. The more important changes wrought in American economic life during that half-century should now be clear to the reader. With economic changes came a different attitude toward economic policy. Although federal and state aid had been granted at various times for internal improvements and industry had received aid from the protective tariff, the nation in general had committed itself during these years to the economic doctrine of *laissez faire*. Faith in this doctrine was never stronger than in the hectic period of economic development following the Civil War. The early popularity of the doctrine was in part a reaction from the innumerable government regulations of industry during the Middle Ages which seemed unduly to hamper the rapid expansion of modern commerce and industry. Late eighteenth- and early nineteenth-century economists, such as Adam Smith and John Stuart Mill, gave it classic expression. Strength was added to the arguments of the economists by the ideas derived from Charles Darwin's *Origin of Species* (1859)—the "survival of the fittest." According to this theory, those best equipped to meet an environment are most likely to survive. If *laissez faire* brought great inequalities of wealth, if many were destroyed or doomed to a life of hardship and suffering, it was as nature determined it. It was a person's own fault if he did not succeed.

The policy of *laissez faire* undoubtedly speeded the development of an expanding nation. It was, of course, strongly advocated by those who had reached the top in the economic struggle. The eighties and nineties saw the golden age of *laissez faire,* but the average citizen's faith in it had already weakened. Particularly had this faith been undermined by the long period of agrarian distress, by the resentment against railroad abuses, by the opposition of the small businessman and manufacturer to the consolidation of industry and capital, and by the example of state control and social experiment in Europe and Australia. There was a growing feeling that America was no longer the land of unlimited opportunity and that *laissez faire* had benefited only a small group who had amassed the major share of the wealth and resources of the nation. A culmination of this discontent came in the first decade of the present century when Theodore Roosevelt, catching the prevailing feeling of unrest, led a vigorous campaign for greater government regulation, a campaign which was duplicated in many of the states.

Preliminary shots had been fired in the Interstate Commerce Act of 1887 and the Sherman Antitrust Act of 1890, which inaugurated a policy of government regulation that was widened and strengthened in the succeeding decades. But the extension of federal activities was not confined simply to restraining harmful practices; the federal government definitely enlarged its own economic interests in many ways, notably by entering the transportation business through the parcel post (1912) and the banking business through the postal saving banks (1912). It sought to aid agriculture, industry, commerce, and labor, particularly through the Department of Agriculture, established in 1889, and the Department of Commerce and Labor, established in 1903 and separated in 1913.

In many ways the breakdown of *laissez faire* was more striking in state legislation than in that of the federal government. The leadership among the states was taken by Wisconsin under the inspiration of La Follette during 1900 to 1905. It was then that Wisconsin became a veritable laboratory for social legislation, strengthening its railroad commission, establishing a public utility commission to regulate rates and determine valuation, and creating an industrial commission to enforce labor legislation and, finally, a tax commission to evolve a more equitable and scientific system of taxation. One of the most important of the Wisconsin laws was that providing for a personal income tax (1911), and her lead was followed by the federal government (1913) and eventually by many states.[1] In practically every state inheritance taxes were also levied. These new taxes, it should be noted, were the result of the mounting expenses, as well as of a change in the attitude of the people.

It is unnecessary to review here the many types of labor legislation and

---

[1] Although an income tax had been imposed during the Civil War (above, p. 509), a second effort was declared unconstitutional in 1895. The income tax of 1913 was made possible by the sixteenth amendment adopted in that year. By 1952 thirty-one states and the District of Columbia were imposing some type of income tax. That in New Hampshire applied only to interest and dividends.

other efforts toward social control characteristic of the first decade of the century or to point out how the demands for social control found their way into party platforms.[2] "Eminent economists," wrote Dr. Beard in 1914, "turned from free trade and *laissez faire* to consider some of the grievances of the working class, and many abandoned the time-honored discussions of 'economic theories,' in favor of legislative programs embracing the principles of state socialism to which Germany and England were already committed. . . . While none of the states went so far as to establish old-age pensions and general sickness and accident insurance, it was apparent from an examination of the legislation of the first decade of the twentieth century that they were well on the paths of nations like Germany, England and Australia."[3]

One aspect of this subject which is sometimes overlooked is the internal as well as external decline of *laissez faire*. That is, private businessmen began to realize that ruthless and unregulated competition might be utterly ruinous. As capitalism matured and competition grew keener, private individuals sought to eliminate "free enterprise" by consolidations and monopolies. It was industrialists, not the government, who first broke down the free competitive system. After that, the government under public pressure began an effort, as Wilson called it, to restore the "new freedom" by government regulation.[4] *Laissez faire* was destroyed by business before the government was called in to restore competition or to regulate monopoly.

CONSERVATION

An important aspect of the decline of *laissez faire* was the rather sudden interest aroused after 1900 in the problem of conservation. Blessed for three centuries with an apparently exhaustless supply of land and raw materials, the American people became prodigal of their heritage and wasteful in their habits. As population began to press seriously upon the land and the cost of raw materials increased, attention was drawn more and more to the conservation of the remaining resources. Investigations showed that our supplies of wood and minerals were not inexhaustible,[5] that four-fifths of the forests

[2] Above, Chapter 1, particularly pp. 28–29.

[3] C. A. Beard, *Contemporary American History*, pp. 304–305.

[4] The attack on *laissez faire* is discussed in more detail in H. U. Faulkner, *The Quest for Social Justice* and *The Decline of Laissez Faire*.

[5] The consumption figures for a single issue of a great metropolitan newspaper furnish an excellent illustration of the rapid use of our natural resources. The Public Service Bureau of the Chicago *Tribune* gave "the approximate figures on the materials that are required to publish the Sunday edition of the Chicago *Tribune*" in 1924 as follows: "Standing timber, 54 acres; sulphur, 21 tons; coal, 665 tons; electric horsepower, 63,000; water, 18,200,000 gallons; limestone, 28 tons; paper, 800 tons." Mr. S. M. Williams of the New York *World* estimated (1924) 400 to 450 tons of newsprint paper as the average of the New York Sunday *World*, with coal consumption varying from 1400 to 1700 pounds of coal per ton of paper and approximately fifty acres of pulpwood (chiefly spruce and balsam) forests cut over.

had been cut down without thought of renewing them, and that most minerals, except coal, would be exhausted by the end of the twentieth century. They showed that in the mining of bituminous coal, one-fourth was left underground permanently lost, and in like manner at least half of the anthracite, while annually millions of gallons of mineral oils evaporated or were lost in pumping. Unscientific methods of lumbering were both denuding the nation of wood and releasing the floods to spread havoc, and soil eroded or was being robbed of its fertility without renewal. Not alone in the processes of production was waste to be found, but also in the use of the finished material. Furthermore, in no highly developed industrial nation was human life more lightly regarded than in the United States. Conservative estimates placed the deaths from industrial accidents in the early 1920's at over 20,000 a year, with industrial injuries of greater or less importance at about 2,000,-000.[6] For every 250,000 tons of coal mined in 1928 (a year of low fatality rates) it was claimed that one man was killed and several were injured, but this condition has been improved. The Interstate Commerce Commission reported for the year 1919 over 2000 railroad employees killed and over 131,-000 injured.

Although the conservation of material and human resources may take many forms, the "conservation movement" in America is generally considered to have commenced with the agitation of such men as Gifford Pinchot and Frederick Haynes Newell and to have been promoted by President Roosevelt. Actually a handful of scientists had for years pointed to the need of conservation. John Wesley Powell of the United States Geological Survey had urged in the seventies the preservation of grasslands as a national resource. Newell, later chief engineer of the Reclamation Service, had written much in the nineties on the need of irrigation and reclamation, and a beginning of federal aid had been made in the Carey Act of 1894 and the Newlands Act of 1902. It was Pinchot, America's first professional forester, who did most to arouse greater interest in forest conservation. Influenced by Pinchot, Roosevelt called a famous conference of governors in 1908.

The result was the appointment of forty state conservation committees, and a national conservation committee, and much publicity for the whole subject. From it came a reaction against the wasteful exploitation of earlier years, a new interest in the more scientific and intelligent use of natural resources, particularly inland waterways, and new legislation to protect the public domain and the subsoil resources on public lands. It was found that under the liberal land laws large corporations had acquired, often by fraudulent methods, a large part of the mineral and forest resources of the country. To prevent a similar fate for the water-power resources, the great power of the

[6] See C. R. Daugherty, *Labor Problems in American Industry*, chap. 5.

future, Roosevelt hastened to withdraw over 172,000,000 acres from public entry. The efforts of public-spirited men to preserve some parts of the public lands for the nation as a whole were hampered by lack of congressional co-operation and by the opposition of private interests. Nevertheless real progress was made.

Progress was made also in the conservation of human resources, as can be seen by surveying the important social legislation passed since the opening of the century and by noting the various federal and state agencies, such as the Women's and Children's Bureau of the Department of Labor and the recently created Department of Health, Education, and Welfare. It can be seen likewise in the more aggressive and definite attitude taken by the churches, Catholic and Protestant alike, on the subject of social and economic justice. Significant as is the conservation movement in the general story of the breakdown of *laissez faire*, it is ironical that it should appear in the years just before the First World War plunged the world into the greatest orgy of waste and destruction which history records up to that time.

INCOMES AND THE DISTRIBUTION OF WEALTH

The need both for conservation and for a more scientific approach to the whole problem of the production and distribution of economic wealth is obvious when one attempts to survey the material well-being of the American people in the years before that war. The Census of 1900 placed the total wealth of the nation at approximately $88,500,000,000. This had more than doubled by 1914 and with it had come an increase in per capita wealth. Significant increases are also to be noted during these years in the national income. No adequate statistics are available before 1909, but the best figures collected since then appear in the accompanying table. In examining the figures due consideration should be given to the rise in prices after 1900 and particularly to the inflation after 1914. When reduced to the price level of 1913, the purchasing power of the $61,000,000,000 national income in 1918, for example, would amount to but $38,800,000,000, and that of the per capita income of $586 would be only $372.

The figures in this table do not necessarily mean that the income of the average wage earner in terms of purchasing power was necessarily increasing. Economists in 1914 were generally agreed on two points: (1) that comparatively few adult workers earned wages which would secure a decent standard of living, and (2) that real wages had advanced but slightly between 1900 and 1914. Douglas, who has made the most intensive study of earnings in the period after 1890, gives an index figure of 98 for the average annual real earnings in all industries (excluding farm labor) for 1897 and 104 for 1914; for all industry (including farm labor) he gives 97 in 1897 and 107 in 1914.

He points out, however, that real *hourly* wages in manufacturing remained almost stationary between 1900 and 1914. As for *unskilled* labor in manufacturing, these years saw a decline in real wages. But by 1917 they had recovered to the level of 1897. In the decade following 1914, however, Douglas believed that there was a gain of 19 per cent in the purchasing power of a full-time week's work and holds that most groups of manual workers en-

NATIONAL INCOME, 1909–1918

Years	National Income (In Billions)	Population (In Millions)	Income per Capita (In Dollars)
1901	28.8	90.37	319
1910	31.4	92.23	340
1911	31.2	93.81	333
1912	33.0	95.34	346
1913	34.4	97.28	354
1914	33.2	99.19	335
1915	36.0	100.43	358
1916	45.4	101.72	446
1917	53.9	103.06	523
1918	61.0	104.18	586

Income in the United States, Its Amount and Distribution, 1909–1919, by the Staff of the National Bureau of Economic Research, Inc., 1921. This table is adapted from Tables 1, 9, and 11, in Vol. I, pp. 13, 64, and 68.

joyed a substantial increase in real wages in the decade following the war. On the other hand, he believes that most groups of non-manual workers, with the notable exception of teachers, experienced a real decline.[7]

From another angle, that is, the proportion of the total national income going to labor, it appears that the share of the wage earners increased slightly, if at all, during the 1920's.[8] Whatever the situation regarding real wages and the share of labor in the national income, there seems to be no question but that the standard of living improved rather steadily during the forty years prior to 1929. Improvement was due primarily to two influences—new inventions that made work easier and living more comfortable, and the large amount of social legislation that went far to protect the health, well-being, and working conditions of the wage earner and his family. His standard indeed improved, but in most cases it remained, as in 1914, below a decent minimum. Furthermore, as a class, the American wage earner, owing to the decline of the organized labor movement in the postwar years,[9] was in a weaker position in 1932 than in 1914.

[7] Summarized in H. U. Faulkner, *Decline of Laissez Faire,* pp. 251 ff., and discussed in detail in Paul H. Douglas, *Real Wages in the United States, 1890–1926,* Tables 25, 59, 147, pp. 111, 174–184, chap. 22.

[8] *Recent Economic Changes,* II, 766–771.

[9] Below, pp. 630 ff.

At least one other aspect of this problem should be noted—the distribution of wealth. Although per capita income and per capita wealth have been greater in the United States than in European countries, the distribution of general wealth, at least until the late 1940's, has not been radically different, a striking and sobering fact when the greater resources, the newness of the country, and its democratic institutions are remembered. According to a careful study made in 1890, seven-eighths of the families held but one-eighth of the wealth, and one per cent of the families owned more than the remaining 99.[10] A decade later there appeared to be little change. A study of estates probated in five Wisconsin counties during 1900 revealed the fact that the poorest two-thirds of the population owned only 5 or 6 per cent of the wealth and the poorest four-fifths scarcely 10 per cent, while the richest one per cent owned half of the property probated. As these Wisconsin counties comprised

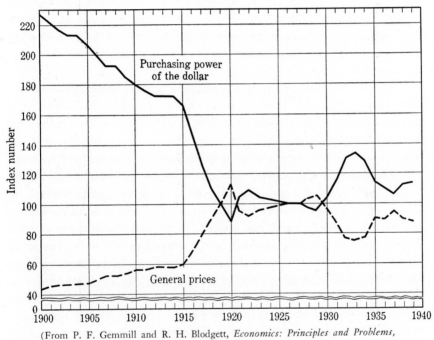

(From P. F. Gemmill and R. H. Blodgett, *Economics: Principles and Problems,* Harper & Brothers.)

GENERAL PRICES AND PURCHASING POWER OF THE DOLLAR, 1900–1940 (1926 = 100).

rural communities and cities including Milwaukee, and as the findings agree with similar studies made at different periods in Massachusetts, they may be taken as typical.[11] They point inevitably to the fact that fully 80 per cent of

[10] C. B. Spahr, *The Present Distribution of Wealth in the United States,* pp. 65–70.
[11] W. I. King, *The Wealth and Income of the People of the United States,* pp. 72–87, 90–115.

the people lived on the margin of existence and that the wealth of the nation was largely owned by the remaining 20 per cent. Little had happened by 1914 or, for that matter, by 1940, to change this situation.[12]

Although the distribution of wealth is far more unequal than that of income, a study of income tax returns only serves to strengthen conclusions obtained from probate records. Taking the year 1920 as fairly indicative (since it included both the last months of the war inflation and the beginning of the subsequent depression), we find that even in this year of partially inflated wages 83 per cent of those over ten years of age gainfully employed did not receive an income amounting to $1000. Yet this was a period when government agencies were putting $2200 or over as a minimum comfort income for a family of five. Although it is extremely difficult, even with the force of government pressure, to secure accurate information on incomes, it appeared that in 1920 less than one per cent of the income receivers had close to 12 per cent of the national income and 10 per cent had 34 per cent. At the same time, whereas the incomes of those receiving between $1000 and $5000 amounted to 64.35 per cent of the total income reported, they paid only 15.43 per cent of the tax.

Despite the discouraging facts revealed by a study of incomes and the distribution of wealth, the American people had never before made more rapid progress toward a better civilization than in the decade preceding the First World War. Not alone was there a tremendous economic development, but great progress was being made in the integration and regulation of economic life. The bitter attacks of the "muckrakers" upon the social, political, and economic ills of the day were but the symbol of the changed attitude of the nation, of its willingness to take sober stock of its resources, to modify the economic brigandage which had ushered in the new century, and to value more highly the scientific approach as the solution of many ills. The attack on the old order was carried on along the entire front. In the states by means of the initiative, referendum, and recall and improved city government an effort was made to rescue the state and local governments from exploiting private interests and return them to the people. The seventeenth amendment was aimed in the same direction in the federal government. An infinite variety of social legislation directed on the one hand against the slums, the exploitation of the labor of women and children, and the waste of life in industry, and on the other toward the improvement of the facilities for education, recreation, and health gave the tone to the new century. The prewar years closed with four notable pieces of federal legislation—the Clayton

[12] A Federal Trade Commission study of estates left between 1912 and 1923 showed that 80 per cent of decedents left estates valued at less than $500 and that more than 90 per cent of all estates amounted to less than $5000. About one per cent of the decedents owned more than 90 per cent of the wealth. P. H. Nystrom, *Economics of Consumption*, p. 152.

Antitrust Act, a new effort to prevent monopolies; the Federal Trade Commission Act, better to control big business; the Federal Reserve Act, to integrate more closely the nation's banking system; and the Underwood Act, the most intelligent tariff since the Civil War.

YEARS OF NEUTRALITY

The famous acts in the first year of the Wilson administration represented the climax of the reform movement of the early years of the century. The First World War, which engulfed Europe in the late summer of 1914 and widened two and one-half years later to include the United States, virtually ended for the time being the drive for social justice and ushered in a period of reaction. Few Americans who followed their newspapers with such intensity in 1914 had any realization of the far-reaching economic effects which the war would bring. For four years most of the European nations devoted their supreme efforts to the task of annihilation. Millions of workers were withdrawn from productive industry to indulge in an orgy of destruction which was to use up the accumulated wealth of decades. To the 7,450,000 men killed in battle must be added a greater number of disabled or brought to an early death by wounds, and the fatalities to the civilian population because of disease and starvation. To the immediate cost of $186,000,000,000 must be added the subsequent payments for pensions, the cost of reconstruction, and other burdens too infinite to estimate. These costs piled up the debts of the warring nations to a figure which could mean only repudiation. For two decades after the conflict the world was cursed by the problems of war debts and inflation. For the moment the war disorganized the financial, commercial, and the industrial systems of the world. But even the expenditure of human life and material wealth was of little avail. The First World War proved but a preliminary struggle to an even greater world conflict.

The early effect of the First World War upon the United States was much like that experienced during the period of the French Revolution and the Napoleonic Wars. The years 1913 and 1914 found this country suffering from a minor depression which was accentuated by the economic disorganization of the first few months of the European conflict. Beginning in 1915, however, there ensued a five-year period of enormous industrial and agricultural expansion caused in the first instance by increased European needs and later augmented by American participation in the war. As Europeans turned from peacetime pursuits the gap had to be filled elsewhere, and the United States, as a century earlier, served as a source of raw materials and food supplies. Unlike her role in the Napoleonic Wars, the part this country now played, because of her industrial development, was an important one as exporter of minerals, semi-manufactured goods, and munitions. In the end, however, whatever gains she may have made from the woes of Europe were canceled by her own participation. The world again proved too small for the United States to escape being drawn into a world conflict.

Although estimates put the increase in gross national product between 1914 and 1918 at only 15 per cent, the story was quite different in the products needed for war.[13] Producers of metals and other minerals were naturally the first to feel the impetus. The production of iron ore increased from 41,439,000 long tons in 1914 to 75,288,000 in 1917; the production of copper from 1,150,-137,000 pounds to 1,886,120,000 pounds, of zinc from 343,000 short tons to 584,600, of bituminous coal from 422,703,000 short tons to 551,790,000, and of petroleum from 265,762,000 barrels to 335,315,000. Agricultural prosperity soon followed as the demand for cotton, wheat, wool, leather, and lumber increased. Cotton, which was a drug on the market in 1915 at 8.5 cents a pound, rose to an average of 35.9 cents during 1920. The production of wheat, which had been 763,380,000 bushels in 1913, rose to 1,025,800,000 in 1915. Poor crops cut it in 1916 and 1917, but the output in both 1918 and 1919 was well over 900,000,000 bushels; the price of wheat rose from 97 cents in 1913 to $2.73 in 1920. The corn crop, which amounted to 2,445,988,000 bushels in 1913, was pushed up to 3,065,233,000 in 1917, a record up to that time. Not only was the production of metals and agricultural products stimulated, but many articles hitherto largely purchased abroad were manufactured here in increased quantities. Of these should be mentioned dyes, potash, chemicals, scientific instruments, and optical goods. The rapid development of the chemical industry, the most important of the "war babies," was, in fact, one of the most significant effects of the war upon American industry.

Since the United States was the largest producer of the chief raw materials and the most convenient source of foodstuffs, foreign purchases were extremely heavy during the war and immediately afterward. As a consequence, foreign commerce increased enormously, notwithstanding the activity of German submarines. For a decade preceding the war American exports had surpassed imports by between $450,000,000 and $500,000,000, a balance of trade which had been offset by the payment of interest and dividends on borrowed capital, by the payment of freight rates to European shippers, by the expenditures of American travelers, and by immigrant remittances. The excess of exports over imports, which had amounted to $435,800,000 in the year ending June 30, 1914, jumped to $3,567,800,000 in 1917. Exports, as will be seen from the accompanying table, considerably more than tripled between 1914 and 1920. As was natural, the great increase came in munitions and foodstuffs; thus the value of explosives exported rose from $6,272,000 in 1914 to $802,789,000 in 1917; of chemicals, dyes, drugs, etc., from $21,924,000 to

---

[13] For natural production indexes, see Simon Kuznets, *National Production in Wartime*, p. 148.

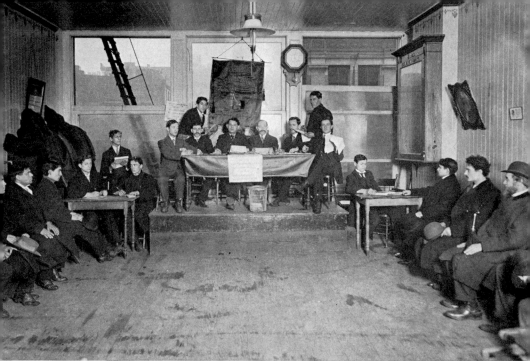

or Union Meeting
the Time of the
akmaker's Strike in
ew York in 1912.

uel Gompers, Pres-
of the American
ration of Labor,
5–1894, 1896–1924.

Train of the Camden and Amboy Railroad Reconstructing the Delaware and
Raritan Canal About 1866 at a Time When Canal Transportation
Was Declining.

Completion of the First Transcontinental Railroad at Promontory Point, Utah,
May 10, 1869.

Poster Advertising the Opening of the Union
Pacific Railroad.

Union Pacific's First Locomotive. It Was Brought to Omaha by Steamboat
from St. Louis, June 5, 1865.

A Crack Pullman Train of the Early Twentieth Century Running Along the
Bank of the Chesapeake and Ohio Canal.

Alfred Stieglitz Has Beautifully Photographed in "The Terminal" Horse Car Transportation in New York in the 1890's.

arles Duryea in His First
Horseless Carriage.

The Wright Brothers' First Flight Near Kitty Hawk, North Carolina,
December 17, 1903.

Black Maria—The First Moving Picture Studio Set Up by Edison for His
Experiments.

Mechanized Agriculture—Twelve McCormick-Deering Sixteen-foot Threshers Cutting a Swath 192 Feet Wide and Capable of Cutting 640 Acres a Day.

Mechanized Agriculture—A Caterpillar Diesel Tractor Pulling a 14-foot Drill and a 14-foot Land Roller in Tandem.

Displaced by Drought and Mechanical Agriculture, the Small Farmer Moves
on in Search of Work.

$181,028,000; of iron and steel, from $251,486,000 to $1,133,746,000; of meat products, from $143,261,000 to $353,812,000; and of wheat from $87,953,400 to $298,180,000. The excess of exports was made possible in three ways. First, the Allied nations liquidated approximately $2,000,000,000 worth of American securities; second, they borrowed in the United States to the limit of their

FOREIGN TRADE OF THE UNITED STATES, 1914–1921 (IN MILLIONS OF DOLLARS)

Year[a]	Exports of Domestic Merchandise	Imports of Merchandise	Excess of Exports over Imports	Percentage of Agricultural Exports	Percentage of Manufactured Exports
1914	2,329.7	1,893.9	435.8	48	47
1915	2,716.2	1,674.2	1,042.0	54	43
1916	4,272.2	2,197.9	2,074.3	36	62
1917	6,227.2	2,659.4	3,567.8	32	66
1918	5,838.7	2,945.7	2,893.0	39	58
1919	7,749.8	3,904.4	3,845.4	53	45
1920	8,080.5	5,278.5	2,802.0	43	52
1921	4,378.9	2,509.1	1,869.8	48	46

[a] Fiscal years ending June 30 to 1918; thereafter calendar years.
Statistical Abstract, 1921, Table 482, pp. 840, 847, 849.

credit; and finally, after the United States entered the war, they purchased with extensive loans furnished by the American government.

Even when the price inflation caused by the war is taken into consideration, the increase in foreign trade was enormous. It was the result not alone of the war needs of Europe but also of an increase in trade with Latin America and Asia where the United States was able to fill the gap made by the elimination of Germany and the preoccupation of Great Britain. The excess of exports over imports, along with the prosperity in this country and the destruction in Europe, helps to explain the shifting of the world's financial center to New York. For the first time in her history the United States became a creditor nation.

The rapid expansion of American commerce did not proceed unhampered. Of the difficulties faced by the United States, inadequate shipping facilities was the most important. Unlike the Napoleonic era when this country had the second largest merchant fleet in the world, the year 1914 found her with a relatively small tonnage. In that year the tonnage of American vessels engaged in foreign trade amounted to a little over a million. The lack of a merchant marine was keenly felt, particularly as the great German steamship lines were driven from the sea at the very time when German submarines were destroying Allied tonnage faster than it could be replaced and when considerable Allied tonnage was being withdrawn from commerce for strictly war purposes. The situation was acute, and as early as 1914 the federal government instituted an active policy for the stimulation of shipping. In that year the laws regarding registry and other matters were modified to allow foreign ships to seek refuge under the neutral flag of the United States, and legislation was passed creating a Bureau of War Risk Insurance in the Treasury Department to insure American vessels and cargoes if insurance could not be otherwise provided on reasonable terms.[14] Two years later (September 7, 1916), Congress authorized the appointment of a United States Shipping Board to promote the development of the merchant marine and to regulate shipping.

With Europe battling in a life-and-death struggle, it was unlikely that America could enjoy unmolested the profits of neutrality. As in the Napoleonic Wars, each side in the struggle was anxious to keep American products from reaching the other. To achieve this purpose both Great Britain and Germany violated neutral rights as they balanced their immediate needs against the displeasure and possible action of the United States. Great Britain, controlling the sea, blockaded German ports and arbitrarily extended the contraband list to include cotton, wool, leather, rubber, copper, and chemicals, which had formerly been free of seizure, and later foodstuffs. She also enforced the theory of "ultimate destination" and seized cargoes bound for the neutral nations of Europe on the grounds that they were destined eventually for the Central Powers. On her part, Germany proclaimed the waters around the British Isles a "war zone" and embarked on a policy of unrestricted submarine warfare which resulted in the loss of American lives and property.

The causes which make for war are extremely complex, and their relative importance is impossible to determine. Much emphasis was given after the First World War to the economic causes for our entry. American economic life, it was pointed out, had become geared more and more to the task of supplying essential war commodities, and these commodities, owing to Britain's control of the seas, had gone to only one side. It was Germany's interference with this commerce that provided the technical cause for our declaration of war on April 17, 1917. Moreover, private loans to Allied borrowers amounted to over $2,500,000,000 before our entry into the war, compared with $45,000,000 to Germany. The Wilson administration had at first frowned on these loans, but in 1915 it stood aside and allowed them to be floated. This action later opened the administration to the charge of developing a background which helped to make inevitable American entry into the war.[15]

---

[14] Extended by an act of October, 1917, to include compensation to sailors and their dependents in case of death or disability.

[15] The attitude of the Wilson administration on the question of war loans was opened up early in 1936 by a Senate committee investigating the munitions industry, headed by Gerald P. Nye. Opposing views may be examined in C. A. Beard, "Solving Domestic Crisis by War," *New*

The United States without doubt had a definite economic interest in the success of the Allies. But this is far from explaining her entry.[16] Incredible blunders of Germany diplomacy and violations of neutral rights were alone sufficient to bring this country into the war without the influence of other factors. American culture and traditions were based on those of Great Britain; her language and legal and constitutional institutions stemmed from the British Isles. Moreover, Allied propaganda was far more successful than that of Germany. Long before 1917 most Americans were convinced of the justice of the Allied cause; they interpreted it as a fight for civilization and liberal institutions. The decision could hardly be otherwise.

ECONOMIC MOBILIZATION

The policy of *laissez faire* which had been gradually crumbling during the first two decades of the century collapsed completely under the stress of war conditions. Economic life in America was so radically affected by the war even before this country entered the conflict that it was felt necessary for the government to interfere actively in private business; with our entrance, centralized supervision and direction of production and distribution were absolutely essential to effective participation. Government control, to an extent never before exercised here, was effected through federal boards, commissions, or corporations, endowed in some instances with very wide powers and sometimes aided by subordinate state or local bodies.

When the United States entered the conflict, the war had been in progress more than two and one-half years. European experience had made American leaders at least aware of the enormity and complexity of the problems of economic mobilization. Primarily, it was a task of integration and co-operation. It meant, first of all, a survey of resources, an estimate of needs, and then a shift of production from peacetime needs to those of war. Fortunately for this country, the rapid expansion of the industries producing metal and munitions for the Allies had laid a foundation for this shift of production. In the second place, it meant the establishment of central governing and purchasing boards to ration raw materials through priority rules, to direct purchasing at fair prices, and to bring some order out of the chaos of competition among manufacturers for raw materials, machinery, and labor.

There were also the problems of standardization, of profit control, of labor policies, of price fixing, of civilian needs, along with the necessity of speed-

Republic, LXXXVI, 127–129 (March 11, 1936), and Newton D. Baker, *Foreign Affairs*, XV, 1–86 (Oct., 1936). The most objective study of why America entered the First World War is in C. C. Tansill, *America Goes to War* (1938).

[16] A recent article based on a survey of more than thirty leading trade and financial papers exonerates American businessmen from warmongering up to 1917. See H. C. Syrett, "The Business Press and American Neutrality, 1914–1917," *Mississippi Valley Historical Review*, XXXII, 215–230 (Sept., 1942).

ing up war production as rapidly as possible. The government itself was also entering the field of production, as in the case of nitrates and shipping. Other pressing problems included the development of more efficient transportation, greater production of food, and the financing of the war. For a nation of immense size, conditioned to individual rather than co-operative action, and with virtually no experience in this type of action, the task was one of almost superhuman proportions. Despite appalling unpreparedness, inevitable inefficiency, blunders, and failures in specific projects, the job as a whole was accomplished. During the nineteen months of our participation in the war, the government maintained a continuous flow of food and munitions to the Allies, raised and armed over 4,000,000 men, transported 2,000,000 to Europe, and put 1,000,000 on the battle lines. In addition it financed the Allied nations during these months.

As the possibility of America's entrance into the war loomed larger, Congress was stirred to action. Legislation in September, 1916, authorized the creation of a United States Shipping Board to promote and regulate the merchant marine, and a Council of National Defense to supervise and integrate the defense program. It was not until October 11, 1916, barely six months before the declaration of war, that this Council, consisting of the Secretaries of War, Navy, Interior, Agriculture, Commerce, and Labor, was organized. At the same time an Advisory Commission of seven experts was set up to cover the fields of munitions and manufacturing, transportation, engineering and education, medicine and surgery, raw materials, supplies, and labor.[17] From this Council and its Advisory Commission eventually evolved numerous subordinate committees or boards to deal with almost every important phase of problems affecting the war. The enormity of the pioneering work which the Council and the Advisory Commission had to do can be seen from the fact that as late as six weeks before war was declared the Army had no plans for the organization or equipment of a large force.

Of all the subdivisions created by the Council of National Defense, the most important was undoubtedly the War Industries Board. Its duties were wide, for it was to "act as a clearing-house for the war industry needs of the Government, and determine the most effective way of meeting them, and the best means and methods of increasing production. . . ."[18] So important was the work done by this Board that the President in the spring of 1918 re-

[17] The first director of the Council was Walter S. Gifford, later president of the American Telephone and Telegraph Company. The first members of the Advisory Commission were Howard V. Coffin, a Detroit industrialist; Daniel Willard, president of the Baltimore and Ohio; Julius Rosenwald, president of Sears, Roebuck & Co.; Dr. Hollis Godfrey, a scientist; Samuel Gompers, president of the A. F. of L.; Dr. Franklin Martin of the American College of Surgeons, and Bernard M. Baruch.

[18] G. B. Clarkson, *Industrial America and the World War*, p. 37.

organized it, gave it enlarged powers, put Bernard M. Baruch at its head, and made it an independent agency directly responsible to himself. Its work was grouped into functional divisions—conservation, priorities, price fixing, requirements, labor, and Allied purchasing. To aid these divisions the Board gradually organized fifty-seven sections of experts on particular industries who acted as a clearinghouse of information. Under powers conferred by Congress on the President and then delegated to this Board, it could determine priorities, virtually fix the prices of the commodities which it purchased, and, if necessary, commandeer manufacturing plants, the latter to be done through orders of the Army and Navy.

FOOD AND FUELS

As the stocks of foodstuffs and fuels declined in the warring nations, their production and conservation in the United States became a matter of extreme importance. The situation led Congress to pass two acts, in August, 1917—the Food Production Act and the Food and Fuel Control Act. The first gave the Department of Agriculture power to stimulate the production and conservation of food products on the farms. The second gave the administration power to control "foods, feeds, fuel including fuel oil and natural gas, and fertilizer and fertilizer ingredients, tools, utensils, implements, machinery, and equipment required for the actual production of foods, feeds, and fuel." It forbade hoarding, willful destruction, and discrimination or unfair practices in sale and distribution, and gave the President power under certain conditions to purchase, store, and sell wheat and other commodities. Even before this act was passed Herbert Hoover was called back from the administration of relief for Belgium to tackle the food problem. He later headed the National Food Administration, set up to enforce the agricultural provisions of the act.

Unlike the War Industries Board, the National Food Administration had many specific powers granted to it by legislative act. Hoover himself preferred voluntary co-operation, but it became necessary, as the war continued, to impose restrictions and use the power granted by Congress. By licensing the manufacture, storage, and distribution of food products, effectual regulations limiting the use of sugar, wheat, meat, butter, and other foods were imposed. The people as a whole were stimulated to self-denial and to the use of substitutes, and meatless and wheatless days were imposed to further this self-denial. While the consumer was urged to curtail, every means was used to stimulate farmers to greater production.

Although the Food Administration had no legal authority to fix agricultural prices, it virtually did so, since its purchases for the Army and Navy, the Allies, Belgian relief, and the Red Cross comprised such a large proportion of the available supplies. It could and did guarantee minimum prices which it would pay and it put them sufficiently high to stimulate production. Some of its purchasing operations were carried on through subsidiary non-profit government corporations. A Food Administration Grain Cooperative, for example, was established to purchase wheat and flour for the United States and her Allies and to maintain the guaranteed price. In similar manner a Sugar Equalization Board was established to buy raw sugar from producers at an agreed price and to supply refineries under arrangements to fix profits and stabilize prices.

The most acute shortage that developed during the war, both for civilian needs and for war industries, was in coal. Under the Fuel Administration, headed by Harry A. Garfield, almost every known means was used to overcome the difficulty. The problem was threefold—production, distribution, and rationing. To stimulate production, operators and miners were urged to eliminate waste and to introduce more efficient methods. The problem of distribution was met in part by introducing a zoning system which served consumers from the nearest mine and eliminated crosshauls. To make the coal go as far as possible, unnecessary illumination and heating were curtailed and in April, 1918, a system of general rationing for domestic users was established. Control over the distribution of fuel oil was instituted in January of that year and was later extended to natural gas and gasoline.

WARTIME CONTROL OF TRANSPORTATION

Preliminary efforts to enlarge the American merchant marine before we entered the war have already been noted. After our entrance the functions of the United States Shipping Board were enlarged to include supervision of the vast shipbuilding program, control of vessels under the jurisdiction of the government, and the training of men for service in the merchant marine. When the United States declared war, Germany was sinking shipping faster than it could be built. Our problem was to reverse this situation and to keep supplies moving on the high seas. In April, 1917, the Shipping Board organized a subsidiary, the Emergency Fleet Corporation, with a capital of $50,-000,000, to undertake the construction of merchant ships. In May Congress authorized the President to take over 600,000 tons of German shipping interned in American ports. In August the government commandeered all steel vessels in process of construction; this added 3,000,000 dead-weight tons. Finally, it took over all American ships of 2500 tons or over, fit for use, but allowed their owners to operate them.

The Emergency Fleet Corporation started with virtually unlimited funds from Congress. Its objective was to build a "bridge of ships" across the Atlantic and its method was mass production from prefabricated parts and materials manufactured according to standardized designs. It expanded old shipyards already working to capacity and built new ones. The largest of these, Hog Island at Philadelphia, had a capacity greater than that of Great Britain in any prewar year. The 61 shipyards of 1917 and their 235 ways had increased by November, 1918, to 341 shipyards and 1284 launching ways, and the number of workmen from 45,000 to 380,000. During the nineteen months of the war 875 vessels were built, totaling over 2,941,000 tons, and by September 1, 1918, the Shipping Board had control of 8,693,579 tons of shipping. American tonnage engaged in foreign trade had increased from 2,185,000 in 1916 to 11,077,000 in 1921.

Government regulation of the railroads has been the accepted policy since 1887, but it was only during the war that the experiment of government operation was tried. The inability of the railroads to cope successfully with the exigencies of war needs, and the absolute necessity of subordinating transportation facilities to the one purpose of winning the war, brought about this step. The position of the roads at the opening of the European conflict was far from strong. For fifteen years the cost of railroad operation in maintenance, materials, and labor had been increasing. On the other hand, attempts to gain higher rates had been unsuccessful until 1914. In 1910 certain of the roads petitioned for a 10 per cent advance in freight rates, but this was refused by the Interstate Commerce Commission, which based its decision on the prosperous year of 1910. Further efforts in 1913 and 1914 were successful, in that the Commission eventually permitted substantial increases, but these came too late to be of much immediate value. The year 1914 was disastrous to the railroads, and 1915 found one-sixth (42,000 miles) of the railroad system of the United States in the hands of receivers. The war brought temporary prosperity with the enormous stimulation of the freight business in 1915 and 1916. But the rising cost of materials and the greater expenditures for wages, necessitated partly by the Adamson Eight-Hour Act of 1916,[19] absorbed much of the profits. The railroads for some time had been buying insufficient equipment and their rolling stock could not meet the pressure of war needs. It was in this predicament that the roads found themselves when the United States entered the war.

As a whole, the railroads did their best to rise to the occasion. Daniel Willard, president of the Baltimore and Ohio and transportation expert to the Advisory Commission of the Council of National Defense, organized a Special Committee of National Defense which elected an executive committee of five, known as the Railroads' War Board. This Board opened offices in Washington and made every effort to co-operate with the government. As the months went on, however, there were increasing complications

[19] Above, p. 466.

due to special Army needs, to the orders of the Priorities Boards, to lack of equipment, to the inability to force all the roads to follow the orders of the Committee, to the impossibility of obtaining joint action among the competing roads, and to labor difficulties brought about by demands for higher wages and the departure of railroad men to join the Army. Above all was the general inefficiency of the whole railroad system. All pointed to the breakdown of private control and the need for government operation. The Esch bill of May, 1917, gave the Interstate Commerce Commission power to regulate freight cars, and finally on December 26, 1917, upon the advice of the Interstate Commerce Commission and after a thorough investigation of the situation, President Wilson issued a proclamation providing for government operation two days later.

The President's proclamation was followed on March 21, 1918, by a Railroad Control Act which provided (1) that each road taken over should receive an annual payment not to exceed its average net operating income for the three years ending June 30, 1917; (2) that a revolving fund of $500,000,000 should be created to finance the operation; (3) that the roads should be returned to their owners within one year and nine months following the ratification of the treaty of peace; (4) that each road should be returned "in substantially as good repair and in substantially as complete equipment as it was at the beginning of government control"; and (5) that the Interstate Commerce Commission should be deprived of its power to suspend rates, but that it should retain most of its other powers.

The Pullman and express companies were also taken over, but not all of the short lines. William G. McAdoo, Secretary of the Treasury, was made Director General of the Railroads.[20] Eventually the whole transportation system was handled through eight administrative divisions at Washington, and for operating purposes the country was divided into seven regional organizations. Over each district was a regional director and over each road a federal manager, the latter in some cases a former railroad president. To the history of transportation control should be added the fact that in July, 1918, the government took over control of the telegraph and telephone systems and placed them under the direction of the Postmaster General; in November it assumed control of marine cables. Radio systems had been taken over at the beginning of the war and placed under the control of the Navy.

In dealing with labor the government found it necessary to take cognizance of the fact that railroad wages were not as high as those in other lines of work. In the absence of legislation to require railroad men to stay on the job, the only other course was to increase wages, which was done on the recommendation of a nonpartisan board of adjustment. Increased rates were neces-

[20] Succeeded by Walter D. Hines, a prominent railroad executive.

sary, and on May 25, 1918, all classes of freight were raised 25 per cent, and passenger fares to three cents a mile.

The gains to the efficient prosecution of the war from government operation were many. Joint use of terminals, equipment, and repair shops; relief of congestion by arbitrary routing; better control of traffic at the source; more efficient handling of troops and war supplies; the elimination of duplicate passenger service; and the standardization of equipment in purchasing—all these aided in carrying on the war. Co-ordinated under a single unit and operated in the public interest, the railroads succeeded in doing a difficult job which they had failed to accomplish as separate and competing properties.[21]

The term "government operation" is hardly accurate. The government exercised some direction, control, and pressure, but in most cases the same executives as before operated the railroads. After the war there was widespread railroad propaganda that "government operation" had been costly and inefficient and that property had not been adequately maintained. It insisted that the excess of operating costs over revenues for the twenty-six months of government control was about $900,000,000. How much of this excess was the result of mounting costs and the previous run-down condition of many railroads which had to be rectified will never be known. That the government erred in not increasing rates and fares fast enough is generaly conceded. However, it made little difference whether the nation paid for its war transportation by increasing rates and fares or by subsidies. In any event, the railroads were given extra compensation after the war and rates and fares were again increased. As to inadequate maintenance, Director General Hines subsequently wrote, "The notion of a broken-down condition of the railroads' properties at the end of Federal control never had any foundation and has been clearly disproved by subsequent events and analyses."[22]

LABOR DURING WARTIME

The greatest immediate effect of the First World War upon labor was to create a shortage which was felt even before our participation. The normal flow of immigration declined from an annual average of about 662,100 during the three years 1912–1914 to about 257,887 for 1915–1918. At the same time thousands of those engaged in industry were called home to serve in the European armies or joined the military forces here. The supply of labor was consequently falling off just at the time when there was an abnormal expansion in industry. After this country entered the war the shortage was of course accentuated by the addition of over 4,000,000 men to our armed forces. This gap in the ranks of labor was partly filled by women—at least 1,000,000

[21] George Soule, *Prosperity Decade*, p. 36.
[22] Walter D. Hines, *War History of American Railroads*, p. 120.

entered industry during the war—but the shortage persisted. The government's chief method of meeting this problem was to expand the activities of the Employment Service of the Department of Labor. This organization, co-operating with state and local agencies, was able to some extent to co-ordinate the task of directing needed workers to defense jobs and decreasing labor turnover. The President in June, 1918, requested all employers engaged in war work to secure their workers through the Employment Service, and in that year it placed over 10,000 workers a day.

As a natural consequence of this shortage the position of labor was at least temporarily strengthened. Dollar wages moved upward rapidly. Great gains were made in securing the eight-hour day, in part because of a law passed in 1912 making the eight-hour day mandatory for those engaged in government contracts. Although the policy of the government labor boards with reference

Year	Wages per Hour	Cost of Living	Real Wages
1913	100	100.0	100.0
1916	111	118.3	93.8
1917	128	142.4	89.9
1918	162	174.4	92.9
1919	184	188.3	97.7
1920	234	208.5	112.2

to unions was to recognize the *status quo,* in actual practice it tended to favor them. Mediation boards found it much easier to supervise collective bargaining where unions existed. Average union membership increased from 2,772,700 in 1916 to 4,125,200 in 1919.

While wages advanced rapidly until the early months of 1920, the gain was more apparent than real, for prices rose even more quickly so that real wages per hour or per piece tended to fall. It is doubtful if in the long run real wages were appreciably bettered by the war, but the fact that some workers were able to buy luxuries for perhaps the first time gave rise to the myth of the "silk-shirted worker." The aggregate earnings of labor, however, undoubtedly increased, but only because of the larger volume of employment which the war made possible. It must be remembered that whatever efforts were made in the First World War to control prices were concerned with government purchases from producers and processors. They did not reach the level of civilian consumers. The accompanying index numbers, compiled by the Department of Labor, give a general picture of the relations between wages and the cost of living during the war years.[23]

[23] *Statistical Abstract, 1931,* p. 347. The figures on wages do not include agricultural labor. Other students have slightly modified these statistics, but in general they represent what happened. Beginning in 1920, it will be noticed, real wages increased and this trend continued throughout the decade.

Led by Gompers and the Executive Committee, which declared that "this is labor's war," the American Federation of Labor threw itself wholeheartedly into the war, removing restrictions and suspending regulations inimical to efficiency, but demanding that the standard of living be not lowered. Gompers was placed upon the Advisory Committee of National Defense, and labor leaders were appointed to most of the war boards organized by the government. Early in the war Gompers, as chairman of the Committee on Labor of the Council of National Defense, called a conference of representatives of both employers and labor at which both sides agreed not to take advantage of the emergency to press their demands in a way which would hinder the prosecution of the war. It was an informal truce for the duration of the conflict, but, surprisingly enough, it worked fairly well. It did not, of course, end labor disputes or even prevent strikes. According to the Department of Labor, 6000 strikes occurred during the nineteen months of the war but most were brief and voluntarily ended by labor.[24]

Early in 1918, in an effort to consolidate the labor policies and the mediation work of the numerous labor boards and committees, the President appointed Secretary of Labor Wilson as Labor Administrator, and under him a War Labor Board and a War Labor Policies Board were established. The latter was to determine the general policies of the government toward hours, wages, and working conditions, and, as far as possible, the relations between capital and labor. The War Labor Board was a judicial body to which disputes between employers and employees could be submitted. Some 1500 disputes were adjudicated by this Board; in a number of cases it prescribed the creation of shop committees and other means by which further controversies might be adjusted. Besides these boards, special commissions were set up for certain industries, and different branches of the War Department had Industrial Service Sections to handle labor problems. Matters of wage adjustment on the railroads were handled, after government control was inaugurated, by a Railroad Wage Commission appointed by the railroad administration. By means of this machinery, by wage increases, and by the loyalty of both leaders and rank and file, labor disturbances were greatly reduced during the war.

Labor's contribution to the winning of the war resulted in the recognition in the peace treaty of certain specific rights for which it had long contended and the provision for a permanent organization to promote the international improvement of labor conditions. In accordance with the treaty, an international labor conference was held in Washington in 1919 which drew up a program to be recommended to the League of Nations. One result was the establishment of the International Labor Organization.

[24] The best brief summary of labor in the First World War is George Soule, *op. cit.*, chap. 3.

In spite of this international recognition, the effect of the war on American labor was detrimental rather than favorable. Gains were made, to be sure, in recognition of the eight-hour day, but real wages were lower in 1919 than in 1913.[25] Some of the most important losses, however, had little to do with wages or working conditions. The weakening of the Socialist party, which by 1912 had grown to sizable proportions, and the disintegration of the I.W.W. and other left-wing elements so necessary to the development of an aggressive labor movement were a misfortune. The growth of intolerance and the decline of personal liberty in the war and postwar years hurt labor more than other classes. There was also a relative economic decline for labor as industrialists and financiers reaped the financial profits of the war.

FINANCING THE FIRST WORLD WAR

After the United States entered the First World War, she assumed the responsibility of financing not only her own participation but the expenses of her Allies as well. The First Liberty Loan Act of April, 1917, authorized the Secretary of the Treasury, on the approval of the President, to make loans to Allied governments up to $10,000,000,000. After that private loans ceased. The problem of whether the war should be paid for immediately out of current taxes or shifted to later years by loans was resolved as usual by compromise. About one-third of the direct cost of the war was met by current taxation, and about two-thirds by loans.

The expenses of the federal government had not greatly increased in the years before the war. The normal net expenses in 1916 ($674,230,020) were less than $35,000,000 in excess of those of 1910. But succeeding years saw a tremendous increase; within two years after the end of the war the federal government's interest charge alone had become greater than the entire cost of running the government before the war. The total direct cost of the war to the United States, including the nine and a half billions lent to the Allies, was about $35,500,000,000, an amount three times the total expenditures of the federal government during the first hundred years of its existence and more than $2,000,000 an hour for the duration of the war. The national debt, which amounted to only $1,000,000,000 before the war, jumped to the unprecedented total of $26,596,701,648 by the end of August, 1919.

To obtain these vast amounts spent at home and lent to the Allies, the government relied chiefly upon loans. Five bond issues were subscribed to by the people, in units of as low as $50 and with interest rates varying from 3½ to 4¼ per cent. The first four issues were known as Liberty Loans; the fifth,

---

[25] Bulletins of the U.S. Bureau of Labor Statistics No. 274, *Union Scale of Wages and Hours of Labor, May 15, 1919,* pp. 47–50, and No. 270, *Retail Prices 1913 to December 1919,* pp. 50–58.

floated after the armistice, was called the Victory Liberty Loan. In the five loans the government asked for $18,500,000,000, received subscriptions for $25,000,000,000, and allotted $21,400,000,000.[26] At the height of war enthusiasm almost $7,000,000,000 was subscribed in a single loan by over 22,000,000 people. Of these war bonds, it is estimated that about $7,000,000,000, or 30 per

AGGREGATE EXPENDITURES AND FOREIGN LOANS OF THE UNITED STATES GOVERNMENT, FISCAL YEARS 1917–1920

Year	Normal Net Expense	Net War Cost (Excess Above Estimated Normal Expenses)	
		Excess Army and Navy	Excess Interest Pensions, Etc.
1917	$ 659,860,650	$ 393,852,949	$ 2,690,164
1918	682,458,285	6,770,295,897	120,952,611
1919	691,858,252	10,917,817,469	379,367,891
1920	826,550,410	1,073,892,747	1,073,392,874
	$2,860,727,597	$19,155,859,062	$1,576,403,540

Year	Net War Cost (Excess Above Estimated Normal Expenses)		Loans to European Governments (Less Repayments)
	Special War Activities	Total War Cost	
1917	$ 33,060,510	$ 429,603,623	$ 885,000,000
1918	1,094,994,128	7,986,242,636	4,739,434,750
1919	2,487,710,885	13,784,896,245	3,470,280,265
1920	1,634,695,094	3,781,980,715	350,291,840
	$5,250,460,617	$25,982,723,219	$9,445,006,855

From Table 3, p. 21, of E. B. Rosa, "Expenditures and Revenues of the Federal Government," *Annals of the American Academy of Political and Social Science*, Vol. XCV, No. 184 (May, 1921).

cent, went to individuals with incomes of $2000 or less, about $10,000,000,000 to individuals with incomes of $2000 or more, and the remainder to corporations including banks.[27] In addition to the Victory and Liberty Loans, war saving certificates of five dollars and war saving stamps of 25 cents were sold to a total of $1,000,000,000. The grand total of the loans floated in these two ways was close to $22,500,000,000.

Not alone was large-scale borrowing resorted to, but also new and heavier taxes were imposed. Contrary to the method pursued during the Civil War, the Democratic Congress, which had reduced the tariff in 1913, refused to consider import duties as an important source of revenue, and scarcely 5 per

[26] *Report of the Secretary of the Treasury, 1920*, pp. 419, 439.
[27] J. M. Clark, *The Cost of the World War to the American People*, p. 137.

cent of the taxes for the war year of 1918 was derived from this source. On the other hand, a comprehensive scheme of taxation was inaugurated. The income tax levied by virtue of the sixteenth amendment in 1913 and raised in 1916 was further increased in 1917. Personal exemptions were reduced to $2000 and $1000 in the case of married and unmarried persons, and the rate was graduated from 6 per cent on the first $4000 above exemption to 63 per cent on incomes of over a million. In addition, there were inaugurated (1) a war excess profits tax on the incomes of corporations, partnerships, and individuals ranging from 15 to 60 per cent, depending on the amount of capital invested in the business; (2) additional taxes upon liquors, beverages, and tobacco; (3) taxes on luxuries and amusements; (4) war taxes on facilities furnished by public utilities; (5) war taxes on instruments and documents of various kinds; and (6) an increase in estate taxes. The effect of these additions to taxation is shown by a comparison of the amounts raised by taxation immediately preceding and during the war, which were as follows: for the fiscal year ending June 30, 1914, $735,000,000; 1915, $692,000,000; 1916, $779,-000,000; 1917, $1,118,000,000; 1918, $4,174,000,000; 1919, $4,648,000,000. The largest single source was the excess profits tax; that and the income tax yielded about two-thirds of the revenue.

With reference to the monetary statistics of wartime, it should again be emphasized that they must be interpreted with reference to the inflation of those years. As already pointed out, there was virtually no suspension of specie payments in the United States, but there was great inflation. This was caused in the first place by the enormous amount of gold which was sent here to finance the purchase of war materials, and which eventually brought to this country almost half of the world's monetary supply of that metal. In the second place, the liberal policies of the Federal Reserve System in extending credit during the war and in assisting through loans in the flotation of Liberty bonds tended toward inflation, as did the vast issue of government bonds which could be used as a reserve against bank note issue. Besides these factors, there was, as in all wars, a rise in commodity prices because of increased demand. Inflation, indeed, was as great as during the Civil War, but it differed in being caused by a plethora of gold and the enormous extension of credit rather than suspension of specie payments and the printing of fiat money.

CONCLUSION

The emphasis in this chapter has been largely placed on the economic policies pursued by the federal government during the First World War. The experience of this war should have influenced, and to some extent did influence, the conduct of the United States in the Second World War. The maze of boards, commissions, and committees set up to integrate the economic efforts of the Second World War may seem superficially to be quite different from those of the earlier struggle, but fundamentally they were engaged in the same effort and in much the same way. On the economic front Wilson's administration achieved its greatest success in industrial expansion and experienced its greatest failure in preventing price and wage inflation. It also failed to develop any policy for reconstruction. Controls over the economic life, which the government had learned to use during the First World War, were more widely extended in the second conflict. Plans for postwar reconstruction, on the other hand, were almost as inadequate in the 1940's as in the 1920's and the policies quite as inept.

America's participation in the First World War was relatively brief, but it was long enough to exert important economic effects. Despite all efforts to "return to normalcy" America could never quite go back to the economic conditions of the prewar days. The industrial expansion of the war years left her with a productive capacity in certain fields far beyond her normal needs. This was particularly true in textiles, leather manufacturing, shipbuilding, and coal mining. The postwar deflation combined with competition from other commodities left these industries in a permanently weak condition. The rapid expansion of the merchant marine left the nation with a fleet of ocean carriers far beyond any possible need. A similar expansion of agricultural production left farmers, after the inevitable collapse, in a worse condition than after the Civil War. Government control and operation of transportation facilities presented the problem of continued operation or return to private owners. In the end the properties were returned, but control was increased. Deflation of wages after the war brought labor struggles of greater proportions than the nation had yet seen. These and other effects will be discussed in the next chapter.

SELECTED READINGS

Soule, George, *Prosperity Decade,* chaps. 1–3.
Faulkner, H. U., *The Decline of Laissez Faire.*
Slosson, P. W., *The Great Crusade and After,* chaps. 1, 2.
Noyes, A. D., *The War Period of American Finance,* chaps. 2–5.
Dixon, F. H., *Railroads and Government,* chaps. 8–14.
Clarkson, G. B., *Industrial America in the World War,* chaps. 12–30.
Lorwin, L. L., *The American Federation of Labor,* chap. 6.
Genung, A. B., "Agriculture in the World War Period," *Yearbook of Agriculture, 1940,* pp. 277–296.

PART V

A NEW SOCIETY

CHAPTER 28

THE GREAT ILLUSION

DEMOBILIZATION

Depression

To describe what happened after the First World War as "reconstruction" would be a travesty on the term. Except for some decisions later made necessary in dealing with railroads and the merchant marine, neither the administration nor Congress gave much thought to postwar planning.[1] Few plans had been formulated to aid the 4,000,000 veterans in search of jobs, to demobilize wartime industry, or to preserve some of the gains of wartime regulation of business. The one fundamental desire was to liquidate the war as quickly as possible and return to prewar policies—or to "normalcy," as Harding called it in the campaign of 1920. Within a month after the armistice half of the uncompleted war contracts were canceled and by the end of the year many of the government control boards had ceased to function. The War Industries Board began removing price controls two days after the armistice.

Despite lack of planning and a military and economic demobilization so rapid as to seem chaotic, the nation not only survived the immediate strain but experienced a continuation of the war prosperity. This is largely explained by the fact that the Treasury continued to spend during 1919 more than it received from the current income of the nation. This money went in loans to the Allies, largely spent in America, in shipbuilding and other industries not yet demobilized, in settlement of business contracts, and in current military expenditures and dismissal pay to soldiers. Although there was unemployment as a result of military demobilization and industrial reconversion, the latter was carried through with unusual speed and the income of

[1] When Wilson was invited late in 1918 to address a Reconstruction Congress of American Industries he could only reply, "You may be sure that I would send a message to the meeting at Atlantic City if I knew what message to send, but frankly I do not. It is a time when we must all thankfully take counsel and apply the wisest action to circumstances as they arise." Quoted by P. A. Samuelson and E. E. Hagen, *After the War—1918–1920*, p. 6, a pamphlet written for the National Resources Planning Board, 1943.

the nation was not affected radically enough to curtail purchasing power. Moreover, two important industries, held back by the war, responded quickly to the coming of peace—the manufacure of automobiles and building construction. With all this went a too generous expansion of bank loans to private individuals, not a little of which went into stock market speculation.

This unusual postwar business activity lasted from late 1918 to the midsummer of 1921. It ended in an acute but fortunately brief depression. The reasons for the crash seem reasonably clear. First was the decline in government spending and the cessation of loans to the Allies. Combined with this was the European situation where the warring nations, impoverished by the struggle, staggering under crushing debts and with exchange rates against them, no longer had either the funds or the credit to make extensive purchases abroad. This, of course, cut the market for American manufacturers and, as we shall see, brought disaster to American farmers. Exports and imports, which reached unheard-of figures in 1919 and 1920, declined radically in 1921.

Moreover, by 1920 the postwar boom had attained unhealthy proportions. Credit expansion had reached the legal limit and the banks were forced to retreat. Prices continued to mount after the war until the inflation began to push those on fixed incomes out of the market. The income of many wage earners, however, had kept pace with the inflation and the total expenditure for consumers' goods held up. Some resistance, nevertheless, was evident. Manufacturers suddenly became convinced that they had produced more than could be sold; wholesalers and retailers looked suspiciously at their inventories and began to cancel orders.

With these adverse factors at work, the business cycle rapidly pursued its downward swing. Cancellation of orders or failure to book new ones reduced output and closed mills, causing reduced wages and unemployment. The depression, which had first appeared in the production of luxuries, especially the silk industry and certain phases of the rubber and automobile industry, soon became general. In only a few industries did business continue normal. Upon no group did the depression fall more heavily than upon the farmers. Encouraged by the war prices and the demand for foodstuffs, many had borrowed heavily to purchase land and equipment in order to increase production, only to be caught in a glutted market in which values were declining to a point below the cost of production. Wheat, which had sold for $2.15 a bushel in December, 1919, dropped to $1.44 in December, 1920; corn from $1.35 to $.68; oats from $.72 to $.47; and cotton from $.36 a pound to $.14.

Labor, which had become accustomed to a higher standard of living, was loath to return to previous wage scales and, where strongly organized, succeeded in maintaining most of what was gained during the war period. Nevertheless, the number of those actively employed declined almost one-third during the depression,[2] and the average hourly wage as reported by the National Industrial Conference Board was as follows: July, 1914, 24.3 cents; peak, 1920, 62.1; December, 1921, 48.2. Capital as a whole probably suffered less than any other group, although, as in previous panics, the small businessman was hit hard. Mercantile and industrial insolvencies, which numbered 6451 in 1919, had more than tripled in 1921. Although bank failures reached 383 in 1921, with liabilities of almost $168,000,000, they were mainly rural banks with small capitalization and did not fundamentally endanger the general banking structure. The deflation, although severe, did not reach the proportions of a panic.

The natural effect of this industrial collapse upon prices was to force them downward. The decline included most commodities, being especially noticeable in foodstuffs and clothing and least apparent in fuel and rent. The partial cessation of normal building during the war, which caused a shortage of living accommodations, and the high cost of building materials explain to some extent the failure of rents to decline. The explanation of the continued high cost of fuel is not so easy, but it was caused among other reasons by increased cost of labor and transportation, by monopoly conditions, and by the continued high profits taken by capital. According to the United States Department of Labor, the average index number of wholesale prices of typical commodities (1913 = 100) was 272 in May, 1920; 148 in June, 1921; 150 in June, 1922; 153 in June, 1923. With all the misery which the postwar depression undoubtedly caused, it had one fortunate effect. It pricked the bubble of inflation and substantially reduced prices. From 1922 to 1929 both retail food prices and the general cost of living remained relatively stationary.

By the end of 1922 deflation had run its course and industry had adjusted itself to a peace basis. Most of the principal industries were again working at close to capacity, the railroads reported record business, and unemployment had largely disappeared. Certain industries, particularly agriculture, failed to respond to the renewed prosperity, and the agricultural unrest remained a significant political and economic factor. That and the unsettled conditions abroad remained in 1923 the chief adverse factors in what appeared to be the opening of a period of greater business activity and more normal conditions.

THE EXPANSIVE TWENTIES

In retrospect the postwar depression seems a perfectly normal effect of the artificial expansion of the war years. More difficult is the problem of explain-

[2] W. I. King (*Employment Hours and Earnings in Prosperity and Depression*, pp. 29–31) believes that there were 4,000,000 unemployed in 1921. W. A. Berridge (*Business Cycles and Unemployment*, p. 59) believes that the unemployment situation in that year was almost twice as acute as in 1908 and at least twice as acute as in 1914–1915.

ing the brevity of the depression and the intense business activity of the 1920's, a period in which the rest of the world was still suffering from the economic postwar recession. Although there was much that was artificial about the economic life of the 1920's, the fact remains that during the six years from 1923 until the stock market crash in the autumn of 1929 large groups of people and certain sections of the country enjoyed an era of prosperity approaching that of wartime. A glance at the accompanying table will show that industrial production almost doubled during the decade and that both the national income and the real income per capita substantially increased.

ECONOMIC GROWTH, 1921–1929

Year	Industrial Production 1933–39 = 100	Wholesale Prices 1926 = 100	National Income (Billions)	Real Income per Capita (1929 Prices)
1921	58	97.6	$59.4	$522
1922	73	96.7	60.7	553
1923	88	100.6	71.6	634
1924	82	98.1	72.1	633
1925	90	103.5	76.0	644
1926	96	100.0	81.6	678
1927	95	95.4	80.1	674
1928	99	96.7	81.7	676
1929	110	95.3	87.2	716

George Soule, *Prosperity Decade*, p. 108. The index figures for industrial production and wholesale prices are from the *Federal Reserve Bulletin* (October, 1945), p. 1049. Those for national income and real income are from Simon Kuznets, *National Income and Its Composition*, National Bureau of Economic Research, 1941, pp. 137, 153.

As for the brevity of the depression and the speed with which the nation pulled out of it, various explanations have been offered. Rapid liquidation of inventories induced manufacturers to resume production and retailers to place orders. Although the volume of consumer spending dropped from 62.9 billions in 1920 to 56.1 billions in 1921, prices dropped even more rapidly. Put in another way, wage rates dropped less than the cost of living. This situation helped to maintain purchasing power. At the same time manufacturers gained from the declining costs of raw materials, which seemed to assure them of profits on finished goods and encouraged them to continue production.

One of the most valid explanations offered for the intense economic activity and the prosperity of the remaining years of the 1920's was increased efficiency. Whereas population gained approximately 12 per cent, industrial production almost doubled; the productivity per worker increased by the same amount, and the national income at least twenty billions. Although the share of wage earners in the total national income increased only slightly, if at all, after 1920, real wages among certain groups showed a substantial advance. The decline in the birth rate, restriction of immigration, and increased application of science to business also helped to promote this efficiency. To many economists it is this last that furnishes the fundamental explanation. "Since 1921," wrote Wesley C. Mitchell, surveying the work of the Committee on Economic Changes, "Americans have applied intelligence to the day's work more effectively than ever before. . . . The whole process of putting science into industry has been followed more intensively than before; it has been supplemented by tentative efforts to put science into business management, trade-union policy and Government administration."[3] New machinery introduced during reconversion, development of mass production and scientific management (advocated earlier by Frederick Winslow Taylor), and rapid expansion of research explain the greater productivity of labor. It is an acceleration of earlier tendencies rather than structural change that provides the key to an understanding of the economic lift of the 1920's.

Although the industrial expansion in this decade was widespread, it rested fundamentally upon the manufacture of automobiles and electrical equipment and the boom in building construction. The first great expansion in automobile production came in the decade and a half from 1914 to 1929. It is estimated that nearly four million jobs were created directly or indirectly by the automobile, and that they probably supported three times that number, a good share of the 17,000,000 increase in population during the decade. Although an appreciable part of the income which went into automobiles was income which would normally have been expended for other commodities, thereby injuring other industries, the fact remains that enough new industry and wealth were created by the motorcar to speed up the whole economic machine. Of the many by-products of the automobile industry which created work and stimulated industry, the most important perhaps was better roads, in the construction of which close to $2,000,000,000 a year was expended even in the depression years of 1930 and 1931.

Next to the automobile, the most important industrial advance was in the manufacture of electric machinery and appliances. The penetration of these products was universal. Industry was turning to electric power and the housewife insisted on such appliances as electric irons, washing machines, vacuum cleaners, and refrigerators. The radio industry also had a phenomenal development in the 1920's, its product increasing in value from $10,648,000 in 1921 to $411,637,000 in 1929. It is little wonder that production of electric power more than doubled during the decade. The electrical industry produced ma-

[3] *Recent Economic Changes*, p. 862.

chinery not only for factories and homes but also for the production of electric power itself. The value of its products almost tripled—from $809,590,000 in 1921 to $2,334,246,000 in 1930.

Outside of the spectacular development of the automobile and electrical equipment industries, the most striking aspect of the prosperous years of the mid-twenties was the extraordinary building boom, one of the greatest in our history. Normal construction retarded during the war years had to be made good, high rents stimulated building, a rapid increase of surplus wealth made it possible, and modern improvements made even recent structures seem out of date. Building construction in 120 cities, which had reached the high point of $919,000,000 in 1916, dropped to $373,000,000 in 1918 and rose to $1,172,-000,000 in 1919, and finally to $3,399,000,000 in 1925, when the high point was reached.[4] Total building in that year amounted to somewhat over $6,000,000,-000. A good share of the building in cities (about one-third) was carried on in New York, where the sky line changed with amazing rapidity, and where the Empire State Building with its eighty-six stories towering 1248 feet into the sky was completed in 1931. In automobiles, new roads, new buildings, and electrical equipment was invested much of the wealth created in this country during the third decade.

The vast expenditures which made possible this boom era were undoubtedly stimulated by the development of "high-pressure" advertising and installment buying. Conservative estimates place the number of automobiles sold on installment in 1927 at around 60 per cent, but other estimates for various years are much higher.[5] Concerning installment buying, Seligman makes the conservative estimate of $4,875,000,000 as the total volume of retail installment sales for 1925.[6] These figures were to increase in subsequent years until 15 per cent of all goods were sold on the installment plan. By the end of the decade there was practically nothing, in the realm of either luxury or necessity, that could not be bought "on time."

Despite the fact that most people were mortgaging their future income through installment buying and spending a disproportionate share of their wages in the purchase and maintenance of automobiles, the fact remains that during the speculative period from 1914 to 1925 the number of savings accounts increased nearly fourfold, from 11,000,000 to 43,000,000 and their amount from $8,000,000,000 to $23,000,000,000. In addition to this it is notable that more than 25,500,000 ordinary life insurance policies and over 76,000,000 industrial policies were in force in the United States by the end of 1926, their total assets amounting to $12,500,000,000. The number of building and loan

---

[4] Given by Bradstreet for 120 identical cities. *New International Yearbook, 1930*, p. 118.

[5] E. R. A. Seligman, *The Economics of Installment Selling* (2 vols., 1927), I, 111, 117; II, 426; and *Recent Economic Changes*, I, 390 ff.

[6] *Ibid.*, I, 117.

policies increased from 3,103,935 to 8,554,352 in the ten years up to 1924, when over 11,000,000 families owned their own homes.

Not all economists were willing to grant unreservedly that this decade was a period of prosperity.[7] Prosperity, if such it was, was exceedingly uneven, for it did not include all sections or all groups. Furthermore, coal mining, cotton manufacturing, shipbuilding, the shoe and leather business, and particularly agriculture were stagnant, or declining. The Middle Atlantic, the East North Central, and the Pacific States seemed prosperous; but New England, which suffered from the textile depression, the South, the agricultural areas of the Middle West, and the Mountain sections, which suffered from the decline in agricultural prices, did not participate greatly in the economic boom. Even in the most prosperous of these years there was considerable unemployment, due in part to technological improvements. In Massachusetts, for example, the wage earners employed in manufacturing declined from the high of 757,-100 in January, 1920, to 509,700 in July, 1928. These were not the only sour notes in the paean of self-congratulatory praise. Some students were quick to point out that, notwithstanding the increase in profits, in wages, and in the consumption of consumers' goods, practically no progress was being made in solving the problems of unemployment or of economic and old-age security. Moreover, the mania for gambling and speculation was a warning signal to the experienced economic navigator. While trusting souls talked glibly of a "New Economic Era" from which panics and depressions were forever banished, and European observers came to America to study the causes of this prosperity, a few realists regarded dubiously the unsound structure being reared and looked forward with apprehension to its collapse.

REVIVAL OF BUSINESS CONSOLIDATION

In spite of state laws and federal enactments passed in the hope of maintaining free competition and protecting the consumer, the consolidation of American business continued with little interruption. The decade following the First World War, in fact, witnessed a significant revival in business consolidation, comparable to that in the years 1897–1904. An intensive study recorded a steadily increasing number of mergers in manufacturing and mining, from 89 in 1919 to 221 in 1928, with the number of merged or acquired concerns increasing correspondingly from 438 to 1038.[8] In actual mergers the iron, steel, and machinery group took the lead, accounting for about one-fifth of all those in mining and manufacturing; but there was hardly an industry which did not show a notable development along this line. Important mergers took place in the automobile industry, in the manufacture of food, in

---

[7] Stuart Chase, *Prosperity, Fact or Myth* (1930), gives both sides of the picture.
[8] Willard Thorpe, in *Recent Economic Changes*, I, 184.

the moving-picture industry, in banking, and most conspicuously, perhaps, in the field of public utilities. Over 3700 utility companies disappeared during 1919–1927, including many municipally operated concerns.[9]

While thousands of utility concerns were going out of existence, the larger ones which remained were being rapidly welded together into huge holding companies. "In 1915," asserts the Federal Trade Commission, "the 16 largest groups controlled about 22.8 per cent [generating capacity of the country], while in 1925 the 16 largest interests consisting of 11 holding-company groups and five independent operating interests, controlled approximately 53 per cent of the country's total."[10] From 1925 until the great depression this process of consolidation, chiefly through holding companies, went on rapidly. The speed with which the nation's electric power resources were consolidated brought the question of the effective control of this industry before the country as a problem of major importance, and the so-called "power trust" became a political issue after 1928.[11] Not only did the depression end the period of utility consolidation, but under the Public Utility Holding Company Act of 1935 many of the fantastic structures erected during the 1920's were broken up.

In previous decades the consolidation of industry was closely identified with the development of the corporate form of ownership. By 1929, however, this form was so typical of American business, both large and small, that the process of consolidation was indicated in the census by a new classification of establishments according to type of management, whether independent or one of a number of plants under unified central control. "The heightened industrial activity of the decade 1919 to 1929," said the census, "was not accompanied by any material alteration in the size of manufacturing establishments in general. The changes which occurred for the most part took other directions. Integration, for example, was accomplished not so much by the concentration of more wage earners in individual plants as by a common superstructure of ownership and control."[12]

The postwar movement toward business consolidation, as is obvious enough, differed also from consolidations of the past in several other aspects. Not only did it include new industries that had appeared since the last era

---

[9] *Ibid.*, p. 187.

[10] Federal Trade Commission, *Electric Power Industry: Supply of Electrical Equipment and Competitive Conditions,* 70th Cong., 1st Sess., Senate Doc. 46, p. 176. The figures of the Federal Trade Commission are based on 1924 production. The Federal Power Commission, reporting as late as 1936, asserted that 90 per cent of the electric generating capacity of the utility industry (book value $13,000,000,000) was controlled by fifty-seven companies. Of these, twelve controlled 49.7 per cent and one of them, the Electric Bond and Share group, controlled 11.5 per cent.

[11] Below, p. 670.

[12] *Census of Manufactures, 1929,* I, 61.

of consolidation, but it also embraced a much larger field than it did prior to 1917. It extended for example, into the automobile industry, into the production of package foods, and into the realm of banking. There was likewise a rapid development of consolidation in retailing as well as in production. The growth of chain stores was particularly notable in the drug, tobacco, and grocery fields, and the small merchant came to feel the same competition from the large corporations that the small manufacturer had faced for decades.[13] The Great Atlantic & Pacific Tea Company, for example, which had 5000 stores in 1922, had 17,500 by 1928, with an annual business of $750,-000,000.

Space forbids a detailed treatment of consolidation in the various fields in which it operated, but special mention should be made of banking, where this trend was particularly evident. In 1921 the number of banks in the nation reached a peak of 30,812. Although the country's wealth and resources increased greatly, the number of banks ten years later had dropped to about 22,000. Of those that no longer existed, some had failed and others had merged with neighboring institutions. The trend toward consolidation was particularly evident in the large cities. The lead was taken during 1928–1930 by the three titans in New York, when the National City Bank joined with the Farmers' Loan and Trust Company, the Guarantee Trust Company with the Bank of Commerce, and the Chase National Bank with the Equitable Trust Company, making the Chase the largest bank at that time in the world. While large-scale mergers occurred among city banks, concentration of resources also took place through the development of chain banking. In California, where chain banking reached its greatest development, a huge holding company, the Transamerica Comporation, controlled the Bank of America of California and other large banks, which in turn had 500 chain banks spreading across the state. When the Pujo Committee insisted in 1919 that a "money trust" existed, financial consolidation was actually in its infancy.[14]

What is the explanation for this extraordinary revival of consolidation during the 1920's? In the first place, the rather widespread industrial prosperity from 1923 to 1929 stimulated the movement. In spite of the fact that many mergers take place to soften bitter competition and precarious prices, it is in times of prosperity that consolidations are more common.[15] The spirit of confidence and the ease of floating security issues may in part explain this. In the second place, the artificial expansion of the war days left American

[13] F. Flügel and H. U. Faulkner, *Readings in the Economic and Social History of the United States,* pp. 600–607.

[14] Above, pp. 447–448.

[15] Willard Thorpe, in *Recent Economic Changes,* I, 183–184.

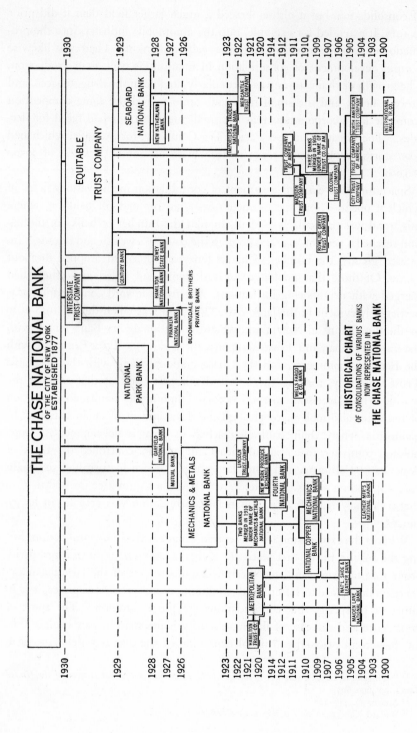

THE CHASE NATIONAL BANK
OF THE CITY OF NEW YORK
ESTABLISHED 1877

HISTORICAL CHART
of CONSOLIDATIONS OF VARIOUS BANKS
NOW REPRESENTED IN
THE CHASE NATIONAL BANK

industry in an overbuilt and overexpanded condition, and salvation was sought by this method. In the third place, the changing attitude of the nation should be noted. The distrust of business consolidation which had been so evident up to 1910 appears to have been considerably lessened by the third decade of the century for a number of reasons: an appreciation of the inevitability of consolidation in a capitalist system, the futility of antitrust legislation to prevent it, the rising standard of living which has made the masses less keen to scent evils in the movement, and finally, the incessant propaganda of big business interests.

It must also be evident that the postwar movement toward concentration of control was greatly stimulated by the holding company, by the old methods of interlocking stockholding and directorates, and by the more recent devices of voting trusts and nonvoting stock. Human ingenuity appears to have been strained to the limit to circumvent the antimonopoly laws, to prevent popular control of great corporations, and to camouflage real earnings. The result, as Laidler suggests, "has led to the development of combinations and trusts—vertical, horizontal and circular—with vaster ramifications, with greater resources than any combinations that have hitherto appeared."[16] Business consolidation naturally involves consolidation of capital. By 1930 the 200 largest corporations controlled nearly half of all non-banking corporate wealth (probably 38 per cent of all business wealth), received 43.2 per cent of the income of all non-banking corporations, and were controlled by approximately 2000 individuals.[17]

The changing attitude toward consolidation was, of course, reflected in the attitude and activities of the federal government, which were essentially conservative during the twenties. In the first place, rather wide exemptions were made in the operation of the antitrust laws.[18] In the second place, the personnel of the Federal Trade Commission became more conservative, its rules of procedure were modified, and its work was rendered less effective. This situation was due in part to President Coolidge's very definite effort to pack the Commission with members little interested in enforcing the law. Finally, the decisions of the Supreme Court have been of such a nature as to make public regulation of business increasingly difficult.

[16] H. W. Laidler, *Concentration of Control in American Industry*, p. 11. He defines a "circular merger" (p. 444) as a "merger of companies producing allied or complementary articles, usually, but not always, composed of those commodities which sell through the same channels or to the same market."

[17] A. A. Berle, Jr., and G. C. Means, *The Modern Corporation and Private Property*, pp. 28 ff.

[18] G. A. Fernby, "Special Privilege Under Our Federal Anti-Trust Laws," *Annals of the American Academy*, CXLVII, 38 (Jan., 1930), has noted twelve exempted groups: labor, farmers, planters, ranchmen, dairymen, nut and fruit growers, railroads, national banks, American steamship lines, those engaged in export business, producers of industrial alcohol, Philippine exporters. It should be noted, however, that the exemption extended to labor by the Clayton Act has been weakened by Supreme Court decisions.

Figuratively speaking, the lid was taken off in 1920 when, in the case against the United States Steel Company,[19] the Court refused to dissolve that corporation, holding that neither mere size, short of actual monopoly, nor the possession of potential power to restrain trade was necessarily a violation of the Sherman Act. This decision was made despite common knowledge that United States Steel had virtually dictated prices in the industry for fifteen years. The earlier hope that regulation might be achieved by extending the principle of public interest over a larger number of activities was scotched when in three decision in two years the Court held that gasoline dealers in Tennessee, employment agencies in New Jersey, and ticket brokers in New York did not fall into the category of "public interest" enterprises.[20] The Court also badly weakened effective regulation of public utilities, long recognized as vitally affecting the public interest, in a number of ways, but particularly by introducing into valuation cases the theory of "reproduction costs."[21] From a relatively simple and just method of determining rates, the Court made the problem extremely difficult and complex, with the consumer always at a disadvantage. The Court also appears to have put its stamp of approval upon trade associations, although the activities of such associations often seem in contravention of the antitrust laws.[22] "It is highly significant," remarks one student tersely, "that in recent years not a single adverse decision had been rendered requiring the dissolution of an actually functioning business merger."[23]

RAILROADS DURING THE POSTWAR PERIOD

One problem of reconstruction Congress could not evade—the future of the railroads. Having taken over control and operation of them during the war with the promise of return in substantially as good condition as when acquired, it could not delay action indefinitely. But the railroads were too important a part of the American economic structure for even a conservative Congress to restore to private owners without serious thought of the future. Wilson in his annual message of 1918 pointed to three possibilities: restoration to the owners under old conditions, complete government control and

---

[19] 251 U.S. 444.

[20] Williams *v.* Standard Oil Co. of La., Docket No. 64, U.S. Court, October Term 1928 (1929); Rupert Ribnick *v.* Andrew F. McBride, 277 U.S. 350 (1928); Tyson *v.* Banton, 273 U.S. 418 (1927). See D. M. Keezer and Stacy May, *Public Control of Business* (1930), pp. 108, 235; also H. S. Raushenbush, "Government Ownership and Control," *Annals of the American Academy,* CXLIX, 133 (May, 1930).

[21] McCurdle *v.* Indianapolis Water Company, 272 U.S. 400 (1926).

[22] Maple Flooring Manufacturers Association *v.* U.S., 268 U.S. 563 (1925); Cement Manufacturers Protective Association *v.* U.S., 268 U.S. 588 (1925).

[23] M. W. Watkins, "The Sherman Act," *Quarterly Journal of Economics,* XLIII, 37 (Nov., 1928).

ownership, or return under new conditions with increased government regulation. "The one conclusion," said he, "that I am ready to state with confidence is that it would be a disservice alike to the country and to the owners of the railroads to return to the old conditions unmodified. These are conditions of restraint without development."

In the active discussion of the future, Director General McAdoo advised continued government operation for five years. Labor, on the other hand, strongly advocated government ownership and worked hard to popularize the "Plumb Plan," which called for the government purchase of the roads and their operation by a board of directors upon which the public, operating officers, and employees would be equally represented. The earnings, after operating expenses, maintenance, and liquidation of the purchase price had been taken care of, were to be divided between the government and the operating company. This ingenious scheme might have gone far toward solving many difficult aspects of the railroad problem, but it was too much of an innovation in the conservative reaction following the war. Finally Congress was spurred to action by the President's threat to return the roads on March 1, 1920, whether Congress legislated or not.

The Transportation Act of February 28, 1920 (the Esch-Cummins Act), made up largely of amendments to the Interstate Commerce Act, increased the Commission to eleven members and gave it new responsibilities and powers. Among other provisions, it guaranteed the roads, for a period of six months after March 1, 1920, a net return equal to one-half the rental paid during government operation. The Interstate Commerce Commission was authorized to divide the country into rate districts, and in each of them to prescribe rates which "under honest, efficient, and economical management" would give a "fair return upon the aggregate value of the railroad property." The duty of appraising the property and determining a "fair return" was left to the Commission, but the return was temporarily fixed for two years at $5\frac{1}{2}$ per cent, with the addition of one-half of one per cent to provide for improvements and additions if the Commission thought best. In order that the weak roads might be preserved without the strong being permitted to reap too great profits, it was stipulated that any carrier receiving in any year a net income in excess of 6 per cent should turn over one-half of the excess to the Interstate Commerce Commission to be held as a revolving fund to be lent to the weak roads. The half retained by the carrier had to be placed in a reserve fund until the sum accumulated amounted to 5 per cent of the value of its property, after which the annual excess income might be used at will. In any year in which the income failed to reach 6 per cent, the reserve might be drawn on for dividends.

The Commission was authorized to work out plans for the consolidation of the roads into not less than twenty nor more than thirty-five systems. At the same time it could permit pooling agreements subject to its supervision. It was given new power in regulating the capitalization of the roads, with the right to prescribe minimum as well as maximum rates. Additional powers were conferred upon it in the control of rolling stock and the use of terminal facilities and in respect to the control of new road construction. Severe strikes in 1919 brought home to the public the importance of uninterrupted transportation, and in the hope of preventing strikes the act created railroad boards of adjustment between one road or group of roads and employees, and in addition created a Railroad Labor Board of nine members, three representing the railroad employers, three representing the public, and three representing labor.

From this somewhat lengthy description of the law it will be seen that the authority of the Commission was considerably increased. More important than this, perhaps, was the evidence of a changing attitude on the part of the public toward the railroads. Up to this time the business of the Commission had been essentially to protect the public from the railroads. By the act of 1920 it also became the Commission's duty to see that the railroads received a fair return on the capital invested and that they were maintained as an essential part of our economic equipment. Although competition was to continue, the act showed a realization of the fact that efficiency would be promoted by further consolidation of many railroad systems.

Many of the innovations introduced by the Transportation Act of 1920 were undeniably desirable, but few of them were successfully applied. The Labor Board, unsatisfactory to management and labor alike, and powerless because its decisions were not binding, was abolished in 1926, and new experiments in labor mediation were tried.[24] Efforts by the Interstate Commerce Commission to enforce the recapture clause of the 1920 act were fruitless in spite of the fact that its constitutionality was upheld by the Supreme Court. Difficulties encountered in applying it, and the relentless opposition of the more prosperous railroads led the Commission in 1930 to ask Congress to

---

[24] The Railroad Labor Act (Watson-Parker Act) of 1926 was amended by the Crosser-Dill Act of 1934. As a result of this legislation, disputes involving the interruption and application of existing agreements covering wages and working conditions may be referred by either party to a National Railroad Adjustment Board created by the legislation. Disputes involving requested changes in wages or working agreements must first be handled in conferences. If no settlement is reached either party may take them to a National Mediation Board. If the parties accept arbitration, an arbitration board is created to decide the dispute. If either party refuses to accept arbitration, the President may appoint an emergency board to investigate. The board is allowed thirty days to report, and no change in the conditions out of which the dispute arose may be made until thirty days after the report is submitted. This can delay a strike for sixty days in the hope that arbitration, investigation, and publicity may overcome the possibility of strikes. The important role played by unions under this act has virtually ended the company unions in the railroads.

modify this part of the act. This action, as we shall see, was taken in 1933.[25]
Great difficulties likewise were met in carrying out the theory of the act of
1920—that railroad consolidation to promote efficiency should be encouraged,
but that at the same time competition, if possible, be maintained. Although
various plans were submitted to the Commission and studies made, it was
not until December, 1929, that the Commission finally offered a tentative
scheme of consolidation into twenty-one systems. Even then little progress
was made. The railroads found it difficult to agree on plans; the Commission
had power only to suggest and approve, not to compel. No important consolidations were made under the act, and in 1940 Congress relieved the Commission of any responsibility regarding consolidations.

RAILROADS DURING THE TWENTIES

Year	Investment in Road and Equipment (In Millions)	Freight Revenue (In Millions)	Passenger Revenue (In Millions)	Passengers Carried (In Thousands)	Taxes (In Millions)
1920	$19,849	$4,421	$1,305	1,269,913	$289
1925	23,231	4,648	1,065	901,963	366
1929	25,405	4,899	876	786,432	403

Interstate Commerce Commission, *Statistics of Railways in the United States* for 1922, 1930, 1931. See
also H. G. Moulton and associates, *The American Transportation Problem*, pp. 28 ff.

A survey of railroad statistics during the 1920's gives conclusive evidence of
the weakened position of the roads. While the investment in rolling stock
and other equipment substantially increased and the burden of taxation grew
heavier, freight revenue increased but slightly and passenger traffic declined
by one-third. The cause for this decline was obviously the rapid development
of privately owned automobiles and motor buses; the failure of freight traffic
to increase notably in a decade of prosperity was attributable to a similar
development of freight trucks. Although domestic airplanes were carrying
over 400,000 passengers by 1930, competition from this source was not yet
significant. Competition from motor vehicles forced roads to abandon mileage and to curtail passenger service. The more progressive railroads operated
buses themselves; others streamlined their trains, installed air-conditioned
cars, and attempted through greater luxury and speed to win back their passenger business. It was obvious that motor transportation was enjoying temporary advantages during the twenties because of the low burden of taxation
under which they operated and the lack of efficient regulation, but these
advantages to some extent disappeared in the thirties.[26]

[25] Below, p. 671.
[26] Below, p. 671.

In spite of this new competition, the general situation of the more prosperous railroads appears to have been about as good in the 1920's as in the years preceding the First World War. It is true that the average return on investment for Class I railways[27] was estimated at only 4.3 per cent for the seven years 1921–1927, but the better-managed and better-situated railroads actually made large profits during certain of these years. In the eight years 1920–1927, Class I railways and their subsidiaries spent over $5,000,000,000 for extensions, additions, and betterments. Until the depression that began in 1929 there was a steady increase in total track mileage, although "first-track" mileage just about held its own. Furthermore, in 1929 the Pennsylvania, the Philadelphia and Reading, the Delaware, Lackawanna and Western, and several other railroads announced plans for electrification and many of these projects were completed in spite of the depression.

EXPANSION OF TRANSPORTATION FACILITIES

The revival of interest in the development of inland waterway transportation and in artificial waterways which occurred in the first decade of the century continued with little abatement, despite the tremendous development of motor vehicle traffic and the fact that railroads continued to improve their facilities and were adequately equipped to handle normal demands. A partial explanation is found in the fact that inland water transportation on the Great Lakes and the contributory canals has shown a notable increase, and in the belief that water transportation is cheaper than rail and should be encouraged.[28] Likewise it is felt that since the United States has the finest inland waterways to be found in any nation in the world, they should be further developed. A great impetus was undoubtedly given by the agricultural distress of the Middle West during the 1920's and early 1930's and by the conviction that cheaper all-water routes to foreign markets would help to remedy the situation.

Two projects have long been discussed: (1) the Lakes-to-the-Gulf Deep Waterway, which would follow the line of the Chicago Sanitary Drainage Canal, the Illinois and Michigan Canal, and the Mississippi River; and (2) the St. Lawrence Ship Canal. The first project, it was hoped, would restore the Mississippi traffic and provide a direct route from the Mississippi Valley

[27] Class I railways are those companies whose individual operating revenues amount to a million dollars or more annually. They represent about 95 per cent of the mileage of the country.

[28] In round numbers, the freight carried on the Sault Ste Marie increased from 62,363,000 tons in 1910 to 92,622,000 in 1929, only to drop to 20,486,000 in 1932. It had grown again by 1950 to 106,140,000. Tonnage on the Erie and other New York canals has barely held its own, increasing from an average of 3,328,000 (1906–1910) to 3,937,952 (1946–1950). The freight carried in 1929 through the Sault Ste Marie alone was more than three times that carried through the Panama Canal. *Statistical Abstract, 1930*, pp. 435, 436, 442.

to South American ports; the latter would connect the great agricultural regions of the Middle West with Europe by a direct all-water route. The Lakes-to-the-Gulf Deep Waterway had the endorsement of successive administrations since Theodore Roosevelt's, and has been aided since 1917 by a succession of legislative acts and appropriations. This whole project has been entangled with the expensive problem of flood control, but the political strength of those desiring both flood control and inland water routes has been great enough to achieve both objects. With the opening in 1933 of the Illinois Waterway, which linked Lake Michigan, the Illinois River, and the Mississippi by canal, the through route from the Great Lakes to the Gulf was made available. In 1924 the federal government went so far as to organize an Inland Waterways Corporation to carry on the operation of government-owned inland, canal, and coastwise water transportation, but particularly to demonstrate the practicability of water transportation on the upper Mississippi. An outstanding event of the year 1929 was the formal opening of the Ohio River Canalization, a project which had been under way for some fifty years and had cost $125,000,000. Both the Mississippi and the Ohio projects provided for a minimum depth of nine feet.

The St. Lawrence Ship Canal project, which also included schemes for a great electric power development, met strong opposition in New York State, where over $200,000,000 had been invested since 1903 in the Barge Canal (an enlargement and improvement of the old Erie Canal) and which demanded an all-American route. It also encountered stiff opposition from the railroads and the various seaport cities of New England and the Middle Atlantic States. After various investigations had been made, Secretary Hoover recommended the St. Lawrence route as cheaper to construct, as a shorter route to northern Europe, and as providing greater savings to the shipper than the New York route. His advocacy of this project failed to accomplish much during his administration as President. His successor, President Franklin D. Roosevelt, urged the Senate in 1934 to ratify the treaty which would make possible the construction of this project, but the Senate failed to act. On the ground that it was necessary for the long-range defense needs of both Canada and the United States it was revived in 1941 in the form of an agreement (requiring only a majority approval of Congress) between the two nations. Up to the end of 1952 Congress had taken no action. Canada has announced her intention of developing this project whether the United States participates or not.

Obviously the St. Lawrence project is tangled in politics and sectional interests which often obscure fundamental factors. That there would be a saving in mileage and possibly in freight costs between the Middle West and the ports of Europe over this route is conceded. From an engineering point of view it is practicable, and there is no doubt that the Middle West sincerely desires it. The project, however, would cost close to a billion dollars (including power projects) and many experts doubt whether it can be justified on purely economic grounds for many years to come.[29] It is doubtful if the savings in transportation would be commensurate with the initial cost and upkeep. The power developments, on the other hand, would be advantageous to Canada and to the northeastern section of the United States.

A third project of much less importance, but one which has received considerable publicity and continual federal appropriations, is a sheltered series of coastal waterways planned to extend from Boston to Brownsville, Texas. It is reminiscent of part of Gallatin's old plan suggested in 1808.[30] A glance at the map will show that a large portion of this project had been completed by the early 1950's. Some of the canals along the Atlantic coast, such as the Delaware and Chesapeake, have developed an active traffic in transporting coal and oil, but much of the mileage

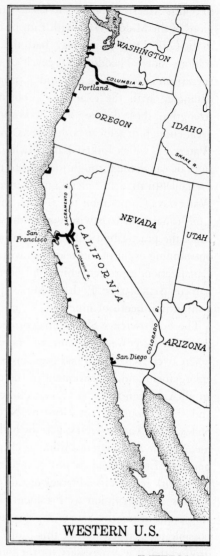

WESTERN U.S.

INTERNAL

has little use except as an inland yacht route to Florida. On the other hand, the Gulf Intracoastal Waterway, extending from St. Marks River in western Florida to Brownsville, Texas, has provided an important route for the transportation of crude petroleum and petroleum products which has steadily increased.

[29] H. G. Moulton, C. S. Morgan, and A. A. Lee, *The St. Lawrence Navigation and Power Project* (1929). See also H. G. Moulton and associates, *The American Transportation Problem*, pp. 505–513.
[30] Above, p. 264.

MIDWESTERN AND EASTERN U.S.

WATERWAYS IN THE 1950's

(From H. U. Faulkner and Tyler Kepner, *America, Its History and People,* Harper & Brothers; and U.S. Army Map Service, Office of the Chief of Engineers, 1948.)

At the opening of the First World War the automobile was just passing out of the experimental stage. Its use was still largely confined to the wealthy and upper middle classes, the number of motor vehicles produced in the United States in 1914 being 569,054, and the number registered 1,258,062. During the next fifteen years the motorcar had its great era of expansion and became a pleasure and business vehicle for all classes of people. Production of passenger cars and trucks increased to 5,621,715 in 1929 and the number registered to 26,501,443.[31] This represented about five-sixths of the world's production, and about one automobile to every five people in the United States. While the automobile undoubtedly affected the steam and interurban electric roads, even to the extent of causing the abandonment of several thousand miles of track, much of the business of the bus and motor truck was new, and these agencies supplemented rather than supplanted the older facilities. For example, there are today in this country 45,000 communities with no important means of transportation other than the motor vehicle.

The agitation for better roads, essentially based on the desire to bring rural transportation on a level with urban, had been stimulated in the late eighties and early nineties by the bicycle craze. It was given increased impetus by the automobile, but the work done prior to World War I was largely in local and state hands.[32] Ignoring the constitutional limitations pointed out by Jackson on the Maysville Road veto,[33] the federal government reverted in 1916 to the old policy which had built the national pike. By the Rural Post Roads Act of 1916, supplemented by subsequent legislation, it has been aiding the states to build primary interstate roads and secondary connecting roads, the states contributing an amount equal to that given by the federal government. Under this stimulus over 300,000 miles of road had been improved by 1950 and the federal government by that time was contributing some $400,000,000 a year. Important as this federal help is in the improvement of highways, the amount appropriated is small in comparison to the total expenditures for county and city roads. It spite of this tremendous advance, little more than one-half of the 3,000,000 miles of rural road in the United States are better than dirt roads. Nevertheless, the effect of the automobile and improved roads upon our economic, social, and intellectual history in stimulating economic life, in providing work and support for millions of people, in speeding the tempo of our civilization, in breaking down rural isolation, and in integrating social and cultural development is almost beyond comprehension.

[31] Owing to the depression the production of motor vehicles dropped to 1,431,494 in 1932 and the automobile registrations to 24,136,879. The year 1933, however, showed a 45 per cent increase in production and an increase in registration. Motor vehicles registered in 1951 numbered 51,913,965.

[32] Above, p. 501.

[33] Above, p. 265.

To those old enough to remember pre-automobile days, many of the effects of the motor vehicle are obvious, but the significance may not be so clear to the present generation of college students. A study of transportation published in the early thirties comments that the diffusion of the automobile "within the population, vertically and horizontally, has been without precedent. It has increased the mobility of people in all classes of society, and given them a control over their own movements that could not have been foreseen

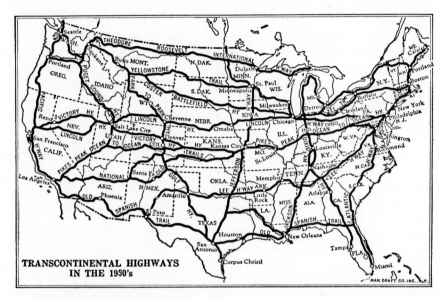

TRANSCONTINENTAL HIGHWAYS
IN THE 1930's

thirty years ago. It is bringing into existence new and integrated transportation systems, both within local communities, which it is helping to transform into larger and more closely knit regional urban areas, and between more distant points. It has multiplied enormously man's potential personal contacts in remote communities, and with his fellow townsmen as well. It is an innovation that has been reshaping many phases of contemporary life."[34] When the saga of the motorcar is finally written, it may well show that the coming of the motor vehicle inaugurated a second industrial and social revolution.

Up to 1917 the story of aviation is largely a story of technical advance.[35] Not until the early 1930's did the airplane become significant in the economic life of the nation; its importance up to that time had been chiefly military. By 1914 the airplane was sufficiently developed to be used in combat service in the First World War, but its main value was in the field of reconnaissance and combat control. A glance at the accompanying table will indicate the

[34] M. W. Willey and S. A. Rice, *Communication Agencies and Social Life*, pp. 39–40.
[35] The early years of aviation history are described above, pp. 501–502.

comparatively trivial commercial importance of aviation in the twenties. Then came a sudden spurt in 1929 to 1931. Unlike most industries and other types of transportation, commercial aviation more than held its own during the depression. A second rapid advance came in the middle thirties and a third boom at the end of the Second World War.

Certain obvious reasons explain the sudden spurt in 1929 which gave aviation a commercial as well as military significance. First of all, the technical groundwork had been laid for the construction and operation of relatively

AIRPLANE PASSENGER AND MAIL TRAFFIC (DOMESTIC)

Year	Passengers	Express and Freight (Pounds)	Mail (Pounds)	Miles Flown
1928	49,713	216,644	4,063,173	10,673,450
1929	173,405	257,443	7,772,014	25,141,499
1930	417,505	468,571	8,513,675	36,945,203
1931	522,345	1,151,348	9,643,211	47,385,987
1932	540,681	1,033,970	7,908,723	50,932,967
1933	493,141	1,510,215	7,362,180	48,771,533
1940	3,185,278	....	10,117,858	119,517,000
1945	7,995,330	30,914,363	65,092,921	247,591,000
1950	17,346,943	151,351,000	47,009,000	364,256,000

Statistical Abstract, 1933, p. 371, for figures through 1932; *ibid., 1940,* p. 457; *ibid., 1952,* p. 530. The figures for express and freight, beginning with 1945, are ton-miles flown; figures for 1940 are not available. Figures for mail, beginning in 1940, are for ton-miles flown.

safe planes. At the same time tremendous interest had been aroused by many spectacular flights during the prosperous twenties when capital was available for the industry and there was business for the planes. Finally, there was the assistance of the government, federal and local. This help cannot be over-estimated. The United States was the chief customer of the manufacturers of aviation supplies. In 1931, for example, 812 of the 2394 planes produced were military units. Actual transportation by air was even more dependent upon government aid than was the manufacturing. The government became interested in aviation first in its military aspects and then in its commercial. In 1918 an experimental Air Mail Service was established jointly by the Post Office Department and the Army. This was soon abandoned, but in the following year the Post Office acting alone inaugurated a mail service between Chicago and Cleveland, which in 1924 was extended to transcontinental proportions. When a government service was finally established on a satisfactory basis, Congress suddenly reversed itself and virtually ordered the Post Office Department to cease carrying air mail and to contract the business to private concerns. The result has been the subsidization of American aviation chiefly by means of post-office air-mail contracts. This particular form of aid got out of bounds by 1934, and when charges of fraud and favoritism were made, the government suddenly revoked its contract, carried the mail itself for a few weeks, and then called for new bids.[36]

In the second period of rapid expansion during the middle thirties aviation' began to free itself from its utter dependence upon government subsidy. After 1934 its chief source of revenue was its passenger traffic. Beginning in 1938 the government received more from postal revenues than it paid to air-mail carriers. In 1940 commercial passenger planes flew over 94,000,000 miles and carried over 3,000,000 passengers over a nation equipped with 2600 airports and landing fields. This was about 10 per cent of the passengers carried on Pullman trains. Planes were carrying one-seventh of the first-class mail and one-fourth of the transcontinental mail. Commercial aviation was rapidly reaching maturity. Its expanding popularity was due primarily to the increasing speed and safety of air flights. By 1940 the time from New York to San Francisco had been cut to fifteen hours. In March, 1940, commercial air lines completed a full year without a fatal accident.

DECLINING POSITION OF AGRICULTURE

Just as the American farmer found himself confronted with a serious economic crises in the years following the Napoleonic and Civil wars, so also after the First World War he was again faced by a somewhat similar situation. While most economic interests recovered rapidly after the deflation of 1920 and 1921, agriculture failed to respond. Two basic factors help to explain this: (1) overproduction in the markets of the world brought on by the demands of the war and by improved agricultural machinery, particularly the gasoline tractor, and (2) the world-wide falling off in demand and the deflation of prices after the war. The first of these produced an agricultural revolution at a time when increased production was hardly necessary. The second, the world-wide deflation, was particularly hard upon agriculture, for in periods of deflation and falling prices raw materials, and especially agricultural products, usually suffer first and worst. Whereas wages and retail prices decline more slowly or possibly resist deflation, the bottom is knocked completely out of agricultural prices and the farmer finds his income out of line with that of other groups. Furthermore, although the income of farmers declined in the 1920's, his taxes increased.

Among other factors operating against the farmer was the new immigration policy of the United States, which cut the flow of immigration and

[36] Estimates for 1932 put the various kinds of federal aid to air transportation at $26,274,000, and contributions from passenger and postal carriers at not more than $15,000,000. In that year the government paid air-mail carriers $19,938,123 but received only $6,016,280 in postal revenue.

tended to keep wages high. The same was true of freight rates and handling costs, which did not decline with the price of agricultural products. There were also dietary and style changes which led people to turn from meats and cereals to vegetables and fruit. Individualistic, the farmer adjusts himself less easily to new conditions. Moreover, he is unable to adjust his production to market demands as quickly as the manufacturer. The war encouraged over-expansion and overemphasis upon the one-crop system, both of which proved ruinous in the postwar years. Finally, before any satisfactory adjustment was achieved, a second period of world-wide depression began in 1929.

In the sudden deflation at the conclusion of the war corn prices in 1921 dropped to a third those of 1919; cotton, wheat, and hogs fell to half the 1919 figure, and beef cattle to almost half. The prices of most agricultural com-modities recovered somewhat during 1923 to 1926, but then dropped again. With the decline in prices, the bankruptcy rate per 1000 farms jumped from 0.21 in 1920 to slightly over 1.20 for the years 1924–1926. In spite of this in-crease, the total farm mortgage debt rose by almost $2,000,000,000 between 1920 and 1928, an increase of 19 per cent from 1920 to 1925 and a rise of one per cent from 1925 to 1928.[37] Under the circumstances a decline in land values was to be expected, but the drop in agricultural land values from $79,000,000,-000 in 1920 to $58,000,000,000 in 1927 was staggering.[38] At the same time, the population on farms declined from 31,614,000 in 1920 to 30,169,000 in 1930, with a net movement from farms during the decade of about 600,000 per year.[39] Expansion of the productive area, which had been rapid during the war, ceased immediately. Between 1919 and 1924, it is estimated, 13,000,000 acres went back to grass, brush, and woodlands.[40] Since the savings of farm-ers customarily are invested in land and buildings, the collapse of farm values and agricultural prices meant the wiping out of lifetime savings and the in-crease in bankruptcy meant a growth in tenancy. For the nation as a whole the growth in tenancy rose from 38 per cent in 1920 to 42 in 1930.[41] More-over, this tenancy was of a discouraging type. Instead of a rung on the ladder upwards to independent ownership, as had often been the case in the past, it was a descent toward the status of the agricultural laborer. One result of the increase in tenancy was a deterioration in land and equipment.

The accompanying table of index figures gives a reasonably accurate pic-ture of the agricultural situation in the prewar and postwar years.

[37] The figures for the three years are $7,857,700,000 in 1920, $9,360,620,000 in 1925, and $9,468,526,000 in 1928.

[38] During this period capital invested in corporations increased from $99,000,000,000 to $134,000,000,000.

[39] *Yearbook of Agriculture, 1934*, p. 699. The figure 600,000 represents roughly the excess of those leaving the farms over those arriving at farms from the cities.

[40] *Ibid., 1928*, p. 393.

[41] The percentage has dropped to 38.7 in 1940 and 26.8 in 1950.

INDEX NUMBERS OF FARM PRICES, PRICES PAID BY FARMERS, FARM WAGES, AND
TAXES, 1910–1929 (1910–1914 = 100)

Date	Prices Received for Farm Products	Prices Paid by Farmers for Commodities Used in		Farm Wages Paid to Hired Labor	Taxes on Farm Property (1914 = 100)
		Living	Production		
1910	103	98	98	97	. . .
1911	95	100	103	97	. . .
1912	99	101	98	101	. . .
1913	100	100	102	104	. . .
1914	102	102	99	101	100
1915	100	107	104	102	102
1916	117	124	124	112	104
1917	176	147	151	140	106
1918	200	177	174	176	118
1919	209	210	192	206	130
1920	205	222	174	239	155
1921	116	161	141	150	217
1922	123	156	139	146	232
1923	134	160	141	166	246
1924	134	159	143	166	249
1925	147	164	147	168	250
1926	136	162	146	171	253
1927	131	159	145	170	258
1928	139	160	148	169	263
1929	138	158	147	170	267
1930	117	148	140	152	266
1931	80	126	122	116	. . .
1932	57	108	107	86	. . .
1933	63	109	108	80	. . .

Yearbook of Agriculture, 1932, p. 900, and *ibid., 1934,* p. 706.

It was inevitable that the agricultural depression would have reverberations in politics and would result in legislation. In May, 1921, Senators and Representatives of both parties from the agricultural states organized the "farm bloc" and led the movement for legislation to aid agriculture. Thoroughgoing legislation, they asserted, was necessary not only to help remedy a very serious situation but also to put the farmers on an equal status with other economic groups protected and favored by the federal government. The result of this agitation led to a considerable amount of legislation which can be roughly grouped under three heads.[42] In the first place, the various tariff measures, including the emergency tariff of 1921, the Fordney-McCumber tariff of 1922, and the Hawley-Smoot bill of 1930, all made an effort to protect agricultural commodities from foreign competition. While these tariffs undoubtedly helped to maintain prices on certain agricultural products, economists were generally agreed that they had no effect upon the prices of high-

[42] A summary of this legislation from 1920 to 1928 is given in J. D. Black, *Agricultural Reform in the United States* (1929), pp. 69–73, and in C. C. Davis, "The Development of Agricultural Policy Since the End of the World War," *Yearbook of Agriculture, 1940,* pp. 297–326.

protein wheat, corn, barley, cotton, and other important commodities. A tariff on agricultural commodities of which there was a large surplus for export helped little, if at all, particularly when a general high tariff policy restricted those markets where an agricultural surplus might be disposed of. The irony of helping an export industry, such as American agriculture, by a tariff was at last becoming evident even to Republican farm leaders, and this time-honored sop no longer satisfied them. The blind spot in the whole agricultural program of the 1920's was the failure of farm leaders to realize that the foreign market for agricultural products was permanently contracted (at least in normal times) and that the shift of the United States from a debtor to a creditor nation made the exportation of the agricultural surplus of less importance to the national welfare.

In the second place, a number of acts were passed, designed to extend better credit to farmers and encourage them in co-operative efforts. These included revival in 1921 of the War Finance Corporation to finance the exportation of agricultural products and handle emergency agricultural credits, the Agricultural Credits Act of 1923,[43] and the Agricultural Marketing Act of 1929. These and other measures were designed to extend the work inaugurated by the Federal Farm Loan Act of 1916. Valuable as these acts might be, they did not effectively remedy the situation, and the more radical of the agricultural group pressed for a third type of legislation which would actually raise prices. This hope was incorporated in the McNary-Haugen bills, twice passed by Congress in 1927 and 1928 and vetoed both times by Coolidge.

While the details of the McNary-Haugen bills differed somewhat, the general method to be employed was the same. The bills provided that a government corporation should purchase certain agricultural products at a price which would yield a fair profit, and that the surplus should be sold abroad at what it would bring, the loss on the foreign sales to be assessed in the form of an equalization fee against every unit of the product sold by the producer. The net price to the producer would be the fixed price minus the equalization fee; the larger the surplus the larger the fee and the smaller the return to the farmer. As the producers of tobacco and cotton sold too great a proportion of these crops abroad to be much interested in the scheme, and as many products were sold abroad in only small quantities, the bills were middle-western measures designed primarily to help the producers of wheat and hogs. The chief significance of the agitation for the McNary-Haugen bills was that it accustomed both farmers and the urban population

[43] This act set up a Federal Intermediate Credit bank in each of the federal land bank districts, with a capitalization of $5,000,000 and the power to issue debentures to ten times that amount; the purpose was to extend personal and collateral credit for periods intermediate between the usual short-term commercial loan and the long-term obligations secured by land.

to the idea of price fixing and prepared the way for the agricultural legislation of the New Deal.

Both parties in 1928 pledged themselves to agricultural relief, and after the veto of the second McNary-Haugen bill the Hoover administration sanctioned the Agricultural Marketing Act of 1929, mentioned above. By this act Congress appropriated $500,000,000 to be loaned by a Federal Farm Board to

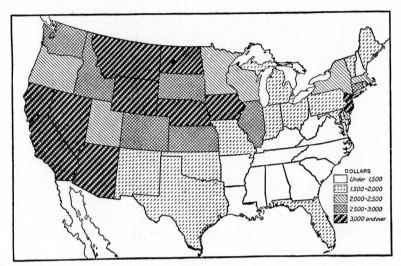

(From *Yearbook of Agriculture, 1930,* p. 245.)

Annual Gross Income per Farm, 1924–1928.

co-operative associations in the hope that this would promote orderly marketing and sound policies and put the farmer in a position to deal more effectively with the whole problem of marketing. Although the Federal Farm Board encouraged co-operatives and through wheat and cotton stabilization corporations attempted to prevent the decline of prices, the effect upon the general agricultural situation was slight. The Board's career was short and disastrous; it ended with the Roosevelt legislation of 1933. The taxpayers were the chief losers.

The body of agricultural legislation passed in the decade and a half after 1915 was considerable in amount and undoubtedly of substantial assistance to the farmers. It is of interest in our economic history because it marked a change in policy. "Prior to 1913," says Malin, "United States agricultural policy was focused upon the problems of production. In that year a new departure was inaugurated which for the first time placed systematic emphasis upon the problems of marketing."[44] A revolution in distribution methods was obviously needed, and the Agricultural Marketing Act distinctly recog-

[44] J. C. Malin, *The United States After the World War,* p. 247.

nized the fact. All the assistance which the government could offer during the twenties, however, could not overcome the two most important handicaps under which the farmer suffered—overproduction and depression conditions at one time or another in most parts of the world.

DECLINE OF ORGANIZED LABOR

Although the international position of labor was stronger after the First World War, the position of American labor was decidedly weaker. The American Federation of Labor, proudly conscious of its war record, laid down at its annual convention in 1919 a "reconstruction program" which called for democracy in industry, abolition of unemployment, higher wages, shorter hours, equal pay to women for equal work, abolition of child labor, the right of public employees to organize and bargain collectively. It also demanded curtailment of the power of the judiciary, government ownership of public and semipublic utilities, development and operation of water power, better federal and state regulation of corporations, absolute freedom of expression and association, extension of workmen's compensation, establishment of government employment agencies and the abolition of those conducted for private profit, the building of model homes by the government and aid in enabling workers to own their homes, and a two-year cessation of immigration.[45]

If labor had any idea that a grateful republic would be sympathetic to this program, it was doomed to speedy disillusionment. In the reaction which settled dismally upon the nation in the postwar years labor found itself attacked from many quarters and its power badly impaired. In the economic depression which inevitably followed in the wake of war expansion, all but the most powerfully organized workers experienced wage decreases. Strikes to prevent deflation or to secure higher wages were generally unsuccessful. The federal government broke up a bituminous coal strike in 1919 by obtaining a sweeping injunction authorized, according to the Attorney General, under the Lever Fuel and Food Control Act of 1917. A railroad shopmen's strike in 1919 collapsed through government opposition and the failure of labor to co-operate, and the steel strike in the same year was unsuccessful. The speed with which the hard-earned gains of labor were disappearing and the ease with which they did so amazed Gompers, and he bitterly denounced the Bourbon policies of American industrialists. Inadequate labor leadership, however, was an important cause.[46] The steel strike of 1919, for example,

---

[45] *Monthly Labor Review*, VIII, 63–72 (March, 1919). See also F. Flügel and H. U. Faulkner, *op. cit.*, pp. 839–842.

[46] Aroused to action, the A. F. of L. Executive Committee, for the first time in its history, officially supported a presidential candidate, La Follette, in 1924, whose consistent labor record could not be ignored. His defeat merely served to convince labor leaders of the correctness of

was a strategic struggle in which the demands of labor were eminently fair, the sympathy of a large element of the public was with them, and the chances for success were at least even. A united front on the part of American labor might have seen a different outcome. In 1919 there were nine labor disturbances, in each of which over 90,000 men were involved, and in that year over 4,000,000 men went on strike.[47] Most of the important conflicts terminated unsuccessfully for labor.

Labor was also experiencing losses in other directions. The depression and the absorption of four million soldiers increased the competition for jobs; corporations, as they saw their profits decline, curtailed their welfare operations; public interest in social legislation declined, and the hand of the judiciary grew heavier. The courts, which during the war had complacently watched constitutional and human rights repeatedly violated, continued to countenance extralegal proceedings, particularly those used to hinder the activities of labor radicals. At the same time, capital, taking a leaf from war experience, increased the use of the labor spy and the *agent provocateur* and called repeatedly upon the state militia.

While organized labor grew weaker, organized capital became stronger. Manufacturers' associations devoted increased attention to combating labor and in many communities secured the close co-operation of chambers of commerce. This effort to break the power of labor and promote the "open shop" was euphemistically called the "American plan" and met with considerable success. A barrage of propaganda asserting that labor was to blame for the high cost of living helped to alienate the sympathy of the middle class so important to the labor movement.

Particularly detrimental to labor were the reactionary decisions of the state and federal judiciary. Federal child labor laws were declared unconstitutional in 1918 and 1922, and in 1923 a minimum-wage law for women in the District of Columbia fell under the ban of the court.[48] Not only was social legislation endangered, but the very existence of labor unions was jeopardized. The Supreme Court in the Danbury Hatters' case (1908, 1915) and in other decisions had held that labor unions and their individual members were responsible without limit for actions of union officers which they had in any

---

their former policy, which, if possible, became more conservative than ever regarding political action. Not until 1952 did the Federation in annual session endorse a presidential candidate, in this case Adlai E. Stevenson.

[47] The number of strikes reported for the year was 3630. See *Monthly Labor Review*, July, 1929. The figures of workmen on strike since the First World War are interesting. The 4,160,348 in 1919 dropped to 1,463,054 in 1920 and to 1,099,247 in 1921, then rose in 1922 during the railroad strike to 1,612,562, but dropped to 756,584 in 1923 and then steadily downward to 329,592 in 1926. From 1927 to 1931 the annual average number of strikes was 763 and the annual average number of strikers involved was 275,000. See table in C. R. Daugherty, *Labor Problems in American Industry*, p. 356.

[48] Above, pp. 470–471.

way sanctioned; in 1915 it declared unconstitutional a state statute aimed to prevent an employer from forcing his employee to agree not to join a union during the latter's term of service ("yellow-dog contract"),[49] and it even upheld a decision that it was illegal to try to organize employees who signed a "yellow-dog contract."[50] It cut the heart out of the protection which Congress intended to give labor in the Clayton Act by declaring a secondary boycott illegal[51] and by permitting suit against an unincorporated union for violation of that act.[52] Particularly dangerous to labor was the growing use of the injunction in labor disputes, a procedure which the A. F. of L. fought consistently and bitterly.

Difficult as it was to counteract the decisions of a conservative judiciary, the activities of the *agent provocateur,* and the decline of public sympathy, organized labor now found its influence undermined in much subtler ways. One of the chief weapons used to disrupt the organized labor movement in the twenties was the "company union." Prior to 1917 not more than a dozen important plants had introduced this system, but by 1927 there were hundreds, with a membership of over 1,400,000. The growth of company unions was particularly rapid in the railway industry after the collapse of the shopmen's strike in 1922, but it was also important in the metal trades and electrical manufacturing establishments. Another subtle weapon directed against organized labor was employee stock ownership. Although the promotion of this can be validated on the grounds that it improves morale, diminishes labor troubles and turnover, and develops a contented personnel, its chief effect was to weaken the organized labor movement, and consequently the power of labor. The leadership in the promotion of stock ownership in the utilities was taken by the American Telephone and Telegraph Company; in the industrial field by such concerns as the Eastman Kodak Company, United States Steel, and Bethlehem Steel; in the rails by the New York Central and the Pennsylvania; and in the oils by the Standard Oil Company.[53] Encouraged chiefly through installment purchases, the number of employee stockholders grew to well over a million, and certain devotees of "Pollyanna economics" extravagantly hailed it as an indication of an "economic revolution" by which the ownership of the nation's wealth was shifting to the wage earner.[54]

That employee stock ownership undoubtedly acts as a palliative in the

[49] Coppage *v.* Kansas, 236 U.S. 1 (1915).

[50] Hitchman Coal and Coke *v.* Mitchell *et al.,* 254 U.S. 229 (1917).

[51] Duplex Printing Press Company *v.* Deering *et al.,* 254 U.S. 443 (1921).

[52] United Mine Workers of America *v.* Coronado Coal and Coke Company, 259 U.S. 344 (1922).

[53] R. F. Foerster and E. N. Dietel, *Employee Stock Ownership in the United States* (1926), pp. 99 ff.

[54] T. N. Carver, *The Present Economic Revolution in the United States* (1925).

conflict between capital and labor is readily conceded, but even the most casual examination quickly dispels the dream that any economic millennium was being achieved through this medium. A Federal Trade Commission investigation made in 1922 and covering a cross section of American business found that employees comprised 7.5 per cent of the common stockholders of corporations in which they were employed, and 3.5 per cent of the preferred stockholders, but held only 1.5 per cent of the common stock and 1.9 of the preferred.[55] A later study made by the Industrial Relations Section of Princeton University found that only 4.26 per cent of the stock of twenty important companies which had vigorously encouraged employee stock ownership was actually owned by employees.[56] When it is realized that a large proportion of this stock is held by superintendents and by the salaried office and executive force, the actual share owned by wage earners appears even smaller. It should furthermore be pointed out that while the actual number of shareholders has increased, the technique whereby a small group may maintain control of an industry has been perfected.[57] The democratization of capital and of business has made little if any progress through employee stock ownership.

It is impossible for any student of labor to ignore the rapid development during the 1920's of a wide range of activities often grouped under the term "welfare capitalism." The impetus for this was generally the desire to paralyze unionization or to develop a more loyal, stable, and efficient working force, but it was also often motivated by a sincere humanitarian concern for the health, safety, and general welfare of the worker. "Welfare capitalism" interested itself in innumerable projects: educational programs, encouragement of workers to own their own homes, low-cost cafeterias, free medical service, profit-sharing devices, vacations with pay, and subsidizing of recreational facilities.[58]

Of all the humanitarian efforts to improve the lot of the worker the most valid and helpful was the establishment of insurance and pension schemes. Various forms of group insurance (in addition to the compulsory workmen's compensation) were widely established, covering disability and death. It was estimated in 1927 that group insurance had been taken out to the extent of $5,600,000,000 covering 4,700,000 employees, one insurance company alone, the Metropolitan, having written it for 2500 firms and 815,000 workers.[59] Also worthy of attention was the development of employee pensions. A survey by

---

[55] Federal Trade Commission, *Report on National Wealth and Income* (1926).
[56] R. F. Foerster and E. N. Dietel, *op. cit.;* and R. W. Dunn, *The Americanization of Labor,* p. 153.
[57] W. Z. Ripley, *Main Street and Wall Street* (1927).
[58] Dunn, *op. cit.,* pp. 193–194.
[59] *Annals of the American Academy of Political and Social Science* (March, 1927), p. 32.

the Pennsylvania Old Age Pension Commission in 1926 revealed the fact that at least 400 firms employing 4,000,000 workers had established pension plans, 88 per cent of which had been started in the previous fifteen years.[60]

Many types of welfare capitalism were helpful and of value to workers, but they indicated that the initiative in improving the condition of labor was shifting from the laborer to the employer and that personal independence and initiative were rapidly being undermined. Obviously the organized labor movement was being outmaneuvered by the employer. The membership of the A. F. of L. dropped from the high point of 4,078,740 in 1920 to 2,532,261 in 1932.[61] These figures tell but a part of the story of the decline of organized labor. The Federation failed miserably in organizing the workers in the automobile factories and in the southern textile mills, it saw strong unions like those of the bituminous coal workers rapidly disintegrate, and it failed badly in making the Amalgamated Association of Iron, Steel and Tin Workers a going concern. Gompers, who died in 1924, passed on his conservative policies to less able leaders, in whose hands they seemed for years to have degenerated into "do-nothingism." The skilled workers who comprised the largest portion of organized labor found their position improving with the decline of prices after World War I and the rising wave of prosperity following the depression of 1921, and were as conservative as their leaders. The more radical element in the ranks of labor who questioned the policies (or, perhaps, lack of them) of the leaders were bitterly assailed by the spokesmen of the Federation and denounced as radicals. By the end of the decade, however, there were indications that the dissatisfied minority, who realized the stagnant position of the organized labor movement, were rapidly increasing and were eager to write a new chapter in American labor history.

IMMIGRATION IN THE 1920's

Closely concerned with the history of American labor since the First World War has been the drastic change in the immigration policy. For decades organized labor had been agitating for greater immigration restrictions, and since the 1880's the laws had gradually tightened. Organized labor, fearful of a declining wage scale and unemployment, was now joined by groups of many types who thought that further large-scale immigration was fraught with danger to American institutions. Nor did employers vigorously oppose restriction, for there was practically no labor shortage in the prosperous years of the middle twenties. Earlier acts which had put every conceivable type of undesirable on the restricted list had failed to prevent large-scale immigra-

[60] Abraham Epstein, *The Problem of Old Age Pensions in Industry* (1926), pp. 18–19.

[61] "Of the 105 international unions in the A. F. of L. 36 lost membership between 1924 and 1929, while 25 remained stationary. . . . These unions included some of the oldest organizations, which had in the past been the very backbone of the Federation." L. L. Lorwin, *The American Federation of Labor* (1933), p. 279.

tion, and the restrictionists now turned to the quota system. In 1921 the so-called "quota law" was passed, limiting immigration in any year to 3 per cent of the number of each nationality in the United States according to the Census of 1910.

This quota did not go far enough for ardent restrictionists, and in 1924 a new law was passed changing the quota to 2 per cent of any nationality residing here in 1890. Canadians and Mexicans were exempt, as were travelers, merchants, seamen, and officials; Japanese were debarred under the 1924 act. This act not only cut the quota of the 1921 act in half,[62] but favored the "old immigration" from northern and western Europe at the expense of the "new immigration" from eastern and southern Europe.[63] The Immigration Act of 1924 also provided that the numerical quota scheme of 2 per cent of 1890 residents should remain in force only until 1927, when a "national-origins" method should be applied. Government scientists were to attempt to find out the real origin of the American people as constituted in 1920 and then apportion the immigration among the nationalities, with the total quota immigration limited to 150,000 a year. So much opposition to this law developed that it did not go into effect until July, 1929.[64]

Whatever may have been the weaknesses of the immigration legislation of the 1920's, it accomplished its objective—the radical curtailment of immigration. From 1927 until 1933 the number of immigrants declined each year. The years 1927 to 1935 saw more aliens leave this country than were admitted.

SELECTED READINGS

Soule, George, *Prosperity Decade,* chaps. 4–13.

Chase, Stuart, *Prosperity, Fact or Myth.*

Laidler, H. W., *Concentration in American Industries,* chap. 23.

Berle, A. A., Jr., and Means, G. C., *The Modern Corporation and Private Property,* chaps. 2–5.

Moulton, H. G., and associates, *The American Transportation Problem,* chaps. 21–31.

Davis, C. C., "The Development of Agricultural Policy Since the End of the World War," *Yearbook of Agriculture, 1940,* pp. 297–326.

Lorwin, L. L., *The American Federation of Labor,* chaps. 8–10.

Perlman, Selig, and Taft, Philip, *History of Labor in the United States, 1896–1932,* chaps. 37–44.

Faulkner, H. U., *From Versailles to the New Deal,* chaps. 4, 8, 9.

[62] The quota for 1923 was placed at 357,803, and that for 1924–1925 at 164,667.

[63] F. Flügel and H. U. Faulkner, *Readings,* pp. 865–868.

[64] Since July 1, 1929, the annual quota of any nationality for each fiscal year has been a number which bears the same ratio to 150,000 as the number of inhabitants in 1920 having that origin bears to the total number of inhabitants in continental United States in 1920. The 1929 law which gives American consuls power to refuse visas to all applicants who may become "public charges" over here helped to cut down immigration radically during the depression.

CHAPTER 29

ECONOMIC COLLAPSE

A CHANGING SOCIETY

AN important crisis, economic or political, often speeds changes in a society which has never been static and forces the acceptance of new points of view and of reforms long needed. Such was the result of the economic depression which began in 1929. The remaining chapters should make clear the effects of this depression and of the Second World War upon the economy of the nation, and at the same time the greater participation of the government in and control of this economy. Enough has already been said in this volume to emphasize the great economic achievements accomplished in the century previous to 1929. They had made the nation economically the greatest in the world. But the economic structure had many inadequacies which the collapse of 1929 made only too evident. It was the effort to reform these inadequacies and the belief that reform could be accomplished which chiefly differentiates this period from that before the catastrophe of 1929.

These efforts, as we shall see, did little to weaken the capitalist economy, but they left small substance to the old theory of *laissez faire*. Under the circumstances the government had no other choice than to assume some guidance and control of the economy by means of a market-price structure which included all shades of competition and monopoly. These efforts operated with varying degrees of effectiveness, but they apparently brought greater stability. They have, along with other influences such as group action, brought higher standards of living. With these has come for most of the people greater protection from economic insecurity. Conflicts as to what the economic society should do, to whose advantage, and in what way have been expressed in part politically. And, of course, many noneconomic values, such as democracy, freedom of the individual, and universal education, have also played a significant role.

THE ECONOMIC CYCLE

The decade of the twenties, which many believed had opened a new and never-ending era of prosperity, closed in the most complete economic collapse in American history. Depressions, of course, are not new phenomena; they have occurred intermittently in the United States, as they have in other parts of the capitalist world. American economic history, in fact, might be written around the story of the recurrent booms and slumps which have characterized our economic life. The crisis years of these cycles (1819, 1837, 1857, 1873, 1884, 1893, 1903, 1907, 1913, 1920, 1929) stand out as key dates. W. C. Mitchell, a leading American authority, states that ". . . the modern view is that crises are but one feature of recurrent 'business cycles.' . . . A crisis is expected to be followed by a depression, the depression by a revival, the revival by prosperity, and prosperity by a new crisis. Cycles of this sort can be traced for at least a century in America."[1]

As these facts became obvious, and as a new school of practical or "institutional" economics as distinguished from the older theoretical one emerged, much study was devoted to the problem of the "business cycle." Some economists or pseudo-economists went so far, in fact, as to organize commercial corporations purporting to inform businessmen, investors, and speculators as to the exact point reached in a cycle at a particular moment. The fact that past cycles had shown certain common tendencies made this seem plausible. A committee appointed by Secretary Hoover in 1921 thus describes the typical cycle:

If we begin the analysis when business is reviving, in general the characteristic features are increased volume of manufacturing, rising stock exchange prices followed by rising commodity prices, then by business expansion and increased demand for credit from both business men and speculators. As the result of the advance of commodity prices, money rates stiffen and credit gradually becomes strained, and these conditions may be accompanied by a curtailment of credit for speculative purposes. Then stock exchange prices fall; for a while longer general business continues to increase unevenly, and transportation facilities are overburdened and deliveries are delayed, the apparent shortage of goods is intensified by speculative buying and duplication of orders by merchants and other buyers until credit expansion nears its limit. Public confidence is then shaken, resulting in widespread cancellation of orders if the cycle is extreme. This is always followed by liquidation of inventories and sharp and irregular fall of prices. During the period of depression, there is always more or less widespread unemployment.[2]

[1] W. C. Mitchell, *Business Cycles and Unemployment*, p. 5.
[2] *Business Cycles and Unemployment*, Report and Recommendations of a Committee of the President's Conference on Unemployment, pp. xii, xiii.

This brief but excellent description does not, of course, deal with the special causes or details of a particular cycle. As we glance back over the history of American panics we note that certain causes have been particularly characteristic of this country.[3] In almost every case depression in America has followed an overexpansion of transportation facilities and land speculation. Thus the panic of 1837 was preceded by a boom in canal building; the panics of 1857, 1873, and 1893, by overexpansion in railroad building; and the depression of the 1930's, by extensive automobile and road building. When good public lands were available speculation in them characterized every boom. Even after these were occupied, there was tremendous speculation in city real estate and building construction in the boom of the 1920's.

While the outstanding causes of these recurrent cycles of prosperity and depression in the United States appear to be much the same, there are always some differences, for history never repeats itself in detail. The difficulty of determining all the factors in a complex economic phenomenon is sometimes increased by the fact that economists differ radically in the emphasis which they put on the various causes. Certain students stress the volume of bank credits, others the price structure; still others interpret the business cycle as dependent upon distribution of income. Marxian socialists base their explanation upon the labor theory of values. Two leading American students, Veblen and Mitchell, center their explanation around the driving impetus of profits. "Profits," says Mitchell, "are the focus of economic activities in a business economy."[4] In the end, he says, the cycles rest upon "this crucial factor—the prospects of profit."[5] Whatever the causes, one thing is clear— the lack of stability in our economic life. The only certain factor is continual change.

The terrific havoc wrought by depressions, particularly that following the crash of 1929, has concentrated attention upon causes and cures. Students with particular theories are inclined to the belief that the elimination of certain causes might solve the problem. For example, those who lay emphasis upon banking credit urge that a better control of banking might prevent depression, those who blame inordinate speculation would carefully police the stock exchange, those who stress the influence of profits would modify the profit system, and so forth. In any case economists in general hold to the belief that scientific study may discern storm signals and thus forestall collapse, or that by means of regulated competition and social legislation serious depressions may be prevented or at least mitigated. Whatever "scientific" eco-

---

[3] See Index under Panics.
[4] *Encyclopaedia of the Social Sciences,* III, 102.
[5] W. C. Mitchell, *op. cit.,* p. 5.

nomics existed in the twenties failed utterly to prevent collapse. The Roosevelt administration after March, 1933, approached the problem through the method of regulated competition and social legislation.

FUNDAMENTAL CAUSES OF THE COLLAPSE OF 1929

Sufficient time has elapsed since the 1920's to construct a reasonably accurate picture of the economic tendencies of that decade. The prosperity of this period, such as it was, seems to have been in part a "carry-over" from the war years. The war, which left Europe impoverished, failed to affect radically the American standard of living. After a brief postwar recession (1920–1921) prosperity returned to many lines of industry and to certain areas of the country. As we have already noted (pp. 607–608), the foundation of this prosperity was primarily the development of the automotive industry and the accompanying boom in road building. Secondly, it was characterized by a boom in urban construction resulting from the scarcity which developed during the war years. Greatly aided by these domestic factors and by an appreciable improvement in general conditions over much of the world, the United States moved into the prosperous years of the middle and later twenties. There was widespread demand, aided and abetted by installment buying, for new products, such as radios and household electric equipment. Favorable trade balances enlarged an already unprecedented abundance of gold and on this basis credit expanded and trade developed. Private loans on a large scale were made to Europe and South America and the proceeds were spent largely in this country.

Despite real evidences of prosperity, sufficiently numerous to give the decade an appearance of a boom era, fundamental flaws in the economic structure existed. Certain industries, notably coal mining, textiles, shipbuilding, railroad equipment, and leather manufactures, failed to revive after the postwar depression. More important was the failure of agriculture to respond to the postwar economic recovery. Overexpansion during the war period, the slowing up of population growth, dietary changes of the American people, increased competition from other parts of the world, and the development of economic nationalism in Europe explain in part the condition of the American farmer. The time-honored role of American agriculture had been twofold: first, to feed the rapidly increasing population of Europe, and second, to provide commodities to exchange with Europe for the capital necessary to develop a new nation. Other new countries were now helping to supply Europe, and as the United States shifted from a debtor to a creditor nation her industry no longer needed foreign loans. What market the farmer still had in Europe was further curtailed by the exorbitantly high Fordney-

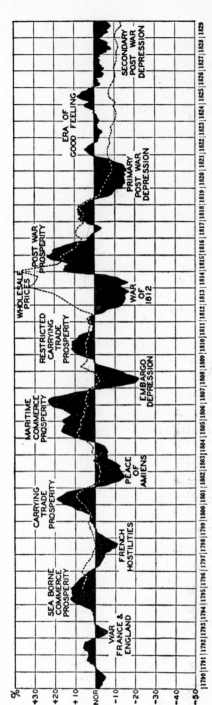
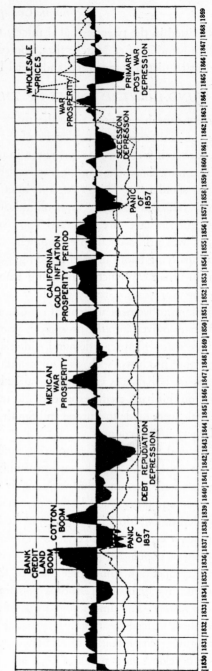

AMERICAN BUSINESS ACTIVITY SINCE 1790.

This graph gives a picture of American business activity from January 1, 1790, until the end of 1952. The dotted line represents the changes in wholesale commodity prices. The graph was compiled from various data by the late General Leonard P. Ayres and the Cleveland Trust Company and is used with the permission of that company.

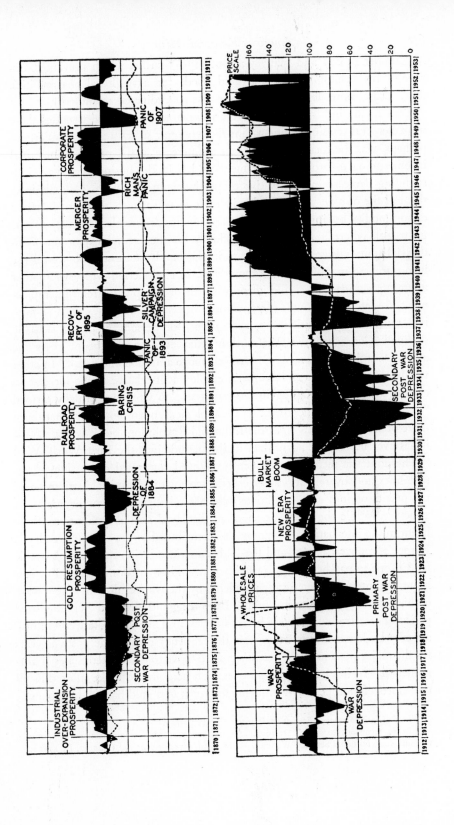

McCumber (1922) and Hawley-Smoot (1930) tariffs, which prevented Europe from exchanging manufactured goods for agricultural commodities. Agriculture more definitely than ever was subordinated to industry.

Even in the industries which were prosperous during the twenties there were elements tending to undermine the economic structure. Most important, perhaps, was the fact that "there was an increase in the proportion of total income going to profits (including those left in the business) and a corresponding decrease in the relative proportion going to wages and salaries— this in spite of a very considerable increase in real wages, reckoned in terms of commodity buying power."[6] The obvious result was the tendency to pile up wealth where it would be used chiefly for the further expansion of industrial units rather than to place it in the hands of those who would use it to purchase manufactured commodities. In conjunction with this another alarming fact was observable: there was little or no upward trend in employment to match the growth of population. In certain industries, such as mining, railroads, and agriculture, the number of persons employed actually declined. Conservative estimates show that even in the boom years the average number of unemployed ran well above a million and a half.[7] In other words, there had been no increase in employment relative to the increase in capital equipment, a failing in large part due to what was usually termed "technological unemployment." "Technological unemployment" has been more or less continuous since the Industrial Revolution, but it is doubtful if it has ever been more acute than in the period since the First World War.

The domestic picture, consequently, showed continued depression in certain lines and overexpansion in others, accompanied by maldistribution of the profits of industry—conditions which tended to weaken the economic structure. While the domestic situation displayed serious weaknesses, those latent in the international economy also contributed to the economic collapse. Europe's impoverishment and the high American tariffs made it impossible for Europe to pay her loans to us either in gold or in commodities. Furthermore, the intense nationalism engendered by the war resulted in a new wave of high tariffs throughout Europe. Even England deserted her long-tried policy of free trade to protect her industries, and she was followed enthusiastically by her colonies. There was the tendency during the postwar years for the major portion of the world's gold to move to the United States, a phenomenon which tended to keep prices high here and to make more difficult the efforts of European governments to return to a gold basis. The economic

---

[6] J. M. Clark, *Strategic Factors in Business Cycles*, p. 106.

[7] In the recession years of 1921, 1922, 1924, and 1927 unemployment estimates ran between two and four millions. See Leo Wolman, "Labor," in *Recent Economic Changes*, II, 478.

distress of Europe reacted to create political instability there; this in turn created uncertainty in international finance, and the whole situation made for world economic insecurity.

CLIMAX OF SPECULATION

Increase in speculation, particularly in stocks, has been a characteristic of so-called "boom eras." The twenties proved no exception. Many reasons account for the speculation of this particular decade. Most segments of American industry and business were prosperous; the wealth of the nation and the real income of large numbers of people were increasing, a situation bound to be reflected in the value of securities. Millions of workers and middle-class people who had never seen a bond or a share of stock until the days of the Liberty Loans and the campaigns for employee stock ownership now became conscious of the stock market. Since the value of American industries actually was increasing, and since this rise was reflected in the price of stocks, almost any purchase meant a profit. Following the lead of the big investors and professional stock market speculators, more and more people entered the market. By the time the frenzy ended, probably a million new customers were buying and selling on the various stock exchanges.

Although many of the new purchasers considered themselves investors rather than gamblers, the effect upon the price of securities was the same. The influx of hundreds of thousands of new purchasers increased the demand for securities and enhanced prices. The sight of these lambs crowding to be shorn was too much for the captains of industry and finance to resist and the business of producing and distributing securities became an important one. "The traditional theory," says Soule, "is that business corporations issue stocks and bonds only when they need additional capital. . . . During this period, however, new securities were manufactured almost like cakes of soap, for little better reason than that there was gain to be made out of their manufacture and sale."[8]

Industries, utilities, railroads, and banks hastened to print new securities to meet the insatiable demand, or split old stock to make it more easily purchasable. Between January 1, 1925, and October, 1929, the number of shares of stock listed on the New York Stock Exchange increased from 443,449,000 to over 1,000,000,000. Upon the bona fide investor who had no desire to speculate but wanted chiefly to invest his savings the bankers and bond houses "palmed off" foreign bonds and "guaranteed" real-estate mortgages, some of which their own employee experts asserted were too risky to purchase. To catch what surplus funds still remained, banks and bond houses organized

[8] George Soule, *Prosperity Decade*, p. 304.

"investment trusts" which were often used to manipulate stocks owned by the sponsors of these trusts. A deterioration and degradation permeated the entire banking and investment business.

The easy money made in speculation as stock prices mounted stimulated increased interest until speculators talked little about actual values and thought only of future accretions. The traditional basis of judging the value of a stock was "ten times earnings." Some stocks in 1929 were selling at fifty times this, or more. The market, as one expert observed, was discounting not only the future but the hereafter. The speculative frenzy was also accentuated by the retirement of the federal war debt at the rate of $800,000,000 a year, which tended to increase the volume of free funds seeking reinvestment, and also by the disproportionately large amount of the national income which went to capital rather than labor. In the end speculation went to incredible lengths; stocks were selling from three to twenty times their book value, thousands abandoned all interest in their legitimate business in order to concentrate on speculation, and the stock exchange became the dominant topic of conversation at business and social gatherings. In earlier times a million-share day on the stock exchange was almost epoch-making. In 1929 the trading on 122 days exceeded 4,000,000 shares, and on 37 exceeded 5,000,-000. So frantic was speculation that the market price of stocks, unlike its behavior in previous cycles, continued to mount for months after it was obvious that business was receding.

It might be supposed that experienced leaders of business and finance, to say nothing of economists, might have predicted the inevitable result. Most of them apparently did not. Optimism was widely prevalent that the country had entered a new era of never-ending prosperity and permanent high level of stock prices.[9] By the time the government began to worry, it was too late. The Federal Reserve Board issued a warning against the volume of margin trading early in 1929 and in February began to raise discount rates. Even the brokerage houses finally raised their requirements to 50 per cent. But any control here was largely nullified by the huge amounts poured into the banks by large corporations and others eager to lend their money on call at interest rates which finally reached 20 per cent. Until the final crash there was never lack of ample funds to finance the speculation.

There could be only one end. The climax came on October 29, 1929.

The big gong had hardly sounded in the great hall of the Exchange at ten o'clock Tuesday morning before the storm broke in full force. Huge blocks of stock were thrown upon the market for what they would bring. . . . Not only were innumerable small traders being sold out, but big ones, too. . . . Again and again the specialist in a stock would find himself surrounded by brokers fighting

[9] Typical statements from these sages are given in Edward Angly, *Oh, Yeah?* (1931).

to sell—and nobody at all even thinking of buying. . . . The scene on the floor was chaotic. . . . Within half an hour of the opening the volume of trading passed three million shares, by twelve o'clock it had passed eight million, by half-past one it had passed twelve million, and when the closing gong brought the day's madness to an end the gigantic record of 16,410,030 shares had been set; . . . the average prices of fifty leading stocks, as compiled by the New York *Times,* had fallen nearly forty points.[10]

THE COURSE OF THE DEPRESSION

The stock market crash of October, 1929, was but the beginning of an economic decline that continued with little interruption until the spring of 1933. Stock prices which had climbed to the most unwarranted heights now dropped to but a small fraction of their former quotations. From September, 1929, to January, 1933, according to the Dow-Jones index, thirty industrial stocks fell from an average of 364.9 to 62.7 dollars per share, a group of twenty public utilities dropped from 141.9 to 28.0 dollars per share, and twenty railroad stocks declined from an average of 180.0 to 28.1 dollars per share. The same story could be told of bank stocks and, as we shall see, of more tangible commodities. When the stock market decline finally hit bottom in July, 1933, some $74,000,000,000, or five-sixths of the September, 1929, value, had disappeared.

Prices of stocks were only a reflection of the business situation as a whole. A general picture is given by the following index numbers compiled by the United States Bureau of Labor Statistics, using 1926 as a base year with an index number of 100:

	Wholesale Prices	Employment	Pay Rolls
1929 average	95.3	97.5	100.5
1930 "	86.4	84.7	81.3
1931 "	73.0	72.2	61.5
1932 "	64.8	60.1	41.6
1933 "	65.9	64.6	44.0

The above index numbers on employment when expressed in terms of human beings meant, according to estimates of the American Federation of Labor, that in October, 1930, there were approximately 4,639,000 unemployed; in October, 1931, the number rose to 7,778,000; in October, 1932, to 11,586,000, and early in 1933 to over 13,000,000. These estimates should be compared to a total labor force in 1919 of somewhat over 48,000,000. They may possibly have been a trifle high, but when it is remembered that a goodly proportion of these unemployed were heads of families upon whose wages others were dependent, it will be seen that the number affected by unemploy-

[10] F. L. Allen, *Only Yesterday,* pp. 333–334.

ment ran into many millions more. A fair estimate of the number on public relief late in 1934 was 17,000,000. In addition to the millions thrown out of work, there were a larger number living on greatly reduced incomes. The index numbers of pay rolls given above show that the total paid in wages was more than cut in half during the first four years of the depression.

As production rests primarily upon the purchasing power of the market it is not at all surprising to find business and industrial activity falling in proportion. One authority puts the nation's industrial production in 1932 at more than 47 per cent below normal,[11] and it was to sink further in the next few months. An estimate of the physical volume of trade, based on the clearing index of business of the Federal Reserve Bank of New York (1926 = 100), shows a drop from 103 in 1929 to 54 in January, 1933.[12]

In agriculture the situation was somewhat different. The general level of production, as the following figures show, did not change so radically for certain of the principal crops:

	Corn (Bu.)	Wheat (Bu.)	Cotton (Bales)
1929	2,622,189,000	806,508,000	14,919,000
1930	2,081,048,000	850,965,000	14,243,000
1931	2,567,306,000	900,219,000	17,097,000
1932	2,908,145,000	726,863,000	12,727,000

The income of the farmers, however, as we have already noted,[13] declined sharply during these years. Between 1929 and 1932 farm values, already severely deflated, suffered a further decline of 33 per cent and the farmers' gross income declined 57 per cent. Remembering that agriculture had been in the throes of a depression ever since the war we see that these figures are extremely significant.

More striking, perhaps, than any of the figures yet given to illustrate the devastation wrought by the depression are those showing the decline in foreign trade:

	Exports (Millions of Dollars)	Imports (Millions of Dollars)
1929	5,241	4,399
1930	3,843	3,061
1931	2,424	2,091
1932	1,611	1,323

For this it is possible to find an abundance of reasons. The most important would include: (1) the decline in purchasing power, not only in the United

[11] Leonard Ayres, *The Economics of Recovery*, p. 5.
[12] C. A. Beard and G. H. E. Smith, *The Future Comes*, p. 9.
[13] Above, pp. 625–630.

States but elsewhere in the markets of the world; (2) the cessation after 1929 of American foreign loans, which had provided funds for some of this international trade; (3) the premium on the American dollar in international exchange, which discouraged the purchase of American goods; and (4) the high tariff policy of the United States, which brought retaliatory tariffs and special discriminations by license or quota devices against American goods. There is no doubt that the collapse in America brought on a depression in Europe which in turn intensified and deepened the economic decline here. Curtailment of American loans forced a similar procedure in England with a freezing of bank credits which ended in precipitating a banking collapse in Germany and Austria. Germany in 1931 defaulted on her war debt; and President Hoover, to prevent a further world economic collapse, effected an agreement for the temporary suspension of intergovernmental debts and reparation payments. Shortly afterward Great Britain abandoned the gold standard for a managed currency and was followed by a number of other European countries; these nations thus had a temporary advantage in international commerce at the expense of the gold standard countries including the United States.

The uprising of the world against the American tariff system came after the Hawley-Smoot Act of 1930, which raised the already high duties of the Fordney-McCumber tariff of 1922. In the new tariff the average of all the schedules went up; one-third of the dutiable items were changed, 890 being increased, including fifty transfers from the free to the dutiable list; 235 were lowered, including seventy-five transfers from the dutiable to the free list. Among the commodities removed from the free list were cement, hides, boots, and shoes. The average rate upon agricultural raw materials, according to a White House statement, was raised from 38.10 to 48.92 per cent, and the rate on other commodities was increased from 31.02 to 34.30 per cent.[14] The general average of the increase may not have been tremendously high, but the general effect appears to have been unfortunate in accelerating a trade decline and in arousing antagonism in other parts of the world. Some opposition developed among farmers and large manufacturers with surpluses to export, and more from bankers with billions invested in foreign loans, the payment of which was largely dependent upon the export trade of the debtor nations. Over a thousand economists petitioned the President not to sign the bill, but Hoover insisted that the new tariff would improve the economic situation and that any striking defects might be eliminated by the flexible

[14] It is estimated that the average for the dutiable articles in the McKinley tariff was 48.4 per cent; in the Wilson-Gorman tariff, 41.3; in the Dingley bill, 46.5; in the Payne-Aldrich, 40.7; in the Fordney-McCumber, 38.5; and in the Hawley-Smoot Bill (based on imports for 1932), 53.2 per cent. Statement of U.S. Tariff Commission.

provision allowing him to make changes upon recommendation of the Tariff Commission.[15]

Regarding the severity of the depression, statistics could be quoted almost without end. By 1934 most students agreed with Colonel Ayres, who maintained that "this depression has been far more severe than any of the 20 major depressions that we have experienced in this country since 1790."[16] On the other hand, there is little unanimity as to the reasons for the unique severity of this particular debacle. One economist has suggested two reasons—the uneven decline in prices and the long-drawn-out series of crises in credit.[17] For various reasons already discussed, agricultural prices slumped rapidly, but the prices of manufactured commodities, influenced by wage agreements and monopoly practices, held up longer. The utter collapse of the buying power of millions of farmers curtailed radically the business of workers and manufacturers and accentuated the depression. The series of credit crises was caused primarily by the weakness of the American banking system and the unsettlement of European finances, which culminated in 1931 when Great Britain went off the gold standard. The fact that 6987 banks in the United States failed in the decade ending in 1930, to which were added 2294 failures in 1931 and 1456 in 1932, explains much.

Another explanation offered for the severity was the large public and private debt which had been built up out of all proportion to the national income.[18] Still another was the large amount invested during the preceding years in such durable goods as automobiles whose replacement could be delayed, thus retarding recovery.[19] Many attributed the severity to the coincidence of much technological unemployment with the coming of the depression. To these may be added certain factors tending to accentuate the depression and delay recovery: world economic conditions; the increasing competition faced by the American farmer from other parts of the world; the collapse of the foreign market for industrial products, emphasized by the establishment of American factories in foreign countries to avoid their tariffs; the collapse of the foreign market as a place for safe investment; the continued concentration of wealth and income; the growing rigidity of the price system (because of increased business consolidation) and the failure of prices in certain lines to respond to deflation; and, finally, the difficulty of putting labor back to work because of labor-saving machinery. It looked as if American agriculture, industry, banking, and labor had indeed entered a new era,

---

[15] F. W. Taussig, "The Tariff Act of 1930," *Quarterly Journal of Economics*, XIV, 1–21 (November, 1930).

[16] Leonard Ayres, *op. cit.*, p. 5.

[17] *Ibid.*, pp. 5 ff.

[18] C. A. Beard and G. H. E. Smith, *op. cit.*, p. 9.

[19] J. M. Clark, *op. cit.*, p. 108.

but not the dazzling "new era" predicted in the dreams of the inflated twenties.

EARLY EFFORTS TOWARD RECOVERY

The depression following the stock market crash of 1929 was not only the most severe in our history but also the first one in which the federal government entered aggressively into the situation to alleviate conditions. During earlier panics the government did little except to safeguard its own credit and sit by until the storms blew over. This was partly because earlier generations did not know what to do, or because, dominated by a *laissez-faire* philosophy, they did not consider it the function of government to interfere in economic life to this extent. This does not mean that depressions did not eventually have an effect in speeding certain reform legislation, but it usually came after the event. By 1929 the days had passed when a government could sit by calmly and let its people suffer without some gesture of help. Too many revolutions had taken place in the world during the previous decade as a result of economic conditions, and too great a change had occurred in the philosophy of governmental functions for any administration to adopt a do-nothing policy.

Despite the fact that the Hoover administration prided itself on its adherence to *laissez faire* and glorified "rugged individualism," it made definite efforts to stay the economic collapse. These gave certain Republicans sympathetic with the "New Deal" an opportunity to claim Hoover as its originator. Be that as it may, the President, after the stock market crash of October, 1929, called a series of White House conferences with railroad presidents, industrial and labor leaders, key men in construction and public utilities, and leaders in national agricultural associations. His objective was to stabilize business by securing declarations favoring the maintenance of normal business activity and prevailing wages. He earnestly urged private business as well as state and municipal governments to aid the situation by increasing, if possible, their normal programs of construction. He also urged this on Congress. The latter responded by increasing appropriations for various types of public works. In the belief that tax reduction would counteract the depression, Hoover asked Congress in December, 1929, for lower income tax rates. Congress responded at once, but the only effect was to create a deficit and a new tax measure in 1932 increasing rates.

Four months before the crash the Agricultural Marketing Act had been passed.[20] Under its authority the Federal Farm Board created a Grain Stabilization Corporation and a Cotton Stabilization Corporation whose purpose it was to raise the prices of those commodities. Beginning in 1930, both

[20] Above, p. 629.

corporations went into the market and by actual purchase of these commodities, or of "futures" in them, succeeded for a brief period in maintaining their prices at levels slightly higher than the world market averages. Almost half a billion was spent to support the prices of farm commodities, but the net result, except for a loss of some $148,000,000 to the American taxpayer, appears to have been nil.

While the Federal Farm Board frantically attempted to stay the decline of agricultural prices, the government, after Congress in 1931 passed a bonus bill over the President's veto, released almost a billion dollars[21] which offered temporary relief to needy veterans but utterly failed to prime the pump of economic recovery. As the depression deepened, the veterans in the following year demanded the remainder of the bonus due them. A "Bonus Expeditionary Force" numbering about 20,000 moved into Washington to bring pressure upon Congress. The Senate refused to comply, and on orders from Hoover federal troops drove the Bonus Army from the city in one of the most tragic incidents of the depression.

The continuance of the depression in conjunction with the coming presidential campaign led to a renewed effort in 1932 on the part of the Hoover administration to improve the economic situation. In January of that year Congress created the Reconstruction Finance Corporation (RFC), with a capital of $500,000,000 and power to incur debts to three times that amount. Its purpose was to loan on security to banks, trust companies, building and loan associations, insurance companies, mortgage and loan companies, agricultural and livestock credit associations, and, with the approval of the Interstate Commerce Commission, to railroads. In July the lending power of the RFC was increased by $1,800,000,000 and its functions were enlarged. It was now empowered to lend to states and to public and private agencies funds to promote self-liquidating projects of public benefit. The RFC proved to be the most valuable effort of the Hoover administration to deal with the depression and Roosevelt extended its functions even more widely. During its first year and a half it loaned about $3,000,000,000. Many criticized the RFC as a method of ladling out credit to the rulers of banks and industries who had already proved themselves incapable of directing the nation's economic life. The fact remains, however, that the RFC saved many a tottering bank, railroad, and insurance company from collapse and eased the strain in one of the most acute periods of the depression.

---

[21] The Bonus Bill of 1924 provided for service certificates which would mature in twenty years and against which a veteran might borrow up to 22½ per cent of the matured value. The act of 1931 raised this to 50 per cent. In 1936 a new Bonus Act was passed over the President's veto; it provided for the redemption of the adjusted service certificates held by the government life insurance fund by means of exchanging them for 3 per cent bonds which in turn might be converted into cash.

Two other acts of less importance but significant in rendering some immediate help and establishing precedents for future action were passed in 1932. One increased the capital stock of the Federal Land Banks by $125,000,000 to augment their resources for lending to farmers. The second was the Home Loan Act, authorized to create not less than eight or more than twelve Home Loan Banks to extend emergency credit to homeowners. Any building or loan association, savings bank, or similar institution might become a member of a Home Loan Bank by subscribing at least one per cent of its own holdings. These amounts might be supplemented by the Treasury up to $125,000,-000. With these funds the Home Loan Banks might lend to home-mortgage institutions against the latter's holdings and thus supply further home mortgages to an amount not specified. Although the RFC and the Home Loan Act were intended to supply emergency credit, many hoped that they might also contribute to start prices upward.

More perhaps than any other in responsible position, Hoover was convinced that America's recovery was closely dependent upon that of the rest of the world. He assumed the leadership in an effort to bolster European economy, and also the initiative in bringing a one-year moratorium on intergovernmental debts. He supported the plan for a World Economic Conference which met after he left office. In all this he took a more realistic view than did his successor, who believed that American recovery could be achieved without European economic entanglements.

THE DEPRESSION AND ECONOMIC THINKING

Efforts of the government to lift the nation out of the slump will be told in the next chapter. In the meantime the despondency, the discontent, and the questionings which arose from years of depression were deep and wide. Forgetting that depressions had frequently occurred in previous years, leaders in all walks of life, including economists, were dumfounded at the speed with which the glittering structure of prosperity had collapsed like a house of cards. Why should this "new era" enjoyed by the richest nation in the world end in disaster?

One effect was to popularize the ideas of the economist Thorstein Veblen, who during the previous thirty years had turned his back on many of the sacred tenets of the classical economics and acidly ridiculed many phases of capitalist civilization. Another effect was a revival of interest in socialism and communism. If capitalism could collapse so easily, many wondered whether there might be something in an economic system based on production for use rather than profit, and a system of public rather than private ownership of the means of production, transportation, and financing. Attention was directed to the experiments in other countries, particularly Russia, where unemployment and depressions were nonexistent. In such areas, the standard of living might still be low, the nation might be controlled by dictators, and civil rights might be unknown. But this situation, it was asserted, was only a temporary stage; high standards of living, civil rights, and personal freedom would come later. Much of the Marxian economics had not stood the test of time. Nevertheless, many whose careers had been blocked by the depression turned for inspiration to the father of "scientific socialism."

In the campaign of 1932 the Socialists polled almost 900,000 votes, but their strength rapidly declined in the face of the many New Deal efforts to bring back prosperity and to reform various aspects of the economic system. The Communist party was never large—perhaps 75,000 at the height of its strength in the late thirties and early forties—but it attracted a host of "fellow travelers" whose influence was greater. Doubtless a few Communists and a larger number of "fellow travelers" worked for the government during this period, but the experiments came not from them but rather from a necessity to do something to revive the economic order, to reform certain economic evils so obvious in the twenties, to bring some hope to the stricken masses, and to save the capitalist system. The proponents and artificers of the New Deal were not dominated by socialism or by Marxian theories, concerning which most of them knew little. Rather they worked from day to day, with slight precedent to guide them, attempting to devise experiments that might work.

If the young economists of the New Deal were captured by any theories, they were those of John Maynard Keynes, the English economist, whose ideas were widely known and discussed by the middle thirties. Keynes was an internationalist rather than a nationalist; a believer in government inter-ference when necessary, not complete *laissez faire*. As he watched the world fail to pull itself out of the depression, he discarded the classic theory that low interest rates on savings would induce enterprisers to invest and thus start the business cycle upwards. Savings, he pointed out, inevitably contract during depression and grow during prosperity. But even in prosperity there is always a limit to the market for goods produced, with the consequent falling off in the demand for savings (capital). Since prosperity is dependent upon continued investment and business expansion, every boom is threatened with collapse, as every depression is threatened with an inability to revive.

To start the cycle upward, he insisted, the government must step in to help sustain buying power by cutting down unemployment and thus lead the way to a resumption of business investment. This might mean "deficit spend-ing," but it would also restore the economic balance. This was what the New Deal, in fact, had already been attempting to do, and now Keynes gave it a highly technical and theoretical underpinning in his famous treatise, *The*

General Theory of Employment, Interest and Money (1936). It became the Bible of the New Deal economists. Keynes upset many aspects of classic economy and tremendously influenced American economic thinking.

POLITICAL REACTIONS

That the economic depression would have its political reactions was obvious. Only one American President, James Monroe, ever politically survived a major economic depression, and he was probably saved only by the fact that there was no strong political party to oppose him. Hoover, as it turned out, was no exception to the rule. The congressional elections of 1930 wiped out the Republican majority in the House and cut their majority in the Senate to the slimmest margin. As the presidential election of 1932 approached, most voters were convinced that the Hoover administration had no policy beyond an effort to cushion the depression—a policy which seemed utterly inadequate. Actually the efforts of the administration had gone beyond that. The chief criticism that can be leveled at them is that they were "too little and too late."

Although the platforms of the two parties in 1932 were much alike and considerable attention was devoted during the campaign to the question of prohibition, there was only one real issue—the depression. Hoover and his spokesmen tried to convince the voters that the Republicans had accomplished all that could be done safely and that a Democratic victory would precipitate an even greater economic collapse. The Democratic candidate, Franklin D. Roosevelt, presented his views on economic problems in a series of speeches. He spoke in general terms but he implied that a change in policies would improve conditions. In brief, he promised a "New Deal." This was enough. The Democrats were overwhelmingly victorious not only in the national but also in state and local elections. For the first time since 1919 the Democratic party had control of both legislative and executive branches. What the "New Deal" would mean in practice no one knew, but if the new administration had any real program with which to meet a major economic catastrophe, its opportunity had come.

SELECTED READINGS

Soule, George, *Prosperity Decade,* chaps. 13, 14.

Mitchell, Broadus, *Depression Decade,* chaps. 1–3.

Faulkner, H. U., *From Versailles to the New Deal,* chaps. 10, 11.

Mitchell, W. C., "Business Cycles," *Encyclopaedia of the Social Sciences,* Vol. III, pp. 92–106.

Clark, J. M., *Strategic Factors in Business Cycles,* pp. 96–124.

CHAPTER 30

THE NEW DEAL

BEGINNINGS OF THE NEW DEAL

IT would be difficult to exaggerate the utter economic collapse and the dark pessimism of the nation when Franklin D. Roosevelt became President on March 4, 1933. General business had sunk to less than 60 per cent of normal; more than one-fourth of the wage earners were unemployed; exports had sunk to close to the lowest point in thirty years. Commodity prices had reached the lowest point since the beginning of the depression. More serious, perhaps, at the moment was the disintegration of the credit and banking structure. More than 1400 banks had failed during 1932 and the situation became worse in the early months of 1933. It reached a climax on February 14 when leading banks in Detroit closed and the state of Michigan declared an eight-day banking moratorium. This action was quickly followed elsewhere until by March 2 there were twenty-one states, besides the District of Columbia, where either moratoria had been established or the banks were operating under special regulation. On the day of Roosevelt's inauguration New York and Illinois declared bank holidays which closed the stock and commodity markets in the country's greatest financial centers.

Roosevelt, whose ideas and plans for meeting the depression had been expressed during the presidential campaigns in only the most general terms, now acted with unexpected speed. He immediately called Congress into special session and on March 6 declared a nation-wide bank moratorium and placed an embargo on the withdrawal or transportation of gold. When Congress met on March 9 it passed an Emergency Banking Act which confirmed the proclamation of the President and gave him emergency powers to regulate transactions in credit, currency, gold and silver, and foreign exchange. It empowered the Secretary of the Treasury to require deposit of all gold and gold certificates and authorized the Comptroller to appoint a conservator for any national bank in difficulty and for the reorganization of such banks. It also provided that national and state banks which were members of the

Federal Reserve System might open under license, and it sought to strengthen the position of the weaker banks by empowering the Reconstruction Finance Corporation to purchase their preferred stock or take it as collateral for loans. To help break the credit impasse, the note-issuing power of the Federal Reserve banks was enlarged. On March 13 the bank moratorium officially came to an end when banks which had obtained licenses reopened. The latter were the solvent banks and those which could be rehabilitated through government aid. Altogether, during the special session of the Seventy-Third Congress, that body passed almost a score of major acts dealing with various aspects of the economic situation, which roughly comprise what the nation came to term the "New Deal."

Before proceeding with a more intensive description of the New Deal, certain general statements may be offered to aid in threading the maze of numerous legislative acts. Two main objectives dominated the entire program —recovery and reform. Sometimes these were interwoven in a single piece of legislation, sometimes separated. The primary objective was to pull the nation out of the disastrous depression, the second was to remedy economic abuses which were all too evident and which had contributed to bring on the catastrophe. In conjunction with these objectives was a third, which looked toward a balance of the economic system—strengthening the weaker segments, such as labor and agriculture, and bringing others, such as finance and industry, under stronger federal control. Said Roosevelt: "What we seek is balance in our economic system—balance between agriculture and industry and balance between the wage earner, the employer and the consumer. We seek also balance that our internal markets be kept rich and large, and that our trade with other nations be increased on both sides of the ledger."

Since these objectives necessitated a certain amount of over-all planning, they inevitably meant extended government supervision, control, and activity. The result was a rapid expansion of the federal bureaucracy but not, as many contended, a movement toward socialism. The New Deal contemplated no fundamental change in the economic system. The essential elements of capitalism remained—private ownership of the means of production and distribution and the profit system. In fact, the main business of the New Deal appeared to be to save capitalism. As it proceeded, a shift of emphasis was discerned which has led students to differentiate between a "First New Deal" and a "Second New Deal." During the first period the administration sought recovery by close co-operation with private enterprise. The effort was to encourage "price rises which would increase profits and seep down in the form of higher wages, to groups which would use their increased purchasing power to stimulate recovery."[1] In the Second New Deal, which began in

[1] Basil Rauch, *The History of the New Deal, 1933–1938*, p. 157.

1935, the administration shifted to permanent recovery by pouring purchasing power into the hands of the less privileged groups and guaranteeing their future through social security.

Among other aspects that should be emphasized is the fact that the New Deal began without any over-all or detailed plan. Much of it was experimental, improvised as the months went on, and with few precedents in this country to base it on. Although the President sought counsel from the leaders of industry and finance, he came to rest mainly on the so-called "brain trust," a group of experts drawn from university circles. Another factor in the situation should be noted. It was not the legislation and policies alone which improved the economic situation; it was in part the improvement of morale and the restoration of confidence inspired by the President's quick and able handling of the bank crisis and his activity in attacking the depression on many fronts.

CURRENCY AND CREDIT

The financial program of the New Deal, as far as it concerned currency and credit, had three objectives—inflation, banking reform, and better supervision of the security and commodity exchanges. In every major depression experienced by the United States there has been a strong demand for inflation. By 1933 the clamor became so insistent that it could not be denied. The arguments for inflation rested, of course, primarily upon the fact that the increased value of the dollar bore heavily upon the debtor class, which includes in one way or another the great majority of the population, and that restoration of currency values to the level at which the debts were contracted was necessary to restore equilibrium between debtor and creditor and thus halt the economic collapse. As Roosevelt said later, "We had determined definitely to seek an increase in all values. Two courses were open: to cut down the debts through bankruptcies and foreclosures to such a point that they would be below property values; or else to increase property values until they were greater than the debts. Obviously the latter course was the only legitimate method of putting the country back on its feet without destroying human values."

Mention has already been made of efforts to expand credit facilities in the Emergency Banking Act of March 9, 1933, and by the Executive Orders forbidding the hoarding of gold and of gold certificates and the export of gold without license from the Treasury. A broader legal basis was established in May by the Farm Relief and Inflation Act (First Agricultural Adjustment Act). It gave the President power, if he desired to exercise it, (1) to require the Federal Reserve banks to expand their credit up to $3,000,000,000; (2) to issue United States notes secured solely on the credit of the United States up to $3,000,000,000, these notes to be used only to retire outstanding federal obligations but to be legal tender for all debts, public and private; (3) to devalue the gold dollar by as much as 50 per cent; (4) to accept silver for six months up to $200,000,000, at a price not exceeding 50 cents an ounce, in payment of war debts due from foreign governments; and (5) to coin silver without limit at any ratio to gold he might decide. This act gave him power to inflate in almost any way he pleased. He could print more paper money, the old demand of the Greenbackers. He could buy more silver, the old cry of the silver group in the 1880's and 1890's.

Under the authority of these two acts inflation may be said to have begun with Executive Orders of March 10, 1933, halting the export of gold except when licensed by the Treasury; of April 5, forbidding the hoarding of gold and gold certificates; and of April 19, forbidding the export of gold. The last is generally regarded as taking the nation off the gold standard. This was technically true, but as the gold was impounded in the Treasury it remained, in the words of economists, a "psychological reserve." This was made more definite by the Gold Repeal Joint Resolution of June 5, which canceled the gold clauses in public and private obligations, making debts payable in legal tender. A rise in prices in the spring and early summer of 1933 halted for the moment further tinkering with the currency, but their decline in the early autumn simultaneously with the marketing of summer crops revived agitation for inflation.

Up to this point the President had used only one of the five powers of inflation given him in the Farm Act by putting $600,000,000 in circulation by Federal Reserve bank purchases of federal securities. In October the administration decided to attempt inflation by reducing the gold content of the dollar. Beginning in September the Treasury offered to accept gold from producers for resale at the world price. When this did not secure the desired result, the President on October 22 announced that the Treasury would buy gold at a price determined by the RFC. Instead of the long-established legal price of $20.67 an ounce, the price was initially set at $31.36 and eventually raised to $34.45 (January 16, 1934). This operation was carried out in practice by giving sellers of gold more paper dollars for the same amount of gold than they had previously received. As long as the government could peg the price of gold in the open market it could theoretically devalue the dollar and raise prices. To the surprise of the advocates of this scheme, prices did not rise proportionately to the depreciation of the dollar; and on December 21 the President ordered the Treasury to purchase at 64½ cents an ounce all of the silver mined in the United States; this price was 21½ cents higher than that at which silver was then selling on the open market.

When the President started the gold purchase plan in October, 1933, he stated that he was "moving toward a managed currency." That he might have even more clear-cut authorization, he asked Congress in January, 1934, for legislation containing specific power to devalue the dollar to between 50 and 60 cents in terms of its former gold content, to manage the dollar within these limits, to impound in the Treasury the gold held in the Federal Reserve banks, to assure to the government the profits that might accrue from devaluing the dollar, and, finally, to use part of this profit to create a $2,000,000,000 fund to stabilize the dollar. Under the authority of the Gold Reserve Act (January, 1934) the value of the dollar was officially fixed in February at 59.06 per cent of its former (1900) value in terms of gold. Three months later it was discovered that while the gold content of the dollar had been reduced by law 40.94 per cent, wholesale commodity prices had risen only 22 per cent. At the insistent clamor of the silver advocates the administration consented to further legislation, and in June, 1934, the Silver Purchase Act was passed, the "ultimate objective" of which was to increase the use of silver in the nation's monetary stock until the proportions were one-quarter in silver to three-quarters in gold.

In the particular method it pursued to raise prices the administration appeared to have been influenced by the school of economists who hold that the price level of commodities is closely influenced by the gold content of the monetary medium. That such a relationship exists no one will deny, but it proved in this case no short cut to inflation. The fact that nine-tenths of the nation's business is conducted on bank credit rather than with money is a partial explanation for the failure of the government's inflation policy to raise prices to the extent expected. It also helps to explain the shift of inflationary efforts from currency to credit and indicates the necessity both of repairing the credit system and of extending credit. This process had begun, in fact, during the Hoover administration with the establishment of the Reconstruction Finance Corporation. The powers of the RFC, as we have seen, were extended under the Emergency Banking Act (p. 655) and again in June, 1934, when the Loans-to-Industry Act authorized direct loans to industrial organizations up to $580,000,000. The latter act aroused considerable criticism on the ground that it was poor economy to attempt to save the weaker units in an already overbuilt industrial system, but the great need of keeping men at work was the important argument for the loans.

A further effort to stabilize the credit situation, and at the same time save the small homeowner, began under Hoover in 1932 with the Home Loan Bank Act, which established federal banks to lend to private banks and building and loan associations on real-estate mortgages. This was supplemented in 1933 by the Home Owner's Loan Act, setting up a corporation which could issue bonds up to $2,000,000,000 to refinance first mortgages on homes whose value did not exceed $20,000. Interest on the bonds was guaranteed and an amendment of 1934 extended this guarantee to the principal. The lending activities of this corporation lasted for three years, when they were taken over by the Federal Housing Administration, which also insured against losses from loans on real estate. Any discussion of inflationary possibilities through extension of credit should also include, as we shall see, consideration of the credit facilities extended to agriculture through various channels.

The tragic shortcomings of the American banking system had been amply demonstrated, during both the boom years of the twenties and the depression years of the thirties. Reform of some sort would have been inevitable under any administration. That adopted by the Democrats was incorporated in the Banking Acts of 1933 and 1935. The most widely discussed and perhaps the most important parts of the Banking Act of 1933 were those which separated security affiliates from the parent banks in the Federal Reserve System and those which set up a Federal Deposit Insurance Corporation to provide insurance on deposits.[2] The provision requiring banks to relinquish their security affiliates confined them again to a strictly banking business, and the insurance scheme was devised to safeguard the almost defenseless depositor. Under the latter all Federal Reserve banks were required to insure, and state banks approved as solvent by the state banking authorities might participate. Other clauses in the act restricted the use of Federal Reserve bank credit for stock market speculation,[3] broadened the power of national banks to establish branch banks in those states that permitted branch banking, and restrained national banks from dealing in the securities of foreign countries and other foreign securities. It forbade private banks that conduct a business of underwriting and promoting the sale of securities from acting as banks of deposit, and established a quick-liquidating procedure for the benefit of depositors in banks that had failed. The act also allowed industrial and savings banks to join the system. Many wished that the act had gone further on the road of banking reform; nevertheless, it was an honest effort to rectify some of the worst abuses which had developed since the establishment of the Federal Reserve System in 1913.

In the Banking Act of 1935 an important effort was made to extend federal power over money and credit. Although the amount insurable under the Federal Deposit Insurance Corporation was reduced, the supervisory powers of that corporation were considerably extended. In the second place, the Federal Reserve Board was reorganized into a seven-member board by eliminating

[2] The amount which could be insured for each account was finally fixed in 1935 at $5000.

[3] For example, Federal Reserve member banks could no longer lend on the stock market "for others," that is, they could not receive idle funds from corporations or individuals placed in the banks for the purpose of lending for stock market speculation.

the Secretary of the Treasury and the Comptroller from ex officio membership, in the hope of lessening political influence and making it more impartial
and disinterested. In the third place, the credit policy of the separate banks
was transferred to a Federal Open Market Committee (already created by
the act of 1933) made up of the seven members of the Board and five regional representatives of the Reserve banks. In the fourth place, the Board
could now vary within certain limits the reserve requirements of the member banks and review periodically the rates charged by the Reserve banks,
and it was required to give its approval to appointments for president and
vice president of each Reserve bank. Finally, certain technical changes enlarged the credit facilities. The Federal Reserve banks, for example, were
authorized to make advances to their members on any satisfactory security,
and member banks might make a larger volume of real-estate loans. The
latter provision allowed loans for ten years up to 60 per cent of the value of
the property and up to a certain proportion of the bank's assets.

The widespread popular resentment against the banks and security houses
which had foisted securities of questionable value upon a gullible public also
brought in 1933 the passage of the Sale of Securities Act, which sought to
protect prospective investors by affording them certain information regarding
new securities sold in interstate commerce. Under this act a concern offering
securities was required to file detailed information with the Federal Trade
Commission (later with a newly created body, the Securities and Exchange
Commission), and even after approval was granted by the Commission sellers might be held liable in civil or criminal suits for untrue statements. This
was a preliminary to another act, the Securities Exchange Act of June, 1934
(amended in 1936 to include unlisted securities), which provided for the
regulation of securities exchanges and established a Securities and Exchange
Commission to supervise them. Both acts were bitterly opposed by the
financial interests and in the second act they succeeded in reducing the liabil-
ity of underwriters, officers, and directors of the concerns issuing securities as
originally provided in the Sale of Securities Act. Regulation of a somewhat
similar type was extended to certain agricultural commodities in 1936 by the
Commodity Exchange Act, which set up a Commodity Exchange Commission to regulate transactions on commodity futures exchanges, to limit short
selling, and to curb manipulation. These acts did not guarantee the safety
of an investment, but they attempted to protect the investor by securing
honest information from corporations regarding new securities and those
listed on the exchanges. Moreover, it was the business of the commissions to
eliminate manipulation and dishonest practices. The result has brought a
marked improvement in the ethics of these exchanges.

One notable contribution of SEC was the preparation of an act passed by

Congress in 1940 for the registration and regulation of investment trusts. Such companies were organized to sell their own stock, the funds from which were invested in a variety of stock, the income (after deducting management expenses) being then distributed to their own stockholders. Such companies were designed for small investors whose time or knowledge was inadequate to look after their own financial interests. The opportunities for the misuse of such funds were many, and strict regulations were necessary. Although a number of investment trusts had been organized in the thirties, the great development came in the forties with hundreds of thousands of investors participating.

A NEW DEAL FOR AGRICULTURE

The preceding discussion of inflationary measures leads naturally to a consideration of agricultural legislation. No group, it was believed, would benefit more from higher prices than the farmers. As the agricultural legislation of the New Deal developed, its major objective was to restore the farmer's purchasing power and his general economic position to that which he had enjoyed during the prewar period, that is, from August, 1909, to July, 1914, a time when the prices the farmer paid were sufficiently in balance with those received for his commodities to maintain a decent standard of living.[4] This was to be done in part by inflation and in part by adjusting farm production to market requirement, both of which methods would prepare the way for establishing "parity prices" and parity income. In addition to this there was a definite policy to aid in debt reduction and provide security against inflation. Also included in the program was general rural relief and the rehabilitation of submarginal farmers. Important for the future was a growing interest in soil conservation and land improvement. This broad program the government followed with an enthusiasm which hardly envisaged the complexities of the agricultural situation.

The program began in earnest in May, 1933, with the Farm Relief and Inflation Act, more commonly known as the First Agricultural Adjustment Act.[5] It moved to cut the surplus and raise the income of the farmers by three methods: (1) by cotton options under which cotton growers were to reduce their cotton acreage at least 30 per cent and for which they were given options

---

[4] As stated specifically in the Farm Relief and Inflation Act the purpose was:

"To establish and maintain such balance between the production and consumption of agricultural commodities, and such marketing conditions therefor, as will reestablish prices to farmers at a level that will give agricultural commodities a purchasing power with respect to articles that farmers buy, equivalent to the purchasing power of agricultural commodities in the base period. The base period in the case of all agricultural commodities except tobacco shall be the pre-war period, August, 1909–July, 1914. In the case of tobacco, the base period shall be the post-war period, August, 1919–July, 1929."

[5] For inflationary features, see above, pp. 656–657.

to purchase an amount of cotton corresponding to the amount they agreed not to raise (cotton which was still held by the former Federal Farm Board) and which the option holders might sell if prices went up; (2) by "rental" or benefit payments under which the government gave bonuses for acreage temporarily taken out of cultivation; and (3) by marketing agreements which might eliminate waste and provide for more scientific marketing. The cost was to be paid by processing taxes levied on products manufactured from the basic commodities concerned.

During the first year the Agricultural Adjustment Administration concentrated on cotton, wheat, corn, hog, and tobacco reduction. The results seemed sufficiently successful for it to enlarge its operation in 1934 to include beef and dairy cattle, peanuts, rye, barley, flax, grain sorghums, sugar beets, and sugar cane; the tobacco and cotton curtailment programs were strengthened by special acts. At the same time the government encouraged submarginal farmers to retire from commercial agriculture and attempted through trade agreements (reciprocal tariffs) to stimulate foreign trade in agricultural commodities.

No part of the New Deal program inspired more widespread criticism than that pertaining to agriculture. The whole idea of curtailing the production of foodstuffs while millions were on the point of starvation seemed to humanitarians little short of insanity. An effort to promote a "scarcity economy" at a time when the opposite was needed seemed incredible. Furthermore, it largely shifted the burden to the hard-pressed consumer. Even from the point of view of scarcity economics, however, there was no clear-cut proof in the early months that the program was successful. Despite government efforts, the violation of acreage reduction contracts, favorable climatic conditions, and more intensive farming produced crops of cotton, corn, and hogs in 1933 not much below those of 1932. While the controlled crops were reduced, farmers turned to other crops. The sudden increase in the cost of foodstuffs brought consumer resistance, and the general rise in prices kept the purchasing power of the farmer's dollar about where it had been. Likewise, American curtailment stimulated foreign agricultural production. Nor were the prospects of increased foreign trade through reciprocal tariffs particularly bright for the farmers because in some cases such tariffs were bound to bring foreign agricultural products in greater competition with domestic products. Despite retarding influences, there was no question as to the fact that the economic conditions of the farmers improved rapidly. The Agricultural Adjustment Administration noted early in 1935 that the purchasing power of farm products in 1934 averaged 73 per cent of the prewar level, as compared with 55 per cent at the low point in March, 1933. Some of this improvement was doubtless the result of a general economic improvement, but it was also due in part to the New Deal program.

Whatever may have been the contributions of the Agricultural Adjustment Act, they were greatly curtailed when in January, 1936, the Supreme Court declared parts of the act unconstitutional on the grounds that it invaded the reserved rights of the states and was an improper use of the taxing power. The strong probability that this might happen had led the government to canvass the possibilities of continuing agricultural relief in some other way, and the method decided upon was soil conservation. The drought of 1934 and the dust storms in the spring of 1935 called attention to the tragic results of soil destruction, and Congress recognized the problem by creating in 1933 a Soil Erosion Service and by enacting in 1935 the Soil Erosion Act. This legislation created the Soil Conservation Service, under the Secretary of Agriculture, to conduct soil erosion surveys and carry out preventive measures. The scope of this work was greatly enlarged after the AAA decision by the Soil Conservation and Domestic Allotment Act (1936), which appropriated $500,-000,000 for the preservation and improvement of soil fertility, the promotion of the economic use and conservation of land, and the protection of rivers and harbors against soil erosion. For two years direct aid might be given to co-operating farmers, after which it was to be extended only to states that had adopted authorizing legislation and a conservation plan acceptable to the Secretary of Agriculture.

The Soil Conservation and Domestic Allotment Act was a makeshift. With the re-election of Roosevelt in 1936 and a more sympathetic Supreme Court, Congress in 1938 passed a new Agricultural Adjustment Act (second AAA). It retained certain features of the old acts and added new ones. As in earlier legislation, its primary aim was to maintain "parity prices," that is, to keep the prices of certain agricultural products (wheat, cotton, corn, tobacco, and rice) at a level in relation to the cost of commodities bought by farmers in 1909–1914.[6] This was to be achieved by the government's setting a "parity price" and a quota each year for the commodity to be raised. If the price fell below this, the government would in part recompense the farmer for the difference between the actual price received and the "parity price." If production in any year was far beyond the amount set by the government, marketing quotas might be established if two-thirds of the farmers producing that commodity agreed. Such agreements would be enforced by penalty taxes for selling beyond the quotas. In determining the amount of a commodity to be raised in a year, the Department of Agriculture was to include a surplus so that in case of drought or other emergency a sufficient quantity would always

---

[6] For tobacco the years 1919–1926 were to be used.

be on hand. This policy, a new feature of the act, was expected to maintain an "ever-normal granary." Another new feature was the establishment of insurance on wheat. The maintenance of soil resources as provided in the Soil Conservation and Allotment Act was retained as a permanent policy.

The second great objective of the New Deal agricultural program, debt reduction and security against foreclosure, was also pushed aggressively. The First Agricultural Adjustment Act aimed to aid the farmers' credit situation by authorizing the Federal Land banks to issue $2,000,000,000 in 4 per cent bonds—the interest but not the principal to be guaranteed by the government —to refinance farm mortgages at an interest rate not to exceed $4\frac{1}{2}$ per cent. To increase efficiency the President in 1933 consolidated the government's various agricultural credit agencies in the Farm Credit Administration. This consolidation, authorized under the Farm Credit Act (June, 1933), grouped the credit facilities into four divisions dealing with land banks, production credit, intermediate credit, and co-operative credit, and considerably enlarged existing facilities.

From providing easier credit facilities the program moved on to the mortgage problem. Congress passed three acts in 1934: (1) the Farm Mortgage Refinancing Act, creating a Federal Farm Mortgage Corporation to aid further in refinancing farm debts; (2) a Farm Mortgage Foreclosure Act, extending the authority of the Land Bank Commissioner to enable him to make loans to farmers for the purpose of enabling them to redeem farm properties owned by them prior to foreclosure; and (3) the Frazier-Lemke Bankruptcy Act, providing that in cases of bankruptcy the farmer might demand a "fair and reasonable" appraisal and might repurchase his property over a period of six years with interest at one per cent. If creditor or mortgagee objected to the settlement the farmer might retain the property for a period of five years at a reasonable rental, bankruptcy proceedings being halted. The Frazier-Lemke Act was declared unconstitutional in 1935 as a violation of the fifth amendment, but a similar act shortening the retention period to three years was upheld in 1936. Within a year and a quarter after the acts had been passed the Farm Credit Administration had made 1,400,000 loans totaling $2,000,000,000. The result was a virtual stoppage of farm foreclosures.

The legislation so far mentioned by no means encompassed the entire program of agricultural aid. The program included the much criticized and not too successful resettlement project of moving farmers from submarginal lands and settling them on subsistence homesteads. It included the Federal Surplus Commodities Corporation to purchase and distribute surplus products among state relief organizations. It rendered great aid to agriculture through flood-control projects (TVA and others), by larger appropriations for interstate highways, and by substantial allotments for rural electrification. Moreover, the reciprocal tariffs (pp. 694–695) sought to aid farmers as well as other economic groups. In fact, it would be difficult to think of any method, unless it be complete socialization, neglected by the federal government to rehabilitate American agriculture.

A survey of the farm legislation passed during the five years 1933–1938 makes clear certain facts. First of all, "economic planning" was carried further with respect to agriculture than to any other economic interest. The government took upon itself the responsibility of attempting to determine both production and prices as well as maintaining soil resources and handling most of the credit resources of the farmers. In the second place, this program was carried out at the expense of the consumer. Agriculture was to be a favored industry, with the taxpayer and consumer paying the bill. This, of course, did not disturb the farmer; he insisted that agriculture was now merely receiving protection as industry had long received it through the protective tariff. Finally, it should be noted that the government entered so definitely into the program of financing agriculture that by 1937 its agencies held about half of the long-term agricultural paper of the country. At the same time private agencies largely abandoned the business of financing agriculture. All this made serious inroads on the so-called "free enterprise" system and was indeed a big step from the *laissez-faire* policies of earlier decades.

INDUSTRY AND THE NEW DEAL

The New Deal's policy toward industry, as implemented in the National Industrial Recovery Act (1933), was almost as revolutionary as its policy toward agriculture. It aimed, said Roosevelt in signing the act, to assure "a reasonable profit to industry and living wages to labor with the elimination of piratical methods and practices which have not only harassed honest business but also contributed to the ills of labor." More simply stated, the NIRA aimed to promote recovery by introducing self-regulation of business, curtailing overproduction, increasing wages, shortening hours of labor, and raising prices. Along with this the act authorized the federal financing of public works to the extent of $3,300,000,000.

To accomplish the purpose, the President was authorized to work out codes of fair competition which industry was to accept voluntarily but which could be enforced through a system of licensing. Theoretically these codes were to be worked out through the co-operation of government, industry, labor, and the consumer. In actual practice they were largely the work of representatives of industry, with some participation from labor where unions were strong. As in the case of the agricultural legislation, the interest of the consumers was largely ignored. Behind the NIRA was the theory that the efforts of the older antitrust acts to maintain unlimited competition had brought disaster and that in their place, at least temporarily, should be substituted an attempt to establish industrial co-operation under government control. Technically the antitrust acts were still in force; actually they were pushed into the background. The background of the NIRA was wider than the depression. Throughout the twenties the nation had taken a more lenient attitude toward monopolies and this was reflected in the attitude of the Supreme Court and the failure of the enforcement agencies to prosecute infringements of the antitrust acts. The government had co-operated closely with big business during the First World War and later with the trade associations. The trade associations in turn had developed a precedent of industrial co-operation and had somewhat modified unbridled competition within the separate industries. And there was, of course, the propaganda of industry that self-regulation would bring better results than government regulation.

To carry out the NIRA a National Recovery Administration (NRA) was set up under the direction of General Hugh S. Johnson as administrator and Donald Richberg as general counsel. These men, with a staff of expert assistants in co-operation with representatives of industry and labor, drew up what were believed to be fair codes, held public hearings, and finally promulgated the codes over the President's signature. As several thousand industries were eligible for codification and the duration of the act was only two years, the first problem was to decide whether it would be better to hammer out a few perfect codes for the basic industries or to formulate as many as possible as quickly as possible in the hope that defects could be eventually ironed out. The latter course was followed: but as a stopgap until separate codes could be drawn, a blanket agreement on hours and wages, known as the President's Reemployment Agreement, was promulgated in July. This blanket code banned child labor, established a working week of thirty-five hours for industrial workers and forty for white-collar workers, and set minimum wages of 40 cents per hour for industry and from $12 to $15 per week for others depending on the size of the community. Employers who would adhere to this temporary agreement (to last six months but later extended to May 1, 1934) would receive the symbol of the Blue Eagle. Unlike the industry codes, the blanket code was not enforceable at law. The pressure of public approval, however, gave it strength and hastened the process of code making in the individual industries. In the meantime Washington took on a hectic atmosphere reminiscent of war days as representatives of industrial trade associations and labor unions flocked to the capital to participate in code making. Eventually over 576 basic codes were approved along with 189 supplementary codes, and the majority of industrial workers operated under the Blue Eagle.

No effort to codify and integrate industry on such a scale had ever before been made in America, and the difficulties were great. The desperate condition in which the nation found itself, however, created, at least in the early months, a willingness to co-operate in carrying the NIRA into effect. Nevertheless, there was criticism from the start. There were frequent charges that the codes were evaded ("chiseling") and that the interests of the consumer were ignored in making the codes. Unorganized and inadequately represented as this group was, their complaint had a strong basis in fact. But as the months went by, criticism also developed rapidly on the part of labor, which insisted that there had been widespread evasion of those parts of the codes applying to labor, especially of the spirit and intention of Section 7 (a) of the NIRA, which guaranteed the right of labor to organize and be represented by persons of their own choosing (below, p. 677). In the end there was considerable opposition also from industry, particularly from the small manufacturer, who felt that the codes favored the larger unit.[7] The barrage of criticism brought the appointment of a National Recovery Review Board to investigate the operation and effect of the NIRA. Dissatisfaction finally culminated in the textile strike of September, 1934, the resignation of Johnson, and the reorganization of the National Recovery Administration. In the face of the criticism the administration claimed that the NIRA had lifted the nation out of its economic slough and put it on the road to recovery. Many opponents, on the other hand, asserted that it had delayed recovery. This is one of those controversial problems the truth of which can never be ascertained. Certainly, as we shall see, labor gained important initial benefits, industry escaped temporarily from the antitrust laws, and there was an improvement in the general economic situation. Only the consumer seemed lost in the shuffle.

Whatever may have been the gains or losses through the organization of industry under the NIRA, the whole question became largely academic when the Supreme Court in the Schechter case (May, 1935) held that the code-making provisions in the NIRA were an invalid transfer of the legislative power from Congress to the President and that the attempt to regulate industry in the manner prescribed was an improper use of the interstate commerce power. The result of the decision, which was unanimous, was quickly to liquidate the NRA. Despite the decision, Congress tried to maintain its principles in one of the nation's most demoralized industries. In the Bituminous Coal Conservation Act (1935) the mining of bituminous coal was declared "af-

[7] This point of view was stressed in the report by the National Recovery Review Board, created in February, 1934, which contended that the NRA was fostering monopoly and that codes were administered by monopolists to oppress small industrialists, distributors, and consumers.

fected with a national public interest" and a commission was set up to formulate a bituminous coal code. The Supreme Court also cracked down on this legislation.

It is clear from a study of the above legislation that during the early years of the New Deal the government was in a mood to soften the antitrust acts in order to restrain unbridled competition. This attitude was also evident in later legislation. The Robinson-Patman Act of 1936 aimed to sharpen and clarify certain prohibitions of the Clayton Act to make illegal the sale of goods where there was discrimination between individuals and localities or where the price was so low as to destroy competition or eliminate a competitor. This new act, which was obviously directed against chain stores, was expected to give relief to the local storekeeper. In the meantime various states had attempted to aid this group by legislation allowing agreements between manufacturers and their distributors or retailers which fixed minimum prices for trade-marked commodities. This was legalized in interstate commerce by the Miller-Tydings Act of 1937, which amended the Sherman Antitrust Act.

Interestingly enough, the attitude of the administration toward monopoly appeared to change about 1938. Believing that the recession of 1937 and 1938 was in part caused by high monopoly prices, President Roosevelt asked Congress for funds for a full investigation by a special committee. The Temporary National Economic Committee's "Investigation of the Concentration of Economic Power" brought up to date the methods used and the extent reached in the concentration of economic power. It was the most thorough examination ever made of the problem of monopoly in this country by any agency, public or private. From its report it was evident that New Deal policies had strengthened and encouraged monopoly development rather than hindered it. The war soon to come had the same effect. It is true that the antimonopoly division of the Attorney General's Office became increasingly active after 1938 in opposing monopoly practices, but the results were slight in a period of close co-operation between government and industry during the Second World War.

REGULATION OF THE POWER INDUSTRY

No American industry was more subject to criticism in the twenties and thirties than the electric power industry. Inflated financial structures which bore little actual relation to the money invested or to the value of the property, and a complicated structure of holding companies imposed one upon the other, so confused the investing and consuming public as to make it difficult for them to determine the financial position of the corporations or the fairness of rates. State utility commissions, except in two or three states, seemed utterly incapable of controlling the situation, partly because the business had outgrown state boundaries. In 1936, as we have noted (p. 610 n.), the twelve largest utility holding companies controlled almost half the power produced in the nation, their lines crossing state boundaries in all directions. In brief, the business of producing and distributing electric power had reached a stage by the early thirties similar to that of the railroads a half-century earlier. The conditions and abuses of the railroads in their early days were being duplicated and were leading again to the same sort of demand for federal control.

Federal regulation had begun in a tentative manner with the Federal Water Power Act of 1920, which set up a Federal Power Commission to exercise administrative control over all power sites erected on public lands of the United States and on navigable rivers. The Commission had the power to license for fifty years concerns desiring to erect such plants, and to require uniform accounting systems; and it was given power over their security issues and over rates for power sold across state boundaries.[8] Perhaps the most important aspect of the utility problem which confronted the nation was whether the authority of this Commission should be extended to cover all companies operating in more than one state and all concerns transporting power across state lines. There was also the question as to whether the federal government itself should enter the field of power production. It was the latter question, as it turned out, which was taken up first.

The problem of government operation could hardly be dodged because the federal government had authorized during the First World War the building of two plants at Muscle Shoals on the Tennessee River to produce nitrates for the manufacture of explosives. To provide electric energy for these plants the Wilson Dam was also authorized; it was completed in 1925, making the total government investment about $145,000,000. Whether the government should operate these plants or turn them over at a nominal cost to private companies was the question before the nation. Urged on by Senator George W. Norris, Congress twice passed bills authorizing enlargement of the plants and government operation; Coolidge pocket-vetoed the first, and Hoover vetoed the second with the words that such a project was not "liberalism" but "degeneration." Roosevelt was known to be more liberal toward government ownership and operation than Hoover, and the power question was a minor factor in the campaign of 1932. Before his inauguration Roosevelt visited Muscle Shoals and announced that he would support a bill for government operation.

One of the most far-reaching and significant acts of the Roosevelt administration, and one that affected agriculture, industry, and other economic interests as well as public utilities, was the Muscle Shoals–Tennessee Valley Development Act (May, 1933). It created a board of three members, known as

[8] As in the case of railroads, this power had been denied by the courts to state commissions.

the Tennessee Valley Authority, to maintain and operate properties owned by the government at Muscle Shoals, Alabama, in the interest of national defense and the development of agriculture and industry in the Tennessee Valley, to improve navigation on the Tennessee, and to control the floodwaters of that river and the Mississippi. The TVA was given wide authority to acquire real estate, build dams and powerhouses, install hydroelectric plants, develop a program of flood control, prevent soil erosion, and aid reforestation, besides manufacturing nitrogen products for fertilizers and explosives. Within a decade the TVA had accomplished all these objectives—one of the most enduring achievements of the New Deal program. The whole project represents an important experiment in the regeneration and development of a geographic region which is also essentially an economic unit. Although the act affected many interests, the chief opposition in the courts came from the public utilities. Despite numerous legal attacks, the act has been upheld by the Supreme Court. So certain was the administration of the success of the TVA experiment that in 1937 Roosevelt in a special message to Congress advocated that six similar regional planning agencies be set up which would cover most of the nation. He did not get even one.

Two years after the Tennessee Valley development was launched, Congress attacked the problem of more effective federal control of power projects and greater protection to the investing and consuming public. The Public Utilities Holding Company Act (1935) was one of the most bitterly fought pieces of New Deal legislation. Among other things it granted to the Federal Power Commission authority to regulate rates and business practices of utilities doing an interstate business, prohibited holding companies beyond the second degree, and required federal sanction through the Securities and Exchange Commission for the issuance of securities, the acquisition of properties, and the handling of other kinds of business. After three years holding companies had to limit their operations to single integrated systems and to business directly connected with the supply of power service to consumers. At the time of its passage, the act was loosely discussed as one which inflicted the "death penalty" upon holding companies. Whatever it did, it apparently did not injure the electric utility business, for it was one of the first to push out of the depression and by 1937 enjoyed the greatest gross revenues of its history. No company died that seemed to have the slightest excuse for living. Opposition by utility companies and the difficulties of reorganization slowed up enforcement, but by 1950 the objects of the act were virtually accomplished.

TRANSPORTATION

No branch of American industrial life felt the depression more than transportation. Much aid had already been extended through the RFC, but Congress in 1933 took a further step by passing the Railroad Emergency Act which set up a Federal Railroad Co-ordinator whose orders, unless revoked by the Interstate Commerce Commission, to whom appeal could be taken, would have the force and effect of the Commission's. With the aid of co-ordinating committees of railroad representatives he was to devise means to avoid waste, to promote financial organization, to reduce fixed charges to the extent required by the public interest, and to improve the credit of the rail-roads. To accomplish these purposes, the antitrust laws, if necessary, might be set aside. The act repealed the famous but unsuccessful recapture clause of the Transportation Act of 1920,[9] but, on the other hand, it sought to remedy one great weakness of the earlier legislation by placing railroad holding cor-porations under the supervision of the Interstate Commerce Act. Although Co-ordinator Joseph B. Eastman and his aids made surveys of the railroad situation and recommendations for improvement—some of which were fol-lowed by the railroads—the most permanent effect of the Emergency Act of 1933, as far as railroads were concerned, appears to have been the modifica-tions of the act of 1920. The office of Federal Railroad Co-ordinator, created as an emergency measure, was discontinued in 1936.

More important than the emergency legislation of 1933 was the Wheeler-Lea Transportation Act of 1940, which enlarged the powers of the ICC to include supervision over water carriers operating in coastwise, inland, and intercoastal trade. The act also relieved the Commission of the necessity of proposing railroad consolidation, but no consolidation could be effected with-out the Commission's approval.

It was not in railroads, however, that the Roosevelt administration made its greatest contribution to the problem of American transportation. One of the recommendations of Co-ordinator Eastman and his staff was for a federal act governing motor vehicles engaged in interstate commerce. By the Motor Carrier Act (1935) such transportation was put under the regulation of the Interstate Commerce Commission and its activities were co-ordinated with those of other carriers. A study of this act reveals regulations suggestive of the earlier legislation regulating railroads. The Commission was empowered to establish just and reasonable rates and prescribe uniform systems of ac-counting, and the carriers were forbidden to grant rebates or to discriminate as to rates, localities, and persons. The Commission also had the power to establish standards for hours of work, safety, and equipment. In brief, a real beginning was made in extending federal control to motor carriers engaged in interstate commerce.

Although the development of commercial aviation was temporarily halted by the depression, the industry did not collapse.[10] On the contrary, it ad-vanced rapidly during the 1930's. The government's problem was not one of

[9] Above, pp. 615–617.
[10] Above, p. 617.

saving aviation, but rather one of improving federal control. Charges of fraud and favoritism in awarding mail contracts led President Roosevelt in 1934 to cancel all these contracts, and for a brief period the Army carried the mail. By the Air Mail Act of 1934 the transportation of mail was returned under new contracts to private carriers, with government supervision divided among the Interstate Commerce Commission, the Secretary of Commerce, and the Postmaster General. Since this type of supervision was too clumsy, Congress in 1938 consolidated much of the control under a Civil Aeronautics Authority, with a semi-independent Air Safety Board to investigate accidents and study safety measures. The work of these two bodies helped to inspire greater efficiency and safety in civil aviation and was popular with private air companies. It was believed to be nonpolitical. Consequently, there was criticism when the President in 1940, under the powers given him to reorganize the government service, consolidated these boards and placed them within the Department of Commerce.

By 1936 a number of factors contributed to direct the nation's attention again to the question of the merchant marine. A succession of maritime disasters called for more thoroughgoing regulation and supervision, acute labor troubles pointed to the need of better working conditions, and the general decline of the merchant marine called for new measures if it was to be saved.[11] This situation was made particularly clear by a report from the Maritime Commission in 1937, which showed that of the 9,000,000 gross tonnage built during the previous decade only 5 per cent had been registered in the United States. Although this country still ranked second in tonnage volume, it ranked fourth in speed and last in age of vessels. At least one-quarter of the tonnage was obsolete and seven-eights would be in that condition by 1942.

To deal with this problem the Merchant Marine Act of 1936 was passed. It ended the construction loans under the old Merchant Marine Act of 1920, dissolved the former United States Shipping Board Merchant Fleet Corporation, and established a new agency known as the United States Maritime Commission. It directed the Commission to survey the American merchant marine to determine what additions and replacements were necessary, to investigate employment and wage conditions, and to consider applications for construction subsidies, at the same time laying down conditions under which they might be granted. The old system of subsidization through mail contracts was to be replaced by direct subsidies. These subsidies were chiefly of two kinds. First, ships might be built on government contract and sold to the shipper (on long-term easy payments) at cost minus the difference between the cost of building here and abroad. Second, operating subsidies might be granted to vessels engaged on essential trade routes, these subsidies to be suf-

[11] Above, p. 542.

ficient to offset the difference in cost between operating American and foreign ships. The Commission was also given power to determine wages, minimum crews, and working conditions, and a Maritime Labor Board was established to mediate labor disputes.

RELIEF AND SECURITY

The detrimental effect of the depression on labor with respect to unemployment and decline in income has already been noted (p. 645). Income decreased more rapidly than the cost of living. There was conclusive evidence of an increase in industrial accidents reflecting a letup in safety and accident-prevention activities; there was a general increase in sweatshop conditions and in the overworking of women and children. Until the tide was turned by the codes of the NIRA there was a lengthening of hours and a weakening of the position of union labor. On the other hand, the long-drawn-out depression, as we shall see, stimulated interest in new forms of legislation.

Toward labor the Roosevelt administration developed a threefold policy. The first and most pressing need was to relieve the unemployment situation; the second was to improve the economic security of the wage earner through unemployment insurance, old-age insurance, and other methods; the third was to strengthen the position of organized labor in the American economic system. The attack on unemployment began almost immediately after Roosevelt's inauguration with an act empowering the President to employ young men in a Civilian Conservation Corps to construct public works in connection with reforestation, flood control, and similar projects, in an effort to relieve unemployment among the younger men. During the first year over 300,000 enrolled in the Civilian Conservation camps. A pet project of the administration, the CCC was maintained as a permanent feature of the New Deal policy until Congress finally ended its appropriations in 1942.

In May came the Emergency Relief Act creating the Federal Emergency Relief Administration and directing the RFC to make available $500,000,000 for emergency relief to the states. Then came the NIRA, which set up a Public Works Administration with an appropriation of $3,300,000,000 to promote construction in the public interest. The PWA spent over $7,000,000,000 during its career, but despite all efforts failed to absorb the millions of unemployed. To speed re-employment Congress in 1935 again made large appropriations for a second public works program and the President by Executive Order established the Works Progress Administration (later called Works Projects Administration) to co-ordinate the entire works program. The WPA initiated many projects outside the limited category of public works.

The WPA continued until the increased economic activity produced by the Second World War solved, at least for the time being, the problem of unemployment. During the seven years from 1935 to 1942, when Congress ordered it liquidated, the WPA spent about $10,500,000,000, plus $2,700,000,000 contributed by sponsors, chiefly local governments. It never solved entirely the unemployment problem, but at the height of its activity in 1938 it provided jobs for 3,800,000, about one-third of the unemployed. At one time or another it employed 8,500,000 persons. Counting dependents of workers, it benefited directly more than 25,000,000 persons. Among the many things accomplished by the WPA were the construction of 122,000 public buildings, 664,000 miles of new roads, 77,000 new bridges, 285 new airports, and 24,000 miles of storm and water sewers, and the repair of thousands of existing facilities. In addition it built parks, playgrounds, reservoirs, and innumerable other things that were greatly needed. Not only did the WPA provide jobs for skilled and unskilled workers in the various building projects, but it helped white-collar workers, including teachers, actors, artists, and writers. It also stretched out through the National Youth Administration to aid high-school and college students to obtain an education.

It was clear from the start that the policy of unemployment relief went beyond made-work jobs and priming the economic pump. It was based on a fundamental belief that human beings had a right to work and that it was better for all to live by work rather than by charity. Nevertheless, this program was bitterly criticized. It was charged with waste and inefficiency, with the expenditure of millions for political purposes, and with failure to accomplish its major objective—the elimination of unemployment. In reply, the administration insisted that the self-respect of millions had been saved by jobs rather than by the "dole," that much needed work had been done, and that the whole program had helped materially to ease the depression.

A real start was likewise made under the PWA on the problem of low-cost housing and slum clearance. To speed this program the Wagner-Steagall Housing Act of 1937 established a United States Housing Authority, with power to make loans and contributions for slum clearance and the building of low-rent houses. The Housing Authority was allowed to lend up to $500,-000,000 (tripled in later years) for housing projects, with a limit of $4000 for a family dwelling in cities with a population up to 500,000 and a $5000 limit for cities above that population. The loans were to be made and the construction done in co-operation with local public housing agencies. By the middle of 1940 the USHA had made contracts for the construction of over 400 housing projects containing almost 150,000 homes. When it is remembered that one-third of the nation is poorly housed, the work of the PWA and later of the USHA seemed but a tiny beginning. Nevertheless, it was a start in the right direction. Moreover, it stimulated private interests to build new housing projects in slum areas. It also established a precedent for federal aid in veterans' housing after the Second World War.

The second great labor objective of the Roosevelt administration—improvement of the security of the wage earner—was provided by many types of legislation. The National Employment Service Act (1933) created a national system of exchanges to co-operate with state employment offices, subsidized in part by the federal government. By a Railroad Retirement Act (1935) the federal government took over the machinery of handling pensions for railroad workers. This was to be done by a pay-roll tax split half and half between worker and employer. Congress in 1936 passed the Walsh-Healey Government Contracts Act providing that public contracts (except for certain specified articles) in excess of $10,000 made by any department or agency of the federal government must include stipulations requiring that the contractor be a manufacturer or regular dealer in the materials for which he is contracting, that he pay not less than the prevailing wages for persons employed in the industry, that he permit no one to work more than eight hours in one day or forty hours in any week, and that he employ no male under sixteen years of age and no female under eighteen. The work, furthermore, must be done under conditions that are not unduly hazardous.

This type of legislation was climaxed in 1938 by the Fair Labor Standards Act (Wages and Hours Act). It proposed to put a floor under wages and a ceiling on hours. Maximum working hours were set at forty-four a week for the first year, forty-two for the second, and forty thereafter. Minimum wages were to start at 25 cents an hour for the first year and be increased to 40 cents over a period of seven years. The act applied to all labor engaged in interstate commerce or the production of goods entering that commerce and was expected at the time to cover from 12,000,000 to 13,000,000 workers. Although the minimum wages under this act bore little relation to a decent American standard of living, the provisions were generally accepted as a step in the right direction. Nevertheless, it was not until 1949 that Congress raised the minimum wages to 75 cents an hour.

One important part of the act, significant because it has compensated somewhat for the failure of the ratification of the child labor amendment, is that concerning child labor. It prohibits the shipment in interstate commerce of goods produced in establishments where "oppressive" child labor is employed. The latter is defined as the employment of minors under sixteen in any occupation covered by the act and the employment of minors between sixteen and eighteen in occupations declared to be hazardous by the chief of the Children's Bureau. Children between fourteen and sixteen may be employed in nonmanufacturing and nonmining occupations under regulations issued by the Children's Bureau when such employment does not interfere with their schooling or their health and well-being. The act has been upheld by the Supreme Court.[12]

More important than the legislation just discussed was the promotion of unemployment insurance, old-age pensions, and other benefits provided for by the Social Security Act of 1935, as amended in 1939 and later. Unemployment insurance had made little progress in the twenties; only one state, Wisconsin, had introduced such a system up to 1934. More rapid progress had been made with old-age pension schemes; by 1929 at least twenty-nine states had some kind of old-age pension law. It was the federal Social Security Act that made their application nation-wide. First the act provided for a system of old-age pensions to aged needy persons over sixty-five years of age through federal grants on a fifty-fifty matching basis with the states, except that the federal government's share in no case would exceed $20 a month. To take care of the future the law provided for a contributory old-age insurance scheme to be paid for by an income tax on employees and a pay-roll tax on employers beginning with one per cent in 1937 and rising each three years until 1949, when the contribution from both would be 3 per cent. Under this scheme the monthly retirement payment was expected to range between $10 and $85, depending on wages earned between January, 1937, and the retirable age. These amounts have been increased by an act of 1952. At the same time the group eligible for insurance was greatly widened. The original act included chiefly wage and salary workers in commerce and industry. By the new act, self-employed other than farmers, regularly employed domestic workers, agricultural laborers, employees of nonprofit organizations, and certain other groups were added. By 1952 it was estimated that 62,300,000 persons were fully insured under the act. This was 73 per cent of all living persons who had held a covered job at any time during the years 1937 to 1952.

In addition to old-age insurance, the Social Security Act also sought to encourage the development of state systems of unemployment insurance that would meet certain minimum requirements. This is accomplished by a special federal tax on pay rolls levied against employers. If the state co-operates by adopting an unemployment insurance system the employer is allowed to deduct 90 per cent of his federal tax from the tax imposed by the state.[13] Other features of the Social Security Act carried appropriations—usually based proportionately on similar appropriations made by the states—to take care of needy dependent children; to promote the health of mothers and

[12] United States *v.* Darby (1941), which overruled Hammer *v.* Dagenhart (1918). See p. 466.

[13] The unemployment insurance systems adopted by the states differed, but in general they provided at the beginning for about half the weekly salary, with a maximum of $15 for a maximum period of sixteen weeks. The benefits followed a waiting period to prove the validity of the unemployment.

children in areas suffering severe economic distress; to provide medical, surgical, and corrective services for crippled children; to aid homeless and neglected children; to rebuild vocationally the physically disabled; to aid the needy blind; and finally, to promote adequate public health service.

This legislation was a notable step forward in the search for social security. Criticism has come chiefly because of its limitations rather than its fundamental purpose. One weakness, the limitation of coverage, was largely eliminated in 1952, as noted above. Since the insurance is based on the income of the worker, those who need it most are likely to get the least. Unemployment insurance likewise does not cover all of the groups included in old-age insurance, and usually the tax is not imposed on employers of less than eight workers. Moreover, the insurance is not adequate to cope with a long period of unemployment. The scheme has been criticized because it fails to deal with the problem of unemployment caused by illness. However, the pension scheme now covers about three-fifths of the workers and continuous efforts have been made, and with some success, to broaden the scope of social security.

THE REVIVAL OF ORGANIZED LABOR

The third labor policy of the New Deal was to strengthen the power of organized workers. The 1920's had seen a serious decline in the membership, prestige, and morale of unions and it was the belief of many that something should be done to restore a better balance in the employer-labor relationship. This effort started with Section 7 (a) of the NIRA, and to labor this section was the crux of the New Deal. Briefly, it provided that employees should have the "right to organize and bargain collectively through representatives of their own choosing, and shall be free from interference, restraint, or coercion of employers of labor, or their agents, in the designation of such representatives or in self-organization." No employee as a condition of employment might be required to join a company union or to refrain from joining a labor organization of his own choosing, and employers had to comply with the code regulations of their industry respecting labor. Indeed, this seemed like a new "charter of liberty" to labor and under the circumstances it is hardly surprising that union membership increased rapidly.

In addition to advantages under Section 7 (a) of the NIRA, labor was expected to benefit under the codes established for the various industries. The first of the codes, somewhat typical of their general character, was that for the cotton textile industry; it forbade the employment of children under sixteen, prohibited the speeding up of work, and established minimum wages of $13 a week in the North and $12 a week in the South. Contrary to the intention of the administration, the minimum wages in the codes tended to become the maximum and as prices of commodities began to swing upward the benefit to labor was doubtful. The banning of child labor, however, was an unquestioned blessing.

The high hopes raised in the minds of labor by the NIRA were never realized. Opposition by many employers, widespread evasion of the codes, and the government's failure through the various labor boards vigorously to enforce the act greatly weakened its operation long before the Supreme Court declared it unconstitutional in 1935. As the fact dawned upon labor that the NIRA was no short cut to the millennium and that in the end its enforcement was primarily their responsibility, the number of strikes increased rapidly. The number of workers directly involved in strikes, which had sunk to 158,114 in 1930, increased to 812,137 in 1933 and to considerably more in 1934. The inability of the National Recovery Administration to enforce Section 7 (a) or the code provisions regarding labor was due not to reluctance but chiefly to inability to cope with the enormity of the task. Congress tried to help by establishing a nonpartisan National Labor Relations Board; and the President, in the face of actual or threatened strikes, appointed special boards of arbitration to handle labor troubles among the longshoremen and the automobile, steel, and textile workers.

The Supreme Court decision which ended the NIRA (p. 667) did not involve the labor provisions and Congress continued them in the National Labor Relations Act (1935). The new act sought to promote equality of bargaining power between employers and employees and to diminish the causes of labor disputes. Specifically, it forbade employers (1) to interfere with, restrain, or coerce employees in the exercise of their rights to collective bargaining, (2) to refuse to bargain collectively, and (3) to dominate or interfere with the formation or administration of a labor organization or to interfere with membership in a labor organization by discrimination with regard to hire or tenure. To enforce the act, a permanent National Labor Relations Board was established. If adequately enforced, the National Labor Relations Act was bound to be extremely significant. It not only encouraged labor organization, but it made collective bargaining compulsory on the employer, and by its wording seemed to doom the company union, the "yellow dog" contract, and the labor spy. Enforcement, of course, was handicapped until the Supreme Court passed judgment, but the act was eventually affirmed when the Court in a single day (April 12, 1937) upheld its constitutionality in five decisions. These cases in general involved the question as to whether certain industries, including steel and men's clothing, were sufficiently concerned with interstate commerce to be covered by the act. With the exception of the Fansteel decision in 1939, which virtually banned sit-down strikes, the Court during succeeding months not only approved the constitutionality of the act by implication but time and again upheld the procedure and decisions of the National Labor Relations Board.

Important as was the National Labor Relations Act and its approval by the Supreme Court, the growth of organized labor depended on other factors as well. First of all was the need of regaining middle-class sympathy, which had been lost in part during the twenties. The depression helped in this because many were convinced that labor had suffered severely and needed greater protection. Help came also from the activities of the Senate Committee on Education and Labor, headed by Robert La Follette, which received special instructions to investigate "violations of the rights of free speech and assembly and undue interference with the right of labor to organize and bargain collectively." As this committee spread on the record the facts pertaining to the use of labor spies, strikebreakers, tear gas, and deadly weapons by supposedly reputable employers and the abridgment of civil liberties in company-controlled towns and regions, the public for the first time realized the difficulties faced by labor in its efforts toward organization.

More important than government aid and encouragement was the ability of labor to help itself. The government might protect and encourage, but labor must do its own organizing. Spurred on by the NIRA and the National Labor Relations Act, organized labor rose to the occasion. Organizing machinery which had grown rusty was put in commission, older leaders were sent into the field, and younger men who had demonstrated their ability were called on. During the first three years of the New Deal organized labor added more than a million and a half to its membership, and in the following years the growth was more rapid.[14] In the drive for labor membership after 1933 it was often found more practical to organize shops on the basis of industry rather than craft, and the A. F. of L. granted many charters to these "federal unions." The new recruits included a large number of workers as yet unacquainted with the conservative traditions of A. F. of L. craft unionism. They gave a more militant tone to organized labor, a tone which was reflected in an overwhelming vote at the annual convention in 1934 to promote industrial unionism in certain "mass industries," particularly steel, automobiles, rubber, radio, and aluminum. Failure of the Executive Committee of the A. F. of L. to pursue this mandate aggressively led certain unions under the leadership of John L. Lewis and the United Mine Workers of America to organize the Committee for Industrial Organization.[15]

[14] Average membership of labor unions was 2,973,000 in 1933, 4,700,000 in 1936, 8,200,999 in 1939, 13,500,000 in 1943, and approximately 15,400,000 in 1947.

[15] The unions composing the original committee suspended from the A. F. of L. in August, 1936, were as follows: United Mine Workers of America; Amalgamated Clothing Workers of America; International Ladies' Garment Workers' Union; United Textile Workers of America; Oil Field, Gas Well and Refinery Workers of America; International Union of Mine, Mill and

Although suspended from membership by the A. F. of L., the C.I.O. unions swung into action. The initial objective of the C.I.O. was the steel industry, but the movement for industrial organization spread so rapidly that, contrary to plans, the first battle was fought in the automobile industry. Following spectacular strikes early in 1937 in the General Motors and Chrysler corporations the C.I.O. succeeded in effecting compromise settlements which recognized the C.I.O. automobile union as the bargaining agency for its own members. In actual practice this meant the recognition of organized labor in practically all of the major units in the hitherto unorganized automobile industry, except the Ford Motor Company. This concern finally gave up in 1941.

As the battle front shifted to steel, the United States Steel Corporation, instead of opposing labor, reversed a lifelong policy to the surprise of all and signed contracts with the C.I.O. Although other steel corporations immediately followed in granting recognition, a few of the more important "independents" did not, and a strike against these companies in the late spring of 1937 resulted in the first important reverse of the C.I.O. But, under the stress of war preparations, even the "independents" agreed later to recognition. In the meantime the C.I.O. spread rapidly. By 1942 it claimed over forty national unions and a membership of 5,000,000, not far behind that of the A. F. of L. Despite efforts both within and without organized labor, the two factions were unable to reconcile their differences. In 1938 the Committee for Industrial Organization changed its name to the Congress of Industrial Organizations, adopted a constitution, and took on a more permanent form. Its early leader, John L. Lewis, resigned the presidency in 1940 and was succeeded by Philip Murray, who had led the drive for organization in the steel industry.

The wave of strikes which accompanied efforts in 1937 to organize the automobile industry was watched with particular interest because for the first time in this country labor used the "sit-down" technique on a wide scale. This refusal by the worker to leave the plant during a strike on the theory that he had a vested interest in his job proved a powerful weapon because it forced the employer to commit the first violence in a strike. Employers, of course, denounced "sit-down" strikes as illegal trespassing on property rights and certain states passed legislation to ban them. The practice ended after the Fansteel decision of 1939. Many of the strikes in the 1930's were also characterized by mass picketing, which sometimes resulted in violence and gave opportunity for agitation for new laws to make labor "more responsi-

Smelter Workers; Federation of Flat Glass Workers of America; Amalgamated Association of Iron, Steel and Tin Workers; International Union United Automobile Workers of America; United Rubber Workers of America. The I.L.G.W.U. later withdrew from the C.I.O. and eventually rejoined the A. F. of L.

Modern Industry—Automobile Body Assembly Line.

mbling Com-
nt Parts for
Electron Gun.

Culver Se[rvice]

The Old and the New—A Southern Pacific Modern Streamliner Alongside of the Tiny "C. P. Huntington" in Operation in the 1860's.

A Trans World Airlines Constellation Outward Bound from New York.

Courtesy of T[WA]

Photo by Brown Brothers

A Parade of Coal Miners at Shenandoah, Pennsylvania, in the Coal Strike
of 1902.

Photo by Brown Brothers

William Green, Late President of the American Federation of Labor, and
John L. Lewis, Founder of the Congress of Industrial Organizations.

Photo by Brown Broth

National Guardsmen Dispersing Strikers with Tear Gas at Greenville, South Carolina, September, 1934.

New York City Transport Workers Marching to a Rally at City Hall to Demand Shorter Hours and Higher Wages, 1951.

International News Pho

Photo by Brown Brothers

A California Oil Field.

Photo by Brown Brothers

New Deal—Excavating a Sewer Tunnel in Chicago, a Project Undertaken
with a WPA Allotment of $42,000,000.

Photo by Brown Broth

New Deal—Jane Addams House, Chicago. A Slum Clearance Project Built Through the United States Housing Administration. It Covers 22 Acres of Land.

New Deal—City Hal at Pawtucket, Rhode Island. This Was PWA Job, One of 31 City Halls and Court houses Erected b PWA.

*Courtesy of Th
National Archive*

War Industry—An Assembly Line Working on Attack Bombers.

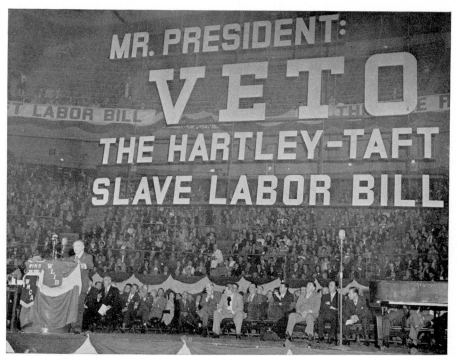

International Ladies Garment Workers' Union President David Dubinsky
Demands a Veto of the Taft-Hartley Bill.

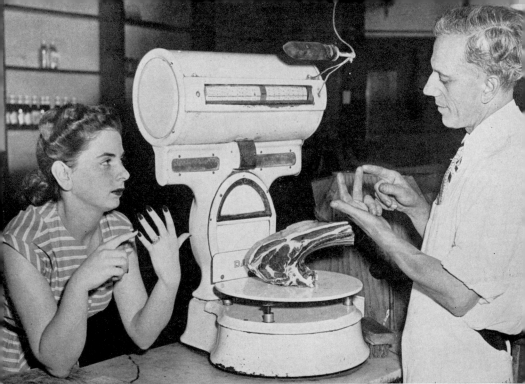

International News Pl

With the End of Price Control the Cost of Meat Skyrocketed to Prices Which Most Scales, Set at a Limit of 75 Cents a Pound, Could Not Handle.

Private Enterprise Contributes to Meet the Postwar Housing Shortage. Planned by Levitt and Sons, This Is the First Section of Levittown, Pennsylvania, a New City of 16,000 Homes Being Built to House the Workers at the United States Steel's New Fairless Works, 1953.

Courtesy of Levitt and

ble." On the whole, labor was able to resist this agitation, at least in the federal legislature, until the war and postwar years.

ECONOMIC IMPLICATIONS OF THE NEW DEAL

The preceding summary of New Deal legislation and policies should clear the ground for certain general comments. The New Deal is significant, it is obvious, as the first real effort made in this country to attack a depression by bringing to bear upon it various economic weapons. In earlier depressions the government had contented itself largely with protecting the credit of the federal government and allowing the nation to work itself out of the depression as best it might. The economic catastrophe following the First World War had developed throughout the world various controls over economic life. The New Deal, so called, was America's way of attacking her own depression, and the majority attitude held that it was superior to the methods of other nations and that it should be given a fair trial.

Efforts to pull the country out of the depression were made in various ways. One was inflation and a managed currency to help debtors and stimulate production. Another was the restoration of confidence by pouring funds into banks, insurance companies, railroads, and industries to prevent bankruptcy and re-establish them on a sounder basis. Still another was the finding of jobs for labor by speeding public works and by a large program of made-work projects. This program of saving the economic structure and finding jobs meant, of course, much deficit spending, but deficit spending was justified on the theory that it would be absorbed in the future economic expansion of the country and that it was as justifiable in the crisis of depression as it was in war. Moreover, the enlarged policy of government spending would act to prime the pump of economic recovery.

In one way the depression produced a reaction not unlike that of earlier economic panics in stimulating reform. Recovery and reform were closely interwoven in the New Deal. The banking structure was not only saved but reformed. The same was true of the electric power industry. Some control of stock exchanges and the dealing in securities was established. The situation gave an opportunity for the TVA and for a wide program of soil and forest conservation as well as the construction, through the WPA and other agencies, of innumerable facilities for the welfare of the people.

Above all, the New Deal moved aggressively toward the conservation of human resources. This included the effort not alone to strengthen organized labor but to find jobs for the unemployed through the CCC, WPA, and National Youth Administration. It was part of this program to establish minimum rates of pay and maximum hours of work and to prohibit child labor. It brought old-age and unemployment insurance, and the other objectives in the Social Security Act. The New Deal was impregnated with the desire for conservation and the ideal of humanitarianism. Said Roosevelt in 1937 in a special message urging the Fair Labor Standards Act, "The time has arrived for us to take further action to extend the frontiers of social progress. . . . One-third of our population, the overwhelming majority of which is in agriculture or industry, is ill-nourished, ill-clad and ill-housed. . . . A self-supporting and self-respecting democracy can plead no justification for the existence of child labor, no economic reason for chiseling workers' wages or stretching workers' hours." It was this aspect of the New Deal that won it the permanent approbation of most of the people, no matter what their political affiliations might be.

Quite as obvious as anything yet said about the New Deal is the fact that the program necessitated an expansion of government activities and a more active participation in the economic and social life of the nation. More definitely and rapidly than ever before the state was deserting the policy of *laissez faire*. As Louis Hacker wrote in 1938:

Today the state is operating to defend the underprivileged, to increase the national income, and to effect a more equitable distribution of that income among the various categories of producers. To achieve these ends not only has the American state taken on the whole job of assuring social security, but it has also become a participant in and an initiator of business enterprise. Our state, in short, has become the capitalist state, where only yesterday it was the *laissez-faire*, or passive, state; it constructs and operates plants; it buys and sells goods and services, lends money, warehouses commodities, moves ships and operates railroads. In one sense, the state is seeking to erect safeguards for the underprivileged against exploitation; in another it is competing with and replacing private enterprise—without, however, parting company with capitalist relations.[16]

So obvious was this change that many asserted that the New Deal marked a revolution in American history. This point of view has been exaggerated. The extension of federal control of business goes back at least to the Interstate Commerce Act of 1887 and the Sherman Antitrust Act of 1890. The control of banking goes back to the earliest years, and the history of humanitarian legislation in state and federal governments long preceded the New Deal. Moreover, the government has protected and aided business as well as regulated it. In a sense there was little that was new in the New Deal; it was largely an extension and continuation of an older method and an older philosophy.[17] Roosevelt asserted that he was trying to save the capitalist system rather than destroy it, and the legislation affecting finance, industry, and

[16] Louis Hacker, *American Problems of Today*, p. vii.
[17] This point of view is developed more fully in H. U. Faulkner, "Antecedents of New Deal Liberalism," *Social Education*, III, 153–160 (March, 1939).

agriculture is indisputable proof. The new element in the New Deal was the acceleration of the decline of *laissez faire.*

SELECTED READINGS

Mitchell, Broadus, *Depression Decade,* chaps. 3–11.

Rauch, Basil, *The History of the New Deal, 1933–1938.*

Hacker, Louis, *American Problems of Today,* chaps. 7–10.

Rozwenc, E. C. (ed.), *The New Deal* (Amherst-Heath Series).

Pasvolsky, Leo, *Current Monetary Issues,* chap. 6

Shultz, W. J., and Caine, M. R., *Financial Development of the United States,* chaps. 28–29.

CHAPTER 31

WORLD ECONOMIC RELATIONS

EXPORT OF AMERICAN CAPITAL, 1914–1940

Efforts were made in an earlier chapter to describe the penetration of American capital into foreign nations in the years between the Spanish-American War and the opening of the First World War. Briefly they show that American investments, direct and portfolio, had increased during these years over five times—from $684.5 million (1897) to $3513.8 million (1914). American capital had moved during this period chiefly into Canada, Mexico, Europe, South America, and Cuba. In Canada American capital had flowed into manufacturing enterprises, particularly pulp, paper, and lumber, into mining, and into the production of electric power. The manufacturing enterprises were mostly branch plants of American concerns. United States investments in Mexico were chiefly in mining, oil production, and railroads. Investments in Europe were largely made in bonds, manufacturing plants, and selling organizations, the most important of the latter being the facilities established by the Standard Oil Company. Investments in South America were chiefly in mining, those in Cuba in sugar production.

As against American investments abroad of $3513.8 million in 1914, foreign investments in the United States amounted to $7200 million, leaving the United States a debtor to the extent of approximately $3686 million.[1] These investments had come chiefly from Europe—over half from Great Britain, with Germany and the Netherlands as the next largest investors. European investments had found their way into almost every type of American enterprise, but over half were in railroads.[2] This flow of European capital to America had been a normal and continuous process since the first colonial settlements, and it had made an important contribution to the development of the United States. By 1914, however, the United States was pro-

[1] Cleona Lewis, *America's Stake in International Investments*, p. 445.
[2] *Ibid.*, p. 546.

ducing surplus capital and was using her own capital resources in the development of other parts of the world.

The First World War not only revealed the large amount of surplus capital in the United States which could be called upon for foreign loans but quickly ended the debtor position of this country. Between the opening of the war in 1914 and the entrance of the United States in 1917 over $2,000,000,-000 in American securities owned in Europe were returned to this country. Much of this was done through the British and French governments, which induced their citizens to lend their American securities or exchange them for domestic loans. Of equal significance in reversing the debtor position of the United States were the dollar loans advanced to foreign governments, mainly the Allied nations of Europe, which reached approximately $2,600,000,000. With American entry into the war, private loans transactions ended.[3] The federal government then took over the problem of financing the last year of the war and aiding in European reconstruction. Under the Liberty Loan Act of 1917 the United States advanced $9,581,000,000 to European governments.[4]

These figures do not tell the whole story or even the most important part. The war left Europe so exhausted economically that during the following years the United States continued to be the great source of capital. The world's financial center shifted from London to New York. With the end of the war restrictions on the international lending operations of private agencies were lifted and the expansion of American investments in the 1920's reached fantastic proportions. Omitting government loans, American foreign investments grew from $3513.8 million in 1914 to $6955.6 in 1919 and $17,-009.6 in 1929. After that, as we shall see, they declined rapidly.[5]

In a study of the debts owed to private American citizens the Department of Commerce in 1930 estimated that one-half of the money lent abroad was in the form of "portfolio investments"—that is, in ownership of foreign securities, public and private, by individuals or institutions in this country—and one-half in "direct investments" made by American corporations in agricultural, industrial, commercial, mining, public utility, and other enterprises abroad. The chief investment areas at that time in order of importance were Europe, Canada, and South America. The migration of billions of American dollars to other parts of the world did not come simply because the prosperity of the 1920's created surplus wealth which high interest rates lured into foreign investment. It came in part because American economic interests were stretching far and wide to extend business. Most of the big American concerns, such as the Ford Motor Company, General Motors, General Electric,

[3] *Ibid.*, p. 355; C. C. Tansill, *America Goes to War*, Appendices A and B.
[4] Reduced to $9386.7 millions by 1922 when negotiations for debt payments were started. Cleona Lewis, *op. cit.*, p. 362.
[5] *Ibid.*, p. 606.

Standard Oil, International Telephone and Telegraph, and International Harvester, set up their own plants or bought control of foreign companies. Many economic factors led to this movement of capital into foreign industries, and of these the high tariffs which developed rapidly in the 1920's were one of the most important. When American manufacturers found it impossible to break through the tariff barriers, they simply set up branch factories abroad to serve foreign markets. Every traveler in Canada, for example, finds there numerous branches of American concerns which represented in 1948 over $6,000,000,000 of American direct investments. Since then they have increased.

While many of the direct investments, notably those in Canada, were perfectly sound and of benefit both to the American investor and to world economic development, the same cannot be said of a large portion of the portfolio investments. Many of them were for nonproductive purposes and were sold by governments or private corporations whose ability to pay was extremely uncertain, to say the least. American investment houses that floated these loans, says Soule, "were often more concerned with their underwriting profits than with the probable safety of the capital."[6] Such institutions searched the world for opportunities to lend money; they literally forced it upon borrowers even when the Department of Commerce and their own experts warned them of the danger. Said one of the more conservative bankers, "I have in mind reports . . . of American bankers and firms competing on almost a violent scale for the purpose of obtaining loans in various foreign money markets overseas. Naturally it is a tempting thing for certain of the European governments to find a horde of American bankers sitting on their doorsteps offering them money. It is rather demoralizing for municipalities and corporations in the same countries to have money pressed upon them. This sort of competition tends to insecurity and unsound practices."[7]

This policy, so typical of the 1920's, was too fantastic to last even if world economic relations had been on a sound and stable basis. Latin America was borrowing more than she could pay even under normal conditions. Europe, impoverished by the war, must meet her obligations with American dollars which could be obtained only by rendering services and exporting commodities. One type of service, the transportation of American commodities on the ocean, was curtailed by the development of a new American merchant marine. Export of foreign commodities to this country was hindered by the high American tariffs. The abnormal situation was maintained chiefly by continued American loans and intense economic activity. With the cessa-

[6] George Soule, *Prosperity Decade*, p. 269.
[7] Thomas W. Lamont of J. P. Morgan & Co., in an address before the International Chamber of Commerce, 1927. Quoted by Cleona Lewis, *op. cit.*, p. 380.

tion of loans and the coming of depression at the end of the decade the structure collapsed.

The United States government during the 1920's showed little comprehension of the international economic problem nor did it offer much leadership. The retreat to isolation was more evident in the political than in the economic field, but it was clear enough here. The return to higher tariffs when the opposite was indicated for a creditor nation was a mistaken policy. From a

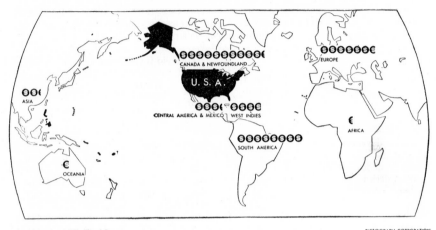

Each symbol represents 200 million dollars

PICTOGRAPH CORPORATION

(From H. U. Faulkner and Tyler Kepner, *America, Its History and People*, McGraw-Hill.)

AMERICAN DIRECT INVESTMENTS, 1940.

conventional point of view the scaling down of the war debts by the United States seemed liberal enough, but the conflicting interests of the various nations prevented a realistic approach and the whole war-debt problem clogged the machinery of economic recovery. The Department of Commerce under Secretary Hoover did excellent work in promoting foreign trade despite the handicap of domestic tariffs, but in general the Department encouraged rather than warned against unwise foreign investments.

The large flow of American capital declined in 1928. With the crash in the following year it dwindled to a tiny trickle. The depression of the 1930's wiped out almost $11,000,000,000 from the equity of American foreign investments. Until the situation was stimulated by the Second World War, the income from direct investments in Latin America was relatively low. United States holdings in Latin-American dollar bonds (most of them government securities) amounted in 1940 to almost $1,000,000,000, but approximately two-thirds of these bonds were in partial or complete default. In continental Europe the situation was even worse. Direct investments there amounted to $1,370,000,000 in 1940, a large amount of which was in the Axis countries.

For years exchange controls had prevented heavy remittances of income from these countries and the withdrawal of capital had been largely halted. The greater proportion of assets were frozen and when liquidation was permitted it was accompanied by heavy losses. Indirect (portfolio) investments there amounted to $636,000,000 at the end of 1940, but 59 per cent was in default. Moreover, the Debt Default Act of 1934 (Johnson Act), which prohibited loans to any government in default in its payments of obligations to the

UNITED STATES LONG-TERM INVESTMENTS IN FOREIGN COUNTRIES, BY TYPES OF INVESTMENT
AND BY GOEGRAPHIC AREAS, DECEMBER 31, 1940
(In Millions of Dollars)

Area	Direct Invest-ments	Portfolio Investments			Grand Total
		Foreign Dollar Bonds	Miscel-laneous Foreign Securities	Total	
Canada and Newfoundland	2,065	1,390	285	1,675	3,740
West Indies	755	74	5	79	834
Central America and Mexico	650	26	...	26	676
South America	1,615	893	5	898	2,513
Europe	1,370	506	130	636	2,006
Asia	460	155	5	160	620
Oceania	135	95	3	98	233
Africa.	105	2	17	19	124
International	25	...	...	...	25
Total	7,180	3,141[a]	450	3,591	10,771

[a] The estimated market value of these holdings was $1,791,000,000.
U.S. Department of Commerce, *Balance of International Payments in the United States in 1940*, p. 51.

United States, automatically ended the possibility of loans to most European governments. The war between China and Japan and the increasing tension throughout that area boded ill for the future of American investments in the Far East.

In the meantime foreign investors looking for an outlet turned to the United States. By the end of 1940 the Department of Commerce listed long- and short-term foreign investments in the United States at $9,695,000,000. This was almost within a billion dollars of American investments abroad and a far different picture from that of a decade earlier.[8]

THE WAR-DEBT PROBLEM AND THE NEUTRALITY ACTS

Although the problem of the debts of the First World War seems academic today, it was closely interwoven with our international policy for two decades. When the United States entered that war, the credit of the Allied nations

[8] U.S. Department of Commerce, *Balance of International Payments in the United States in 1940*, p. 56.

was exhausted and these loans were necessary to win the war. They were, however, supposedly made in good faith, with the expectation that they would be repaid. They had reached such staggering proportions that in 1922 the United States established a World War Foreign Debt Commission to take up with each nation the question of refunding the debt. Long before this the debtor nations had begun a vigorous campaign for cancellation of the debts. They argued that these loans should be considered as part of America's contribution to the common cause, that this money had enabled the Allies to hold off the enemy until the United States had time to prepare for war, and that the money was largely spent in the United States and so had aided this country as well as the Allies. Moreover, the debtor nations insisted that they could not pay in gold since there was not enough gold in Europe and what existed was needed to support their currencies. As for paying their debts in goods, that was impossible because of the high tariff policy of the United States.

In this country the official attitude was to make large reductions in the amounts owed but to insist upon payment. Gradually over a period of seven years arrangements were made with fifteen European nations by which the total principal was fixed at $11,522,000,000 to be paid during a period of sixty-two years; the interest amounted to $10,621,000,000, and the grand total to $22,143,000,000. The annual payments were to vary from an average of $204,000,000 during the first decades to $414,000,000 during the last ten years. These arrangements involved a 23 per cent reduction of the British debt, a 46 per cent reduction of the Belgian debt, 52 per cent of the French, and 75 per cent of the Italian. While these reductions appear extremely liberal, it must be remembered that the debts were contracted during the high-price period of wartime, that most of the money was used to purchase American commodities, and that the reductions merely tended to cancel wholly or in part the postwar deflation, on the basis of which the debts were to be paid.

Whether they were liberal or not, the agitation in Europe for complete cancellation continued. This was in part due to the fact that a large part of the reparations obtained from Germany came to the United States for the payment of Allied debts. The Treaty of Versailles originally fixed German reparations at $33,000,000,000, but it quickly became evident that Germany could not meet her payments. Not only so, but the draining of gold from Germany brought disastrous inflation in that country, and attempts to collect reparations in goods upset the economy of the creditor nations. A committee headed by Charles G. Dawes adopted a plan in 1924 by which Germany's annual payments were scaled down and an effort was made to balance her budget. This effort lasted as long as American loans in gold poured into Germany. The gold went immediately to France and England in reparations and then completed the circle by being returned to the United States in debt payments. This curious situation existed until American loans to Germany began to dry up.

The collapse of the Dawes Plan led to another attempt to revamp the reparations program by a committee under the chairmanship of Owen D. Young. The Young Plan radically reduced the German debt and provided that the size of certain yearly payments would be conditional upon a reduction of the Allied debts by the United States. This joining of reparation payments and Allied debts the United States would not officially recognize; but, practically speaking, such a connection existed, since four-fifths of the German payments eventually found their way to the United States. How close the connection was became evident in 1931 when the economic situation forced Germany to default and, to avoid a world economic collapse, President Hoover in June, 1931, after consultation with Allied governments, declared a moratorium for one year on all government debts and reparations payments. By June, 1933, only Finland made full payment of her interest; Britain, Italy, Latvia, Czechoslovakia, Rumania, and Lithuania paid a small part in silver as token, and Belgium, France, Hungary, Poland, and Estonia defaulted. After 1934 only Finland paid interest.

It was evident by 1932 that the whole war-debt problem would have to be reconsidered. The obvious possibilities were three: further postponement of payment, further reduction, or outright cancellation. There was considerable sentiment in this country for each of these plans, because many now felt with Secretary of the Treasury Mellon that "the entire foreign debt is not worth as much to the United States in dollars and cents as a prosperous Europe as a customer." Others believed that the money was not worth the harvest of hatred and suffering being reaped, and still others (who proved to be right) felt that the United States would never collect the money anyway and might as well let it go on the best terms possible. At the other extreme was the sentiment, expressed by Coolidge, that the Allied nations had "hired it" (the money) and should pay it back. The most that can be said about the whole business of reparations and war debts was that it provided an experience that proved of some value in later years.

Resentment over the European attitude regarding war debts along with other factors led in 1934 to the Debt Default Act. It was also one of the many causes which produced a program to maintain America's neutrality in future wars. A Senate investigation of the munitions industry greatly strengthened the belief (although it did not prove it) that the United States had been drawn into the First World War because of the close economic relations which had bound her to one group of belligerent nations. Determined if possible to prevent the recurrence of certain influences tending to break down neutrality, Congress passed three Neutrality Acts culminating in that of May, 1937. In addition to requiring all persons engaged in the manufacture of munitions to register with the Secretary of State and to export only under license, the act provided for mandatory embargoes on loans, munitions, and implements of war to foreign belligerents or to factions in a civil strife of such proportions as to threaten the peace of the United States. It prohibited American citizens from traveling on belligerent vessels except under conditions prescribed by the President; it forbade the transportation of munitions by American merchantmen, established the National Munitions Control Board, with which all manufacturers and exporters of munitions must register, restricted the use of American ports as bases of supply in wartime, allowed the President to exclude belligerent submarines and armed merchantmen from American ports, and prohibited the arming of American merchantmen. The act of 1937 also gave the President optional power for two years to embargo other commodities than loans and munitions, and when such embargo was proclaimed all trade in these commodities must be in accordance with the "cash and carry" principle. In other words, America's ownership in such commodities must end before they left our shores and they must be transported by foreign ships. The Neutrality Acts represented the climax of a sentiment toward isolationism which had been growing since the First World War. For the sake of peace the country had abandoned a policy as old as the nation itself, that of "freedom of the seas." Whether even this could keep America out of an impending European war was soon to be determined.

THE PROBLEM OF INTERNATIONAL TRADE

Three aspects of the American position in international trade between the two world wars should be emphasized. The first was its changing character. As already noted,[9] the proportion of exports of raw materials and foodstuffs declined while that of semimanufactured and finished manufactured commodities increased. At the same time the proportion of the imports of raw materials increased and that of manufactured commodities declined. This reflected the continued industrialization of the United States and also made clear the fact that this country was approximating the position of such industrialized nations as Great Britain, Germany, and Japan. In international trade the United States had become an importer of raw materials and an exporter of manufactured goods and so a competitor of other industrialized nations.

Despite what has been said, it should be emphasized, in the second place, that foreign trade did not attain the significance in the over-all economic life of this country as in that of most other nations. The possession of most essen-

[9] Above, pp. 543–547.

tial raw materials, the high industrial development, and the extensive buying
power of the American people made the nation less dependent upon foreign
trade for her economic prosperity. At no time during these years did the value
of either imports or exports represent more than 8 per cent of the national income. This does not mean that a rise or decline in the exports of certain commodities or the prices paid for them did not affect in an important way
groups of American producers. On the one hand the decline of the European

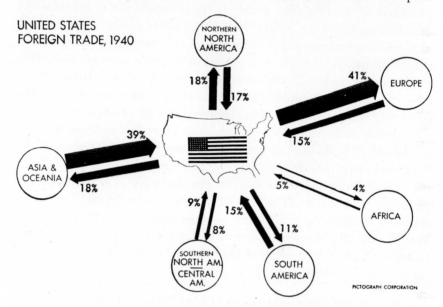

UNITED STATES
FOREIGN TRADE, 1940

(From H. U. Faulkner and Tyler Kepner, *America, Its History and People*, McGraw-Hill.)

market for certain American foodstuffs hurt our agriculture. The cotton
growers, for example, depended heavily upon exports. On the other hand
many industries profited from an active foreign market. The chief exports
during the two decades were machinery, petroleum, automobiles, iron and
steel products, and cotton.

The fact that international trade did not play such an important part in
American economic life as in that of certain other nations likewise does not
mean that American imports were not significant. Despite her large resources
of raw materials, there were commodities—notably raw silk, tin, and crude
rubber—which the United States did not have. There were others, such as
sugar, copper, paper and pulp, hides and skins, of which this country did not
produce sufficient for her needs. And there were coffee, tropical fruits, and
other luxuries which she was eager to buy. The above represent the chief imports. About 66 per cent of the imports consisted of raw materials and semi-
manufactured commodities for use in industry. Most of the rest consisted of

raw or processed food; only 6 per cent of the total value of imports comprised finished manufactured goods (other than food) ready for direct consumption. Next to Great Britain, the United States at the end of the 1920's was the chief importing nation of the world. It is hardly necessary to point out that the large purchases made by the United States in Canada, Cuba, Brazil, Japan, and the East Indies enabled those areas to buy in Europe and elsewhere and so helped to bolster the whole structure of international trade.

A third aspect of the American position was the continued excess of exports over imports. This was not a new phenomenon; with the exception of one year (1893), it had been continuous since 1889. What was new was the fact that this so-called "favorable balance of trade" was now combined with America's position as a creditor nation. In brief, the United States was developing a creditor position by both foreign loans and an excess of exports. The resulting situation was by no means a healthy one, at least from the long-term point of view. In an extended period of an unequal balance of trade, creditor balances can be paid only in gold or in goods. Gold was largely disappearing from the debtor nations and the free flow of goods was obstructed by high tariffs. In such a situation the balances due the creditor lead generally to foreign loans or to investments abroad. This was what was happening in the 1920's, when American trade was to no small extent supported by such loans. This could not go on indefinitely, for the continued export of capital by the creditor nation merely accentuated an already unhealthy situation. Conditions were in the making which led to the almost complete debacle of international trade at the end of the decade.

Many statesmen and economists were by no means blind to the dangers lurking in the area of international commerce. These dangers were not alone the results of the unusual position of the United States; they were the heritages of the First World War. Embargoes, quotas, and other impediments of trade, natural during wartime, had been revived after the war by various nations in an effort to restore internal economic life or protect their trade balances. The League of Nations sponsored numerous conferences aiming to end such restrictions and to reverse the developing high-tariff policies, but with few tangible results. The United States was persuaded to participate in at least two of these conferences, including the International Economic Conference of 1927. Here she joined in signing the conference report that "the time has come to put an end to the increase in tariffs and move in the opposite direction." Instead of following this policy, the Hoover administration sponsored the Hawley-Smoot tariff.

The shift in American policy finally came with the Democratic platform of 1932 and the subsequent victory of Franklin D. Roosevelt. The platform advocated not only lower tariffs but also "an international economic conference to restore international trade and facilitate exchange." Such a conference was arranged by the League of Nations to meet at London in 1933. Here the American delegation headed by Secretary of State Hull came out strongly for a modification of all unnecessary trade barriers. Certain of the European nations led by France insisted that a policy of tariff reductions must be accompanied by monetary stabilization. President Roosevelt, who in preliminary conferences had agreed to this, now reversed himself and refused to participate in plans for currency stabilization. At that time he was convinced that the shortest road to recovery was through rising prices produced by currency inflation.

Roosevelt's attitude brought the London Economic Conference to an untimely end. Nevertheless, the Roosevelt administration on its own part strove vigorously to improve international relations and revive foreign commerce. Its policy, as enthusiastically pushed by Secretary of State Cordell Hull, was one of tariff reductions through reciprocal trade agreements. It was made possible by the Reciprocal Trade Agreements Act of 1934, which authorized the President for a period of three years to negotiate trade agreements without action of Congress and gave him power to raise and lower tariff rates by not more than 50 per cent. This act, it should be noted, was an amendment to the Tariff Act of 1930. The latter, the Hawley-Smoot Act, remained as the basic tariff of the country, but the President was allowed to modify it for the purpose of expanding American export trade and alleviating the current depression. The Trade Agreements Act was subsequently renewed each time that it ran out. The fifth extension, made by a Republican Congress in 1948, was for one year and was designed to curtail the power of the executive branch in the making of future tariffs. The victory of the Democrats in the elections of 1948, however, brought in 1949 a three-year renewal without the Republican restrictions. Between 1934 and the end of 1948 trade agreements were concluded with twenty-nine countries.

The reciprocal trade agreements were concerned not alone with promoting trade through tariff reductions, but also with breaking down the quota systems and with pledges not to increase tariffs or remove items from existing free lists ("duty bindings" and "free-list bindings"). The latter were extremely significant in reversing a world-wide tendency toward higher tariffs and the intense economic nationalism which had been a characteristic of the postwar decades. Also significant was the fact that the trade agreements provided for most-favored-nation treatment in the matter of duty concessions and administration of customs, and in some cases for quotas and other factors.[10] In other words, concessions made to one country applied to others with which the United States had most-favored-nation agreements.

---

[10] The most-favored-nation treatment did not apply to the Cuban treaty of 1934 or generally to arrangements made by various countries with their colonies.

It was extremely difficult to determine the effect of the trade agreements before the outbreak of the Second World War and it has been virtually impossible since 1939, despite the fact that the twenty-nine countries with whom agreements were made included eight of America's ten best customers (1937) and absorbed about two-thirds of her foreign trade. Total foreign trade increased from 1934 to 1937, then decreased in 1938 and 1939, but revived again in 1940 with the coming of war. How much of this early increase was the result of improved economic conditions and how much it was due to trade agreements no one can tell. Statisticians have shown that between the years 1934–1935 and 1938–1939 American exports to trade agreement countries rose by 63 per cent while exports to non-trade agreement countries rose by only 32 per cent. In the same years imports from agreement countries rose 22 per cent and from non-agreement countries 13 per cent. This pattern, however, might also have been followed without trade agreements. That these agreements ended some discriminations against the United States and liberalized the movement of goods by removing trade barriers there can be no doubt. One careful student summarizes the findings by asserting that "it is reasonable to conclude that the United States has enjoyed a gain in trade, as compared with the volume of trade that would have been transacted if there had been no trade agreements program. As a stop-loss device, the program has been important."[11]

Implicit in the trade agreement program was the hope of improving international relations. The program was pushed with particular vigor in Latin America, where it became an integral part of the "good-neighbor policy." In addition to the trade agreements the Roosevelt administration attempted to improve international relations and the domestic economic situation by resuming diplomatic relations with Russia (1933). This move came after sixteen years of nonrecognition and was accompanied by a special commercial agreement.

SELECTED READINGS

Mitchell, Broadus, *Depression Decade,* chap. 11.

Lewis, Cleona, *America's Stake in International Investments,* chaps. 17–18.

Williams, B. H., *Economic Foreign Policy of the United States,* chaps. 1–4.

Moulton, H. G., and Pasvolsky, Leo, *War Debts and World Prosperity,* Part V.

Sayre, F. B., *The Way Forward: The American Trade Agreement Program,* chaps. 4, 8, 14.

Beckett, Grace, *The Reciprocal Trade Agreements Program,* chap. 6.

[11] Grace Beckett, *The Reciprocal Trade Agreements Program* (1941), p. 113.

CHAPTER 32

THE SECOND WORLD WAR

PREPARATION FOR WAR

THE outbreak of the Second World War in August, 1939, had two immediate effects upon the United States. First, it quickly ended any hope of maintaining the isolation characteristic of the period since the First World War and drew the nation back again into a world orbit. In the second place, it pulled the country out of the economic doldrums into which it had sunk with the recession of 1937. It is true that most Americans had hoped until Pearl Harbor (December 7, 1941) that the country might avoid war, but the strong belief of the great majority in the justice of the Allied cause soon ended all pretense of neutrality. Convinced that Britain and her allies were fighting the cause of this country as well as their own, the United States adopted an official policy of helping them in every way short of war. This policy, combined with Axis victories during the first years of the war, made it necessary to embark on a large-scale defense program. Aid to the nations fighting Germany and military preparedness at home changed the whole economic picture in America.

Within three weeks after the outbreak of war the President called a special session of Congress to revise the Neutrality Acts (p. 691) to allow the belligerents to purchase arms and munitions in this country. The President's request was granted, but all sales to combatants had to be made on a cash basis with deliveries in their own ships (cash-and-carry plan), except sales to their territories far distant from the war zones. Because of Britain's supremacy on the seas, this meant that war goods would go only to the Allies, except for Japan, not yet in the war. As Germany invaded one small European nation after another, the American government froze the assets of these nations in the United States in order to protect the property of American nationals abroad. This was also done with German assets after our entry into the war. In the meantime, with private loans abroad declining because of unwillingness to take risks or prevented by the Debt Default Act and the Neutrality Acts, aid to other nations devolved upon the government. After the war began virtually all loans to foreign governments were made by the RFC through the Export-Import Bank or by other means.

A second step in breaking down the Neutrality Acts was taken in January, 1941, when the President called for "all-out aid" to the embattled democracies and asked for power to sell, exchange, loan, or lend any war equipment to any nation whose defense he might think vital to the defense of the United States. Bitterly opposed by those who believed that this was a definite step toward war, the legislation requested was finally granted after two months' debate. So also was the President's request for large grants to implement the Lend-Lease Act. This act virtually nullified both the "cash and carry" principle and the Debt Default Act of 1934. Between March, when lend-lease began, and the end of the year almost $750,000,000 worth of materials were sent to the Allies. As a result of the Lend-Lease Act and other legislation and of Executive Orders the United States actively engaged in large-scale economic warfare before she entered the fighting war. It was also clear that the administration was determined to reassert the old American principle of "freedom of the seas" which had been relinquished in the Neutrality Acts. At the famous Atlantic conference in August, 1941, President Roosevelt and Prime Minister Churchill made "freedom of the seas" part of the Atlantic Charter.

The demands of lend-lease added new impetus to the development of a war economy already stimulated by a defense program which had begun seriously in 1938. This program was stepped up after the European war began and particularly after the evacuation of Dunkirk and the fall of France. Congress in 1940 voted $17,692,000,000 for various types of defense, and appropriations in 1941 reached the staggering figure of approximately $50,000,000,000. Congress in 1940 committed itself to a two-ocean navy and for the first time in American history to a system of compulsory peacetime conscription. The heavy appropriations of 1941 were accompanied by the heaviest tax bill in our history up to that time, a bill which it was hoped would raise the total federal tax income to $13,000,000,000.

The execution and co-ordination of the vast defense program was a tremendous task and the setting up of the administrative organization brought confusion and many false starts. It began in 1939 with a War Resources Board, to make an over-all survey of the problem. Then, as in the First World War, the President established in 1940 a Council of National Defense, composed of six Cabinet members, with a National Defense Advisory Commission to aid it. After the invasion of the Netherlands, the President created the Office of Emergency Management, which was superior to the National

Defense Advisory Commission and soon absorbed its functions. The OEM had two principal agencies. One was the Office of Production Management, which was concerned with production, priorities, purchases, materials, labor, contract distribution, and civilian supply—in brief, the production of commodities for war and civilian use. The other main agency was the Office of Price Administration, whose duties were chiefly to control prices.

In January, 1941, the President raised the Office of Production Management to the top position in handling war production, with William S. Knudsen, president of General Motors, as director, and Sidney Hillman, president of the Amalgamated Clothing Workers (C.I.O.), as associate director. But progress under the OPM was still too slow and in September the President created a new defense organization known as the Supply, Priorities, and Allocations Board (SPAB). Its chairman was Vice President Wallace and its executive director was Donald Nelson. Other members were Secretaries Stimson and Knox, OPM Directors Knudsen and Hillman, Lend-Lease Supervisor Harry Hopkins, and Price Administrator Leon Henderson. Except for the President, this Board had the final direction of defense production when Pearl Harbor at last took the nation into the war.

The impact of the European war in 1939 affected the American economy almost overnight. Said Price Administrator Henderson in reviewing the early weeks, "Memories of the First World War—memories of insatiable demand, of shortages, of inflation—were rekindled and there was an immediate and sharp increase in buying. The businessman who customarily bought one carload put in orders for three. Prices rose precipitately, basic commodities and basic raw materials both jumping about 25 per cent in the single month of September. The rise in prices itself evoked widespread accumulation of inventories and further fed the stream of buying. A speculative boom was on."[1] But the American economy was soon influenced by much more than fear of shortages and hopes of profits. Revision of the Neutrality Acts to allow the cash-and-carry plan, the Lend-Lease Act, and the large-scale defense program gave a more substantial basis.

First of all, industrial production approximately doubled between August, 1939, and December, 1941.[2] Since a substantial portion of this production was sold to the Allied nations, the situation was reflected in an increase of exports from approximately $3,177,000,000 in 1939 to $5,147,000,000 in 1941. But the European war and the domestic defense program were by no means the only cause for the skyrocketing of industrial production to heights hardly dreamed of in 1929. The increase in consumers' goods (25 per cent between August,

[1] Office of Price Administration, *First Quarterly Report,* for Period Ended April 30, 1942, p. 1.
[2] Using the average of 1935-1939 as 100, the Federal Reserve Board puts the index figure of industrial production in 1938 at 88 and that of December, 1941, at 167.

1939, and August, 1941) was also large. The latter is explained by increased employment, zooming pay rolls, and the desire of wage earners to acquire commodities denied them during the bleak depression days of the 1930's. The early years of the war had not yet solved the unemployment problem, but the number of nonagricultural workers had increased from 35,321,000 in April, 1940, to 41,036,000 in December, 1941. At the same time the index figures of pay rolls showed an increase approximately equal to that of industrial production.[3]

What made the economic picture brighter, particularly for wage earners in the durable goods industries, was that income moved ahead more rapidly than prices. Average hourly earnings increased from 73.4 cents in 1940 to 87.1 in December, 1941, and average weekly earnings, resulting in part from the increased number of hours, went up from $29.88 to $38.62.[4] At the same time the cost of goods purchased by wage earners increased less than 10 per cent. The farmers profited by a far greater differential between the prices they received for their products and the cost of commodities they purchased. The failure of retail prices to move upward rapidly immediately after the European war broke out was probably the result of the fact that production in 1939 was still far below capacity. The wholesale price index did not advance perceptibly until August, 1940, or seriously until February, 1941, when it began to spread out to include retail prices.

When war came with Pearl Harbor, the nation was by no means adequately prepared. Defense production was still in the formative stage and the administrative organizations had not yet been established on a basis of high efficiency. However, the preliminary work had been done and the pattern of defense production laid out. With war the machinery of production slipped into high gear more speedily than was expected by even the most optimistic. Preparedness during the years 1940 and 1941 paid off in 1942 in what to many seemed a "miracle of production."

PRODUCTION FOR WAR

The chief sinews of war are men, money, and materials. In the end the United States found an adequate supply of all three. Manpower was obtained mainly through the Selective Service Act of 1940 as amended and broadened after Pearl Harbor. Money came through increased taxation and great loan drives. Despite the enormous cost of the Second World War, the nation, as we shall see, experienced no great difficulty in financing the struggle. The main problem was that of materials. This involved not only the production

[3] Tables and graphs on the economic effect of the war are collected in Broadus Mitchell, *Depression Decade*, pp. 446–453.
[4] *Ibid.*, p. 389.

of raw materials of every kind, including food, but the conversion of civilian manufacturing to wartime production, the building of new facilities for manufacturing arms and munitions, and the establishment of systems of priorities, allocations, and rationing. It was also concerned with every phase of the labor problem.

Implicit in any adequate handling of production and distribution of war materials is efficient administration. Reorganization and realignment of administrative agencies continued during the war, but relative stabilization was secured by 1942. On January 7 of that year the President co-ordinated the activities of the Office of Production Management and other governmental agencies concerned with production into the War Production Board with Donald M. Nelson at its head.[5] The Board handled the battle of production during the war. Except for the purely military aspects, defense efforts as a whole were largely grouped under the Office of Emergency Management (p. 696), a framework within the Executive Office of the President. Among the principal agencies under OEM were the War Production Board, the Office of Civilian Defense, the Office of Defense Transportation, the Office of Lend-Lease Administration, the Office of Scientific Research and Development, the National War Labor Board, the Board of Economic Warfare, and the War Shipping Administration. This array of agencies, and many others, which appeared and disappeared during the war, were often confusing, but they show much similarity to those created during the First World War.

The first and most important problem of the WPB and its predecessors was the conversion of existing facilities to war production and the increase of those facilities. The latter was brought about largely by the federal government, which spent about $16,000,000,000 in the construction of war plants through the Defense Plants Corporation. At least five-sixths of the new plant construction during the war was done by government financing and this comprised the newest and best of the manufacturing facilities. At the end of the war the federal government owned over 90 per cent of the facilities for producing synthetic rubber, aircraft, magnesium, and ships; 70 per cent of the aluminum capacity; and 50 per cent of the facilities for building machine tools. It had also constructed plants for steel, high octane gasoline, and chemicals, to say nothing of 3800 miles of oil pipes (the "Big Inch" and "Little Inch") to carry petroleum to the east coast.

Conversion to war production necessitated the shifting of tools, equipment, facilities, man-hours, and floor space and to a large extent the retooling of

---

[5] Other members during the early years of the war were the Secretaries of War, Navy, and Agriculture, the Federal Loan Administrator (Jesse Jones), the officer in charge of War Department production (Lt. Gen. William S. Knudsen), the Administrator of the Office of Price Administration (Leon Henderson), the Chairman of the Board of Economic Welfare (Vice President Wallace), and the Defense Aid Administrator (Harry Hopkins).

industry. Two years of preparation and of selling equipment to the Allies had its effect; with America's entry into the war the whole program proceeded with unexpected speed. The United States, said Donald Nelson toward the end of May, 1942, "is actually doing things today which were unthinkable a year ago. It is executing programs which sounded utterly fantastic no more than six months ago." Thousands of factories hitherto engaged in manufacturing peacetime products turned to war production. The great automobile industry, for example, converted itself almost entirely to the manufacture of airplanes, tanks, trucks, jeeps, and other war needs. Industrial production (1935–1939 = 100) rose to 239 in 1943, and durable manufactured goods to 360. Production of machinery quadrupled, and transportation equipment (automobiles, aircraft, railroad equipment, and ships) increased seven times. As summarized by J. A. Krug, later Chairman of the WPB: "In 1939 . . . this country devoted less than 2% of its total national output to war, and about 70% to satisfying immediate civilian needs, the remaining 28% going to civilian government expenditures, capital formation, and exports. By 1944, war outlay had mounted to 40%, and the civilian share—though just as large in physical quantity—represented only half of our total output."[6]

During the five years of defense preparation and war (July 1, 1940, to July 31, 1945) the nation spent $186,000,000,000 for munitions production. The result was amazing. At the time of Pearl Harbor the armed forces possessed only 1157 planes suitable for combat and about the same number of usable tanks. During the five years of production the nation produced 86,338 tanks, 297,000 airplanes, 17,400,000 rifles, carbines, and side arms, vast quantities of artillery equipment and munitions, 64,500 landing vessels, and thousands of navy ships, cargo ships, and transports. During these five years the United States merchant fleet quadrupled, navy fire power increased tenfold. By mid-1944 it was estimated that the combined war production of Great Britain, Canada, and the United States was four times as high as that of the Axis powers. So well was production going that by the late summer of 1944 the WPB felt safe in ordering cutbacks in war production and allowing some resumption of the manufacture of civilian goods. It should be remembered that not all of this tremendous production was used in this country. From March 11, 1941, to December 1, 1945, goods transferred and services rendered under lend-lease amounted to approximately $49,096,000,000. Of this, about 60 per cent went to the United Kingdom and 22 per cent to Russia.

Obviously the spectacular munitions production depended to no small extent upon the increased production of raw materials and the ability to distribute them. The index for mineral production (1935–1939 = 100) rose to 148

---

[6] J. A. Krug, *Production: Wartime Achievements and the Reconversion Outlook*, WPB Document No. 334 (October 9, 1945), p. 4.

in 1942—"particularly noteworthy," said Secretary of the Interior Ickes, "because the nation skimmed much of the 'cream' from its mineral resources during the First World War." The production of fuels (coal and oil) also reached new levels with the index figure at 145 in 1944. The history of agricultural production is quite as remarkable. Production here increased each year from 1938 to 1944 with the index reaching 136 in the latter year.[7]

No area of American economy met the challenge of war more successfully than transportation. Inability of the railroads to cope with the situation in the First World War had forced the government to take over and operate a large part of the system. In the Second World War the railroads did such a superb job under the direction of the Office of Defense Transportation that the government found it unnecessary to extend further controls. Railroads reported that they had moved two and a half times the number of ton-miles of freight in 1944 that they had in 1939, and four and a half times the passenger traffic. This enormous increase was handled with practically the same number of locomotives as in 1939 and but a slight increase in freight or passenger cars. The Office of Defense Transportation under Joseph B. Eastman (until 1944) not only supervised the railroads but had jurisdiction over air transport, inland and coastwise shipping, pipe-line facilities, and rubber-borne transportation.

Despite the notable records of manufacturers, miners, farmers, and transportation workers, serious shortages of both military and civilian commodities existed at one time or another. The early difficulties had to do chiefly with manufacturing facilities, but this problem was largely solved by mid-1943. By that time the needs for most classes of military goods were being fully satisfied and the peak of the munitions program was reached in the last two months of that year. Shortages of raw materials, however, were more acute and persistent, although the bottlenecks shifted as time went on. The first great shortage, that of aluminum, brought the government into action with a program of government-built but privately operated expansion which quadrupled production over that in the prewar years.

Aluminum shortage for war needs vanished by the end of 1942, but shortages appeared in iron, ships, rubber, gasoline, fuel oil, and other commodities. Although the United States at that time had an ample supply of iron resources and a productive capacity greater than that of any nation in the world, the fantastic demand for steel products outdistanced the supply. The shortage was explained in part by failure to obtain scrap metal and this in turn was ascribed to the low ceiling on scrap prices. Fortunately, as time went on the situation improved through increased capacity, better utilization of scrap metal, and the channeling of steel into war production rather than

[7] The index figures in this section are from the *Statistical Abstract, 1947,* pp. 629, 816.

civilian commodities. Steel was in acute demand not only for munitions but for the building of ships for both the Navy and the merchant marine. The shortage of merchant ships was caused chiefly by the successful German submarine campaign in the Atlantic, which destroyed over 600 Allied cargo ships by the end of 1942. A shipbuilding program which launched 3,000,000 tons of merchant shipping in 1942 and 9,000,000 in 1943, combined with a successful Allied attack on the submarine menace, overcame this problem in 1943. No sooner was the submarine menace under control than the increased needs of 5,000,000 soldiers overseas again strained shipping facilities to the limit.

One of the most disastrous aspects of the German submarine activities was the interference with the transportation of gasoline and fuel oil, most of which was normally moved from the Gulf ports to the eastern seaboard by tankers. Reduction of civilian use by strict rationing, the construction by the government of huge pipe lines from the oil fields to the east coast, and increased production made available a sufficient supply for military needs. Quite different from the aggressive efficiency with which the government handled the aluminum, shipping, and oil situations was its muddling slowness in meeting the rubber shortage. After Japan's conquest of the East Indies had closed the source of virtually all the natural rubber used by the United States and her Allies, it was clear to anyone that immediate and decisive steps must be taken. The solution was obvious—the production of synthetic rubber by methods known to all rubber chemists. Existing rubber stocks were frozen and tires rationed, but it was six months after Pearl Harbor before the government organized a synthetic rubber program. Confusion, divided responsibility, and politics all slowed up the program. The delay seems to have been caused largely by the insistence of the farm bloc that rubber be manufactured from agricultural products as well as from oil. Action finally came after the President appointed a special committee headed by Bernard M. Baruch to investigate the problem and later a National Rubber Conservation Director to put a program into action. With the aid of government-built synthetic plants, production by mid-1944 had reached the rate of 836,000 tons a year compared with prewar imports of natural rubber ranging from 550,000 to 650,000 tons a year. This took care of the expanding military needs but left little for civilians.

RATIONING AND PRICE CONTROL

Perhaps the greatest failure in the First World War was the lack of adequate rationing or price control (p. 594). During the nineteen months of that conflict the price index (1914 = 100) rose to 162. During the Second World War, in which American participation was twice as long, the price index (1939 = 100) rose only to 133. Failure adequately to control prices in the earlier conflict substantially increased the cost of the war and reduced the standard of living of millions of people. As America began to feel the impact of the Second World War, the government at once realized the importance of the price problem. Some efforts to protect and acquire strategic raw materials had been made even before the Division of Price Stabilization, under the National Defense Advisory Commission, was established in May, 1940 (p. 697). The Division of Price Stabilization became increasingly important and was made an executive agency known as the Office of Price Administration in August, 1941.

The OPA, however, had little power in the prewar days. It could set up price schedules and through publicity, informal agreements, requests, and warnings sometimes bring compliance. It could not impose penalties. Nevertheless, its influence was great for it supplied government purchasing agencies with fair price schedules which they could follow. After the coming of war, Congress by the Emergency Price Control Act of January, 1942, gave the OPA statutory power to control prices and rents and set forth specific penalties for violations. That the pressure for inflation was great there could be no doubt. Both the government and consumers were intensive buyers and there was not sufficient of most commodities to go around. Although industry was actually producing more consumers' goods than before the war, the income of consumers had grown tremendously and thus increased the demand.

In 1942 the OPA estimated that income payments for that year would approximate $117,000,000,000, of which $31,000,000,000 would be returned to the government either in taxes or in individual savings in the form of war bonds or stamps, leaving a balance of $86,000,000,000 available for spending on civilian goods and services. At the same time it estimated that goods and services produced during the year would total approximately $69,000,000,000, leaving $17,000,000,000 of purchasing power as an "inflationary gap" to threaten the price structure. Governmental policies to close this "gap" and thus hold back the inflation included increased taxes, wide efforts to promote bond sales, curtailment of installment buying, rationing, and price control. The last two methods were the responsibility of the OPA.

Within a month after the war started the OPA began the rationing program with tires (January 5, 1942). In May it began to ration gasoline on the east coast and in December extended it to the entire nation. In similar manner rationing was imposed on fuel oil in the East in the fall of 1942 and made nation-wide in the late winter of 1943. Shortages in food first occurred in sugar and coffee. During normal prewar years Americans consumed close to 8,000,000 tons of sugar, two-thirds of which was imported from the Philippines, Hawaii, and Cuba. With war the Philippine supply was cut off, that of Hawaii seriously reduced, and that from Cuba curtailed by lack of shipping and submarine activities. At the same time, the demand was enlarged by lend-lease shipments and the increased use of sugar in manufacturing alcohol for explosives. Coffee, most of which is imported from Brazil, also became temporarily scarce because of large shipments to the Allies and interference with shipping. Rationing of sugar began in May, 1942, with the issuing of stamp books to consumers, and coffee was rationed in November, although the latter restriction was discontinued eight months later.

By the end of 1942 the armed forces and lend-lease were absorbing 25 per cent of the foodstuffs produced in this country, particularly canned, bottled, frozen, and dried vegetables, fruits, juices, and soups. As these commodities began to disappear from grocers' shelves, the country was not surprised when Food Administrator Claude Wickard on December 27 ordered Price Administrator Henderson to ration them. Consumers registered in February for Ration Book No. 2, and on March 1, 1943, the rationing of various kinds of canned and packaged goods went into operation under a "point system." Four weeks later rationing under the same system was extended to include meats and fats. Under the point system coupons were valued for a certain number of points and the amount of goods that could be purchased was determined by the point value assigned to each commodity by the OPA. By mid-1943 rationing covered 95 per cent of the food supply and insured a fairer distribution, but it by no means solved the problem of shortages. The OPA was also assigned the task of controlling rents in defense areas and establishing price ceilings on all commodities affecting the cost of living. Both jobs were difficult and complicated. Nevertheless the OPA by mid-1943 had designated 456 defense-rental areas and had established control over most of them by freezing rents at the March, 1942, level.

Prices were established on a community, zone, or national basis and often at the producer, wholesaler, or retail level. Probably no government agency ever affected more intimately the lives of so many people as the OPA and it received more than its share of criticism. The fundamental necessity of its work was understood, however, and the great mass of patriotic Americans loyally supported it. Unfortunately a small minority attempted to evade these regulations, and a "black market," particularly in gasoline and meats, existed at various times and places, which the OPA found itself inadequately equipped to prevent. Despite the difficulties, the OPA did a remarkable job. It not only saved the taxpayers billions of dollars in the cost of the war, but it prevented widespread chaos and suffering which would inevitably have followed failure to ration commodities and impose price control.[8]

[8] Leon Henderson resigned as Administrator of OPA in January, 1943. He was succeeded by Prentiss M. Brown, formerly Senator from Michigan, who in turn was followed in October by Chester A. Bowles.

Among the many complications involved in the battle against inflation was the control of wages and the special protection which the farmers had received on prices. President Roosevelt, who took the lead in the fight against inflation, asked Congress in the autumn of 1942 for full power to regulate farm prices. This was granted, along with the power to stabilize wages and salaries. The President followed with an order directing (1) the National Labor Board to limit wages and salaries, (2) the OPA to fix ceilings on retail and wholesale prices and on rents not yet curbed, and (3) the Department of Agriculture and the OPA to co-operate to hold down farm prices. To supervise all this control he created an Office of Economic Stabilization and as its head appointed James F. Byrnes, who resigned from the Supreme Court to accept the position.

LABOR IN THE WAR

Regarding labor the federal government faced three major problems. The first was to obtain an adequate supply of trained workers for the war industries. The second was to develop a sound and successful policy for handling labor disputes. The third was the difficult job of determining a wage policy which would dovetail with government efforts to control prices.

The first and primary task, that of developing an adequate supply of labor, seemed at the beginning an insuperable job. It was necessary not only to replace approximately 12,000,000 men and women drawn into the armed forces but to take care of the need for greater war production. Nevertheless, this task was eventually accomplished. Between 1940 and 1945 the labor force increased from 54,000,000 to 64,000,000—almost 20 per cent. This additional 10,000,000, plus those who filled the gaps made by workers drawn into the armed forces, were recruited from many sources. First of all, the new demand largely absorbed the 9,000,000 unemployed in 1939. It drew from youth of school age, from aged workers who had retired, and above all from the ranks of women. The number of women working outside the home increased by 5,000,000 during the war. Women factory workers doubled between 1939 and 1944.

Even with this additional force, the job of war production plus the maintenance of civilian production at prewar levels could never have been done without a willingness to work longer and harder. In the years 1939 to 1944 the average week increased from 37.7 to 45.2 hours (20 per cent) in manufacturing; from 32.4 to 39.5 hours in construction, and from 32.3 to 43.9 hours in mining. At the same time, said the WPB, "productivity—output per man-hour—climbed sharply, as volume increased, manufacturing methods improved, and workers responded to appeals to move the munitions to the fighting fronts faster and faster."[9]

[9] J. A. Krug, *op. cit.*, p. 2.

Obviously the addition of millions of new wage earners and the shift of millions of others from their regular jobs to new ones in war industries created many problems. One of the most difficult was the training for new jobs. This involved "refresher courses" for adults, vocational training for youth, and enlargement of apprentice training in virtually every factory in the land. Another problem was the movement of workers into defense areas, which resulted in a housing shortage, crowded conditions and increased sickness, and high rates of absenteeism. Long hours exhausted all but the hardiest. Many women were doing factory work in addition to their home duties; men also tried to add war work to their regular jobs.

As in the First World War, the federal government understood the need of close co-operation with labor and set up machinery to maintain it at all stages (p. 595). One method was to put labor representatives in all important defense agencies. Even before America's entry into the war, labor had a place on the Advisory Commission of the Council of National Defense. As already noted, Sidney Hillman, president of the Amalgamated Clothing Workers, was appointed associate director of the Office of Production Management when that body was set up to prepare for defense and possible war. The war policies of the federal government with relation to labor were carried out chiefly through two bodies: the War Manpower Commission and the National War Labor Board. The War Manpower Commission was "to establish basic national policies to assure the most effective mobilization and maximum utilization of the nation's manpower in the prosecution of the war." It had supervision of job recruiting and job training in war industries and the placement of workers where they were most needed. It performed a useful function in deciding over-all policies and in the end had virtual control over the Selective Service system in determining draft deferments.

Quite as important and much better known was the national War Labor Board. Established to function as a sort of "supreme court for labor disputes," it had the final power over labor conflicts. Refusal to obey it left government seizure and operation as the only alternative. It was a twelve-member body with equal representation from the public, the employer, and labor. With its twelve regional offices and its subsidiary boards, it ironed out thousands of difficult disputes and did a valuable service. It was recognized as a body of strategic importance in the war effort and had the confidence of the public. It became increasingly unpopular with labor, however, after it was given the responsibility of stabilizing wages.

PRICES AND WAGES

As a whole, labor gave excellent support to the war effort. Leaders of organized labor pledged a no-strike policy and urged their membership to the fullest co-operation. There were numerous strikes, most of them unauthorized or "outlaw," but on the whole the pledge was kept as far as responsible labor leaders were concerned. There were some exceptions, notably John L. Lewis and his United Mine Workers, whose interruptions of coal production will be noted below. From January 1, 1942, to August 14, 1945, the Department of Labor records 14,647 "work stoppages" involving 6,728,000 workers and 35,998,000 man-hours lost. The average length of the stoppages in 1943 was 5 days and in 1944 was 5.6 days. The time lost, however, was but one-tenth of one per cent of the total working time (1943–1944). Considering rising prices, the strain of speed-up, and longer hours, the total record was unusually good.

The chief friction arose over wages. On the theory that wage control should follow price control, the administration ordered the national War Labor Board in 1942 to stabilize wages at a level equal to the rise in the cost of living up to that time. When 180,000 workers of the Bethlehem, Youngstown, Inland, and Republic Steel companies sought a dollar-a-day raise, the WLB granted them 15 per cent on the theory that this represented the rise in the cost of living between January 1, 1941, and May, 1942. This was known as the "Little Steel formula" and was followed thereafter by the WLB. Labor economists presented data to prove that prices had gone up more than 15 per cent, that they were continuing to rise, and that the profits of farmers and industries were increasing. The WLB, however, refused to abandon its figure, insisting that the actual "take-home" pay equaled the rise in the cost of living. Nevertheless, it softened its policy by allowing vacation pay, higher wages for overtime, and other indirect ways of increasing income.

Friction between the policies of the WLB and the unions demanding higher wages became acute in 1943 and 1944 and many efforts were made to break through the "Little Steel formula." The most successful were those of the United Mine Workers, led by John L. Lewis, who suspended work four times in 1943 and forced the government to take over the mines and to grant miners substantial increases. Threat of a railway strike in December of that year also brought government seizure of the railroads and government operation for three weeks until the wage disputes were adjusted. Strikes and threats of strikes during wartime aroused resentment. The reaction of Congress was the War Labor Disputes (Smith-Connally) Act of 1943, passed over the President's veto. It extended for the duration of the war plus six months.

The War Labor Disputes Act aimed primarily to prevent interruption of war production. It strengthened the power of the WLB, authorized the President to take possession of any industry producing materials needed in the war effort, and forbade any person to promote strikes, lockouts, or other interruption in production after the government had taken possession. Workers contemplating a strike in private industries were required to notify the government, and the WLB was to hold a ballot within thirty days to determine whether the workers would strike. The act also forbade corporations, banks, and labor organizations to contribute to any election involving federal officials. Since there were more strikes and more workers involved in strikes in 1944 than in 1943, it appeared that this legislation had little immediate effect. It was significant, however, in showing the strong antiunion feeling in Congress and the growing strength of the antiunion group. It marked a definite shift in congressional attitudes toward labor and was a portent of more such legislation in the postwar years.

FINANCING THE WAR

The problem of financing the Second World War was greater than that of the First World War; the struggle was longer and the amounts involved relative to the capacity of the country were greater. But as a whole, the job was better done. Experience in the earlier conflict may have helped. Closer government connection with various segments of the economic life, including banking, made it easier. Better control of inflation kept expenses down and left the consumer with a larger surplus to invest in government securities, and these the government was able to sell at lower interest rates. Taxation was more far-reaching and yielded relatively larger returns.

It was fortunate that all this was so, for the cost of the war was stupendous. The budgetary expenses for the fiscal years 1941–1945 amounted approximately to $317.6 billion, of which $281.5 billion (88.6 per cent) was spent directly for war. Federal expenditures climbed from $12.8 billion in the fiscal year 1941 to $100 billion in 1945. The public debt in 1941 was $48.9 billion; in 1945 it was almost $258.7 billion. Of the $281.5 billion direct cost of the war, $159.6 went to the Army and $88.4 billion to the Navy, the remainder being spent by the United States Maritime Commission, the War Shipping Administration, and various government departments or administrative units. Of these vast expenditures for war and other government needs, about 43 per cent was obtained from taxes and other non-borrowing sources during the period July 1, 1940, through December 31, 1945. This was a better record than that of the First World War, when less than one-third of the total expenditures came from such sources.

War financing may be said to have begun with the Revenue Act of 1940, designed to produce larger funds for the defense program. No new forms of taxation were introduced, but the law either increased the rates or broadened the base of almost all existing sources of revenue. In general this was true of later finance measures. One innovation came in the Public Debt Act of 1941, which made interest on future issues of securities of the government subject to all federal income taxes. A more important innovation came in the current Tax Payment Act of 1943, which provided for withholding income taxes at the source on wages and salaries, thus introducing a new "pay-as-you-go" plan. Tax receipts for the fiscal years 1941–1945 were approximately $138.5 billion, of which income and excess profits taxes from individuals approximated 36.2 per cent, from corporations 34.2 per cent, and the remaining 29.6 per cent from other sources, such as internal revenue, employment taxes, and tariffs.[10] It is interesting to note that the number of individuals, estates, and trusts paying taxes increased from 7,633,000 in 1939 to 43,602,000 in 1943. In the latter year about 284,000 corporations also paid taxes.

Between May 1, 1941, the day that President Roosevelt bought the first Savings Bond of Series E, until the last dollar from savings bonds sold during the Victory Loan was deposited with the Treasurer of the United States on January 3, 1946, the Treasury sold $185.7 billion of securities to finance the war. Of this amount the seven War Loans and the final Victory Loan took care of approximately $156.9 billion. About two-thirds of this amount ($102.2 billion) was purchased by corporations, one-third by individuals ($43.3 billion), and the remainder by commercial banks and treasury investment accounts.

THE TWO WARS

The administration in the Second World War drew heavily on the experience of the earlier conflict. The President himself had been Assistant Secretary of the Navy in the First World War and was acquainted with the problem faced by his colleagues and the administrative bodies set up to carry on the struggle. In certain positions Roosevelt's war Cabinet eventually surpassed that of Wilson. Moreover, with peacetime conscription and the decision to build a two-ocean navy, defense preparations had begun earlier and more intensely in the period before the second war.

Where the second struggle surpassed the first, however, was chiefly in financing and economic controls. As noted in a previous paragraph, a larger percentage of the cost of the war was handled by taxes rather than passing the burden on to future generations. More important, perhaps, was the superior handling of rationing on the consumer level and the efforts to control wages and prices. The latter prevented a runaway inflation and saved billions for the taxpayer, to say nothing of distributing the burden of war more evenly upon the nation as a whole. The Second World War was carried on more efficiently than any other in our history.

[10] These and other figures in this section are taken from those collected by J. R. Craf, *A Survey of the American Economy, 1940–1946* (1947), pp. 120–136.

SELECTED READINGS

Craf, J. R., *A Survey of American Economy, 1940–1946.*
Harris, S. E., *Price and Related Controls in the United States,* chaps. 1–7.
Nelson, Donald, *Arsenal of Democracy,* chaps. 9–16.
Stettinius, E. R., Jr., *Lend Lease, Weapon for Victory,* chaps. 15–28.
Baxter, J. P., 3rd, *Scientists Against Time,* chaps. 20–28.

CHAPTER 33

THE POSTWAR YEARS

POSTWAR REACTION

Except in international relations, where the United States seemed to have largely repudiated her earlier policy of isolation, the years after the Second World War resembled those after the earlier conflict. The nation in 1945 had the same desire to liquidate the war as quickly as possible and the same overwhelming urge to return to its brand of "normalcy" as it had in 1918. Reconversion was pushed quickly and successfully. Decontrol was also pushed quickly, but with a resulting unfortunate inflation. Among the immediate results of inflation was serious labor unrest and a wave of strikes as after the First World War, and then antilabor legislation. All this was accompanied not alone by economic uncertainty but by a revival of intolerance and reaction.

During the war the government made many promises to veterans by the Servicemen's Readjustment Act of 1944 ("G.I. Bill of Rights"), which it fulfilled with considerable success. Except for this, any over-all program of social or economic reconstruction was as lacking as after the First World War. The congressional elections of 1946 brought an antiadministration Congress for the first time in fourteen years and thus ended any possibility of close co-operation on the part of all branches of government in dealing with domestic problems or developing a wise policy of reconstruction. The program of the new Congress, as far as it had one, was primarily to reduce taxation and pass antilabor legislation. The former was of doubtful wisdom at a time when the nation was embarking on a program of European aid and would soon be engaged in rearmament. The latter was too much tinged with bitterness and revenge to produce objective results. Congress not only was little concerned with a wise program of reconstruction but on the contrary seemed interested rather in weakening some of the more intelligent New Deal legislation and reviving the past. This tendency was delayed by the unexpected Democratic victory of 1948, but renewed by the Republican victory in 1952.

RECONVERSION AND DECONTROL

Reconversion in a sense began as early as late 1943 and early 1944 when the War Production Board began to cut back orders on certain war goods that were ahead of schedule and to allow resumption of production of civilian commodities. Dissension over the problem of cutbacks between military and civilian personnel in the government was, in fact, one of the causes for the resignation of Donald Nelson, head of WPB (January, 1942, to September, 1944), and the appointment of his successor, Julius A. Krug. It also brought, in October, 1944, the establishment of the Office of War Mobilization and Reconversion headed successively by James F. Byrnes, Fred M. Vinson, and John W. Snyder. This organization was to unify the programs and establish the policies regarding the use of natural resources and manpower until the end of the war and in the meantime take over the responsibility and planning for demobilization and reconversion.

There can be no doubt as to the efficiency and speed of reconversion. The productive machinery of the nation, of which at least 50 per cent had been devoted to the war effort, shifted over to civilian production with amazing success. By mid-1947 the job of conversion was practically finished. The impetus came from a market eager to overcome shortages which had accumulated for three and one-half years. With equal speed the administrative war agencies were disbanded. Exclusive of Army and Navy units, approximately 165 emergency war agencies had been established between late 1939 and the middle of 1946. Some of these were absorbed in existing departments or agencies; other were eliminated. By the latter date not more than a dozen of the main agencies remained. As to the wisdom of this speed, some reservations can be made. The rapid elimination of price controls, as we shall see, proved disastrous. Even on the purely military level, as it turned out, restraint would have been better. In less than three years the nation revived a program of rearmament and began to build larger military forces.

The most satisfying aspect of the reconversion picture was the transition with relatively little unemployment. Instead of unemployment, the number of workers actually increased. According to the President's Council of Economic Advisers, total employment increased between 1945 and 1952 from almost 54,000,000 to over 61,000,000.[1] Many factors help to explain this fortunate situation. First of all was the continuation of the war prosperity. The "temporary props" for this prosperity were mainly three: business expenditure for reconversion and for new construction and equipment; heavy con-

[1] *The Economic Report of the President* (January, 1953), p. 177.

sumer spending, much of it for commodities unobtainable during the war; and heavy export of goods and services at an annual record rate of $20,000,-000,000 compared with imports of only $8,000,000,000. Since at least half of this export trade was financed by the federal government, some of this prosperity was artificially maintained by the taxpayers. Also fundamental in the whole picture was the enlarged productivity of the nation. It might be noted in this connection that the railroads spent an average of a billion dollars a year in rehabilitation during the eight years following the war.

Congress by the "G.I. Bill of Rights" had done much to ease the unemployment problem for the veterans as well as to extend aid in other ways. The act provided hospitalization, unemployment benefits, aid in obtaining jobs, and loans for homes, farms, and business. It also took tens of thousands of veterans out of the labor market by aiding them to continue their education for a period up to four years. The employment situation was, of course, aided by the maintenance of a peacetime Army and the retirement from industry or agriculture of many who considered their wartime participation as merely temporary.

SHORTAGES AND INFLATION

Perhaps the two most important problems which faced the nation in the postwar years were shortages of consumer goods and inflation. The war had lasted more than three and one-half years, twice as long as the First World War, and shortages were more acute. Although production of civilian goods was larger during wartime than before, few commodities were adequate to meet the demand. Fortunately the rapid reconversion of industrial plants largely solved this problem. Within two years after V-J Day most shortages had been overcome.

Among those which persisted into 1948 were automobiles and houses. By the end of 1948, automobile production had actually reached a rate of 5,000,-000 a year, but it could not supply the demand. More acute was the housing shortage. Except for the Army and defense workers, the construction of housing had practically ceased for four years. The Office of Mobilization and Reconversion estimated that over 3,000,000 people would be seeking new homes in the two postwar years 1946 and 1947. Government agencies set their sights for the yearly construction of from one to one and a half million housing units a year, but actual production fell far below. Retarding factors were shortages of raw materials and labor and the high cost of construction. It is also possible that continuance of rent controls may have been a minor factor in keeping new capital from housing construction. Congress in 1946 aided by providing $400,000,000 for subsidies to speed production of bottleneck materials and authorized large loans to promote home building. Veterans were given preference and might receive direct aid in the G.I. Bill of Rights.

During the 1940's the birth rate was high and the population had increased in the decade by 19,000,000. The nation's population in 1950 was approximately 150,700,000. However, permanent nonfarm dwellings had increased from the end of the war through 1950 by over 4,871,000. Shortages still remained in certain large urban areas, but generally the situation was under control. This was also true by mid-1950 of most other commodities. By that time but a relatively small proportion of our economic activity could be attributed to the shortages created by the war. Not only were shortages of necessary commodities overcome, but certain vital needs such as the expansion of rural electrification were being met. And there were new commodities, notably television, introduced. By 1953 at least 47 per cent of wired homes had television receivers.

Of greater significance than shortages for the future welfare of the nation was the problem of inflation. Most shortages were eventually overcome, but the disastrous results of inflation were far more permanent. For the policy makers of 1945 and 1946, history had no lessons. With virtually no price control on the retail level, many prices during and after the First World War almost doubled. About half of this rise occurred after the war. Inflation lasted until mid-1920, when high prices combined with the end of heavy government spending brought a collapse, a shakedown of prices, and a new start. The consumers' price index for moderate-income families in large cities as prepared by the Bureau of Labor Statistics of the Department of Labor (1935–1939 = 100) rose from 70.7 in 1913 to 107.5 in 1918, then continued upward to 143.3 in 1920, only to drop to 127.7 in 1921.

As already noted, the price history during the Second World War was different from that of the earlier struggle because of more extensive rationing and price control. In terms of the above index, the figure rose from 100.2 in 1940 to 129 on June 15, 1945. This was inflation, but not to the extent of that after the First World War, particularly when the greater length of the last war is remembered. After the Second World War ended and controls were lifted, the experience was much the same. The price index for the year 1945 was 128.6 with food at 139.1; it reached 189.7 in 1952 with food at 231.4 and apparel at 202.5 (see graph). The extent of this inflationary spiral was by no means the result solely of the too rapid ending of priorities and price control, although that may have been the predominating influence. Shortages of badly needed commodities and pent-up buying power were also fundamental. Some blame perhaps may be attributed to the financial wartime policies of the federal government, which left too much excess buying power in the hands of civilians. Undoubtedly one important cause of the inflation was the fact that the government continued to loan heavily abroad to provide the chief support of the United Nations Relief and Rehabilitation activities, and later to implement the European Relief Program (Marshall Plan).

In any event, these influences pointed to a continuation of controls. Nevertheless, even before V-J Day the War Production Board began to lift priori-

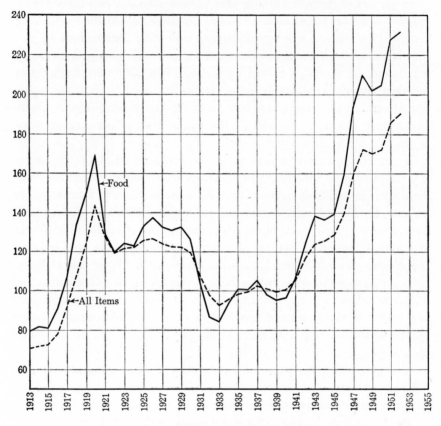

COST OF LIVING, 1913–1952 (1935–1939 = 100).

ties on hundreds of materials, and this process continued until the WPB went out of existence in November of 1945. The day after Japan surrendered, the OPA removed gasoline, fuel oil, and certain canned goods from the ration list. During the rest of the year the OPA struggled to control prices, but widespread opposition and the growth of the black market led the administration to end the rationing of other commodities before the end of the year —butter, meats, shoes, automobiles, and tires. By the time the life of the OPA was to run out in June, 1946, President Truman had become sufficiently worried over the extent of inflation to urge Congress to extend its life. Congress responded with a bill so useless in the opinion of the President that he vetoed it as a "choice between inflation with a statute and inflation without one." Congress then passed a new act continuing OPA for a year, but the main business of the Office was to decontrol all prices except those on agricultural commodities, now shifted to the Department of Agriculture, and those on rents.

All price controls had been lifted by the end of 1946 except those on sugar, rice, and rents; a year later only rents remained and on these a 15 per cent increase had been allowed, if the tenant agreed. With the Republican victory in the congressional elections of 1946, the Democrats for the first time in fourteen years lost control of the legislative branch. Truman, who had found little Democratic interest in maintaining price control, found less in the Republican-dominated legislature. The inflation continued and with it severe labor disputes aimed to raise wages. At a special session of Congress called in November, 1947, Truman asked for wide powers to control inflation as well as for aid to Europe. Congress replied by granting some minor powers which the President accurately described as "pitifully inadequate."

As the President predicted, these minor powers were of little use. The inflation continued throughout the larger part of 1948 and the Eightieth Congress adjourned without further legislation to check it. When the President found that the platform of both major parties favored action on a number of problems left unsolved, including housing and inflation, he recalled Congress in special session in July to deal with them. To his request for wide powers to control inflation Congress again responded only with authority to curb consumer installment buying and to increase the amount of cash Federal Reserve banks must keep on hand, thus curbing their ability to grant business loans.

Thus the situation remained until mounting inflation and the Korean War brought the Defense Production Act of September, 1950. This act again granted almost complete control over prices, wages, credit, and rationing. The President appointed Charles E. Wilson, president of the General Electric Company, as Defense Mobilization Director, and under him established an Economic Stabilization Agency with two divisions, one for prices and one for wages. It was well into 1951, however, before such action brought results. By mid-1952 prices began to show some stabilization and ceilings were suspended on many types of commodities in the retail area. However, at least 76 per cent of the wholesale market transactions were still under active price control in late 1952. With the advent of the Eisenhower administration early in the next year, all federal price controls including rents were ended. The result was higher prices.

It may be added that the Eisenhower administration found no easy solution to many other problems, notably that of agriculture. Nor did it cover itself in case of future difficulties in industry. The twenty-year-old Reconstruction Finance Corporation, which had done so much for industry was junked in 1953, except for a small remnant to aid "little business" (Small Business Administration).

The question immediately arises as to why the inflation, as after the First World War, did not contribute to bring on a depression. Why did economic activity and prosperity continue after 1945? At least four explanations may be offered: first, the heavy expenditures for reconversion and for new construction and equipment; second, heavy consumer spending, in part from war savings, for commodities unobtainable during the war; and third, the heavy exports of goods and services often double the value of imports—goods for which the government largely paid. Finally, organized labor had succeeded in achieving wage levels in line with rising prices.

LABOR AFTER THE WAR

Although widespread discontent existed over rising prices and bitter criticism was directed against Congress for failure to act, the unorganized consumers had little influence. The only powerful group which exerted pressure for counter-inflationary action was organized labor. When it failed, it turned its energies to obtain higher wages. Labor, moreover, was the one group able to defend itself. Membership, as in the First World War, grew in strength and continued to mount after the war was over. Membership of 8,500,000 in 1940 increased to 15,400,000 in 1947.

In a demand for wage increases adequate to meet the rising prices, thousands of strikes were called in the last half of 1945 and in 1946. The latter year turned out to be the stormiest year in American labor history with some 4700 strikes involving 4,700,000 workers. This wave of strikes was led by some of the larger C.I.O. unions in such mass-production industries as automobile manufacturing, electric equipment, meat packing, and steel, and were generally successful in achieving wage increases approximately equal to the inflation. Continued rising prices quickly threw the 1946 wage scales out of line, and new strikes or threats of strikes brought a second round of increases in 1947. With prices still high in 1948, a third round followed. Although leadership in obtaining wage increases was often in the hands of the automobile and steel workers and the miners, the efforts quickly extended to workers in other industries. Union success in obtaining higher wages was not alone the result of strong organizations. These were years of prosperity, high industrial profits, and full employment. Many factors worked for the benefit of labor.

Criticism of labor which had resulted during the war in the War Labor Disputes Act (p. 708) grew in the postwar years as the result of numerous strikes and repeated efforts to raise wages. As had happened before, labor was now blamed for the high prices and inflation. Labor disclaimed the responsibility, pointed to the essential causes of inflation—shortages of commodities, a backlog of buying power, continued heavy purchases by the government, and failure of the government to maintain brakes of various kinds. Organized labor also pointed out that it had been the chief group to oppose ending controls after the war. Wage earners maintained further (and with much truth) that the profits of industry were so large that wages could be increased without raising the retail price of the product. In any event, workers insisted that they could protect themselves against inflation only by higher wages and, if necessary, strikes to obtain them.

Although unions had grown in numerical strength during the war and in their ability to obtain higher wages, their position in other ways had declined. While they had lost much of the good will of the public that had been conspicuous in the 1930's, their natural opponents had grown in economic and political strength. As after the First World War, the years after the recent war were characterized by reaction and conservatism. The crusade for reform had largely ended. Many felt that the strikes during wartime were unpatriotic and the postwar strikes inflationary. The persistent propaganda of antilabor groups that the National Labor Relations Act had given the workers too much strength and that a better balance should be established was finally having its effect. On its part labor had failed to maintain good public relations or to explain its position as successfully as had its opponents.

While labor lost prestige with the general public, its strength relative to management also declined. The reputation of business leaders, which had been badly deflated during the depression, had revived as a result of their contribution to the war effort. Their confidence had also increased with profits and prosperity. The same was true of the strength of the Republican party, which had won control of Congress in the mid-term elections of 1946. Neither the A. F. of L. nor the C.I.O. had officially backed either party, but the Political Action Committee sponsored by the C.I.O. had supported the Roosevelt candidacy since 1936, as had the American Labor party and the Liberal party, whose backing came largely from labor. It seemed evident that the majority of organized workers had thrown in their lot with the Democrats. This was even more evident in the Eisenhower-Stevenson presidential campaign of 1952, when both the A. F. of L. and the C.I.O. officially backed the Democratic candidate.

The changing attitude toward labor evident in the War Labor Disputes Act (1943) continued after the war. The Lea Act (1946) forbade "featherbedding" practices in the Musicians Union, and in the same year the Hobbs Anti-Racketeering Act curbed certain activities in the Teamsters Union.

Congress also passed the Case bill, which contained many restrictions later incorporated in the Taft-Hartley Act, but failed to pass it over the President's veto. Although Congress passed legislation to restrict unions, it ignored until 1949 the repeated suggestion of the President to increase the minimum wages of the Fair Labor Standards Act (p. 675). This was the record of Democratic Congresses, and it was not likely to be reversed after the Republicans took over early in 1947. Legislation to curb and weaken unions became, in fact, a major item in the Eightieth Congress.

LABOR-MANAGEMENT RELATIONS ACT

The theory behind the Labor-Management Relations Act of 1947 (Taft-Hartley Act) was that labor had become so powerful under the National Labor Relations Act that the employer was no longer able to bargain on equal terms and that the balance must be restored. In addition there was the belief that certain labor practices were injurious and should be banned. Many argued that if these objectives were accomplished, industrial peace would be promoted. The old National Labor Relations Act had stated that certain acts of employers which interfered with workers' rights to join unions and bargain collectively were unfair and that workers might appeal to a National Labor Relations Board against employers violating such acts. The new Taft-Hartley Act retained these provisions, but it also forbade certain "unfair" labor practices against which employers, workers, or even other unions might appeal to a new NLRB set up by the act.

The list of "unfair" labor practices forbidden were many. (1) No one may interfere with the right of a person not to join a union. (2) A union may not discriminate against a worker or influence an employer to discharge him because he is not a union member. (3) A union may not refuse to bargain collectively. (4) Certain strikes and secondary boycotts are declared unfair labor practices. For example, workers are forbidden to strike to force an employer to join an employers' association or to force one employer to cease dealing with another (secondary boycott).[2] (5) The act also forbids jurisdictional strikes. (6) Unions having union-shop contracts with employers are forbidden to charge "excessive or discriminatory" initiation fees. (7) "Featherbedding," that is, the attempt to compel an employer to pay for services not actually performed, is made an unfair labor practice. (8) It is also an unfair labor practice under the act for a union having a contract to strike without giving notice, sixty days before its expiration, of a desire to change the agreement and bargain with the employer. If no agreement is

---

[2] As interpreted by this act, a secondary boycott generally concerned a situation in which workers refuse to handle materials produced by nonunion workers or made in a shop where a labor dispute is in progress. Secondary boycotts involving picketing, but not strikes, appeared to be legal.

reached with the employer within thirty days after the notice was sent, the union must notify the Federal Mediation and Conciliation Service and the state mediation board, if such a board exists.

Responsibility for enforcement of the new law was placed with the National Labor Relations Board, now increased from three to five members. It may issue "cease and desist" orders or its general council may ask for injunctions from federal courts forbidding violations of the law. Refusal to obey may be punished by fine, imprisonment, or both. The services of the NLRB, which includes handling petitions from unions for elections and receiving complaints against unfair practices of employers, are open only to unions which fulfilled two primary conditions. First, each local, national, or international union must file certain information regarding itself such as the constitution, bylaws, annual financial statements, and names and salaries of all officers. Second, each officer of a local or national union must file annually a sworn statement that he is not a member of the Communist party or affiliated with it and that he does not believe in the overthrow of the government by force or unconstitutional means.

One blow at labor which was warded off was a strong demand to ban any contract providing that all workers hired by a concern be union members. A compromise was written into the law forbidding a *closed* shop but allowing a *union* shop. In other words, the law allowed an employer to hire anyone, union member or not, as he pleased. However, if the majority of all the workers in a shop vote in favor of a union shop, the nonunion worker must join the union thirty days after he has been hired. While the union shop was saved, labor lost severely when the act revived (if it did not encourage) the use of the injunction. Labor had fought against the injunction for half a century; the Clayton Antitrust Act (p. 467) had tried to limit its use, and the Norris-LaGuardia Act had forbidden it in labor disputes except under unusual circumstances. In one blow the act swept away the gains achieved by decades of struggle. Not only was the use of the injunction revived, but employers might sue unions for violation of contract or for damages resulting from a secondary boycott. In such suits unions were bound by the acts of their agents, but the courts could not fine individual members, only the union as a body.

As to money earned by workers, the employer was forbidden to deduct dues from workers' pay (checkoff system) unless each individual gave written permission. The employer might, however, deduct payments to union welfare funds, but on condition that new contracts provided for equal representation of labor and management in administration of the fund. The act forbade the use of union funds in any election for federal office.

The act also provided a method of delaying strikes which might "imperil the national health and safety." In the event of such a strike or threat of strike, the President was empowered to appoint a "board of inquiry" to investigate the dispute and make its findings public. Upon receipt of the report the President might seek an injunction in a federal court to restrain the union from striking for eighty days. The act also forbade strikes by employees of the federal government. In the hope of providing assistance in ironing out labor disputes, the act took the United States Conciliation Service out of the Department of Labor and made it an independent body under the same name of Federal Mediation and Conciliation Service. It could offer its services but could compel no one to accept them or to abide by its decisions.

Such were the main provisions of the most important legislation aimed definitely to curtail the power of labor. Truman vetoed the bill as an act discriminating against labor in a "consistent pattern of inequality" which would surround collective bargaining with "bureaucratic procedures" and "time-consuming legislation." Congress passed it over his veto. Labor asserted that the act nullified essential rights won by a century of struggle and reduced labor to a status of slavery. Their opponents insisted that it merely restored bargaining equality and ended abuses recognized as harmful to both labor and the public. In the heat of conflict, both sides undoubtedly exaggerated, but there is no question that the act went further than eliminating abuses and restoring equality; it took away hard-won gains and reduced labor to an inferior position. The unexpected victory of the Democratic party in 1948, pledged to a repeal of the act, presaged at least drastic revisions. But Congress was little interested and only one minor revision was secured. In the elections of 1952 the Democrats promised repeal and the Republicans the retention of the act, but with amendments.

In the meantime, general prosperity and the demand for labor not only prevented decline in union membership but allowed some increase. The Department of Labor in 1953 estimated union membership at between 16,-500,000 and 17,000,000 members (including over 600,000 affiliates in Canada) of which 9,500,000 million were in the A. F. of L. and 5,000,000 in the C.I.O. with the rest scattered in the Railroad Brotherhoods, in unions ousted by the C.I.O. as Communist dominated, and in various other independent organizations. Organized labor blamed the Taft-Hartley Act for the slowdown in growth, but other factors contributed. Easily organized workers were already in the fold; many others were not interested in joining and in some cases voted down affiliation. One difficulty faced by labor during this period, particularly by the C.I.O., was the problem of a few Communist-dominated unions. The C.I.O. in 1949-1950 ousted eleven such unions, and generally set up rival unions to attract membership. Late in 1952, Philip

Murray, president of the C.I.O. for sixteen years, and William Green, president of the A. F. of L. for twenty-seven years, died. They were succeeded respectively by Walter Reuther and George Meany.

IMMIGRATION

The position of labor with regard to immigration was not greatly changed during the postwar years. The McCarran-Walter Act of 1952 amended and codified previous legislation but kept in general the quota system of 1924, which thus maintained the maximum number of immigrants, now 154,657, virtually unchanged. It removed the ban on Asian and Pacific peoples but limited the number to 2000. It was bitterly criticized by many as restricting the immigration from eastern and southern Europe, as limiting Asian and Pacific immigrants to 2000, and also as opening the security measures to overzealous interpretation. It reinforced the methods of keeping out "subversives" and gave the Attorney General the power to deport Communist and Communist-front people even after they had acquired United States citizenship. Congress passed the act over President Truman's veto, but in the Senate only by one vote more than the necessary majority.

Congress, however, did pass in 1948 a Displaced Persons Act which allowed displaced and homeless persons from Europe to be admitted. While charged against the quota, the act permitted 50 per cent of the quota for future years to be mortgaged by such persons, that is, they had preferred treatment to that amount in the future. During the three years the act was in force some 315,000 such persons were admitted. Another law operating from 1945 to 1948 allowed the entrance (above the quota) of alien wives, husbands, and children of citizen members of the armed forces. The number as admitted was about 119,700. As a result of much agitation a new bill was enacted in 1953 allowing the entrance within three years of 214,000 refugees, mainly from Europe.

ECONOMIC CO-OPERATION THROUGH THE UNITED NATIONS AND THE MARSHALL PLAN

Reactionary and unimaginative as were many of the postwar domestic policies of the United States, quite the contrary was true of her international economic activities. Not only did this country take the leadership in the organization of the United Nations, but she provided similar leadership before the war was over in launching various economic organizations which were destined to become special agencies of the Economic and Social Council of the United Nations. After the United Nations was established, the Economic and Social Council became one of its most important organs. By the beginning of 1949 this Council had established commissions on human rights, on the status of women, on economic and employment problems, on transportation and communication, on population, on fiscal matters, on statistics, and on population. It had set up special economic commissions on Europe and Asia. In addition to the commissions, various specialized agencies or committees having to do with international economic co-operation were attached to the Council. On these commissions and specialized agencies largely rested the world's hopes of future economic co-operation.

One of the specialized agencies of the United Nations, the International Labor Organization, had been part of the League of Nations. It had maintained its structure during the war and in 1946 it affiliated with the United Nations. It continued through its regional conferences and its industry committees to work for improved labor conditions throughout the world. Largely through the influence of the United States, four other specialized agencies were set in motion during the war. At the Bretton Woods Conference of 1944 an International Bank of Reconstruction and Development with a capital of $9,000,000,000 was planned. Its purpose was to lend money for reconstruction in war-torn areas and in less developed countries, and to guarantee loans made by governments and private agencies. An International Monetary Fund of $8,800,000,000 was also proposed to stabilize world currencies and facilitate world trade. A Food and Agricultural Organization was established to improve the world's agricultural production and raise the standard of living, and an International Civil Aviation Organization to establish international rules for civil aviation governing the safety and supervision of air navigation. Possibilities of important economic co-operation were also implicit in such agencies as the United Nations Educational, Scientific and Cultural Organization and the World Health Organization, and more obviously in the International Trade Organization. To these organizations the United States was the chief contributor.

The International Trade Organization was founded to promote international trade in the hope of maintaining a balanced and expanding world economy. Although the charter of the ITO was not finally completed until the Havana conference of 1948, a beginning was made at the Geneva conference in 1947, where a General Agreement on Tariffs and Trade (GATT) was effected. At that conference the twenty-three key trading nations participating concluded 123 trade agreements, including nineteen general trade agreements by the United States. Subsequent GATT conferences were held at Annecy, France (1949), and Torquay, England (1951), which brought further tariff cuts and reciprocal arrangements. By that time American tariffs had reached the lowest levels since the early years of the Republic. Since 1934 the United States had followed a policy of lower tariffs. To a certain extent other countries have co-operated. On the other hand, foreign nations in the postwar years have curtailed imports from this country by raising tariffs, establishing quotas and licensing systems to enforce them, and other controls of various types.

It is too soon to measure the possibilities of international economic co-operation through the instrumentalities of the United Nations. In the final analysis they will depend upon the success of the UN in preserving peace and easing the political and ideological friction between nations. Unfortunately, this friction increased rather than declined in the years after the war. Russia, violating the Yalta and Potsdam agreements, imposed her will and, as far as practical, her economic and political systems upon at least seven of the nations of eastern Europe and upon eastern Germany. Not content with this string of satellites, she sought to win control of Greece and to press for power at various points in the Near and Far East. President Truman expressed his opinion that "it must be the policy of the United States to support free peoples who are resisting attempted subjection to armed minorities or by outside pressure" and Congress in 1947 voted $250,000,000 to aid Greece and $150,000,000 for Turkey. This was largely military aid, but the "Truman Doctrine" was broadened in the same year by the so-called Marshall Plan. At a Harvard commencement Secretary of State Marshall suggested the willingness of the United States to undertake a policy "against hunger, poverty, desperation and chaos" and toward a "revival of a working economy in the world so as to permit the emergence of political and social conditions in which free institutions can exist." For such a plan the initiative, he said, must come from Europe.

The Marshall Plan meant the economic co-operation of European nations and a program which would include the pooling of resources, the breaking down of economic barriers, and the assessment of needs on a continent-wide basis. With amazing speed the idea was taken up and conferences were held to initiate the program. Russia, asserting it was an American plan to enslave western Europe and bring it under economic control, refused to co-operate, and her satellite states obediently but reluctantly followed. Sixteen European nations, however, co-operated in the plan, and early in April, 1948, the United States voted $6,098 billion to implement the Marshall Plan for one year, with relatively small amounts going to China ($338 million for economic aid, $125 million for military aid) and to Greece and Turkey for military aid ($275 million). The program was to be handled by an Economic Co-operation Administration and to head it the President appointed Paul G. Hoffman.

The European Recovery Program included Trieste and the French, British, and American zones in Germany as well as sixteen nations. Its purpose was not alone to save many Europeans from virtual starvation but also to help them rehabilitate their agriculture and industry and stabilize their monetary and financial systems in the hope of making them self-supporting. In addition there was the desire to prevent the misery and chaos which might lead to Communist domination. The program got under way slowly and American exports during the spring and summer were largely food and agricultural products. By the late autumn and early winter, however, industrial products, including those which would aid in long-term industrial revival, predominated. The Marshall Plan, administered by the Economic Co-operation Administration (ECA), was a long-term economic gamble, but it proved successful. Within three and one-half years, for example, the industrial production of France and western Germany surpassed that of the prewar level. Even food production was up 9 per cent above the prewar level, while goods and services in the co-operating nations as a whole were up 15 per cent above the prewar days. Not only so, but the program brought the economic life of the co-operating nations closer together through the freer movement of goods, co-operation in a European Payments Union, and the Schuman Plan, which unified the six major steel- and coal-producing countries into a unified marketing area.

Altogether the ECA spent about $12,000,000,000, primarily in economic aid, of which $5,500,000,000 went for industrial products, $5,200,000,000 for food and other agricultural commodities, and $800,000,000 for freight costs. On their part the European nations contributed $9,000,000,000. After the North Atlantic Treaty was signed in 1949, the United States began to appropriate large amounts to help rearm the free nations. In 1951 Congress abolished the ECA and put further economic help into the hands of the Mutual Security Administration and military aid in the hands of the Department of Defense. Between July, 1945, and the end of 1952 the United States government's grants and credits to foreign governments (chiefly European) amounted to over 37.6 billion, of which about 27.8 billion were gifts, and about 9.9 billion were obligations to repay. This included not only economic help but some military aid, as well as contributions to UNRA, a large loan to Great Britain, and other loans through the Export-Import Bank.

FOREIGN ECONOMIC RELATIONS

In foreign trade (merchandise, gold, and silver) the United States maintained a total excess of exports over imports from 1889 through 1933. From 1934 through 1940 imports were higher than exports. With 1941 and the heavy contributions made by the United States government to Allied nations the excess of exports became very large. As far as the balance of payments is concerned, the picture of international transactions is somewhat different. Here the United States shows an excess from 1930 on, except for the years 1942 through 1945 and 1950. The excess after the end of the war (except

1950) came despite the large contributions in kind or in cash through lend-lease, UNRRA, and other channels. These international transactions, of course, include movements of capital invested and the return on these investments.

The problem of the investment position of the United States is a difficult one, particularly since the middle 1930's. Government documents and estimates disagree, and the question of evaluating property in the warring countries is impossible. If short-term obligations are included, it would appear that from 1939 to 1945 foreign investments in this country were as large, if not larger, than ours abroad. After the end of the war, however, this country again assumed the position that it had held in the 1920's and most of the 1930's.

A BACKWARD GLANCE

For three and a half centuries the drama of American history has been unfolding for us. We have seen one generation of frontiersmen after another push their way westward until they conquered a continent and left for their children an unsurpassed heritage. We have seen a primitive agricultural people broaden its interests under the stimulus of limitless raw materials and become a nation whose economic life has widened into almost every activity. And we have seen an economically dependent people achieve first political, then economic independence, until finally the nation assumed a strong economic and political role which made it the decisive factor in two world wars. It has been a history of the opening and exploitation of a region enormously rich in raw materials and overflowing with possibilities. The United States became the only nation with resources and wealth sufficiently great to give important aid in the reconstruction of many nations after these two great wars.

The task of developing a continent our people met with confidence, buoyancy, and optimism. But the methods were often crude and wasteful. Much of value was needlessly squandered and lost forever. Irreparable inroads were made in our most valuable raw materials. Much of this took place in a period which many have called an "era of *laissez faire*." But complete *laissez faire* in the economic realm is impossible and has never entirely existed. It was utterly absent in the colonial period, when legislation governed almost all aspects of economic life. It grew during the nineteenth century, but even in those years high tariffs and state and federal aid to transportation cut deeply into such a philosophy, as did the control of banking by state or federal governments. By the twentieth century *laissez faire* had largely ended. By this time economic problems had become too complicated to be solved automatically by such a policy.

Many obvious causes contributed to the decline of *laissez faire*. One was continued demand of economic groups for government aid and protection. Another was the disregard of the public interests and the monopoly practices of big business which finally forced government regulation. Business itself first cracked the existing structure of *laissez faire* when it combined to save itself from the ruin of unrestricted competition. And, of course, as the over-all economic and social life became more intricate, controls became necessary and inevitable if the delicate structure of society was to be held together.

As our nation grew older we experienced many of the economic and social problems of the older industrial nations of Europe. As we grew rapidly and almost chaotically into a mighty manufacturing nation, population increased and concentrated in cities. There economic groups became more differentiated and class feeling became stronger. Fortunately, as the nation grew to maturity many early faults were rectified. The waste of natural resources has been checked, the standard of living has improved, and the income of the people has changed to the benefit of the lower-income groups. This has been particularly evident in the quarter-century since 1929. Measured in 1952 prices, the average annual income after taxes increased from $1000 in 1929 to $1500 in 1952. Moreover, since 1935–1936 the real income of families and single persons in the lowest two-fifths of the income range has increased 90 per cent, while the income in the top fifth has increased about 40 per cent. This marks a general improvement in social progress.

The last quarter-century has indeed been a notable one in American economic history. Measured in 1952 prices the output of all goods and services in 1929 was $172,000,000,000; in 1952 it was $345,000,000,000. While industrial production doubled, agricultural output rose 50 per cent. At the same time the number of workers having civilian jobs increased from 48,000,000 to 61,-000,000. While the work week dropped from forty-eight to forty hours, each worker turned out on the average 80 per cent more goods and services. Money spent in durable equipment on farms and in factories doubled during the period, as did the number of automobiles, while household equipment saw a similar increase. Twelve million nonfarm homes were built, chiefly since the end of the war, while homeownership increased from 48 per cent in 1930 to 55 per cent in 1952.

While advances on a percentage basis similar to these may have happened in certain areas in previous quarter-centuries, such development in a mature economy seems amazing. As to the future, predictions are of dubious value. If international tensions subside and the nation can drastically cut its expenditures for defense, if atomic energy can be shifted from destructive purposes to the needs of a peaceful world, we may look forward to a ceaseless economic development and a continued improvement in the standard of living. But this can be accomplished only in a free world functioning through unselfish and intelligent leadership dedicated both to the encouragement of private initiative and to the wise control of our economic system.

SELECTED READINGS

The Economic Report of the President Submitted to Congress, January, 1952, pp. 1–31.

Millis, H. A., and Brown, E. C., *From the Wagner Act to Taft-Hartley,* chap. 16.

Slichter, S. H., *The American Economy.*

Slichter, S. H., *What's Ahead for American Business?*

Condliffe, J. B., and Hutcheson, H. H., *Point Four and the World Economy,* Foreign Policy Association Headline Series, No. 79.

BIBLIOGRAPHY

BIBLIOGRAPHY

Prefatory Note

THE literature of American economic history has grown rapidly in recent years. The chief output originates from government economists and statisticians who issue scores of studies each year with the imprint of the various government departments. Three private organizations are also prolific—the National Industrial Conference Board, supported largely by industrialists; the National Bureau of Economic Research, subsidized by the Rockefeller Foundation; and the Brookings Institution. The quantitative studies of the NBER are of a high level, as are the specialized treatments of the Brookings Institution. The Harvard Studies in Business History, the series of the Smith College Council of Industrial Studies, and other groups sponsored by educational institutions have added to the output.

Research will be aided by H. P. Beers, *Bibliographies in American History: Guide to Materials for Research* (1942), and by the annual volume of bibliography sponsored by the American Historical Association and prepared by Grace G. Griffin *et al.*, *Writings in American History*. The latter covers the years 1906–1940, and 1948. Allen Johnson and Dumas Malone (eds.), *Dictionary of American Biography* (20 vols., 1928–1937, with a supplementary volume in 1944), has many biographies of men significant in economic life. Students of economic history will find important articles in E. R. A. Seligman and Alvin Johnson (eds.), *Encyclopaedia of the Social Sciences* (15 vols., 1930–1935), and a short cut to information in J. T. Adams and R. V. Coleman (eds.), *Dictionary of American History* (5 vols., 1940). Two historical atlases useful in economic history are C. O. Paullin, *Atlas of the Historical Geography of the United States* (1932), and C. L. and E. H. Lord, *Historical Atlas of the United States* (1944). L. M. Hacker, R. Modley, and G. R. Taylor, *The United States: A Graphic History* (1937), and Harold U. Faulkner and the Graphics Institute, *Visual History of the United States* (1953), are useful collections of pictorial statistical graphs with comments. Absolutely necessary is Henrietta M. Larson, *Guide to Business History* (1948).

Louis M. Hacker, *The Triumph of American Capitalism* (1940), and T. C. Cochran and William Miller, *The Age of Enterprise* (1942), are suggestive economic interpretations of American history. The Hacker volume, mainly on the period before 1865, emphasizes the rise of capitalism rather than the westward movement as the dominating influence, while Cochran and Miller stress the influence of business enterprise. Charles and Mary Beard, *Rise of American Civilization* (2 vols., 1927), emphasizes the influence of economic sections, as does F. J.

Turner, *The Significance of Sections in American History* (1932). Single-volume economic histories of the United States by Kirkland, Shannon, McGrane, and Bining are written by scholars primarily historians, those by Wright and by Bogart and Kemmerer are by economists. The co-operative volume edited by H. F. Williamson depends upon both groups. Books of readings in American economic history include the following: G. S. Callender, *Selections from the Economic History of the United States, 1765–1860* (1909), with enlightening introductory notes; E. L. Bogart and C. M. Thompson (eds.), *Readings in the Economic History of the United States* (1916), and F. Flügel and H. U. Faulkner (eds.), *Readings in the Economic and Social History of the United States, 1773–1829* (1929). The latter does not cover the colonial period but contains greater material on the post-Civil War era. More specialized than the above is N. S. B. Gras and H. M. Larson, *Casebook in American Business History* (1939). Note should be made here of the Amherst Series, "Problems in American Civilization," edited by G. R. Taylor *et al.*, which contain items in economic history and are of great value in teaching.

Of the great co-operative works, that of Allen Johnson (ed.), *Chronicles of America* (50 vols., 1918–1921), now brought down to date under the editorship of Allan Nevins, has numerous volumes devoted largely to phases of economic history. A. M. Schlesinger and D. R. Fox (eds.), *History of American Life* (13 vols., 1927–1948), contains economic as well as social history. In process of publication by Rinehart & Company is a nine-volume series, *The Economic History of the United States* (Henry David, H. U. Faulkner, L. M. Hacker, C. P. Nettels, and F. A. Shannon, eds.), of which five volumes have appeared. They contain full bibliographies.

On the economic interpretation of history the following are among the most useful studies: E. R. A. Seligman, *The Economic Interpretation of History* (1922); H. See, *The Economic Interpretation of History* (1929); and M. M. Bober, *Karl Marx's Interpretation of History* (1927). Two valuable studies emphasizing responsibility of the state in the economic life of the pre-Civil War period have appeared in Oscar and Mary F. Handlin, *Commonwealth: A Study of the Role of Government in the American Economy: Massachusetts, 1774–1861* (1947), and Louis Hartz, *Economic Policy and Democratic Thought: Pennsylvania, 1776–1860* (1948).

1. *Physiographic Factors and Natural Resources*

The interest of thinkers on the influence of geography upon history has been traced through the ages by H. E. Barnes, *The New History and the Social Studies* (1925), chap. 2. Perhaps the most famous contribution was made by H. T. Buckle, *History of Civilization in England* (1884), in his epoch-making introduction. The subject has been brilliantly followed by H. B. George, *The Relations of Geography and History* (1901). An economist's point of view may be found in Achille Loria, *Economic Foundations of Society* (1898). The best work on American history has been done by F. J. Turner in his famous studies; by Ellen C.

Semple, *American History and Its Geographic Conditions* (rev. ed. by C. F. Jones, 1933) and *Influence of Geographic Environment* (1911); and by A. B. Hulbert, *Soil and Its Influence on the History of the United States* (1930). In this area help can be found in some of the recent works of J. C. Malin, *Essays in Historiography* (1946), *The Grassland of North America, Prolegomena to Its History* (1947) and "Soil, Animal, and Plant Relations of the Grassland Historically Reconsidered," *Scientific Monthly,* LXXVI, 207–220 (April, 1953).

A preliminary discussion of products and resources is to be found in Livingston Farrand, *Basis of American History* (1904), Vol. II of the American Nation Series, and in Ellsworth Huntington, *The Red Man's Continent* (1919), in the Chronicles of America Series. Further figures and facts are obtainable in C. R. Van Hise, *Conservation of Natural Resources in the United States* (1910), revised in 1930 under the editorship of Loomis Havemeyer; in C. G. Gilbert and J. E. Pogue, *America's Power Resources* (1921); in R. S. Kellogg, *The Timber Supply of the United States* (1909); in J. R. Smith, *Men and Resources: A Study of North America and Its Place in World Geography* (1937); and in John Ise, *United States Forest Policy* (1920) and *United States Oil Policy* (1927). On soils C. E. Kellogg, *The Soils That Support Us* (1941), is an excellent introduction. In 1938 the Department of Agriculture devoted its entire yearbook to this subject under the title *Soils and Men.* See also F. A. Shannon, *The Farmer's Last Frontier,* chap. 1, and J. F. Dewhurst *et al., America's Needs and Resources* (1947). Two pleas for conservation are Fairfield Osborn, *Our Plundered Planet* (1948), and William Vogt, *Road to Survival* (1948). On present and future resources see The President's Materials Policy Commission, *Resources for Freedom* (5 vols., 1952).

Numerous excellent textbooks on economic geography are available, including J. R. Smith and O. M. Phillips, *North America* (1940); H. H. McCarty, *The Geographic Basis of American Economic Life* (1940); E. Huntington and S. W. Cushing, *Principles of Human Geography* (2nd ed., 1922); and E. Huntington and F. E. Williams, *Business Geography* (1926). On the effect of climate on man, see E. Huntington, *Civilization and Climate* (1924).

A stimulating book is R. H. Whitbeck and O. J. Thomas, *The Geographic Factor: Its Rôle in Life and Civilization* (1932). Revealing observations of the effect of physical environment on social, political, and economic life are frequently found in Ernest Gruening (ed.), *These United States* (2 vols., 1923–1924). Interesting on frontier disease is R. C. Buley, "Pioneer Health and Medical Practices in the Old Northwest to 1840," *Mississippi Valley Historical Review,* XX, 497–520 (March, 1934). One of the ablest of the specialized studies of climatic influence is Louis C. Hunter, "Seasonal Aspects of the Economic Life of the Ohio Valley Before the Age of Big Business," in *Smith College Studies in History,* Vol. XIX, Nos. 1–2 (Oct., 1933–Jan., 1934).

2. *Economic Background of Colonization*

For Europe on the eve of expansion, see E. P. Cheyney, *European Background of American History* (1904) and *The Dawn of a New Era* (1936). For general accounts of the late Middle Ages, see Carl Stephenson, *Mediaeval History* (1935); J. W. Thompson, *Economic and Social History of Europe in the Late Middle Ages, 1300–1530* (1931); E. Lipson, *The Economic History of England* (3 vols., 1915–1931); and the early chapters of Curtis Nettels, *The Roots of American Civilization* (1938).

The story of the Commercial Revolution is summarized in W. C. Abbott, *Expansion of Europe* (2 vols., 1918), and in L. B. Packard, *The Commercial Revolution* (1927). Readable accounts of discovery and exploration are given in G. K. Jayne, *Vasco da Gama and His Successors* (1910); J. P. O. Martins, *The Golden Age of Prince Henry the Navigator* (1914); J. N. L. Baker, *History of Geographical Discovery and Exploration* (1932); and J. Bartlett Brebner, *The Explorers of North America, 1492–1806* (1933). Albert H. Lybyer, "Influence of the Ottoman Turks upon the Routes of Oriental Trade," *Annual Report of the American Historical Association* (1914), Vol. I, pp. 125–133, clears up certain misconceptions. New light has also been thrown on Venice and the shifting trade routes by F. C. Lane, "Venetian Shipping During the Commercial Revolution," *American Historical Review,* Vol. XXXVIII, No. 2 (Jan., 1933), and *Venetian Ships and Shipbuilders of the Renaissance* (1934). The best life of Columbus is S. E. Morison, *Admiral of the Ocean Sea* (1942). Leading sources are in Cecil Jane (ed.), *Select Documents Illustrating the Four Voyages of Columbus* (1903–1933), with an essay on Columbus. Recent scholarship regarding Columbus is reviewed in C. E. Nowell, "The Columbus Question," *American Historical Review,* XLIV, 802–822 (July, 1939).

Walter Prescott Webb in *The Great Frontier* (1952) deals with the world effect of exploration and colonization. See also J. G. Gillespie, *The Influence of Overseas Expansion on England* (1920).

Richard Hakluyt, *Principall Navigations, Voyages, Traffiques, and Discoveries of the English Nation* (16 vols., 1885–1890), is indispensable for the background of English exploration and settlement. The early chapters of Louis M. Hacker, *The Triumph of American Capitalism* (1940), survey brilliantly the economic background of colonization. On the influence of the Protestant Revolt, see R. H. Tawney, *Religion and the Rise of Capitalism* (1926).

The British background is developed in the monumental work of William Cunningham, *The Growth of English Industry and Commerce* (5th ed., 1910–1912), and in W. E. Lingelbach, *The Merchant Adventurers of England* (1902).

3. *The Colonization of America*

A detailed account of the Spanish colonial system is W. Roscher, *The Spanish Colonial System* (1904). Excellent summaries of Spain in America are Bernard Moses, *The Establishment of Spanish Rule in America* (1898); E. G. Bourne, *Spain in America* (1904), in the American Nation Series; William R. Shepherd, *Latin America* (1914), especially good on the transplanting of Spanish culture; and William S. Robertson, *History of the Latin American Nations* (1922). Spanish civilization in America is competently described by H. I. Priestley, *The Coming of the White Man* (1929), Vol. I of A History of American Life. Salvador de Madariaga, *The Rise of the Spanish American Empire* (1948), is a fresh interpretation. The spectacular features of the early years of Spain in America are covered in the classic volumes of W. H. Prescott, *The Conquest of Mexico* (1843) and *The Conquest of Peru* (1847). A recent study is F. A. Fitzpatrick, *The Spanish Conquistadores* (1943). Further light on the economic aspects of New Spain may be gleaned from C. H. Haring, *Trade and Navigation Between Spain and the Indies in the Time of the Hapsburgs* (1918), and L. B. Simpson, *The Encomienda in New Spain* (1929). A source of never-failing interest is covered in C. H. Haring, *The Buccaneers in the West Indies* (1910), and P. A. Means, *The Spanish Main* (1935). A competent textbook is M. W. Williams, *The People and Politics of Latin America* (rev. ed., 1938). An unusually excellent survey of the colonial period of both the North and South American colonies is V. B. Holmes, *A History of the Americas* (1950).

On France in America, consult R. G. Thwaites, *France in America* (1904), in the American Nation Series; W. B. Munro, *Crusaders of New France* (1918), in the Chronicles of America Series (chaps. 8–11 are best on New France); H. I. Priestley, *The Coming of the White Man;* the histories of Francis Parkman, especially *Pioneers of France in the New World* (1865), *The Old Régime in Canada* (1874), *Montcalm and Wolfe* (2 vols., 1884), and *A Half Century of Conflict* (2 vols., 1892). An important contribution is A. L. Burt, *The Old Province of Quebec* (1933). French explorations are emphasized in Justin Winsor, *Cartier and Frontenac* (1894) and *The Mississippi Valley* (1895). Carl Wittke, *History of Canada* (rev. ed., 1941), is an excellent recent text, as is Edgar McInnis, *Canada: A Political and Social History* (1947).

On the Dutch in New York, see J. R. Brodhead, *History of New York* (2 vols., 1871); T. A. Janvier, *The Dutch Founding of New York* (1903); J. H. Innes, *New Amsterdam and Its People* (1902); A. C. Flick (ed.), *History of the State of New York* (1933); and M. W. Goodwin, *Dutch and English on the Hudson* (1919), Chronicles of America.

The bibliography on the English colonies is extensive, ranging from single-volume introductions—like those of C. L. Andrews, *The Colonial Period* (1912), in the Home University Library; E. B. Greene, *The Foundations of American Nationality* (1922); M. W. Jernegan, *The American Colonies, 1492–1750* (1929); Carl Becker, *Beginnings of the American People* (1915); C. M. Andrews, *The Fathers of New England* (1919), Chronicles of America Series, chap. 4; and Louis B. Wright, *The Atlantic Frontier* (1947)—to more detailed works of several volumes. Among the latter are the scholarly volumes of H. L. Osgood, *The American Colonies in the Seventeenth Century* (3 vols., 1904–1907) and *The American Colonies in the Eighteenth Century* (4 vols., 1924–1925); Charles M. Andrews, *The Colonial Period in American History* (4 vols., 1934–1937); and Edward Channing, *History of the United States,* Vols. I–III (1905–1912). The great cooperative work of Justin Winsor, *Narrative and Critical History of America* (8 vols., 1888–1889), is invaluable. The most noteworthy study by an Englishman is that of J. A. Doyle, *English Colonies in America* (5 vols., 1882–1907). A new major effort of interpretation is Lawrence H. Gipson, *The British Empire Before the Revolution,* of which six volumes had appeared by 1950. Interestingly written and historically sound are the two volumes by J. T. Adams, *The Founding of New England* (1921) and *Revolutionary New England* (1923). A successful effort to emphasize the social history and picture the life of the common man has been made by T. J. Wertenbaker, *The First Americans* (1927), and J. T. Adams, *Provincial America* (1927), Vols. II and III in A History of American Life. The textbook by Curtis Nettels, *The Roots of American Civilization* (1938), emphasizes the economic phase. For the important simultaneous history of the West Indies, see F. W. Pitman, *The Development of the British West Indies, 1700–1763* (1917).

The more purely economic aspect is touched on in William B. Weeden, *Economic and Social History of New England* (2 vols., 1891), and Philip A. Bruce, *Economic History of Virginia in the Seventeenth Century* (2 vols., 1895). On land tenure, see B. W. Bond, Jr., "Quit Rent System in the American Colonies," in the *American Historical Review,* October, 1912, and V. F. Barnes, "Land Tenure in English Colonial Charters in the Seventeenth Century," *Essays in Colonial History* (1931), pp. 4–40.

4. *Colonial Agriculture and Labor*

The best bibliographies of American agriculture are those by Louis Bernard Schmidt, *Topical Studies and References on the Economic History of American Agriculture* (rev. ed., 1923), and E. E. Edwards, *A Bibliography of the History of Agriculture in the United States,* Dept. of Agriculture, Misc. Pub. No. 84 (1930). On Indian agriculture the following are useful: P. A. Bruce, *Economic History of Virginia in the Seventeenth Century,* Vol. I (1895); L. Farrand, *Basis of American History* (1904), in the American Nation Series; J. W. Powell, "The North American Indians," in N. S. Shaler, *The United States of America,* Vol. I (1897); and G. K. Holmes, "Aboriginal Agriculture: The North American Indian," in Bailey's *Cyclopedia of American Agriculture,* Vol. IV (1909).

Adequate and scholarly are the treatments by Lyman Carrier, *The Beginnings of American Agriculture* (1923); P. W. Bidwell and J. I. Falconer, *History of Agriculture in the Northern United States Before 1860* (1925); and L. C. Gray, *History of Agriculture in the Southern United States to 1860* (2 vols., 1933). The ablest summary of our agricultural history is the article by E. E. Edwards, "American Agriculture—The First 300 Years," *Yearbook of Agriculture, 1940,* pp. 171–276. Old but still usable for its detail is C. L. Flint, "Agriculture in the United States, 1607–1860," in *Eighty Years' Progress* (1861). Virginian agriculture is exhaustively handled by Bruce, *Economic History of Virginia,* and suggestively treated by T. J. Wertenbaker, *The Planters of Colonial Virginia* (1922) and *The Old South* (1942), and E. Q. Hawk, *Economic History of the South* (1934). Joseph Schafer, *The Social History of American Agriculture* (1936), and A. O. Craven, *Soil Exhaustion as a Factor in the Agricultural History of Virginia and Maryland, 1606–1860* (1926), are also suggestive. Glimpses of northern agriculture are given in Weeden, *Economic and Social History of New England.* Among the special studies are those of M. Jacobstein, *The Tobacco Industry in the United States,* Columbia University Studies in History, Economics and Public Law, Vol. XXVI, No. 3 (1907), and L. G. Connor, "A Brief History of the Sheep Industry," in the *Annual Report of the American Historical Association* (1918). The most valuable and interesting contemporary account is the anonymously published *American Husbandry* (2 vols., 1775), reprinted and edited in 1939 by Harry Carman for the Columbia University Press. That a few colonial farmers were intensely interested in scientific farming is evident in C. R. Woodward, *Ploughs and Politicks, Charles Read of New Jersey and His Notes on Agriculture* (1941). Other source material may be found in L. B. Schmidt and E. D. Ross, *Readings in the Economic History of American Agriculture* (1925). T. J. Wertenbaker, *The First Americans* (1927), and J. T. Adams, *Provincial America* (1927), give pictures of an essentially agrarian society.

The results of much earlier investigation have been brought together by U. B. Phillips in *American Negro Slavery* (1921) and in *Life and Labor in the Old South* (1929). More detailed studies in special fields are those of J. R. Brackett, *The Negro in Maryland* (1889); J. C. Ballagh, *Slavery in Virginia* (1902); E. R. Turner, *The Negro in Pennsylvania, Slavery—Servitude—Freedom, 1639–1861* (1910); and L. J. Greene, *The Negro in Colonial New England, 1620–1776* (1942). Source material appears in Elizabeth Donnan, *Documents Illustrative of the Slave Trade to America* (3 vols., 1930–1932). On the conditions of white servitude are the investigations of E. I. McCormac, *White Servitude in Maryland* (1904), Johns Hopkins Studies; J. C. Ballagh, *White Servitude in Virginia* (1895), *ibid.;* J. S. Bassett, *Servitude and Slavery in the Colony of North Carolina* (1896), *ibid.;* C. A. Herrick, *White Servitude in Pennsylvania* (1926); and K. F. Geiser, *Redemptioners and Indentured Servants in Pennsylvania* (Supplement to the *Yale Review,* 1901). See also A. E. Smith, "The Transportation of Convicts to the American Colonies in the Seventeenth Century," *American Historical Review,* Vol. XXXIX, No. 2 (Jan., 1934). One of the best treatments of the indentured servants is in Edward Eggleston, *The Transit of Civilization,* pp. 293–307. A more recent study is Marcus W. Jernegan, *Laboring and Dependent Classes in Colonial America, 1607–1783* (Chicago, 1931). The most valuable single volume is A. E. Smith, *Colonists in Bondage: White Servitude and Convict Labor in America, 1607–1776* (1947). T. J. Wertenbaker, *Patrician and Plebeian in Virginia* (1910) and *Planters of Colonial Virginia* (1922), throws considerable light on class structure in that colony. An excellent summary of plantation labor appears in L. C. Gray, *History of Agriculture in the Southern States to 1860* (2 vols., 1933), chap. 16. A specialized work of high scholarship is R. B. Morris, *Government and Labor in Early America* (1946).

5. *Colonial Commerce and Industry*

Curtis Nettels, *The Roots of American Civilization* (1938), has excellent material, and L. M. Hacker, *The Triumph of American Capitalism* (1940), an intelligent interpretation. W. T. Baxter, *The House of Hancock* (1945), gives a

detailed picture of business in Boston in the eighteenth century as he describes
the rise and fall of the Hancock fortune.

A standard work on commerce is that of Emory R. Johnson, T. W. Van Metre,
G. G. Huebner, and D. S. Hanchitt, *History of Domestic and Foreign Commerce
of the United States* (2 vols., 1915), based on monographs by various collaborators
and published in the Contributions to American Economic History by the Carne-
gie Institution of Washington. Vol. I contains a useful bibliography. Important
in their special field are M. S. Morriss, *Colonial Trade of Maryland, 1689–1715*,
Johns Hopkins University Studies, Series XXXII, No. 3 (1914); C. P. Gould,
Money and Transportation in Maryland, 1720–1765 (1915); and C. C. Crittenden,
The Commerce of North Carolina, 1763–1789 (1936). Enlightening is J. S.
Bassett, "The Relation Between the Virginia Planter and the London Merchant,"
Annual Report of the American Historical Association (1901), Vol. I, pp. 553–575.

English colonial policy can be best studied in the works of G. L. Beer, *Origins
of British Colonial Policy, 1578–1660* (1908), *British Colonial Policy, 1754–1765*
(1907), and *The Old Colonial System* (1913). See also H. E. Egerton, *British
Colonial Policy* (2d ed., 1909), and for a brief but most enlightening survey,
C. M. Andrews, *The Colonial Period* (1912), in the Home University Library.
Two valuable articles by C. M. Andrews are "Colonial Commerce," *American
Historical Review*, Vol. XX (Oct., 1914) and "Anglo-French Commercial Rivalry,
1700–1750," *ibid.*, Vol. XXI (July, 1915). The most recent scholarship on this
subject is Lawrence A. Harper, *The English Navigation Laws* (1939).

On mercantilism, consult Gustav Schmoller, *The Mercantile System and Its Historical Significance* (1896), and E. F. Heckscher, *Mercantilism* (2 vols., 1936).
Edward Channing, in his *History of the United States* (Vol. II, 1908), devotes
chap. 17 to "Colonial Industry and Commerce." The somewhat desultory volume
of William B. Weeden contains much information.

On colonial finance see the textbooks by Dewey and by Shultz and Caine (bibliography in the latter, pp. 721–745) and also C. P. Nettels, *Money Supply of
the American Colonies Before 1720* (Madison, Wis., 1934). On the medium of
exchange in Virginia see P. A. Bruce, *Economic History of Virginia in the Seventeenth Century* (2 vols., 1907), Vol. II, chap. 19; on Massachusetts consult the
detailed study of A. M. Davis, *Currency and Banking in the Province of Massachusetts Bay* (2 vols., 1900–1901) and *Colonial Currency Reprints, 1682–1751*
(4 vols., 1911).

Treatments of the slave trade are to be found in W. W. Claridge, *History of
the Gold Coast* (1915); U. B. Phillips, *American Negro Slavery* (1921); and
W. E. B. Du Bois, *The Suppression of the American Slave Trade* (1896). On
piracy, see G. F. Dow and J. H. Edmonds, *The Pirates of the New England Coast,
1630–1730* (1923), and G. F. Dow, *Slave Ships and Slavery* (1927); on privateering, Edgar S. Maclay, *History of American Privateers* (new ed., 1924), and J. F.
Jameson (ed.), *Privateering and Piracy in the Colonial Period* (1924), a source
book.

The best single volume on colonial manufacturing is that by V. S. Clark, *History of Manufactures in the United States, 1607–1860* (1916), published by the

Carnegie Institution in its series on American economic history. It contains an extensive bibliography. Two books, now out of date but containing a mass of interesting detail not easily accessible elsewhere, are J. L. Bishop, *A History of American Manufactures from 1608–1860* (3 vols., 1886), and A. S. Bolles, *Industrial History of the United States* (1887). Brief accounts are contained in Malcolm Keir, *Manufacturing* (1928), under specific industries. Consult also E. L. Lord, *Industrial Experiments in the British Colonies of North America* (1898) in Johns Hopkins Studies in Historical and Political Science, Vol. XVII, and R. M. Tryon, *Household Manufactures in the United States, 1640–1860* (1917). See also Weeden and Bruce, and for the South E. Q. Hawk, *Economic History of the South* (1934), and Kathleen Bruce, *Virginia Iron Manufacture in the Slave Era* (1931).

On the fur trade see Katherine Coman, *Economic Beginnings of the Far West* (1912), and H. A. Innis, *The Fur Trade in Canada* (1930). Very suggestive is the latter's "Interrelations Between the Fur Trade of Canada and the United States," *Mississippi Valley Historical Review,* Vol. XX, No. 3 (Dec., 1930). A. T. Volwiler, *George Crogham and the Westward Movement, 1741–1782* (1926), and V. W. Crane, *The Southern Frontier, 1670–1732* (1928), deal with special regions, and the well-known study by C. A. Alvord, *The Mississippi Valley in British Politics* (2 vols., 1917), shows the influence of the fur trade upon imperial policy.

The best studies on whaling and the fisheries are those of R. McFarland, *A History of the New England Fisheries* (1911), and W. S. Tower, *A History of American Whale Fishing* (1920), University of Pennsylvania Studies, No. 23. See also C. B. Hawes, *Whaling* (1924), and E. O. Hohman, *The American Whalemen* (1928). A collateral industry is studied in R. G. Albion, *Forests and Sea Power* (1926).

Special studies on manufacturing include M. T. Copeland, *The Cotton Manufacturing Industry of the United States* (1912); B. E. Hazard, *The Organization of the Boot and Shoe Industry in Massachusetts Before 1873* (1921); A. H. Cole, *The American Wool Manufacture* (2 vols., 1926), and A. C. Bining, *British Regulation of the Colonial Iron Industry* (1933). An interesting article is that by Curtis Nettels, "The Menace of Colonial Manufacturing," *New England Quarterly,* IV, 230–269. On the influence of slave labor upon industry, read M. W. Jernegan, "Slavery and the Beginnings of Industrialism in the American Colonies," *American Historical Review,* Vol. XXV (Jan., 1920). The seaports engaged in foreign commerce are described in Carl Bridenbaugh, *Cities in the Wilderness* (1938).

A comparison of European industrial life during the same period is extremely valuable. Material with special reference to England may be found in George Unwin, *Industrial Organization in the Sixteenth and Seventeenth Centuries* (1904).

6. Frontier Expansion Before the Revolution

Most of the studies of the significance of the westward movement in American history rest upon the pioneer work of Professor F. J. Turner, scattered in various articles published in magazines and the publications of historical societies. The most complete collection of references on the westward movement is that of F. J. Turner and F. Merk, *List of References on the History of the West* (rev. ed., 1922). Consult also E. E. Edwards, "References on the Significance of the Frontier in American History," U.S. Dept. of Agriculture, Biographical Contributions No. 25 (1935). A few of Professor Turner's essays have been collected in *The Frontier in American History* (1921) and *Significance of Sections in American History* (1933). Attempts to integrate a part of the story have been made by F. L. Paxson, *History of the American Frontier, 1763–1893* (1924), a Pulitzer Prize book; by Dan E. Clark, *The West in American History* (1937); by R. E. Riegel, *America Moves West* (rev. ed., 1947); and by Ray A. Billington, *Westward Expansion* (1949) with full bibliography. Concerning Turner and the Turnerian interpretation, read the brilliant essay by M. E. Curti, "The Section and the Frontier in American History," *Methods in the Social Sciences* (1931), pp. 353–367, and the able introductory essay by Fulmer Mood in *The Early Writings of Frederick Jackson Turner* (1938). In recent years Turner's emphasis on the frontier has been under some fire, particularly by L. M. Hacker in his pamphlet, *The Farmer Is Doomed* (1933), and in the *Nation*, 137, 109–110 (July 26, 1933). It has also been criticized in D. R. Fox (ed.), *Sources of Culture in the Middle West* (1934) and his *Ideas in Motion* (1935). See particularly G. W. Pierson, "The Frontier and Frontiersmen of Turner's Essays," *Pennsylvania Magazine*, LXIV, 449–478 (Oct., 1940), and "The Frontier and American Institutions," *New England Quarterly*, XV, 224–255 (June, 1942). See also B. F. Wright, Jr., "Political Institutions and the Frontier," in D. R. Fox, *Sources of Culture*, and Murray Kane, "Some Considerations on the Frontier Concept of Frederick Jackson Turner," *Mississippi Valley Historical Review*, Vol. XXVII (Dec., 1940). More extensive bibliographies on the Turnerian thesis and later aspects of the frontier are given for chapters 10 and 18.

The conflict between France and England is recounted by Parkman in a style so brilliant that history and literature join hands. The story of the frontier advance and Indian conflicts is told in Theodore Roosevelt, *The Winning of the West* (4 vols., 1889–1896), but with little attempt at interpretation. Detailed but dry are the narratives of Justin Winsor, *Mississippi Basin* (1895) and *Wesward Movement* (1897). C. W. Alvord, *The Mississippi Valley in British Politics* (2 vols., 1917), is a brilliant piece of research and essential to any understanding of colonial history. Since Turner and Alvord's work, the most significant contribution to frontier history is that of Walter P. Webb, *The Great Plains* (1931). This book touches only lightly on the colonial period, but on the plains frontier of the nineteenth century it deals illuminatingly with such important influences as water, fences, firearms, and windmills. See also his *The Great Frontier* (1952).

The expansion of Virginia is treated in Osgood and Bruce. On New England consult L. K. Mathews, *Expansion of New England* (1909); Osgood; C. F. Adams, A. C. Goodell, Jr., M. Chamberlain, and E. Channing, "Genesis of the New England Town," in *Massachusetts Historical Society Proceedings*, 2nd Series,

Vol. VII, and the second essay in Turner's *Frontier in American History,* entitled "The First Official Frontier of the Massachusetts Bay." Important on the New England township system are the excellent monograph by R. H. Akagi, *The Town Proprietors of the New England Colonies* (1924), and F. M. Woodward, *The Town Proprietors in Vermont: the New England Town Proprietorship in Decline* (1936).

The best introduction to the advance into the Piedmont is Turner's essay on "The Old West," chap. 3 in his *Frontier in American History.* There is also much information in Roosevelt. More detailed on certain sections are Archibald Henderson, *The Conquest of the Old Southwest* (1920); C. L. Skinner, *Pioneers of the Old Southwest* (1919), in the Chronicles of America Series; H. E. Bolton, *The Spanish Borderlands* (1921), in the same series; and F. W. Halsey, *The Old American Frontier* (2 vols., 1901). See also F. J. Turner, "State Making in the Revolutionary Era," in *American Historical Review,* Vol. I. Important additions to the westward movement of the period include K. P. Bailey, *The Ohio Company of Virginia and the Westward Movement, 1748–1792* (1939); S. J. and E. H. Buck, *The Planting of Civilization in Western Pennsylvania* (1939); W. S. Lister, *The Transylvania Company* (1935); T. P. Abernethy, *Western Lands and the American Revolution* (1937); and the biographies by John Bakeless, *Daniel Boone* (1939), C. S. Driver, *John Sevier* (1932), and L. K. Koontz, *Robert Dinwiddie* (1941).

The part which certain nationalities played in this advance may be studied in G. D. Bernheim, *German Settlements in North and South Carolina* (1872); A. B. Faust, *The German Element in the United States* (1909); Oscar Kuhns, *The German and Swiss Settlements of Colonial Pennsylvania* (1901); H. J. Ford, *The Scotch-Irish in America* (1915); and C. A. Hanna, *The Scotch-Irish* (1902). Americans of Irish descent have done much in recent years to "debunk" what they consider to be the "Scotch-Irish myth" and to emphasize the great contributions of the immigrants from southern Ireland. This material can be found in the publications of the American Irish Historical Society, and in M. J. O'Brien, *A Hidden Phase of American History* (1919). The first serious effort to determine the national origin of the colonial population was made by the Twelfth Census in *A Century of Population Growth, 1790–1900* (1909), based on the inaccurate criterion of names. Corrected estimates are in American Council of Learned Societies, *Report of Committee on Linguistics and National Stocks in the Population of the United States,* and *Annual Report of the American Historical Association,* I, 103–441 (1931).

Maps showing the settlements at various periods may be found at the end of Vol. II of Channing's *History of the United States* and in *Harper's Atlas of American History* (1920). Farrand and Semple give maps showing portages and routes of travel. For pictorial material, examine Clark Wissler, C. L. Skinner, and W. Wood, *Adventurers in the Wilderness* (1925), and R. H. Gabriel, *The Lure of the Frontier* (1929), both in the Pageant of America. Excellent readings are I. F. Woestemeyer and J. M. Gambrill, *The Westward Movement* (1939).

7. *Economic Causes of the Revolution*

The leading books on mercantilism and British colonial policy—those of Beer, Johnson, Harper, Egerton, and others—have already been cited in the bibliography for chapter 5. To these should be added W. S. McClellan, *Smuggling in the American Colonies* (1912), and A. M. Schlesinger, *The Colonial Merchants and the American Revolution* (1918). Among the special studies are C. H. Van Tyne, *The Causes of the War of Independence* (1922), an excellent recapitulation of the political and intellectual causes; H. E. Egerton, *Causes and Character of the American Revolution* (1923), a conservative and scholarly restatement by an Englishman; and C. M. Andrews, *The Colonial Background of the Revolution* (1924). See also J. T. Adams, *Revolutionary New England* (1923); C. A. Barker, *The Background of the Revolution in Maryland* (1940); Carl Becker, *The Eve of the Revolution* (1918), Chronicles of America; and E. B. Greene, *The Revolutionary Generation* (1943). The most recent effort to integrate all the causes is John C. Miller, *Origins of the American Revolution* (1943), based on a re-examination of the sources.

An interesting study of the background of the war, with good chapters on Boston of that time, is that by the Englishman Henry Belcher, *The First American Civil War* (2 vols., 1911). The situation in that city is also studied in C. M. Andrews, *Boston Merchants and the Non-Importation Movement* (1917), and in W. T. Baxter, *The House of Hancock* (1945), primarily an economic study. Other cities are treated in V. D. Harrington, *New York Merchants on the Eve of the Revolution* (1935), and L. Sellers, *Charleston Business on the Eve of the Revolution* (1934). On the western phase, read C. W. Alvord, *The Mississippi Valley in British Politics* (2 vols., 1917). In Louis M. Hacker, "The First American Revolution," *Columbia University Quarterly,* Vol. XXVII, No. 3 (1935), the theses of Channing, Andrews, and Van Tyne are questioned and the point is brilliantly developed that the Revolution resulted from the constricted opportunities of colonial merchant capitalism. This thesis is largely repeated in his *Triumph of American Capitalism* (1940), chaps. 11, 12.

The intellectual background of the colonial period can best be studied in V. L. Parrington, *The Colonial Mind, 1620–1800* (1927), Vol. I of *Main Currents in American Thought;* in Max Savelle, *Seeds of Liberty* (1948); in Merle Curti, *The Growth of American Thought* (1943); and in Michael Kraus, *Inter-Colonial Aspects of American Culture with Special Reference to the Northern Towns* (1928).

To the source books already noted should be added S. E. Morison, *The American Revolution, 1764–1788, Sources and Documents* (1923).

8. *Economic Aspects of the Revolution*

An excellent résumé of the financial aspect of the war is given in D. R. Dewey, *Financial History of the United States* (10th ed., 1928). More detailed studies are those of W. G. Sumner, *Finance and Financiers of the American Revolution*

(2 vols., 1891); C. J. Bullock, *Finances of the United States, 1775–1789,* University of Wisconsin Bulletins (1895); R. V. Harlow, "Aspects of Revolutionary Finance, 1775–1783," *American Historical Review,* XXXV, 46–68 (Oct., 1929); W. B. Norton, "Paper Money in Massachusetts During the Revolution," *New England Quarterly,* Vol. VII (March, 1934); E. P. Oberholtzer, *Life of Robert Morris* (1903); and Charles E. Russell, *Haym Salomon and the Revolution* (1930), a popular biography.

Material on the economic background can be found in V. S. Clark; W. B. Weeden; E. R. Johnson *et al.;* S. E. Morison, *Maritime History of Massachusetts, 1783–1860* (1921); Allan Nevins, *The American States During and After the Revolution, 1775–1789* (1924), especially chaps. 10 and 11; Thomas C. Cochran, *New York in the Confederation* (1932); H. J. Eckenrode, *The Revolution in Virginia* (1916); R. A. East, *Business Enterprise in the American Revolutionary Era* (1938); and R. F. Upton, *Revolutionary New Hampshire* (1936). Most illuminating on the social aspects is J. F. Jameson, *The American Revolution Considered as a Social Movement* (1926). See also Michael Kraus, *Inter-Colonial Aspects of American Culture on the Eve of the Revolution with Special Reference to the Northern Towns* (1928). Of interest is O. W. Stephenson, "The Supply of Gunpowder in 1776," *American Historical Review,* XX, 271–281 (Jan., 1925), and E. C. Burnett, "Observations of London Merchants on American Trade," *ibid.,* XVIII, 773–780 (July, 1913).

On the westward movement, see Roosevelt and Henderson, already cited; E. L. Sparks, *The Expansion of the American People* (1900); Justin Winsor, *The Westward Movement, 1763–1798* (1897); W. S. Lester, *The Transylvania Colony* (1934), more objective than Henderson; and E. C. Semple, *American History and Its Geographic Conditions* (1903), chaps. 4 and 5.

The part played by the loyalists is set forth in C. H. Van Tyne, *Loyalists in the American Revolution* (1902). Also see A. C. Flick, *Loyalism in New York* (1901); I. S. Harrell, *Loyalism in Virginia* (1926); C. H. Ambler, *Sectionalism in Virginia* (1910); and H. B. Yoshpe, *The Disposition of Loyalist Estates in the Southern District of New York* (1939). Sources on this period are in S. E. Morison, *The American Revolution, 1764–1788, Sources and Documents* (1923).

The most authoritative study of the economic phases of the movement for the Constitution is that by C. A. Beard, *An Economic Interpretation of the Constitution of the United States* (1913). His conclusions must be reckoned with by any student of this period. Attention to social and economic conditions, as well as to the political story, is given in Merrill Jensen, *The New Nation* (1950); A. C. McLaughlin, *The Confederation and the Constitution* (1905), American Nation Series; Max Farrand, *The Fathers of the Constitution* (1921), Chronicles of America Series; and J. B. McMaster, *History of the People of the United States,* Vol. I, chap. 1. See also the old and popularly written but still valuable volume by John Fiske, *The Critical Period* (1888). The basic history of Shays's Rebellion upon which historians have largely relied is G. R. Minot, *History of the Insurrection in Massachusetts* (1810). A recent study is F. R. Mullaly, *The Massachusetts In-*

surrection of 1786–1787 (1947), a Smith College master's thesis. See also J. P. Warren, "The Confederation and the Shays Rebellion," *American Historical Review*, XI, 42–67 (Oct., 1905), W. A. Dyer, "Embattled Farmers," *New England Quarterly*, IV, 460–481 (July, 1931), and L. N. Newcomber, *The Embattled Farmer* (1953). Able interpretative chapters are those in Charles and Mary Beard, *The Rise of American Civilization* (1927), Vol. I, chaps. 5 and 6; Curtis Nettels, *The Roots of American Civilization*, chap. 24; and Louis Hacker, *The Triumph of American Capitalism*, chaps. 13–14.

9. *Finance and Tariff*

Hamilton's reports may be found in *American State Papers, Finance*, Vol. I. The most satisfactory textbooks for the general student are those of D. R. Dewey, and of Shultz and Caine. On currency, see A. B. Hepburn, *History of Coinage and Currency in the United States* (rev. ed., 1915); J. L. Laughlin, *History of Bimetallism in the United States* (4th ed., 1897); and David K. Watson, *History of American Coinage* (1899). Interesting sidelights on the financial operations of the first Congress are to be found in E. S. Maclay (ed.), *Journal of William Maclay* (1890), republished in 1927 with an introduction by Charles A. Beard.

On the national bank controversy there is an extended literature. In addition to the valuable accounts in many of the general histories, more detailed studies are to be found in Ralph C. H. Catterall, *The Second Bank of the United States* (1903); Charles A. Conant, *History of Modern Banks of Issue* (1896; rev., 1915); William G. Sumner, *History of Banking in the United States* (1896); William MacDonald, *Jacksonian Democracy* (1906), in the American Nation Series; and John S. Bassett, *Life of Andrew Jackson*, Vol. II (1911; rev., 1916, 1 vol.). Also see David Kinley, *History, Organization and Influence of the Independent Treasury of the United States* (1893). The revival of interest in the Jacksonian period by the wide reading of A. M. Schlesinger, Jr., *The Age of Jackson* (1946), has developed new specialized literature on the second Bank of the United States, such as Bray Hammond, "Jackson, Biddle, and the Bank of the United States," *Journal of Economic History*, VII, 1–23 (May, 1947) and "Banking in the Early West: Monopoly, Prohibition and *Laissez Faire*," *ibid.*, VIII, 1–25 (May, 1948). W. B. Smith, *Economic Aspects of the Second Bank of the United States* (1953) is the ablest defense of the bank. Another recent article of interest on early banking is W. S. Lake, "The End of the Suffolk System," *Journal of Economic History*, VII, 183–207 (Nov., 1947).

On the economic collapse of 1837, consult R. C. McGrane, *The Panic of 1837* (1924), "Some Aspects of American State Debts in the Forties," *American Historical Review*, XXXVIII, 673–686 (July, 1933), and *Foreign Bondholders and American State Debts* (1935). On the general history of business cycles during these years, read W. B. Smith and A. H. Cole, *Fluctuations in American Business, 1790–1860* (1935).

The conflict of economic theories during these years can be best studied in the writings of publicists, economists, and statesmen; but some short cuts can be found in E. L. Bradsher, *Mathew Carey* (1912); H. D. H. Kaplan, *Henry Charles Carey* (1931); R. G. Stone, *Hezekiah Niles as an Economist* (1933); and Dumas Malone, *Public Life of Thomas Cooper, 1783–1839* (1926). See also Joseph Dorfman, *The Economic Mind in American Civilization* (1946), Vol. I.

For the tariff, consult Percy W. L. Ashley, *Modern Tariff History* (3rd ed., 1920; Edward Stanwood, *American Tariff Controversies in the Nineteenth Century* (1903); and F. W. Taussig, *Tariff History of the United States* (7th ed., 1923). There is no definitive life of Hamilton. To the early studies by F. S. Oliver, W. G. Sumner, and J. T. Morse has been added Nathan Schachner, *Alexander Hamilton* (1946), probably the best. For the other great Secretary of these years, see Henry Adams, *Life of Albert Gallatin* (1880); J. A. Stevens, *Albert Gallatin* (1917); and Cheng Tseng Mai, *Fiscal Policies of Albert Gallatin* (1930). The most recent life of America's great banker is H. E. Wildes, *Lonely Midas: The Story of Stephen Girard* (1943). See also K. L. Brown, "Stephen Girard, Promoter of the Second Bank of the United States," *Journal of Economic History,* Vol. II, No. 2 (Nov., 1942).

For a general economic interpretation of the period, read Charles A. Beard, *The Economic Origins of the Jeffersonian Democracy* (1915), and Charles and Mary Beard, *The Rise of American Civilization* (2 vols., 1927).

10. *Westward Expansion from the Revolution to the Civil War*

The most complete bibliography of the westward movement during this period is that by F. J. Turner and F. Merk, *List of References on the History of the West* (rev. ed., 1922). Besides the source books already cited, see such valuable contemporary accounts as Harriet Martineau, *Society in America* (1837); J. W. Monette, *History of the Discovery and Settlement of the Valley of the Mississippi* (1846), by an early inhabitant of the valley; Timothy Flint, *Recollections of the Last Ten Years* (1826) and *History and Geography of the Mississippi Valley* (1832); J. M. Peck, *Guide for Emigrants to the West* (1837); R. G. Thwaites (ed.), *Journals of Lewis and Clark* (1904–1905) and *Early Western Travels* (32 vols., 1904–1907).

For an interpretation of the movement the essays of F. J. Turner are important. In his *Rise of the New West* (1906), American Nation Series, the westward movement is interwoven with the political history. See also his "The Significance of the Section in American History," *Wisconsin Magazine of History,* VII, 255–280 (March, 1925), and his *The United States: 1830–1850* (1934).

Excellent chapters appear in Edward Channing, *A History of the United States* (1921), Vol. V, chap. 2; and J. B. McMaster, *History of the People of the United States* (6 vols., 1883–1896), Vol. II, pp. 144 ff.; Vol. III, pp. 100–142, 459–496; Vol. IV, pp. 381–428; Vol. V, pp. 160 ff. The work of McMaster, in the opinion of Channing, is "the best bit of writing" on the subject "that has been done." The story of this period has now been skillfully integrated in the single volumes of Paxson, Clark, Riegel, and Billington.

The movement into the Old Northwest is developed in F. W. Halsey, *Old New*

York Frontier (1901); L. K. Mathews, *Expansion of New England* (1909); Beverley W. Bond, Jr., *The Civilization of the Old Northwest* (1934); and R. C. Buley, *The Old Northwest Pioneer* (2 vols., 1950); that into the Southwest in U. B. Phillips, "Origin and Growth of the Southern Black Belts," *American Historical Review,* IX, 798, and C. L. Skinner, *Pioneers of the Old Southwest* (1919), Chronicles of America Series. See also Everett Dick, *The Dixie Frontier* (1948). For western New York, see Paul D. Evans' chapter in A. C. Flick (ed.), *History of the State of New York* (1934), Vol. VI. Most important for the region beyond the Mississippi is W. P. Webb, *The Great Plains* (1931), an original and significant approach. Consult also K. Coman, *Economic Beginnings of the Far West* (2 vols., 1912); C. Goodwin, *The Trans-Mississippi West* (1922); M. R. Werner, *Brigham Young* (1925); L. H. Greer, *Utah and the Nation* (1929) and *The Founding of an Empire* (1947); M. R. Hunter, *Brigham Young, the Colonizer* (1940); J. H. Evans, *Charles Coulson Rich, Pioneer Builder of the West* (1936), a biography of a Mormon leader; and Rena Stanley, *A Biography of Perley P. Pratt* (1937), another important Mormon. See also Y. O. Larson, "The Story of the Perpetual Emigration Fund," *Mississippi Valley Historical Review,* XVII, 184–194 (Sept., 1931). For the advance into Southern California read R. G. Cleland, *Pathfinders* (1929), and for early California his *History of California, The American Period* (1922), and Owen C. Coy, *The Great Trek* (1931). R. P. Bieber, "California Gold Mania," *Mississippi Valley Historical Review,* XXV, 3–28 (June, 1948), is an interesting article.

On Oregon, consult J. Schafer, *History of the Pacific Northwest* (1905); C. J. Brosnan, *Jason Lee, Prophet of the New Oregon* (1932); and the sources edited by A. B. Hulbert and others: *Where Rolls the Oregon* (1933), *The Call of the Columbia* (1934), *The Oregon Crusade* (1935), and *Marcus Whitman, Crusader* (3 vols., 1936–1941). See also the recent article by C. H. Ambler, "The Oregon Country, 1810–1830: A chapter in Territorial Expansion," *Mississippi Valley Historical Review,* XXX, 3–24 (June, 1943).

On the diplomatic background of the Mississippi Valley, see F. J. Turner, "Policy of France Toward the Mississippi Valley," *American Historical Review,* X, 249–279 (Jan., 1905), and A. P. Whitaker, "New Light on the Treaty of San Lorenzo," *Mississippi Valley Historical Review,* XV, 435–454 (March, 1929).

The land policy of the United States may be studied in P. J. Treat, *The National Land System, 1785–1820* (1910); in B. H. Hibbard, *A History of the Public Land Policies* (1924); in R. M. Robbins, *Our Landed Heritage: The Public Domain, 1776–1936* (1942); and in Thomas Donaldson, *The Public Domain, Its History with Statistics* (1884). A. M. Sakolski, *The Great American Land Bubble* (1932), is a popular treatment of an important topic. Exhaustive research on land speculation is revealed in P. W. Gates, *The Illinois Central Railroad and Its Colonization Work* (1934), and his article, "Land Policy and Tenancy in the Prairie States," *Journal of Economic History,* I, 60–82 (May, 1941). Of varying usefulness are W. E. Peters, *Ohio Lands and Their Subdivisions* (1918); A. E.

Sheldon, *Land Systems and Land Policies in Nebraska* (1936); and R. L. Lokken, *Iowa Public Land Disposal* (1942).

The safety-valve theory is questioned in F. A. Shannon, "The Homestead Act and the Labor Surplus," *American Historical Review,* XLI, 637–651 (July, 1936); and in Carter Goodrich and Sol Davison, "The Wage Earner and the Westward Movement," *Political Science Quarterly,* L, 161–185 (June, 1935), and LI, 61–116 (March, 1936); also in Goodrich and Davison, "The Frontier Safety Valve: A Rejoinder," *ibid.,* LIII, 268–271, and Murray Kane, "Some Considerations on the Safety Valve Doctrine," *Mississippi Valley Historical Review,* XXIII, 69–188 (Sept., 1936). The theory is defended in Joseph Schafer, "Concerning the Frontier as a Safety Valve," *Political Science Quarterly,* LII, 407–420 (Sept., 1937), and "Was the West a Safety Valve for Labor?" *Mississippi Valley Historical Review,* XXIV, 299–314 (Dec., 1937). A criticism of the Turner thesis beyond the safety-valve theory is undertaken in Murray Kane, "Some Considerations of the Frontier Concept of Frederick Jackson Turner," *ibid.,* XXVII, 379–400 (Dec., 1940). See also C. H. Danhof, "Farm-Making Costs and the Safety-Valve: 1850–1860," *Journal of Political Economy,* XLIX, 317–359 (June, 1941).

For geography and routes of travel, see E. C. Semple, *American History and Its Geographic Conditions* (1903). On routes to the interior, read A. B. Hulbert, *Paths of Inland Commerce* (1920), Chronicles of America Series; and for pictorial source material, see R. H. Gabriel, *The Lure of the Frontier* (1929), Vol. II in the Pageant of America.

11. *The Agricultural Era*

Bibliographies include E. E. Edwards, "Guide for Courses in the History of American Agriculture," Dept. of Agriculture, Bibliographical Contribution No. 35 (1939); E. E. Edwards, "Bibliography of the History of American Agriculture," Dept. of Agriculture, Bibliographical Contribution No. 32; and L. B. Schmidt, *Topical Studies and References on the Economic History of American Agriculture* (rev. ed., 1937). The best condensed account is E. E. Edwards, "American Agriculture—the First 300 Years," *1940 Yearbook of Agriculture,* with excellent bibliography.

The standard treatise on agriculture in the North during this period is P. W. Bidwell and J. I. Falconer, *History of Agriculture in the Northern United States, 1620–1860* (Carnegie Institution, 1925), equipped with an exhaustive bibliography. There are many articles of exceptional value in Vol. IV of Bailey's *Cyclopedia of American Agriculture.* A short and popular account is that by A. H. Sanford, *The Story of Agriculture in the United States* (1916). Among the best of the early accounts are those of C. L. Flint, "Agriculture in the United States," in *Eighty Years' Progress* (1869); also in the *Annual Report, U.S. Department of Agriculture* (1872), and in the *First Annual Report of the Massachusetts Board of Agriculture* (1854). See also the Introduction to the volume on Agriculture in the *Eighth Census of the United States* (1860), and W. N. Brewer, "Report on the Cereal Production of the United States" in the *Tenth Census* (1880), volume on Agriculture, Part II. For source material, consult L. B. Schmidt and E. D. Ross, *Readings in the Economic History of American Agriculture* (1925); H. J. Carman (ed.), *Jesse Buel* (1947), selections from an agricultural reformer; and the books of readings already cited.

On New England farming of this period, read P. W. Bidwell, "Rural Economy in New England at the Beginning of the Nineteenth Century," in *Transactions of the Connecticut Academy of Arts and Sciences,* Vol. XX (1916), and "The Agricultural Revolution in New England," in the *American Historical Review,* Vol. XXVI, No. 4 (1921). Also consult Elizabeth Ramsay, *History of Tobacco Production in the Connecticut Valley,* Smith College Studies in History, Vol. XV, Nos. 3–4 (1930); M. R. Pabst, *Agricultural Trends in the Connecticut Valley Region of Massachusetts, ibid.,* Vol. XXVI, Nos. 1–4 (1941); and H. F. Wilson, *The Hill Country of Northern New England* (1936).

On southern agriculture the most exhaustive study is that by Lewis C. Gray, *History of Agriculture in the Southern United States to 1860* (Carnegie Institution, 2 vols., 1933). Valuable also are M. B. Cairnes, *The Slave Power* (1863); M. B. Hammond, *The Cotton Industry* (1897); A. B. Hart, *Slavery and Abolition,* in the American Nation Series; F. L. Olmsted, *Journeys and Explorations in the Cotton Kingdom* (1861); James A. B. Scherer, *Cotton as a World Power* (1916), a study in the economic interpretation of history; M. Jacobstein, *The Tobacco Industry in the United States,* Columbia University Studies, Vol. XXVI, No. 3 (1907); and for an interesting general picture, U. B. Phillips, *Life and Labor in the Old South* (1929). Excellent chapters will be found in McMaster, Vol. VII, chap. 76; in Rhodes, Vol. I, chap. 4; and in E. Q. Hawk, *Economic History of the South,* chaps. 8 and 9. Important are A. O. Craven, *Soil Exhaustion as a Factor in the Agricultural History of Virginia and Maryland, 1660–1860* (1925); his "The Agricultural Reformers of the Ante-Bellum South," *American Historical Review,* XXXIII, 302–314 (Jan., 1928); and his *Edmund Ruffin, Southerner; a Study in Secession* (1932). A first-class biography in the field of agricultural history is W. T. Hutchinson, *Cyrus Hall McCormick* (2 vols., 1930–1935). The story of the reaper has also been told by an admiring grandson in Cyrus McCormick, *The Century of the Reaper* (1931). An exceedingly valuable study on the effects of labor-saving machinery is Leo Rogin, *The Introduction of Farm Machinery in Its Relation to the Productivity of Labor in Agriculture of the United States* (University of California Publications in Economics, 1931). Jeanette Mirsky and Allan Nevins have fully told the story of the cotton gin in *The World of Eli Whitney* (1952).

On the public domain, see I. Donaldson, *The Public Domain* (1884); L. H. Haney, *A Congressional History of Railways in the United States,* Vol. I, to 1850 (1908); Vol. II, 1850–1887 (1918), Bulletin of the University of Wisconsin (1910); R. T. Hill, *The Public Domain and Democracy,* Columbia University Studies, Vol. XXXVIII (1910); the Annual Reports of the Commissioner of the General Land Office from 1860 to 1900; P. J. Treat, *The National Land System, 1785–1820*

(1910); R. G. Wellington, *The Political and Sectional Influence of the Public Lands, 1828–1842* (1914); George M. Stephenson, *The Political History of the Public Lands from 1840–1862* (1917); B. H. Hibbard, *A History of the Public Land Policies* (1924); and R. M. Robbins, *Our Landed Heritage: The Public Domain, 1776–1936* (1942). *The Centennial History of Illinois,* Clarence W. Alvord, editor-in-chief, contains much valuable material. See especially S. J. Buck, *Illinois in 1818* (1917), and T. C. Pease, *The Frontier State, 1818–1848* (1922). A. M. Sakolski, *The Great American Land Bubble* (1932), deals with speculation on the public domain. Also see Homer Hoyt, *One Hundred Years of Land Values in Chicago, 1830–1930* (1933), and the bibliography on land policy in the preceding chapter.

Many European travelers commented on agriculture; see especially Morris Birkbeck, *Notes on a Journey in America* (1818), and James Flint, *Letters from America* (1822), reprinted in R. G. Thwaites (ed.), *Early Western Travels,* Vol. IX.

12. *The Merchant Marine and Foreign Commerce*

The standard history of American commerce is the co-operative work of E. R. Johnson, T. W. Van Metre, G. G. Huebner, and D. S. Hanchett, *History of Domestic and Foreign Commerce of the United States* (published by the Carnegie Institution in 2 vols., 1915, reprinted in 1 vol. in 1922). It contains an extensive bibliography. On the European background of the War of 1812, E. F. Hecksher, *The Continental System* (1922), is the best.

Possibly the best short account of the American merchant marine in the nineteenth century is that by J. R. Soley, one-time Assistant Secretary of the Navy, in Vol. I of N. S. Shaler (ed.), *The United States of America* (1897). Good chapters are also included in A. S. Bolles, *Industrial History of the United States* (1878). The ground is covered in more detail in W. J. Abbot, *The Story of Our Merchant Marine* (1919); W. Bates, *American Marine* (1893); C. E. Cartwright, *The Tale of Our Merchant Marine* (1924); A. H. Clark, *The Clipper Ship Era, 1843–1849* (1911); and K. S. Latourette, *Voyages of American Ships to China, 1784–1844* (1927). Delightfully written are R. D. Paine, *The Old Merchant Marine* (1919), Chronicles of America Series; and S. E. Morison, *Maritime History of Massachusetts, 1783–1860* (1921), the latter containing valuable bibliographies.

The best work on a single port is that by R. G. Albion, *The Rise of New York Port* (1939). John Robinson and George F. Dow, *Sailing Ships of New England,* Marine Research Society *Publications* (Second Series, 1924, and Third Series, by Dow alone, 1928), gives beautiful reproductions of pictures of sailing ships in the famous Peabody Collection at the Essex Institute in Salem. A little-known phase of this subject can be studied in L. D. Baldwin, "Shipbuilding on the Western Waters, 1793–1817," *Mississippi Valley Historical Review,* XX, 29–44 (June, 1933), in A. B. Hulbert, "Western Shipbuilding," *American Historical Review,* XXI, 720–733 (July, 1916), and above all in L. C. Hunter's exhaustive study of *Steamboats on the Western Rivers* (1949).

On the whale fisheries, see W. S. Tower, *History of the American Whale Fish-*

ery (1907); T. Jenkins, *A History of the Whale Fisheries* (1921); C. B. Hawes, *Whaling* (1924); G. F. Dow, *Whale Ships and Whaling* (1925), Marine Research Society; E. O. Hohman, *The American Whalemen* (1928); R. McFarland, *A History of New England Fisheries* (1907); and F. R. Hart, "The New England Whale Fisheries," Colonial Society of Massachusetts *Publications,* Vol. XXVI, *Transactions 1924–26,* pp. 65–79, with interesting pictures of whaling captains. Much information on the early merchant marine is available in the numerous books bearing the imprint of the Essex Institute of Salem, Massachusetts. On privateering, see bibliography for Chapter 5; also E. S. Maclay, *A History of American Privateers* (1924), scholarly and well written; George Coggeshall, *History of the American Privateers and Letters-of-Marque During Our War with England in the Years 1812, 13, and 14* (1856); and Nathaniel Hawthorne (ed.), *The Yarn of a Yankee Privateer* (1926).

On early subsidization, consult Royal Meeker, *History of Ship Subsidies* (1905); M. M. McKee, *Ship Subsidy Question in United States Politics* (1922), in Smith College Studies VIII, No. 1; and the thorough study of J. G. B. Hutchins, *The Maritime Industries and Public Policy, 1789–1914* (1941). R. H. Dana, *Two Years Before the Mast,* a classic of the sea, gives an interesting picture of the early California trade and of conditions on shipboard, and life on a whaler is dramatically pictured in Melville's *Moby Dick.* Joseph Hergesheimer, *Java Head* (1919), a story of social life in Salem in the forties, pictures the decline of Salem in the Oriental trade. Foreign commerce in the early nineteenth century as carried on by Massachusetts merchants is well told and illustrated through source materials in K. W. Porter, *The Jacksons and the Lees* (2 vols., 1937).

The basic causes of the War of 1812 are discussed in J. W. Pratt, *The Expansionists of 1812* (1925); his failure to emphasize the agricultural causes sufficiently is rectified in G. R. Taylor, "Agrarian Discontent in the Mississippi Preceding the War of 1812," *Journal of Political Economy,* XXXIX, 471–505 (Aug., 1931). A history of the changing interpretations of the causes of the War of 1812 is given in W. H. Goodman, "The Origin of the War of 1812," *Mississippi Valley Historical Review,* XXVIII, 171–186 (Sept., 1941). On the embargo, consult W. W. Jennings, *The American Embargo, 1807–1809* (1921), and L. M. Sears, *Jefferson and the Embargo* (1927).

13. *The Rise of the Factory System*

Except for agriculture, which the volume does not include, the most useful economic history of the period from 1815 to 1865 is that of G. R. Taylor, *The Transportation Revolution* (1951), Vol. IV in Rinehart's Economic History of the United States Series. It has full bibliographies. The best study of manufacturing during this period is that by V. S. Clark, *History of Manufacturers in the United States, 1607–1860* (new ed., 1929), published by the Carnegie Institution of Washington and containing an extensive bibliography. Of the older books, the most valuable is that by J. L. Bishop, *History of American Manufacturers from 1608–1860* (3 vols., 1866), containing detailed accounts of specific industries in the early stage. Much information, not easily obtained elsewhere, is crammed into A. S. Bolles, *Industrial History of the United States* (1878). See also *Eighty Years' Progress* (1869), articles under the various manufacturing industries. On the English background the following are excellent: J. H. Clapham, *An Economic History of Modern Europe* (3 vols., 1926–1938), and Arthur Redford, *The Economic History of England, 1760–1860* (1931).

The census reports of the government will be found useful, as will also such special reports as those of Alexander Hamilton, *Report on Manufactures,* in F. W. Taussig, *State Papers and Speeches on the Tariff,* and of Louis McLane, *Report on Manufactures* (2 vols., 1833), House Doc. No. 308, 22nd Cong., 1st Sess. Much that is interesting and instructive is obtainable from the accounts of foreign travelers, extracts from which are contained in books of readings already cited.

On the tariff, consult Taussig, Ashley, and Stanwood, cited for Chapter 9.

On cotton, see James A. B. Scherer, *Cotton as a World Power* (1916); James L. Watkins, *Production and Price of Cotton for One Hundred Years,* U.S. Department of Agriculture, Division of Statistics, Miscellaneous Series, Bulletin No. 9 (1895); Broadus Mitchell, *The Rise of Cotton Mills in the South* (1921), Johns Hopkins University Studies in Historical and Political Science, 39th Series, and his *William Gregg, Factory Master of the Old South* (1928); M. T. Copeland, *The Cotton Manufacturing Industry in the United States* (1912); Caroline F. Ware, *The Early New England Cotton Manufacture* (1931); and E. H. Knowlton, *Pepperell's Progress* (1948). Few adequate histories of specific industries have yet been written, but among those available are A. H. Cole, *The American Wool Manufacture* (2 vols., 1926); C. B. Kuhlmann, *Development of the Flour-Milling Industry in the United States* (1929); L. H. Weeks, *A History of Paper Manufacturing in the United States, 1690–1916* (1916); F. J. Allen, *The Shoe Industry* (1916); Howard and Ralph Wolf, *Rubber: A Story of Glory and Greed* (1936); and Rudolph A. Clemon, *The American Livestock and Meat Industry* (1923).

The history of two relatively small but long-lived New England industries has been well told in C. W. Moore, *Timing a Century: History of the Waltham Watch Company* (1945), and in G. S. Gibb, *The Whitesmiths of Taunton: A History of Reed and Barton* (1943). The study by Felicia J. Deyrup, *Arms Makers of the Connecticut Valley,* Smith College Studies in History, Vol. XXXIII (1948), has interest not only as the history of an important small metal industry, but because of the long interrelationship between government and business. See also Blanche E. Hazard, "Organization of the Boot and Shoe Industry in Massachusetts Before 1875," *Quarterly Journal of Economics,* Vol. XXVII (Feb., 1913). Constance M. Green's chapter on "Light Manufactures and the Beginnings of Precision Manufacture Before 1861" in H. F. Williamson (ed.), *The Growth of American Economy,* is the best summary of this subject. One early New England industry, the manufacture of textile machinery, is now well covered in T. R. Navin, *The Whiten Machine Works Since 1831* (1950), and G. S. Gibb, *The Sacco-Lowell Shops* (1950).

Specialized studies of the heavy industries include A. C. Bening, *The Pennsyl-*

vania Iron Manufacture in the Eighteenth Century (1938); Kathleen Bruce, *Virginia Iron Manufacture in the Slave Era* (1930); and L. C. Hunter, "Influence of the Market upon Technique in the Iron Industry of Western Pennsylvania up to 1860," *Journal of Economic and Business History*, I, 241–281 (Feb., 1929).

The rise of the factory system may be studied in excellent histories of three New England factory towns: Vera Shlakman, *Economic History of a Factory Town: A Study of Chicopee, Massachusetts,* Smith College Studies in History, Vol. XX, Nos. 1–4 (1935); C. M. Green, *Holyoke, Massachusetts* (1939); and M. T. Parker, *Lowell, a Study in Industrial Development* (1940).

14. *Internal Transportation and Communication to 1860*

George Taylor's volume, cited in the last chapter, is notable for its chapters on transportation. One of the most interesting studies of American transportation is the four-volume work by Seymour Dunbar, *History of Travel in America* (1915), somewhat diffuse but well written and illustrated with many rare prints. An indispensable companion volume is that issued by the Carnegie Institution under the editorship of B. H. Meyer of the Interstate Commerce Commission and written by C. E. MacGill *et al., History of Transportation in the United States Before 1860* (1917), with a good bibliography. Shorter accounts may be found in E. R. Johnson and T. W. Van Metre, *Principles of Railway Transportation* (1922); C. E. Carter, *When Railroads Were New* (1909); and Slason Thompson, *A Short History of American Railways* (1925). Helpful is Malcolm Keir, *The March of Commerce* (1927), Vol. IV in the Pageant of America, and R. E. Riegel, *America Moves West* (rev. ed., 1947). Excellent chapters are those in J. B. McMaster, *History of the People of the United States,* Vol. IV, chap. 33, and Vol. V, chap. 44. See also A. B. Hulbert, *Paths of Inland Commerce* (1920), in the Chronicles of America. F. A. Cleveland and F. W. Powell, *Railroad Promotion and Capitalization in the United States* (1909), throws light on the early years.

For older accounts, see the chapters on travel and transportation in *Eighty Years' Progress* (1869); H. S. Tanner, *A Description of the Canals and Railroads of the United States* (1840); H. V. Poor, *Manual of Railroads* (1881), Introduction; and the *Census of 1880,* Vol. IV on Transportation. Mark Twain, *Life on the Mississippi* (1883), and Mark Twain and C. D. Warner, *The Gilded Age* (1873), are history as well as humor. Interesting accounts of traveling conditions by coach, canal, and railway are to be found in the travels of Dickens, Martineau, the Trollopes, and other European commentators.

The literature on special phases is rapidly growing. T. B. Searight, *The Old Pike* (1894), and A. B. Hulbert, *The Old National Pike* (1901) and *Historic Highways* (15 vols., 1902–1905), are valuable for turnpikes. Helpful are the two popular books on river steamboating: F. E. Dayton, *Steamboat Days* (1925), and G. L. Eskew, *The Pageant of the Packets* (1929); and the material on this subject cited for Chapter 12.

On canals, consult the *Preliminary Report of the Inland Waterways Commission,* 60th Cong., 1st Sess., Senate Doc. No. 325 (1908), and read A. F. Harlow,

Old Towpaths (1926). See also A. B. Hulbert, *Historic Highways,* Vols. XIII and XIV; E. L. Bogart, "Early Canal Traffic and Railroad Competition in Ohio," *Journal of Political Economy,* Vol. XXI; W. F. Dunaway, *History of the James River and Kanawha Company,* Columbia University Studies in History, Economics and Public Law, Vol. CIV, No. 2 (1922); C. L. Jones, *Economic History of the Anthracite Tidewater Canals,* University of Pennsylvania Series in Politics, Economics and Public Law, No. 22 (1908); W. S. Sanderlin, *The Great National Project: A History of the Chesapeake and Ohio Canal* (Johns Hopkins Studies, 1946); E. L. Bogart, *Internal Improvements and State Debts in Ohio* (1924); E. J. Benton, *The Wabash Trade Route in the Development of the Old Northwest* (1903); J. W. Putnam, *The Illinois and Michigan Canal* (1918); N. E. Whitford, *History of the Canal System of the State of New York* (2 vols., 1906); and Christopher Roberts, *The Middlesex Canal* (1938).

On sections, the following deal with the South: U. B. Phillips, *History of Transportation in the Eastern Cotton Belt to 1860* (1908); R. S. Cotterill, "The Beginnings of Railroads in the Southwest," *Mississippi Valley Historical Review,* VIII, 318–326 (June, 1921); "Southern Railroads and Western Trade," *ibid.,* III, 427–441 (March, 1917); and "Southern Railroads," *ibid.,* X, 153–172 (Sept., 1923). On the Middle West: W. F. Gebhard, *Transportation and Industrial Development in the Middle West,* Columbia University Studies, Vol. XXXIV, No. 1 (1900); Charles H. Ambler, *History of Transportation in the Ohio Valley* (1932). On New England: George P. Baker, *The Formation of the New England Railroad Systems* (1937); Thelma M. Kistler, *The Rise of Railroads in the Connecticut River Valley,* Smith College Studies in History, Vol. XXIII, Nos. 1–4 (1938); and E. C. Kirkland, *Men, Cities, and Transportation* (2 vols., 1948). On Railroads beyond the Mississippi: R. E. Riegel, "Trans-Mississippi Railroads During the Fifties," *Mississippi Valley Historical Review,* X, 153–173 (1923), and his *History of Western Railroads* (1926). W. J. Lane, *From Indian Trail to Iron Horse* (1939), is the history of transportation in New Jersey. For government aid, see H. L. Haney, *Congressional History of Railroads in the United States to 1850* (1908).

The history of several of the early railroads has been written; such books include Edward Hungerford, *The Story of the Baltimore and Ohio Railroad, 1827–1927* (2 vols., 1928). *A Century of Progress, History of the Delaware and Hudson Company, 1823–1923* (1925); and *Men of Erie* (1946); F. W. Stevens, *The Beginnings of the New York Central Railroad* (1926); S. M. Derrick, *Centennial History of South Carolina Railroad* (1930); F. B. C. Bradlee, *The Boston and Maine Railroad* (1921); H. W. Schotter, *The Growth and Development of the Pennsylvania Railroad* (1927); and Paul W. Gates, *The Illinois Central Railroad and Its Colonization Work* (1934). A. F. Harlow, *Old Waybills* (1934), is an interesting popular history of the express companies. On the Santa Fe Trail, read Katherine Coman, *Economic Beginnings of the Far West* (2 vols., 1912); R. L. Duffus, *The Santa Fé Trail* (1930); Josiah Gregg, "Commerce of the Prairies," in R. G. Thwaites (ed.), *Early Western Travels* (1905), Vol. XX; and M. G.

Fulton (ed.), *Diary and Letters of Josiah Gregg: Southwestern Enterprises, 1840–1847* (1941). A little-known phase is treated in L. B. Lesley, *Uncle Sam's Camels* (1929). The experiences of a newspaper correspondent on the first overland trip of the Butterfield Mail have been printed by the Huntington Library: W. L. Ormsby, *The Butterfield Overland Mail* (1942).

J. A. Miller, *Fares, Please!* (1941), is a spirited popular account of street railroads from horsecars to streamliners. A. D. Turnbull, *John Stevens: An American Record* (1928), is the biography of an early railroad experimenter, and W. J. Lane, *Commodore Vanderbilt* (1942), is the life of an early transportation entrepreneur. The early story of the telegraph is now available in the excellent book: Carleton Mabee, *The American Leonardo: A Life of Samuel F. B. Morse* (1943), a Pulitzer Prize book, and in R. L. Thompson, *Wiring a Continent: The History of the Telegraph Industry in the United States, 1832–1866* (1947).

Transportation maps may be found in MacGill, in McMaster, in *Harper's Atlas of American History,* in C. O. Paullin, *Atlas of the Historical Geography of the United States* (1932), and in C. L. Lord and E. H. Lord, *Historical Atlas of the United States* (1943).

15. *Population and Labor*

A convenient statistical summary is the census monograph, *A Century of Population Growth* (1909). This should be supplemented by W. S. Thompson and P. K. Whelpton, *Population Trends in the United States* (1933). A suggestive treatment of the development of the metropolitan economy in America is given in the last chapter of N. S. B. Gras, *An Introduction to Economic History* (1922).

On immigration, consult the *Preliminary Report of the Eighth Census* (1862), reproduced in part in Bogart and Thompson. The most voluminous and valuable collection of material is the *Report of the Immigration Commission* (42 vols., 1911), summarized in two volumes of abstracts. Edith Abbott, *Historical Aspects of the Immigration Problem* (1926), contains excellent contemporary material. Two important recent books are M. L. Hansen, *The Atlantic Migration, 1607–1860* (1940), emphasizing the European background, and C. F. Wittke, *We Who Built America* (1939), discussing the contribution of many of the non-English groups. Other studies should be noted: J. R. Commons, *Races and Immigrants in America* (1907); H. P. Fairchild, *Immigration* (1925); and G. M. Stephenson, *History of American Immigration, 1820–1924* (1926).

The most detailed account of the history of free labor during this period is given in John R. Commons (ed.), *History of Labor in the United States* (2 vols., 1918). Important source material upon which the first volume of this work is based appears in J. R. Commons *et. al., Documentary History of American Industrial Society,* Vols. III–VIII. Shorter accounts based largely on the work of Commons and his associates are in Mary Beard, *A Short History of the American Labor Movement* (1920); Herbert Harris, *American Labor* (1939); and M. S. Clark and S. F. Simon, *The Labor Movement in America* (1938). From the left-wing point of view the following are helpful: James O'Neal, *The Workers in*

Bibliography 757

American History (4th ed., 1921); Anthony Bimba, *The History of the American Working Class* (1927); and A. M. Simons, *Social Forces in American History* (1912). P. S. Foner, *History of the Labor Movement in the United States* (1947) would substitute a Marxian interpretation for that of the Commons school. Edith Abbott, *Women in Industry* (1910), contains good chapters on conditions surrounding the early mill operatives, as does Vera Shlakman, *Economic History of a Factory Town: A Study of Chicopee, Massachusetts,* Smith College Studies in History, Vol. XX, Nos. 1–4 (1935). Norman Ware, *The Industrial Worker, 1840–1860* (1924), is invaluable for the period after 1840. An early but still useful book is R. T. Ely, *The Labor Movement in America* (1886). The Bureau of Labor Statistics has a valuable study, *History of Wages in the United States from the Colonial Times to 1928* (1929).

Perhaps the best summary of communistic experiments is to be found in Morris Hillquit, *History of Socialism in the United States* (5th ed., 1910). More detailed studies are those of J. H. Noyes, *History of American Socialism* (1870); Charles Nordhoff, *The Communistic Societies of the United States from Personal Visit and Observation* (1875); and W. A. Hinds, *American Communities and Co-operative Commonwealths* (rev. ed., 1908). A picture of Brook Farm is given in O. B. Frothingham, *George Ripley* (1882), and of the Florence community in A. E. McBee, *From Utopia to Florence 1830–1852,* Smith College Studies in History, Vol. XXXII, 1947. Commons *et al., Documentary History of American Industrial Society,* has material on co-operatives, communal societies, and land reform. See also H. S. Zahler, *Eastern Workingmen and National Land Policy, 1829–1892* (1941); R. M. Robbins, "Horace Greeley, Land Reform and Unemployment," *Agricultural History,* VII, 18–41; and J. G. Raybeck, "The American Workingman and the Antislavery Crusade," *Journal of Economic History,* III, 152–163 (Nov., 1943). Some idea of the intellectual ferment and reform drive during these years may be found in E. M. Schuster, *Native American Anarchism,* Smith College Studies in History, Vol. XVII, Nos. 1–4 (1932).

16. *Economic Causes of the Civil War*

Besides other source books, already cited, see the first two volumes of the *Documentary History of American Industrial Society* (1910), the whole work prepared under the direction of J. R. Commons and associates. The introduction to the first two volumes on slavery by Professor Phillips is, in the opinion of Channing, "the best brief survey of the system that has been written." Other sources are scattered through Hunt's *Merchants' Magazine and Commercial Review* (New York, 1839–1870), Niles' *Weekly Register* (Baltimore, 1811–1849), and *De Bow's Review* (intermittently in various places 1846–1880).

Short studies of slavery are included in the standard histories—e.g., J. F. Rhodes, *History of the United States,* Vol. I, chap. 4, and Vol. III, chap. 1; J. B. McMaster, *History of the People of the United States,* Vol. VII, chap. 76; Edward Channing, *History of the United States,* Vol. V, chap. 5; and Allan Nevins, *Ordeal of Union* (2 vols., 1947). Thumbnail sketches of various phases of southern economic history are included in Vol. V of *The South in the Building of the Nation* and Alfred H. Stone's article, "The Negro in the South," Vol. X. An interesting and well-balanced résumé with an excellent bibliography appears in A. B. Hart, *Slavery and Abolition,* in the American Nation Series. Histories of the American Negro include those of Ulrich B. Phillips, *American Negro Slavery* (1918), an expansion of many earlier studies; Benjamin Brawley, *A Short History of the American Negro* (1919) and *A Social History of the American Negro* (1921). Invaluable are Frederic Bancroft, *SlaveTrading in the Old South* (1931); C. S. Sydnor, *Slavery in Mississippi* (1933); R. B. Flanders, *Plantation Slavery in Georgia* (1933); C. S. Davis, *The Cotton Kingdom in Alabama* (1939); and W. E. B. Du Bois, *Suppression of the African Slave Trade* (1896). See also Minnie C. Boyd, *Alabama in the Fifties* (1931), and R. S. Cotterill, *The Old South* (1936).

The best studies of southern civilization in the days before the war are those by Ulrich B. Phillips, *Life and Labor in the Old South* (1929), and Clement Eaton, *A History of the Old South* (1949). New light on the part played by the small and middle-class white farmer is given in F. L. and H. C. Owsley, "The Economic Basis of Society in the Late Ante-Bellum South," *Journal of Southern History,* Vol. VI, No. 1 (Feb., 1940), and in Blanche H. Clark, *The Tennessee Yeoman, 1840–1860* (1942). One phase of the slave system has been illustrated in J. S. Bassett, *The Southern Plantation Overseer as Revealed in His Letters* (1925), a study based on letters written to President James K. Polk by his plantation overseers. In Francis P. Gaines, *The Southern Plantation, a Study in the Development and Accuracy of a Tradition* (1924), a truer perspective regarding the plantation is attained. R. B. Russel, *Economic Aspects of Southern Sectionalism, 1840–1861* (1923), University of Illinois Studies in the Social Sciences, Vol. XI, Nos. 1–2, clarifies the background of the Civil War, as does J. G. Van Deusen, *Economic Basis of Disunion in South Carolina,* Columbia University Studies (1928), and R. H. Shryock, *Georgia and the Union in 1850* (1926). Important in understanding southern history is A. O. Craven, *Soil Exhaustion as a Factor in the Agricultural History of Virginia and Maryland, 1606–1860* (1925). The problem of soil, climate, and resources is also stressed in F. J. Turner, *The Significance of Sections in American History* (1932); in R. B. Vance, *Human Geography of the South: a Study in Human Resources and Human Adequacy* (1932); and in C. W. Ramsdell, "The Natural Limits of Slavery Expansion," *Mississippi Valley Historical Review,* XVI, 151–171 (Sept., 1929). On the social background, see G. S. Johnson, *A Social History of the Sea Islands* (1925); A. C. Cole, *The Irrepressible Conflict* (1930); and Allan Nevins, *Ordeal of Union* (2 vols., 1947).

The contemporary material on slavery is large. Very valuable are the works of J. E. Cairnes, *The Slave Power* (2nd ed., enlarged, London and Cambridge, 1863), an impersonal study by a famous English economist; Hinton R. Helper, *The Impending Crisis of the South* (1857), the best-known denunciation of the system by a Southerner; and J. S. Buckingham, *The Slave States of America* (1842), by an English traveler. Typical defenses of slavery are those of Professor C. F. Mc-Cay of Columbia, South Carolina, in *Eighty Years' Progress* (1869), *and The Pro-Slavery Argument* (1852) by several writers. See also Daniel R. Goodloe, *An Inquiry into the Causes Which Retard the Southern States* (1848), and T. R. Kettell, *Southern Wealth and Northern Profits* (1861). See also G. H. Barnes, *Antislavery Impulse, 1830–1844* (1933), and D. L. Dumond, *The Secession Movement, 1860–1861* (1931).

A mine of information on life and conditions in the prewar South is J. D. B. DeBow (ed.), *The Industrial Resources of the Southern and Western States* (3 vols., 1852–1853); and the various works of Frederick L. Olmsted, the "best-known writer on conditions in the south prior to the outbreak of the Civil War," including *Journey in the Seaboard Slave States* (1859), *A Journey Through Texas* (1857), *A Journey Through the Back Country* (1860), and *The Cotton Kingdom* (1861), reprinted and edited by A. M. Schlesinger (1953). Interesting also are the observations of the famous actress, Frances Kemble, *Journal of a Residence on a Georgia Plantation in 1838–1839* (1863); of Edward Ingle, *Southern Side-lights* (1896); and of J. B. Angel, *Reminiscences of James Burrill Angell* (1912), who in Chapter II tells of a horseback journey and winter spent in the South in 1850 and 1851. Mrs. Harriet Beecher Stowe's *Uncle Tom's Cabin* (first published in 1852) should be read for its tremendous historical significance as an influence upon the generation which fought the Civil War, and also her *Key to Uncle Tom's Cabin* (1853).

The best study of cotton is that by M. B. Hammond, *The Cotton Industry*, Publications of the American Economic Association, New Series, No. 1 (1897). A more recent book, previously cited, is James A. B. Scherer, *Cotton as a World Power* (1916). See also A. H. Stone, "The Cotton Factorage System of the Southern States," *American Historical Review*, XX, 557–565 (April, 1915). For the "cotton triangle" trade as it centered in New York, read R. G. Albion, *The Rise of New York Port*, chap. 6. The whole background has been excellently summed up in W. E. Dodd, *The Cotton Kingdom* (1919), in the Chronicles of America. Results of the latest research are summarized in L. M. Hacker, *The Triumph of American Capitalism* (1940).

17. *The Civil War*

The digested material on the economic history during the Civil War is still meager. An over-all picture of living conditions at the outbreak of this war is E. W. Martin, *The Standard of Living in 1860, American Consumption Levels on the Eve of the Civil War* (1942). The most satisfactory study of the South is that by John C. Schwab, *The Confederate States of America* (1901), a financial and industrial history devoting special attention to the financial phase and containing a good bibliography. What Schwab has done for the South E. D. Fite has done for the North in his *Social and Industrial Conditions in the North During the Civil War* (1910), but with more emphasis upon the social and industrial and less upon the financial. Popular accounts of the nonmilitary aspects of the Civil War are given in Nathaniel Stephenson, *The Day of the Confederacy* (1919) and *Abraham Lincoln and the Union* (1918), both in the Chronicles of America. Important also are the later chapters in A. C. Cole, *The Irrepressible Conflict* (1934), and J. G. Randall, *The Civil War and Reconstruction* (1937), chaps. 27, 28. Further summaries of conditions in the South appear in J. F. Rhodes, *History of the United States* (1905), Vol. V, chaps. 27 and 28, and in his *History of the Civil War, 1861–1865* (1917), chaps. 11 and 12.

The financial history of the period is of special interest. That of the North is summarized in Davis R. Dewey, *Financial History of the United States* (10th ed., 1928); and in more detail in A. S. Bolles, *Financial History of the United States,* Vol. III, 1861–1885 (1886); also in W. C. Mitchell, *History of the Greenbacks* (1903); in Don C. Barrett, *The Greenbacks and the Resumption of Specie Payments, 1862–1879* (1931); and in A. M. Davis, *The Origin of the National Banking System* (1910). On the finances of the Confederacy, see the book by John C. Schwab previously mentioned, and the following articles: "Finances of the Confederacy," *Political Science Quarterly,* VII, 38–56 (1892); "The Confederate Foreign Loan," *Yale Review,* I, 175–186 (1893); "The Financier of the Confederate States," *Yale Review,* II, 288–301 (1894), in part a review of Henry D. Capers, *The Life and Times of C. G. Memminger* (1894); and J. L. Sellers, "An Interpretation of Civil War Finance," *American Historical Review,* XXX, 282–297 (Jan., 1925), and his "Economic Incidence of the Civil War in the South," *Mississippi Valley Historical Review,* XIV, 179–191 (Sept., 1927). See also his chap. 19 in *Cambridge Modern History,* Vol. VII. For prices during the war, consult the Report by Mr. Aldrich for the Committee on Finances and Prices, Wages, and Transportation, *Senate Reports,* 52nd Cong., 2nd Sess., 1892–1893, special session, March 4, 1893, Vol. III, four parts. See also E. P. Oberholtzer, *Jay Cooke* (2 vols., 1907), and Henrietta Larson, *Jay Cooke, Private Banker* (1936). The story of the most important single industry developed during these years is told in scholarly fashion in Paul H. Giddens, *The Birth of the Oil Industry* (1938).

The influence of railroads on the course of the Civil War may be traced in E. A. Pratt, *The Rise of Rail Power* (1916), chaps. 2, 3, and 4. On an important topic read L. B. Schmidt, "The Influence of Wheat and Cotton on Anglo-American Relations During the Civil War," *Iowa Journal of History and Politics,* XVI, 400–439 (July, 1918), and Frank L. Owsley, *King Cotton Diplomacy* (1931), chap. 19. On the efforts to break the blockade, see Francis B. C. Bradlee, *Blockade Running During the Civil War and the Effect of Land and Water Transportation on the Confederacy* (1925); James R. Soley, *The Blockade and the Cruisers* (1890); and William M. Robinson, *Confederate Privateers* (1928). The European attitude is developed in D. Jordan and E. S. Pratt, *Europe and the American Civil War* (1931).

The story of the most important labor leader of the Civil War era is Jonathan Grossman, *William Sylvis, Pioneer of American Labor* (1945).

18. *The Last Frontier*

The history and significance of the westward movement since the Civil War have never been adequately summarized, although much has been done since F. J. Turner in 1893 pointed out the "Significance of the Frontier in American History," in the American Historical Association *Annual Report*. The most complete bibliography of the period is in F. J. Turner and F. Merk, *List of References on the History of the West* (rev. ed., 1922). The earliest phases of the trans-Mississippi West are developed in Katherine Coman, *Economic Beginnings of the Far West* (2 vols., 1912), and the more recent in F. L. Paxson, *The Last American Frontier* (1910); H. E. Briggs, *Frontiers of the Northwest* (1940); and W. J. Ghent, *The Early Far West: A Narrative Outline, 1540–1850* (1931). Note also the texts of Paxson, Clark, and Billington.

On the miners' frontier, S. E. White, *The Forty-Niners* (1920), Chronicles of America, and R. G. Cleland, *California: The American Period* (1939), tell the early history of California; and Owen C. Coy, *The Grand Trek* (1931), the story of the forty-niners. The early days in Nevada are recounted in C. H. Shinn, *Story of the Mine* (1896), and E. Lord, *Comstock Mining* (U.S. Geological Survey, IV, 1883); Mark Twain's *Roughing It* gives an intimate picture of a stagecoach journey to the Far West and of the boom period in the Nevada silver mines. C. B. Glasscock, *The Big Bonanza* (1931), and Oscar Lewis, *Silver Kings* (1947), are popularly written. On mining, consult W. J. Trimble, *The Mining Advance into the Inland Empire*, University of Wisconsin Bulletin, No. 638 (1914), and T. A. Rickard, *A History of American Mining* (1932).

On ranching and the cow country, E. S. Osgood, *The Day of the Cattleman* (1929), E. E. Dale, *The Range Cattle Industry* (1930), W. P. Webb, *The Great Plains* (1931), and Everett Dick, *The Sod House Frontier* (1937), are valuable and significant studies. Osgood is particularly valuable on the business and financial aspects of ranching, and Webb on the importance of firearms, barbed wire, and water as the background of plains settlement. Also important are Louis Pelzer, *The Cattleman's Frontier* (1936); O. B. Peake, *The Colorado Range Cattle Industry* (1937); P. A. Rollins, *The Cowboy* (1936); W. C. Barnes, *The Story of the Range* (1926); E. D. Branch, *The Cowboy and His Interpreters* (1926); R. A. Clemens, *The American Livestock and Meat Industry* (1923); and J. G. McCoy, *Historic Sketches of the Cattle Trade of the West and Southwest* (new ed., 1932), the latter by one of the pioneer cattlemen. E. E. Dale, *Cow Country* (1942), is a collection of essays on the Great Plains area. Intimate pictures of cowboy life are to be found in the books of Will James, but perhaps the most complete picture of ranching is that by Emerson Hough, *The Story of the Cowboy* (2 vols., 1897). See also F. L. Paxson, "The Cow Country," *American Historical Review,* XXII, 65–84, and the following articles in the *Mississippi Valley Historical Review:* E. E. Dale, "The Ranchman's Last Frontier" (June, 1923); Louis Pelzer, "A Cattlemen's Commonwealth on the Western Range" (June, 1926); R. S. Fletcher, "End of the Open Range in Eastern Montana" (Sept., 1929); and

Harold Briggs, "The Development and Decline of Open Range Ranching in the Northwest" (March, 1934). See also C. M. Lowe, "History of the Cattle Industry in the Southwest," *Southwestern Historical Quarterly,* Vol. XX (July, 1916). A popular summary is Emerson Hough, *The Passing of the Frontier* (1918), in the Chronicles of America. The life of Henry Miller, a cattle baron of California, is interestingly told in E. F. Treadwell, *The Cattle King* (1931).

On the public land policy, consult McLoughlin and Hart, *Cyclopedia of American Government* (1914), articles on Public Land, Land Grants, Homestead Act, etc., also G. M. Stephenson, *The Political History of the Public Lands from 1840 to 1862* (1917), and B. H. Hibbard, *A History of the Public Land Policies* (1924). T. Donaldson, *Public Domain* (1881), although inaccurate, is the only available detailed account up to that time. See also the *Public Land Report* (1880) and the *Report With Appendix* (1905). The most significant recent book is R. M. Robbins, *Our Landed Heritage; The Public Domain, 1776–1936* (1942). Important special studies are F. A. Shannon, "The Homestead Act and the Labor Surplus," *American Historical Review,* XLI, 637–651 (July, 1936); P. W. Gates, "The Homestead Law in an Incongruous Land System," *ibid.,* pp. 652–681; and R. M. Robbins, "The Public Domain in the Era of Exploitation, 1862–1901," *Agricultural History,* XIII, 97–118 (April, 1939). See also G. T. Du Bois and G. S. Mathews, *Galusha A. Grow, Father of the Homestead Act* (1917). Certain aspects of the fencing problem are presented in E. W. Hayter, "Barbed Wire Fencing—A Prairie Invention," *Agriculture History,* XIII, 180–207 (Oct., 1939) and "The Fencing of Western Railroads," *ibid.,* XIX, 163–167 (July, 1945).

The Indian Wars are recounted in N. A. Miles, *Serving the Republic* (1911), and F. L. Paxson, *The Last American Frontier.* On the Indian, see F. E. Leupp, *The Indian and His Problem* (1910), and G. E. E. Lindquist, *The Red Man in the United States* (1923).

Material on the contribution of the railroads to the opening of the West may be found in H. K. White, *Union Pacific Railway* (1898); J. P. Davis, *Union Pacific Railway* (1894); E. V. Smalley, *The Northern Pacific Railway* (1883); *Memoirs of Henry Villard* (2 vols., 1904); Henrietta Larson, *Jay Cooke, Private Banker* (1936); J. G. Pyle, *Life of James J. Hill* (2 vols., 1917); F. L. Paxson, "The Pacific Railroads and the Disappearance of the Frontier," *American Historical Association Annual Report* (1907), I, 105–118; R. C. Overton, *Burlington West; a Colonization History of the Burlington Railroad* (1941); and particularly J. B. Hedges, "The Colonization Work of the Northern Pacific," *Mississippi Valley Historical Review* (Dec., 1926). See also Hedges' *Henry Villard and the Railways of the Northwest* (1930). The contribution to settlement by railroads in the Middle West is developed in P. W. Gates, *The Illinois Central Railroad and Its Colonization Work* (1934).

On Turner and the "safety-valve" theory, see the bibliography for Chapter 10.

Two recent articles on western bibliography should be noted: E. D. Ross, "A Generation of Prairie Historiography," *Mississippi Valley Historical Review,* XXXIII, 391–410 (Dec., 1946), and H. E. Briggs, "An Appraisal of Historical

Writings on the Great Plains Region Since 1920," *ibid.,* XXXIV, 83–100 (June, 1947).

19. *The Agrarian Revolution*

See the bibliography for Chapters 11 and 18. The latter has a partial bibliography on the ranchers' frontier, the last farmers' frontier, and other aspects of agricultural history. The files of *Agricultural History* (1918–   ), published by the Agricultural History Society, will be found invaluable. The *Annual Reports* of the United States Department of Agriculture are a mine of information. Particularly important are the historical articles in the *1940 Yearbook*. These have been gathered together as *Yearbook* Separate No. 1783 and printed under the title "An Historical Survey of American Agriculture." For the earlier years, consult the Introduction to the volume on Agriculture in the *Eighth Census,* the special reports on *The Cereals,* on *Flour Milling,* and on *Meat Production;* and in the *Tenth Census,* Vol. III, the report on *Tobacco.* In Vol. V, pp. xvi–xxvii of the same census, there is a brief review of the *Agricultural Progress of Fifty Years, 1850–1900.* See also volumes on *Agriculture* in the recent census volumes.

The best brief historical summary is E. E. Edwards, "American Agriculture— The First 300 Years," pp. 171–276 of the *1940 Yearbook of Agriculture,* also issued as *Yearbook* Separate No. 1730. The standard volume on the post-Civil War period is Fred A. Shannon, *The Farmer's Last Frontier: Agriculture, 1860–1897* (1945). Harold Berger and H. H. Landsberg, *American Agriculture, 1899–1939: A Study of Output, Employment and Productivity* (1942), is largely statistical. N. S. B. Gras, *History of Agriculture* (1925), is suggestive. *The Agricultural Problem in the United States* (1920), by the National Industrial Conference Board, Inc., is an interesting survey. For the years 1897–1917, see H. U. Faulkner, *The Decline of Laissez Faire* (1951), chaps. 12, 13.

On farm machinery, see H. N. Casson, *The Romance of the Reaper* (1908); H. W. Quintance, *The Influence of Farm Machinery on Production and Labor* (1904), Publications of the American Economic Association, 3rd Series, Vol. V, No. 4; and Leo Rogin, *The Introduction of Farm Machinery in Its Relation to the Productivity of Labor in the Agriculture of the United States* (1931). On the reaper, see W. T. Hutchinson, *Cyrus Hall McCormick* (2 vols., 1930–1935), and Cyrus McCormick, *The Century of the Reaper* (1931). Helpful is O. E. Baker, *A Graphic Summary of Farm Machinery Facilities, Roads and Expenditures,* U.S. Dept. of Agriculture Misc. Pub. 264 (1937).

The history of government aid in the problems of agriculture may be found in the following: A. P. Chew, *The Response of Government to Agriculture* (1937); W. L. Wanlass, *The United States Department of Agriculture; a Study in Administration* (1920); A. C. True, *A History of Agricultural Extension Work in the United States, 1785–1923,* U.S. Dept. of Agriculture Misc. Pub. 15 (1928), his *A History of Agricultural Education in the United States, 1785–1925,* U.S. Dept. of Agriculture Misc. Pub. 36 (1929), and his "Agricultural Experiment Stations in the United States," *Yearbook of Agriculture, 1939,* pp. 513–548. On the problems of credit, consult A. C. Wiprud, *The Federal Farm Loan System in Operation* (1921); Clara Elliot, *The Farmers' Campaign for Credit* (1927); and E. S. Sparks, *History and Theory of Agricultural Credit in the United States* (1932). Government aid to agricultural science is skillfully integrated in T. S. Harding, *Two Blades of Grass: A History of Scientific Development in the U.S. Department of Agriculture* (1947). See also J. C. Bailey, *Seeman A. Knapp: Schoolmaster of American Agriculture* (1945).

On irrigation, see George Thomas, *The Development of Institutions Under Irrigation* (1920); R. P. Teale, *The Economics of Land Reclamation in the United States* (1927); J. W. James, *Reclaiming the Arid West* (1917); and P. B. Sears, *Deserts on the March* (1935).

The history of certain specific aspects of agriculture may be found in R. A. Clemen, *The American Livestock and Meat Industry* (1923); A. H. Cole, "The American Rice-Growing Industry," *Quarterly Journal of Economics*, XLI, 595–643 (Aug., 1927); L. G. Connor, "A Brief History of the Sheep Industry in the United States," *American Historical Association Annual Report* (1918), pp. 89–197; C. B. Kuhlman, *The Development of the Flour-Milling Industry in the United States* (1929); C. W. Larson *et al.*, "The Dairy Industry," *Yearbook of Agriculture, 1922*, pp. 281–394; C. E. Leighty *et al.*, "The Corn Crop," *ibid.*, pp. 161–226; C. R. Ball *et al.*, "Wheat Production and Marketing," *ibid., 1921*, pp. 77–160; W. W. Garner *et al.*, "History and Status of Tobacco Culture," *ibid., 1922*, pp. 395–468; A. M. Ageslato *et al.*, "The Cotton Situation," *ibid., 1921*, pp. 323–406; E. W. Brandes *et al.*, "Sugar," *ibid., 1923*, pp. 151–228; E. W. Sheets *et al.*, "Our Beef Industry," *ibid., 1921*, pp. 227–322; D. A. Spencer *et al.*, "The Sheep Industry," *ibid., 1923*, pp. 229–310; and C. E. Pirlee, *History of the Dairy Industry* (1926). Two recent studies have helped to fill out the Webbs' study of the Plains area: J. C. Malin, *Winter Wheat in the Golden Belt of Kansas: A Study in Adaptation to Subhumid Geographical Environment* (1944), and Theodore Saloutas, "The Spring-Wheat Farmer in a Maturing Economy, 1870–1920," *Journal of Economic History*, VI, 173–190 (Nov., 1946).

Two phases of southern agriculture are presented in M. B. Hammond, *The Cotton Industry* (1897), in the Publications of the American Economic Association, and by M. Jacobstein, *The Tobacco Industry* (1907), Columbia University Studies, Vol. XXVI, No. 3. For southern tenancy, consult R. P. Brooks, *The Agrarian Revolution in Georgia, 1865–1912* (1914), and for a general picture of the whole country, E. A. Goldenweiser and L. E. Truesdale, *Farm Tenancy in the United States,* Census Monograph No. 4, 1920 Census (1924), and L. C. Gray *et al.*, "Farm Ownership and Tenancy," *Department of Agriculture Yearbook, 1923*, pp. 507–600. The "ladder theory" is questioned by Lawanda F. Cox, "Tenancy in the United States, 1865–1900," *Agricultural History*, XVIII, 97–105 (July, 1944). See also her "The American Agricultural Wage Earners, 1865–1900," *ibid.*, XXII, 95–114 (April, 1948). See also Harry Schwartz, *Seasonal Farm Labor in the United States* (1945).

20. *Development of the Industrial Revolution*

The bases for the study of manufacturing since the Civil War are the census reports, especially Vol. VII of the *Twelfth Census of the United States* and the *Abstract of the Thirteenth Census.* Companion volumes of equal value are the *Reports on Manufactures* for 1905 and 1914. Essential for industrial developments but unwieldy to handle is the *Report of the Industrial Commission* (19 vols., 1902), particularly the *Final Report* in Vol. XIX. Extracts from this report are included in the *Readings* by Bogart and Thompson and by Flügel and Faulkner. The only comprehensive secondary account is V. S. Clark, *History of Manufacturers in the United States,* Vol. II, 1860–1893; Vol. III, 1893–1928 (1929). An older book which covers part of this period is C. M. Depew (ed.), *One Hundred Years of American Commerce* (2 vols., 1895). More recent descriptive accounts are Malcolm Keir, *Manufacturing* (1928); E. B. Alderfer and H. E. Michl, *Economics of American Industry* (1942); and H. T. Worshaw (ed.), *Representative Industries in the United States* (1928). N. S. B. Gras, *Industrial Evolution* (1930), is a valuable study of special industries.

For this and the next six chapters, the student will find summaries of the material for the years 1897 to 1917 in H. U. Faulkner, *The Decline of Laissez Faire* (1951), Vol. VII in Rinehart's Economic History of the United States Series. Longer accounts of special industries may be traced in encyclopedias, especially the *Encyclopaedia of the Social Sciences,* and in the following books: T. M. Young, *The American Cotton Industry* (1903); P. H. Nystrom, *Textiles* (1916); M. T. Copeland, *The Cotton Manufacturing Industry in the United States* (1912); B. F. Lement, *The Cotton Textile Industry of the Southern Appalachian Piedmont* (1933); J. H. Burgy, *The New England Cotton Textile Industry. A Study in Industrial Geography* (1932); T. R. Smith, *The Cotton Industry of Fall River, Massachusetts* (1944); S. L. Wolfbein, *The Decline of a Cotton Textile City: A Study of New Bedford* (1944); A. H. Cole, *The American Wool Manufacture* (2 vols., 1926); W. C. Wyckoff, *American Silk Manufacture* (1880); C. B. Kuhlman, *The Development of the Flour-Milling Industry in the United States* (1929); F. J. Allen, *The Shoe Industry* (1916); B. E. Hazard, *The Organization of the Boot and Shoe Industry in Massachusetts Before 1875* (1921); H. N. Casson, *The Romance of Steel* (1907); J. R. Smith, *Story of Iron and Steel* (1913); J. V. Woodworth, *American Tool Making and Interchangeable Manufacturing* (1905), and A. O. Backert (ed.), *The A B C of Iron and Steel* (4th ed., 1921). Indispensable for the iron industry is B. J. Hendrick, *Andrew Carnegie* (2 vols., 1932). R. C. Epstein, *The Automobile Industry* (1928), emphasizes the commercial and financial aspects of the industry, and E. D. Kennedy, *The Automobile Industry* (1941), is more inclusive. Malcolm MacLauren, *The Rise of the Electric Industry During the Nineteenth Century* (1943), is for the general reader.

The lumber industry is treated from two aspects in J. E. Defebaugh, *History of the Lumber Industry of America* (4 vols., 1906–1909), and in John Ise, *United*

States Forest Policy (1920). The latter's United States Oil Policy (1927) is the best on that subject. See also Paul Giddens, The Birth of the Oil Industry (1938). For other industries, see the following: L. T. Sutherland, Fifty Years of Portland Cement (1923); William Haynes and E. L. Gordy (eds.), Chemical Industries' Contribution to the Nation, 1635–1935 (1935); Howard and Ralph Wolf, Rubber: A Story of Glory and Greed (1936), an excellent history; R. A. Clemen, The American Livestock and Meat Industry (1923); J. H. Collins, The Story of Canned Foods (1924); A. P. Van Gelder and Hugo Schlatter, History of the Explosives Industry in America (1927); B. B. Hampton, History of the Movies (1931); and C. E. Puffer, Air Transportation (1941). The coal industry, hitherto largely neglected by historians, has been finally approached in H. N. Eavenson, The First Century and a Quarter of American Coal Industry (1942), largely statistical. See also Harold Barger and S. H. Schurr, The Mining Industry, A Study of Output, Employment and Production (1944). A six-volume history of the chemical industry is in progress, of which three volumes had appeared by 1945. Volumes II and III by William Haynes covers the years 1912–1922.

Efforts have been made through index numbers to measure the extent of industrial growth and volume of production. The most widely used are those established by E. E. Day and Woodlief Thomas, The Growth of Manufactures, 1899–1923, Census Monograph VIII, 1928, based in part on the "Harvard Index" of Warren M. Persons. Three products of the National Bureau of Economic Research covering the same field are F. C. Mills, Economic Tendencies in the United States (1932); Solomon Fabricant, The Output of Manufacturing Industries (1940); and Harold Barger and S. H. Schurr, The Mining Industry (1944).

A popular history of many inventions is given in W. Kaempffert, History of American Inventions (2 vols., 1924).

21. Consolidation of Business

Some of the most important source material on industrial and financial concentration is to be found in the various investigations made by the state and federal legislatures. Of these the most valuable are: Preliminary Report of the Industrial Commission on Trusts and Industrial Combinations. Vol. I of the Commission's Report (1900); Final Report of the Industrial Commission, Vol. XIX of the Commission's Report (1902); Report of the Special Committee on Railroads Appointed Under a Resolution of the Assembly of February 28, 1879, to Investigate Alleged Abuses in the Management of Railroads Chartered by the State of New York, Assembly Doc. No. 38, 1880 (Hepburn Committee), especially informative on rebates; Report of the Committee Pursuant to House Resolutions 429 and 504 to Investigate the Concentration of the Control of Money and Credit (1913) (Pujo Committee). See also the Thirteenth Census Abstract, chap. 10, and the Abstract of the Census of Manufactures, 1914, chaps. 6 and 7. The Commission of Corporations and, since 1914, the Federal Trade Commission have made many valuable reports on specific industries. Excerpts from their reports on the tobacco industry, the steel industry, the International Harvester Company, the meat-packing industry, and the concentration of electrical power are given in Flügel and Faulkner, *Readings,* chap. 14.

General studies of the trust movement include J. W. Jenks and W. E. Clark, *The Trust Problem* (5th ed., 1929), a standard and scholarly work; Eliot Jones, *The Trust Problem in the United States* (1921); C. R. Van Hise, *Concentration and Control* (rev. ed., 1914); R. T. Ely, *Monopolies and Trusts* (1900); John Moody, *The Truth About the Trusts* (1904), with valuable statistical information by an expert; and John Moody, *The Masters of Capital* (1919), in the Chronicles of America. Essential to any understanding of business concentration is J. C. Bonbright and G. C. Means, *The Holding Company* (1932), and A. A. Berle, Jr., and G. C. Means, *The Modern Corporation and Private Property* (1932). A valuable survey is by H. R. Seager and C. A. Gulick, Jr., *Trust and Corporation Problems* (1929), primarily historical. On the Federal Trade Commission, G. C. Henderson, *The Federal Trade Commission* (1924), is exhaustive up to that date. It should be supplemented by T. C. Blaisdell, Jr., *The Federal Trade Commission* (1932). Recent important discussions of the general problem are given in M. W. Watkins, *Industrial Combinations and Public Policy* (1927); D. M. Keezer and Stacy May, *The Public Control of Business* (1930); and A. R. Burns, *The Decline of Competition* (1936). In a class by itself as the most important description of recent concentration is H. W. Laidler, *Concentration in America Industry* (1931). On the Webb Export Act, read L. T. Fournier, "The Purposes and Results of the Webb-Pomerene Act," *American Economic Review,* Vol. XXII, No. I (March, 1932). Sources are collected in W. Z. Ripley, *Trusts, Pools, and Corporations* (rev. ed., 1916).

Other studies which should not be neglected include National Industrial Conference Board, *Mergers in Industry* (1929); W. I. Thorpe, *The Integration of Industrial Operation,* Census Monograph III (1928); and two monographs done by Walton Hamilton for the Temporary National Economic Committee: *Patents and Free Enterprise,* Monograph 31 (1941), and *Antitrust in Action,* Monograph 16 (1941). Also on the legal aspect is W. H. Taft, *The Anti-Trust Act and the Supreme Court* (1914).

The heaviest guns in the early antitrust agitation were fired by Henry Demarest Lloyd in his unsparing denunciation of monopoly, *Wealth Against Commonwealth* (1894). See also C. Lloyd, *Life of Henry Demarest Lloyd* (2 vols., 1912), for a survey of the growth of antitrust feeling. In later years Woodrow Wilson lifted his voice in favor of competition and small business in his *New Freedom* (1913), a collection of campaign speeches.

In C. C. Regier, *The Era of the Muckrakers* (1932), and in Louis Filler, *Crusaders for American Liberalism* (1939), can be found a résumé of the literature of protest; two of the most famous of the "muckrakers" contribute a wealth of interesting material in Charles Edward Russell, *Bare Hands and Stone Walls* (1933), and Lincoln Steffens, *Autobiography of Lincoln Steffens* (2 vols., 1931).

A general discussion of the social unrest leading to reform legislation is that by H. U. Faulkner, *The Quest for Social Justice* (1931), Vol. XI in the History of American Life Series.

Special industries may be studied in Ida M. Tarbell, *History of the Standard Oil Company* (2 vols., 1904), a pioneer work based on firsthand research; in G. H. Montague, *Rise and Progress of the Standard Oil Company* (1903), a defense of the oil monopoly; in H. R. Mussey, *Combination in the Mining Industry* (1905); in Abraham Berglund, *The United States Steel Corporation* (1907), Columbia University Studies in History, Economics and Public Law, Vol. XVIII, No. 3; in H. L. Wilgus, *A Study of the United States Steel Corporation* (1901); in Arundel Cotter, *The United States Steel—A Corporation with a Soul* (1921); in the *Report of the Commissioner of Corporations on the Steel Industry* (3 parts, 1911); and in Eliot Jones, *The Anthracite Coal Combination,* Harvard Economic Studies, Vol. II (1914). See also *Report to the President on the Anthracite Coal Strike of May–October, 1902,* by the Anthracite Coal Strike Commission, Bulletin of the Department of Labor, No. 46 (1903), especially Appendix J; and *Report of the United States Coal Commission Transmitted Pursuant to the Act Approved Sept. 22, 1922* (1925).

Most of the biographies of the industrial giants of the period are "official," and not always objective. These include J. W. Jenkins, *J. W. Duke, Master Builder* (1927); I. M. Tarbell, *The Life of Elbert H. Gary* (1925); B. J. Hendrick, *Life of Andrew Carnegie* (2 vols., 1932); George Harvey, *Henry Clay Frick, the Man* (1928); and Carl Hovey, *The Life of J. Pierpont Morgan* (1912). Critical but based on sound research are the much more satisfactory Lewis Corey, *The House of Morgan* (1930); F. L. Allen, *The Great Pierpont Morgan* (1949); J. T. Flynn, *God's Gold* (1931), on Rockefeller; Harvey O'Connor, *Mellon's Millions* (1933); and Matthew Josephson, *Robber Barons: The Great American Capitalists, 1861–1901* (1934). Allan Nevins, *John D. Rockefeller: The Heroic Age of American Business* (2 vols., 1940), is a detailed and fair study, as is his subsequent book on Rockefeller, *Study in Power* (2 vols., 1953). Useful also is Gustave Myers, *History of Great American Fortunes* (3 vols., 1910). F. L. Allen, *Lords of Creation* (1935), presents the story of consolidation in popular form.

On the "money trust" see the report of the Pujo Committee; John Moody, *Masters of Capital;* Berle and Means, *Modern Corporation and Private Property,* all three cited above; and L. P. Brandeis, *Other People's Money* (1914).

22. The Labor Movement to 1914

Among the briefer histories of the labor movement published since 1920 are G. S. Watkins, *An Introduction to the Study of Labor Problems* (1922); Selig Perlman, *A History of Trade Unionism in the United States* (1922); N. J. Ware, *The Labor Movement in the United States* (1929), covering the period from 1860 to 1895 and dealing chiefly with the Knights of Labor; Leo Wolman, *Growth of American Trade Unions 1880–1923* (1924), and his *Ebb and Flow in Trade Unionism* (1936); Malcom Kier, *Labor's Search for More* (1937); M. S. Clark and

S. F. Simon, *The Labor Movement in America* (1938); Herbert Harris, *American Labor* (1939); F. R. Dulles, *Labor in America* (1949); and Mark Starr and H. U. Faulkner, *Labor in America* (rev. ed., 1949). The most detailed account is that by J. R. Commons *et al., History of Labour in the United States* (2 vols., 1918). This has recently been continued in *History of Labor in the United States, 1896–1932* (2 vols., 1933–1935), of which the first volume, by D. D. Lescohier and Elizabeth Brandeis, covers labor conditions and employer policies, and the second, by Selig Perlman and Philip Taft, covers labor movements. A recent excellent general textbook is C. R. Daugherty, *Labor Problems in American Industry* (6th ed., 1952). L. L. Lorwin, *The American Federation of Labor* (1933), is the first adequate effort to deal with that organization. For the Negro, see C. H. Wesley, *Negro Labor in the United States* (1927).

For the official attitude of the American Federation of Labor, see D. J. Saposs, *Readings in Trade Unionism* (1925). Carroll D. Wright, "Historical Sketch of the Knights of Labor," *Quarterly Journal of Economics,* pp. 127–168 (Jan., 1887), is an excellent contemporary account of that movement. A more recent account is the Ware volume cited above and Powderly's autobiography, *The Path I Trod,* edited by H. J. Carman, Henry David, and P. N. Guthrie (1940). The best of the histories and interpretations by labor leaders are those of T. V. Powderly, *Thirty Years of Labor, 1859–1889* (1890), by the Grand Master of the Knights of Labor and particularly interesting on that organization ; G. E. McNeill (ed.), *The Labor Movement, the Problem of Today* (1887), by one of the earliest state labor officials; and John Mitchell, *Organized Labor* (1903), by the one-time president of the United Mine Workers of America. No study of American labor would be complete without reading Samuel Gompers, *Seventy Years of Life and Labor: An Autobiography* (2 vols., 1925). The best biography of Gompers is R. H. Harvey, *Samuel Gompers, Champion of the Toiling Masses* (1935). An interesting episode is described in D. L. McMurry, *Coxey's Army* (1929).

There are numerous studies by experts, many of whom have received their inspiration from the researches and training of J. R. Commons. Among the best are J. R. Commons, *Trade Unionism and Labor Problems,* First Series (1905) and Second Series (1921), collections of readings; J. R. Commons, *Labor and Administration* (1913); J. R. Commons and J. B. Andrews, *Principles of Labor Legislation* (4th ed., 1936); W. Jett Lauck and Edgar Sydenstricker, *Conditions of Labor in American Industries* (1917); D. D. Lescohier, *The Labor Market* (1919); and Hayes Robins, *The Labor Movement and the Farmer* (1922). W. B. Catlin, *The Labor Problem in the United States and Great Britain* (1926), is a scholarly interpretation. Also of value is Florence Peterson, *Survey of Labor Economics* (1947). Important also are F. Frankfurter and N. Greene, *The Labor Injunction* (1930); Edward Berman, *Labor and the Sherman Act* (1930); and N. J. Ware, *The Boycott in American Trade Unions,* Johns Hopkins Studies, Series 34, No. 1 (1916). A standard volume on wages is P. H. Douglas, *Real Wages in the United States* (1930). See also U.S. Bureau of Labor Statistics, *History of Wages in the United States from Colonial Times to 1928* (1929), and Paul F. Brissenden,

Earnings of Factory Workers, 1899 to 1927: An Analysis of Payroll Statistics, Dept. of Commerce, Bureau of Census, Census Monograph X (1929). An interesting study by an industry lawyer is W. G. Merritt, *Destination Unknown* (1951).

On the labor of women and children, there is now a large amount of material. Pioneer government work was done in the *Report on Condition of Woman and Child Wage-Earners in the United States* (19 vols., 1910–1912), published by the United States Department of Labor, 61st Cong., 2nd Sess., Senate Documents, Vols. 86–104, and subsequent reports by the Women's Bureau and Children's Bureau of the Department of Labor. Other studies include Adelaide M. Anderson, *Women in the Factory* (1922), and J. A. Hill, *Women in Gainful Occupations, 1870–1920,* Census Monograph IX (1929).

On the more radical developments, the books of P. F. Brissenden, *The I.W.W., a Study of American Syndicalism,* Columbia University Studies, Vol. LXXXIII (1919), and J. G. Brooks, *American Syndicalism: The I.W.W.* (1913), the latter emphasizing the philosophy of the movement and its international aspect, will be found valuable. The Brissenden book has now been supplemented and continued by J. S. Gambs, *The Decline of the I.W.W.* (1932). Carleton H. Parker, *The Casual Laborer and Other Essays* (1920), and John Spargo, *Syndicalism, Industrial Unionism and Socialism* (1913), are illuminating. For some radical developments, see George Soule, *The New Unionism in the Clothing Industry* (1920); D. J. Saposs, *Left Wing Unionism* (1920); Anthony Bimba, *The Molly McGuires* (1932); and Nathan Fine, *Labor and Farmer Parties in the United States 1828–1928* (1928). J. A. Fitch, *The Causes of Industrial Unrest* (1924), is a sane study of the psychological background. Henry David, *The Haymarket Riot* (1936), is a detailed study of that episode. P. S. Foner, *History of the Labor Movement in the United States* (1947), is a left-wing interpretation.

The immigration problem may be studied in J. R. Commons, *Races and Immigrants in America* (1907), an excellent early survey; J. W. Jenks and W. J. Lauck, *The Immigration Problem* (1917), a scholarly presentation summarizing the findings of the Immigration Commission; I. A. Hourwich, *Immigration and Labor* (1922); John P. Gavit, *Americans by Choice* (1922); F. J. Warne, *The Tide of Immigration* (1916); Grace Abbott, *The Immigrant and the Community* (1917); National Industrial Conference Board, Inc., *Immigration Problems in the United States* (1923); and two collections of source materials by Edith Abbott. For statistics, see the Report of the Immigration Commission, containing *Statistical Review of Immigration, 1820–1910,* and *Distribution of Immigrants, 1850–1900,* 61st Cong., 3rd Sess., Senate Document No. 756, Vol. XX (1911). Two excellent summaries are G. M. Stephenson, *History of American Immigration, 1820–1924* (1926), and R. L. Garis, *Immigration Restriction* (1927).

Three significant reports on specific strikes are the *Report to the President on the Anthracite Coal Strike of May–October, 1902,* by the Anthracite Coal Commission (1903); *Report of Strike of Textile Workers in Lawrence, Massachusetts* (1912), 62nd Cong., 2nd Sess., No. 870; *Report of the Steel Strike of 1919* by the Commission of Inquiry of the Interchurch World Movement.

The number of studies of specific unions is rapidly growing. For coal mining there is Arthur Elliott, *Coal Miners' Struggle for Industrial Status* (1926), and McAlister Coleman, *Men and Coal* (1943), the latter written with spirit and understanding. On the I.L.G.W.U. the standard of the work is high: Louis Levine, *The Women's Garment Workers: A History of the International Ladies' Garment Workers Union* (1924), and Benjamin Stolberg, *Tailor's Progress: The Story of a Famous Union and the Men Who Made It* (1944). Rose Pesotta, *Bread upon the Waters* (1944), is the story of a worker, officer, and organizer in that union. The fine volume by Joel Seidman, *The Needle Trades* (1942), tells the story of both the I.L.G.W.U. and the Amalgamated Clothing Workers (men's clothing). C. H. Green, *The Headwear Workers: A Century of Trade Unionism* (1944), is the history of the United Hatters, Cap and Millinery Workers International Union. Other union histories include H. J. Lahne, *The Cotton Mill Worker* (1944); Jacob Loft, *The Printing Trades* (1944); H. S. Roberts, *The Rubber Workers* (1944); Herman Schulter, *The Brewing Industry and the Brewery Workers' Movement in America* (1910); E. C. Robbins, *Railway Conductors* (1914); B. R. Brazeal, *The Brotherhood of Sleeping Car Porters* (1946); V. H Jensen, *Lumber and Labor* (1945); and Stuart Jamieson, *Labor Unionism in American Agriculture* (1945), which synthesizes much of the work done on agricultural labor (U.S. Dept. of Labor, Bureau of Labor Statistics Bulletin No. 836).

The position of Negroes in the labor movement may be studied in C. H. Wesley, *Negro Labor in the United States* (1927); in his "Organized Labor and the Negro," *Journal of Negro Education* (July, 1939); in H. R. Clayton and G. F. Mitchell, *Black Workers and the New Unions* (1939), and in the Brazeal volume just noted.

On farm labor see also Harry Schwartz, *Seasonal Farm Labor in the United States* (1945), and Lawanda F. Cox, "The American Agricultural Wage Earner," *Agricultural History,* XXII, 95–114 (April, 1948).

23. *Transportation and Communication, 1860–1914*

In addition to the various railroad magazines, Hunt's *Merchant's Magazine,* 1835–1870, and the *Commercial and Financial Chronicle* since 1870 will be found useful; also the yearly reports of the Interstate Commerce Commission. Short résumés are E. R. Johnson and T. W. Van Metre, *Principles of Railway Transportation* (1922); C. F. Adams, Jr., *Railroads: Their Origin and Problems* (1878; rev. ed., 1893); A. T. Hadley, *Railroad Transportation* (1886); F. L. McVey, *Railway Transportation* (1921); I. L. Sharpman, *The American Railroad Problem* (1921); Eliot Jones, *Principles of Railway Transportation* (1924); and Slason Thompson, *History of American Railways* (1925). Exceedingly valuable are the standard studies by W. Z. Ripley, *Railroads, Rates and Regulations* (1912) and *Railroads; Finance and Organizations* (1915). For the reconstruction period in the South, see Carl Russell Fish, *The Restoration of the Southern Railroads* (1919), in University of Wisconsin Studies in the Social Sciences and History, No. 2.

On special phases, consult L. H. Haney, *A Congressional History of Railroads in the United States, 1850–1887* (1910); S. J. Buck, *The Granger Movement* (1913) and the *Agrarian Crusade* (1920), in Chronicles of America; F. Cleveland and F. W. Powell, *Railroad Promotion and Capitalization* (1909); W. F. Gephart, *Transportation and Industrial Development in the Middle West,* Columbia University Studies (1909); M. B. Hammond, *Railway Rate Theories of the Interstate Commerce Commission* (1911); Leonor F. Loree, *Railroad Freight Transportation* (1922); Frank H. Dixon, *Railroads and Government; Their Relations in the United States, 1910–1921* (1922); W. J. Cunningham, *American Railroads: Government Control and Reconstruction* (1922); and I. L. Sharfman, *The Interstate Commerce Commission* (5 vols., 1931–1937). Two excellent discussions of general problems are D. P. Locklin, *Economics of Transportation* (rev. ed., 1938), and Stuart Daggett, *Principles of Inland Transportation* (rev. ed., 1941). The most important recent book is Harold Barger, *The Transportation Industries 1889–1946, a Study of Output, Employment and Productivity* (1951).

The history of certain of the specific railroads has been written—e.g., H. S. Mott, *Story of the Erie* (1900); C. F. Adams, *Chapters of Erie* (1886); F. C. Hicks, *High Finance in the Sixties* (1929), chapters on the early history of the Erie; and Edward Hungerford, *Men of Erie: A Story of Human Effort* (1946), which adds later history to the earlier volumes. Other studies include Grenville Dodge, "How We Built the Union Pacific," *Senate Doc. 447, 61st Cong., 2nd Sess.;* Nelson Trottman, *History of the Union Pacific* (1923); E. V. Smalley, *History of the Northern Pacific* (1883); Stuart Daggett, *Chapters in the History of the Southern Pacific* (1922); Edward Hungerford, *The Story of the Baltimore and Ohio Railroad 1827–1928* (2 vols., 1928); Milton Reizenstein, *The Economic History of the Baltimore and Ohio Railroad, 1827–1853* (1897); F. W. Stevens, *The Beginnings of the New York Central Railroad* (1926); S. M. Derrick, *Centennial History of the South Carolina Railroad* (1930); F. B. C. Bradlee, *The Boston and Maine Railroad* (1921); H. W. Shotter, *The Growth and Development of the Pennsylvania Railroad Company* (1927) and L. F. Lorce, *A Century of Progress, History of the Delaware and Hudson Company* (1925). R. E. Riegel, *Story of Western Railroads* (1926), is a condensed account of the trans-Mississippi railroads, and J. I. Bogan, *The Anthracite Railroads* (1927), provides a similar treatment for the railroads serving northeastern Pennsylvania. Two recent studies of New England railroads are A. F. Harlow, *Steelways of New England* (1945), and E. C. Kirkland, *Men, Cities and Transportation* (2 vols., 1948). Biographies which throw much light on early railroad building are H. G. Pearson, *An American Railroad Builder* (1911), relating the career of J. M. Forbes; E. P. Oberholtzer, *Jay Cooke, Financier of the Civil War* (2 vols., 1907); H. M. Larson, *Jay Cooke, Private Banker* (1936); J. G. Pyle, *Life of J. J. Hill* (2 vols., 1917); George Kennan, *E. H. Harriman* (2 vols., 1922); J. B. Hedges, *Henry Villard and the Railways of the Northwest* (1930); and the *Memoirs of Henry Villard* (2 vols., 1904). John Moody, *The Railway Builders* (1919), Chronicles of America, is chiefly biographical. A. D. Turnbull, *John Stevens: An American Record* (1928), deals with an important railroad pioneer.

Two legislative reports giving insight into early abuses are those of the "Hepburn Committee," New York State Assembly Document No. 38 (1880), and of the "Cullom Committee," Senate Reports, 49th Cong., 1st Sess., Serial Number 2356 (2 vols.). See also the *Report of the Industrial Commission on Transportation* (1902).

On waterways, consult the bibliography for Chapter 14. H. J. Moulton, *Waterways vs. Railways* (1912) and *American Transportation Problems,* chaps. 21–22, defend the economic advantages of railroads as against internal waterways. A. F. Harlow, *Old Towpaths* (1926), writes interestingly of the decline of canal transportation; Mildred H. Hartsough, *From Canoe to Steel Barge on the Upper Mississippi* (1934), traces transportation changes on the Mississippi; and N. E. Whitford, *History of the Barge Canal of New York State* (1922), tells of the revival of one early system. The history and problems of the Panama Canal are adequately handled in D. C. Miner, *The Fight for the Panama Route* (1940), and N. J. Pendleford, *The Panama Canal in Peace and War* (1942).

Three excellent books on the history of the automobile are R. C. Epstein, *The Automobile Industry* (1928), which emphasizes the financial aspect; E. D. Kennedy, *The Automobile Industry* (1941), which covers many phases; and L. H. Seltzer, *A Financial History of the Automobile Industry* (1928). The history of the better-road movement is given in C. L. Dearing, *American Highway Problems* (1941). Keith Sward, *The Legend of Henry Ford* (1948), is the best study of Ford and Garet Garrett, *The Wild Wheel* (1952), an excellent interpretation.

Perhaps the best study on the recent history of highways is the joint report by the U.S. Bureau of Public Roads, U.S. Dept. of Agriculture and the Conn. State Highways Dept., *Report of a Survey of Transportation of the State Highway System of Connecticut* (1926). Mark Sullivan, *Our Times,* Vol. II, has a popular but excellent account of the early development of automobiles and airplanes in the United States. A popular history of the express business has been done by A. F. Harlow, *Old Waybills* (1934).

Street railways may be studied in chap. 6 of Stuart Daggett, *Principles of Inland Transportation* (rev. ed., 1934); in D. F. Wilcox, *Analysis of the Electric Railway Problem* (1921); and in E. S. Mason, *The Street Railways in Massachusetts* (1932). A popular but valuable account is J. A. Miller, *Fares, Please* (1941).

On aviation, C. E. Puffer, *Air Transportation* (1941), is outstanding. Also adequate on its phase is J. H. Frederick, *Commercial Air Transportation* (1942). Popular accounts of the early years are Eric Hodgins and F. A. Magoun, *Sky High* (1935), and H. L. Smith, *Airways* (1941).

An early history of the telephone is H. N. Casson, *History of the Telephone* (1910). T. A. Watson, *The Birth and Babyhood of the Telephone* (1926), is an account of the early years written by Bell's assistant. M. R. Danilian, *A. T. & T.* (1939), is exhaustive and critical. A. W. Page, *The Bell Telephone System* (1941), is a description of the operation and problems by a vice president of the A. T. & T. Horace Coon, *American Tel & Tel* (1939), is an interesting appraisal.

For the history and organization of the postal system, see D. C. Roper, *The United States Post Office* (1907), by a one-time First Assistant Postmaster-General, and A. F. Harlow, *Old Post Bags* (1928). See also K. M. Moon and J. Phillips, *John A. Moon, Father of the Parcel Post* (1941). On telegraph history R. L. Thompson, *Wiring a Continent* (1947), is excellent up to 1866. After that the bibliography is meager. See A. F. Harlow, *Old Wires and New Waves: The History of the Telegraph, Telephone and Wireless* (1936); James D. Reid, *The Telegraph in America* (1886); Federal Communications Commission, "Corporate History of the Western Union Telegraph Company," 73 Cong., 2nd Sess., House Report No. 1273, Part III, No. 4 (1935); and H. H. Goldin, "Governmental Policy and the Domestic Telegraph Industry," *Journal of Economic History*, VII, 53–68 (May, 1947).

24. *Financial History Since 1860*

The *Annual Report on the Finances* by the Secretary of the Treasury forms an essential part of the material for detailed study of federal finances. Special reports of value include that of the Special Commissioner of the Revenue, 1869, giving the results of David A. Wells's investigation of the money cost of the Civil War; the *National Monetary Commission Report* (1908–1910); and the "Money Trust Investigation" (Pujo Committee), 1912–1913.

Besides the textbooks on financial history of Dewey, and Schultz and Caine, the student is referred to two other books, each of which provides a valuable synthesis of finance and business trends: G. W. Edwards, *The Evolution of Finance Capital* (1938), and F. C. Mills, *Economic Tendencies in the United States* (1932). Other volumes useful for various phases of the subject are A. B. Hepburn, *History of Coinage and Currency in the United States* (rev. ed., 1915); A. D. Noyes, *Forty Years of American Finance* (1909), and the continuation, *The War Period in American Finance, 1908–1925* (1926).

On the struggle for the gold standard, see W. C. Mitchell, *A History of the Greenbacks* (1903), which contains useful tables; J. Laurence Laughlin, *History of Bimetallism in the United States* (4th ed., 1897); and Don C. Barrett, *The Greenbacks and Resumption of Specie Payments, 1862–1879* (1931). On a special phase, see Neil Crothers, *Fractional Money* (1930).

Of the general textbooks on money and banking the following are excellent: C. F. Dunbar, *Theory and History of Banking* (5th ed., 1916); J. T. Holdsworth, *Money and Banking* (3rd ed., 1921); H. P. Willis and G. R. Edwards, *Banking and Business* (rev. ed., 1925), and F. A. Bradford, *Money and Banking* (1935).

On the Federal Reserve system, consult W. Kemmerer, *The A B C of the Federal Reserve System* (11th ed., 1938); H. Parker Willis, *The Federal Reserve System* (1923), by an expert influential in its plan and organization; H. P. Willis and W. H. Steiner, *Federal Reserve Banking Practice* (1926); P. M. Warburg, *The Federal Reserve System* (2 vols., 1930), a history and criticism; S. E. Harris, *Twenty Years of the Federal Reserve Policy* (2 vols., 1933), exhaustive on this phase; J. L. Laughlin, *The Federal Reserve Act, Its Origins and Problems* (1933), best on the history of the act; W. O. Weyforth, *The Federal Reserve Board* (1933); C. O. Hardy, *Credit Policies of the Federal Reserve System* (1932); and C. S. Tibbetts, *State Banks and the Federal Reserve System* (1929). Special topics on banking are adequately developed in A. M. Davis, *The Origins of the National Banking System* (National Monetary Commission Report, 1910); G. C. Barnett, *State Banks and Trust Companies Since the Passage of the National Banking Act* (1911); L. C. Helderman, *National and State Banks, a Study of Their Origins* (1931); and J. C. Smith, *The Development of Trust Companies in the United States* (1927). Serious study of the American banking situation would necessitate an examination of the work of both the Pujo Committee and the National Monetary Commission (Aldrich Commission).

On commercial crises and business depressions much has recently been written: O. M. W. Sprague, *History of Crises Under the National Banking System,* Senate Document No. 538, 61st Cong., 2nd Sess. (1910); Alvin H. Hansen, *Cycles of Prosperity and Depression, 1902–1908* (1921), University of Wisconsin Studies in the Social Sciences and History, No. 5; W. C. Schluter, *Economic Cycles and Crises* (1933); Hudson B. Hastings, *Cost and Profits: Their Relation to Business Cycles* (1923), Pollak Foundation for Economic Research, No. 3; J. A. Schumpeter, *Business Cycles* (2 vols., 1939); W. C. Mitchell, *Business Cycles* (1913), Memoirs of the University of California, Vol. III; Warren M. Persons, *Forecasting Business Cycles* (1931); Thorstein B. Veblen, *Theory of Business Enterprise* (1904); National Bureau of Economic Research, Inc., *Business Cycles and Unemployment* (1923), pp. xxvii–xl, and 1–405 in Conference on Unemployment (Washington, 1921); Report of Joint Commission of Agricultural Inquiry, *The Agricultural Crisis and Its Causes* (1921), House of Rep., 67th Cong., 1st Sess., Report No. 408; and W. C. Shluter, *The Pre-War Business Cycle, 1907–1914* (1923). An outline of general conditions is given in W. L. Thorp, *Business Annals* (1926). Also valuable is A. F. Burns, *Production Trends in the United States Since 1870* (1934), and M. G. Myers, *The New York Money Market* (1931).

Much of interest is contained in the autobiographies of two men who were in the thick of the currency controversies of the period: Hugh McCulloch, *Men and Measures of Half a Century* (1889), by a Secretary of the Treasury who served under Lincoln, Johnson, and Arthur; and John S. Sherman, *Recollections of Forty Years* (1895), by Hayes's Secretary of the Treasury. Allan Nevins, *Grover Cleveland, A Study in Courage* (1932), is the best study of Cleveland. A racy account of a leading banker of the period is J. K. Winkler, *The First Billion, The Stillmans and the National City Bank* (1933). On the leading financier of these years, Carl Hovey, *The Life of J. Pierpont Morgan* (1912), is conventional, and Lewis Corey, *The House of Morgan* (1930), is critical. Much of interest is in Henry Clews, *Fifty Years in Wall Street* (1908).

Since the life insurance companies became an increasingly important source of investment funds, their history should be examined. Fortunately, the bibliography is rapidly expanding. The best of the recent studies are L. I. Dublin, *A Family of Thirty Million. The Story of the Metropolitan Life Insurance Company* (1943);

Shepard B. Clough, *A Century of American Life Insurance: A History of the Mutual Life Insurance Company of New York, 1843–1943* (1946); and Marquis James, *The Metropolitan Life: A Study in Business Growth* (1947).

25. Domestic and Foreign Commerce

The chief sources for this subject are the various publications of the Department of Commerce. The best study of distribution costs is the work of the Twentieth Century Fund, Inc., *Does Distribution Cost Too Much?* (1939). Two helpful textbooks on marketing are L. D. H. Weld, *The Marketing of Farm Products* (1919), and C. S. Duncan, *Marketing, Its Problems and Methods* (1921). On specific problems dealt with in this chapter, see E. R. A. Seligman, *The Economics of Installment Buying* (2 vols., 1927); W. S. Hayward and Percival White, *Chain Stores, Their Management and Operation* (1925); Frank Presbrey, *The History and Development of Advertising* (1929); R. M. Hower, *The History of an Advertising Agency: N. W. Ayer and Son at Work, 1869–1949* (1949); F. E. Melder, *State and Local Barriers to Interstate Commerce in the United States* (1937); G. R. Taylor, E. L. Bertis, and F. V. Waugh, *Barriers to Internal Trade in Farm Products,* Department of Agriculture (1939); and D. H. Jacobson, *Our Interests as Consumers* (1941). T. D. Clark, *Pills, Petticoats and Plows: The Southern Country Stores* (1944), gives a good picture of rural retailing; R. M. Howes, *History of Macy's of New York, 1858–1919* (1943), does the same thing for urban retailing.

To the bibliography given under Chapter 12 should be added J. H. Frederick, *Development of American Commerce* (1932), a brief but serviceable textbook; Julius Klein, *Frontiers of Trade* (1929), a product of the optimistic twenties; W. S. Culbertson, *Commercial Policy in War Time and After* (1919) and *International Economic Policies* (1925); Ethel Dietrich, *World Trade* (1939); and P. V. Horn, *International Trade* (rev. ed., 1945).

Besides the general books on the American merchant marine listed under Chapter 12, see R. Meeker, *History of Ship Subsidies* (1905); J. E. Sangstad, *Shipping and Shipbuilding Subsidies,* Trade Promotion Series No. 129, Bureau of Domestic and Foreign Commerce (1932); L. W. Maxwell, *Discriminatory Duties and the American Merchant Marine* (1926); P. M. Zeis, *American Shipping Policy* (1938); and J. G. B. Hutchins, *The American Maritime Industries and Public Policy, 1789–1914* (1941).

On the tariff, consult Ashley, Stanwood, and Taussig. Also see C. W. Wright, *Wool Growing and the Tariff; a Study in the Economic History of the United States* (1910), Harvard Economics Studies, Vol. V. On the Fordney-McCumber tariff, see F. W. Taussig, "The Tariff Act of 1922," and A. H. Cole, "The Textile Schedules in the Tariff of 1922," both articles in the *Quarterly Journal of Economics,* Vol. XXXVII, No. 1 (Nov., 1922); and W. S. Culbertson, "The Making of Tariffs," in *Yale Review* (Jan., 1923). On the Hawley-Smoot bill, see F. W. Taussig, "The Tariff Act of 1930," *Quarterly Journal of Economics,* XLV, 1–21 (Nov., 1930). An excellent symposium covering the many aspects of the subject is

"Tariff Problems of the United States," *Annals of the American Academy of Political and Social Science,* Vol. CXLI (Jan., 1929).

26. Economic Imperialism

For background, the diplomatic histories of Latané and Wainhouse, of Sears, of Bemis, or of Bailey will be found satisfactory.

The best general survey of the movement of capital in and out of the United States is Cleona Lewis, *America's Stake in International Investments* (1938). Particularly useful are the annual reports (beginning in 1923) of the Department of Commerce on "The Balance of International Payments of the United States." Other useful volumes on economic imperialism are B. H. Williams, *Economic Foreign Policy of the United States* (1929); Achille Villate, *Economic Imperialism and International Relations During the Last Fifty Years* (1923); L. H. Jenks, *Migration of British Capital to 1875* (1927); and Herbert Feis, *Europe the World's Banker 1870–1914* (1930). An important study is C. T. Bullock, J. H. Williams, and R. S. Tucker, "The Balance of Trade of the United States," *The Review of Economic Statistics,* Vol. I (1919). Other studies of various economic phases appear in the following: F. M. Halsey, *Investments in Latin America and the British West Indies,* Department of Commerce Special Agent Series, No. 169 (1918); Francis W. Hirst and George Paish, *The Credit of Nations and the Trade Balance of the United States* (1910), National Monetary Commission Publications, No. 2, Senate Doc. No. 579. Of particular reference to American imperialism is Scott Nearing and Joseph Freeman, *Dollar Diplomacy* (1925), highly critical, which should be supplemented by R. W. Dunn, *American Foreign Investments* (1929); Max Winkler, *Investments of United States Capital in Latin America* (World Peace Foundation, 1929), and his *Foreign Bonds, an Autopsy* (1933); and C. F. Remer, *Foreign Investments in China* (1933). J. F. Rippy, *Latin America and the Industrial Age* (1944), is an excellent introduction to the subject of Latin-American economic relations with the outside world.

Valuable material can be found in biographical studies of those who played a leading part in the drama of expanding imperialism: C. S. Olcott, *William McKinley* (2 vols., 1916); H. F. Pringle, *Theodore Roosevelt* (1931); *Theodore Roosevelt, an Autobiography* (1913); H. F. Pringle, *The Life and Times of William Howard Taft* (2 vols., 1939); R. S. Baker, *Life and Letters of Woodrow Wilson* (8 vols., 1927–1939); H. C. Hill, *Roosevelt and the Caribbean* (1927); Tyler Dennett, *John Hay* (1933); and J. C. Jessup, *Elihu Root* (2 vols., 1938). Strong arguments against imperialism are presented in G. F. Hoar, *Autobiography of Seventy Years* (1913). The reminiscences of a bitter anti-imperialist Senator, interesting and containing information not easily available, are given in R. F. Pettigrew, *The Course of Empire* (1920). F. H. Harrington, "The Anti-Imperialist Movement in the United States, 1898–1900," *Mississippi Valley Historical Review,* XXII, 211–223 (Sept., 1935), describes the opposition to expansion.

The material on Latin America has become voluminous. Good general books include D. G. Munro, *The Latin American Republics: A History* (1942); C. L.

Jones, *The Caribbean Interests of the United States* (1916) and *Caribbean Backgrounds and Prospects* (1931); G. H. Stuart, *Latin America and the United States* (4th ed., 1943), an excellent study. A result of the latest scholarly research on the economic background of the Spanish-American War is J. W. Pratt, *Expansionists of 1898* (1936). Walter Millis, *The Martial Spirit: A Study of Our War with Spain* (1931), is the best one-volume account. S. F. Bemis, *The Latin American Policy of the United States* (1943), is a defense of our policy in that area.

On Cuba, Leland H. Jenks, *Our Cuban Colony: A Study in Sugar* (1928), is the best single volume as far as it carries the story. Harry F. Guggenheim, *The United States and Cuba* (1934), is a defense of the American domination by the Ambassador of the United States during a part of the Machado regime. The most valuable economic survey in the 1930's is Foreign Policy Association, *Problems of the New Cuba* (1935). D. A. Lockmiller, *Magoon in Cuba: A History of the Second Intervention, 1906–1909* (1938), defends the Magoon administration. On Puerto Rico, B. W. and J. W. Diffie, *Porto Rico: A Broken Pledge* (1931), is extremely critical of American occupation. Victor A. Clark *et al., Porto Rico and Its Problems* (1930), is a scientific and intelligent survey. Also valuable is A. D. Gayer, P. T. Homan, and E. K. James, *The Sugar Economy of Puerto Rico* (1938). R. G. Tugwell, *The Stricken Land* (1947), is a survey of political and economic conditions by a New Deal governor. On the Virgin Islands, see L. K. Zabriskie, *The Virgin Islands of the United States of America* (1918), and C. C. Tansill, *The Purchase of the Danish West Indies* (1932).

American penetration in specific areas is covered in the following books. On Santo Domingo and Haiti the best single volume is M. M. Knight, *The Americans in Santo Domingo* (1928). See also U. S. Senate Select Committee, *Inquiry into Occupation and Administration of Haiti and Santo Domingo* (67th Cong., 1922); Carl Kelsey, "American Intervention in Haiti and Santo Domingo," *Annals of the American Academy of Political and Social Science,* C, 109–202; "American Occupation of Haiti," *Foreign Policy Reports,* Vol. V, Nos. 19–20 (1919); and A. C. Millspaugh, *Haiti Under American Control, 1915–1930* (World Peace Foundation, 1931). On Central America, see Carleton Beals, *Banana Gold* (1932); C. D. Kepner and J. H. Soothill, *The Banana Empire* (1935); and C. D. Kepner, *Social Aspects of the Banana Industry* (1936).

The story of Panama from various angles is discussed in the following: Philippe Bunau-Varilla, *Panama, Its Creation, Destruction and Resurrection* (1913), by the arch-conspirator of the affair; E. R. Johnson, *The Panama Canal and Commerce* (1916); M. W. Williams, *Anglo-American Isthmian Diplomacy, 1815–1915* (1916); J. F. Rippy, *The Capitalists and Colombia* (1931); and D. C. Miner, *The Fight for the Panama Route* (1940). W. L. McCain, *The United States and the Republic of Panama* (1937), tells a full story of our relations with that country.

To understand the relations between the United States and Mexico it is necessary to comprehend the Mexican scene. Two books showing a real understanding of Mexican civilization and tradition are Carleton Beals, *Mexican Maze* (1931), and Ernest Gruening, *Mexico and Its Heritage* (1928). American relations with Mexico are adequately handled in C. W. Hackett, *Mexican Revolution and the United States, 1910–1926* (World Peace Foundation, 1926), and J. F. Rippy, *The United States and Mexico* (rev. ed., 1931).

Among the best books on the Philippines are D. C. Worcester, *The Philippines Past and Present* (2 vols., 1914); C. B. Elliott, *The Philippines* (2 vols., 1917); F. B. Harrison, *The Corner-stone of Philippine Independence* (1922), by an anti-imperialistic governor-general; J. S. Reyes, *Legislative History of America's Economic Policy Toward the Philippines* (1923); and J. R. Hayden, *The Philippines: A Study in National Development* (1942), the most useful general treatment. Pedro E. Ahelarde, *American Tariff Policy Towards the Philippines* (1947), is an objective study by a native of the Philippines.

On the Far East, Tyler Dennett, *Americans in Eastern Asia* (1922), covers the history to 1901; it should be supplemented with M. J. Bau, *The Open Door Doctrine and Relations to China* (1923), and Tyler Dennett, *John Hay* (1933). P. J. Treat, *Japan and the United States, 1853–1921* (2nd ed., 1928), is an authoritative study. See also the excellent volume by A. W. Griswold, *The Far Eastern Policy of the United States* (1938). Aspects of dollar diplomacy are covered in H. K. Norton, *China and the Powers* (1927); J. W. Overlach, Foreign Financial Control in China (1919); and C. F. Remer, *Foreign Investments in China* (1933). H. D. Croly, *Willard Straight* (1924), is a biography of the agent of the Morgan bankers in China.

27. *America and the First World War*

An effort to present a picture of American life during the decade and a half preceding the First World War is H. U. Faulkner, *The Quest for Social Justice* (1931), and on the economic side, his *The Decline of Laissez Faire* (1951). The rise and decline of progressivism is developed in John Chamberlain, *Farewell to Reform* (1932). C. C. Regier, *The Era of the Muckrakers* (1932), is the best on this episode. See also Louis Filler, *Crusaders for American Liberalism* (1939), for a more complete picture of the reform movement as it functioned in the literature of exposure.

A standard volume on conservation is that of L. Havemeyer (ed.), *Conservation of Natural Resources in the United States* (1930). Other studies are C. G. Gilbert and J. E. Pogue, *America's Power Resources* (1921); Benton MacKaye, *Employment and Natural Resources* (1919), Publications of the Department of Labor; F. L. Lane, *Conservation Through Engineering* (1920), Bulletin 705, Department of the Interior, United States Geological Survey. A wealth of material is to be found in the *Proceedings of the Conference of Governors* (1909); in the *Annals of the American Academy of Political and Social Science,* Vol. XXXIII, No. 3 (1909); and in John Ise, *The United States Forest Policy* (1920). R. M. Robbins, *Our Landed Heritage,* has material on the history of land conservation. Gifford Pinchot, *Breaking New Ground* (1947), is the autobiography of the first professional forester in America and a leader in the conservation movement.

Excellent studies of income have been made by the Staff of the National Bureau of Economic Research, Inc., *Income in the United States, Its Amount and Distribution, 1909–1919*, Vol. I, *Summary* (1921); Vol. II, *Detailed Report* (1922); also their *Distribution of Income by States in 1919*, Publication No. 3 (1922). See also W. I. King, *The Wealth and Income of the People of the United States* (1917); David Friday, *War, Profits and Prices* (1920); Federal Trade Commission, *National Wealth and Income* (1926); and the publications of the Treasury Department on income statistics. Important government investigations are the *Aldrich Report on Prices, Wages, and Transportation*, Senate Document 1394, 52nd Cong., 2nd Sess., March, 1893; *Investigation Relative to Wages and Prices of Commodities*, 61st Cong., 3rd Sess., Senate Document 847 (1911); and the *Report of the Massachusetts Commission on the Cost of Living* (1910). The Department of Labor studies the cost of living and reports regularly in the *Monthly Labor Review*. One of its most indispensable studies is *History of Wages in the United States from Colonial Days to 1928* (1929).

Other important studies on wages and standard of living include Robert Hunter, *Poverty* (1904); John Ryan, *A Living Wage* (1906); R. C. Chapin, *The Standard of Living Among Workingmen's Families in New York City* (1909); F. H. Streightoff, *The Standard of Living Among the Industrial People of America* (1911); Whitney Coombs, *The Wages of Unskilled Labor in the Manufacturing Industries in the United States, 1890–1920* (1926); P. F. Brissenden, *Earnings of Factory Workers 1899–1927*, Census Monograph X (1929); and Paul H. Douglas, *Real Wages in the United States, 1890–1926* (1930). Some of Douglas' conclusions have been challenged by A. H. Hansen in *American Economic Review*, XX, 747–752 (Dec., 1930), and in other numbers. Consult also Leo Wolman, "Consumption and the Standard of Living," *Recent Economic Changes* (1929), I, 13–78, and Morris A. Copeland, "The National Income and Its Distribution," *ibid.*, II, 757–839.

Detailed studies of the war are to be found in the series, "Problems of War and Reconstruction," edited by F. G. Wickwire, and including G. O. Smith, *The Strategy of Minerals* (1919); W. F. Willoughby, *Government Organization in War Time and After* (1919); and E. L. Bogart, *War Costs and Their Financing* (1921). On the American section of the Carnegie series on the *Economic and Social History of the World War* the following volumes are important: W. G. Leland and N. D. Mereness, *Introduction to the American Official Sources for the Economic and Social History of the World War* (1926); W. D. Hines, *War History of American Railroads* (1928); and J. M. Clark, *The Cost of the World War to the American People* (1931). On the cost of the war, in addition to the works of Bogart and of Clark cited above, see J. H. Hollander, *War Borrowing* (1919); E. L. Bogart, *Direct and Indirect Cost of the Great World War* (1919); E. R. A. Seligman, "The Cost of the War and How It Was Met," *American Economic Review*, Vol. IX (Dec., 1919); and especially E. B. Rosa, "Expenditures and Revenues of the Federal Government," in the *Annals of the American Academy of Political and Social Science*, Vol. XCV, No. 184 (May, 1921).

For a brief summary of finance, consult A. D. Noyes, *War Period in American Finance: 1908–1925* (1926). America's participation in the war is told rather fully in B. Crowell and R. F. Wilson, *How America Went to War* (6 vols., 1921). On labor, read Samuel Gompers, *Seventy Years of Life and Labor* (2 vols., 1925), and U.S. Dept. of Labor, Wages and Hours Division, *War Time Policies on Wages, Hours and Other Labor Standards in the United States, 1917–1918* (1942). On transportation, see F. H. Dixon, *Railroads and Government, Their Relations in the United States* (1922). G. B. Clarkson, *Industrial America and the World War* (1923), is an excellent summary. Two recent important studies on special phases are C. O. Hardy, *War Time Control of Prices* (1940), and W. C. Mullendore, *History of the United States Food Administration, 1917–1919* (1941). Extremely valuable is B. M. Baruch, *American Industry in the War* (1941), a reprint of his Report of the War Industries Board and of the Commodity Section submitted to the President on March 3, 1921. Both W. G. McAdoo, Secretary of the Treasury, and D. F. Houston, Secretary of Agriculture, wrote their memoirs.

For the life of the people during wartime read Preston Slosson, *The Great Crusade and After: 1914–1928* (1930), Vol. XII in the History of American Life Series; and Mark Sullivan, *Our Times*, Vol. V (1933). A discussion of the economic background of America's entrance into the war is given in C. Hartley Grattan, *Why We Fought* (1929), and C. C. Tansill, *America Goes to War* (1936). H. C. Syrett, "The Business Press and American Neutrality, 1914–1917," *Mississippi Valley Historical Review*, XXXII, 215–230 (Sept., 1945), finds no proof that American businessmen were eager for war. A good general history of the Wilson administration is F. L. Paxson, *Pre-War Years, 1913–1917* (1936) and *America at War, 1917–1918* (1939).

28. The Great Illusion

Probably the two most important books on American economic life during the decade of the twenties are *Recent Economic Changes* (2 vols., 1927), the report of the Committee on Recent Economic Changes of the President's Conference on Unemployment, and *Recent Social Trends* (2 vols., 1933), the report of the President's Research Committee on Social Trends. The best brief summary is George Soule, *Prosperity Decade from War to Depression, 1917–1929* (1947), Vol. VIII in Rinehart's Economic History of the United States Series. A good survey of the legislative history during the same period is J. C. Malin, *The United States After the World War* (1930). Likewise consult Nathan Fine, *Labor and Farmer Parties in the United States, 1828–1928* (1928). P. W. Slosson, *The Great Crusade and After, 1914–1928* (1930) is a clever integration of postwar social history. F. L. Paxson, *Postwar Years* (1948), attempts an integration of political, economic, and social history of the period 1918–1923. A unique and valuable piece of research is R. S. and H. M. Lynd, *Middletown* (1929.)

Important books on business consolidation include H. R. Seager and C. A. Gulick, Jr., D. M. Keezer and Stacy May, F. A. Fetter, J. L. Bonbright and G. C. Means, H. W. Laidler, A. A. Berle, Jr., and G. C. Means, all cited in the bibliography for Chapter 21, and W. Z. Ripley, *Main Street and Wall Street* (1927). These books should, of course, be supplemented in particular by the reports of the Federal Trade Commission on the Radio Industry, on the Control of Power Companies, etc. Useful also is the National Industrial Conference Board, *Public Regulation of Competitive Practices* (1925), and "The Anti-Trust Laws of the United States," *Annals of the American Academy,* Vol. CXLVII (1930). Two invaluable studies by the Temporary National Economic Committee which reach back into the 1920's are Walton Hamilton, *Antitrust in Action* (1941), and Clair Wilcox, *Competition and Monopoly in American Industry* (1941).

An excellent start in the study of recent transportation is afforded by the chapters in *Recent Economic Changes* and *Recent Social Trends*. These should be followed by H. G. Moulton and associates, *The American Transportation Problem* (1933). Important studies of railroads include W. J. Cunningham, *American Railroads: Government Control and Reconstruction Problems* (1922); F. H. Dixon, *Railroads and Government: Their Relations in the United States* (1922); D. P. Locklin, *Railroad Regulation Since 1920* (1928); H. D. Wolfe, *The Railroad Labor Board* (1927); Rogers McVeagh, *The Transportation Act, 1920* (1923); and W. N. Leonard, *Railroad Consolidation Under the Transportation Act of 1920* (1946). Perhaps the best study in its field is H. G. Moulton, C. G. Morgan, and A. L. Lee, *The St. Lawrence Navigation and Power Project* (1929), a critical appraisal. Enthusiastically favorable is Tom Ireland, *The Great Lakes–St. Lawrence Deep Waterway to the Sea* (1934). On the merchant marine, see National Industrial Conference Board, Inc., *The American Merchant Marine Problem* (1929); American Bureau of Shipping, *The American Merchant Marine;* and the volumes of Maxwell and of Zeis, cited for Chapter 25. On transportation (automobiles, air, highways, and mail) see the books listed for Chapter 23.

Besides the chapter by E. G. Nourse in *Recent Economic Changes,* and the *Yearbook of the Department of Agriculture* for the years after the war, probably J. D. Black, *Agricultural Reform in the United States* (1929), is the most useful on this period. Also useful, particularly as a statistical summary, is Harold Barger and H. H. Landsberg, *American Agriculture, 1899–1939: A Study of Output, Employment and Productivity* (1942). T. W. Shultz, *Agriculture in an Unstable Economy* (1945), gives a general picture of the problems faced by agriculture. An excellent summary with bibliography is C. C. Davis, "The Development of Agricultural Policy Since the End of the World War," *Yearbook of Agriculture, 1940,* pp. 297–326. Valuable also is the symposium, "The Agricultural Situation in the United States" in the *Annals of the American Academy of Political and Social Science,* Vol. CXVII (1925). Other useful books of interpretation and otherwise which should be mentioned include Isaac Lippincott, *What the Farmer Needs* (1928); Wilson Gee, *Place of Agriculture in Our Life* (1930) and *American Farm Policy* (1934); E. R. A. Seligman, *The Economics of Farm Relief* (1929); and the National Industrial Conference Board, *The Agricultural Problem in the United States* (1926).

An invaluable study of organized labor is L. L. Lorwin, *The American Federa-*

tion of Labor (1933). Standard discussions of labor history covering this decade are in Vols. III and IV of J. R. Commons *et al., History of Labour in the United States*. Vol. III, by D. D. Lescohier and Elizabeth Brandeis, deals with working conditions and labor legislation; Vol. IV, by Selig Perlman and Philip Taft, with the general history of labor. Specialized studies particularly pertinent to the twenties include G. James *et al., Profit Sharing and Stock Ownership for Employees* (1926); R. F. Foerster and E. H. Dietel, *Employee Stock Ownership in the United States* (1926); R. W. Dunn, *The Americanization of Labor* (1927); H. W. Laidler and Norman Thomas (eds.), *New Tactics in Social Conflict* (1926); *Report on the Steel Strike of 1919 by the Commission of Inquiry, the Interchurch World Movement* (1920); W. J. Lauck, *Political and Industrial Democracy, 1776–1926* (1926); and Abraham Epstein, *The Problem of Old Age Pensions in Industry* (1926). Exhaustive studies of wages have been made by the National Industrial Conference Board, and by P. H. Douglas, *Real Wages in the United States, 1890–1926* (1930). See also D. J. Ahearn, Jr., *The Wages of Farm and Factory Laborers, 1914–1944* (1945). Valuable for the study of current labor history is the *American Labor Yearbook*, published annually during these years; the *American Federationist*, the official organ of the A. F. of L.; and the *Monthly Labor Review*, published by the Department of Labor of the United States government. For further labor material, see the bibliography for Chapters 15 and 22.

29. *Economic Collapse*

For the economic background of the crash of 1929, the student is referred to the bibliography for the last chapter. Among the books of particular value are *Recent Economic Changes* and *Recent Social Trends*. Others are F. C. Mills, *Economic Tendencies in the United States* (1932); National Industrial Conference Board, *The Banking Situation in the United States* (1933); H. W. Laidler, *Concentration in American Industry* (1931); and A. A. Berle, Jr., and G. C. Means, *The Modern Corporation and Private Property* (1932). The most useful single volume which attempts to integrate the economic history of the pre-depression years is George Soule, *Prosperity Decade* (1947). H. U. Faulkner, *From Versailles to the New Deal* (1950), is a political and economic history in the Chronicles of America.

The most useful study of the causes of the depression of 1920–1921 is a pamphlet prepared by Paul A. Samuelson and Everett E. Hagen for the National Resources Planning Board, *After the War—1918–1920* (1943). On the crash of 1929 perhaps the best single account is F. W. Hirst, *Wall Street and Lombard Street* (1931). Ferdinand Pecora, *Wall Street Under Oath* (1939), is the summary of the revelations obtained by the Senate committee investigating the stock market—United States Senate Committee on Banking and Currency, "Stock Exchange Practices," 72nd Cong., 1st Sess. The depression after 1929 brought new studies and new evaluations of the forces operating in the business cycle. These include J. M. Clark, *Strategic Factors in Business Cycles* (1934); W. C. Schluter, *Economic Cycles and Crises* (1933); J. A. Schumpeter, *Business Cycles* (2 vols., 1933);

W. M. Persons, *Forecasting Business Cycles* (1931); J. M. Keynes, *The General Theory of Employment, Interest and Money* (1936); and A. H. Hansen, *Fiscal Policy and Business Cycles* (1941). A summary of the main theories as they existed in the late twenties is given in W. C. Mitchell's article, "Business Cycles," *Encyclopaedia of the Social Sciences*, III, 92–106.

30. *The New Deal*

The most satisfactory summary of the New Deal is Broadus Mitchell, *Depression Decade* (1947), Vol. IX in the Economic History of the United States Series. It has a full and discriminating bibliography. Basil Rauch, *The History of the New Deal, 1933–1938* (1944), is a brief, straightforward chronological account. Dixon Wecter, *The Age of the Great Depression* (1948), is a social history of the period. Denis Brogan, *The Era of Franklin D. Roosevelt* (1950), is a lively account.

The New Deal theoreticians give their viewpoint in R. G. Tugwell, *The Battle for Democracy* (1935); H. L. Ickes, *The New Democracy* (1934); D. R. Richberg, *The Rainbow* (1936); and A. A. Berle, Jr., and others, *America's Recovery Program* (1934). Those with more conservative economic views criticize the program in such books as William McDonald, *The Menace of Recovery* (1934); D. V. Brown and others, *The Economics of the Recovery Program* (1933); L. P. Ayres, *The Economics of Recovery* (1933); and the Columbia University Commission, *Economic Reconstruction* (1934); more radical criticism may be found in Norman Thomas, *The Choice Before Us* (1934) and *Human Exploitation in the United States* (1934). For a British appraisal, see Editors of the Economist, *The New Deal* (1937). An important appraisal from an ex-New Dealer is Raymond Moley, *After Seven Years* (1939). Any study of sources must include F. D. Roosevelt, *The Public Papers and Addresses of Franklin D. Roosevelt* (5 vols., 1938), edited and collected by Samuel I. Rosenman.

On agriculture, see H. A. Wallace, *America Must Choose* (1934), by the Secretary of Agriculture; Wilson Gee, *American Farm Policy* (1934), a sympathetic description; E. G. Nourse, J. S. Davis, and J. D. Black, *Three Years of the Agricultural Adjustment Administration* (1937), an objective and exhaustive study; S. E. Johnson, *Wheat Under the Agricultural Adjustment Act* (1934); H. I. Richards, *Cotton and the AAA* (1936); D. C. Blaisdell, *Government and Agriculture* (1940); and the annual reports of the Department of Agriculture, particularly that of 1940. A popular presentation of the agricultural problem is Stuart Chase, *Rich Land, Poor Land* (1936). For background see Theodore Saloutos and J. D. Hicks, *Discontent in the Middle West, 1900–1939* (1951).

Excellent on money and banking are Leo Pasvolsky, *Current Monetary Issues* (1933); National Industrial Conference Board, Inc., *The New Monetary System of the United States* (1934); J. I. Bogen and M. Nadler, *The Banking Crises* (1933). Later summaries of monetary policy in this period are A. W. Crawford, *Monetary Management Under the New Deal* (1940); B. G. Johnson, Jr., *The Treasury and Monetary Policy, 1933–1938* (1939); and J. D. Paris, *Monetary*

Policies of the United States, 1932–1938 (1938). On the London Monetary Conference see Moley, cited above, and J. P. Nichols, "Roosevelt's Monetary Diplomacy in 1933," *American Historical Review,* LVI, 295–317 (Jan., 1951).

On the NRA perhaps the most objective is L. S. Lyon *et al., The National Recovery Administration* (1935). See also L. S. Lyon and Victor Abramson, *Government and Economic Life* (2 vols., 1939–40). A vivid description of the career of the NRA by its first administrator is H. S. Johnson, *The Blue Eagle from Egg to Earth* (1935). His successor, Donald Richberg, has also written of it in *The Rainbow* (1936). On the Tennessee Valley experiment see David Lilienthal, *TVA —An Experiment in Democracy* (1944).

For labor, the following are excellent: C. R. Daugherty, *Labor Under the NRA* (1934); Emanuel Stein *et al., Labor and the New Deal* (1934); and G. E. Sokolsky, *Labor's Fight for Power* (1934). The conflict between the A. F. of L. and the C.I.O. is told in Edward Levinson, *Labor on the March* (1938), and J. R. Walsh, *C.I.O., Industrial Unionism in Action* (1937), both sympathetic with the C.I.O. See also R. R. R. Brooks, *Unions of Their Own Choosing* (1939), and Twentieth Century Fund, *Labor and Government* (1935). For the background of the social security legislation, see E. M. Burns, *Toward Social Security* (1936); P. H. Douglas, *Social Security in the United States* (1937); and Maxwell Stewart, *Social Security* (1937). On unemployment and relief: Doris Carothers, *Chronology of the Federal Emergency Relief Administration, May 12, 1933, to December 31, 1935,* WPA Research Monograph VI (1937); T. E. Whiting and T. J. Woofter, Jr., *Summary of Relief and Federal Work Program Statistics 1933– 1940* (1941); WPA Administration, *Five Years of Rural Relief* (1938) and *Urban Workers on Relief* (2 vols., 1936–1937). See also H. L. Ickes, *Back to Work: The Story of PWA* (1935), and U.S. Federal Works Agency, Federal Emergency Relief Administration, *Final Statistical Report* (1942).

Many important articles appeared in the journals, including Bernard Flexner, "The Fight on the Securities Act," *Atlantic Monthly,* CLIII, 232–250 (Feb., 1934); F. A. Southard, Jr., "American Industry Abroad Since 1929," *Journal of Political Economy,* XLI, 530–547 (Aug., 1933); R. B. Westerfield, "The Banking Act of 1933," *ibid.,* pp. 721–749 (Dec., 1933); H. H. Preston and V. W. Bennett, "Agricultral Credit Legislation of 1933," *ibid.,* XLII, 6–33 (Feb., 1934); J. H. Taggart and L. D. Jennings, "The Insurance of Bank Deposits," *ibid.,* pp. 508–516 (Aug., 1934); S. D. Zagoroff, "The External Depreciation of the Dollar and Its Effect upon the Price Level in the United States," *ibid.,* pp. 641–653 (Oct., 1934); R. L. Dewey, "Merchant Marine Act of 1936," *American Economic Review,* XXVII, 239–252 (June, 1937), and his "Transportation Act of 1940," *ibid.,* XXXI, 15–26 (March, 1941).

31. *World Economic Relations*

The annual pamphlets published after 1923 by the Department of Commerce on the *Balance of International Payments of the United States* are invaluable. Also essential is *The United States in the World Economy,* U.S. Dept. of Commerce, Economic Series No. 23 (1923). The debtor and creditor position of the United States is discussed in J. W. Angell, *Financial Foreign Policy of the United States* (1933), and more exhaustively treated in Cleona Lewis, *America's Stake in International Investments* (1938). See also the volumes of Dunn, Winkler, Remer, and Overlach cited for Chapter 26. An excellent appraisal of the problem is J. T. Madden, Marcus Nadler, and H. C. Sauvain, *America's Experience as a Creditor Nation* (1937).

On the war debt problem, H. G. Moulton and Leo Pasvolsky, *War Debts and World Prosperity* (1932), is exhaustive, and Carl Bergmann, *The History of Reparations* (1927), is a narrative of negotiations by a German participant. On the problem of international trade, see B. H. Williams, *Economic Foreign Policy of the United States* (1929) and *American Diplomacy* (1936); Ethel Dietrich, *World Trade* (1939) and *Far Eastern Trade of the United States* (1940). F. W. Taussig, *International Trade* (1927), is theoretical as well as historical; W. A. Brown, Jr., *The International Gold Standard Reinterpreted, 1914–1934* (1940), is a history of the gold standard; and a League of Nations document, *International Currency Experience, Lessons of the Inter-War Period* (1944), ably deals with currency and exchange controls. The following are concerned with cartels during this period: L. R. Edminister, *International Control of Raw Materials* (1930); Irvin Hexner, *International Cartels* (1945); and W. F. Notz, *Representative International Cartels, Combines and Trusts* (1929), a government report. Wendell Berge, *Cartels* (1944), is by a former head of the Antitrust Division of the Department of Justice. A recent study is G. W. Stocking and M. W. Watkins, *Cartels or Competition* (1948). On the tariff during the Roosevelt administration, see F. B. Sayre, *The Way Forward: The American Trade Agreement Program* (1939); J. D. Larkin, *Trade Agreements; a Study in Democratic Methods* (1940); Grace Beckett, *The Reciprocal Trade Agreements Program* (1941); and J. C. Pearson, *The Reciprocal Trade Agreements Program: The Policy of the United States and Its Effectiveness* (1942). Material on the "good-neighbor policy" may be found in H. C. Herring, *Good Neighbors* (1941); H. B. Hinton, *Cordell Hull* (1942); G. H. Graham, *Latin America and the United States* (3rd ed., 1938); Mordecai Ezekiel, *Economic Relations Between the Americas* (Carnegie Endowment for International Peace, 1941); J. F. Rippy, *Latin America in World Politics* (1938), and H. J. Trueblood, *Progress of American Cooperation* (Foreign Policy Reports, Vol. XV, No. 23, 1940).

32. *The Second World War*

Many of the important facts in the story of American war production and economic control are brought together in J. R. Craf, *A Survey of American Economy, 1940–1946* (1947). On war production the best sources are the reports of the chairman of the War Production Board. The work of the WPB has been told by the chairman in Donald Nelson, *Arsenal of Democracy: The Story of American War Production* (1946); the story of aid to the Allies in E. R. Stettinius, Jr., *Lend Lease: Weapon for Victory* (1944); and that of scientific research in J. P.

Baxter, III, *Scientists Against Time* (1946). See also the bimonthly *Reports to Congress of the Smaller War Plants Corporation; Economic Concentration and World War II* (1946), and U.S. Office of Facts and Figures, *Report to the Nation: The American Preparation for War* (1942).

On price control the essential documents are the *Quarterly Reports* of the Office of Price Administration. General discussions of this subject include Meyer Jacobstein and H. G. Moulton, *Effects of the Defense Program on Prices, Wages and Profits,* a Brookings Institution pamphlet (1941); Seymour E. Harris, *Prices and Related Controls in the United States* (1945) and *Inflation and the American Economy* (1945). One aspect of the work of the OPA is studied in R. F. Campbell, *The History of Basic Metals Price Control in World War II* (1948).

The financial development may be studied from the Secretary of the Treasury, *Annual Report on the State of the Finances;* the status of agriculture from the annual outlook issues of *The Agricultural Situation* published by the Bureau of Agricultural Economics of the United States Department of Agriculture; and the history of labor from the monthly surveys in the *Monthly Labor Review* of the Bureau of Labor Statistics of the United States Department of Labor. Full-length studies of agriculture during the war have appeared in W. W. Wilcox, *The Farmer in the Second World War* (1947), and in Bela Gold, *Wartime Economic Planning in Agriculture* (1949).

Other economic studies include H. M. Somers, *Presidential Agency: OWMR* (1950), a scholarly study of the Office of War Mobilization and Reconversion; R. H. Connery, *The Navy and Industrial Mobilization in World War II* (1951); J. P. Miller, *Pricing of Military Procurements* (1949); and David Novick, Melvin Anshen and W. C. Truppner, *Wartime Production Controls* (1949). See also *Civilian War Transport: A Record of the Control of Domestic Traffic Operations by the Office of Defense Transportation, 1941–1946* (1948), and Bureau of Demobilization, Civilian Production Administration, *Industrial Mobilization for War,* Vol. I, Program and Administration (1947), an excellent official history of the WPB. Eliot Janeway, *The Struggle for Survival* (1951), appraises the economic management of war.

33. *The Postwar Years*

The postwar years have not yet been adequately synthesized, although annual summaries of various topics may be found in the encyclopedia yearbooks. On the prospects of reconversion a useful document is J. A. Krug, *Production: Wartime Achievements and the Reconversion Outlook,* WPA Document No. 334 (1945). Perhaps the most useful of the economic surveys are the *Economic Reports of the President Submitted to Congress* twice yearly (January and July) since January, 1947, and prepared by the Counsel of Economic Advisers.

Contemporary studies on reconversion prospects are in Twentieth Century Fund, *America's Needs and Resources* (1947), for statistics before and after the war and in *Rebuilding the World Economy* (1947). On the prospects of private investments abroad, consult Cleona Lewis, *The United States and Foreign Invest-*

ment Problems (1948). See also H. G. Moulton, *Controlling Factors in Economic Development* (1949); Sumner Slichter, *The American Economy* (1948) and *The Future of American Business* (1951); and Mordekai Ezekiel (ed.), *Towards World Prosperity Through Industrial and Agricultural Expansion* (1947).

Various writers have contributed in Katherine Lumpkin (ed.), *Labor in Postwar America* (1949), to survey and interpret recent labor history. The best discussion of the Labor-Management Relations Act is in Harry A. Millis and Emily C. Brown, *From the Wagner Act to Taft-Hartley* (1950). It is more briefly described in D. I. Ashe and George Rifkin, *The Taft-Hartley Act* (1947), a Rand School pamphlet. J. B. S. Hardman and M. F. Neufeld (eds.), *The House of Labor* (1951), interprets the American labor movement from various angles.

The most important economic unit of the United Nations has been explained in Herman Finer, *The United Nations Economic and Social Council* (World Peace Foundation, 1949). In Organization for European Economic Cooperation, *European Recovery Program: Second Report* (1950), is a report on the work of the first two years. The Point Four Program is surveyed in J. B. Condliffe and H. H. Hutcheson, *Point Four and the World Economy* (1950), and in U.S. International Development Advisory Board, *Report to the President,* "Partners in Progress" (1951). Foreign Aid is fully covered in W. A. Adams, Jr., and Redners Opie, *American Foreign Assistance* (1953).

John Gunther, *Inside U.S.A.* (rev. ed., 1951), is a suggestive report on the nation in the postwar years.

INDEX

INDEX